THE OXFORD HANDBOOK OF

THE ARCHAEOLOGY OF INDIGENOUS AUSTRALIA AND NEW GUINEA

THE OXFORD HANDBOOK OF

THE ARCHAEOLOGY OF INDIGENOUS AUSTRALIA AND NEW GUINEA

Edited by

IAN J. MCNIVEN *and* BRUNO DAVID

OXFORD
UNIVERSITY PRESS

Oxford University Press is a department of the University of Oxford. It furthers
the University's objective of excellence in research, scholarship, and education
by publishing worldwide. Oxford is a registered trade mark of Oxford University
Press in the UK and certain other countries.

Published in the United States of America by Oxford University Press
198 Madison Avenue, New York, NY 10016, United States of America.

© Oxford University Press 2023

All rights reserved. No part of this publication may be reproduced, stored in
a retrieval system, or transmitted, in any form or by any means, without the
prior permission in writing of Oxford University Press, or as expressly permitted
by law, by license, or under terms agreed with the appropriate reproduction
rights organization. Inquiries concerning reproduction outside the scope of the
above should be sent to the Rights Department, Oxford University Press, at the
address above.

You must not circulate this work in any other form
and you must impose this same condition on any acquirer.

Library of Congress Cataloging-in-Publication Data
Names: McNiven, Ian J., author, editor. |
David, Bruno, 1962– author, editor.
Title: The Oxford handbook of the archaeology of Indigenous Australia and New Guinea /
edited by Ian J. McNiven and Bruno David.
Description: New York : Oxford University Press, 2023. |
Series: Oxford handbooks series | Includes bibliographical references and index. |
Identifiers: LCCN 2023033884 (print) | LCCN 2023033885 (ebook) |
ISBN 9780190095611 (hardback) | ISBN 9780190095642 (epub) |
ISBN 9780190095628
Subjects: LCSH: Aboriginal Australians–Antiquities. |
Indigenous peoples–New Guinea–Antiquities. | Australia–Antiquities. |
New Guinea–Antiquities. | Excavations (Archaeology)–Australia. |
Excavations (Archaeology)–New Guinea.
Classification: LCC DU124.A57 O96 2023 (print) | LCC DU124.A57 (ebook) |
DDC 994–dc23/eng/20230808
LC record available at https://lccn.loc.gov/2023033884
LC ebook record available at https://lccn.loc.gov/2023033885

DOI: 10.1093/oxfordhb/9780190095611.001.0001

Printed by Integrated Books International, United States of America

CONTENTS

List of Contributors   xi

1. Conceptualizing and Framing Archaeologies of Indigenous Australia and New Guinea   1
   IAN J. MCNIVEN AND BRUNO DAVID

PART I: APPROACHING THE PAST

2. 'The Thick Darkness of Pre-Historic Times': Antiquarian Archaeology in Nineteenth-Century Colonial Victoria   53
   IAN J. MCNIVEN

3. History of Archaeology in Papua New Guinea: The Early Years up to 1960   85
   GLENN R. SUMMERHAYES

4. The Development (and Imagined Reinvention) of Australian Archaeology in the Twentieth Century   109
   CHRIS URWIN AND MATTHEW SPRIGGS

5. Encountering the Past: Ancestors with Agency in Australian Archaeology   137
   CLAIRE SMITH, LIAM M. BRADY, AND CHRISTOPHER WILSON

6. Oral Tradition, History, and Archaeohistory of Indigenous Australia   157
   IAIN DAVIDSON, HEATHER BURKE, PEARL CONNELLY, STEPHEN PORTER, HAZEL SULLIVAN, LANCE SULLIVAN, ISABEL TARRAGÓ, AND LYNLEY A. WALLIS

7. Museum Collections and Their Legacies   187
   LINDY ALLEN

vi CONTENTS

PART II: COLONIZING SAHUL

8. Island Hopping to Sahul   215
   KASIH NORMAN, SUE O'CONNOR, AND MICHAEL BIRD

9. Australia's First People: Oldest Sites and Early Culture   241
   CHRIS CLARKSON, KASIH NORMAN, SUE O'CONNOR,
   JANE BALME, PETER VETH, AND CERI SHIPTON

10. Interactions with Megafauna   273
    CHRIS N. JOHNSON, JOE DORTCH, AND TREVOR H. WORTHY

11. What Does DNA Tell Us about Past Connections and
    the Settlement of Sahul?   301
    ELIZABETH MATISOO-SMITH AND ANNA L. GOSLING

PART III: CONSTRUCTED LANDSCAPES
AND WATERSCAPES

12. Enhanced Ecologies and Ecosystem Engineering: Strategies
    Developed by Aboriginal Australians to Increase the Abundance
    of Animal Resources   329
    IAN J. MCNIVEN, TIINA MANNE, AND ANNIE ROSS

13. The Coming of the Dingo   361
    JANE BALME AND SUE O'CONNOR

14. Fire and the Transformation of Landscapes   381
    CASSANDRA ROWE, JANELLE STEVENSON, SIMON CONNOR,
    AND MATTHEW ADELEYE

15. Stone-Walled Fish Traps of Australia and New Guinea as
    Expressions of Enhanced Sociality   413
    IAN J. MCNIVEN AND ARIANA B. J. LAMBRIDES

16. The Meaning of Ditches: An Ethnography of Field Systems
    and Other Networks in a New Guinea Landscape   449
    CHRIS BALLARD

17. Engaging and Designing Place: Furnishings and the Architecture
    of Archaeological Sites in Aboriginal Australia   473
    BRUNO DAVID, JEAN-JACQUES DELANNOY, CHRIS URWIN,
    JOANNA FRESLØV, RUSSELL MULLETT, AND CHRISTINE PHILLIPS

PART IV: LONG-TERM CHRONOLOGICAL TRENDS AND CULTURAL CHANGE

18. Persistence of Complexity: Continuation of Intensification, Population Change, and Sociostructural Change in Current Debates in Australian Archaeology   497
    HARRY LOURANDOS AND ANNIE ROSS

19. Past Aboriginal Populations and Demographic Change Using Radiocarbon Data and Time-Series Analysis   523
    ALAN N. WILLIAMS, SEAN ULM, AND MIKE SMITH

20. The Big Flood: Responding to Sea-Level Rise and the Inundated Continental Shelf   541
    JONATHAN BENJAMIN AND SEAN ULM

21. Dating Rock Art: A Kimberley Perspective   559
    HELEN GREEN, DAMIEN FINCH, ANDREW GLEADOW, RÉKA-H. FÜLÖP, AND ZENOBIA JACOBS

PART V: CULTURAL DYNAMICS AND NETWORKS

22. Coral Sea Cultural Interaction Sphere   591
    IAN J. McNIVEN

23. Mortars and Pestles Make the Mid-Holocene Occupation of New Guinea and the Bismarck Archipelago Visible   617
    PAMELA SWADLING

24. Axe Quarrying, Production, and Exchange in Australia and New Guinea   641
    ANNE FORD AND PETER HISCOCK

25. Flaked Stone Tools of Holocene Sahul: Case Studies from Northern Australia and Papua New Guinea   669
    TIM RYAN MALONEY

26. Shell Valuables and Exchange Systems in New Guinea   693
    KATHERINE SZABÓ

viii CONTENTS

27. Boundaries, Relationality, and Style Provinces in Australian Rock Art 717
   MADELEINE KELLY AND LIAM M. BRADY

28. Australian Indigenous Ochres: Use, Sourcing, and Exchange 743
   JILLIAN HUNTLEY

PART VI: SPECIALIZED SOCIETIES

29. Maritime Coastal and Island Societies of Australia and New Guinea 773
   MICHAEL ROWLAND, BEN SHAW, AND SEAN ULM

30. Swamp and Delta Societies of the Papuan Gulf, Papua New Guinea 803
   CHRIS URWIN, JAMES W. RHOADS, AND JOSHUA A. BELL

31. The Archaeology of Social Transformation in the New Guinea Highlands 831
   DYLAN GAFFNEY AND TIM DENHAM

32. Below the Sky, Above the Clouds: The Archaeology of the Australian High Country 861
   JOANNA FRESLØV AND RUSSELL MULLETT

33. Murray River Societies in Australia through the Lens of Bioarchaeology 889
   JUDITH LITTLETON, SARAH KARSTENS, AND HARRY ALLEN

34. Beyond the Barriers: A New Model for the Settlement of Australian Deserts 917
   PETER VETH, JO MCDONALD, AND PETER HISCOCK

PART VII: CEREMONIES AND RITUALS

35. Historicizing the 'Dreaming': An Archaeological Perspective from Arid Australia 949
   MIKE SMITH

36. Rock Art Modification and Its Ritualized and Relational Contexts 969
   LIAM M. BRADY, ROBERT G. GUNN, AND JOAKIM GOLDHAHN

37. Dugongs and Turtles as Kin: Relational Ontologies and Archaeological Perspectives on Ritualized Hunting by Coastal Indigenous Australians 993
   IAN J. MCNIVEN

PART VIII: VISITORS AND COLONIZERS

38. Cross-Cultural Interaction Across the Arafura and Timor Seas: Aboriginal People and Macassans in Northern Australia   1023
   CHRIS URWIN, LYNETTE RUSSELL, AND LILY YULIANTI FARID

39. Whaling and Sealing in Nineteenth-Century Australia   1043
   MARTIN GIBBS AND LYNETTE RUSSELL

40. Fatal Frontier: Temporal and Spatial Considerations of the Native Mounted Police and Colonial Violence Across Queensland   1057
   LYNLEY A. WALLIS, HEATHER BURKE, BRYCE BARKER, AND NOELENE COLE

41. The Archaeology of Agrarian Australia   1079
   ALISTAIR PATERSON

42. 'Prehistory' and the Indigenous Archaeology of Missions and Reserves in Australia and New Guinea   1101
   JEREMY ASH

Index   1131

Contributors

Matthew Adeleye, Postdoctoral Research Associate, Australian National University; Australian Research Council Centre of Excellence for Australian Biodiversity and Heritage

Harry Allen, Honorary Research Fellow, University of Auckland

Lindy Allen, Honorary Fellow, University of Melbourne

Jeremy Ash, Research Fellow, Monash University; Australian Research Council Centre of Excellence for Australian Biodiversity and Heritage

Chris Ballard, Associate Professor, Australian National University

Jane Balme, Professor Emerita, University of Western Australia

Bryce Barker, Professor, University of Southern Queensland

Joshua A. Bell, Curator of Globalization, Smithsonian National Museum of Natural History

Jonathan Benjamin, Professor, Flinders University; Australian Research Council Centre of Excellence for Australian Biodiversity and Heritage

Michael Bird, Distinguished Professor, James Cook University; Australian Research Council Centre of Excellence for Australian Biodiversity and Heritage

Liam M. Brady, Associate Professor and Australian Research Council Future Fellow, Flinders University

Heather Burke, Professor, Flinders University

Chris Clarkson, Professor, University of Queensland; Australian Research Council Centre of Excellence for Australian Biodiversity and Heritage

Noelene Cole, Honorary Senior Research Fellow, James Cook University; Australian Research Council Centre of Excellence for Australian Biodiversity and Heritage

Pearl Connelly, Mitakoodi people, Queensland

Simon Connor, Fellow, Australian National University; Australian Research Council Centre of Excellence for Australian Biodiversity and Heritage

Bruno David, Professor, Monash University; Australian Research Council Centre of Excellence for Australian Biodiversity and Heritage

Iain Davidson, Emeritus Professor, University of New England

Jean-Jacques Delannoy, Professor, Université Savoie Mont Blanc; Australian Research Council Centre of Excellence for Australian Biodiversity and Heritage

Tim Denham, Professor, Australian National University

Joe Dortch, Senior Adjunct Research Fellow, University of Western Australia

Lily Yulianti Farid, Post-Doctoral Research Fellow, Monash University

Damien Finch, Research Fellow, University of Melbourne

Anne Ford, Associate Professor, University of Otago

Joanna Fresløv, Senior Research Advisor, GunaiKurnai Land and Waters Aboriginal Corporation

Réka-H. Fülöp, Research Scientist, Australian Nuclear Science and Technology Organisation

Dylan Gaffney, Research Fellow, University of Oxford

Martin Gibbs, Professor, University of New England

Andrew Gleadow, Emeritus Professor of Earth Sciences, University of Melbourne

Joakim Goldhahn, Rock Art Australia Ian Potter Kimberley Chair, University of Western Australia

Anna L. Gosling, Research Fellow, University of Otago

Helen Green, Research Fellow, University of Melbourne; Australian Research Council Centre of Excellence for Australian Biodiversity and Heritage

Robert G. Gunn, Independent consultant

Peter Hiscock, Professor, University of Wollongong

Jillian Huntley, Senior Research Fellow, Griffith University

Zenobia Jacobs, Professor, University of Wollongong; Australian Research Council Centre of Excellence for Australian Biodiversity and Heritage

Chris N. Johnson, Professor, University of Tasmania; Australian Research Council Centre of Excellence for Australian Biodiversity and Heritage

Sarah Karstens, Honorary Research Fellow, University of Auckland

Madeleine Kelly, Researcher, Monash University; Australian Research Council Centre of Excellence for Australian Biodiversity and Heritage

Ariana B. J. Lambrides, Australian Research Council DECRA Fellow, James Cook University; Australian Research Council Centre of Excellence for Australian Biodiversity and Heritage

Judith Littleton, Professor, University of Auckland

Harry Lourandos, Adjunct Professor, James Cook University

Tim Ryan Maloney, Research Fellow, Griffith University

Tiina Manne, Associate Professor, University of Queensland; Australian Research Council Centre of Excellence for Australian Biodiversity and Heritage

Elizabeth Matisoo-Smith, Professor of Biological Anthropology, University of Otago

Jo McDonald, Professor, University of Western Australia

Ian J. McNiven, Professor of Indigenous Archaeology, Monash University; Australian Research Council Centre of Excellence for Australian Biodiversity and Heritage

Russell Mullett, GunaiKurnai Elder, GunaiKurnai Land and Waters Aboriginal Corporation

Kasih Norman, Researcher, University of Wollongong; Australian Research Council Centre of Excellence for Australian Biodiversity and Heritage

Sue O'Connor, Distinguished Professor, Australian National University; Australian Research Council Centre of Excellence for Australian Biodiversity and Heritage

Alistair Paterson, Professor, University of Western Australia

Christine Phillips, Senior Lecturer, RMIT University

Stephen Porter, Gamilaraay people, New South Wales

James W. Rhoads, Honorary Research Fellow, University of Western Australia

Annie Ross, Associate Professor, The University of Queensland

Cassandra Rowe, Research Fellow, James Cook University; Australian Research Council Centre of Excellence for Australian Biodiversity and Heritage

Michael Rowland, Adjunct Associate Professor, James Cook University

Lynette Russell, Laureate Professor, Monash University; Australian Research Council Centre of Excellence for Australian Biodiversity and Heritage

Ben Shaw, Senior Lecturer, Australian National University ; Australian Research Council Centre of Excellence for Australian Biodiversity and Heritage

Ceri Shipton, Lecturer, University College London; Australian Research Council Centre of Excellence for Australian Biodiversity and Heritage

Claire Smith, Professor, Flinders University

Mike Smith, Director of Research and Development, National Museum of Australia

Matthew Spriggs, Emeritus Professor, Australian National University

Janelle Stevenson, Research Fellow, Australian National University; Australian Research Council Centre of Excellence for Australian Biodiversity and Heritage

Hazel Sullivan, Yalarrnga people, Queensland

Lance Sullivan, Yalarrnga people, Queensland

Glenn R. Summerhayes, Professor, University of Otago

Pamela Swadling, Research Affiliate, Australian National University

Katherine Szabó, Pre-Construct Archaeology Ltd, Cambridge; Australian Research Council Centre of Excellence for Australian Biodiversity and Heritage

Isabel Tarragó, Wangkamahdla people, Queensland

Sean Ulm, Distinguished Professor, James Cook University; Australian Research Council Centre of Excellence for Australian Biodiversity and Heritage

Chris Urwin, Research Fellow, Monash University; Australian Research Council Centre of Excellence for Australian Biodiversity and Heritage

Peter Veth, Laureate Professor, University of Western Australia; Australian Research Council Centre of Excellence for Australian Biodiversity and Heritage

Lynley A. Wallis, Professor, Griffith University

Alan N. Williams, EMM Consulting Pty Ltd, St Leonards, New South Wales; Australian Research Council Centre of Excellence for Australian Biodiversity and Heritage

Christopher Wilson, Research Fellow, University of Tasmania; Australian Research Council Centre of Excellence for Australian Biodiversity and Heritage

Trevor H. Worthy, Associate Professor, Flinders University

CHAPTER 1

CONCEPTUALIZING AND FRAMING ARCHAEOLOGIES OF INDIGENOUS AUSTRALIA AND NEW GUINEA

IAN J. MCNIVEN AND BRUNO DAVID

INTRODUCTION

TODAY, mainland Australia, often considered the world's largest island, is surrounded by some 8000 near and offshore islands. The Australian mainland is separated from New Guinea—the third-largest island on Earth, itself surrounded by hundreds of islands—by a 150 km-wide continental shelf known as Torres Strait. During periods of low sea level, the continental shelf that *separates* Australia and New Guinea with sea waters, comes to *connect* it with a land bridge, such as it did during the Last Glacial Maximum. Whereas politically Australia is a single nation-state, New Guinea is divided into two, Indonesia in the west and Papua New Guinea in the east. Although Australia and New Guinea take in only 6% of the world's landmass and 0.5% of the population, collectively they represent 20% of its linguistic diversity (Dixon 2011; Foley 2000). However, none of the above has always been so, and it is the role of archaeology and its kin disciplines—geomorphology, palaeoecology, palaeo-genetics, linguistics, and so on—to systematically and reliably figure out that long cultural and environmental history. That project of archaeology is not only to fill in the factual gaps of when, where, and what happened in the past (often framed as data-building through the application of increasingly better methods) but also to conceptualize and reconceptualize what we know or think we know ('theory'). For example, should we really conceive of the cultural landscape and seascape of Sahul (Australia, New Guinea, and their intervening islands and exposed continental shelf) during the Last Glacial Maximum as a *connection* between Australia and New Guinea, and as a *separation* following the drowning of the continental shelf before and after the

Last Glacial Maximum? Or did the waters facilitate rather than inhibit connections, and if so, when, where, and how? The specifics cannot be assumed, for it is the task of archaeology not to assume, but to determine exactly what happened, where, when, and how, and, ultimately, to try to understand why.

Australia and New Guinea are archaeologically connected on two broad conceptual and epistemological fronts. The first relates to shared recent histories of Southeast Asian and then European 'discovery', colonialism, and independence and nationhood that together span the past c. 500 years. The second concerns ongoing scientific understandings of the connected biogeography of the two landmasses over some 65,000 years of human occupation. Long before Spanish and Dutch (and then French and English) seafarers began to chart the shores of Australia and New Guinea in the sixteenth and seventeenth centuries, the idea of a Great Southern Land had prevailed in the European imagination. The Ancient Greeks reasoned on the existence of an antipodal continent and second habitable world in a Southern Hemisphere that acted as a counterbalance to the known inhabited world (*oikoumene*) of Europe, Africa, and western Asia in the Northern Hemisphere (Romm 1992; Stallard 2016). For the early Greeks working in the Pythagorean tradition (including Pythagoras of Samos: c. 570–490 BCE), the Earth was a sphere with latitudinal zones in a cosmos physically structured as moral geography (e.g., Huffman 2018). The word 'Antipodes' was coined to describe an imagined Southern Hemisphere where people stood with their feet opposite to those of the Northern Hemisphere (e.g., Stallard 2010). For centuries before its European discovery, the peoples of the Antipodes, Australia, and New Guinea had been conjured in opposition to Europeans.

By the early sixteenth century, with improvements in long-distance sailing technologies, European cosmographers and cartographers began to search for the unknown southern continent (Stallard 2016: 13). In 1532, French cartographer Oronce Finé published his world map depicting the hypothetical landmass of 'Terra Australis' (Southern Land) as a discrete island (Richardson 2006: 14). In 1545, the Spaniard Ynigo Ortiz de Retez sailed along the northwest coast of New Guinea and called it 'Nueva Guinea' in recognition of perceived physical similarities between the peoples he observed and peoples of Guinea in west Africa (Pouwer 1999: 159). Soon after, a partly chartered and imagined New Guinea ('Nueva Guinea'/'Nova Guinea') started appearing on Spanish (from the 1550s) and Dutch (from the 1560s) maps (Douglas 2019). In the early seventeenth century, the coastlines of northern, western, and southern Australia were surveyed by Dutch mariners and the landmass designated New Holland ('Hollandia Nova') by the Dutch cartographer Joan Blaeu in 1648 (Clancy 1995: Maps 6.11–6.22; Schilder 1972: 42; Stallard 2016: 17). Mapping the coastlines of the eastern half of New Guinea and Australia took place following British and French expeditions of the eighteenth century (Clancy 1995: Maps 6.30–6.43). 'Torres's Straits' appeared on Samuel Dunn's 1772 published map after James Cook confirmed the seaway's existence in 1770 (Douglas 2019). Yet Stallard (2016: 233–236) argues that New Guinea and Australia were rarely considered part of the elusive Terra Australis of the South Pacific by the Dutch, British, or French. Following his circumnavigation of Australia in 1801–1802 and demonstration of a single landmass, British mariner Matthew Flinders posited the name 'Australia' (after the Latin word *australis*, meaning 'southern') for the continental island, in recognition of Terra Australis, the long-sought Great Southern Land (Flinders 1814: iii; Stallard 2016: 231–232).

British colonial invasion of Australia began in 1788 with the arrival of the First Fleet at Botany Bay and later Port Jackson (known today as Sydney). Colonial settlement of what became other major cities and colonies in Australia occurred mostly in the early nineteenth century: Hobart (1804), Brisbane (1824), Perth (1829), Melbourne (1835), Adelaide (1836), and Darwin (1869). In 1901, the various British colonies were federated as six states into the Commonwealth of Australia, with the Northern Territory and the Australian Capital Territory separating in 1911. In marked contrast, the eastern half of New Guinea obtained nationhood with the declaration of Papua New Guinea in 1975. Prior to this independence, the southern half of eastern New Guinea was the protectorate of British New Guinea (1884) and then the Territory of Papua (1904). The northern half of eastern New Guinea became German New Guinea (1899), and New Guinea (1921) under the control of Australia after World War I. After World War II, eastern New Guinea became The Territory of Papua and New Guinea (1949), and later Papua New Guinea (1972), also under Australian control. The major colonial settlement of Port Moresby was established in 1873. Today, Papua New Guinea is divided into twenty-two provinces, including the National Capital District (Port Moresby) and the Autonomous Region of Bougainville. The western half of New Guinea became part of the Dutch East Indies in 1824, which eventually became formalized as Netherlands New Guinea (1895–1962). Dutch colonial towns included Merauke (1902) and Hollandia (now the regional capital Jayapura) (1910). Between 1962 and 1969, the Republic of Indonesia increasingly assumed control of western New Guinea (Irian Barat/West Irian), later renamed Irian Jaya (1973), and then Papua (2002), with a new provincial subdivision of West Papua consisting of the Birds Head and Bomberai Peninsulas and nearby islands in 2007 (Pouwer 1999). The Indigenous independence movement refers to all of western New Guinea as West Papua (Antonopoulos & Cottle 2019; Kluge 2020).

In contrast to Australia and Indonesian Papua/West Papua, the nation of Papua New Guinea is governed by its local Indigenous citizens. The British colonization of Australia was founded on a negation of Indigenous land ownership (the doctrine of *terra nullius*— land belonging to no one) and displacement of Indigenous peoples for British settlement. During peak British colonial expansion in the nineteenth century, tens of thousands of Aboriginal people died through disease and murder (often in massacres). Estimates of the number of Aboriginal people killed in Queensland by the paramilitary Native Police force range from 41,000 (Evans & Ørsted-Jensen 2014) to over 100,000 (Burke, Barker, Wallis, Craig, & Combo 2020: 321). Across Australia, local Aboriginal communities violently resisted British invasion, often through the guerrilla tactics of killing and maiming of livestock and strategic killing of pastoralists (Reynolds 1981). In contrast, the impact of colonialism on Torres Strait Islanders in Far North Queensland was in many ways far less devastating, as the desire for land acquisition was relatively minor (Beckett 1987).

The Indigenous or First Nations population of Australia comprises two major groups—Aboriginal peoples and Torres Strait Islanders, collectively divided into hundreds of local community groups, organizations, and corporate entities (Langton 2018). In 2016, the number of First Nations Australians was estimated to be just under 800,000, of whom 71,000 identified as having Torres Strait Islander heritage (ABS 2018). Overall, First Nations peoples represent 3.3% of the total population of Australia, the majority (61%) of whom live in New South Wales and Queensland (ABS 2018). At the point of British colonization in 1788, it is estimated that the Aboriginal and Torres Strait Islander population of Australia was at least 750,000 (White & Mulvaney 1987) and probably well over a million (Bradshaw et al. 2021). The legacies of colonialism and economic marginalization and disadvantage for First Nations Australians is revealed starkly by a median age of twenty-three, compared to thirty-eight for Australia's non-Indigenous population (ABS 2018). The population of Papua New Guinea is estimated to be 9–10 million, nearly all (>99%) of whom are Indigenous (Bourke & Allen 2021; NSO 2015). The median age of people in Papua New Guinea is twenty-one (NSO 2015). The population of Indonesian Papua/West Papua is 4.5 million, many of whom are immigrants from large-scale transmigration programs involving peoples from other parts of Indonesia (especially Java) over the past half-century (Antonopoulos & Cottle 2019; Kusumaryati 2018: 5).

Sahul

During periods of lower sea level in the last glacial cycle (Late Pleistocene), the continental shelves of Australia and New Guinea were exposed to form a large, single continental landmass: Sahul (Figure 1.1). The term derives from 'Sahull', the name given to a shoal south of Timor that first appeared on Dutch cartographer Johannes Jansson's 1633 map *Indiae Orientalis Nova Descriptio* (Ballard 1993; see Clancy 1995: Map 6.6). At that same location, Flinders (see earlier) identified the 'Great SAHUL shoal' on a map published in 1814 (Flinders 1814, III: Plate XVI). Beneath the label, Flinders added: 'This shoal is said to be dry in some parts. The Malays of Makassar formerly came to fish upon it for Trepang' (see later). According to Ballard (1993: 19), it was Rhys Jones (1977) who expanded the term 'Sahul' to take in the continental shelf of Australia (and by implication New Guinea) in his introductory chapter to *Sunda and Sahul: Prehistoric Studies in Southeast Asia, Melanesia and Australia*. In this sense, continental Sahul was relationally conceived in contradistinction to Sunda, the Pleistocene landmass of Southeast Asia. Jones (1977: 2) added that the Sunda and Sahul 'continental shelves' were separated by the intervening islands of Wallacea, a biogeographic zone long named in honour of Charles Darwin's counterpart in evolutionary theory: Alfred Russel Wallace (1869). In the same *Sunda and Sahul* volume, physical anthropologist Alan Thorne (1977: 187) made the explicit statement that Sahul was 'the landmass embracing Australia and New Guinea'.

CONCEPTUALIZING AND FRAMING ARCHAEOLOGIES 5

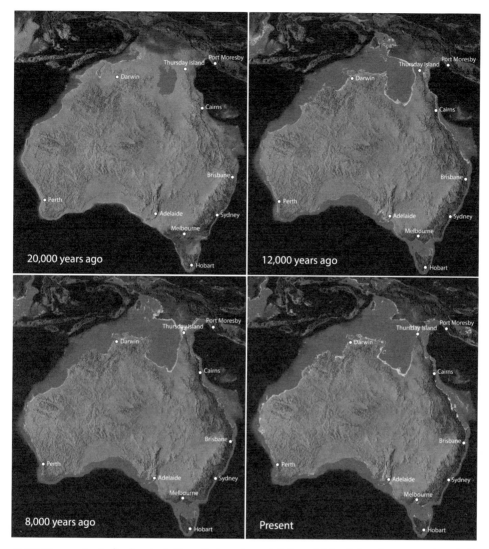

FIGURE 1.1. Australia (centre), New Guinea (top right), and Island Southeast Asia (top left) at different sea levels. Full exposure of continental shelves occurred during the Last Glacial Maximum at c. 20,000 years ago, resulting in Australia and New Guinea joining as a single landmass to form the island continent of Sahul. Subsequent sea-level rise flooded continental shelves, leaving a landbridge across Torres Strait at c. 12,000 years ago, formation of Torres Strait by 8000 years ago, and present sea levels and coastal configurations reached in the past 1000 years.

(Modelling and images courtesy of Michael Bird and Damian O'Grady, James Cook University.)

The epistemological value and impact of the concept of Sahul for the region's archaeology were immediate, exemplified by Peter White and James O'Connell's influential 1982 text, *A Prehistory Australia, New Guinea and Sahul*. Following Jones (1977), White and O'Connell (1982: 6) pointed out that the concept of Sahul not only had 'biogeographic' integrity but avoided the chauvinism ('cartographic imperialism'—Ballard

1993: 20) of terms such as 'Greater Australia' which subsume the identity of New Guinea. Biogeographically, Sahul encapsulated the long evolutionary isolation and characteristic fauna beyond the eastern end of the African-European-Asian landmass, especially its marsupial mammals and bird life of friarbirds, cockatoos, and other distinctive taxa (Wallace 1869; White & O'Connell 1982: 12). White and O'Connell (1982: 6–17) also emphasized that Sahul is a landmass of great environmental diversity and extremes, with an arid/semiarid zone comprising two-thirds of Australia and tropical forests covering more than 90% of New Guinea. Average annual rainfall ranges from less than 10 cm in some desert regions of Central Australia to 10 m in some highlands regions of New Guinea.

White and O'Connell (1982: 3) also noted that 'for at least 80% of the time during which humans have occupied the area, Australia and New Guinea were subsumed into the single continent of Sahul. For about the first 40,000 years, the people of Sahul have a common history'. Nevertheless, as Ballard (1993: 21) has remarked, 'any significant cultural continuity between New Guinea and Australia during the Pleistocene still remains to be demonstrated'. While recent DNA research does indeed point to an ancient biological separation between human populations of both regions (Bergström et al. 2016; Malaspinas et al. 2016), cultural comparisons between the two regions have often relied on an essentialized dichotomy between so-called hunter-gatherers (Australia) versus agriculturalists (New Guinea) (David & Denham 2006). Yet the absence and presence of agriculture in Australia and New Guinea, respectively, cannot be ignored, and it is seen by some to underpin deviating historical trajectories between the two regions over the past c. 10,000 years (Allen & O'Connell 1995 and Yen 1995 in particular; cf. Harris 1995).

PEOPLE ON THE OTHER SIDE OF WHOSE WORLD?

Harry Lourandos (1980a, 1980b, 2008) has long pointed out that cultural, and especially subsistence, differences between New Guinea and Australia are not only clinal but also show considerable overlap (see also Denham 2008; Denham, Donohue, & Booth 2009; Harris 1977, 1995). On this issue, Paul Roscoe (2002: 153–154) reveals that perhaps 10% of New Guinea's '1,000 or so cultures' derive at least 75% of their calories from foraging. More profoundly, and following a point raised by Lourandos (1980b), Roscoe (2002: 159) also emphasized that across New Guinea, 'There appears to be no clear correlation between dependence on wild or domesticated resources on the one hand and sociocultural form and complexity on the other. Many of the region's cultivators have a sociocultural complexity no greater than that of foragers dependent on hunting for their meat protein, while foragers with access to rich aquatic resources rival the sociocultural complexity of the most intensive agriculturalists in the Highlands'. Roscoe (2002: 160) concludes that labelling certain groups of people as 'hunter-gatherers' has little intrinsic heuristic value, and that 'it might be less misleading and more useful to describe them as *practicing*, for example, "hunting and gathering"—*among other things*—rather than referring to them *as* "hunters and gatherers," thereby surrendering to the Western tendency to reduce people to, or essentialize them as, their socioeconomic occupations (doctor, lawyer, forager, farmer)'. This echoes in many ways Claude Lévi-Strauss's prescient warning at the influential 'Man the Hunter' conference in Chicago in 1966 (Lee & Devore 1968), where he emphasized that 'It is very narrow if we insist upon limiting the category [of 'hunter-gatherers'] to those few tribes who live exclusively by hunting and gathering' (Lévi-Strauss 1968: 344). Lévi-Strauss pointed out that most 'hunter-gatherers' also undertook some cultivation, and in 'many parts of Europe' the collection of wild mushrooms 'is a full-fledged gathering activity' (1968: 344). As such, 'the object of our studies' is not to think of hunting and gathering as a type of people but rather as a 'certain type of behaviour' (1968: 344). This view has been voiced many times since, both internationally and in Australia, especially in relation to Australian Aboriginal relations to plant communities and Country. Examples include Clark's (1972: viii) ecological thinking that views relations among people, plants, and animals as 'far too complex to be explained in terms of an elementary dichotomy'; and Hynes and Chase (1982: 38), who noted that Aboriginal:

> knowledge and manipulation of plants is neither simple nor 'pre-agricultural', and can only be understood by detailed study of the particular cultural and biological systems within which they operate. . . . Most importantly, some plant communities may have been not merely modified but created by Aboriginal cultural activity. Aboriginal interactions with plants are the outcome of strategies which include not only physical resource exploitation, but as well systems of locality and territoriality that recognize ties between particular individuals and groups and particular home environments.
>
> The categorizing of certain human groups as hunters and gatherers has resulted in the view that they operate within 'wild' environments to obtain 'wild' resources, as opposed to the 'domestic' environments and resources of agricultural and horticultural peoples. . . . simple unilinear theories of development based on resource activities are no longer acceptable in anthropology.

Hynes and Chase's solution is to think through the concept of 'domiculture' rather than pigeonholing Aboriginal resourcing practices as 'hunting and gathering' in opposition to 'agriculture'. The onus is for researchers to describe the particular ecological relations among plants, animals, people, and so forth, rather than forcing such relations into preformulated categories that invariably fail to do justice to the existential and operational depths of cultural practices. It is, in other words, for the researcher to embrace a more anthropological archaeology that does better justice to the practices in question by aiming to interrogate precisely how those particular practices are embedded in relations between 'things', and where those relations include everything within one's purview including more (or other)-than-human actors. Thinking in terms of a domicultural logic rather than through 'hunting and gathering' versus 'agriculture' brings to the fore the relational, or 'domestic', dimensions of how people and their worlds are co-constructed in meaningful social practice and worldviews (ontologies). Further, to paraphrase Hynes and Chase (1982: 49), describing the particular relations between plants and people, rather than pigeonholing cultural groups into 'hunter-gatherers' versus 'agriculturalists', 'give[s] us a basis for explaining domicultural processes as integral components in Aboriginal life-systems and allow us to uncouple Aboriginal influence on plants and sites from linear, pre-agricultural models'. It is in that same logic that David (2017: 221) points out that 'it makes little or no sense whatsoever' to assume that one group of people can be understood by reference to another group 'simply because they, too, hunt and gather items of food (after all, we cannot meaningfully understand our own cultural expressions and creativity by reducing ourselves to "food buyers"). People make sense of their world in many ways other than through generic methods of obtaining food. This is the stuff of culture, and reducing [Aboriginal cultural practices] to notions of "hunter-gatherers" is entirely inappropriate' when trying to understand peoples and cultures. Understanding the history of Australia and New Guinea by investigating each issue of interest, and in doing so questioning the preformulated conceptual categories through which they have hitherto been known—that is, by reflecting on the biases and blindspots that have been brought into the frame from the onset—can only benefit a greater and culturally more inclusive understanding.

As noted earlier, such interrogations can take many forms. Ballard (1993: 21), for example, has noted that limiting a 'common history' of New Guinea and Australia to Pleistocene land-bridge (Sahul) times negates the capacity of waterways to facilitate interactions, as seen during the Holocene after the formation of Torres Strait around 8000–9000 years ago. When the Holocene Arafura and Coral Seas that today 'separate' Australia and New Guinea are conceptualized as 'connecting' the two landmasses instead, new opportunities to visualize maritime relations between the two regions emerge, including the possibility and ways by which the human histories of Australia and New Guinea may have always, or periodically, been linked (see Lilley 2000).

In light of this, the scope of this Handbook should include the archaeology of Indigenous Australia, Papua New Guinea, and Indonesian Papua/West Papua. Unfortunately, little published archaeological research is available for Indonesian Papua/West Papua. In their comprehensive 'Archaeological Review of Western New Guinea', Duncan Wright and colleagues (2013: 25) noted that 'archaeological information for the region is scarce due to limited investigations, limited publication and the multilingual nature of publications. Consequently, little archaeological information about western New Guinea has percolated into the mainstream literature'. Furthermore, the 'archaeological record of wNG [western New Guinea] is too fragmented to be presented chronologically or thematically' (Wright et al. 2013: 33). As such, this Handbook focuses mainly on the archaeology of Indigenous Australia and Papua New Guinea, awaiting new results from the western half of New Guinea in future years (see Gaffney & Tolla in press).

It is nevertheless clear that the archaeological history of Indonesian Papua/West Papua articulates in critical ways with the major cultural domains of Papua New Guinea in the east and Island Southeast Asia in the west (Spriggs 1998). On a deeper (Late Pleistocene) time-scale, western New Guinea formed the northwest section of Sahul and was one of the likely entry points for initial human colonization (Birdsell 1977). Evidence of people in Papua New Guinea c. 40,000–50,000 cal BP (based on radiocarbon dating; Summerhayes et al. 2010) and Australia 65,000 years ago (based on luminescence dating; Clarkson et al. 2017) indicates that the current earliest radiocarbon dates of c. 26,000 cal BP from archaeological excavations for people in Indonesian Papua/West Papua (Pasveer 2004) and c. 37,000 cal BP for anthropic burning as registered in buried sediments (Haberle et al. 1991; Hope 1998) are underestimates for initial human presence by a factor of nearly two.

Structuring the Handbook

We have structured the Handbook into eight thematic sections. We deliberately avoided a geographical approach that would have seen the volume largely consisting of regional chapters. Our aim is to showcase the intellectual depth and breadth of the archaeology of Indigenous Australia and New Guinea by highlighting a broad range of conceptual and empirical approaches to the past. In this sense, the goal is to create a volume that also helps promote emerging research standards and agendas into the future. We outline each of the Handbook's eight major themes as contexts for the forty-one specialist chapters.

I. Approaching the Past

The distinctive forms of Indigenous archaeology practiced in Australia and New Guinea signal not only the unique character of the archaeological records of both major land masses but also the changing nature of colonial relations between archaeologists and local Indigenous peoples over the past 200 years. Until the 1980s, archaeological research in Australia and New Guinea was undertaken with little concern for, or involvement with, local Indigenous communities (cf. Colley 2002; B. Griffiths 2018; T. Griffiths 1996; Smith 2004; Taylor 2017). Yet early archaeological practices in the two countries varied considerably, in large part due to the different forms of colonial relations in each area. In Australia, Aboriginal peoples especially were subjected to colonial invasion and settler colonialism whereby European occupation was predicated upon removal, relocation, murder, and massacre of local Aboriginal families and communities along with the appropriation of property. During the second half of the nineteenth century, European intellectual and antiquarian curiosity turned to the 'origins' of Aboriginal peoples. This intellectual gaze was viewed through the lens of social evolutionism and its underlying racial, and racist, hierarchies of cultural development and worthiness. In such a view, Aboriginal primitivism and primordialism prevailed in the European imagination. Aboriginal peoples came to be seen as living representatives of primitive Europeans, as evidenced by fossil Neanderthal and early modern human ('Cro-Magnon') skeletal remains and artefacts being uncovered in Europe. The focus of nineteenth-century antiquarianism was the State of Victoria in southeast Australia, where interest by British colonists developed in the wake of frontier violence and the dispossession of Aboriginal lands (see Chapter 2: McNiven). In Papua New Guinea, archaeological research had a different historical trajectory reflecting more an interest in oral traditions (i.e., taking into account local Indigenous perspectives, if not epistemologies, from the onset) (e.g., Golson 1968), as well as the German and British mercantile colonial interests that in practice did not usually feature the dispossession of Indigenous lands. Here antiquarian interests have a shorter history mostly dating back to the early twentieth century, and they were often directly linked to European museums, universities, and local missionary enterprises. During the first half of the twentieth century in Australia, institutionalized archaeology (primarily museum-based) demonstrated the potential of excavations to reveal deep, even if usually assumed to be not particularly ancient, stratigraphic cultural sequences and chronological change. These early excavations laid the foundations for the development and formalization of 'prehistoric' archaeology in Australian universities in the 1960s (Chapter 4: Urwin & Spriggs). Similar developments in New Zealand and Australia set the scene for the beginnings of modern archaeological research in Papua New Guinea in the 1960s and early 1970s (see Chapter 3: Summerhayes).

Archaeological approaches to Indigenous pasts have changed radically over the past six decades both in Australia and New Guinea. In addition to exponential improvements in scientific techniques, such as dating and sourcing methods, there has also been a seismic shift in the social and ethical dimensions of archaeological practice. These latter changes have come about through widespread social change, including from Indigenous peoples advocating strongly for a greater say in how their heritage is to be researched, interpreted, and presented to the world. Whereas in the past Indigenous archaeological sites in Australia and New Guinea were seen largely as the exclusive domain of archaeologists, most practicing archaeologists today understand and appreciate that cultural heritage belongs to the local descendant Indigenous communities whose ancestors are the subjects of investigation. Such recognition should also bring with it an understanding that the concept of 'stakeholder' is not appropriate when thinking of First Nations peoples' interests and concerns about archaeological research on traditional lands. Rather, and subject to consent from local representative groups, Traditional Owners are *hosts* for non–Traditional Owner archaeologists who may be privileged to work on Country as *guests* (McNiven & Russell 2005). Such opportunities entail a moral and ethical imperative for researchers to assume the role of respectful guests within Indigenous host communities. In this guise, archaeologists are guided by local Indigenous cultural protocols. Sometimes the research will be founded on approved consultations and permissions; sometimes on more inclusive collaborations; and sometimes on deeper partnerships built on mutual respect and deep two-way initiatives and aspirations.

Since the late 1980s in particular, some archaeologists and Traditional Owner groups have developed deeper collaborations that explore the potentials of articulating archaeological methods with Indigenous perspectives. Such endeavours often operate across multiple ontological standpoints (cf. Nakata's [2007] concept of the 'cultural interface'; Nakata & David [2010]) and have guided research initiatives by both Indigenous and non-Indigenous researchers, including the editors of this Handbook and their colleagues and graduate students (e.g., Ash, Manas, & Bosun 2010; Brady, Bradley, & Kearney 2016; David 2002; David et al. 2021; Grainer et al. 1992; Bradley & McNiven 2019; McNiven & Russell 2005; McNiven 2016; Urwin 2019; Wright, van der Kolk, & Dauareb community 2019). The quest for a decolonized practice of Indigenous archaeology that articulates with Indigenous viewpoints on research agendas, practices, interpretative frameworks, and communication protocols is one pursued by numerous archaeologists and Indigenous groups in Australia beyond Monash University, notably at Flinders University (e.g., Fowler, Roberts, McKinnon, O'Loughlin, & Graham 2014; Pollard et al. 2020; Roberts et al. 2005; Smith & Wobst 2005; Smith et al. 2019) and the University of Western Australia (e.g., Moro Abadia & Porr 2021; Porr 2018). Despite these achievements, opportunities, and will, archaeologists with Indigenous heritage remain under-represented in universities both in Australia and New Guinea. It is in this context that the voice of Christopher Wilson of the Ngarrindjeri Nation of South Australia at Flinders University, for example, is important (see Chapter 5: Smith, Brady, & Wilson).

Indigenous archaeologies have provided opportunities for archaeologists to engage in innovative ways with various forms of 'tangible' (material records) and 'intangible' (non-material forms, such as oral traditions, dances, songs, etc.) cultural heritage that better express Indigenous views, interests, and aspirations. Research into 'oral histories' and traditions, often presented in Aboriginal ways as 'story' that prioritize not just a linear past but embedded perspectives and the richness of experience in which they are located, including how they are expressed in both archaeological and environmental records, is producing new insights into the potential temporal depth of Indigenous knowledge that challenge the epistemological authority of archaeology as the only tool to access the deep past and as the only way of understanding the past. Two high-profile examples are the many oral traditions that may be linked to postglacial sea-level rise at least 7000 years ago (Nunn & Reid 2016), and a Gunditjmara story from western Victoria that is thought to relate to the eruption of Budj Bim (volcano) dated by geologists to 37,000 years ago (Matchan, Phillips, Jourdan, & Oostingh 2020). For most non-Indigenous researchers, the potential time depth of Indigenous oral traditions measured in many thousands of years seems inconceivable, especially when most Westerners would have trouble recounting the names of their own great-grandparents. Yet orality has its own methods and epistemologies, where memories often rely on ritualized narratives and landscape mnemonics. As has been said many times before (e.g., Kelly 2016), for most Indigenous peoples without traditions of writing, (hi)story is less about when and more about where. Yet care is needed when archaeologists attempt to 'interpret', 'decode', and 'translate' what are seen as metaphorical and symbolic dimensions of oral traditions into the so-called realist perspectives of Western science, as if archaeology had a superior standpoint from which to view the world. The challenge for archaeology is to ensure that the cultural integrity of oral traditions is not diminished (colonized) by ontologically chauvinistic acts of scientific judgement and reinscription (Chapter 6: Davidson et al.). At the same time, the challenge for Indigenous communities is to decide on what types of archaeological research (processes and results) are to be entered into, with respectful cross-cultural methodologies and multiple perspectives in mind. While deep-time oral traditions may capture the limelight, for many Indigenous communities it is archaeo-logical explorations of material expressions of oral histories and traditions relating to re-cent times and events that often have high social and cultural relevance and significance and that are thus often sought for (e.g., Ash, Manas, & Bosun 2010; David et al. 2004, 2012; Harrison 2004; McNiven 2016: 32–33; Roberts et al. 2016).

Recent years have seen archaeologists increasingly turn to old excavation assemblages in museums for reanalysis, although in Australia such reanalyses have been going on since at least the early 1980s (e.g., Cundy 1990; Smith 1982). Interest in these legacy collections reflects a combination of financial considerations (undertaking new excavations is expensive and time-consuming), advances in archaeological analyt-ical techniques, and the failure to analyse excavated assemblages long accumulated in museum and university stores and, dare we say, private garages. Such reanalyses have often shed considerable new insights (e.g., for Kenniff Cave, central Queensland, see Richardson 1992). In some cases, the time difference between the old and new analyses is only a few decades, such as with midden assemblages excavated by McNiven (1990) for his PhD thesis that were reanalysed and reinterpreted by Smith (2016) for her PhD thesis (see Smith & McNiven 2019). In other situations, reanalysis and reinterpreta-tion of legacy collections has called for the reexcavation of sites in partnership with local Indigenous communities, employing fine-grained excavations and new dating techniques, along with new interpretative frameworks informed by local Indigenous perspectives (e.g., for Cloggs Cave in GunaiKurnai Country in eastern Victoria, see David et al. 2021; Flood 1974, 1980).

Legacy collections in museums include more than excavated assemblages from archae-ological sites. The majority of Indigenous archaeological objects in Australian museums are surface-collected stone artefacts. Poor geographical provenance for many of these is a hindrance to traditional archaeological analyses. However, in some cases, provenance is specific enough to allow broad-scale regional analyses of artefact distributions, such as in McBryde's (1978, 1984, 1986) classic sourcing of Victorian stone axes and reconstructions of exchange networks. Irrespective of provenance details, and for better or for worse, these collections are the legacy of the formative years of Australian archaeology, and their poor provenance and biases towards particular types of objects are intrinsic sources of historical information on paradigms of the time. More importantly, these collections are the cultural heritage of Indigenous communities, providing new research challenges to assist communities in reinterpreting, recontextualizing, reinscribing, reassembling, and reconnecting with their collections (see Chapter 7: Allen).

II. Colonizing Sahul

Many First Nations Australians reject archaeological understandings of their origins couched in terms of arrival, colonization, and temporal specificity, and instead identify strongly with the succinct statement that 'we have always been here' (Griffiths & Russell 2018: 43). Sometimes such a perspective can be at odds with an approach that posits an Aboriginal presence in Australia of c. 65,000 years. Yet Griffiths and Russell (2018: 43) point out that a number of Aboriginal people state that '65,000 years is forever'. Others have said 'that on arriving here some 65,000 years ago, their ancestors became Aboriginal, and therefore Aboriginal people have always been here' (Griffiths & Russell 2018: 43). Alternatively, archaeologist Mark Grist, of the Werigia, Wamba Wamba, and Nyeri Nyeri people of northwest Victoria, states: 'I believe that we all originated from early primates in Africa. Yes, I am a believer of evolutionary theory and yes, I am an Aboriginal man. Equally I believe that I come from a group of people that have always had a deep spiritual connection to this country we now call Australia. I am comfortable where I sit in the scheme of things. I think that it is far too easy for non-Aboriginal people to believe that all Aboriginal people think that they have always had their origins in Australia. I accept that hominids evolved out of Africa' (Dugay-Grist 2006: 372). The late Herman Mandui, Head of Archaeology at the Papua New Guinea National Museum, noted that 'In Papua New Guinea there are many different perspectives on "knowing the past"' but also acknowledged '50,000 years' worth of archaeological heritage' (Mandui 2006: xvi, 379–380). The challenge is not to embrace methods and perspectives of historicism where multiple viewpoints meet, but where they do not.

John Mulvaney's pioneering excavations at Kenniff Cave in central Queensland in the early 1960s represent the first unambiguously dated Pleistocene archaeological sequence in Australia (Mulvaney & Joyce 1965). Around the same time, Sue Bulmer published the first Pleistocene date for human occupation in Papua New Guinea (Bulmer 1964). Initially, Mulvaney's earliest date for Kenniff Cave was 12,900 ± 170 BP (Mulvaney 1962: 137), soon to be followed by an even earlier date of 16,130 ± 140 BP (Mulvaney 1964), and Bulmer's was 10,350 ± 140 BP for Kiowa rock shelter in the Eastern Highlands. Over the ensuing decades, early dates for Indigenous sites around Australia and New Guinea have been progressively pushed further and further back in time. Today, the earliest chronometrically dated archaeological sites in Sahul are c. 65,000 years old (Madjedbebe: Clarkson et al. 2017) in Australia and c. 43,000–49,000 cal BP (Ivane Valley: Summerhayes et al. 2010) in Papua New Guinea. Earliest dates for Aboriginal occupation have an inherent public appeal and continue to redefine the importance of Aboriginal people and culture in the nation's deep-time history and identity, but they have unfortunately also reignited the flames of racism in some quarters (Griffiths 2018; Griffiths & Russell 2018). At the same time, claims for earliest dates and great antiquity require close scientific scrutiny and analysis in the spirit of peer review, as much of this research is done at the cutting edge of technological know-how (O'Connell et al. 2018; Roberts et al. 1998; see later). One of the consequences of the ever-increasing antiquity for Indigenous occupation of Australia and New Guinea is that Sahul reveals some of the earliest evidence for modern humans out of Africa. Significantly, the cultural repertoire of the earliest peoples of Sahul not only repositions Sahul as a centre of cultural innovation but also helps redefine the cultural capacities of *Homo sapiens* as they left Africa (see Chapter 9: Clarkson et al.). One extraordinary area of early innovation is the construction of seagoing vessels and associated navigational and seascape knowledge that ferried the earliest colonists from Southeast Asia to the Sahul landmass (see Chapter 8: Norman, O'Connor, & Bird). The cultural flexibility and adaptability of the colonizing peoples of Sahul is demonstrated by the wide range of environments they successfully moved into (from coasts to mountains from the tropical north to the temperate south). One persistent question, however, is how the earliest occupants of Sahul interacted with the megafauna then present. Despite the persistent lack of reliable archaeological evidence for interactions between people and megafauna across Sahul, a range of views exist among palaeozoologists on the role people played in megafaunal extinctions (see Chapter 10: Johnson, Dortch, & Worthy). While ancient DNA has the potential to shed novel insights into the degree of isolation and longevity of megafaunal populations across different parts of the continent, and thus new insights into the extinction debate, it is modern and ancient human DNA studies and what they can tell us about the origins and spread of people across Australia and New Guinea that the most profound insights may lie in the near future (see Chapter 11: Matisoo-Smith & Gosling).

III. Constructed Landscapes and Waterscapes

All peoples, past and present, live *in* environments, not *off* environments. Separating people from their environments represents a distinct dualist viewpoint that emanates from the Enlightenment and that underpins much (but not all) modern scientific reasoning (note, however, that much continental philosophical thinking, including most phenomenological philosophy since Heidegger and some of his predecessors, goes beyond such dualisms). Yet people inhabit landscapes of their own making. Dwelling and inhabitation is an ongoing process of embedded presencing in place; archaeologically and through related disciplines (geomorphology, palaeoecology, etc.), dimensions of such cultural presencing can be investigated by studying the ways that environments, and places generally, have been modified (e.g., David & Thomas 2008; Ingold 1993; McNiven 2018a; Thomas 1996). Here the culture/nature duality breaks down as a dominant Cartesian perspective of an external environment (consisting of non-scient 'objects' in contradistinction from meaning-making 'subjects' with agency) that is under this formulation subjectively perceived but not agential, fails to capture the world and lived experience of many Indigenous (and non-Indigenous) peoples both in Australia and New Guinea and beyond (see e.g., Descola 2013). For many Indigenous peoples, and for whole philosophical schools within even dominant Western traditions, the environment has no prediscursive reality or reality beyond culture. As such, to understand culture is to understand place as a lived condition.

Until recently, most regionally focused PhDs in Australian archaeology routinely included a chapter on 'environmental background'. Such seemingly obligatory chapters often reflected developments in processual archaeology, where the structural complexity of cultural systems and cultural change were adaptively linked to 'natural' environmental diversity and change. In some cases, vegetation patterns and associated plant and animal resources were thought or understood to have been altered by Aboriginal landscape firing practices, introduced to the national lexicon by Australian archaeologist Rhys Jones (1969) with the alluring label of 'fire-stick farming'. Jones (1969: 224) pointed out (in the gendered language of the day) that it was a myth to see Aboriginal peoples 'like most other hunters and gatherers the world over, as passive slaves of the environment, in contrast to the impact of agricultural or industrial man, who is seen as the master of nature, the initiator of ecological change'. Through deliberate landscape burning, Aboriginal Australians 'may have increased his food supply and thus probably his population' (Jones 1969: 227). It is now clear that Aboriginal peoples across the Australian continent employed a wide range of practices to strategically and deliberately increase animal habitats (niche construction), including to artificially enhance food supplies (see Chapter 12: McNiven, Manne, & Ross; see also Sutton & Walshe 2021). But as First Nations peoples keep on reminding us, landscape management is also more than this (as also recognized by Jones in his 'fire-stick farming'), incorporating Aboriginal notions of keeping Country healthy by 'cleaning' the ground of leaf and thick grass cover that form dense habitats for snakes and thus inhibit safe travel across Country, for example. Across New Guinea, animal food supplies increased in many regions with the introduction of pigs and chickens during the Late Holocene. Although no archaeological evidence is available to indicate that Aboriginal peoples introduced new domestic animals for food into Australia, it is becoming increasingly clear that the introduction of the dog (dingo) around 3500 years ago had major social, cultural, and environmental consequences for Aboriginal peoples of mainland Australia (see Chapter 13: Balme & O'Connor).

Palynologists have been looking for potential evidence of the impacts of Aboriginal burning practices on vegetation changes well into the Late Pleistocene ever since Peter Kershaw (1974) identified possible anthropogenic burning at 38,000 years ago in north Queensland (e.g., see Clark 1983; individual chapters in David, Haberle, & Walker 2012). Yet separating out the impacts of Aboriginal burning practices from natural fires and climate drivers remains challenging in paleoenvironmental studies (see Chapter 14: Rowe, Stevenson, Connor, & Adeleye). At the same time, that the scale and complexity of Aboriginal burning practices has transformed Australian environments over tens of thousands of years has generated considerable public interest, debate, hundreds if not thousands of academic and popular articles, and award-winning books (e.g., Gammage 2012; Pascoe 2014).

In many ways, it was archaeologist Harry Lourandos in his 1980 PhD thesis 'Forces of Change: Aboriginal Technology and Population in South Western Victoria' from the University of Sydney who most influentially broke through the paradigm of environmental determinism in Australian archaeology. Lourandos (1980a, 1980b) argued on both theoretical and empirical grounds that archaeologically observable Late Holocene changes in so-called hunter-gatherer societies signal not only social and environmental factors, but that environments can also be modified by people. As such, people adapt to environments that are often the products of cultural modification.

Lourandos studied ethnographic accounts and archaeological sites and land and waterscapes of Aboriginal societies in southwest Victoria to illustrate how people and their landscapes mutually constitute each other. He drew on the 1840s ethnographic accounts of George Augustus Robinson, Chief Protector of Aborigines for the Port Phillip District. Robinson recorded freshwater fishing facilities, focused on eels, that ranged from small brush weirs across streams through to extensive systems of excavated trenches that in some cases stretch for kilometres in length (see McNiven & Bell 2010). An iconic example of the specialized eeling trenches that Robinson documented is the Toolondo site, where Lourandos (1980a, 1980b) recorded a 3 km-long channel system that connected Budgeongutte Swamp (within the natural range of eels) to Clear Swamp (further to the northwest and outside the natural range of eels) (Figure 1.2). According to Lourandos (1980b: 254), the 'size and construction of these drains points to their operation as more than mere eel harvesting devices'. In a series of thought-provoking and archaeologically revolutionary articles, Lourandos argued that the engineered, hydrologic

FIGURE 1.2. Section of a 3 km-long channel excavated by Aboriginal people to allow water and eels to extend from Budgeongutte Swamp to enter Clear Swamp (background) at Toolondo, southwest Victoria. Archaeological excavation trench (Pit T II) by Harry Lourandos in February 1976.

(Courtesy of Barengi Gadjin Land Council Aboriginal Corporation. Photograph: Harry Lourandos.)

gradient-sensitive channel systems at Toolondo operated as 'artificial water controls, the drainage systems operated as a form of swamp management, coping with excess water during floods and retaining water in times of drought. This would have served to counteract the effect of variations in water availability on the distribution, and therefore the availability, of eels in these marginal areas of their range. An extension of eel range, by providing access to further inland swamps and waterways, would have led to an increase in the annual production of eels' (Lourandos 1980b: 254). These engineered, landscape-scale fishing systems have since been described by Heather Builth (2002, 2014) as 'aquaculture'.

Hydrological engineering and fishing facilities of southwest Victoria also include stone-walled structures and excavated channels that have been dated back to c. 6600 cal BP (McNiven et al. 2012, 2015; see also Builth 2014; Coutts, Frank, & Hughes 1978). In addition to profound ecological knowledge and engagements, and monumental-scale social inscriptions of Country across generations (with implications for signalling ancestral-descendant connections in place), the scale of these facilities also implies high investments in cooperative labour. Lourandos (1980b) emphasized the social dimensions of these earthen and stone fishing facilities, and how the artificially increased availability of fish (especially eels) underwrote higher population densities and increased 'social complexity' and ecologies, expressed in large-scale interregional sociopolitical and ceremonial gatherings amidst the growing material installations that are also social markers. The sociality of small- and large-scale fishing facilities similarly apply in freshwater and marine contexts, such as with tidal fish-trapping complexes (see Chapter 15: McNiven & Lambrides).

The sociality of engineered fishing facilities sits within the broader topic of hydrological engineering, which in New Guinea encompasses large-scale networks of ditches associated with agricultural field systems. As is well known, the highlands of New Guinea was a centre of agricultural innovation in the Early Holocene (Denham 2018; Golson 1977). However, the modification of swamp systems to manage and control water by engineering kilometres of excavated ditch systems signalled much more than hydrologic skills and labour investments. In many cases, such as among the Huli of the Southern Highlands, extensive systems of elaborate ditches are the cumulative result of multiple named generations of labour and social investments through which people cosmologically and physically marked the land, managed access to places and resources, and fostered territorial relations (e.g., Ballard 1995). As the inherited landscapes of their ancestors, Huli ditch systems express 'multiple and layered' social, historical, symbolic, and cosmological dimensions that challenge archaeologists to explore the 'fluid ontologies' and associated rituals and symbolism of wetlands and waterscapes (see Chapter 16: Ballard).

Since the first decade of the twenty-first century, revolutionary insights into the scale and complexity of Aboriginal stone structures have extended beyond fishing facilities to engineered and modified rock shelters. In some cases, small rock shelters have revealed the addition of stone walls that doubled as both extra new habitats and traps for targeted animal (food) species (e.g., Wallis & Matthews 2016). Such engineering is now known to extend back into the Pleistocene, and in some cases to have included the transport and removal of tonnes of rock to increase the available space within rock shelters (Chapter 17: David et al.). For decades, such radical processes of architectural engineering have been hiding in plain sight to archaeologists, and have only become apparent through a paradigm change, and the new subdiscipline of archaeomorphology that came with it (e.g., Delannoy et al. 2013).

IV. Long-Term Chronological Trends and Cultural Change

Lourandos's (1980b) reconceptualization of Aboriginal relations as recursive and mutually transformative had major implications for the ways Australian archaeologists explored and explained long-term cultural change. Prior to Lourandos, Australian archaeology was dominated by environmentally deterministic approaches whereby archaeologically observable cultural change was usually tied closely and causally to environmental change (but see, e.g., Bowdler 1976). While in many respects such adaptationist interpretations remain dominant, in the 1980s and 1990s Lourandos precipitated a paradigmatic shift and fostered a new generation of archaeologists in the wake of what became known as the 'Great Intensification Debate' (see chapters in David, Barker, & McNiven 2006; Lourandos 1983; Lourandos & Ross 1994). Lourandos used anthropologically informed theory to argue that long-term cultural changes within so-called hunter-gatherer societies were not always responses to environmental change, but also to internal socio-demographic dynamics (and hereby the normative distinction between 'hunter-gatherers' and 'agriculturalists' was questioned). Critical to this new approach to Australian archaeology was the idea that sociodemographic changes were not only a shared attribute of so-called hunter-gatherers and agricultural societies, but that such changes often encompassed strategic modifications of the environment. One of the important consequences of this shift in attitudes was a conceptual blurring of hunter-gatherers and agriculturalists; a blurring that increased the comparability of Australian and New Guinea societies (Lourandos 1997, 2008). Although attempts have been made to critique intensification as promoting teleological progress (i.e., cultural complexity culminating in the Late Holocene being explained by its functional outcomes rather than through the historical foundations and causes from which it came; see Bird & Frankel 1991) and continental homogenization (underplaying regional diversity; Ulm 2013), its critics have not sufficiently recognized that the intensification arguments had not argued for an absence of complexity in the more distant past, but rather that major transformations can be seen in the archaeological record and these required explanation beyond environmental adaptation. The relevance of key points made in the intensification arguments for the archaeology of Australia and New Guinea endures (Chapter 18: Lourandos & Ross).

Examination of the numerical occurrence of the close to a thousand then-published radiocarbon dates from archaeological sites for blocks of time was an analytical tool used by Lourandos (1983, 1993; David & Lourandos 1997; Lourandos & David 1998) as a proxy to chart long-term changes in the occupational intensity of regions through time. In these endeavours, the original source of every carbon date was individually related to its stratigraphic context and assessed for taphonomic reliability before incorporation into the database. This approach has since been elaborated in scale, comprehensiveness, and sophistication by Alan Williams and colleagues (2018) to model long-term trends in 'demography'. Although many long-term chronological trends in dates and occupational intensity have been tied plausibly to environmental changes linked to changes in resource availability and reliability, large increases in dates and occupational intensity in the Late Holocene are seen to 'decouple' from environmental change; this point was originally made by Lourandos (1980b) (Chapter 19: Williams, Ulm, & Smith). Significantly, sophisticated dates-as-data modelling by Williams and colleagues (2018) revealed significant increases in population at the end of the Pleistocene, which they relate to the well-known process of 'demographic packing' (cf. the 'concertina effect' of Hall 1999: 177) associated with a dramatic decrease (c. 20%) in the size of the Australian landmass resulting from postglacial sea-level rise, where 90% of the continental shelf was flooded between 15,000 and 8000 years ago (e.g., McNiven 1999: 165; Morwood 1987: 343). Such modelling raises questions of the nature of Aboriginal occupation of the continental shelf prior to its inundation, which is being pursued with tantalizing results and implications (Chapter 20: Benjamin & Ulm).

One area of archaeological research in Australia that has long frustrated attempts at understanding long-term changes in rock art are limitations in dating. Unlike buried occupation deposits, rock art panels have traditionally been difficult to date chronometrically. Rock art provides unique windows into the artistic world of peoples and their symbolic, social, and cosmological logic. As such, insights into the past based primarily on excavation of occupation deposits and analysis of portable materials such as stone artefacts and animal bones under-represent the social worlds of peoples of the past. Although rich rock art traditions are found across many parts of Australia and New Guinea, the Kimberley region of northern Western Australia contains one of the richest assemblages of rock art in the world. It has long been thought that degrees of weathering, stylistic differences, and superpositions indicate that Kimberley rock art extends from the ethnographic present back into the Late Pleistocene. An influential idea was developed in detail in Lewis's published BA Honours thesis (1983, 1988), that the formal similarities between the Gwion paintings of the Kimberley and Dynamic Figures of Arnhem Land indicate social interactions between the two regions. Since the intervening region is now covered by the drowned Joseph Bonaparte Gulf, the art was reasoned to date to a time prior to the postglacial inundation, and must therefore be Pleistocene in age. The later art (e.g., Wandjina in the Kimberley, X-ray in Arnhem Land) had become regionally distinctive, giving further credence to the chronological model of widespread preinundation cultural practices and postinundation regionalization. However, it has only been with major advances in dating techniques, and at the University of Melbourne the meticulous separation of organic components from datable mud-wasp nests beneath and over the art (e.g., Finch et al. 2020), that the art's Late Pleistocene antiquity was conclusively shown (Chapter 21: Green, Finch, Gleadow, Fulop, & Jacobs).

V. Cultural Dynamics and Networks

Despite the continental scale of Australia and New Guinea and the ethnographic recording of over 1000 language groups for both areas, small-scale and large-scale social networks directly and indirectly connected groups across hundreds and in some cases thousands of kilometres (e.g., Hughes 1977; Mulvaney 1976; Pétrequin & Pétrequin 2006; Skelly & David 2017). All of these networks helped maintain and control complex sociopolitical and ceremonial relations often cemented through material exchanges and trade. The social entanglements associated with the movement of objects is illustrated by one set of gift exchange objects that formally passed through the hands of 134 individuals over a distance of less than 300 km in the Ports Keats region of the Northern Territory in the 1950s (Falkenberg 1962: 152–157).

In a classic paper, McCarthy (1939: Map 16) synthesized a wide range of ethnographic information to map out what he termed 'trunk trade routes' that not only criss-crossed the Australian continent but extended northwards into New Guinea via Torres Strait and into the islands of Southeast Asia through Makassan trepangers (see also Mulvaney 1976). His best-known trade route map plotted the trans-continental movement of tropical pearl (*Pinctada* sp.) and baler (*Melo* sp.) shell body adornments, with examples known to have travelled 2000 km from northwest Australia to the South Australian coastline (McCarthy 1939: Map 14; see also Akerman & Stanton 1994). Baler shell trade and sea crossings also connected south-central New Guinea with Cape York Peninsula via Torres Strait (e.g., Lawrence 1994). Such maritime trade was part of major interactions and the sharing of objects and ideas between north Queensland and New Guinea that have recently been conceptualized as the Coral Sea Cultural Interaction Sphere (Chapter 22: McNiven; McNiven 2022).

The interregional congregations reported from the nineteenth and twentieth centuries brought to the fore an understanding that it was not only material goods that were exchanged but also ideas. Widely distributed object types thus do not necessarily indicate object exchange, for technological know-how and stylistic preferences could also move with the times: contiguous groups may transmit knowledge that enabled their neighbours to then make their own examples (e.g., Mulvaney 1976; Paton 1994; Williams 1977). The large-scale proliferation of small, intricately flaked backed artefacts (including 'geometric microliths') across much of mainland Australia, especially between c. 4000 and 1000 cal BP, reveals information exchange and social inclusiveness by multiple neighbouring communities through shared technologies and possession and use of a mutually recognizable object form that was put to multiple purposes (Hiscock 2021; McNiven 2011; Robertson, Attenbrow, & Hiscock 2009). Across many parts of New Guinea, especially the highlands, a proliferation in the manufacture and use of distinctively shaped stone mortars and pestles during the Mid-Holocene again expresses, at least in part, social connectivities (Chapter 23: Swadling).

Chronological and spatial changes in the movement of objects and ideas map out the changing history of social, political, and religious networks and relationships. Marine shell beads excavated from 30,000-year-old levels of the Riwi rock shelter in northern Western Australia indicate geographical ties with the now-submerged Pleistocene coastline some 500 km away (Balme & Morse 2006). At Matenbek rock shelter in New Ireland, off the northeast coast of New Guinea, 18,000–20,000-year-old obsidian artefacts have been sourced to outcrops located 350 km away in New Britain (Summerhayes 2009). However, most archaeological evidence for interregional exchanges and the movement of objects dates to the past 5000 years. For example, although ground-edge axes were an innovation in northern Australia at least 60,000 years ago (Clarkson et al. 2017), the large-scale movement of axes (over 1000 km in some cases) as part of exchange networks across many parts of Australia and New Guinea is restricted to the Late Holocene (Chapter 24: Ford & Hiscock). The incorporation of symbolically loaded, 'valuable and socially prestigious' flaked stone points within expanding exchange systems across northern Australia during the Mid- to Late Holocene has been argued to represent a social change towards increasing 'interconnectedness' that may also have been a socioeconomic strategy to decrease foraging risk associated with environmental fluctuations and unpredictability (Chapter 25: Maloney). In Papua New Guinea, rich ethnographies on marine shell valuables that were carried inland along river valleys up into the highlands, and transported in canoes across archipelagos and along hundreds of kilometres of coastline, document historically contingent endpoints of changes in craft specialization and symbolic meaning and value over hundreds and in some cases thousands of years (Chapter 26: Szabó).

The mapping of rock art style provinces provides another archaeological approach to documenting and understanding long-term changes in the distribution and sharing of object forms and motifs (e.g., see the Kimberley–Arnhem Land example cited earlier). Ethnographic observations reveal that spatial continuities and discontinuities in rock art styles may express a wide range of social, political, cosmological, and ritual domains that can be difficult to disentangle when approached archaeologically. What is clear is that the past 3000 years witnessed an efflorescence of stylistic diversity in rock art across Australia linked to regional developments in corporate group identity and territorial and ritual/religious place-marking and place-making strategies that helped demarcate social differences and similarities at a range of geographical scales (David 2002; David & Wilson 2002). New ethnographic readings of the role of boundaries in Aboriginal societies reveal that the spatial distribution of rock art motifs may be 'relational and multilayered' and 'overlapping and intersecting in the landscape', facilitating social differentiation and interaction in the process (Chapter 27: Kelly & Brady). Understanding the complexities of social boundaries and interactions is further enhanced when spatial analyses of rock art motifs are combined with characterization and sourcing of rock art pigments (Chapter 28: Huntley). The analytical potential of such integrated investigations to explain spatial patterning of rock art across New Guinea and its offshore islands is only beginning to be realized (e.g., Tsang et al. 2022; see also Lamb et al. 2021; Specht et al. 2021).

VI. Specialized Societies

The Indigenous cultures of Australia and New Guinea are diverse, ranging from those of the sandy deserts of Central Australia (where population densities are as low as one person per 90 km^2), to the maritime peoples of Torres Strait (island population densities of up to 200 people per km^2), to the highland valley societies of New Guinea (population densities of up to 175 people per km^2) (Brown 1978: 102; Meggitt 1962: 32; Mullins 1992: Table 2). The highest population densities appear to occur in areas where subsistence combines foraged and hunted marine animals with agricultural crops. The issue of population densities and food availability is complicated also by artificial enhancement of resources and their habitats, as practiced to varying degrees by all Indigenous societies across Australia and New Guinea (e.g., Beaton 1982; Gott 1982; Hallam 1975; Hynes & Chase 1982).

One way of exploring this diversity is through the characteristics of the major habitats in which people dwell. Here we have identified four broad but highly specialized environmental zones that feature across Australia and New Guinea: coasts and offshore islands; highlands; large, low-lying rivers and their deltas; and deserts (see also Keen 2004; Peterson 1976). Coastal and even more so island societies are the most recent to have developed given that current coastlines (totalling some 60,000 km for Australia) formed around 7000–8000 years ago with the flooding of the continental shelf and end of the postglacial sea-level rise. Yet since the end of this major phase of marine transgression, sea levels and marine environments and associated ecosystems continued to fluctuate, creating dynamic archaeological records documenting myriad responses to the changing conditions. Over the past half century, most coastal archaeological research has taken place across the northern half of Australia, with specialist maritime societies ('Saltwater peoples') limited to far northern Australia (Hall & McNiven 1999; McDonald 2015; McNiven 2004; Sharp 2002; Ulm 2011). In some situations, where the continental shelf is narrow, and Pleistocene coastlines are near modern coastlines, Australia and New Guinea have produced some of the earliest evidence in the world of the modern human use of marine resources (e.g., Gosden & Robertson 1991; Veth et al. 2017). As expected given taphonomic issues relating to land and seascape dynamics, most coastal midden sites date to the Late Holocene (but see, e.g., Richards 2012), which furnish rich assemblages of cultural materials that have generated considerable debate on cultural change and marine specialization in Australia and Papua New Guinea (Chapter 29: Rowland, Shaw, & Ulm). This period also saw the emergence of the Lapita Cultural Complex in northeast Papua New Guinea, whose impacts on the colonization of the islands of the western Pacific is well known but connections and influences along the south coast of New Guinea and in north Queensland are only beginning to be revealed (e.g., David et al. 2011; Kirch 1997; McNiven et al. 2011; Skelly & David 2017; see also Chapter 22: McNiven). Post-Lapita developments along the south coast of Papua New Guinea are critical to understanding the emergence of highly specialized river delta and swamp societies within the past 1000 years (e.g., Barker et al. 2012; see Chapter 30: Urwin, Rhoads, & Bell).

Mountainous regions of Australia are concentrated along the eastern margin (Great Dividing Range) and through the centre of New Guinea (Central Ranges). The New Guinea highlands are more elevated than the Australian highlands, with highest peaks at Puncak Jaya in Indonesian Papua/West Papua (4884 m above sea level [a.s.l.]) and Mount Kosciuszko in New South Wales (2228 m a.s.l). Glaciers are found in mountainous Indonesian Papua/West Papua, but not in Papua New Guinea or mainland Australia and its nearby islands. In contrast to Australia, during the early colonial period, mountain regions of New Guinea were heavily populated with over one million people, a fact only realized by the outside world in the twentieth century (Brown 1978; Gammage 1998). Whereas numerous detailed ethnographies have documented New Guinea highland societies, ethnographic records on Aboriginal peoples of the Australian High Country are meagre due to its proximity to the early phase of colonial invasion, before the development of anthropology. The Papua New Guinea highlands have also revealed the earliest evidence for people in New Guinea, with stone artefacts and charred plant foods in the Ivane Valley at c. 2000 m a.s.l. dated to 43,000–49,000 cal BP (Summerhayes et al. 2010). However, the focus of archaeological attention in the highlands of Papua New Guinea has been intensive agricultural systems, with the region now recognized as one of a small group of locations in the world for the independent development of plant domestication and agriculture (e.g., Denham 2018; Golson 1977; Golson et al. 2017). Yet agricultural developments over the past 10,000 years had a complex and 'patchy' history of elaboration through time, including introduction of pigs (of Southeast Asian origin and used ethnographically in prestige ceremonial displays, ritual exchanges, competitive cycles, and wealth accumulation; see e.g. Rappaport 1968) within the past c. 2000 years and sweet potato (of South American origin) within the past 500 years (Chapter 31: Gaffney & Denham).

Although little archaeological research has occurred across the High County and alpine regions of southeastern Australia compared to the New Guinea highlands, available excavation evidence hints at intensified use by Aboriginal groups during the Late Holocene following initial and transitory use of elevated areas and foothills in the Late Pleistocene. And just as connections between coastal and mountainous regions via river valley corridors in New Guinea involved the elaboration of exchange systems in the Late Holocene (e.g., coastal movement of inland stone axes and inland movement of marine shells), in the southeastern highlands of Australia, the Late Holocene saw an intensification of connections with the coast taking place through ceremonial gatherings that ritually celebrated and expressed the special spiritual and cosmological significance of the High Country (see Chapter 32: Fresløv & Mullett). Although currently the occupation of alpine and subalpine mainland Australia is only archaeologically known from the Mid- to Late Holocene, longer sequences from southwest Tasmania show that here alpine environments were used seasonally during the Late Pleistocene (Allen 1996; Cosgrove, Allen, & Marshall 1990).

Riverine and desert zones and associated societies reveal how seasonal variations in the availability of water can dramatically contribute to the structure of social and cultural practices. The largest river system in Australia is the Murray River (2508 km) and its major tributary the Darling River (1472 km) in the southeast of the continent. In Papua New Guinea, the two major waterways are the Sepik River (1146 km), and the Fly River (1060 km) and its major tributary the Strickland River (824 km), with headwaters on the northern and southern sides of the Central Ranges, respectively. The density of people and social groups is much greater along the Sepik River compared to the Fly-Strickland Rivers (Lutkehaus et al. 1990; Swadling 1983). Most of the Sepik River has seen little or no archaeological research, and almost the entire length of the Fly-Strickland River system is an archaeological blank slate (Swadling 1983, 1990, 1997). In marked contrast, the Murray-Darling River system has seen extensive archaeological research, and this includes the Willandra Lakes World Heritage Area that contains the renown 40,000-year-old Lake Mungo burials (including the world's oldest-known cremation). Significantly, most published archaeological research on the Murray-Darling River system concerns human remains which are abundant in the many large pre-European contact Aboriginal cemeteries found along the lower and middle sections of the Murray River. The high number of cemeteries and complex mortuary practices were expressions of corporate group identity and land ownership by the large number of people and cultural groups that lived along the Murray River corridor (Pardoe 1988). The cluster of burials at Kow Swamp in northern central Victoria date to at least c. 15,000–10,000 cal BP and represent the world's oldest known cemetery (Macumber 1977; Stone & Cupper 2003). Bioarcheological analysis of human remains reveals that Murray River populations of the Mid- to Late Holocene were characterized by extensive relatedness and gene flow, and regional variability in pathologies and diet (Chapter 33: Littleton, Karstens, & Allen).

Deserts are a feature of Australia but not New Guinea. Australia's deserts are dry arid environments that cover 35% of the continent, with characteristic hot days and cold nights. Despite the seeming harshness of Australia's deserts, Aboriginal peoples thrived through deep ecological knowledge supported by myriad technologies and social networking strategies (e.g., Yengoyan 1976) that included the development of multifunctional tools and symbolic landscapes expressed through songlines, ceremonies, and diverse rock art styles. Such knowledge extended to the management and manipulation of environments by complex mosaic firing practices that increased biodiversity and food production (e.g., Bliege Bird, Bird, Codding, Parker, & Jones 2008). Sparse archaeological knowledge combined with Euro-centric misunderstandings of the capacity of Australian deserts to support viable communities underpinned early thinking of a recency of desert occupation by Aboriginal people (Gould 1977). However, improved desert archaeological and palaeoenvironmental records combined with new sophisticated and anthropologically nuanced understandings of desert strategies inform a new dynamic model for the settlement of some Australian deserts by c. 60,000 years ago (Chapter 34: Veth, McDonald, & Hiscock).

VII. Ceremonies and Rituals

Archaeologies of Australia and New Guinea have until recently been largely dominated by environmental paradigms that focus attention on settlement and subsistence patterns. Although such a focus is in keeping with international trends in 'prehistory', it clashes with the rich ethnographies of Australia and New Guinea, where the complex and elaborate ceremonial and ritual lives of peoples is documented, sometimes in great detail (e.g., Dussart 1989; Haddon 1935; Rappaport 1968; Taylor 1996; Thomson 1949). In the late nineteenth century, when antiquarian archaeologies of Aboriginal Australia were tied closely to ethnographic encounters, knowledge, and curiosities, research interest extended to ritual rock shelter sites in Victoria (Chapter 2: McNiven), an interest only recently reinvigorated in southeastern Australia (e.g., Clark 2007; David et al. 2021). Rock art similarly caught the antiquarian's eye in Australia, although it was at first linked less to ethnographic observations and more to social evolutionary, racial migration theories (McNiven & Russell 1997). Somewhat ironically, Baldwin Spencer and Frank Gillen's (1899) classic ethnography of the Arrernte of Central Australia included descriptions of rock art sites associated with increase/maintenance ceremonies that had little immediate impact on Australian archaeology but was famously analogically (mis) used by Salomon Reinach (1903) to construct a magico-religious interpretation of the newly discovered Upper Palaeolithic cave art of France and Spain (Palacio-Pérez 2010).

The extraordinary cultural diversity of Australia and New Guinea known from ethnography and directly from Indigenous peoples is expressed also in the wide range of ceremonies and rituals undertaken by all groups. These ceremonies and rituals relate to all aspects of life and the universe and have varying social, political, moral, spiritual, and cosmological significance. Ceremonies and rituals are central to the reproduction of life and continuity of spiritual forces that orchestrate the world, as well as structuring and connecting people and things within and between cultural groups. Across Australia and New Guinea, many rituals focus on ensuring the continuity of spiritual forces that structure and support life, such as through food resources, water, and the elements. Within the Australian context, many ceremonies and rituals are known ethnographically to be part of clan-based responsibilities to maintain cosmological forces and associated spiritual and ancestral beings of the Dreaming, and all relate to Law, the rules of life passed down from the originary creative beings. These cosmological and creative forces and beings are known through Dreaming narratives, and they can involve varying degrees of secrecy progressively revealed through life and following appropriate kin relationships. They are often led by highly initiated and knowledgeable religious experts in specific parts of the landscape ('sites'). Those sites serve as the focal points of sacred and often secret ceremonies and rituals of renewal and growth.

The richness of ethnographic records for Australia and New Guinea present archaeologists with extraordinary opportunities to understand not only the potential materiality of ceremonies and rituals but also their long-term history and emergence. Indeed, it is the materiality of these practices that provides archaeologists with an opportunity to understand the chronological depth of associated ceremonies and rituals from which to model historical emergence (David 2002, 2006). Beyond rock art, archaeologists in Australia and New Guinea have tended not to take up these opportunities due to a disciplinary focus on subsistence and technology and environmental adaptations. However, a few archaeologists, mostly with strong backgrounds in social anthropology, have explored these opportunities to historicize material expressions of the Dreaming (including but not limited to rock art sites) and hunting rituals.

Most archaeological research on understanding the material and historical dimensions and expressions of the Dreaming in Australia has focused on rock art sites. Critically, these studies do not impose a Western chronology on the Dreaming (which is considered timeless and eternal in Aboriginal ontologies), but are rather concerned with investigating the emergence of archaeologically recognizable forms of ethnographic Dreaming practices. For example, David, McNiven, Attenbrow, Flood, and Collins (1994) documented post-European contact elaborations of rock art representations of Dreaming beings by the Wardaman of the Northern Territory as an assertion of land ownership in response to colonial invasion (see also Kelly & Wardaman Indigenous Protected Area 2021). In north Queensland, David and Wilson (1999) argued that the near absence of occupational materials within sites on the top of Ngarrabullgan (Mt Mulligan) by Djungan people over the past 600 years provides an age for inception of avoidance practices associated with recognition of the presence of dangerous spirit beings or 'devils' known in Dreaming narratives. Within the arid zone, considerable archaeological attention has been given to dating and historicizing human expressions of the Dreaming, with analysis of Dreaming-associated sites and materials (e.g., ceremonial gatherings, rock art, stone arrangements, and ochre) consistently revealing Late Holocene ages (see Chapter 35: Smith). Is an archaeology that does not incorporate what is most meaningful to the community truly an appropriate way of depicting and historicizing a people in a postcolonial world? Those story places by definition have narratives, and those narratives connect people with each other, with places, and have chronologies that are in effect life stories with ongoing meaningfulness today and into the future. They give sense and structure to the lived world, and therefore they also give structure to social actions and to their resulting archaeological records. Investigating place through archaeology is thus a means to investigate not simply human actions as adaptations, but more poignantly how the world is rendered intelligible in social relations, cultural knowledge, and meaning. It gives rise to the possibility of an archaeology of places that hold special significance to local Indigenous communities, places that may be marked by more or less outstanding features without necessarily holding *occupational* deposits, what has elsewhere been called an 'archaeology of natural places' (Bradley 2000) that are really cultural. This is an exciting avenue for the future of archaeology in Australia and New Guinea, especially given the richness of oral traditions that relate to people and place, and that relate people to place as Country.

Ritual modification of rock art is another expression of human engagement with agentive and animate worlds that in some cases relates to Dreaming narratives and forces of renewal. Archaeological research on processes of ritual modification creates new understandings of the dynamic and agentive ontological status of rock art beyond concerns with dating and stylistic historicism. Although archaeologists generally acknowledge that most, if not all, rock art production is a ritual act, there is often a confusion between its role in 'ritual' (in the sense of repeated, socially circumscribed behaviour) and 'religious ritual' (in the sense that it engages with broader cosmological understandings of the way the world operates, and that often assumes social ceremonies). There has also been a focus on the timing of the creation of rock art motifs, at the expense of postproduction engagements with rock art, including with preexisting motifs and places. Physical modification of rock art motifs through the performative and repetitive actions of superimposition, remarking, retouching, repainting, and recarving represent material expressions of such engagements and ritualization amenable to archaeological enquiry (see Chapter 36: Brady, Gunn, & Goldhahn).

In Australia, archaeologies of ritual have also investigated the ontological status of people and animals and people-animal dualities through rock art and hunting practices. Key to this approach has been a recognition that a Western ontological separation of people and animals is a product of Enlightenment philosophy that is not recognized in Indigenous ontologies (Descola 2013). Anthropological research has long revealed that Aboriginal and New Guinean ontologies are founded on the corporeal and metaphysical dimensions of people and animals as potentially and situationally blurred, permeable, mutable, and even transformable (as in the influential concepts of 'metamorphosis' and 'coming into being' in Australian anthropology, for example). Sentience, agency, morality, and sociality can be as much features of animals and spirit-beings as of people in Australian and New Guinean worldviews, and beings of animal form can signify human qualities, and vice versa. Approaching rock art through local Aboriginal or New Guinea ontological perspectives provides opportunities to see with 'new' (for the archaeologist) interpretative eyes, a particularly important approach due to the rapprochement and greater relevance that this implies between the time of its creation and ontologically descendent interpretation.

Torres Strait Islanders of northeast Australia have strong traditions of hunting dugongs and marine turtles. These totemic animals are infused with ritual and spiritual significance, and it is thus of no surprise to find that the hunting and consumption of dugongs and turtles is imbued with embedded social protocols and meaning. Rituals of dugong and turtle hunting are known ethnographically from numerous Indigenous coastal communities of northern Australia and New Guinea (e.g., Bradley 1991; Haddon 1935; Landtman 1927; Thomson 1934). Despite this pervasiveness, the archaeological exploration of dugong and, to a lesser extent, turtle hunting rituals has largely focused on Torres Strait. Much of this focus stems from the remarkable materiality of dugong-hunting rituals, especially in the form of large mounded structures of arranged dugong bones dating to the past c. 800 years (e.g., David et al. 2009; McNiven & Bedingfield 2008; McNiven & Feldman 2003; Skelly et al. 2011; Wright et al. 2021). Amongst the dense bone assemblages are ear bones (locally referred to as 'radar' bones by some Torres Strait Islanders today) extracted from skulls that were used to communicate with and draw dugongs and hunters together, to bring hunting success (e.g., McNiven 2010). Much scope exists to extend such archaeological understandings to shrines associated with turtle hunting and increase/maintenance rituals in Torres Strait and beyond (e.g., Minnegal 1984) to shed rare insights into fundamental kin relationships between people and animals and reciprocal moral and social obligations between hunters and prey (Chapter 37: McNiven). Archaeological explorations of relational ontologies have ethical and moral implications as they draw archaeologists away from secularizing the past with techno-environmental models of adaptation into more conceptually challenging domains more commensurate with local Indigenous worldviews (e.g., for the inappropriateness of a ritual/secular dichotomy relating to 'middens', see McNiven & Wright 2008).

VIII. Visitors and Colonizers

Most chapters in this volume concern the pre-European colonial and settlement histories of Australia and Papua New Guinea. For both countries, postcontact histories are usually taken as the period after British colonial annexation and settlement in the late eighteenth and nineteenth centuries. However, early European contacts with Indigenous peoples of New Guinea and Australia, albeit coastal and fleeting, extend back to the sixteenth and seventeenth centuries, respectively. Yet contact between 'outsiders' from Island Southeast Asia and Indigenous peoples of Australia and New Guinea have much deeper histories. For example, Indigenous peoples of New Guinea were first contacted by ancestral 'Austronesians' from Island Southeast Asia by at least 3500–4000 years ago, and more recently also by visiting seafaring traders more than 1000 years ago (Spriggs 2011; Swadling 1996; Szabó et al. 2020). The degree to which these multiple phases of interaction, as documented so far in the archaeology, actually represent more or less independent pulses versus continuous processes that call on experiences or social memories of past connections to rejuvenate as new forms of interaction remains to be determined. Similarly, Aboriginal peoples of northern Australia were first contacted by traders from Indonesia sometime between 500 and 1000 years ago (e.g., Clarke 2000). The history of these visits, specifically by Makassan trepang fishers to northern Australia, was a focus for some of the earliest 'historical' archaeology in Australia, with the pioneering excavations of Campbell Macknight in the 1960s (Macknight 1976). Archaeological research about these visits is important both for better understanding the (hi)story of Aboriginal societies and for a better recognition that outsider visits to Australia and interactions with Indigenous communities did not commence with British colonial invasion (e.g., Macknight 1976; McNiven 2017; Mulvaney 1969; Rowland 2018; Swadling 1996). Archaeological evidence of dozens and perhaps hundreds of Makassan trepang processing sites across northern Australia demonstrate negotiations between Makassans and numerous Aboriginal groups over a number of centuries before British colonization. Aboriginal peoples were negotiating largely peaceful (as documented in historical records) and successful international relations long before the British began violently imposing their presence in 1788. Remarkably, and despite close to sixty years of focused research, the archaeology of Makassan (and broader Island Southeast Asian) visits to northern Australia remains in its infancy, with the legacies of exchanges of goods and ideas echoing through to contemporary generations in northern Australia and Indonesia. While available archaeological and historical evidence points to an elaborate trepang industry operating since c. 1700 CE, rock art depictions of Makassan sailing ships (*praus*) in Arnhem Land of northern Australia hint at earlier visits and potentially pre-1700s objects and cross-cultural influences (Chapter 38: Urwin, Russell, & Yulianti Farid; see also e.g., Taçon et al. 2010).

Most archaeology relating to outside visitors in Australia and New Guinea concerns the impacts and cultural transformations associated with British colonialism. Within Australia, settler colonialism and pan-continental invasion have created a diverse range of archaeological projects striving to shed light on the divergent experiences and actions of First Nations Australians encountering nineteenth-century colonial powers. A common theme in all these archaeological projects is the rewriting and overcoming of silences in mainstream histories by listening to contemporary Indigenous testimonies and letting the material (archaeological) record associated with late eighteenth- to early twentieth-century ancestors tell new stories of agency and experience. One challenging area with enormous potential for new insights through archaeological investigation is Indigenous involvement in sealing, whaling, and pearling industries. In such cases, documentary silences concern Indigenous peoples and colonists who were operating often well before and well away from pastoral and urban settlements. In the case of sealers, such cooperative work arrangements involved Aboriginal women and men from different cultural backgrounds working together in southern waters, creating new and often hybrid ('creolized') social and cultural formations that present conceptual challenges for archaeological investigation through dualistic gender and essentialized ethnic categories (Russell 2005). New social formations involving Indigenous agency, entrepreneurship, and exploitation extended to whaling, both shore-based and also ship-based with 'chequerboard crews' (i.e., multicultural) (Russell 2012). These novel social formations also integrated Aboriginal spiritual, ritual, social, and subsistence relationships with whales that have been under-researched by archaeologists (see Chapter 39: Gibbs & Russell). Such concerns could be extended to Queensland's late nineteenth-century commercial maritime industries associated with the exploitation of dugongs (e.g., Daley, Griggs, & Marsh 2008), pearlshells (e.g., Ganter 1994; McPhee 2004; see also Paterson & Veth 2020), and sugarcane plantation industries (e.g., Barker & Lamb 2011; Fatnowna 1989; Hayes 2002; Moore 2001) that variably involved local Indigenous communities working and living with British, Pacific Islander, and East Asian migrants, amongst others. The potential for archaeological research on cross-cultural endeavours, such as through whaling ships and coastal communities in Papua New Guinea, to contribute to better understanding of both history and the present is likewise considerable (e.g., Gray 1999; Specht 1975).

A key dimension of frontier interactions in Australia is the horrific and shameful violence and massacres that continue to be keenly felt by descendant families and communities. Across Australia, frontier violence resulted in the death of Aboriginal peoples and invading colonists, with Aboriginal people representing over 99% of casualities. Across the islands of Torres Strait in Far North Queensland, British colonial annexation occurred late (1870s) compared to the rest of Australia (1788), with low-level attempts of forced resource use and settlement often successfully thwarted by violent resistance (e.g., McNiven 2018b; Mullins 1994). For Aboriginal peoples of other regions of Queensland dealing with the rapidly expanding pastoral frontier of the late nineteenth century, resistance was met brutally by establishment of the paramilitary Native Police force (see earlier). The social and cultural complexities and tragedies of the Native Police and trackers, with their use of Aboriginal recruits, is often minimally apparent in archival records but coming to light with oral histories of recruit descendants and archaeological investigations of the many Native Police camps across Queensland (Chapter 40: Wallis, Burke, Barker, & Cole). In many areas of Australia, Aboriginal people found employment on pastoral properties where their intimate knowledge of resources, especially water, was crucial to the success of cattle and sheep industries. For many Aboriginal people, working on pastoral properties provided an opportunity to remain on homelands and on Country to continue to undertake a wide range of cultural practices (e.g., Godwin & L'Oste-Brown 2002; Merlan 1998). Cultural continuity included opportunities to innovate, with representations of new subject matters such as horses, sheep, guns, clay pipes, and ships in rock art, and the uptake and repurposing of metal, glass, and ceramic for tools, providing excellent examples (e.g., Ash, Brooks, David, & McNiven 2008; Kelly & Wardaman Indigenous Protected Area 2021; Perston et al. 2022). Archaeological research combined with the recording of oral histories has provided fundamental insights into how Aboriginal people on pastoral properties, or in the vicinity of such properties, lived their lives and adaptively innovated during periods of tumultuous social and cultural change in the nineteenth and early twentieth centuries (Chapter 41: Paterson).

One aspect of colonialism that brought mixed blessings for many Indigenous communities across New Guinea and Australia was Christian missions. In the Australian context, missions often operated as part of government or government-sanctioned reserves that were established for Aboriginal communities displaced through frontier violence and exclusion from lands due to pastoral and settlement expansion. Unfortunately, many reserves operated as institutions of forced assimilation and Westernization ('civilizing'), where cultural practices (e.g., languages) were banned with the fear of severe punishment and families torn apart by inhumane policies of child removal. Yet such places also operated as refuges of safety away from the violence of colonial persecution and exploitation. But colonial control and surveillance failed to suppress Aboriginal agency, with many people covertly undertaking cultural practices, often hidden in plain sight (e.g., Berndt, Berndt, & Stanton 1993; Kenny 2007; L'Oste-Brown et al. 1995; Lydon 2009). A number of First Nations communities in Australia have successfully been granted legal ownership of their old mission sites and reactivated use of cemeteries. Such acts of reclamation allow contemporary First Nations communities to take control of their ancestors' remains and memories and to reinscribe institutional infrastructure as Indigenous. (There has been a problematic tendency in much of Australia to consider 'Aboriginal and Torres Strait Islander sites' only those archaeological places that predate European invasion; yet more recent Aboriginal and Torres Strait Islander sites, many with cross-cultural interactions, are also present.)

Generalizing about mission experiences for Indigenous peoples of New Guinea and Australia glosses over considerable differences in the evangelizing approaches of a multitude of Christian denominations and the extraordinary cultural diversity of Indigenous 'recipient' communities. For example, the arrival of the London Missionary Society (LMS) to Torres Strait in 1871 involved the strategic use of Pacific Islander missionaries who understood Melanesian lifeways on islands. The enduring legacy of the LMS in Torres Strait is celebrated each year on the 1st of July with the 'Coming of the Light' Christian-based festivities. Archaeologies of missions across Australia have included recordings of oral histories of association and attachment that help contextualize material evidence of domestic control and regimentation. In addition, archaeological research often reveals that the materiality of Christianity—and as often emphasized, with some denominations including the LMS more so than others—expressed syncretism with local cultural traditions and practices often left silent in official mission records either deliberately or due to ignorance. Although New Guinea archaeology has not embraced mission archaeology to the extent seen in Australia, it holds considerable potential to expand understandings of relationships among evangelism, colonialism, and identity, especially if set within the context of local community research agendas, epistemologies, and worldviews (see Chapter 42: Ash).

Conclusion

Today the archaeology of Indigenous Australia and New Guinea is as diverse in approach, ideas, and aspirations as it has ever been. At various times in the past, we have heard, and read, that Australian and New Guinea archaeology has 'lost its way', that it has lost its sense of direction and unity. But in truth, other than previously having a much smaller cohort of trained practitioners, it has always been variant and divergent, in the intellectual priorities it has chased, in the actions and interests of its individuals, in its academic departments and schools of thought, and in its mavericks. In this, much understated has been the variability of approaches that the different university departments have brought to the fold, both in their educational curricula and in their research directions. We often hear that Australian and New Guinea archaeology is different to that of other parts of the world such as the United Kingdom, the United States, South Africa, France, and so forth. What makes archaeology in this part of the world distinct is a heightened sense of awareness that the past is actually the present, that the artefacts, sites, and landscapes are not just an archaeological 'playground', but living Aboriginal, Torres Strait Islander, and New Guinean heritage, to borrow a phrase so influentially and challengingly presented to the Australian Archaeological Association by the Tasmanian Aboriginal community back in 1982 (Langford 1983). More than any other, this was a turning point that came to define Australian archaeology as we know it today (arguably archaeology in Papua New Guinea was already shaping through a national system governed by Indigenous Papua New Guineans, in a context where 97% of the country is owned by Indigenous communities). What we do not give enough credit for is the healthy diversity of views, approaches, and aspirations that the over-1000 professional archaeologists and ten major Indigenous archaeology departments bring to the fold. There is not just one style of Australian and New Guinean Indigenous archaeology, but many, a topic whose institutional and disciplinary genealogies would be worthy of further exploration. The archaeological practices of the teaching and research departments at the Australian National University, Flinders University, James Cook University, La Trobe University, Monash University, Sydney University, the University of New England, the University of Papua New Guinea, the University of Queensland, and the University of Western Australia (let alone the archaeological practices of other institutions such as museums and regulatory bodies) are not all quite the same, nor have they ever been, and this is a good thing, bringing a healthy dose of variety to the discipline.

The pairing of Australia and New Guinea for this volume was underpinned by sometimes contiguous and shared, sometimes common but separated, and sometimes divergent biogeographies, European exploration and colonialism, and long-term Indigenous histories spanning at least c. 65,000 years. For more than 80% of the human history of both areas, Australia and New Guinea were a single landmass now known as Sahul. Nevertheless, approaches to the archaeology of Indigenous pasts in the two areas have often differed due to dichotomous views of cultural developments linked to a perceived fundamental difference between agricultural (New Guinea) and hunter-gatherer (Australia) societies. Needless to say, this is despite the long recognition that Aboriginal peoples have long been aware of farming, planting, and/or in some places aquacultural practices (e.g., Hallam 1975; Lourandos 1980b); that in New Guinea there are plenty of examples of hunting and gathering practices, including among societies who do not practice agriculture as conventionally defined (e.g., Roscoe 2002); and that sago-production in New Guinea (e.g., Rhoads 1980) (Figure 1.3), and fishing generally (e.g., Testart 1982), do not easily fit into the agriculture versus hunting-gathering framework. Somewhat ironically, the categorization of Australian and New Guinea societies has often been relative to each other, as scaled understandings of Australian so-called hunter-gatherer cultural dynamics and complexities were often framed in relation to perceptions of New Guinea agricultural dynamics and complexities, and vice versa (e.g., Allen & O'Connell 1995; Murray & White 1985). A central driving force in reorienting Australian archaeology to more socially sensitive perceptions of cultural change, expressed most clearly in the Intensification debate, was pointing out the similarities and overlaps between ethnographically known Indigenous societies of Australia and New Guinea (Lourandos 1980b, 1988, 2008).

Over the past two decades, the archaeologies of Indigenous Australia and New Guinea have in many ways been brought closer together by archaeological research

FIGURE 1.3. Archaeological fieldwork with Keipte Kuyumen clan members, Upper Kikori River (highlands foothills of Papua New Guinea), 2007–2009.[1]

findings in Torres Strait and the adjacent coasts of Papua New Guinea and mainland Queensland to the north and south, respectively. Central to this rapprochement has been the recovery of Lapita pottery on the south coast of Papua New Guinea dating to c. 2900–2600 cal BP, pottery in Torres Strait dating back to c. 2600 cal BP, and pottery on Lizard Island to the south dating to between c. 2000 and 3000 cal BP (e.g., Carter 2004; David et al. 2011; McNiven et al. 2006, 2011; Tochilin et al. 2012; Ulm & McNiven 2021). Pottery in all three regions appears to have been locally made, indicating shared technologies underpinned by cultural interactions and possibly migrations involving more than 1000 km of coastline (Chapter 22: McNiven). Significantly, these dated pottery finds were made by archaeologists with experience in all three broad regions of Papua New Guinea, Torres Strait, and Australia. Such collective experience supports a desired outcome of this volume: that archaeological research in Australia and New Guinea continues to be practiced by increasing numbers of archaeologists who work not just within but across geographical and disciplinary boundaries. Indeed, as these new pottery finds were emerging, the importance of Australian and Papua New Guinean archaeologists working closer together to understand common histories across Torres Strait was emphasized by Ian Lilley, who has broad expertise in the archaeology of both countries (e.g., Carter & Lilley 2008; Lilley 2000, 2019).

The presence of many and varied Indigenous groups across Australia and New Guinea, coupled with research processes founded on collaborations and partnerships, ensures that the future of Indigenous archaeology in the region will be vibrant and diverse. Although in the past, conceptual developments in the archaeology of Australia and New Guinea tended to often be imported from overseas (especially Europe and North America), combined anthropology-archaeology departments and collaborative research partnerships with Traditional Owner groups have accelerated homegrown developments in disciplinary practices and ideas, so that today there is a much greater awareness of the presence and significance of local Indigenous epistemologies, ontologies, and ethics. Local Indigenous archaeologies are creating more culturally and socially inclusive forms of community research and community (hi)story, with relevance also to many other parts of the world. The international relevance of Australia and New Guinea's socially oriented archaeological practices is increased by similar experiences of colonialism by most Indigenous communities across the world, where archaeological approaches to the past also continue to take on the challenging task of decolonization. While many important developments have been made in recrafting archaeology as an anti-colonial process that works for and not against Indigenous communities, the process remains ongoing as colonialism and its diverse legacies, and community life and Country, are front and centre of the daily lives of most Indigenous peoples.

ACKNOWLEDGMENTS

This volume was mostly assembled as the COVID-19 pandemic engulfed the world. As such, well over 100 people, including authors, reviewers, copyeditors, and production staff, have gone the extra yards to ensure its completion, and we are greatly thankful to all. Thank you to Oxford University Press for taking onboard this ambitious publication, and especially to Timothy Allen, Robert Cavooris, Victoria Harris, Camilla Helsing, and Benjamin Leonard. We thank also the following people who kindly reviewed chapters: Harry Allen, Lee Arnold, Val Attenbrow, Bryce Barker, Tim Bayliss-Smith, Rebecca Bliege Bird, Heather Burke, John Bradley, Adam Brumm, Emilie Chalmin, Chris Clarkson, Melanie Fillios, Michael-Shawn Fletcher, Richard Gillespie, Laurence Goldman, Tartyn Gooley, Tom Griffiths, Giles Hamm, Nathan Jankowski, Shimona Kealy, Matthew Leavesley, Chantal Knowles, Bastien Llamas, Jane Lydon, Campbell Macknight, Paul Memmott, Monica Minnegal, Ian Moffatt, Patrick Moss, Sue O'Connor, Donald Pate, Alistair Paterson, Christina Pavlides, Rachel Popelka-Filcoff, Martin Porr, Amy Roberts, Lynette Russell, Lyndall Ryan, Ben Shaw, Rob Skelly, Glenn

Summerhayes, Peter Sutton, Pamela Swadling, Paul Taçon, Luke Taylor, Fenja Theden-Ringl, Chris Urwin, Peter Veth, and Duncan Wright. Last but not least, thank you to Claire Smith and Sean Ulm for helpful comments on aspects of this introductory chapter. This work was supported by the Australian Research Council Centre of Excellence for Australian Biodiversity and Heritage (CE170100015).

NOTE

1. In 2006, members of the Keipte Kuyumen clan sent a letter to request archaeological research on clan lands, to document sago-pounder manufacture by Wero, the last of the master stone-sago makers in the community. Following an initial meeting and planning field trip in 2007, the following years documented: (A) The extraction of chert nodules from the inland limestone cliffs at the quarry site of Tobakarowi. (B) The making of sago-pounders and other stone tools by Wero Sisira at Karobayu. Here his two brothers, Mauke Umari and Kuto Umari, and brother's son and prodigy Michael Mauke are instructed on the skills of stone tool-making using the Tobakarowi chert nodules. PNG National Museum archaeologist Nick Araho (right) documents the process. (C) Wero Sisira with the finished and hafted chert sago-pounders at Karobayu. (D) Sinama Uke (left) and Maureen Harry (right) preparing the sago-starch flour (the key local staple food) which they had earlier processed from felled sago palms (*Metroxylon sagu*) with the sago-pounders. The hollow bamboo sections will be filled with sago flour as cooking containers. (E) The anticipation and planning of the inland expedition to obtain the chert is educational, socially structured, and rich in preparation, including ritual instruction. Here clan members discuss the planning at the Karobayu camp area. (F) Such sojourns are also opportunities to pass on ancestral stories and knowledge about legendary ancestral beings. Here Wero Sisira recounts the one-eyed fish-being ancestral clan story to Michael Mauke, where it resides at the remote location of Fokopi. Documenting the past at the request of the community is an opportunity for community Elders and leaders to tell the stories of the ancestors, ancestral beings, and sacred story-places to the younger generations, as a way of caring for clan lands and their numinous life forces, into the future. (Photos by Bruno David and Bernard Sanderre.) Note that many of the depicted activities are highly gendered, and some can remain largely or entirely invisible in the archaeological record. While sago-pounder production (male) and use (female) would be relatively easily detectable archaeologically by the stone artefacts and their use-wear/residues, much of the post-pounding sago flour processing (female) would not be detected unless micro-bioarchaeological techniques are employed.

REFERENCES

ABS. (2018). Estimates of Aboriginal and Torres Strait Islander Australians. Canberra: Australian Bureau of Statistics. https://www.abs.gov.au/statistics/people/aboriginal-and-tor res-strait-islander-peoples/estimates-aboriginal-and-torres-strait-islander-australians/lat est-release

Akerman, K., & Stanton, J. (1994). *Riji and jakuli: Kimberley pearl shell in Aboriginal Australia*. Darwin: Northern Territory Museum of Arts and Sciences.

Allen, J. (Ed.) (1996). *Report of the Southern Forests Archaeological Project*. Bundoora: La Trobe University.

Allen, J., & O'Connell, J. F. (Eds.) (1995). *Transitions: Pleistocene to Holocene in Australia and Papua New Guinea. Antiquity, 69*(265), 649–862.

Antonopoulos, P., & Cottle, D. (2019). Forgotten genocide in Indonesia: Mass violence, resource exploitation and struggle for independence in West Papua. In F. Jacob (Ed.), *Genocide and mass violence in Asia: An introductory reader* (pp. 160–188). Oldenbourg: De Gruyter.

Ash, J., Brooks, A., David, B., & McNiven, I. J. (2008). European-manufactured objects from the 'early mission' site at Totalai, Mua (Western Torres Strait). *Memoirs of the Queensland Museum. Cultural Heritage Series, 4*(2), 473–492.

Ash, J., Manas, L., & Bosun, D. (2010). Lining the path: A seascape perspective of two Torres Strait missions, northeast Australia. *International Journal of Historical Archaeology, 14*(1), 56–85.

Ballard, C. (1993). Stimulating minds to fantasy? A critical etymology for Sahul. In M. A. Smith, M. Spriggs, & B. Fankhauser (Eds.), *Sahul in review: Pleistocene archaeology in Australia, New Guinea and Island Melanesia* (pp. 17–23). Occasional Papers in Prehistory No. 24. Canberra: Department of Prehistory, Research School of Pacific Studies, The Australian National University.

Ballard, C. (1995). *The death of a great land: Ritual, history and subsistence revolution in the Southern Highlands of Papua New Guinea* (PhD thesis). Australian National University, Canberra.

Balme, J., & Morse, K. (2006). Shell beads and social behaviour in Pleistocene Australia. *Antiquity, 80*(310), 799–811.

Barker, B., & Lamb, L. (2011). Archaeological evidence for South Sea Islander traditional ritual practice at Wunjunga, Ayr, central Queensland coast. *Australian Archaeology, 73*(1), 69–72.

Barker, B., Lamb, L., David, B., Korokai, K., Kuaso, A., & Bowman, J. (2012). Otoia, ancestral village of the Kerewo: Modelling the historical emergence of Kerewo regional polities on the island of Goaribari, south coast of mainland Papua New Guinea. In S. G. Haberle & B. David (Eds.), *Peopled landscapes: Archaeological and biogeographic approaches to landscapes* (pp. 157–176). Terra Australis 34. Canberra: ANU E Press.

Beaton, J. M. (1982). Fire and water: Aspects of Australian Aboriginal management of cycads. *Archaeology in Oceania, 17*(1), 51–58.

Beckett, J. (1987). *Torres Strait Islanders: Custom and colonialism*. Cambridge: Cambridge University Press.

Bergström, A., Nagle, N., Chen, Y., McCarthy, S., Pollard, M. O., Ayub, Q., . . . Tyler-Smith, C. (2016). Deep roots for Aboriginal Australian Y chromosomes. *Current Biology, 26*(6), 809–813.

Berndt, R. M., Berndt, C. H., with Stanton, J. E. (1993). *A world that was: The Yaraldi of the Murray River and the lakes, South Australia*. Carlton: Melbourne University Press at the Miegunyah Press.

Bird, C. F., & Frankel, D. (1991). Chronology and explanation in western Victoria and southeast South Australia. *Archaeology in Oceania, 26*(1), 1–16.

Birdsell, J. B. (1977). The recalibration of a paradigm for the first peopling of Greater Australia. In J. Allen, J. Golson, & R. Jones (Eds.), *Sunda and Sahul* (pp. 113–168). London: Academic Press.

Bliege Bird, R., Bird, D. W., Codding, B. F., Parker, C. H., & Jones, J. H. (2008). The 'fire stick farming' hypothesis: Australian Aboriginal foraging strategies, biodiversity, and anthropogenic fire mosaics. *Proceedings of the National Academy of Sciences, 105*(39), 14796–14801.

Bourke, R. M. & Allen, B. (2021). Estimating the population of Papua New Guinea in 2020. Development Policy Centre Discussion Paper 90. Canberra: Crawford School of Public Policy, The Australian National University.

Bowdler, S. (1976). Hook, line, and dilly bag: An interpretation of an Australian coastal shell midden. *Mankind, 10*, 248–258.

Bradley, J. J. (1991). 'Li-Maramaranja': Yanyuwa hunters of marine animals in the Sir Edward Pellew Group, Northern Territory. *Records of the South Australian Museum, 25*(1), 91–110.

Bradley, J., & McNiven, I. J. (2019). 'Why those old fellas stopped using them?': Socio-religious and socio-political dimensions of stone-walled tidal fish trap use and dis-use amongst the Yanyuwa of northern Australia. *The Journal of Island and Coastal Archaeology, 14*(3), 337–355.

Bradley, R. (2000). *An archaeology of natural places.* London: Routledge.

Bradshaw, C. J., Norman, K., Ulm, S., Williams, A. N., Clarkson, C., Chadœuf, J. . . . Weyrich, L. S. (2021). Stochastic models support rapid peopling of Late Pleistocene Sahul. *Nature Communications, 12*(1), 1–11.

Brady, L. M., Bradley, J. J., & Kearney, A. J. (2016). Negotiating Yanyuwa rock art: Relational and affectual experiences in the southwest Gulf of Carpentaria, northern Australia. *Current Anthropology, 57*(1), 28–52.

Brown, P. (1978). *Highland peoples of New Guinea.* Cambridge: Cambridge University Press.

Builth, H. (2002). *The archaeology and socioeconomy of the Gunditjmara: A landscape analysis from southwest Victoria, Australia* (PhD thesis). Flinders University, Adelaide.

Builth, H. (2014). *Ancient Aboriginal aquaculture rediscovered.* Saarbrucken, Germany: LAP Lambert Academic Publishing.

Bulmer, S. (1964). Radiocarbon dates from New Guinea. *Journal of the Polynesian Society, 73*(3), 327–328.

Burke, H., Barker, B., Wallis, L., Craig, S. & Combo, M. (2020). Betwixt and between: Trauma, survival and the Aboriginal troopers of the Queensland Native Mounted Police. *Journal of Genocide Research, 22*(3), 317–333.

Carter, M. (2004). *North of the cape and south of the Fly: The archaeology of settlement and subsistence on the Murray Islands, eastern Torres Strait* (PhD thesis). James Cook University, Townsville.

Carter, M., & Lilley, I. (2008). Between the Australian and Melanesian realms: The archaeology of the Murray Islands and consideration of a settlement model for Torres Strait. In J. Conolly & M. Campbell (Eds.), *Comparative island archaeologies* (pp. 69–83). British Archaeological Reports 1829. Oxford: Archaeopress.

Clancy, R. (1995). *The mapping of* Terra Australis. Macquarie Park, NSW: Universal Press.

Clark, G. (1972). Foreword. In E. S. Higgs (Ed.), *Papers in economic prehistory* (pp. vii–x). Cambridge: Cambridge University Press.

Clark, I. D. (2007). The abode of malevolent spirits and creatures: Caves in Victorian Aboriginal social organization. *Helictite, Journal of Australasian Speleological Research, 40*(1), 3–10.

Clark, R. L. (1983). Pollen and charcoal evidence for the effects of Aboriginal burning on the vegetation of Australia. *Archaeology in Oceania, 19*(1), 32–37.

Clarke, A. (2000). The moormans' trowsers: Aboriginal and Macassan interactions and the changing fabric of Indigenous social life. In S. O'Connor & P. Veth (Eds.), *East of Wallace's Line: Studies of past and present maritime cultures of the Indo-Pacific region* (pp. 315–335). Rotterdam: A.A. Balkema.

Clarkson, C., Jacobs, Z., Marwick, B., Fullagar, R., Wallis, L., Smith, M., . . . Florin, S. A. (2017). Human occupation of northern Australia by 65,000 years ago. *Nature*, *547*(7663), 306–310.

Colley, S. (2002). *Uncovering Australia: Archaeology, Indigenous people and the public*. Crows Nest, NSW: Allen & Unwin.

Cosgrove, R., Allen, J., & Marshall, B. (1990). Palaeo-ecology and Pleistocene human occupation in south central Tasmania. *Antiquity*, *64*(242), 59–78.

Coutts, P. J. F., Frank, R. K., & Hughes, P. (1978). Aboriginal engineers of the Western District, Victoria. *Records of the Victorian Archaeological Survey 7*. Melbourne.

Cundy, B. (1990). *An analysis of the Ingaladdi assemblage: Critique of the understanding of lithic technology* (PhD thesis). Australian National University, Canberra.

Daley, B., Griggs, P., & Marsh, H. (2008). Exploiting marine wildlife in Queensland: The commercial dugong and marine turtle fisheries, 1847–1969. *Australian Economic History Review*, *48*(3), 227–265.

David, B. (2002). *Landscapes, rock art and the Dreaming*. London: Leicester University Press.

David, B. (2006). Archaeology and the Dreaming: Toward an archaeology of ontology. In I. Lilley (Ed.), *Archaeology of Oceania: Australia and the Pacific islands* (pp. 48–68). Oxford: Wiley-Blackwell.

David, B. (2017). *Cave art*. London: Thames & Hudson.

David, B., Barker, B., & McNiven, I. J. (Eds.) (2006). *The social archaeology of Australian Indigenous societies*. Canberra: Aboriginal Studies Press.

David, B., & Denham, T. (2006). Unpacking Australian prehistory. In B. David, B. Barker, & I. J. McNiven (Eds.), *The social archaeology of Australian Indigenous societies* (pp. 52–71). Canberra: Aboriginal Studies Press.

David, B., Fresløv, J., Mullett, R., GunaiKurnai Land and Waters Aboriginal Corporation, Delannoy, J.-J., McDowell, M., . . . Russell, L. (2021). 50 years and worlds apart: Rethinking the Holocene occupation of Cloggs Cave (East Gippsland, SE Australia) five decades after its initial archaeological excavation and in light of GunaiKurnai world views. *Australian Archaeology*, *87*(1), 1–20.

David, B., Haberle, S. G., & Walker, D. (2012). Peopled landscapes: The impact of Peter Kershaw on Australian Quaternary science. In S. G. Haberle & B. David (Eds.), *Peopled landscapes: Archaeological and biogeographic approaches to landscapes* (pp. 3–23). Terra Australis 34. Canberra: ANU E Press.

David, B., Lamb, L., Delannoy, J.-J., Pivoru, F., Rowe, C., Pivoru, M., . . . Pivoru, R. (2012). Poromoi Tamu and the case of the drowning village: History, lost places and the stories we tell. *International Journal of Historical Archaeology*, *16*(2), 319–345.

David, B., & Lourandos, H. (1997). 37,000 years and more in tropical Australia: Investigating long-term archaeological trends in Cape York Peninsula. *Proceedings of the Prehistoric Society*, *63*, 1–23.

David, B., McNiven, I., Attenbrow, V., Flood, J., & Collins, J. (1994). Of Lightning Brothers and white cockatoos: Dating the antiquity of signifying systems in the Northern Territory, Australia. *Antiquity*, *68*(259), 241–251.

David, B., McNiven, I. J., Crouch, J, Hewitt, G., Skelly, R., Barker, B., & Courtney, K. (2009). Koey Ngurtai: The emergence of a ritual domain in Western Torres Strait. *Archaeology in Oceania*, *44*(1), 1–17

David, B., McNiven, I., Manas, L., Manas, J., Savage, S., Crouch, J., . . . Brady, L. (2004). Goba of Mua: Archaeology working with oral tradition. *Antiquity*, *78*(299), 158–172.

David, B., McNiven, I. J., Richards, T., Connaughton, S., Leavesley, M., Barker, B., & Rowe, C. (2011). Lapita sites in the Central Province of mainland Papua New Guinea. *World Archaeology*, *43*(4), 580–597.

David, B., & Thomas, J. (Eds.) (2008). *Handbook of landscape archaeology*. Walnut Creek, CA: Left Coast Press.

David, B., & Wilson, M. (1999). Re-reading the landscape: Place and identity in NE Australia during the late Holocene. *Cambridge Archaeological Journal*, *9*(2), 163–188.

David, B., & Wilson, M. (Eds.) (2002). *Inscribed landscapes: Marking and making place*. Honolulu: University of Hawai'i Press.

Delannoy, J.-J., David, B., Geneste, J.-M., Katherine, M., Barker, B., Whear, R. L., & Gunn, R. G. (2013). The social construction of caves and rockshelters: Chauvet Cave (France) and Nawarla Gabarnmang (Australia). *Antiquity*, *87*(335), 12–29.

Denham, T. (2008). Traditional forms of plant exploitation in Australia and New Guinea: The search for common ground. *Vegetation History and Archaeobotany*, *17*(2), 245–248.

Denham, T. (2018). *Tracing early agriculture in the Highlands of New Guinea: Plot, mound and ditch*. London: Routledge.

Denham, T., Donohue, M., & Booth, S. (2009). Horticultural experimentation in northern Australia reconsidered. *Antiquity*, *83*(321), 634–648.

Descola, P. (2013). *Beyond nature and culture*. Chicago: University of Chicago Press.

Dixon, R. M. W. (2011). *The languages of Australia*. Cambridge: Cambridge University Press.

Douglas, B. (2019). Mapping the once and future strait: Place, time, and Torres Strait from the sixteenth century to the Pleistocene. *History and Anthropology*. DOI: 10.1080/02757206.2019.1607849.

Dugay-Grist, M. (2006). Shaking the pillars. In I. Lilley (Ed.), *Archaeology of Oceania: Australia and the Pacific Islands* (pp. 367–379). Malden, MA: Blackwell.

Dussart, F. (1989). *Warlpiri women's yawulyu ceremonies: A forum for socialization and innovation* (PhD thesis). Australian National University, Canberra.

Evans, R., & Ørsted-Jensen, R. (2014). 'I cannot say the numbers that were killed': Assessing violent mortality of the Queensland frontier. Unpublished paper presented at The Australian Historical Association 33rd Annual Conference, University of Queensland, St Lucia, Australia, 7–11 July 2014.

Falkenberg, J. (1962). *Kin and totem: Group relations of Australian Aborigines in the Port Keats District*. Oslo: Oslo University Press.

Fatnowna, N. (1989). *Fragments of a lost heritage*. R. Keesing (Ed.). North Ryde, NSW: Angus & Robertson.

Finch, D., Gleadow, A., Hergt, J., Levchenko, V. A., Heaney, P., Veth, P., . . . Green, H. (2020). 12,000-year-old Aboriginal rock art from the Kimberley region, Western Australia. *Science Advances*, *6*(6). doi/10.1126/sciadv.aay3922.

Flinders, M. (1814). *A voyage to Terra Australis*. 3 vols. London: G. and W. Nicol.

Flood, J. (1974). Pleistocene man at Cloggs Cave: His tool kit and environment. *Mankind*, *9*(3), 175–188.

Flood, J. (1980). *The moth hunters: Aboriginal prehistory of the Australian Alps*. Canberra: Australian Institute of Aboriginal Studies.

Foley, W. A. (2000). The languages of New Guinea. *Annual Review of Anthropology*, *29*(1), 357–404.

Fowler, M., Roberts, A., McKinnon, J., O'Loughlin, C., & Graham, F. (2014). 'They camped here always': 'Archaeologies of attachment' in a seascape context at Wardang Island (Waraldi/

Wara-dharldhi) and Point Pearce Peninsula (Burgiyana), South Australia. *Australasian Historical Archaeology, 32*, 14–22.

Gaffney, D., & Tolla, N. (Eds.) (in press). *The archaeology and material culture of western New Guinea.* Terra Australis. Canberra: ANU Press.

Gammage, B. (1998). *The sky travellers: Journeys in New Guinea 1938–1939.* Carlton South: Melbourne University Press.

Gammage, B. (2012). *The biggest estate on Earth: How Aborigines made Australia.* Sydney: Allen & Unwin.

Ganter, R. (1994). *The pearl-shellers of Torres Strait: Resource use, development and decline, 1860s–1960s.* Carlton: Melbourne University Press.

Godwin, L., & L'Oste-Brown, S. (2002). A past remembered: Aboriginal 'historical' places in central Queensland. In R. Harrison & C. Williamson (Eds.), *After Captain Cook: The archaeology of the recent indigenous past in Australia* (pp. 191–212). Archaeological Methods Series 8, Archaeological Computing Laboratory. Sydney: University of Sydney.

Golson, J. (1968). Introduction to Taurama archaeological site Kirra Beach. *Journal of the Papua and New Guinea Society, 2*, 67–71.

Golson, J. (1977). No room at the top: Agricultural intensification in the New Guinea Highlands. In J. Allen, J. Golson, & R. Jones (Eds.), *Sunda and Sahul: Prehistoric studies in southeast Asia, Melanesia and Australia* (pp. 601–638). London: Academic Press.

Golson, J., Denham, T., Hughes, P., Swadling, P., & Muke, J. (Eds.) (2017). *Ten thousand years of cultivation at Kuk Swamp in the Highlands of Papua New Guinea.* Terra Australis 46. Canberra: Australian National University Press.

Gosden, C., & Robertson, N. (1991). Models for Matenkupkum: Interpreting a Late Pleistocene site from southern New Ireland, Papua New Guinea. In J. Allen & C. Gosden (Eds.), *Report of the Lapita Homeland Project* (pp. 20–45). Occasional Papers in Prehistory No. 20. Canberra: Department of Prehistory, Research School of Pacific Studies, The Australian National University.

Gott, B. (1982). Ecology of root use by the Aborigines of southern Australia. *Archaeology in Oceania, 17*(1), 59–67.

Gould, R. A. (1977). Puntutjarpa Rockshelter and the Australian Desert Culture. *Anthropological Papers of the American Museum of Natural History, 54*(1), 1–187.

Grainer, J., David, B., Cribb, R., White, B., & Kuhn, H. (1992). Nurrabullgin—'a mountain, once seen, never to be forgotten'. *Rock Art Research, 9*(1), 74–77.

Gray, A. C. (1999). Trading contacts in the Bismarck Archipelago during the whaling era, 1799–1884. *The Journal of Pacific History, 34*(1), 23–43.

Griffiths, B. (2018). *Deep time Dreaming: Uncovering ancient Australia.* Carlton: Black.

Griffiths, B., & Russell, L. (2018). What we were told: Responses to 65,000 years of Aboriginal history. *Aboriginal History, 42*, 31–53.

Griffiths, T. (1996). *Hunters and collectors: The antiquarian imagination in Australia.* Cambridge: Cambridge University Press.

Haberle, S. G., Hope, G. S., & DeFretes, Y. (1991). Environmental change in the Baliem valley, montane Irian Jaya, Republic of Indonesia. *Journal of Biogeography, 18*(1), 25–40.

Haddon, A. C. (1935). *Reports of the Cambridge Anthropological Expedition to Torres Straits. Vol. I. General ethnography.* Cambridge: Cambridge University Press.

Hall, J. (1999). The impact of sea level rise on the archaeological record of the Moreton region, southeast Queensland. In J. Hall & I. J. McNiven (Eds.), *Australian coastal archaeology* (pp. 169–184). Research Papers in Archaeology & Natural History, No. 31. Canberra: ANH Publications, Australian National University.

Hall, J., & McNiven, I. J. (Eds.) (1999). *Australian coastal archaeology*. Research Papers in Archaeology & Natural History, No. 31. Canberra: ANH Publications, Australian National University.

Hallam, S. (1975). *Fire and hearth: A study of Aboriginal usage and European usurpation in south-western Australia*. Canberra: Australian Institute of Aboriginal Studies.

Harris, D. R. (1977). Subsistence strategies across Torres Strait. In J. Allen, J. Golson, & R. Jones (Eds.), *Sunda and Sahul: Prehistoric studies in Southeast Asia, Melanesia and Australia* (pp. 421–463). London: Academic Press.

Harris, D. (1995). Early agriculture in New Guinea and the Torres Strait divide. In J. Allen & J. F. O'Connell (Eds.), *Transitions: Pleistocene to Holocene in Australia and Papua New Guinea. Antiquity*, 69(265), 848–854.

Harrison, R. (2004). *Shared landscapes: Archaeologies of attachment and the pastoral industry in New South Wales*. Sydney: UNSW Press.

Hayes, L. (2002). The tangible link: Historical archaeology and the cultural heritage of the Australian South Sea Islanders. *Australasian Historical Archaeology*, 20, 77–82.

Hiscock, P. (2021). Small signals: Comprehending the Australian microlithic as public signalling. *Cambridge Archaeological Journal*, 31(2), 313–324.

Hope, G. (1998). Early fire and forest change in the Baliem Valley, Irian Jaya, Indonesia. *Journal of Biogeography*, 25(3), 453–461.

Huffman, C. (2018). Pythagoras. In E. N. Zalta (Ed.), *Stanford encyclopedia of philosophy*. Stanford, CA: Stanford University. https://plato.stanford.edu/entries/pythagoras/

Hughes, I. (1977). *New Guinea Stone Age trade: The geography and ecology of traffic in the Interior*. Terra Australis 3. Canberra: Department of Prehistory, Research School of Pacific Studies, ANU.

Hynes, R. A., & Chase, A. K. (1982). Plants, sites and domiculture: Aboriginal influence upon plant communities in Cape York Peninsula. *Archaeology in Oceania*, 17(1), 38–50.

Ingold, T. (1993). The temporality of the landscape. *World Archaeology*, 25(2), 152–174.

Jones, R. (1969). Fire-stick farming. *Australian Natural History*, 16(7), 224–228.

Jones, R. (1977). Sunda and Sahul: An introduction. In J. Allen, J. Golson, & R. Jones (Eds.), *Sunda and Sahul: Prehistoric studies in Southeast Asia, Melanesia and* Australia (pp. 1–9). London: Academic Press.

Keen, I. (2004). *Aboriginal economy and society: Australia at the threshold of colonisation*. South Melbourne: Oxford University Press.

Kelly, L. (2016). *The memory code: The traditional Aboriginal memory technique that unlocks the secrets of Stonehenge, Easter Island and ancient monuments the world over*. Sydney: Allen & Unwin.

Kelly, M. A., & Wardaman Indigenous Protected Area. (2021). Resistance and remembering through rock art: Contact-period rock art in Wardaman country, Northern Australia. *Archaeology in Oceania*, 56(3), 173–195.

Kenny, R. (2007). *The lamb enters the Dreaming: Nathanael Pepper and the ruptured world*. Melbourne: Scribe.

Kershaw, A. P. (1974). A long continuous pollen sequence from north-eastern Australia. *Nature*, 251, 222–223.

Kirch, P. V. (1997). *The Lapita peoples: Ancestors of the Oceanic world*. Cambridge: Blackwell.

Kluge, E. (2020). West Papua and the international history of decolonization, 1961–69. *The International History Review*, *42*(6), 1155–1172.

Kusumaryati, V. (2018). *Ethnography of a colonial present: History, experience, and political consciousness in West Papua* (PhD thesis). Harvard University, Cambridge, Massachusetts.

Lamb, L., Barker, B., Leavesley, M., Aubert, M., Fairbairn, & Manne, T. (2021). Rock engravings and occupation sites in the Mount Bosavi region, Papua New Guinea: Implications for our understanding of the human presence in the Southern Highlands. *Archaeology in Oceania*, *56*(3), 304–321.

Landtman, G. (1927). *The Kiwai Papuans of British New Guinea*. London: Macmillan and Co.

Langford, R. (1983). Our heritage—Your playground. *Australian Archaeology*, *16*(1), 1–6.

Langton, M. (2018). *Welcome to Country: A travel guide to Indigenous Australia*. Richmond, VA: Hardie Grant Travel.

Lawrence, D. (1994). Customary exchange across Torres Strait. *Memoirs of the Queensland Museum*, *34*(2), 241–446.

Lee, R. B., & DeVore, I. (Eds.) (1968). *Man the hunter*. Chicago: Aldine.

Lévi-Strauss, C. (1968). Future agenda. In R. B. Lee, & I. DeVore (Eds.), *Man the hunter* (pp. 344–345). Chicago: Aldine.

Lewis, D. (1983). *Art, archaeology and material in Arnhem Land* (BA Honours thesis). Australian National University, Canberra.

Lewis, D. (1988). *The rock paintings of Arnhem Land, Australia*. BAR International Series 415. Oxford: British Archaeological Reports.

Lilley, I. (2000). So near and yet so far: Reflections on archaeology in Australia and Papua New Guinea, intensification and culture contact. *Australian Archaeology*, *50*, 36–44.

Lilley, I. (2019). Lapita: The Australian connection. In S. Bedford & M. Spriggs (Eds.), *Debating Lapita: Distribution, chronology, society and subsistence* (pp. 105–114). Terra Australis 52. Canberra: Australian National University Press.

L'Oste-Brown, S., & Godwin, L. (with Henry, G., Mitchell, T., & Tyson, V.) (1995). '*Living under the Act*': *Taroom Aboriginal Reserve 1911–1927*. Cultural Heritage Monograph Series No. 1. Brisbane: Department of Environment and Heritage.

Lourandos, H. (1980a). *Forces of change: Aboriginal technology and population in southwestern Victoria* (PhD thesis). University of Sydney, Sydney.

Lourandos, H. (1980b). Change or stability? Hydraulics, hunter-gatherers and population in temperate Australia. *World Archaeology*, *11*(3), 245–266.

Lourandos, H. (1983). Intensification: A late Pleistocene-Holocene archaeological sequence from southwestern Victoria. *Archaeology in Oceania*, *18*, 81–94.

Lourandos, H. (1988). Palaeopolitics: Resource intensification in Aboriginal Australia and Papua New Guinea. In T. Ingold, D. Riches, & J. Woodburn (Eds.), *Hunters and gatherers: History, evolution and social change* (pp. 148–160). Oxford: Berg.

Lourandos, H. (1993). Hunter-gatherer cultural dynamics: Long- and short-term trends in Australian prehistory. *Journal of Archaeological Research*, *1*(1), 67–88.

Lourandos, H. (1997). *Continent of hunter-gatherers: New perspectives in Australian prehistory*. Cambridge: Cambridge University Press.

Lourandos, H. (2008). Constructing 'hunter-gatherers', constructing 'prehistory': Australia and New Guinea. *Australian Archaeology*, *67*, 69–78.

Lourandos, H., & David, B. (1998). Comparing long-term archaeological and environmental trends: North Queensland, arid and semi-arid Australia. *The Artefact*, *21*, 105–114.

Lourandos, H., & Ross, A. (1994). The great 'intensification debate': Its history and place in Australian archaeology. *Australian Archaeology, 39*, 54–63.

Lutkehaus, N., Kaufmann, C., Mitchell, W. E., Newton, D., Osmundsen, L., & Schuster, M. (Eds.) (1990). *Sepik heritage: Tradition and change in Papua New Guinea*. Bathurst: Crawford House Press.

Lydon, J. (2009). *Fantastic dreaming: The archaeology of an Aboriginal mission*. Lanham, MD: AltaMira Press.

Macknight, C. C. (1976). *The voyage to Marege'*. Melbourne: Melbourne University Press.

Macumber, P. G. (1977). The geology and palaeohydrology of the Kow Swamp fossil hominid site, Victoria, Australia. *Journal of the Geological Society of Australia, 24*(5–6), 307–320.

Malaspinas, A-S., Westaway, M. C., Muller, C., Soussa, V. C., Lao, O., Alves, I., . . . Willerslev, E. (2016). A genomic history of Aboriginal Australia. *Nature, 538*, 207–214.

Mandui, H. (2006). What is the future of our past? Papua New Guineans and cultural heritage. In I. Lilley (Ed.), *Archaeology of Oceania: Australia and the Pacific Islands* (pp. 379–382). Malden, MA: Blackwell.

Matchan, E. L., Phillips, D., Jourdan, F., & Oostingh, K. (2020). Early human occupation of southeastern Australia: New insights from ^{40}Ar/^{39}Ar dating of young volcanoes. *Geology, 48*(4), 390–394.

McBryde, I. (1978). Wil-im-ee Moor-ring: Or, where do axes come from?: Stone axe distribution and exchange patterns in Victoria. *Mankind, 11*(3), 354–382.

McBryde, I. (1984). Kulin greenstone quarries: The social contexts of production and distribution for the Mount William site. *World Archaeology, 16*(2), 267–285.

McBryde, I. (1986). Artefacts, language and social interaction: A case study from South-Eastern Australia. In G. N. Bailey & P. Callow (Eds.), *Stone Age prehistory: Studies in memory of Charles McBurney* (pp. 77–93). Cambridge: Cambridge University Press.

McCarthy, F. D. (1939). 'Trade' in Aboriginal Australia, and 'trade' relationships with Torres Strait, New Guinea and Malaya. *Oceania, 9*(4), 405–439, *10*(1), 80–104, *10*(2), 171–195.

McDonald, J. (2015). I must go down to the seas again: Or, what happens when the sea comes to you? Murujuga rock art as an environmental indicator for Australia's north-west. *Quaternary International, 385*, 124–135.

McNiven, I. J. (1990). *Prehistoric Aboriginal settlement and subsistence in the Cooloola Region, coastal southeast Queensland* (PhD thesis). University of Queensland, Brisbane.

McNiven, I. J. (1999). Fissioning and regionalisation: The social dimensions of changes in Aboriginal use of the Great Sandy Region, southeast Queensland. In J. Hall & I. J. McNiven (Eds.), *Australian coastal archaeology* (pp. 157–168). Research Papers in Archaeology & Natural History, No. 31. Canberra: ANH Publications.

McNiven, I. J. (2004). Saltwater people: Spiritscapes, maritime rituals and the archaeology of Australian indigenous seascapes. *World Archaeology, 35*(3), 329–349.

McNiven, I. J. (2010). Navigating the human-animal divide: Marine mammal hunters and rituals of sensory allurement. *World Archaeology, 42*(2), 215–230.

McNiven, I. J. (2011). Backed artefacts as a material dimension of social inclusiveness. *Australian Archaeology, 72*, 71–72.

McNiven, I. J. (2016). Theoretical challenges of Indigenous archaeology: Setting an agenda. *American Antiquity, 81*(1), 27–41.

McNiven, I. J. (2017). Edges of worlds: Torres Strait Islander peripheral participation in ancient globalizations. In T. Hodos (Ed.), *The Routledge handbook of globalization and archaeology* (pp. 319–334). New York: Routledge.

McNiven, I. J. (2018a). Inhabited landscapes. In S. L. López Varela (Ed.), *The encyclopedia of archaeological sciences* (pp. 1–5). Society for Archaeological Sciences. Malden, MA: Wiley Blackwell.

McNiven, I. J. (2018b). Ritual mutilation of Europeans on the Torres Strait maritime frontier. *Journal of Pacific History, 53*(3), 229–251.

McNiven, I. J. (2022). Beyond bridge and barrier: Reconceptualising Torres Strait as a co-constructed border zone in ethnographic object distributions between Queensland and New Guinea. *Queensland Archaeological Research, 25,* 25–46.

McNiven, I. J., & Bedingfield, A. C. (2008). Past and present marine mammal hunting rates and abundances: Dugong (*Dugong dugon*) evidence from Dabangai Bone Mound, Torres Strait. *Journal of Archaeological Science, 35*(2), 505–515.

McNiven, I. J., & Bell, D. (2010). Fishers and farmers: Historicising the Gunditjmara freshwater fishery, western Victoria. *The La Trobe Journal, 85,* 83–105.

McNiven, I. J., Crouch, J., Richards, T., Gunditj Mirring Traditional Owners Aboriginal Corporation, Dolby, N., & Jacobsen, G. (2012). Dating Aboriginal stone-walled fishtraps at Lake Condah, southeast Australia. *Journal of Archaeological Science, 39*(2), 268–286.

McNiven, I. J., Crouch, J., Richards, T., Sniderman, K., Dolby, N., & Gunditj Mirring Traditional Owners Aboriginal Corporation. (2015). Phased redevelopment of an ancient Gunditjmara fish trap over the past 800 years: Muldoons Trap Complex, Lake Condah, southwestern Victoria. *Australian Archaeology, 81,* 44–58.

McNiven, I. J., David, B., Richards, T., Aplin, K., Asmussen, B., Mialanes, J., . . . Ulm, S. (2011). New direction in human colonisation of the Pacific: Lapita settlement of south coast New Guinea. *Australian Archaeology, 72,* 1–6.

McNiven, I. J., Dickinson, W. R., David, B., Weisler, M., von Gnielinski, F., Carter, M. & Zoppi, U. (2006). Mask Cave: Red-slipped pottery and the Australian-Papuan settlement of Zenadh Kes (Torres Strait). *Archaeology in Oceania, 41*(2), 49–81.

McNiven, I. J., & Feldman, R. (2003). Ritually orchestrated seascapes: Bone mounds and dugong hunting magic in Torres Strait, NE Australia. *Cambridge Archaeological Journal, 13,* 169–194.

McNiven, I. J., & Russell, L. (1997). 'Strange paintings' and 'mystery races': Kimberley rock art, diffusionism and colonialist constructions of Australia's Aboriginal past. *Antiquity, 71,* 801–809.

McNiven, I. J., & Russell, L. (2005). *Appropriated pasts: Indigenous peoples and the colonial culture of archaeology.* Lanham, MD: AltaMira Press.

McNiven, I. J., & Wright, D. (2008). Ritualised marine midden formation in western Zenadh Kes (Torres Strait). In G. Clark, F. Leach, & S. O'Connor (Eds.), *Islands of inquiry: Colonisation, seafaring and the archaeology of maritime landscapes* (pp. 133–147). Terra Australis 29. Canberra: Pandanus.

McPhee, E. (2004). Archaeology of the pearlshelling industry in Torres Strait. *Memoirs of the Queensland Museum – Culture, 3*(1), 363–377.

Meggitt, M. J. (1962) *Desert people: A study of the Walbiri Aborigines of Central Australia.* London: Angus & Robertson.

Merlan, F. (1998). *Caging the rainbow: Places, politics, and Aborigines in a north Australian town.* Honolulu: University of Hawaii Press.

Minnegal, M. (1984). A note on butchering dugong at Princess Charlotte Bay. *Australian Archaeology, 19,* 15–20.

Moore, C. (2001). The South Sea Islanders of Mackay, Queensland, Australia. In J. Fitzpatrick (Ed.), *Endangered peoples of Oceania: Struggles to survive and thrive* (pp. 167–181). Westport, CT: Greenwood Press.

Moro Abadia, O., & Porr, M. (Eds.) (2021). *Ontologies of rock art: Images, relational approaches, and Indigenous knowledges.* London: Routledge.

Morwood, M. J. (1987). The archaeology of social complexity in south-east Queensland. *Proceedings of the Prehistoric Society, 53*(1), 337–350.

Mullins, S. (1992). Torres Strait's pre-colonial population: The historical evidence reconsidered. *Queensland Archaeological Research, 9*, 38–42.

Mullins, S. (1994). *Torres Strait: A history of colonial occupation and culture contact 1864–1897.* Rockhampton: Central Queensland University Press.

Mulvaney, D. J. (1962). Advancing frontiers in Australian archaeology. *Oceania, 33*(2), 135–138.

Mulvaney, D. J. (1964). The Pleistocene colonization of Australia. *Antiquity, 38*(152), 263–267.

Mulvaney, D. J. (1969). *The prehistory of Australia.* New York: Frederick A. Praeger.

Mulvaney, D. J. (1976). The chain of connection: The material evidence. In N. Peterson (Ed.), *Tribes and boundaries in Australia* (pp. 72–94). Social Anthropology Series No. 10. Canberra: Australian Institute of Aboriginal Studies.

Mulvaney, D. J., & Joyce, E. B. (1965). Archaeological and geomorphological investigations on Mt. Moffatt station, Queensland, Australia. *Proceedings of the Prehistoric Society, 31*, 147–212.

Murray, T., & White, J. P. (Eds.) (1985). Trends towards social complexity in prehistoric Australia and Papua New Guinea. I & II. *Archaeology in Oceania, 20*(2), 41–72 & *20*(3), 73–104.

Nakata, M. (2007). *Disciplining the savages: Savaging the disciplines.* Canberra: Aboriginal Studies Press.

Nakata, M., & David, B. (2010). Archaeological practice at the cultural interface. In J. Lydon & U. Z. Rizvi (Eds.), *Handbook of postcolonial archaeology* (pp. 429–443). Walnut Creek, CA: Left Coast Press.

NSO. (2015). *Papua New Guinea 2011 national report. National population and housing census 2011.* Waigani: National Statistical Office.

Nunn, P. D., & Reid, N. J. (2016). Aboriginal memories of inundation of the Australian coast dating from more than 7000 years ago. *Australian Geographer, 47*(1), 11–47.

O'Connell, J. F., Allen, J., Williams, M. A., Williams, A. N., Turney, C. S., Spooner, N. A., . . . Cooper, A. (2018). When did *Homo sapiens* first reach Southeast Asia and Sahul?. *Proceedings of the National Academy of Sciences of the USA, 115*(34), 8482–8490.

Palacio-Pérez, E. (2010). Salomon Reinach and the religious interpretation of Palaeolithic art. *Antiquity, 84*(325), 853–863.

Pardoe, C. (1988). The cemetery as symbol. The distribution of prehistoric Aboriginal burial grounds in southeastern Australia. *Archaeology in Oceania, 23*(1), 1–16.

Pascoe, B. (2014). *Dark emu black seeds: Agriculture or accident?* Broome: Magabala Books.

Pasveer, J. M. (2004). *The Djief hunters: 26,000 years of rainforest exploitation on the Bird's Head of Papua, Indonesia.* Leiden: A.A. Balkema.

Paterson, A., & Veth, P. (2020). The point of pearling: Colonial pearl fisheries and the historical translocation of Aboriginal and Asian workers in Australia's Northwest. *Journal of Anthropological Archaeology, 57*, 101143.

Paton, R. (1994). Speaking through stones: A study from northern Australia. *World Archaeology, 26*(2), 172–184.

Perston, Y., Wallis, L. A., Burke, H., McLennan, C., Hatte, E., & Barker, B. (2022). Flaked glass artifacts from nineteenth-century Native Mounted Police camps in Queensland, Australia. *International Journal of Historical Archaeology, 26*, 789–822.

Peterson, N. (1976). The natural and cultural areas of Aboriginal Australia: A preliminary analysis of population groupings with adaptive significance. In N. Peterson (Ed.), *Tribes and boundaries in Australia* (pp. 50–71). Social Anthropology Series No. 10. Canberra: Australian Institute of Aboriginal Studies.

Pétrequin, A.-M., & Pétrequin, P. (2006). *Objets de pouvoir en NouvelleGuinée: Approche enthnoarchéologique d'un system de signes sociaux*. Saint-Germain-en-Laye: Musée d'Archéologie Nationale.

Pollard, K., Smith, C., Willika, J., Copley Snr., V., Copley Jnr., V., Wilson, C., Poelina-Hunter, E., & Ah Quee, J. (2020). Indigenous views on the future of public archaeology in Australia. A conversation that did not happen. *AP: Online Journal in Public Archaeology, 10*, 31–52.

Porr, M. (2018). Country and relational ontology in the Kimberley, Northwest Australia: Implications for understanding and representing archaeological evidence. *Cambridge Archaeological Journal, 28*(3), 395–409.

Pouwer, J. (1999). The colonisation, decolonisation and recolonisation of west New Guinea. *The Journal of Pacific History, 34*, 157–179.

Rappaport, R. A. (1968). *Pigs for the ancestors: Ritual in the ecology of a New Guinea people*. New Haven, CT: Yale University Press.

Reinach, S. (1903). L'art et la magie. A propos des peintures et des gravures de l'age du Renne. *L'Anthropologie, 14*, 257–266.

Reynolds, H. (1981). *The other side of the frontier: Aboriginal resistance to the European invasion of Australia*. Sydney: University of New South Wales Press.

Rhoads, J. W. (1980). *Through a glass darkly: Present and past land-use systems among Papuan sagopalm users* (PhD thesis). Australian National University, Canberra.

Richards, T. (2012). An Early Holocene Aboriginal coastal landscape at Cape Duquesne, southwest Victoria, Australia. In S. G. Haberle & B. David (Eds.), *Peopled landscapes: Archaeological and biogeographic approaches to landscapes* (pp. 65–102). Terra Australis 34. Canberra: ANU E Press.

Richardson, N. (1992). Conjoin sets and stratigraphic integrity in a sandstone shelter: Kenniff Cave (Queensland, Australia). *Antiquity, 66*(251), 408–418.

Richardson, W. A. R. (2006). *Was Australia chartered before 1606? The Jave la Grande inscriptions*. Canberra: National Library of Australia.

Roberts, A., Hemming, S., Trevorrow, T., Trevorow, G., Rigney, M., Rigney, G., Agius, L., & Agius, R. (2005). 'Nukun and kungun Ngarrindjeri Ruwe' (Look and listen to Ngarrindjeri Country): Investigation of Ngarrindjeri perspectives of archaeology in relation to Native Title and heritage matters. *Australian Aboriginal Studies, 2005*/1, 45–53.

Roberts, A., Mollenmans, A., Agius, Q., Graham, F., Newchurch, J., Rigney, L. I., . . . Wanganeen, K. (2016). 'They planned their calendar . . . they set up ready for what they wanted to feed the tribe': A first-stage analysis of Narungga fish traps on Yorke Peninsula, South Australia. *The Journal of Island and Coastal Archaeology, 11*(1), 1–25.

Roberts, R., Bird, M., Olley, J., Galbraith, R., Lawson, E., Laslett, G., . . . Hua, Q. (1998). Optical and radiocarbon dating at Jinmium rock shelter in northern Australia. *Nature, 393*(6683), 358–362.

Robertson, G., Attenbrow, V., & Hiscock, P. (2009). Multiple uses for Australian backed artefacts. *Antiquity, 83*(320), 296–308.

Romm, J. S. (1992). *The edges of the Earth in ancient thought: Geography, exploration, and fiction*. Princeton, NJ: Princeton University Press.

Roscoe, P. (2002). The hunters and gatherers of New Guinea. *Current Anthropology, 43*(1), 153–162.

Rowland, M. J. (2018). 65,000 years of isolation in Aboriginal Australia or continuity and external contacts? An assessment of the evidence with an emphasis on the Queensland coast. *Journal of the Anthropological Society of South Australia, 42,* 211–240.

Russell, L. (2005). Kangaroo Island sealers and their descendants: Ethnic and gender ambiguities in the archaeology of a creolised community. *Australian Archaeology, 60*(1), 1–5.

Russell, L. (2012). *Roving mariners: Australian Aboriginal whalers and sealers in the Southern Oceans 1790–1870*. Albany: State University of New York Press.

Schilder, G. (1972). New cartographical contributions to the coastal exploration of Australia in the course of the seventeenth century. *Imago Mundi, 26,* 41–44.

Sharp, N. (2002). *Saltwater people: The waves of memory*. Crows Nest, NSW: Allen & Unwin.

Skelly, R., & David, B. (2017). *Hiri: Archaeology of long-distance maritime trade along the south coast of Papua New Guinea*. Honolulu: University of Hawaiʻi Press.

Skelly, R., David, B., McNiven, I. J., & Barker, B. (2011). The ritual dugong bone mounds of Koey Ngurtai, Torres Strait, Australia: Investigating their construction. *International Journal of Osteoarchaeology, 21*(1), 32–54.

Smith, A., McNiven, I. J., Rose, D., Brown, S., Johnston, C., & Crocker, S. (2019). Indigenous knowledge and resource management as world heritage values: Budj Bim Cultural Landscape, Australia. *Archaeologies, 15*(2), 285–313.

Smith, A. D. (2016). *Archaeological expressions of Holocene cultural and environmental change in coastal southeast Queensland* (PhD thesis). University of Queensland, Brisbane.

Smith, C., & Wobst, H. M. (Eds.) (2005). *Indigenous archaeologies: Decolonizing theory and practice*. London: Routledge.

Smith, C., Burke, H., Gorman, A., Ralph, J., Pollard, K., Wilson, C., . . . Jackson. G. (2019). Pursuing social justice through collaborative archaeologies in Aboriginal Australia. *Archaeologies, 15*(3), 536–569.

Smith, L. (2004). *Archaeological theory and the politics of cultural heritage*. London: Routledge.

Smith, M. A. (1982). Devon Downs reconsidered: Changes in site use at a lower Murray Valley rockshelter. *Archaeology in Oceania, 17*(3), 109–116.

Smith, T., & McNiven, I. J. (2019). Aboriginal marine subsistence foraging flexibility in a dynamic estuarine environment: The late development of Tin Can Inlet (southeast Queensland) middens revisited. *Queensland Archaeological Research, 22,* 1–38.

Specht, J. (1975). Smoking pipes and culture change on Buka Island, Papua New Guinea. *The Journal of the Polynesian Society, 84*(3), 356–364.

Specht, J., Torrence, R., & Mulvaney, K. (2021). Petroglyphs and place: Complex histories at four sites in New Britain. *Archaeology in Oceania, 56*(3), 196–228.

Spencer, W. B., & Gillen, F. J. (1899). *The native tribes of Central Australia*. London: Macmillan.

Spriggs, M. (1998). The archaeology of the Bird's Head in its Pacific and southeast Asian context. In J. Miedema, C. Ode, & R. A. Dam (Eds.), *Perspectives on the Bird's Head of Irian Jaya, Indonesia. Proceedings of the Conference, Leiden, 13–17 October 1997* (pp. 931–940). Amsterdam: Rodopi.

Spriggs, M. (2011). Archaeology and the Austronesian expansion: Where are we now? *Antiquity, 85*(328), 510–528.

Stallard, A. J. (2010). Origins of the idea of Antipodes: Errors, assumptions, and a bare few facts. *Terrae Incognitae, 42*(1), 34–51.

Stallard, A. J. (2016). *Antipodes: In search of the Southern Continent.* Clayton: Monash University Publishing.

Stone, T., & Cupper, M. L. (2003). Last Glacial Maximum ages for robust humans at Kow Swamp, southern Australia. *Journal of Human Evolution, 45*(2), 99–111.

Summerhayes, G. R. (2009). Obsidian network patterns in Melanesia: Sources, characterisation and distribution. *Bulletin of the Indo-Pacific Prehistory Association, 29*, 110–124.

Summerhayes, G. R., Leavesley, M., Fairbairn, A., Mandui, H., Field, J., Ford, A., & Fullagar, R. (2010). Human adaptation and plant use in highland New Guinea 49,000 to 44,000 years ago. *Science, 330*, 78–81.

Sutton, P., & Walshe, K. (2021). *Farmers or hunter-gatherers? The Dark Emu debate.* Melbourne: Melbourne University Press.

Swadling, P. (1983). *How long have people been in the Ok Tedi region?* PNG National Museum Record 8. Boroko: Trustees of the PNG National Museum.

Swadling, P. (1990). Sepik prehistory. In N. Lutkehaus, C. Kaufmann, W. E. Mitchell, D. Newton, L. Osmundsen, & M. Schuster (Eds.), *Sepik heritage: Tradition and change in Papua New Guinea* (pp. 71–86). Bathurst: Crawford House Press.

Swadling, P. (1996). *Plumes from paradise.* Boroko: Papua New Guinea National Museum.

Swadling, P. (1997). Changing shorelines and cultural orientations in the Sepik-Ramu, Papua New Guinea: Implications for Pacific prehistory. *World Archaeology, 29*(1), 1–14.

Szabó, K., David, B., McNiven, I. J., & Leavesley, M. (2020). Preceramic shell-working, Caution Bay and the Circum New Guinea Archipelago. In T. D. Thomas (Ed.), *Theory in the Pacific, the Pacific in theory: Archaeological perspectives* (pp. 123–144). Routledge.

Taçon, P. S. C., May, S. K., Fallon, S. J., Travers, M., Wesley, D., & Lamilami, R. (2010). A minimum age for early depictions of Southeast Asian Praus in the rock art of Arnhem Land, Northern Territory. *Australian Archaeology, 71*(1), 1–10.

Taylor, L. (1996). *Seeing the inside: Bark painting in western Arnhem Land.* Oxford: Clarendon Press.

Taylor, R. (2017). *Into the heart of Tasmania: A search for human antiquity.* Carlton: Melbourne University Press.

Testart, A. (1982). *Les chasseurs-cueilleurs ou l'origine des inégalités.* Paris: Société d'Ethnographie, Université Paris X-Nanterre.

Thomas, J. (1996). *Time, culture and identity: An interpretive archaeology.* London: Routledge.

Thomson, D. F. (1934). The dugong hunters of Cape York. *The Journal of the Royal Anthropological Institute of Great Britain and Ireland, 64*, 237–263.

Thomson, D. F. (1949). *Economic structure and the ceremonial exchange cycle in Arnhem Land.* Melbourne: Macmillan.

Thorne, A. G. (1977). Separation or reconciliation? Biological clues to the development of Australian society. In J. Allen, J. Golson, & R. Jones (Eds.), *Sunda and Sahul: Prehistoric studies in Southeast Asia, Melanesia and Australia* (pp. 187–204). New York: Academic Press.

Tochilin, C., Dickinson, W. R., Felgate, M. W., Pecha, M., Sheppard, P., Damonc, F. H., . . . Gehrels, G. E. (2012). Sourcing temper sands in ancient ceramics with U-Pb ages of detrital zircons: A southwest Pacific test case. *Journal of Archaeological Science, 39*, 2583–2591.

Tsang, R., Pleiber, W., Kariwiga, J., Plutniak, S., Forestier, H., Taçon, P. S. C., . . . Leavesley, M. G. (2022). Rock art and long-distance prehistoric exchange behavior: A case study from

Auwim, East Sepik, Papua New Guinea. *The Journal of Island and Coastal Archaeology, 17*(3), 432–444.

Ulm, S. (2011). Coastal foragers on southern shores: Marine resource use in northeast Australia since the Late Pleistocene. In N. F. Bicho, J. A. Haws, & L. G. Davis (Eds.), *Trekking the shore: Changing coastlines and the antiquity of coastal settlement* (pp. 441–461). New York: Springer.

Ulm, S. (2013). 'Complexity' and the Australian continental narrative: Themes in the archaeology of Holocene Australia. *Quaternary International, 285,* 182–192.

Ulm, S., & McNiven, I. (2021). Excavating Jiigurru. In B. Mitchell & R. Ridgway (Eds.), *Connections across the Coral Sea: A story of movement* (pp. 30–33). South Brisbane: Queensland Museum.

Urwin, C. (2019). Excavating and interpreting ancestral action: Stories from the subsurface of Orokolo Bay, Papua New Guinea. *Journal of Social Archaeology, 19*(3), 279–306.

Veth, P., Ward, I., Manne, T., Ulm, S., Ditchfield, K., Dortch, J., & Kendrick, P. (2017). Early human occupation of a maritime desert, Barrow Island, north-west Australia. *Quaternary Science Reviews, 168,* 19–29.

Wallace, A. R. (1869). *The Malay Archipelago.* London: Macmillan.

Wallis, L. A., & Matthews, J. (2016). Built structures in rockshelters of the Pilbara, Western Australia. *Records of the Western Australian Museum, 31,* 1–26.

White, J. P., & Mulvaney, D. J. (1987). How many people? In D. J. Mulvaney & J. P. White (Eds.), *Australians to 1788* (pp. 115–117). Broadway, NSW: Fairfax, Syme & Weldon.

White, J. P., & O'Connell, J. F. (1982). *A prehistory of Australia, New Guinea and Sahul.* Sydney: Academic Press.

Williams, A. N., Ulm, S., Sapienza, T., Lewis, S., & Turney, C. S. M. (2018). Sea-level change and demography during the Last Glacial Termination and Early Holocene across the Australian continent. *Quaternary Science Reviews, 182,* 144–154.

Williams, F. E. (1977). *'The Vailala madness' and other essays.* London: C. Hurst & Company.

Wright, D., Denham, T., Shine, D., & Donohue, M. 2013. An archaeological review of western New Guinea. *Journal of World Prehistory, 26*(1), 25–73.

Wright, D., van der Kolk, G., & Dauareb community. (2019). Ritual pathways and public memory: Archaeology of Waiet zogo in Eastern Torres Strait, far north Australia. *Journal of Social Archaeology, 19*(1), 116–138.

Wright, D., Carro, S. C. S., Nejman, L., van der Kolk, G., Litster, M., Langley, M.C., . . . Repu, C. (2021). Archaeology of the Waiat mysteries on Woeydhul Island in Western Torres Strait. *Antiquity, 95*(381), 791–811.

Yen, D. E. (1995). The development of Sahul agriculture with Australia as bystander. In J. Allen & J. F. O'Connell (Eds.), *Transitions: Pleistocene to Holocene in Australia and Papua New Guinea. Antiquity, 69*(265), 831–847.

Yengoyan, A. A. (1976). Structure, event and ecology in Aboriginal Australia: A comparative viewpoint. In N. Peterson (Ed.), *Tribes and boundaries in Australia* (pp. 121–132). Social Anthropology Series No. 10. Canberra: Australian Institute of Aboriginal Studies.

PART I

APPROACHING THE PAST

CHAPTER 2

'THE THICK DARKNESS OF PRE-HISTORIC TIMES'

Antiquarian Archaeology in Nineteenth-Century Colonial Victoria

IAN J. MCNIVEN

INTRODUCTION

THE past three decades have seen numerous publications documenting the rapid development of archaeology in Australia during the second half of the twentieth century (e.g., Allen 2019; Colley 2002; du Cros 2002; Griffiths 2018; Horton 1991; Murray & White 1981; Smith 2007; Spriggs 2020; Taylor 2017; see also Urwin & Spriggs, this volume). This scholarship broadened the scope of Australian archaeological historiography beyond intellectual developments of the late nineteenth and early twentieth centuries when archaeological approaches to Australia's Aboriginal past emerged with the rise of 'prehistoric archaeology' as a formal discipline of Western science (e.g., Griffiths 1996; Horton 1991; McNiven & Russell 2005; Mulvaney 1958a, 1958b, 1961, 1977). While it may seem like the intellectual development of Australian archaeology over the past 150 years has been well charted, the complexities and legacies of nineteenth-century archaeology remain poorly understood. Over the past twenty-five years, new histories of nineteenth-century archaeology in Australia have emerged that include case studies drawn from Victoria (Griffiths 1996; McNiven & Russell 2005). This chapter provides a focused account of the social and conceptual context of nineteenth-century archaeology in Victoria, detailing the broad range of ethnographically informed site types that attracted antiquarian interest and scholarship on Aboriginal origins.

It is now known that Aboriginal occupation of Victoria extends back at least 30,000–40,000 years (Hewitt & Allen 2010; Richards, Pavlides, Walshe, Webber, & Johnston 2007). This archaeological insight relies on chronometric dating techniques, such as radiocarbon dating which was introduced to Australian archaeology with a date of 1177±175 BP obtained on charcoal collected from a marine shell midden at Goose Lagoon located 1.2 km inland and 6 km west of Port Fairy, western Victoria, in the early 1950s (Gill 1955: 53–54, 1968: 162). For nineteenth-century antiquarians in Victoria, approaching the question of Aboriginal antiquity presented not only technical but also philosophical and ideological challenges.

INTERSECTING DISCOURSES: NINETEENTH-CENTURY ARCHAEOLOGIES IN AUSTRALIA

The practice of archaeology in Australia during the nineteenth century was a dimension of the global development of anthropological theories of human evolutionary progress. Bruce Trigger (1984: 358) identified 'three different social contexts' of the international development of archaeology: 'nationalist, colonialist, and imperialist or world-oriented'. Despite the clear heuristic value of these 'social contexts', Trigger acknowledged that 'as ideal types, they also fail to express the varying intensity with which the characteristics of each type are realised in specific cases' (1984: 358). *Nationalist* archaeologies have dominated the historical development of the discipline of archaeology as nation states attempted to create ancient historical pedigrees, often to assert and glorify cultural and ethnic distinctiveness albeit with political overtones. *Imperialist* archaeologies similarly arose in the nineteenth century and were associated with nation states constructing extra-regional and even global narratives of history in support of thinly veiled nationalist agendas of cultural, social, and racial superiority and political dominance.

In many respects, imperialist archaeologies provide the overarching framework for European understandings of the origins of Australia's First Nations peoples. During the first half of the nineteenth century, biblical views of the history and development of people dominated European understandings of humanity. John Mulvaney (1958a: 144, 1961) noted that before the publication of Charles Darwin's *On the Origin of Species* in 1859, 'acceptance of the Mosaic time scale [i.e., 6000 years] imposed a closed system of dating for Australia as for the rest of the world. As all varieties of men had developed since Adam, practically no time was left for their differentiation'. In the second half of the nineteenth century, biblical views were replaced in many intellectual circles by the paradigm of social evolutionism.

In the 1860s, European intellectual understandings of, and theorizing on, the origins and development of peoples and cultures across the globe changed fundamentally with formalization of the paradigm of social evolutionism in John Lubbock's *Prehistoric Times* (1865) and Edward Tylor's *Primitive Culture* (1865). Mulvaney (1958b: 299) rightly claimed that both of these volumes 'profoundly influenced contemporary thought'. Social evolutionism formalized speculative views of the unilinear development of humans from apes to so-called primitive hunter-gatherers ('savages'), to pastoralists and agriculturalists ('barbarians'), and finally through to cities and civilization (i.e., Europeans). In this schema, British colonists placed Australian Aboriginal peoples, especially Tasmanians, at the bottom of this imaginary evolutionary ladder and themselves at the top of the ladder. As a result, 'many eminent Victorians treated Australia as a museum of primeval humanity and a storehouse of fossil culture' (Mulvaney 1958b: 297).

Colonialist archaeologies are associated mostly with settler colonial states where Indigenous peoples have been invaded by Europeans. In a nutshell, 'while the colonisers had every reason to glorify their own past, they had no reason to extol the past of the peoples they were subjugating and supplanting. Indeed, they sought by emphasizing the primitiveness and lack of accomplishments of these peoples to justify their own poor treatment of them. . . . Modern native peoples were seen as comparable only to the earliest and most primitive phases of European development and as differentiated from Europeans by possessing no record of change and development and hence no history' (Trigger 1984: 360). Trigger (1984: 360–363) noted that the earthen mounds of the southeast United States and the site of Great Zimbabwe in southern Africa provide classic examples of nineteenth-century colonialist archaeologies, whereby the Indigenous origins of these sites was silenced by theories of external cultural origins.

Ian McNiven and Lynette Russell (2005) elaborated a conceptual framework to investigate and understand the historical development of colonialist archaeologies in settler colonial states, focusing on Australia. They posited that the 'colonial culture of archaeology' is 'founded upon and underwritten by a series of deep-seated colonialist and negative representational tropes of Indigenous peoples developed as part of European philosophies of imperialism over the last 2,500 years' (McNiven & Russell 2005: 2). Within the context of Australia, McNiven and Russell (2005: 7) argued that the colonial culture of archaeology comprised the 'two intricately related concepts' of 'disassociation and appropriation'. That is, Australian Aboriginal archaeological sites were attributed to other 'races' (in some cases Europeans), exemplified by rock paintings of the Kimberley region of Western Australia (McNiven 2011; McNiven & Russell 1997) and stone circles in Victoria (Russell & McNiven 1998).

SOCIAL CONTEXT OF ARCHAEOLOGY IN COLONIAL VICTORIA

The colony of Victoria was established in 1851 after separation from the colony of New South Wales which was established in 1788 with the beginnings of British settlement of the Australian continent at Sydney. Victoria became a state in the federation of the Commonwealth of Australia in 1901. Prior to 1851, the colony was known as the Port Phillip District of New South Wales. Melbourne, the capital of the district and later colony, was established in 1835 in the midst of rapid and violent expropriation of

Aboriginal lands across the colony for settler properties (Broome 2005; Critchett 1990). Immediately prior to European invasion, the region of Victoria was home to 50,000–100,000 Aboriginal people divided into at least forty language groups (Broome 2005; Butlin 1983: 144). By 1861, over 500,000 outsiders had moved into Victoria (Powell 1970: 59). By 1881, 51,000 km^2, or 22% of the area of Victoria, had been 'granted and sold' to colonists, mostly for agriculture and pastoralism (Powell 1970; Rusden 1883: 590). Survival for Aboriginal peoples in post-1850 frontier Victoria meant refuge on government reserves and church missions (Broome 2005). It was only after Aboriginal dispossession that wide-scale colonial agrarian land use and disturbance (e.g., ploughing), and diggings associated with gold rushes in the 1850s, that considerable archaeological evidence accumulated of Aboriginal occupation of Victoria. Antiquarian archaeology in Victoria rose out of the ashes of colonial invasion.

The recovery of, and interest in, archaeological evidence of Aboriginal activity across Victoria during the second half of the nineteenth century was not independent of the rise of Melbourne as a major metropolitan centre and hub of European intellectual culture in Australia. This status originally owed much to the rise of a 'squattocracy'—a wealthy class of pastoralists across rural Victoria, particularly the Western District— who maximized their squatting privileges to amass fortunes. These colonial aristocrats often visited Melbourne for financial reasons, and for leisure they centred on the men-only Melbourne Club (est. 1838) (de Serville 1980). Following the discovery of gold in Victoria in 1851, gold rush income profoundly invigorated Melbourne and its upper-class elite, expressed through the establishment of numerous intellectual institutions— University of Melbourne (1853), Royal Society of Victoria (1854), Public Library (1854), Philosophical Institute (1855), National Museum of Victoria (1858), and Museum of Art (1861) (de Serville 1991). By 1861, Melbourne had become the intellectual centre of the Australian colonies with the city boasting a 90% literacy rate (Roe 1974: 59). The British historian Asa Briggs (1993: 278) remarked that Melbourne was described as the 'Paris of the Antipodes' and listed it as one of the great cities of the nineteenth-century Victorian era. Of relevance to this chapter, Melbourne, as an internationally recognized social, cultural, and intellectual hub, included

> educated men with an interest in Aboriginal culture. These were public officials, advocates, guardians and protectors, who acted as both field observers and collectors and as metropolitan theorists and public intellectuals. The group and their emerging ethnographic conversation included pastoralists, protectors and explorers. Although most were familiar with and accustomed to life in regional locations, all also had homes in the city of Melbourne, where they met and attended lectures and other functions.
>
> (Boucher & Russell 2012: 155)

Compared to the rest of Australia, Melbourne metropolitan elites also stood out as 'these men often inflected their ethnographic enquiry with humanitarian and social justice concerns' (Boucher & Russell 2012: 155; see also Mitchell & Curthoys 2015: 200). Yet these men subscribed to the 'dying race' ethos where Aboriginal extinction was seen as an inevitable albeit regrettable outcome of colonial settlement and the cost of progress and civilization. Out of this ethos 'developed an imperative to salvage the culture, customs and life ways via ethnographic enquiry' (Boucher & Russell 2012: 155). Leigh Boucher (2015: 89–90) adds, 'in the 1850s the colony abounded with ethnographic lectures, displays of Aboriginal artefacts (and bodies), performances of Aboriginal ceremonies, and—perhaps most importantly—a steady population of middle-class men who claimed expertise'.

It is no coincidence that ethnographic inquiry and anthropological thinking in Australia centred on Melbourne during the second half of the nineteenth century. According to A. Peter Elkin (1975: 1), five of the ten nineteenth-century 'founders of social anthropology in Australia' were based in Victoria, including the two internationally renowned anthropologists—Alfred Howitt and Baldwin Spencer (see later). The Melbourne/Victorian intellectual milieu produced most of the classic nineteenth-century ethnographic texts on Aboriginal Australians, despite the fact that none of the authors of these texts were professionally employed as anthropologists. In some cases, texts were by antiquarians employed as government officials linked to paternalistic governance of Aboriginal people, such as the monumental, two-volume *The Aborigines of Victoria* (1878) assembled over sixteen years by Robert Brough Smyth, mining engineer and member of various government welfare Boards to manage Victorian Aboriginal people. Volume 1, written by Smyth, incorporated considerable information elicited from William Thomas, who was Assistant Protector (1839–1849), Guardian (1850–1867), and welfare Board member (Christie 1979; Standfield 2015). Volume 2 features a series of lengthy and informative appendices authored by government officials, including 'Notes and Anecdotes of the Aborigines of Australia' with archaeological interest by Philip Chauncy (District Surveyor at the Victorian gold-mining town of Ballarat). The volumes were reviewed in the journal *Nature* and described as 'an "epoch-making" event in the progress of ethnological studies' (Keane 1879: 549). In the mid-1880s, another Board member, Edward M. Curr (squatter and Chief Inspector of Stock), assembled and edited the equally monumental four-volume *The Australian Race* (1886–1887) (Furphy 2013).

Two Victorian pastoralists with a keen interest in Victorian Aboriginal peoples and their history also wrote classic ethnographies: James Dawson's *Australian Aborigines* (1881) and Peter Beveridge's *The Aborigines of Victoria and Riverina* (published posthumously in 1889). Dawson was from the Western District of Victoria and a Local Guardian of the Aborigines and, along with his daughter Isabella (who was fluent in the local Gunditjmara language), developed close relationships with Aboriginal peoples (Critchett 1981). Beveridge was a squatter whose property was located near the town of Swan Hill on the Murray River in northwest Victoria.

The late nineteenth century and turn of the twentieth century saw Victorians publish three ethnographic texts of international standing: Alfred Howitt and Lorimer Fison's *Kamilaroi and Kurnai* (1880), Baldwin Spencer and Frank Gillen's *The Native Tribes of Central Australia* (1899), and Alfred Howitt's *The Native Tribes of South-East Australia*

(1904). Howitt was a Police Magistrate and Warden of the Goldfields in Gippsland (eastern Victoria), and Fison was a Wesleyan missionary based in Fiji and Melbourne. Spencer was Professor of Biology at the University of Melbourne, and Gillen was Special Magistrate and Sub-Protector of the Aborigines in Alice Springs, South Australia. Anthropological doyens, Edward Tylor at Oxford University in England and Lewis Henry Morgan in the United States, enthusiastically endorsed *Kamilaroi and Kurnai* for publication (Gardner & McConvell, 2015: 207–208; Mulvaney 1970). The British anthropologist James Frazer (1909: 151) described *Kamilaroi and Kurnai* as 'a document of primary importance in the archives of anthropology' whose value 'can hardly be overestimated'. Of *The Native Tribes of South-East Australia*, Frazer (1909: 169–170) declared: 'it must always remain an anthropological classic'. Frazer's (1899: 81) praise for *The Native Tribes of Central Australia* could not have been stronger: 'I cannot but regard it as one of the most valuable contributions ever made to the early history of mankind'. Such praise was the shared view of the international anthropological elite (Kuklick 2006; Stocking 1995: 96). At the same time, it needs to be kept in mind that Spencer was an advocate of social evolutionism: 'the Australian aborigine may be regarded as a relic of the early childhood of mankind left stranded in a part of the world where he has, without the impetus derived from competition, remained in a low condition of savagery' (Spencer 1901: 12).

Victorian Aboriginal Origins and Antiquity: Multiple Approaches

In keeping with the rest of Australia, insights into 'Aboriginal origins' and 'antiquity' in Victoria during the nineteenth century were considered within the broader context of the origins of the 'Australian race' and viewed largely through the lens of social evolutionism. Three approaches with different epistemological underpinnings were employed: anthropological, geological (including oral histories), and archaeological. Most antiquarians, however, were sympathetic to Smyth's (1878, I: lxv) lament that the 'origin of the Australian race is still hidden from us. We cannot yet penetrate the thick darkness of pre-historic times'.

Anthropological Approaches

Anthropological approaches to the origins of Aboriginal Australians focused on characteristics of contemporary Aboriginal peoples (cultural/linguistic and physiological) to determine whether the so-called 'Australian race' was a 'pure', single race or a mixed race who amalgamated either before entering Australia or after. For example, based on similarities in cultural practices, languages, and physical features, Curr (1886, I: 152, 158,

187; 1887, III: 680–681) elaborated a theory of a single colonization of mainland Australia by Africans 'crossed by some other race' with subsequent and 'quite inconsequential and recent infusion of Malay blood here and there on the north coast'. Tasmania, in contrast, represented a separate colonization event by peoples of 'mixed' African descent (Curr 1887, III: 604). Beveridge (1889: 105–106) stated simply that lack of archaeological evidence 'denoting the former existence of a higher order of men' suggested that contemporary Aboriginal 'people are descended from a primitive race' who were immigrants akin to 'the long-extinct pre-historic races of Europe'.

In his paper read before the Royal Society of New South Wales in 1889, Rev. John Mathew of Coburg in Melbourne went against the single colonization theory of Aboriginal origins and elaborated his famous trihybrid model. Mathew (1889) categorized contemporary Aboriginal cultural/linguistic and physiological variability into three separate groups and migration waves. He proposed that Australia was first colonized by Papuans (represented mostly now by Tasmanians), followed by immigration ('invasion') of Dravidians (sourced to India) and then Malays (both represented now by mainland Australians). Mathew (1889: 382) put no dates on these migrations, stating simply that they occurred 'at a very early period of the world's history'. Victoria had importance as the departure point for Papuans entering Tasmania using the 'string of islands' across Bass Strait as 'stepping stones' (perhaps walking across 'dry land' at lower sea level), a view said to be consistent with linguistic similarities between Victoria and Tasmania (Mathew 1889: 356, 364, 370, 382).

Geological Approaches

The most compelling evidence presented by nineteenth-century antiquarians for a deep antiquity to Aboriginal occupation of Victoria concerns linking Aboriginal people to ancient geological events, namely volcanic eruptions and sea-level changes and the formation of Bass Strait.

In his 1881 book *Australian Aborigines*, James Dawson recorded oral histories from Western District Aboriginal people of a time when a number of the region's volcanoes were active (1881: 101–102). Further oral histories associated with specific volcanoes in the Western District were published in Melbourne's *Argus* newspaper 1897 (Anon. 1898a: 56). Howitt (1898: 753) commented that 'if any reliance may be placed upon aboriginal tradition, the affirmative belief in the presence of man in Victoria during the Newer Volcanic Era [Late Pleistocene] is much strengthened' (see also Howitt 1904: 17). John Gregory, Professor of Geology at the University of Melbourne, in his highly influential paper 'The Antiquity of Man in Victoria', critically evaluated these oral histories, concluding that 'the evidence of the aboriginal traditions gives no certain support to the view that man witnessed any of the volcanic eruptions in Victoria' (1904: 133–138, 140). This conclusion reflected a dismissal of the epistemological veracity of Aboriginal oral histories and his entrenched view that archaeological evidence supported only recent Aboriginal occupation of Victoria.

More recently, the Gunditjmara of southwest Victoria have made public their 'old story' of how the being Budj Bim released molten rock and laid down to form the landscape feature that Europeans call the Mt Eccles volcano (Gunditjmara People & Wettenhall 2010). Recent geochronological dating of the eruption of Budj Bim to 37,000 years ago indicates the potential age of this oral history (Matchan, Phillips, Jourdan, & Oostingh 2020; see also Wilkie, Cahir, & Clark 2020).

The proposition that Aboriginal occupation of Victoria, and by extension the rest of mainland Australia, must predate the formation of Bass Strait if the ancestors of Aboriginal Tasmanians walked across a dry Bass Strait remains as plausible and convincing today as it did when first proposed in the late nineteenth century. Bonwick (1870: 248) assumed, following Huxley's proposition that no culture loses the 'art of navigation', that the absence of seagoing canoes of the ethnographically known Tasmanians indicated that their ancestors were similarly incapable of crossing the 'boisterous Bass's Straits'. As such, he advanced the hypothesis that the ancestors of the Tasmanians walked to Tasmania across a land bridge that once joined Victoria and Tasmania 'many, many thousands of years' ago (Bonwick 1870: 215, 249, 252, 258–259, 261, 263). This land bridge subsequently became inundated by 'subsidence' of land, after which the ancestors of mainland Australians entered the continent bearing a slightly different culture to that of the Tasmanians (Bonwick 1870: 259, 264–265).

The hypothesis of colonization of Tasmania via a land bridge long since submerged by land subsidence followed by arrival of another group to mainland Australia was similarly advanced by Smyth (1878, I: lxx–lxxii) and in more sophisticated form by Howitt (1898). Howitt (1898: 751) added that the 'origin' of the 'Tasmanians' 'demand a vast antiquity' and that of the 'Australians' 'a very long period of at least prehistoric time'. Etheridge (1891: 266) concluded his critical evaluation of archaeological evidence to the question of 'Has man a geological history in Australia?' with a reference to the separation of Tasmanians and mainland Australians by the formation of Bass Strait, stating 'herein lies one of the strongest proofs of man's early existence on the Island Continent of Australia'. Aligning himself with the wrong side of history, Gregory (1904: 138) dismissed the Bass Strait hypothesis, giving precedence to what he considered to be a lack of convincing archaeological evidence for Aboriginal occupation of Australia beyond a few hundred years.

Archaeological Approaches

Nineteenth-century antiquarians in Victoria agreed that an important source of information on the antiquity of Aboriginal occupation was physical evidence in the form of artefacts and sites on the landscape. While in some cases sites were clearly 'prehistoric', in other cases the boundary between archaeological site and ethnographic site was blurred as many sites were used within living memory. The ethnographically informed approach ensured that the range of sites examined and discussed was both diverse and comprehensive: burials (e.g., ground interments), implement sites (e.g., stone axes, flaked stone artefacts, and fossil bone artefacts), occupation sites (e.g., earthen 'oven' mounds, shell middens, and stone huts), resource extraction sites (e.g., stone axe quarries, and fishtraps), and ceremonial sites (e.g., stone arrangements, ritual caves, and rock art). In some cases, sites were fanciful such as megalithic henges and fossilized footprints. While most sites were examined to reveal insights into the history of Victorian Aboriginal peoples, it was also common to expand discussions to broader questions of the origins of the 'Australian race'.

Burials and Craniometry

Victoria's antiquarians during the nineteenth century expressed only minor interest in Aboriginal skeletal remains. In marked contrast, Aboriginal skeletal remains excavated from cemeteries along the Murray River in northern Victoria have been the focus of twentieth-century archaeological studies of ancient burial practices and pathology in Australia (see Littleton, Karstens, & Allen, this volume). Nineteenth-century reports of Aboriginal human remains tended to be ad hoc, superficial, and based on serendipitous disturbance of graves during agricultural practices such as ploughing or construction of drainage channels. Descriptions of human remains tended to be in the context of burial practices as an extension of what was known through ethnographic observations. However, in some cases, antiquarian interest extended to further (purposeful) disturbance of burial sites to recover more human remains to better understand and contextualize burial practices. Chauncy (1878: 234) reported that up to six 'skeletons' had been recovered from an oven mound in southwest Victoria, while Beveridge (1889: 37) mentioned that twenty-eight 'skeletons' had been excavated from an oven mound on the Murray River in northern Victoria.

Worsnop (1897: 105) provided a rare comment on the potential age of disturbed Aboriginal burials in Victoria. The graves were uncovered at 'more than 6ft.' (1.8 m) below the surface during excavation of drainage channels in the Condah Swamp region of southwest Victoria in 1892. The graves were located below a layer of peat and 'were probably ancient, as the peat accumulates slowly' (Worsnop 1897: 105).

Academic interest in the physical remains of Aboriginal Victorians focused on the broader question of the origins of the so-called Australian race and the extent to which Aboriginal skulls revealed morphological features of primitiveness and evolutionary evidence for closer proximity to apes compared to Europeans. As Antje Kühnast (2012: 172) cogently remarked, 'In the wake of Darwinian evolutionary theorising Australian Aboriginal human remains became coveted pieces of evidence in European evolutionary discourse'. This discourse was the grander narrative of 'racial origins' informed by the paradigm of social evolutionism. Victoria's role in this nineteenth-century imperialist enterprise was to contribute further examples of the 'Australian race'.

Two Victorian skulls had international prominence. The first example featured in the most important description of a human fossil skull find of the nineteenth century—the remains of 'Neanderthal man', unearthed in a cave in the Neander Valley in Prussia (Germany) in 1856. In his description, famous English evolutionist Thomas Huxley (1863: 155) compared the 'Neanderthal skull' to a number of 'Aboriginal skulls', including one taken from 'Western Port' located immediately southeast of Melbourne and housed at the time in the Museum of the Royal College of Surgeons of England in London. The Western Port skull had been taken by physician and naturalist Edmund Hobson in the early 1840s and sent to the famous comparative anatomist Richard Owen at the Royal College of Surgeons in 1844 (Owen 1853: 823; Turnbull 2017: 91). Although the Neanderthal skull revealed some resemblances to the Aboriginal skulls, it also shared attributes in common with a more recent prehistoric (Mesolithic) skull from Denmark. The lack of a clear morphological proximity between the Neanderthal skull (a demonstrated early form of human from the past) and an Aboriginal skull (an assumed early form of human in the present) puzzled Huxley as it did not fit with expectations of racial ranking and development underpinning the social evolutionism paradigm. To offset this anatomical anomaly, Huxley reminded readers that both Neanderthals and Aboriginal people were 'savages' that used tools fashioned from stone and bone (cited in Lyell 1863: 89–90) (for further discussion, see McNiven & Russell 2005: 58–62).

The second example concerned remains of a recently deceased Aboriginal man of the 'Warrnambool tribe' in southwest Victoria. The remains were sent to Wilhelm Keferstein at the Göttingen Zoological Museum (Germany) by famous colonial botanist Ferdinand von Müller of the Botanical Gardens in Melbourne and Warrnambool (Keferstein 1865; Kühnast 2012: 173). As with Huxley in England, Keferstein (1865) countered the unexpected finding of morphological similarities between the skulls and skeleton of Aboriginal people and Europeans by 'recourse to colonial discourse on the alleged inferiority of Aboriginal culture and intellect' (Kühnast 2012: 174).

Chauncy (1878: 241) examined two Aboriginal skulls removed from an oven mound 'near Fiery Creek' in southwest Victoria and similarly found results contradictory to social evolutionist doctrine. He suggested that the 'conclusion that the Australian skull is unquestionably inferior in development to the European has been arrived at on insufficient data. . . . Bad heads in the European type are not uncommon, but cannot be accepted as fair examples of the race' (Chauncy 1878: 241).

Implement Sites

Stone Axes

Stone axes were the Aboriginal object that caught the attention of antiquarians in nineteenth-century Victoria. An early insight into their potential antiquity was a stone axe recovered at 'a depth of twenty-two inches [56 cm] from the surface, while trenching for a garden' in Ballarat, central Victoria, in 1864 (Anon. 1864: 120) (Figure 2.1a). The 'bluestone' (basalt) axe exhibited a hafting groove and was compared to a detailed account of similarly shaped stone tools ('stone mauls') associated with copper mining by Native Americans at Lake Superior in North America quoted at length from *Prehistoric Man* by Daniel Wilson (1862, I: chap 8, fig. 11). While Anon. (1864) avoided speculating on the potential age of the axe, Bonwick (1870: 215–216) proffered that it 'would sanction the idea of considerable antiquity'.

That stone axes were a focus of interest in colonial documentation of Victorian Aboriginal material culture is revealed by the nonillustrated *Catalogue of the Objects of Ethnographic Art in the National Gallery* of Victoria published in 1878. Of the nearly 300 Victorian ethnographic and archaeological objects listed, 30% are stone axes (N = 85 of which only 7 are hafted) (Anon. 1878: 6–34).

Smyth (1878, I: 371) noted that 'great numbers' of 'highly-polished stone axes', both complete and broken, 'are found in nearly all parts of the colony'. Indeed, Smyth (1878) remains the most comprehensive illustrated catalogue of ground-edge axes published for Victoria. He lists nearly forty locations in Victoria, mostly in the southwest (Western District) and southeast (Gippsland), where axes had been found archaeologically (Smyth 1878, I: 361, 368–376). Smyth included ethnographic examples of Victorian stone axe with wooden handles in his catalogue of archaeological axes to reveal morphological and technological similarities between past and present (Figure 2.1b, 1c). Remarkably, Davis (1894: 582) reported that stone axes, 'some in handles', were recovered following ploughing of paddocks near Mt William axe quarry (see later) located immediately north of Melbourne.

Smyth expressed mixed and contradictory views on the antiquity of stone axes in Victoria. In his Introduction to *The Aborigines of Victoria*, he stated 'wherever the soil is dug or ploughed over any considerable area, old tomahawks are turned up, thus showing the immense period of time that the land has been occupied by the native race' (1878, I: lvii). Further into the volume Smyth changed tune. He pointed out that 'it is remarkable that no stone hatchet, chip of basalt, or stone knife has been found anywhere in Victoria except on the surface of the ground or a few inches beneath the surface' (Smyth 1878, I: 364). Furthermore, 'though some hundreds of square miles of alluvia have been turned over in mining for gold, not a trace of any work of human hands has been discovered' (Smyth 1878, I: 364). And, 'if only small portions of the alluvia in Victoria had been excavated—if the country had not been occupied for twenty years by many thousands of miners, who have washed the gravels down to the bed-rock in innumerable shallow gullies—the non-discovery of relics might have been easily accounted for; but in this country the spots most likely to conceal them have been laid bare' (Smyth 1878, I: 365). Smyth's conclusions on lack of evidence for antiquity were supported by MacPherson (1886: 119) and Etheridge (1891: 265).

Yet, even when subsurface stone axes were found, the potential for antiquity was dismissed. Smyth (1878, I: 361) made no comment on the likely antiquity of the Ballarat axe (Anon. 1864). Howitt (1898: 752, 1904: 16) declared that a stone axe uncovered in 1870

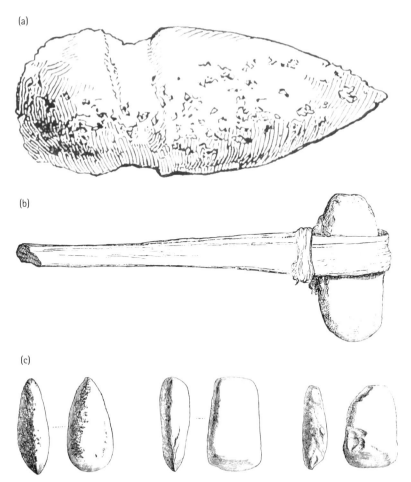

FIGURE 2.1. Stone axes from Victoria. A: archaeological stone axe unearthed in Ballarat, central Victoria, in 1864 (L = 20 cm) (Anon. 1864: fig. 1). B: ethnographic axe made from 'greenstone (dense diorite)' with 'wooden handle' from Lake Tyers, Gippsland, eastern Victoria (L = 38 cm) (Smyth 1878, I: 366, fig. 177). C (left): archaeological axe made from 'black greenstone' and collected from Coranderrk, southern central Victoria (L = 17 cm) (Smyth 1878, I: 369, fig. 184); C (middle): archaeological axe made from 'metamorphic sandstone' and collected from Lake Tyers, Gippsland, eastern Victoria (L = 17 cm) (Smyth 1878, I: 369, fig. 185); C (right): archaeological axe made from 'metamorphic sandstone' and collected from Lake Tyers, Gippsland, eastern Victoria (L = 15 cm) (Smyth 1878, I: 369, fig. 186).

by gold miners in the Upper Dargo River of Gippsland (eastern Victoria) at a depth of 'about 2 feet below the surface' from 'shingly alluvium' did 'not necessarily imply any great antiquity'.

A different view on the antiquity of subsurface stone axes in Victoria was published by The Royal Anthropological Society of Australasia (RASA) in its 'official organ'—the journal *Science of Man*. The RASA argued that stone axes recovered from Warrnambool in southwest Victoria were 'thousands of years' old as they had been recovered from under 'sand-drift rock', evidenced a heavily weathered surface (i.e., 'enamelled with a silecious [sic] glaze'), and that they 'are in shape quite distinct from the tomahawk of the last century' (i.e., 'heavier' and 'grooved') and also to those found in shell 'middens' and mounded 'ovens' (Anon. 1898a: 54, 1898b: 41, see also Archibald 1894). Similar axes found 'between 3 and 4 feet' below the surface nearby at Panmure, and 'under twenty feet of alluvium by gold miners . . . in the valley of the Mitchell river' in Gippsland, were presented as corroborating evidence for antiquity (Anon. 1898a: 55, 1898b: 41).

While the RASA made a plausible argument that heavy, grooved axes were older and dissimilar in form to recent Aboriginal stone axes in Victoria, social evolutionists in England went one step further and argued that ground-edge axes were a discordant stone artefact technology of Aboriginal Australians. In *Pre-Historic Times*, John Lubbock (1865) contrasted what he famously termed the 'Palaeolithic period' (characterized by flaked implements such as knives and scrapers) with the 'Neolithic period' (characterized by 'polished' implements such as 'celts' and ground-edge axes). As detailed in McNiven (2020), Edward Tylor (1865: 193, 201) pointed out that Lubbock's division was problematic for understanding Australian Aboriginal stone tool technologies, which possessed an anomalous mixture of the 'Un-ground Stone Age' (cf. Palaeolithic) and the 'Ground Stone Age' (cf. Neolithic) (see also Mulvaney 1958b: 303). To account for this discordance and potential challenge to the integrity of the social evolutionism paradigm, Tylor posited that Aboriginal Australians learnt the art of ground-edge axe use from contact with outsiders of a 'Malay or Polynesian source' (1865: 201). By recourse to external contact and diffusion, the essentialized core of Aboriginal technology as 'Palaeolithic' was maintained and 'necessary to keep Aboriginal Australians in their primordial place' (McNiven 2006: 91).

Smyth (1878, I: lv) took exception to the social evolutionists' take on Aboriginal stone artefact technologies representing a mixture of the 'Neolithic period' and the 'Palaeolithic period of Europe'. He argued that Aboriginal technology with flaked and ground implements 'seem to press strongly against the theories of Sir John Lubbock' (Smyth 1878, I: lv). Furthermore, the Australian evidence indicated that 'there is no method by which we can distinguish a difference of period if we examine stone implements' (Smyth 1878, I: 360). Mulvaney (1977: 264) suggested that Smyth's anti-Lubbock stance 'encouraged a bleak nationalism . . . [which] . . . was not an atmosphere in which to nurture prehistoric research'. Yet such 'nationalism' was a courageous stance against the monolithic edifice of social evolutionism and luminaries such as Lubbock.

Remarkably, issues of stone axe antiquity and chronological changes in form remain unresolved in Victorian archaeology as few stone axes have been recovered using modern excavation techniques. However, the dating (albeit limited) of Victorian axes to the Late Holocene is consistent with southern Australia more broadly (Ford & Hiscock this volume; Frankel 2017: 188).

Flaked Stone Artefacts

Although Victoria was a focus of flaked stone artefact collection and classification in Australia during the first half of the twentieth century (e.g., Mulvaney 1977: 264), such interest emerged in the late nineteenth century, pushed by Smyth (1878, I: 361–364), who listed a range of locations in Victoria, mostly in the southwest, where 'chips' occur. More significantly, Smyth (1878, I: 358) 'produced the first detailed, systematic stone tool classification' of Aboriginal stone artefacts, listing eleven functional types (e.g., hatchets, knives, adzes) (Mulvaney 1977: 263–264). This approach laid the foundations for Kenyon and Stirling's (1901) elaborated classification system of fifty-two types of 'Aboriginal stone implements', which focused on Victoria. Kenyon and Stirling's paper was read before the Royal Society of Victoria by Baldwin Spencer in 1900, who subsequently used the system to arrange the Aboriginal stone artefact displays at the National Museum of Victoria (Spencer 1901).

In terms of antiquity, Smyth (1878 I: 364–365) argued forcefully that no convincing evidence of buried stone artefacts (both stone axes and 'chips') of antiquity have been recovered from Victoria. In support of Smyth, MacPherson (1886: 117–119) added that even where subsurface stone artefacts had been found, rapid deposition rates of flood sediments and dune deposits, as recorded historically, obviated conclusions on antiquity. Gregory (1904) similarly subscribed to rapid deposition to dismiss associations between deeply buried artefacts and antiquity. He concluded that 'the oldest bed in which stone implements have been found need not be more than a few centuries old. The evidence is overwhelming that the implements occur only in the superficial layers or in beds such as river silts and sand dunes, which may accumulate with extreme rapidity' (Gregory 1904: 141). As such, 'the general evidence seems to me to point to the conclusion that the aborigines have resided in Victoria for but a short period' (Gregory 1904: 141).

Despite doubts cast on the antiquity of recorded subsurface artefacts in Victoria by Smyth, MacPherson, and Gregory, others continued to support the view that subsurface artefacts were the most fruitful avenue of research to demonstrate antiquity. For example, Davis (1894: 584) argued that 'the period of the first occupation of the continent by the Australian race . . . must be ascertained by the position in the soil of less perishable monuments. Their stone implements, almost indestructible in their character, are surer guides, in considering this question, than any other of their works of art'. Ferguson (1894: 87, 89–90) suggested that subsurface stone artefacts eroding from terraces flanking the Wannon and Hopkins Rivers in southwest Victoria may represent 'relics of man' laying 'undisturbed for thousands of years'. In the past twenty years, excavations have revealed stone artefacts in Victoria dated to 30,000–40,000 years ago, all within 1.5 m of the ground surface (Hewitt & Allen 2010; Richards, Pavlides, Walshe, Webber, & Johnston 2007).

Fossil Bone Artefacts

A reputed bone tool was recovered from a depth of 72 m below the surface in a gold mining shaft by employees of the Great Buninyong Estate Mine to the immediate south of Ballarat in central Victoria in 1897 (de Vis 1899; Hart 1899). The object is a 15.4 cm-long, fossilized fragment of the distal half of a rib bone of a giant extinct diprotodontid

(Nototheres, cf. *Nototherium mitchelli*) and revealed (pre-fossilization) flaking and chop marks which de Vis considered had to be of cultural origin and not from gnawing by a carnivore such as the (now extinct) marsupial lion (*Thylacoleo carnifex*). Charles de Vis (1899: 86) of the Queensland Museum considered the bone 'to be the first to record the presence and indicate the condition of man in Australia in an age so remote, we cannot but feel a profound interest'. The great age of the bone object was indisputable given its association with bones of other extinct animals (e.g., giant kangaroos) and its recovery from clays located beneath a basalt lava flow (de Vis 1899; Hart 1899). But the artefactual status of 'The Buninyong Bone' implement was short lived. Gregory (1904: 124) concluded that the lingering question of potential carnivore modification plus the absence of associated stone artefacts indicated 'that we cannot accept the high antiquity of man in Victoria on the evidence of this bone alone'. The hypothesis of carnivore agency was demonstrated conclusively by a detailed comparative study of marsupial lion gnawing damage to bones by Spencer and Walcott (1911). History repeated itself in the twentieth century with a large incisor from an extinct Diprotodon excavated from Spring Creek in southwest Victoria, whereby a series of incisions initially interpreted as made by a stone tool (Vanderwal & Fullagar 1989) have been reinterpreted as the result of animal gnawing, probably by a spotted-tailed quoll (*Dasyurus maculatus*) (Langley 2020).

OCCUPATION SITES

Earthen (Oven) Mounds

Earthen mounds average around 10 m in diameter and 0.5 m in height (Williams 1988), with one large example located on 'Connewarren Estate . . . measuring 39 yards [36 m] across, 6 feet [1.8 m] deep in the middle, and estimated to contain over 1500 cubic yards [1147 m³] of earth' (Soilleux 1891: 42) (Figure 2.2a). They comprise occupation deposits (e.g., bones, shells, stone artefacts), cooking features (e.g., charcoal), and sometimes burials (e.g., skeletal remains), and occur mostly across western and northern Victoria (e.g., Frankel 2017: 151–160; Williams 1988). Informative nineteenth-century overviews of the form, location, structure, and function of these sites (usually referred to as 'oven mounds'), infused with ethnographic observations, are available for the Western District of southwest Victoria (e.g., Chauncy 1878: 233–234, 241; Dawson 1881: 103–104; MacPherson 1885; Smyth 1878, I: 239–240, 364, 368–369, 371; Soilleux 1891) and the Murray River region of northern Victoria (e.g., Beveridge 1869, 1884: 37–40, 1889: 31–37; Curr 1883: 236–239).

The content of 'oven mounds' attracted considerable antiquarian attention during the nineteenth century as sources of ground-edge axes and burials. Indeed, these sites mark the beginning of subsurface archaeological investigation of Aboriginal occupation sites in Australia, albeit through shovel excavation. A landmark excavation was James Dawson's sectioning of 'Aboriginal mounds' in the Western District in 1869 (Figure 2.2b). He observed that 'throughout the faces of the crosscuttings which were dug in different

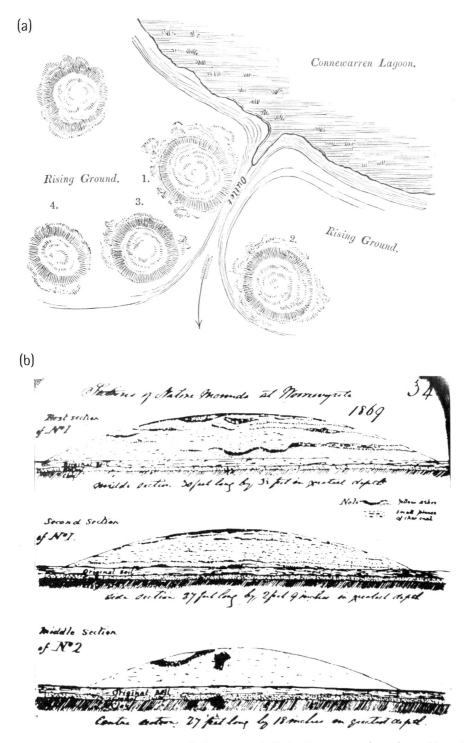

FIGURE 2.2. A: Earthen oven mounds (*Mirrn-yong*), 'Lake Connewarren', southwest Victoria (from Chauncy, 1878: 233, fig. 247). B: James Dawson's section drawings of two Aboriginal mounds excavated in southwest Victoria in 1869 (Dawson scrapbook, p. 34, microfilm, State Library of Victoria. Original in the possession of the Dawson family).

directions a complete history of the growth of these mounds was exhibited as shown in the first and second sections of No. 1 where the marks of old fires or hearths are directly traceable by saucer shaped streaks and layers of yellow coloured wood ashes intermixed with small pieces of charcoal' (Dawson scrapbook pp. 34–35 cited in Williams 1988: 16; see also Madden 2010).

Smyth (1878, I: 368–369) surmised that a heavily weathered stone axe recovered from an oven mound at Lake Condah in southwest Victoria must have been buried for 'an immense period of time'. Chauncy (1878: 232–233) suggested that large mounds accumulated over 'the course of centuries' and 'must be of great antiquity'. He advanced that 'some of the largest of these mounds be scientifically examined, with a view of ascertaining whether they contain any relics or implements differing from those in use at the present time' (Chauncy 1878: 234). Assumptions on the accumulation rates of ash similarly informed MacPherson's (1885: 58–59) conclusion that some large oven mounds in southwest Victoria may 'drive us back into a much greater antiquity than 400 years'. MacPherson (1885: 59) added that if 'great antiquity is claimed' for the 'Australian race', then 'we shall have to regard the building of ovens and the accumulation of the mounds of ashes as comparatively modern innovations'. Curr (1886, I: 207) posited that 'many huge ovens or cinder-heaps' found along the Murray River provide 'abundant proof that the period which has elapsed since our Blacks completed their occupation of this southern portion of the continent is a long one'. Modern archaeological research demonstrates that the tradition of earthen mounds in Victoria is indeed a recent 'innovation', with the earliest Western District mounds dated to c. 2400 years ago (Coutts & Witter 1977: table 1), and the earliest Murray River mounds dated to c. 4000 years ago (Berryman & Frankel 1984).

Shell Middens

Victorian Aboriginal shell middens, both marine and freshwater, attracted only minor antiquarian interest during the nineteenth century. Smyth (1878, I: xxxvi, 241) pointed out that 'middens are found on the banks of nearly all the rivers and large lakes and marshes in Victoria, and on the sea-coast'. Chauncy (1878: 234) noted that with the 'large shell-mounds on the coast, especially near Cape Otway . . . It must have taken ages for the fish-eating natives of the coast to build up such heaps'. He advocated that 'some of the largest of these mounds be scientifically examined, with a view of ascertaining whether they contain any relics or implements differing from those in use at the present time'. Smyth (1878, I: xxxvi, 241) similarly spoke of 'ancient shell-mounds' and large midden deposits, indicating that 'they must have been the resort of the natives during very long periods'. He added that as little is known about shell mounds owing to the lack of disturbance by colonists, 'future archaeologists will find abundant fields for research' (Smyth 1878, I: 242). Curr (1886, I: 206–207) posited that 'long lines of mussel shells' buried up to 0.6 m below the surface within 'the banks of the Murray' River in central northern Victoria provide further support for the conclusion that 'the Australian race is of vast antiquity'. Gregory (1904: 142) dismissed Curr's conclusions, stating that 'a single flood may deposit a couple of feet of silt'. Modern archaeological research in Victoria has revealed coastal (marine) shell middens dated back to 11,000 years ago (Richards 2012), and mussel shell middens on the banks of the Murray River dated back to 15,000 years ago (Garvey 2017) and perhaps over 16,000 years ago (Coutts 1980: 10).

STONE HOUSES

Aboriginal stone houses in Victoria did not attract antiquarian interest until the late nineteenth century. The sites are mostly U- or C-shaped structures (3–4 m across) with low walls of basalt blocks that once supported domed-roofed structures of branches, thatch, and mud. Ethnographic and archaeological evidence concur that these structures are domestic houses, with a distribution restricted to lava flows in southwest Victoria (for a detailed overview, see McNiven, Dunn, Crouch, & Gunditj Mirring 2017). Chauncy (1878: 234–235) briefly mentioned examples of stone houses located 'south of Lake Purrumbete' in southwest Victoria. Further to the west in the Lake Condah region, Worsnop (1897: 78, 105–106) reported clusters of up to twenty stone houses. Numerous stone houses in southwest Victoria have been archaeologically excavated since the 1970s, most revealing glass and metal artefacts, indicating occupation in the mid-nineteenth century (see McNiven, Dunn, Crouch, & Gunditj Mirring 2017). Unequivocal archaeological evidence for precontact use of stone houses in southwest Victoria has yet to be obtained.

RESOURCE EXTRACTION SITES

Stone Axe Quarries

The interest of nineteenth-century antiquarians in ground-edge axes also explains considerable interest in stone axe quarries (Smyth 1878: 359, 378). Axe quarries were recorded at Mt Hope (Smyth 1878: lvii, 378), Mt William (Davis 1894, 1898; Howitt 1904: 311–312; Le Souëf 1878: 298–299; Smyth 1878: lvii, 181, 370; Worsnop 1897: 99), and Wartook (Worsnop 1897: 99). The focus of this interest was the large stone axe quarry (Wil-im-ee Moor-ing) at Mt William located immediately north of Melbourne within Wurundjeri country. In 1854, William Blandowski, recently appointed Government Zoologist of Victoria, visited the quarry complex, noting: 'the quarries which extend over an area of upwards of 100 acres, present an appearance somewhat similar to that of a deserted gold field, and convey a faithful idea of the great determination displayed by the aboriginals' (Blandowski 1855: 50, 56; see also Darragh 2009). Smyth (1878: 181) added, 'the quarry is extensive, and hundreds of tons of stone have been taken from it'. Geologist George Ulrich from the University of Melbourne surmised that 'from the amount of broken stone covering a large area, this quarry must have been in use for a very lengthened period' (Ulrich 1875: 21). Following a visit to the Mt William 'axe-quarries' in 1893, Davis (1894: 582) concluded from the 'heaps of small chips I should say they were worked from recent times back for hundreds of years, and formed a flourishing industry' (see also Davis 1898: 113). Gregory (1904: 128) read the Mt William evidence differently, implying a shallow antiquity as 'no great amount of stone has been removed'. No archaeological dates are available (published) on the age of the Mt William axe quarry or any other tool stone quarry in Victoria. To date, archaeological research has focused on petrographic characterization of quarries and surface-collected stone axes across Victoria to document patterns of exchange (e.g., McBryde 1984, 1986; see also Ford & Hiscock this volume).

Fish Traps

In 1841, George Augustus Robinson, Chief Protector of Aborigines in the Port Phillip District, recorded an extraordinary Aboriginal freshwater aquaculture channel system in southwest Victoria. The system featured what appeared to be a maze of kilometres of excavated channels covering an area of '15 acres' (6 ha) 'resembling the work of civilized man but which on inspection I found to be the work of the Aboriginal natives, purposefully constructed for catching eels' (cited in Clark 1998: 308). W. Augustus Miles, Commissioner of Police, Sydney, discussed Robinson's findings in his 1854 paper in the *Journal of the Ethnological Society*. He stated that 'these earth-works were for purposes of irrigation, and evidently indicate a higher state than that of the present race' (Miles 1854: 10). An advocate of degeneration, Miles associated these earthworks with a more advanced pre-Aboriginal 'race', with an essentialized, pejorative flourish that 'the Australian native has no settled industrial pursuit; it is not in his nature' (Miles 1854: 11).

At the end of the nineteenth century, Thomas Worsnop (1897: 104–106) published the first detailed account of large-scale, stone-walled fish trapping structures made by the Gunditjmara people of southwest Victoria. In marked contrast to Miles, Worsnop (1897: 104) noted that 'an aboriginal work of great ingenuity and some engineering skill has lately been discovered at the Great Condah Swamp' in southwest Victoria. He noted similar traps at 'Lake Condah' and 'Darlot's Creek' to the immediate south (Richards 2011). This practice of stone-walled fish trap construction was, according to Worsnop (1897: 105), 'of undoubted antiquity, but to what remote period in time it owes its origin no one will ever know. Its stands as a dateless monument of incredible labor visible through the volcanic *debris* discharged from Mounts Eccles and Napier, and the work and its design were worthy of their builders'. The Gunditjmara practice of stone-walled fish trap construction is known to date back at least 6,600 years ago (McNiven et al. 2012) and to have included landscape-scale aquaculture systems (Builth 2014). The scale, complexity, and age of these systems form the material basis of the Budj Bim Cultural Landscape World Heritage Area (Brown, Rose, McNiven, & Crocker 2017; Smith et al. 2019).

CEREMONIAL SITES

Ritual Caves

It is axiomatic in modern archaeology that caves and rock shelters have the potential to contain archaeological deposits of Aboriginal activity over many thousands of years. Indeed, 'classic archaeology begins' in Australia with the controlled excavation of deeply stratified deposits in Ngaut Nguat (aka Devon Downs) rock shelter on the lower Murray River in South Australia by Norman Tindale and Herbert Hale in 1929 (Hale & Tindale 1930; Horton 1991: xvii). It took another three decades before controlled archaeological excavation of rock shelter sites occurred in Victoria (Mulvaney 1962), with subsequent excavations revealing occupation deposits dated back to c. 26,000 years ago (Bird & Frankel 2005: 71).

Understandings of the potential of caves and rock shelters to reveal Aboriginal antiquity did not exist in nineteenth-century Victoria. Interest by antiquarians in Victoria centred on these sites as the domain of spiritual beings who sometimes attracted ritual veneration (Clark 2007). For example, Hull (1846: 28) noted that a cave at 'Cape Schanck' located south of Melbourne was 'once the residence of *Pungil* [Bunjil], the God of the natives, who they believe came out of the sea—formed it, and much delighted in it. There are no paintings or marks, but apparently a wide alter and decayed steps in the recess'. In southwest Victoria, Bonwick (1970: 112) was informed that 'some spirit, Punyil [Bunjil], once resided in one' of the near-coastal Bridgewater Caves 'and was accustomed to descend therefrom and walk the shore'. In 1857, Bonwick followed up on a rumour of 'rude attempts at drawings' in the cave but found nothing (1970: 112).

Near Port Campbell in southwest Victoria were sea caves in the coastal cliffs, one of which is associated with a blow-hole. According to Chauncy (1878: 268–269), 'for ages past the natives were in the habit, whenever they approached this air-hole, to throw a piece of wood into it to propitiate the demon supposed to reside within its profound and mysterious depths'. When government Superintendent La Trobe and his team visited the cave in the mid-1840s, 'they found an enormous pile of wood, which must have been the accumulation of ages, as the natives had to carry the pieces of wood from the distant forest. The men set fire to the pile, which lit up and displayed a magnificent vaulted chamber' (Chauncy 1878: 269; Clark 2007: 6).

Rock Art

Although nearly two hundred rock art sites have been recorded in Victoria (Gunn 1984; Gunn & Goodes 2022), this site type attracted little antiquarian interest in the nineteenth century, with 'very few' examples recorded (Mathew 1899: 138). Mathew (1897) provides the only detailed nineteenth-century description of an Aboriginal rock art site in Victoria (see also Tugby & Tugby 1980; Worsnop 1895: 140). The rock shelter is located in the Victoria Range of western Victoria and is now known as Billimina (formerly Glenisla 1). Found by Europeans in ~1860, the site featured a large panel with dozens of figurative (e.g., people, macropods, and lizard) and nonfigurative (e.g., lines) paintings executed in red ochre. Much of the site had been defaced by settler graffiti (Mathew 1897: 31). Excavations at the site in 1975 revealed occupation dating back to at least 10,000 years ago, with a major increase in site use and ochre deposition within the past 2000 years (Bird & Frankel 2005: 45–46, 60; McNiven, David, & Lourandos 1999: 84).

Megalithic Stone Circles

Stone arrangements used for ceremonial purposes by Aboriginal Victorians attracted little nineteenth-century antiquarian attention and only moderate archaeological interest by twentieth-century archaeologists (e.g., Lane & Fullagar 1980). Chauncy (1878: 235–236) briefly described 'rows of large stones' on 'a little basalt islet in Lake Wongan' in southwest Victoria. Knowing little about the function of such sites, he speculated somewhat flippantly that it 'was possibly executed for the purpose of carrying on some mystic rites, or probably only for the amusement of running between the rows of stones and up the hill and down again' (Chauncy 1878: 236).

The Mt Elephant stone circle site in southwest Victoria has the dubious status of attracting the most international attention of any archaeological site in nineteenth-century Victoria (for detailed discussion, see Griffiths 1996: 40–41; McNiven & Russell 2005: 104–113; Russell & McNiven 1998). Following what appears to have been a misreading of a description of a large circular arrangement of small stones as an English megalithic structure, publications and illustrations began appearing in the late 1860s and 1870s of a series of large henge-like megalithic structures in the Mt Elephant district of southwest Victoria (Figure 2.3). But the megalithic structures were fanciful. Chauncy (1878: 235) pointed out that 'there are no such circles, and never were'. MacPherson (1885: 55) added that the megalithic sites 'were works of imagination'. While twentieth-century surveys indicate that some Aboriginal stone arrangements in southwest Victoria feature stones weighing 500–1000 kg (Lane & Fullagar 1980: 135, 140), none are of megalithic form as depicted in the Mt Elephant site illustration.

Interpreting the fanciful representation of megalithic structures at Mt Elephant as simply a mistake ignores the broader context of colonialist archaeologies in Australia. Disassociating Indigenous peoples from their heritage was a popular colonial trope employed in Australia, the Americas, and Africa (see McNiven & Russell 2005, for details). In the case of Mt Elephant, disassociation was achieved by stating that local Aboriginal people knew nothing about the sites and by linking the sites with the known European tradition of megaliths. Mt Elephant was a rare example from nineteenth-century Victoria where the British colonial imagination was drawn to undermining the validity

FIGURE 2.3. 'Stone Circles near Mount Elephant' as depicted in the *Illustrated Sydney News and New South Wales Agriculturalist and Grazier*, 31 March 1877.

of Aboriginal Victorians as original occupiers of the land to help ease the moral burden of violent colonial expropriation of Indigenous lands and peoples.

FOSSILIZED HUMAN IMPRESSIONS

The final site for discussion is one of the most bizarre archaeological sites in the history of Australian Indigenous archaeology. In the 1890s, *Science of Man* (Journal of the Royal Anthropological Society of Australasia) published a series of articles on fossilized impressions of human feet and buttocks within sandstone exposed during quarrying at Warrnambool in southwest Victoria (e.g., Anon. 1891, 1898a, 1898b, 1898c, 1899a, 1899b, 1899c; Archibald 1894; McDowell 1899; Officer 1893; see also Griffiths 1996: 60–62). In 1873, 'footprints of men, birds, and other animals, had been found in the quarries' and were 'known to many residents' of Warrnambool (Anon. 1898a: 54–55). The new finds of 1890 were found 'about a mile from the sea, and at a depth of about 50 feet [15 m]' (Officer 1893: 34). They were interpreted as representing 'impressions' left by a man and women sitting together at the base of a sand dune (Anon. 1898a: 55). Some of the impressions were taken to the local Warrnambool Museum, while a block with the male feet was 'built into the walls of the Town Hall' in Warrnambool (Gregory 1904: 130). Speculation on the age of the imprints ranged from 'Miocene Tertiary' to 'Pleistocene age' to 'recent' (Anon. 1898a: 54; Officer 1893: 38). Gregory (1904: 130–133) critically discussed the 'human impressions' in 'Warrnambool sandstone' at length and concluded that the empirical evidence 'is not convincing'. But in many respects, enthusiasm for the Warrnambool impressions site was more about ideology than substance, pushed by The Royal Anthropological Society of Australasia to promote the view that an ancient human presence in Australia may predate the arrival of the ancestors of mainland Aboriginal peoples (Berclouw 2001; Mulvaney 1958b: 304–305).

CONCLUSION

Colonial Victoria played host to a dynamic intellectual culture interested in understanding the antiquity of Aboriginal occupation using information obtained from a broad range of archaeological sites. Although most of this intellectual activity took place in Melbourne, many metropolitan intellectuals had rural connections across the colony that provided much needed ethnographic and archaeological data. As archaeology was closely aligned with anthropology, the boundaries between both disciplines in colonial Victoria were blurred as archaeological questions related to site function were answered by observing and talking to local Aboriginal peoples. In some respects such a close association created a historical stasis such that archaeological evidence was seen as conforming to ethnography and hence Aboriginal history was seen as unchanging. In rare instances, antiquarians looked beyond the lens of ethnography and recognized difference in some archaeological objects such as stone axes that differed in form (and degree of weathering) to those known ethnographically. Yet historical stasis and dynamism were independent of the additional issue of antiquity, as it was recognized that Aboriginal occupation of Victoria could date to the remote past irrespective of whether cultural practices changed through time.

Nineteenth-century arguments for a remote antiquity to Aboriginal occupation of Victoria considered archaeological and geological evidence. Archaeological evidence included large, grooved stone axes differing in form to those used in recent/ethnographic time, stone axes exhibiting weathered surfaces consistent with considerable age, and stone axes buried in sediments of possible Pleistocene age. Geological evidence centred on Aboriginal oral histories of ancient volcanic eruptions and the presumed pedestrian colonization of Tasmania by peoples from Victoria before the formation of Bass Strait. Despite such evidence (albeit indirect) for antiquity, the twentieth century begins with Gregory's (1904: 144) pronouncement that in many respects framed and constrained Victorian archaeology for the next half a century—'there is no evidence of the long occupation of Victoria by man'. In the 1950s, Mulvaney (1957: 32, 35) noted that Victorian researchers believed in an 'absence of stratified sites in this State' and that 'excavation could reveal nothing that could not already be deduced from surface collecting' (see Griffiths 1996: 66–79).

It is difficult to know to what extent Gregory's denial of antiquity was more ideologically subjective than objective. Kuklick (2006: 565) notes that the implications of his conclusions for Aboriginal people's presence in Australia were clear; shallow antiquity 'meant that their claims to its ownership were no more legitimate than those of Europeans'. Although a brilliant geologist, Gregory was known for his intellectual and social 'conservativism', which he revealed openly in his 1925 book *The Menace of Colour: A Study of the Difficulties Due to the Association of White and Coloured Races* (Leake & Bishop 2009: 282). In this book, Gregory (1925: 159) detailed his support for the Australian federal government's White Australia Policy (est. 1901), adding that 'Australia will avoid great dangers if it can maintain the whole continent for the white race'.

Antiquarians in colonial Victoria operated within the paradigm of social evolutionism as a dimension of imperialist and colonialist archaeologies. Indeed, Victorian antiquarians saw Aboriginal peoples as a primitive and primordial form of humanity, that is, 'living fossils'. Far from simply following social evolutionism, antiquarians constructed information to support and energize the paradigm. Yet such complicity was not without critique. Cracks emerged with some antiquarians pointing out empirical inconsistencies, such as the absence of so-called primitive features in Aboriginal skulls and the incongruous mixture of so-called Palaeolithic and Neolithic stone tool types. Mulvaney (1977: 264) suggested that some of this critique 'encouraged a bleak nationalism', yet such critique was valid. Advocacy for the exceptionalism of Aboriginal cultural development went hand in hand with the crumbling edifice of social evolutionism and its unilinear framework to pave the way for the development and professionalization of archaeology in Australia in the twentieth century.

Although underpinned by the racist and colonialist paradigm of social evolutionism, with occasional bizarre outcomes (Mt Elephant stone circles and Warrnambool impressions), Victorian antiquarians laid the foundations for an ethnographically informed archaeology of Aboriginal Australians. This archaeological approach to the antiquity of Aboriginal occupation drew on a diverse range of site types and the fruits of excavation to reveal a past that could be materially different to the present.

ACKNOWLEDGMENTS

This chapter was improved by critical readings by Tom Griffiths and Chris Urwin.

REFERENCES

Allen, H. (2019). The first university positions in prehistoric archaeology in New Zealand and Australia. *Bulletin of the History of Archaeology, 29*(1), 1–12.

Anon. (1864). Ancient mining tools: Singular discovery of a stone implement or weapon at Ballarat. *Dicker's Mining Record, 3*(7), 120–121.

Anon. (1878). *Catalogue of the objects of ethnographic art in the National Gallery, published by the direction of the Trustees of the Public Library & Museums of Victoria.* Melbourne: Mason, Firth & M'Cutcheon.

Anon. (1891). Papers. *The Victorian Naturalist, 8*(6), 82–84.

Anon. (1898a). Evidence collected to establish the discovery of the most ancient men in Australia. *Science of Man, 1*(3), 54–56.

Anon. (1898b). The discovery of the most ancient or Tertiary men in Australia, by Mr. Archibald. *Science of Man, 1*(2), 40–41.

Anon. (1898c). Further evidence to establish discoveries in Warrnambool quarries. *Science of Man, 1*(4), 86–87.

Anon. (1899a). The relics of primitive men found in Australia. *Science of Man, 2*(2), 32–33.

Anon. (1899b). A fossil bone found under twenty feet of rock and other ancient things, from Warrnambool. *Science of Man, 2*(6), 95–96.

Anon. (1899c). Ancient men in Australia. *Science of Man, 2*(10), 196.

Archibald, J. (1894). Notes on the antiquity of the Australian Aboriginal race, founded upon the collection in the Warrnambool Public Museum. *Transactions of the Royal Geographical Society of Australasia (Victorian Branch), 11*, 22–25.

Berclouw, M. (2001). Dr Allan Carroll and the 'Science of Man'. *Critical Studies in Education, 42*(2), 1–26.

Berryman, A., & Frankel, D. (1984). Archaeological investigations of mounds on the Wakool River near Barham, New South Wales. *Australian Archaeology, 19*, 21–30

Beveridge, P. (1869). Aboriginal ovens. *Journal of the Anthropological Society of London, 7*, clxxxvii–clxxxix.

Beveridge, P. (1884). Of the Aborigines inhabiting the great lacustrine and riverine depression of the Lower Murray, Lower Murrumbidgee, Lower Lachlan, and Lower Darling. *Journal and Proceedings of the Royal Society of New South Wales, 17*, 19–74.

Beveridge, P. (1889). *The Aborigines of Victoria and Riverina.* Melbourne: M. L. Hutchinson.

Bird, C., & Frankel, D. (2005). *An archaeology of Gariwerd: From Pleistocene to Holocene in Western Victoria.* Tempus 8. St. Lucia: Anthropology Museum, The University of Queensland.

Blandowski, W. (1855). Personal observations made in an excursion towards the central parts of Victoria, including Mount Macedon, McIvor, and Black Ranges. *Transactions of the Philosophical Society of Victoria, 1*, 50–74.

Bonwick, J. ([1858] 1970). *Western Victoria: Its geography, geology, and social condition.* Geelong: Thomas Brown. New Edition, C. E. Sayers (Ed.). Melbourne: William Heinemann.

Bonwick, J. (1870). *Daily life and origin of the Tasmanians.* London: Sampson Low, Son, & Marston.

Boucher, L. (2015). The 1869 *Aborigines Protection Act*: Vernacular ethnography and the governance of Aboriginal subjects. In L. Boucher & L. Russell (Eds.), *Settler-colonial governance in nineteenth century Victoria* (pp. 63–94). Canberra; Australian National University Press.

Boucher, L., & Russell, L. (2012). 'Soliciting sixpences from township to township': Moral dilemmas in mid-nineteenth-century Melbourne. *Postcolonial Studies, 15*(2), 149–165.

Briggs, A. (1993). *Victorian cities.* Berkeley: University of California Press.

Broome, R. (2005). *Aboriginal Victorians: A history since 1800.* Crows Nest, NSW: Allen & Unwin.

Brown, S., Rose, D., McNiven, I., & Crocker, S. (2017). *Australia's nomination of Budj Bim Cultural Landscape. World Heritage nomination for inscription in the UNESCO World Heritage List.* Canberra: Department of Environment and Energy.

Builth, H. (2014). *Ancient Aboriginal aquaculture rediscovered*. Saarbrucken, Germany: LAP Lambert.

Butlin, N. G. (1983). *Our original aggression: Aboriginal populations of southeastern Australia 1788–1850*. Sydney: George Allen & Unwin.

Chauncy, P. (1878). Appendix A: Notes and anecdotes of the Aborigines of Australia. In R. B. Smyth, *The Aborigines of Victoria*, Vol. 2 (pp. 221–288). Melbourne: John Currey, Government Printer.

Christie, M. F. (1979). *Aborigines in colonial Victoria 1835–86*. Sydney: Sydney University Press.

Clark, I. D. (Ed.) (1998). *The journals of George Augustus Robinson, Chief Protector, Port Phillip Aboriginal Protectorate, Volume Two: 1 October 1840–31 August 1841*. Melbourne: Heritage Matters.

Clark, I. D. (2007). The abode of malevolent spirits and creatures-caves in Victorian Aboriginal social organization. *Helictite, 40*(1), 3–10.

Colley, S. (2002). *Uncovering Australia: Archaeology, Indigenous people and the public*. Crows Nest: Allen & Unwin.

Coutts, P. J. F. (1980). Victoria Archaeological Survey report of activities 1978–79. *Victoria Archaeological Survey, 10*, 1–56.

Coutts, P. J. F., & Witter, D. C. (1977). New radiocarbon dates for Victorian archaeological sites. *Records of the Victorian Archaeological Survey, 4*, 59–73.

Critchett, J. (1981). Introduction. Facsimile of James Dawson's 1881 *Australian Aborigines* (pp. 1–9). Canberra: Australian Institute of Aboriginal Studies.

Critchett, J. (1990). *A distant field of murder: Western District frontiers 1834–1848*. Carlton: Melbourne University Press.

Curr, E. M. (1883). *Recollections of squatting in Victoria then called the Port Phillip District (from 1841 to 1851)*. Melbourne: George Robertson.

Curr, E. M. (1886–1887). *The Australian race. Its origins, languages, customs, place of landing in Australia, and the routes by which it spread itself over that continent*. 4 vols. Melbourne: John Ferres, Government Printer.

Darragh, T. A. (2009). William Blandowski: A frustrated life. *Proceedings of the Royal Society of Victoria, 121*(1), 11–60.

Darwin, C. (1859). *On the origin of species by means of natural selection*. London: John Murray.

[Davis, C. H.] (1894). A visit to the Aboriginal stone-hammer quarries, Mt William, Lancefield, Victoria. *The Bankers' Magazine of Australasia*, March, 582–585.

Davis, C. H. (1898) A visit to the Aboriginal stone-hammer quarries Mt. William, Lancefield, Victoria. *Science of Man, 1*(5), 113–115.

Dawson, J. (1881). *Australian Aborigines: The languages and customs of several tribes of Aborigines in the Western District of Victoria, Australia*. Melbourne: George Robertson.

De Serville, P. (1980). *Port Phillip gentlemen and good society in Melbourne before the gold rushes*. Melbourne: Oxford University Press.

De Serville, P. (1991). *Pounds and pedigrees: The upper class in Victoria 1850–80*. Melbourne: Oxford University Press.

De Vis, C. W. (1899). Remarks on a fossil implement and bones of an extinct kangaroo. *Proceedings of the Royal Society of Victoria, 11*(1), 81–90.

Du Cros, H. (2002). *Much more than stones and bones: Australian archaeology in the late twentieth century*. Carlton South: Melbourne University Press.

Elkin, A. P. (1975). R. H. Mathews: His contribution to Aboriginal studies. Part 1. The founders of social anthropology in Australia. *Oceania, 46*(1), 1–24.

Etheridge, R. (1891). Has man a geological history in Australia. *Proceedings of the Linnean Society of New South Wales*, *5*(2), 259–266.

Ferguson, W. H. (1894). Evidence of the antiquity of man in Victoria. *The Victorian Naturalist*, *11*(2), 87–90.

Frankel, D. (2017). *Between the Murray and the sea: Aboriginal archaeology in southeastern Australia*. Sydney: Sydney University Press.

Frazer, J. G. (1899). Observations on central Australian totemism. *The Journal of the Anthropological Institute of Great Britain and Ireland*, *28*(3/4), 281–286.

Frazer, J. G. (1909). Howitt and Fison. *Folklore*, *20*(2), 144–180.

Furphy, S. (2013). *Edward M. Curr and the tide of history*. Canberra: Australian National University E Press.

Gardner, H., & McConvell, P. (2015). *Southern anthropology—A history of Fison and Howitt's Kamilaroi and Kurnai*. Hampshire: Palgrave Macmillan.

Garvey, J. (2017). Australian Aboriginal freshwater shell middens from late Quaternary northwest Victoria: Prey choice, economic variability and exploitation. *Quaternary International*, *427*, 85–102.

Gill, E. D. (1968). Radiocarbon dating. *The Victorian Naturalist*, *85*(6), 161–164.

Gill, E. D. (1955). Aboriginal midden sites in western Victoria dated by radiocarbon analysis. *Mankind*, *5*(2), 51–55.

Gregory, J. W. (1904). The antiquity of man in Victoria. *Proceedings of the Royal Society of Victoria*, *17*(1), 120–144.

Gregory, J. W. (1925). *The menace of colour: A study of the difficulties due to the association of white and coloured races*. London: Seeley, Service & Co.

Griffiths, B. (2018). *Deep time Dreaming: Uncovering ancient Australia*. Carlton: Black Inc.

Griffiths, T. (1996). *Hunters and collectors: The antiquarian imagination in Australia*. Cambridge: Cambridge University Press.

Gunditjmara People, & Wettenhall, G. (2010). *The people of Budj Bim: Engineers of aquaculture, builders of stone house settlements and warriors defending country*. Ballarat: em PRESS.

Gunn, R. G. (1984). The rock art areas of Victoria: An initial comparison. *Aboriginal History*, *8*(1/2), 189–202.

Gunn, R. G., & Goodes, J. R. (2022). A short story of Gariwerd: The rock art management chapter. In P. S. C. Taçon, S. K. May, U. Frederick, & J. McDonald (Eds.), *Histories of Australian rock art research* (pp. 113–130). Terra Australis 55. Canberra: ANU Press.

Hale, H. M., & Tindale, N. B. (1930). Notes on some human remains in the lower Murray valley, South Australia. *Records of the South Australian Museum*, *4*(2), 145–218.

Hart, T. S. (1899). The bone clay and associated basalts at the Great Buninyong Estate Mine. *Proceedings of the Royal Society of Victoria*, *12*(1), 74–80.

Hewitt, G., & Allen, J. (2010). Site disturbance and archaeological integrity: The case of Bend Road, an open site in Melbourne spanning Pre-LGM Pleistocene to Late Holocene periods. *Australian Archaeology*, *70*, 1–16.

Horton, D. (1991). *Recovering the tracks: The story of Australian archaeology*. Canberra: Aboriginal Studies Press.

Howitt, A. W. (1898) On the origin of the Aborigines of Tasmania and Australia. In A. Liversidge (Ed.), *Report of the Seventh Meeting of the Australasian Association for the Advancement of Science held at Sydney, 1898* (pp. 723–758). Sydney: AAAS.

Howitt, A. W. (1904). *The native tribes of south-east Australia*. London: Macmillan & Co. Ltd.

Howitt, A. W., & Fison, L. (1880). *Kamilaroi and Kurnai*. Melbourne: George Robertson.

[Hull, W.] Colonial Magistrate (1846). *Remarks on the probable origin and antiquity of the Aboriginal natives of New South Wales.* Melbourne: William Clarke, Herald Office.

Huxley, T. H. (1863). *Evidence as to man's place in nature.* London: Williams & Norgate.

Keane, A. H. (1879). Review of *The Aborigines of Victoria* by R. Brough Smyth. *Nature, 19*(494), 549–552.

Keferstein, W. (1865). *Bemerkungen über das skelett eines Australiers vom stamme Warrnambool.* Dresden: Druck von E. Blochmann und Sohn.

Kenyon, A. S., & Stirling, D. L. (1901). Australian Aboriginal stone implements: A suggested classification. *Proceedings of the Royal Society of Victoria, 13*(2), 191–200.

Kühnast, A. (2012). Racialising bones and humanity: The scientific abuse of Australian Aboriginal human remains in nineteenth-century German physical anthropology. In S. Ritter & I. Wigger (Eds.), *Racism and modernity: Festschrift for Wulf D. Hund* (pp. 162–178). Berlin: Lit Verlag.

Kuklick, H. (2006). 'Humanity in the chrysalis stage': Indigenous Australians in the anthropological imagination, 1899–1926. *The British Journal for the History of Science, 39*(4), 535–568.

Lane, L., & Fullagar, R. L. K. (1980). Previously unrecorded Aboriginal stone alignments in Victoria. *Records of the Victorian Archaeological Survey, 10,* 134–151.

Langley, M. C. (2020). Re-analysis of the 'engraved' Diprotodon tooth from Spring Creek, Victoria, Australia. *Archaeology in Oceania, 55*(1), 33–41.

Leake, B. E., & Bishop, P. (2009). The beginnings of geography teaching and research in the University of Glasgow: The impact of J. W. Gregory. *Scottish Geographical Journal, 125*(3–4), 273–284.

Le Souëf, A. A. C. (1878). Notes on the natives of Australia. In R. B. Smyth (Ed.), *The Aborigines of Victoria,* Vol. 2 (pp. 289–299). Melbourne: John Currey, Government Printer.

Lubbock, J. (1865). *Pre-historic times: As illustrated by ancient remains, and the manners and customs of modern savages.* London: Longman, Green.

Lyell, C. (1863). *The geological evidences of the antiquity of man with remarks on theories of the origin of species by variation.* London: John Murray.

MacPherson, P. (1885). The oven-mounds of the Aborigines of Victoria. *Journal and Proceedings of the Royal Society of New South Wales, 18,* 49–59.

MacPherson, P. (1886). Stone implements of the Aborigines of Australia and some other countries. *Journal of the Royal Society of New South Wales, 19,* 113–119.

Madden, R. (2010). James Dawson's scrapbook: Advocacy and antipathy in colonial Western Victoria. *La Trobe Journal, 85,* 55–69.

Matchan, E. L., Phillips, D., Jourdan, F., & Oostingh, K. (2020). Early human occupation of southeastern Australia: New insights from $^{40}Ar/^{39}Ar$ dating of young volcanoes. *Geology, 48*(4), 390–394.

Mathew, J. (1889). The Aborigines of Australia. *Journal and Proceedings of the Royal Society of New South Wales, 23,* 335–449.

Mathew, J. (1897). Note on Aboriginal rock painting in the Victoria Range, County of Dundas, Victoria. *Proceedings of the Royal Society of Victoria, 9,* 29–33.

Mathew, J. (1899). *Eaglehawk and Crow: A study of the Australian Aborigines.* London: David Nutt; Melbourne: Melville, Mullen & Slade.

McBryde, I. (1984). Kulin greenstone quarries: The social contexts of production and distribution for the Mt. William site. *World Archaeology, 16*(2), 267–285.

McBryde, I. (1986). Artefacts, language and social interaction: A case study from south-eastern Australia. In G. N. Bailey & P. Callow (Eds.), *Stone Age prehistory: Studies in memory of Charles McBurney* (pp. 77–93). Cambridge: Cambridge University Press.

McDowell, J. (1899). Foot marks in rocks. *Science of Man*, 2(11), 216.

McNiven, I. J. (2006). Colonial diffusionism and the archaeology of external influences on Aboriginal culture. In B. David, B. Barker, & I. J. McNiven (Eds.), *The social archaeology of Indigenous societies* (pp. 85–106). Canberra: Aboriginal Studies Press.

McNiven, I. J. (2011). The Bradshaw debate: Lessons learned from critiquing colonialist interpretations of Gwion Gwion rock paintings of the Kimberley, Western Australia. *Australian Archaeology*, 72, 35–44.

McNiven, I. J. (2020). Primordialising Aboriginal Australians: Colonialist tropes and Eurocentric views on behavioural markers of modern humans. In M. Porr & J. Matthews (Eds.), *Interrogating human origins: Decolonisation and the deep human past* (pp. 96–111). Oxon: Routledge.

McNiven, I. J., Crouch, J., Richards, T., Gunditj Mirring Traditional Owners Aboriginal Corporation, Dolby, N., & Jacobsen, G. (2012). Dating Aboriginal stone-walled fish traps at Lake Condah, southeast Australia. *Journal of Archaeological Science*, 39(2), 268–286.

McNiven, I. J., David, B., & Lourandos, H. (1999). Long-term Aboriginal use of western Victoria: Reconsidering the significance of recent Pleistocene dates for the Grampians-Gariwerd region. *Archaeology in Oceania*, 34(2), 83–85.

McNiven, I. J., Dunn, J. E, Crouch, J., & Gunditj Mirring Traditional Owners Aboriginal Corporation. (2017). Kurtonitj stone house: Excavation of a mid-nineteenth century Aboriginal frontier site from Gunditjmara country, southwest Victoria. *Archaeology in Oceania*, 52(3), 171–197.

McNiven, I. J., & Russell, L. (1997). 'Strange paintings' and 'mystery races': Kimberley rock art, diffusionism and colonialist constructions of Australia's Aboriginal past. *Antiquity*, 71, 801–809.

McNiven, I. J., & Russell, L. (2005). *Appropriated pasts: Indigenous peoples and the colonial culture of archaeology*. Lanham, MD: AltaMira Press.

Miles, W. A. (1854). How did the natives of Australia become acquainted with the demigods and daemonia, and with the superstitions of the ancient races? And how have many Oriental words been incorporated in their dialects and languages? *Journal of the Ethnological Society*, 3, 4–50.

Mitchell, J., & Curthoys, A. (2015). How different was Victoria? Aboriginal 'protection' in a comparative context. In L. Boucher & L. Russell (Eds.), *Settler-colonial governance in nineteenth century Victoria* (pp. 183–201). Canberra: Australian National University Press.

Mulvaney, D. J. (1957) Research into the prehistory of Victoria: A criticism and a report on a field survey. *Historical Studies*, 8, 32–43.

Mulvaney, D. J. (1958a). The Australian Aborigines 1606–1929: Opinion and fieldwork. Part I: 1606–1859. *Historical Studies-Australia and New Zealand*, 8, 131–151.

Mulvaney, D. J. (1958b). The Australian Aborigines 1606–1929: Opinion and fieldwork. Part II: 1859–1929. *Historical Studies-Australia and New Zealand*, 8, 297–314.

Mulvaney, D. J. (1961). Anthropology in Victoria 100 years ago. *Proceedings of the Royal Society of Victoria*, 73, 47–50.

Mulvaney, D. J. (1962). Archaeological excavations on the Aire River, Otway Peninsula, Victoria. *Proceedings of the Royal Society of Victoria*, 75(1), 1–15.

Mulvaney, D. J. (1970). The anthropologists as tribal elder. *Mankind*, 7(3), 205–217.

Mulvaney, D. J. (1977). Classification and typology in Australia. In R. V. S. Wright (Ed.), *Stone tools as cultural markers: Change, evolution and complexity* (pp. 262–268). Canberra: Australian Institute of Aboriginal Studies.

Murray, T., & White, J. P. (1981). Cambridge in the bush? Archaeology in Australia and New Guinea. *World Archaeology, 13*(2), 255–263.

Officer, C. G. W. (1893). The discovery of supposed human footprints on aeolian rock at Warrnambool. *Victorian Naturalist, 9*, 32–39.

Owen, R. (1853). *Descriptive catalogue of the osteological series contained in the Museum of the Royal College of Surgeons of England. Volume 2: Mammalia Placentalia.* London: Taylor & Francis.

Powell, J. M. (1970). *The public lands of Australia Felix.* Melbourne: Oxford University Press.

Richards, T. (2011). A late nineteenth-century map of an Australian Aboriginal fishery at Lake Condah. *Australian Aboriginal Studies, 2011*(2), 64–87.

Richards, T. (2012). An Early-Holocene Aboriginal coastal landscape at Cape Duquesne, southwest Victoria, Australia. In S. G. Haberle & B. David (Eds.), *Peopled landscapes: Archaeological and biogeographic approaches to landscapes* (pp. 63–102). Terra Australis 34. Canberra: ANU E-Press.

Richards, T., Pavlides, C., Walshe, K., Webber, H., & Johnston, R. (2007). Box Gully: New evidence for Aboriginal occupation of Australia south of the Murray River prior to the last glacial maximum. *Archaeology in Oceania, 42*(1), 1–11.

Roe, J. (1974). *Marvellous Melbourne: The emergence of an Australian city.* Sydney: Hicks Smith & Sons.

Rusden, G. W. (1883). *History of Australia.* Vol. III. London: Chapman & Hall.

Russell, L., & McNiven, I. J. (1998). Monumental colonialism: Megaliths and the appropriation of Australia's Aboriginal past. *Journal of Material Culture, 3*, 283–299.

Smith, A., McNiven, I. J., Rose, D., Brown, S., Johnson, C., & Crocker, S. (2019). Indigenous knowledge and resource management as World Heritage values: Budj Bim Cultural Landscape, Australia. *Archaeologies: Journal of the World Archaeological Congress, 15*(2), 285–313.

Smith, C. (2007). A brief history of Australian archaeology. In C. Smith & H. Burke (Eds.), *Digging it up down under: A practical guide to doing archaeology in Australia* (pp. 1–19). New York: Springer.

Smyth, R. B. (1878). *The Aborigines of Victoria: With notes relating to the habits of the natives of other parts of Australia and Tasmania. Compiled from various sources for the Government of Victoria.* 2 Vols. Melbourne: John Ferres, Government Printer.

Soilleux, G. (1891). Blackfellows' mounds. *Transactions of the Historical Society of Australasia, 1*, 40–44.

Spencer, B. (1901). *Guide to the Australian ethnographical collection in the National Museum of Victoria.* Melbourne: R. S. Brain, Government Printer.

Spencer, B., & Gillen, F. J. (1899). *The native tribes of central Australia.* London: Macmillan & Co.

Spencer, B., & Walcott, R. H. (1911). The origin of cuts on bones of Australian extinct marsupials. *Proceedings of the Royal Society of Victoria, 24*(1), 92–123.

Spriggs, M. (2020). Everything you've been told about the history of Australian archaeology is wrong!. *Bulletin of the History of Archaeology, 30*(1), 1–16.

Standfield, R. (2015). 'Thus have been preserved numerous interesting facts that would otherwise have been lost': Colonisation, protection and William Thomas's contribution to *The Aborigines of Victoria*. In L. Boucher & L. Russell (Eds.), *Settler-colonial governance in nineteenth century Victoria* (pp. 47–62). Canberra: Australian National University Press.

Stocking, G. W. (1995). *After Tylor: British social anthropology 1888–1951.* Madison: The University of Wisconsin Press.

Taylor, R. (2017). *Into the heart of Tasmania: A search for human antiquity.* Melbourne: Melbourne University Press.

Trigger, B. G. (1984). Alternative archaeologies: Nationalist, colonialist, imperialist. *Man, 19*(3), 355–370.

Tugby, D., & Tugby, E. (1980). The Rev. John Mathew and painted rock: Perception and cognition in the recording and reproduction of an Aboriginal rock painting in the Grampians, Victoria. *The Artefact, 5*(3 & 4), 123–143.

Turnbull, P. (2017). *Science, museums and collecting the dead in colonial Australia.* Cham, Switzerland: Palgrave Macmillan.

Tylor, E. B. (1865). *Researches into the early history of mankind and the development of civilisation.* London: John Murray.

Ulrich, G. H. F. (1875). *A descriptive catalogue of the specimens in the Industrial and Technological Museum (Melbourne) illustrating the rock system of Victoria.* Melbourne: Mason, Firth & McCutcheon.

Vanderwal, R., & Fullagar, R. (1989). Engraved Diprotodon tooth from the Spring Creek Locality, Victoria. *Archaeology in Oceania, 24*(1), 13–16.

Wilkie, B., Cahir, F., & Clark, I. D. (2020). Volcanism in Aboriginal Australian oral traditions: Ethnographic evidence from the Newer Volcanics Province. *Journal of Volcanology and Geothermal Research, 403,* 1–11.

Williams, E. (1988). *Complex hunter-gatherers: A late Holocene example from temperate Australia.* BAR International Series 423. Oxford: BAR.

Wilson, D. (1862). *Prehistoric man: Researches into the origin of civilisation in the Old and the New World.* Vols. 1 & 2. Cambridge: Macmillan & Co.

Worsnop, T. (1895). The prehistoric arts of the Aborigines of Australia. In J. Shirley (Ed.), *Report of the Sixth Meeting of the Australasian Association for the Advancement of Science, held at Brisbane, Queensland, January, 1895* (pp. 135–148). Sydney: AAAS.

Worsnop, T. (1897). *The prehistoric arts, manufactures, works, weapons, etc., of the Aborigines of Australia.* Adelaide: C. E. Bristow, Government Printer.

CHAPTER 3

HISTORY OF ARCHAEOLOGY IN PAPUA NEW GUINEA

The Early Years up to 1960

GLENN R. SUMMERHAYES

INTRODUCTION

AUGUST 1959 to May 1960 marked a major milestone for archaeology in Papua New Guinea with the first modern excavations undertaken by Sue Bulmer (see Figure 3.1), a master's student at the University of Auckland. The preliminary results were published in *American Anthropologist* less than five years later (Bulmer & Bulmer 1964) with the reporting of the first radiocarbon dates the same year (Bulmer 1964). The excavated sites were Yuku and Kiowa located in the highlands of Papua New Guinea. The Bulmers demonstrated the presence of stratified deposits with changing technology, and occupation beginning in the Pleistocene and continuing through to the Holocene. They argued for initial occupation by hunter-gatherers with later use by agriculturalists.

This series of radiocarbon dates also provided estimates for the time spans of the three technological phases posited for Kiowa based on the large stone implements. Phase A (Levels 6–12), represented by pebble and flake tools, may be provisionally dated to between c. 10,300 and 4800 BP. Phase B (Levels 3–5), during which oval/lenticular axe-adze blades and waisted blades are first evident at Kiowa, would have begun c. 6000 BP and lasted until at least 6100 BP and probably later. Phase C (Level 2), in which the planilateral axe-adze blade appeared, began sometime after 4800 BP and lasted until recent times (see Bulmer 1964: 327–329 for details).

For the first time, archaeological excavations provided a time depth to early occupation of Papua New Guinea with later phases of agricultural settlement in the Holocene. Since then, much archaeological research has been undertaken with the earliest occupation now extended to 50,000 years ago (Summerhayes et al. 2010). Yet archaeological research has its roots some fifty years before Bulmer's excavations with a search for

FIGURE 3.1. A: Otto Meyer at the mission, Watom, with Lapita pottery (Meyer 1932: 185) (Reproduction from the Summerhayes collection). B: Rodolf Pöch (Reproduction courtesy of the Archive of the University of Vienna. Archiv der Universität Wien, Bildarchiv / Signatur: 106.I.2580). C: Charles Monckton (Monckton 1922: frontpiece) (Reproduction from the Summerhayes Collection). D: Sue Bulmer, digging at Wanelek, Kaironk Valley, 1972 (Reproduction from the Bulmer Collection, Otago University, Courtesy of Summerhayes).

human origins going back much earlier. European exploration of Southeast Asia and the western Pacific led to much speculation on where the inhabitants of New Guinea and adjacent islands originated. Eighteenth- and nineteenth-century models based mostly on linguistic data, physical observations of the people, and limited by the intellectual milieu of the day (see McNiven, this volume) posited that many of the peoples of the Pacific originated from Asia. Subsequent observations of people and collections of material culture, and in particular stone tools, by missionaries, government officials, and early anthropologists, led to the first archaeological models attempting to explain the origins of New Guinea peoples and cultures. This chapter presents a review of the earliest excavations undertaken in what is today known as Papua New Guinea, and the first archaeological observations based on material culture. The chapter is not intended to be an exhaustive review of every material object collected by whom and when, but will guide the reader through the important collections and observations. The first excavations will be addressed, followed by general trends in modelling the past through ancient material culture. For an overview of the archaeology of western New Guinea (Indonesia), see Wright et al. (2013).

THE EARLY EXCAVATIONS

The earliest archaeological excavations in Papua New Guinea occurred over 100 years ago: one undertaken by a priest (Otto Meyer on Watom Island), the other by an anthropologist (Rudolf Pöch at Wanigela). See Figure 3.1 for images of Meyer and Pöch.

Watom Island

The German missionary Father Otto Meyer belonged to the Sacred Heart Mission and from 1902 was based in Rakival village where he set up the Reber Mission, on Watom Island, located off the northeastern tip of New Britain (Meyer 1932). Meyer was an extraordinary priest, undertaking scientific research and publishing thirty papers on many topics besides archaeology, including anthropology, linguistics, zoology, and botany (Meyer 1932). Heavy rain and unusually strong northwesterly winds exposed buried pottery on the coastal beachfront in the usually calm Reber Bay, capturing his attention (Meyer 1909a). Meyer subsequently conducted research, including a number of excavations in 1909, 1922, and 1924, reporting the finds in the journal of *Anthropos* (see Meyer 1909b) (mostly a summary of finds) as well as producing a number of unpublished reports which contained more detail of what was found (see Anson 2000 for translations of these reports; Howes 2017). Meyer's finds were mostly around the Rakival village at locations he designated Maravot, Vunaburigai, and Kainapirina (see Specht 1968; Meyer n.d. in Anson 1983: Appendix 1, and Anson 2000 for further details).

Meyer recorded and described the stratigraphy of the excavations and recognized early on that the pottery had been redeposited into the sea from further inland (Anson 2000: 12). An early understanding of the site's formation was hugely important for later archaeologists in understanding the cultural sequence. Meyer not only reported on pottery but also stone tools, including basalt and slate points, obsidian flakes, plus human skeletal remains and faunal material. Faunal remains included pig teeth, bones of bird and reef fish, snails, and marine shells of a variety of species, some used for artefacts such as *Conus* disks, *Trochus* fishhooks, and *Terebra* drills (Meyer 1910). The reports provided one of the first glimpses into the subsistence patterns of these early inhabitants, whose antiquity was unknown to Meyer.

How did Meyer interpret the presence of pottery? It is important to note that the inhabitants of Watom in the early twentieth century did not produce or use pottery. More important still, no pottery was made in this region, or anywhere in New Britain or nearby New Ireland, within living memory. Indeed, we now know that this absence went deep into the past, at least 2000 years. The presence of pottery was therefore a conundrum to Meyer. The finds generated much speculation and there was some talk that it could have originated from South America, with Evan Stanley, the geologist for the 1920 New Guinea Expedition, proposing that it may have originated from Peru. This expedition was a resource-finding mission whose results formed part of a major 1923 report to the League of Nations on the administration of New Guinea which was then a Class 'C' Mandated Territory. Stanley wrote about the possible Peruvian origin on hearsay when in Rabaul in 1921–1922 (Stanley 1923: 7). He attributed the pottery's presence on Watom Island to possibly Spanish or Portuguese visitors. However, Meyer in his unpublished report written in the 1930s (Meyer n.d.; Anson 2000: 20) stated that Stanley, after actually seeing the pottery and talking to Meyer, changed his mind and considered it to be older.

Other interpretations were made on this pottery. Dermot Casey, an Honorary Ethnologist at the National Museum of Victoria (NMV) in Melbourne, saw similarities with assemblages from Southeast Asia. Meyer had sent a small number of sherds to the NMV for their collection, with a further several hundred pieces subsequently loaned to the Museum (and returned) (Casey 1936: 94). Casey, on examination of the sherds, described the stamped impressed designs with lime infill for the first time and noted that the vessels ranged in size (Casey 1936: 96). See Figure 3.2 for Watom Lapita pottery from the NMV. Casey again noted that pottery was presently unknown on Watom and east New Britain, and it is unlike that presently made in Collingwood Bay or Finschhafen (Casey 1936: 94). He did note, however, similarities between the use of stamped impressions with wares reported from Malaya (Casey 1936: 95), but with similarities in designs on gauze fabric from Peru (Casey 1936: 97). He made the important point that the motifs with 'interlocking branched (cymose) key patterns . . . seem to be derived from plaited basketwork' with similarities to basket ware and fabrics from Indonesia and China, and rattan mats from South Sumatra and Borneo, although he again makes the case for the closest designs to be found on a gauze fabric from Peru (Casey 1936: 97).

Fr Patrick O'Reilly, a French Marist priest, visited New Britain and Bougainville in 1934–1935 and met with Meyer. He took with him a selection of sherds back to the Musée de l'Homme in Paris. In an unpublished paper translated and published by Anson (2000), O'Reilly argued for differences in the pottery and divided the sherds into what he called 'Melanesian' and 'non-Melanesian', the latter referring to the lime-filled dentate stamped ceramics, and the former to those with various forms of applique and incision. Thus, O'Reilly saw this pottery typology as representing different cultures.

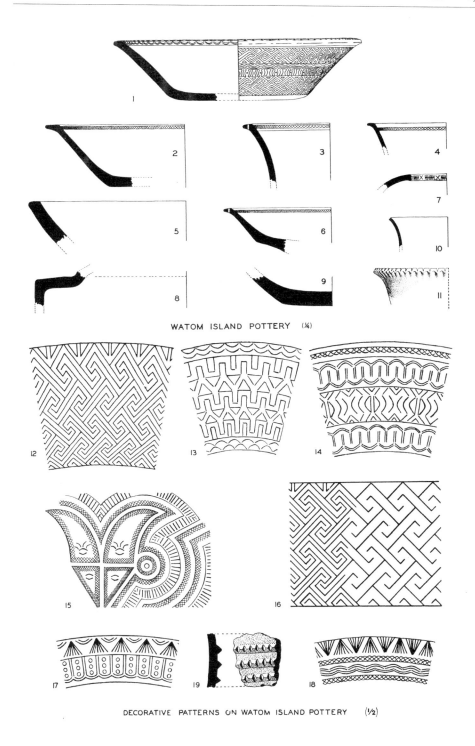

FIGURE 3.2. Lapita pottery from Watom housed at the National Museum of Victoria (Casey 1936: Plate VIII) (Reproduction from the Summerhayes Collection).

Many years later, Specht (1968) argued that the two decorative styles of pottery could well represent functional differences within a society, a point borne out by subsequent research. Certainly, applied and relief ware did bear similarities with pottery from Vanuatu, Buka, New Caledonia, and Fiji. For more detail on Fr O'Reilly, see Dotte-Sarout and Howes (2019).

The pottery excavated and described by Meyer is what we know today as Lapita, and his finds were of monumental importance to later studies and critical in showing a link with similar decorated pottery from Tonga (McKern 1929), and Fiji and New Caledonia (Gifford 1951; Gifford & Shutler 1956). The highly visible dentate-stamped designs on the pottery were shown to be similar with other finds reported from islands between Watom and Tonga. 'Search and find' expeditions for dentate-stamped pottery subsequently included MacLachlan's work in Fiji and the New Hebrides (Vanuatu) which was based on surface collections (MacLachlan 1938, 1939, 1940a, 1940b), as were Lenormand's (1948) and Avias's (1949, 1950) finds in New Caledonia. However, it was Avias and O'Reilly who noticed a similarity between the pottery from Watom and the Ile des Pins off the south coast of New Caledonia. Excavations by Gifford in Fiji and later accompanied by Shutler in New Caledonia led to the similarity being extended to Site 13 in New Caledonia, Sigatoka in Fiji, and Tonga (Gifford & Shutler 1956: 94).

Watom is now probably the most extensively excavated Lapita site, with further fieldwork by Specht in 1965–1967 (1968, 2003), Green and Anson in 1985 (as part of the Lapita Homeland Project) (for a list of the extensive number of publications from this excavation, see Anson et al. 2005), and in 2008/2009 by Anson, Buckley, and Petchey (Petchey et al. 2016). It is now one of over 290 sites with Lapita pottery that has been identified across the western Pacific dating to between c. 3300 and c. 2300 cal BP, marking a major colonization event out of Near Oceania and into Remote Oceania (areas east of the Solomon Chain) (see Bedford at al. 2019 for an update).

Wanigela

Excavations at Wanigela in Collingwood Bay, southeast Papua New Guinea, were undertaken by Rudolf Pöch, an Austrian anthropologist (Howes 2017). In the late nineteenth century, the southern part of Papua New Guinea had been known as 'British New Guinea' and later the 'Territory of Papua'. This region was more commonly known as 'Papua', as distinct from 'German New Guinea', which included areas to the north and the Bismarck Archipelago. Pöch was in Papua and New Guinea collecting for the Museum für Völkerkunde in Vienna. At the Cape Nelson administration station he saw some of the pottery that had been unearthed in the levelling of Wanigela for the construction of the mission station. His interest in the pottery led him to join the Resident Magistrate on a visit to Wanigela in December 1905 to undertake excavations.

The villagers were originally located further inland and in 1898 moved to the coast to avoid attacks from interior peoples. Yet they moved again in 1904 as the swamps were seen as unhealthy for the missionaries (see Ambrose et al. 2012: 15 for further

HISTORY OF ARCHAEOLOGY IN PAPUA NEW GUINEA 91

information). They were subsequently moved to the new mission located about a mile away (Chignell 1911: 19; Monckton 1905: 32). When clearing this new location, which included felling trees, a series of mounds were located, some 4–5 m high and 15–30 m in length (Chignell 1911: 20). The subsequent levelling was undertaken by a lay missionary, Mr Percy J. Money, and the local inhabitants (men, women, and children). Money had sent material he dug to the Australian Museum in Sydney, while Pöch noted that the local inhabitants had subsequently dug up some of the other mounds to obtain objects for sale (Pöch 1907a: 69). The mounds that were levelled were used to 'fill in swamps' (see Chignell 1911: 19; Arthur Kent Chignell was a missionary sent to Wanigela in 1907). Charles Monckton, who arrived in New Guinea in 1895 and became the New Guinea Resident Magistrate of the Northern Division, was also at the mission and surveyed the new Mission station at Rainu, noting material unearthed in the levelling (Monckton 1922: 117; see Monckton 1905 as well for a detailed description; see Figure 3.1 for an image of Monckton). Rainu was the village area covering the mounds north of the church, while Oreresan was the area south of the church (see Chignell 1911: 20). As noted by Monckton

> In some excavations carried out by the mission and natives of Rainu, in Collingwood Bay, an interesting discovery was made of an old village site of a forgotten people, and a quantity of broken and ancient pottery found of curious and unique designs and shapes. The pottery was much superior to any now made or in use, and there is no tradition or record of the people by whom it was made. Among human remains, at a depth of 4 feet, two fragments of carved shell were found, placed, I think, originally in a grave. (1905: 33)

Pöch excavated using a more systematic approach, cutting a 'transverse section' through the mound with all finds bagged to their respective layers (Pöch 1907a: 68). These finds were sent back to the museum in Vienna. The mound was interpreted by Pöch as a rubbish heap where people were occasionally buried. Apart from pot sherds and ceramic handles, Pöch also found pig bones and shell, the latter either a food refuse or used as tools (Pöch 1907a: 69). Human remains were also found in association with the finds (see later). The excavated pottery, as noted by Pöch, was unlike that used by the recent people of Wanigela. It was thick-walled pottery, some with angular rings which would have been pedestalled bowls, some with triangular cut-outs. One sherd was like the narrow neck of a flask. Some sherds were handles. Importantly, modern Wanigela pottery production is completely different, being thinner walled with different decorative techniques (Pöch 1907a: 70). A further description with illustrations of the pottery is given in a subsequent article (Pöch 1907b) and also found in a travelogue published in English (Pöch 1907c).

Similar observations were made by British anthropologists Charles Seligmann and Thomas Joyce (1907: 334), who examined the pottery collected by Monckton and donated to the British Museum in 1905. They also noted that the pottery was far superior than those made at the turn of the century (Seligmann & Joyce 1907: 333). The forms differed and included some with handles, some with cut-out decoration. One was probably a spindle whorl, or a weight of a pump drill, and three others were 'necks of bottle-shaped vases' (Seligmann & Joyce 1907: 334). This form of vessel was unknown from contemporary New Guinea.

There was a twist to the story of the Wanigela pottery sent to the British Museum. Remarkably, shortly afterwards, a monumental tome by Neil G. Munro on *Prehistoric Japan* was published. The first edition came out in 1905 with most copies destroyed by fire before their distribution, and a second edition was subsequently published in 1911 (Munro 1911). This was the first book written in English on Japanese archaeology. The volume was profusely illustrated with pottery, leading Joyce to argue for similarities between pottery from Collingwood Bay and Jomon Japan (Joyce 1912). Both wares have meandering relief, incised concentric circles, and 'ribbon'-like handle. However, the similarities ended there.

These early excavations and collections not only produced pottery but also non-ceramic material, including adze blades made from ophicalcite, which could be quarried and found in the northern Goropu Range, part of the Owen Stanley Range of Papua, and c. 60 km inland from Collingwood Bay (Seligmann & Joyce 1907: 331). Club heads were also noted along with unique carved *Conus* shells.

Carved *Conus* shells were found by Pöch (1907a), Money and Chignell (see Chignell 1911: 20), and Monckton (1905; Seligman & Joyce 1907: 329), with thirteen in all recovered from the ancient mounds of Wanigela in the early twentieth century (Ambrose et al. 2012: 113). Of these thirteen, six were sent to the Australian Museum by Money; four to the British Museum by both Monckton ($n = 3$) and Chignell ($n = 1$), one to the Horniman Museum in London by Chignell, one to Cambridge Museum by Seligmann, and another to the Museum für Völkerkunde in Vienna by Pöch (see Ambrose et al. 2012: Table 1). These carved or engraved *Conus* shells were unique to this region, being mostly curvilinear in design, with one having a bird design, and another a rectilinear pattern. The shells collected by Monckton from the clearance and the single shell collected by Pöch were associated with human remains (Monckton 1905: 33; 1922: 117; Pöch 1907b).

The mounds of Collingwood Bay and the nearby offshore northern Massim Islands were later researched by Peter White (briefly) (White 1965; White et al. 1970a), and Brian Egloff who undertook extensive fieldwork for his PhD in the late 1960s and early 1970s (Egloff 1970, 1971, 1972, 1978, 1979). We now know that these mounds represent two different time periods. The bulk of the material comes from the 'Expansion Phase' (1000 to 500 BP—Ambrose et al. 2012), including the engraved shells and relief pottery. The pottery with the unusual forms (pedestalled bows—some with triangular cut-outs), one like the neck of a flask, and handles, are older in age and originate from what has been termed heuristically as the 'Early Phase', dating from 1500 to 1000 BP (see Ambrose et al. 2012: 128).

Wanigela from a Regional Perspective

The archaeological material from Wanigela was initially interpreted as the product of people other than the ancestors of the present-day inhabitants. In fact, Pöch saw the pottery as originating from people who inhabited the Massim region to the east. As mentioned, by comparing the pottery excavated to contemporary pottery, Pöch, Monckton, and Seligmann/Joyce noted that the excavated material was superior to the pottery made by the people inhabiting Collingwood Bay at the beginning of the twentieth century. Yet Pöch and Monckton were wrong to suggest that the excavated pottery was a better or superior ware. The pottery was technologically different and much was slab constructed rather than using the coil and ring techniques of today's pottery. Thus, the archaeology was seen as external to the current inhabitants, and in hindsight they were partially right. New Guinea is not inhabited by a homogenous group of people— but is heterogeneous and diverse culturally, linguistically, and physically. When the missionaries moved to the coastal strip of Collingwood Bay, people living in the interior moved with them. Warfare at this time was rampant in the region, and the mission proved a safe refuge.

Connections with the Massim, the islands immediately to the east of the southeast New Guinea mainland, were also evident with the presence of the engraved *Conus* shells mentioned earlier. Pöch, on the basis of similarities in engraved *Conus* shells between Wanigela and the Trobriand Islands (Massim region), argued that 'the vanished pottery-making settlements in question were possibly a colony founded by tribes from the Massim district' (Pöch 1907a: 71). To Pöch these influences from across the sea correlated with a society of chiefs. Pöch (and Monckton and Seligmann/Joyce), however, did not have a grasp of absolute chronology as their insights were before the first use of radiocarbon dating by archaeologists in the 1950s (see later discussion).

German ethnographer Otto Finsch (1914) and British anthropologist Alfred Haddon (1932) also offered opinions on the significance of the Wanigela finds. Similar to Pöch, Finsch, in his 1914 classic 'Südseearbeiten' viewed the pottery as coming from people more culturally superior than today's inhabitants, although Pöch explicitly said a 'higher culture'. Finsch based his opinions on the peculiar forms of pottery, including the narrow-necked vessels, and those with handles, but in particular the various ornaments in raised and open work which he saw as a highly developed technique (Finsch 1914: 269). Like Finsch, Haddon when discussing a 'prehistoric sherd' from the Mailu District (south coast of southeast mainland Papua New Guinea), also focussed on pot decoration, pointing out that the 'most striking form of ornament is that obtained by means of open work' (Haddon 1932: 112). He also noted the unique nature of some vessel forms, in particular the three necks of bottle shaped 'vases' which were not found in any of the modern pottery producing areas (Haddon 1932: 112).

We know now that many of the pottery forms described by Pöch, Haddon, Monckton, and Finsch are found in Lapita assemblages, some 3000 years old, and with a non-utilitarian or ceremonial function (Summerhayes 2000). Similar ware, which also have distinct affinities with earlier Lapita wares, were excavated in 2004 by Vincent Kewibu on Goodenough Island (Massim region) and dated to 1520–1320 cal BP, known here as the Early Phase, strengthening arguments for connections between people of southeast mainland Papua New Guinea and islands to the east.

Similarities between pottery across this region were also made many years ago by Leo Austen (1939/40), a government official, who first noticed stylistic similarities between Collingwood Bay prehistoric pottery and sherds lying scattered across the Trobriand Islands (Ambrose et al. 2012: 129). Austen noted that the Trobriands pottery was found on top of stone structures with disarticulated human remains. Stone structures are found on many Massim Islands as far as Rossell Island (Armstrong 1928), but as noted by Egloff, structures with human remains were much later in time and had a restricted distribution being found on Goodenough Bay, Milne Bay, and South Cape (Egloff 1970: 154; see also Lindt 1887: 78; Riesenfeld 1950: map IV; and Seligmann 1910: 463–465). The age of these structures was unknown to these authors. One stone structure, a stone circle located inland of Goodenough Bay at Boianai, was excavated by the Territory of Papua's Government Anthropologist Francis Edgar Williams (1931). The excavation revealed burials and is one of the earliest attempts at archaeological excavation in Papua New Guinea.

Similarities between the raised spiral designs on the Wanigela pottery and the designs found on the engraved *Conus* shells discussed earlier can be further explained by their contemporaneity, as we now know both are associated with the Expansion Phase (1000 to 500 BP). This sharing of spiral designs is yet another example of cultural connections across this region.

Rock art provides another example of cultural connection across the region. For example, a stone slab with spiral designs was collected from Boianai (Goodenough Bay) and donated to the Australian Museum (Etheridge 1908). Etheridge (a curator at the Australian Museum) noted similarities between the spiral designs on the stone slab and those carved on recent wooden lime spatulas of the Massim region. More recently, similarities in stone carving designs have been noted between Goodenough Bay and nearby Normandy Island (Egloff 1970: 154).

But are the spirals found on the *Conus* shells similar to rock art found at Goodenough Bay? Etheridge (1908: 27) noted that spirals on rock art but does not make a connection between the two. Finding similarities in the use of patterns between regions can be fraught with interpretative difficulty. Golson (1972: 584) had made connections between the spiral design on shells and the Dong Son cultures of Southeast Asia. Prehistoric connections between Southeast Asia and southeast Papua New Guinea were also made by other archaeologists some fifty years ago. Based on the presence of a 'stylistic marker'—the curvilinear scroll—Bill Solheim (1968) saw connections between Sa-huynh-Kalanay pottery and pottery from Mailu on the southeast Papuan Coast. The 'curvilinear scroll' was found on Dong Son bronzes as well, leading art historians to invoke Bronze Age inspiration in South Pacific art (Badner 1972; Fraser 1972). Massim art was argued to have been Dong Son inspired. Considering that Dong Son bronzes were found in western New Guinea (Indonesia), such claims could not be discounted without adequate archaeological research. As Jack Golson wisely argued in 1967 (Golson 1972), such connections should *not* be assumed but argued within the archaeological data developing at that time. Indeed, we now know after further archaeological research that over a millennium separates the Dong Son and the spiral design forms on archaeological material culture in southeast Papua New Guinea. The designs are indigenous to the Massim region, and their presence on shells, pots, and rocks could well be connected.

FURTHER COLLECTING IN PAPUA NEW GUINEA

Systematic excavation and surface collection of archaeological objects was rare in Papua New Guinea during the early twentieth century. Many objects were either dug from the ground or collected from the surface by miners, government officials, or missionaries. Most of these were stone objects and seen as remnants of an unknown people. Early collections were made in southeast Papua New Guinea, which produced a wealth of other forms of material culture, including many examples of obsidian tools. Obsidian originated from only a handful of sources in Papua New Guinea (Manus, west New Britain, and Fergusson Island) (for more detail, see Summerhayes 2009). Formal tool types were rarely observed ethnographically. Although formal tool types had been found in contemporary communities, such as Manus where stemmed tools were used as ceremonial spear points, most obsidian was distributed as cores or flakes with no formal technologies. Many pieces of obsidian in southeast Papua New Guinea and offshore islands were unearthed by miners, some at great depth. In the early twentieth century, the majority of obsidian pieces were found near the Mamba River and Collingwood Bay, although a single obsidian piece was found on Misima Island (obsidian spear head), while numerous pieces were found from Goodenough Bay, and from Murua. The find locations no doubt reflect the work of miners, missionaries, and officials and also the presence of Barton and Monckton, who kept up a keen interest in these finds (Barton 1908; Monckton 1905; see earlier discussion). Captain Barton arrived in New Guinea in 1899 and became the Administrator of British New Guinea from 1904 to 1907. Monckton also recorded an obsidian axe dug up from Yodda Creek (northern Kokoda Valley), found with a pestle and mortar, the latter dug out c. 12 feet [c. 3.7 m] below the surface. Following previous interpretations based on comparisons with present day people and their material culture, Monckton reckoned the excavated stone objects were made by a 'forgotten race' (Monckton 1905: 31; Monckton 1922: 116; see also Seligmann & Joyce 1907: 328–329). On the obsidian axe he said:

> The first discovery of this nature was made by the miner, William Ivory, who dug up from under the debris of a pre-historic forest and a stratum of gold-bearing gravel an obsidian battle-axe, where the thing must have lain for untold centuries. Obsidian (volcanic glass) is not used or worked by the Papuans, and the shape of the axe was exactly that of an ancient Saxon or Danish axe, and certainly not that of any weapon or tool used by savages. This axe was given by me to the Hon. David Ballantine, by whom later it was presented to the British Museum.
>
> (Monckton 1922: 116–117)

Seligman noted (incorrectly) similarities with obsidian from Rapa Nui (Easter Island) and argued that the excavated objects from Yodda Creek could be a 'relic of the period when the ancestors of the Polynesians were passing through Melanesia to reach their homes in the Eastern Pacific' (Seligman 1915: 162). Similar obsidian objects were found further afield in west New Britain, such as stemmed tools from Talasea (see Araho et al. 2002). Another obsidian piece that was unique was called a 'fishhook' and recorded from Lihir Island (off the east coast of New Ireland). This 'fishhook' and the stemmed tools from Talasea found their way to Australia and were accessioned into the Museum of Victoria (Casey 1939: 146, 148).

Monckton also was prodigious in recording many large pestles, again found by gold digging in southeast Papua New Guinea: 'several large pestles found by them in digging their gardens; while miners there worked out many more large bowls, pestles, and curiously carved objects with pestles ends, such as birds with outstretched wings and snake heads. Huge stone two-handed swords were also discovered' (Monckton 1922: 118).

In 1906, Monckton recorded finding northeast of Mount Albert Edward a 'stone pillar, about three feet in diameter and four in height, very weather worn, and crowned by an enormous and very eroded stone bowl' (Monckton 1922: 118). Similar mortars cut into boulders of rock have been seen by the author in New Hanover, New Ireland Province, northeast Papua New Guinea.

One pestle in particular stood out, a bird-headed form 36 cm in length reported in detail by Captain Barton (1908) and now in the British Museum. It was found some 12 m above the bed of the Aikora River (an offshoot of the Gira in the Yodda Goldfields) and excavated under 3 m of alluvium (Barton 1908: 2). Bird pestles will be further discussed later.

Many finds were made outside southeast Papua. All have a common theme: much of what was collected was not made by the inhabitants of today but by a previous unknown people. The first expeditions by the Germans and British noted stone objects left behind by previous occupants of the country (see Neuhauss 1911). Richard Neuhauss, while recording societies along the north and northeast coast of New Guinea, also played an important role in collecting material remnants of the past (Claas & Roscoe 2009). He was a German anthropologist who visited New Guinea (in particular the Huon coastline and the northern coastline) from 1908 to 1910, and he wrote a chapter titled 'Vorebevölkerung', which literally means 'pre-population', in his classic three-volume *Deutsch Neu-Guinea* (1911: 136–148). In this tome, Neuhauss discussed the possibility of an earlier population along parts of the northeast coast of New Guinea and the presence of what is translated from German as ethnographic objects, such as pestles and mortars, intricately carved stone figurines, stone spatulas, ceramics, pottery sherds and ceramic rings, plus obsidian. He noted the presence of pestles and mortars on the east coast of the Huon Peninsular and environs: 'Several were found far inland, west of Sattelberg. One I discovered in the village square of the small village of Ago on the coast between Finschhafen and Cape King Wilhelm. Another was found at a depth of 30 cm deep in the bed of a stream at Logaueng, south of Langemak Bay near Finschhafen' (Neuhauss 1911: 137, translated from the original German).

The Logaueng mortar was taken from a stream bed *in situ*. Pot sherds with obsidian were also found at the same village. Nearby, Neuhauss found weathered human bone in a rock shelter; some of the long bones were split, which he reckoned was to obtain marrow. From Bukaua, on the south coast of the Huon Peninsula, he found a serpentine figurine (Neuhauss 1911: 145). These objects suggested to Neuhauss that they were made by previous inhabitants of this area as the present inhabitants knew nothing of their origin, saying they have always been there. Despite their earlier origins, Neuhauss recognized that much of this material culture was re-used by the present inhabitants for ritual/religious purposes. For example, pestles were used in taro magic (Neuhauss 1911: 138), and ceramic rings and one of the stone figurines from Bukaua were used in pig magic.

The widespread nature and importance of these finds in understanding the past was noted in the 1939 volume of the journal *Oceania*: 'A considerable portion of our knowledge of ancient peoples has been gained from the study of fragments of stone vessels, implements and ornaments which has survived them' (Murphy 1938: 37). The author, John Murphy, was an Officer in the Department of District Services and Native Affairs of the Territory of New Guinea. Of note was his comment that many such 'relicts' were found across the Mandated Territory, including his own finds. These he saw as follows: 'Here we find, fashioned in stone, a fragmental history of a people who apparently inhabit no part of the island to-day, nor have they, perhaps, for a thousand years past. Practically anywhere in the Mandated Territory relics and fragments are found' (Murphy 1938: 37). Furthermore, 'They appear to have been made from the country rock, and usually take the form of plain or decorated bowls, some with pedestals, and some without; mortars and pestles; effigies of birds and of the male genitalia. They have been dug up in creek-beds or in gardens, and in many cases have been, for generations, in the possession of various native communities who use them in feasts and rituals' (Murphy 1938: 37).

Murphy made a number of important points, some of which will be further discussed. First is a description of what is a unique obelisk in the central Highlands: 'At its edge was found a large white pillar of limestone standing upright. It measured eleven feet high [3.4 m], was two feet [0.6 m] square in cross-section, and was accurately cut. What its purpose is and who put it there is a mystery. There is no other stone or rock nearby and the natives have no opinion to offer' (Murphy 1938: 38).

Secondly, he recorded stone vessels (called *kuru* by the Waghi people of Mount Hagen) used in festivals and buried in a secret place when not in use. This is important when considering the context of subsequent excavations of such objects (Murphy 1938: 38).

Thirdly, he noted the wide distribution of mortars, bird effigies (see earlier), and club heads were not the product of the present inhabitants:

> Effigies of birds, fragments of vessels and mortars, and a variety of club heads have been found in this part of the country. But the natives certainly do not make them. Nor are stone relics confined to this area alone. Roughly two hundred miles [c.320 km] to the south-east, near Otibanda, on the edge of the Kukukuku country,

fragments of mortars and pestles and the heads of a cockatoo and a cassowary have been found. These are faithful reproductions showing attention to detail and skill in execution, and are now in the Australian Museum, Sydney.

(Murphy 1938: 38–39)

Lastly, while recognizing that certain people still made stone tools and subsequently distributed them, for instance the stone adze blades and pineapple-shaped stone club heads made by the Kukukuku, or the Hagen-made axes, he made the point that many people in New Guinea did not (Murphy 1938: 39).

A full summary of archaeologically known stone objects recovered from Papua New Guinea is provided by Chinnery (1919), the Government Anthropologist of New Guinea. He noted that they were of an unknown origin, with many dug up by ancestors of the people he collected them from, which to him and his colleagues represented peoples of an earlier 'unknown race'. Chinnery also includes those pestles and mortars described by Neuhauss from the northeast coast of New Guinea (1911: 136–148) (see earlier) and reviews the arguments for previous peoples who made this material. Further descriptions and comments on the same objects were provided by Edge-Partington (1902).

Following on from John Murphy's observations earlier, reports of mortars and/or pestles were common. Miles (1935, 1938) reports the 1933 finding of a pestle and mortar in Infuntera Creek near a gold mine, and another stone mortar from Edie Creek. Both mortars had star-shaped rims. Gerald Miles was the curator at the Cranmore Ethnographical Museum in Kent, England, which acquired the mortars. The private museum closed in 1940, and its collections were transferred to the British Museum.

More mortars, along with perforated disks and stone figurines, were reported from the Annaberg-Atemble area located along the Ramu River (Kasprusch 1940/41; England 1946). Father Alios Kasprusch SVD (Society of Divine Word) was a long-standing priest and missionary based at Annaberg before World War II. England was a plantation manager before the war, a member of ANGAU (the Australian New Guinea Administrative Unit) during the war, and afterwards was a notable character along the Sepik River and saw miller, publican, trader, and crocodile shooter based at Angoram (Tudor 1968: 68–69). One mortar was found 'halfway in the ground' by missionaries clearing space for the Atemble mission, located on a hill 50 m high (Kasprusch 1940/41: 649). The mortar is some 60 cm high with a human face carved into it. Both Kaprusch and England noted that the origin of these objects is unknown to the present inhabitants and were made by people who had either died out or 'migrated away' (Kasprusch 1940/41: 651; England 1946: 233). Kasprusch noted that these stones must have been imported as stone was not available locally. He also called this stone mortar 'prehistoric' ('prähistorische') because as with other mortar finds, the local inhabitants were unaware of the origin. People around Atemble referred to the stone mortars as ghost stones (*masalai*) (Kasprusch 1940/41: 651) and used them in fertility magic: 'The Ramu natives ascribe to mortars some kind of mysterious powers and even consider them as the habitation of spirits and bestow on them a kind of lower cult' (Kasprusch 1973: 157). Kasprusch also reported a second large stone mortar with carved human face some four hours' walk from

Annaberg Mission at Vrimsebu, near the foothills of the Schrader Ranges (Kasprusch 1940/41: 653). Other mortars of varying sizes were also found in the surrounding area (Kasprusch 1940/41: 654, 1973: 159).

Mortars and pestles were also reported from the Wahgi and lower Chimbu Valleys by Father Nilles, who was based in the highlands with Father Ross. In 1936, a mortar was recovered while clearing the ground at Mingende located 24 km west of the Wahgi junction with the Chimbu River (Nilles 1944: 15). The mortar was made of locally available diorite, suggesting local manufacture. However, as with all reported mortars, the present population had no idea of its manufacture (Nilles 1944: 15).

Bird pestles were found in a number of locations, including northeast New Guinea, the highlands (one pestle having two legs) (Casey 1939: 143), the Sepik River (Kasprusch 1940/41, 1973), and the islands of the Bismarck Archipelago (see Swadling, this volume). Georg Höltker (1951) wrote a comprehensive review article on bird-headed pestles and published an image of a unique 'cockatoo' headed implement excavated from the Watut gold diggings (1951: 243). He also reported and published images of a stone human head supposedly from the Huon Gulf and collected by Vogt (Höltker 1951: 249). Höltker was a German priest and missionary who worked for many years in New Guinea, and also as an ethnologist based at various institutions. He was the first editor of *Anthropos* and published a number of publications on New Guinea. For an up-to-date review of bird-head pestles, see Swadling, this volume. The original function of mortars is seen in terms of nut preparation, rather than their use as magical items by recent communities. Pestles were also viewed as part of a megalithic culture linking Bougainville, New Ireland, and New Guinea more broadly with the Malay Archielago (McCarthy 1938: 47).

Of importance in the history of understanding the archaeology of Papua New Guinea is a short article by Adam (1946), published in *Mankind* (*The Journal of the Anthropological Society of NSW*), which examined the contents of the works by Kasprusch (1940/41) and Höltker (1940/1941), both written in German and inaccessible to many. Leonhard Adam was a German-born anthropologist based in Melbourne who worked primarily on Australian Aboriginal material culture (Sloggett 2016). Höltker's 1940/41 paper was over fifty pages in length and looked at the archaeology of New Guinea by focussing on stone club heads, and axes and adzes from the Massim. He presented a classification system for stone club heads, arguing that many of the perforated stones were produced from 'earlier Papuan populations' (and re-used), and of the same age as the mortars. Höltker's (1940/41) paper was intended as preparatory work for a larger study on the 'pre- and early history of New Guinea', which never eventuated (Höltker 1940/41: 681). As Adam noted, the paper 'is indeed a valuable source of information for those who wish to study the prehistory of New Guinea generally' (Adam 1946: 254). Furthermore,

> Since there is no clear indication of the stratification of prehistoric cultures in New Guinea, the preliminary classification of all those objects which are not the work of recent natives, i.e. all those objects which belong to cultures extinct before the arrival of white observers, as just 'prehistoric', must suffice as a working hypothesis.

It is probable, however, that further studies will lead to the establishment of various prehistoric cultural strata.

(Adam 1946: 255)

Aitape Skull, Leask, and Amateur Archaeology

Although archaeological excavations by Pöch, Meyer, and Williams were rare in the early days of Papua New Guinea archaeology, there are other examples. The first involved the finding of what has been called the Aitape skull. In April 1929, human cranial fragments were found by P. S. Hossfeld 13 km inland from Sissano Lagoon on the north coast of Papua New Guinea (Fenner 1944; Hossfeld 1949). Hossfeld was part of a petroleum survey (see Nason-Jones 1930) when he located the remains on the bank of the Panari Creek eroding from soft blue mudstone we know today as remnants of a Mid-Holocene inland lagoon (Hossfeld 1965). Subsequent morphological analyses suggest similarities with population further south in Australia (Durband & Creel 2011). These were the only human remains predating the Late Holocene up until the last twenty years.

Excavations were also undertaken by an amateur archaeologist during World War II. Maurice Leask made the most of his service in New Guinea, making a number of remarkable archaeological discoveries (Pretty 1967: 3). The first was the finding in 1945 of a dentate-stamped sherd, called the 'Aitape Sherd'. The details of the recovery by Leask are still unknown. We know he enlisted in the Australian Infantry Forces and was attached to the Army Education Services. After Leask's death near Ballarat, a country town in Victoria, Australia, in 1963, the sherd, along with Leask's major collection from Cape Wom near Wewak, was recovered and sent to Graeme Pretty, a curator at the South Australian Museum in Adelaide. Pretty found the sherd in a bag labelled 'Aitape Area'. It is a rim sherd with dentate decoration and a channelled lip. The decoration is 'Middle Lapita' in style, which dates to the early third millennium BP (see image in Swadling et al. 1988: 19, fig. 44). Leask also recorded obsidian tool scatters at Cape Wom just west of Wewak, and at the aerodrome just 10 km to the southeast (Leask 1947). Obsidian was also recorded along the Aitape coast, with the largest pieces found (just over 5 cm) at Sapi Village on Tumelo Island and Vokau village just out of Aitape town (Leask 1945/46: 99). He also recorded pottery around St Anne mission (just south of Aitape), c. 270 m inland, which he suggested could have been a trading village (Leask 1945/46: 100). Leask had also earlier reported and published on the remnants of a 'kitchen midden' found on a summit overlooking the south coast of Papua at an undisclosed location (due to war time censorship), but undoubtedly in the Port Moresby area (Leask 1943a). The site was a 'slightly raised mound' with the remains found 'in situ to a depth of 12 inches [30 cm]' (Leask 1943a: 236). He collected shells and bones and sent these for identification, these being the first examination of faunal materials recorded from archaeological context in Papua New Guinea. He also visited and wrote about rock art sites (engravings and paintings), two of which were previously recorded by F. E. Williams (1931). The first, Rouna, is a rock shelter located on the Laloki River Gorge 1.2 km upstream, while the second, Wureva Yani rock shelter, is found 0.8 km below the falls. He also recorded for the first time two other rock shelters located in the same area (Leask 1943b). These reports recorded details of the sites with no explanation or interpretation. Within the next fifteen years such a situation was to change with the advent of modern archaeological research.

The Beginning of Modern Archaeology

Many of the observations described herein were not made in a vacuum but with regional models of migrations in the background made by linguists and anthropologists alike. Every published paper reporting these archaeological excavations or collections of artefacts had one thing in common: the belief that the makers of these archaeological objects were from a 'prehistoric', unknown population unrelated to the present-day inhabitants. Here prehistoric was equated with anything not used by present-day populations (see also Berndt 1954: 556). Berndt, for example, emphasized that in the Eastern Highlands the people did not use stone mortars as mortars, nor did they use stone club heads as stone-headed clubs (Berndt 1954: 570); a point he found surprising as the neighouring Kukukuku did manufacture and use stone-headed clubs (with wooden handles). Many of these objects, Berndt argued, and as seen from numerous examples presented earlier, were re-used with different functions from spiritual/magic to being mirrors when holding water. Höltker made the same point, as did others, that the inhabitants had no knowledge of the origins of stone pestles and mortars and used them for 'magic stones' (fertility) (Höltker 1951: 236).

The models invoking waves of migrating peoples both within New Guinea (also see Haddon 1920) and external (see Chinnery 1919) were a product of the time. Chinnery provided a useful review of these models in his 1919 article on 'Stone-work in the Gold Fields of British New Guinea'. The ideas of Pöch and Haddon, based on physical descriptions of the inhabitants of New Guinea, were discussed by Chinnery, as were the diffusionist models propounded by Elliot Smith (1916) and Perry (1923). Perry argued for a historical connection from Indonesia to Easter Island, and areas in between based on the presence of stone megaliths. Perry coined the term 'stone-using immigrants', which was used some thirty years later in Riesenfeld's 1950 compendium *The Megalithic Cultures of Melanesia*. Riesenfeld wrote an incredibly detailed book, over 700 pages in length, reviewing all the archaeological evidence found in excavations, collections, and also the records of stone structures, to base his model about a group of stone-using migrants. Based on the distribution of material culture, he also argued that pestles and mortars were introduced into the New Guinea highlands from the north and east coastal regions of New Guinea by a new population of seafaring peoples. This was the scenario when Sue Bulmer, aided by her husband Ralph, undertook the first modern excavations in New Guinea in the late 1950s. These excavations provided information unobtainable by writers of the past—time depth (using radiocarbon dating).

After the Bulmer initial excavations, archaeology in Papua New Guinea picked up speed, due to a number of factors. First was the appointment in 1961 of Jack Golson to the Australian National University. Golson was the driving force in developing the future of archaeology of Papua New Guinea, and he sent a number of PhD scholars to various parts of the country. His major aim was to develop a 'programme of research in the archaeologically underdeveloped fields of Australian and Southwest Pacific Prehistory and with a particular commitment to Papua New Guinea' (Golson 2006: 110). Critical in the success was the employment of Ron Lampert whom Golson sent in 1966 to make an archaeological reconnaissance of the country, looking for potential fieldwork sites (Lampert 1966). Many of the field projects arose out of that survey. The ANU produced many PhDs in Papua New Guinea archaeology. Peter White visited a number of areas, including Collingwood Bay and Kosipe, before focussing on central highland sites for his PhD. His work at Kosipe led to a 26,000-year-old sequence for the Papuan Highlands (White et al. 1970b). Jim Specht worked on Watom Island as noted earlier, and also Buka Island for his PhD. Other PhDs soon followed, laying the temporal framework by which we work today. Secondly, the National Museum and Art Gallery of PNG was developed to monitor the country's cultural heritage, including its archaeology. Lastly, the University of Papua New Guinea was established in 1965 while under the Australian Administration. The university subsequently employed Jim Allen in 1969 to teach archaeology to the next generation of New Guinea students.

Conclusion

Understanding the ancient past of Papua New Guinea in the first half of the twentieth century was limited by the intellectual and scientific milieu of the time. Although excavations were first undertaken over 100 years ago, uncovering a rich array of archaeological materials, along with the numerous finds by missionaries, government officials, and anthropologists, the significance of these finds was only made apparent from the late 1950s with the arrival of professional archaeologists, incorporating new scientific techniques, in particular radiocarbon dating, which provided a time depth hitherto unimagined. Modern scientific techniques in dating, palaeo-environmental reconstructions, and sourcing studies of pottery and stone, for example, went hand in hand with major changes in archaeological theory and practice (see Spriggs 2019). These scientific techniques, not available to our predecessors, can be used in the reanalysis of these legacy collections. Archaeological research from the first half of the twentieth century is still important today. It not only informs us of where we have been but also points to potential new areas of research through revisiting fieldwork areas and/or the reanalysis of earlier collections.

Acknowledgements

I thank both Ben Shaw and Dylan Gaffney for constructive comments on this chapter. I also thank Rob Skelly and two other referees for their suggestions. A special dedication to two leading archaeologists of New Guinea, Pam Swadling and the late Susan Bulmer, both trailblazers in the field. Lastly, a thanks to Ian McNiven for great patience.

References

Adam, L. (1946). Comments on some recent contributions to the prehistory of New Guinea. *Mankind*, *3*(9), 252–258.

Ambrose, W., Petchey, F., Swadling, P., Beran, H., Bonshek, L., Szabo, K., Bickler, S., & Summerhayes, G. (2012). Engraved prehistoric *Conus* shell artifacts from southeastern Papua New Guinea: Their antiquity, motifs and distribution. *Archaeology in Oceania*, *47*, 113–132.

Anson, D. (1983). *Lapita pottery of the Bismarck Archipelago and its affinities* (PhD thesis). University of Sydney, Sydney.

Anson, D. (2000). Appendix 1: The archaeological excavations of Father Otto Meyer on Watom Island. In R. C. Green, An introduction to investigations on Watom Island, Papua New Guinea. *New Zealand Journal of Archaeology*, *20*, 12–27.

Anson, D., Walter, R., & Green, R. C. (2005). *A revised and redated event phase sequence for the Reber-Rakival Lapita site, Watom Island, East New Britain Province, Papua New Guinea*. University of Otago Studies in Prehistoric Anthropology No. 20. Dunedin: University of Otago.

Araho, N., Torrence, R., & White, J. P. (2002). Valuable and useful Mid-Holocene obsidian artefacts from West New Britain, Papua New Guinea. *Proceedings of the Prehistoric Society*, *68*, 61–81.

Armstrong, W. E. (1928). *Rossel Island: An ethnological study*. Cambridge: Cambridge University Press.

Austen, L. (1939/40). Megalithic structures in the Trobriand Islands. *Oceania*, *10*, 30–53.

Avias, J. (1949). Contribution a la prehistoire de l'Oceanie les tumuli des plateaux de fer en Nouvelle-Caledonie. *Journal de la Societe des Oceanistes*, *5*, 15–50.

Avias, J. (1950). Poteries canaques et poteries prehistoriques en Nouvelle-Caledonie. *Journal de la Societe des Oceanistes*, *6*, 111–140.

Badner, M. (1972). Some evidence of Dong-son derived influence in the art of the Admiralty Islands. In N. Barnard (Ed.), *Early Chinese art and its possible influence in the Pacific Basin* (pp. 597–630). 3 vols. New York: Intercultural Press.

Barton, F. R. (1908). Note on stone pestles from British New Guinea. *Man*, *8*, 1–2.

Bedford, S., Spriggs, M., Burley, D., Sand, C., Sheppard, P., & Summerhayes, G. (2019). Debating Lapita: Distribution, chronology, society and subsistence. In S. Bedford & M. Spriggs (Eds.), *Debating Lapita: Chronology, society and subsistence* (pp. 5–33). Terra Australis 52. Canberra: ANU E Press.

Berndt, R. M. (1954). Contemporary significance of pre-historic stone objects in the Eastern Central Highlands of New Guinea. *Anthropos*, *49*, 553–587.

Bulmer, S. (1964). Radiocarbon dates from New Guinea. *Journal of the Polynesian Society*, *73*, 327–328.

Bulmer, S., & Bulmer, R. (1964). The prehistory of the Australian New Guinea Highlands. *American Anthropologist, 66*, 39–76.

Casey, D. (1936). Ethnological notes. *Memoirs of the National Museum of Victoria, 9*, 90–97.

Casey, D. A. (1939). Some prehistoric artefacts from the Territory of New Guinea. *Memoirs of the National Museum of Victoria, 11*, 143–150.

Chignell, A. K. (1911). *An outpost in Papua*. London: Smith, Elder & Co.

Chinnery, E. W. P. (1919). Stone-work and goldfields in British New Guinea. *The Journal of the Royal Anthropological Institute of Great Britain and Ireland, 49*, 271–291.

Claas, U., & Roscoe, P. (2009). Hot air and the colonialist 'other': The 'German-English-Dutch Airship Expedition' to New Guinea. *Journal of the Royal Anthropological Institute, 15*(1), 131–150.

Dotte-Sarout, E., & Howes, H. (2019). Lapita before Lapita: The early story of the Meyer/O'Reilly Watom Island archaeological collection. *Journal of Pacific History, 54*, 354–378.

Durband, A. C., & Creel, J. A. (2011). A reanalysis of the early Holocene frontal bone from Aitape, New Guinea. *Archaeology in Oceania, 46*, 1–5.

Edge-Partington, J. (1902). Stone-headed clubs from the outer coast of British New Guinea. *Man, 2*, 58–59.

Egloff, B. (1970). The rock carvings and stone groups of Goodenough Bay, Papua. *Archaeology and Physical Anthropology of Oceania, 5*, 147–156

Egloff, B. (1971). Archaeological research in the Collingwood Bay area of Papua. *Asian Perspectives, 14*, 60–64.

Egloff, B. J. (1972). The sepulchral pottery of Nuamata Island, Papua. *Archaeology and Physical Anthropology in Oceania, 7*, 146–163.

Egloff, B. J. (1978). The Kula before Malinowski: A changing configuration. *Mankind, 11*, 429–435.

Egloff, B. J. (1979). *Recent prehistory in southeast Papua*. Terra Australis 4. Canberra; Department of Prehistory, Research School of Pacific Studies, Australian National University.

Elliot Smith, G. (1916). *The migrations of early culture*. Manchester: University Press.

England, P. (1946). The Ramu stones: Notes on stone carvings found in the Annaberg-Atemble area, Ramu Valley, New Guinea. *Mankind, 3*, 233–236.

Etheridge, R. (1908). Ancient stone implements from the Yodda valley goldfield, north-east British New Guinea. *Records of the Australian Museum, 7*(1), 24–28

Fenner, F. J. (1944). Fossil human skull fragments of probable Pleistocene age from Aitape, New Guinea. *Records of the South Australian Museum, 6*, 335–354.

Finsch, O. (1914). *Sudseearbeiten*. Hamburg: L. Friederichsen & Co.

Fraser, D. (1972). Early Chinese artistic influence in Melanesia? In N. Barnard (Ed.), *Early Chinese art and its possible influence in the Pacific Basin* (pp. 631–654). 3 vols. New York: Intercultural Press.

Gifford, E. W. (1951). *Archaeological excavations in Fiji*. Anthropological Records 13(3). Berkeley: University of California.

Gifford, E. W., & Shutler, R. (1956). *Archaeological excavations in New Caledonia*. Anthropological Records 18(1). Berkeley: University of California.

Golson, J. (1972). Both sides of the Wallace Line: New Guinea, Australia, Island Melanesia and Asian prehistory. In N. Barnard (Ed.), *Early Chinese art and its possible influence in the Pacific Basin* (pp. 533–597). 3 vols. New York: Intercultural Press.

HISTORY OF ARCHAEOLOGY IN PAPUA NEW GUINEA   105

Golson, J. (2006). Prehistory: A late arrival. In B. V. Lal & A. Ley (Eds.), *The Coombs: A house of memories* (pp. 109–116). Canberra: Australia National University Press.

Haddon, A. C. (1920). Migrations and cultures in British New Guinea. *The Journal of the Anthropological Institute of Great Britain and Ireland, 50*, 237–280.

Haddon, A. C. (1932). A prehistoric sherd from the Mailu District, Papua. *Man, 32*, 111–114.

Höltker, G. (1940/41). Einiges über steinkeulenköpfe und steinbeile in Neuguinea. Tatsachen und probleme in Ausschnitten und perspektiven. *Anthropos, 35 / 36*(4/6) 681–736.

Höltker, H. (1951). Die Steinvögel in Melanesien. In *Südseestudien Etudes Sur L'Oceanie / South Sea Studies: Gedenkschrift zur erinnerung an Felix Speiser* (pp. 235–265). Basel: Museum für Völkerkunde.

Hossfeld, P. S. (1949). The stratigraphy of the Aitape skull and its significance. *Transactions of the Royal Society of South Australia, 72*, 201–207.

Hossfeld, P. S. (1965). Radiocarbon dating and palaeoecology of the Aitape fossil remains. *Proceedings of Royal Society of Victoria, 78*, 161–165.

Howes, H. (2017). Early German-language analyses of potsherds from New Guinea and the Bismarck Archipelago. *Journal of Pacific Archaeology, 8*(1), 35–46.

Joyce, T. A. (1912). Note on prehistoric pottery from Japan and New Guinea. *The Journal of the Royal Anthropological Institute of Great Britain and Ireland, 42*, 545–546.

Kasprusch P. A. (1940/41). Der große 'prähistorische' Steinmörser in Atemble am mittleren Ramu River in Neuguinea. *Anthropos, 35 / 36*, 647–654.

Kasprusch, A. (1973). *The tribes of the Middle Ramu and Upper Keram Rivers (North-East New Guinea).* Studia Instituti Anthropos Vol. 17. Bonn: Sumptibus Instituti Anthropos St Augustin Bei Bonn.

Lampert, R. (1966). Archaeological reconnaissance in Papua and New Guinea. Uncirculated mimeographed paper for limited circulation.

Leask, M. F. (1943a). A kitchen midden in Papua. *Oceania, 13*, 235–242.

Leask, M. F. (1943b). Rock engravings and paintings of the Sogeri District of Papua. *Mankind, 3*, 116–119.

Leask, M. (1945/1946). Obsidian and its use in the stone implements of New Guinea. *The Victorian Naturalist, 62*, 98–100.

Leask, M. F. (1947). Tools of a canoe-building industry from Cape Wom, northern New Guinea. *Oceania, 17*, 300–309.

Lenormand, M. (1948). Decouvert d'un gisement de poteries a l'Ile des Pins. *Etudes Melanesiennes, 3*, 54–58.

Lindt, J. W. (1887). *Picturesque New Guinea.* London: Longmans Green & Co.

MacLachlan, R. (1938). Native pottery from central and southern Melanesia. *Journal of the Polynesian Society, 47*, 64–89.

MacLachlan, R. (1939). Native pottery of the New Hebrides. *Journal of the Polynesian Society, 48*, 32–55.

MacLachlan, R. (1940a). Three pottery sherds from the New Hebrides. *Journal of the Polynesian Society, 49*, 172.

MacLachlan, R. (1940b). Native pottery of the Fiji Islands. *Journal of the Polynesian Society, 49*, 243–271.

McCarthy, F. D. (1938). A comparison of the prehistory of Australia with that of Indo-China, the Malay Peninsula and the Netherlands East Indies. In *Proceedings of the Third Congress of the Prehistorians of the Far East* (pp. 30–50). Singapore: Government Printing Office.

McKern, W. C. (1929). *Archaeology of Tonga*. Bulletin No.60. Honolulu: Bernice P. Bishop Museum.

Meyer, O. (1909a). Funde prahistorischer topferei und ateinmesser auf Vuatom, Bismarck Archipel. *Anthropos, 4*, 251–252.

Meyer, O. (1909b). Nachtrag. *Anthropos, 4*(4), 1093–1095.

Meyer, O. (1910). Funde von menschen- und tierknochen, von prahistorischer topferei und steinwerkzeugen auf Vatom, Bismarck-Archipel. *Anthropos, 5*(4), 1160–1161.

Meyer, O. (1932). Missionar und wissenschaft. In J. Hüskes (Ed.), *Pioniere der Sudsee: Werden und wachsen der Herz-Jesu-Mission von Rabaul zum goldenen jubiläum 1882–1932* (pp. 185–196). Hiltrup Salzburg: Missionare vom hlst. Herzen Jesu

Meyer, O. (n.d.). Report on the excavations of Father Otto Meyer at Watom Islands lodged at the Musee de l'Homme. Translated by D. Anson. In D. Anson (1983). Appendix 1 in *Lapita pottery of the Bismarck Archipelago and its affinities* (PhD thesis). University of Sydney, Sydney.

Miles, G. P. L. (1935). A stone pestle and mortar from the Upper Ramu River. *Man, 35*, 185.

Miles, G. P. L. (1938). Another stone mortar from New Guinea. *Man, 38*, 96.

Monckton, C. A. W. (1905). Appendix D: Northeastern Division. In *British New Guinea. Annual Reports for the year ending 30th June 1905* (pp. 31–34). The Parliament of the Commonwealth of Australia. Melbourne: Government Printer.

Monckton, C. A. W. (1922). *Last days in New Guinea*. London: Bodley Head.

Munro, N. G. (1911). *Prehistoric Japan*. Second Edition. Yokohama: Privately Printed.

Murphy, J. (1938). Stone workers of New Guinea: Past and present. *Oceania, 9*, 37–40.

Nason-Jones, J. (1930). *The geology of the Finsch coast area*. London: Harrison & Sons.

Neuhauss, R. (1911). *Deutsch Neu-Guinea*. Band 1. Berlin: Verlag Dietrich Reimer.

Nilles, J. (1944). Natives of the Bismarck Mountains, New Guinea Part 2. *Oceania, 15*, 1–18.

Perry, W. J. (1923). *Children of the sun*. London: Methuem & Co.

Petchey, P., Buckley, H., Walter, R., Anson, D., & Kinaston, R. (2016). The 2008–2009 excavations at the SAC locality, Reber-Rakival Lapita site, Watom Island, Papua New Guinea. *Journal of Indo-Pacific Archaeology, 40*, 12–31.

Pöch, R. (1907a). Einige bemerkenswerte ethnologika aus Neu-Guinea. *Mitteilungen der Anthropologischen Gesellschaft in Wien, 37*, 57–71.

Pöch, R. (1907b). Ausgrabungen alter topfscherben in Wanigela (Collingwood-Bay). *Mitteilungen der Anthropologischen Gesellschaft in Wien, 37*, 137–139.

Pöch, R. (1907c). Travels in German, British and Dutch New Guinea. *The Geographical Journal, 30*, 609–616.

Pretty, G. (1967). The Maurice Leask collection of stone blades and pottery from Cape Wom, North-East New Guinea. *Journal of the Anthropological Society of South Australia, 5*, 3–4.

Riesenfeld, A. (1950). *The megalithic cultures of Melanesia*. Leiden: E. J. Brill.

Seligmann, C. G. (1910). *The Melanesians of British New Guinea*. Cambridge: Cambridge University Press.

Seligmann, C. G. (1915). Note on an obsidian axe or adze blade from Papua. *Man, 91*, 161–162.

Seligmann, C. G., & Joyce, T. A. (1907). On prehistoric objects in British New Guinea. In H. Balfour et al. (Eds.), *Anthropological essays presented to Edward Burnett Tylor* (pp. 325–341). Oxford: Claredon Press.

Sloggett, R. (2016). Recalibrating meaning and building context for collections of distantiated stone tools. *World Archaeology, 48*(2), 311–324.

Solheim, W. G. II (1968). Possible routes of migration into Melanesia as shown by statistical analysis of methods of pottery manufacture. In *Asian and Pacific Archaeology Series No. 2* (pp. 139–166). Honolulu: Social Science Research Institute, University of Hawaii.

Specht, J. (1968). Preliminary report of excavations on Watom Island. *The Journal of the Polynesian Society, 77*, 117–134.

Specht, J. (2003). Watom Island and Lapita: Observations on the Reber-Rakival localities. In C. Sand (Ed.), *Pacific archaeology: Assessments and prospects* (pp. 121–134). Noumea: Le Cahiers de l'Archeologie en Nouvelle–Caledonie 15.

Spriggs, M. 2019. Towards a history of Melanesian archaeological practices. In M. Leclerc and J. Flexner (Eds.), *Archaeologies of Island Melanesia: Current approaches to landscapes, exchange and practice* (pp. 9–31). Canberra: Terra Australis 51. ANU E-Press.

Stanley, E. R. (1923). Appendix B. Government of the Commonwealth of Australia report on the salient geological features and natural resources of the New Guinea Territory including notes on dialectics and ethnology. In *Report to the League of Nations on the Administration of the Territory of New Guinea from 1st July 1921 to 30th June 1922* (pp. 1–93). Melbourne: Commonwealth of Australia.

Summerhayes, G. R. (2000). *Lapita interaction*. Terra Australis No.15. Canberra: Centre of Archaeology, Australian National University

Summerhayes, G. R. (2009). Obsidian network patterns in Melanesia—Sources, characterisation and distribution. *Bulletin of the Indo-Pacific Prehistory Association, 29*, 110–124.

Summerhayes, G. R., Leavesley, M., Fairbairn, A., Mandui, H., Field, J., Ford, A., & Fullagar, R. (2010). Human adaptation and use of plants in highland New Guinea 49,000–44,000 years ago. *Science, 330*, 78–81.

Swadling, P., Hauser-Schaublin, B., Gorecki, P., & Tiesler, F. (1988). *The Sepik-Ramu: An introduction*. Port Moresby: National Museum with Gordon & Gotch.

Tudor, M. (1968). So now they have buried Peter England. *Pacific Island Monthly* 39 (3) (March), 68–69.

White, J. P. (1965). An archaeological survey in Papua New Guinea. *Current Anthropology, 6*, 334–335.

White, J. P., de S. Disney, H. J., & Yaldwyn, J. C. (1970a). Prehistoric Papuan engraving. *Australian Natural History, 16*, 344–345.

White J. P., Crook K. A. W., & Ruxton, B. P. (1970b). Kosipe: A Pleistocene site in the Papua Highlands. *Proceedings of the Prehistoric Society, 36*, 152–170.

Williams, F. E. (1931). Papuan petrographs. *The Journal of the Royal Anthropological Institute of Great Britain and Ireland, 61*, 121–155.

Wright, D., Denham, T., Shine, D., & Donohue, M. (2013). An archaeological review of western New Guinea. *Journal of World Prehistory, 26*(1), 25–73.

CHAPTER 4

THE DEVELOPMENT (AND IMAGINED REINVENTION) OF AUSTRALIAN ARCHAEOLOGY IN THE TWENTIETH CENTURY

CHRIS URWIN AND MATTHEW SPRIGGS

MAKING SENSE OF THE HISTORY OF AUSTRALIAN ARCHAEOLOGY

RECENT books such as Billy Griffiths's *Deep Time Dreaming* (2017a, 2018) and Rebe Taylor's *Into the Heart of Tasmania* (2017: 171–205) have brought aspects of the history of Australian archaeology to large and nonspecialist readerships (see also Colley 2002). Griffiths's (2018) wide-ranging history details some of the key figures and events that helped transform the discipline between 1956 and the 1990s. Among other case studies, Griffiths (2018) explores Isabel McBryde's extensive archaeological surveys in the New England region of New South Wales (NSW), the excavations of Rhys Jones in Tasmania, and the ethnoarchaeological research conducted successively by Carmel Schrire and Betty Meehan in Arnhem Land. These investigations commenced in the 1960s, led by a 'new breed' (Jones & Megaw 2000: 14) of mostly overseas-trained archaeologists, among whom John Mulvaney looms large in disciplinary histories. Griffiths suggests that '[t]he modern era of archaeological investigation began on Friday 13 January 1956' (2017b: 106, 2018; see also Colley 2002: 4; Murray & White 1981). On this day, the Melbourne and Cambridge-educated archaeologist began excavating a rock shelter site at Tungawa (then known as Fromm's Landing) on the Murray River in South Australia. The excavations have subsequently been lauded for combining 'environmental data about river levels with archaeological information, history and ethnography' (Griffiths 2017b: 107; see also McBryde 1964: 5). Other founding events have been proposed for the discipline. Horton (1991: 349), for example, attributed the 'flowering of Australian archaeology' to the 1970s, following the discovery of 25,000- to 32,000-year-old archaeological deposits and Aboriginal ancestral remains at Lake Mungo in NSW (Bowler, Jones, Allen, & Thorne 1970).

In commencing his history of the discipline with events of the late 1950s, Griffiths (2018: 5) aimed to investigate 'the dramatic discovery of Australia's deep history' while disassociating 'the discipline of archaeology from the skulduggery' of the previous era.[1] In his approach, Billy Griffiths (2017b, 2018) follows Tom Griffiths's (1996) earlier exploration of the motivations and activities of stone artefact collectors and antiquarians in the state of Victoria. The Victorian stone artefact collectors—some of whom were affiliated with the National Museum of Victoria (NMV)—removed large quantities of stone artefacts from Aboriginal places and (until the mid-1940s) believed that the presence of Aboriginal people in Australia had no significant antiquity (Griffiths 1996; see also Mulvaney 1957, 1961, 1986: 100). For Griffiths (1996), the era of amateur collecting ceased in the 1960s, making way for an era of professional archaeological enquiry and state-legislated protection of Aboriginal places. Mulvaney (1957, 1961: 88; 1986) himself asserted that excavations prior to the 1960s were of 'indifferent quality' and that collectors destroyed archaeological sites to acquire 'a cabinet collection'. There was only one clear exception to his rule: the excavations of Hale and Tindale (1930) in 1929 at Tartanga and Ngaut Ngaut (Devon Downs) on the Murray River, which were based on 'stratigraphy and a recognition of cultural change' (Mulvaney 1960: 54, 1961: 65; Figure 4.1).[2]

Certainly, Australian archaeology enjoyed something of a 'golden age' in the 1960s–1970s (Colley 2002: 4). New and relatively secure sources of funding, maturing scientific techniques such as palynology and radiocarbon dating, and an influx of trained researchers accelerated the progress of archaeological research (see Allen 2019; Colley 2002; Davidson 1983; Griffiths 2018; Megaw 1966; Moser 1995b; Mulvaney 1961: 100–101; Murray & White 1981: 256). This era also saw the development of new university courses in archaeology within Australia, legislation aimed at protecting archaeological sites, and improvements in disciplinary ethics. By 1964, professional archaeologists were teaching and researching at the University of New England, Sydney University, and The Australian National University (ANU) (Megaw 1966). The first museum archaeologist, London Institute of Archaeology trained Ian Crawford, was appointed to the Western Australian Museum in Perth in 1961. Perhaps most importantly, the Australian Institute of Aboriginal Studies (AIAS, now the Australian Institute of Aboriginal and Torres Strait Islander Studies or AIATSIS) was founded in 1961 and provided considerable funding for archaeological fieldwork and analysis in its early years. However, as Spriggs (2020) has pointed out, the history of Australian archaeology has been oversimplified. As archaeological research accelerated from 1960 onwards, the newcomers produced and reproduced a history of archaeology that was divided along lines of worthy 'professionals' (researchers from the 1960s onwards) and inept 'amateurs' (pre-1960s researchers) (e.g., see Murray & White 1981).[3] The narrative emerged from a need. Beginning in the 1960s, archaeologists felt it necessary to establish themselves and attract university funding by proving that their work was innovative, ethical, and relevant to Australian society.

But there are problems with dividing and disassociating pre-1960s archaeologies (whether good, bad, or ugly) from later developments. First, defining the eras in terms of professionalization is essentially meaningless. If the term *professional* refers to people trained and employed to conduct a specific job, then there were no professional archaeologists continuously employed in Australia until the early 1960s (see Spriggs 2021).[4] Further, as we explore in this chapter, the two eras are difficult to divide, and aspects of archaeological thought and practice with continued salience developed in Australia well before the 1960s. If we are to perpetuate histories of Australian archaeology that commence c. 1960, we cannot properly identify the intellectual baggage, biases, and trajectories of our discipline. How have recent histories of archaeology in Australia built on (and subsequently silenced) methodological and theoretical contributions made prior to and during the 1960s? In this chapter, we examine some key moments and projects that helped transform Australian archaeology in the early decades of the twentieth century and in the 1940s, 1960s, and 1980s.[5] Each example has implications for how we understand certain aspects of the development of archaeology more recently and thus how we might reflect on our practice.

Geologists, Museum Workers, and Independent Scholars in the Early to Mid-Twentieth Century

In the early to mid-twentieth century, Australian archaeology developed steadily, driven by the theories and fieldwork of earth scientists, independent scholars, and museum workers. At the turn of the twentieth century, palaeontologists such as Robert Etheridge (1890; David & Etheridge 1889) and geologists such as John W. Gregory (1904) and Daniel J. Mahony (1912) reviewed the evidence for Aboriginal antiquity. In the absence of direct dating methods such as radiocarbon, they were looking for evidence of Aboriginal artefacts deposited in geological strata or alongside the remains of extinct (mega) fauna. Gregory—who was then Professor of Geology at the University of Melbourne—published a review of the evidence for the 'antiquity of man in Victoria' with the state's Royal Society. His paper reveals that, at the turn of the twentieth century, members of the Society were debating the relevance of several lines of evidence for the antiquity of Aboriginal presence in Victorian landscapes (Gregory 1904):

1. The reported presence of Aboriginal artefacts in or below distinctive geological strata, especially of volcanic tuff in western Victoria;

2. Aboriginal oral traditions that describe volcanic eruptions in western Victoria and sea-level changes;
3. The depth of cultural deposits, including shell middens;
4. Possible fossil footprints found in a piece of sandstone quarried from a depth of 54 feet below the surface near Warrnambool.

In the early 1900s, the lack of reliable geological (or archaeological) dating techniques hindered the search for Aboriginal antiquity. Both Etheridge (1890) and Gregory (1904: 141) underestimated the potential age of deep cultural deposits in 'river silts and sand dunes'. Gregory (1904: 144) had concluded that 'the geological evidence suggests that man has not been resident in Victoria for any prolonged period'. He indicated that this opinion was, at the time, 'in opposition to preconceived anthropological opinion' and contradicted *'the obvious probabilities of the case'* (Gregory 1904: 144, our emphasis). He hoped his paper would serve as a call for future research into the chronology of Aboriginal occupation. However, McNiven (this volume) has shown that Gregory's improbable conclusion was influenced by deep-seated racial prejudice. Like many colonists in this era, he believed that Aboriginal people were an inferior (and dying) race (see Gregory 1925). Among Victoria's scholarly community, Gregory's (1904: 129; cf. Casey, 1940; Mahony, Baragwanath, Wood Jones, & Kenyon 1936: 1341) surficial view of Aboriginal antiquity seems to have prevailed into the 1940s (see further discussion in Griffiths 1996: 72, 77–80; McNiven 2001: 214–215).

By 1932, the experienced archaeologist Dermot Casey had been appointed honorary ethnologist at the NMV. Early in 1934, the Anthropological Society of Victoria had been founded, with Casey on its organizing committee. In May of that year, the University of Melbourne Council, at the behest of Professor Frederic Wood-Jones, announced a donation of £500 towards a 'Victorian Archaeological Survey' over the next two years. Casey was appointed to lead it a few days later, and his archaeological qualifications for the position were listed in the Melbourne press: 'He attended a London University course in archaeology, and was assistant to the keeper of the London Museum (Dr R. E. M. Wheeler). He conducted investigations into Roman and prehistoric ruins while abroad. Mr Casey is a fellow of the Royal Archaeological Institute'.[6] It is not clear how much effort Casey actually put in on the Survey, although he was certainly active in museological matters and in researching Australian and New Guinea stone artefacts over the next several years (Spriggs 2021).

As others have observed (Du Cros 1984, 1993; Griffiths 2017b: 105; Mulvaney 1961; Smith 2007: table 1.2), there were several attempts at systematic (and sometimes stratigraphic) excavation prior to the 1960s. In 1929, the South Australian Museum workers Herbert Hale and Norman Tindale (1930) excavated at Tartanga and at Ngaut Ngaut (Devon Downs) rock shelter. The location of the 1929 excavations had been determined by wide-ranging surveys by staff and affiliates of the South Australian Museum conducted from 1925 to 1928 (see Sheard 1927; Sheard, Mountford, & Hackett 1927; Tindale & Mountford 1936; also Mulvaney 1960: 53–56).[7] The excavation at Ngaut Ngaut uncovered 12 well-defined and culturally rich strata spanning 6 metres in depth (Hale &

Tindale 1930; see also Smith 2000). In much the same way as archaeologists discuss their results in excavation reports today, the excavators used stratigraphic fluctuations in the distribution of shellfish, crustacean, animal bone, and stone artefact deposits to infer several distinct superimposed 'industries' (Hale & Tindale 1930: 204). By correlating the changes found at Ngaut Ngaut with the nearby Tartanga beds (which they believed, based on geological inference, to be a more ancient deposit), Hale and Tindale (1930: 175) identified six 'cultural phases'. In the 1940s, H. V. V. Noone (1949: 146; see also Casey 1940: 27; Davidson 1935: 146) remarked that theirs was the 'only productive excavation' in the country but that it required 'stratigraphic confirmation from material found elsewhere'.

In Tasmania, the Devonport-based history teacher Archibald L. Meston conducted excavations at Rocky Cape from 1931 to 1938 in a midden 'just over fifteen feet deep' (Meston 1949: 147; Jones 1971: 45–49; Figure 4.1). Meston (1956: 8) identified 'no stratification layers and no evidence of changed culture'. As Griffiths (2019), Taylor (2017),

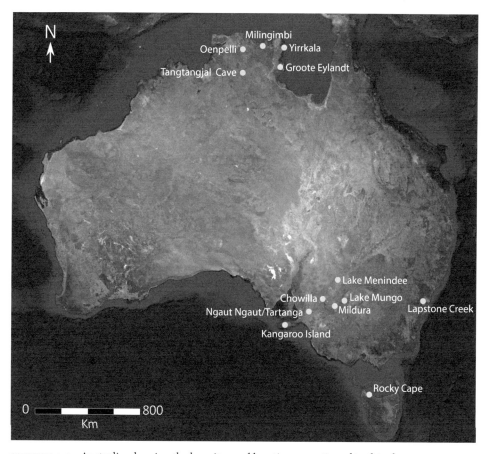

FIGURE 4.1. Australia, showing the key sites and locations mentioned in this chapter.

(Satellite image courtesy of the U.S. Geological Survey.)

and Struwe (2006) have shown, the example of the Tasmanians and their enduring stone artefacts was used from the 1860s into the twentieth century to anchor theories of social evolution (see also McNiven & Russell 2005: chap. 3; Murray 1992). As Griffiths (2019) points out: 'According to the evolutionary hierarchies made popular by Edward Burnett Tylor and William J. Sollas, the Tasmanians were an extreme example of the human condition: a datum point from which to speculate about the essence and evolution of humankind'. Meston's (1956) reading of the Rocky Cape sequence followed these earlier theories in suggesting that Tasmanian culture was unchanging (e.g., see Struwe 2006). However, stone artefacts excavated from the site enabled Norman Tindale to identify change, and to start connecting Tasmania's cultural history with that of mainland Australia (and Southeast Asia) (see Tindale 1937a, 1937b). Tindale visited Tasmania in April 1936 to view rock art that Meston (1934) had just published in the journal *Antiquity*; he also examined the excavation profile at Rocky Cape and the stone artefacts that had been dug out 'some years ago' (Tindale 1937b: 34). Noticing that stone artefacts from basal strata in the excavation profile were patinated, he sorted the collection into what he thought were Older (patinated) and Newer (less patinated) stone artefacts (Tindale 1937b: 34). Following the earlier observations of Henry Balfour, he identified 'typological differences' (Tindale 1937a, 1937b: 34; see also Taylor 2017: 172–175) between the two sets of stone artefacts and started to correlate the Older and Newer artefacts with three of the industries he and Hale had identified at Ngaut Ngaut/Tartanga.

Despite his pioneering attempts to identify culture change and correlate stone artefact typologies and stratigraphy across space, Tindale (1957: 41–44; see also Tindale 1937a; Tindale & Birdsell 1941) invoked the idea that various races or 'archaeological cultures' displaced one another through time to explain changing 'industries'. Straying from the relative security of stratigraphic correlations, he suggested that large stone artefacts (e.g., large unifacial pebble 'tools') found in surface deposits on Kangaroo Island and Tasmania predated the Ngaut Ngaut/Tartanga industries.[8] He suggested that these were the 'crude' tools the first migrants to Australia brought with them. For Tindale (1937a: 55), they were an 'old culture' possibly connected with 'the Upper Palaeolithic of Malaya'. Tindale and Birdsell (1941: 1) suggested that 'the Australian aborigines are not derived from a single ethnic group, but result from the blending . . . of three discrete ethnic elements, which may be called 'Southern', 'Northern', and 'Tasmanoid'.[9] This trihybrid theory has been thoroughly disproved but endures among white nationalist elements of Australian society (see Grounds & Ross 2010; McNiven & Russell 2005: 92). The idea that an early industry comprising mostly large stone artefacts was followed by an industry of smaller stone artefacts proved highly influential in Australian archaeology, well past the 1960s (see Lampert 1980; Bowler, Jones, Allen, & Thorne 1970; Jones 1973; Flood 1974). Tindale was also far from the last archaeologist to propose a close correlation between large unifacial stone artefacts found in Australia and those found in excavations in Southeast Asia (see Bowdler & Tan 2003; McBryde 1976; McCarthy 1941).

As can be seen from the examples given here, many of the earliest archaeological investigations were conducted by museum workers and independent scholars, often in interdisciplinary teams (see Hale & Tindale 1930: 217–218). As Professor Joseph L.

Shellshear (1937: 169) put it: 'the science of prehistory is of necessity confined to the correct interpretation of the material objects found. . . . The layers of the soil in these ancient sites are, as it were, leaves of a book. . . . To read the book aright requires the labour [of] many minds and hands. The services of the geologist, the ethnologist, the surveyor, the anthropologist, the botanist, the zoologist, the soil analyst, and many others are essential'.

In 1936, the Australian-born Shellshear returned to Sydney and took up an honorary position in the Anthropology Department of the Australian Museum. He was an anatomist who had gained archaeological field experience in the Netherlands, before teaching at the University of Hong Kong. By the time of his arrival in NSW, three Australian Museum ethnologists had already conducted excavations in the region: William W. Thorpe, Elsie Bramell, and Frederick D. McCarthy (see McCarthy 1934, 1948, 1978; Kahn 1993: 3). Thorpe was the Australian Museum ethnologist from 1906 to 1932, and he was a founding member of the Anthropological Society of NSW in 1928 along with C. C. Towle. Thorpe worked with the Society to excavate a rock shelter site at Burrill Lake in 1930 (Thorpe 1931; see also Du Cros 1984, 1993). The Burrill Lake excavations featured 'a testable hypothesis, excavation methodology and analysis of the material' (Du Cros 1984: 6). Yet the hypothesis under examination was that of J. S. Falkinder (1932: 69), who posited that the 'Tasmanian race' originated in Melanesia and was pushed into Tasmania from the Australian mainland 25,000–15,000 years ago by successive migrations of supposedly more advanced people.

After Thorpe's death in 1932, Elsie Bramell and Frederick D. McCarthy also worked with the Society to excavate a rock shelter near Emu Plains in 1934 (McCarthy 1934), and McCarthy worked with C. C. Towle to excavate the Lapstone Creek site in 1935–1936 (McCarthy 1948, 1978; Nelson 2007). Following this pioneering research, the Trustees of the Australian Museum funded Shellshear (1937: 173), Bramell, and McCarthy to survey 'rock shelters, kitchen middens, rock carvings, and other features on the shores of Port Hacking, George's River, the Hawkesbury River, and the Gosford and Newcastle areas'. They recorded about 400 rock shelters during their surveys and launched what was to become a long program of advocacy for legislative protection of cultural heritage in NSW. Bramell had been employed at the Australian Museum since 1932. In 1935, she had graduated with a Master's degree in anthropology from the University of Sydney, making her the most qualified museum anthropologist in the country. Her contribution to the Museum and to Australian archaeology was to some extent silenced by her marriage to McCarthy in 1940 (but see McCarthy, Bramell, & Noone 1946; McCarthy 1942: 93–94), at which time she was required to resign her position in accordance with NSW Public Service rules (see Bowdler & Clune 2000: 29).

The excavations at Lapstone Creek were for McCarthy (1948) what Ngaut Ngaut/ Tartanga had been for Tindale. McCarthy identified differences in stone artefact technology between the lower and upper deposits. Backed Bondi points were only found in the lower-level assemblage (termed the Bondaian industry). Stone artefacts in the upper levels (termed the Eloueran industry) contained many small backed adze blades (Elouera) and edge ground stone artefacts. McCarthy (1943a, 1943b; 1948: 28–29) applied this sequence of industries to other pre-1948 excavations and surface sites in NSW. He understood these sites in terms of 'Bondaian' and 'Eloueran culture', based on the Lapstone Creek sequence (McCarthy 1948: 28–29).

Extensive survey programs and pioneering excavations conducted in South Australia and NSW in the first half of the twentieth century laid the foundations for the later explosion of archaeological research. Early analysts demonstrated the potential of excavation to reveal technological change through time (see Attenbrow 2008: 494–493), but explanations for these changes differed (e.g., Tindale and Birdsell's trihybrid theory, described above). As McNiven and Russell (2005: 165–173) have explored, theories of hyperdiffusionism proliferated in some circles in Australia in the early 1900s. The English-based but Australian-born anatomist and ethnologist Grafton Elliott Smith (1915), along with William Perry (1923), advanced the idea that supposedly advanced technologies such as ground-edge axes were diffused to Aboriginal people by a 'heliolithic culture'. Those conducting systematic research into the archaeological record of Indigenous Australian societies mostly resisted hyperdiffusionism (e.g., see Kenyon 1930: 71; McCarthy 1940: 184). However, scholars such as McCarthy (1944) suggested that key aspects of material culture (e.g., tanged axes, geometric microliths) had diffused to Aboriginal Australia from New Guinea (see McNiven 2006). As Dermot Casey (1940: 26) argued at a meeting of the Congress of Prehistorians of the Far East in 1938: 'There is no element of their [Aboriginal] culture which cannot reasonably be supposed to be either original, or to have evolved or developed in Australia, or to have come by diffusion from New Guinea'; no 'heliolithic' echoes there!

During the 1940s, more sophisticated approaches to archaeological interpretation developed, often taking an approach that today would be labelled cultural ecology. Spriggs (2020: 5–7) refers to several of the major interpretive projects of the time, including Thomas D. Campbell and Herbert V. V. Noone's (1943; see also Campbell, Cleland, & Hossfeld 1946) research into Aboriginal sites in the Woakwine Range region of South Australia, which was based on fieldwork conducted in 1943–1945. Their analyses combined ethnohistory, observation of locally available animal and plant foods, midden contents, and estimates of required meat weight per person to calculate population figures. Campbell, Cleland, and Hossfeld (1946: 445) succinctly summarized the aims of their paper: 'The present work was planned to amplify previous investigation into more of an ecological approach; that is by correlating available recorded information of the once living aboriginal with an intensive study of the present day remnants of his material culture and indigenous environment. By this means we can learn something of his reactions and adjustments to his particular geographical circumstances; and, in short, endeavour to reconstruct a picture of his ways of living'.

Also notable was a wide-ranging paper by NMV geologist and palaeontologist Robert A. Keble (1947), 'Notes on Australian Quaternary Climates and Migration', which examined the entry of humans into Australia and their subsequent dispersal. As Spriggs (2020: 5) notes, this broad survey gave detailed consideration to the stratigraphy of Ngaut Ngaut and Tartanga and to instances of artefacts below volcanic deposits in Victoria, their stratigraphic context and dating. Keble reexcavated the key site of Bushfield in western Victoria, conducted geological, zoological, palaeobotanical, palaeontological, and mineralogical studies of the deposit, and dated the site based on climatic indicators from these as well as discussion of Aboriginal traditions of volcanic activity. Discussion followed on whether cut marks on megafaunal bones were caused by humans or by marsupial carnivores, before reconstruction maps of the Sahul Shelf at two different stages of the Glacial period prior to the modern sea-level being reached were presented (Keble 1947: 65, 67). The date by which the Torres Strait had formed was estimated correctly at 8000 years ago, and Keble (1947: 74) contended that settlement of Australia was between 21,000 and 15,000 years ago, correlated with very specific climatic conditions that dictated probable migration routes across the continent.

Cross-Cultural Research and Historicizing Rock Art in Arnhem Land (1940s)

Archaeological research took several turns in the 1940s. In this era, archaeologists working in Arnhem Land (the northeast corner of Australia's Northern Territory) documented rock art and excavated archaeological sites with Aboriginal people. Sydney University-trained anthropologists Frederick McCarthy (1949: 319) and Neil W. G. MacIntosh (1951) explored the potential of archaeology as a means to historicize ethnographically known cross-cultural interactions and rock art production. In McCarthy's (1949: 319) words: 'Apart . . . from the general problem of the antiquity of man in Australia is the complementary one of establishing the historical relationships between our stone implement cultures, rock paintings and engravings, stone arrangements, and other traits throughout the continent'.

McCarthy's research in northern Australia took place during the American-Australian Expedition to Arnhem Land (McCarthy & Setzler 1960; Setzler & McCarthy 1950). The 1948 expedition was led by the ethnographer and filmmaker Charles P. Mountford (1956), who had played a key role in the South Australian Museum surveys of the 1920s. Mountford had successfully courted project funding from the National Geographic Society during his film and lecture tour of the United States in 1945–1946. The expedition aimed to bring together Australian and American researchers to study the art, ethnology, and music of Aboriginal people (Mountford 1956; see also May 2009, 2011: 174–175; Specht 2012; Thomas 2010). McCarthy led the archaeological component of the expedition with Frank Setzler, Curator of Anthropology at the Smithsonian Institution. The pair conducted twenty-four excavations in the regions of Groote Eylandt, Yirrkala, Oenpelli (now called Gumbalanya), and Milingimbi (Figure 4.1). McCarthy had spent time in 1937 and 1938 in museums and on excavations in Indonesia and the Malay Peninsula (see Kahn 1993: 3). Based on McCarthy's experiences in Southeast Asia, and on earlier findings of Macassan pottery in Arnhem Land by Ronald M. Berndt and Catherine H.

Berndt (1947), the pair knew there was potential to recover 'dateable objects of Malay or European origin in direct association with an aboriginal horizon' (McCarthy & Setzler 1960: 215). Their investigations followed the earlier research of the professionally trained U.S. archaeologist/anthropologist Daniel S. Davidson (1935: 153) whose excavations with Wardaman people in 1930 suggested to him that Aboriginal people had 'undoubtedly lived in this region for thousands of years.'[10,11]

It is an underappreciated aspect of the history of Australian archaeology that Aboriginal people participated in the excavations and rock art recording of McCarthy and Setzler in 1948 (e.g., see May 2009: fig. 4.3). Photographs taken by Setzler (McCarthy & Setzler 1960: plate 4A–C) depict Aboriginal people excavating at the 'Macassar Well' site on Milingimbi Island (Figure 4.2). During excavation of the Macassar Well shell midden, a tanged implement was found, which the Aboriginal fieldworkers apparently did not recognize (McCarthy & Setzler 1960: 238). We speculate that McCarthy (1944: 271) sought Indigenous interpretations of this item to establish whether tanged axes had diffused to Aboriginal Australia via New Guinea. Interactions in and around the dig sites also demonstrated continuities of practice. McCarthy and Setzler (1960: 250) recorded that '[Aboriginal] women still gather on this midden to pound cycad nuts in season on mortars similar to those found in the midden' at the Macassar Well site. Aboriginal people exercised discretion regarding what knowledge they shared and which 'ethnographic' items they sold to expedition members (May 2009: 63–64). The archaeological team 'collected' hundreds of Aboriginal and Macassan ancestral remains. Some of these remains were covertly stolen by Setzler (Thomas & Bijon 2018; Griffiths 2018: 151–152), an action that has caused ongoing distress to Arnhem Land communities. Some sixty years later, local Aboriginal leaders successfully negotiated the repatriation of their ancestral remains from the Smithsonian Institution (see May 2009; Thomas & Bijon 2018).

Through excavation, the archaeologists attempted to establish links between buried deposits and rock art (McCarthy & Setzler 1960; see also Clarke & Frederick 2011: 141). At a rock shelter in the Oenpelli region, McCarthy and Setzler (1960: 218–219) identified 'a direct connection between the occupational deposits in the floors of the rock shelters and the paintings on their walls and ceilings'. Although the deposits could not be dated, they read changing cultural practices into the rock art. Their analyses of motif superimpositions suggested that the rock art had been produced via 'a succession of techniques' (McCarthy & Setzler 1960: 219). As Clarke and Frederick (2011) have explored, McCarthy recorded hundreds of rock art motifs during the expedition and introduced systematic methods (such as drawing the rock art motifs using a grid) to this form of archaeology. However, the precise relationship between buried deposits of red, yellow, and white ochre and 'the various painting techniques or periods' eluded McCarthy and Setzler (1960: 219). Clarke and Frederick (2011) picked up some of the strands of this early research in the Groote Eylandt region in the 1990s. Using modern archaeological techniques such as radiocarbon dating, they were able to 'begin the kind of integrated interpretation that McCarthy sought all those years ago' (Clarke & Frederick 2011: 156) in close collaboration with local Indigenous families.

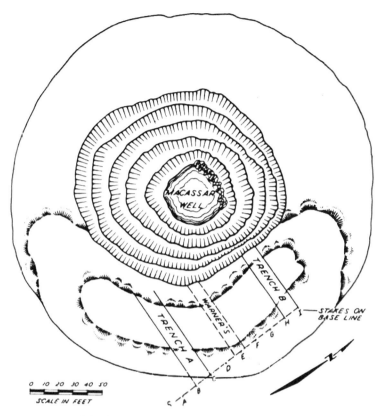

FIGURE 4.2. Diagram of the 'Macassar Well' site on Milingimbi Island, excavated by Frederick McCarthy, Frank Setzler, and local Aboriginal people (from McCarthy & Setzler 1960: fig. 2). The zone they excavated was an Aboriginal shell midden located immediately east of a freshwater spring. The spring was identified as 'Macassar' on the basis that it was surrounded by a grove of exotic tamarind trees. One of the trenches depicted had previously been excavated by W. Lloyd Warner (1937) in 1927–1928.

In 1949, Macintosh (1951, 1952) commenced archaeological research in Arnhem Land on an expedition led by anthropologist Adolphus Peter Elkin (1952). Macintosh and journalist John Thompson excavated the floor of the 7-metre-long Tangtangjal (then called Tandandjal) Cave. The cave site comprised a rock art gallery and several stone arrangements (Macintosh 1951: 181). Macintosh systematically recorded the rock art gallery, as well as that of the nearby site of Torriya Kuta-luk (then called Doria Gudaluk, or Beswick Creek Cave). In each instance, Macintosh (1951: 179, 1952: 256; see also Gunn & Whear 2007) visited the sites with Jawoyn people and seems to have explicitly sought their permission to excavate. The motif interpretations made by Macintosh (1951, 1952, 1977) and a Jawoyn man called Lamjerroc (Elkin 1952) have since become a classic case study of the importance of informed ethnography for rock art studies (see Brady, Gunn, Smith, & David 2018; Gunn & Whear 2007; Smith, Domingo, & Jackson 2016).[12]

The excavations were extensive and provided an opportunity to relate layers of cultural materials with events and phases of rock art production. Macintosh (1951: 195) was struck by obvious patterns in the vertical and horizontal distribution of white and red ochre. A 0.5-cm-thick layer of soil containing ash and red and white ochre was found at the interface of the lowermost strata: layers 3 and 4. Macintosh assessed the distribution of white and red ochre within 12 discrete zones of the upper layers (1 and 2). Ochre was absent from layer 3, which, along with changing concentrations of charcoal with depth, suggested to Macintosh (1951: 196) that there had been a hiatus in site use: 'The hiatus between two time periods is here seen again in the use of ochre; but whereas in the earlier period red is concentrated towards the inner wall of the cave . . . in the later period white is predominant towards the inner wall and red towards the mouth of the cave'.

In 1929, Hale and Tindale (1930: 208–211) had attempted to identify a sequence of rock art engravings by piecing together the history of site formation (rock fall events) at Ngaut Ngaut. Two decades later, research in Arnhem Land demonstrated the potential of historicizing the production of rock art by correlating sequences of motif production (including colour use) with ochre found buried in the ground. Novel techniques such as ochre sourcing and highly fine-grained radiocarbon chronologies are realizing that promise now (see, e.g., Chalmin & Huntley 2018; David et al. 2013). If histories of Australian archaeology are to ignore or deride the 1940s as a 'dark age' (*sensu* Mulvaney 1961), we stand to lose several aspects of our history. We risk ignoring the presence, influence, and interpretations of Aboriginal people during early archaeological fieldwork (see also Davidson 1935). We also risk denying ethically problematic interactions in the history of archaeology (see further discussion below). Finally, this example illustrates the fact that archaeologists were asking nuanced questions of the material cultural record (not simply seeking Aboriginal 'antiquity'). Here the archaeologists attempted to historicize the sequence by which caves were adorned with ochre through time. The key differentiation between the 1940s and 1970s was not in the questions nor necessarily in scientific rigour, but in terms of *ethics* and *technology*.

The Overlap of So-Called Amateur and University Research in the Willandra Lakes Region (1960s)

We now move to the 1960s era in the Willandra Lakes and Mildura regions to examine the overlap of emerging university 'professionals' with so-called amateurs (locals with no formal training in archaeology/anthropology). Although this was not the first time Australian research reached international scholarly audiences (e.g., see Wood Jones 1944), the 1960s–1970s research conducted at Lake Mungo in the Willandra Lakes region quickly became emblematic of Australian archaeology (see Griffiths 2018: 120–149;

Horton 1991: 349; Figure 4.1). Lake Mungo itself is an ancient lake that has been dry for some 10,000 years. Jim Bowler completed his PhD study on the lake's geomorphology in 1970. During fieldwork for his doctoral research in July 1968, Bowler (1970: 121–124) found a human burial eroding from the large eroded dune or 'lunette' situated on the eastern margin of Lake Mungo. From his knowledge of the local stratigraphy and of dates already received (but not yet published) from the ANU radiocarbon-dating laboratory (see Polach, Lovering, & Bowler 1970; Bowler 1970: table 4.2),[13] Bowler recognized that the burial was ancient.

Excavations and initial radiocarbon dating demonstrated that the Mungo I individual (aka Mungo Lady) had lived sometime in the period 32,000–25,000 years ago. Bowler and colleagues (1970; see also Barbetti & Allen 1972; Bowler, Thorne, & Polach 1972) published the finds in *World Archaeology* and described the highly active erosional landscape as a 'living site'. The excavations were seen as a triumph of modern, university-based archaeology and were underpinned by radiocarbon dates from the ANU laboratory. The investigations conducted by Bowler (1970) acted as a primer for the PhD research of Harry Allen (1972: 3). Allen conducted extensive surveys and excavations in the Darling Basin and Wilcannia regions from 1969 to 1971. Overlapping these projects were the wide-ranging surveys, collections, and excavations conducted by Sir Robert Blackwood, Ken N. G. Simpson, Dermot Casey, and Edmund Gill for the NMV along the Murray River (see Blackwood & Simpson 1973; Gill 1973). In the early 1960s, the Murray River-side location of Chowilla (30 km upstream of the town of Renmark in South Australia) had been proposed as the site for a large dam. The NMV project aimed to salvage sites of cultural heritage and natural historical importance within the vast proposed lake upstream of Chowilla (see Gill 1973: 1). However, these concentrated research programs were not entirely novel. Local independent scholars had already surveyed innumerable sites within c. 160 localities in the region (mostly on large agricultural 'stations' and lakes) in the period 1960–1970 and had conducted a controlled excavation of Aboriginal shell middens at Red Cliffs in 1965–1969.

The Mildura and District Anthropological Group (MDAG) comprised members of the Anthropological Society of Victoria living in the Mildura region (Thomas 1964: 105). The group was built around Hallett ('Hal') F. Thomas, who was an agriculturalist and merchant from Irymple South. The other active members were Noel Connard, Desmond Keen, Peter Thatcher, and Tom Thomson. Outside the immediate group, Mrs. H. McCredden of Cuthero Station was the most significant donor of stone artefacts to the MDAG. The group formally began their activities in 1960, the scale of which is quite remarkable. Thomas (1964: 105) described their work as 'a detailed survey of the remaining indications of Aboriginal occupation within a one hundred mile radius of the Mildura Post Office'. Throughout the 1960s, the group conducted day trips to at least seventy different stations in Victoria and NSW within their identified study area. They also collected from the shores of lakes on the Darling Anabranch (e.g., Nearie, Popiltah, Travellers, Yelta) and in the Willandra Lakes region (e.g., Mungo, Garnpang), as well as from water sources on the Murray River (e.g., Lake Gol Gol, Lake Hattah, Lake Iraak, Lake Ranfurly, Lake Victoria, Karadoc Swamp, and Kings Billabong).[14]

Evidently, the trips were social affairs, conducted by friends and acquaintances on their weekends. Thomas (1960–1970) documented and mapped these activities meticulously. He produced a logbook that described each of the 246 field trips the group undertook and wrote at least 'three lengthy written reports' to the Anthropological Society of Victoria.[15] The group collected cultural materials and megafaunal bones that they came across on their field trips. The bulk of these collections were donated to the NMV, latterly Museums Victoria, in several lots by Thomas and his family between 1978 and 2019.

Thomas was closely associated with several departments of the NMV. On the second official trip of the MDAG in March 1960, Hal Thomas and Tom Thomson visited the south side of Lake Gol Gol with three members of the Museum: Charles W. Brazenor (Director), Aldo Massola (Curator of Anthropology), and Mr. R. Boswell (a senior preparator) (Thomas logbook, 5 March 1960). The Museum staff visited Lake Victoria and Karadoc Swamp with the MDAG over the following two days. One can get a snapshot of the shared interests of the MDAG and the NMV from these three days. The group examined the contents of Aboriginal hearth sites containing 'baked box-flat grey clay' balls, some of which had the 'imprint of the palm of a human hand' (Thomas logbook, 5 March 1960). They also inspected the impacts of agricultural activity on Aboriginal burial grounds at Lake Victoria (Thomas logbook, 6 March 1960) and examined 'several strata, or layers, of mussel-charcoal deposit' exposed at Karadoc Swamp (Thomas logbook, 7 March 1960). The group excavated Aboriginal ancestral remains during these three days; these excavations are part of a long and well-documented history of white settlers removing Aboriginal remains from the large burial grounds present in the Murray River region. The MDAG believed (without irony) that their collections of skeletal remains and stone artefacts were made for the purpose of salvage and conservation. We discuss this legacy further at the conclusion of this chapter.

The MDAG published their archaeological research only once, in *Mankind*, the journal of the Anthropological Society of NSW. Their study, sole-authored by Hal Thomas (1964), documented 93 Aboriginal scarred trees at Lake Gol Gol in NSW, about 90 km southwest of Lake Mungo. Their recording methods were systematic, and their analyses nuanced. Thomas (1964: 112) referred to the trees as 'frame-trees', dismissing other possible terms (e.g., 'carved' or 'cut'), which he thought implied methods of incision that were not evident on the Lake Gol Gol trees. The MDAG drew each 'frame' and mapped their spatial distribution and orientation (probably following McCarthy [1945]) (Figure 4.3). Based on their observations, Thomas (1964) suggested that Aboriginal people had made the modifications both before and after settler intrusion: 'There are certainly marks just inside the perimeter of one or two of the frames that may be attributable to blows from a stone axe, but there are also marks in several frames that have obviously been made by steel axes' (Thomas 1964: 117). Thomas (1964: 115–118) proposed a ceremonial interpretation for the site, suggesting that it was made during a period in which Indigenous ceremonial practices were changing rapidly in response to settler invasion (and the arrival of disease). He drew on similarities between the Lake Gol Gol site and a Bora ground at 'Banaway' (now Collymongle) in NSW (see Black 1944: 33), to suggest that the Wathi Wathi and Tati Tati peoples of the Murray River region

FIGURE 4.3. Hal F. Thomas (left) and another member of the MDAG measuring scarred trees at Lake Gol Gol, sometime between July 1961 and May 1964 (Thomas 1964: 105). Source: First Peoples Department, Museums Victoria [XP30079].

(The photographer is unknown.)

adopted ceremonial practices through contact with Aboriginal communities from central-eastern NSW (Thomas 1964: 119). The study remains an important reference for scarred trees in the Murray-Darling River region but has seldom been cited (but see Massola 1969: 121; McCarthy 1967: 157). The group feared for the survival of the ceremonial ground and, more broadly, for Aboriginal cultural heritage across the region. After a field trip on 8 July 1961, Thomas (1961: 94) recorded: 'we were somewhat dismayed to note the rapid strides being made by the new settlers [at Lake Gol Gol]. . . . Much timber—mainly box—has been felled since we were last in the vicinity. . . . Much of the country now being cleared has old Aboriginal camp-sites, burial grounds, etc., upon it, and it seems certain that these will now disappear for ever. Although we have done some work in this area . . . much more could have been done had we realized just how quickly the new owners of the land were going to get on with the job'.

In 1965–1969, the group expanded their activities to include systematic excavation. The site they selected for their two excavations was a large shell midden deposit at Red Cliffs. In a report on the excavations sent to Jim Bowler on 11 December 1973,[16] Thomas described the location as being c. 4 km east of Red Cliffs within the 'Cliffside Public Park and Recreation Reserve'.[17] The two discrete excavations were dug to depths of c. 140 and 200 cm in excavation units measuring 8–15 cm. The deposits contained two species of bivalve mussels (*Alathyria jacksoni* and *Velesunio ambiguus*), another species of bivalve (*Corbiculina angasi*), and river and land snails. The MDAG noted the presence of a 'camp-site' comprising lumps of fire baked clay and charred sandstone 'cooking stones' 'on the surface of, or partly buried in, the ground in close proximity to the "digs".[18] In his notes to Bowler, Thomas[19] drew on his knowledge of the distribution and arrangement of the shells within the deposit to rule out various nonanthropogenic explanations for the accumulation, including that they were natural riverine shell beds later exposed by rapid subsidence. Gill (1969: 185) and later Bowler (1980: 25, fig 2.5) assisted the MDAG by acquiring radiocarbon dates on shells excavated from the deposit.

On various occasions in the period 1965–1969, the MDAG was visited at their Red Cliffs excavations by Adolphus Peter Elkin, John Mulvaney, Edmund Gill, Dermot Casey, and Aldo Massola. Notably, Blackwood, Casey, and Gill (then Assistant Director of the NMV) visited from 30 April to 2 May 1965.[20] On this trip, they visited Keira Station, the Red Cliffs excavations, Lake Hattah National Park, and Lake Victoria in the vicinity of the proposed Chowilla dam development. The dam development had been approved by federal and state governments in 1963, and the visit was presumably devised by Blackwood and Gill as a reconnaissance of the area. The NMV salvage project commenced in 1967, and the earlier investigations of Thomas and the MDAG certainly influenced project design. Many of the Aboriginal burial sites and cultural materials that were documented and 'salvaged'—such as Berribee Station, Lake Victoria, Neds Corner Station, Talgarry Station, Dunedin Park Station, and Boy Creek—had been foci of the MDAG's earlier surveys and collections.

So, what impact did the MDAG have on archaeological (and geological) research in the region? Evidently, Gill and Bowler were willing to spend research funds to clarify the antiquity of the Red Cliffs shell deposits. Bowler visited Thomas at his Irymple home on several occasions during his late 1960s and early 1970s research (Donnie Byrne personal communication, 2019). Bowler (personal communication, 2020) believed the long sequence of shell deposits had great potential for unravelling the history of the Murray River. Red Cliffs was the first directly dated midden deposit for the entire lower Murray River region (see Clark & Hope 1985) and demonstrated the potential antiquity of shell middens in the region. As a result, Gill (1969: 185) concluded that 'Murray River tribes were present from at least 11,250 years ago'.

Allen (1972: 134), on the other hand, was unaware of the surveys of the MDAG, believing that he had conducted 'the first major archaeological survey of the Darling Basin'. Allen can be excused for this belief, as the MDAG's reports were mostly inaccessible. Their surveys were far more expansive but less systematic than those of Allen (1972: 134), who aimed to document the 'variety and distribution of the sites and their faunal and implement contents'. However, Allen's (1972: 124–128) review of published examples of scarred trees east of the Darling River Valley would have benefitted from Thomas's (1964) published insights. The AIAS deemed the notebooks and collection cards of the MDAG important enough that, in the mid-1960s, they granted Thomas money to have the logbooks and collection cards transcribed. Sometime prior to 1979, Thomas provided copies of his logbooks to the Victorian Archaeological Survey. His contribution was acknowledged by W. V. Houghton, the Minister for Conservation for Victoria,[21] who told Thomas: 'your work has not been wasted and will provide a valuable basis for continuing field work in the north-west of Victoria'.

THE GOOD, THE BAD, AND THE UGLY: CAN OUR DISCIPLINE LEARN FROM ITS HISTORY?

In this chapter, we have focussed on often-neglected aspects of the history of Australian archaeology from the early 1900s up to the early 1970s. Developments from these early events and projects, along with Aboriginal land rights and political activism in the preceding decades would lead—in the 1980s—to a revolution of control in Australian archaeology. This change of ethics and project direction in archaeology has been well documented (see McNiven & Russell 2005: 187–190, 211–218; Allen 1983; Smith 1999). Aboriginal activism within archaeology and consequent changes in disciplinary ethics (described below) followed high-profile and effective Aboriginal assertions of their rights to land in the early 1960s (see Attwood & Markus 1999; Reynolds 1995). Of course, Aboriginal people had asserted their rights to land ever since invasion (e.g., see Goodall 1996), but protests in the 1960s were especially influential in garnering national support from 'sympathetic whites' (Powell 1982: 235). In 1976, the Australian Parliament passed the Aboriginal Land Rights (Northern Territory) Act, a key piece of legislation that resulted from increasing Indigenous activism through the 1960s and early 1970s.

One of archaeology's defining moments came in 1982, when Ros Langford (1983) of the Palawa (Tasmanian Aboriginal) community addressed the attendees of the Australian Archaeological Association conference in Hobart. Langford (1983: 2) demanded that researchers should not view Aboriginal heritage as their 'playground', and that archaeological research should take place only on the terms of Aboriginal communities. Langford was reacting, in part, to what some Palawa peoples regarded as unconsultative research and disempowering rhetoric employed by archaeologists in Tasmania during the 1960s to 1980s (see Taylor 2017: 191–208). In the Mildura region, it was Mutthi Mutthi Elder Alice Kelly who led the reassertion of control by Aboriginal people over archaeological research into their ancestors (see Griffiths 2018: 133–137). In 1973, Kelly asked that the excavation of ancestral remains at Lake Mungo cease. Local Aboriginal people knew that Europeans had long been disinterring their ancestors from the large cemeteries situated on the shores of lakes and waterways in the Mildura region (Mark Dugay-Grist in Faulkhead & Berg 2010: 82–83). The most disturbing (and best documented) example was the large-scale collecting of Aboriginal ancestral remains by Murray Black for medical research in the 1940s and 1950s (see Faulkhead & Berg 2010; Jones 2010; Russell 2010). While their activities were by no means the same as those of Murray Black (see Pardoe 2013 for critical discussion), the MDAG, the NMV, and the ANU all removed partly eroded burials from their resting places for scientific research.

These excavations continue to cause distress to the Aboriginal community (for instance, see Jim Berg in Faulkhead & Berg 2010: 16–17). The deceptive activities of Frank Setzler (and to a lesser extent, McCarthy) in Arnhem Land are certainly among the darker chapters of this part of archaeology's history.

Ethics and practice changed rapidly within archaeology in direct response to powerful Indigenous assertions of their rights to land and control of their cultural heritage. By 1983, the power dynamics of archaeological research had changed in the Mildura region. Excavations of Aboriginal burials took place only at the request of the community, at times when development or erosion disturbed ancestral remains (Clark & Hope 1985: 68–69; Pardoe 1985, 2013). The AIAS employed Colin Pardoe in 1984 to 'survey and measure the . . . naturally eroding burials' with Aboriginal communities in riverine NSW and Victoria. The new program of collaborative research was founded on 'complete acceptance of Aboriginal ownership of their ancestors' remains' (Pardoe 2013), and results were communicated directly to the relevant communities via short reports. In the mid-1980s, repatriations of the ancestral remains collected by Murray Black, the MDAG, and the ANU started to flow back to the Traditional Owners.[22] Gunditjmara Elder and cultural heritage worker Jim Berg was instrumental in agitating for these changes in Victoria and NSW through the legal system (see Faulkhead & Berg 2010). The repatriations of ancestral remains from the Smithsonian Institution to the Arnhem Land communities occurred only much later in 2010 (see Thomas & Bijon 2018). However, archaeologists working in Arnhem Land in the interim sought to decolonize research in the region, placing control in the hands of the families and communities who own the places, the past, and the ancestral remains (see, e.g., Clarke 2002; Clarke & Frederick 2011). Progress was made through the activism of Aboriginal people, who caused archaeologists to reflect differently about the discipline's history, including its early history of supporting racialist and social evolutionary ideas (see Bowdler 1992; Faulkhead & Berg 2010; McBryde 1985; Moser 1995a). Stories of the bad and the ugly in Australian archaeology were important then, as they are today, but we should not forget the vast strides made in cross-cultural research during the 1980s. They remind us where we came from (see McNiven & Russell 2005).

Parallel to the dark or murky aspects of early archaeological practice, there were also significant advances. As we explored in the introduction to this chapter, recent histories of Australian archaeology tend to suggest that extensive and systematic survey and excavation programs belong almost exclusively to the post-1960s era. Yet, large numbers of archaeological sites had been recorded prior to 1950, particularly in NSW (e.g., McCarthy 1942, 1945) and South Australia (e.g., Sheard 1927; Sheard, Mountford, & Hackett 1927). Independent scholars, members of local anthropological societies, geologists, and museum workers drove this era of research, and so-called amateur scholars continued to make key contributions well into the 1960s era of professionalized university-based research. Changes in the material cultural record of Aboriginal societies were demonstrated by c.1930, and Tindale and McCarthy developed and applied their own cultural phases during the 1930s–1940s to provide some archaeological order to disparate parts of the continent. Overseas advances in archaeological science were quickly taken up in Australia, demonstrating the international archaeological networks that existed throughout the first half of the twentieth century (Spriggs 2020: 7–9). Nuanced approaches to historicizing the production of rock art emerged in the late-1940s, at a time when Aboriginal people were contributing to archaeological excavations and the interpretation of material culture. We have only just begun to scratch the surface of this complex cross-cultural history (see also Smith 2007; Spriggs 2020).

The idea that nuanced or insightful archaeology commenced in 1956, 1960, or 1970 is incorrect. The notion that, in the 1960s, Australian archaeology was becoming the domain of professional university-based researchers is more accurate, as the balance of archaeological efforts shifted from museums towards the new university departments. So-called amateurs were often derided inaccurately by university scholars; people such as Campbell, Gill, Hossfeld, McCarthy, Mountford, and Tindale continued to make important contributions spanning both the earlier and later years of the century and to link the developments of the 1960s and later back to earlier valuable investigations, theories, and ideas. With hindsight we can appreciate the battle fought by the generation of the 1960s to establish archaeology as a valued discipline within Australian universities and understand the need they felt to distance themselves from past archaeological practices. But it was clearly unjust of Mulvaney (1971: 229) to relegate earlier efforts to the 'byways of antiquarianism and the haphazard fringes of lunacy' or for McBryde (1964: 5) to describe them as merely 'random digging and collecting'. Our hope is that the present generation of archaeologists will seek to (re)engage with all aspects of the at times difficult, complex, and fascinating history of Australian archaeology. Telling the kind of 'messy' stories we have outlined here will play a role in cultivating a culture of reflexivity within the discipline.

ACKNOWLEDGMENTS

We thank Harry Allen for insightful feedback on an earlier version of this manuscript. Thanks also to the First Peoples Department at Museums Victoria for permission to conduct research using their archives and the State Ethnohistory Collection. Robert McWilliams, Mary Morris, and Melanie Raberts generously shared their knowledge with CU about the MDAG collection. Thanks to Donnie Byrne (Hal Thomas's daughter), Penny Byrne (his granddaughter), and Jim Bowler for providing personal recollections and reflections.

NOTES

1. Elsewhere, Griffiths (2017b: 10–15; following Mulvaney 1993a: 112) explains that he sought to disassociate the two eras 'to move away from early evolutionary perspectives to depict archaeology as a careful, systematic and creative craft, anchored in the belief that Aboriginal peoples have their own history and that this can be recovered through archaeological techniques' (Griffiths, 2017b: 12–13).
2. Spriggs (2020: 11) notes that Mulvaney (1993a, 1993b, 2011) later watered down this critical rhetoric at a time when archaeology was becoming better established in Australian universities.

3. Richards, Howes, and Govor (2019) make similar (and convincing) arguments that 'modern' archaeology in the Pacific was a product of gradual developments that began in the mid-1800s.

4. Spriggs (2020, 2021) notes that earlier Australian practitioners such as Dermot Casey had held professional positions overseas, in his case with Mortimer Wheeler in England in the late 1920s to 1930s and in British India in 1944–1955, while D. S. Davidson, who conducted fieldwork in Australia in 1930–1931 and 1938–1940, held a 1928 PhD from the University of Pennsylvania and taught there almost continuously from 1924 to 1946.

5. In discussing the development of 'Australian archaeology', our focus is the archaeology of Australia's Indigenous societies. For brief explorations of the development of historical archaeology in Australia, see Bowdler and Clune (2000: 30) and Smith (2007).

6. Quotation from *Melbourne Argus*, 17 May 1934, p. 10. See also *Melbourne Age*, 17 May 1934, p. 7.

7. These affiliates included Charles P. Mountford, who also surveyed and conducted initial auger sampling and excavation at the Fromm's Landing rock shelters in 1952 with students from the University of Adelaide. Mountford subsequently alerted Mulvaney (1960: 55) to the site's potential for stratigraphic excavation.

8. Taylor (2017: 180) incorrectly asserts that Tindale assigned the Older series of stone artefacts from Rocky Cape to a pre-Ngaut Ngaut/Tartanga industry called the Kartan. This error was probably introduced by Mulvaney (1961: 98), who misinterpreted Tindale's (1957: 4) ambiguous statement that the Kartan was 'an earlier stratum in a Tasmanian culture sequence'. Tindale (1937a: 56) was in fact referring to surface finds of large pebble artefacts (not the Older industry of Meston's Rocky Cape collection).

9. Tindale and Birdsell's (1941) initial ethnological research took place as part of the Harvard and Adelaide Universities' Anthropological Expedition of 1938–1939, which was funded by the Carnegie Corporation (New York).

10. In his excavations, Davidson (1935: 153) identified 'an indication of stratification . . . between the quartzite spear-heads which were so abundant throughout the deposits, except at the very bottom, and several scrapers, adze points and a questionable type of small adze point, which were at or near the bottom'.

11. The anthropologist Donald Thomson (1939) also made a contribution to archaeology in Arnhem Land, publishing a pioneering ethnoarchaeological study: 'The Seasonal Factor in Human Culture Illustrated from the Life of a Contemporary Nomadic Group' (see Allen & Rowe 2014, for discussion).

12. Macintosh (1951, 1952) published his interpretations of various motifs made in 1949 and 1952. These motif interpretations differed significantly (by 90%) from those of Lamjerroc (Elkin 1952).

13. According to Bowler (1970: table 4.2), two of the twenty radiocarbon dates were taken from deposits 'associated with early human occupation'. The earlier research of Tindale (1955) and Tedford (1955) c. 160 km to the northwest at Lake Menindee had already demonstrated the layered and potentially ancient stratigraphy of lake lunettes in the Darling River Basin. Tindale's research of June 1939 and 1953 was of an exemplary standard for the time, identifying three distinct layers in the eroding lakeshore dune deposits and attempting to correlate them with particular stone industries and associations with extinct fauna.

14. Lake Mungo had not yet been named, but the MDAG's records show that they collected from the shores of the ancient lake while collecting on the properties of 'Mungo' and 'Zanci'.

15. Letter, Hal F. Thomas to the secretary of the Australian Institute of Aboriginal Studies, 7 June 1964. Archives of the First Peoples Department, Museums Victoria.
16. Manuscript XM7192. Letter, Hal F. Thomas to 'Jim', 11 December 1973. Held in the First Peoples Ethnohistory Collection at Museums Victoria (Victorian State Collection). XM references given hereafter are from the same collection. 'Jim' is Jim Bowler, and the notes were written specifically for him. This fact is confirmed by a separate letter in the same collection (XM7189).
17. Manuscript XM7198. Seven-page manuscript entitled 'Notes on the Shell Deposit at Red Cliffs, Victoria' and dated 10 December 1973.
18. Manuscript XM7192.
19. Manuscript XM7192.
20. Manuscript XM7193. Two-page manuscript entitled 'Report on Visit to Northern Victoria'.
21. Manuscript XM7190. Letter, W. V. Houghton to Hal F. Thomas, 22 November 1979.
22. Faulkhead & Berg (2010: xxi; see also Pardoe 2013) note that the repatriation debates of the 1980s and 1990s were complex and often 'simplified and represented as a battle between Western-based research or science and the cultural beliefs of Indigenous peoples', but there were in fact 'many voices', which should not be reduced to polar opposites. See Mulvaney (1981, 1991) for examples of the arguments mounted by 'Western-based' archaeologists opposed to comprehensive repatriation.

REFERENCES

Allen, H. (1972). *Where the crow flies backwards: Man and land in the Darling Basin* (PhD thesis). Australian National University, Canberra.

Allen, H. (2019). The first university positions in prehistoric archaeology in New Zealand and Australia. *Bulletin of the History of Archaeology, 29*(1), 1–12.

Allen, H., & Rowe, P. (2014). Assessing Thomson's model of seasonal change. *Ethnoarchaeology, 6*(1), 61–77.

Allen, J. (1983). Aborigines and archaeologists in Tasmania. *Australian Archaeology, 16*, 7–10.

Attenbrow, V. (2008). Ethnographic and archaeological collections by F. D. McCarthy held in the Australian Museum. In N. Peterson, L. Hamby, & L. Allen (Eds.), *Makers and making of Indigenous Australian museum collections* (pp. 472–507). Melbourne: Melbourne University Press.

Attwood, B., & Markus, A. (1999). *The struggle for Aboriginal rights.* Sydney: Allen & Unwin.

Barbetti, M., & Allen, H. (1972). Prehistoric man at Lake Mungo, Australia, by 32,000 years BP. *Nature, 240*(3), 46–48.

Berndt, R. M., & Berndt, C. H. (1947). Discovery of pottery in north-eastern Arnhem Land. *Journal of the Royal Anthropological Institute of Great Britain and Ireland, 77*, 133–138.

Black, L. (1944). *The bora ground.* Melbourne: Robertson & Mullen Ltd.

Blackwood, R., & Simpson, K. N. G. (1973). Attitudes of Aboriginal skeletons excavated in the Murray Valley region between Mildura and Renmark, Australia. *Memoirs of the National Museum of Victoria, 34*, 99–150.

Bowdler, S. (1992). Unquiet slumbers: The return of the Kow Swamp burials. *Antiquity, 66*, 103–106.

Bowdler, S., & Clune, G. (2000). That shadowy band: The role of women in the development of Australian Archaeology. *Australian Archaeology, 50*, 27–35.

Bowdler, S., & Tan, D. (2003). A comparison of stone industries from Southeast Asia and Australia: Some preliminary results. In A. Karlström, & A. Källén (Eds.), *Fishbones and glittering emblems: Southeast Asian archaeology 2002* (pp. 37–48). Stockholm: Museum of Far Eastern Antiquities.

Bowler, J. M. (1970). *Late Quaternary environments: A study of lakes and associated sediments in southeastern Australia* (PhD thesis). Australian National University, Canberra.

Bowler, J. M. (1980). Quaternary chronology and palaeohydrology in the evolution of mallee landscapes. In R. R. Storrier & M. E. Stannard (Eds.), *Aeolian landscapes in the semi-arid zone of south eastern Australia: Proceedings of a conference held at Mildura, Victoria, Australia on October 17–18, 1979* (pp. 17–36). Wagga Wagga: Riverina College of Advanced Education.

Bowler, J. M., Jones, R., Allen, H., & Thorne, A. G. (1970). Pleistocene human remains from Australia: A living site and human cremation from Lake Mungo, western New South Wales. *World Archaeology, 2*(1), 39–60.

Bowler J. M., Thorne, A. G., & Polach, H. (1972). Pleistocene man in Australia: Age and significance of the Mungo skeleton. *Nature, 240,* 48–50.

Brady, L., Gunn, R. G., Smith, C., & David, B. (2018). Rock art and ethnography in Australia. In B. David & I. J. McNiven (Eds.), *The Oxford handbook of the archaeology and anthropology of rock art* (pp. 545–564). Oxford: Oxford University Press.

Campbell, T. D., Cleland, J. B., & Hossfeld, P. S. (1946). Aborigines of the lower south east of South Australia. *Records of the South Australian Museum, 8*(3), 445–502.

Campbell, T. D., & Noone, H. V. V. (1943). Some Aboriginal camp sites in the Woakwine Range Region of the south east of South Australia. *Records of the South Australian Museum, 7*(4), 371–395.

Casey, D. A. (1940). The present state of our knowledge of the archaeology of Australia. In *Proceedings of the Third Congress of Prehistorians of the Far East* (pp. 22–29). Singapore: Government Printing Office.

Chalmin, E., & Huntley, J. (2018). Characterizing rock art pigments. In B. David & I. J. McNiven (Eds.), *The Oxford handbook of the archaeology and anthropology of rock art* (pp. 885–910). Oxford: Oxford University Press.

Clark, P., & Hope, J. (1985). Aboriginal burials and shell middens at Snaggy Bend and other sites on the central Murray River. *Australian Archaeology, 20,* 68–89.

Clarke, A. (2002). The ideal and the real: Cultural and personal transformations of archaeological research on Groote Eylandt, Northern Australia. *World Archaeology, 34*(2), 249–264.

Clarke, A., & Frederick, U. (2011). Making a sea change: Rock art, archaeology and the enduring legacy of Frederick McCarthy's research on Groote Eylandt. In M. Thomas & M. Neale (Eds.), *Exploring the legacy of the 1948 Arnhem Land expedition* (pp. 135–155). Canberra: ANU E Press.

Colley, S. (2002). *Uncovering Australia: Archaeology, Indigenous people and the public.* Crows Nest: Allen & Unwin.

David, B., Barker, B., Petchey, F., Delannoy, J.-J., Geneste, J.-M., Rowe, C., Ecclestone, M., Lamb, L., & Whear, R. (2013). A 28,000 year old excavated painted rock from Nawarla Gabarnmang, Northern Australia. *Journal of Archaeological Science, 40*(5), 2493–2501.

David, T. W., & Etheridge, R. (1889). Report on the discovery of human remains in the sand and pumice bed at Long Bay, near Botany. *Records of the Geological Survey of New South Wales, 1*(1), 9–16.

Davidson, D. S. (1935). Archaeological problems of Northern Australia. *The Journal of the Royal Anthropological Institute of Great Britain and Ireland, 65,* 145–183.

Davidson, I. (1983). Beating about the bush? Aspects of the history of Australian archaeology. *Australian Archaeology, 17*, 136–144.

Du Cros, H. (1984). Burrill Lake rockshelter: An early use of a research design in Australian prehistory. *Australian Archaeology, 19*, 1–7.

Du Cros, H. (1993). Female skeletons in the closet: A historical look at women in Australian archaeology. In H. Du Cros & L. Smith (Eds.), *Women in archaeology: A feminist critique* (pp. 239–244). Occasional Papers in Prehistory 23. Canberra: Department of Prehistory, Australian National University.

Elkin, A. P. (1952). Cave-painting in southern Arnhem Land. *Oceania, 22*(4), 245–255.

Etheridge, R. (1890). Has man a geological history in Australia? *Proceedings of the Linnean Society of New South Wales, Second Series, 5*, 262–265.

Falkinder, J. S. (1932). The extinct Tasmanians. *Mankind, 1*, 79–81.

Faulkhead, S., & Berg, J. (2010). *Power and the passion: Our ancestors return home*. Melbourne: Koorie Heritage Trust.

Flood, J. M. (1974). Pleistocene man at Cloggs Cave: His tool kit and environment. *Mankind, 9*, 175–188.

Gill, E. D. (1973). Geology and geomorphology of the Murray River region between Mildura and Renmark. *Memoirs of the National Museum of Victoria, 34*, 253–273.

Gill, E. D. (1969). Some aspects of prehistory in Victoria. *Victorian Historical Magazine, 40*(4), 173–189.

Goodall, H. (1996). *Invasion to embassy: Land in Aboriginal politics in New South Wales, 1770–1972*. Sydney: Allen & Unwin.

Gregory, J. W. (1904). The antiquity of man in Victoria. *Proceedings of the Royal Society of Victoria, 17*, 120–144.

Gregory, J. W. (1925). *The menace of colour: A study of the difficulties due to the association of white and coloured races*. London: Seeley, Service & Co.

Griffiths, B. (2019). The archive of the earthy: Reading Rocky Cape. *Journal of Colonialism and Colonial History, 20*(2). doi:10.1353/cch.2019.0014.

Griffiths, B. (2017a). 'The dawn' of Australian archaeology: John Mulvaney at Fromm's Landing. *Journal of Pacific Archaeology, 8*(1), 100–111.

Griffiths, B. (2017b). *Deep time dreaming: Uncovering ancient Australia* (PhD thesis). University of Sydney, Sydney.

Griffiths, B. (2018). *Deep time dreaming: Uncovering ancient Australia*. Melbourne: Black Inc.

Griffiths, T. (1996). *Hunters and collectors: The antiquarian imagination in Australia*. Cambridge: Cambridge University Press.

Grounds, S., & Ross, A. (2010). Constant resurrection: The trihybrid model and the politicisation of *Australian Archaeology, 70*, 55–67.

Gunn, R. G., & Whear, R. L. (2007). Tangtangjal cave revisited. *The Artefact, 30*, 16–28.

Hale, H. M., & Tindale, N. B. (1930). Notes on some human remains in the lower Murray Valley, South Australia. *Records of the South Australian Museum, 4*(2), 145–218.

Horton, D. R. (1991). *Recovering the tracks: The story of Australian archaeology*. Canberra: Aboriginal Studies Press.

Jones, R. L. (2010). Medical schools and Aboriginal bodies. In S. Faulkhead & J. Berg (Eds.), *Power and the passion: Our ancestors return home* (pp. 50–54). Melbourne: Koorie Heritage Trust.

Jones, R. M. (1973). Emerging picture of Pleistocene Australians. *Nature, 246*, 278–281.

Jones, R. M. (1971). *Rocky Cape and the problem of the Tasmanians* (PhD thesis). University of Sydney, Sydney.

Jones, R. M., & Megaw, V. (2000). Confessions of a wild colonial boy. *Australian Archaeology*, *50*, 12–26.

Kahn, K. (1993). Frederick David McCarthy: An appreciation. *Records of the Australian Museum Supplement, 17*, 1–5.

Keble, R. A. (1947). Notes on Australian Quaternary climates and migrations. *Memoirs of the National Museum of Victoria, 15*, 28–81.

Kenyon, A. S. (1930). Stone structures of the Australian Aborigines. *Victorian Naturalist, 47*, 71–75.

Lampert, R. J. (1980). Variation in Australia's Pleistocene stone industries. *Journal de la Société des Océanistes, 68*, 190–206.

Langford, R. F. (1983). Our heritage—your playground. *Australian Archaeology, 16*, 1–6.

Macintosh, N. W. G. (1951). Archaeology of Tandandjal Cave, South-west Arnhem Land. *Oceania 21* (3), 178–204.

Macintosh, N. W. G. (1977). Beswick Creek cave two decades later: A reappraisal. In P. J. Ucko (Ed.), *Form in indigenous art* (pp. 191–197). Canberra: Australian Institute of Aboriginal Studies.

Macintosh, N. W. G. (1952). Paintings in Beswick Creek Cave, Northern Territory. *Oceania, 22*(4), 256–273.

Mahony, D. J. (1912). On the bones of the Tasmanian devil and other animals associated with human remains near Warrnambool: With a note on the dune sand. *The Victorian Naturalist, 29*, 43–46.

Mahony, D. J., Baragwanath, W., Wood Jones, F., & Kenyon, A. S. (1936). Fossil man in the state of Victoria, Australia. *Report of the International Geological Congress, Washington 1933*(2), 1335–1342.

Massola, A. (1969). *Journey into Aboriginal Victoria*. Melbourne: Rigby.

May, S. K. (2009). *Collecting cultures: Myth, politics, and collaboration in the 1948 Arnhem Land expedition*. Lanham, MD: AltaMira Press.

May, S. K. (2011). Piecing the history together: An overview of the 1948 Arnhem Land expedition. In M. Thomas & M. Neale (Eds.), *Exploring the legacy of the 1948 Arnhem Land expedition* (pp. 171–188). Canberra: ANU E Press.

McBryde, I. (1964). Archaeology in Australia—Some recent developments. *The Record (University of New England Union), 6*(1), 5–7.

McBryde, I. (1976). Seelands and Sai Yok pebble tools: A further consideration. *Australian Archaeology, 4*, 58–73.

McBryde, I. (Ed.) (1985). *Who owns the past? Papers from the annual symposium of the Australian Academy of the Humanities*. Melbourne: Oxford University Press.

McCarthy, F. D. (1940). Aboriginal stone arrangements in Australia. *The Australian Museum Magazine, 7*(6), 184–188.

McCarthy, F. D. (1944). Adzes and adze-like implements from eastern Australia. *Records of the Australian Museum, 21*(5), 267–271.

McCarthy, F. D. (1943a). An Analysis of the knapped implements from eight Elouera industry stations on the south coast of New South Wales. *Records of the Australian Museum, 21*, 127–153.

McCarthy, F. D. (1967). Australia: 1964–1966. *Asian Perspectives, 10*, 137–159.

McCarthy, F. D. (1942). Catalogue of the Aboriginal relics of New South Wales. Part I. Rock engravings. *Mankind, 3*(3), 91–99.

McCarthy, F. D. (1945). Catalogue of the Aboriginal relics of New South Wales. Part III. Carved trees. *Mankind, 3*(7), 199–206.

McCarthy, F. D. (1948). The Lapstone Creek excavation: Two culture periods revealed in eastern New South Wales. *Records of the Australian Museum, 22*(1), 1–34.

McCarthy, F. D. (1978). New light on the Lapstone Creek excavation. *Australian Archaeology, 8*, 49–62.

McCarthy, F. D. (1949). The prehistoric cultures of Australia. *Oceania, 19*(4), 305–319.

McCarthy, F. D. (1934). A rock-shelter near Emu Plains. Results of excavation. *Mankind, 1*(10), 240–241.

McCarthy, F. D., (1943b). The trimmed coroid and knapped implements of the Bathurst District, N. S. Wales. *Records of the Australian Museum, 21*, 199–209.

McCarthy, F. D. (1941). Two pebble industry sites of Hoabinhian I type on the north coast of New South Wales. *Records of the Australian Museum, 21*, 21–27.

McCarthy, F. D., Bramell, E., & Noone, H. V. V. (1946). *The stone implements of Australia.* Australian Museum Memoir 9. Sydney: Australian Museum.

McCarthy, F. D., & Setzler, F. M. (1960). The archaeology of Arnhem Land. In C. P. Mountford (Ed.), *Records of the American-Australian scientific expedition to Arnhem Land 1948: 2, anthropology and nutrition* (pp. 215–295). Melbourne: Melbourne University Press.

McNiven, I. J. (2001). Collectors and diggers: The early years of Aboriginal archaeology. In C. Rasmussen, *A museum for the people: A history of Museum Victoria and its predecessors* (pp. 214–217). Melbourne: Scribe Publications.

McNiven, I. J. (2006). Colonial diffusionism and the archaeology of external influences on Aboriginal culture. In B. David, B. Barker, & I. J. McNiven (Eds.), *The social archaeology of Australian Indigenous societies* (pp. 163–200). Canberra: Australian Institute of Aboriginal and Torres Strait Islander Studies.

McNiven, I. J. (this volume). 'The thick darkness of pre-historic times': Antiquarian archaeology in nineteenth century colonial Victoria. I. J. McNiven & B. David (Eds.), *The Oxford handbook of the archaeology of Indigenous Australia and New Guinea.* Oxford: Oxford University Press.

McNiven, I. J., & Russell, L. (2005). *Appropriated pasts: Indigenous peoples and the colonial culture of archaeology.* Lanham, MD: AltaMira Press.

Megaw, V. (1966). Australian archaeology—How far have we progressed? *Mankind, 6*(7), 306–312.

Meston, A. L. (1934). Aboriginal rock-carvings in Tasmania. *Antiquity, 8*, 179–184.

Meston, A. L. (1956). Miscellaneous notes on the culture of the Tasmanian Aboriginal. *Memoirs of the National Museum of Victoria, 20*, 1–9.

Meston, A. L. (1949). The Tasmanians—A summary. *Records of the Queen Victoria Museum Launceston, 2*, 145–150.

Moser, S. (1995a). The Aboriginalisation of archaeology: The contribution of the Australian Institute of Aboriginal Studies to the Indigenous transformation of the discipline. In P. J. Ucko (Ed.), *Theory in archaeology: A world perspective* (pp. 150–177). London: Routledge.

Moser, S. (1995b). *Archaeology and its disciplinary culture: The professionalisation of Australian prehistoric archaeology* (PhD thesis). University of Sydney, Sydney.

Mountford, C. P. (Ed.). (1956). *Records of the American-Australian expedition to Arnhem Land 1948: Art, myth and symbolism.* Melbourne: Melbourne University Press.

Mulvaney, D. J. (1960). Archaeological excavations at Fromm's Landing, on the lower Murray River. *Proceedings of the Royal Society of Victoria, 72*, 53–85.

Mulvaney, D. J. (1986). Archaeological retrospect. *Antiquity, 60*, 96–107.

Mulvaney, D. J. (1993a). Australian anthropology: Foundations and funding. *Aboriginal History, 17*(2), 105–128.

Mulvaney, D. J. (2011). *Digging up a past*. Sydney: UNSW Press.

Mulvaney, D. J. (1991). Past regained, future lost: The Kow Swamp Pleistocene burials. *Antiquity, 65*, 12–21.

Mulvaney, D. J. (1971). Prehistory from antipodean perspectives. *Proceedings of the Prehistoric Society, 37*, 228–252.

Mulvaney, D. J. (1957). Research in the prehistory of Victoria: A criticism and a report on a field survey. *Historical Studies—Australia and New Zealand, 8*, 32–43.

Mulvaney, D. J. (1993b). Sesqui-centenary to bicentenary: Reflections of a museologist. *Records of the Australian Museum, Supplement, 17*, 17–24.

Mulvaney, D. J. (1961). The Stone Age of Australia. *Proceedings of the Prehistoric Society, 27*, 56–107.

Mulvaney, D. J. (1981). What future for our past? Archaeology and society in the eighties. *Australian Archaeology, 13*, 16–27.

Murray, T. (1992). Tasmania and the constitution of the 'dawn of humanity'. *Antiquity, 66*(252), 730–743.

Murray, T., & White, J. P. (1981). Cambridge in the bush? Archaeology in Australia and New Guinea. *World Archaeology, 13*, 255–263.

Nelson, R. C. (2007). The Lapstone Creek rockshelter: The story continues. *Australian Archaeology, 65*, 37–43.

Noone, H. V. V. (1949). Some implements of the Australian Aborigines with European parallels. *Man, 49*, 111–146.

Pardoe, C. (1985). Cross-cultural attitudes to skeletal research in the Murray-Darling region. *Australian Aboriginal Studies, 2*, 63–67.

Pardoe, C. (2013). Repatriation, research and reburial: Rhetoric and practice in Australia. In L. N. Stutz & S. Tarlow (Eds.), *The Oxford handbook of the archaeology of death and burial* (pp. 733–761). Oxford: Oxford University Press.

Perry, W. J. (1923). *The children of the sun: A study in the early history of civilization*. London: Methuen.

Polach, H. A., Lovering, J. F., & Bowler, J. M. (1970). ANU radiocarbon date list IV. *Radiocarbon, 12*(1), 1–18.

Powell, A. (1982). *Far country: A short history of the Northern Territory*. Melbourne: Melbourne University Press.

Reynolds, H. (1995). *Fate of a free people*. Melbourne: Penguin.

Richards, M., Howes, H., & Govor, E. (2019). Origins of Archaeology in the Pacific: The emergence of and application of archaeological field techniques. *Journal of Pacific History, 54*(3), 307–329.

Russell, L. (2010). Reflections on Murray Black's writings. In S. Faulkhead & J. Berg (Eds.), *Power and the passion: Our ancestors return home* (pp. 56–59). Melbourne: Koorie Heritage Trust.

Setzler, F. M., & McCarthy, F. D. (1950). A unique archaeological specimen from Australia. *Washington Academy of Sciences Journal, 40*(1), 1–5.

Sheard, H. L. (1927). Aboriginal rock shelters and carvings—three localities on the lower Murray. *Transactions of the Royal Society of South Australia, 51*, 138–140.

Sheard, H. L., Mountford, C. P., & Hackett, C. J. (1927). An unusual disposal of an Aboriginal child's remains from the lower Murray. *Transactions of the Royal Society of South Australia, 51*, 173–176.

Shellshear, J. L. (1937). An appeal for the preservation of prehistoric remains in Australia. *Australian Museum Magazine, 6*(5), 169–175.

Smith, C. (2007). A brief history of Australian archaeology. In C. Smith & H. Burke (Eds.), *Digging it up down under: A practical guide to doing archaeology in Australia* (pp. 1–19). New York: Springer.

Smith, C., Domingo, I., & Jackson, G. (2016). Beswick Creek Cave six decades later: Change and continuity in the rock art of Doria Gudaluk. *Antiquity, 90*(354), 1613–1626.

Smith, G. E. (1915). *The migrations of early culture: A study of the significance of the geographical distribution of the practice of mummification as evidence of the migrations of peoples and the spread of certain customs and beliefs.* Manchester: Manchester University Press.

Smith, L. (1999). The last archaeologist? Material culture and contested identities. *Australian Aboriginal Studies, 2*, 25–34.

Smith, M. A. (2000). The opening chapter of the romance of excavation in Australia: Reflecting on Norman Tindale's archaeology. *Historical Records of Australian Science, 13*(2), 151–160.

Specht, R. L. (2012). American-Australian scientific expedition to Arnhem Land (1948): Its long-range impact. *The Open Ecology Journal, 5*, 53–83.

Spriggs, M. (2021). 'Casey did very good work for Wheeler and you are lucky to have him': Dermot Casey's underappreciated importance in Australian archaeology. *Historical Records of Australian Science, 32*, 1–14.

Spriggs, M. (2020). Everything you've been told about the history of Australian archaeology is wrong! *Bulletin of the History of Archaeology, 31*(1), 1–16.

Struwe, R. (2006). An ambitious German in early twentieth century Tasmania: The collections made by Fritz Noetling. *Australian Archaeology, 62*(1), 31–37.

Taylor, R. (2017). *Into the heart of Tasmania: A search for human antiquity.* Melbourne: Melbourne University Press.

Tedford, R. H. (1955). Report on the extinct mammalian remains at Lake Menindee, New South Wales. *Records of the South Australian Museum, 11*, 299–305.

Thomas, H. F. (1960–1970). The abridged logbook of the Mildura and District Anthropological Group (Volumes 1–10). Unpublished reports produced for the Australia Institute of Aboriginal Studies. Accessed at the Museums Victoria Library (Melbourne).

Thomas, H. F. (1964). A possible Aboriginal ceremonial ground at Lake Gol Gol, N. S. W. *Mankind, 6*(3), 105–120.

Thomas, M. (2010). A short history of the 1948 Arnhem Land expedition. *Aboriginal History, 34*, 143–170.

Thomas, M., & Bijon, B. (2018). *Etched in bone* [Documentary film]. Red Lily Productions.

Thomson, D. (1939). The seasonal factor in human culture illustrated from the life of a contemporary nomadic group. *The Proceedings of the Prehistoric Society, 5*, 209–221.

Thorpe, W. W. (1931). A rock shelter at Lake Burrill, N.S. Wales. *Mankind, 1*, 53–55.

Tindale, N. B. (1955). Archaeological site at Lake Menindee, New South Wales. *Records of the South Australian Museum, 9*, 269–298.

Tindale, N. B. (1957). Culture succession in south eastern Australia from late Pleistocene to the present. *Records of the South Australian Museum, 13*, 1–49.

Tindale, N. B. (1937a). Relationship of extinct Kangaroo Island Culture with cultures of Australia, Tasmania and Malaya. *Records of the South Australian Museum, 6*, 39–60.

Tindale, N. B. (1937b). Tasmanian Aborigines on Kangaroo Island. *Records of the South Australian Museum, 6*, 29–37.

Tindale, N. B., & Birdsell, J. B. (1941). Tasmanoid tribes in north Queensland. *Records of the South Australian Museum, 7*, 1–9.

Tindale, N. B., & Mountford, C. P. (1936). Results of the excavation of Kongarati Cave near Second Valley, South Australia. *Records of the South Australian Museum, 5*(4), 487–502.

Warner, W. L. (1937). *A black civilisation: A social study of an Australian tribe*. New York: Harper & Brothers.

Wood Jones, F. (1944). The antiquity of man in Australia. *Nature, 3877*, 211–212.

CHAPTER 5

ENCOUNTERING THE PAST

Ancestors with Agency in Australian Archaeology

CLAIRE SMITH, LIAM M. BRADY, AND
CHRISTOPHER WILSON

INTRODUCTION

OVER three decades ago, Nicholas and Andrews (1997: 3) defined Indigenous archaeology as 'archaeology with, for, and by Indigenous peoples'. During the 1990s and early 2000s, Indigenous archaeology emerged as a subfield of archaeology. Like any new field of endeavor, its immediate concerns were focused on articulating its aims and goals and on how it might be practiced in the real world. The core themes that have emerged since then include the following: (1) identifying and expunging archaeology's colonialist underpinnings (Atalay 2006; Nicholas & Andrews 1997; Porr & Matthews 2017; Silliman 2005; Smith & Wobst 2005); (2) the repatriation of ancestral remains (Lippert 2008; Loring 2008; Wilson 2009); (3) ethical research practices (Atalay 2008; Jackson & Smith 2005; Kato 2017; Menzies & Wilson 2020; Nicholas 2007; Wiynjorroc, Manabaru, Brown, & Warner 2005); (4) meaningful collaborations and partnerships (Brady 2009; Colwell-Chanthaphonh 2012; Colwell-Chanthaphonh & Ferguson 2007; Colwell-Chanthaphonh et al. 2010; Smith et al. 2019; Wilson 2007); (5) cultural and intellectual property rights and Indigenous ownership and control of cultural heritage (McNiven & Russell 2005; Nicholas & Bannister 2004; Smith, Copley & Jackson 2018; Watkins 2000); and (6) sharing the benefits of archaeological research in the pursuit of social justice (Atalay 2012; Smith & Jackson 2007; Zimmerman & Branam 2014). With a few notable exceptions (e.g., David 2006; Nicholas 2003; Silliman 2010; Wilson 2007), theoretical considerations have, for the most part, lagged behind practical concerns.

While early efforts to explore themes relating to 'encountering the past' emerged in Australia with the work of archaeologists such as Isabel McBryde (e.g., 1986, 1995), more concerted efforts began during the 1990s and early 2000s when Indigenous archaeology emerged as a subfield of archaeology. Coincidentally, these increasing concerns with Indigenous archaeology emerged during an important decade for Indigenous affairs and reconciliation efforts through mechanisms such as the Aboriginal and Torres Strait Islander Commission's ten-year plan for Reconciliation, and the representation of Indigenous Australia at high-profile events such as the Sydney Olympics. Yet despite these developments in the Indigenous archaeology space, theoretical considerations have, for the most part, lagged behind practical concerns. Recently, however, archaeological interest has emerged in developing new interpretative theoretical frameworks shaped by Indigenous worldviews (Brady & Bradley 2014; Brady, Bradley, & Kearney 2016; McNiven 2016a, 2016b; Porr 2018; Porr & Matthews 2016; Supernant, Baxter, Lyons, & Atalay 2020). While this work is breaking new ground, this area of archaeological enquiry is still severely undertheorized. In this chapter, we aim to contribute to this space by doing a 'deep dive' into some of the theoretical concepts in Indigenous archaeologies further highlighted by Ian McNiven in his 2016 article 'Theoretical Challenges of Indigenous Archaeology: Setting an Agenda'. McNiven took up the challenge of articulating an interpretive theoretical agenda for Indigenous archaeology that would integrate Indigenous worldviews. One of the concepts he focused on is Indigenous relationality (knowledge and lived experiences) of *encountering the past*. McNiven argued that the creation of understandings and interpretations of the past that are more central to Indigenous ontologies would further advance archaeological practice by understanding the intangible forces (e.g., ancestral presences, and spiritual and metaphysical agency) that guide and shape Indigenous negotiations and relationships with artefacts. Moreover, he contended that 'tangible ancestral presence subverts the encountering of archaeological materials from the objectivist notion of discovery by people to a constructivist notion of revelation by the ancestors' (McNiven 2016a: 30). As part of his overall argument, he introduced the concept of the 'social catchment' to capture the spiritual dimensions of a place or site as well as the equally meaningful socialized spaces between artefacts and features. We further propose the concept of 'ancestral agency'.

In this chapter, we apply McNiven's conceptualization of how the past is encountered to our own work with Aboriginal people in Ngarrindjeri Country, South Australia; Jawoyn Country in the Barunga region of the Northern Territory (encompassing the communities of Barunga, Beswick, and Manyallaluk); and Yanyuwa Country in the southwest Gulf of Carpentaria, also in the Northern Territory (Figure 5.1). Through the lens of encountering the past, our chapter focuses on the notions of living landscapes, revelation by the ancestors, and ancestral remains as people, not objects. All three are underpinned by the concept of ancestors having and exerting agency that ultimately shapes how the 'archaeological record' is interpreted. Our positions in the interpretive process are influenced by the subjectivities and individual standpoints that each of us brings to the research (see Moreton-Robinson 2013; Nakata 2007). Christopher Wilson is a proud Ngarrindjeri man and a proud Australian with European heritage, including Irish and British ancestry on his mother's side. Though he is closely related

FIGURE 5.1. Map of Australia showing the Aboriginal communities whose knowledge is shared in this chapter.

to Kaurna people, identity is multidimensional. Ngarrindjeri always identify with the father's line. Educated in both Aboriginal and Western knowledge systems, his dual-cultural standpoint influences his choice to complement traditional archaeological narratives with other ways of 'telling'. Claire Smith is a non-Indigenous archaeologist who grew up in a working-class area of Newcastle, NSW, in the 1960s and 1970s. Her standpoint is embedded in a strong sense of social justice and a concern with human rights and the ethics of archaeological practice. Liam M. Brady is Canadian with parents from Ireland and Trinidad and Tobago, and came to Australia in 2001 to begin his PhD. He was trained from the outset by Ian McNiven and Bruno David, and has embedded his research (PhD–present) with Aboriginal and Torres Strait Islanders in the host-guest model of partnership archaeology that centres on Indigenous power, control, and ownership of archaeological research. His standpoint has been further influenced by working with anthropologist John Bradley, who introduced him to the complexities of archaeological interpretations when placed alongside Aboriginal worldviews.

LIVING LANDSCAPES

> *For many Indigenous people, ancestors have agency and prescience and actively mediate and orchestrate interactions between living people (including archaeologists) and archaeological materials.*
>
> (McNiven 2016a: 30)

While European traditions of knowledge draw a clear distinction between culture and nature, in Indigenous traditions there is no such thing as a 'natural' environment as all nature is imbued with cultural qualities (see Burke & Smith 2010). Indigenous Australians conceptualize landscapes (along with seascapes and skyscapes) as living, sentient, and capable of responding to actions and events, both positive and negative. What the West calls 'natural worlds', for Aboriginal people, are actually complex cultural worlds. They are inhabited by Ancestral Beings (sometimes referred to by other Aboriginal people as Dreamings) and other spiritual beings who have their own agency and who watch over, and monitor, people's behaviours and management of lands. They hold knowledge about Aboriginal lifeworlds, and they are part of a relational world where 'all things are connected'. For Aboriginal people in the Barunga region of the Northern Territory, Australia, the world around them is inhabited by three forms of spiritual beings:

1. Ancestral Beings ('Dreamings'), who created the world, its people, animals, and plants, and transformed parts of their bodies into features of the landscapes and seascape.
2. *Mimi* spirits, independent beings that have family structures that mirror those of Aboriginal society but who were never humans or creators of the physical world; and
3. 'Old People', relatives and other people who have died but whose spirits continue to exist in the present.

Ancestral Beings: The Original Creators

Ancestral Beings first existed during the creation era known as the 'Dreaming' or 'Dreamtime' where they undertook epic journeys across the landscape and seascape. While the terms 'Dreaming' or 'Dreamtime' are not appropriate to use today (see Wolfe 1991), for some Indigenous Australians, they are the closest terms in English that capture the concept at a point in time when there was limited Western knowledge and understanding about this time. Some Ancestral Beings simply lived their own lives, but others were the creators of people, animals, and the land. As they travelled, their actions and interactions formed the topographic features of landscapes and seascapes. Through their actions these ancestors created distinct features of the landscape—rivers, waterholes, hills, and boulders. For example, an Ancestral Being who was a snake could create a river as it slithered through the land. Another Ancestral Being that was a goanna may have created a river with a different shape (Mizoguchi & Smith 2019: 149–155).

The Ancestral Past engenders the concept of living landscapes in which ancestors with agency have the capacity to mediate interactions between living peoples. In contrast to Western notions of linear time, the Ancestral Past is embedded in an interlinked conceptualization of time in which the past continuously impacts upon the present. The Ancestral Past exists in, and somehow directs, the present, and also exists in the future. In a sense, it is timeless; it exists apart from time. Morphy (1998: 68) describes the Ancestral Past as existing independently of linear time and the temporal sequence of historical events: 'Indeed, the Dreaming is as much a dimension of reality as a period of time. It gains its sense of time because it was there in the beginning, underlies the present and is a determinant of the future; it is time in the sense that once there was only Dreamtime. But the Dreamtime has never ceased to exist and from the viewpoint of the present ... is as much a feature of the future as it is of the past' (Morphy 1998: 68).

The world was created by Ancestral Beings and is guarded by them in the present. Phenomena that Europeans would classify as natural, such as strong winds or floods, are understood by Aboriginal people to be cultural as these phenomena can result from the actions of Ancestral Beings. These concepts relate to metaphysical relationships between humans, country, and the spiritual realm as interconnected. For example, 'country is a living body, a living landscape and must be healthy for people to be healthy'. Jawoyn woman Joslyn McCartney describes the contemporary presence of the creation being, *bolung*, also known as the rainbow snake:

> That *bolung* is alive. I think so because when you go and touch anything that they own you feel a big wind blowing and you know you have touched something that you shouldn't have touched. Or when you go and *bogi* (swim) down the river you feel that yourself, that someone there, that you interrupt that *bolung*, that you shouldn't be going into the water. When we see all the flying fox around we know that the *bolung* is there. He is watching over them because they are his children ... Those 1998 floods at Katherine Gorge (also known as Nitmiluk) ... probably something happened that made that *bolung* real angry and he made more rain and flooded the whole area. [This can happen] if people touch something that doesn't belong to them. They [people] have to leave it as it is. That *bolung* will come and probably take them away. Rain and wind. Sometimes, different sweat [from people], he can smell it.
>
> One time all the Rembarrnga mob bin go dancing la Nitmiluk (Katherine Gorge). Might be that *bolung* was upset by all the different [unfamiliar] sweat from all the different people and that wind bin blowing. They [the people] bin get frightened now. It is on a DVD la [at] Jawoyn [Association]. You can't see the wind blowing, strong wind. My grandson was there. Kienan Martin, he was there. He came back and told me. It was a warning, I think, to tell them to get away. They were dancing on the top ground, but probably they should have been dancing on the sand ground. Probably that was a place when they did ceremony before and that *Bolung* didn't want them to be there because he sent a big wind down the river. They got a lot of sacred area around there that people can't go. There is a sacred area that only men can

go. He saw the dancing and he didn't want them to be there. They know that *bolung* is like a rainbow serpent, a snake. Old people know that he can get real angry. He was always there.

(Joslyn McCartney, 13 July 2021)

When this story was relayed to a Jawoyn woman, Jasmine Willika, who is studying archaeology at Flinders University, she responded in terms of her own recent participation in an archaeological fieldtrip in southwest Queensland: 'That is interesting. What happened at that ceremony site at [name withheld], there was a strong wind. I couldn't even move. I couldn't talk. Nothing. There were a few other stone circles on top. I followed the people up to the top and there was nothing there. No wind. That feeling wasn't there. I thought maybe that was a meeting ground on top and the ceremony ground was down below' (Jasmine Willika, 13 July 2021).

For archaeologists, one challenge is to identify tangible evidence of Ancestral Beings, especially if they are considered to be part of the 'archaeological record'. There are physical clues, but archaeologists need to be taught *how to read them*. The actions of Ancestral Beings have physical mnemonics that not only signify past actions but also their continued existence in the present. After their journeying during the Ancestral Past, the Ancestral Beings sat down in one place and became a living part of that place forever. Sometimes their bodies form part of the landscape. A hill may be a women's breast. A pile of stones may be someone's tears, and yellow or red rocks the excreta of an Ancestral Being. A stony mountain may be destitute of vegetation because of a devastating fire caused by Ancestral Beings. These features make Aboriginal lands a living landscape, encompassing Ancestral Beings who may be slumbering but are not dead (see Mizoguchi & Smith 2019: 149–155).

As shown in Figure 5.2 (left), Ancestral Beings sometimes placed their bodies on the rock as paintings. Such paintings are found across much of the continent (see, for example, Mangolamara, Karadada, Oobagooma, Woolagoodja, & Karadada 2018 for the Kimberley) and are greatly valued by Aboriginal people because they are the physical embodiment of Ancestral Beings. Mostly, the power held by Ancestral Beings in rock art is inert, unactivated. However, some paintings are potent. They cannot be looked upon by particular people because they would make those people sick. Similarly, some places can only be accessed by people with particular rights or knowledge. Living landscapes—with or without archaeological signatures such as paintings—need to be traversed with care, and the Aboriginal knowledge surrounding them treated with respect.

Mimis: Long, Tall, Skinny People

The second form of spiritual being that inhabits the worlds of Aboriginal people in the Barunga region are *mimis*, spirit creatures who live in family groups in a similar manner to Aboriginal people. *Mimis* live their own lives in landscape and rarely interact with

FIGURE 5.2. Left: Image of the Ancestral Being known as Luma Luman, who placed her body on the rock at Doria Gudaluk (Beswick Creek Cave) near Barunga, Northern Territory (photo by C. Smith, published courtesy of Traditional Owner Esther Bulumbara and Junggayi/Custodians Nell Brown and Guy Rankin; original permission to publish this image granted by Phyllis Wiynjorroc and Peter Manaburu). Right: Giant lanterns of a *mimi* figure, created for the annual Sport and Cultural Festival at Barunga, Northern Territory.

(photo by C. Smith, published courtesy of Traditional Owner Esther Bulumbara and Junggayi/Custodians Nell Brown and Guy Rankin.)

humans. They can harm people, or they can be playful, especially with children. Joslyn McCartney recalls:

> That *mimi*, him real, I. When they have meeting or Christmas Party at Nitmiluk and we all stayed at the Cicada Lodge. That was the first time we sleep there. I sleep myself. The next morning they said 'All them piccaninni [children] come around there and the kids wanted to play with them'. They got a shock that the *mimis* came around there and they were playing with kids. All the kids told their parents 'We had somebody here, playing'. All the kids bin look, they saw the *mimi*. The parents just heard what the kids said. They said to their parents 'We had visitors here, last night they bin come'. Might be them little one *mimi* bin come around. Those kids they weren't frightened. They told their parents the next day. The parents were asleep when the *mimi* came but the kids were still awake, talking.
>
> (Joslyn McCartney, 13 July 2021)

The living landscapes that contain the bodies of Ancestral Beings are also inhabited by *mimis*. There is also tangible evidence of *mimis*. Aboriginal people know what they look like. They are very skinny and if they turn their side to you, you might not see them. *Mimis* are depicted in rock art and various forms of contemporary art (e.g., Figure 5.2 [right]). Unlike Ancestral Beings, *mimis* do not place their body on the rock, creating an image of themselves. However, sometimes they are identified as the creators of rock art located in highly unreachable places, such as high on a cliff face. The inaccessible placement of these paintings is cited as proof that the art could not have been made by humans and, therefore, must have been created by *mimis*.

Old People: 'Those People Are Listening Now. They're Not Deaf'

The third form of spiritual being that inhabits the worlds of Aboriginal people from Barunga are the 'Old People'—dead relations and other deceased persons whose spirits still roam the landscapes that they used to live in. When Barunga people visit places in the landscape they have not been to for some time, they call out in Aboriginal language to the Old People whose spirits still inhabit these places, telling the spirits that they do not wish to disturb them. If they wish to do something special, such as retouch rock paintings, they ask permission from the Old People, making sure that they do not incur their wrath through showing disrespect. Senior Traditional Owner Phyllis Wiynjorroc (see Figure 5.3) says: 'Those people are listening now. They're not deaf'. Joslyn McCartney explains the protocols for Jawoyn Country around Barunga:

> We sing out to the old people telling them we might have visitors and to watch after us. When we go to that Country we call out to let them know that we are here. When we call we ourselves know that the old people are still around roaming around the Country. All our ancestors are still around. If you feel weird or something, you probably know that they are near you. You can't see them but you have a feeling. You know those old people are still watching. They look after us, I, as well. Make sure that we don't do anything silly. We know that they are still there on that Country. Especially when you enter Country, and you want to look at that art or painting on the rock. You have a feeling that they are there to make sure that we do the right thing, I, for them. Make sure that we don't break any rules.
>
> (Joslyn McCartney, 13 July 2021)

Unlike Ancestral Beings or *mimis*, the Old People do not seem to have the capacity to leave material traces of their lives as spirits. However, they are able to exert agency on the world around them, shaping how people might engage with their Country. Claire Smith was with Peter Manabaru (see Figure 5.3) the day her father died. In response to her question: What happens after you die? Peter replied, 'You stay around your family to look after them' (Peter Manabaru, personal communication, 6 December, 2006). The belief that Old People have agency in relation to their family members is also apparent in this conversation with Esther Bulumbara about deceased Traditional Owners Phyllis Wiynjorroc and her brother Lamjerroc, Esther's grandfather:

> They are still around. A couple of mob [people] went to the waterfall, fishing there (Beswick Falls). They heard that old lady Phyllis say 'Go back home. You mob go home now' and they had to get their fishing lines and their kids. They were frightened. All the Bulumbara and Bush family. Raelene and Crystal and their kids. That olgaman [old lady] said: 'Go back home'. That voice was just there, next to them. And my grandfather, I, Lamjerroc. Those grandkids saw Phyllis but they didn't old Lamjerroc. They just heard that voice. It was a bit late for fishing there. Around one

FIGURE 5.3. Senior Traditional Owner of Bagala lands, Phyllis Wiynjorroc (left) and Senior Junggayi/Custodian Peter Manaburu (right), both now deceased/Old People.

(Photos by C. Smith, published courtesy of Traditional Owner Esther Bulumbara and Junggayi/Custodians Nell Brown and Guy Rankin.)

or two o'clock. Probably she wanted to look after them. Sometimes family come and warn you if something bad might happen. Might be if they had stayed one kid might walk away by himself and get lost.

(Esther Bulumbara, 14 July and 21 July 2021)

The Aboriginal lands around Barunga are inhabited by at least three forms of spirit beings—ancestral beings, *mimis* and the Old People—each with a capacity to actively mediate and orchestrate interactions between living people (including archaeologists) and the environments they inhabit. It is likely that the Old People have prescience, a capacity to foretell or predict possible futures and to nudge their families in directions that keep them safe. When the existence of these three forms of spirit beings is considered together, the overarching lesson is that both archaeological practice and interpretations need to take into account the presence of spiritual beings in living landscapes. This consideration is discussed further in the following sections.

REVELATION BY THE ANCESTORS

Tangible ancestral presence subverts the encountering of archaeological materials from the objectivist notion of discovery by people to a constructivist notion of revelation by the ancestors.

(McNiven 2016a: 30)

In the southwest Gulf of Carpentaria region where Liam Brady works with Yanyuwa families, and with anthropologists John Bradley and Amanda Kearney, the *ngabaya* spirit beings are a constant presence in collaborative rock art research. During this time, the *ngabaya* have played a critical role in revealing and concealing rock art sites. The *ngabaya* are different from the creative Ancestral Beings. In the Yanyuwa language, the term *ngabaya* can be glossed as a 'spirit' or a 'ghost'. In Aboriginal English, the *ngabaya* are also referred to as 'devil' or 'debildebil' (Bradley et al. 2006; see also Brady, Bradley, & Kearney 2016). The *ngabaya* can be many things: the spirits of deceased kin who, upon death, return to their traditional Country—the places that they owned or managed, and where they once lived, hunted, and foraged. They are a constant presence in the landscape, where they are the 'invisible companions of the living' (Brady, Bradley, & Kearney 2016: 32). Other *ngabaya* are simply spirit beings not associated with deceased kin; they can be named such as the *namurlangjangkyu* who inhabit Vanderlin Island (see later) or *jududubanji* in Garrwa Country near to the Northern Territory/Queensland border. They can be tricksters and cause illness and even death. There are *ngabaya* who sing, dance, and do all the things that living people do such as wear clothes and drive cars. However, amongst all of this is the certainty that *ngabaya* exist and have agency—they have the power to do things, create fear and humour, and are often responsible for the things that do not have an explanation such as noises in the night or finding what was once lost.

The agency of the *ngabaya* in our rock art research has been one of the central features of Yanyuwa interpretations of the successes and failures of our surveys for sites and motifs (e.g., Brady & Bradley 2014; Brady, Bradley, & Kearney 2016). One of the most recent examples of *ngabaya* agency came in 2019 when our research team visited Vanderlin Island to survey for rock art sites in the Liwingkinya landscape, near the freshwater lake known as Walala (Lake Eames). Traveling by helicopter with the senior *ngimirringki* (owners, or 'bosses') and *jungkayi* (guardians) for this area, we arrived at Liwingkinya, where we began surveying the tall sandstone rockstacks, many with shelters at their base, that dominate the area. Upon visiting one site, we encountered two side-by-side red hand stencils high up on the roof of a shallow shelter. What made these motifs distinctive was their fresh, exceptionally bright appearance, as though they had been created very recently. Their exceptional condition was a stark contrast to the faded and deteriorated motifs we had been recording throughout the day. When we returned to where one of the senior *ngimirringki*, Mavis Timothy, was waiting for us, we explained what the two hand stencils looked like, emphasizing their fresh, bright appearance, and she responded: 'From yesterday perhaps, or maybe early this morning those hand prints, the spirit beings [*namurlanjanyngku*] heard your words, when you spoke and sang for this Country, so that was what they did, they felt good, so the spirit beings from this place put their hand prints in the cave for you, they are newly made, they are not from a long time ago' (Mavis Timothy, cited in Bradley, Kearney, & Brady 2021: 117).

Mavis's explanation was embedded into a much larger relational sphere. On the night prior to our travels, three senior Yanyuwa women and Bradley sang the ancestral songline (a song that describes the travels and activities of Ancestral Beings in the

Ancestral Past) for this part of Vanderlin Island. Singing the songline had 'woken up the spirit beings', the *namurlanjanyngku*, who were happy that people were coming back onto Country, and in their anticipation for our arrival they inscribed the landscape with their marks. What becomes clear in this example is that the Yanyuwa interpretation of our encounter with the hand stencils is embedded in a relational context, where song, Country, kin, and spirit beings are brought together to make sense of symbols found on Country (see Bradley, Kearney, & Brady 2021, for further details; see also Brady, Bradley, & Kearney 2016, 2018, for other examples).

The process of *ngabaya* revealing and concealing motifs in the Yanyuwa landscape also presents a challenge for archaeologists, one that confronts the objectivist notions that typically underpin investigations of the archaeological record. In the case of rock art, there have been many times when senior Yanyuwa men and women have directed the research team to places on the islands where they remember seeing rock art when they were younger. Yet in many instances, upon our arrival and survey of the sites, we have been unable to find the motifs. Scientific reasoning could be applied as an explanation: granular disintegration of the rock face over time eventually removed the painting, feral animals could have rubbed out the lower-most paintings, or the harsh coastal regime deteriorated the paintings to a point where they could no longer be seen. However, when Yanyuwa knowledge and understanding is applied to the presence or absence of known paintings, there is a power shift—from the dominant position of Western science as an explanatory framework for different phenomena to one that is entangled in a complex network of social and cultural understandings. That is, explanations that for the Yanyuwa are the only one and true way of engaging with things in Country.

The Agency of Elders

Clearly, the treatment of human remains provides rare windows into past ontologies.

(McNiven 2016a: 34)

In Australia the discipline of archaeology has graduated three Indigenous archaeologists with doctoral degrees since 2017 and this section is part of a wider movement that seeks to infiltrate unfiltered Indigenous voices into disciplinary discussions which have been led by Ngarrindjeri archaeologist Christopher Wilson (see also Pollard et al. 2020)

One of the most significant issues relate to the debate about ancestral remains and care for the 'dead'. Over the last two decades observations, insights, and thoughts have offered insight into what is known as 'repatriation and reburial of ancestral remains', a domain that encompasses a broad range of human skeletal, tissue, hair, and biological materials identified as Aboriginal in origin. Repatriation and reburial have been highly debated topics in our discipline and in the study of the human past, and intersect with museum studies, bioarchaeology, DNA studies, forensics, human anatomy and physical anthropology, archaeology, heritage management, and governance of cultural institutions of our states and territories. The key point of contention for me is the issue of consent and how this process is guided by traditions and cultural practices. This guidance relates to the metaphysical spiritual and celestial realms partly tangible and mostly intangible but deeply theoretical and in reference to data sets and repositories which are the complex ecosystems of cultural knowledge and authority.

Translating Ngarrindjeri Epistemologies

Sharing intimate cultural reflections on lived experiences and professional practices are part of Indigenous ontologies, particularly for Aboriginal people like Wilson who were born onto Country. It is an expression of how ancestors and how their material record is now available for descendants to reclaim and recover as part of a global practice of resolution, cultural justice, and healing. Below these are captured in the first person in an interview between Smith and Wilson for this paper:

My sentiments are best captured in the first person; the first account and first attempt at expression and relationality in situ at the moment when deeply engaged in the thought, reflection, and discussion in conversation with another person (a co-author in this case and senior academic/researcher). This is how the discussion unfolded in the space of an hour via telephone without environmental factors impacting my responses.

Your *miwi* (wisdom, located in the lower stomach and the entrance of the umbilical cord) encapsulates both your physical and spiritual connection to the world around. For me, growing up, I knew it was there, but I did not know what it was called. I was only told about it when I was an adult. I think if you reach that point in life and you show interest and that you are willing to learn, you get access to that knowledge. It is not about rights to knowledge or accessing knowledge because you want to know, which is the Western tradition. It is about you being ready to accept that knowledge. That knowledge was communicated through oral tradition, but it was held back until you are ready. It raises the question: Is there cultural danger in having this knowledge for the written record? That information would be accessible to people outside of the community. People were aware of the breakdown of the knowledge, so transferring that knowledge on to researchers was a logical way of keeping that knowledge so it can be passed on. That is part of the responsibility, to pass on knowledge. Of course, Aboriginal people had agency at that point. They knew about the objects that were in museums. Aboriginal people have been witnesses to what unfolded through colonialism, and the impacts that it had were the burdens that people took on. Of course, they were aware of the impacts. People were physically moved off their lands and into marginal spaces such as missions. For Ngarrindjeri Raukkan, Point McLeay mission site, was on Ngarrindjeri Country. It was a key Ngarrindjeri meeting place. I feel that there must have been some cultural reason behind the mission being there. So a lot of families still stayed together. There were good relationships with locals as well. Even though they weren't at a particular place, they were still connecting to that place (cf. Watkins 2006 for Native Americans).

They could talk about their Country. If you are in someone else's Country, you can't speak for that Country, and you are not going to speak in reference to your own Country unless you are asked.

Today, we say 'Where are you from?' as a greeting. This is a continuation of that traditional way of relating people to their Country. I was in a museum meeting and people were talking about being caretakers. That made sense to me. A museum can be a respectful way of viewing not just the objects, but the stories and knowledge that come with them. There are so many different stories, and the knowledge transfer isn't just about Aboriginal people. Knowledge can also come from non-Aboriginal people. The Elders passed on that knowledge to non-Aboriginal people whom they respected to care for that knowledge properly. Therefore, the transfer of knowledge from those non-Aboriginal people is very much a continuation of the wishes of those Elders (but see Smith, Copley Snr., & Jackson 2018, for the complexities of this transfer in regard to Ngadjuri people in South Australia). That ongoing transfer of knowledge is a continuation of the agency of those Elders. It is their agency in the past informing what we do today. That is very much the Elders speaking back. We define culture as contemporary in which the past and the future are together. There are always elements of the past in the present, and we are always thinking about the future.

If we think about human remains that are in a museum, they are not just bones; they are ancestral remains. They are people, not objects (see e.g., Hemming 2003). Their spirit is still there. For Ngarrindjeri, their spirit would go up to the Milky Way and become a star. But if their bones are taken, there has been a disturbance, a disconnection. The normal transition to the spirit realm is not possible without appropriate interment or cultural processes. There is no disagreement in the community around that stuff. That is across all the communities that I know. There are communities who do testing, might be radiocarbon dating and other kinds of research, invasive or non-invasive, and there are communities who ask the museums to be caretakers. In the end it is about knowledge. That person is still giving knowledge in their afterlife; that is how I look at it. If that person wasn't alive and didn't end up in that position, it would not be possible. Those Old People still have some form of agency in that. Maybe not in a consent form. Their history has been captured in their body, and that is what researchers try to find out—the person's history, where they are from, what they ate, who are their relations.

We just completed a project about *Ngartjis* (totems) (see Wilson et al. 2022). Some were animals and some were plants. *Ngartji* also means "close friend." It makes sense that you also have knowledge around certain plants and that is how people allocated that knowledge. It was based on your family and kin relationships. Some people show capacity over time, starting from when they are young to when they are adults. That idea really crystalized for me when I was at a recent museum committee meeting. I went into the meeting thinking, 'These are the reasons why I am not ready,' but the Elders on the committee said, 'We nominate Chris. You have been preparing yourself for a long time. You have dedicated your life to this area' (see Hemming et al. 2020; Wilson 2007, 2009). I wasn't sure that I was ready, but this is what they want me to do.

We moved around quite a bit when I was a kid, and there is resilience in that. It is difficult, challenging. You have to make new friends, adapt to new schools, but you also have a network of family to support you. Also, when I got to high school, I knew a lot of people from the area. I had connections throughout the area, on Ngarrindjeri or Kaurna Country. The meeting of the waters at the Coorong, where the river and sea meet. That is about birthing and life. In my family, women are the important people, the life-givers. They are also the strongest people in the family. They do look after the extension of the family. There are a lot of restrictions on Aboriginal people through colonization, so we had to adapt. Like, when young people are locked up, a lot of family go to visit them, to keep them connected. A lot of my aunts still look after me. They check me from time to time and let me know that they are proud of me, and they let me know that I am on the right track. And they might do that through Facebook or a mobile phone. People get locked into thinking about that mode of communication, but what is important is what is communicated, not the communication tool. I think we get lost in that—what is traditional, what is not. Because the technology is modern, it can take attention from a traditional practice, or that there is knowledge, values, and belief systems that are passed on.

What does this all mean? I am a Ngarrindjeri archaeologist. When I am working on Ngarrindjeri projects, there is a sense of urgency or priority. It makes sense for me to be at that end. I might do some work in other places, but it still comes back to being a Ngarrindjeri archaeologist. I have had invitations to work in the Kimberley (Western Australia) and other places, but so far it has never worked out. By identifying as a Ngarrindjeri archaeologist, there are things that I don't get to do, but that is okay. I am focusing on the normal responsibilities that I would have as a Ngarrindjeri man. In whatever form that comes in. Sometimes we can't define it; it comes from the ancestors. That is where the *miwi* comes in. Sometimes your head and your heart are in conflict, or one might lead you down the wrong path. Your heart might be your personal desire, but your head might be more about what the community needs. You might be conflicted in how you feel. That is where the *miwi* comes into it; you need to come back to the *miwi* to centre yourself and do the right thing.

DISCUSSION

Indigenous archaeology is in a constant state of 'becoming'. In 2023, it is not the same as it was when Nicholas and Andrews (1997: 3) defined it as 'archaeology with, for, and by Indigenous peoples'. Nor is it the same entity that George Nicholas later portrayed as 'an expression of archaeological theory and practice in which the discipline intersects with Indigenous values, knowledge, practices, ethics, and sensibilities, and through collaborative and community-originated or -directed projects, and related critical perspectives' (Nicholas 2008: 1660). From this perspective, Indigenous archaeology seeks to engage and empower Indigenous peoples in the protection, preservation, and management of their cultural heritage and to correct perceived inequalities in modern archaeology.

While this social justice commitment remains core to Indigenous archaeology, it is now complemented by new epistemologies that incorporate the non-material aspects of Indigenous knowledges into archaeological narratives and interpretations of the past. This is part of a new global movement that seeks to obtain interpretations of the past that are more closely aligned with the knowledge systems of the people who created the archaeological material and cultural landscapes (e.g., McNiven 2016a; Porr 2018), more grounded in emotional connections to people, place, and objects (Supernant et al. 2020; Hodgins 2021), and which draw on Indigenous science and cultural knowledge to address critical challenges faced by the world today (e.g., Atalay 2020; Hopkins et al. 2019). In a sense, this chapter is an attempt to replace the Western, colonial blinkers that can derail our interpretations of the past with richer, more nuanced, more *appropriate* Indigenous understandings of Indigenous cultural materials and landscapes. As Jasmine Willika (personal communication, 13 July 2021) states: 'If you or I focused on Western knowledge, how can you see what is in front of you when you are on Country with Traditional Owners?'

Embedded in an Indigenous approach to encountering the past, our study raises several questions for the practice of Indigenous archaeology. How might our learnings from Aboriginal people about encountering the past inform archaeological practice in the present? If archaeologists are to meaningfully contribute to an interpretive theoretical framework for Indigenous archaeology, they must be willing and able to embrace methodological openness as a strategy to encountering the archaeological record, and to bridging the gap or space between archaeological and Indigenous conceptualizations of the world. As Brady and Kearney (2016: 644) have noted, '[I]t is in this gap that we might be able to better hear the articulations of those with whom we collaborate and those for whom the 'past' matters in ways the archaeologist can never conceive of'. This process involves abandoning preconceived ideas about materiality, and instead focusing on other aspects of Indigenous life-worlds, such as kinship, social organization, epistemology, and ontology, to explain and understand the archaeological record. In terms of practice, archaeologists need to draw on the skills and cultural knowledge of Aboriginal people who can safely guide their fieldwork in living landscapes. This is a matter of protection as well as respect and protocol. In addition, an understanding of living landscapes needs to be embraced more fully into interpretations of archaeological material. Taken together, these actions have the potential to reset how we do archaeology. An important next step is for Aboriginal people and archaeologists (including Aboriginal archaeologists) to determine the methods required for such a reorientation of archaeology as a discipline.

How might archaeologists apply ethnographic observations concerning Ancestral Beings whose bodies are in rock art or paintings by *mimis* in inaccessible locations to understanding similar material in the past? The problems with the uncritical use of direct ethnographic analogy to inform interpretation of the past are well recognized (see Currie 2016; McGranaghan 2017; Domingo May, & Smith 2016; McNiven 2016b; Politis 2015). However, one fruitful approach is to focus on 'the local, empirically tractable ways in which particular ethnographic analogies may be licensed' (Currie 2016:

84) and to develop 'empirical demonstrations of applicability based on fine-grained, incremental chrono-stratigraphic backtracking of specific cultural practices' (McNiven 2016a: 33). Fine-grained analyses have the capacity to identify the material correlates of human behaviours and of Aboriginal belief systems. If anchored chronologically, these insights have the potential to trace the emergence of, and developments in, these belief systems through time. In fact, this is one of the ways in which archaeology can be of use to Indigenous people who are interested in scientific interpretations of their pasts: 'Saliently, archaeological data must operate as epistemologically equivalent to ethnographic data in order to resist the tendency to cast back a rich, textured ethnographic case study wholesale into the murky waters of prehistory. Only when this status is afforded archaeological data . . . is it possible to reveal the ways in which past conditions diverged from ethnographic ones' (McGranaghan 2017: 1).

How can an understanding of living landscapes inhabited by spiritual beings be used to enrich archaeological understandings of the past? Aboriginal people exist in living landscapes that are imbued with meaning, redolent with power, and potentially dangerous. Many of the places of significance associated with spirit beings cannot be identified by traditional archaeological methods, and knowledge concerning them is held in the hands of Traditional Owners and Custodians. In this way, the living heritage of the land is linked to the living heritage of oral traditions, rituals, and Indigenous knowledge systems. The existence of these beings in the landscape and the possibility that they could be wakened or that their attention could be attracted makes the process of traversing the land a matter of great care. Informed by cultural protocols, this careful, culturally directed traversing of the landscape necessarily involves avoiding particular places, leaving those places with little or no artefactual evidence of human occupation. So, what can archaeologists analyse in the absence of material culture? One way forward is suggested by McNiven's (2016a: 31) argument that material invisibility and a non-artefactual archaeological record is the 'material (tangible) expression of . . . intangible avoidance practices and new symbolic attachments to such sites'. Considered from this perspective, the absence of tangible artefacts may signal the presence of intangible values relating to foci of power (and danger) in the landscape, and a hiatus in site occupation in excavated deposits may indicate a change in the symbolic attachments attributed to that place.

This chapter contributes to theorizing Australian archaeology and approaches to working with Indigenous communities. We ask archaeologists to ask themselves: 'How does my work contribute to positive change and restorative justice'? After all, the investigation of the human past is a heritage matter situated within the humanities. We may like to reflect on the humanitarian aspect of our role in the construction and subsequent deconstruction of a past which is both objective and subjective. The emergence of Indigenous people who are formally trained in archaeology is more a political achievement by Indigenous subjects than it is an achievement of the discipline, since the individuals are agents for change whilst disciplinary and institutional structures largely serve to subjugate them. This situation poses new challenges for the discipline. Jawoyn woman Jasmine Willika articulates the cultural risks faced by Indigenous people who are archaeologists—simultaneously embedded in two, often conflicting, knowledge systems—highlighting a disciplinary responsibility to protect them: 'As Aboriginal people we are becoming focussed on Western knowledge by being trained as archaeologists. Sometimes we go out to sites and there are no cultural protocols. That can be dangerous for us. We should be thinking about 'How can we keep other Aboriginal archaeologists safe when they are working on someone else's Country?' Making our work safe, not only for Aboriginal archaeologists but also for other archaeologists working there' (Jasmine Willika, personal communication, 13 July 2021).

ACKNOWLEDGMENTS

Christopher Wilson thanks the Ngarrindjeri Aboriginal Corporation, Flinders University, South Australia Museum, the Australian Research Council's Centre of Excellence for Australian Biodiversity and Heritage, and Flinders University for their ongoing support of his research. Claire Smith thanks all the people with whom she works at Barunga, Beswick, and Manyallaluk, especially Joslyn McCartney, Jean Tiati, Traditional Owner Esther Bulumbara, and Junggayi/Custodians Nell Brown and Guy Rankin. She also thanks Jasmine Willika for sharing her knowledge and experiences. Liam M. Brady thanks the Yanyuwa community, the *li-Anthawirrayarra* Sea Rangers, and Elders past and present who invited him to work with them on rock art recording projects across Yanyuwa Country. Finally, we thank all the Old People who watch over us. We also thank the reviewers, particularly Duncan Wright.

REFERENCES

Atalay, S. (2006). Indigenous archaeology as decolonizing practice. *American Indian Quarterly*, *30*(3–4), 280–310.

Atalay, S. (2008). Multivocality and Indigenous archaeologies. In J. Habu, C. Fawcett, & J. M. Matsunaga (Eds.), *Evaluating multiple narratives. Beyond nationalist, colonialist, imperialist archaeologies* (pp. 29–44). New York: Springer.

Atalay, S. (2012). SHARE(ing) the benefits of anthropological research. *American Anthropologist*, *114*(1), 144–145.

Atalay, S. (2020). Indigenous science for a world in crisis. *Public Archaeology* https://doi.org/ 10.1080/14655187.2020.1781492.

Bradley, J. J., Holmes, M., Marrngawi, D. N., Karrakayn, A. I., Wuwarlu, J. M., & Ninganga, I. (2006). *Yumbul Yumbulmantha ki-Awaru (All kinds of things from country): Yanyuwa ethnobiological classification*. St Lucia: Aboriginal and Torres Strait Islander Studies Unit, University of Queensland.

Bradley, J., Kearney, A., & Brady, L. M. (2021). A lesson in time: Yanyuwa ontologies and meaning in the southwest Gulf of Carpentaria, northern Australia. In O. Moro Abadía & M. Porr (Eds.), *Ontologies of rock art: Images, relational approaches and Indigenous knowledge* (pp. 117–134). London: Routledge.

Brady, L. M. (2009). (Re)engaging with the (Un)known: collaboration, Indigenous knowledge, and reaffirming Aboriginal identity in the Torres Strait islands, NE Australia. *Collaborative Anthropologies, 2,* 33–64.

Brady, L. M., & Bradley, J. (2014). Reconsidering regional rock art styles: Exploring cultural and relational understandings in northern Australia's Gulf country. *Journal of Social Archaeology, 14*(3), 361–382.

Brady, L. M., Bradley, J. J., & Kearney, A. J. (2016). Negotiating Yanyuwa rock art: Relational and affectual experiences in the southwest Gulf of Carpentaria, northern Australia. *Current Anthropology, 57*(1), 28–52.

Brady, L. M., Bradley, J. J., & Kearney, A. J. (2018). Rock art as cultural expressions of social relationships and kinship. In B. David & I. J. McNiven (Eds.) *Oxford handbook of the archaeology and anthropology of rock art* (pp. 671–694). Oxford: Oxford University Press.

Brady, L. M., & Kearney, A. (2016). Sitting in the gap: Ethnoarchaeology, rock art, and methodological openness. *World Archaeology, 48*(5), 632–655.

Burke, H., & Smith, C. (2010). Vestiges of colonialism: Manifestations of the culture/nature divide in Australian heritage management. In P. Messenger & G. Smith (Eds.), *Cultural heritage management, policies, and issues in global perspective* (pp. 21–37). Gainesville: University Press of Florida.

Colwell-Chanthaphonh, C. (2012). Archaeology and Indigenous collaboration. In I. Hodder (Ed.), *Archaeological theory today* (2nd ed., pp. 267–291). Cambridge: Polity Press.

Colwell-Chanthaphonh, C., & Ferguson T. J. (Eds.) (2007). *Archaeological practice: Engaging descendant communities*. Walnut Creek, CA: AltaMira Press.

Colwell-Chanthaphonh, C., Ferguson, T. J., Lippert, D., McGuire, R. H., Nicholas, G. P., Watkins, J. E., & Zimmerman, L. J. (2010). The premise and promise of Indigenous archaeology. *American Antiquity, 75*(2), 228–238.

Currie, A. (2016). Ethnographic analogy, the comparative method, and archaeological special pleading. *Studies in History and Philosophy of Science Part A, 55*, 84–94.

David, B., (2006). Archaeology and the Dreaming: Towards an archaeology of ontology. In I. Lilley (Ed.), *Archaeology in Oceania* (pp. 48–68). Oxford: Blackwell.

Domingo, I., May, S. K., & Smith, C. (2016). Communicating through rock art: An ethnoarchaeological perspective. In O. Buchsenschutz, C. Jeunesse, C. Mordant, & D. Vialou (Eds.), *Signes et communication dans les civilisations de la parole* (pp. 9–26). Actes des Congress des sociétés historiques et scientifiques Paris: Edition electronique du CTHS.

Hemming, S. (2003). Objects and specimens: Conservative politics and the SA Museum's Aboriginal Cultures gallery. *Overland, 171*, 64–69.

Hemming, S., Rigney, D., Sumner, M., Trevorrow, L., Rankine Jr, L., Berg, S. & Wilson, C. (2020). Ngarrindjeri repatriation: Kungun Ngarrindjeri Yunnan (listen to Ngarrindjeri People speaking). In C. Fforde, C. T McKeown, & H. Keeler (Eds.), *The Routledge companion to Indigenous repatriation: Return, reconcile, renew* (pp. 147–164). Abington, Oxon: Routledge.

Hodgins, E., (2021). Review of K. Supernant, J. E. Baxter, N. Lyons, & S. Atalay (Eds.) (2020). *Archaeologies of the heart. Antiquity*, 1–2. doi:10.15184/aqy.2021.97.

Hopkins, D., Joly, T. L., Sykes, H. V., Waniandi, A., Grant, J., Gallagher, L. . . . . Bailey, M. (2019). "Learning together": Braiding Indigenous and Western knowledge systems. *Journal of Ethnobiology, 39*(2), 315–336.

Jackson, G., & Smith, C. (2005). Living and learning on Aboriginal lands: Decolonising archaeology in practice. In C. Smith & H. M. Wobst (Eds.), *Indigenous archaeologies: Decolonising theory and practice* (pp. 326–349). London: Routledge.

Kato, H. (2017). Archaeological heritage and Hokkaido Ainu: Ethnicity and research ethics. In C. Hillerdal, A. Karlström, & C.-G. Ojala (Eds.), *Archaeologies of "us" and "them": Debating history, heritage and indigeneity* (pp. 218–232). London: Routledge.

Lippert, D. (2008). Not the end, not the middle, but the beginning: Repatriation as a transformative mechanism for archaeologists and Indigenous peoples. In C. Colwell-Chanthaphonh & T. J. Ferguson (Eds.), *Archaeological practice: Engaging descendant communities* (pp. 119–130). Walnut Creek, CA: AltaMira Press.

Loring, S. (2008). The wind blows everything off the ground: New provisions and new directions in archaeological research in the north. In T. Killion (Ed.), *Opening archaeology: Repatriation's impact on contemporary research and practice* (pp. 181–194). Santa Fe, NM: School for Advanced Research.

McBryde, I. (1986). Australia's once and future archaeology. *Archaeology in Oceania, 21*(1), 13–28.

McBryde, I. (1995). Dream the impossible dream? Shared heritage, shared values, or shared understanding of disparate values. *Historic Environment, 11*(2&3), 8–14.

Mangolamara, S., Karadada, L., Oobagooma, J., Woolagoodja, D., & Karadada, J. (2018). *Nyara pari kala niragu (Gaambera), Gadawara ngyaran-gada (Wunambal), Inganinja gubadjoongana (Woddordda): We are coming to see you.* Derby: Dambimangari Aboriginal Corporation & Wunambal Gaambera Aboriginal Corporation.

McGranaghan, M. (2017) Ethnographic analogy in archaeology: Methodological insights from southern Africa. In T. Spear (Ed.), *Oxford research encyclopedia of African history.* https://oxfordre.com/africanhistory/view/10.1093/acrefore/9780190277734.001.0001/acrefore-9780190277734-e-213

McNiven, I. J., & Russell, L. (2005). *Appropriated pasts.* Walnut Creek, CA: AltaMira Press.

McNiven, I. J. (2016a). Theoretical challenges of Indigenous archaeology: Setting an agenda. *American Antiquity, 81*(1), 27–41.

McNiven, I. J. (2016b). Ethnoarchaeology, epistemology, ethics. *World Archaeology, 48*(5), 683–686.

Menzies, D., & Wilson, C. (2020). Indigenous heritage narratives for cultural justice. *Historic Environment, 32*(2), 64–69.

Mizoguchi, K., & Smith, C. (2019) *Global social archaeologies. Making a difference in a world of strangers.* London: Routledge.

Moreton-Robinson, A. (2013). Towards an Australian Indigenous women's standpoint theory. A methodological tool. *Australian Feminist Studies, 28*(78), 331–374.

Morphy, H. (1998). *Aboriginal art.* London: Phaidon Press.

Nakata, M. (2007). *Disciplining the savages: Savaging the disciplines.* Canberra: Aboriginal Studies Press.

Nicholas, G. P. (2003). A necessary tension: Integrating processual, postprocessual, and other approaches to the past. In T. Peck, E. Siegfried, & G. Otelaar (Eds.), *Indigenous peoples and archaeology* (pp. 14–129). Calgary: University of Calgary Press.

Nicholas, G. P. (2007). Education and empowerment: Archaeology with, for, and by the Shuswap Nation. In G. Nicholas & T. D. Andrews (Eds.), *At a crossroads: Archaeology and first peoples in Canada* (pp. 85–104). Burnaby: Archaeology Press, Simon Fraser University.

Nicholas, G. P. (2008). Native peoples and archaeology. In D. Pearsall (Ed.), *Encyclopedia of archaeology* (pp. 1660–1669). New York: Academic Press.

Nicholas, G. P., & Andrews, T. D. (Eds.) (1997). *At a crossroads: Archaeology and first peoples in Canada.* Burnaby, BC: Archaeology Press, Simon Fraser University.

Nicholas, G. P., & Bannister, K. (2004). Copyrighting the past? Emerging intellectual property rights issues in archaeology. *Current Anthropology, 45*(3), 327–350.

Politis, G. (2015). Reflections about contemporary ethnoarchaeology. *Pyrenae, 46*(1), 41–83.

Pollard, K., Smith, C., Willika, J., Copley Sr., V., Copley Jnr., V., Wilson, C., Poelina-Hunter, E., & Ah Quee, J. (2020). Indigenous views on the future of public archaeology in Australia. A conversation that did not happen. *AP: Online Journal in Public Archaeology*, *10*, 31–52.

Porr, M. (2018). Country and relational ontology in the Kimberley. *Cambridge Archaeological Journal*, *28*(3), 395–409.

Porr, M., & Matthews, J. (2016). Thinking through story: Archaeology and narratives. *Hunter Gatherer Research*, *2*(3), 249–274.

Porr, M., & Matthews, J. M. (2017). Post-colonialism, human origins and the paradox of modernity. *Antiquity*, *91*(358), 1058–1068.

Silliman, S. W. (2005). Culture contact or colonialism? *American Antiquity*, *70*(1), 55–74.

Silliman, S. W. (2010). Indigenous traces in colonial spaces: Archaeologies of ambiguity, origin, and practice. *Journal of Social Archaeology*, *10*(1), 28–58.

Smith, C., Burke, H., Gorman, A., Ralph, J., Pollard, K., Wilson, C., . . . Jackson. G. (2019). Pursuing social justice through collaborative archaeologies in Aboriginal Australia. *Archaeologies*, *15*(3), 536–569.

Smith, C., Copley, V. Sr., & G. Jackson, G. (2018). Intellectual soup: On the reformulation and repatriation of Indigenous knowledge. In V. Apaydin (Ed.), *Shared knowledge, shared power* (pp. 1–28). New York: Springer.

Smith, C., & Jackson, G. (2007). The ethics of collaboration. Whose culture? Whose intellectual property? Who benefits? In C. Colwell-Chanthaphonh & T. J. Ferguson (Eds.), *Collaboration in archaeological practice: Engaging descendent communities* (pp. 171–191). Walnut Creek, CA: AltaMira Press.

Smith, C., & Wobst, H. M. (Eds.) (2005). *Indigenous archaeologies: Decolonizing theory and practice*. London: Routledge.

Supernant, K., Baxter, J. E., Lyons, N., & Atalay, S. (Eds.) (2020). *Archaeologies of the heart*. Cham: Springer.

Watkins, J. E. (2000). *Indigenous archaeology: American Indian values and scientific practice*. Walnut Creek, CA: AltaMira Press.

Watkins, J. E. (2006). Communicating archaeology: Words to the wise. *Journal of Social Archaeology*, *6*, 100–118.

Wilson, C. (2007). Indigenous research and archaeology: Transformative practices in/with/for the Ngarrindjeri community. *Archaeologies*, *3*(3), 320–334.

Wilson, C. (2009). Implications and challenges of repatriating and reburying Ngarrindjeri Old People. *Museum International*, *61*(1–2), 37–40.

Wilson C, Roberts A, Fusco D (2022) New data and syntheses for the zooarchaeological record from the lower Murray River Gorge, South Australia: Applying a *ngaio* lens. *Australian Archaeology* 88: 200–214.

Wiynjorroc, P., Manabaru, P., Brown, N., & Warner, A. (2005). We just have to show you: Research ethics blekbalawei. In C. Smith & H. M. Wobst (Eds.), *Indigenous archaeologies: Decolonizing theory and practice* (pp. 316–327). London: Routledge.

Wolfe, P. (1991). On being woken up: The Dreamtime in anthropology and in Australian settler culture. *Comparative Studies in Society and History*, *33*(2), 197–224.

Zimmerman, L. J., & Branam, K. (2014). Collaborating with stakeholders. In J. Balme & A. Paterson (Eds.), *Archaeology in practice: A student guide to archaeological analyses* (pp. 1–25). Chichester: John Wiley and Sons.

CHAPTER 6

······

ORAL TRADITION, HISTORY, AND ARCHAEOHISTORY OF INDIGENOUS AUSTRALIA

······

IAIN DAVIDSON, HEATHER BURKE,
PEARL CONNELLY, STEPHEN PORTER,
HAZEL SULLIVAN, LANCE SULLIVAN,
ISABEL TARRAGÓ, AND LYNLEY A. WALLIS

INTRODUCTION

WHEN considering either Australia or Sahul, a chapter on oral history and tradition of Indigenous societies could be very long. Many studies have recorded the spoken or sung traditions of the many peoples of Australia and Papua New Guinea (e.g., Berndt & Berndt 1989; Parker 2001; Wiessner & Tumu 1998); some from people who live by tradition, albeit mediated by the non-Indigenous person who collected and translated the material (e.g., Sutton 2009: Chap. 7; Warner [1937]1964: 519–565), some reconstructed from knowledge disrupted by the invasion of non-Indigenous people (e.g., Dixon & Duwell 1990; Haddon 1901–1935), but generally reported or reconstructed by non-Indigenous people (Hercus 1980; Roth 1897). There are accounts of life and social structure among Aboriginal people, again, almost entirely seen through the eyes of anthropologists (e.g., Myers 1986; Spencer & Gillen 1899), and of the often-violent encounters between Aboriginal and non-Aboriginal people (e.g., Burke, Barker, Wallis, Craig, & Combo 2020; Hercus & Sutton 1986). Only recently have Aboriginal people at the heart of such studies been included as co-authors.

Sometimes Aboriginal oral histories are quite intimate, personal accounts of events (Davidson et al. 2020), and all such histories documented here have been discussed between Aboriginal and non-Aboriginal authors.[1] Such accounts have been used to build up pictures of the lives of people in Sahul, including their reactions to outsiders at various times and places, and especially to shed light on the role of oral histories and traditions as fundamental to the ways in which Aboriginal and New Guinea peoples have seen and see their own pasts, without the intervention of outsiders. There are many examples which collect orally transmitted myths, such as Berndt and Berndt (1989) and Organ (1994) for Australia, or Lawrie (1970) for Torres Strait and Landtman (1917) for New Guinea. In addition, most works of anthropology include accounts of the tradition as people recounted them either in Australia (e.g., Myers, 1986: Chaps. 2–3) or in New Guinea (e.g., West 2006: Chap. 3). There are fewer that assess what part of the oral tradition and history has been passed on to people in the twenty-first century. This chapter's contribution is a discussion of the second group.

The significance of the legal verdict in the *Mabo v. Queensland (no. 2)* (1992) case by the High Court of Australia (Attwood 1996), which recognized Aboriginal peoples' Native Title rights through the processes of a non-Aboriginal law and court, is that a culture dependent on written text finally recognized the ongoing authority of oral tradition. Consequently, histories now need to consider not only written accounts and archaeological evidence but also oral traditions. In this chapter we assess some works that contribute, through the use of oral traditions, to understanding the past of Australia, knowing that clarification will have implications for understanding Sahul.

Oral evidence—history and tradition—is one of the three central pillars for writing about the past. The others are history written from documents and archaeohistory, itself a history of deep time (see Davidson 2016) constructed from the material evidence of archaeology. Archaeological evidence is generally independent of, and distinct from, both oral accounts and written texts (Davidson, forthcoming). All history begins with oral history (Atkinson 2002), but archaeohistories are constructed from facts based on material evidence, with gaps between the facts embroidered on the basis of theoretical assumptions (Davidson, forthcoming).

The concept is familiar to archaeologists through the intersection of material and oral evidence with ethnography (e.g., Kearney, Brady, & Bradley 2018)—the subject of ethnoarchaeology (Davidson 1988) (and see discussion of the principles in McNiven and Russell [2005, especially 243–247], which looks forward to a more complete integration of understanding from archaeology with that from oral history). For people dedicated to archaeology of a remote past, ethnographic analogy may be used with or without tyranny (Belfer-Cohen & Goring-Morris 2009; Wobst 1978), but it may be that 'tyranny' is not the only option.

There are two different approaches to the use of ethnographic information in archaeological approaches to the past. One uses behaviour and knowledge of modern people, evidence from the present, to supplement evidence from the past and to provide a fuller story of that past (an objective identified by Brady & Kearney 2016)—implicitly providing an interpretation of the past and ultimately making it some sort of reflection of the present (for a recent Australian example, see Cane 2013). The other sets up behaviour and knowledge of modern people as the outcome reached through the processes of archaeohistory (in the manner of Irwin 1978) as a way to elucidate the complexities of historical emergence, in particular situations, of modern patterns of

ORAL TRADITION, HISTORY, AND ARCHAEOHISTORY   159

society, technology, economy, and morality (e.g., Davidson 2014a, 2014b). The obligation to 'make archaeological approaches to the past more meaningful and relevant to Indigenous communities' is an important component of this approach (McNiven 2016). Geoff Irwin (1978), for example, used archaeological evidence to demonstrate how Mailu Island in southeast Papua New Guinea went from being an unspecialized village to a central place for the production and distribution of pottery, with concomitant social and political changes; oral tradition had only recorded the central place condition (Malinowski 1915). The intention is to use the second approach in this chapter—one in which archaeology shows the pattern of changes in the past that may be complementary to and provide certainty (e.g., radiocarbon dates) about those described in oral tradition (Urwin, Hua, & Arifeae 2021). Archaeology contributes to the historical knowledge of Indigenous communities, rather than simply using their, often spiritual, traditions as if they were literal versions of history. The interaction has to work in both directions.

In addition to its theoretical contribution, this chapter addresses an issue that involves oral knowledge in quite literal ways: the possibility that historical rising sea level is mentioned in oral histories around Australia (Nunn & Reid 2015; Nunn 2018). This argument may be taken to include oral accounts—histories—from a time when no one was specifically documenting changing sea levels, yet took it for granted that there was a time when water levels were different (Davidson & Roberts 2008; Plomley 1971).

Oral History, Oral Tradition, and Ethnography

After extensive analysis of oral traditions of Enga people in Highland New Guinea, Polly Wiessner, an American anthropologist, and Akii Tumu, an Enga artist and director of the Enga Museum (1998), demonstrated that some oral traditions, whatever other influences on their contents, recount narratives of earlier historical events. In doing so, they also showed that oral histories fade and that the amount of information diminishes with increasing time, and the functions of oral evidence change. The authors, anthropologist and Enga, recorded three main categories of oral evidence: (1) myth, including origin myths for cults; (2) historical traditions, including genealogies (between eight and fourteen generations) and tribal origin traditions; and (3) other forms, including poems, formulas, and songs (Wiessner & Tumu 1998: 26–42). The authors interviewed people in their own language, obtaining histories of twenty-three Enga tribes and of six immigrant tribes (Wiessner & Tumu 1998: 7).

The type of historical detail available for Enga history within the song cycles of the oral tradition appears to be unique in New Guinea, and similar compilations have not yet been attempted in Australia. However, some accounts of what are said to be original conditions of communities around Australia have been reconstructed by consulting the earliest accounts written by non-Aboriginal observers based on their oral interactions with Aboriginal peoples (Keen 2003). Some such accounts have been published as compilations of 'tales', without much introspection about their value as sources of Aboriginal history (Parker 2001). While oral accounts may or may not record events of the past accurately, they begin with passing on verbally an account of something observed or imagined in the past. It is rare that events are ever described in writing at the moment they occurred, even in cases where writing must have been available. For all other events writing did not yet exist or those experiencing it had no knowledge of it. At some stage the oral transmission was written down and thus became part of the 'written record', taking on a different role and meaning. Ian Keen's (2003) compilation, and the sources on which it was based, are derived from that written record of Aboriginal people close to the time Whites first wrote about them.

Robert Tonkinson recorded one example of the emergence of an oral tradition in Australia. In his experience, one 'dream-spirit ritual' was composed by ten men with a common cultural background who shared ritual culture and who combined the common elements of it into a single new ritual. In general such rituals were short-lived, but Tonkinson suggested that some came to characterize the deeper 'Dreamtime' as follows: 'Over time, and with cultural transmission, the composers were quickly forgotten and Aborigines of later generations came to regard them as being Dreamtime creations' (Tonkinson 1974: 85–86). This is an example of extracting from the ethnography a process of relevant generality. That principle is that the particular understanding of a place by an individual was situated within what was possible of the cultural discussion of the place by conversations between that individual and other senior people in the community (among many examples, see Myers 1986: Chap. 5). Such a process could account for the manner in which ritual knowledge passed from being particular discussions between individuals to a more general belief, widely distributed in society, and sanctified.

Although both archaeology and oral traditions begin with the evidence of the past, in material evidence and social relations, only the material evidence survives largely unchanged. When archaeologists write archaeohistories using such evidence, they are aware of the constraints arising from the evidence archaeology relies on. Although the evidence of archaeology is always physical and incomplete, it takes the form of facts, albeit ones that can be interpreted in various ways. Such evidence only becomes archaeohistory by filling in—embroidering—the gaps shaped by the interpreted facts arising from that evidence. For the past beyond the reach of oral histories, archaeologists have been sole creators of much of the written historical narrative, even in Australia with its rich legacy of oral traditions preserved in songlines (Flood 1995: 10; Neale 2017; Smith 2017; Tonkinson 1974, 1978). In some instances, Aboriginal members of research teams were able to identify plants that were the same as those found in the archaeological record from 65,000 years before (Clarkson et al. 2017; Florin et al. 2020). For more recent times archaeologists have often turned to oral traditions (e.g., Davidson 2014b) to provide the principles that guide the embroidery. Students of societies in Sahul will find many other bibliographies of previous work in other chapters in this volume.

Historians and archaeohistorians both interact with oral knowledge (Minc 1986; Nunn & Reid 2015; Vansina 1985), often in interesting ways. We need to establish what might be meant by 'oral histories,' because usage in some disciplines makes no sense for our discussion. For example, Robert Perks and Alistair Thomson (1998: ix) cited Grele (1996: 63) to say that oral history is 'the interviewing of eye-witness participants in the events of the past for the purposes of historical reconstruction'. Jan Vansina (1973: 171–172) outlined the ways in which different sorts of oral tradition might be biased. In this chapter we focus on the variety of history that people-without-writing hold in their minds (Neale & Kelly 2020), tell in their stories, and sing as songs to their peers, as well as to people of the next generation, often prompted by the material evidence, land or sea (e.g., Kelly in Chap. 5 of Neale and Kelly 2020). Here there is more than one category of oral knowledge as a result of variation on different time-scales, but it is informal story-telling about the past. In contrast, Leah Minc (1986) argued that there is an important category of oral knowledge which should be called a tradition. For Minc, there were two categories of oral tradition: secular traditions, including folktales, songs, and histories, which lean on repetition to be continued and have plenty of potential for variation; and sanctified oral traditions that must be correctly reproduced and that include the elaboration of ritual. Importantly, while oral traditions as recorded appear to be immutable at the time of recording, there is a case that they have also been the subject of discussion and negotiation within their cultural context, particularly when the birth of a tradition was observed, as in the example from Tonkinson. Arguably when material evidence comes to be fixed permanently and associated with ritual, as is argued for rock art (Ross & Davidson 2006), oral tradition and archaeology seem to merge.

Personal Cases of Oral Histories

There are many outcomes from initial interactions between non-Aboriginal and Aboriginal people, most of which were bad for Aboriginal peoples. In western Queensland many types of colonial interventions led to disrupted Aboriginal communities. Yet oral traditions were retained despite non-Aboriginal people often thinking none survive; this is probably typical for many other regions. Such knowledge is not necessarily of the sort that has usually been the stock-in-trade for non-Aboriginal anthropologists. Our research (with Stephen Porter, Figure 6.1B) among Gamilaraay people around Moree in New South Wales showed that substantial knowledge of plants (forty-five species) and animals (thirty species), as well as of some technological items (a fish trap modelled on a traditional form shown in Figure 6.1A), had been passed on orally within the community. This knowledge has been passed on despite considerable disruptions and lack of access to Country (Cotter, Davidson, Porter, Wilson, & Duncan 2004), where 'Country' is the key concept that Aboriginal groups use to identify where they are from (as discussed by Peter Sutton in 1995).

Of Country, Margo Neale (Neale & Kelly 2020: 48) wrote: 'It is this capacity of Aboriginal people to adapt to change that has enabled their survival for millennia. These [sacred] objects are portals to the places where the knowledge resides in Country, and thus Country can be accessed through them via song and performance, even from a distance. They are not *about* Country: they *are* Country'.

Deborah Bird Rose (1996: 7), an anthropologist who worked in the Northern Territory over many years, wrote: 'People talk about country in the same way that they would talk about a person: they speak to country, sing to country, visit country, worry about country, feel sorry for country, and long for country. People say that country knows, hears, smells, takes notice, takes care, is sorry or happy'.

In northwest Queensland, parts of the Yalarrnga (known as Yulluna in Native Title documents) community between Boulia and Mt Isa (the Sullivan family), and of the Mitakoodi from Cloncurry (the Connelly family), retain enough orally transmitted traditional knowledge of plants and animals in their Countries for it to be included in books (Ah Sam 2006; Connelly & Wallis 2013; Sullivan c. 1994; Sullivan c. 2005). Pearl Connelly provided information about at least twenty-six medicinal plants she learned about from her grannies (Connelly & Wallis 2013) (Figure 6.1C shows Pearl Connelly with a branch of the species *Santalum lanceolatum*, Northern Sandalwood, which has medicinal properties). This information provides the cultural background within which other Aboriginal knowledge should be considered; different classes of stone artefacts need to be assessed in the context of the resource distributions understood from work such as that of Pearl Connelly. Mrs Hansen, mother of Wangkamahdla woman Isabel Tarragó, passed on to her daughter knowledge of 'looking after Country', places, and plants that she had visited and curated with her husband, Jack Hansen, during the mid-twentieth century at the times when, so far as the pastoral station knew, they were on 'walkabout'. The word 'walkabout' allowed Aboriginal people to continue to look after Country without revealing to the station managers that they were maintaining their traditions. For Mrs Hansen and her husband, this included the maintenance of *pituri* (native tobacco) groves and experience of how the plant was collected for processing (Figures 6.1 D and 6.1 E).

Undoubtedly much traditional knowledge has been lost by Aboriginal communities, but clearly much has also been retained and passed on unknown by non-Aboriginal people, perhaps precisely because that communication was oral. Aboriginal people remain actors in their own Country so long as they retain some level of access to their land and its resources. Access is key and most highly politicized. As Aboriginal people remember and document orally, Gamilaraay worked successively as shepherds, stockmen, shearers, and cotton chippers on their own Country, even as the economy created these roles and then took each of them away. Yalarrnga and Mitakoodi people both worked in the pastoral industry and lived on cattle stations within their own Countries. For example, Pearl Connelly's husband worked cutting wood and fencing. Within those intimate environments, people also retold family histories of interactions with the invaders; in particular, the Yalarrnga passed on stories of their interactions with the Native Mounted Police such as we recount here and elsewhere (Davidson et al. 2020; see also Wallis, Burke, Barker, & Cole this volume).

ORAL TRADITION, HISTORY, AND ARCHAEOHISTORY 163

FIGURE 6.1. (A) Fish trap in a bucket, Caroona, New South Wales. In 2004, Vic Porter and friend (now deceased) were making fish traps. Stephen asked his father, Vic, to make one. They demonstrated it using sticks and reeds, and then using chicken wire (photograph by Maria Cotter, 2004). (B) Stephen and Vic (photograph by Stephen Porter, 2021). (C) Pearl Connelly with branch of Northern Sandalwood, *Santalum lanceolatum*, the Bush Plum, on Mitakoodi Country near Cloncurry, northwest Queensland (photograph by Lynley A. Wallis, 2013). (D) Isabel Tarragó and her mother, Mrs Hansen, in front of a Pituri bush, *Duboisea hopwoodei*, at the top of a Simpson Desert dune, west central Queensland (photograph by Iain Davidson, 1982). (E) The sort of bunch of leaves harvested to prepare the drug for smoking (photograph by Iain Davidson, 1982).

It is arguable that it is the knowledge that Aboriginal people were telling each other about their lives on their own Country that was and is partly responsible for non-Aboriginal people fearing to grant them access rights (based on Native Title determinations) to their appropriated lands. As Native Title determinations repeatedly demonstrate, individuals retain ritual knowledge orally that connects them to their Country and justifies their legal rights to lands. The commonalities of their ritual knowledge generally demonstrate a complex geography of connection which ties in to that known from other accounts (e.g., Roth 1897, 1904). Thus, for example, Wangkamahdla woman, Mrs Hansen, sang songs learned in ceremony and told traditional stories with sand drawings (to her daughter Isabel Tarragó and to Iain Davidson) for the Country between Alice Springs (Central Australia) and the Simpson Desert, extending as far as Dajarra (northwest Queensland). These songs were about the 'protection of the place', 'knowledge of Country', and 'looking after' Country (Figure 6.2). Yalarrnga man Tom Sullivan told stories (to his nephew Lance Sullivan, and to Iain Davidson and Heather Burke a generation earlier) about the Country between Dajarra and Cloncurry (see inset in Figure 6.3, top). These stories overlap with each other, the evidence from Walter Roth, and the message sticks retained in the Queensland Museum (Davidson, Tarragó, & Sullivan 2004). Arguably no archaeology of the region could be complete without taking into account such linkages, spread over 500 km.

Research in the Selwyn Ranges of central western Queensland has shown the importance of the interconnections by demonstrating that hatchets mined near Mt Isa passed through the ranges on their way south to the Great Australian Bight (cf., Davidson et al. 2005; Tibbett 2001, 2003). These hatchets were part of the movement of materials, generally described as trade, which united much of eastern Australia in a huge network

FIGURE 6.2. (Left) Mrs Hansen singing songs about looking after Country for her daughter, Isabel Tarragó, near Mitaka, Glenormiston Station, west central Queensland (photograph by Iain Davidson, 1982). (Right) Wonomo Waterhole (northwest Queensland) 2017 with Val Punch and Hazel Sullivan and Lance Sullivan (photograph by Iain Davidson, 2017).

ORAL TRADITION, HISTORY, AND ARCHAEOHISTORY 165

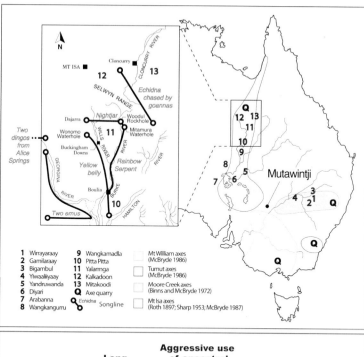

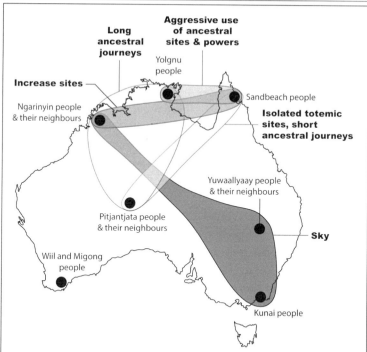

FIGURE 6.3. (Top) The map was originally produced for Davidson et al. (2005.) The inset shows the overlapping oral traditions for Tom Sullivan, Yalarrnga, and Mrs Hansen, Wangkamadla (Davidson et al. 2004). (Bottom) Australia showing the 'subtle variations' in reported beliefs called 'The Dreaming' in different parts of Australia, according to Keen (2003: 13).

of relationships (McBryde 1987; McCarthy 1939; Mulvaney 1976) that could only be documented through a combination of oral traditions and archaeological evidence.

Similar long-distance links are evident in the trade in the Mudlunga ceremony in northwest Queensland, including the transmission in a single language as it crossed into Country of people who spoke other languages. According to oral tradition recorded by Roth (1897), this ceremony began northwest of Boulia (central western Queensland) in 1893. It subsequently passed through Killalpaninna east of Lake Eyre (northeast South Australia) in 1901, where the songs were learned, orally, by Mick McClean Irinyili and recounted later to linguist Luise Hercus (1980). The same ritual was reported by Frank Gillen (writing to Spencer on 11 March 1898) as arriving in Alice Springs after starting in the Saltwater Country to the northeast (Mulvaney, Morphy, & Petch 1997).[2] This starting point was Wagaya Country according to Mick Maclean (Hercus 1980). Several authors contributed to knowledge of the elements of the main ritual as it traversed well-established routes via oral transmission: Routes and destinations 'figured prominently in mythologies describing the travels of ancestral beings in the Dreaming' (McBryde 1987: 268). 'McCarthy (1939: 422–423) suggested that each local group through whose territory the Dreaming track passed, "owned" part of the total story associated with the larger Dreaming track. Associations through links in the Dreaming tracks between territories provided predictable patterns of human movement and economic activities' (Davidson et al. 2005: 110).

Further, analysis of the paints (ochre pigments) and paintings in the Selwyn region by archaeologists was assisted by Kalkadoon man Alf Barton. When compared to the recording of oral accounts by Roth (1897: 132), these analyses showed that '[t]he coincidence in chronology of the trade in stone artefacts and of the creation of the paintings suggests that these two forms of non-utilitarian activity were part of a single set of cultural relationships mediated by the symbolic system represented by the paintings' (Davidson et al. 2005: 122). Much of the reason for exchange of materials was social rather than to fill a resource gap. This sociality was what the oral tradition shows—that the fundamental currency was and is knowledge of the relationship between people and Country.

Two things follow from this analysis. First, that Aboriginal people in the Selwyn region retain knowledge of the geographic extent of the movements of their families within their lifetimes; second, they do this partly through their ritual knowledge of earlier times and distant places retained in oral tradition. Longer connections and wider territories of climatic and environmental variation become important parts of the survival of communities across Australia. The people of northwest Queensland participated in the wide networks that were deemed essential to the operation of Aboriginal societies in sparsely occupied regions (Yengoyan 1968). Such networks were maintained in ceremonies that brought otherwise dispersed people together during times of plenty, as was happening at Wonomo Waterhole in January 1879 when pastoralists intruded, leading to their deaths. As a consequence, there were extensive settler and Native Mounted Police reprisals against local Aboriginal people (Davidson et al. 2020: 729). All of this links the fragmentary personal elements of oral traditions with archaeological evidence to construct an archaeohistory of widespread interactions across Australia from north to south and probably east to west.

In terms of ritual knowledge, the key concepts are the Dreaming and associated Songlines. The Dreaming is a cosmological system that Bill Stanner referred to as having 'subtle (and probably important) variations' (Stanner [1962] 1979a). Such variation is discerned in Keen's (2004) compilation of early evidence of this cosmology around Australia (see Figure 6.3, bottom, and Table 6.1). Furthermore, conceptualization of the Dreaming has its own history within anthropology and as an institution in its own right (David 2002; Hiscock & Faulkner 2006). The concept underpins various Aboriginal belief systems that are about the relations between people and place, about the creation of those places, and about the relations between people in consequence of that history of creation and their place in it (Neale & Kelly 2020). The Dreaming also refers to a time that Stanner memorably referred to as 'everywhen' (Stanner [1953] 1979b: 24).

The term 'Dreaming' was developed to counter claims by Lutheran missionaries that the Arrernte (also known as Aranda) of Central Australia conceptualized what we would now call a High God (for historical context on this development in terms of non-Aboriginal knowledge of Aboriginal religion, see Hiatt 1996: Chap. 6). According to Patrick Wolfe (1991), the name 'The Dreamtime' originated as a translation of the Arrernte word *alcheringa* by Frank Gillen in correspondence with Baldwin Spencer (Mulvaney, Morphy, & Petch 1997). It was then applied to a variety of different manifestations because of the knowledge limitations of non-Aboriginal researchers when gathering data about Aboriginal religion. As an all-encompassing concept, the Dreaming permitted non-Aboriginal society to simplify what is still a complex cosmology. Among the beliefs were those of the Euahlayi of northern New South Wales, who, unlike the Arrernte, did have a High God, Baiame (Parker in Keen 2004), contradicting the original purpose of using the term 'The Dreamtime'. It became, in

Table 6.1. Cosmological beliefs all called 'Dreaming' (from Keen 2003).

	Emphasis on the sky	Isolated totemic sites, short ancestral journeys	Emphasis on long ancestral journeys linking sites	'Increase' sites	Aggressive use of ancestral sites and powers
Kûrnai	X				
Yuwaaliyaay	X				
Pitjantjatjara		X	X		
Wiil/Miŋong					
Sandbeach		X		X	X
Ngarinyin	X		X	X	
Yolngu			X		X

fact, a widespread oral tradition among anthropologists and Aboriginal communities to use the word 'Dreamtime' to refer to Aboriginal religious practices whatever they were. Both parties agreed that the word could be used for Aboriginal spiritual beliefs generally, despite what Bill Stanner called 'variations', because that was the cultural practice of anthropologists. Aboriginal peoples know their beliefs anyway. Yet Keen's (2003) compilation shows that there was great variation (and some convergence) across Australia.

Indigenous Oral Traditions in Relation to Non-Indigenous Histories

Elsewhere we have set out in detail the interaction between oral histories and traditions and non-Indigenous histories about northwest Queensland (in papers and blogs, see Davidson et al. 2020).[3] The circumstances of that interaction were those of massacres of Yalarngga people following the killing of four pastoral workers (the most well-known of them called Molvo) at Wonomo Waterhole in 1879. The waterhole (Figure 6.3, right), on Suleiman Creek, was the start of a Dreaming track associated with the fish called yellowbelly, or golden perch (Davidson, Tarragó, & Sullivan 2004), and therefore was probably a place for ceremonies.

After detailed discussion of oral history told to Davidson and Burke by different members and generations of the Sullivan family twenty-eight years apart, study of the primary published text about the events (Fysh 1933), and investigation of associated archaeological evidence, we concluded (Davidson et al. 2020: 738):

> . . . in this context part of the victory [of the non-Aboriginal invaders] is precisely because the history was written and in consequence could be spread to readers who would not have been party to an oral history. The victors in colonial situations also promulgate a belief that the losers, being non-literate, have no memory of the trauma and no version of events. When the losers are from a small-scale society, as here, the intention of the colonists is to wipe them out. As a result, the victors assume their version is all there is, and the consumers of their printed history have no means of knowing otherwise. In contrast, we have shown that there is a quite detailed oral history three generations deep of events from 1879.

One consequence of the destruction of the agency of Aboriginal people in the public domain has been that their histories have generally remained relatively local unless formalized by anthropologists into histories that are European in form but Aboriginal in content. Suppose we are correct in surmizing that, before 1879 the Yalarrnga had already heard of the killing habits of the invaders conveyed in oral accounts from Myall Creek (New South Wales) and surrounds, through Lake Eyre and north to Wonomo (Davidson et al. 2018). We can be fairly certain that this knowledge, along with much of the rich mythologies of the Yalarrnga people, was lost as a result of nineteenth-century massacres. Although Roth (1897: 41–42) recorded details, such as vocabulary, social relations, and oral traditions, of many of the peoples of northwest Queensland, he did not record any about the Yalarrnga. Davidson suggested that this omission might have been because at that time Yalarrnga had to be approached through influential White pastoralist Alexander Kennedy, with whom Roth had no desire to interact (Davidson 2008: 128). Consequently, what remained were various written accounts of the Wonomo killings and subsequent events that were regarded by the invaders as history—what Hudson Fysh's book called *Taming the North* (Fysh 1933). For Fysh, and for Alexander Kennedy who told Fysh his side of the story, that was success.

Local Native Mounted Police officer at the time, Ernest Eglinton, presumably a 'typical' White officer, led 'dispersals' of Aboriginal people in the region after the events at Wonomo, together with Kennedy. Eglinton had a son, Willie, with a Yalarrnga woman, Ruby, who survived one of those massacres. Eglinton, and doubtless others like him in different places, moved on from their Aboriginal partners,[4] to marry and father children with non-Aboriginal wives. The forgetting began when the White officers left the Native Mounted Police and resumed 'normal' lives in which their intimacy with Aboriginal women, known only through the oral histories of those involved (and children known only in the bush), was no longer mentioned. Accounts of the terrible history of the Wonomo events, written about by the invaders, were also preserved in the oral histories of the Sullivan family (and probably others).

Oral Traditions and Surviving the Present

One of the challenges when trying to elicit historical information from oral traditions is that the information has to remain relevant to the listeners or it will be forgotten, just as the names of the original composers of Dreaming songs are forgotten, as described elsewhere by Tonkinson. Names may be left unspoken but known in many situations, or forgotten because they were not spoken, or there may be a prohibition about them being spoken (such as when people die). As the time between present and past lengthens, oral information appears more unchanging, as if it had always been (even when it has been demonstrably changed or lost). The classic case here is genealogies written down by some person (often an anthropologist), who revisited a generation or more later. On the subsequent visit the genealogy still recorded the same number of generations with the earliest having been dropped (Goody & Watt [1963] 1968). This culling reveals a limit on memory but also the importance of the material record that documented the change and provided a context for more information to be remembered subsequently (for the importance of rock art and rock art sites in this respect, see Davidson 2023). People cannot remember all of the events of their past, and as such, need a device to retain important memories. Yolngu man, Narritjin, working with anthropologist Howard

Morphy (1991: 251) in northeastern Arnhem Land of the Northern Territory, suggested that 'given enough bark on which he could represent everything, topography was the basis on which he would organize the painting', knowing, probably, that there could never be such a large piece of bark, and implying that there could have been other ways of organizing things. There are changes in the functions of memories and consideration of the factors that impact on the memories carried down to the present.

Stephen Sutton and colleagues (2020) have outlined the importance of memories of past events on an island in northern Sumatra, Indonesia, affected by the tsunamis (locally called *smong*) of 2004. Here, on the island of Simeulue, in the north of Aceh Province, the songs, stories, and memories of grandmothers seem to have kept alive for over one hundred years the knowledge of how to survive a *smong*, principally by reducing it to a formula to remember appropriate actions ('if there is a big earthquake and the sea recedes—run to the mountain. Don't wait just run') (Sutton, Paton, Buergelt, Sagala, & Meilianda 2020: 6).

Patrick Nunn (2018) also argued that oral histories, particularly of peoples around the Pacific Ocean, celebrate and warn about events in the past, especially of the sea-level rise about 10,000 years ago that had particular significance to the societies where the stories are maintained. That may be true, and is considered in more detail later, but how many such events can people recall, and to which ones do they give salience? The beauty of Sutton's argument is that *smong* happened previously and the retained knowledge, continually passed on, was preserved because it saved lives. In contrast, sea-level rise at the end of the 'Last Glacial Period'[5] was a one-off process that has not been repeated in the lifetimes of whole generations of people (Williams, Ulm, Sapienza, Lewis, & Turney 2018); thus, retaining knowledge about it would have served no practical advantage.

For Aboriginal people in Australia, oral traditions similarly contain knowledge of values for survival. Some, from the 'Old Times', appear to offer knowledge only of Creation myths, but probably also define the directions and natures of social connections. Some provide a philosophy of living in the world. Deborah Bird Rose (1984, 1994) documented the presence across northern Australia of mythology about Ned Kelly (a nineteenth-century bushranger/outlaw from southeast Australia, well-known for his improvized armour and his conflicts with police) and Captain James Cook (an eighteenth-century British maritime explorer of eastern Australia, said to exemplify the British attitude to their first knowledge of eastern Australia). In both cases, these famous White people were also known mythologically in non-Aboriginal communities. These myths seem to account for the similarities and differences between Aboriginal and non-Aboriginal communities, and suggest that 'Aboriginal people's search for a moral European communicates the challenging and provocative possibility that colonizer and colonized can share a moral history' (Rose 1984: 175). The point here is that oral traditions contain all of several features: personal histories recounting real events in spite of the presence of non-Aboriginal people which might otherwise not be easily explained; songs and stories which fit within the general cultural context of the society; songs and stories about the Creation of the world; and moral guidance.

Oral Traditions, Geography, and the Long-Term History from Other Sources

Some oral histories claim to report on the time before writing (Nunn & Reid 2015; Nunn 2018). They involve the memories of participants and others about their perceptions of events of particular significance. Once such oral accounts are written down, and those perceptions are taken out of play, the text tends to take on an air of certainty and is more difficult to change. That implies a capacity to change oral histories, and more belief in written ones.[6] It is clear that oral histories are subject to change (as are written histories), some of it observable, such as variations to Enga myths from the New Guinea Highlands within living memory to incorporate events such as the discovery of gold by colonial prospectors (Wiessner & Tumu 1998: 27).

Without archaeological evidence the oral testimony about any event depends on the relationship between the teller—be that in song or story—and the listener (or the reader of the written oral history). Texts appear to stand alone, and some literary specialists debate whether they can be assessed without any consideration that there were authors. Texts can be read at any time and in any place by anyone, and when printed, by many people at the same or different times and in different places. With oral histories we must not forget the hearer(s) is(are) as necessary as the teller, but once the history is codified through writing we can no longer appreciate the oral text except as a written text that is full of narrative conventions (cf., Tonkinson's 1974 'forms and procedures' of the Jigalong mob) mixed in with the realistic descriptions that belong to the time the oral text was written down (Irene 2005).

It is a tradition for anthropologists and linguists to interpret Dreaming stories in terms that suit their academic narrative, and some supposedly traditional stories can be shown to have nontraditional origins. Claims by Margaret Sharpe and Dorothy Tunbridge (2003), and others, for the identification of extinct animals in northern Australian Dreaming stories based only on the oral traditions do not seem to be substantiated and, in any case, the 'odds that a depiction of a megafaunal species could be identified with certainty are extremely low' (Lewis 2017: 97). Similarly, Robert Dixon claimed that a Dreaming story he recorded from Yidnyji elder Dick Moses provided evidence of a volcanic eruption that caused the creation of Lake Eacham, southwest of Cairns in North Queensland (Irvine & Dixon 1991: 41). This story turned out to be less convincing when examined closely (as in the reproduction of the text Dixon used by David 2002: 109–110). Bruno David (2002: 91) summed up the underlying issues:

> Many (hi)stories in any cultural tradition are undoubtedly based on historical events, the knowledge of which has been modified through the ages. But to isolate a handful of cosmogonic stories from any culture as proof of folk memory because

they remind the scientist of past geological events dating back 10,000 years or more is a dubious endeavour. It also belittles the ability of Indigenous peoples to observe and interpret their own surroundings—to infer a prior molten state and even fiery origin for rocks (lava) with surficial flow marks, for example. This is not to say that there may not be some historical basis for some of the Dreaming stories, but determining what is historical from cosmogonic or heuristic reality is another matter.

Importantly, most cultural knowledge has been derived from real events, but trying to work out the past events solely on the basis of the modern relaying of that knowledge can be a difficult process, as is the case here. The issue is really a matter of the author's belief system. Some authors argue that the oral traditions describe the historical information that they are interested in, rather than some other event; others question how we would establish that there is information that can be pinpointed and how we would identify that which can be pinpointed from that which cannot.

A recent study of oral traditions by Patrick Nunn and Nick Reid (2015) looked at Australian Aboriginal myths that seem to refer to catastrophic effects of sea-level rise, back to c. 13,000–7,000 years ago in some cases. That sea-level rise initially isolated Tasmania from the rest of Sahul (Lambeck & Chappell 2001) and then the large island of Australia from New Guinea (Yokoyama, Purcell, Lambeck, & Johnston 2001). The world is currently experiencing the fastest rate of sea-level rise since that time, and we know that some part of it has been caused by anthropogenic climate change (Frederikse et al. 2020). Sea-level rise in the twentieth century is of the order of 20 cm since 1900, and it will be much greater in the future. As inhabitants of the mainland, we go to the beach from time to time and see the water come in and out. Even with our understanding of tides, we are not well-equipped to know whether the sea is coming in more now than it did at this time last year, though it would be relatively easy for us to make such a measurement with the necessary technology and some forethought. Such changes may be more obvious for those who depended on the products of the seashore. Yet this sort of rise, and especially its causes and consequences, would be invisible without the sophisticated direct and indirect monitoring and instrumental recording worldwide that is now available. A 20 cm rise over 120 years would not register among people who only periodically visit the coast and have no written records, and who have no expectation that sea level would rise or fall, and no means of recording past sea levels to compare to those of the present. On small islands the effects would be more obvious, though not dramatic, and might be appreciated initially through salinization of (aquifer) drinking supplies.[7] There are often traditions about what conditions were like in the past, but it is often difficult to argue from them alone that the factual basis from which such memories are derived corresponds to the explanation non-Indigenous people would have of those phenomena.

Western scientific knowledge of higher and lower sea levels was not current in the nineteenth century (but appears to have been resolved between 1961 and 1998, as in Fairbridge 1961; Pillans, Chappell, & Naish 1998).[8] As such, it may be that Indigenous people who live closely with the sea, and possess undersea sacred sites (e.g., for the Yolngu in Arnhem Land see Morphy & Morphy 2006), may keep alive stories of sea-level change that predate instrumental observations of similar changes made by Western geoscientists. The difference between oral traditions and scientific ones lies in the question of establishing past sea-level changes by any means other than direct experience. We do not doubt that it was true because of the weight of scientific evidence, just that it used to be difficult to convince anyone who had not lived through it. In the same way, indeed, modern Indigenous people find it difficult to convince some modern politicians who continue to deny the reality of the climate crisis.

For most places, sea-level rise would have been slow, not even steady, as natural climatic fluctuations occurred, and its most obvious effects would still be subtle: some seepage within a mangrove swamp, for example, not a sudden and massive inundation. Yet several of the stories quoted by Nunn and Reid (2015) describe the sea 'rushing' in (Table 6.2). We might expect 'rushing' in very specific circumstances if a bay was protected by a sill which was breached and then eroded. We can think of two such places: (1) Port Philip Bay, south of Melbourne; and (2) Botany Bay, south of Sydney. In both there is a sill and an Indigenous story that the sea rushed in, which is quite a good test of the veracity of the association between sea-level rise and these stories. Unfortunately, seven of the ten stories associated with rushing sea in Nunn and Reid's account have not been noted to involve a sill, and one that does has no story of water rushing in. On balance the overall argument presented by Nunn and Reid (2015) does not seem very plausible.

The extreme examples of sea-level rise for Australia are the isolation of Tasmania by Bass Strait and the separation of New Guinea at Torres Strait coupled with the inundation of the huge Arafura Plain to the west. Around 1831—when there was no geological, environmental, or archaeological evidence on the matter—George Augustus Robinson recorded a story from the original Tasmanians (Davidson & Roberts 2008). Robinson's words, as transcribed by Brian Plomley (1971), noted that the Tasmanians 'have a tradition that this Island was settled by emigrants from a far country, that they came here on land, that the sea was subsequently formed'. Since that time we know for a variety of reasons that the people of Tasmania have a common past with those of the mainland partly because of our knowledge of sea-level change, partly because of common features of the archaeology. For example, archaeology has shown that Tasmanians, in common with mainland Aboriginal people, produced rock art in the form of hand stencils and engravings (Davidson 1936; Dix 2016; Sims 2013), as well as other forms of art (Roth 1899). This rock art similarity seems likely to be explicable in terms of a continuation from behaviour that was present before isolation (Davidson & Roberts 2008: 27). Apart from the somewhat dubious statement about sea-level change by Robinson, there does not seem to have been a major oral tradition on either side of Bass Strait that refers to the social trauma of separation.

What is it about the claims by people such as Patrick Nunn and Nick Reid that people find believable? Do the collected oral traditions from several places contain information about events or processes that we now know took place at least 7000 years ago? We

174 IAIN DAVIDSON ET AL.

Table 6.2. Davidson's analysis of the content of narratives about sea-level change reported by Nunn and Reid (2015).

	Tool	Animal	Rushing	Myth	Sill
Spencer Gulf	Y	Y	Y	Y	
Kangaroo Island			Y	Y	
MacDonell Bay				Y	
Port Philip Bay			Y		Y
Gippsland			Y		
Botany Bay & Georges R			Y		Y
Moreton and Stradbroke Island				Y	
Hinchinbrook and Palm Island				Y	
Cairns–Great Barrier Reef				Y	
Gulf of Carpentaria & Wellesley Island	y	Y	Y	Y	
Elcho Island	Y			Y	
Goulburn Island	Y			Y	
Cape Don			Y	Y	
Bathurst and Melville Island				Y	
Brue Reef				Y	
Rottnest, Carnac & Garden Island			Y		
Cape Chatham			Y		
Oyster Harbour		Y		Y	Y
Bremer Bay	Y	Y	Y	Y	Y
Eucla				Y	
Fowler's Bay	Y		Y	Y	

have no doubt that there would have been stories of this sort in response to those events, and others responding to similar events. The important point is that if histories are constantly revealed, then sometimes stories can emerge which correspond, with hindsight, with what is now known. Sometimes the stories imply a binary choice in which one option appeals to one group of people, another to the other group, but often new understanding of processes makes one of those accounts more unlikely. In reality, whether or not the Aboriginal accounts refer to the sea-level change that Western science has now established, both Aboriginal and non-Aboriginal stories continue to be reasonable accounts of the way the world exists within two different cultural systems with different ways of explaining the world (David et al. 2012).

Detailed Western scientific investigation of the history of postglacial inundation of South Australia's Spencer Gulf and the formation of its many islands shows compelling similarity with Narungga traditional narratives of sea-level rise (Roberts, Mollenmans, Rigney, & Bailey 2020). But the authors acknowledge that there are also versions of the narratives which say nothing about inundation. The analysis has revealed 'deeper complexities' and demonstrates that people have interpreted the facts of the oral traditions together with other aspects of local cultural contexts.

One other approach to the question of oral traditions would be to look at multiple lines of evidence. The first is to take a category such as claimed sea-level change and enquire a bit more thoroughly into the nature of oral traditions. The sorts of questions that might be asked include the following: What led to oral traditions being preserved when the events or processes described do not appear to include information that saves people or society (as in the example from Stephen Sutton and colleagues mentioned earlier)? Are oral traditions present in all places where the impacts of change might have been felt? We have already seen that Bass Strait might be a case where an oral tradition of separation might be expected, and it is arguable that the Arafura Sea might be another.

Another approach is to investigate what major changes are not represented in an oral tradition. Here the example might be language. Linguists have learned over many years of analysis that Aboriginal languages of Australia fall into two major groups: a single family of more recent Pama-Nyungan languages across about 80% of Australia (Blake 1988; Bouckaert, Bowern, & Atkinson 2018; Evans 1988), and a large number of earlier non-Pama-Nyungan languages in twenty families in the region predominantly in central northern Australia (Evans 2005). Is it not strange that the huge expansion of Pama-Nyungan language does not appear in the oral histories (McConvell & Bowern 2011)? Why? Perhaps it was so gradual that no one noticed the change. Likewise, consider Torres Strait and the language changes of New Guinea—and the drowning of the Arafura Sea. In that region there are more than twenty major language groups, many of which appear unrelated to each other and to Australian languages (Pawley 2007). It is not enough for us to seek a reconciliation of archaeological evidence and oral tradition which, after the event, fits with Western models of how the world works. It is not surprising that, in retrospect, there is a fit, but there are other events and processes that people lived through and talked to each other about that do not seem to appear in the oral traditions. We also have to ask about major experiences that oral tradition might have reported and consider why they are not there.

DISCUSSION

Davidson (2016) suggested that there are three principal genres of historical knowledge: (1) history from documents; (2) archaeohistory, or the historical narrative derived from archaeological evidence; and (3) oral histories and traditions among the people who often become the objects of historical or archaeohistorical research. These three

176 IAIN DAVIDSON ET AL.

Table 6.3. The different approaches to the past and the ways in which they affect what we know.

	A time period in the past	Events or acts in that time period	Interpretation of those events or acts	The uses of historical interpretations
History from documents	Conventional understanding— constrained by what is recorded in documents.	Named actors are generally visible. Constrained by the documents that endure.	Constrained within known patterns of behaviour important enough to write about.	Generally about the process of how modern events came to be written about and then evolved.
Archaeohistory	Extends back further (as far back as chronometric dating techniques have the capacity to reveal).	Named actors are never visible. Constrained by the material evidence that endures.	Often involves interpretation of material evidence of behaviour. Often that which was not otherwise recorded.	Generally about the process of how modern events emerged as a result of material changes.
Oral history	Cannot tell exactly which period it refers to. Typical construction of history in societies focused on family histories is 50–100 years (3–4 generations) (Rose 1984) but can be longer in some (Wiessner).	Named actors are sometimes visible. Details many changes that do not endure.	Generally no documents and nothing material. Not about the content per se, but its orientation and purpose.	Often small-scale accounts of what happened to individuals in their interactions with other individuals.
Oral tradition	Generally has specific times removed.	Agents are often mythologized, but individually named actors generally drop away, so ancestors can be included who were not likely to be present, such as Cook or Kelly.	Often makes very old events appear to be the result of behaviour that appears modern. Present events, if deemed memorable, will also be incorporated. Often involves a moral purpose.	Often about how modern events evolved but may be unconstrained by material evidence. Specific historical events may be unreliable.

genres have different effects on the different ways we understand history (Table 6.3): 'The word "history" has many meanings . . . It refers generally to 1) a time period in the past; 2) events or acts in that time period; 3) the interpretation of those events or acts in terms of the actions of people and the institutions they constitute; and 4) the uses of such interpretations' (Davidson 2016: 892).

All narratives, whether archaeohistorical, oral, or historical, are themselves tightly constrained because they are narratives. Anthropologists find this, too, for they deal with narratives but are charged with disentangling the social relationships described within them (Kearney, Brady, & Bradley 2018). Sometimes those are oral narratives about the actions of the people who have accompanied the narrator—as with the stories told by Mrs Hansen to her daughter, Isabel, by Tom Sullivan and Clem Sullivan to their nephew Lance, or those recounted to Amanda Kearney and colleagues. Sometimes those narratives have been subtly altered so that the agency of mere mortals is less visible, as with the stories reported by Tonkinson. At all times the narrators are conscious that those agents were operating in a real world of other actors, plants, animals, and landscape. That is part of the significance of the information passed on in the Gamilaraay community and recounted to Stephen Porter, or in the Mitakoodi community and told to Lynley Wallis by Pearl Connelly.

Myths all over the world include the actions of fictional characters who shaped events and landscapes. This is because a narrative about that shaping requires actors to do it. Oral histories, like everything else in a narrative, require that there be agents, and often these were named ancestral beings, such as Achilles, Moses, Krishna, Beowulf, or the Rainbow Serpent. They require an account of a series of events; there are almost always actors or agents, including gods and heroes but also other mythologized individuals (Landau 1993). In practice, the possible interactions between agents and events are limited as a result of the nature of narrative: Misia Landau (1984) outlined six different scenarios for human evolution; Christopher Booker (2004) outlined seven basic plots for literature; and Jonathan Phillips (2012) outlined eight basic plots for storytelling in the earth sciences. Those constraints determine much of what can be narrated about the agency of ancestral beings towards each other, towards plants, animals, and landscapes, and towards people. It is reasonable to expect that oral telling begins from events that could be seen to happen, but it is not necessarily reasonable that the oral account remained unchanged from the moment of first telling to the present. Leah Minc (1986) has argued that in those contexts where the oral tradition transmits survival information, as in the Indonesian example from Sutton and colleagues (2020), the narrative becomes ritualized and invariant.

In Davidson et al. (2020: 723), we presented an argument about the interplay between narratives written from different sources of evidence in the context of discussing massacres of Yalarrnga and other people in Queensland:

> Oral histories are unlikely to be precise about chronology, become more generalised over longer durations, and are prone to processes of mythologising (Curthoys 2003; Morphy & Morphy 1984). At the same time they can be highly accurate for high emotion events, position people in relation to present day concerns, and are continuously reconsolidated through storytelling (Moshenska 2010; Thomson 2011: 85–90). As two alternative forms of "cultural construction through history" (Hill 2015: 139) we are particularly concerned here with the power relations created through orality and writing in colonial contexts. The archaeology results from similar processes, and tells a different but complementary story, without emotion, and generally without evidence about individuals.

Oral traditions arise from the ritualization of an oral account through the growing unimportance of the identity of the composers as time goes by within the known cultural context, in the manner described by Tonkinson (1974, 1978). Even archaeohistories involve the slow gestation of the narratives that see the light of day, lovingly constructed first with discussions in fieldwork and on to the final publication, frequently in the context of what is already known and expected (Joyce 2008: 4–6). Such oral traditions among archaeologists are constantly negotiated, in the manner of archaeology students sharing a drink after work (for a history of similar approach, see Cooper & Yarrow 2012). Anthropologists likewise encounter several different contexts of their lives which have an impact on the way they tell the story of the people they work with (West 2005). In the same way, the penetration of the concept of 'Dreamtime' following Frank Gillen, as a tradition within anthropology, has the characteristics of the cultural context within which anthropologists have operated unreflectively. The use of the same word has given the appearance of uniformity across Australia, despite the awareness of demonstrable variations in form.

Many years ago, one of us defined a number of possible roles for anthropologists interacting with Aboriginal communities: 'Are the conclusions the result of much thought about a few events—the social anthropologist as philosopher illustrating general truths through selected instances? Or are they empirical generalizations from many events—the social anthropologist as "scientist"? Or are they the result of casting the explanations by informants in the context of western semiotic theory—the social anthropologist as decoder?' (Davidson 1995: 892). That issue still remains, but the solution was the one we have found here and was hinted at in that earlier analysis: 'Yolngu have their own interests' (Davidson 1995: 892).

Peter Sutton's (2009: Chap. 7) analysis has shown that the history of anthropological knowledge depended on relationships between the White people who wrote down stories and customs revealed through their close friendships with Aboriginal people: Lancelot Threlkeld wrote about the Awabakal in the Hunter Valley of New South Wales on the basis of his relationship with Biraban in the 1830s; Lloyd Warner wrote about the Murngin people (who would be called Yolngu now) of Arnhem Land through the revelations of his friend Mahkarolla in the 1920s; beginning in 1927, Ursula McConnell recorded the knowledge of the Wik people from western Cape York Peninsula principally working with Bambegan; likewise, over a long period between 1932 and 1959, Bill Stanner recorded the insights of Durmugam, a Nangiomeri man from the coastal parts of the Daly River. Peter Sutton 2009 (186–187) mentioned seven other relationships between other anthropologists and the Aboriginal agents communicating their culture to them. In all cases, it is the Aboriginal people who choose to tell their oral stories and who are the geniuses. Those named chose what to tell and what not to tell—they are the code switchers, not anthropological luminaries such as Frank Gillen, Walter Roth, Lloyd Warner, Ursula McConnell, or Donald Thomson. In the cases we have highlighted here, the oral information passed on within communities is the history missing from texts written only by non-Aboriginal people. Archaeologists may find different facts and tell other stories, but both are true under the assumptions being made (David et al. 2012).

There is an atmosphere of decolonization of historical studies at present, in response to the known cliché that histories are written by the victors. In historical disciplines, it has been non-Indigenous people who have written the stories, sometimes trying to take into account the actions of Indigenous people. Even with that recognition, it has been rare until recently to recognize the fundamental importance of the agency of Indigenous people—in this case the oral histories of Aboriginal people describing events within their own families and communities. The consequence is that there is now a more general recognition of people once regarded as minorities. Just as historians dependent on written texts have to counter charges from a narrow-minded public and their politicians that there is only one history and they should not attempt to change it, so archaeology must face similar reactionary forces. In the past, archaeology has often engaged in narrative construction about the people it studies from a distant past, rather than working with the people whose history archaeology has written (an issue addressed in Porr and Matthews 2020). The important point is that archaeohistory has always had an emphasis on the material evidence, often absent from oral tradition. In the end, archaeology and archaeohistory depend on the archaeological material evidence interpreted on its merits, together with theoretical assumptions by archaeologists—their cultural context. Those archaeologists now come from much more diverse backgrounds, including, of course, Indigenous peoples whose past is being studied. Which materials they regard as important have changed over time, particularly as popular perceptions have changed. The new diversity of people studying the past will bring new sensitivity to oral traditions and scepticism about previously unexpected assumptions of the culture of archaeology. This will include the recognition that, just as earlier scholars ignored the oral traditions of Indigenous peoples because that was what they did, so will this new generation of archaeologists find that there are oral histories from scholarly communities and reflectiveness about the prior telling of the archaeohistories that they were brought up with. They will not be wrong. Just different.

CONCLUSION

The oral tradition of any people must have been based on facts—events and processes—as they were perceived by people, filtered through the cultural values of those who created the tradition. Archaeologists aim to use their own work to contribute to the traditional and historical knowledge of Indigenous communities, rather than simply using the often spiritual, Indigenous traditions to interpret evidence as if it were a literal version of history.

It is sometimes possible to take a series of oral traditions from different peoples and, by comparing them, construct a history of their interactions. Generally, oral traditions cannot be taken as literal versions of past events, as they have been altered by changing cultural values. Archaeology studies the material evidence of events and processes from the past, which may include places, landscapes and seascapes. It can often be embroidered to produce a richer archaeohistory by deriving principles from oral traditions of the place.

This chapter describes instances in which modern Aboriginal people have revealed traditional knowledge. These reflect the cultural contexts that have been passed on traditionally among peoples, including Wangkamahdla, Yalarrnga, Mitakoodi, and Gamilaraay peoples. Part of the reason why these traditions were passed on is that they were, at some stage, ritualized in a process that has generally made them easier to pass on and more valuable for survival.

There seem to be several oral traditions around Australia that correspond with modern knowledge among non-Indigenous people about sea-level changes. We suggest that it is complicated to make an argument that these all refer to the same events of scientifically known sea-level change, because there are several occasions where landscapes and seascapes have been affected in ways that need to be remembered.

As Indigenous people study both archaeology and their oral traditions, they will create a new culture of archaeology. The new diversity of people studying the past will produce different stories about the past. History and archaeohistory will be different, and it will be up to for Indigenous peoples to decide whether oral traditions also change.

Acknowledgments

This work involved interactions and help from many people. The paper was mostly written by Davidson and results from ideas that include those he learned and discussed 'after work' with all his companions in the field, especially Heather Burke, Scott Mitchell, Lynley Wallis, and the late Tom Sullivan. All of those ideas come from working with a variety of Aboriginal people, who are authors as surely as if they had written the sentences themselves.

This chapter would not have been possible without the invitations from Ian McNiven and Bruno David and from Shawn Rowlands, Paige West, Ann McGrath, and Dan Smail. Important contributions were also made by Quentin Mackie, Mark Moore, Annie Ross, June Ross, Martin Thoms, Sean Ulm, and Peter White. Helen Arthurson commented on an earlier draft. All of these people, and the three reviewers, made it easier to express the ideas—thank you—but none should be blamed for the way we have used their work.

Notes

1. All the Aboriginal authors of this paper have expressed a preference to be referred to as Aboriginal or by their language group names: Gamilaraay (Stephen Porter), Mitakoodi (Pearl Connelly), Wangkamahdla (Isabel Tarragó), and Yalarrnga (Hazel Sullivan and Lance Sullivan).
2. But the date was not 1901 as suggested in Mulvaney (1976: 90–91) and repeated in Davidson et al. (2005).
3. Details of this history are described and discussed in the following blogs: https://archaeolo gyonthefrontier.com/2020/07/13/murdering-molvo-part-i; https://archaeologyonthefront ier.com/2020/08/13/murdering-molvo-part-ii/

4. The child of Ernest Eglinton and Ruby was Willie Sullivan, the father of Tom and Hazel Sullivan, Val Punch, and Dorrie Prowse and grandfather of Lance Sullivan. Eglinton then married a White woman and they had a family; one of their grandchildren, Ian Keays, knew nothing of this violent history until he contacted us (personal communication).
5. This is how oral traditions continue beyond their relevance. The glaciers of the last 2 million years are barely relevant to Sahul, but it became traditional within the archaeological and geological worlds to refer to climatic variations in terms of glacial stages in Europe.
6. ID thanks Dr James Knight for his observations in relation to Tindale's work (Knight 2003). Once Tindale had written down Kaurna traditions, his written word was taken to have more authority than oral traditions of the people themselves.
7. Such accounts were the preoccupation of the Kulkalgal people of the Torres Strait island of Masig.
8. Fairbridge (1961: 99) wrote that 'through geological eyes we might regard the present M.S.L. [Mean Sea Level] as ephemeral as a fleeting ray of sunshine on a wintery afternoon'.

REFERENCES

Ah Sam, M. (2006). *Mitakoodi bush tucker*. Thuringowa: Black Ink Press.

Atkinson, A. (2002). *The commonwealth of speech*. Melbourne: Australian Scholarly Publishing.

Attwood, B. (1996). Mabo, Australia and the end of history. In B. Attwood (Ed.), *In the age of Mabo* (pp. 100–116). Sydney: Allen & Unwin.

Belfer-Cohen, A., & Goring-Morris, N. (2009). The tyranny of the ethnographic record, revisited. *Paleorient*, 35(1), 81–82.

Berndt, R. M., & Berndt, C. H. (1989). *The speaking land*. Ringwood: Penguin.

Blake, Barry J. (1988). Redefining Pama-Nyungan. *Aboriginal Linguistics*, 1, 1–90.

Booker, C. (2004). *The seven basic plots*. London: A&C Black.

Bouckaert, R. R., Bowern, C., & Atkinson, Q. D. (2018). The origin and expansion of Pama–Nyungan languages across Australia. *Nature Ecology & Evolution*, 2(4), 741–749.

Brady, L. M., & Kearney, A. (2016). Sitting in the gap: Ethnoarchaeology, rock art and methodological openness. *World Archaeology*, 48(5), 642–655.

Burke, H., Barker, B., Wallis, L., Craig, S., & Combo, M. (2020). Betwixt and between: Trauma, survival and the Aboriginal troopers of the Queensland Native Mounted Police. *Journal of Genocide Research*, 22(3), 317–333.

Cane, S. (2013). *First footprints*. Sydney: Allen & Unwin.

Clarkson, C., Jacobs, Z., Marwick, B., Fullagar, R., Wallis, L., Smith, M., Roberts, R. G., Hayes, E., Lowe, K., Carah, X., & Florin, S. A. (2017). Human occupation of northern Australia by 65,000 years ago. *Nature*, 547(7663), 306–310.

Connelly, P., & Wallis, L. (2013). *Kar-kar: Mitakoodi traditional medicinal plant uses of the Cloncurry region*. Mount Isa: Southern Gulf Catchments.

Cooper, A., & Yarrow, T. (2012). 'The age of innocence': Personal histories of the 1960s 'Digging Circuit' in Britain. *International Journal of Historical Archaeology*, 16(2), 300–318.

Cotter, M., Davidson, I., Porter, S., Wilson, J., & Duncan, B. (2004). Documenting Aboriginal ecological knowledge in northern New South Wales. Poster presented at Australian Archaeological Association Conference, Armidale, NSW.

Curthoys, A. (2003). Constructing national histories. In B. Attwood & S. Foster (Eds.), *Frontier conflict* (pp. 185–200). Canberra: National Museum of Australia.

David, B. (2002). *Landscapes, rock-art and the Dreaming.* London: Leicester University Press.

David, B., Lamb, L., Delannoy, J.-J., Pivoru, F., Rowe, C., Pivoru, M., Frank, T., Frank, N., Fairbairn, A., & Pivoru, R. (2012). Poromoi Tamu and the case of the drowning village. *International Journal of Historical Archaeology, 16*(2), 319–345.

Davidson, D. S. (1936). Aboriginal Australian and Tasmanian rock carvings and paintings. *American Philosophical Society Memoirs, 5,* 1–151.

Davidson, I. (1988). The naming of parts: Ethnography and the interpretation of Australian prehistory. In B. Meehan & R. Jones (Eds.), *Archaeology with ethnography: An Australian perspective* (pp. 17–32). Canberra: Department of Prehistory, Australian National University.

Davidson, I. (1995). Paintings, power, and the past. Review of *Ancestral connections* by H. Morphy. *Current Anthropology, 36*(5), 889–892.

Davidson, I. (2008). Ethnological studies and archaeology of North West Central Queensland. In R. McDougall & I. Davidson (Eds.), *The Roth family, anthropology and colonial administration* (pp. 121–132). Walnut Creek, CA: Left Coast Press.

Davidson, I. (2014a). Hunter gatherers in Australia. In V. Cummings, P. Jordan, & M. Zvelebil (Eds.), *Oxford handbook of the archaeology and anthropology of hunter gatherers* (pp. 368–404). Oxford: Oxford University Press.

Davidson, I. (2014b). It's the thought that counts. In M. Porr & R. Dennell (Eds.), *East of Africa* (pp. 243–256). Cambridge: Cambridge University Press.

Davidson, I. (2016). Review of long history, deep time: Deepening histories of place. In A. McGarth & M. A. Jebb (Eds.), Aboriginal History, *40,* 317–324.

Davidson, I. (2023). Humans making history through continuities and discontinuities in art. *Cambridge Archaeological Journal,* 1–18.

Davidson, I., Burke, H., Sullivan, L., Wallis, L. A., Artym, U., & Barker, B. (2020). Cultural conflict in text and materiality. *World Archaeology, 51*(5), 724–740.

Davidson, I., Burke, H., Wallis, L. A., Barker, B., Hatte, E., & Cole, N. (2018). Connecting Myall Creek and Wonomo. In J. Lydon & L. Ryan (Eds.), *Remembering the Myall Creek massacre, 1838–2018* (pp. 100–111). Sydney: New South Press.

Davidson, I., Cook, N. D. J., Fischer, M., Ridges, M., Ross, J., & Sutton, S. A. (2005). Archaeology in another country. In I. Macfarlane, M.-J. Mountain, & R. Paton (Eds.), *Many exchanges: Archaeology, history, community and the work of Isabel McBryde* (pp. 101–128). Aboriginal History Monographs 11. Canberra: Aboriginal History.

Davidson, I., & Roberts, D. (2008). 14, 000 BP—on being alone: The isolation of Tasmania. In D. A. Roberts & M. Crotty (Eds.), *Turning points in Australian history* (pp. 18–31). Sydney: UNSW Press.

Davidson, I., Tarragó, I., & Sullivan, T. (2004). Market forces. In V. Donovan & C. Wall (Eds.), *Making connections: A journey along Central Australian Aboriginal trading routes* (pp. 12–23). Brisbane: Arts Queensland.

Dix, S. (2016). New Aboriginal hand stencil discoveries at the Freycinet National Park, Tasmania. *Australian Archaeology, 82*(1), 76–79.

Dixon, R. M. W., & Duwell, M. (Eds.) (1990). *The honey-ant men's love song and other Aboriginal song poems.* Brisbane: University of Queensland Press.

Evans, N. (1988). Arguments for Pama-Nyungan as a genetic subgroup, with particular reference to initial laminalization. *Aboriginal Linguistics, 1,* 90–110.

Evans, N. (2005). Australian languages reconsidered: A review of Dixon (2002). *Oceanic Linguistics, 44,* 242–286.

Fairbridge, R. W. (1961). Eustatic changes in sea level. *Physics and Chemistry of the Earth, 4,* 99–185.

Flood, J. (1995). *Archaeology of the Dreamtime.* Sydney: Angus & Robertson.

Florin, S. A., Fairbairn, A. S., Nango, M., Djandjomerr, D., Marwick, B., Fullagar, R., Smith, M., Wallis, L. A., & Clarkson, C. (2020). The first Australian plant foods at Madjedbebe, 65,000–53,000 years ago. *Nature Communications, 11*(924), 1–8.

Frederikse, T., Landerer, F., Caron, L., Adhikari, S., Parkes, D., Humphrey, V. W., Dangendorf, S., Hogarth, P., Zanna, L., Cheng, L., & Wu, Y. H. (2020). The causes of sea-level rise since 1900. *Nature, 584*(7821), 393–397.

Fysh, H. (1933). *Taming the north.* Sydney: Angus & Robertson.

Goody, J., & Watt, I. ([1963] 1968). The consequences of literacy. In J. Goody (Ed.), *Literacy in traditional societies* (pp. 1–27). Cambridge: Cambridge University Press.

Grele, R. J. (1996). Directions for oral history in the United States. In D. K. Dunaway & W. K. Baum (Eds.), *Oral history* (pp. 62–84). Walnut Creek, CA: Altamira Press.

Haddon, A. C. (Ed.) (1901–1935). *Reports of the Cambridge Anthropological Expedition to Torres Straits.* Vols. 1–5. Cambridge: Cambridge University Press.

Hercus, L. A. (1980). How we danced the Mudlunga. *Aboriginal History, 4*(1), 4–32.

Hercus, L. A., & Sutton, P. (Eds.) (1986). *This is what happened.* Canberra: Australian Institute of Aboriginal Studies.

Hiatt, L. R. (1996). *Arguments about Aborigines.* Cambridge: Cambridge University Press.

Hill, J. (2015). Violent encounters. In J. G. Cusick (Ed.), *Studies in culture contact* (pp. 139–161). Center for Archaeological Investigations, Occasional Paper No. 25. Carbondale: Southern Illinois University Press.

Hiscock, P., & Faulkner, P. (2006). Dating the Dreaming? *Cambridge Archaeological Journal, 16*(2), 209–222.

Irene, J. F. de J. (2005). Convention versus realism in the Homeric epics. *Mnemosyne, 58*(1), 1–22.

Irvine, T., & Dixon, R. M. W. (1991). *Words of our country.* St. Lucia: University of Queensland Press.

Irwin, G. J. (1978). Pots and entrepôts. *World Archaeology, 9*(3), 299–319.

Joyce, R. A. (2008). *The languages of archaeology.* John Wiley & Sons.

Kearney, A., Brady, L. M., & Bradley, J. (2018). A place of substance: Stories of Indigenous place meaning in the southwest Gulf of Carpentaria, Northern Australia. *Journal of Anthropological Research, 74*(3), 360–387.

Keen, I. (2003). Aboriginal economy and society at the threshold of colonisation. *Before Farming, 3*(2), 1–24.

Keen, I. (2004). *Aboriginal economy and society.* Melbourne: Oxford University Press.

Knight, J. R. (2003). *Testing Tindale tribes* (PhD thesis). University of New England, Armidale.

Lambeck, K., & Chappell, J. (2001). Sea level change through the Last Glacial cycle. *Science, 292*(5517), 679–686.

Landau, M. (1984). Human evolution as narrative. *American Scientist, 72*(3), 262–268.

Landau, M. (1993). *Narratives of human evolution.* New Haven, CT: Yale University Press.

Landtman, G. (1917). *The folk-tales of the Kiwai Papuans.* Acta Societatis Scientiarium Fennicae 47. Helsingfors: Finnish Society of Literature.

Lawrie, M. (1970). *Myths and legends of Torres Strait.* St Lucia: University of Queensland Press.

Lewis, D. (2017). Megafauna identification for dummies. *Rock Art Research, 34*(1), 82–99.

Malinowski, B. (1915). The natives of Mailu. *Transactions and Proceedings of the Royal Society of South Australia, 39,* 494–706.

McBryde, I. (1987). Goods from another country: Exchange networks and the people of the Lake Eyre basin. In D. J. Mulvaney & J. P. White (Eds.), *Australians to 1788* (pp. 252–273). Sydney: Fairfax, Syme & Weldon.

McCarthy, F. D. (1939). 'Trade' in Aboriginal Australia, and 'trade' relationships with Torres Strait, New Guinea and Malaya. *Oceania*, 9(4), 405–439, 10(1), 80–104, 10(2), 171–195.

McConvell, P., & Bowern, C. (2011). The prehistory and internal relationships of Australian languages. *Language and Linguistics Compass*, 5(1), 19–32.

McNiven, I. J. (2016). Ethnoarchaeology, epistemology, ethics. *World Archaeology*, 48(5), 683–686.

McNiven, I. J, & Russell, L. (2005). *Appropriated pasts*. Lanham, MD: Altamira Press.

Minc, L. D. (1986). Scarcity and survival. *Journal of Anthropological Archaeology*, 5, 39–113.

Morphy, H. (1991). *Ancestral connections*. Chicago: University of Chicago Press.

Morphy, H., & Morphy, F. (1984). The 'myths' of Ngalakan history. *Man*, 19(3), 459–478.

Morphy, H., & Morphy, F. (2006). Tasting the waters. *Journal of Material Culture*, 11(1–2), 67–85.

Moshenska, G. (2010). Working with memory in the archaeology of modern conflict. *Cambridge Archaeological Journal*, 20(1), 33–48.

Mulvaney, D. J. (1976). 'The chain of connection'. In N. Peterson (Ed.), *Tribes and boundaries in Australia* (pp. 72–94). Canberra: Australian Institute of Aboriginal Studies.

Mulvaney, D. J., Morphy, H., & Petch, A. (Eds.) (1997). *My dear Spencer*. Melbourne: Hyland House.

Myers, F. R. (1986). *Pintupi country, Pintubi self*. Canberra: Australian Institute of Aboriginal Studies.

Neale, M. (Ed.) (2017). *Songlines: Tracking the Seven Sisters*. Canberra: National Museum of Australia Press.

Neale, M., & Kelly, L. (Eds.) (2020). *Songlines. The power and the promise*. Melbourne: Thames & Hudson.

Nunn, P. D. (2018). *The edge of memory*. London: Bloomsbury.

Nunn, P. D., & Reid, N. J. (2015). Aboriginal memories of inundation of the Australian coast dating from more than 7000 years ago. *Australian Geographer*, 47(1), 1–37.

Organ, M. (1994). Australian Aboriginal Dreaming stories. *Aboriginal History*, 18(1/2), 123–144.

Parker, K. L. (2001). *Australian legendary tales*. London: The Folklore Society.

Pawley, A (2007). Recent research on the historical relationships of the Papuan languages, or, what does linguistics say about the prehistory of Melanesia. In J. S. Friedlaender (Ed.), *Genes, language, and culture history in the Southwest Pacific* (pp. 36–58). Oxford: Oxford University Press.

Perks, R., & Thomson, A. (1998). Introduction. In R. Perks & A. Thomson (Eds.), *The oral history reader* (pp. ix–xiii). London: Routledge.

Phillips, J. (2012). Storytelling in Earth sciences. *Earth-Science Reviews*, 115(3), 153–162.

Pillans, B., Chappell, J., & Naish, T. R. (1998). A review of the Milankovitch climatic beat. *Sedimentary Geology*, 122(1–4), 5–21.

Plomley, N. J. B. (Ed.) (1971). *Friendly mission: The Tasmanian journals and papers of George Augustus Robinson 1829–1834. A supplement*. Hobart: Tasmanian Historical Research Association.

Porr, M., & Matthews, J. (Eds.) (2020). *Interrogating human origins*. London: Routledge.

Roberts, A. L., Mollenmans, A., Rigney, L.-I., & Bailey, G. (2020), Marine Transgression, Aboriginal narratives and the creation of Yorke Peninsula/Guuranda, South Australia. *The Journal of Island and Coastal Archaeology*, 15(3), 305–332.

Rose, D. B. (1984). The saga of Captain Cook. *Australian Aboriginal Studies*, 2, 24–39.

Rose, D. B. (1994). Ned Kelly died for our sins. *Oceania*, 65(2), 175–186.

Rose, D. B. (1996). *Nourishing terrains*. Canberra: Australian Heritage Commission.

Ross, J., & Davidson, I. (2006). Rock art and ritual. *Journal of Archaeological Method and Theory*, 13(4), 305–341.

Roth, H. L. (1899). *The Aborigines of Tasmania*. Second edition. Halifax, England: F. King & Sons.

Roth, W. E. (1897). *Ethnological studies among the North-West-Central Queensland Aborigines*. Brisbane: Government Printer.

Roth, W. E. (1904). *Domestic implements, arts, and manufactures*. North Queensland Ethnography, Bulletin No 7. Brisbane: Home Secretary's Department.

Sharpe, M., & Tunbridge, D. (2003). Traditions of extinct animals, changing sea-levels and volcanoes among Australian Aboriginals. In R. Blench & M. Spriggs (Eds.), *Archaeology and language I* (pp. 345–361). London: Routledge.

Sims, P. (2013). No reprieve for Tasmanian rock art. *Arts*, 2(4), 182–224.

Smith, M. (2017). The metaphysics of songlines. In M. Neale (Ed.), *Songlines: Tracking the Seven Sisters* (pp. 216–221). Canberra: National Museum of Australia Press.

Spencer, W. B., & Gillen, F. J. (1899). *Native tribes of Central Australia*. London: Macmillan.

Stanner, W. E. H. (1979a). Religion, totemism and symbolism (1962). In W. E. H. Stanner (Ed.), *White man got no Dreaming* (pp. 106–143). Canberra: Australian National University Press.

Stanner, W. E. H. (1979b). The Dreaming (1953). In W. E. H. Stanner (Ed.), *White man got no Dreaming* (pp. 23–40). Canberra: Australian National University Press.

Sullivan, D. (c. 1994). *English, Kalkadoon illustrated language book*. Mt. Isa: Kalkadoon Language Prints.

Sullivan, L. (c. 2005). *Ngiaka Yalarrnga*. Townsville: Lance Sullivan.

Sutton, P. (1995). *Country*. Aboriginal History Monograph Series 4. Canberra: Aboriginal History.

Sutton, P. (2009). *The politics of suffering*. Melbourne: Melbourne University Press.

Sutton, S. A., Paton, D., Buergelt, P., Sagala, S., & Meilianda, E. (2020). Sustaining a transformative disaster risk reduction strategy. *International Journal of Environmental Research and Public Health*, 17(21), 7764.

Thomson, A. (2011). Memory and remembering in oral history. In D. A. Ritchie (Ed.), *The Oxford handbook of oral history* (pp. 77–95). Oxford: Oxford University Press.

Tibbett, K. (2001). Thesis abstract. Stone axe trade and exchange on an inland sea: An archaeological and petrological analysis of stone axe exchange networks in the Lake Eyre Basin. *Australian Archaeology*, 52, 66.

Tibbett, K. (2003). Hammer dressed stone hatchets in the Lake Eyre Basin. *Archaeology in Oceania*, 38(1), 37–40.

Tonkinson, R. (1974). *The Jigalong mob*. Menlo Park, CA: Cummings.

Tonkinson, R. (1978). *The Mardudjara*. New York: Holt, Rinehart & Winston.

Urwin, C., Hua, Q., & Arifeae, H. (2021). Combining oral traditions and Bayesian chronological modelling to understand village development in the Gulf of Papua (Papua New Guinea). *Radiocarbon*, 63(2), 647–667.

Vansina, J. (1985). *Oral tradition as history*. Madison: University of Wisconsin Press.

Vansina, J. (1973). *Oral tradition*. Translated by H. M. Wright. London: Routledge & Keegan Paul.

Warner, W. L. ([1937] 1964). *A black civilization*. New York: Harper Torchbooks.

West, P. (2005). Holding the story forever. *Anthropological Forum, 15*(3), 267–275.

West, P. (2006). *Conservation is our government now.* Durham, NC: Duke University Press.

Wiessner, P., & Tumu, A. (1998). *Historical vines: Enga networks of exchange, ritual, and warfare in Papua New Guinea.* Washington, DC: Smithsonian Institution Press.

Williams, A. N., Ulm, S., Sapienza, T., Lewis, S., & Turney, C. S. (2018). Sea-level change and demography during the last glacial termination and early Holocene across the Australian continent. *Quaternary Science Reviews, 182,* 144–154.

Wobst, H. M. (1978). The archaeo-ethnology of hunter-gatherers or the tyranny of the ethnographic record in archaeology. *American Antiquity, 43*(2), 303–309.

Wolfe, P. (1991). On being woken up. *Comparative Studies in Society and History, 33*(2), 197–224.

Yengoyan, A. A. (1968). Demographic and ecological influences on Aboriginal marriage sections. In R. B. Lee & I. DeVore (Eds.), *Man the hunter* (pp. 185–199). Chicago: Aldine.

Yokoyama, Y., Purcell, A., Lambeck, K., & Johnston, P. (2001). Shore-line reconstruction around Australia during the Last Glacial Maximum and Late Glacial Stage. *Quaternary International, 83–85,* 9–18.

CHAPTER 7

MUSEUM COLLECTIONS AND THEIR LEGACIES

LINDY ALLEN

INTRODUCTION

MUSEUMS worldwide have vast holdings of Indigenous collections, including an estimated 250,000 organic objects from Australian Indigenous people (Jones 2007: 5). Museums also hold an extraordinarily larger number of objects from across the Pacific and an inestimable quantity of stone artefacts and archaeological assemblage material. These collections have been a fundamental component of the research practice of material culture and technology, especially within the fields of archaeology and anthropology (e.g., Allen 2020; Allen 2011; Allen & Akerman 2015; Allen, Babister, Bonshek, & Goodall 2018; Attenbrow 2010; Chaloupka & Guiliani 2005; Hamby 2011; Holdaway & Stern 2004; Langley, Lister, Wright, & May 2018; Wesley & Lister 2015; Wright, Langley, May, Johnson, & Allen 2016). Furthermore, since the 1970s, these collections have been an active and pivotal point of reference for Indigenous people and source communities seeking their cultural patrimony (Peers & Brown 2003: 1). This chapter considers the fundamental importance of museum collections and their legacies in this context, and investigates how the application of an Indigenous lens to, and a critical analysis of, what are perceived as essentially 'hollow' or 'empty' forms has seen new life and meanings breathed into collections. The intention is to provide a nuanced understanding of the complexities associated with museum collections and the multidimensional nature of the engagement of Indigenous people with their cultural patrimony. This engagement has contributed to reshaping and reframing the enduring legacies of museum collections. Moreover, the collections have gained a potency and agency in the present that has the capacity to exert significant influence into the future.

A paradigm shift in museums in Australia emerged as a consequence of Indigenous activism in the 1970s (see Bolton 2003; Edwards & Stewart 1980; Kelly & Gordon 2003).[1] This shift saw a recalibration of the moral horizon in museums marked by the inclusion rather than the exclusion of Indigenous people. This moral and ethical imperative was enshrined in major policy frameworks and documents of the peak museum industry bodies, such as *Continuous Cultures, Ongoing Responsibilities* (Museums Australia 2005) and its predecessor, *Previous Possessions, New Obligations* (Council of Australian Museum Associations 1993; see also Griffin 1996). These documents resulted in a 'national policy framework to provide consistency in guiding the development of partnerships between museums and Indigenous people' (Kelly & Gordon 2003: 163). The paradigm shift developed as a global phenomenon with legislative changes in the United States such as the National American Graves Protection and Repatriation Act (NAGPRA) 1990 and the National Museum of the American Indian Act 1989. Other changes with relevance to museum-based practice included the World Archaeological Congress (WAC) adopting a Code of Ethics in 1990 that acknowledged 'obligations to indigenous peoples', as well as the Vermillion Accord on Human Remains in 1989 and the Tamaki Makau-rau Accord on the Display of Human Remains and Sacred Objects in 2005 (see https://worldarc.org/code-of-ethics; Phillips & Allen 2010).

'De-centering the West' is at the heart of current global calls to 'decolonize museums', refocusing and re-centering attention on the questions of who owns the past and who has the right to interpret the past (e.g., Clifford 2013; Hicks 2020). However, this decolonizing discourse often gives little or no acknowledgment to previous generations of activists who effected changes in museums over decades. These changes included commitments to prioritizing Indigenous voices in the interpretation and management of collections, the appointment of Indigenous curators and directors throughout Australia and the Pacific, and collaborations between Indigenous communities and museums in establishing cultural centres and keeping places (e.g., Gordon 1981; Phillips 2003; Museums Victoria 2021; Poll 2020; Sculthorpe 1989; Edwards & Stewart 1980). The major museum developments of the late 1990s and early 2000s that foregrounded Indigenous narratives and curation and co-curation in exhibitions include Te Papa Tongarewa in Wellington, New Zealand, the Bunjilaka Aboriginal Centre at Melbourne Museum, and the National Museum of Australia in Canberra that opened in 1998, 2000, and 2001, respectively (see Message 2006; Museum Victoria 2000). Art historian and curator Ruth Phillips (2005) coined the term 'the second museum age' to capture what had, by the new millennium, become a global movement.

Giving primacy to Indigenous ontologies and decolonizing narratives are global trends (see Archibald, Xiiem, Lee-Morgan, & De Santolo 2019; Moreton-Robinson 2015), with the issue of decolonizing well embedded in broader issues of sovereignty and treaty-making in Australia. These issues have been embraced by the broader GLAM sector within Australia;[2] peak industry bodies have responded, and the reforms they seek herald the arrival of what might be described as a 'third museum age'. The Australian Museums and Galleries Association (AMaGA) released its *Indigenous Roadmap* (Janke 2018) and now has on-line programs, training, and webinars available for its members. Similarly, the United Kingdom's Museums Association (n.d.) has an on-line 'decolonising kit' that addresses 'why it's time to disrupt the dominant and excluding museum narratives'. Yet, museums remain the primary target for the 'decolonizing' narrative, their collections constituting visible, viable, and compelling evidence of the sovereignty of Indigenous people. The discourse often casts museums as embedded in their colonial pasts, reticent and intransigent in handing over authority to Indigenous people. That is, museums are seen as operating as they did in the nineteenth and early twentieth centuries when collections were developed for posterity and for future generations. In this old guise, the interests of the broader public were paramount and devoid of any social conscience or moral compass regarding the concerns and aspirations of the descendants of those from whom the collections came. That 'future generations' might be descendants of the individuals from whom these things came originally 'was undoubtedly inconceivable at the time collections were assembled' (Peers & Brown 2003: 1). Anthropology, one of the Western canons of museums, is also a target for this discourse, seen 'as the epitome of arrogant, intrusive colonial authority [whose] scientific authority [is] understood as modes of colonial domination from the other side of the structural power imbalance' (Clifford 2013: 213).

The intention here is not to dismiss the claims or positions taken in relation to 'decolonising museums', but rather to broaden the discussion regarding Indigenous people engaging with their cultural patrimony in museums. As Harrison, Byrne, and Clark (2013: 5) note, the aim is to move 'beyond what could be interpreted as an asymmetrical and broadly neocolonial engagement [and] develop new models for understanding the networks of social and material interactions that center on the space of the museum collection'. This chapter moves beyond the discourse of museums as 'contact zones' and 'sites of friction' (see Clifford 1997; Karp, Kratz, Szwaja, & Ybarra-Frausto 2006) and focuses more on how museums operate as sites of 'persuasion' (Morphy 2006) and places of 'hybrid possibilities and political negotiation' (Clifford 1997: 213). In doing so, the paper builds on the work of similar-minded researchers (e.g., Bolton 2003; Clifford 1997, 2013; Golding & Modest 2013; Gosden & Knowles 2001; Harrison et al. 2010; Harrison, Byrne, & Clark 2013; Herle 2003; Horwood 2019; Karp, Kratz, Szwaja, & Ybarra-Frausto 2006; Peers & Brown 2003; Sandell 2003; Sleeper-Smith 2009).

This chapter seeks to re-center the decolonizing discourse to look at the interventions that have led to museum collections being reenvisioned, repositioned, and reactivated in the present and for posterity, particularly through the engagement of Indigenous people with their cultural patrimony. These interventions involve a sensitive and critical approach to reframing and scrutinizing collections—deconstructing, reconnecting, and reassembling dispersed elements within and between museums, and disentangling the artificial layers of 'noise' that disguise their essential nature and histories (see Thomas 1991, 2018; Hamby 2008; Harrison, Byrne, & Clark 2013; Allen & Hamby 2016; Nugent & Sculthorpe 2018; Torrence, Bonshek, Clark, Davies, Philp, & Quinnell 2020). These interventions combine to return the essence or 'feelings' that archaeologist Denis Byrne identifies as missing in relation to Australia's immovable cultural heritage. He notes that an absence of Indigenous people in interpreting cultural sites devalues 'social context, past and present, hollows it out and deforms it [such that] what you are left with are things minus feeling' (2008: 231). This sentiment equally applies to the nation's moveable cultural heritage, much of which resides in museums. Without such interventions, museum collections remain, like cultural sites, essentially and effectively isolated from any context within which their broader significance might be understood.

While privileging Indigenous pedagogies, the new curatorial 'praxis' that began emerging in museums in the late 1970s has been a collaborative, cross-cultural, and, at times, cross-disciplinary venture, with the sharing of 'skills, knowledge and power to produce something of value to both parties' (Peers & Brown 2003:4) (see also Allen & Hamby 2010; Bolton 2003; Chan 2019; Clifford 1997, 2013; Golding & Modest 2013; Gosden & Knowles 2001; Harrison, Byrne, & Clark 2013; Herle 2003; Horwood 2019; Sleeper-Smith 2009; Stanton 2011). This new praxis should not, however, be read as museums retaining power and authority, or as paternalistic patronage, or maintaining control and acting as 'gate-keepers'. Alternatively, museums are effective collaborators and partners in this cross-cultural space.

This model of collaboration sits in stark contrast to the essentially partisan approaches championed by proponents of the decolonizing discourse, while recognizing that the authority of Indigenous people is critical to reassembling and reinterpreting collections within culturally appropriate pedagogies. The legacy of separating and systematizing collections according to the Western museological canons of the past—science, archaeology, anthropology, and ethnography—is, however, pervasive, and significantly compromises the endeavors of source communities whose interests are in *all* things associated with their Old People, their country, and their history. In contrast to classic museological practice, Indigenous people make no ontological distinction between organic artefacts and stone tools that would require them to be stored and managed separately. This separation within museums is founded on the assumption that stone tools are generally considered to come from the distant past and that organic artefacts are thought to be relevant to the more recent past. To Indigenous people, their connection to place is the context, not time. In contrast, Western researchers see organic and lithic artefacts as incommensurably different ontological and epistemological domains. The consequence of these distinctions is that cultural links between different classes of objects are missed, ignored, or not even considered as relevant to Indigenous people by museums.

These inherent complexities are perhaps the least understood aspect of museum collections and pose the greatest challenges for Indigenous people engaging with their cultural patrimony. Collections require decoding and deciphering, and even recoding in order to render them comprehensible to Indigenous people. For many museum objects, any threads of original documentation or context as to their histories and context will have been obscured or removed entirely through the imposition of institutional schema and their dispersal within museums. Such decontextualization is often worse for those objects obtained through exchanges between other museums and even private collectors. The systemization of collections according to 'types', with little or no relevance to Indigenous pedagogies, and the propensity of museums to 'habitually reinvent cataloguing systems'[3] have resulted in multiple generations of cataloguing systems adding layer upon layer of complexities and obscuring any original context, meanings, and histories or associations and connections between objects.

Untangling these layers of disassociation is generally beyond the remit (and responsibility) of Indigenous people. Much like the process of an archaeological excavation, the process of reassociation is painstaking and necessitates specific expertise and methodologies, drawing particularly on the curatorial experiences and disciplinary knowledge of museum staff who know the idiosyncrasies of generations of museum cataloguing systems (see Attenbrow 2010; Attenbrow & Cartwright 2014; Harrison, Torrence, Byrne, & Clark 2010; Harrison, Byrne, & Clark 2013; Herle 2003; Karp, Kratz, Szwaja, & Ybarra-Frausto 2006; Nugent & Sculthorpe 2018; Peers & Brown 2003, 2015; Peterson, Allen, & Hamby 2008; Thomas 2018; Torrence et al. 2020). This positioning should not, however, be read as museums retaining power and authority, but rather as taking responsibility to address what are otherwise 'hollow' and 'deformed' entities. In many cases, objects carry hints or traces in their fabrication, form, and materials that to an informed eye can assert particular contexts, meanings, and significance within culturally appropriate pedagogies. As will be shown below, even with little or no recovery of any semblance of a history or context, object collections can be framed within a broader history of collecting or positioned as evidence and reminders of colonial domination.

The Impact of Collecting and Museum Practices on Collections

The pivotal starting point for any dialogue and engagement with museums for Indigenous people is having confidence that they are seeing all relevant collections. This is difficult given the nature of museum collection cataloging systems and the complexities involved in validating object records. As noted above, multiple factors contribute to obscuring the origin and significance of many objects, in particular the absence or disassociation of 'original' documentation together with the consequences of the systemization of collections according to Western pedagogies. As a rule, the older the collection, the more likely it will have been subjected to systematic reordering multiple times. Recovering the threads of the histories and origins of objects can also involve interrogating the motivations and biases of collectors. Peterson, Allen, and Hamby (2008: 2) note that objects are 'sometimes gathered in an encounter measured only in minutes and shaped by the choices made by the collectors about what to collect, [along with] . . . the decisions made by Aboriginal people about what to relinquish, and to their lived experience at the time'. Museum collections inherently exhibit a predominance of certain 'types' of objects that caught the interest and imagination of collectors, be it weapons collected by male amateur collectors or stone tools avidly sought by and exchanged amongst the 'antiquarian' collectors of the 'Victorian stone circle' during the nineteenth and early twentieth centuries (Griffiths 1996: 66; Russell 2001).

Further layers of complexities relate to the history of the dispersal of collections (often through exchange with other museums and private collectors) during the nineteenth and early twentieth centuries (see Cochrane & Quanchi 2011; Griffiths 1996; Hamby 2008; Leo 2008; O'Hanlon & Welsch 2004; Sloggett 2016; Torrence & Clark 2016; Torrence et al. 2020). Although multiple numbers and codes on objects are the key indicator of such histories, often little or no information accompanies these numbers, making it almost impossible to trace their origins. Those objects in collections considered 'duplicates' were a particular focus for intermuseum exchanges, with the global networks of exchange enabling museums to develop world-class ethnographic and natural science collections. Groups of objects without any original documentation or history are often classed as 'orphan' collections or 'orphan' objects. As such, they rarely receive serious attention, and so they are relegated to the class of 'unprovenanced' and are essentially put into the 'too hard basket' and ignored.

The historical neglect of so-called orphan collections and objects renders them virtually invisible as they are rarely shown to Indigenous people or researchers visiting museums. This neglect can contribute to the harm Indigenous people feel in relation to museums, as the absence of object information is often a source of disquiet and distrust. Although making objects (not of a secret/sacred nature) available on-line could ameliorate this potential distrust, few museum collections are accessible in this way. Waanji artist Judy Watson and Palawa archaeologist, artist, and scholar Julie Gough have both undertaken extensive research on museum collections in Australia and overseas, with Gough describing her experiences of viewing objects as being a 'quietly conducted, reunion with objects . . .like a monitored prison visit' (2016: 90). Gough (2016: 90) adds:

> [T]here is no one fixed Indigenous position on museums. Immersion at [the Museum of Archaeology and Anthropology, University of Cambridge] propelled me from an anxiety about the overwhelming excess of collections toward working out what can be undertaken personally. . . . From accessing, withdrawing, making and re-entering the museum to exhibit my response, I feel part of a positive movement—empowered to actively encourage others to access their objects.

Unfortunately, at a broad level, the opportunity to browse collections and discover has been curtailed significantly as museums adhere to strict risk-averse protocols for accessing their storerooms.

REFRAMING ARCHAEOLOGICAL AND LITHIC COLLECTIONS

Interest in stone artefact collections by Gough and many other Indigenous people sits in stark contrast to the consideration given to such collections by museums. These collections are generally given little or no attention and, in fact, are seriously neglected. Such neglect is common in museums across the world, which archaeologist Terry Childs attributes to the challenges of 'lack of storage space for new and existing collections, insufficient professional staff to manage collections, and inadequate funding to support good preservation and access to collections, rising collections and increasing numbers of orphan collections' (Childs 2011: 19). As a result, many Indigenous people are discontented with museums, given that these collections are viewed as critical markers of their ancestors who left these stone tools on the ground surface when passing through their country. Gough (2018: 49) notes:

> Walking in Tasmania my heart leaps when I see objects handmade by our Old People, resting where they put them; I am then walking in their path. But these are rare to find today unless you go right off the beaten track. Others beat me there, to ship more than 15,000 Tasmanian stone tools to museums around the world.[4]

For Gough, viewing stone artefacts from Tasmania in the Museum of Archaeology and Anthropology (MAA) at the University of Cambridge was particularly poignant. It resulted in Gough's *The Lost World (Part 2)* project, where she photographed thirty-five of these stone artefacts and visited sites or vicinities where they were collected. Gough (2016: 49) explains that filming their 'return . . . [and the] response to our exiled objects reconnected me with Country'. Furthermore, Gough attempted to 'return' and reconnect these objects to place in a very unexpected way in the exhibition at the MAA in 2013 by including a live webcam feed of the stone tools on display to the Contemporary Art Tasmania Gallery in north Hobart:

> I realized that the sound of the places where I 'returned' the photographs of the artefacts should be an intrinsic component of the outcome. Sound promised something real, albeit intangible, to the captive stone tools, in a manner of a 'return'. I installed the artefacts in a cabinet adjacent to a window blind onto which the film work was projected. This proximity enabled the artefacts to hear the contemporary captured at the places where they had been removed generations ago.
>
> (Gough 2016: 61)

Stone artefacts, more so than other objects in museums, tend to have the names of the places where they were collected written onto their 'bodies'; these notations being the most obvious remnants of cataloguing systems of various museum and often private collectors. However, Watson (2014: 3) identifies this inscription as an act of 'vandalism, a sacrilege, and infliction of control by another, dominating culture'. She feels the 'tattooing of numbers and scarification of labels onto objects in some way takes away from their natural beauty and form. It diminishes them to be curiosities within a museum. They are a token from another, stranger culture. Not able to exist for themselves or their people, they are branded and assigned to a forlorn existence within the holding collection' (Watson 2014: 2). Watson (2014: 1) further observes that 'by writing onto the object, the collector asserts their ownership and authority, stamping it onto the cultural item [and] can be read as a form of colonization, sterilization and desecration'. However, while museums are dogged by vast numbers of objects devoid of any documentation or related material and contextual information, inscriptions on stone artefacts are often the only clues to their provenance and history. These 'tattoos' provide clues for exploring connections to museums and to collectors, and hopefully then back to the places where they were collected, thus maximizing the potential of being linked directly to source communities.

VISITING COLLECTIONS, VISITING ANCESTORS

The 'museum' for those Indigenous people and source communities seeking their cultural property and patrimony centres on the storerooms where they encounter the collections directly face-to-face. In this way, the 'museum' becomes a field site where Indigenous people turn attention on themselves, thus subverting the 'ethnographic gaze' (Fienup-Riordan 2003; Herle 2003). At its broadest reading, this cultural patrimony 'represents the discontinuity with their own history and cultural practices wrought by the intrusions of colonisation' (Nakata 2001). As is evident in the previous discussion of the experiences of Judy Watson and Julie Gough, exposure to museum collections is, in itself, confronting for many Indigenous people. Most Indigenous people will have little or no idea of what they will see or find, how they will feel, or even how they will be received by curators. Entering the storeroom can be overwhelming, with row upon row of objects on shelves, in cabinets, boxes, and crates, some perhaps stacked to the ceiling requiring navigation of what could be described as the 'motherload'[5] of Indigenous cultural capital from across the globe. The profound silence of the space is broken only by 'noise' emanating from the objects that are heard or sensed by the visitors who are listening and looking hard for familiar forms or 'faces'. The experience can also be unsettling for many Indigenous people with the anticipation of not recognizing their own objects or people, or of being in proximity or exposed to objects they should not see. Such exposure includes objects belonging to their customary neighbours, enemies, or total strangers on the other side of the world, who cannot provide the permissions or appropriate cultural protocols to ensure cultural protection and safety to all in this space during face-to-face encounters.

Anthropologist Diane Hafner (2010: 265) explains how these collections can provoke mixed feelings during visits to the storerooms:

> Both objects and images reveal the connections between individuals and aspects of their past . . . certain images or objects will interest some people more than others; they may provoke differing emotional responses; some may engage personal memory and knowledge in ways that others do not. Thus engaging with the museum objects is fraught with multiple potentialities for people such as the Lamalama. While the process has been overwhelmingly positive, the seemingly simple act of

touching and looking at the Thomson materials inevitably involves some confrontation with the sometimes painful circumstances of their history.

The Lamalama are sandbeach people from southeastern Cape York Peninsula in north Queensland. They have made several pilgrimages over three decades to see the Donald Thomson Collection at Museums Victoria in Melbourne,[6] working with the author and Hafner, and, for a much longer time, with anthropologist and linguist, Professor Bruce Rigsby. Their quest was to recover their past from the photographs taken by, and the objects collected by, the anthropologist Donald Thomson in the late 1920s and early 1930s. A dugong rope was a particularly poignant signifier for the Lamalama and their identity as 'Dugong Hunters of Cape York' (see Thomson 1934), but more so, because the man he most likely acquired it from, Harry Liddy (1903–c.1970), is an iconic figure for the Lamalama. In 1963, Liddy attempted the 400 km walk overland from Bamaga (at the tip of Cape York Peninsula) back to Port Stewart from where he and his countrymen were removed by the Queensland government in 1961 (see Rigsby & Jolly 1994). The Queensland government deceived the Lamalama into thinking that they were being moved temporarily to Bamaga for medical treatment, but instead the move was permanent so that pastoralists could take up leases on their country around Princess Charlotte Bay. As they boarded the government launch for Bamaga, their houses were burned and their dogs shot.

Thomson collected the dugong rope, no doubt a very rare, precious, and symbolic object for the Old People at Port Stewart, and one they felt was important to part with for posterity (see Jones 2018b). These ropes would not be easily replaced, as a significant amount of fibre must be procured from the inner bark of the hibiscus plant, and then beaten, shredded, and plied into rope (as recorded photographically by Thomson). This rope would have been made for Harry Liddy by the one Old Man with the appropriate skills, expertise, and responsibility. Harry Liddy can be seen with other senior Port Stewart men in photographs taken by Thomson of the butchering of a dugong prior to the distribution of the meat to families. When Harry left Bamaga, he carried with him his dugong rope, a most critical part of his identity as a dugong hunter. For Lamalama community members visiting the museum, encountering the rope triggered the retelling of Harry Liddy's story, which continues to loom large in the minds of Lamalama. Karen Liddy says, 'Every week my grandparents would try to walk home . . . [and in 1964] my grandfather died of a broken heart' (Davies & Earl 2018). 'In a letter to a white friend, [Harry Liddy] lamented that he had been hunted down "like a kangaroo" with dogs and taken back to Bamaga by the police and trackers' (Rigsby & Jolly 1994: 619). This story resides within this dugong rope and is inextricably linked to this one Old Man from Port Stewart, the senior dugong man and last clan leader for that mob when they still lived on their country. For the Lamalama, the rope symbolizes Harry Liddy and all of the Old People at Port Stewart in the late 1920s who remained on this last vestige of their traditional country around the southeastern coast of Princess Charlotte Bay where dugong live and feed.

In the late 1980s, Lamalama Elders who were only a generation removed from the Old People from whom the objects in the Donald Thomson Collection were derived and who appear in Thomson's photographs, left Bamaga and moved back to Port Stewart to establish an outstation, Moojeeba. Seeing the Donald Thomson Collection was amongst the highest priorities at the time for Lamalama Elder, Sunlight Bassani, who was the key driver in securing title to parcels of land within their clan estates in Princess Charlotte Bay (under Queensland's Aboriginal Land Act 1991 and the Commonwealth's Native Title Act 1993). Lamalama cultural patrimony in this collection was a critical element in legally proving their connections to country (see Allen 2016; Allen & Hamby 2010; Hafner 2010; Hafner, Rigsby, & Allen 2007; Rigsby, Allen, & Hafner 2015). Sunlight Bassani highlighted the importance of the Donald Thomson Collection in his correspondence with the Queensland Department of Aboriginal Affairs in January 1990, where he sought funding for Lamalama Elders to travel to Melbourne to visit the museum:

> Professor Donald Thomson first visited our old people at Port Stewart in 1928, and his Collection includes many photographs, notes and artefacts, such as spears, fish nets and a Bora mask. The Lamalama people would like to see these items and learn more about our old people and their history. We believe that this information can help the Lamalama people strengthen their position with respect to gaining some form of secure title to their country around Port Stewart.
>
> (Bassani 1990: 1)

Within weeks of sending this letter, Sunlight and his wife Florrie Bassani (Harry Liddy's daughter), together with Bobby and Daisy Stewart, travelled to Melbourne to see the Donald Thomson Collection.[7] They were accompanied by three younger Lamalama people, a strategy that Sunlight repeated in the six subsequent visits made over the next twenty or so years. Building on the Elders' knowledge of the 'proper Lamalama way', and drawing on the cultural capital embedded in the Port Stewart material in the Donald Thomson Collection to fill in gaps caused by their enforced relocation to the tip of Cape York, was Sunlight's vision for 'future proofing' the maintenance of cultural knowledge and practice. These visits with younger people laid the foundation for 'growing up' the next generation of Lamalama leaders. These leaders include Gavin Bassani and Alison Liddy, who participated in the first Lamalama visit to Melbourne in February 1990 and who, with others, take responsibility for the collection and also for caring for their country through the Indigenous Land and Sea Ranger program (see Davies & Earl 2018). Photographs of their Old People on country taken by Donald Thomson, which were central to the taking of oral evidence in land claims, are now part of a Lamalama curated display at the Ranger Station Visitor Centre at the Moojeba outstation at Port Stewart.

Reconnecting Collections and Recovering Legacies

Visiting collections in a museum, either located far from source communities or dispersed across multiple institutions globally, presents major logistical and financial challenges for many Indigenous people. An earlier and largely overlooked example is that of the Gogodala of the lower Fly River in the Western Province of Papua New Guinea (PNG), whose cultural patrimony was located in twenty museums across eight countries, little having survived in PNG itself (see Crawford 1981). In the early 1970s, the PNG National Cultural Council (NCC) sponsored a project to find and document this distributed material. At the same time, the NCC developed and built the Gogodala Cultural Centre at Balimo 'to house, preserve, and promote art and cultural activities of these lagoon dwellers' (Crawford 1980: 13).[8] The Gogodala did not visit museums, nor were collections physically returned or repatriated to them; instead, they worked with the extensive documentation sourced and collated by Tony Crawford. These collections proved to be the singular inspiration for an extraordinary cultural transformation and revival of practices absent for decades; their sacred objects and other paraphernalia inside the men's house having been burned by missionaries in the 1930s. As anthropologist Marilyn Strathern (1981: 11) observed, 'Tracing records of every Gogodala artifact known from museums throughout the world . . . became the basis of the cultural revival, since they provided the visual stimulus and key to making the people think of ways in which to recreate their lost world after the mission impact'.

Anthropologist Nicholas Thomas identified the highly problematic nature of research on the origins of objects perceived or purported to be from the voyages of Captain James Cook (1728–1779). Thomas found that the traces and connections of the associated objects had been either misread or not interrogated fully to ensure clarity and certainty about their provenance. He revealed how misreading and misrepresenting objects can create and perpetuate provenance myths:

> Given the many publications dedicated to Cook-voyage collections and related themes, it might be assumed that artefacts have by now been conclusively identified and wider questions answered. This is not the case. The material, visual, oral and documentary evidence is fragmented, widely dispersed, often unavailable online and difficult to interpret. Many publications include errors of fact or interpretation: museum artefacts are often incompletely documented or misattributed, in some cases in publicly accessible catalogues. Many fanciful claims have been made for relics' and artefacts' Cook-voyages provenances. And historians have occasionally been misled by outright hoaxes . . . current research into the collections made in the course of early expeditions continues to expose previously unsuspected complexities.
>
> (Thomas 2018: 6)

Deconstructing and disentangling the multiple artificial layers imposed on collections can allow reconstruction of the biographies of objects and collections (Gosden & Marshall 1999). Such reconstruction is critical in revealing a multitude of stories relating to the original use, purpose, and origin of objects, to the networks of exchange along which objects travelled, and the specific nature of the encounters and exchanges between people. The latter includes revealing the agency of Indigenous people in these transactions (e.g., Herle & Philp 2020), an aspect of collections largely ignored in the discourse of decolonizing museums that asserts that all collections are essentially ill-gotten booty. Rather, as Knowles (2011: 236) observes, 'the object has locus for a set of stories, a life history, which connects makers, owners, interpreters and others and can be used to elicit local agency at a certain moment in time'.

It is a unique feature of museum collections to enable Indigenous people to remember and recover knowledge that might otherwise 'languish on the edges of their memories' (Rigsby 1990: 2 cited in Allen 2016). This memory recovery is a critical aspect in the agency of collections in the present, as tangible evidence of the lives of individuals, families, clans, or so-called tribes and their lifeways. Object collections and the memories they trigger survive outside of the oral record; yet they have the capacity to reinvigorate and recover the oral record. For Indigenous people, collections are imprinted with the remnants and residues of the past—of people, places, and events—and for them they bear the marks of parents, aunts, uncles, grandparents, and many generations before them. These ancestors are omnipresent, etched into the fabric of the objects or present in still and moving images, sound recordings, documents, and other components of museum collections. As such, when Indigenous people enter museum storerooms, it is usual for them to speak to their ancestors, often with song and in language. For Indigenous people, these objects are envisioned beyond the walls of the museum—in another time and space—in the hands of those who made or owned them, touched and used them, carried, treasured, and cared for them, traded and exchanged them, sang for them, and so on. In the case of photographs and recordings, Indigenous people see and hear their ancestors in a particular place and point in time. The agency of these collections, particularly how they enact the agency of people associated with them in the past in the present, is extraordinary. It also exists in spite of the nefarious events that may have led to their collection and destiny as museum collections.

In 2000, Indigenous scholar and Daygurrgurr elder, the late Dr Joe Gumbula,[9] visited the Donald Thomson Collection at Museums Victoria's (MV's) main campus, Melbourne Museum, for the first time, to view restricted men's ceremonial material from eastern Arnhem Land housed in a purpose-built storeroom within the main storeroom for the Australian Indigenous collections. Just over a year later, he returned to examine in greater detail the extent of his clan's cultural patrimony—that of the Gupapuyngu Daygurrgurr clan from eastern Arnhem Land in the Northern Territory. He spent 2003 in Melbourne and was able to take his time in searching this and other collections at the museum. From this work emerged the Gupapuyngu Legacy Project,[10] where Gumbula sought to identify, document, and collate the visual and cultural history of the Gupapuyngu Daygurrgurr clan in museum and archive collections worldwide.

He also had a very particular quest to locate works by his father, Djäwa Dhäwirriŋu (c.1905–1980), an internationally renowned bark painter and leader at the Miliŋimbi Mission Station in the 1950s and 1960s. Amongst a remarkable set of bark paintings at MV, collected by Edgar Wells in his time as Mission Superintendent at Miliŋimbi between 1949 and 1959, was a single work by Djäwa of the ancestor, Murayana, the iconic ancestral figure for the Daygurrgurr clan. Murayana holds spears and a spearthrower, his body painted with the iconic Daygurrgurr sacred design or *madayin minytji*, and he is depicted on Gumbula and Djäwa's ancestral homeland of Djiliwirri, the final resting place of Murayana on the Arnhem Land mainland to the east of Miliŋimbi in Buckingham Bay. This painting would prove to be a profound discovery for Gumbula, its impact continuing in the present with his brothers insisting on seeing the painting whenever they visit the museum. Of the Daygurrgurr bark paintings in the Donald Thomson Collection, only one captured Gumbula's attention at this time—a small painting he attributed to Narritj Narritj,[11] who was a powerful leader in the early days of the mission and his paternal grandfather.

Gumbula first patiently trawled through some 2000 or so photographs taken by Donald Thomson across Arnhem Land. He was looking to find his father, whom he remembered as having a distinctive shock of white hair, but without success. On realizing his father was a young man at the time, he recalibrated his frame of reference, looking again and identifying Djäwa in an extraordinary sequence of images that, with the Murayana painting, would set the trajectory of his work and thinking from this point onward. Amongst the photographs catalogued under the title ARNHEM LAND— DJALAMBU—MORTUARY PRACTICES (many having no individuals named or dates or places identified), ten images immediately stood out to Gumbula. The images were randomly placed within the category of *djalambu*—a secondary burial ritual where the bones of a person are broken up and placed inside a hollow log or *dupun*, which is then raised up on a prepared ground and left to the elements. Three young men in the foreground in the images he identified as Djäwa, his older brother, Dawaranygulil, and his younger brother, Lipundja #1. Gumbula reordered the sequence based on his knowledge from Djäwa of the order in which the ceremony is conducted. Being separated and scattered within the larger sequence had rendered them almost invisible, but Gumbula's keen and well-educated eye drew the images out from relative obscurity, disentangling and reassociating them accordingly in the right order. By 'filling out' their context, Gumbula, in his mind, situated the images back on country with the sounds of people talking and singing and the sights and smells of the place itself.

The singular importance of these photographs was clearly apparent to Gumbula— it was the last *djalambu* that the Daygurrgurr clan conducted at Djiliwirri—and was conducted for his great-grandfather, Nuwa, Djäwa's father's father. The old man at the centre of the proceedings was Narritj Narritj, Djäwa's father, who was seated on the ground breaking up bones. The realization that this photograph captured the actual event that his father had talked about was incredible; its importance to Gumbula and his family was immeasurable. However, on reflection, Gumbula expressed disappointment that Djäwa had never mentioned that Thomson was present at Djiliwirri on this occasion, and, more so, that he had not mentioned that Thomson photographed the *djalambu*. Gumbula knew that the mortuary ceremony had taken place during the mission time when deceased Yolŋu were given Christian burials (with some customary rites) in the mission graveyard, but the exact timing of the events at Djiliwirri had been unknown. For Gumbula, it was significant that Thomson had been a witness to this event. As a result, Thomson was now firmly embedded in a shared history with Daygurrgurr people.

The *djalambu* for Nuwa continues to loom large in the Daygurrgurr psyche as a defining moment in their history. The discovery of the photographs proved a catalyst for a number of events that would follow, most importantly, the return of Djäwa's direct descendants, spanning six generations, to Djiliwirri in 2004, and again the following year, after an absence of many years. On arrival, Gumbula and his oldest brother, now also deceased, called out the 'big names', talking to their country and their ancestors, making it safe for all to be there. This process was also to safeguard the objects and photographs I had brought from the Donald Thomson Collection at Gumbula's request, to be shared and documented with those family members present.

Then in 2011 a new thread emerged in this story when discussions were initiated with the Daygurrgurr about conservation treatments for two bark paintings collected by Donald Thomson—one collected at Buckingham Bay in 1937, and for the second, information was missing. A close examination of these paintings more than a decade after Gumbula first saw them prompted him to revisit the *djalambu* photographs taken at Djiliwirri. In the early 2000s, Gumbula had not considered the paintings particularly remarkable, no doubt due to the poor and unstable condition of the bark and pigments. However, after a week of deliberations with the author and objects conservator, Samantha Hamilton, at Melbourne Museum in 2012, Gumbula and his brother, Milaypuma Gaykamaŋu,[12] concluded that the paintings were done at Djiliwirri (in Buckingham Bay) during the time of the *djalambu*, a ceremony 'that would go on for a month' (Gumbula personal communication, 20 August 2011). These works were immediately repositioned as significant 'history' paintings. Gumbula explained that the photographs and paintings together 'tell of the story beyond the ceremony—while also being evidence of the story. . . [and] Ngarritj Ngarritj [who] was in his seventies by this time, and was highly respected and had high power—[it was the] last moment to say to his sons [he was] giving them the law . . . they were young—in their twenties' (Gumbula personal communication, 2 April 2012).

No connections had been made previously between the *djalambu* photographs before Gumbula undertook his research, let alone between the images and the bark paintings, all of which now had a clear association, and one that cast their importance in a totally new light. The brothers used the Yolŋu word *miŋgurr* to describe the positioning these works were now afforded (i.e., commanding 'high respect') and asserted that they had this status, in fact, when they were painted. Gumbula pointed out the sections of the paintings with remnants of the important final layer of white pigment. According to Gumbula, the work was done in this way 'when you want the paintings perfectly done—[for] the image is to shine . . . [and now] the old paintings that remain, they are the history' (Gumbula personal communication, 2 April 2012). Although the status of *mingurr* was originally applied to execution of the bark paintings, that status was now of a different order as a testament to the past and events that transpired at Djiliwirri. Gumbula asked for the photographs again, looking closely at each image and reading the detail. He concluded that the bark painting with the provenance of Buckingham Bay was in fact to Djiliwirri, and the other had been executed at the same time. He also believed that Narritj Narritj had painted these barks with the assistance of his three sons, all of whom would later achieve status as master painters, as well as Mayanygila, a Djambarrpuyŋu man. While Mayanygila was not identifiable in the *djalumbu* sequence of photographs, he would have been present given his role of *djunggayi* for the Daygurrgurr clan at that time. This role required him to ensure that the *djalambu* and everything associated with it was done the right way, including who had the authority to paint these works for Thomson. Late 1937 was the date recorded by Thomson for collecting one of the paintings, and at least one photograph was dated 16 October 1937, which Gumbula identified as being the first in the sequence of performances for *djalambu*. Based on this information, it was concluded that the mortuary ritual commenced in mid-October 1937 and continued through to around mid-November. While it is unclear how long Thomson spent at Djiliwirri, as no field notes have been directly matched to this time, the second bark painting and the other nine photographs can be dated to this window of time and provenanced to Djiliwirri.

DISCUSSION

Gumbula's project demonstrates the 'complex and fluid relationship between people, images and things' (Edwards & Hart 2004: 1), which is the nature of the engagement of Indigenous people with museum collections. For the Daygurrgurr Elders, connecting loose threads in a collection previously considered well documented[13] was a remarkable journey. It began with establishing links between the photographs, then between the two paintings, next between the photographs and the paintings, and lastly by establishing a direct link to a seminal point in time and pivotal event in Daygurrgurr history. Placing Narritj Ngarritj and his three sons at their ancestral homeland of Djiliwirri in late 1937 where they conducted the final rites for Nuwa on country was not an ending that anyone imagined or anticipated. The museum 'field study' took these disjointed elements and, in connecting them, established the broader context within which they needed to be considered, thus 'filling' out what some would consider, at face value, 'hollow' remnants of the past. The bark paintings were restored to their place of importance where their lives began seventy-five years before, but they took on additional values for the Daygurrgurr as both 'history paintings' and inalienable possessions enabled by the cultural and intellectual capital the brothers brought to the interrogation of the collection.

The success of the project also stemmed from an active and ongoing dialogue and research partnership with the museum, which, as Hafner (2010: 265) notes, fosters an environment of trust whereby a 'familiarity and understanding can allow the freedom of responses to occur'. Gumbula's recalibration of the status or *mingurr* of the bark paintings was totally unexpected, particularly given his lack of engagement with them nearly a decade earlier. His assessment then had no doubt been influenced by the poor physical condition of the works with significant loss of pigment, particularly the white that makes it 'shine' as well as the splits in the bark sheets. The cautionary note here for museums is not to be persuaded that something is unimportant based on its condition and/or lack of documentation—often the primary criterion for museums to dispose of or destroy collections. The profound postscript to this story is that in 2015, Milaypuma requested a burial shroud screenprinted with an image of one of the bark paintings be made for Gumbula's funeral at Milinjimbi. The use of the bark painting image in this way confirms the status attributed to these works by the brothers. Milaypuma requested that, prior to screenprinting the cloth, the image be digitally enhanced with the missing or damaged sections of the design 'restored'. This process demonstrates the fluidity of the engagement of Indigenous people with collections and the agency and relevance that these objects can assert in the present.

This project also demonstrates the unpredictable nature of the legacies embedded in museum collections and how they can be realized for Indigenous people in the present. While Gumbula's example is exceptional, it demonstrates the importance of reassembling all the parts and critically examining and interrogating all records. In this case, the parts included objects, photographs, field notes, and genealogies. Another critical element was the relevant museum catalogue documentation, with Gumbula wishing to know what Thomson knew and recorded. Such information required the specific skills and knowledge of the 'museum' (i.e., the author as curator). This process of information assembly served to 'fill' out what had been rendered 'hollow forms' (after Byrne 2008) by virtue of the cataloguing processes applied by Thomson initially and then by the museum. The intersection of this process with the oral record was the catalyst for detailed examination of all the elements of the record from multiple perspectives, at times prompting very robust discussion.

In many instances, the process of museum engagement for Indigenous people is complicated by the fragile nature of Indigenous knowledge due to the passage of time and the consequences of colonial history. Yet museum collections do serve as a trigger to memory, and in the absence of such encounters, it is possible that 'certain knowledge of incidents or events would never be discussed and perhaps even be forgotten' (Allen & Hamby 2010: 211). The relevance of museum collections to a specific group or individual may not be immediately apparent or recognizable, but the form of an object, its decoration, construction, and materials, may provide clues to connections or bear the signature style or elements that particularly knowledgeable individuals can interpret and identify. The work of Wiradjiri artist Jonathon Jones is pertinent here, having developed a specialized eye for decorated shields from southeastern Australia through close examination of examples in many museum collections across the world. Working from known works of named artists, Jones can identify specific styles and attribute the maker and provenance to shields with little or no associated documentation. Jones's extensive knowledge, built up over many years, led to his attribution of a shield in the British

Museum (OC1980.0.721) to a Taungurung man at Coranderrk Aboriginal Station near Healesville based on a photograph taken by the nineteenth-century photographer Charles Walter:

> Along with identifying regional styles it is also possible to match master carvers' hands. For instance, the broad shield has a unique design of interlocking bands of concentric diamonds and triangles with rounded corners threaded together by a series of zigzagging lines. The design bears a striking resemblance to a shield photographed with a man known as Guangnurd or Redman of the 'Goulbourne tribe', which refers to Taungerong [sic] people whose land includes the Goulburn River.
>
> (Jones 2015: 78)

Nicholas Thomas's caution against misreading or misrepresenting the connections of objects in museum collections and ensuring myths are neither created nor perpetuated (see Nugent & Sculthorpe 2018; Thomas 2018) highlights the critical importance of getting things right and putting them back in the right order, as it was for the Daygurrgurr and others (see above). Similarly, it was important for the Lamalama to learn more about their past through the Port Stewart component of the Donald Thomson Collection. This knowledge not only helped secure legal title to their estates (land and sea) but helped build a future that ensured younger people grew up knowing the 'proper Lamalama way', a process mediated by the tangible and visible proof in the Donald Thomson Collection. This process was particularly potent given that Lamalama Elders, like the Daygurrgurr men, could draw on knowledge gained from their own lived experience, being only a generation removed from the Old People of Thomson's time and growing up on country. For Gumbula, his reflection on the importance of museum collections is captured in his statement, 'everything is telling us who we are' (2010: 1), and in his undertaking to uncover this legacy in museums 'for our young people, it is a collaboration for the future' (Gumbula 2010: 2). Furthermore, it was important to Gumbula that future generations knew what he did and what he uncovered in the Donald Thomson Collection. In this connection, Gumbula asked the author 'how will they know I have been here' (personal communication, 2012), conscious of the legacy he had created by restoring the connections between the photographs, the bark paintings, and the *djalambu* at Djiliwirri. Ironically, recording knowledge of this process of assembly will depend on the rigor of current museum processes.

Interrogating the remnants of various museum cataloguing systems to recover clues as to the origins of objects and object collections requires specific knowledge of museum processes to uncover and recover some of the threads of their histories. These threads include cataloguing numbers, codes, and notes written on objects in different hands, the handwriting itself, and the institutional history of inks, chalks, and pencils used for such inscriptions. Writing place names on the surfaces of stone artefacts is commonplace, and Gough used this information to re-connect the Cambridge collections in her exhibition at Cambridge to sites in Tasmania. Filling out these somewhat 'hollow' forms was further enhanced by introducing 'the sound-hearing element [which] was an emotionally moving aspect of the project—the closest to an actual "return" that I was able to achieve' (Gough 2016: 61).

Conclusion

This chapter has explored the multidimensional nature of the legacies of museum collections and the varied and diverse experiences and understandings of Indigenous people who have sought out their cultural patrimony in such institutions. As a result of these experiences, many Indigenous people have come to see museum collections as a unique and vast reservoir of data embodying knowledge of customary practices, beliefs, encounters, exchanges, and events in the past, all imbued with the essence of their Old People and their country. The significant challenge for future curators is not to be constrained by the classic pedagogy of museums that separates collections physically and ontologically. Indigenous people have taken the lead on this front, casting their gaze broadly across museums to find a myriad of connections between objects and their Old People and their country. Scholarship challenging the old siloed nature of collections, such as the role of Indigenous people in the collection of natural science collections (see Olsen & Russell 2019), is emerging, in contrast to classic approaches to research on collections by archaeologists and anthropologists, which have tended to reinforce these Western colonial constructs.

Reconstructing and reassembling collections is, as discussed here, no easy task and involves the deconstruction of the colonial processes to which they have been exposed during their lives as museum objects. The disassociation of information and collections overall and the imposition of generations of idiosyncratic cataloguing systems, each one displacing the last and further distancing collections from any relevant order or context relating to their origins, have rendered museum collections difficult to read, especially the capacity to confirm provenance. Jonathon Jones (Jones 2018a: 281–284) believes that this process of disassociation is 'designed to control and subjugate, these collections often have limited acquisition records [and w]e are left to ponder, who, what, when and where'. As such, museums are seen as complicit in the disempowerment of Indigenous people and source communities in respect of their cultural patrimony, thus fueling the ever-present contested nature of relationships between Indigenous people and museums and the perception that museums continue to operate as trophy houses and agents of ongoing colonial domination.

Despite these issues, this chapter has shown the value of situating the interrogation of collections within a multidimensional dialogic pedagogy, with responsibility on museums to provide the specialized tools and knowledge to tackle the issues posed by the systemization of collections particularly. The challenge for museums is to reestablish, reassemble, and restore, wherever possible, some semblance of an order from which stories and histories relevant to these collections can emerge and be reframed within Indigenous pedagogies. The case studies discussed here reveal the capacity of museums to tackle this problem of assembly through a collaborative research model involving specific interventions and a critical reading of the record, as well as a good deal of imagination and luck.

For Indigenous people, their engagements with their cultural patrimony within museums have often yielded outcomes that could never have been anticipated or imagined. These engagements have also revealed a potency and capacity in collections to exert influence both in the present and into the future, albeit within an engineered cultural landscape that is the museum storeroom. In this sense, Indigenous people have developed strategies to safeguard themselves and others while in that space. At the same time, the collections are read as critical markers of the presence of their ancestors in the landscape. Stone artefacts provide a poignant example of such presence, having been left on the ground surface by ancestors when passing through country and/or forced to depart their country due to colonial invasion. In some instances, objects including stone artefacts were stolen or removed without permission. In other situations, objects were traded and bartered, photographs taken, and written recordings made of associated stories and histories. The collections provide a window to these processes and many other pasts that Indigenous people can uniquely contextualize for relevance in the present. Gough achieved this contextualization with the use of digital technologies linking stone tools on display in Cambridge directly with the places in Tasmania where the objects were obtained, thus reinvesting the objects with the sounds and sense of those places.

Gough's solution can be read as an example of Clifford's (1997: 213) contention that museums can be places of 'hybrid possibilities and political negotiation'. Yet Gough also allows us to understand these stone artefacts as moments of contestation where the history of their collection and removal from country evidences (or laments) a time when Palawa walked and lived on country without interference. Gough reveals the capacity of collections to provoke differing and competing views and perspectives, where multiple interpretations and narratives emerge from or are read into these objects. What emerges from the discussion here is that the fundamental essence of the Old People and their country endures well beyond and apart from the lives of these objects in museum collections. Through Indigenous ontologies and epistemologies, these objects can be placed back in time while also being reimagined and enabled in the present. In this way, some of the hollow and misshapen forms have been restored or emerged to the class of inalienable possessions, like the Daygurrgurr bark paintings.

Notes

1. The watershed moment was the UNESCO Regional Seminar on the Role of Museums in Preserving Indigenous Cultures held in Adelaide (South Australia) in March 1978 (see Edwards & Stewart 1980; Stanton 2011). Indigenous delegates from Australia and the Pacific Rim demanded 'representation throughout the museum world—in collections, at senior management level and on boards of trustees' (Stanton 2011). As John Stanton (2011) observed, the 'UNESCO seminar spawned an immediate response from curators of Indigenous collections in the region, with representatives of communities and museums

from Papua New Guinea, New Caledonia and New Zealand joining their Australian counterparts at the Conference of Museum Anthropologists [COMA] held in Melbourne the following year'.

2. GLAM stands for Galleries, Libraries, Archives, and Museums; and the policies and protocols developed by the other components of this sector have drawn on those developed by museums; see *National Policy Framework for Aboriginal and Torres Strait Islander Library Services and Collections* (National and State Libraries Australasia 2007).

3. A phrase used by Chantal Knowles in recent discussions (personal communication, 7 May 2020).

4. In 1923, the Pitt-Rivers Museum in Oxford received over 13,000 stone artefacts collected in Tasmania by the British geologist, Ernest Westlake, and Hobart resident, Joseph Paxton Moir (see Taylor 2012; Taylor, Jones, & McCarthy 2014).

5. The term is used here in the metaphorical sense, meaning something of great value and in great abundance.

6. Donald Thomson (1901–1970) was a Melbourne-based anthropologist. The Donald Thomson Collection is on long-term loan to Museums Victoria from the University of Melbourne (the artefact component), and the Thomson family (the images and manuscript component). Thomson went to Port Stewart in the late 1920s and early 1930s, resulting in a collection of over 100 objects, around 600 black and white photographs, mostly on glass plates, and extensive field notes (see Allen 2008, 2016). Early visits by the Lamalama were to the storerooms at 328 Swanston Street. All of the collection was relocated to Melbourne Museum in the late 1990s.

7. Travel to Melbourne takes two days, and involves a four-hour drive from Coen (where they live) to Cairns, staying overnight, and flying three to six hours to Melbourne Tullamarine airport (depending on stopovers), then around half an hour's drive to the city to the museum.

8. The then Papua New Guinea Chief Minister, the late Mr. [Sir] Michael Somare, officially opened the Gogodala Cultural Centre on 29 August 1974 (Crawford 1980: 13).

9. According to the wishes of the family and Yolŋu cultural protocol, Dr Gumbula (1954–2015) is used here and not his Yolŋu name.

10. The University of Melbourne appointed Gumbula the Inaugural Liya-Ngarra'mirri Visiting Fellow (2003), during which time he initiated intensive research on collections at Museums Victoria.

11. Five paintings in the Donald Thomson Collection relate to the Gupapuyngu Daygurrgurr clan: DT36, DT39, DT46, DT47, and DT93.

12. Travel for Gumbula and Gaykamangu was funded by University of Melbourne's Cultural and Community Relations Committee.

13. The Donald Thomson Collection was curated by Donald Thomson in a two-storey terrace house on the University of Melbourne's Carlton campus. After his death in 1970, the collection was transferred to Museums Victoria under a loan agreement. In the absence of any formal cataloguing process at the university, data relating to some items was not tracked or was lost prior to this transferal.

References

Allen, L. (2008). Tons and Tons of Valuable Material: the Donald Thomson Collection. In N. Peterson, L. Allen, & L. Hamby (Eds.), *The Makers and Making of Indigenous Australian Museum Collections* (pp.387–418). Melbourne: Melbourne University Publishing.

Allen, H. (2020). Archaeology of the recent: Wooden artefacts from Anbangbang and Djuwarr 1, western Arnhem Land. *Australian Archaeology, 86*(1), 1–13.

Allen, H. (2011). Thomson's spears: Innovation and change in eastern Arnhem Land projectile technology. In Y. Musharbash & M. Barber (Eds.), *Ethnography and the production of anthropological knowledge: Essays in honour of Nicolas Peterson* (pp. 69–88). Canberra: ANU Press.

Allen, H., & Akerman, K. (2015). Innovation and change in northern Australian spear technologies: The case for reed spears. *Archaeology in Oceania, 50*, 83–93.

Allen, L. (2016). On the edges of their memories: Reassembling the Lamalama cultural record from museum collections. In J.-C. Verstraete & D. Hafner (Eds.), *Land and language in Cape York Peninsula and the Gulf Country* (pp. 435–454). Culture and Language Use Series: Studies in Anthropological Linguistics. Amsterdam/Philadelphia: John Benjamins.

Allen, L., Babister, S., Bonshek, E., & Goodall, R. (2018). Finding the signatures of glass beads: A preliminary investigation of Indigenous artefacts from Australia and Papua New Guinea. *Journal of the Anthropological Society of South Australia, 42*, 48–80.

Allen, L., & Hamby, L. (2010). Pathways to knowledge: Research, agency and power relations in the context of collaborations between museums and source communities. In R. Harrison, R. Torrence, S. Byrne, & A. Clark (Eds.), *Unpacking the collections: Networks of material and social agency in the museum* (pp. 209–230). One World Archaeology. New York: Springer.

Allen, L., & Hamby, L. (Eds.). (2016). *Makarrata–Bringing the past into the future*. Canberra: Australian National University and Museum Victoria.

Archibald, J., Xiiem, Q. Q., Lee-Morgan, J. B. J., & De Santolo, J. (2019). *Decolonizing research: Indigenous storywork as methodology*. London: Zed Books.

Attenbrow, V. (2010). *Sydney's Aboriginal past: Investigating the archaeological and historical records*. Sydney: UNSW Press.

Attenbrow, V., & Cartwright, C. (2014). An Aboriginal shield collected in 1770 at Kamay Botany Bay: An indicator of pre-colonial exchange systems in south-eastern Australia. *Antiquity, 88*, 883–895.

Bassani, S. (1990). Correspondence to Ross Rolfe, Director of Aboriginal Affairs, Brisbane. 15 January. On file Museum Victoria, Melbourne.

Bolton, L. (2003). The object in view: Aborigines, Melanesians and museums. In L. Peers & K. Brown (Eds.), *Museums and source communities: A Routledge reader* (pp. 42–54). London: Routledge.

Byrne, D. (2008). A critique of unfeeling heritage. In L. Smith & N. Akagawa (Eds.), *Intangible heritage* (pp. 229–252). Hoboken, NJ: Routledge.

Chaloupka, G., & Guiliani, P. (2005). Strands of time. In L. Hamby (Ed.), *Twined together: Kunmatj njalehnjaleken* (pp. 3–17). Gunbalanya: Injalak Arts and Crafts.

Chan, K. (Ed.) (2019). *Kambek: Reconnecting collections*. Brisbane: Queensland Museum.

Childs, S. T. (2011). Archaeological collections management in the United States: Developing a path to sustainability. In C. Smith & T. Murray (Eds.), *Caring for our collections: Developing sustainable, strategic collection management approaches for archaeological assemblages* (pp. 19–36). Melbourne: Museum Victoria in association with La Trobe University.

Clifford, J. (1997). Museums as contact zones. In J. Clifford (Ed.), *Routes: Travel and translation in the twentieth century* (pp. 188–219). Cambridge, MA: Harvard University Press.

Clifford, J. (2013). *Returns: Becoming Indigenous in the twenty-first century*. Cambridge, MA: Harvard University Press.

Cochrane, S., & Quanchi, M. (Eds.). (2011). *Hunting the collectors: Pacific collections in Australian museums, art galleries and archives*. Brisbane: Australian Association of the Advancement of Pacific Studies.

Council of Museums Association. (1993). Previous possessions, new obligations: Policies for museums in Australia and Aboriginal and Torres Strait Islander peoples. https://www.amaga.org.au/sites/default/files/uploaded-content/website-content/SubmisssionsPolicies/previous_possessions_policy_2000.pdf. Accessed 16 December 2020.

Crawford, A. (1980). *Gogodala: Lagoon dwellers of the Gulf.* Land and People Series 3. Port Moresby: Gordon & Gotch.

Crawford, A. (1981). *Aida: Life and ceremony of the Gogodala.* Bathurst: National Cultural Council of PNG in association with Robert Brown & Associates.

Davies, A., & Earl, C. (2018). Life on the land with the Lamalama rangers—A picture essay. *The Guardian*, 20 December. https://www.theguardian.com/environment/2018/dec/20/life-on-the-land-with-the-lama-lama-rangers-a-picture-essay. Accessed 20 October 2020.

Edwards, E., & Hart, J. (Eds.) (2004). *Photographs objects histories: On the materiality of images.* London: Routledge.

Edwards, R., & Stewart, J. (Eds.) (1980). *Preserving Indigenous cultures: A new role for museums.* Canberra: Australian Government Publishing Service.

Fienup-Riordan, A. (2003). Yup'ik Elders in museums: Fieldwork turned on its head. In L. Peers & A. Brown (Eds.), *Museums and source communities: A Routledge reader* (pp. 28–41). London: Routledge.

Golding, V., & Modest, W. (2013). *Museums and communities: Curators, collections and collaborations.* Bloomsbury: London.

Gordon, P. (1981). 'From ignorance to doubt', my first year in the Australian Museum. *Conference of Museum Anthropologists, 7*(March), 15–16.

Gosden, C., & Knowles, C. (2001). *Collecting colonialism: Material culture and colonial change.* London: Berg.

Gosden, C., & Marshall, Y. (1999). The cultural biography of objects. *World Archaeology, 31*(2), 169–178.

Gough, J. (2016). The possessed past—museums: Infiltration and outreach and The Lost World (Part 2). In K. von Zinnenburg Carroll (Ed.), *The importance of being anachronistic: Contemporary Aboriginal art and museum reparations* (pp. 51–100). Australia: Discipline in Collaboration with Third Text Publications.

Gough, J. (2018). *Fugitive history: The art of Julie Gough.* Crawley: University of Western Australia Press.

Griffin, D. (1996). Previous possessions, new obligations: A commitment by Australian museums. *Curator, The Museum Journal, 39*, 45–62.

Griffiths, T. (1996). *Hunters and collectors: The antiquarian imagination in Australia.* Melbourne: Cambridge University Press.

Gumbula, J. N. (2010). *Makarr-Garma: Aboriginal collections from a Yolŋu perspective.* Sydney: Macleay Museum, University of Sydney.

Hafner, D. (2010). Viewing the past through ethnographic collections: Indigenous people and materiality of images and objects. *Museum History, 3*(2), 257–279.

Hafner, D., Rigsby, B., & Allen, L. (2007). Museums and memory as agents of social change. *The International Journal of the Humanities, 5*(6), 87–94.

Hamby, L. (2008). The reluctant collector: Lloyd Warner. In N. Peterson, L. Allen, & L. Hamby (Eds.), *The makers and making of Indigenous Australian museum collections* (pp. 355–386). Melbourne: Melbourne University Publishing.

Hamby, L. (2011). Held by the teeth: Biting-bags from Milingimbi. *Journal of Australian Studies, 35*(4), 511–527.

Harrison, R., Byrne, S., & Clark, A. (Eds.). (2013). *Reassembling the collection: Ethnographic museums and Indigenous agency*. Santa Fe: School for Advanced Research Press.

Harrison, R., Torrence, R., Byrne, S., & Clark, A. (Eds.). (2010). *Unpacking the Collections: Networks of material and social agency in the museum*. New York: One World Archaeology (Springer).

Herle, A. (2003). Objects, agency and museums: Continuing dialogues between the Torres Strait and Cambridge. In L. Peers & A. K. Brown (Eds.), *Museums and source communities: A Routledge reader* (pp. 194–207). London: Routledge.

Herle, A., & Philp, J. (2020). *Recording Kastom: Alfred Haddon's journals from the Torres Strait and New Guinea, 1888 and 1898*. Sydney: Sydney University Press.

Hicks, D. (2020). *The Brutish Museum: The Benin bronzes, colonial violence and cultural restitution*. London: Pluto Press.

Holdaway, S., & Stern, N. (2004). *A record in stone: The study of Australia's flaked stone artefacts*. Canberra: Aboriginal Studies Press & Museum Victoria.

Horwood, M. (2019). *Sharing authority in the museum: Distributed objects, reassembled relationships*. Museums in Focus. New York: Routledge.

Janke, T. (2018). *First peoples: A roadmap for enhancing Indigenous engagement in museums and galleries*. Canberra: Australian Museums and Galleries Association.

Jones, J. (2015). A symphony of lines: Reading south-east shields. In L. Bolton & G. Sculthorpe (Eds.), *Indigenous Australia: Enduring civilisations* (pp. 74–78). London: Trustees of the British Museum.

Jones, J. (2018a). Bringing life to death. In C. Leahy, J. Ryan, I. Crombie, & M. Patty (Eds.), *Colony: Australia 1770–1861 / frontier wars* (pp. 274–287). Melbourne: National Gallery of Victoria: Thames and Hudson.

Jones, M. (2018b). Linking items, connecting content: The Donald Thomson Collection. In C. Fuchs & C. Angel (Eds.), *Organisation, representation and description through the digital age: Information in libraries, archives and museums* (pp. 102–116). Berlin: De Gruyter Saur.

Jones, P. (2007). *Ochre and rust: Artefacts and encounters on Australian frontiers*. Kent Town: Wakefield Press.

Karp, I., Kratz, C., Szwaja, L., & Ybarra-Frausto, T. (Eds.). (2006). *Museum frictions: Public cultures, global transformations*. Durham, NC: Duke University Press.

Kelly, L., & Gordon, P. (2003). Developing a community of practice: Museums and reconciliation in Australia. In R. Sandell (Ed.), *Museums, society, inequality* (pp. 153–174). London: Routledge.

Knowles, C. (2011). 'Objects as ambassadors': Representing nation through museum exhibitions. In R. Harrison, R. Torrence, S. Byrne, & A. Clark (Eds.), *Unpacking the collections: Networks of material and social agency in the museum* (pp. 231–248). One World Archaeology. New York: Springer.

Langley, M., Lister, M., Wright, D. & May, S. (Eds.). (2018). *The archaeology of portable art: Southeastern Asia, Pacific and Australian perspectives*. New York: Routledge.

Leo, D. (2008). The ark of Aboriginal relics: The collecting practices of Dr LP Winterbotham. In N. Peterson, L. Allen, & L. Hamby (Eds.), *The makers and making of Indigenous Australian museum collections* (pp. 77–110). Melbourne: Melbourne University Publishing.

Message, K. (2006). *New museums and the making of culture*. Oxford: Berg Oxford International Publishing.

Moreton-Robinson, A. (2015). *The white possessive: Property, power and Indigenous sovereignty*. Minneapolis: University of Minnesota Press.

Morphy, H. (2006). Sites of persuasion: *Yingapungapu* at the National Museum of Australia. In I. Karp, C. Kratz, L. Szwaja, & T. Ybarra-Frausto (Eds.), *Museum frictions: Public cultures/ global transformations* (pp. 469–499). Durham, NC: Duke University Press.

Museum Victoria. (2000). *Bunjilaka: The Aboriginal Centre at Melbourne Museum.* Melbourne: Museum Victoria.

Museums Victoria. (2021). Creating First Peoples with community—Bunjilaka. museumsvictoria. com.au. Accessed 16 January 2021.

Museums Association. (UK). n.d. https://www.museumsassociation.org/museums-practice/ decolonising-museums. Accessed 5 March 2020.

Museums Australia. (1993, revised 2005). *Continuous cultures, ongoing responsibilities—Principles and guidelines for Australian museums working with Aboriginal and Torres Strait Islander cultural heritage.* Electronic document, http://www.museumsaustralia.org.au/dbdoc/ccor_final_ feb_05.pdf.

Nakata, M. (2001). 'Cracks in the Mask': Media review. http://muse.jhu.edu/journals/cp/summ ary/v013/`3.2nakata.htm. Accessed September 2013.

National and State Libraries Australasia. (2007). *National policy framework for Aboriginal and Torres Strait Islander library services and collections.* http://www.nsla.org.au/publications/ policies/2007/pdf/NSLA.Policy-20070129-National.Policy.Framework.for.Indigenous. Services.pdf.

Nugent, M., & Sculthorpe, G. (2018). A shield loaded with history: Encounters, objects and exhibitions. *Journal of Australian Historical Studies*, 49(1), 28–43.

O'Hanlon, M., & Welsch, R. (Eds.). (2004). *Hunting the gatherers: Ethnographic collectors, agents and agency in Melanesia, 1870s–1930s.* Oxford: Berghahn.

Olsen, P., & Russell, L. (2019). *Australia's first naturalists: Indigenous people's contribution to early zoology.* Canberra: National Library of Australia.

Peers, L., & Brown, A. K. (Eds.). (2003). *Museums and source communities: A Routledge reader.* London: Routledge.

Peers, L., & Brown, A. K. (2015). *Visiting with the ancestors: Blackfoot shirts in museum spaces.* Edmonton: Athabasca University Press.

Peterson, N., Allen, L., & Hamby, L. (Eds.). (2008). *The makers and making of Indigenous Australian museum collections.* Melbourne: Melbourne University Publishing.

Phillips, C., & Allen, H. (Eds.). (2010). *Bridging the divide: Archaeology into the 21st century.* Walnut Creek, CA: Left Coast Press.

Phillips, R. (2003). Community collaborations in exhibitions: Toward a dialogic paradigm. In L. Peers & A. K. Brown (Eds.), *Museums and source communities: A Routledge reader* (pp. 155–170). London: Routledge.

Phillips, R. (2005). Re-placing objects: Historical practices for the second museum age. *The Canadian Historical Review*, 86(1), 83–110.

Poll, M. (2020). *Written in stone.* Sydney: Macleay Museum, University of Sydney.

Rigsby, B. (1990). Letter to Ross Rolfe, Department of Aboriginal Affairs, Brisbane, 29 January, 5 pages. Copy held at Museums Victoria.

Rigsby, B., Allen, L., & Hafner, D. (2015). The legacy of Norman B. Tindale at Princess Charlotte Bay in 1927: Lamalama engagement with museum collections. *Journal of the Anthropological Society of South Australia*, 39, 1–25.

Rigsby, B., & Jolly, L. (1994). *Liddy, H. Encyclopedia of Aboriginal Australia. Vol. 1* (pp. 618–619). Canberra: Aboriginal Studies Press.

Russell, L. (2001). *Savage imaginings: Historical and contemporary representations of Australian Aboriginalities*. Kew: Australian Scholarly Publications.

Sandell, R. (Ed.). (2003). *Museums, society, inequality*. London: Routledge.

Sculthorpe, G. (1989). What has Aboriginalisation meant at the Museum of Victoria? *Conference of Museum Anthropologists, 22*(April), 17–24.

Sleeper-Smith, S. (Ed.). (2009). *Contesting knowledge: Museums and Indigenous perspectives*. Lincoln: University of Nebraska Press.

Sloggett, R. (2016). Recalibrating meaning and building context for collections of distantiated stone tools. *World Archaeology, 48*(2), 311–324.

Stanton, J. (2011). Ethnographic museums and collections: From the past into the future. In D. Griffin & L. Paroissien (Eds.), *Understanding museums: Australian museums and museology*. https://nma.gov.au/research/understanding-museums/JStanton_2011.html.

Strathern, A. (1981). Introduction. In A. Crawford, *Aida: Life and ceremony of the Gogodala* (pp. 11–13). Bathurst: National Cultural Council of PNG in Association with Robert Brown & Associates.

Taylor, R. (2012). A journey of 13,033 stones: The Westlake Collection and Papers. *Collections— A Journal for Museums and Archives Professionals, 8*(1), 7–38.

Taylor, R. with Jones, M. & McCarthy, G. (2014). Stories in stone: An annotated history and guide to the collections and papers of Ernest Westlake (1855–1922), Rebe Taylor, with Michael Jones and Gavan McCarthy—Stories in stone: An annotated history and guide to the collections and papers of Ernest Westlake (1855–1922). westlakehistory.info. Accessed 15 February 2021.

Thomas, N. (1991). *Entangled objects: Exchange, material culture, and colonialism in the Pacific*. Cambridge, MA: Harvard University Press.

Thomas, N. (2018). A case study of identity: The artefacts of the 1770 Kamay (Botany Bay) encounter. *Australian Historical Studies, 49*(1), 4–27.

Thomson, D. (1934). The dugong hunters of Cape York. *Journal of the Royal Anthropological Institute of Great Britain and Ireland, 64*, 237–262.

Torrence, R., Bonshek, E., Clark, A., Davies, S., Philp, J., & Quinnell, M. (2020). Regimes of value in museum practices: A networked biography of the MacGregor field collection from British New Guinea. *Museum History Journal, 13*(2), 111–131.

Torrence, R., & Clark, A. (2016). Excavating ethnographic collections: Negotiations and cross-cultural exchange in Papua New Guinea. *World Archaeology, 48*(2), 181–195.

Watson, J. (2014). Found with bones. In D. Young (Ed.), *Written on the body* (pp. 1–3). St Lucia: University of Queensland Anthropology Museum.

Wesley, D., & Lister, M. (2015). Small, individually nondescript and easily overlooked. *Australian Archaeology, 80*, 1–16.

Wright, D., Langley, M., May, S., Johnstone, I., & Allen, L. (2016). Painted shark vertebrae beads from the Djawumbu-Madjawarrnja complex, western Arnhem Land. *Australian Archaeology, 82*(1), 43–54.

PART II

COLONIZING SAHUL

CHAPTER 8

ISLAND HOPPING TO SAHUL

KASIH NORMAN, SUE O'CONNOR, AND MICHAEL BIRD

INTRODUCTION

THE expansion of *Homo sapiens* through the Wallacean archipelago entailed the first great maritime migration undertaken by modern humans, resulting in the peopling of Sahul (the Pleistocene landmass encompassing Australia, New Guinea, and the Aru Islands). Today, Wallacea forms part of larger Island Southeast Asia, but during the Late Pleistocene the archipelago was located between the continents of Sunda (the continent now comprising the Malay Peninsula, Sumatra, Borneo, Java, and Bali) and Sahul. The region formed the first large permanent water barrier that *H. sapiens* encountered on their eastward dispersal from Africa. Despite many decades of research in the region, the archaeology, fossil record, and genetic legacy of Wallacea remain in many respects both unique and deeply enigmatic for a number of reasons. First, the region has the highest known concentration of archaic hominin species outside of Africa, some of which may still have been present when *H. sapiens* reached the archipelago. Second, a successful dispersal across Wallacea required *H. sapiens* to develop and/or adapt a maritime economy and voyaging technology. Third, the evidence for an initial *H. sapiens* presence in Wallacea is considerably younger than the fossil and archaeological evidence to the west and east of the archipelago. Finally, the scale of Wallacea and the number of islands and island groups mean that much of the archipelago remains archaeologically poorly known. In this chapter we review the earliest evidence for *H. sapiens* in the region. We then review the environments they encountered and evidence for the earliest economies. Evidence for possible overlaps with archaic hominins is also examined. Finally, we review the modelling contributions made to our understanding of dispersal pathways through Wallacea, identify research gaps and outline directions for future research.

Dispersals East from Africa

Fossil evidence for *H. sapiens* in Greece, Arabia, Israel, and China (Groucutt et al. 2018; Grün et al. 2005; Harvati et al. 2019; Liu et al. 2015) demonstrates that dispersals from Africa occurred well before the genetic window for the major Out of Africa event at 72–51 ka (Malaspinas et al. 2016; Mallick et al. 2016; Pagani et al. 2016). This finding is consistent with at least two *H. sapiens* migrations Out of Africa (Lahr & Foley 1994; Timmermann & Friedrich 2016). Evidence for the eastern reach of the Out of Africa dispersals—and their timing—has proved more contentious, with our understanding of the nature of the *H. sapiens* expansion into Sunda and on to Sahul continuing to evolve. A southern dispersal from Africa along the coastlines of the Indian Ocean to Sunda is one possibility (Balme et al. 2009; Lahr & Foley 1994; Stringer 2000). Archaeological evidence from India places an early *H. sapiens* population in the subcontinent at the time of the Toba super eruption (Sumatra, Indonesia). That is, bracketing ages for the lowest artefacts are 86.0–73.2 ka and 71.4–59.0 ka on feldspar minerals[1] (Clarkson et al. 2020; Petraglia et al. 2007) (Figures 8.1–8.2; Table 8.1), although skeletal evidence is required to definitively demonstrate an association with *H. sapiens*. In Eastern Asia at Fuyan Cave in southern China, a calcite floor capping was found to overlie modern human teeth. Direct dating of a small stalagmite that formed directly on the calcite capping provided a minimum U-series age of 82.3–76.7 ka for the deposition of the teeth (Figures 8.1–8.2; Table 8.1) (Liu et al. 2015). The Fuyan evidence extends the very early eastward migration of *H. sapiens* into East Asia at the onset of Marine Isotope Stage (MIS) 5a (82–71 ka), broadly contemporaneous with the evidence from the Indian subcontinent. Taken together, the Indian and Chinese evidence indicates a wide geographical distribution of *H. sapiens* in Asia at this time.

In Southeast Asia, a cranial element (designated TPL-1) at the site of Tam Pa Ling in Laos (Demeter et al. 2012), represents the oldest fossil evidence for *H. sapiens* immediately north of Sunda. Cranial and skeletal elements were found encased in slope-wash deposits, meaning that thermoluminescence (TL), optically stimulated luminescence (OSL), and radiocarbon dates in association with the skeletal and cranial elements provide minimum ages only. Direct U-series dating on the skull gave an older estimate than the associated ages. As U-series dates the time of uranium uptake in the bones (which may be substantially delayed), rather than the time of death of the individual, the direct date must also be viewed as providing a minimum age (Figures 8.1–8.2 and Table 8.1) (Demeter et al. 2012; Shackelford et al. 2018).

Providing associated ages for the Tam Pa Ling fossils has proved challenging. Radiocarbon samples adjacent to the TPL-1 cranial element are clearly at the radiocarbon barrier (Demeter et al. 2012). Dating of quartz minerals at the site is hampered by the OSL traps being close to saturation in the deeper samples (Shackelford et al. 2018). Feldspar mineral grains from the same sediment samples have returned older burial ages than those of quartz. Compared to quartz, feldspar minerals saturate at a higher dose, meaning feldspars can date burial events further back in time.

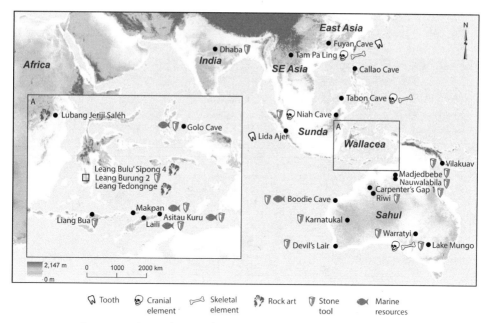

FIGURE 8.1. Location of sites discussed in text. Topographic and bathymetric data obtained from GEBCO 2014 Grid, version 20150318, http://www.gebco.net.

Sediments overlying additional cranial and skeletal elements (TPL-3 and 4) found at Tam Pa Ling give ages of 58–38 ka (quartz minerals) and 86–54 ka (feldspar minerals) from the same sediment sample (Shackelford et al. 2018). Taken together, the direct U-series age for TPL-1 and associated feldspar age for the lowest Tam Pa Ling remains indicates *H. sapiens* had reached Southeast Asia by early MIS 4 (71–57 ka) (Figures 8.1–8.2; Table 8.1).

Sunda to Sahul

The earliest evidence for a human presence in Sunda is on the island of Sumatra at the site of Lida Ajer. Today, Sumatra forms part of Island Southeast Asia, but it formerly comprised part of the western margin of the Sunda continent. Lida Ajer is adjacent to the southern (coastal) dispersal route from Africa, falling near a modelled least cost pathway for early migration into the region (Field & Lahr 2005). *H. sapiens* teeth were collected from breccia deposits at the site in the 1880s. Flowstones, breccia, and faunal elements recorded in association with the modern human teeth have subsequently been dated (Figures 8.1–8.2; Table 8.1) (Westaway et al. 2017). Direct dating of the teeth themselves is yet to be undertaken, but the associated ages of 78.0–58.0 ka demonstrate a modern human presence on the western edge of Sunda roughly contemporaneous with

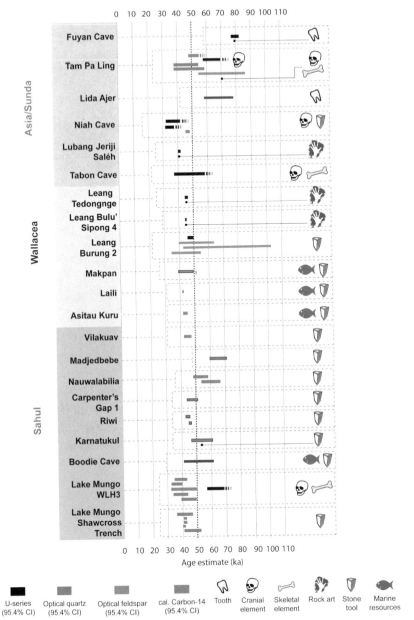

FIGURE 8.2. Age estimates for the earliest evidence for *H. sapiens* in East and Southeast Asia, Sunda, Wallacea, and Sahul. All age ranges are given at the 95.4% CI. Individual age estimates for each site (demarcated by dashed box) are shown in stratigraphic order. Dates that represent a minimum age estimate for the directly dated sample are stippled. Ages that represent a minimum age due to their position in relation to the fossil/artefact(s) (e.g., higher in the stratigraphic profile, or overlying rock art), are indicated by a line and dot. Bayesian modelled ages are outlined. Bayesian modelled ages (Lida Ajer and Boodie Cave) include samples from multiple independent techniques.

Table 8.1. *Homo sapiens* skeletal and archaeological sites showing an early presence in the region. All age ranges are expressed at the 95.4% CI. Radiocarbon samples have been calibrated using Calib Rev 8.1.0 (Stuiver et al. 2021), the IntCal20 (Reimer et al. 2020), and the SHCal20 (Hogg et al. 2020) atmospheric curves for charcoal and Marine20 for shell (Heaton et al. 2020). Ages marked with an asterisk (*) are considered minimum dates for modern humans and are discussed in the main text. Individual ages for each site are given in order of depth (shallowest to deepest).

Site	Region	Sample(s)	Sample material	Technique(s)	Age (ka)	Source
Dhaba	India	Dhab1-OSL1	Feldspar minerals	MET-pIRIR	86.0–73.2	Clarkson et al. (2020)
Fuyan Cave	Southern China (East Asia)	FYS-S2	Stalagmite	U-series	82.3–76.7*	Liu et al. (2015)
Tam Pa Ling	Laos (SE Asia)	TPL b	Charcoal	Radiocarbon	53.0–47.0[a]	Demeter et al. (2012)
Tam Pa Ling	Laos (SE Asia)	TPL-1	Bone (human skull)	U-series	69.6–57.6*	Demeter et al. (2012)
Tam Pa Ling	Laos (SE Asia)	TPLOSL-1	Quartz minerals	SG-OSL	54.0–38.0[b]*	Demeter et al. (2012)
Tam Pa Ling	Laos (SE Asia)	TPLOSL-10	Quartz minerals	SG-OSL	58.0–38.0[b]*	Shackelford et al. (2018)
Tam Pa Ling	Laos (SE Asia)	TPLOSL-10	Feldspar minerals	pIR-IRSL	86.0–54.0*	Shackelford et al. (2018)
Lida Ajer	Sumatra (ISEA - Sunda)	Modelled age	Flowstone, straw stalactite, tooth, and feldspar and quartz minerals	U-series, coupled U-series/ESR, pIR-IRSL, and red TL	78.0–58.0	Westaway et al. (2017)
Niah Cave	Borneo (ISEA - Sunda)	Deep Skull	Bone (human skull)	U-series	41.9–32.1*	Barker et al. (2007)
Niah Cave	Borneo (ISEA - Sunda)	Deep Skull	Bone (human skull)	U-series	37.5–31.5*	Barker et al. (2007)
Niah Cave	Borneo (ISEA - Sunda)	OxA-V-2076-15	Charcoal	Radiocarbon	47.8–46.4	Barker et al. (2007)
Lubang Jeriji Saléh	Borneo (ISEA - Sunda)	LJS2.4	Speleothem (overlying rock art)	U-series	28.6–23.6[c]*	Aubert et al. (2018)
Lubang Jeriji Saléh	Borneo (ISEA - Sunda)	LJS2.5	Speleothem (underlying rock art)	U-series	51.8–48.7[c]	Aubert et al. (2018)
Lubang Jeriji Saléh	Borneo (ISEA - Sunda)	LJS1	Speleothem (overlying rock art)	U-series	41.7–40.0*	Aubert et al. (2018)
Tabon Cave	Palawan Island	IV-2000-T-197	Bone (human tibia)	U-series	58.0–37.0*	Détroit et al. (2004)
Leang Bulu Bettue	Sulawesi (ISEA - Wallacea)	3612	Bovid tooth	U-series	40.0–39.6	Brumm et al. (2017)

(*continued*)

Table 8.1. Continued

Site	Region	Sample(s)	Sample material	Technique(s)	Age (ka)	Source
Leang Burung 2	Sulawesi (ISEA - Wallacea)	STRAW-08-R2 (Layer A)	straw stalactite	U-series	49.6–45.8[d]	Brumm et al. (2018)
Leang Burung 2	Sulawesi (ISEA - Wallacea)	LB2-OSL12 (Layer A)	Feldspar minerals	pIRIR	63.0–39.0[d1]	Brumm et al. (2018)
Leang Burung 2	Sulawesi (ISEA - Wallacea)	LB2-OSL11 (Layer A)	Feldspar minerals	pIRIR	102.0–42.0[d]	Brumm et al. (2018)
Leang Burung 2	Sulawesi (ISEA - Wallacea)	LB2-OSL13 (Layer B)	Feldspar minerals	pIRIR	54.0–34.0[d1]*	Brumm et al. (2018)
Leang Bulu' Sipong 4	Sulawesi (ISEA - Wallacea)	BSP4.3.5	Speleothem (overlying rock art)	U-series	44.9–43.9*	Aubert et al. (2019)
Leang Tedongnge	Sulawesi (ISEA - Wallacea)	LTed3	Speleothem (overlying rock art)	U-series	45.8–45.1*	Brumm et al. (2021)
Laili	East Timor (ISEA - Wallacea)	LA35-001	Charcoal	Radiocarbon	44.2–43.0	Hawkins et al. (2017)
Asitau Kuru	East Timor (ISEA - Wallacea)	SANU-56310	Marine shell	Radiocarbon	45.0–42.4	Shipton et al. (2019)
Makpan	Alor Island (ISEA - Wallacea)	Modelled age	Charcoal and marine shell	Radiocarbon	49.2–39.1	Kealy et al. (2020)
AAXF Vilakuav	PNG (Sahul)	Wk-27072	Charcoal	Radiocarbon	47.3–42.6	Summerhayes et al. (2010)
Madjedbebe	NW Australia (Sahul)	Modelled age	Quartz minerals	SG-OSL	70.7–59.3	Clarkson et al. (2017)
Nauwalabila	NW Australia (Sahul)	K168	Quartz minerals	OSL	64.2–42.6[e]	Roberts et al. (1994)
Nauwalabila	NW Australia (Sahul)	K169	Quartz minerals	OSL	73.7–46.9[e]	Roberts et al. (1994)
Carpenter's Gap 1	NW Australia (Sahul)	Modelled age	Charcoal	Radiocarbon	51.0–43.8	Maloney et al. (2018)
Riwi	NW Australia (Sahul)	Modelled age Layer 12 (end/middle transition)	Charcoal	Radiocarbon	46.4–44.6	Wood et al. (2016)
Riwi	NW Australia (Sahul)	Modelled age Layer 12 end	Quartz minerals	SG-OSL	45.3–42.5	Wood et al. (2016)
Boodie Cave	NW Australia (Sahul)	Modelled age	Marine shell, charcoal and quartz minerals	Radiocarbon and SG-OSL	61.4–41.0	Veth et al. (2017)
Karnatukul	Western Australia (Sahul)	Modelled age	Charcoal	Radiocarbon	60.7–46.4[f]*	McDonald et al. (2018)

Lake Mungo WLH3	SE Australia (Sahul)	M3T 61.2 m (Upper Mungo unit)	Quartz minerals	SG-OSL	42.5–34.5	Jankowski et al. (2020)
Lake Mungo WLH3	SE Australia (Sahul)	M1R 0.37 m (Lower Mungo Unit)	Quartz minerals	SG-OSL	43.1–33.5	Jankowski et al. (2020)
Lake Mungo WLH3	SE Australia (Sahul)	Mean of multiple samples	Bone (human) and teeth (human)	U-series and ESR	68.0–56.0[g]	Thorne et al. (1999)
Lake Mungo WLH3	SE Australia (Sahul	MG-1 (grave infill)	Quartz minerals	SG-LM-OSL	49.9–31.9[h]	Olley et al. (2006)
Lake Mungo WLH3	SE Australia (Sahul)	M1T 35.2 m (Lower Mungo Unit)	Quartz minerals	SG-OSL	48.8–38.8	Jankowski et al. (2020)
Lake Mungo Trench	SE Australia (Sahul)	ST 1.95 m	Quartz minerals	SG-OSL	46.2–35.8[i]	Jankowski et al. (2020)
Lake Mungo Trench	SE Australia (Sahul)	SANU-46314	Fish otolith	Radiocarbon	42.5–41.1[i]	Long et al. (2018)
Lake Mungo Trench	SE Australia (Sahul)	SANU-46316	Fish otolith	Radiocarbon	42.8–41.3[i]	Long et al. (2018)
Lake Mungo Trench	SE Australia (Sahul)	SANU-46317	Fish otolith	Radiocarbon	42.1–40.2[i]	Long et al. (2018)
Lake Mungo Trench	SE Australia (Sahul)	ST 2.40 m	Quartz minerals	SG-OSL	51.8–40.6[i]	Jankowski et al. (2020)

[a] Sample age is likely to be outside calibration range and is given at 1σ.

[b] Quartz minerals are interpreted as minimum ages.

[c] The two samples derive from the calcium carbonate deposits overlying and underlying the rock art, and represent minimum and maximum ages.

[d] It remains unclear if the stone tools in the lowest part of the assemblage (Layers A and B) were created by *H. sapiens* or an archaic hominin species.

[d1] Anomalously young basal age likely due to fluctuations in the uranium-enriched water table. The 'dose-rate corrected' ages for samples LB2-OSL12 and LB2-OSL13 are used here.

[e] The two lowest ages bracket the basal artefacts.

[f] Artefacts occur in the site at deeper levels that are devoid of charcoal and remain undated.

[g] Age of the human remains (WLH3) may be affected by uranium loss, with the associated sediments giving younger ages.

[h] Quartz sample dates the grave infill of WLH3.

[i] The two OSL ages bracket the lowest cultural material with intervening radiocarbon ages. The lowest OSL sample (ST 2.40 m) was collected from sterile deposit, with the lowest artefacts coming from spit 15, from which a radiocarbon age of 42.1–40.2 ka derives (sample B4/15/4).

that shown at Tam Pa Ling (Figures 8.1–8.2; Table 8.1). The existing archaeological and skeletal record for *H. sapiens* on Borneo (formerly northeast Sunda) is younger. Basal archaeological deposits and direct dating of human remains at Niah Cave returned ages post *c.* 50 ka (Barker et al. 2007) (Figures 8.1–8.2; Table 8.1), well into MIS 3 (57–29 ka). In contrast, Palawan Island (formerly part of a land bridge between Sunda and the southern Philippines) contains older evidence. Here, direct dating of *H. sapiens* skeletal and cranial elements at Tabon Cave (Figures 8.1–8.2; Table 8.1) (Détroit et al. 2004) places modern humans off the northeast margin of Sunda by late MIS 4 or early MIS 3. As noted for Tam Pa Ling, the direct U-series ages must be viewed as minimum dates for the Tabon Cave modern human skeletal elements.

While the early geographic range of modern humans on Sunda appears to have been extensive, inferring spatial-temporal patterns must be done with caution. Higher sea levels during the Holocene inundated once low-lying continental lands (Hall 2009), with areas of higher elevation now comprising densely forested islands. There is some evidence that a range of ecosystems existed across Sunda during the Last Glacial Period (Oxygen Isotope Stages 2–4). Substantial rainforest contraction during the Last Glacial Period likely led to the expansion of savannah through central Sunda. A savannah 'corridor' has been inferred from a range of proxy data, potentially dividing rainforest regions in Sumatra and Borneo, and facilitating human dispersal southward through the Pleistocene continent (Bird et al. 2005; Wurster et al. 2010). Two of the oldest fossil and archaeological sites to have survived marine flooding, Lida Ajer (Sumatra) and Niah Cave (Borneo), are both located in regions that were densely forested throughout the Last Glacial Period (Barker et al. 2007; Westaway et al. 2017). This has led to speculation that *H. sapiens* at these sites likely formed part of a population that had either been established in Sunda for some time or brought technological and subsistence rainforest adaptations with them as they migrated into the region (Rabett 2018).

Whatever the economies practised by *H. sapiens* dispersing through Sunda, once they reached the continent's easternmost extent, they were confronted with the vast Wallacean archipelago, rich in marine resources but containing many islands comparatively depauperate in terrestrial fauna (O'Connor et al. 2017). An expansion into Wallacea almost certainly necessitated a transition to, or inclusion of, a marine-focused economy. Isotopic analyses on human teeth from Timor and Alor Islands show an early reliance on marine resources, with use of terrestrial (including closed forest canopy) environments occurring later (Roberts et al. 2020). The early use of pelagic (open ocean) and/or coastal resources is also evident in the faunal records of many of the earliest archaeological sites across Wallacea, Melanesia, and Sahul (Hawkins et al. 2017; Kealy et al. 2020; Leavesley & Allen 1998; Leavesley et al. 2002; O'Connor et al. 2011; Shipton et al. 2019; Veth et al. 2017). While the diets of *H. sapiens* appear to have become largely marine dominant with their dispersal across Wallacea, they also retained subsistence strategies adapted to terrestrial environments. Supporting evidence from terrestrial faunal remains occurs on Flores at the inland site of Liang Bua (Sutikna et al. 2016; 2018) and on Sulawesi at the inland site of Leang Bulu Bettue (Brumm et al. 2017). This evidence is also supported by rock art paintings of terrestrial animals at Maros-Pangkep

(Aubert et al. 2019; Brumm et al. 2021). While *H. sapiens* clearly embraced a maritime lifestyle, what is less certain is both the speed at which people transitioned from mainland Sunda to island Wallacea, and the pace and duration of the maritime migration to Sahul.

The continuum of ancient fossil sites across East, Southeast, and Island Southeast Asia indicates that *H. sapiens* had reached Sunda by MIS 4 (71–57 ka) (Demeter et al. 2012; Détroit et al. 2004; Liu et al. 2015; Shackelford et al. 2018; Westaway et al. 2017). However, the archaeological record for Wallacea currently suggests a substantial delay in dispersal into the archipelago from Sunda, which may be due to a number of factors. First, the earliest excavated archaeological evidence for *H. sapiens* in Wallacea is found at Liang Bua on the island of Flores (Sutikna et al. 2018), Makpan Cave on Alor Island (Kealy et al. 2020), and Laili and Asitau Kuru in Timor Leste (Hawkins et al. 2017; Shipton et al. 2019). All of these sites have age estimates consistent with the onset of occupation after *c.* 50 ka (Figures 8.1–8.2; Table 8.1). The exception to this trend is the archaeological site of Leang Burung 2 on the island of Sulawesi (Brumm et al. 2018). Here the lowest artefacts in a deep archaeological sequence have bracketing ages of 63–39 ka and 102–42 ka (Figures 8.1–8.2; Table 8.1). Due to this antiquity and lack of skeletal remains, the makers of these stone tools could be either *H. sapiens* or a late surviving archaic species, which has been inferred from stone tool evidence to occur on Sulawesi (Van den Bergh et al. 2016a). Second, the general pattern for a later onset of occupation by *H. sapiens* in Wallacea may indicate a variety of factors complicating the transition from interior environments to a maritime economy. One such factor, for example, could be a delay in the development of maritime skills and technologies required to make the island crossings and thrive in the new environment. Alternatively, population increase coming into MIS 3 may have been slow; ecological modelling shows that a large founding population deriving from Wallacea was necessary to successfully people Sahul (Bradshaw et al. 2019).

The pace of the maritime dispersal across Wallacea is also important. Following an optimal foraging strategy, *H. sapiens* could theoretically have crossed the ~1000 km-wide archipelago to Sahul in as little as ~2000 years (O'Connell & Allen 2012; Norman et al. 2018). Under this model, the push of diminishing resources on occupied islands, added to the pull of untapped resources on the next island, served to drive highly mobile maritime-based foragers to journey rapidly through Wallacea. Indeed, the existing Wallacean archaeological record (that can be confidently attributed to modern humans) points to a delayed entry and then rapid dispersal across the archipelago.

This interpretation of delayed entry to, followed by rapid dispersal across, Wallacea is complicated by several factors. In contrast to the Wallacean archaeological record, the earliest evidence for *H. sapiens* in Sahul is generally older (Figures 8.1–8.2; Table 8.1), particularly in Australia's northwest. The site of Madjedbebe in Western Arnhem Land has age estimates that place modern humans in the continent by MIS 4 (71–57 ka) (Clarkson et al. 2017), overlapping with evidence for Lida Ajer at the modelled 95.4% CI. The archaeological sites of Nauwalabila, Boodie Cave, and Karnatukul all have age estimates for an initial appearance of modern humans that are older than the earliest evidence found in Wallacea (Figures 8.1–8.2; Table 8.1)(McDonald et al. 2018; Roberts et al. 1994; Veth et al. 2017). Inclusion of the Sahul evidence presents an alternative interpretation for a *H. sapiens* dispersal from Sunda. Under this scenario, on reaching Wallacea, *H. sapiens* experienced little delay in adapting to maritime environments and island-hopped rapidly eastward, reaching Sahul within a few thousand years.

In addition to the pace of dispersal, the scale of human movement is also significant. The diversity of mitochondrial lineages found in Sahul today indicates that a founding population of at least 200–300 people reached the continent (Bird et al. 2018). Demographic modelling based on hunter-gatherer ethnographic data shows that a viable founding population (i.e., one that avoids extinction) for Sahul had to be in the range of 1300–1500 individuals, crossing in groups containing greater than 100 individuals, all within a period of less than 1000 years (Bradshaw et al. 2019). This modelling implies that a minimum of several hundred people were present on Wallacean islands adjacent to Sahul prior to journeying. Large groups of modern humans present on the final stepping-stone islands to Sahul should presumably leave a clear and detectable archaeological signature. However, detecting this archaeological signature is complicated by the presence of more than one species of hominin.

ARCHAIC ENCOUNTERS

Detecting the onset of the *H. sapiens* dispersal is more complicated across Wallacea than across many other parts of the world. This complexity is due to the presence of three archaic hominins (*Homo erectus*, *Homo floresiensis*, and *Homo luzonensis*) who reached the region in advance of modern humans. Where possible windows of overlap exist, interpreting which species is responsible for depositing the archaeological record is far from straightforward (Brumm et al. 2018; Sutikna et al. 2018; Van den Bergh et al. 2016a). This issue is not the case for *H. erectus* on Sunda, which was probably extinct well before the arrival of *H. sapiens* (Rizal et al. 2020). Fossil remains for *H. erectus* are found on Java (southeast Sunda) from 1.5 Ma (Zaim et al. 2011) until the Late Pleistocene (Indriati et al. 2011; Rizal et al. 2020; Swisher et al. 1994; Yokoyama et al. 2008). The butchering of rhinoceros on the island of Luzon (northern Philippines), dated to 0.7 Ma (Ingicco et al. 2018), shows a deep time depth for archaics to the north of Wallacea. The archaic species *H. luzonensis* persisted on Luzon at Callao Cave into the Late Pleistocene, with the type fossil returning a direct age of 68.7–64.7 ka (Mijares et al. 2010; Détroit et al. 2019). As this date represents a minimum age, the species may have died out much earlier. Finally, the diminutive *H. floresiensis* is found on the island of Flores in southern Wallacea by ~700 ka (Brumm et al. 2016; Van den Bergh et al. 2016b), persisting as late as 75–55 ka (Sutikna et al. 2016).

The evidence for a fourth archaic species in the region—Denisovans—is more enigmatic. Denisovan skeletal remains are found only in Tibet and the Altai region of Siberia (Chen et al. 2019; Jacobs et al. 2019a; Douka et al. 2019; Reich et al. 2010). Conversely, modern human populations in the Sunda and Sahul region have the highest (DNA) concentrations of Denisovan ancestry worldwide (Jacobs et al. 2019b; Mondal et al. 2019; Malaspinas et al. 2016; Mallick et al. 2016). Of these, New Guinean and Australian Indigenous peoples have the greatest percentage of Denisovan heritage (Jacobs et al. 2019b; Mallick et al. 2016; Mondal et al. 2019; Reich et al. 2011). The genetic legacy originates from a Denisovan group distinct from the Altai population (Browning et al. 2018; Mondal et al. 2019; Jacobs et al. 2019b). This distinction has led some to infer that introgression (i.e., transfer of genetic code from one species to another) occurred on Sunda, or possibly further east on the islands of Wallacea and northern Sahul (Jacobs et al. 2019b; Teixeira & Cooper 2019), though this inference is not currently supported by fossil evidence.

Within the network of possible archaic and modern human interactions and timelines, archaeological sites within Island Southeast Asia dating to less than 50 ka are attributed to *H. sapiens* (Aubert et al. 2018; Hawkins et al. 2017; O'Connor et al. 2011). The reasons for this attribution are two-fold. First, the most recent skeletal evidence for archaics in Island Southeast Asia is ~65 ka (Detroit et al. 2019; Sutikna et al. 2016), with no fossil evidence for a continuing archaic presence beyond this time. Second, archaeological sites in Wallacea dating to after *c.* 50 ka often possess evidence for complex cultural behaviours typically attributed to modern humans, while those predating *c.* 50 ka do not. However, it should be noted that U-series ages on calcite overlying rock art at sites on the islands of Borneo and Sulawesi are minimum ages only (Aubert et al. 2014; 2019; Brumm et al. 2021). The true age of the paintings could be far greater than the earliest minimum age of 45.8–45.1 ka (Brumm et al. 2021). Behavioural and cultural signatures associated with *H. sapiens* and found across Island Southeast Asia and Sahul include (1) maritime resource exploitation and technology (Langley et al. 2016; O'Connor et al. 2011; Veth et al. 2017); (2) the use of pigments and parietal art (Aubert et al. 2014, 2018); (3) manufacture of personal adornments (Brumm et al. 2017; Langley et al. 2016); (4) the controlled use of fire (Barker et al. 2007; Morley et al. 2017; Summerhayes et al. 2010), and (5) a broad-spectrum diet (Barker et al. 2007; Florin et al. 2020). These cultural signatures have traditionally been thought to be the exclusive preserve of modern humans. It is important to note that this assumption has recently been challenged on several fronts (see Porr & Matthews 2020). For example, dating of Palaeolithic rock art in Spain potentially points to a *Homo neanderthalensis* origin (Hoffmann et al. 2018, but cf. Pons-Branchu et al. 2020), as does the manufacture of personal adornments in the form of an eagle talon necklace in Croatia (Radovčić et al. 2015). Exploitation of marine and coastal resources has now also been demonstrated for *H. neanderthalensis* at the site of Figueira Brava in Portugal (Zilhão et al. 2020). In turn, if evidence for a late Denisovan introgression in New Guinea (northern Sahul) (Jacobs et al. 2019b) stands the test of time, this would have to indicate the use of maritime technology. It is becoming increasingly clear that blanket assumptions cannot be made about sites containing complex material culture. Concomitantly, archaeological sites with basal ages exceeding *c.* 50 ka but lacking such evidence should not automatically be assigned an archaic origin.

In addition to the presence of multiple hominin species, the size of the maritime region and the number of islands and island groups make the search for the wavefront of *H. sapiens* dispersal challenging. Fortunately, there are several likely migration routes through the island networks, and a focus on islands along these dispersal corridors may facilitate detection of the earliest traces of *H. sapiens* in Wallacea.

ISLAND HOPPING AND DISPERSAL CORRIDORS

The maritime migration passage of *H. sapiens* through Wallacea to Sahul was possible through two major stepping stone island corridors—termed the northern and southern routes (Figure 8.3) (Birdsell 1977). Passage along these island corridors was greatly facilitated during the Last Glacial Period when falling sea levels substantially increased exposure of land (Lambeck & Chappell 2001) and the Wallacean archipelago was framed on either side by the expanded continental landmasses. The number of islands within the Wallacean and Philippine archipelagos also increased with the Last Glacial Period sea-level fall, enlarging existing islands and exposing others (Kealy et al. 2016; Robles et al. 2015). The northern route through Wallacea entailed a passage

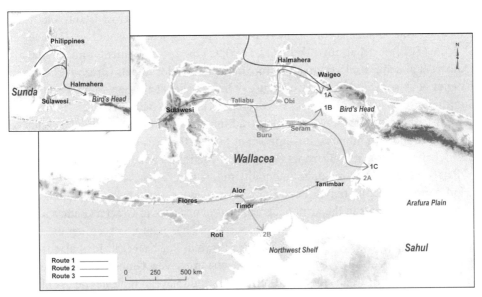

FIGURE 8.3. Wallacean archipelago with Birdsell's (1977) northern and southern routes marked. The Morwood and Van Oosterzee (2009) dispersal model is extended to reach the Bird's Head (shown here as Route 3). Topographic and bathymetric data obtained from GEBCO 2014 Grid, version 20150318, http://www.gebco.net.

from Sunda (in the region now comprising eastern Borneo) to Sulawesi, with eastward maritime migration through the Sula and Moluccan archipelagos, terminating at either the Bird's Head of New Guinea (Route 1A, 1B) or the Sahul Arafura Plain (Route 1C). A southern route required *H. sapiens* to cross from Sunda at what is now Bali and to disperse along the Banda Island Arc, which includes the islands of Lombok, Flores, Alor, and Timor (among others). A southern route dispersal terminated with landfall at the now submerged Sahul northwest continental shelf (Route 2B), or the Arafura Shelf with a crossing from Tanimbar Island (Route 2A). Building on Birdsell's model, an early intervisibility analysis (meaning the ability of someone standing on one island to see to the next) for Wallacea found the northern route to be fully intervisible, while the southern route's final large crossing from Timor to Sahul was blind (Irwin 1992; but cf. Butlin 1993).

Intervisibility of stepping stone islands is considered a potentially important variable in dispersal models (Irwin 1992). That is, *H. sapiens* following an intervisible island corridor decreased the risk of commencing a maritime voyage into an unknown environment towards an invisible destination. Based on the shorter crossing distances between islands on the northern route (Birdsell 1977) and Irwin's (1992) intervisible northern corridor, the northern route has long been considered the likely dispersal corridor for the peopling of Sahul (O'Connell & Allen 2012; but cf. O'Connor 2007). Half a century from Birdsell's (1977) initial identification of the island migration corridors, our understanding of the Wallacean dispersal remains largely dependent on a range of modelling outputs.

First-generation models (Birdsell 1977; Field et al. 2007; Irwin 1992; O'Connell & Allen 2012) focused on variables such as maritime travelling distance, intervisibility, least cost principles, and optimal foraging theory. Second-generation models (Bird et al. 2019; Kealy et al. 2018; Norman et al. 2018), while continuing to include these variables in many instances, have investigated a number of more complex factors. These new variables include real-world hunter-gatherer population dynamics such as survivorship and fertility, and more complex physical world variables such as modelling the impact of ocean currents on maritime dispersal. The value of both first- and second-generation models is their ability to generate a range of testable predictions for the initial dispersal pathways of *H. sapiens* through Wallacea.

Contrary to some first-generation models (e.g., Irwin 1992), second-generation dispersal models have repeatedly demonstrated the potential viability of both the northern and southern routes to Sahul (Bird et al. 2018, 2019; Kealy et al. 2017, 2018; Norman et al. 2018). Irwin's findings that the final step of the southern route lacked intervisibility with Sahul was initially overturned when Kealy et al. (2017) modelled intervisibility corridors for Wallacea. Their results showed that intervisibility with Sahul existed from sea level (i.e., while voyaging), but not from the final stepping stone islands of Roti and Timor. Kealy et al.'s (2017) initial findings were partially amended when Norman et al. (2018) developed a visual connectivity analysis for greater Island Southeast Asia to calculate intervisibility across the region's archipelagos. The results of the connectivity analysis demonstrated that intervisibility existed from multiple high points across Timor and

Roti islands to a now-submerged string of palaeo-islands and from these to Sahul's northwest shelf. Intervisibility from sea level would not be possible until voyagers were almost upon the palaeo-island chain. These findings were replicated shortly after by Bird et al. (2018) who highlighted that intervisibility did not exist to the Sahul palaeo-island chain from Timor and Roti's coastlines, but only from areas of high elevation, as found by Norman et al. (2018). The combined results of all four intervisibility studies demonstrate that northern and southern intervisible corridors existed through Wallacea, albeit with one important caveat. *H. sapiens* dispersing along the southern route could only see the outer palaeo-island chain of the northwest Sahul shelf from high points across the islands of Roti and Timor, with visibility from the coastline and maritime crafts nonexistent until very close to final landfall. This caveat has implications for the nature of a crossing to Sahul using the southern route. Voyaging would require preplanning, with the direction of travel based on the already known location of the palaeo-island chain, which from a coastal and voyaging vantage point were hidden below the horizon. In contrast, an intervisible corridor through the northern route has now been shown for terrestrial and maritime vessel vantage points.

Recent dispersal models, while incorporating intervisibility and minimum travel distance, have increasingly investigated the effects of population demographics on migration, and the implications of random and intentional maritime voyaging. Results have consistently shown a northern entry to Sahul through the Bird's Head of New Guinea to have far higher probabilities for a successful peopling of the continent (Bird et al. 2019; Kealy et al. 2018; Norman et al. 2018). However, the southern route is also possible under certain dispersal conditions. Norman et al. (2018) generated a suite of agent-based simulations incorporating intervisibility, island carrying capacity, realistic survival, fertility and longevity rates, and population 'fissioning' rates and territory size drawn from hunter-gatherer populations. They modelled the 'push' to colonize new islands caused by population growth and by populations competing with one another for resources. The results of the agent simulations showed that the northern route was utilized by populations under all model scenarios, and the probability of a successful dispersal through the north far outranked a southern migration. However, if populations dispersed into Wallacea at the entry to the southern route (i.e., Bali), then the agent population divided, dispersing both north into Sulawesi towards the Bird's Head and east along the southern route towards the northwest shelf. This split led Norman et al. (2018) to conclude that while the northern route held the highest probability of success, a dispersal event into Wallacea may have led to dual migrations into Sahul at both New Guinea and the Australian northwest shelf.

Subsequently, Kealy et al. (2018) developed a computational cost surface model for sea travel through Wallacea, essentially adapting the least-cost models of Field and Lahr (2005) and Field et al. (2007) to a maritime setting. Their model incorporated voyaging distance between islands, intervisibility from a maritime craft at sea level, and the impact of island uplift along the northern route on island visibility in the past. Kealy et al.'s (2018) results again demonstrated the northern route to be the most likely, with final landfall at the Bird's Head overwhelmingly favoured. Following this work, Bird et al. (2019) developed dispersal models incorporating coastal intervisibility, population projections based on hunter-gatherer demography, and marine craft random and directed drift modelling. They similarly found a northern dispersal leading to a successful peopling event of Sahul was far more probable, and most importantly, that such an event was extremely unlikely to have been accidental. Comparison between random and optimal voyaging demonstrated the chance of a successful dispersal event to Sahul predicated on nondirected random voyaging to be vanishingly small. In contrast, intentional guided voyaging along the northern route in climatically optimal windows resulted in the successful peopling of Sahul in 70–90% of simulations, and ~50% of simulations for the southern route (with longer voyaging times required). The necessity of intentional voyaging to reach Sahul supports recent findings that 1300–1500 people would need to cross to establish a successful and viable founding population (Bradshaw et al. 2019). Taken together, these results suggest that a large group of people intentionally voyaged to Sahul and that this migration required planning, provisioning, and construction of many seaworthy vessels. It also raises interesting questions about the dispersal pathways taken by *H. sapiens* along the island corridors, and the location and number of peopling events into Sahul. Recent genetic studies have helped to clarify these matters.

Dispersal Corridors: The Genetic Evidence

At this time, the genetic record reflects some conflict concerning the likelihood of a northern or southern route expansion into Sahul, or concerning the possibility that both functioned as gateways into the continent. Genetic evidence from New Guinea and Australia strongly suggests a common ancestral population (Malaspinas et al. 2016), with little indication of gene flow into Sahul after the initial peopling event(s) (Bergström et al. 2016; Nagle et al. 2017; Tobler et al. 2017). While genomic data suggest a single migration event (Malaspinas et al. 2016), recent mitochondrial DNA evidence concludes that settlement occurred via both the northern and southern routes (Nagle et al. 2017; Pedro et al. 2020). Genetic evidence from the modern New Guinean population genome for an earlier Out of Africa event at ~120 ka remains intriguing, pointing to the possibility either (1) that a very ancient dispersal into the Bird's Head (Pagani et al. 2016) occurred or (2) that *H. sapiens* entering New Guinea carried this early signal and it remained preserved in the modern population due to relative isolation. As a whole, the genetic evidence for the peopling of Sahul indicates that *H. sapiens* migrating into Wallacea likely followed complex dispersal patterns through the archipelago. This dispersal seems to have resulted in the ancestral population diverging along both major island chains to Sahul, with peopling events at both northwest Australia and New Guinea (Pedro et al. 2020; Nagle et al. 2017; Yuen et al. 2019).

Geographical Gaps and Chronological Caveats

A number of possible reasons exist for the lag seen in the presence of *H. sapiens* in the Wallacean archaeological record (compared to Sahul). First, archaeological research with a Late Pleistocene focus has traditionally occurred on several large islands on the southern route and on Sulawesi and the North Malaku island group on the northern route. Along the northern route, the Peleng, Sula, and Maluku (or Moluccan) island groups have historically suffered a dearth of archaeological research into their Late Pleistocene history (Kealy et al. 2018), though this neglect is now beginning to change (Shipton et al. 2020). While Golo Cave in the North Maluku islands (Bellwood et al. 1998) has a basal occupation date of 36.5–35.2 ka cal. BP (calibrated using Calib Rev 8.1.0 (Stuiver et al. 2021) and the Marine20 curve for shell (Heaton et al. 2020)), this site is unusual for its antiquity. The limited archaeological exploration across large areas of the northern route is a possible explanation for this paucity of early dates. Future work may uncover very early evidence for modern humans in this region given that both modelling and genomic research points to its significance (Bird et al. 2019; Kealy et al. 2018; Nagle et al. 2017; Norman et al. 2018; Pedro et al. 2020).

Second, the minimum U-series age of 58.0–37.0 ka (Table 8.1) from the skeletal remains at Tabon Cave on Palawan Island (Figure 8.1), hints at another explanation for the lack of an early bridging chronology in Wallacea. It remains possible that instead of initially entering Wallacea through eastern Sulawesi and/or Bali, *H. sapiens* first dispersed north from Borneo to the Philippines. Entry to northern Wallacea via Mindanao (southern Philippines) would require island-hopping along the intervisible Sangihe Islands corridor to reach the northern tip of Sulawesi (Norman et al. 2018) (Figure 8.3). Such a dispersal model has been previously hypothesized from biogeographic factors (Morwood & Van Oosterzee 2009), though the model terminates at northern Sulawesi. However, from that point it is possible to skim the northern rim of the Wallacean archipelago, crossing from Sulawesi to Halmahera, possibly using the small stepping stone island of Maju. From Halmahera there exists comparatively easy passage to Waigeo Island and the Bird's Head of New Guinea (Figure 8.3). Such a dispersal pathway would result in a lag in the Wallacean archaeological and skeletal records for *H. sapiens* and would produce the archaeological pattern that presently exists in the region.

Finally, the search for a pre-50 ka *H. sapiens* occupation in the Wallacean archipelago requires the use of dating techniques that can extend deep into the past. At ancient tropical sites, environmental conditions often result in intensive weathering of organic materials such as charcoal, causing chemical alteration and loss of elemental carbon (Bird et al. 2002; Clarkson et al. 2018). This loss results in ^{14}C samples beyond a certain age threshold not surviving chemical pretreatment, and underscores the need for alternative dating methods in tropical sites with very ancient occupation. Cases such as the archaeological site of Karnatukul in the Australian arid zone highlight the issue of organic sample preservation. Artefacts at the site occur at depths devoid of charcoal (McDonald et al. 2018). Furthermore, the temporal limit of the radiocarbon method is also problematic for testing the timing of *H. sapiens* dispersals through Wallacea to Sahul. Radiocarbon dating can provide, in theory and in circumstances of exceptional preservation, reliable ages up to *c.* 55 ka if using specific pretreatment methods (Higham et al. 2009; Reimer et al. 2020; Wood 2015). However, even 0.5% contamination by modern material in an ancient sample approaching 40–50 ka will generate an age ~10 ka below the true age of the sample (Wood 2015). Radiocarbon continues to be an extremely valuable chronological tool in Wallacean archaeology. However, it is important to acknowledge the issues deriving from poor preservation of ancient organic samples, the temporal limits caused by the upper bound of the technique, and the impact on the age of even minuscule amounts of contamination by modern carbon. These three factors place limitations on the utility of radiocarbon dating in understanding the timing of the initial *H. sapiens* dispersal into Wallacea.

Building robust chronologies in Wallacean archaeology requires the application of multiple dating techniques, preferably used in tandem. Use of optical chronologies paired with U-series and/or radiocarbon has become increasingly common over the past half-decade (Brumm et al. 2018; Kealy et al. 2020; Shipton et al. 2019, Sutikna et al. 2016; Van den Bergh et al. 2016a; Westaway et al. 2017). The use of paired chronologies has expanded our understanding of early *H. sapiens* and archaic hominins in Wallacea considerably. However, while the ability to extend chronologies well past *c.* 40–50 ka makes optical techniques attractive, these are not a panacea, coming with their own set of caveats and limitations. This issue is highlighted at the site of Leang Burung 2 in Sulawesi, where fluctuations in the uranium-enriched water table have introduced uncertainty into the optical ages for the lowest phase of occupation (Brumm et al. 2018). At Tam Pa Ling in Laos, the saturation threshold of quartz minerals means age estimates from this material must be taken as minimum ages only (Shackelford et al. 2018). Despite the challenges, optical and U-series techniques remain vital in a debate focused on *H. sapiens* either (a) arriving at ~50 ka (at the very point that contamination and survival of carbon become critical), or (b) arriving pre-50 ka (beyond the radiocarbon barrier).

The use of U-series to date calcite crusts overlying rock art is a method that has continued to push back the timing for the first appearance of symbolic expressions by *H. sapiens* (Aubert et al. 2014, 2018, 2019; Brumm et al. 2021). Rock art remains arguably (cf. Hoffman et al. 2018) a cultural signature exclusive to modern humans, and thus it functions as a relatively unambiguous signal for the appearance of *H. sapiens* in Wallacea. The earliest minimum U-series ages for rock art at Leang Tedongnge (45.8–45.1 ka) (Brumm et al. 2021) now matches the earliest ages for archaeological sites in Wallacea that are attributed to *H. sapiens* (Liang Bua ~45 ka, Laili 44.2–43.0 ka, Makpan 49.2–39.1 ka, and Asitau Kuru 45.0–42.4 ka) (Hawkins et al. 2017; Kealy et al. 2020; Shipton et al. 2019; Sutikna et al. 2018). As the minimum U-series ages date the formation of the calcite crusts over the rock art, the true age of the paintings could be far older and may exceed the earliest dates obtained on excavated archaeological deposits. Future research programs seeking to detect an early—and currently elusive—*H. sapiens* presence in Wallacea will need to make use of all available dating techniques and modelling outputs.

Dispersal Paths and Stepping Stone Islands: Directions for Future Research across Wallacea

Recent years have seen a suite of dispersal models developed for Wallacea that highlight the efficacy of both the northern and southern routes, and in particular the importance of the under-researched northern route. The predictive nature of these dispersal models allows archaeologists to target specific islands and test the model outputs. Two recent models have sought to pinpoint major stepping stone islands in the Wallacean dispersal (Kealy et al. 2018; Norman et al. 2018). These islands are defined in two ways: the first acts as a migration 'bottleneck', meaning a large number of modelled dispersal pathways funnel through the island; the second is termed a 'gateway', meaning those islands that form the final stepping stones before crossing to Sahul. Focusing research efforts on Wallacean islands that fall into these categories should increase the likelihood of detecting an early modern human presence in the archipelago. Islands along the northern route flagged by both models include the Taliabu group, Buru, Obi, and Seram, with the first acting as a bottleneck island and the last as a major gateway island into New Guinea (northern Sahul). The dense rainforests of the northern route islands are unlikely to have been an impediment to early *H. sapiens*, who appear to have successfully exploited these environments while dispersing through Sunda (Barker et al. 2007; Westaway et al. 2017). Unlike the northern route, southern route islands form a clear linear corridor, with the majority of islands technically forming a dispersal bottleneck. The major gateway islands for the south are Timor and Roti, adjacent to the Australian northwest shelf. Islands along this dispersal pathway have not experienced the same dearth of research seen for the northern route. Extensive archaeological research programs investigating both archaic hominins and early *H. sapiens* are ongoing on Flores, Alor, and Timor-Leste (O'Connor et al. 2011, 2017; Kealy et al. 2020; Sutikna et al. 2016, 2018), to name a few.

The importance of Timor and its smaller sister island of Roti for a southern dispersal has been noted by both Norman et al. (2018) and Bird et al. (2018). Extensive research programs on Flores, Timor-Leste, and Alor have yielded the earliest evidence so far found for *H. sapiens* in Wallacea (Hawkins et al. 2017; Kealy et al. 2020; O'Connor et al. 2011; Shipton et al. 2019; Sutikna et al. 2018). West Timor remains archaeologically unknown, while pioneering early research undertaken several decades ago on Roti Island dates initial occupation to the terminal Pleistocene, and potentially to the onset of the

Last Glacial Maximum (Mahirta 2003; Mahirta et al. 2004). Future research into the Wallacean dispersal would benefit from targeting the bottleneck and gateway islands highlighted in recent dispersal models, especially those where little to no archaeological research has been undertaken.

CONCLUSIONS

This chapter clearly demonstrates that understanding of the archaeological, fossil, and genetic record for Wallacea is rapidly evolving. Despite the pace of discovery, much remains to be clarified about the early movements of *H. sapiens* in this important part of the world. Intriguingly, it is plausible that *H. floresiensis* inhabited Flores when *H. sapiens* reached Wallacea, with a possible Denisovan presence under debate. The potential for a late survival of archaics adds complexity to the task of assigning species to early archaeological sites in the region. This complexity is heightened by both the uncertainty surrounding when *H. sapiens* first reached Wallacea and their choice of the earliest dispersal pathways through the archipelago. The lack of a bridging chronology in Wallacea that links the Sunda and Sahul skeletal and archaeological evidence likewise remains intriguing. The possibility exists that *H. sapiens* initially circumvented Wallacea, moving from Sunda to the Philippines, and from there skimmed only the northern rim of the Wallacean archipelago to reach the Bird's Head of New Guinea. Alternatively, recent models for a dispersal through Wallacea to Sahul have highlighted several islands about which we know little archaeologically, but are pivotal to the major migration corridors to Sahul, hinting at significant gaps in our understanding of the region.

NOTE

1. Here and throughout the text, age ranges are expressed at the 95.4% CI (confidence interval).

REFERENCES

Aubert, M., Brumm, A., Ramli, M., Sutikna, T., Saptomo, E. W., Hakim, B., et al. (2014). Pleistocene cave art from Sulawesi, Indonesia. *Nature*, *514*(7521), 223–227.

Aubert, M., Lebe, R., Oktaviana, A. A., Tang, M., Burhan, B., Jusdi, A., et al. (2019). Earliest hunting scene in prehistoric art. *Nature*, *576*(7787), 442–445.

Aubert, M., Setiawan, P., Oktaviana, A. A., Brumm, A., Sulistyarto, P. H., Saptomo, E. W., et al. (2018). Palaeolithic cave art in Borneo. *Nature*, *564*(7735), 254–257.

Balme, J., Davidson, I., McDonald, J., Stern, N., & Veth, P. (2009). Symbolic behaviour and the peopling of the southern arc route to Australia. *Quaternary International*, *202*(1–2), 59–68.

Barker, G., Barton, H., Bird, M., Daly, P., Datan, I., Dykes, A., et al. (2007). The 'human revolution' in lowland tropical Southeast Asia: The antiquity and behavior of anatomically modern humans at Niah Cave (Sarawak, Borneo). *Journal of Human Evolution*, 52(3), 243–261.

Bellwood P., Nitihaminoto G., Irwin, G., Gunadi, A. W., & Tanudirjo, D. (1998). 35,000 years of prehistory in the northern Moluccas. In G. J. Bartstra (Ed.), *Bird's Head approaches: Irian Jaya studies—A programme for interdisciplinary research* (pp. 233–275). Rotterdam: A. A. Balkema Publishers.

Bergström, A., Nagle, N., Chen, Y., McCarthy, S., Pollard, M. O., Ayub, Q., et al. (2016). Deep roots for Aboriginal Australian Y chromosomes. *Current Biology*, 26(6), 809–813.

Bird, M. I., Beaman, R. J., Condie, S. A., Cooper, A., Ulm, S., & Veth, P. (2018). Palaeogeography and voyage modeling indicates early human colonization of Australia was likely from Timor-Roti. *Quaternary Science Reviews*, 191, 431–439.

Bird, M. I., Condie, S. A., O'Connor, S., O'Grady, D., Reepmeyer, C., Ulm, S., et al. (2019). Early human settlement of Sahul was not an accident. *Scientific Reports*, 9(1), 1–10.

Bird, M. I., Taylor, D., & Hunt, C. (2005). Palaeoenvironments of insular Southeast Asia during the Last Glacial Period: A savanna corridor in Sundaland? *Quaternary Science Reviews*, 24(20–21), 2228–2242.

Bird, M. I., Turney, C. S. M., Fifield, L. K., Jones, R., Ayliffe, L. K., Palmer, A., et al. (2002). Radiocarbon analysis of the early archaeological site of Nauwalabila I, Arnhem Land, Australia: Implications for sample suitability and stratigraphic integrity. *Quaternary Science Reviews*, 21(8–9), 1061–1075.

Birdsell, J. B. (1977). The recalibration of a paradigm for the first peopling of Sahul. In J. Allen, J. Golson, & R. Jones (Eds.), *Sunda and Sahul: Prehistoric studies in Southeast Asia, Melanesia and Australia* (pp. 113–167). London: Academic Press.

Bradshaw, C. J., Ulm, S., Williams, A. N., Bird, M. I., Roberts, R. G., Jacobs, Z., et al. (2019). Minimum founding populations for the first peopling of Sahul. *Nature Ecology and Evolution*, 3(7), 1057–1063.

Browning, S. R., Browning, B. L., Zhou, Y., Tucci, S., & Akey, J. M. (2018). Analysis of human sequence data reveals two pulses of archaic Denisovan admixture. *Cell*, 173(1), 53–61.

Brumm, A., Hakim, B., Ramli, M., Aubert, M., van den Bergh, G. D., Li, B., et al. (2018). A reassessment of the early archaeological record at Leang Burung 2, a Late Pleistocene rock-shelter site on the Indonesian island of Sulawesi. *PloS one*, 13(4), p.e0193025.

Brumm, A., Langley, M. C., Moore, M. W., Hakim, B., Ramli, M., Sumantri, I., et al. (2017). Early human symbolic behavior in the Late Pleistocene of Wallacea. *Proceedings of the National Academy of Sciences*, 114(16), 4105–4110.

Brumm, A., Oktaviana, A. A., Burhan, B., Hakim, B., Lebe, R., Zhao, J. X., et al. (2021). Oldest cave art found in Sulawesi. *Science Advances*, 7(3), p.eabd4648.

Brumm, A., Van Den Bergh, G. D., Storey, M., Kurniawan, I., Alloway, B. V., Setiawan, R., et al. (2016). Age and context of the oldest known hominin fossils from Flores. *Nature*, 534(7606), 249–253.

Butlin, N. G. (1993). *Economics and the Dreamtime: A hypothetical history.* Cambridge: Cambridge University Press.

Chen, F., Welker, F., Shen, C. C., Bailey, S. E., Bergmann, I., Davis, S., et al. (2019). A late Middle Pleistocene denisovan mandible from the Tibetan plateau. *Nature*, 569(7756), 409–412.

Clarkson, C., Harris, C., Li, B., Neudorf, C. M., Roberts, R. G., Lane, C., et al. (2020). Human occupation of northern India spans the Toba super-eruption~ 74,000 years ago. *Nature Communications*, 11(1), 1–10.

Clarkson, C., Jacobs, Z., Marwick, B., Fullagar, R., Wallis, L., Smith, M., et al. (2017). Human occupation of northern Australia by 65,000 years ago. *Nature, 547*(7663), 306–310.

Clarkson, C., Roberts, R. G., Jacobs, Z., Marwick, B., Fullagar, R., Arnold, L. J., & Hua, Q. (2018). Reply to comments on Clarkson et al. (2017) Human occupation of northern Australia by 65,000 years ago. *Australian Archaeology, 84*(1), 84–89.

Demeter, F., Shackelford, L. L., Bacon, A. M., Duringer, P., Westaway, K., Sayavongkhamdy, T., et al. (2012). Anatomically modern human in Southeast Asia (Laos) by 46 ka. *Proceedings of the National Academy of Sciences, 109*(36), 14375–14380.

Détroit, F., Dizon, E., Falguères, C., Hameau, S., Ronquillo, W., & Sémah, F. (2004). Upper Pleistocene Homo sapiens from the Tabon cave (Palawan, The Philippines): Description and dating of new discoveries. *Comptes Rendus Palevol, 3*(8), 705–712.

Détroit, F., Mijares, A. S., Corny, J., Daver, G., Zanolli, C., Dizon, E. (2019). A new species of *Homo* from the Late Pleistocene of the Philippines. *Nature, 568*(7751), 181–186.

Douka, K., Slon, V., Jacobs, Z., Ramsey, C. B., Shunkov, M. V., Derevianko, A. P., et al. (2019). Age estimates for hominin fossils and the onset of the Upper Palaeolithic at Denisova Cave. *Nature, 565*(7741), 640–644.

Field, J. S., & Lahr, M. M. (2005). Assessment of the southern dispersal: GIS-based analyses of potential routes at oxygen isotopic stage 4. *Journal of World Prehistory, 19*(1), 1–45.

Field, J. S., Petraglia, M. D., & Lahr, M. M. (2007). The southern dispersal hypothesis and the South Asian archaeological record: Examination of dispersal routes through GIS analysis. *Journal of Anthropological Archaeology, 26*(1), 88–108.

Florin, S. A., Fairbairn, A. S., Nango, M., Djandjomerr, D., Marwick, B., Fullagar, R., et al. (2020). The first Australian plant foods at Madjedbebe, 65,000–53,000 years ago. *Nature Communications, 11*(1), 1–8.

Groucutt, H. S., Grün, R., Zalmout, I. A., Drake, N. A., Armitage, S. J., Candy, I., et al. (2018). *Homo sapiens* in Arabia by 85,000 years ago. *Nature Ecology and Evolution, 2*(5), 800–809.

Grün, R., Stringer, C., McDermott, F., Nathan, R., Porat, N., Robertson, S., et al. (2005). U-series and ESR analyses of bones and teeth relating to the human burials from Skhul. *Journal of Human Evolution, 49*(3), 316–334.

Hall, R. (2009). Southeast Asia's changing palaeogeography. *Blumea-Biodiversity, Evolution and Biogeography of Plants, 54*(1–2), 148–161.

Harvati, K., Röding, C., Bosman, A. M., Karakostis, F. A., Grün, R., Stringer, C., et al. (2019). Apidima Cave fossils provide earliest evidence of *Homo sapiens* in Eurasia. *Nature, 571*(7766), 500–504.

Hawkins, S., O'Connor, S., Maloney, T. R., Litster, M., Kealy, S., Fenner, J. N., et al. (2017). Oldest human occupation of Wallacea at Laili Cave, Timor-Leste, shows broad-spectrum foraging responses to late Pleistocene environments. *Quaternary Science Reviews, 171*, 58–72.

Heaton, T. J., Köhler, P., Butzin, M., Bard, E., Reimer, R. W., Austin, W. E., et al. (2020). Marine20—the marine radiocarbon age calibration curve (0–55,000 cal BP). *Radiocarbon, 62*(4), 779–820.

Higham, T., Brock, F., Peresani, M., Broglio, A., Wood, R., & Douka, K. (2009). Problems with radiocarbon dating the Middle to Upper Palaeolithic transition in Italy. *Quaternary Science Reviews, 28*(13–14), 1257–1267.

Hoffmann, D. L., Standish, C. D., García-Diez, M., Pettitt, P. B., Milton, J. A., Zilhão, J., et al. (2018). U-Th dating of carbonate crusts reveals Neandertal origin of Iberian cave art. *Science, 359*(6378), 912–915.

Hogg, A. G., Heaton, T. J., Hua, Q., Palmer, J. G., Turney, C. S., Southon, J., et al. (2020). SHCal20 Southern Hemisphere calibration, 0–55,000 years cal BP. *Radiocarbon, 62*(4), 759–778.

Indriati, E., Swisher III, C. C., Lepre, C., Quinn, R. L., Suriyanto, R. A., Hascaryo, A. T., et al. (2011). The age of the 20 meter Solo River Terrace, Java, Indonesia and the survival of *Homo erectus* in Asia. *PloS one*, 6(6), p.e21562.

Ingicco, T., van den Bergh, G. D., Jago-On, C., Bahain, J. J., Chacón, M. G., Amano, N., et al. (2018). Earliest known hominin activity in the Philippines by 709 thousand years ago. *Nature*, 557(7704), 233–237.

Irwin, G. (1992). *The prehistoric exploration and colonisation of the Pacific*. Cambridge: Cambridge University Press.

Jacobs, G. S., Hudjashov, G., Saag, L., Kusuma, P., Darusallam, C. C., Lawson, D. J., et al. (2019b). Multiple deeply divergent Denisovan ancestries in Papuans. *Cell*, 177(4), 1010–1021.e32.

Jacobs, Z., Li, B., Shunkov, M. V., Kozlikin, M. B., Bolikhovskaya, N. S., Agadjanian, A. K., et al. (2019a). Timing of archaic hominin occupation of Denisova Cave in southern Siberia. *Nature*, 565(7741), 594–599.

Jankowski, N. R., Stern, N., Lachlan, T. J., & Jacobs, Z. (2020). A high-resolution late Quaternary depositional history and chronology for the southern portion of the Lake Mungo lunette, semi-arid Australia. *Quaternary Science Reviews*, 233, 106224.

Kealy, S., Louys, J., & O'Connor, S. (2016). Islands under the sea: A review of early modern human dispersal routes and migration hypotheses through Wallacea. *The Journal of Island and Coastal Archaeology*, 11(3), 364–384.

Kealy, S., Louys, J., & O'Connor, S. (2017). Reconstructing palaeogeography and inter-island visibility in the Wallacean Archipelago during the likely period of Sahul colonization, 65–45 000 years ago. *Archaeological Prospection*, 24(3), 259–272.

Kealy, S., Louys, J., & O'Connor, S. (2018). Least-cost pathway models indicate northern human dispersal from Sunda to Sahul. *Journal of Human Evolution*, 125, 59–70.

Kealy, S., O'Connor, S., Mahirta, Sari, D. M., Shipton, C., Langley, M. C., Boulanger, C., et al. (2020). Forty-thousand years of maritime subsistence near a changing shoreline on Alor Island (Indonesia). *Quaternary Science Reviews*, 249, 106599.

Lahr, M. M., & Foley, R. (1994). Multiple dispersals and modern human origins. *Evolutionary Anthropology: Issues, News, and Reviews*, 3(2), 48–60.

Lambeck, K., & Chappell, J. (2001). Sea level change through the last glacial cycle. *Science*, 292(5517), 679–686.

Langley, M. C., O'Connor, S., & Piotto, E. (2016). 42,000-year-old worked and pigment-stained Nautilus shell from Jerimalai (Timor-Leste): Evidence for an early coastal adaptation in ISEA. *Journal of Human Evolution*, 97, 1–16.

Leavesley, M., & Allen, J. (1998). Dates, disturbance and artefact distributions: Another analysis of Buang Merabak, a Pleistocene site on New Ireland, Papua New Guinea. *Archaeology in Oceania*, 33(2), 63–82.

Leavesley, M. G., Bird, M. I., Fifield, L. K., Hausladen, P. A., Santos, G. M., & Di Tada, M. L. (2002). Buang Merabak: Early evidence for human occupation in the Bismarck Archipelago, Papua New Guinea. *Australian Archaeology*, 54(1), 55–57.

Liu, W., Martinón-Torres, M., Cai, Y. J., Xing, S., Tong, H. W., Pei, S. W., et al. (2015). The earliest unequivocally modern humans in southern China. *Nature*, 526(7575), 696–699.

Long, K., Wood, R., Williams, I. S., Kalish, J., Shawcross, W., Stern, N., & Grün, R. (2018). Fish otolith microchemistry: Snapshots of lake conditions during early human occupation of Lake Mungo, Australia. *Quaternary International*, 463, 29–43.

Mahirta, K. P. A. (2003). *Human occupation on Rote and Sawu Islands, Nusa Tenggara Timur* (Doctoral dissertation). Australian National University, Canberra.

Mahirta, K. P. A., Aplin, K. P., Bulbeck, D., Boles, W. E., & Bellwood, P. (2004). Pleistocene occupation site on Roti Island, Nusa Tenggara Timur, Indonesia. In S. G. Keates & J. M. Pasveer (Eds.), *Modern quaternary research in Southeast Asia: Quaternary Research in Indonesia*, 18 (pp. 361–394). London: A. A. Balkema Publishers.

Malaspinas, A. S., Westaway, M. C., Muller, C., Sousa, V. C., Lao, O., Alves, I., et al. (2016). A genomic history of Aboriginal Australia. *Nature*, 538(7624), 207–214.

Mallick, S., Li, H., Lipson, M., Mathieson, I., Gymrek, M., Racimo, F., et al. (2016). The Simons genome diversity project: 300 genomes from 142 diverse populations. *Nature*, 538(7624), 201–206.

Maloney, T., O'Connor, S., Wood, R., Aplin, K. and Balme, J. (2018). Carpenters Gap 1: A 47,000 year old record of indigenous adaption and innovation. *Quaternary Science Reviews*, 191, 204–228.

McDonald, J., Reynen, W., Petchey, F., Ditchfield, K., Byrne, C., Vannieuwenhuyse, et al. (2018). Karnatukul (Serpent's Glen): A new chronology for the oldest site in Australia's Western Desert. *PloS one*, 13(9), p.e0202511.

Mijares, A. S., Détroit, F., Piper, P., Grün, R., Bellwood, P., Aubert, M., et al. (2010). New evidence for a 67,000-year-old human presence at Callao Cave, Luzon, Philippines. *Journal of Human Evolution*, 59(1), 123–132.

Mondal, M., Bertranpetit, J., & Lao, O. (2019). Approximate Bayesian computation with deep learning supports a third archaic introgression in Asia and Oceania. *Nature Communications*, 10(1), 1–9.

Morley, M. W., Goldberg, P., Sutikna, T., Tocheri, M. W., Prinsloo, L. C., Saptomo, E. W., et al. (2017). Initial micromorphological results from Liang Bua, Flores (Indonesia): Site formation processes and hominin activities at the type locality of *Homo floresiensis. Journal of Archaeological Science*, 77, 125–142.

Morwood, M. J., & Van Oosterzee, P. (2009). *A new human: The startling discovery and strange story of the Hobbits of Flores*. New York: Left Coast Press.

Nagle, N., Ballantyne, K. N., Van Oven, M., Tyler-Smith, C., Xue, Y., Wilcox, S., et al. (2017). Mitochondrial DNA diversity of present-day Aboriginal Australians and implications for human evolution in Oceania. *Journal of Human Genetics*, 62(3), 343–353.

Norman, K., Inglis, J., Clarkson, C., Faith, J. T., Shulmeister, J., & Harris, D. (2018). An early colonisation pathway into northwest Australia 70-60,000 years ago. *Quaternary Science Reviews*, 180, 229–239.

O'Connell, J. F., & Allen, J. (2012). The restaurant at the end of the universe: Modelling the colonisation of Sahul. *Australian Archaeology*, 74(1), 5–31.

O'Connor, S. (2007). New evidence from East Timor contributes to our understanding of earliest modern human colonisation east of the Sunda Shelf. *Antiquity*, 81(313), 523–535.

O'Connor, S., Louys, J., Kealy, S., & Samper Carro, C. S. (2017). Hominin dispersal and settlement east of Huxley's Line, the role of sea level changes, island size, and subsistence behavior. *Current Anthropology*, 58(S17), S567–S582.

O'Connor, S., Ono, R., & Clarkson, C. (2011). Pelagic fishing at 42,000 years before the present and the maritime skills of modern humans. *Science*, 334(6059), 1117–1121.

Olley, J. M., Roberts, R. G., Yoshida, H., & Bowler, J. M. (2006). Single-grain optical dating of grave-infill associated with human burials at Lake Mungo, Australia. *Quaternary Science Reviews*, 25(19–20), 2469–2474.

Pagani, L., Lawson, D. J., Jagoda, E., Mörseburg, A., Eriksson, A., Mitt, M., et al. (2016). Genomic analyses inform on migration events during the peopling of Eurasia. *Nature*, 538(7624), 238–242.

Pedro, N., Brucato, N., Fernandes, V., André, M., Saag, L., Pomat, W., et al. (2020). Papuan mitochondrial genomes and the settlement of Sahul. *Journal of Human Genetics, 65*(10), 875–887.

Petraglia, M., Korisettar, R., Boivin, N., Clarkson, C., Ditchfield, P., Jones, S., et al. (2007). Middle Paleolithic assemblages from the Indian subcontinent before and after the Toba super-eruption. *Science, 317*(5834), 114–116.

Pons-Branchu, E., Sanchidrián, J. L., Fontugne, M., Medina-Alcaide, M. Á., Quiles, A., Thil, F., & Valladas, H. (2020). U-series dating at Nerja cave reveal open system. Questioning the Neanderthal origin of Spanish rock art. *Journal of Archaeological Science, 117*, 105–120.

Porr, M., & Matthews, J. (Eds.). (2020). *Interrogating human origins: Decolonisation and the deep human past.* New York: Routledge.

Rabett, R. J. (2018). The success of failed *Homo sapiens* dispersals out of Africa and into Asia. *Nature Ecology and Evolution, 2*(2), 212–219.

Radovčić, D., Sršen, A. O., Radovčić, J., & Frayer, D. W. (2015). Evidence for Neandertal jewelry: Modified white-tailed eagle claws at Krapina. *PloS one, 10*(3), p.e0119802.

Reich, D., Green, R. E., Kircher, M., Krause, J., Patterson, N., Durand, E. Y., et al. (2010). Genetic history of an archaic hominin group from Denisova Cave in Siberia. *Nature, 468*(7327), 1053–1060.

Reich, D., Patterson, N., Kircher, M., Delfin, F., Nandineni, M. R., Pugach, I., et al. (2011). Denisova admixture and the first modern human dispersals into Southeast Asia and Oceania. *The American Journal of Human Genetics, 89*(4), 516–528.

Reimer, P. J., Austin, W. E., Bard, E., Bayliss, A., Blackwell, P. G., Ramsey, C. B., et al. (2020). The IntCal20 Northern Hemisphere radiocarbon age calibration curve (0–55 cal kBP). *Radiocarbon, 62*(4), 725–757.

Rizal, Y., Westaway, K. E., Zaim, Y., van den Bergh, G. D., Bettis, E. A., Morwood, M. J., et al. (2020). Last appearance of *Homo erectus* at Ngandong, Java, 117,000–108,000 years ago. *Nature, 577*(7790), 381–385.

Roberts, P., Louys, J., Zech, J., Shipton, C., Kealy, S., Carro, S. S., et al. (2020). Isotopic evidence for initial coastal colonization and subsequent diversification in the human occupation of Wallacea. *Nature Communications, 11*(1), 1–11.

Roberts, R. G., Jones, R., Spooner, N. A., Head, M. J., Murray, A. S. and Smith, M. A., (1994). The human colonisation of Australia: optical dates of 53,000 and 60,000 years bracket human arrival at Deaf Adder Gorge, Northern Territory. *Quaternary Science Reviews, 13*(5–7), 575–583.

Robles, E., Piper, P., Ochoa, J., Lewis, H., Paz, V., & Ronquillo, W. (2015). Late Quaternary sea-level changes and the palaeohistory of Palawan Island, Philippines. *The Journal of Island and Coastal Archaeology, 10*(1), 76–96.

Shackelford, L., Demeter, F., Westaway, K., Duringer, P., Ponche, J. L., Sayavongkhamdy, T., et al. (2018). Additional evidence for early modern human morphological diversity in Southeast Asia at Tam Pa Ling, Laos. *Quaternary International, 466*, 93–106.

Shipton, C., O'Connor, S., Jankowski, N., O'Connor-Veth, J., Maloney, T., Kealy, S., & Boulanger, C. (2019). A new 44,000-year sequence from Asitau Kuru (Jerimalai), Timor-Leste, indicates long-term continuity in human behaviour. *Archaeological and Anthropological Sciences, 11*(10), 5717–5741.

Shipton, C., O'Connor, S., Kealy, S., Syarqiyah, I. N., Alamsyah, N., & Ririmasse, M. (2020). Early ground axe technology in Wallacea: The first excavations on Obi Island. *PloS one, 15*(8), p.e0236719.

Stringer, C. (2000). Coasting out of Africa. *Nature, 405*(6782), 25–27.

Stuiver, M., Reimer, P. J., & Reimer, R. W. (2021). CALIB 8.2 [WWW program] at http://calib. org. Accessed 29 January 2021.

Summerhayes, G. R., Leavesley, M., Fairbairn, A., Mandui, H., Field, J., Ford, A., & Fullagar, R. (2010). Human adaptation and plant use in highland New Guinea 49,000 to 44,000 years ago. *Science, 330*(6000), 78–81.

Sutikna, T., Tocheri, M. W., Faith, J. T., Awe, R. D., Meijer, H. J., Saptomo, E. W., & Roberts, R. G. (2018). The spatio-temporal distribution of archaeological and faunal finds at Liang Bua (Flores, Indonesia) in light of the revised chronology for *Homo floresiensis. Journal of Human Evolution, 124,* 52–74.

Sutikna, T., Tocheri, M. W., Morwood, M. J., Saptomo, E. W., Awe, R. D., Wasisto, S., et al. (2016). Revised stratigraphy and chronology for *Homo floresiensis* at Liang Bua in Indonesia. *Nature, 532*(7599), 366–369.

Swisher, C. C., Curtis, G. H., Jacob, T., Getty, A. G., & Suprijo, A. (1994). Age of the earliest known hominids in Java, Indonesia. *Science, 263*(5150), 1118–1121.

Teixeira, J. C., & Cooper, A. (2019). Using hominin introgression to trace modern human dispersals. *Proceedings of the National Academy of Sciences, 116*(31), 15327–15332.

Thorne, A., Grün, R., Mortimer, G., Spooner, N. A., Simpson, J. J., McCulloch, M., et al. (1999). Australia's oldest human remains: Age of the Lake Mungo 3 skeleton. *Journal of Human Evolution, 36*(6), 591–612.

Timmermann, A. & Friedrich, T. (2016). Late Pleistocene climate drivers of early human migration. Nature, doi: 10.1038/nature19365

Tobler, R., Rohrlach, A., Soubrier, J., Bover, P., Llamas, B., Tuke, J., et al. (2017). Aboriginal mitogenomes reveal 50,000 years of regionalism in Australia. *Nature, 544*(7649), 180–184.

Van den Bergh, G. D., Kaifu, Y., Kurniawan, I., Kono, R. T., Brumm, A., Setiyabudi, E., et al. (2016b). *Homo floresiensis*-like fossils from the early Middle Pleistocene of Flores. *Nature, 534*(7606), 245–248.

Van den Bergh, G. D., Li, B., Brumm, A., Grün, R., Yurnaldi, D., Moore, M. W., et al. (2016a). Earliest hominin occupation of Sulawesi, Indonesia. *Nature, 529*(7585), 208–211.

Veth, P., Ward, I., Manne, T., Ulm, S., Ditchfield, K., Dortch, J., et al. (2017). Early human occupation of a maritime desert, Barrow Island, North-West Australia. *Quaternary Science Reviews, 168,* 19–29.

Westaway, K. E., Louys, J., Awe, R. D., Morwood, M. J., Price, G. J., Zhao, J. X., et al. (2017). An early modern human presence in Sumatra 73,000–63,000 years ago. *Nature, 548*(7667), 322–325.

Wood, R. (2015). From revolution to convention: The past, present and future of radiocarbon dating. *Journal of Archaeological Science, 56,* 61–72.

Wood, R., Jacobs, Z., Vannieuwenhuyse, D., Balme, J., O'Connor, S., & Whitau, R. (2016). Towards an accurate and precise chronology for the colonization of Australia: The example of Riwi, Kimberley, Western Australia. *PloS one, 11*(9), p.e0160123.

Wurster, C. M., Bird, M. I., Bull, I. D., Creed, F., Bryant, C., Dungait, J. A., & Paz, V. (2010). Forest contraction in north equatorial Southeast Asia during the Last Glacial Period. *Proceedings of the National Academy of Sciences, 107*(35), 15508–15511.

Yokoyama, Y., Falguères, C., Sémah, F., Jacob, T., & Grün, R. (2008). Gamma-ray spectrometric dating of late Homo erectus skulls from Ngandong and Sambungmacan, Central Java, Indonesia. *Journal of Human Evolution, 55*(2), 274–277.

Yuen, L. K., Littlejohn, M., Duchêne, S., Edwards, R., Bukulatjpi, S., Binks, P., et al. (2019). Tracing ancient human migrations into Sahul using hepatitis B virus genomes. *Molecular Biology and Evolution, 36*(5), 942–954.

Zaim, Y., Ciochon, R. L., Polanski, J. M., Grine, F. E., Bettis III, E. A., Rizal, Y., et al. (2011). New 1.5 million-year-old *Homo erectus* maxilla from Sangiran (Central Java, Indonesia). *Journal of Human Evolution, 61*(4), 363–376.

Zilhão, J., Angelucci, D. E., Igreja, M. A., Arnold, L. J., Badal, E., Callapez, P., et al. (2020). Last Interglacial Iberian Neandertals as fisher-hunter-gatherers. *Science, 367*(6485), eaaz7943.

CHAPTER 9

AUSTRALIA'S FIRST PEOPLE
Oldest Sites and Early Culture

CHRIS CLARKSON, KASIH NORMAN, SUE O'CONNOR, JANE BALME, PETER VETH, AND CERI SHIPTON

INTRODUCTION

THE archaeology of Australia is remarkable for many reasons. First, it is the driest occupied continent on Earth with a unique and diverse flora and fauna that gave rise to specialist adaptations and cultural practices unseen anywhere else in the world. Second, as an island continent, it has developed its own cultural trajectory largely isolated from the developments in Eurasia. Third, it has a remarkably long history of *Homo sapiens* occupation dating to at least 65,000 years ago (or 65 ka, with 'ka' meaning kiloanni or thousands of years ago), with some of the earliest known innovations in certain forms of technology, economy, and symbolism. Fourth, the journey to Sahul (the Pleistocene continent of mainland Australia, Tasmania, New Guinea, and the Aru Islands) was the earliest long-distance maritime voyage undertaken, and it must have involved considerable planning, manufacture of ocean-going vessels, and quite likely, a large founding population (Balme 2013; Bird et al. 2018; Bradshaw et al. 2019, 2021; Davidson & Noble 1992; O'Connell, Allen, & Hawkes 2010). Finally, while Australia remained a continent of hunter-gatherers throughout its long history, complexity arose in many times and places, perhaps reaching its zenith in the Late Holocene (Lourandos & Ross 1994). The story of Aboriginal people in Australia is one of innovation, resilience, unique cultural development, and continual change.

In this chapter, we review what is known about the oldest archaeological sites in Australia (>45 ka) and the cultures, technology, and beliefs of early Aboriginal societies. We first examine the long-running debate over the age of the earliest sites in Australia and then describe each of the oldest sites currently known across the continent. We then look at what is known about early demography and settlement of the continent. Finally, we outline important insights into early technology, subsistence economy, and symbolism from the Australian archaeological record, many of which have only recently come to light.

DEBATES ABOUT DATES

The chronology of first occupation of Australia has been a topic of fierce debate for several decades, often termed the 'long versus short chronology'. With improvements in dating and the excavation of an increasing number of sites, the known antiquity of occupation of Australia by people has increased by approximately 10,000 years every decade since the 1960s (Hiscock 2017) (Figure 9.1). Prior to the 1960s, Australia was thought by many to have been occupied for little more than a few thousand years (cf., Etheridge 1890 and Sollas 1911; see McNiven, Antiquarian archaeology, this volume), but by the 1960s, Mulvaney's pioneering archaeological work at Kenniff Cave in central Queensland had extended the known age of occupation back to at least 16 ka (Mulvaney & Joyce 1965; see Urwin & Spriggs, this volume). By the mid-1970s, the accepted radiocarbon (^{14}C) chronology for first occupation of Australia was extended 20,000 years further to c. 40 ka (Jones 1999).

The debate over a long versus short chronology was first aired when two archaeological sites in northern Australia were dated using luminescence techniques to c. 50–60 ka (Roberts, Jones, & Smith 1990; Roberts et al. 1994a). Proponents for a longer chronology emphasized that the earliest known archaeological sites in Australia had reached the limits of radiocarbon dating, so if older sites existed, alternative dating techniques were required (Chappell, Head, & Magee 1996; Jones 1999; Roberts, Jones, & Smith 1994b). Those espousing a short occupation chronology, however, suggested that the earliest known sites were roughly correct, and that their dating to c. 45,000 ka, at the limits of radiocarbon dating, was simply a coincidence (Allen 1994; Allen & O'Connell 2003; O'Connell et al. 2018). Adherents of the short chronology have suggested site formation issues exist with many sites older than 45 ka, but they have steadily revised the barrier for accepted ages over the last several decades from c. 35–40 ka (Allen & Holdaway 1995; O'Connell & Allen 1998), to c. 45 ka (Allen & O'Connell 2003), to 47–48 ka (Allen & O'Connell 2014), with their currently accepted upper margin at ~50 ka (O'Connell et al. 2018). This is now in line with the original published thermoluminescence (TL) age for Malakunanja II (now Madjedbebe) of 52 ± (6, 9) ka (Roberts et al. 1990), and it is consistent at the 95.4% confidence interval with the new optically stimulated luminescence (OSL) chronology of 68.7–50.4 ka for Phase 2 of Madjedbebe for first peopling of the continent (Clarkson et al. 2017).

An important element in this debate is the limitations of various dating techniques. While greater precision is possible with radiocarbon (i.e., uncertainty ranges are typically small and in the order of decades to centuries for Late Pleistocene samples), the

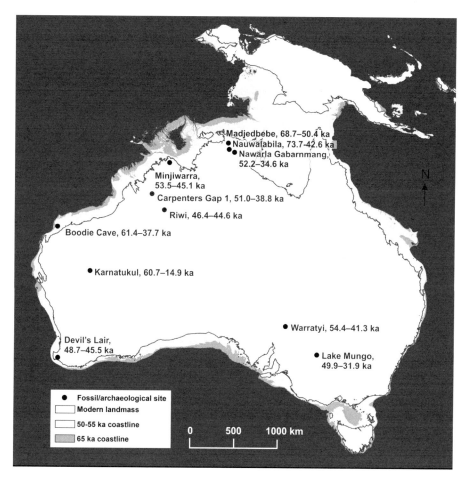

FIGURE 9.1. Map showing ages for earliest occupation of sites in Australia that are older than 45 ka and that are discussed in text. Age ranges are given at 95.4% confidence. Where available Bayesian modelled start (bottom) and end (top) ages are provided for initial occupation phases. See Table 9.1 for more detail. Topographic and bathymetric data were obtained from GEBCO 2014 Grid, version 20150318, http://www.gebco.net. The edge of the continental shelf is indicated at –120 m below present sea level (bpsl) and –75 m bpsl, consistent with both first human arrival c. 65 ka, and the Last Glacial Maximum.

upper limit (radiocarbon barrier) of this technique is 50–55 ka depending largely on the pretreatment method employed (Bird et al. 1999; Fairbanks et al. 2005; Rodríguez-Rey et al. 2015; Turney et al. 2001). However, even 0.5% contamination by modern material in an ancient sample approaching 40–50 ka will generate an age ~10 ka below its true age (Wood 2015). Loss of elemental carbon and chemical weathering due to harsh environmental conditions can also affect the age of the sample or result in it not surviving chemical pretreatment (Bird et al. 2002; Clarkson et al. 2018). This reinforces the need for dating methods that are both resistant to these processes, and that can reliably assess the age of sites beyond c. 50 ka.

Many of the oldest sites in Australia are dated with optical techniques, often in conjunction with radiocarbon dating where charcoal and other organic material is available. Whereas the radiocarbon method dates organic materials through measuring the extent of decay of radioactive ^{14}C since death, optical techniques measure the accumulation of electrons in the crystal traps of quartz or feldspar minerals since last exposure to sunlight (Jacobs & Roberts 2007). Although the confidence intervals for age estimates are generally larger, optical techniques can date the time of last exposure to sunlight of sediments to time depths far beyond the radiocarbon barrier. The advent of single-grain OSL dating has provided a useful additional means of examining the adequacy of sunlight bleaching, and for determining postdepositional mixing complications that can go undetected in traditional (multiple-grain) OSL studies (Roberts et al. 1998a). These factors make OSL a critical dating method in Australia where organic materials do not survive well, given that quartz is abundant in most sites. Ultimately, building robust chronologies in Australia (and elsewhere) requires the routine use of several dating techniques, ideally used in conjuction.

Modelled age ranges provided throughout the text for earliest occupation across Australia are given at the 95.4% confidence interval (CI). Where discussed, individual radiocarbon samples have been calibrated using Calib Rev 8.1.0 (Stuiver et al. 1993) and the SHCal20 (Hogg et al. 2020) atmospheric curve for charcoal and Marine20 for shell (Heaton et al. 2020). A number of the published Bayesian modelled start and end ranges for the cultural phases (discussed in text and supplied in Table 9.1) were originally derived using IntCal13 or SHCal13 calibrations of ^{14}C datasets. While beyond the scope of this chapter, with the release of the updated SHCal20 curve these original phase model estimates require revision.

AUSTRALIA'S OLDEST SITES

At present, the earliest evidence for the peopling of Australia is found at the archaeological sites of Madjedbebe and Nauwalabila I in western Arnhem Land in northcentral Australia (Figure 9.1; Table 9.1). Intriguingly, the archaeological record for the Wallacean archipelago is younger than the oldest sites in Sahul (see Norman et al., this volume; Norman et al. 2018). However, fossil sites for *Homo sapiens* in East, Southeast, and Island Southeast Asia (islands that formerly comprised the Pleistocene continent of Sunda) have age estimates that are older or overlapping at 95.4% probability with the earliest Australian evidence (Demeter et al. 2012; Liu et al. 2015; Shackelford et al. 2018; Westaway et al. 2017). It should also be noted that the earliest age estimates for Australian archaeological sites sit within the confidence intervals for some of the oldest Sahul mtDNA haplogroups (M29'Q: 42–67 ka, M27: 40–62 ka, Fu et al. (2013) mutation rate) regardless of the mutation rate used (Pedro et al. 2020).

Outside of Arnhem Land, the earliest evidence for human occupation occurs in Western Australia at the coastal site of Boodie Cave (Veth et al. 2017), and in the arid

Table 9.1. Age estimates for earliest occupation across Australia.

Site	Region	Sample(s)	Sample Material	Technique(s)	Age (ka) (95.4% CI)	Source
Madjedbebe	Central northern Australia	Bayesian modelled age (Phase 2 start and end)	Quartz minerals	SG-OSL	68.7–50.4[a]	Clarkson et al. (2017)
Nauwalabila 1	Central northern Australia	K168	Quartz minerals	OSL	64.2–42.6[b]	Roberts et al. (1994a)
		K169	Quartz minerals	OSL	73.7–46.9[b]	
Nawarla Gabarnmang	Central northern Australia	Bayesian modelled age (Period 1 start and end)	Charcoal	Radiocarbon	52.2–34.6	David et al. (2019)
Minjiwarra	NW Australia	Shfd17121	Quartz minerals	OSL	53.5–45.1[c]	Veth et al. (2019)
Carpenters Gap 1	NW Australia	Bayesian modelled age (Phase 1 start and end)	Charcoal	Radiocarbon	51.0–38.8	Maloney et al. (2018)
Riwi	NW Australia	Bayesian modelled age (Layer 12 middle/end transition)	Charcoal	Radiocarbon	46.4–44.6[d1]	Wood et al. (2016)
Riwi	NW Australia	Bayesian modelled age (Layer 12 start)	Quartz minerals	SG-OSL	50.9–46.0[d2]	Wood et al. (2016)
Boodie Cave	Western Australia	Bayesian modelled age (Phase SU8 start to SU6 end)	Marine shell, charcoal, and quartz minerals	Radiocarbon and SG-OSL	61.4–37.7	Veth et al. (2017)
Karnatukul	Western Australia	Bayesian modelled age (Phase SU6 start and end)	Charcoal	Radiocarbon	60.7–14.9[e]	McDonald et al. (2018)
Devil's Lair	SW Australia	Bayesian modelled age	Charcoal, teeth, and quartz minerals	Radiocarbon, ESR-EU, and OSL	48.7–45.5[f1]	Tobler et al. (2017)
		Bayesian modelled age	Charcoal, teeth, and quartz minerals	Radiocarbon, ESR-EU, OSL, and U-series	51.7–47.3[f2]	

(*continued*)

Table 9.1. Continued

Site	Region	Sample(s)	Sample Material	Technique(s)	Age (ka) (95.4% CI)	Source
Warratyi	South Australia	Bayesian modelled age (SU4 start and end)	Avian eggshell and quartz minerals	Radiocarbon and SG-OSL	54.4–41.3	Hamm et al. (2016)
Lake Mungo WLH3	SE Australia	M3T 61.2 m (Upper Mungo Unit)	Quartz minerals	SG-OSL	42.5–34.5[91]	Jankowski, Stern, Lachlan, & Jacobs (2020)
		M1R 0.37 m (Lower Mungo Unit)	Quartz minerals	SG-OSL	43.1–33.5[92]	Jankowski et al. (2020)
		Mean of multiple samples	Bone (human) and teeth (human)	U-series and ESR	68.0–56.0[h]	Thorne et al. (1999)
		MG-1 (grave infill)	Quartz minerals	SG-LM-OSL	49.9–31.9[i]	Olley, Roberts, Yoshida, & Bowler (2006)
		M1T 35.2 m (Lower Mungo Unit)	Quartz minerals	SG-OSL	48.8–38.8[93]	Jankowski et al. (2020)
Lake Mungo Shawcross Trench	SE Australia	ST 1.95 m (Mungo B trench) (Spit 13)	Quartz minerals	SG-OSL	46.2–35.8[j]	Jankowski et al. (2020)
		B5/13/4 (Spit 13)	Fish otolith	Radiocarbon	42.5–41.1	Long et al. (2018)
		B4/14/2 (Spit 14)	Fish otolith	Radiocarbon	42.8–41.3	Long et al. (2018)
		B4/15/4 (Spit 15)	Fish otolith	Radiocarbon	42.1–40.2[k]	Long et al. (2018)
		ST 2.40 m (Mungo B Trench) (Spit 17)	Quartz minerals	SG-OSL	51.8–40.6[l]	Jankowski et al. (2020)

Note: Where available the Bayesian modelled start and end ages for the top and bottom of the initial occupation phase are given. Where multiple individual ages are given for a single site, they are shown in stratigraphic order (shallowest to deepest). Ages are shown at 95.4% confidence. Radiocarbon results on charcoal have been calibrated using Calib Rev 8.1.0 (Stuiver et al. 1993) and the SHCal20 (Hogg et al. 2020) atmospheric curve.

[a] Published Bayesian start and end ages at the 95.4% CI, random-only errors.

[b] The two lowest ages bracket the basal artefacts.

[c] Date in association with a single artefact.

[d1] Published Bayesian modelled age range for first definitive occupation of the site (lowest hearth feature) (transition between mid Layer 12 and top Layer 12).

[d2] Published Bayesian modelled age ranges for the base and top of Layer 12 (very low levels of cultural material continue to the base of Layer 12).

[e] Both of the deepest age estimates from Karnatukal are from the base of SU6. Stone tools (N = 4) occur in the site at deeper levels which are devoid of charcoal and remain undated.

[f1] Age for onset of occupation of the cave.

[f2] Age for lowest artefacts (N = 6). Four artefacts are on calcrete, a material available within the cave, and two on quartz.

[g1-3] The WLH burial was found at the interface between the Upper and Lower Mungo Units, and the SG-OSL age estimates are considered bracketing ages for the burial.

[h] Age of the human remains (WLH3) may be affected by uranium loss, with the associated sediments giving younger ages.

[i] Quartz sample dates the grave infill of WLH3.

[j] Upper bracketing age for lowest artefacts.

[k] Radiocarbon age estimate derives from the same spit as the lowest artefact.

[l] Age estimate from sterile deposit below lowest artefact.

interior at Karnatukul rock shelter (McDonald et al. 2018) (Figure 9.1; Table 9.1). Archaeological sites in the Kimberley are slightly younger and have modelled start ages for onset of occupation that overlap extensively with one another (Maloney, O'Connor, Wood, Aplin, & Balme 2018; Norman et al. 2022; Veth et al. 2019; Wood et al. 2016) (Table 9.1). This pattern is replicated in southwest and southeastern Australia, with occupation appearing virtually synchronously across the southern half of the mainland (Figure 9.1; Table 9.1) (Hamm et al. 2016; Tobler et al. 2017; Turney et al. 2001).

While the date of first arrival of people in Australia is vigorously debated, Hiscock (2017) has pointed out the risks of settling on an arrival age too soon in the search process. Ages for first occupation are susceptible to sampling effects, with increasing research effort likely to result in finding older sites. However, older sites will become increasingly difficult to find as we approach the true age of arrival. This process is asymptotic, or in other words, beyond a certain point ever-increasing research effort results in diminishing returns—a phenomenon Hiscock depicts graphically as a 'discovery curve'. Hiscock argues that the discovery curve for ancient Australian sites is flattening, though it may still be too early to settle on a firm arrival date. We must be mindful here also of the Sippil-Rongis effect, or the palaeontological precept that the oldest known fossil will not represent the first appearance of a taxon (Kircher & Weil 2000). Hence, no site currently known is likely to represent the true age of the initial peopling of the continent. This age difference, whatever it might be, is emphasized even further when it is remembered that first settlement of Greater Australia would have taken place on coastlines now submerged on the edge of the continental shelf. Whether the rate of increase in the age of sites in Australia will continue, or begin to slow, remains to be seen, but Hiscock suggests that the following decades may see a further flattening of the curve, with an upper bound on the first occupation of Australia perhaps falling somewhere below 75 ka.

Madjedbebe

Madjedbebe is currently Australia's oldest known archaeological site (Figures 9.1 and 9.2a) (Clarkson et al. 2017; but see O'Connell et al. 2018 and Williams, Spooner, McDonnell, and O'Connell 2021 for contrary views and replies by Smith, Ward, & Moffat 2020, 2021). The site is known for its abundant contact rock art (May, Wesley, Goldhahn, Litster, & Manera 2017), as well as its long excavation history and abundant evidence for early Aboriginal cultures (Clarkson et al. 2015, 2017, 2018; Kamminga & Allen 1973; Roberts et al. 1990, 1998b). Madjedbebe is a 50 m-long rock shelter located at the foot of an outlier of the western Arnhem Land plateau, within Mirarr Country. Twenty 1 × 1 m squares were excavated to a maximum depth of 4 m between 1979 and 2015. The three-dimensional coordinates of ~11,000 artefacts and other archaeological features (hearths, burials, and pits) were recorded with an estimated 164,000 artefacts recovered from the excavation. Macrobotanical remains were recovered by flotation (Florin et al. 2020, 2021), and a detailed radiocarbon and OSL chronology

FIGURE 9.2. Some of Australia's oldest known archaeological sites. (a) Madjedbebe (photograph by Gundjeihmi Aboriginal Corporation with permission); (b) Riwi (photograph by Jane Balme). (c) Carpenter's Gap 1 (photograph by Susan O'Connor with permission from the Bunuba Dawangarri Aboriginal Corporation); (d) Karnatukul (photograph by Jospehine McDonald with permission from the Mungarlu Ngurrakatja Rirraunkaja Proscribed Body Corporate); (e) Boodie Cave (photograph by Peter Veth); (f) Nawarla Gabarnmang (photograph by Bruno David).

was developed for the site (Clarkson et al. 2017). Bayesian analysis divided the site into seven phases, with Phases 2–7 firmly associated with human occupation. Geoarchaeological analyses of the organic and inorganic components of the deposit established only small-scale postdepositional disturbance at the site. Artefacts were analysed for usewear and residues, and detailed technological analysis of stone artefacts is ongoing.

Artefacts occur in three dense bands in Phases 2, 4, and 6–7, with fewer artefacts in intervening phases. Each band corresponds to a change in raw material use, stone working technology, and climatic conditions. Phase 1 (start 87.4–73.0 ka, end 76.6–65.4 ka), corresponding to the end of Marine Isotope Stage 5 and the beginning of Marine Isotope Stage 4, has very few artefacts and is of uncertain cultural origin. Phase 2 (start 68.7–61.3 ka, end 55.1–50.4 ka) is associated with a cool, dry Marine Isotope Stage 4 (71–57 ka) climate (Florin et al. 2021, 2022) and low sea levels, with the nearest shoreline ~300 km to the north. A large and dense stone artefact assemblage rich in exotic raw materials occurs in this phase, with evidence of points and thinning flakes, discoidal cores, edge-ground axes, and flakes from ground edges and ground surfaces, and large numbers of grindstones of various kinds (Hayes et al. 2022) (Figures 9.3e–h and 9.4). Large quantities of ground ochre are also found in this phase. Phase 3 (start 54.0–49.2 ka, end 30.1–26.0 ka) has a variable but wetter Marine Isotope Stage 3 (57–29 ka) climate with higher sea levels and a stronger monsoon with infrequent use of exotic raw materials and local quartz dominant. Phase 4 (start 28.9–24.6 ka, end 14.2–12.2 ka) corresponds to dry Marine Isotope Stage 2 conditions (Florin et al. 2021, 2022), including the peak of the Last Glacial Maximum, very low sea levels, and a retreat of the coastline to >300 km away.

Contention around the age of Madjedbebe centres on whether artefacts could have moved down through sandy sediments over time as a result of bioturbation from termites, trampling, or seasonal wetting and drying (Allen 2017; Allen & O'Connell 2020' O'Connell et al. 2018; Williams et al. 2021). As pointed out in the original study and subsequently (Clarkson et al. 2017, 2018; Smith et al. 2020, 2021), artefacts cannot have moved down through the profile en masse due to (1) the existence of tightly packed rubble in the front several metres of the excavation; (2) the distinctive nature of Phase 2 raw materials, including artefacts that are technologically distinct from the higher levels; (3) an absence of termite-related features or clay particles associated with termite galleries; (4) low dispersion in the ages of individual grains from Phase 2, indicating little postdepositional mixing; (5) trampling experiments in sediments from the site which indicate small-scale movements of artefacts only (Marwick, Hayes, Clarkson, & Fullagar 2017); (6) no size sorting of artefacts or sediments as expected of termite bioturbation; (7) peaks in magnetic susceptibility indicating heightened human activity and burning associated with pulses in stone artefact discard incompatible with widespread mixing; (8) the presence of intact cultural features in Phase 2, including hearths; (9) artefact refits within but not between Phases 2 and 4; and (10) artefact associations such as ground ochre wrapped in mica sheets. Williams et al. (2021) most recently speculated that fine particles may have moved through the sequence by termites without altering the position of sand grains, thus preserving low overdispersion in OSL ages from the site. But if this were true, then the association between artefacts and dated sand grains would also be preserved. Consequently, while all archaeological sites undergo some degree of postdepositional alteration, there is currently no sustainable evidence upon which to dismiss the Madjedbebe chronology and its associated artefactual sequence.

Nauwalabila 1

The rock shelter site of Nauwalabila 1 is Australia's second-oldest known site and is located in Deaf Adder Gorge around 70 km south of Madjedbebe, in western Arnhem Land (Figure 9.1). The site formed under a large fallen boulder in a gently sloping sand apron near the foot of the western edge of the Arnhem Land escarpment. The site was excavated several times in the 1970s and 1980s down to 3 m depth by Rhys Jones, Mike Smith, Ian Johnson, Richard Roberts, and Jo Kamminga (Jones & Johnson 1985; Kamminga & Allen 1973; Roberts et al. 1994a). Around 30,200 artefacts were recovered, with the lowest artefacts bracketed by OSL ages of 73.7–46.9 ka and 64.2–42.6 ka (Jones & Johnson 1985; Roberts et al. 1994a). No artefacts were found in the lowest spit, and downward movement of artefacts into the lowest artefact-bearing compact rubble is unlikely. Radiocarbon dates closely track OSL ages down to around 1 m depth, but diagenesis and chemical alteration of charcoal resulted in increasing divergence between radiocarbon and luminescence ages with greater depth (Bird et al. 2002), illustrating the problems with radiocarbon dating charcoal from tropical sand sheets mentioned earlier (Clarkson et al. 2018).

The occupational sequence at Nauwalabila 1, like Madjedbebe, reveals a series of changes in raw materials and technology through time. The earliest peak is dominated by quartz and quartzite artefacts, with a silcrete flake and a possible thinning flake in Spit 71 (CC's unpublished reanalysis), as well as ground ochre, grindstones, and edge-ground axe fragments in the lowest zone of occupation (Jones & Johnson 1985).

As with Madjedbebe, O'Connell and Allen (1998, 2004) and O'Connell et al. (2018) view the Nauwalabila 1 chronology as an erroneous outlier in their post-50 ka settlement model of Sahul. They argue the lowest artefacts at the site were likely displaced downwards into the basal rubble as a result of the formation of a termite stone line. In their detailed consideration of the geoarchaeological evidence, Smith et al. (2020) argue that such an interpretation of the deepest stone artefacts on subsurface termite stone lines at both Madjedbebe and Nauwalabila 1 is not consistent with the archaeology or geomorphology on a number of grounds. These include lack of a fine-grained mantle overlying a stone layer, lack of substantial paedogenesis above a stone layer, no direct evidence for termite activity, no >10 ka time steps in sedimentation above the stone layer that would allow time for a stone line to form, and no size sorting of artefacts with depth. The problems O'Connell and Allen note with the radiocarbon chronology at Nauwalabila 1 are also much more likely the result of contamination and chemical degradation of charcoal samples in tropical sand sheets below c. 1 m depth, rather than displacement and disturbance by termites. Bird et al. (2002), in their thorough reanalysis of the sedimentology and radiocarbon and luminescence chronologies, conclude that there is no evidence that there has been significant vertical displacement of artefacts relative to the surrounding sand matrix, and that both the radiocarbon and luminescence chronologies suggest occupation of the site before 50,000 years ago.

Nawarla Gabarnmang

This site is located on top of the Arnhem Land Plateau, about 180 m above the plateau's plains. It is a large (32 × 23 m), pillared gallery-like rock shelter with an intricately painted ceiling (David et al. 2011, 2019; Gunn 2018) (Figures 9.1 and 9.2f). Since human arrival, the site and the pillars have been extensively reworked. Seven areas were excavated between 2010 and 2012, with excavation proceeding to bedrock typically at 78–80 cm depth. Extensive radiocarbon dating and analysis of the cultural assemblage were undertaken for Squares ILM and F (David et al. 2019). The lowest stratigraphic layer (SU5) is undated and culturally sterile. The deepest layer with human occupation (SU4) has a modelled Bayesian start age of 52.2–45.6 cal. ka BP (calibrated Before Present) on charcoal, making Nawarla Gabarnmang the earliest dated use of the Arnhem Land Plateau. Spanning 52.2–34.6 cal. ka BP, the lowest occupation peak contains over 500 stone artefacts, including thinning flakes, ground ochre, and rare exotic stone raw materials.

Minjiwarra

Minjiwarra is a large, vertically cut fluvial bank feature of up to 6 m height located on the western flank of the Drysdale River, northern Kimberley (Veth et al. 2019) (Figure 9.1). This prominent sedimentary feature has well-marked alternating layers of dark red, orange, and grey sands with a low density of *in situ* artefacts. The bank feature is located several kilometres upstream of a constricted passage, where the Drysdale River follows a fault line of the rock art–rich Warton Sandstone, before discharging into the Timor Sea. Ongoing erosion of the alluvial bank feature has created a near-continuous scatter of artefacts lying on a basal carbonate pavement. This exposed pavement scatter continues for a kilometre along the edges of the river channel, with more recent Late Holocene artefacts such as pressure-flaked Kimberley points and associated bifacial thinning flakes eroding from paler sediment tongues at each end (see Maloney 2015; Moore 2015). A sediment column was sampled approximately halfway along the face of the bank feature and OSL samples recovered from the boundaries of the lowest five stratigraphic units (Veth et al. 2019, Table 3, Figure 7). These OSL ages ranged from c. 7.7 ka to as early as c. 50 ka, with SU9, a culturally sterile layer, dated to 82.50–64.6 ka (Shfd17118–Shfd17122). The interface of Stratigraphic Units 8 and 9, which has *in situ* stone artefacts, returned an age of 53.5–45.1 ka. The stone artefacts were largely made on local river bed materials, including igneous, mudstone, quartz, and silicified sandstones. Tools from the excavated assemblage included scrapers and an edge-ground axe, and from the lag deposits along the riverbed a variety of edge-ground axes and bifacial points. The presence of sediments covering the last 70,000 years, with artefacts from 53.5–45.1 ka and through the Last Glacial Maximum (21.4–17.8 ka), stands in contrast to rock shelter deposits from the region which appear often to have had pre-Holocene deposits removed by large-scale erosional processes (Veth et al. 2019: 117).

Carpenters Gap 1

Carpenters Gap 1 is a rock shelter in the Napier Range of the southern Kimberley (Figures 9.1 and 9.2c). Five square metres of the shelter have been excavated (O'Connor 1995). A Bayesian-modelled radiocarbon chronology indicates an initial occupation phase (SU8) with modelled start and end ages of 51.0–43.8 ka and 44.4–38.8 ka, respectively (Maloney et al. 2018). The 65 stone artefacts from the lowest phase are dominated by locally available crystal quartz with occasional small (10.42±7.8 mm) hornfels pieces. Focalized platforms are common and bipolar flaking is evident. A single edge-ground axe flake was recovered from this phase (Hiscock, O'Connor, Balme, & Maloney 2016), as well as an ochred bone artefact, which has been interpreted as a possible nose ornament (Langley, O'Connor, & Aplin 2016). Organic materials are exceptionally well-preserved. Faunal remains in the earliest occupation phase suggest that people were mainly eating reptiles with some freshwater turtle and fish. From ~41.4 ka there are fewer freshwater species and higher quantities of reptiles and smaller arid-adapted species, suggesting greater use of the plains away from the range (Maloney et al. 2018: 222).

Carpenters Gap 1 is also rare amongst Australian sites in having remarkably well-preserved macrobotanic remains, even in its oldest levels. The macrobotanics are thought to predominantly represent food remains, so they provide rare insight into the annual timing of site occupation and changes in vegetation and plant resources within the site's foraging catchment over time (Dilkes-Hall, O'Connor, & Balme 2019). In the initial occupation phase there are low numbers of macrobotanics, in keeping with the low numbers of stone artefacts and minimal evidence of site use more generally. The seeds of monsoonal rainforest taxa, such as *Terminalia* spp. and *Vitex* cf. *glabrata*, dominate this earliest phase and show use of the site during the wet season. Abundant palm phytoliths from two different taxa also occur in the initial occupation phase and then disappear entirely in the levels coinciding with the Last Glacial Maximum (Wallis 2001: 113). Palms require a permanent water source to survive and their nearest occurrence today is at least 40 km north, suggesting wetter conditions prevailed around the site at the time of first occupation.

From about 41.4 ka to 27.1 ka there is a change in the macrobotanic record that parallels that seen in the faunal remains, with an overall increase in the quantity of material recovered and increase in the diversity of taxa represented, showing that people were using a greater variety of ecological zones around the site to obtain their food (monsoon rainforest, savannah, and riparian) (Dilkes-Hall et al. 2019). The presence of parenchyma remains suggests that roots and tubers were also exploited (Dilkes-Hall et al. 2019). The most common seeds recovered from first occupation until c. 27 ka are *Terminalia* spp., *Vitex* cf. *glabrata*, and cf. *Grewia breviflora*, fruit-bearing trees that produce in the wet season months (November–April) (Kenneally, Edinger, & Willing 1996: 88; Wheeler 1992: 167, 794). This suggests that early occupation of Carpenters Gap 1 was in many ways akin to that recorded in the ethnography (Blundell 1975: 113, 128), with caves and rock shelters being the preferred campsites during the monsoonal

Riwi

Riwi, a limestone cave in the South Lawford Range, is another site in the southern Kimberley (Figures 9.1 and 9.2b). However, unlike Carpenters Gap 1, the site is not near a permanent water source. Excavations of three square metres within the cave, and one along the dripline, document intermittent occupation from 46.4 to 44.6 ka (where the deepest hearth lies) to the present (Wood et al. 2016). The cave has painted rock art on its walls and ceiling and deeply incised grooves concentrated at its entrance. Although it is not yet possible to date the rock art, the presence of ochre throughout all occupation layers suggests that paintings may have been consistently created from first occupation. Pleistocene occupation at Riwi was intermittent and probably primarily during the wet monsoon season or at other times when surface water was available and the ephemeral creek near the front of the cave flowed. Because of the alkaline environment, bone and charcoal have preserved throughout the sequence, but other organic remains are only preserved for the Holocene. The Pleistocene technology consists of flaked artefacts made of locally available stone, as well as a range of bone artefacts (Balme et al. 2018; Langley, Balme, & O'Connor 2021). When the site was first occupied, the dietary fauna was dominated by reptiles and small to medium-sized wallabies. A major change about 34 ka, when wallabies are replaced by large macropods, may indicate longer drought periods in the region accompanying the onset of the Last Glacial phase. At about the same time, there is also a clear change in the type of hearths made at the site. Between 45 ka and about 35 ka, shallow single-use hearths were combusted at Riwi, using wood from the eucalypt savanna of the valley floor, suggesting that occupation during this phase was 'intermittent, with enough time between site visits to allow for these flat, open-air, single use hearths to be covered by natural, rapid aeolian deposition' (Whitau, Vannieuwenhuyse, Dotte-Sarout, Balme, & O'Connor 2017).

Boodie Cave

Boodie Cave is a limestone shelter on Barrow Island located on the arid northwest Australian coastline (Figures 9.1 and 9.2e). The site registers first human occupation by 61.4–41.0 ka (Phase SU8 start) (Veth et al. 2017: SI Table A5), with a discontinuity straddling the Last Glacial Maximum, and then abandonment by 6.8 ka when the island became separated from the mainland (Veth, Ditchfield, & Hook 2014). Positioned near the edge of the Australian continental shelf, the site is well located to detect past use of the now-drowned coastal plains. There is evidence for a mixed coastal and arid plains fauna indicative of a maritime desert adaptation. The dietary and utilitarian shellfish species found at the cave were transported over the emergent continental shelf to the site. By 42 ka, coastal foragers collected and transported to the site four taxa of shellfish from mangrove, mudflat, and rocky substrates up to 15 km over the coastal plain (Veth et al. 2017). Whereas three shellfish species are dietary (*Terebralia*, *Tellina*, and *Nerita*), the fourth taxon (*Melo* sp.) is a robust, much larger gastropod commonly used for water carrying, ornamentation, and shell artefact production (Balme & Morse 2006). *Nerita*, *Tellina*, and *Terebralia* could have been safely transported in wet clumps for later consumption at Boodie Cave (Veth et al. 2017). Boodie Cave also contains many modified shell fragments, including dentate pieces likely to have been used for marine mammal butchering, chisels, and polished edge scrapers. The presence of shell tools is expected, given the lack of hard rocks in the vicinity. Twenty-two fragments of tusk shell (scaphopod) with consistent wear patterns probably served as personal ornaments such as beads in a necklace. The presence of dietary shellfish from the earliest occupation levels of Boodie Cave (albeit in small quantities), and from karstic sites to the north in Timor Leste and Borneo (Barker 2017; O'Connor, Ono, & Clarkson 2011), demonstrate the maritime competencies of people entering Sahul (Kealy, Louys, J., & O'Connor 2016). The early colonists of the now-submerged shelf of Greater Australia did not remain coastally tethered, but instead rapidly adapted to the marsupial fauna and arid zone plants of northwest Australia's extensive maritime deserts.

Karnatukul

Karnatukul is located in the remote Carnarvon Ranges of the Little Sandy Desert (Figures 9.1 and 9.2d). It was the first Pleistocene site to have been dated in the Western Desert (O'Connor, Veth, & Campbell 1998). With more recent excavations (McDonald et al. 2018), a new record is now available with a Bayesian modelled start date for initial occupation of 60.7–46.4 ka with occupation continuing through the Last Glacial Maximum. The two deepest radiocarbon samples (base of SU6) return calibrated age estimates beyond the radiocarbon barrier. Four artefacts, along with microdebitage fragments, were found in deposits underlying the lowest organic samples (McDonald et al. 2018). The pre–Last Glacial Maximum assemblages from Karnatukul show a preference for 'exotic' high-quality chert (McDonald et al. 2018). The oldest assemblage includes an ironstone scraper and a backed chert artefact (Figures 9.3c and 9.4) dating to 45.6–41.6 cal. ka BP. This backed artefact is the earliest example of geometric microlith technology in Australia (McDonald et al. 2018).

Devil's Lair

Devil's Lair is a limestone cave in the tall Karri forests of the Leeuwin-Naturaliste region of southwestern Australia (Figure 9.1). In contrast to the other early Sahul sites that are all either in the monsoonal north, arid, or semiarid areas, Devil's Lair is in the cooler temperate part of the continent and has a Mediterranean climate. Excavations, primarily undertaken in the 1970s, opened an area 5 × 1.5 m to a depth of about 6.5 m in one 50 × 50 cm square. A U-series age on flowstone collected from near the base of the deposit dates the lowest sterile layers to 64.8–61.6 ka (Turney et al. 2001: 11). Six stone artefacts thought to have washed into the cave were found in sediments between Layers 32 and 38 with a Bayesian modelled age of 51.7–47.3 ka (Tobler et al. 2017), and they could indicate a human presence in the region (Dortch 1979). Four of these six artefacts are made of calcrete, a material available within the cave, while two very small artefacts are made from quartz (Dortch 2004: 96). It is possible, as Dortch speculates, that these lowest artefacts derive from overlying sediments, though this would require almost a metre of vertical downward movement. The earliest clear evidence for human occupation of the cave is contained in a thick organic layer (Layer 30 lower) that has been interpreted by Balme, Merilees, and Porter (1978) as representing the creation of an opening sufficiently large to allow people to enter the cave (Balme et al. 1978; Turney et al. 2001). Using OSL and ABOX-SC radiocarbon ages, the Bayesian modelled date for the earliest evidence of occupation of the cave is 48.7–45.5 ka (Tobler et al. 2017; Turney et al. 2001).

Today, Devil's Lair is only 5 km from the sea, but 50 ka the sea was c. 30 km away from the site (Balme et al. 1978). Vegetation shifts associated with these sea level changes have been identified from the charcoal (Dortch 2004) and faunal remains (Balme et al. 1978). This evidence suggests that, when first occupied, the environment around the cave was more open than it is today and consisted of open woodland species (Dortch 2004). The stone artefacts in these early occupation levels are unretouched flakes, and the prey species suggest a diverse selection of small to large game, including macropods, bandicoots, and possums (Balme et al. 1978; Dortch & Wright 2010).

Warratyi

Warratyi is an arid zone rock shelter located in the Lake Eyre Basin at the northern end of the Flinders Ranges in South Australia. It contains some of the earliest evidence for arid zone occupation by people (Figure 9.1). Two 2 × 1 m trenches have been excavated to a maximum depth of 1 m, with a modelled start age of 54.4–46.4 ka for the lowest occupation phase (SU4) (Hamm et al. 2016). The 129 artefacts that represent the lithic technology of the early occupation are mostly local quartz, with a few imported quartzite and silcrete pieces (Hamm et al. 2016). Phase SU4 also contains one of the earliest examples of red ochre pigment use for the arid zone. The early phase of occupation includes a single bone fragment attributed to *Diprotodon optatum*, as well as eggshell fragments from *Genyornis newtoni* (Hamm et al. 2016). This site is one of the few examples anywhere in Sahul to demonstrate human association with extinct megafauna.

Lake Mungo

Lake Mungo is located in southeastern Australia on the edge of the arid zone and forms part of the larger Willandra Lakes system (Figure 9.1). The site contains both

AUSTRALIA'S FIRST PEOPLE 257

a rich Late Pleistocene cultural history and an extensive palaeoenvironmental record for the semiarid desert margin. The earliest known burials for Australia's First Peoples are located at Lake Mungo. They comprise the cremation burial of a young woman (known as Mungo I or WLH1) (Bowler, Jones, Allen, & Thorne 1970) and a fully articulated body buried with large quantities of red ochre (Mungo III or WLH3) (Bowler & Thorne 1976). The burials were found eroding out of the stratigraphic boundary between two well-defined sedimentary units. Both sets of remains were dug into the Lower Mungo Unit and capped by the Upper Mungo Unit. Early direct radiocarbon ages for the cremation (Bowler et al. 1970) and U-series and coupled U-series/ESR direct age estimates on the ochred burial (Thorne et al. 1999) are in conflict with the burial age of the Lower and Upper Units within which the remains were encased. The radiocarbon ages for the cremation are considerably younger, and the U-series and coupled U-series/ESR direct age estimates on the ochred burial are far older, than TL and OSL ages obtained from the Lower and Upper Mungo Units (Bowler & Price 1998; Bowler et al. 2003; Jankowski et al. 2020; Oyston 1996). Age estimates on the underlying and overlying Mungo Units are in agreement with optical ages on the ochred burial grave fill (Olley et al. 2006). The younger radiocarbon age for the cremation burial has been interpreted to be the result of contamination by young carbon, while the older ages for the ochred burial are possibly the result of uranium migration (Bowler et al. 2003). The most recent single-grain OSL ages for the Mungo sedimentary Units further constrain the age of the burials to between 42.5 and 34.5 ka (Upper Mungo Unit) and 43.1–33.5 ka (Lower Mungo Unit, close to the interface) (Jankowski et al. 2020). This dating is consistent with ages for the Mungo Units from previous TL and OSL dating programs (Bowler & Price 1998; Bowler et al. 2003; Olley et al. 2006; Oyston 1996).

Excavations at the Mungo B Trench (close to the burials) found evidence for human habitation in the form of stone tools, charcoal, and burnt animal bone (Bowler et al. 2003; Shawcross 1998). The earliest evidence of human habitation takes the form of eleven silcrete flakes excavated from the Mungo B Trench below a layer of gravel and barrier sands with bracketing single-grain OSL ages of 51.8–40.6 ka and 46.2–35.8 ka (Bowler et al. 2003; Jankowski et al. 2020; Shawcross 1998). Radiocarbon dates from fish otoliths from the intervening deposit provide an age estimate of 42.1–40.2 cal. ka BP from the same spit as the lowest artefact (Spit 15) (Long et al. 2018) (Table 9.1).

Lake Mungo experienced high lake level conditions from ~64 to 32 ka, in phase with the broader palaeoenvironmental trends across the region (Jankowski et al. 2020). Studies on fish otoliths dated to between c. 45 and 35 ka indicate that lake-full conditions likely prevailed at this time (Long et al. 2018). The Mungo burials and oldest artefacts date to the onset of a period when people were increasingly exploiting the freshwater resources of the Willandra lakes and rivers, as indicated by the peak in mussel exploitation during this time (Stern 2015; Stern, Tumney, Fitzsimmons, & Kajewski 2013).

POPULATION SIZE

Archaeologists have long pondered the likely size of Aboriginal populations at the time of the initial peopling of Australia as well as upon European arrival. Only with the rise of genetic analyses of modern populations has it become possible to estimate founding population size in Australia and identify periods of demographic growth. Population size at the time of European invasion nevertheless remains uncertain, with estimates ranging from hundreds of thousands to even millions of people.

Genetic and demographic modelling suggests that founding population sizes were likely large, and that voyaging to Sahul from Island Southeast Asia was therefore probably not accidental (Bird et al. 2018; Bradshaw et al. 2019; Moore 2001). Based on the number of females required to found the 9–10 Aboriginal mitochondrial lineages in Australia, Bird et al. (2018) estimate a founding population size in the order of at least 72–100 individuals, but see 200–300 people as a more likely estimate. Using a stochastic, age-structured model based on the demographic rates of hunter-gatherer societies and modelled carrying capacity of northern Sahul, Bradshaw et al. (2019) estimated a founding population size in the order of at least ~1300 individuals to avoid extinction upon making landfall in Sahul. Founding populations of hundreds of people would point to a deliberate, planned, provisioned, multivessel journey to Sahul from eastern Wallacea that was unparalleled at this point in human history (Leppard 2015).

High coverage and mtDNA analyses of Aboriginal genomes suggest that Australian populations diverged from Papuans ~37 ka and became internally geographically structured by around 10–32 ka (Malaspinas et al. 2016; Tobler et al. 2017), with population expansions noticeable after the Last Glacial Maximum (Pedro et al. 2020) and in the Holocene ~10 ka (Malaspinas et al. 2016).

Most recently, Bradshaw et al. (2021) developed a demographic simulation using real-world data about long-distance dispersal of people, human survival, fertility rates, and the chance of natural disasters. These were employed in combination with principles of human ecology and behaviour, and with anthropological, ecological, and environmental data to model the peopling of Sahul. The simulation model explored multiple possible entry points along the northwest coast of Sahul (assuming sea crossings from island southeast Asia) as well as a range of possible entry times. Bradshaw and colleagues found that the ancestors of Indigenous Australians and New Guineans could have settled Sahul in as little as 5000 years, with the population potentially growing to 6.5 million in that time, and an estimated 3 million in Australia alone (including the now submerged continental shelf). Furthermore, contrary to expectations (Bowdler 1977), the study found that modelled populations did not exclusively follow coastlines when moving through Sahul but also well-watered inland routes (see also Bird et al. 2016; Crabtree et al. 2021; Horton 1981), pausing only briefly to enter the driest parts of central Australia. Strongest support was found for the arrival of people either 50,000 or 75,000 years ago, with the average establishment rate of 1 km per year. Models of this kind challenge old assumptions and provide useful predicitions for where early archaeological sites may be found.

Technology

The first people of Sahul were innovative and dynamic, and some of the innovations in technology are firsts on a global stage (Figures 9.3 and 9.4). These firsts include examples of the oldest edge-ground axes in the world. At Madjedbebe, resin-hafted waisted edge-ground hatchet heads (Figures 9.3e and 9.4) and many flakes from their edges appear in Phase 2 (68.7–50.4 ka) (Table 9.1) and strongly resemble recent Aboriginal stone axes, though morphological diversity is present in the Pleistocene (Akerman 2014; Clarkson et al. 2017; Dortch 1977). Similar early examples occur across other regions of northern Australia, with axe technology present in the initial phase of occupation (51.0–38.8 ka) at Carpenters Gap 1 (Hiscock et al. 2016; Maloney et al. 2018), by 35.4±0.4 cal ka BP at Nawarla Gabarnmang (Geneste et al. 2010), and by c. 40 ka at Sandy Creek

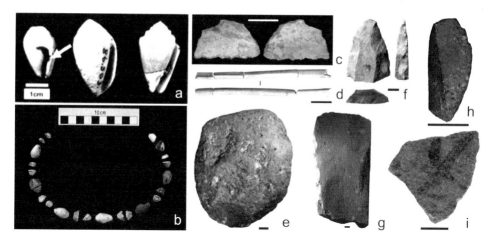

FIGURE 9.3. Examples of early innovative technological and symbolic behaviours in Australia. Unless otherwise indicated, scale bar is 1 cm. (a) Close-up of *Conus* sp. perforated shell bead from Mandu Mandu rock shelter, 40.4–36.0 cal. ka BP; (b) shell beads in hypothetical necklace arrangement, Mandu Mandu, 40.4–36.0 cal. ka BP (a and b with permission Nganhurra Thanardi Garrbu Aboriginal Corporation); (c) oldest backed artefact from Karnatukul, 45.6–41.6 cal. ka BP (with permission from the Mungarlu Ngurrakatja Rirraunkaja Proscribed Body Corporate); (d) presumed ochred nose bone or awl from Carpenter's Gap 1, Phase 1 (51.0–38.8 cal. ka BP) (with permission from the Bunuba Dawangarri Aboriginal Corporation). (e) oldest edge-ground axe from Madjedbebe, Phase 2 (68.750.4 ka); (f) unifacial point tip from Madjedbebe, Phase 2; (g) whetstone from Madjedbebe, Phase 2; (h) ground ochre crayon from Madjedbebe, Phase 2 (e–h with permission from the Gundjeihmi Aboriginal Corporation); (i) fragment of dynamic art motif, Nawarla Gabarnmang, 27.7–26.9 cal. kaBP (courtesy of Bruno David).

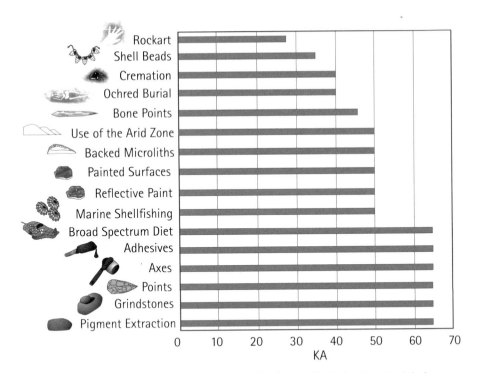

FIGURE 9.4. Chronological evidence for a range of early complex behaviours in Sahul.

in Cape York Peninsula (Morwood & Trezise 1989), indicating the existence of a distinctive Pleistocene tropical techno-cultural zone. Edge-ground axes were likely developed to access the many important resources (bark, wood, resin, etc.) and high-ranked foods sequestered within or high up in trees (honey, eggs, insects, possums, nuts, fruit, and flowers), justifing the substantial time investment involved in their manufacture (Dickson 1972; Sillitoe & Hardy 2003). Axes may also have played an important symbolic role in the deep past, of the kind summarized by Sharp (1952), Brumm (2010), and Akerman (2014) (see Ford & Hiscock, this volume). Other signs of early technological innovation are also known from Australia, such as the early use of stone points carefully crafted through the removal of thinning flakes at Madjedbebe (Clarkson et al. 2017) and Nawarla Gabarnmang (David et al. 2019) (Figure 9.4).

The first people in Australia were investing heavily in other kinds of grinding technology as well, as seen in the appearance of a very large grindstone assemblage in the deepest occupation layer (Phase 2) at Madjedbebe. These tools show traces of processing a wide range of substances, including soft and hard plants, ochre, axes, and seeds, making these the oldest known seed-grinding tools outside of Africa (Clarkson et al. 2017) and the oldest whetstones in the world (Figures 9.3g and 9.4) (Hayes et al. 2022). The heavy investment in grinding stones most likely indicates that some important foods required extensive processing to make them edible, and that axes were resharpened at habitation sites as well as in production areas. Pleistocene grinding tools are also well attested in parts of southern Australia (Fullagar & Field 1997; Fullagar et al. 2015).

Another application of grinding technology is to create bone artefacts. A variety of bone artefacts which have been manufactured by scraping followed by careful grinding are present from the earliest levels at most sites where the bone is well-preserved (Figure 9.4). Bone points made from macropod fibulae were recovered from the initial phase of occupation at Carpenters Gap 1 (Figure 9.3d) and Riwi (Langley et al. 2016; Balme et al. 2018), and the second phase of occupation at Warratyi (SU3), which has an associated age of 44.9–36.1 ka (Hamm et al. 2016).

Flakes from rejuvenating the ground edges and surfaces of edge-ground axes and grinding stones are a persistent feature of lithic technology for Arnhem Land as well as the earliest occupied sites in the Kimberley. However, from ~52 to 28 ka at Madjedbebe there is a shift in stone raw material use away from silcrete to quartz, with bipolar technology becoming more frequent and thinning flakes dropping out (Clarkson et al. 2017). This second phase accords with the technological record of sites to the west and further south, with bipolar knapping of quartz characterizing the initial phase of occupation (Phase 1) at Carpenters Gap 1 (Maloney et al. 2018), and small quartz flakes the dominant artefacts at the beginning of the Warratyi cultural sequence (SU4) (Table 9.1) (Hamm et al. 2016). Tiny backed mircoliths are also an innovation first appearing in the arid zone at Karnatukul at 45.6–41.6 cal ka BP (Figures 9.3c and 9.4). Backed artefacts make sporadic appearances in the Pleistocene at Warratyi, Walkunder Arch Cave in north Queensland (Cambell 1982) and at GRE8 and OLH in the Riversleigh area of the Gulf of Carpentaria (Slack, Fullagar, Field, & Border 2004), before becoming common across the southern two-thirds of Australia in the late Hoocene.

SUBSISTENCE ECONOMY

The innovative and flexible nature of dispersing early modern humans is further evident in the plants utilized in the earliest layers at Madjedbebe (Florin et al. 2020, 2022). These charred remains contain several kinds of tubers, nuts, seeds, palms, and fruits, representing a broad diet that included low-ranked foods, some of which required extensive processing, including grinding (Figure 9.4). There is also abundant evidence for early use of new and difficult environments around Australia. These include early use of monsoon, riparian, and savannah resources in the first phase of occupation at Madjedbebe and Carpenters Gap 1, with the earliest use of the arid zone occurring at Karnatukul and Warratyi rock shelters (Figure 9.4) (Hamm et al. 2016; McDonald et al. 2018).

Extensive use of inland lakes and waterways is evident at the Willandra Lakes by ~40 ka when there appears to have been a focus on the freshwater resources of the lake system (Long et al. 2018; Stern et al. 2013). Exploitation of freshwater mussels and Golden Perch peaks between ~40 and 36 ka, and then declines before people renew their focus on the Willandra Lakes system in the Last Glacial Maximum (Bowler et al. 2012). Early use of marine resources is found at Boodie Cave, with a small volume of shellfish transported inland over 15 km to the site by ~42 ka (Veth et al. 2017).

Overall, the early archaeological record from Australia points to early modern humans exploiting a broad range of plant and animal resources, and employing highly flexible and innovative economies. This pattern is consistent with the notion that early Aboriginal populations were engaged in ecological plasticity as 'generalist-specialists' capable of occupying new and extreme environments for the first time (Roberts & Stewart 2018).

Symbolism

The evidence for symbolic expression was once thought to be almost entirely absent in early Southeast Asia and Australia and that behavioural modernity was in some sense lacking or differently expressed in these regions (Habgood & Franklin 2008; O'Connell & Allen 2007). In the last two decades, a wealth of new information has come to light demonstrating clear evidence for early symbolic expression (Langley, Clarkson, & Ulm 2011, 2019).

Evidence for personal adornment comes from a bone point most likely used as an ochred nose bone or awl found at Carpenters Gap 1 in semiarid northern Australia and dating from 51.0 to 38.8 ka (Phase 1) (Figures 9.3d and 9.4) (Langley et al. 2016; Maloney et al. 2018). At Mandu Mandu rock shelter (Figures 9.3a, b and 9.4) on the central west coast of Australia, twenty-two shell beads made from *Conus* sp. radiocarbon date to 40.4–36.0 cal. ka BP (Balme & Morse 2006; Morse 1993).

Early use of ground ochre pigment, presumably for artistic or symbolic activities of some kind, is widespread across Australia and occurs in the earliest cultural horizons of all the sites shown in Figures 9.1 and 9.4 (Balme et al. 2018; Bowler et al. 2003; Clarkson et al. 2017; David et al. 2019; Hamm et al. 2016; Maloney et al. 2018; O'Connor & Fankhauser 2001). The earliest examples come from Madjedbebe, where more than 3.5 kg of ground ochre was found in the earliest occupation layer (Phase 2) (Figures 9.3h and 9.4). Ochre traces are also common on Phase 2 grindstones from Madjedbebe (Clarkson et al. 2017; Hayes et al. 2022). The mixing of ground mica with ochre to make reflective paint is attested on ochred rock slabs from the site dated to c. 50–40 ka, as well as a bundle of exotic yellow ochre wrapped in cut sheet mica from Phase 2 (Figure 9.4). Ground ochre pigment is found in the earliest cultural levels at Nauwalabila 1, while the earliest pictograph for the continent was excavated at the plateau site of Nawarla Gabarnmang (Figures 9.3i and 9.4). It fell from the ceiling c. 28 ka, so the pre-existing painting on the small fallen stone tablet must be older (David et al. 2013). Ochre is present in the oldest known burial in Australia (Mungo III) (Bowler & Thorne 1976), while at the site of Warratyi in the arid zone, worked red ochre and ochre residue on a silcrete flake were found in the lowest occupation phase (54.4–41.3 ka).

CONCLUSION

The successful expansion through the Wallacean archipelago of Southeast Asia to Sahul is testament to the remarkable ingenuity of the First Australians. The maritime skills that were vital to support onward movement through Wallacea to Sahul were honed in the equatorial island communities from which these early mariners came. Once in Sahul, a wider range of technological skills appear to have been quickly invented and were no doubt essential for movement through the myriad unique environments of Sahul with its marsupial fauna and very hard timbers. The current evidence shows a lag between occupation of Arnhem Land in Marine Isotope Stage 4 (71–57 ka), perhaps due to very dry conditions in the south (DeDekker et al. 2019), and first occupation across the rest of the continent in early Marine Isotope Stage 3 (57–29 ka). Once outside of Arnhem Land, people appear to have rapidly occupied diverse environments, from coasts (Boodie Cave) to forests (Devil's Lair), to the semiarid Willandra Lakes (Mungo) and the arid centre (Karnatukul and Warratyi).

The flaked stone technology in many early sites was largely unspecialized and not unlike that of Island Southeast Asia at the time. However, at Madjedbebe, highly specialized composite tools, such as edge-ground axes and stone points, are present from the onset of occupation. Ground bone artefacts occur in the very earliest occupation layers at Carpenters Gap 1 and Riwi, showing that bone was an important raw material in the technological repertoire following arrival in Sahul. The Riwi and Carpenters Gap 1 bone tools were used for a diverse array of purposes such as piercing and awling, and as projectiles and for personal decoration.

The application of grinding to axes to form a sharp edge appears to be a local invention in Sahul, perhaps in response to Sahul's hardwoods. The objects made from these hardwoods have not survived, but it can be assumed that they played important roles. The lack of spread of edge-ground axes to the southern part of the continent until the Holocene might indicate the relative importance of wooden objects in the north, or the early spread of the technology across the north may indicate greater cultural interactions there during the Pleistocene.

Rock art has an antiquity in excess of 45.8–45.1 ka on the island of Sulawesi in Island Southeast Asia (Brumm et al. 2021). The presence of ochre in early northern Sahul suggests that this aspect of symbolic behaviour was present from the onset of occupation in Australia, too, although we do not yet have firm dates for rock art of equivalent age in Sahul, nor do we know the nature of early rock art depictions in Sahul.

Sahul was a unique and diverse Pleistocene supercontinent in terms of its natural and cultural history. On present evidence from Arnhem Land in central northern Australia, an early peopling event occurred in MIS 4, perhaps followed by a substantial delay in southward dispersal, with the remainder of the continent rapidly peopled in early MIS 3. The cultures of early Australians were clearly complex, innovative, and diverse, showing an early familiarization with and exploitation of local resources using technologies that were novel on a global scale. Much work remains to be done to better understand this fascinating period and the many cultural, technological, and symbolic dimensions of the first Australians.

REFERENCES

Akerman, K. (2014). Observations on edge-ground stone hatchets with hafting modifications in Western Australia. *Australian Archaeology, 79*(1), 137–145.

Allen, J. (1994). Radiocarbon determinations, luminescence dating and Australian archaeology. *Antiquity, 68*(259), 339–343.

Allen, J. (2017). Yes, Virginia, there is a Santa Claus: He just doesn't bring presents to children who don't believe in him. *Australian Archaeology, 83*(3), 163–165.

Allen, J., & Holdaway, S. (1995). The contamination of Pleistocene radiocarbon determinations in Australia. *Antiquity, 69*(262), 101–112.

Allen, J., & O'Connell, J. (2003). The long and the short of it: Archaeological approaches to determining when humans first colonised Australia and New Guinea. *Australian Archaeology, 57*(1), 5–19.

Allen, J., & O'Connell, J. (2014). Both half right: Updating the evidence for dating first human arrivals in Sahul. *Australian Archaeology, 79*(1), 86–108.

Allen, J., & O'Connell, J. (2020). A different paradigm for the initial colonisation of Sahul. *Archaeology in Oceania, 55*(1), 1–14.

Balme, J. (2013). Of boats and string: The maritime colonisation of Australia. *Quaternary International, 285*, 68–75.

Balme, J., Merilees, D., & Porter, J. (1978). Late Quaternary mammal remains spanning 30,000 years, from excavations in Devil's Lair, Western Australia. *Journal of the Royal Society of Western Australia, 61*(2), 33–65.

Balme, J., & Morse, K. (2006). Shell beads and social behaviour in Pleistocene Australia. *Antiquity, 80*(310), 799–811.

Balme, J., O'Connor, S., Maloney, T., Vannieuwenhuyse, D., Aplin, K., & Dilkes-Hall, I. E. (2018). Long-term occupation on the edge of the desert: Riwi Cave in the southern Kimberley, Western Australia. *Archaeology in Oceania, 54*(1), 35–52.

Barker, G., Hunt, C., Barton, H., Gosden, C., Jones, S., Lloyd-Smith, L., . . . O'Donnell, S. (2017). The 'cultured rainforests' of Borneo. *Quaternary International, 448*, 44–61.

Bird, M. I., Ayliffe, L. K., Fifield, L. K., Turney, C. S. M., Cresswell, R. G., Barrows, T. T., & David, B. (1999). Radiocarbon dating of 'old' charcoal using a wet oxidation, stepped-combustion procedure. *Radiocarbon, 41*(2), 127–140.

Bird, M. I., Beaman, R. J., Condie, S. A., Cooper, A., Ulm, S., & Veth, P. (2018). Palaeogeography and voyage modeling indicates early human colonization of Australia was likely from Timor-Roti. *Quaternary Science Reviews, 191*, 431–439.

Bird, M. I., O'Grady, D., & Ulm, S. (2016). Humans, water, and the colonization of Australia. *Proceedings of the National Academy of Sciences, 113*(41), 11477–11482.

Bird, M. I., Turney, C. S. M., Fifield, L. K., Jones, R., Ayliffe, L. K., Palmer, A., . . . Robertson, S. (2002). Radiocarbon analysis of the early archaeological site of Nauwalabila I, Arnhem Land, Australia: Implications for sample suitability and stratigraphic integrity. *Quaternary Science Reviews, 21*(8–9), 1061–1075.

Blundell, V. (1975). *Aboriginal adaptation in northwest Australia* (PhD thesis). University of Wisconsin-Madison, Wisconsin.

Bowdler, S. (1977). The coastal colonisation of Australia. In J. Allen, J. Golson, & R. Jones (Eds.), *Sunda and Sahul: Prehistoric studies in Southeast Asia, Melanesia and Australia* (pp. 205–246). London: Academic Press.

Bowler, J. M., Gillespie, R., Johnston, H., & Sporcic, K. (2012). Wind v water: Glacial maximum records from the Willandra Lakes. In S. G. Haberle & B. David (Eds.), *Peopled landscapes: Archaeological and biogeographic approaches to landscapes* (pp. 271–296). Terra Australis 34. Canberra: ANU ePress.

Bowler, J. M., Johnston, H., Olley, J. M., Prescott, J. R., Roberts, R. G., Shawcross, W., & Spooner, N. A. (2003). New ages for human occupation and climatic change at Lake Mungo, Australia. *Nature, 421*(6925), 837.

Bowler, J. M., Jones, R., Allen, H., & Thorne, A. G. (1970). Pleistocene human remains from Australia: A living site and human cremation from Lake Mungo, western New South Wales. *World Archaeology, 2*(1), 39–60.

Bowler, J. M., & Price, D. M. (1998). Luminescence dates and stratigraphic analyses at Lake Mungo: Review and new perspectives. *Archaeology in Oceania, 33*(3), 156–168.

Bowler, J. M., & Thorne, A. G. (1976). Human remains from Lake Mungo: Discovery and excavation of Lake Mungo III. In R. L. Kirk & A. G. Thorne (Eds.), *The origin of the Australians* (pp. 127–138). Canberra: Australian Institute of Aboriginal Studies.

Bradshaw, C. J., Norman, K., Ulm, S., Williams, A. N., Clarkson, C., Chadoeuf, J., . . . Saltré, F. (2021). Stochastic models support rapid peopling of Late Pleistocene Sahul. *Nature Communications, 12*(1), 1–11.

Bradshaw, C. J., Ulm, S., Williams, A. N., Bird, M. I., Roberts, R. G., Jacobs, Z., . . . Saltré, F. (2019). Minimum founding populations for the first peopling of Sahul. *Nature Ecology & Evolution, 3*(7), 1057–1063.

Brumm, A. (2010). 'The falling sky': Symbolic and cosmological associations of the Mt William greenstone axe quarry, central Victoria, Australia. *Cambridge Archaeological Journal, 20*(2), 179–196.

Brumm, A., Oktaviana, A. A., Burhan, B., Hakim, B., Lebe, R., Zhao, J. X., . . . Aubert, M. (2021). Oldest cave art found in Sulawesi. *Science Advances, 7*(3), p.eabd4648.

Campbell, J. B. (1982). New radiocarbon results for north Queensland prehistory. *Australian Archaeology, 14*(1), 62–66.

Chappell, J., Head, J., & Magee, J. (1996). Beyond the radiocarbon limit in Australian archaeology and Quaternary research. *Antiquity, 70*(269), 543–552.

Clarkson, C., Jacobs, Z., Marwick, B., Fullagar, R., Wallis, L., Smith, M., . . . Florin, S. A. (2017). Human occupation of northern Australia by 65,000 years ago. *Nature, 547*(7663), 306–310.

Clarkson, C., Roberts, R. G., Jacobs, Z., Marwick, B., Fullagar, R., Arnold, L. J., & Hua, Q. 2018. Reply to comments on Clarkson et al. (2017). 'Human occupation of northern Australia by 65,000 years ago'. *Australian Archaeology, 84*(1), 84–89.

Clarkson, C., Smith, M., Marwick, B., Fullagar, R., Wallis, L. A., Faulkner, P., . . . Carah, X. (2015). The archaeology, chronology and stratigraphy of Madjedbebe (Malakunanja II): A site in northern Australia with early occupation. *Journal of Human Evolution, 83*, 46–64.

Crabtree, S.A., White, D.A., Bradshaw, C.J., Saltré, F., Williams, A.N., Beaman, R.J., . . . Ulm, S. (2021). Landscape rules predict optimal superhighways for the first peopling of Sahul. *Nature Human Behaviour, 5*(10), pp.1303–1313.

David, B., Barker, B., Petchey, F., Delannoy, J.-J., Geneste, J.-M., Rowe, C., . . . Whear, R. (2013). A 28,000 year old excavated painted rock from Nawarla Gabarnmang, northern Australia. *Journal of Archaeological Science, 40*(5), 2493–2501.

David, B., Delannoy, J.-J., Mialanes, J., Clarkson, C., Petchey, F., Geneste, J.-M., . . . Chalmin, E. (2019). 45,610–52,160 years of site and landscape occupation at Nawarla Gabarnmang, Arnhem Land plateau (northern Australia). *Quaternary Science Reviews, 215*, 64–85.

David, B., Geneste, J.-M., Whear, R. L., Delannoy, J.-J., Katherine, M., Gunn, R. G., . . . Rowe, C. (2011). Nawarla Gabarnmang, a 45,180±910 cal BP site in Jawoyn country, southwest Arnhem Land plateau. *Australian Archaeology, 73*(1), 73–77.

Davidson, I., & Noble, W. (1992). Why the first colonisation of the Australian region is the earliest evidence of modern human behaviour. *Archaeology in Oceania, 27*(3), 135–142.

De Deckker, P., Arnold, L. J., van der Kaars, S., Bayon, G., Stuut, J. B. W., Perner, K., . . . Demuro, M. (2019). Marine Isotope Stage 4 in Australasia: A full glacial culminating 65,000 years ago–Global connections and implications for human dispersal. *Quaternary Science Reviews, 204*, 187–207.

Demeter, F., Shackelford, L. L., Bacon, A. M., Duringer, P., Westaway, K., Sayavongkhamdy, T., . . . Wang, H. (2012). Anatomically modern human in Southeast Asia (Laos) by 46 ka. *Proceedings of the National Academy of Sciences, 109*(36), 14375–14380.

Dickson, F. P. (1972). Ground edge axes. *Mankind, 8*(3), 206–211.

Dilkes-Hall, I. E., O'Connor, S., & Balme, J. (2019). People-plant interaction and economic botany over 47,000 years of occupation at Carpenter's Gap 1, south central Kimberley. *Australian Archaeology, 85*(1), 30–47.

Dortch, C. E. (1977). Ancient grooved stone axes from an alluvial terrace on Stonewall Creek, Kimberley, Western Australia. *Journal of the Royal Society of Western Australia, 60*(1), 23–30.

Dortch, C. E. (1979). Devil's Lair, an example of prolonged cave use in south-western Australia. *World Archaeology, 10*(3), 258–279.

Dortch, J. (2004). *Palaeo-environmental change and the persistence of human occupation in south-western Australian forests.* Oxford: Archaeopress.

Dortch, J., & Wright, R. (2010). Identifying palaeo-environments and changes in Aboriginal subsistence from dual-patterned faunal assemblages, south-western Australia. *Journal of Archaeological Science, 37*, 1053–1064.

Etheridge, R. (1890). Has man a geological history in Australia. *Proceedings of the Linnean Society of New South Wales, 5*, 259–266.

Fairbanks, R. G., Mortlock, R. A., Chiu, T. C., Cao, L., Kaplan, A., Guilderson, T. P., . . . Nadeau, M. J. (2005). Radiocarbon calibration curve spanning 0 to 50,000 years BP based on paired 230Th/234U/238U and 14C dates on pristine corals. *Quaternary Science Reviews, 24*(16–17), 1781–1796.

Florin, S. A., Fairbairn, A. S., Nango, M., Djandjomerr, D., Marwick, B., Fullagar, R., . . . Clarkson, C. (2020). The first Australian plant foods at Madjedbebe, 65,000–53,000 years ago. *Nature Communications, 11*(1), 1–8.

Florin, S. A., Roberts, P., Marwick, B., Patton, N. R., Shulmeister, J., Lovelock, C. E., . . . Fullagar, R. (2021). Pandanus nutshell generates a palaeoprecipitation record for human occupation at Madjedbebe, northern Australia. *Nature Ecology & Evolution, 5*(3), 295–303.

Florin, S. A., Fairbairn, A. S., Nango, M., Djandjomerr, D., Hua, Q., Marwick, B., . . . Clarkson, C. (2022). 65,000 years of changing plant food and landscape use at Madjedbebe, Mirarr country, northern Australia. *Quaternary Science Reviews, 284*, 1–16.

Fu, Q., Mittnik, A., Johnson, P. L., Bos, K., Lari, M., Bollongino, R., . . . Ronchitelli, A. M. (2013). A revised timescale for human evolution based on ancient mitochondrial genomes. *Current Biology, 23*(7), 553–559.

Fullagar, R., & Field, J. (1997). Pleistocene seed-grinding implements from the Australian arid zone. *Antiquity, 71*(272), 300–307.

Fullagar, R., Hayes, E., Stephenson, B., Field, J., Matheson, C., Stern, N., & Fitzsimmons, K. (2015). Evidence for Pleistocene seed grinding at Lake Mungo, south-eastern Australia. *Archaeology in Oceania, 50*, 3–19.

Geneste, J.-M., David, B., Plisson, H., Clarkson, C., Delannoy, J.-J., Petchey, F., & Whear, R. (2010). Earliest evidence for ground-edge axes: 35,400±410 cal BP from Jawoyn Country, Arnhem Land. *Australian Archaeology, 71*(1), 66–69.

Gunn, R. G. (2018). *Art of the ancestors: Spatial and temporal patterning in the ceiling rock art of Nawarla Gabarnmang, Arnhem Land, Australia.* Oxford: Archaeopress.

Habgood, P. J., & Franklin, N. R. (2008). The revolution that didn't arrive: A review of Pleistocene Sahul. *Journal of Human Evolution, 55*(2), 187–222.

Hamm, G., Mitchell, P., Arnold, L. J., Prideaux, G. J., Questiaux, D., Spooner, N. A., . . . Coulthard, V. (2016). Cultural innovation and megafauna interaction in the early settlement of arid Australia. *Nature, 539*(7628), 280–283.

Hayes, E., Fullagar, R., Marwick, B., Field, J., Matheson, C., Wallis, L., . . . Clarkson, C. (2022). 65,000-years of continuous grinding stone use at Madjedbebe, Northern Australia. *Scientific Reports, 12* (1),1–17. DOI: 10.1038/s41598-022-15174-x

Heaton, T. J., Köhler, P., Butzin, M., Bard, E., Reimer, R. W., Austin, W. E., . . . Reimer, P. J., (2020). Marine20—the marine radiocarbon age calibration curve (0–55,000 cal BP). *Radiocarbon, 62*(4), 779–820.

Hiscock, P. (2017). Discovery curves, colonisation and Madjedbebe. *Australian Archaeology, 83*(3), 168–171.

Hiscock, P., O'Connor, S., Balme, J., & Maloney, T. (2016). World's earliest ground-edge axe production coincides with human colonisation of Australia. *Australian Archaeology, 82*(1), 2–11.

Hogg, A. G., Heaton, T. J., Hua, Q., Palmer, J. G., Turney, C. S., Southon, . . . Pearson, C. (2020). SHCal20 Southern Hemisphere calibration, 0–55,000 years cal BP. *Radiocarbon, 62*(4), 759–778.

Horton, D. (1981). Water and woodland: The peopling of Australia. *Australian Institute of Aboriginal Studies, 16*, 21–27.

Jacobs, Z., & Roberts, R. G. (2007). Advances in optically stimulated luminescence dating of individual grains of quartz from archeological deposits. Evolutionary Anthropology: Issues, News, *and Reviews: Issues, News, and Reviews, 16*(6), 210–223.

Jankowski, N. R., Stern, N., Lachlan, T. J., & Jacobs, Z. (2020). A high-resolution late Quaternary depositional history and chronology for the southern portion of the Lake Mungo lunette, semi-arid Australia. *Quaternary Science Reviews, 233*, 106–224.

Jones, R. (1999). Dating the human colonization of Australia: Radiocarbon and luminescence revolutions. *Proceedings of the British Academy, 99*, 37–66.

Jones, R., & Johnson, I. (1985). Deaf Adder Gorge: Lindner Site, Nauwalabila 1. In R. Jones (Ed.), *Archaeological research in Kakadu National Park* (pp. 165–228). Canberra: Australian National Parks and Wildlife Service.

Kamminga, J., & Allen, H. (1973). *Report of the archaeological survey.* Alligator Rivers Environmental Fact-Finding Study. Darwin: Government Printer for Alligator Rivers Region Environmental Fact-Finding Study.

Kealy, S., Louys, J., & O'Connor, S. (2016). Islands under the sea: A review of early modern human dispersal routes and migration hypotheses through Wallacea. *The Journal of Island and Coastal Archaeology, 11*(3), 364–384.

Kenneally, K. F., Edinger, D. C., & Willing, T. (1996). *Broome and beyond: Plants and people of the Dampier Peninsula, Kimberley, Western Australia.* Como: Department of Conservation and Land Management.

Kirchner, J. W., & Weil, A. (2000). Delayed biological recovery from extinctions throughout the fossil record. *Nature, 404*(6774), 177.

Langley, M. C., Balme, J., & O'Connor, S. (2021). Bone artefacts from Riwi Cave, south-central Kimberley: Reappraisal of the timing and role of osseous artefacts in northern Australia. *International Journal of Osteoarchaeology* DOI: 10.1002/oa.2981.

Langley, M. C., Clarkson, C., & Ulm, S. (2011). From small holes to grand narratives: The impact of taphonomy and sample size on the modernity debate in Australia and New Guinea. *Journal of Human Evolution, 61*(2), 197–208.

Langley, M. C., Clarkson, C., & Ulm, S. (2019). Symbolic expression in Pleistocene Sahul, Sunda, and Wallacea. *Quaternary Science Reviews, 221*, 105883.

Langley, M. C., O'Connor, S., & Aplin, K. (2016). A >46,000-year-old kangaroo bone implement from Carpenter's Gap 1 (Kimberley, northwest Australia). *Quaternary Science Reviews, 154*, 199–213.

Leppard, T. P. (2015). The evolution of modern behaviour and its implications for maritime dispersal during the Palaeolithic. *Cambridge Archaeological Journal, 25*(4), 829–846.

Liu, W., Martinón-Torres, M., Cai, Y. J., Xing, S., Tong, H. W., Pei, S. W., . . . Li, Y. Y. (2015). The earliest unequivocally modern humans in southern China. *Nature, 526*(7575), 696–699.

Long, K., Wood, R., Williams, I. S., Kalish, J., Shawcross, W., Stern, N., & Grün, R. (2018). Fish otolith microchemistry: Snapshots of lake conditions during early human occupation of Lake Mungo, Australia. *Quaternary International, 463*, 29–43.

Lourandos, H., & Ross, A. (1994). The great 'intensification debate': Its history and place in Australian archaeology. *Australian Archaeology, 39*(1), 54–63.

Malaspinas, A. S., Westaway, M. C., Muller, C., Sousa, V. C., Lao, O., Alves, I., . . . Heupink, T. H. (2016). A genomic history of Aboriginal Australia. *Nature, 538*(7624), 207–214.

Maloney, T., O'Connor, S., Wood, R., Aplin, K., & Balme, J. (2018). Carpenters Gap 1: A 47,000 year old record of indigenous adaption and innovation. *Quaternary Science Reviews, 191*, 204–228.

Maloney, T. R. (2015). *Technological organisation and points in the southern Kimberley* (PhD thesis). Australian National University, Canberra.

Marwick, B., Hayes, E., Clarkson, C., & Fullagar, R. (2017). Movement of lithics by trampling: An experiment in the Madjedbebe sediments, northern Australia. *Journal of Archaeological Science, 79*, 73–85.

May, S. K., Wesley, D., Goldhahn, J., Litster, M., & Manera, B. (2017). Symbols of power: The firearm paintings of Madjedbebe (Malakunanja II). *International Journal of Historical Archaeology, 21*(3), 690–707.

McDonald, J., Reynen, W., Petchey, F., Ditchfield, K., Byrne, C., Vannieuwenhuyse, D., . . . Veth, P. (2018). Karnatukul (Serpent's Glen): A new chronology for the oldest site in Australia's Western Desert. *PloS one, 13*(9), 1–35.

Moore, J. H. (2001). Evaluating five models of human colonization. *American Anthropologist, 103*(2), 395–408.

Moore, M. W. (2015). Bifacial flintknapping in the northwest Kimberley, Western Australia. *Journal of Archaeological Method and Theory, 22*(3), 913–951.

Morse, K. (1993). Shell beads from Mandu Mandu Creek rock-shelter, Cape Range peninsula, Western Australia, dated before 30,000 bp. *Antiquity, 67*(257), 877–883.

Morwood, M. J., & Trezise, P. J. (1989). Edge-ground axes in Pleistocene greater Australia: New evidence from SE Cape York Peninsula. *Queensland Archaeological Research, 6*, 77–90.

Mulvaney, D. J., & Joyce, E. B. (1965). Archaeological and geomorphological investigations on Mt. Moffatt station, Queensland, Australia. *Proceedings of the Prehistoric Society, 31*, 147–212.

Norman, K., Inglis, J., Clarkson, C., Faith, J. T., Shulmeister, J., & Harris, D. (2018). An early colonisation pathway into northwest Australia 70–60,000 years ago. *Quaternary Science Reviews, 180*, 229–239.

Norman, K., Shipton, C., O'Connor, S., Malanali, W., Collins, P., Wood, R., . . . Jacobs, Z. (2022). Human occupation of the Kimberley coast of northwest Australia 50,000 years ago. *Quaternary Science Reviews, 288*, 1–20.

O'Connell, J. F., & Allen, J. (1998). When did humans first arrive in greater Australia and why is it important to know? Evolutionary Anthropology: *Issues, News, and Reviews, 6*(4), 132–146.

O'Connell, J. F., & Allen, J. (2004). Dating the colonization of Sahul (Pleistocene Australia–New Guinea): A review of recent research. *Journal of Archaeological Science, 31*(6), 835–853.

O'Connell, J. F., & Allen, J. (2007). Pre-LGM Sahul (Pleistocene Australia-New Guinea) and the archaeology of early modern humans. In O. Bar Yosef & C. Stringer (Eds.), *Rethinking the human revolution* (pp. 395–410). Cambridge: McDonald Institute for Archaeological Research.

O'Connell, J. F., Allen, J., & Hawkes, K. (2010). Pleistocene Sahul and the origins of seafaring. In A. Anderson, J. H. Barrett, & K. V. Boyle (Eds.), *The global origins and development of seafaring* (pp. 57–68). Cambridge: McDonald Institute for Archaeological Research.

O'Connell, J. F., Allen, J., Williams, M. A., Williams, A. N., Turney, C. S., Spooner, N. A., . . . Cooper, A. (2018). When did *Homo sapiens* first reach Southeast Asia and Sahul? *Proceedings of the National Academy of Sciences, 115*(34), 8482–8490.

O'Connor, S. (1995). Carpenters Gap rockshelter 1: 40,000 years of Aboriginal occupation in the Napier Range, Kimberley, WA. *Australian Archaeology, 40*, 58–59.

O'Connor, S., & Fankhauser, B. (2001). One step closer: An ochre covered rock from Carpenters Gap Shelter 1, Kimberley region, Western Australia. In A. Anderson, I. Lilley, & S. O'Connor (Eds.), *Histories of Old Ages: Essays in honour of Rhys Jones* (pp. 287–300). Canberra: Australian National University.

O'Connor, S., Ono, R., & Clarkson, C. (2011). Pelagic fishing at 42,000 years before the present and the maritime skills of modern humans. *Science, 334*(6059), 1117–1121.

O'Connor, S., Veth, P., & Campbell, C. (1998). Serpent's Glen Rockshelter: Report of the first Pleistocene-aged occupation sequence from the Western Desert. *Australian Archaeology, 46*(1), 12–22.

Olley, J. M., Roberts, R. G., Yoshida, H., & Bowler, J. M. (2006). Single-grain optical dating of grave-infill associated with human burials at Lake Mungo, Australia. *Quaternary Science Reviews, 25*(19–20), 2469–2474.

Oyston, B. (1996). Thermoluminescence age determinations for the Mungo III human burial, Lake Mungo, southeastern Australia. *Quaternary Science Reviews, 15*(7), 739–749.

Pedro, N., Brucato, N., Fernandes, V., André, M., Saag, L., Pomat, W., . . . Sudoyo, H. (2020). Papuan mitochondrial genomes and the settlement of Sahul. *Journal of Human Genetics, 65*(10), 875–887.

Roberts, P., & Stewart, B. A. (2018). Defining the 'generalist specialist' niche for Pleistocene *Homo sapiens*. *Nature Human Behaviour*, *2*(8), 542–550.

Roberts, R., Bird, M., Olley, J., Galbraith, R., Lawson, E., Laslett, G., . . . Hua, Q. (1998a). Optical and radiocarbon dating at Jinmium rock shelter in northern Australia. *Nature*, *393*(6683), 358–362.

Roberts, R., Yoshida, H., Galbraith, R., Laslett, G., Jones, R., & Smith, M. (1998b). Single-aliquot and single-grain optical dating confirm thermoluminescence age estimates at Malakunanja II rock shelter in northern Australia. *Ancient TL*, *16*(1), 19–24.

Roberts, R. G., Jones, R., & Smith, M. A. (1990). Thermoluminescence dating of a 50,000-year-old human occupation site in northern Australia. *Nature*, *345*(6271), 153.

Roberts, R. G., Jones, R., Spooner, N. A., Head, M. J., Murray, A. S., & Smith, M. A. (1994a). The human colonisation of Australia: Optical dates of 53,000 and 60,000 years bracket human arrival at Deaf Adder Gorge, Northern Territory. *Quaternary Science Reviews*, *13*(5–7), 575–583.

Roberts, R. G., Jones, R., & Smith, M. A. (1994b). Beyond the radiocarbon barrier in Australian prehistory. *Antiquity*, *68*(260), 611–616.

Rodríguez-Rey, M., Herrando-Pérez, S., Gillespie, R., Jacobs, Z., Saltré, F., Brook, B. W., . . . Miller, G. H. (2015). Criteria for assessing the quality of Middle Pleistocene to Holocene vertebrate fossil ages. *Quaternary Geochronology*, *30*, 69–79.

Scarlett, N. H. (1985). *A preliminary account of the ethnobotany of the Kija people of Bungle outcamp*. Canberra: Center for Resource and Environmental Studies.

Shackelford, L., Demeter, F., Westaway, K., Duringer, P., Ponche, J. L., Sayavongkhamdy, T., . . . Sénégas, F. (2018). Additional evidence for early modern human morphological diversity in Southeast Asia at Tam Pa Ling, Laos. *Quaternary International*, *466*, 93–106.

Sharp, L. (1952). Steel axes for stone-age Australians. *Human Organization*, *11*(2), 17–22.

Shawcross, W. (1998). Archaeological excavations at Mungo. *Archaeology in Oceania*, *33*(3), 183–200.

Sillitoe, P., & Hardy, K. (2003). Living lithics: Ethnoarchaeology in highland Papua New Guinea. *Antiquity*, *77*(297), 555–566.

Slack, M. J., Fullagar, R. L., Field, J. H., & Border, A. (2004). New Pleistocene ages for backed artefact technology in Australia. *Archaeology in Oceania*, *39*(3), 131–137.

Smith, M. A., Ward, I., & Moffat, I. (2020). How do we distinguish termite stone lines from artefact horizons? A challenge for geoarchaeology in tropical Australia. *Geoarchaeology*, *35*(2), 232–242.

Smith, M., Ward, I., & Moffat, I. (2021). Letter to the editors on termite stone lines. *Geoarchaeology*, *36*(2), 363–365.

Sollas, W. J. (1911). *Ancient hunters and their modern representatives*. New York: Macmillan.

Stern, N. (2015). The archaeology of the Willandra: Its empirical structure and narrative potential. In A. McGrath & M. A. Jebb (Eds.), *Long history, deep time: Deepening histories of place* (pp. 221–240). Canberra: ANU Press.

Stern, N., Tumney, J., Fitzsimmons, K. E., & Kajewski, P. (2013). Strategies for investigating human responses to changes in landscape and climate at Lake Mungo in the Willandra Lakes, southeast Australia. In A. McGrath & M. A. Jebb (Eds.), *Archaeology in environment and technology: Intersections and transformations* (pp. 221–240). Canberra: ANU Press.

Stuiver, M., & Reimer, P. J. (1993). Extended 14C data base and revised CALIB 3.0 14C age calibration program. *Radiocarbon*, *35*(1), 215–230.

Thorne, A., Grün, R., Mortimer, G., Spooner, N. A., Simpson, J. J., McCulloch, M., . . . Curnoe, D. (1999). Australia's oldest human remains: Age of the Lake Mungo 3 skeleton. *Journal of Human Evolution*, *36*(6), 591–612.

Tobler, R., Rohrlach, A., Soubrier, J., Bover, P., Llamas, B., Tuke, J., . . . O'Loughlin, I. (2017). Aboriginal mitogenomes reveal 50,000 years of regionalism in Australia. *Nature*, *544*(7649), 180–184.

Turney, C. S., Bird, M. I., Fifield, L. K., Roberts, R. G., Smith, M., Dortch, C. E., . . . Dortch, J. (2001). Early human occupation at Devil's Lair, southwestern Australia 50,000 years ago. *Quaternary Research*, *55*(1), 3–13.

Veth, P., Ditchfield, K., & Hook, F. (2014). Maritime deserts of the Australian northwest. *Australian Archaeology*, *79*(1), 156–166.

Veth, P., Ditchfield, K., Bateman, M., Ouzman, S., Benoit, M., Motta, A. P., . . . Balanggarra Aboriginal Corporation. (2019). *Minjiwarra*: Archaeological evidence of human occupation of Australia's northern Kimberley by 50,000 BP. *Australian Archaeology*, *85*(2), 115–125.

Veth, P., Ward, I., Manne, T., Ulm, S., Ditchfield, K., Dortch, J., . . . Demuro, M. (2017). Early human occupation of a maritime desert, Barrow Island, North-West Australia. *Quaternary Science Reviews*, *168*, 19–29.

Wallis, L. A. (2001). Environmental history of northwest Australia based on phytolith analysis at Carpenter's Gap 1. *Quaternary International*, *83–85*, 103–117.

Westaway, K. E., Louys, J., Awe, R. D., Morwood, M. J., Price, G. J., Zhao, J. X., . . . Compton, T. (2017). An early modern human presence in Sumatra 73,000–63,000 years ago. *Nature*, *548*(7667), 322–325.

Wheeler, J. R. (Ed.) (1992). *Flora of the Kimberley region*. Perth: Department of Conservation and Land Management.

Whitau, R., Vannieuwenhuyse, D., Dotte-Sarout, E., Balme J., & O'Connor, S. (2017). Home is where the hearth is: Anthracological and microstratigraphic analyses of Pleistocene and Holocene combustion features, Riwi Cave (Kimberley, Western Australia). *Journal of Archaeological Method and Theory*, *25*(3), 739–776.

Williams, M. A., Spooner, N. A., McDonnell, K., & O'Connell, J. F. (2021). Identifying disturbance in archaeological sites in tropical northern Australia: Implications for previously proposed 65,000-year continental occupation date. *Geoarchaeology*, *36*(1), 92–108.

Wood, R. (2015). From revolution to convention: The past, present and future of radiocarbon dating. *Journal of Archaeological Science*, *56*, 61–72.

Wood, R., Jacobs, Z., Vannieuwenhuyse, D., Balme, J., O'Connor, S., & Whitau, R. (2016). Towards an accurate and precise chronology for the colonization of Australia: The example of Riwi, Kimberley, Western Australia. *PloS One*, *11*(9), p.e0160123.

CHAPTER 10

INTERACTIONS WITH MEGAFAUNA

CHRIS N. JOHNSON, JOE DORTCH, AND TREVOR H. WORTHY

INTRODUCTION

THE vertebrate fauna of Pleistocene Australia and New Guinea (hereafter Sahul) included many now-extinct large animals, collectively referred to as the Pleistocene megafauna. Sahul's Pleistocene megafauna was a diverse assemblage that included at least twenty genera of large mammals, four genera of large birds, and three genera of large reptiles that are now wholly extinct (Wroe et al. 2013). Many of these extinct genera were unlike any living animals: Sahul now has nothing like the rhino-sized mega-herbivores *Diprotodon* and *Palorchestes*, or the giant land-turtle *Ninjemys*. Other megafauna were closely related to living species and resembled them except in being much larger. Thus, there were scaled-up Pleistocene versions of the living grey kangaroos *Macropus*, the koala *Phascolarctos*, and monitor lizards, which are now represented by species up to 15 kg but in the Pleistocene included *Varanus (Megalania) priscus*, a giant that may have weighed more than 1000 kg (Molnar 2004).

The disappearance of these animals reduced not only the taxonomic diversity and size range of the vertebrate fauna of Sahul, but also the diversity of trophic relationships in the continent's ecosystems. For example, many of the extinct mega-marsupials were browsers that fed on the leaves and stems of woody shrubs and small trees. Nowadays, the complete absence of large browsers is a conspicuous gap in the native ecology of Sahul. Given the vast extent of shrublands in inland Australia, the lack of shrub-eating marsupials would seem a baffling evolutionary anomaly if we knew nothing of the continent's recent history of extinctions.

Sahul's Pleistocene megafauna, and the mystery of its extinction, is significant to archaeology in several ways. The megafauna might have provided an important resource for the first human occupants of the continent, influencing the pattern and tempo of the spread of humans across Sahul and helping to shape the cultures of the continent's first peoples. Exploitation by people could also have had significant effects on the abundance and distribution of megafaunal species, perhaps contributing to their extinction. It has been argued that extinction of megafauna, especially the large herbivores, might then have triggered changes in vegetation and fire regimes that in turn affected people (Flannery 1994). Given the environmental and archaeological implications of these claims, the extinction of the megafauna has been at the centre of some of the liveliest controversies in the archaeology of Sahul, concerning the cause or causes of extinction and the magnitude of environmental impacts of newly arrived people. In this chapter, we update and review the evidence on these issues, focussing on what is known and what still remains uncertain about the interactions of people and megafauna.

THE PLEISTOCENE MEGAFAUNA

Definitions

The term *megafauna* is often defined as animals above a body mass of 45 kg (Martin 1984). This arbitrary threshold is strongly influenced by the distribution of body sizes of mammals in continental North America and Eurasia, as well as by the attractiveness of a round number (i.e., 100 lb). We do not use a fixed body-mass criterion to define the megafauna, but rather consider it to be the set of extinct Pleistocene vertebrates that were either very large compared to all living species (this part of the definition corresponds, roughly, to a body-mass threshold of 45 kg) or were large compared to living relatives from the same genera or families. This definition recognizes that in the late Quaternary, from around 130 ka (thousand years ago), large-bodied species were generally more at risk of extinction than their smaller relatives (Smith, Elliott Smith, Lyons, & Payne 2018), but that the body-size thresholds at which extinction became likely varied for different groups (Johnson 2002). In Sahul, for example, the Pleistocene kangaroos (Macropodidae) ranged in mass from ~1 to 250 kg, and nearly all species heavier than 40 kg went extinct (Johnson 2002), while the megapodes (Megapodiidae, mound-building birds) ranged from ~1.5 to 8 kg, and all species over 3 kg went extinct (Shute, Prideaux, & Worthy 2017). Despite differences in absolute size, we consider the extinct members of both groups to have been megafauna. In this chapter, we discuss the terrestrial megafauna only, leaving aside freshwater species because of lack of information and marine species because of their more limited relevance to archaeology.

Evolution and Diversity

Mammals

The most megafauna-rich group of Pleistocene vertebrates was the kangaroos (Macropodidae). The kangaroos diversified rapidly from about 10 Ma (million years ago) as the climate of Sahul underwent a long period of cooling and drying (Celik et al. 2019). The open grasslands and shrublands that developed with climate drying provided high biomass of plant material accessible to large ground-dwelling grazers and browsers. In response, the number of macropodid genera increased from four, four, and five in the early, middle, and late Miocene (23.03–5.33 Ma), respectively, to 15 in the Pliocene (5.33–2.58 Ma), and 18 in the Pleistocene (2.58–0.0117 Ma) (Black, Archer, Hand, & Godthelp 2012).

During the Pleistocene, the climate of Sahul passed through regular cycles of alternating cool and dry versus warmer and wetter conditions under the control of global glacial-interglacial cycles. These cycles accentuated the development of dry grasslands and shrublands and drove repeated expansions and contractions of arid vegetation types. The success of mega-kangaroos in these conditions is exemplified by the short-faced kangaroos (subfamily Sthenurinae). Sthenurine diversity evidently doubled through the Pleistocene (Prideaux 2004), peaking at four genera and twenty-one species. The short-faced kangaroos were evidently browsers, as confirmed in detail for the largest sthenurine, *Procoptodon goliah* (250 kg; Figure 10.1a), which is known only from the Pleistocene and browsed predominantly on chenopod shrubs (Prideaux et al. 2009).

The other major radiation of megafaunal mammals was the marsupial suborder Vombatiformes. The number of known genera in the Vombatiformes increased from four, nine, and ten in the early, middle, and late Miocene to 13 in the Pliocene and 14 in the Pleistocene (Black et al. 2012). Body size also increased in most lineages, culminating in the Pleistocene *Diprotodon optatum* (Figure 10.1b), which, at around 2700 kg, was the largest-known marsupial (Wroe, Crowther, Dortch, & Chong 2004). The Vombatiformes included carnivores (the thylacoleonids, or 'marsupial lions' [Figure 10.1c]), grazers (the wombats), mixed feeders (the diprotodontids), and specialized browsers (koalas and palorchestids). The palorchestids, which may have exceeded 1000 kg in the Pleistocene *Palorchestes azael* (Figure 10.1d), took browsing to an extreme. *Palorchestes azael* had massive forearms that were made rigid by a fixed elbow joint; it may have stood on its hind legs and used its powerful forearms and heavy claws to rip the lower branches and foliage from trees (Richards, Wells, Evans, Fitzgerald, & Adams 2019). Sahul also supported large insectivorous mammals, in the form of several echidnas that were substantially larger than the living species.

Birds

The biggest birds of Sahul were the herbivorous dromornithids, or mihirungs. They were most diverse in the mid-late Miocene (12–7 Ma) with two genera and three species, including *Dromornis stirtoni* in which males may sometimes have exceeded 600 kg, making them the world's largest-known birds (Handley, Chinsamy, Yates, & Worthy 2016). By the Pleistocene, there was only one species of mihirung, *Genyornis newtoni* (see Worthy, Handley, Archer, & Hand 2016). *Genyornis newtoni* was comparatively small but was nonetheless an impressive bird: The largest individuals probably exceeded 260 kg (Grellet-Tinner, Spooner, Handley, & Worthy 2017). The long decline of the mihirungs was possibly due to ecological competition from the increasingly diverse large herbivorous marsupials (Murray & Vickers-Rich 2004), but it is also correlated

FIGURE 10.1. (a) *Procoptodon goliah*; (b) *Diprotodon optatum*; (c) *Thylacoleo carnifex*; (d) *Palorchestes azael*.

(images: Gabriel Ugueto)

with the increasing variability of resources as aridity intensified through the Pliocene and Pleistocene. Sahul is well known for its ratites, the emu (*Dromaius*) and cassowaries (three species of *Casuarius*), which at 40–60 kg are the next-largest birds in Sahul after the mihirungs. They survived, whereas the mihirungs are extinct. This difference in fate could be related not only to the mihirung's greater size, but also to differences in breeding potential. Continental ratites breed at one year of age and produce many chicks annually; in contrast, recent work on the mihirung *Dromornis stirtoni* shows that it may not have matured until ten years of age (Chinsamy-Turan, Worthy, & Handley, 2019).

The other group of megafaunal birds was the megapodes, or mound-builders. As well as its six genera of living megapodes, Sahul in the Pleistocene had at least three genera of extinct large megapodes (Shute et al. 2017). At 8 kg, *Progura gallinacea* was the largest, but the 6 kg *Latagallina naracoortensis* was still more than twice the mass of the living malleefowl, *Leipoa ocellata*, or brush-turkey, *Alectura lathami*. Megapodes incubate their eggs using environmental sources of heat, often in raked-up mounds of composting organic material. The extinct species all lack the specialized flattened claws of the extant digging taxa, so they may not have built mounds (Shute et al. 2017). In contrast, they probably buried their eggs in shallow scrapes in warm sites such as sand on northern dune slopes where incubation would rely on solar heating.

Reptiles

The biggest terrestrial reptile in Sahul was *Varanus (Megalania) priscus*, but snakes of the family Madtsoiidae also achieved great size: *Wonambi naracoortensis* may have been 5–6 m long. As well, there were at least two large herbivorous reptiles, both of them horned and club-tailed turtles from the family Meiolaniidae (Gaffney 1992).

Sources of Information

Three main types of data inform us on the distribution, diversity, and time of extinction of the megafauna of Sahul: fossil skeletal remains; fossil eggshell; and dung fungi.

Fossils: skeletal remains

Dated records of fossil vertebrates from the Quaternary of Sahul have been compiled in the FosSahul database (Peters et al. 2019; Rodríguez-Rey et al. 2016). FosSahul has 11,871 entries, of which 27% (3205) are considered to be megafauna. While this data resource is large, it is limited by the low reliability of many published ages. FosSahul includes quality ratings of ages, on the basis of which only 14% are considered 'reliable'. Sahul's megafaunal fossils are mostly older than 40 ka (40,000 years ago), and so they are close to or beyond the limit of radiocarbon dating, which in any case usually cannot be applied directly because bones of this age contain too little endogenous carbon. Other techniques, such as optically stimulated luminescence (OSL) and uranium-series (U-series) dating, are needed, but they are technically difficult and depend on complex assumptions (Rodríguez-Rey et al. 2015).

A further limitation is that the distribution of megafaunal fossil sites is biased, being concentrated in the southeastern quarter of Australia (Figure 10.2). The absence of information from much of the rest of Sahul mainly reflects lack of suitable fossil sites. As a result, the diversity of Pleistocene megafauna (and, therefore, the scale of total diversity loss by the end of the Pleistocene) is underrepresented. The fossil record is also biased towards the last 120,000 years. All well-dated fossils older than 120,000 years are from just three locations: the Leeuwin-Naturaliste Region in Western Australia, the Naracoorte area in South Australia, and the Cuddie Springs site in New South Wales.

Fossils: eggshell

Across large areas of the southern arid and semiarid zones, abundant fragments of eggshell from extinct large birds can be collected as they are exposed by deflation of sand dunes. The abundance of shells, together with the fact that they can be directly dated, means they provide a spatial and temporal record of the presence of megafaunal

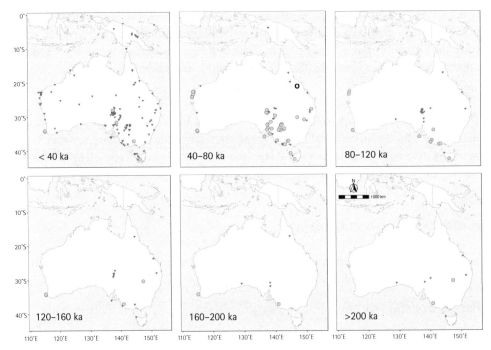

FIGURE 10.2. Locations of sites with dated remains of megafaunal taxa in Sahul through the Quaternary, recorded in FosSahul 2.0 (Peters et al. 2019). Circles are high-quality (A* and A) dates (Rodríguez-Rey et al. 2015); triangles are low-quality (B and C) dates. The 40–80 ka panel shows the location of the Walker Creek site (open circle) described by Hocknull et al. (2020).

birds that is more continuous than the information supplied by skeletal fossils. A series of studies attributed the shells to *Genyornis newtoni* (Miller et al. 1999, 2005, 2016). However, recent analysis (Grellet-Tinner, Spooner, & Worthy 2016; Grellet-Tinner et al. 2017) concluded that the shells were more characteristic of large megapodes, which probably buried their eggs in the sand dunes from which the fragments can now be recovered.

Dung fungi

Several genera of fungi are solely associated with herbivore dung (Baker, Bhagwat, & Willis 2013) and produce spores that can be used as a proxy to indicate the presence and abundance of large herbivores through time. Two overseas studies have confirmed that dung fungi can record the timing of extirpation of large herbivores: the extinction of woolly mammoths *Mammuthus primigenius* on St Paul Island, Alaska, 5600 years ago, a date verified by fossils and environmental DNA (Graham et al., 2016); and the historically known introduction of large herbivores to the sub-Antarctic Enderby Island in the mid-nineteenth century and the eradication of those herbivores about 125 years later (Wood, Wilmshurst, Turney, & Fogwill 2016). Dung fungi have been used to infer extinction of Pleistocene mega-herbivores at several sites in Sahul (see below).

RELATIONSHIPS OF MEGAFAUNA AND PEOPLE

People probably interacted with Sahul's megafauna in several ways. The eggs of large ground-nesting birds could have provided a valuable food resource, being large and easy to collect; the flightless adults were probably also vulnerable to hunting. Some of the large reptiles, and likewise the giant echidnas, were presumably slow-moving and easy to hunt. The large marsupials would also have been valuable food resources. As well as being hunted for food, the megafauna could have supplied materials—eggshell, scutes, hides, pelts, sinews, teeth, bones, and claws—that might have been valuable as tools, clothing, and ornaments. Some of these items may have been valued for symbolic or ritual reasons. A few megafaunal species, especially the marsupial lion *Thylacoleo carnifex*, could have been dangerous to people as well as competitors for prey. Because of their economic value, charisma, or danger, megafauna might have evoked strong emotional responses and might therefore have been incorporated into cosmologies, ceremonies, and artistic expressions.

In turn, exploitation by people could have had large demographic impacts on megafaunal species. Big animals generally have low population growth rates, making them demographically sensitive to hunting and therefore likely to decline even under low rates of hunting by people (Johnson 2002). Species with highly susceptible life-stages, such as the egg in large ground-nesting birds, might have been especially vulnerable. Flannery (1994) speculated that megafaunal animals were easy to kill because of naivete to human hunters, as is characteristic of animals that evolved in the absence of people. This naivete cannot be determined, but there is no doubt that Sahul's fauna would have been vulnerable to hunting because of two uniquely human traits: the capacity for sophisticated forms of cooperative hunting conferred by intelligence and language; and the capability of causing death at a distance due to the ability to employ missile technology (e.g., spears and clubs).

The following sections review evidence on interactions of people and megafauna in Sahul. We first consider whether there was temporal overlap of people and megafauna in Sahul: Were megafauna still present when humans arrived, and if so, how soon after human arrival did megafauna go extinct?

Temporal Overlap

Human arrival

When people arrived in Sahul remains uncertain and contested. The earliest archaeological evidence is dated to 'around 65 ka' (and 'conservatively 59.3 ka') at Madjedbebe in Arnhem Land (Clarkson et al. 2017: 309), although this dating has been disputed

(O'Connell et al. 2018). Several other sites were evidently first occupied around 51–50 ka (David et al. 2019; Hamm et al. 2016; Turney et al. 2001; Veth et al. 2017; Veth et al. 2019). Most archaeologists consider that people could have spread across Sahul quite quickly, perhaps travelling first along coastlines, then reaching inland regions via major waterways and lake systems (Bird, O'Grady, & Ulm 2016). Studies in the western third of the continent demonstrate rapid occupation over large distances: there is at least one archaeological site dated to 50–48 ka in each of five regions spread along a transect from tropical savannah in the north to deserts and temperate forests in the south (Dortch et al. 2019). Elsewhere, people were present in now-arid South Australia by 49 ka (Hamm et al. 2016) and in the southeast by 50–46 ka (Bowler, Wyrwoll, & Lu 2001). It seems likely that people were present in all biomes by 45 ka, if not 50 ka (Allen & O'Connell 2014; Bird et al. 2013), except for Tasmania where occupation depended on the appearance of a land bridge c. 43 ka. Taking all these dates into account, current evidence suggests it is reasonable to take 50 ka as the approximate starting point for a possible period of *widespread* overlap of people and megafauna across most of Sahul.

Megafaunal extinctions

Two studies have conducted comprehensive reviews of the fossil record of Sahul to interpret the timing of megafaunal extinctions at a continental scale, and they have arrived at different conclusions.

In the first study, Wroe et al. (2013) listed all species of megafauna known from Sahul during the Pleistocene according to evidence that they were extant in the periods pre-400 ka, 400–126 ka (Middle Pleistocene), 126–51 ka (Late Pleistocene, pre-human period), 51–39 ka (Late Pleistocene 'extinction window', as inferred by Roberts et al., 2001), and post-39 ka. Wroe et al. (2013) found a decline in the number of species known to be extant through these successive periods. In particular, only a minority of all Pleistocene megafauna species were represented by fossils dated to the Late Pleistocene (126–12 ka), and of these only about half could be confirmed as extant at the beginning of the extinction window at 51 ka. Wroe et al. (2013) therefore argued that the megafauna disappeared in a staggered sequence over several hundred thousand years and was already much reduced by the time people arrived.

In the second study, Saltré et al. (2016) analysed a database of exact ages on fossils of Pleistocene megafauna (FosSahul 1.0; Rodríguez-Rey et al. 2016) to estimate the ages of extinction for as many taxa as possible. They used only high-quality dates, and included only taxa with sufficient numbers of dates to enable them to fit uncertainty ranges to their estimates of time of extinction. They were able to estimate the most likely age ranges of extinction for twelve genera of mammalian megafauna, as well as megafaunal birds dated predominantly from eggshell ('*Genyornis*' but considered by Grellet-Tinner, Spooner, and Worthy [2016] to have been one or more genera of megapodes). These estimates lay between 61 and 35 ka, with a peak in probability of extinction at 42 ka. In short, they found no evidence for gradual decline through the Middle to Late Pleistocene but strong evidence for synchronized extinction soon after the arrival of humans.

Why did these two groups of researchers come to such different conclusions? There could be two main reasons.

First, Saltré et al. (2016) accounted for uncertainties in estimating time of extinction from the incomplete data provided by the fossil record. Wroe et al. (2013) did not do this, which means their inferences could have been distorted by the Signor-Lipps Effect (SLE). The SLE is a bias, caused by incomplete sampling, that makes extinctions appear to be spread through long periods of time even if they were truly synchronous. This bias could have been important in Wroe et al.'s analysis because so many of the species on their list were poorly sampled. For example, they included seven kangaroo species known only as single records from the same Middle Pleistocene site in a region of the Nullarbor Plain with few other fossil sites (Prideaux et al. 2007b). We can have no certainty as to when these species went extinct, but Wroe et al. (2013) considered them all to have been extinct before the Late Pleistocene. The strength of the SLE could have been reinforced by Wroe et al.'s choice to make their time bins progressively narrower in the approach to final extinction of the megafauna. Other things being equal, the probability that a species which is truly extant is detected in a given time period will be reduced as the period is defined more narrowly.

Second, Saltré et al. (2016) worked at genus rather than species level, and they were able to resolve extinction dates for only about half of all known genera of Pleistocene megafauna because the remainder did not have sufficient dated records. Perhaps the time of extinction was correctly estimated for those genera, but they had been losing species through long intervals preceding disappearance of their last surviving species. Add to this the possibility (not currently verifiable) that some other genera had gone extinct earlier in the Pleistocene, and it could be that the true pattern of diversity decline looked more like the gradual attenuation pictured by Wroe et al. (2013) than the abrupt crash inferred by Saltré et al. (2016).

The possibility of a gradual loss of diversity can be tested by examining trends in faunal composition and diversity at well-sampled sites with fossil records spanning the Middle and Late Pleistocene, when, according to Wroe et al. (2013), megafaunal decline was well underway. The most useful places for this testing are Naracoorte in South Australia and the Leeuwin-Naturaliste area in Western Australia. Both are limestone karst landscapes with complex systems of caves, some of which have vertical entrances that open into deep chambers. Animals may accidentally fall into these shafts to die in the caves and be preserved. These systems therefore act as passive pitfall traps that steadily accumulate samples of the local vertebrate fauna over long periods.

At Naracoorte, several studies have found no trend in diversity of the megafaunal assemblage over the last 500 ka (Grün, Moriarty, & Wells 2001; Moriarty, McCulloch, Wells, & McDowell 2000; Prideaux et al. 2007a). A detailed analysis through a sequence from 530 to 200 ka found that while the abundance of large relative to small mammals fluctuated, there was no evidence of a declining trend in the representation of large-bodied species through time (Prideaux et al. 2007a). Instead, variations in the composition of the assemblage appear to have been due to shifts in the geographic ranges of some species away from the region under dry conditions and their return during wetter conditions. The megafaunal species recorded during the 500–200 ka interval remained present in the Late Pleistocene (Prideaux et al. 2007a).

In the Leeuwin-Naturaliste region of coastal southwestern Australia, two limestone caves have well-studied accumulations of vertebrate fossils through long periods: Tight Entrance Cave spans the period 150 ka–30 ka, and Kudjal Yolgah Cave covers 80 ka to the past few thousand years. All Pleistocene megafaunal species known from the region (Prideaux et al. 2007b) are represented in the Late Pleistocene accumulations in these two caves, and all remained extant in levels dated to ~48 ka at Tight Entrance (Prideaux et al. 2010) and 80–41 ka at Kudjal Yolgah (Jankowski, Gully, Jacobs, Roberts, & Prideaux 2016), but were absent from younger levels. At Tight Entrance, Prideaux et al. (2010) evaluated the relative abundance of megafauna by calculating their percentage contribution to the total mammalian assemblage (tallied as minimum number of individuals present in each stratum) and found no general and consistent decline in relative abundance of extinct megafaunal taxa between 143 ka and 48 ka (Figure 10.3a).

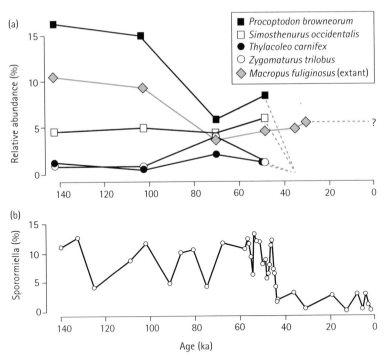

FIGURE 10.3. Trends in megafaunal populations through the past 140 ka, with timing of decline or disappearance: (a) relative abundance (percentage of total individuals in each sample) of species at Tight Entrance Cave, southwest western Australia (Prideaux et al. 2010), showing four megafaunal species that disappeared between 48 and 35 ka and one large kangaroo, the western grey *M. fuliginosus*, that remains extant. Note that the fossil sequence terminates at 31 ka; (b) abundance of spores of the dung fungus *Sporormiella* in a marine core from southwest western Australia, as a percentage of the pollen sum (van der Kaars et al. 2017).

There are very few other fossil sites in Sahul with sequences that could reveal trends in megafaunal diversity and relative abundance through long periods of the Pleistocene. That case was made for fluvial deposits in the Kings Creek catchment in the Darling Downs of southeastern Queensland, where initial analysis through a sequence thought to represent the last glacial cycle suggested a gradual decline of megafaunal diversity (Price & Webb 2006). However, dating of the sequence showed that the three main fossil-bearing units were deposited within a short period of time around 120–110 ka, possibly extending to 80 ka (Price et al. 2011).

The estimate of 42 ka (Saltré et al. 2016) as the age of the peak probability of extinction of megafaunal genera has been supported by three other independent data series. Two studies tracked fluctuations in spores of dung fungi through long and continuous sediment cores that sample the past 130 ka. Both revealed the consistent presence of spores from the beginning of the last glacial cycle until sudden falls at 42 ka in northeastern Australia (Rule et al. 2012) and 43 ka in southwestern Australia (van der Kaars et al. 2017) (Figure 10.3b). The fact that dung fungi were consistently present in these records before 43 ka suggests that populations of large herbivores were generally stable in the face of major climate changes from the previous interglacial and through most of the last glacial period (Rule et al. 2012), while the falls just before 40 ka indicate an unprecedented reduction in herbivore biomass. The same pattern—apparent stability through the previous interglacial and last glacial cycle before abrupt decline soon after 50 ka—is shown by the occurrence of eggshells of extinct large birds. These are consistently present, along with emu eggshells, in dune systems in arid and semiarid southern Australia from 140 ka until 50 ka, but then they disappear by approximately 45 ka, while deposition of emu eggshells continued to the present (Miller et al. 2005, 2016).

Duration of overlap

Saltré et al.'s (2016) analysis suggested that 13.5 kyr elapsed between the arrival of people and the completion of megafaunal extinction at the scale of the entire continent. That is an estimate of the upper limit of possible duration of human-megafaunal interaction because that overlap could have been composed of a series of shorter intervals at different times in different places. For southeastern Australia, Saltré et al. (2019) estimated durations of overlap between 1 and 8 ka at the scale of 1° x 1° grid cells (i.e., within spatial units of roughly 10,000 km^2). It is possible that overlap was even shorter at finer spatial scales that would reflect joint occupation of the same landscapes and habitats, but at present our data on human settlement and megafaunal extinction are too coarse-grained and ill-matched to assess the duration of overlap at these fine spatial scales anywhere in Sahul.

Wroe et al. (2013) cited evidence for several species of megafauna remaining extant after 39 ka, and they suggested that these species may not have gone extinct until the Last Glacial Maximum, around 20 ka. However, Johnson et al. (2016) argued that this interpretation depended on dates with low technical reliability. For example, all published dates on *Diprotodon optatum* younger than 40 ka are technically unreliable (Rodríguez-Rey et al. 2015; Johnson et al. 2016), while the species' survival until ~42 ka is attested by a series of reliable ages. A long period of coexistence of people and megafauna was recently suggested by an age of 33–37 ka on remains of the diprotodontid marsupial *Zygomaturus trilobus* at Willandra Lakes in western New South Wales (Westaway, Olley, & Grün 2017). Given evidence for a human presence in the area from about 50 ka, this implies 17 ka or more of regional coexistence. In our view, however, the age proposed for this specimen is unreliable. The age determination was based on OSL-dating of sand surrounding a specimen collected decades earlier. The OSL method is very sensitive to water content of and radiation dose-rate for sediments; these quantities could not be determined at the time of sample collection. Measured water content >30% is common in lacustrine sediments (Fu, Cohen, & Arnold 2017), but Westaway et al. (2017) assumed a value of 5% for water content. This estimate is likely to be too low and would lead in turn to underestimation of age. Hocknull et al. (2020) rejected the OSL age for this specimen for similar reasons.

Direct Evidence of Interaction

Archaeology and palaeontology

Human–megafaunal interaction can be recorded in the archaeological and palaeontological records by two main kinds of evidence. First, megafaunal remains associated with archaeological materials might suggest that the remains had been transported by people and thus supply evidence of exploitation; at the very least, such evidence would show that people and megafauna had been in the same place at the same time and so would imply some behavioural interaction. Second, remains of megafauna from either archaeological or palaeontological sites might show modifications such as cut marks or characteristic patterns of charring indicating the animals were used by people. Currently, four site studies reveal one or both kinds of evidence.

Lake Menindee, western New South Wales

Early reports of this site described the remains of nine genera of megafauna associated with archaeological materials that included artefacts, hearths, and human burials (Tedford 1955, 1967; Tindale 1955). Evidence for exploitation consisted of the burnt remains of megafaunal taxa in several hearths and two artefacts made from split pieces of massive bone (Tindale 1955). Initial dating suggested the human and megafaunal materials in association were deposited between 23 and 31 ka. Re-dating of some of the megafauna-bearing units gave older ages but still supported overlap of megafauna with people: The base (oldest-age) levels with megafauna yielded OSL ages ranging from 58.4 to 51 ka, and a hearth containing a charred piece of macropodid tibia of megafaunal size was dated to 45.1 ka (Cupper & Duncan 2006). Cupper and Duncan (2006) suggested this bone might have belonged to an older fossil deposit and was unintentionally incorporated into the hearth as it was constructed. This hypothesis seems unlikely in light of Tedford's observations of other hearths with burnt megafaunal remains, which indicate a pattern of consumption of megafauna at the site. Unfortunately, no taphonomic analyses have been made on Tedford and Tindale's collections, nor have there been more extensive investigations of this important human–megafauna horizon.

Cuddie Springs, western New South Wales

The Cuddie Springs site, in an ancient ephemeral lake on the riverine plains of western NSW, contains megafauna bones along with flaked stone artefacts in sediments that lie below a deflation pavement of stone artefacts and unmodified cobbles, and above a highly consolidated deposit of sand and bone fragments, which in turn sits above older and taphonomically distinct megafaunal deposits lacking artefacts (Field, Wroe, Trueman, Garvey, & Wyatt-Spratt 2013; Fillios, Field, & Charles 2010). The deposits that enclose artefacts and megafauna remains have been dated to c. 50–30 ka (Field et al. 2013; Grün et al. 2010). The sediments are composed of fine silts and clays, and the artefacts and bones are undamaged and unweathered, indicating low-energy deposition (Field, Fillios, & Wroe 2008). Dating of megafaunal tooth enamel using electron spin resonance gave ages older than the corresponding radiocarbon and luminescence dates on sediments, suggesting re-deposition of those remains (Grün et al. 2010). In contrast, Field et al. (2013) found support for an earlier study of rare earth elements in bones adsorbed from groundwater cumulatively after deposition (Trueman, Field, Dortch, Charles, & Wroe 2005), suggesting most bones had not been re-worked. We interpret the site as providing evidence for human–megafauna association for some time between 50 and 36 ka. Functional analyses indicate that stone artefacts surrounding the bones were used for butchery, but none of the megafaunal bones is clearly modified by people, so the main evidence for interaction is the implication that megafauna and humans coexisted in the same landscape.

Warratyi rock shelter, Flinders Ranges

This human-occupation site contains a cultural sequence starting around 49 ka, which includes a *Diprotodon optatum* bone (a partial radius of a juvenile), along with eggshell fragments of an extinct megapode, at a level dated at approximately 46 ka and associated with stone artefacts (Hamm et al. 2016). The bone is without carnivore tooth marks, and the shelter is on a steep, rocky escarpment that would presumably have been inaccessible to *D. optatum*. Hamm et al. (2016) infer that the bone was probably carried to the shelter by people. The eggshell must also have been transported to the site because the eggs would originally have been laid in sand. There are no cut marks or other signs of human modification on the bone. The existence of this bone is tantalizing, but a larger sample will be needed to confirm the nature of human–megafauna interaction.

Burnt 'Genyornis' eggshells

Some eggshells of extinct megafaunal birds (most probably megapodes) show distinct patterns of charring that indicate cooking over campfires (Miller et al. 2016). Of nearly 2000 collections of megafaunal eggshell made at many locations in southern and western Australia, 206 contained some charred shell. All burnt megapode shells dated from 53.9 to 43.4 ka, at which time deposition of the megapode shell ceased (Miller et al. 2016). Collections of emu eggshell from the same sites also include a proportion that are burnt. Charring of emu shell first appears around 55 ka, at the same time as the onset of charring of megapode shell, but charred emu shell continued to be deposited until near the present. This evidence indicates that eggs of both emu and extinct megapodes were collected and eaten across a large area from as early as 55 ka, and exploitation of megapode eggs continued until those species went extinct just before 43 ka.

Several other cases of association of megafaunal remains and artefacts have been reported but have been subsequently discounted by more intensive study or are now considered highly uncertain. At Lancefield Swamp in Victoria, Gillespie et al. (1978) described an accumulation of megafaunal bones that also included two stone tools just above a level dated at 31 ka. A thorough reinvestigation concluded that the megafaunal remains were largely deposited between approximately 80 and 45 ka and there was no primary association of archaeological material and megafaunal remains (Dortch et al. 2016). Similarly, at Cloggs Cave in eastern Victoria, Flood (1974) reported megafaunal remains (the sthenurine kangaroo *Simosthenuris occidentalis*) dated to c. 23 ka (uncalibrated), but reinvestigation of the site has shown that the megafaunal remains were deposited between 52 and 47 ka, well before the first evidence of human use of the cave at c. 23 ka (Delannoy et al. 2020). Association of megafaunal remains with human occupation was suggested at Nombe rock shelter in the highlands of Papua New Guinea (Flannery, Mountain, & Aplin 1983), but there is evidence of re-working of sediments at the site (Flannery, Marti, & Szalay 1996), and it awaits thorough reinvestigation and especially redating of relevant levels (Denham & Mountain 2016). Seton Rock Shelter on Kangaroo Island contains megafaunal remains associated with the oldest evidence of human occupation (Hope, Lampert, Edmondson, Smith, & van Tets 1977; McDowell, Prideaux, Walshe, Bertuch, & Jacobsen 2015), but the megafaunal evidence consists only of several isolated tooth fragments; these small volumes of material could indicate that the fragments are intrusive, and not in primary association with archaeological material (McDowell et al. 2015).

There are very few suggestions that marks on megafaunal bones have been made by people, and the most promising of these—a *Diprotodon* incisor recovered from the Spring Creek site in southwestern Victoria that has a row of incisions along one edge (Vanderwal & Fullagar 1989)—was recently reinterpreted as being due to animal scavenging, not human modification (Langley 2020).

Rock art

Contact and interaction between people and megafauna might also be recorded as rock paintings or engravings of extinct megafauna. The survival of such evidence is unlikely but not impossible considering the antiquity of figurative rock art in parts of Southeast Asia (Aubert et al. 2019). Many claims have been made for depictions of now-extinct Pleistocene megafauna in the rock art of Arnhem Land and the Kimberley regions of northern Australia (Akerman 1998; Gunn, Douglas, & Whear 2011; Murray &

Chaloupka 1984; Murray et al. 2013; Walsh 2000). However, Lewis (2017) argued that none of these examples is convincing. There are three general problems. First, while it is possible that some artworks created during the likely period of human–megafaunal contact in northern Australia have survived to the present, none of the claimed megafauna paintings has yet been dated to that period. Second, in many cases the animals depicted in paintings are interpreted as megafauna because they show body proportions that are unlike those of living animals, but that broadly resemble reconstructions of megafaunal species. This is a weak basis of inference because distortion of shape may have been a point of artistic style or convention or could in some cases be an illusory result of the superimposition of separate paintings. Third, the 'megafaunal' paintings typically lack crucial anatomical detail that would allow unambiguous identification of their subjects. For example, two Arnhem Land paintings have been considered to represent the marsupial lion *Thylacoleo*, because while the subjects appear to be large carnivores, the proportions of the legs and placement of the tail are inconsistent with the thylacine, *Thylacinus cynocephalus* (which is accurately depicted in many Arnhem Land paintings; Chaloupka 1993). Nonetheless, the paintings of the purported *Thylacoleo* lack details, particularly the enlarged opposable thumb with long claw, which would support positive identification as *Thylacoleo*.

The most detailed analysis of any of these claims has been applied to a painting of a large bird in a western Arnhem Land rock shelter that was originally interpreted as a probable *Genyornis* (Gunn et al. 2011). Welch (2016) reinterpreted this painting as being a stylized representation of an emu or bustard, rather than a *Genyornis*. Further doubt was cast on the *Genyornis* attribution by interpretation of the style and geomorphological context of the painting suggesting it is between 8000 and 1500 years old (Bednarik 2013; Welch 2016). Dating of the collapsed overhang that once covered the rock wall indicates that the surface on which the image was painted became exposed only around 13.8 ka (Barker et al. 2017). If these ages are correct, the painting is probably too young to be a depiction of a living *Genyornis*, and that attribution now seems unlikely.

Interpretation of the Evidence of Interaction

To summarize the information presented above, there is evidence that people interacted with megafauna during the period 50–40 ka, but that evidence is rare. Three general interpretations of this shortage of evidence are possible.

1. *The evidence of interaction is rare because interaction was rare*

In this case, human-megafauna interaction is unlikely to have been significant for either the people or the animals. But why would interaction have been rare?

One suggestion is that megafauna had mostly disappeared before the arrival of people in Sahul (O'Connell & Allen 2015). However, our review of the fossil evidence (see above) showed that many of the megafaunal species that had existed earlier in the Pleistocene were still extant when people arrived in Sahul. Well-dated fossil sites confirm that the first people of Sahul would have encountered many species of giant mammals (Hocknull et al. 2020; Saltré et al. 2016), several large Pleistocene birds (Grellet-Tinner et al. 2016; Miller et al. 2005; Shute et al. 2017), and giant reptiles (Hocknull et al. 2020; Price et al. 2015). Further, the distribution of well-dated fossil sites shows megafauna continued to be widespread in the Late Pleistocene (Figure 10.2).

A variant of this idea is that the animals were present when people arrived but then rapidly declined for reasons unrelated to people, so that in most places overlap was brief or nonexistent. Such a decline might have been caused by an event such as widespread drought. There is some evidence for such an event. For example, beach ridges at Lake Frome and Lake Eyre reveal falls in water levels from about 48 ka, perhaps indicating a weakening of monsoonal influence and onset of aridification. Cohen et al. (2015) suggested that this change in climate was the reason megafaunal birds disappeared from that region. However, in other parts of the continent, there is no evidence for a major drying of the climate at this time (Barrows et al. 2020; Lewis et al. 2020). Kemp, Tibby, Arnold, and Barr (2019) assembled hydrological records spanning the interval 57–29 ka from across Australia and concluded that in most of Australia conditions were relatively wet, compared to now, between ~50 and 40 ka. There are indications of a drying trend from about 45 ka, but until ~37 ka conditions remained wetter than they had been before 50 ka. It is also relevant to note that many megafauna species were evidently adapted to aridity (Prideaux et al. 2007b).

A refinement of the idea of drought-caused decline is that a synergistic effect of climate change and humans was responsible for the disappearance of megafauna. Perhaps a deteriorating climate caused the decline and fragmentation of populations of megafaunal animals, and people were responsible for either accelerating that decline or extirpating remnant populations. This hypothesis is supported by analysis of the geographic pattern of megafaunal disappearance in southeastern Australia (Saltré et al. 2019), which found that the spatial pattern of megafaunal decline is best explained by the spread of people in combination with local declines in rainfall reconstructed from a palaeoclimate model. This pattern suggests that extinction most likely occurred when people and animals concentrated their activity at the same sources of water (Saltré et al. 2019). However, Saltré et al. (2019) also found that in some areas human–megafaunal coexistence lasted up to 8000 years. Therefore, there should have been many opportunities for interaction, so this analysis does not by itself explain the rarity of evidence of such interaction.

Another possibility is that even though megafaunal animals were available, people made little use of them. However, it seems implausible that the first people of Sahul would have ignored a resource as seemingly valuable as the megafauna, especially in light of ethnographic evidence and foraging theory suggesting that people generally regard large vertebrates as valuable prey (Broughton, Cannon, Bayham, & Byers 2011; Wolfe & Broughton 2020; cf. Bird, Codding, Bird, Zeanah, & Taylor 2013). It is however possible that people used megafauna as part of a broad-spectrum diet that included many other resources, and in which megafauna were not especially prominent. The early populations of *Homo sapiens* in Wallacea, the people who went on to occupy Sahul, had broad diets that were initially based on coastal resources but that expanded to include a wide range of plant and terrestrial resources as occupation became more widespread (Roberts et al. 2020). At the oldest known occupation site in Sahul, Madjedbebe, people made use of a wide range of plant resources, including some that require sophisticated processing (Florin et al. 2020).

2. *Evidence of interaction is rare because much of it was either not preserved or remains undiscovered*

Certain biases in the archaeological record work against the retention of evidence of human–megafaunal interaction (Langley, Clarkson, & Ulm 2011). Most archaeological evidence for the Pleistocene comes from rock shelters and caves. These are rare features in most landscapes, and it is not clear that those sites with evidence of use by people were occupied frequently. Open sites were probably more important as bases for regular foraging and hunting activities, and therefore as sites where evidence of exploitation of megafauna was formed. Because of more limited preservation, open sites do not figure substantially in the early archaeological record of Sahul (Langley et al. 2011). A second possible explanation for the absence of kill sites from the archaeological record is that large animals may have been butchered at locations peripheral to the more obvious occupation sites. Further, the oldest occupied rock shelters in Sahul are typically in sandstone landscapes, as are the few open sites older than 40 ka (Langley et al. 2011). Sandstones give rise to acid conditions that result in poor preservation of organic material, and therefore low survival of the remains of animals used by people.

Added to these biases is the small size of both the archaeological and palaeontological samples from the period of probable human–megafauna overlap in Sahul. Only thirty-five archaeological sites in Sahul have been dated to 40 ka or older, representing 2% of the dated sites for the continent. The fossil record for Sahul is also sparse and (as noted earlier) geographically uneven, due to the combined effects of a small palaeontological workforce, the difficulty of obtaining exact ages on fossil remains pre-40 ka, and climatic and geomorphological conditions that result in poor preservation of Quaternary fossils across most of the continent. In addition, the excavations conducted by archaeologists are typically far smaller than would be considered adequate by palaeontologists wishing to describe the large-vertebrate faunas associated with those sites.

The case of *Diprotodon* illustrates the limited scope of the combined archaeological and palaeontological sample of Sahul's megafauna. *Diprotodon* is one of the best-sampled taxa of megafauna from Sahul, but we have a total of only ten reliable ages on it for the period 50 to 40 ka (Hocknull et al. 2020; Peters et al. 2019)—that is, one age per 1000 years during the likely period of human–megafauna overlap. In comparison, mastodons and mammoths in the United States are represented by eighty-eight and seventy-nine dated specimens, respectively, during the likely period of overlap with people (15–10 ka), amounting to ~18 ages/1000 years for each taxon (Wolfe & Broughton 2020). In other words, the intensity of knowledge of North American megafauna with undoubted evidence of exploitation by people is roughly 18 times higher than for Sahul. Only one of the *Diprotodon* ages from the 50–40 ka period is associated with archaeology, giving a 9:1 ratio of ages from palaeontological versus archaeological contexts. This ratio is within the range calculated for mastodons and mammoths in the United States (44:1 and 7:1, respectively; Wolfe & Broughton, 2020). This comparison suggests that our failure thus far to find more than one case of *Diprotodon* associated with archaeology is predictable, given the limited sample of archaeological excavations.

There is only one taxon, the extinct megapodes, for which we have a large statistical sample of remains through the period of possible human–megafauna overlap, and that case provides clear evidence for exploitation by people (Miller et al. 2016).

3. *The evidence of interaction is rare because people caused rapid extinction of megafauna*

Modelling of the impacts of hunting by people on populations of megafauna suggests that it could have caused extinction within 1000 years (Alroy 2001). A model of human–*Diprotodon* interaction suggested that even quite low rates of hunting could have driven local populations of *Diprotodon* extinct within 500 years (Brook & Johnson 2006). These time spans would reduce the archaeological and palaeontological visibility of exploitation in two ways.

First, an interaction that lasted several hundred years would represent a small proportion of the duration of the archaeological record of Sahul. Therefore, a small fraction only of the total archaeological sample could contain evidence of interaction, and a correspondingly large total archaeological sample would be needed to detect it (Surovell & Grund 2012). As noted above, the early archaeological sample of Sahul is small. Second, a decline extending over several centuries, as in some of the scenarios of light hunting modelled by Brook and Johnson (2006), would encompass many generations of the animals concerned, despite being rapid on archaeological and palaeontological timescales. In that case, most individuals in a hunted population would have died of causes other than hunting even as hunting gradually pushed the population to extinction. The probability that any of the few remains recovered from the period of overlap would show signs of having been killed by people would be reduced accordingly.

These explanations are not consistent with the evidence reviewed earlier for prolonged overlap of humans and megafauna, at large spatial scales. That inconsistency could possibly be reconciled by allowing for complex spatial relationships between human and megafaunal populations. For example, lags in the dispersal of people into some regions could have resulted in later survival of megafauna in those places, allowing extended temporal overlap at very large scales even if contact was followed by rapid local extinction. It is also possible that megafaunal populations might have persisted in the same regions with people if human occupation was initially patchy and was only gradually extended to achieve complete coverage of landscapes. In that case, an extended series of local extinctions, resulting from brief overlap in each case, could ultimately have eliminated megafauna.

In summary, there are many ways to think about the problem of the scarcity of evidence of human–megafaunal interaction. Many of the factors we have described are not mutually exclusive and may well have acted in combination to reduce the availability of evidence. For example, it might be that evidence of interaction is rare because megafauna were not the predominant element of the diets of the earliest peoples to occupy Sahul, but hunting by people—which mostly took place at sites where either no archaeological or palaeontological evidence was formed, or where that evidence was not preserved over the ensuing 40 kyr, or where Sahul's small and overstretched cadre of archaeologists and palaeontologists has not yet discovered it—nevertheless sent megafaunal populations into rapid declines, which were worsened by drought, thus ensuring extinction. Given the complexity of overlapping factors affecting the availability of evidence, it is not possible to draw any strong inferences from the small quantity of evidence of interaction that we currently have on the frequency and importance of the true level of interaction. That is only possible in the one case where evidence is abundant: the megapodes whose eggs were exploited over large areas of southern Australia in the few thousand years immediately preceding their extinction around 43 ka (Miller et al. 2016).

There is another possible interpretation of the shortage of evidence of direct human–megafaunal interaction that we have not yet mentioned: People caused the extinction of megafauna indirectly by radically modifying their habitats. We discuss this hypothesis in the next section.

The Megafaunal Extinction Debate

Why the Pleistocene megafauna of Sahul are now extinct has been debated for more than a century. This debate has been reviewed many times (Horton 1984; Flannery 1994; Johnson 2006; Johnson et al. 2016; O'Connell & Allen 2015; Wroe & Field 2006; Wroe et al. 2013), and we will not revisit it at length here. However, the debate is significant in regard to interpretation of human–megafauna interaction because megafaunal extinction could, in theory, have been a result of such interactions. We therefore provide a brief overview of the hypotheses.

The main hypotheses on megafaunal extinction have been as follows: It was caused either by habitat change due to anthropogenic burning, by direct hunting of megafauna by people, by climate change, or by some combination of all these primary causes. Of these possibilities, the fire hypothesis can now be discarded, for three main reasons (Johnson 2016).

First, there appears to be too little evidence that the arrival of people in Sahul caused large changes in fire regimes and consequent changes in vegetation. Many charcoal records from the Late Pleistocene show evidence of changes in fire activity, but these changes are best explained by climate and there is little indication of widespread increase in burning around 50 ka (Kershaw et al. 2006; Mooney et al. 2010). Second, the few detailed records of megafaunal extinction that can be matched with charcoal records from the same locations do not find the expected sequence of increased fire closely followed by megafaunal decline and extinction. For example, in southwest Western Australia, two studies, one of fossils and the other of dung fungi, agree in finding that the region's megafauna went extinct soon after 48 ka, but in neither case did this coincide with a change in charcoal and by implication fire frequency (Prideaux et al. 2010; van der Kaars et al. 2017). Another study that matched changes in dung fungi with charcoal and pollen did find an increase in charcoal close to the time of megafaunal extinction, but the rise in charcoal closely followed dung–fungi decline rather than the other way around (Rule et al. 2012). Third, reconstructions of the ecology of some extinct megafauna suggest they were unlikely to have been strongly affected by fire. For example, the giant kangaroo *Procoptodon goliah* evidently browsed mainly on chenopod shrubs, and its distribution matched that of chenopod shrublands (Prideaux et al. 2009), but chenopod shrublands have low flammability, their distribution is not strongly affected by fire, and there is no evidence that they contracted at the time *P. goliah* went extinct.

This lack of evidence of changes in fire regimes leaves hunting and climate as contending or complementary hypotheses. The idea that hunting at least contributed to megafaunal extinction is supported by recent evidence (reviewed above) that the megafaunal assemblage was widespread and diverse when humans arrived but was extinct by 40 ka. This extinction date implies a quite rapid decline following human arrival, especially if we take the view, discussed earlier, that human occupation did not become widespread across Sahul until approximately 50 ka or possibly later (despite evidence for considerably earlier settlement at some sites, exemplified by Madjedbebe). The idea that hunting was involved in megafaunal extinction is also supported by the general observation that the extinct animals were likely to have been susceptible to overhunting, for three reasons: their large body size and therefore low population growth rates; the fact that most lived on the ground in open habitats and would thus have been highly exposed to hunters; and in some cases, their possession of highly vulnerable life-stages (the egg in large ground-nesting birds and reptiles).

There are two distinct views on the role of climate as a cause of megafaunal extinction. One view is that long-term deterioration of climate through much of the Pleistocene caused gradual attenuation of the megafauna. However, as we have shown, the evidence for such gradual decline of megafauna is not strong. As far as we can tell, the abundance, distribution, and diversity of megafauna were sustained through the climate fluctuations and stresses of the Pleistocene, and the megafauna did not go into decline until the Late Pleistocene. The other view, most recently argued by Hocknull et al. (2020), is that unprecedented drought during the last glacial cycle wiped out the megafauna within a short period of time. This view faces the difficulty that in some parts of the continent with comparatively rich fossil data, water availability was moderate or even favourable during the period of megafaunal extinction, at least in comparison with the present day (Barrows et al. 2020; Kemp et al. 2019). Therefore, it seems unlikely that climate change could have been the sole or predominant cause of megafaunal extinction on a continental scale.

It remains possible that interactions between the impacts of hunting and fluctuations in climate may be needed to explain both the spatial and temporal pattern of megafaunal decline and the ultimate result. Saltré et al.'s (2019) modelling of extinction dynamics in southeastern Australia supported that view and provided a plausible narrative of extinction in which megafauna disappeared because of the intensified impacts of hunting on populations forced to concentrate around limited water sources during periods of low rainfall. It should be noted, however, that this analysis was conducted at a spatial resolution ($1° \times 1°$) that was coarse compared with the ecological scales at which those interactions might have taken place; that it used modelled rather than empirical data on water availability; and that (because of the scarcity of fossils) all megafaunal species were treated as a single category, with no distinctions possible among taxa differing in water requirements.

CONCLUSION

Understanding the nature of interaction between people and megafauna remains a significant gap in knowledge of Australian archaeology, and our main conclusion must be that there is a great need of more primary data. This is true in archaeology but perhaps even more so in palaeontology. The focus should be on building large fossil databases, along with good proxy data on environmental changes and climate variables, for regions in which archaeological history is also relatively well known, so that we can analyse spatial and temporal relationships of people and animals along with environmental change in the same landscapes. This work will demand intensive and multidisciplinary research into several large-area samples. It is a considerable challenge but worth undertaking considering that the outcome will be stronger data on the megafaunal species that were present in the early archaeological history of Sahul, and a more nuanced and secure understanding of the interaction of people, megafauna, and environmental change across the continent.

ACKNOWLEDGMENTS

For responding to queries, we thank Richard Cosgrove, Judith Field, Michelle Langley, Matthew MacDowell, Katharina Peters, and Gavin Prideaux. We also thank Katharina Peters for supplying Figure 10.2, and Gabriel Ugueto for the images in Figure 10.1.

REFERENCES

Akerman, K. (1998). A rock painting, possibly of the now extinct marsupial *Thylacoleo* (marsupial lion), from the north Kimberley, Western Australia. *The Beagle: Records of the Museums and Art Galleries of the Northern Territory, 14*, 117–121.

Allen, J., & O'Connell, J. F. (2014). Both half right: Updating the evidence for dating first human arrivals in Sahul. *Australian Archaeology, 79*, 86–108.

Alroy, J. (2001). A multispecies overkill simulation of the end-Pleistocene megafaunal mass extinction. *Science, 292*, 1893–1896.

Aubert, M., Lebe, R., Oktaviana, A. A., Tang, M., Burhan, B., Hamrullah, . . . Brumm, A. (2019). Earliest hunting scene in prehistoric art. *Nature, 576,* 442–445.

Baker, A. G., Bhagwat, S. A., & Willis, K. J. (2013). Do dung fungal spores make a good proxy for past distribution of large herbivores? *Quaternary Science Reviews, 62,* 21–31.

Barker, B., Lamb, L., Delannoy, J.-J., David, B., Gunn, R. G., Chalmin, E., . . . Hoerle, S. (2017). Archaeology of JSARN–124 site 3, central-western Arnhem Land: Determining the age of the so-called '*Genyornis*' painting. In B. David, P. S. C. Taçon, J.-J. Delannoy, & J.-M. Geneste (Eds.), *The archaeology of rock art in western Arnhem Land, Australia* (pp. 423–497). Terra Australis 47. Canberra: ANU Press.

Barrows, T. T., Fitzsimmons, K. E., Mills, S. C., Tumney, J., Pappin, D., & Stern, N. (2020). Late Pleistocene lake level history of Lake Mungo, Australia, *Quaternary Science Reviews, 238,* 106338.

Bednarik, R. G. (2013). Megafauna depictions in Australian rock art. *Rock Art Research, 30,* 197–215.

Bird, D. W., Codding, B. F., Bird, R. B., Zeanah, D. W., & Taylor, C.J. (2013). Megafauna in a continent of small game: Archaeological implications of Martu Camel hunting in Australia's Western Desert. *Quaternary International, 297,* 155–166.

Bird, M. I., Hutley, L. B., Lawes, M. J., Lloyd, J. O. N., Luly, J. G., Ridd, P. V., . . . Wurster, C. M. (2013). Humans, megafauna and environmental change in tropical Australia. *Journal of Quaternary Science, 28*(5), 439–452.

Bird, M. I., O'Grady, D., & Ulm, S. (2016). Humans, water, and the colonization of Australia. *Proceedings of the National Academy of Sciences, 113*(41), 11477.

Black, K. H., Archer, M., Hand, S., & Godthelp, H. (2012). The rise of the Australian marsupials: A synopsis of biostratigraphic, phylogenetic, palaeoecologic and palaeobiogeographic understanding, in J. A. Talent (Ed.), *Earth and life* (pp. 983–1078). Dordrecht: Springer.

Bowler, J. M., Wyrwoll, K.-H., & Lu, Y. (2001). Variations of the northwest Australian summer monsoon over the last 300,000 years: The paleohydrological record of the Gregory (Mulan) Lakes System. *Quaternary International, 83–85,* 63–80.

Brook, B. W., & Johnson, C. N. (2006). Selective hunting of juveniles as a cause of the imperceptible overkill of the Australasian Pleistocene 'megafauna'. *Alcheringa, Special Issue 1,* 39–48.

Broughton, J. M., Cannon, M. D., Bayham, F. E., & Byers, D. A. (2011). Prey body size and ranking in zooarchaeology: Theory, empirical evidence, and applications from the Northern Great Basin. *American Antiquity, 76*(3), 403–428.

Celik, M., Cascini, M., Haouchar, D., van der Burg, C., Dodt, W., . . . Phillips, M. J. (2019). A molecular and morphometric assessment of the systematics of the *Macropus* complex clarifies the tempo and mode of kangaroo evolution. *Zoological Journal of the Linnean Society, 186,* 793–812.

Chaloupka, G. (1993). *Journey in time.* Sydney: Reed Books.

Chinsamy-Turan, A., Worthy, T. H., & Handley, W. D. (2019). Growth strategies linked to prevailing environmental conditions in Australia giant flightless mihirung birds (Aves: Dromornithidae). *Society of Vertebrate Paleontology, October 2019, Abstracts of Papers, 79th Annual Meeting, Brisbane Convention and Exhibition Centre.* Brisbane, Queensland, Australia.

Clarkson, C., Jacobs, Z., Marwick, B., Fullagar, R., Wallis, L., Smith, M., . . . Pardoe, C. (2017). Human occupation of northern Australia by 65,000 years ago. *Nature, 547,* 306–310.

Cohen, T. J., Jansen, J. D., Gliganic, L. A., Larsen, J. R., Nanson, G. C., May, J.-H., . . . Price, D. M. (2015). Hydrological transformation coincided with megafaunal extinction in central Australia. *Geology, 43,* 195–198.

Cupper, M. L., & Duncan, J. (2006). Last glacial megafaunal death assemblage and early human occupation at Lake Menindee, southeastern Australia. *Quaternary Research, 66*(2), 332–341.

David, B., Delannoy, J.-J., Mialanes, J., Clarkson, C., Petchey, F., Geneste, J.-M., . . . Castets, G. (2019). 45,610–52,160 years of site and landscape occupation at Nawarla Gabarnmang, Arnhem Land plateau (northern Australia). *Quaternary Science Reviews, 215*, 64–85.

Delannoy, J-J., David, B., Fresløv, J., Mullett, R., GunaiKurnai Land and Waters Aboriginal Corporation, Green, H. . . . Wong, V. N. L. (2020). Geomorphological context and formation history of Cloggs Cave: What was the cave like when people inhabited it? *Journal of Archaeological Science: Reports, 33*, 102461.

Denham, T. I. M., & Mountain, M.-J. (2016). Resolving some chronological problems at Nombe rock shelter in the highlands of Papua New Guinea. *Archaeology in Oceania, 51*(S1), 73–83.

Dortch, J., Balme, J., McDonald, J., Morse, K., O'Connor, S., & Veth, P. (2019). Settling the West: 50 000 years in a changing land. *Journal of the Royal Society of Western Australia, 102*, 30–44.

Dortch, J., Cupper, M., Grün, R., Harpley, B., Lee, K., & Field, J. (2016). The timing and cause of megafauna mass deaths at Lancefield Swamp, south-eastern Australia. *Quaternary Science Reviews, 145*, 161–182.

Field, J., Fillios, M., & Wroe, S. (2008). Chronological overlap between humans and megafauna in Sahul (Pleistocene Australia-New Guinea): A review of the evidence. *Earth Science Reviews, 89*, 97–115.

Field, J., Wroe, S., Trueman, C. N., Garvey, J., & Wyatt-Spratt, S. (2013). Looking for the archaeological signature in Australian megafaunal extinctions. *Quaternary International, 285*, 76–88.

Fillios, M., Field, J., & Charles, B. (2010). Investigating human and megafauna co-occurrence in Australian prehistory: Mode and causality in fossil accumulations at Cuddie Springs, *Quaternary International, 211*(1), 123–143.

Flannery, T. F. (1994). *The future eaters.* Melbourne: Reed.

Flannery, T. F., Martin, R., & Szalay, A. (1996). *Tree kangaroos, a curious natural history.* Melbourne: Reed Books.

Flannery, T. F., Mountain, M.-J., & Aplin, K. (1983). Quaternary kangaroos (Macropodidae: Marsupialia) from Nombe Rock Shelter, Papua New Guinea, with comments on the nature of megafaunal extinction in the New Guinea Highlands. *Proceedings of the Linnean Society of New South Wales, 107*, 75–97.

Flood, J. (1974). Pleistocene man at Clogg's Cave: His tool kit and environment. *Mankind, 9*, 175–188.

Florin, S. A., Fairbairn, A. S., Nango, M., Djandjomerr, D., Marwick, B., Fullagar, R., . . . Clarkson, C. (2020). The first Australian plant foods at Madjedbebe, 65,000–53,000 years ago. *Nature Communications, 11*(1), 924.

Fu, X., Cohen, T. J., & Arnold, L. J. (2017). Extending the record of lacustrine phases beyond the last interglacial for Lake Eyre in central Australia using luminescence dating. *Quaternary Science Reviews, 162*, 88–110.

Gaffney, E. S. (1992). *Ninjemys*, a new name for 'Meiolania' oweni (Woodward), a Horned Turtle from the Pleistocene of Queensland. *American Museum Novitates, 3049*, 1–10.

Gillespie, R., Horton, D. R., Ladd, P., Macumber, P. G., Rich, T. H., Thorne, R., & Wright, R. V. S. (1978). Lancefield Swamp and the extinction of the Australian megafauna. *Science, 200*(4345), 1044.

Graham, R. W., Belmecheri, S., Choy, K., Culleton, B. J., Davies, L. J., Froese, D., . . . Wooller, M. J. (2016). Timing and causes of mid-Holocene mammoth extinction on St. Paul Island, Alaska. *Proceedings of the National Academy of Sciences, 113*(33), 9310–9314.

Grellet-Tinner, G., Spooner, N. A., Handley, W. D., & Worthy, T. H. (2017). The *Genyornis* Egg: Response to Miller et al.'s commentary on Grellet-Tinner et al., 2016. *Quaternary Science Reviews, 161*, 128–133.

Grellet-Tinner, G., Spooner, N. A., & Worthy, T. H. (2016). Is the '*Genyornis*' egg of a mihirung or another extinct bird from the Australian dreamtime? *Quaternary Science Reviews, 133*, 147–164.

Grün, R., Eggins, S., Aubert, M., Spooner, N., Pike, A. W. G., & Müller, W. (2010). ESR and U-series analyses of faunal material from Cuddie Springs, NSW, Australia: Implications for the timing of the extinction of the Australian megafauna. *Quaternary Science Reviews, 29*(5–6), 596–610.

Grün, R., Moriarty, K., & Wells, R. (2001). Electron spin resonance dating of the fossil deposits in the Naracoorte Caves, South Australia, *Journal of Quaternary Science, 16*(1), 49–59.

Gunn, R. G., Douglas, L. C., & Whear, R. L. (2011). What bird is that? Identifying a probable painting of *Genyornis newtoni* in western Arnhem Land. *Australian Archaeology, 73*, 1–12.

Hamm, G., Mitchell, P., Arnold, L. J., Prideaux, G. J., Questiaux, D., Spooner, N. A., . . . Johnston, D. (2016). Cultural innovation and megafauna interaction in the early settlement of arid Australia. *Nature, 539*(7628), 280–283.

Handley, W. D., Chinsamy, A., Yates, A. M., & Worthy, T. H. (2016). Sexual dimorphism in the late Miocene mihirung *Dromornis stirtoni* (Aves: Dromornithidae) from the Alcoota Local Fauna of central Australia. *Journal of Vertebrate Paleontology, 36*(5), e1180298.

Hocknull, S. A., Lewis, R., Arnold, L. J., Pietsch, T., Joannes-Boyau, R., Price, G. J., . . . Lawrence, R. A. (2020). Extinction of eastern Sahul megafauna coincides with sustained environmental deterioration. *Nature Communications, 11*(1), 2250.

Hope, J. H., Lampert, R. J., Edmondson, E., Smith, M. J., & van Tets, G. F. (1977). Late Pleistocene faunal remains from Seton Rock Shelter, Kangaroo Island, South Australia. *Journal of Biogeography, 4*(4), 363–385.

Horton, D. (1984). Red kangaroos: Last of the Australian megafauna. In P. S. Martin & R. G. Klein (Eds.), *Quaternary extinctions: A prehistoric revolution* (pp. 639–680). Tucson: University of Arizona Press.

Jankowski, N. R., Gully, G. A., Jacobs, Z., Roberts, R. G., & Prideaux, G. J. (2016). A late Quaternary vertebrate deposit in Kudjal Yolgah Cave, south-western Australia: Refining regional late Pleistocene extinctions. *Journal of Quaternary Science, 31*(5), 538–550.

Johnson, C. (2006). *Australia's mammal extinctions: A 50,000 year history*. Melbourne: Cambridge University Press.

Johnson, C. N. (2002). Determinants of loss of mammal species during the Late Quaternary 'megafauna' extinctions: Life history and ecology, but not body size. *Proceedings of the Royal Society B-Biological Sciences, 269*(1506), 2221–2227.

Johnson, C. N. (2016). Fire, people and ecosystem change in Pleistocene Australia. *Australian Journal of Botany, 64*(8), 643–651.

Johnson, C. N., Alroy, J., Beeton, N. J., Bird, M. I., Brook, B. W., Cooper, A., . . . Bradshaw, C. J. A. (2016). What caused extinction of the Pleistocene megafauna of Sahul? *Proceedings of the Royal Society B-Biological Sciences, 283*, 20152399.

Kemp, C. W., Tibby, J., Arnold, L. J., & Barr, C. (2019). Australian hydroclimate during Marine Isotope Stage 3: A synthesis and review. *Quaternary Science Reviews, 204*, 94–104.

Kershaw, P., van der Kaars, S., Moss, P., Opdyke, B., Guichard, F., Rule, S., & Turney, C. (2006). Environmental change and the arrival of people in the Australian region. *Before Farming, 2006/1*, 1–24.

Langley, M. C. (2020). Re-analysis of the "engraved" *Diprotodon* tooth from Spring Creek, Victoria, Australia. *Archaeology in Oceania*, *55*(1), 33–41.

Langley, M. C., Clarkson, C., & Ulm, S. (2011). From small holes to grand narratives: The impact of taphonomy and sample size on the modernity debate in Australia and New Guinea. *Journal of Human Evolution*, *61*(2), 197–208.

Lewis, D. (2017). Megafauna identification for dummies: Arnhem Land and Kimberley 'megafauna' paintings. *Rock Art Research*, *34*, 82–99.

Lewis, R. J., Tibby, J., Arnold, L. J., Barr, C., Marshall, J., McGregor, G., . . . Yokoyama, Y. (2020). Insights into subtropical Australian aridity from Welsby Lagoon, North Stradbroke Island, over the past 80,000 years. *Quaternary Science Reviews*, *234*, 106262.

Martin, P. S. (1984). Prehistoric overkill: The global model. In P. S. Martin & R. G. Klein (Eds.), *Quaternary extinctions* (pp. 354–403). Tucson: University of Arizona Press.

McDowell, M. C., Prideaux, G. J., Walshe, K., Bertuch, F., & Jacobsen, G. E. (2015). Re-evaluating the Late Quaternary fossil mammal assemblage of Seton Rockshelter, Kangaroo Island, South Australia, including the evidence for late-surviving megafauna. *Journal of Quaternary Science*, *30*(4), 355–364.

Miller, G. H., Fogel, M. L., Magee, J. W., Gagan, M. K., Clarke, S. J., & Johnson, B. J. (2005). Ecosystem collapse in Pleistocene Australia and a human role in megafaunal extinction. *Science*, *309*, 287–290.

Miller, G. H., Magee, J. W., Johnson, B. J., Fogel, M. L., Spooner, N. A., McCulloch, M. T., & Ayliffe, L. K. (1999). Pleistocene extinction of *Genyornis newtoni*: Human impact on Australian megafauna. *Science*, *283*, 205–208.

Miller, G., Magee, J., Smith, M., Spooner, N., Baynes, A., Lehman, S., . . . DeVogel, S. (2016). Human predation contributed to the extinction of the Australian megafaunal bird *Genyornis newtoni* ~ 47ka. *Nature Communications*, *7*, 10496.

Molnar, R. E. (2004). *Dragons in the dust: The paleobiogy of the giant monitor lizard Megalania*. Bloomington: Indiana University Press.

Mooney, S. D., Harrison, S. P., Bartlein, P. J., Daniau, A. L., Stevenson, J., Brownlie, K. C., . . . Williams, N. (2010). Late Quaternary fire regimes of Australasia. *Quaternary Science Reviews*, *30*(1–2), 28–46.

Moriarty, K. C., McCulloch, M. T., Wells, R. T., & McDowell, M. C. (2000). Mid-Pleistocene cave fills, megafaunal remains and climate change at Naracoorte, South Australia: Towards a predictive model using U-Th dating of speleothems. *Palaeogeography, Palaeoclimatology, Palaeoecology*, *159*(1), 113–143.

Murray, D. C., Haile, J., Dortch, J., White, N. E., Haouchar, D., Bellgard, M. I., . . . Bunce, M. (2013). Scrapheap challenge: A novel bulk-bone metabarcoding method to investigate ancient DNA in faunal assemblages. *Scientific Reports*, *3*, 3371.

Murray, P., & Chaloupka, G. (1984). The dreamtime animals: Extinct megafauna in Arnhem Land rock art. *Archaeology in Oceania*, *19*, 105–116.

Murray, P. F., & Vickers-Rich, P. (2004). *Magnificent mihirungs: The colossal flightless birds of the Australian dreamtime*. Bloomington & Indianapolis: Indiana University Press.

O'Connell, J. F., & Allen, J. (2015). The process, biotic impact, and global implications of the human colonization of Sahul about 47,000 years ago. *Journal of Archaeological Science*, *56*, 73–84.

O'Connell, J. F., Allen, J., Williams, M. A. J., Williams, A. N., Turney, C. S. M., Spooner, N. A., . . . Cooper, A. (2018). When did *Homo sapiens* first reach Southeast Asia and Sahul? *Proceedings of the National Academy of Sciences USA*, *115*(2018), 8482–8490.

Peters, K. J., Saltré, F., Friedrich, T., Jacobs, Z., Wood, R., McDowell, M., . . . Bradshaw, C. J. A. (2019). FosSahul 2.0, an updated database for the Late Quaternary fossil records of Sahul. *Scientific Data, 6*(1), 272.

Price, G. J., Louys, J., Cramb, J., Feng, Y.-X., Zhao, J.-X., Hocknull, S. A., . . . Joannes-Boyau, R. (2015). Temporal overlap of humans and giant lizards (Varanidae; Squamata) in Pleistocene Australia. *Quaternary Science Reviews, 125*, 98–105.

Price, G. J., & Webb, G. E. (2006). Late Pleistocene sedimentology, taphonomy and megafauna extinction on the Darling Downs, southeastern Queensland. *Australian Journal of Earth Sciences, 53*, 947–970.

Price, G. J., Webb, G. E., Zhao, J.-X., Feng, Y.-X., Murray, A. S., Cooke, B. N., . . . Sobbe, I. H. (2011). Dating megafaunal extinction on the Pleistocene Darling Downs, eastern Australia: The promise and pitfalls of dating as a test of extinction hypotheses. *Quaternary Science Reviews, 30*(7), 899–914.

Prideaux, G. J. (2004). *Systematics and evolution of the sthenurine kangaroos.* University of California Publications in Geological Sciences, Volume 146. Berkeley: University of California Press.

Prideaux, G. J., Ayliffe, L. K., DeSantis, L. R. G., Schubert, B. W., Murray, P. F., Gagan, M. K., & Cerling, T. E. (2009). Extinction implications of a chenopod browse diet for a giant Pleistocene kangaroo. *Proceedings of the National Academy of Sciences, 106*(28), 11646–11650.

Prideaux, G. J., Gully, G. A., Couzens, A. M. C., Ayliffe, L.K., Jankowski, N. R., & Jacobs, Z. (2010). Timing and dynamics of Late Pleistocene mammal extinctions in southwestern Australia. *Proceedings of the National Academy of Sciences, 107*(51), 22157–22162.

Prideaux, G. J., Long, J. A., Ayliffe, L. K., Hellstrom, J. C., Pillans, B., Boles, W. E., . . . Warburton, N. M. (2007b). An arid-adapted middle Pleistocene vertebrate fauna from south-central Australia. *Nature, 445*(7126), 422–425.

Prideaux, G. J., Roberts, R. G., Megirian, D., Westaway, K. E., Hellstrom, J. C., & Olley, J. M. (2007a). Mammalian responses to Pleistocene climate change in southeastern Australia, *Geology, 35*(1), 33–36.

Richards, H. L., Wells, R. T., Evans, A. R., Fitzgerald, E. M. G., & Adams, J. W. (2019). The extraordinary osteology and functional morphology of the limbs in Palorchestidae, a family of strange extinct marsupial giants. *PLOS ONE, 14*(9), e0221824.

Roberts, P., Louys, J., Zech, J., Shipton, C., Kealy, S., Carro, S. S., . . . O'Connor, S. (2020). Isotopic evidence for initial coastal colonization and subsequent diversification in the human occupation of Wallacea. *Nature Communications, 11*(1), 2068.

Roberts, R. G., Flannery, T. F., Ayliffe, L. K., Yoshida, H., Olley, J. M., Prideaux, G. J., . . . Smith, B. L. (2001). New ages for the last Australian megafauna: Continent-wide extinction about 46,000 years ago. *Science, 292*, 1888–1892.

Rodríguez-Rey, M., Herrando-Pérez, S., Brook, B. W., Saltré, F., Alroy, J., Beeton, N., . . . Bradshaw, C. J. A. (2016). A comprehensive database of quality-rated fossil ages for Sahul's Quaternary vertebrates. *Scientific Data, 3*, 160053.

Rodríguez-Rey, M., Herrando-Perez, S., Gillespie, R., Jacobs, Z., Saltre, F., Brook, B. W., . . . Bradshaw, C. J. A. (2015). Criteria for assessing the quality of Middle Pleistocene to Holocene vertebrate fossil ages. *Quaternary Geochronology, 30*, 69–79.

Rule, S., Brook, B. W., Haberle, S. G., Turney, C. S. M., Kershaw, A. P., & Johnson, C. N. (2012). The aftermath of megafaunal extinction: Ecosystem transformation in Pleistocene Australia. *Science, 335*(6075), 1483–1486.

Saltré, F., Chadoeuf, J., Peters, K. J., McDowell, M. C., Friedrich, T., Timmermann, A., . . . Bradshaw, C. J. A. (2019). Climate-human interaction associated with southeast Australian megafauna extinction patterns. *Nature Communications, 10*(1), 5311.

Saltré, F., Rodriguez-Rey, M., Brook, B. W., Johnson, C. N., Turney, C. S. M., & Alroy, J., . . . Bradshaw, C. J. A. (2016). Climate change not to blame for late Quaternary megafauna extinctions in Australia. *Nature Communications, 7*, 10511.

Shute, E., Prideaux, G. J., & Worthy, T. H. (2017). Taxonomic review of the late Cenozoic megapodes (Galliformes: Megapodiidae) of Australia. *Royal Society Open Science, 4*(6), 170233.

Smith, F. A., Elliott Smith, R. E., Lyons, S. K., & Payne, J. L. (2018). Body size downgrading of mammals over the late Quaternary. *Science, 360*(6386), 310.

Surovell, T. A., & Grund, B. S. (2012). The associational critique of Quaternary overkill and why it is largely irrelevant to the extinction debate. *American Antiquity, 77* (4), 672–687.

Tedford, R. H. (1967). *The fossil Macropodidae from Lake Menindee, New South Wales.* University of California Publications in Geological Sciences 64. Berkeley: University of California Press.

Tedford, R. H. (1955). Report on the extinct mammalian remains at Lake Menindee, New South Wales. *Records of the South Australian Museum, 11*, 299–305.

Tindale, N. B. (1955). Archaeological site at Lake Menindee New South Wales. *Records of the South Australian Museum, 11*, 269–298.

Trueman, C. N. G., Field, J. H., Dortch, J., Charles, B., & Wroe, S. (2005). Prolonged coexistence of humans and megafauna in Pleistocene Australia. *Proceedings of the National Academy of Sciences of the United States of America, 102*(23), 8381.

Turney, C. S. M., Bird, M. I., Fifield, L. K., Roberts, R. G., Smith, M., Dortch, C. E., . . . Cresswell, R. G. (2001). Early human occupation at Devil's Lair, Southwestern Australia 50,000 years ago. *Quaternary Research, 55*(1), 3–13.

Van der Kaars, S., Miller, G. H., Turney, C. S. M., Cook, E. J., Nürnberg, D., Schönfeld, J., . . . Lehman, S. J. (2017). Humans rather than climate the primary cause of Pleistocene megafaunal extinction in Australia. *Nature Communications, 8*, 14142.

Vanderwal, R., & Fullagar, R. (1989). Engraved *Diprotodon* tooth from the Spring Creek Locality, Victoria. *Archaeology in Oceania, 24*(1), 13–16.

Veth, P., Ditchfield, K., Bateman, M., Ouzman, S., Benoit, M., Motta, A. P., . . . Harper, S. (2019). Minjiwarra: Archaeological evidence of human occupation of Australia's northern Kimberley by 50,000 BP. *Australian Archaeology, 85*(2), 115–125.

Veth, P., Ward, I., Manne, T., Ulm, S., Ditchfield, K., Dortch, J., . . . Kendrick, P. (2017). Early human occupation of a maritime desert, Barrow Island, North-West Australia. *Quaternary Science Reviews, 168*, 19–29.

Walsh, G. (2000). *Bradshaw art of the Kimberley.* Brisbane: Takarakka Nowan Kas Publications.

Welch, D. (2016). That bird is not *Genyornis. Australian Archaeology, 82*, 184–191.

Westaway, M. C., Olley, J., & Grün, R. (2017). At least 17,000 years of coexistence: Modern humans and megafauna at the Willandra Lakes, South-Eastern Australia. *Quaternary Science Reviews, 157*, 206–211.

Wolfe, A. L., & Broughton, J. M. (2020). A foraging theory perspective on the associational critique of North American Pleistocene overkill. *Journal of Archaeological Science, 119*, 105162.

Wood, J. R., Wilmshurst, J. M., Turney, C. S. M., & Fogwill, C. J. (2016). Palaeoecological signatures of vegetation change induced by herbivory regime shifts on subantarctic Enderby Island. *Quaternary Science Reviews, 134*, 51–58.

Worthy, T. H., Handley, W. D., Archer, M., & Hand, S. J. (2016). The extinct flightless mihirungs (Aves, Dromornithidae): Cranial anatomy, a new species, and assessment of Oligo-Miocene lineage diversity. *Journal of Vertebrate Paleontology, 36*(3), e1031345.

Wroe, S., Crowther, M., Dortch, J., & Chong, J. (2004). The size of the largest marsupial and why it matters. *Proceedings of the Royal Society of London B, 271*, S34–S36.

Wroe, S., & Field, J. (2006). A review of the evidence for a human role in the extinction of Australian megafauna and an alternative interpretation. *Quaternary Science Reviews, 25*, 2692–2703.

Wroe, S., Field, J. H., Archer, M., Grayson, D. K., Price, G. J., Louys, J., . . . Mooney, S. D. (2013). Climate change frames debate over the extinction of megafauna in Sahul (Pleistocene Australia-New Guinea). *Proceedings of the National Academy of Sciences, 110*(22), 8777–8781.

CHAPTER 11

WHAT DOES DNA TELL US ABOUT PAST CONNECTIONS AND THE SETTLEMENT OF SAHUL?

ELIZABETH MATISOO-SMITH AND
ANNA L. GOSLING

INTRODUCTION

UNDERSTANDING the human settlement of Sahul has a significant impact on a number of debates and discussions regarding human evolution and history more generally. The archaeological evidence of early human settlement has implications for the timing, genetic composition, and dispersal routes taken by the ancestors of modern peoples. Genetic data from Sahul is providing new evidence of interactions between modern humans and several possible populations or even different species of now extinct hominins, which challenges some key concepts in our understanding of human evolution. The genetic data from animals and humans from Australia and New Guinea are also adding to our understanding of the impact of human arrival on local ecosystems, the possible impacts of climate change on human behaviour, and for assessing levels of interaction within the region and externally.

Because of the deep antiquity of human occupation of Sahul, the genomes of the Indigenous peoples of New Guinea and Australia have been of interest to investigators since the first use of genetics to understand Out-of-Africa migrations (Stoneking, Bhatia, & Wilson 1986; Stoneking, Jorde, Bhatia, & Wilson 1990). Major advances in technology have seen available data increase markedly over the years. Early studies focused on small mitochondrial fragments (Redd & Stoneking 1999; Tommaseo-Ponzetta, Attimonelli, De Robertis, Tanzariello, & Saccone 2002; Friedlaender et al. 2007; Vilar et al. 2008; Nagle et al. 2017a) and microsatellite markers, or short repetitive

DNA sequences found throughout known genomes[1] (Friedlaender et al. 2008). With the rise of high-throughput DNA sequencing technology, complete mitochondrial genomes consisting of ~16.5 thousand nucleotides or base pairs (Ingman & Gyllensten 2003; Tobler et al. 2017; Nagle et al. 2017b), and genome-wide data consisting of tens of thousands of individual nucleotide readings from throughout the genome (Wollstein et al. 2010; Lazaridis et al. 2014; Qin & Stoneking 2015), can now be generated. With subsequent decreases in DNA sequencing costs with further advances in technology, we are now in the position where there are high-depth whole-genome data—all ~3 billion base pairs that make up the human genome—are available (Malaspinas et al. 2016; Pagani et al. 2016; Mallick et al. 2016). These new molecular tools provide amazing opportunities for understanding human variation and for reconstructing the past, particularly with the ability to include ancient genome data, or aDNA, obtained from archaeological and historic tissues (bones, teeth, hair).

Until recently (~2016), relatively little genomic data was available from the populations of Sahul. Indigenous Australians were notably absent from important studies of global human variation, such as the Thousand Genomes Project and the Human Genome Diversity Project, while only a modest number of New Guinea individuals were included in the latter. With significant reduction in the costs of sequencing technology, and the ever-increasing recognition of the complexity of the demographic history of the region (in particular, the recent findings of hominin introgression—see below), there has been an explosion of published genomic sequences (see Table 11.1 and refs therein) and much better understanding of the mitochondrial DNA (mtDNA) and Y chromosome variation in the region.[2] This higher resolution of data is enabling researchers to explore more nuanced questions surrounding the peopling of the continent, as well as questions surrounding the evolution of *Homo sapiens* more broadly.

While Australia has now been relatively well sampled geographically, perhaps with the exception of Tasmania, New Guinea has relatively poor coverage in terms of where samples have been obtained (see Table 11.1). In particular, the western half of New Guinea (Indonesian Papua) is poorly represented, and is highly important in understanding the initial peopling of Sahul. Unfortunately, early studies often provided poor information regarding provenance of samples, and while linguistic affiliation and genetic ancestry do not always correlate, having as much contextual information as possible helps when reconstructing relationships and interactions in the past. However, we note that in some cases, communities may not wish for highly specific information regarding their DNA samples to be made publicly available.

Much needed discussions regarding the ethical issues related to working with genomic data obtained from both ancient and modern populations are currently taking place around the world. Ethical issues are of particular importance when working with data obtained from Indigenous remains and communities given sensitivities associated with legacies of colonialism (Bardill et al. 2018; Anonymous 2020). The recent rise in the number of genetic studies involving Indigenous samples in Australia and New Guinea (see refs in Table 11.1) raises issues that perhaps require even more engaged discussion. Many Indigenous samples were collected decades ago and remain in

Table 11.1. Genetic data currently available for Australia and New Guinea. Where available, geographic or other population defining data are provided.

	n	Population	Reference
Whole genomes			
Australia	10	Ancient genomes (up to 1540 years BP): 7x Queensland (1x Flinders Island, 2x Cairns, 3x Mapoon, 1x Weipa), 3x New South Wales (2x Barnham, 1x Willandra Lakes)	Wright et al. (2018)
	83	Indigenous Australians: 18x NW Australia, 10x NE Australia, 10x NE central Australia, 8x SE Australia, 24x western central Australia, 14x SW Australia	Malaspinas et al. (2016)
	2	Indigenous Australians	Pagani et al. (2016)
	2	Indigenous Australians	Mallick et al. (2016)
New Guinea	31	17x New Britain, 7x Korowai, 7x PNG (undefined)	Jacobs et al. (2019)
	35	Bismarck Archipelago (but most Austronesian speakers)	Vernot et al. (2016)
	25	5x from Bunde area, 5x from Hundiawa, 5x from Mendi, 5x from Tari, 5x from Marawaka	Malaspinas et al. (2016)
	6	3x Koinanbe, 3x Kosipe	Pagani et al. (2016)
	17	15x 'Papuans', 2x Bougainville	Mallick et al. (2016)
SNP arrays			
Australia	10	8x Northern Territory, 2x 'cell cultures'	Reich et al. (2011)
	38	Riverine, New South Wales	McEvoy et al. (2010)
New Guinea	45	6x Port Moresby, 24x Koinambe, 15 Kosipe	Malaspinas et al. (2016)
	381	Pulled from a library of nearly 800 samples: 82x Madang, 525x Highlands, 158x New Guinea South Coast	Bergström et al. (2017)
	20	Papuans	Qin & Stoneking (2015)
	16	16x Papuans	Lazaridis et al. (2014)
	37	22x Bougainville, 17x Papuans	HGDP-CEPH
	25	Southern Highlands (Huli & Angal-Kewa languages)	Wollstein et al. (2010)
Mitogenomes			
Australia	41	*Ancient* (up to 1540 years BP): 24x Queensland (4x Cairns, 1x Flinders Island, 11x Mapoon, 1x from Stanley Island, 7x Weipa), 4x New South Wales (2x Barnham, 1x Bourke, 1x Willandra Lakes) *Modern*: 16x New South Wales (4x Barnham, 7x Bourke, 2x Riverine, 3x Willandra). Also, first reporting of the mitogenomes from Malaspinas et al. (2016), n=83	Wright et al. (2018)

(continued)

Table 11.1. Continued

	n	Population	Reference
	111	Historically collected hair samples from Point Pearce (South Australia); Koonibba (South Australia), Cherbourg (Queensland)	Tobler et al. (2017)
	127	Genographic collections (103x Queensland, 14x New South Wales, 6x Victoria, 2x Tasmania, 2x Western Australia)	Nagle et al. (2017b)
	1	1x Arnhem Land	Friedlaender et al. (2007)
	5	Indigenous Australians from Kalumburu, NW Australia	Hudjashov et al. (2007)
	8	5x NSW (Riverine), 3x Northern Territory (Walpiri)	van Holst Pellekaan, Ingman, Roberts-Thomson, & Harding (2006)
	20	Indigenous Australians from Northern Territory	Ingman & Gyllensten (2003)
New Guinea	281	New Britain (32x Anem, 28x Ata, 42x Nakanai), Bougainville (29x Buin, 11x Buka, 26x Siwai, 38x Nagovisi, 41x Nasioi, 34x Torau)	Duggan et al. (2014)
	14	3x Highlands (1x Bundi, 1x Fringe Highlands, 1x Garaina). 1x Coastal (1x Markham), 5x New Britain (2x Nakanai, 1x Mangseng, 1x Kove, 1x Melamela), 2x New Ireland (2x Madak), 3x West New Guinea (1x Mondobo, 1x Kol, 1x Pomio)	Friedlaender et al. (2007)
	4	Highlanders from Bundi region	Hudjashov et al. (2007)
	21	10x coastal PNG, 11x Highlands	Ingman & Gyllensten (2003)
mtDNA HVR			
Australia	594	502 newly reported individuals + 92 previously reported by Ballantyne et al. (2012). 77x Northern Territory, 18x Victoria, 90x New South Wales, 391x Queensland, 7x Tasmania, 5x Western Australia, 6x South Australia	Nagle et al. (2017a)
	32	Indigenous Australians from Kalumburu, NW Australia	Hudjashov et al. (2007)
	49	26x New South Wales (Riverine), 23x Northern Territory (Walpiri)	van Holst Pellekaan et al. (2006)
	54	Walbiri (Northern Territory), samples, historic blood collection	Huoponen, Schurr, Chen, & Wallace (2001)
	13	9x Tasmania, 4x Victoria	Presser, Stoneking, & Redd (2003)
	200	95x Arnhem Land, 105x NW Australia	Redd & Stoneking (1999)
New Guinea	432	Massim	van Oven et al. (2014)
	219	Wewak and Yangoru districts of East Sepik Province	Vilar et al. (2008)

Table 11.1. Continued

	n	Population	Reference
	48	Highlanders from Bundi area	Hudjashov et al. (2007)
		Samples from Frieldaender's Southwest Pacific Collection, primarily from the Bismarck Archipelago	Friedlaender et al. (2007)
	202	21x Central Highlands, 73x Fringe Highlands, 43x lowland riverine plain, 64x coastal	Tommaseo-Ponzetta et al. (2002)
Y chromosome			
Australia	1175	Genographic collections (119x Queensland; 19x New South Wales, 4x Victoria, 1x Western Australia; 1x Tasmania); Forensic Science South Australia collection (757); Victorian Police Forensic Services Department collection (182); Northern Territory Forensic Centre Aboriginal database (77x Northern Territory, 5x South Australia, 10x Queensland)	Nagle et al. (2017a)
	13	Genographic collection (9x Queensland; 4x Western Australia)	Bergström et al. (2016)
	757	Forensic Science South Australia collection	Taylor et al. (2012)
	95	60x Arnhem Land, 35x Sandy Desert	Kayser et al. (2001)
New Guinea	389	Massim	van Oven et al. (2014)
	147	147x Admiralty Islands	Kayser et al. (2008)
	162	West Papua and Bird's Head (24x Baham, 19x Ekari, 24x Maibrat, 8x Moi, 5x Tehit, 12x Hatam, 22x Karon, 11x Mantion, 10x Moskona, 5x Irarutu, 2x Onin, 10x Wandamen, 10x Biak)	Mona et al. (2007)
	214	183x West New Guinea, 14x Southern Highlands, 17x Eastern Highlands, 16x Northern Coast, 15x Southern Coast	Kayser et al. (2003)
	132	31x coast, 31x Highland, 54x Trobriand Islands, 16x Tolai New Britain	Kayser et al. (2001)
	157	37x PNG highlands, 42x Tolai New Britain, 23x PNG coast/Roro, 55x Trobriands	Hagelberg et al. (1999)

historic collections in colonial museums overseas, where there may be no requirements for community consultation (Prendergast & Sawchuk 2018). Often, contextual data regarding sample origin may be minimal or lacking, and tracing descendant communities may be impossible, given the history of genocide and forced disassociation from place and culture. There is some hope that the application of genomics can start to help reconnect Indigenous peoples with their ancestral remains (see, for example, Wright et al. 2018), but Indigenous communities are often underrepresented in comparative genomic databases (Caron et al. 2020). This means that until such data exist, the full benefit of answering questions regarding the past, but also for addressing contemporary health disparities experienced by Indigenous communities, cannot be achieved (Robertson et al. 2018). Genomic research involving Indigenous peoples and their ancestors should only be done with full community support and engagement, which includes having open discussions and developing specific agreements regarding benefit sharing and issues such as who has access to data and who controls that access (Hudson et al. 2020). Establishing the necessary relationships to undertake genomic research to address this situation and allow communities to reap the benefits of genomic research requires the establishment of trust, which can take a significant amount of time, commitment, and cultural understanding. The questions being asked and the methods applied need to be addressed fully and openly if we are to move forward towards truly collaborative and, ideally, co-designed and community-driven research (Guglielmi 2019; Claw et al. 2018).

The Journey from Africa to Sahul

Data from Australia and New Guinea have long been critical to debates about the process of human evolution and the dispersal of modern human populations across the globe. Of special note were the Australian physical anthropologist Alan Thorne and Milford Wolpoff, who were the main proponents of the Regional Continuity Model, long held up as the alternative to the Replacement Model for modern human origins. Their argument was based on morphological comparisons and recognition of what they called a morphological clade, linking the mid-Pleistocene *Homo erectus* remains from Indonesia (Sangiran 17 specifically) and the Late Pleistocene and Early Holocene *Homo sapiens* material from Australia (Thorne & Wolpoff 1981). It was the mitochondrial DNA evidence published by Cann, Stoneking, and Wilson (1987) that, at the time, appeared to provide the evidence that supported the Out-of-Africa replacement scenario over the Regional Continuity Model. Interestingly, as ancient DNA from extinct hominin remains has become available over the past 10 years, data show that while a majority of the DNA can be traced back to Africa, gene flow between modern humans and other extinct hominin populations (i.e., Neanderthals and Denisovans) was maintained to a minor degree. Thus, there is some 'multiregional' aspect to the Out-of-Africa story of human origins (Stringer 2014). Again, it is the evidence of genetic data from Sahul that is central to our understanding of the relationships and interactions between a range of populations in the Late Pleistocene.

Introgression with Extinct Hominins—Neanderthal and Denisovan DNA in Our Genomes

In 2010, the first Neanderthal genome was published, which showed that all non-African populations carried about 2–4% Neanderthal DNA in their nuclear genomes (Green et al. 2010). Later that year, David Reich and colleagues announced the recovery of ancient DNA from a tiny finger bone found in an archaeological excavation at Denisova Cave in southern Siberia (Reich et al. 2010). The team was able to sequence the entire genome (at low coverage of 1.9x) of this individual. They also recovered mtDNA from a second sample from the cave, from an adult molar, that was excavated from the same archaeological layer as the finger bone. The mtDNA differed from that of the finger bone at two positions, which indicated that it was from a second individual from the same population. When the nuclear genome was compared to Neanderthal and to modern human genomes, the result indicated that Denisovans appeared to be a sister-group to Neanderthals, but one that had a distinct population history. They shared a common ancestor with Neanderthals over 600,000 years ago and with modern humans over 800,000 years ago. Perhaps most interesting was the fact that Melanesian genomes (specifically peoples from mainland New Guinea and Bougainville) have as much as 4.8% Denisovan DNA, a result much higher than seen in European and Asian populations. Levels of Denisovan DNA in the genomes of Indigenous Australian peoples have been detected at similar levels as found in Melanesian genomes (Malaspinas et al. 2016).

Subsequent studies of additional DNA material from Denisova Cave and various modern human populations have revealed a complex picture. Browning, Browning, Zhou, Tucci, and Akey (2018) showed that two distinct Denisovan lineages could be detected among Asian populations, compared to only one in Oceanians. However, a later, relatively large genomic study of island Southeast Asia and New Guinea indicated that more than one Denisovan lineage contributed to modern human genomes in this region (Jacobs et al. 2019). This finding was consistent with a further study, which used Approximate Bayesian Computation with deep learning to find evidence for a third introgression[3] event with a further extinct hominin (Mondal, Bertranpetit, & Lao 2019). Melanesian populations carry DNA from two deeply divergent Denisovan lineages, designated D1 and D2, that themselves are estimated to have diverged over 350,000 years ago (Jacobs et al. 2019). These two lineages are distinct from a third Denisovan lineage (D0) that is found in modern East Asian and Siberian populations. The dates for these two introgression events in Melanesians have been estimated to be around 30 KYA for D1 and 45 KYA for D2. If correct, these dates have implications for determining where this admixture occurred. The fact that lineage D1 is found only in populations from Papua New Guinea and adjacent islands in Near Oceania has been interpreted as being indicative of at least one Denisovan population making it into Wallacea (Jacobs et al. 2019). This, of course, would suggest that Denisovans had some form of watercraft or other technological means of crossing major water barriers. In addition to the Denisovan introgression, Jacobs et al. (2019) found some limited evidence of a possible additional archaic signature (less than 1%) in Melanesian genomes, which might indicate either *Homo erectus* or possibly *Homo floresiensis* introgression. This idea has been explored through genomic analyses of modern 'pygmy' populations from Flores in Indonesia, close to where the *Homo floresiensis* fossils were found. However, there was no evidence to support additional genetic input from a diverged hominin group, such as *Homo floresiensis* (Tucci et al. 2018). We agree that there is currently no genetic or archaeological evidence to suggest a direct Denisovan presence in Sahul (Teixeira & Cooper 2019) or even Wallacea, though the possibility cannot be rejected. More ancient DNA from the region is necessary to specifically address this possibility.

Early ancient DNA studies by Adcock et al. (2001) attempted to use samples from Indigenous Australian remains, including the apparently gracile individuals from Lake Mungo (dated to ~40–45 KYA) and Willandra Lakes (dated to ~10 KYA) as well as robust individuals from Kow Swamp (dated to 15–8 KYA), to suggest that the emergence of our species did not occur solely in Africa. However, this study has been impossible to replicate with next-generation sequencing technology, and many of the samples, including all Pleistocene samples, proved to have no viable endogenous DNA. Thus, the reported results were likely to have been due to contamination (Heupink et al. 2016). Unfortunately, DNA preservation in island Southeast Asia and the Sahul region is poor due to their hot and wet conditions, so it is unlikely that DNA can be obtained from archaeological remains of any hominins (humans, Denisovans, or early hybrids) from a time period earlier than a few thousand years, unless the context and preservation are unusual or aDNA detection and analysis technology change substantially.

Arrival in Sahul

A long-standing debate in human evolution relates to the number of dispersals and directions of those dispersals of modern humans out of Africa (O'Connell et al. 2018). Cann et al. (1987) showed that all non-African populations could be traced back to the L3 mitochondrial lineage, which soon after departure from East Africa split into the two major branches, or macro-haplogroups, labelled M and N. The distribution of the M and M-derived lineages are found primarily in South Asian populations, while the N lineages are found throughout Europe and Asia. This split has been interpreted as representing two migration routes out of Africa, one carrying the M lineages following the south coast of Asia and the other heading north, carrying N and N-derived lineages into Europe and Asia. The mtDNA lineages found in populations from Sahul, however, belong to both M and N macro-haplogroups (see Figure 11.1). There are three possible explanations for this result: (1) There were two migrations of distinct populations to Sahul; (2) the descendant populations from the M and N dispersals merged somewhere in East or Southeast Asia prior to arrival; or (3) there was only a single dispersal event from Africa and the patterns that resulted from other demographic factors. The increasing amount of data from whole-genome studies is shedding further light on this debate.

The similarities in the amount of Neanderthal and Denisovan DNA found in all populations from Sahul suggest that all populations share a similar settlement history in terms of the timing of initial settlement and source population. Analyses of 300 genomes from 142 populations that are part of the Simons Genome Diversity Project were used to test theories regarding the likelihood of more than one Out-of-Africa migration contributing to the genomes of modern humans (Mallick et al. 2016). The data, which

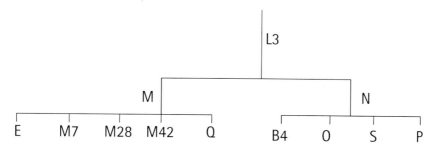

FIGURE 11.1. Mitochondrial phylogeny showing major haplogroups found in the Sahul region. Note that all Sahul lineages derive from the L3 (Out-of-Africa) lineage and from there, from either macrohaplogroup M or N.

included genomic data from Indigenous Australian, New Guinean, and Andamanese populations, indicated that there was no evidence in these genomes for an early, separate dispersal event along the south coast of Asia into Sahul. Instead, Mallick et al. (2016) argue that the modern human ancestry of all non-Africa populations derives from a single, common ancestral population that left Africa about 60 KYA. Divergence dates based on whole-genome data (Malaspinas et al. 2016) suggest that the ancestors of all Sahul populations split from Eurasian populations approximately 58 KYA (51–72 KYA at 95% confidence), which fits with estimates for the Out-of-Africa migration event. All currently available genetic data support the continuous settlement of Sahul and confirm that all living Indigenous Australians descend from these earliest arrivals (Rasmussen et al. 2011; Malaspinas et al. 2016; Bergström et al. 2016; Tobler et al. 2017; Nagle et al. 2017a, 2017b; Wright et al. 2018). In terms of the timing of the earliest arrivals in Australia, the genetic estimates do not support archaeologically based suggestions of very early settlement around 65 KYA, as suggested by Clarkson et al. (2017), or earlier, but they are not inconsistent with their more conservative estimate of 59.3 KYA. Mitochondrial and Y chromosome estimates of arrival time also fit into this general timeframe, if not a bit more recently, given that settlement of Sahul was unlikely to have occurred before the divergence date of mitochondrial haplogroup P, which is estimated at 60 KYA (Nagle et al. 2017b), and the fact that the Sahul K* and C* Y chromosome lineages are estimated to have diverged from their closest South Asian lineages around 54 KYA (Bergström et al. 2016). Given the current limitations and variations regarding molecular dating, however, we would be confident in the suggestion that the settlement of Sahul occurred at least 50 KYA and likely sometime between 50 and 60 KYA.

There has been a significant amount of archaeological research investigating the number of migrations and identifying likely or possible pathways of entry into Sahul, with numerous possible northern and southern routes identified (Birdsell 1977; Allen & O'Connell 2008; Kealy, Louys, & O'Connor 2018; Bird et al. 2019). Again, recent genetic data can also provide some evidence to address these questions, though the results of different genetic studies are not always consistent.

In their analysis of mitogenomes, Tobler et al. (2017) suggest evidence of a single population arriving in Sahul that rapidly dispersed along both the west and the east coasts, reaching southern Australia by 49–45 KYA. It should be noted that this analysis did not include any DNA samples from New Guinea. Nagel et al. (2017a), however, found that the distribution of mtDNA haplotypes from both New Guinea and Australia suggest at least two entry points to Sahul—with a northern route via the Bird's Head of New Guinea that dispersed along the north and east coasts of Sahul and a southern route that dispersed along the west coast (see Figure 11.2). Mitochondrial Haplogroup P, which is the most common haplogroup in Indigenous Australian populations (about 44%), is

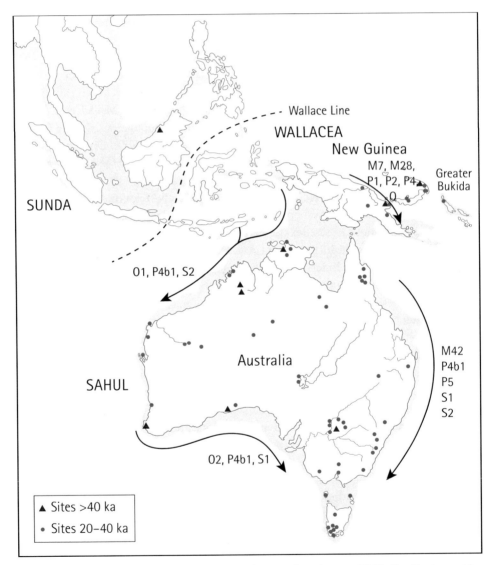

FIGURE 11.2. Map of possible Sahul dispersal routes based on mtDNA distributions. Also shown are archaeological sites dated earlier than 40 KYA (triangles) and those dated to between 20 and 40 KYA (dots).

widely distributed in both New Guinea and Australia and could have dispersed with both groups. Haplogroups O, S, and the M42 subgroups a and b, on the other hand, are found only in Australia, while Q is likely a New Guinea haplogroup. Within Australia, Haplogroup O is found only on the west and northwest coasts, while Haplogroup S is primarily in the west and northwest, but it is also found on the east coast (Nagle et al. 2017a, 2017b). Haplogroup Q1 and Q2 lineages are primarily restricted to New Guinea populations, but both have been found in Queensland, though only in individuals who have known Torres Strait Island maternal ancestry (Wright et al. 2018). It appears from the genetic data that the arid, central region of Australia created or maintained a genetic barrier that explains the clear east/west genetic structure observed in modern Indigenous Australian populations (Malaspinas et al. 2016).

EVIDENCE OF ADAPTATION FROM WHOLE-GENOME DATA

Over the past five years, the rapidly accumulating whole-genome data has allowed researchers to address questions other than population origins and dispersal within Sahul. Investigations of the regions of the Denisovan genomes that are still carried in Indigenous Australian and Melanesian populations indicate positive selection associated with the immune system and metabolic processes, such as glucose production and lipid and carbohydrate metabolism (Vernot et al. 2016; Browning et al. 2018; Jacobs et al. 2019; Zammit et al. 2019). When looking at genomic regions that show evidence of selection within modern Australian genomes, Malaspinas et al. (2016) identified population-specific differences in genes associated with thyroid hormones, which they suggest may be related to adaptation to desert temperatures, and genes influencing serum urate levels, which might be related to protecting against dehydration. They note that further studies would be necessary to determine if these variants are associated with any specific phenotypic traits in Indigenous Australian populations. Unfortunately, when populations encounter new and different environments, these positively selected traits can become deleterious (Zammit et al. 2019; Matisoo-Smith & Gosling 2018).

GENETIC ISOLATION AND DIVERSIFICATION WITHIN SAHUL

Genetic data currently indicate that Indigenous Australian and Melanesian populations have been isolated from one another for a significant amount of time, perhaps very soon after the initial settlement of Sahul. Estimated dates of divergence based on mtDNA all centre around 30 KYA (Nagle et al. 2017b), with dates between 48 and 53 KYA based on Y chromosome data (Bergström et al. 2016) or between 25 and 40 KYA for whole-genome data (Malaspinas et al. 2016). All of these estimates indicate genetic isolation significantly before the Holocene sea-level changes that physically separated the two landmasses with the creation of Torres Strait around 8000–9000 years ago.

Diversification within New Guinea

The island of New Guinea is the most linguistically diverse region in the world and, combined with its deep history, would be expected to reveal significant genetic diversity. Unfortunately, most of the genetic data that we have for New Guinea comes from Papua New Guinea (PNG), which represents only the eastern half of the island and, thus, might underestimate the level of diversity present. Tommaseo-Ponzetta et al. (2002) sampled 202 individuals from Western New Guinea, though, as expected given the date of publication, their analyses were restricted to the short portion of mtDNA known as the hyper-variable region (HVR). Mona et al. (2007) provided some Y chromosome data ($n = 163$ individuals) from the Bird's Head region of northwest New Guinea, but, again, the data are now out of date. While it is difficult to compare HVR data to those of whole mitogenomes, results differed from those available at that time from PNG. In particular, no differences were found between Highlands and coastal populations. In addition, no evidence exists of Haplogroup B, which is often considered a marker of Austronesian ancestry. This result is not too surprising, as Tommaseo-Ponzetta and colleagues did not obtain DNA samples from either the north coast or the Bird's Head Region, which is where Austronesian languages are spoken on the western half of the island.

Over 300 high-coverage whole genomes now exist from the PNG mainland and from the islands in the Bismarck Archipelago, along with an increasing number of samples for which there is a large amount of SNP data.[4] Analyses of these data show significant genetic structure across the region, as might be expected given both the deep time and the extreme topographical geography of the region. The greatest genetic differentiation within PNG appears between the mainland populations and those of the Bismarck Archipelago (Bergström et al. 2017; Jacobs et al. 2019). New Britain and New Ireland (the two major islands of the Bismarck Archipelago) were never connected to the New Guinea mainland, even during periods of lowest sea levels during the Pleistocene. The islands were occupied as early as 40 KYA and were presumably settled from the mainland, likely from the Huon Peninsula (Leavesley et al. 2002). While later Austronesian arrivals in the islands of the Bismarck Archipelago clearly had an impact on the genetic makeup of the populations (Friedlaender et al. 2007), it appears that once settled, the people of New Britain and New Ireland likely had little interaction or genetic exchange with communities on the mainland. Highland and Lowland populations from PNG differentiate from each other genetically, which does not seem to be solely explained by the later Southeast Asian (Austronesian) influences on coastal populations. All Highland populations studied by Bergström et al. (2017) form a clade distinct from Lowland populations, and greater genetic diversity is seen in Western Highland populations compared to those of the Eastern Highlands. While there is little to no evidence of non-Sahul admixture in Highland populations, interestingly, Highland populations do not appear to begin to diversify genetically until around 10 KYA, despite the extreme geography and linguistic variation in the region. This timing for genetic diversification coincides with the dates for the emergence of agriculture and origin of taro cultivation at Kuk Swamp in the Western Highlands (Denham et al. 2003) and also with the spread of the Trans-New Guinea languages across the region (Pawley, Attenborough, Golson, & Hide 2005). The Y chromosome data also provide evidence of a Trans-New Guinea language expansion at the same time (Mona et al. 2007).

The final major demographic impact identified in New Guinea relates to the arrival of Austronesian peoples in the Mid- to Late Holocene. The most obvious marker of this arrival is the appearance of archaeological sites associated with the Lapita Cultural Complex, which first appeared in the Bismarck Archipelago around 3350 years ago (Kirch 2017; Summerhayes et al. 2010). There were many years of debate regarding the arrival of Lapita peoples on the mainland of New Guinea, but several Lapita sites have been recently recorded on both the north and south coasts (David et al. 2011; Gaffney et al. 2015; McNiven et al. 2011). There is no doubt that we see genetic evidence of the arrival of Southeast Asian people, or their recent descendants from the Bismarck Archipelago, on the mainland at some point in the Mid- to Late Holocene, though not necessarily directly associated with Lapita settlers. It is possible that there were Mid-Holocene interactions with island Southeast Asia prior to and after the Lapita period. Such contact is most clearly indicated by the presence of mtDNA lineages belonging to Haplogroups B and E and to Y chromosome Haplogroup O, which are found throughout the Bismarck Archipelago and at low frequency in coastal populations on the New Guinea mainland (Kayser 2010).

Evidence of Southeast Asian contact is also indicated by the arrival of a number of plant and animal species on the mainland of New Guinea, including the dog, pig, and the Pacific rat (*Rattus exulans*), as well as the sweet potato, paper mulberry, and several other important food or utilitarian plants (Storey, Clarke, Ladefoged, Robins, & Matisoo-Smith 2013). Genetic analyses of these commensal species are helping to reconstruct the complexity of interactions in the New Guinea region. MtDNA data from archaeological dog remains suggest that there were multiple introductions of dogs to New Guinea in prehistory (Greig et al. 2018; see also Balme & O'Connor, this volume). These include the ancestors of New Guinea Singing dogs, closely related to dingoes, and two other, likely later, dog introductions, as indicated by mtDNA recovered from archaeological dog remains from the south coast of New Guinea at the sites of Taurama (dated to between 1000 and 2000 years ago), which has one haplogroup, and dog remains from Bogi 1 (dated to ~2100 years ago) and Edubu 1 (dated to ~2400 years ago), both of which have another haplogroup.

Analyses of sweet potato DNA (Roullier, Benoit, McKey, & Lebot 2013) indicate that plants introduced and grown in New Guinea today came from historic transfers; they were likely carried by Dutch sailors from the Caribbean region to the Dutch East Indies (the batata lineage) and by the Spanish who brought the kamote lineage to the

Philippines from Central America. Both the batata and kamote varieties were incorporated into island Southeast Asian trade networks and reached New Guinea during the historic period (the past 400–500 years). These two lineages are distinct from the sweet potato variety that was introduced to Polynesia prior to the European arrival (Roullier et al. 2013). Paper mulberry (*Broussonetia papyrifera*), found in New Guinea today, is thought to be an Austronesian introduction and can be traced ultimately back to Taiwan (Olivares et al. 2019). While many of these island Southeast Asian commensal species are found along the south coast of New Guinea, none appear to have been introduced to the Australian mainland, and, to date, there has been no published report on the presence of Lapita pottery in Australia.

Interestingly, analysis of variation in Hepatitis B virus (HBV) genomes has also been used to address the question of the timing and number of human dispersal events in Sahul (Yuen et al. 2019). Hepatitis B has a deep evolutionary history associated with human populations and was thought to be carried by modern humans as they dispersed across the globe from Africa. Indigenous Australians carry a unique HBV subgenotype known as C4, which has not been found in any other population. Melanesians carry a different lineage, known as C3, which has also only been found in populations from Near Oceania or their descendant populations in the Pacific. By dating the divergence of these two lineages, Yuen and colleagues determined that the two lineages were indeed ancient but represented two independent migration pathways into Sahul. The C4 lineage they argue arrived in Sahul via Timor approximately 44–51 KYA, while the C3 virus likely arrived on the north coast of New Guinea from Halmahera between 44 and 46 KYA. Although the dates for arrival in Sahul are slightly more recent than those based on human DNA, the HBV data are consistent with the dispersal routes suggested by the mtDNA haplogroup distributions and are consistent with multiple early population arrivals in Sahul.

Diversification within Australia

The first Indigenous Australian genome was sequenced in 2011 (Rasmussen et al. 2011), and at the time of writing this chapter, more than 300 Indigenous Australian genomes have been sequenced and studied (see Table 11.1). Whole-genome data allow for reconstruction of demographic change over time. Unfortunately, as we know from historical records, the European arrival had a devastating impact on the Indigenous population. As a result, we undoubtedly have lost a significant amount of the variation that was present, as has been documented in other colonized peoples (Llamas et al. 2016). As noted previously, ancient DNA analyses, while challenging given the environmental conditions and the impact on DNA preservation, are providing some evidence of variation in the past.

Tobler et al. (2017) found significant geographic structure based on analysis of mtDNA obtained from 111 historic hair samples; this result was also indicated at the whole-genome level in comparisons between ancient and modern genomes (Wright et al. 2018). There is strong evidence of an east–west divide along the continent, which is seen in nuclear and mtDNA. The greatest differentiation appeared to be eastern versus western populations, with the analyses of Wright et al. (2018) showing a further trifurcation within the east between northeastern Queensland, northwestern Queensland, and New South Wales. Most importantly, particularly for the issue of repatriation of human remains or for those from the stolen generations who are trying to reconnect to and find the location of their ancestry, Wright et al. (2018) were able to show that with whole-genome data there was enough regional structure that individuals could reliably be traced to their ancestral homeland, within a few hundred kilometres. Wright et al. (2018) also found that identification of Place and Country was not reliable using mtDNA alone, with results of known-source samples indicating the wrong location 7% of the time. They thus warn against the sole use of mtDNA for repatriation of museum samples.

Australian Indigenous ancient mtDNA data does not provide evidence of any major population bottleneck events prior to the European arrival, but they do indicate some degree of population expansion that coincides with the Mid-Holocene climatic optimum (9–6 KYA) (Tobler et al. 2017). Again, the whole-genome data also provide evidence of a population expansion in northeastern Australia during the Holocene, which appears to be associated with the spread of the Pama-Nyungan languages (Malaspinas et al. 2016). There has long been the suggestion of a Mid-Holocene population influx based on the linguistic data, the sudden appearance of backed-blade, small-tool technologies, and the arrival of the dingo (Bowdler 1981; Hiscock 1994). In 2013, in their analysis of genome-wide SNP data from Australia, New Guinea, and island Southeast Asia, Pugach, Delfin, Gunnarsdóttir, Kayser, and Stoneking (2013) reported evidence of gene flow from the Indian subcontinent that they dated to approximately 141 generations, or 4230 years ago. They suggested that this gene flow may have been related to the arrival of the dingo, but they argue that the data indicated that such contact did not proceed through island Southeast Asia. Yet more recent analyses of Indigenous Australian nuclear or mitogenome sequences have failed to find any evidence of Indian admixture. Y chromosome analyses of dingoes (Sacks et al. 2013) and mtDNA of dingoes and New Guinea singing dogs (Savolainen, Leitner, Wilton, Matisoo-Smith, & Lundeberg 2004; Greig, Walter, & Matisoo-Smith 2016; Greig et al. 2018; Ardalan et al. 2012) suggest that dingoes are derived from early East Asian village dogs rather than being more directly related to wild Indian dogs or Indian wolves, as has been suggested based on morphological characteristics (Gollan 1985). Until proven otherwise, there is little genetic evidence to suggest that there were any direct Holocene connections between India and Australia or Sahul more generally prior to the European arrival.

While the commensal approach has been used extensively to track the mobility and migrations of Pacific peoples, it has not been applied in the same way to Australia. Though Indigenous Australians may not have been agriculturalists, in the strict sense of the word, they did modify and manage their landscapes in ways that can leave genetic signatures that will tell us about ancient behaviours. Perhaps the most commonly recognized impacts of people on Sahul landscapes are hunting and habitat modification associated with burning. Such impacts have been implicated as a cause or major contributor to the extinction of the Australian megafauna dated to between 39 and 52 KYA (Stuart 2015; van der Kaars et al. 2017). The debate as to whether this and other major extinction events were human induced or the result of natural climate change is ongoing (Johnson et al., 2016; see also Johnson, Dortch, & Worthy, this volume). Ancient DNA analyses of faunal remains could be used to reconstruct the demographic history of various species to determine if they were already in decline prior to the climate change, as has been demonstrated elsewhere (Allentoft et al. 2014). Llamas et al. (2014) were able to obtain mtDNA from two extinct kangaroo species that were directly dated to 46–50 and 40–45 KYA, but these samples were recovered from high-altitude caves in Tasmania, which provide unusually good DNA preservation conditions. Alternative aDNA approaches such as bulk bone metabarcoding, which target smaller pieces of DNA extracted from otherwise unidentifiable bone from mixed-midden contexts, combined with high-throughput sequencing, have allowed for the identification of faunal species in contexts dating back to 40 KYA (Murray et al. 2013; Haouchar et al. 2014). This type of aDNA study can identify the presence of a species; however, due to the small amount of DNA targeted, the capacity to draw conclusions about the genetic diversity within the species and shed light on population history is limited. These issues are being addressed by other types of analyses, including isotope, proteomic (ZooMS), and coprolite studies (Price et al. 2017; Buckley, Cosgrove, Garvey, & Prideaux 2017; Westaway et al. 2019).

DNA analyses have, however, been able to provide some evidence of human modification of the Australian landscape. In an exciting multidisciplinary study, Rossetto et al. (2017) used DNA from extant samples of *Castanospermum australe* (Fabaceae), a tree commonly referred to as the Black Bean or the Moreton Bay Chestnut, to demonstrate and track human-mediated dispersal of an important food plant. In an excellent example of the value of a multidisciplinary approach that involved ethnographic, bibliographic, ecological, and genetic research, the team was able to show that the genetic distribution of *C. australe* in northern New South Wales was unlikely to be the result of natural, waterborne seed dispersal. Instead, the distribution and pattern of genetic variation observed were consistent with a recent and deliberate human-mediated dispersal, which was also supported by local Indigenous oral traditions. The seeds of the Black Bean are highly toxic, but when processed to neutralize toxins, they were a reliable and highly nutritious food source that could be either ground into a 'meal' or otherwise stored for up to several months. Indigenous Australian communities were known to transfer the seeds or seedlings beyond their natural coastal, riparian dispersal zone so that they could be utilized in those new environments, specifically in northern NSW, in the higher elevations in the inland rainforests. This study could be expanded geographically to identify interaction and mobility networks more widely, and it demonstrates the value of such mixed-method approaches for better understanding how and why people interacted and modified 'wild' landscapes of the past. Such research requires collaboration with Indigenous communities to help produce more culturally meaningful and relevant interpretations of genetic information. For this reason, we strongly encourage engagement with Indigenous communities at the start of the research design process, including identification of hypotheses that may be overlooked by those trained solely in Western science, rather than after data have been obtained (Adams et al. 2014). Such collaborative, partnership approaches will help increase the relevance of genomic research to Indigenous communities, with flow-on benefits for general public engagement with science more broadly.

CONCLUSION

The recent technological developments in genomic research are dramatically increasing our understanding of the evolution and dispersal history of our species. Recent whole-genome data are challenging many long-held hypotheses about interactions between human populations, and between our immediate ancestors and other extinct hominin groups. Attempts to use genetic data to understand the settlement history of Sahul have had impacts on questions regarding modern human origins well beyond the geographic region. In particular, genomic data from Australia and New Guinea have driven interpretations about the routes taken during the Out-of-Africa migrations that led to human expansion across the globe and have been key to finding that multiple populations of Denisovans contributed to the genomes of modern populations in the Asia and Pacific regions (Teixeira & Cooper 2019).

The accumulation of new genetic data from Australia and New Guinea is providing clearer indication of the size, diversity, and number of populations that settled the region beginning 50 to 60 KYA. Such data and analyses, we suggest, support the likelihood of multiple groups arriving on the landmass of Sahul, but all likely came from the same diverse Sunda-based source population in Southeast Asia. There is little genetic evidence to support the concept of a Mid-Holocene population arriving in Australia bringing the dingo or driving linguistic or technological changes observed in the archaeological record. To some extent, it has been the relative geographic isolation of Sahul for tens of thousands of years that has meant that evidence of past interactions has not been swamped by the genetic signature of major, more recent, large population expansions, as has been demonstrated in the spread of Neolithic Steppe populations into northern and western Europe (Haak et al. 2015), or by the Han expansion in east and Southeast Asia (Wen et al. 2004). Interestingly, despite this relative isolation, we see evidence of significant demographic expansion in the Early Holocene that seems to be associated with the spread of particular linguistic groups—comparable to processes identified in Europe and Asia. It is clear, however, that the most recent population arrivals, those of the past 400–500 years (e.g., Europeans), have had a significant impact on Indigenous Australian populations, which is reflected in the genomic data collected to date. In this regard, the recent technological developments and their application to ancient DNA studies may help to provide information that can link both the living and the dead to their ancestral homelands and communities and help to start the healing of deep wounds inflicted by European colonialism.

The power of multidisciplinary approaches for understanding the past and explaining current genetic patterns observed in people, plants, and animals cannot be overstated. It is heartening to see that Indigenous communities and researchers are increasingly engaged and involved in collaborative genetic and genomic studies, not only in Australia and New Guinea but worldwide. The benefits of such research partnerships are clear, but this kind of work is hard and often takes much more time than many Western scientists are used to. Social and ethical concerns of Indigenous communities regarding data management and use may challenge some existing policies regarding ownership of data and public access (Kowal, Llamas, & Tishkoff 2017). Therefore, these issues need to be negotiated carefully and fully prior to collecting samples or processing samples that are already in labs, museums, or other collections (Beaton et al. 2017; Claw et al. 2018; Fox, Rallapalli, & Komor 2020). The commitment made by some major science funding agencies and publishers to seeing evidence of such community engagement is a positive step (Anonymous 2020), but we would hope that the benefits of such engagement are more of an enticement rather than overcoming a perceived hurdle required for obtaining funding or publishing results. Reconstructing population histories and patterns of integration in the past is a complex undertaking, and the genetic data that have been accumulating in the past decade or two are showing that we have underestimated that level of complexity. The greater the diversity of perspectives and approaches that contribute to our models, the greater will be our interpretations and their social and cultural relevance. The end result will be the exploration of research questions that will increase our understanding of the past to move towards a more positive future for all.

NOTES

1. The genome is the entire genetic component of a living organism. The nuclear genome refers to the DNA or genetic material found in the nucleus of each cell. This is the DNA that forms the chromosomes and, thus, is inherited from both parents. During cell division, the chromosomes inherited from each of the parents recombine to form the unique DNA sequence combination that makes up the genome of each of their offspring. Each person's nuclear DNA represents all of their recent ancestry in that they inherit, on average, about 50% of their DNA from each parent, which means they share about 25% of their DNA with each grandparent, 12.5% with each great grandparent, and so on. The genome can be studied at a number of levels—whole-genome sequencing, in which each of the 6.4 billion bases of DNA is sequenced, or by just looking at particular regions or markers within the genome. Genome sequence data obtained via current technology, often referred to as next-generation sequencing or NGS, is most commonly reported with the average 'depth' of coverage, or how often each base is likely to have been sequenced where, for example, 3x coverage reports that, on average, each base position has been recovered and sequenced from three unique pieces of the DNA obtained from a sample.

2. In addition to the nuclear genome, we each also have a mitochondrial genome (sometimes referred to as the mitogenome), which refers to the DNA that is found in the mitochondria within a cell. Mitochondria sit outside of the nucleus and provide energy and respiration for the cell. Mitochondrial DNA (mtDNA) is inherited solely from the mother and therefore

represents only maternal ancestry from the past (e.g., your mother's mother's mother's lineage). Geneticists can also study the strict paternal ancestry of an individual by looking at the DNA variation on the nonrecombining portion of the Y chromosome (the NRY) because each man inherited his Y chromosome directly from his father.

3. Introgression refers to gene flow between different species or populations. If populations shared a recent common ancestor, but remained separated either geographically or behaviourally long enough for their gene pool (the DNA within the group) to change, it is possible to identify the mixing of two groups and the 'introgressed' DNA.

4. Single-nucleotide polymorphisms, or SNPs, are single base-pair changes in DNA. Known mutations that are population specific have been targeted in these SNP analyses. Because most of the genomes that have been used to design these chip analyses are from European and Asian populations, they are not good at identifying novel, population-specific variations from other geographic regions.

REFERENCES

Adams, M. S., Carpenter, J., Housty, J. A., Neasloss, D., Paquet, P. C., Service, C., . . . Darimont, C. T. (2014). Toward increased engagement between academic and indigenous community partners in ecological research. *Ecology and Society, 19*(3), 5.

Adcock, G. J., Dennis, E. S., Easteal, S., Huttley, G. A., Jermiin, L. S., Peacock, W. J., & Thorne, A. (2001). Mitochondrial DNA sequences in ancient Australians: Implications for modern human origins. *Proceedings of the National Academy of Sciences of the United States of America, 98*(2), 537–542.

Allen, J., & O'Connell, J. (2008). Getting from Sunda to Sahul. In G. Clark, B. F. Leach, & S. O'Connor (Eds.), *Islands of inquiry: Colonisation, seafaring and the archaeology of maritime landscapes* (pp. 31–46). Canberra: ANU Press.

Allentoft, M. E., Heller, R., Oskam, C. L., Lorenzen, E. D., Hale, M. L., Gilbert, M. T. P., . . . Bunce, M. (2014). Extinct New Zealand megafauna were not in decline before human colonization. *Proceedings of the National Academy of Sciences of the United States of America, 111*(13), 4922–4927.

Anonymous. (2020). Editorial: Necessary voices. *Nature Genetics, 52*, 135.

Ardalan, A., Oskarsson, M., Natanaelsson, C., Wilton, A. N., Ahmadian, A., & Savolainen, P. (2012). Narrow genetic basis for the Australian dingo confirmed through analysis of paternal ancestry. *Genetica, 140*(1), 65–73.

Ballantyne, K. N., Van Oven, M., Ralf, A., Stoneking, M., Mitchell, R. J., Van Oorschot, R. a. H. & Kayser, M. (2012). MtDNA SNP multiplexes for efficient inference of matrilineal genetic ancestry within Oceania. *Forensic Science International: Genetics, 6*(4), 425–436.

Bardill, J., Bader, A. C., Garrison, N. A., Bolnick, D. A., Raff, J. A., Walker, A., & Malhi, R. S. (2018). Advancing the ethics of paleogenomics. *Science, 360*(6387), 384–385.

Beaton, A., Hudson, M., Milne, M., Port, R. V., Russell, K., Smith, B., . . . Wihongi, H. (2017). Engaging Maori in biobanking and genomic research: A model for biobanks to guide culturally informed governance, operational, and community engagement activities. *Genetics in Medicine, 19*(3), 345–351.

Bergström, A., Nagle, N., Chen, Y., McCarthy, S., Pollard, Martin O., Ayub, Q., . . . Tyler-Smith, C. (2016). Deep roots for Aboriginal Australian Y chromosomes. *Current Biology, 26*(6), 809–813.

Bergström, A., Oppenheimer, S. J., Mentzer, A. J., Auckland, K., Robson, K., Attenborough, R., . . . Tyler-Smith, C. (2017). A Neolithic expansion, but strong genetic structure, in the independent history of New Guinea. *Science, 357*(6356), 1160–1163.

Bird, M. I., Condie, S. A., O'Connor, S., O'Grady, D., Reepmeyer, C., Ulm, S., . . . Bradshaw, C. J. A. (2019). Early human settlement of Sahul was not an accident. *Scientific Reports, 9*(1), 8220.

Birdsell, J. B. (1977). The recalibration of a paradigm for the first peopling of greater Australia. In J. Allen, J. Golson, & R. Jones (Eds.), *Sunda and Sahul: Prehistoric studies in Southeast Asia, Melanesia and Australia* (pp. 113–167). London: Academic Press.

Bowdler, S. (1981). Hunters in the highlands: Aboriginal adaptations in the eastern Australian uplands. *Archaeology in Oceania, 16*(2), 99–111.

Browning, S. R., Browning, B. L., Zhou, Y., Tucci, S., & Akey, J. M. (2018). Analysis of human sequence data reveals two pulses of archaic Denisovan admixture. *Cell, 173*, 1–9.

Buckley, M., Cosgrove, R., Garvey, J., & Prideaux, G. J. (2017). Identifying remains of extinct kangaroos in Late Pleistocene deposits using collagen fingerprinting. *Journal of Quaternary Science, 32*(5), 653–660.

Cann, R. L., Stoneking, M., & Wilson, A. C. (1987). Mitochondrial DNA and human evolution. *Nature, 325*, 31–36.

Caron, N. R., Chongo, M., Hudson, M., Arbour, L., Wasserman, W. W., Robertson, S., . . . Wilcox, P. (2020). Indigenous genomic databases: Pragmatic considerations and cultural contexts. *Frontiers in Public Health, 8*, 111.

Clarkson, C., Jacobs, Z., Marwick, B., Fullagar, R., Wallis, L., Smith, M., . . . Pardoe, C. (2017). Human occupation of northern Australia by 65,000 years ago. *Nature, 547*, 306–310.

Claw, K. G., Anderson, M. Z., Begay, R. L., Tsosie, K. S., Fox, K., & Garrison, N. A. (2018). A framework for enhancing ethical genomic research with Indigenous communities. *Nature Communications, 9*(1), 2957.

David, B., McNiven, I. J., Richards, T., Connaughton, S. P., Leavesley, M., Barker, B., & Rowe, C. (2011). Lapita sites in the Central Province of mainland Papua New Guinea. *World Archaeology, 43*(4), 576–593.

Denham, T. P., Haberle, S. G., Lentfer, C., Fullagar, R., Field, J., Therin, M., . . . Winsborough, B. (2003). Origins of agriculture at Kuk Swamp in the Highlands of New Guinea. *Science, 301*(5630), 189–193.

Duggan, A. T., Evans, B., Friedlaender, F. R., Friedlaender, J. S., Koki, G., Merriwether, D. A., . . . Stoneking, M. (2014). Maternal history of Oceania from complete mtDNA genomes: Contrasting ancient diversity with recent homogenization due to the Austronesian expansion. *The American Journal of Human Genetics, 94*, 1–13.

Fox, K., Rallapalli, K. L., & Komor, A. C. (2020). Rewriting human history and empowering Indigenous communities with genome editing tools. *Genes, 11*(1), 88.

Friedlaender, J. S., Friedlaender, F. R., Hodgson, J. A., Stoltz, M., Koki, G., Horvat, G., . . . Merriwether, D. A. (2007). Melanesian mtDNA complexity. *PLoS One, 2*(2), e248.

Friedlaender, J. S., Friedlaender, F. R., Reed, F. A., Kidd, K. K., Kidd, J. R., Chambers, G. K., . . . Weber, J. L. (2008). The genetic structure of Pacific islanders. *PLoS Genetics, 4*(1), e19.

Gaffney, D., Summerhayes, G. R., Ford, A., Scott, J. M., Denham, T., Field, J., & Dickinson, W. R. (2015). Earliest pottery on New Guinea mainland reveals Austronesian influences in Highland environments 3000 years ago. *PLoS One, 10*(9), e0134497.

Gollan, K. (1985). Prehistoric dogs in Australia: An Indian origin? In V. Misra & P. Bellwood (Eds.), *Recent advances in Indo-Pacific prehistory* (pp. 439–443). Oxford: IBH Publishing Company.

Green, R. E., Krause, J., Briggs, A. W., Maricic, T., Stenzel, U., Kircher, M., . . . Paabo, S. (2010). A draft sequence of the Neandertal genome. *Science, 328*(5979), 710–722.

Greig, K., Gosling, A. L., Collins, C., Boocock, J., McDonald, K., Addison, D. J., . . . Matisoo-Smith, E. (2018). Tracking dogs across the Pacific: Ancient mitogenomes reveal a complex history of origins and translocations. *Scientific Reports, 8*, 9130.

Greig, K., Walter, R., & Matisoo-Smith, E. A. (2016). Dogs and people in Southeast Asia and the Pacific. In M. Oxenham & H. R. Buckley (Eds.), *The Routledge handbook of bioarchaeology in Southeast Asia and the Pacific Islands* (pp. 462–482). New York: Routledge.

Guglielmi, G. (2019). Facing up to genome injustice. *Nature, 568*(7752), 290–293.

Haak, W., Lazaridis, I., Patterson, N., Rohland, N., Mallick, S., Llamas, B., . . . Reich, D. (2015). Massive migration from the steppe was a source for Indo-European languages in Europe. *Nature, 522*(7555), 207–211.

Hagelberg, E., Kayser, M., Nagy, M., Roewer, L., Zimdahl, H., Krawczak, M., . . . Schiefenhovel, W. (1999). Molecular genetic evidence for the human settlement of the Pacific: Analysis of mitochondrial DNA, Y chromosome and HLA markers. *Philosophical Transactions of the Royal Society B: Biological Sciences, 354*(1379), 141–152.

Haouchar, D., Haile, J., McDowell, M., Murray, D., White, N., Allcock, R., . . . Bunce, M. (2014). Thorough assessment of DNA preservation from fossil bone and sediments excavated from a late Pleistocene-Holocene cave deposit on Kangaroo Island, South Australia. *Quaternary Science Reviews, 84*, 56–64.

Heupink, T. H., Subramanian, S., Wright, J. L., Endicott, P., Westaway, M. C., Huynen, L., . . . Lambert, D. M. (2016). Ancient mtDNA sequences from the First Australians revisited. *Proceedings of the National Academy of Sciences of the United States of America, 113*(25), 6892–6897.

Hiscock, P. (1994). Technological responses to risk in Holocene Australia. *Journal of World Prehistory, 8*(3), 267–292.

Hudjashov, G., Kivisild, T., Underhill, P. A., Endicott, P., Sanchez, J. J., Lin, A. A., . . . Forster, P. (2007). Revealing the prehistoric settlement of Australia by Y chromosome and mtDNA analysis. *Proceedings of the National Academy of Sciences of the United States of America, 104*(21), 8726–8730.

Hudson, M., Garrison, N. A., Sterling, R., Caron, N. R., Fox, K., Yracheta, J., . . . Carroll, S. R. (2020). Rights, interests and expectations: Indigenous perspectives on unrestricted access to genomic data. *Nature Reviews Genetics, 21*(6), 377–384.

Huoponen, K., Schurr, T. G., Chen, Y. S., & Wallace, D. C. (2001). Mitochondrial DNA variation in an Aboriginal Australian population: Evidence for genetic isolation and regional differentiation. *Human Immunology, 62*(9), 954–969.

Ingman, M., & Gyllensten, U. (2003). Mitochondrial genome variation and evolutionary history of Australian and New Guinean Aborigines. *Genome Research, 13*(7), 1600–1606.

Jacobs, G. S., Hudjashov, G., Saag, L., Kusuma, P., Darusallam, C. C., Lawson, D. J., . . . Cox, M. P. (2019). Multiple deeply divergent Denisovan ancestries in Papuans. *Cell, 177*(4), 1010–1021.e1032.

Johnson, C. N., Alroy, J., Beeton, N. J., Bird, M. I., Brook, B. W., Cooper, A., . . . Bradshaw, C. J. A. (2016). What caused extinction of the Pleistocene megafauna of Sahul? *Proceedings of the Royal Society B: Biological Sciences, 283*(1824), 20152399.

Kayser, M. (2010). The human genetic history of Oceania: Near and Remote views of dispersal. *Current Biology, 20*, R192–R201.

Kayser, M., Brauer, S., Weiss, G., Schiefenhovel, W., Underhill, P., Shen, P. D., . . . Stoneking, M. (2003). Reduced Y-chromosome, but not mitochondrial DNA, diversity in human populations from West New Guinea. *American Journal of Human Genetics, 72*(2), 281–302.

Kayser, M., Brauer, S., Weiss, G., Schiefenhovel, W., Underhill, P. A., & Stoneking, M. (2001). Independent histories of human Y chromosomes from Melanesia and Australia. *American Journal of Human Genetics*, 68(1), 173–190.

Kayser, M., Choi, Y., van Oven, M., Mona, S., Brauer, S., Trent, R. J., . . . Stoneking, M. (2008). The impact of the Austronesian expansion: Evidence from mtDNA and Y chromosome diversity in the Admiralty Islands of Melanesia. *Molecular Biology and Evolution*, 25(7), 1362–1374.

Kealy, S., Louys, J., & O'Connor, S. (2018). Least-cost pathway models indicate northern human dispersal from Sunda to Sahul. *Journal of Human Evolution*, 125, 59–70.

Kirch, P. V. (2017). *On the road of the winds: An archaeological history of the Pacific Islands before European contact*. Berkeley: University of California Press.

Kowal, E., Llamas, B., & Tishkoff, S. (2017). Consent: Data-sharing for Indigenous peoples. *Nature*, 546(7659), 474.

Lazaridis, I., Patterson, N., Mittnik, A., Renaud, G., Mallick, S., Kirsanow, K., . . . Krause, J. (2014). Ancient human genomes suggest three ancestral populations for present-day Europeans. *Nature*, 513(7518), 409–413.

Leavesley, M. G., Bird, M. I., Fifield, L. K., Hausladen, P. A., Santos, G. M., & Tada, M. L. D. (2002). Buang Merabak: Early evidence for human occupation in the Bismarck Archipelago, Papua New Guinea. *Australian Archaeology*, 54, 55–57.

Llamas, B., Brotherton, P., Mitchell, K. J., Templeton, J. E. L., Thomson, V. A., Metcalf, J. L., . . . Cooper, A. (2014). Late Pleistocene Australian marsupial DNA clarifies the affinities of extinct megafaunal kangaroos and wallabies. *Molecular Biology and Evolution*, 32(3), 574–584.

Llamas, B., Fehren-Schmitz, L., Valverde, G., Soubrier, J., Mallick, S., Rohland, N., . . . Haak, W. (2016). Ancient mitochondrial DNA provides high-resolution time scale of the peopling of the Americas. *Science Advances*, 2(4), e1501385.

Malaspinas, A.-S., Westaway, M. C., Muller, C., Sousa, V. C., Lao, O., Alves, I., . . . Willerslev, E. (2016). A genomic history of Aboriginal Australia. *Nature*, 538, 207–214.

Mallick, S., Li, H., Lipson, M., Mathieson, I., Gymrek, M., Racimo, F., . . . Reich, D. (2016). The Simons Genome Diversity Project: 300 genomes from 142 diverse populations. *Nature*, 538(7624), 201–206.

Matisoo-Smith, E., & Gosling, A. L. (2018). Walking backwards into the future: The need for a holistic evolutionary approach in Pacific health research. *Annals of Human Biology*, 45(3), 175–187.

McEvoy, B. P., Lind, J. M., Wang, E. T., Moyzis, R. K., Visscher, P. M., Pellekaan, S. M. V., & Wilton, A. N. (2010). Whole-genome genetic diversity in a sample of Australians with deep Aboriginal ancestry. *American Journal of Human Genetics*, 87(2), 297–305.

McNiven, I. J., David, B., Richards, T., Aplin, K., Asmussen, B., Mialanes, J., . . . Ulm, S. (2011). New direction in human colonisation of the Pacific: Lapita settlement of south coast New Guinea. *Australian Archaeology*, 72, 1–6.

Mona, S., Tommaseo-Ponzetta, M., Brauer, S., Sudoyo, H., Marzuki, S., & Kayser, M. (2007). Patterns of Y-chromosome diversity intersect with the trans-New Guinea hypothesis. *Molecular Biology and Evolution*, 24, 2546–2555.

Mondal, M., Bertranpetit, J., & Lao, O. (2019). Approximate Bayesian computation with deep learning supports a third archaic introgression in Asia and Oceania. *Nature Communications*, 10(1), 246.

Murray, D. C., Haile, J., Dortch, J., White, N. E., Haouchar, D., Bellgard, M. I., . . . Bunce, M. (2013). Scrapheap challenge: A novel bulk-bone metabarcoding method to investigate ancient DNA in faunal assemblages. *Scientific Reports*, 3, 3371.

Nagle, N., Ballantyne, K. N., van Oven, M., Tyler-Smith, C., Xue, Y., Wilcox, S., . . . The Genographic Consortium (2017a). Mitochondrial DNA diversity of present-day Aboriginal Australians and implications for human evolution in Oceania. *Journal of Human Genetics*, 62(3), 343–353.

Nagle, N., van Oven, M., Wilcox, S., van Holst Pellekaan, S., Tyler-Smith, C., Xue, Y., . . . Ziegle, J. S. (2017b). Aboriginal Australian mitochondrial genome variation—an increased understanding of population antiquity and diversity. *Scientific Reports*, 7, 43041.

O'Connell, J. F., Allen, J., Williams, M. A. J., Williams, A. N., Turney, C. S. M., Spooner, N. A., . . . Cooper, A. (2018). When did *Homo sapiens* first reach Southeast Asia and Sahul? *Proceedings of the National Academy of Sciences of the United States of America*, 115(34), 8482–8490.

Olivares, G., Peña-Ahumada, B., Peñailillo, J., Payacán, C., Moncada, X., Saldarriaga-Córdoba, M., . . . Seelenfreund, A. (2019). Human mediated translocation of Pacific paper mulberry [*Broussonetia papyrifera* (L.) L'Hér. ex Vent. (*Moraceae*)]: Genetic evidence of dispersal routes in Remote Oceania. *PLoS One*, 14(6), e0217107.

Pagani, L., Lawson, D. J., Jagoda, E., Mörseburg, A., Eriksson, A., Mitt, M., . . . Metspalu, M. (2016). Genomic analyses inform on migration events during the peopling of Eurasia. *Nature*, 538(7624), 238–242.

Pawley, A., Attenborough, R., Golson, J., & Hide, R. (2005). *Papuan pasts: Cultural, linguistic and biological histories of Papuan-speaking peoples*. Canberra: Pacific Linguistics.

Prendergast, M. E., & Sawchuk, E. (2018). Boots on the ground in Africa's ancient DNA 'revolution': Archaeological perspectives on ethics and best practices. *Antiquity*, 92(363), 803–815.

Presser, J. C., Stoneking, M., & Redd, A. J. (2003). Tasmanian Aborigines and DNA. *Papers and Proceedings of the Royal Society of Tasmania*, 136, 35–38.

Price, G. J., Ferguson, K. J., Webb, G. E., Feng, Y.-x., Higgins, P., Nguyen, A. D., . . . Louys, J. (2017). Seasonal migration of marsupial megafauna in Pleistocene Sahul (Australia-New Guinea). *Proceedings of the Royal Society B: Biological Sciences*, 284(1863), 20170785.

Pugach, I., Delfin, F., Gunnarsdóttir, E., Kayser, M., & Stoneking, M. (2013). Genome-wide data substantiate Holocene gene flow from India to Australia. *Proceedings of the National Academy of Sciences of the United States of America*, 110(5), 1803–1808.

Qin, P., & Stoneking, M. (2015). Denisovan ancestry in east Eurasian and Native American populations. *Molecular Biology and Evolution*, 32(10), 2665–2674.

Rasmussen, M., Guo, X., Wang, Y., Lohmueller, K. E., Rasmussen, S., Albrechtsen, A., . . . Willerslev, E. (2011). An Aboriginal Australian genome reveals separate human dispersals into Asia. *Science*, 333(6052), 94–98.

Redd, A. J., & Stoneking, M. (1999). Peopling of Sahul: mtDNA variation in Aboriginal Australian and Papua New Guinean populations. *American Journal of Human Genetics*, 65(3), 808–828.

Reich, D., Green, R. E., Kircher, M., Krause, J., Patterson, N., Durand, E. Y., . . . Pääbo, S. (2010). Genetic history of an archaic hominin group from Denisova Cave in Siberia. *Nature*, 468(7327), 1053–1060.

Reich, D., Patterson, N., Kircher, M., Delfin, F., Nandineni, M., Pugach, I., . . . Stoneking, M. (2011). Denisova admixture and the first modern human dispersals into Southeast Asia and Oceania. *American Journal of Human Genetics*, 89(4), 516–528.

Robertson, S. P., Hindmarsh, J. H., Berry, S., Cameron, V. A., Cox, M. P., Dewes, O., . . . Wilcox, P. (2018). Genomic medicine must reduce, not compound, health inequities: The case for hauora-enhancing genomic resources for New Zealand. *The New Zealand Medical Journal*, 131(1480), 81–89.

Rossetto, M., Ens, E. J., Honings, T., Wilson, P. D., Yap, J.-Y. S., Costello, O., . . . Bowern, C. (2017). From songlines to genomes: Prehistoric assisted migration of a rain forest tree by Australian Aboriginal people. *PLoS One, 12*(11), e0186663.

Roullier, C., Benoit, L., McKey, D. B., & Lebot, V. (2013). Historical collections reveal patterns of diffusion of sweet potato in Oceania obscured by modern plant movements and recombination. *Proceedings of the National Academy of Sciences of the United States of America, 110*(6), 2205–2210.

Sacks, B. N., Brown, S. K., Stephens, D., Pedersen, N. C., Wu, J.-T., & Berry, O. (2013). Y Chromosome analysis of dingoes and Southeast Asian village dogs suggests a Neolithic continental expansion from Southeast Asia followed by multiple Austronesian dispersals. *Molecular Biology and Evolution, 30*(5), 1103–1118.

Savolainen, P., Leitner, T., Wilton, A. N., Matisoo-Smith, E., & Lundeberg, J. (2004). A detailed picture of the origin of the Australian dingo, obtained from the study of mitochondrial DNA. *Proceedings of the National Academy of Sciences of the United States of America, 101*(33), 12387–12390.

Stoneking, M., Bhatia, K., & Wilson, A. C. (1986). Mitochondrial DNA variation in Eastern Highlanders of Papua New Guinea. In D. F. Roberts & G. DeStefano (Eds.), *Genetic variation and its maintenance* (pp. 87–100). Cambridge: Cambridge University Press.

Stoneking, M., Jorde, L. B., Bhatia, K., & Wilson, A. C. (1990). Geographic variation in human mitochondrial DNA from Papua New Guinea. *Genetics, 124*(3), 717–733.

Storey, A. A., Clarke, A. C., Ladefoged, T., Robins, J., & Matisoo-Smith, E. (2013). DNA and Pacific commensal models: Applications, construction, limitations, and future prospects. *Journal of Island and Coastal Archaeology, 8*(1), 37–65.

Stringer, C. (2014). Why we are not all multiregionalists now. *Trends in Ecology and Evolution, 29*(5), 248–251.

Stuart, A. J. (2015). Late Quaternary megafaunal extinctions on the continents: A short review. *Geological Journal, 50*(3), 338–363.

Summerhayes, G., Matisoo-Smith, E., Mandui, H., Allen, J., Specht, J., Hogg, N., & McPherson, S. (2010). Tamuarawai (EQS): An early Lapita site on Emirau, New Ireland, PNG. *Journal of Pacific Archaeology, 1*, 62–75.

Taylor, D., Nagle, N., Ballantyne, K. N., van Oorschot, R. A. H., Wilcox, S., Henry, J., . . . Mitchell, R. J. (2012). An investigation of admixture in an Australian Aboriginal Y-chromosome STR database. *Forensic Science International: Genetics, 6*(5), 532–538.

Teixeira, J. C., & Cooper, A. (2019). Using hominin introgression to trace modern human dispersals. *Proceedings of the National Academy of Sciences of the United States of America, 116*(31), 15327–15332.

Thorne, A. G., & Wolpoff, M. H. (1981). Regional continuity in Australasian Pleistocene hominid evolution. *American Journal of Physical Anthropology, 55*(3), 337–349.

Tobler, R., Rohrlach, A., Soubrier, J., Bover, P., Llamas, B., Tuke, J., . . . Cooper, A. (2017). Aboriginal mitogenomes reveal 50,000 years of regionalism in Australia. *Nature, 544*(7649), 180–184.

Tommaseo-Ponzetta, M., Attimonelli, M., De Robertis, M., Tanzariello, F., & Saccone, C. (2002). Mitochondrial DNA variability of West New Guinea populations. *American Journal of Physical Anthropology, 117*(1), 49–67.

Tucci, S., Vohr, S. H., McCoy, R. C., Vernot, B., Robinson, M. R., Barbieri, C., . . . Green, R. E. (2018). Evolutionary history and adaptation of a human pygmy population of Flores Island, Indonesia. *Science, 361*(6401), 511–516.

van der Kaars, S., Miller, G. H., Turney, C. S. M., Cook, E. J., Nürnberg, D., Schönfeld, J., . . . Lehman, S. J. (2017). Humans rather than climate the primary cause of Pleistocene megafaunal extinction in Australia. *Nature Communications, 8*(1), 14142.

van Holst Pellekaan, S. M., Ingman, M., Roberts-Thomson, J., & Harding, R. M. (2006). Mitochondrial genomics identifies major haplogroups in Aboriginal Australians. *American Journal of Physical Anthropology, 131*(2), 282–294.

van Oven, M., Brauer, S., Choi, Y., Ensing, J., Schiefenhövel, W., Stoneking, M., & Kayser, M. (2014). Human genetics of the Kula Ring: Y-chromosome and mitochondrial DNA variation in the Massim of Papua New Guinea. *European Journal of Human Genetics, 22*(12), 1393–1403.

Vernot, B., Tucci, S., Kelso, J., Schraiber, J. G., Wolf, A. B., Gittelman, R. M., . . . Akey, J. M. (2016). Excavating Neandertal and Denisovan DNA from the genomes of Melanesian individuals. *Science, 352*(6282), 235–239.

Vilar, M., Kaneko, A., Hombhanje, F., Tsukahara, T., Hwaihwanje, I., & Lum, J. (2008). Reconstructing the origin of the Lapita Cultural Complex: mtDNA analyses of East Sepik Province, PNG. *Journal of Human Genetics, 53*(8), 698–708.

Wen, B., Li, H., Lu, D., Song, X., Zhang, F., He, Y., . . . Jin, L. (2004). Genetic evidence supports demic diffusion of Han culture. *Nature, 431*(7006), 302–305.

Westaway, M. C., Price, G., Miscamble, T., McDonald, J., Cramb, J., Ringma, J., . . . Collard, M. (2019). A palaeontological perspective on the proposal to reintroduce Tasmanian devils to mainland Australia to suppress invasive predators. *Biological Conservation, 232*, 187–193.

Wollstein, A., Lao, O., Becker, C., Brauer, S., Trent, R. J., Nurnberg, P., . . . Kayser, M. (2010). Demographic history of Oceania inferred from genome-wide data. *Current Biology, 20*(22), 1983–1992.

Wright, J. L., Wasef, S., Heupink, T. H., Westaway, M. C., Rasmussen, S., Pardoe, C., . . . Lambert, D. M. (2018). Ancient nuclear genomes enable repatriation of Indigenous human remains. *Science Advances, 4*(12), eaau5064.

Yuen, L. K. W., Littlejohn, M., Duchêne, S., Edwards, R., Bukulatjpi, S., Binks, P., . . . Locarnini, S. (2019). Tracing ancient human migrations into Sahul using Hepatitis B virus genomes. *Molecular Biology and Evolution, 36*(5), 942–954.

Zammit, N. W., Siggs, O. M., Gray, P. E., Horikawa, K., Langley, D. B., Walters, S. N., . . . Grey, S. T. (2019). Denisovan, modern human and mouse TNFAIP3 alleles tune A20 phosphorylation and immunity. *Nature Immunology, 20*(10), 1299–1310.

PART III

CONSTRUCTED LANDSCAPES AND WATERSCAPES

CHAPTER 12

ENHANCED ECOLOGIES AND ECOSYSTEM ENGINEERING

Strategies Developed by Aboriginal Australians to Increase the Abundance of Animal Resources

IAN J. MCNIVEN, TIINA MANNE, AND ANNIE ROSS

INTRODUCTION

ANTHROPOLOGICAL and archaeological conceptualizations of 'traditional' Aboriginal societies as hunter-gatherers tend to take a static view of relationships with the environment such that social, economic, technological, and especially subsistence activities were structured by 'natural' environmental conditions. As archaeologist Harry Lourandos (2008: 73) points out, this notion of 'passive' environmental engagement was contrasted with 'dynamic' and 'active' environmental engagement and modification by agriculturalists in places such as New Guinea. While nineteenth-century views on passive environmental engagement emphasized simplicity, savagery, naturalness, wilderness, primitivism, unstructured nomadism, and essentialism (see Head 2000; McNiven & Russell 1995, 2005; Taylor 1990), during the twentieth century the complexities of environmental adaptation were emphasized: seasonality and structured mobility (e.g., Thomson 1939), population density and homeostatic systems (e.g., Birdsell 1953), drainage basins and tribal boundaries (e.g., Tindale 1974), drainage divisions and culture areas (e.g., Peterson 1976), population size and island biogeography (e.g., Jones 1977), food selection and optimal foraging (e.g., O'Connell & Hawkes 1981), and risk minimization and technological organization (e.g., Hiscock 1994) (see also Veth, O'Connor, & Wallis 2000). While it is true that 'people cannot live outside of their environment' (Veth et al. 2000: 58), the critical question is: Who or what is responsible for producing the environment and its resources?

For over 40 years, Lourandos (1976, 1997, 2008) has been instrumental in reconceptualizing archaeological understandings of Australian Aboriginal relationships with the environment (see Lourandos & Ross, this volume). Lourandos rejected the notion of passive environmental engagement and used anthropological theory and ethnographic and archaeological evidence to present a dynamic view of Aboriginal–environmental interactions, centred on the empirical reality of dynamic environmental engagement in which Aboriginal people actively manipulated local ecologies to increase the availability of specific food resources. Such targeted manipulations were not seen as a naturalized outcome of long-term occupation and environmental familiarity, but as a result of social demands whereby new social arrangements (e.g., interregional gatherings) required food resource abundance beyond 'natural' availability. In this light, Aboriginal people were reconceptualized as not adapting their society to the environment but as adapting the environment to their society (Lourandos 1997).

Since Lourandos began his paradigmatic makeover of Australian archaeology, numerous other examples of Aboriginal resource enhancement practices have been documented. Some have been known for some time as oddities, or anomalies of Aboriginal hunting and gathering practices. For others, new paradigmatic eyes have revealed a broader process of resource enhancement and 'ecosystem engineering' (Bliege Bird, Tayor, Codding, & Bird 2013) beyond exceptionalism. In addition to these environmentally oriented insights, increasing archaeological attention has been given to the sociopolitical and socioritual dimensions of plant and animal food management and enhancement practices. Sociopolitical dimensions include issues of land ownership and accessibility and have been critical to Lourandos's work, particularly in relation to resource enhancement in support of large-scale interregional gatherings (e.g., Lourandos 1988; see also Bradley 2006; McNiven & Lambrides, this volume). Socioritual dimensions include 'increase' or 'maintenance' rituals where the fertility, abundance, and accessibility of certain plant and animal foods are intimately linked to those individuals with the appropriate rights and responsibilities to seek the intervention and agency of spiritual/ancestral beings and their powers (e.g., Kearney, Bradley, & Brady 2019; McNiven 2016; Sutton & Walshe 2021: Chap. 2; see also McNiven, this volume). Indeed, sociopolitical and socioritual dimensions pervade all of the enhancement strategies discussed in this chapter. As anthropologist Richard Baker (1993: 126) notes,

> In recent years there has been a long overdue acknowledgment by 'western' scientists of the existence of indigenous systems of ecological knowledge. It is important when examining these systems that we do not lose sight of the fact that they are holistic packages of knowledge and that the excitement of discovering individual examples does not blind us from seeing how each example is part of a complete body of information.

This chapter provides a synthesis of evidence to support Lourandos's contention that Aboriginal environmental enhancement was both widespread and commonplace. Critical to understanding the importance of this evidence is a broadened understanding of the concept of 'hunter-gatherers'. We consider how the concept of 'hunter-gatherers' has been reconceptualized by anthropologists and archaeologists over the past four decades, blurring boundaries between hunter-gatherers and agriculturalists, especially between Australia and New Guinea. We show that such blurring encompasses active manipulation and enhancement of ecologies to increase animal (terrestrial and aquatic) food abundance. We then review numerous examples of animal resources management that have characterized, and continue to characterize, Australian Indigenous lifeways. Our chapter focuses on food resources and not the protected rearing and movement of 'pets' such as the dingo (*Canis dingo*) across mainland Australia (e.g., Brumm 2021; Balme & O'Connor, this volume) and cuscus (*Spilocuscus maculatus*) in Torres Strait (e.g., McNiven & Hitchcock 2004: 111–112).

Hunter-Gatherers Redefined

All human societies are sustained by modifications to the 'natural' environment. Indeed, such is the pervasiveness of these modifications that Lesley Head (2008) asks the question: 'Is the concept of human impacts past its use-by date?' In terms of subsistence regimes, the degree and intensity of modification range widely between societies across the world. At one end of the gradient is subtle manipulation of 'natural' ecosystems by many small-scale hunter-gatherer societies. At the other end is the dramatic and large-scale removal of natural vegetation and replacement with agricultural fields of domesticated crops irrigated by artificially constructed water channels underpinning large-scale, state-based urban societies.

Traditionally, discussions of scales of human landscape modifications have been couched in terms of hunter-gatherers versus agriculturalists (Erickson 2006; Lightfoot, Cuthrell, Striplen, & Hyljema 2013). This dichotomous approach has its intellectual roots in social evolutionary theories that underpinned the disciplinary birth of anthropology in the eighteenth- and nineteenth- centuries. Social evolutionism proposed that long-term human cultural changes can be conceived in terms of stages of development, progressing from hunter-gatherers, to agriculturalists and pastoralists, to state-based civilizations (Adams 1998). European societies were seen as the pinnacle of development, and hunter-gatherer societies as the most primitive and least developed. The links between social evolutionism and philosophical justification and legitimization of European settler colonialism, especially in the Americas and Australia, have been well discussed by anthropologists (e.g., Jones 1992; McNiven & Russell 2005).

Over the past 40 years, the supposed reality of the dichotomy between hunter-gatherers and agricultural societies has been undermined by anthropological and archaeological scholarship on two fronts. First, the reality of hunter-gatherers has been questioned, given that the concept was invented as a hypothetical category of primordial society by the ancient Greeks and elaborated as a spurious founding principle of social evolutionism (McNiven & Russell 2005: 38–41; Warren 2021). Second, the integrity of hunter-gatherers has been questioned based on mounting empirical evidence that all so-called hunter-gatherers were also food producers. This latter point is the focus and key message of this chapter.

Critics of the 'hunter-gatherer' label point out that previous representations of hunter-gatherers and agricultural societies have emphasized polarized cultural differences (see later discussion). New understandings have emerged revealing major cultural overlaps between so-called hunter-gathering and agricultural societies in four key areas. First, the social complexity of many hunter-gatherers not only overlaps with, but in some cases rivals that of, many small-scale agricultural societies (Keeley 1995: 268; Price & Brown 1985; Roscoe 2002: 159). Second, most (if not all) hunter-gatherer societies manipulated their environments, sometimes such that plants and animals were intensively managed in ways more commonly associated with small-scale agricultural societies (Harris 1989; Smith 1998, 2001; Terrell et al. 2003: 328). Examples of manipulation processes associated with plants and animals include *landscape burning* (e.g., Bliege Bird et al. 2013; Field, Kealhofer, Cosgrove & Coster 2016; Gottesfeld 1994; Lewis 1982: 49–50, 56; Smith & Wishnie 2000), *transplanting* (e.g., Hynes & Chase 1982; Shipek 1989: 163–165; Yasuoka 2013), and *replanting* (e.g., Fowler 1986: 93; Hynes & Chase 1982; Shipek 1989: 161–162). Third, hunter-gatherer manipulations encompassed hydrological engineering, including construction of *irrigation channels* to facilitate watering of wild plants (e.g., Lawton, Wilke, DeDecker, & Mason 1976; Liljeblad & Fowler 1986: 417–418; Steward 1930), artificially excavated *transport canals* (e.g., Luer 1998; Widmer 1988; Wheeler 1995), excavation of *aquaculture channels* linked to fish growing/holding ponds (e.g., Builth 2014; Lourandos 1980), and the *construction of weirs* to extend the duration of seasonally available freshwater habitats for fish, birds, reptiles, and aquatic plants (Gunn 1908; Jackson & Barber 2016). Fourth, the uptake of agriculture, and the use and development of domesticated plants by many societies, includes plant manipulation practices well-known to many hunter-gatherers. Such intensively manipulated hunter-gatherer landscapes undermine romanticized notions that hunter-gatherers lived 'in harmony with nature' with little or no impact on their 'wilderness' environment (Denevan 1992; Hames 2007; Krech 1999; Lepofsky & Lertzman 2008; Ross, Pickering-Sherman, Snodgrass, Delcore, & Sherman 2011). These manipulations discredit the notion that 'hunters and gatherers rely upon a mode of subsistence characterized by the *absence of direct human control* over the reproduction of exploited species, and little or no control over the reproduction of exploited species, and little or no control over other aspects of population ecology such as the behaviour and distribution of food resources' (Panter-Brick, Layton, & Rowley-Conwy 2001: 2, original emphasis). Jack Golson (1977: 50) notes that the idea that 'hunter-gatherer economies . . . [were] passive, parasitic and totally dependent on nature, has been demolished. There is now an appreciation of the fact that hunter-gatherer groups managed their environment'.

Hunter-gatherer environmental manipulations involve modifying local ecologies to increase production of certain resources. Such manipulations are contrasted with more extreme modifications involving radical transformation of local ecologies, including replacing local plant and animal communities with introduced domesticated crop fields and animal pastures, and terraforming landscapes to transform local hydrologies for water storage (e.g., dams and reservoirs) and water movement (e.g., irrigation channels). In the case of hunter-gatherers, local ecologies are not radically *altered* but selectively and strategically *enhanced*. Resource enhancement involves practices that work *with* local ecological processes and ecosystems. It is for this reason that resource-enhancement practices are usually sustainable and reversible—and challenging to identify in the archaeological record. If these kinds of practices no longer take place, it takes little time for environments to revert to a premodified 'natural' state. Enhanced landscapes bear the cultural imprint not just of human agency but of individual societies strategically manipulating environments into culturally relevant and meaningful 'constructed landscapes' (McNiven 2008) and even 'domesticated landscapes' (Erickson 2006; Terrell et al. 2003; Yen 1989). In most cases, while manipulation targets specific ecological processes for strategic enhancement of specific resources, the impacts of these manipulations may be broad-scale and unintentional (see McNiven 2008). In some cases, strategic enhancement of selected resources results in decreases in other plants and associated animals (e.g., increasing grasslands and reducing shrub/tree vegetation through fire to attract kangaroos—see later discussion).

An important upshot of new understandings of hunter-gatherer social and ecological complexity and deep ecological knowledge is that agriculture is no longer seen as a natural progression *from* a hunting and gathering way of life. Complex hunter-gatherer societies, initially seen as being on the cusp of moving to agriculture, are now acknowledged as cultural endpoints in their own right, as much as agricultural and state-based societies (Smith 2001: 25). Additionally, the two categories have lost much of their explanatory power in terms of comparative studies of societies. A more fruitful and meaningful approach to comparative studies is selection of a particular set of cultural practices, such as manipulation of the environment, to explore the form and scale of such manipulations and transformations by different societies.

During the 1960s and 1970s, a range of publications presented historical and ethnographic evidence that challenged the long-standing view that Aboriginal Australians were passive hunter-gatherers who only exploited the natural availability of food resources (e.g., Campbell 1965; Hallam 1975; Harris 1977; Irvine 1970; Jones 1969; Lourandos 1976). In some cases, the evidence for practices that deliberately and artificially increased the production of key food resources was presented in a progressionist, social evolutionary guise as an incipient form of, or step towards, agriculture. Alastair Campbell (1965: 211), for example, phrased discussions in terms of 'the elementary nature of the food production'. Norman Tindale (1974: 94) similarly stated that 'it has been generally assumed that the aborigines [sic] have always been a non-agricultural people and this may be true, yet some practices suggest that the very first steps may have been taken in areas along a path or paths leading to gardening, irrigation, and the partial domestication of animals'. In a significant conceptual development, David Harris (1977) reconfigured discussions by undermining the dichotomous division between agriculturalists and hunter-gatherers through ethnographic documentation of a 'subsistence gradient' and 'subsistence continuum' over a distance of 1000 km between southern Cape York Peninsula (northeast Australia) and southern Papua New Guinea via Torres Strait.

In the context of Australian and New Guinea archaeology, Lourandos (1980: 258–259, original emphasis) first drew attention to the 'false dichotomy between hunter-gatherer and food-producer', particularly in terms of 'population densities', and the '*continuum* of economies spanning the two original classes' involving 'artificial manipulation and expansion of ecological niches'. Importantly, Lourandos (1980: 258) emphasized that he was 'not suggesting that high-density Australian hunter-gatherers were but "one step away" from food production, but rather that there were effective methods of artificial niche expansion in Australian economies, and that the roughly comparable population density of the two areas has been achieved by different means'.

Lourandos's reconceptualizations resonated immediately with some Australian archaeologists. David Frankel (1982: 45) remarked that nineteenth-century historical evidence of tillaging and gardening of yam-daisy in Victoria challenged the 'traditional dichotomy between "hunter-gatherer" and "farmer"' (see Gott 1982, 1983). Peter White and James O'Connell (1982: 217) similarly concluded that there exists 'a strong suggestion that "hunting and gathering" is an inadequate characterization of subsistence patterns [in Australia]'. More broadly in terms of subsistence strategies, White & O'Connell (1982: 20) stated that 'the contrasts which are usually seen between New Guinea and Australia have been over-emphasized' and that 'a continuum of practices is evident' between Highland agriculturalists of New Guinea and Western Desert hunter-gatherers of Australia (see also David & Denham 2006; Lourandos 1988, 2008). More broadly, Eugene Hunn and Nancy Williams (1982: 1) opined that 'We can firmly reject the stereotype of hunter-gatherers as passive "food collectors" in opposition to active, food-producing agriculturalists'.

In many cases, the boundary between intensively manipulated (enhanced) landscapes and transformed (replaced) landscapes is difficult to differentiate. This situation is illustrated well by those societies that practise mixed subsistence strategies of hunting and gathering along with small-scale cultivation of plants and husbanding of animals. Thus, Ian Keen (2004, 2021) remarked that examples of 'radical intervention in the ecology' by Australian Aboriginal people 'change our picture of Aboriginal hunting, gathering, and fishing as a mode of subsistence'. Furthermore, he notes that 'although I have used the expression "hunters and gatherers" to characterize Aboriginal subsistence practices, it might be more appropriate to classify Aboriginal subsistence production as that of hunter-gatherer-cultivators' (2004: 96). Rupert Gerritsen (2008) and Bill Gammage (2011) similarly cite overwhelming historical and ethnographic evidence for Aboriginal cultivation, and Ross et al. (2011) have made observations of hunter-gatherers and small-scale agriculturalists employing significant environmental modification techniques in the management of resources. This kind of evidence has reached a wider audience through Bruce Pascoe's (2014) book *Dark Emu Black Seeds: Agriculture or Accident?*, winner of the 2016 NSW Premier's Literary Award for Book of the Year (see Lourandos 2021; McNiven 2021; Porr & Vivian-Williams 2021; Sutton & Walshe 2021 for discussion of Pascoe's important book).

Enhanced Terrestrial Resources (Mammals, Reptiles, Birds, and Insects)

Aboriginal Australians deliberately modified terrestrial animal populations by increasing absolute and/or relative animal numbers by concentrating existing populations to specific locations to aid capture. Strategies included habitat extension through manipulation of specific environmental features to create new resources (food and shelter) for selected animals. Such practices operated at a variety of scales, ranging from large-scale (landscape) alterations (e.g., vegetation burning), medium-scale alterations (e.g., maintenance of waterholes), to micro-scale alterations (e.g., creating new shelters for specific animal species). Other strategies included animal translocation and restocking, along with protected rearing of young animals.

Landscape Burning

It is well accepted and broadly known that Aboriginal people altered the 'natural' state of environments through burning. The notion of Aboriginal people deliberately and strategically manipulating ecosystems through fire management was labelled 'firestick farming' by archaeologist Rhys Jones (1969). Pollen core evidence from north Queensland reveals evidence of Aboriginal landscape burning back to 45,000 years ago (Turney et al. 2001). While the scale of impact of Aboriginal landscape burning has been debated, with views ranging from major impact (e.g., Bowman 1998; Flannery 1990) to minor impact (e.g., Horton 1982; Mooney et al. 2011) and even no impact at all (Williams, Mooney, Sisson & Marlon 2015), detailed ethnographic studies reveal that Aboriginal firing regimes in some areas have had a major impact on ecosystems (see Rowe et al. this volume). Aboriginal burning practices varied seasonally and in scale across the continent but with broadly similar results: to expand grasslands to increase mammal populations (e.g., kangaroos), to increase mosaic patterning of plant communities, to enhance vertebrate biodiversity and abundance, to enhance growing conditions, to increase production of selected and prized plant foods (e.g., yams, cycads), and to increase food stocks for selected birds, and so on (Bird, Bliege Bird, & Parker 2005: 458; Bliege Bird, Bird, Codding, Parker, & Jones 2008; Bowman, Walsh, & Prior 2004; Burbidge & McKenzie 1989: 167; Hallam 1975, 1989; Russell-Smith et al. 1997: 175, 177).

In Central Australia, Brian Bolton and Peter Latz (1978) document how frequent mosaic burning by Aboriginal people increased favourable habitats and population numbers of the western hare-wallaby (*Lagorchestes hirstus*) in the Tanami Desert. The replacement of these frequent and low-impact, low-intensity anthropogenic burns with infrequent and highly destructive, high-intensity natural burns has caused the wallaby's near extinction. Latz (1995: 32) also reports that the greater bilby (*Macrotis lagotis*) 'only flourish under this system' of Aboriginal mosaic burning. Similarly, in the

Western Desert of Western Australia, Rebecca Bliege Bird and colleagues document how mosaic burning by Martu Aboriginal people creates 'landscape patchiness' and increases populations of sand monitor lizards, an important food resource (Bliege Bird et al. 2013).

There are countless ethnohistorical accounts of Aboriginal burning creating grassland or other ecosystems that favour specific food fauna. But did such deliberate burning occur well into the past? It is important to address arguments that ancient Aboriginal burning had no impact on ecosystems, given the widespread ethnohistorical evidence to the contrary. Williams et al. (2015) argue that past macro-scale environmental impacts on ecosystems trumped fire impacts. Comparing data on human population change against data on carbonized particle counts in palynological cores, Williams et al. point out that there is no correlation between increasing/changing numbers of people and increasing/changing quantities of charcoal (Williams et al. 2015: 55). Ecosystem changes, they argue, align solely with climatic and environmental changes.

There are many studies that disagree with Williams et al.'s views, and it is beyond the scope of this chapter to canvass them all. We agree with Bliege Bird, Bird, & Codding (2016; see also Bliege Bird et al. 2008; Mooney et al. 2011; Petty 2012; Russell-Smith, Whitehead, & Cooke 2010; Zeanah, Codding, Bliege Bird, & Bird 2017), who provide data to support the prevalence of anthropogenic burning throughout Australia, and for the bulk of the period of human occupation, albeit in varying intensities across landscapes and time. Bliege Bird et al. (2016) conclude that models using only population density figures and charcoal particle numbers are too simplistic to explain the complex relationships between Aboriginal people and fire: they argue that 'detecting the human-climate-fire interaction requires multiple measures of both fire regime and climate' (Bliege Bird et al. 2016: 1).

It is clear that interrelationships between people and fire are multiscalar. Climate *does* have an influence on fire frequency and intensity; nevertheless, because anthropogenic fires target an increase in food species, their regimes will differ from those generated by climate alone (Bliege Bird et al. 2016: 6–7): 'human-fire-climate dynamics are increasingly recognized as playing an important role in shaping [vegetation] community structure in ecosystems characterized by high interannual and interseasonal variability in precipitation. ENSO cycling plays an important role in Australian fire regimes in the absence of people . . . but would not be predicted in an analysis that decouples climate and human drivers of fire regime dynamics' (see also Zeanah et al. 2017).

So Aboriginal fire-stick farming has played a role in the management of terrestrial plant and animal resources across much of Australia and throughout the period of Aboriginal occupation of the continent. Fire, however, is only one way in which people manipulated ecosystems to boost prey numbers.

Waterhole Enhancement

Across inland New South Wales, Mary Gilmore (1935: 21) noted that Aboriginal people maintained the availability of drinking water in natural 'soaks' by ensuring they were kept open and clean 'for themselves [Aboriginal people] and for the kangaroos and emus that were their chief suppliers of meat, eggs, and oil'. Once Aboriginal people ceased maintaining the soaks, they dried up and were filled with sand (Gilmore 1935: 22). The implication of soak management is clear—through Aboriginal agency, water holes were maintained as extra sources of drinking water for kangaroos and emus, and this artificially enhanced the habitats, and increased the local populations, of these animals.

In many cases, a range of practices were employed to increase the availability of freshwater sources that would concomitantly increase the availability of local animals, especially in arid regions. The most obvious example of this process of water enhancement is excavation of wells (up to 7 m deep in the Simpson Desert) to access and expose aquifers (e.g., Hercus & Clarke 1986). Elsewhere in the Simpson Desert, channels were excavated to divert rainfall run-off into depressions (Hercus & Clarke 1986: 58). Latz (1995: 30) records that the Aboriginal people of Central Australia would use fire 'to bare the ground in such a way as to increase run-off and ensure a greater water storage in claypans and small lakes'. In the same region, grooves were chipped into rocks to create small channels to divert rainwater into natural rock holes (Tindale & Lindsay 1963: 65). Rowlands & Rowlands (1969) described a number of Aboriginal earthen dams constructed across drainage lines to create artificial ponds of freshwater in arid and semiarid regions (see also Kimber 1984: 19). Similar damming practices have been documented ethnographically across northern tropical Australia (Jackson & Barber 2016: 390) (see also later discussion). In other cases, water sources were created by pounding away at a rock surface to create a depression that would hold rainwater (see Duncan-Kemp 1961: 179, 185; Tindale & Lindsay 1963: 62). Gilmore (1933: 35) described one such 'dew pond or reservoir' located on the top of a granite outcrop near Wagga Wagga in southern New South Wales. Similar granite outcrop waterholes (*gnamma*) in Western Australia were thought to have been 'enlarged' by Aboriginal people (Bayly 1999: 20). Constructed water holes on granite outcrops 'also attracted animals such as macropods and reptiles, many of which also contributed to Aboriginal diets' (Bindon 1997: 175).

Archaeological evidence for such management of waterholes is rare. Yet there is tangible evidence in the notebooks of early European explorers for widespread waterhole management in savannah regions that was well-entrenched in local culture long before the arrival of Europeans (Preece 2013). Pyke et al. (2021) have undertaken similar studies of ethnohistorical records of Aboriginal resource management techniques in an effort to determine the existence of such knowledge in precontact times. Like Preece, Pyke et al. were able to document that a range of water management practices were in place throughout Australia before the arrival of the first European explorers. Consequently, while archaeological evidence for these practices is rare, their existence prior to European arrival is unarguable.

Shelter Creation

The best-documented example of this process is the construction of rock block structures for small animals to use as shelter. Lynley Wallis and Jacqueline Matthews

(2016) discuss a range of archaeologically known stone block structures found in both large and small rock shelters in the Pilbara region of Western Australia. They argue that in addition to a range of cultural functions, some stone structures may have functioned as 'enhanced animal habitats' as originally posited by Peter Bindon and Mancel Lofgren (1982): 'fissures and niches were walled to encourage habitation by small game and perhaps to aid in making their capture more certain. In our interpretation the walls can be regarded both as a hunting device and as a strategy to increase the resource potential of the area' (Bindon & Lofgren 1982: 123). Bindon & Lofgren (1982: 124) hypothesize that such resource enhancement may have related to provisioning attendees at ceremonial gatherings, as indicated by nearby stone arrangements and large stone artefact scatters ('campsites'). In short, the 'walled shelters both increased the number of animals available and made their location more certain' (Bindon & Lofgren 1982: 124).

Artificially constructed stone structures to create additional habitats for lizards have been documented archaeologically in the Esperance region of southern Western Australia. Myles Mitchell (2016: 63, 218) documents a number of 'lizard traps' (*Karda Mia*) consisting of large slabs of granite (2–3 m in length) propped up around 10–15 cm above granite bedrock by the insertion of granite rocks (Figure 12.1). These 'artificially created habitats' were targeted at lizards who would take refuge under the slabs (Mitchell 2016: 63; see also Gunn 2006: 36). Although recent research found little correlation between lizard traps and higher abundance of lizards (Guislain, Knapp, Lullfitz, & Speldewinde 2020), the function of these structures to enhance lizard populations may have been tied closely to local landscape firing regimes (see Bindon 1997: 175; Bliege Bird et al. 2013). As with stone structures in the Pilbara region, the Esperance region stone structures blur the boundary between trap and artificial niche construction. Similar to Bindon & Lofgren (1982), Mitchell (2016: 63, 229) argues that some lizard habitat structures are found near stone arrangements and may have been constructed to help provision local interregional ceremonial gatherings.

In the King George Sound region of northern Western Australia, George Grey (1841, II: 289, 466) observed that the tops of grass trees (*Xanthorrea* sp.) were broken off purposefully to induce death and subsequent decay of the trunk, a known preferred habitat for highly nutritious *bardi* or witchetty grubs (the large wood-eating larvae of several species of moths). Individual grass trees can produce more than 100 grubs (Grey 1841, II: 288).

Clearly, Aboriginal Australians implemented a range of artificial constructions to encourage the expansion of animal ranges and numbers. But this was not the only way in which animals were husbanded.

Translocations

Limited numbers of ethnographic recordings document deliberate translocation of terrestrial animals by Indigenous Australians. Michael Terry (1974: 135) states that amongst some desert groups, 'when kangaroos and other game are plentiful, some tribes maim

FIGURE 12.1. A lizard trap (*Karda Mia*) recorded by Esperance Tjaltjraak Cultural Rangers. These sites are a common feature across the granite country of southern Western Australia. Scale in 10 cm units.

(Photograph: David Guilfoyle.)

them and move them into territory in which there is enough fodder of one kind or another to keep them alive. They then kill them at their leisure and as they need them'. Elizabeth Williams (1998: 78 citing Reuther 1981) reports that the Diyari (Diari) desert people of northeast South Australia translocated 'rats and caterpillars... from one area to another so as to increase [food] stocks in particular regions'. Aboriginal women in southwest Queensland enticed native bees to establish a new hive in a hollow in a gum tree by draping the tree 'with bunches of yellow flowering punjilla' obtained from a punjilla shrub located 8 km away (Campbell 1965: 208; Duncan-Kemp 1961: 148).

In southwest Torres Strait, a population of agile wallabies (*Macropus agilis*) is located on the small island of Giralag (Cameron, Cogger, & Heatwole 1984). As the size of Giralag is below the carrying capacity threshold for long-term viability of agile wallaby populations, it is likely the wallabies are the result of the introduction of breeding stock by local Kaurareg Aboriginal people, perhaps from mainland Cape York 30 km to the southeast (McNiven & Hitchcock 2004: 117–119). In the 1930s or 1940s, a breeding pair of 'wallabies' (perhaps agile wallabies) from Cape York Peninsula was introduced to the residential island of Mua in central western Torres Strait in a failed attempt to establish a viable population (McNiven & Hitchcock 2004: 119). Archaeological excavations at a series of sites on Mua have revealed teeth of agile wallaby dating to within the past 1400 years (Ash & David 2008: 337; David et al. 2004: 166; David, McNiven, & Weisler 2008:

409; Harris, Barham, & Ghaleb 1985: 16), possibly reflecting earlier examples of wallaby translocation (McNiven & Hitchcock 2004: 119).

Tom Heinsohn (2001) provides a detailed synthesis of known and potential translocations of 'non-domesticated terrestrial vertebrates' in the 'Circum New Guinea Archipelago'. He posits that translocations included unintentional 'stowaways' on boats (e.g., rodents and geckos) and intentional 'ethnotramps' that were deliberately moved 'as pets or for food, trade or ceremonial purposes' (Heinsohn 2001: 156, 2010). Many ethnotramps were released deliberately into their new translocation environments to establish new populations 'as part of a "game park" strategy' (Heinsohn 2001: 156). Translocated species include the agile wallaby, which was 'probably introduced in pre-historic times as escaped or liberated captives carried for food or trade purposes' from the adjacent mainland to the various islands of southeast Papua New Guinea (Heinsohn 2001: 161). Archaeological evidence in Papua New Guinea suggests the translocation of the northern common cuscus (*Phalanger orientalis*) to New Ireland around 24,000 years ago, and the Admiralty cuscus (*Spilocuscus kraemeri*) and the common spiny bandicoot (*Echymipera kalubu*) from the mainland 270 km across the sea to the Admiralty Islands around 15,000 years ago (Flannery & White 1991; Leavesley 2005, 2006: 195–196; Spriggs 1997: 53–55).

Thus, there is both ethnohistorical and archaeological evidence for the deliberate movement of species into new habitats to expand the range of food resources. This practice went hand in hand with restocking in areas where species numbers had declined.

Restocking

Restocking involved moving specific animal species from one location to another where that species has been depleted. Gilmore (1934: 165) recorded that Aboriginal people in the New South Wales Riverina assisted in the regeneration of areas hit hard by 'drought' and critical reductions in food:

> To assist in replenishment of areas, possums would be caught in the land of plenty, and, when rains came these were loosed in the trees in places too far for them to travel back from. This was done in order that they might breed in the renewing locality. Possums were the great stand-by as they could be carried and transported, and could live in trees, having the dew and the leaves as food and drink, when there was no grass and no water for kangaroos and emus.

For Central Australian Aboriginal groups across the southern half of the Northern Territory, Latz noted that many sacred sites were not only restricted areas for religious reasons but also acted as plant and animal sanctuaries:

> Scattered throughout the area would be many sacred sites, most of which would be sanctuaries for plants and animals . . . and therefore have no direct advantage as a food source. These areas would, however, be vitally important for the long-term

viability of an area as immediately after droughts they would be a source of plants and animals to restock depleted areas, thereby ensuring a more rapid recovery of the home range's biota.

(Latz 1995: 22)

These sanctuaries covered many square kilometres (up to 3 km in radius) and some-times contained large waterholes which would help support local animal populations (Latz 1995: 69).

Finding archaeological evidence in support of the longevity of restocking practices has been challenging. Although there is some evidence for restocking of marine re-sources (see later discussion), reliable archaeological evidence for restocking of terres-trial fauna in Australia is currently nonexistent. The same is true for protected rearing.

Protected Rearing

Ethnographic examples of protected rearing of animals as food sources are rare. Ben Kerwin and Gavan Breen (1981: 295–297) recorded that Yandruwandha people of the Innamincka area on the edge of the Strzelecki Desert of South Australia would 'herd' young pelicans into a 'yard' on a lake edge, and over a period of 2–3 weeks they picked off the ever-fattening birds (who continued to be fed naturally by their parents) until all were eaten, whereupon the process was repeated. Tindale (1974: 109) reported that amongst rainforest peoples of north Queensland, wild cassowary chicks were tethered within camps until tame and then reared for up to a year when the large and fat birds were killed and eaten.

Summary

It is clear that a variety of forms of animal husbandry existed in Australia at or well before the time of European colonization. It is probable that much, or all of this, commenced in the distant past, with some archaeological evidence existing for certain elements of artificial terrestrial faunal management across the continent. Landscape burning had the greatest influence on faunal distribution patterns, but more subtle, local influences were also at play, including deliberate manipulation of water sources and the provision of artificial shelter to extend the range of animal habitat. Similar patterns existed for freshwater resources.

ENHANCED FRESHWATER RESOURCES (FISH AND CRAYFISH)

Aboriginal Australians deliberately modified freshwater resources to increase the avail-ability of specific animals in these ecosystems.

Translocation

Gilmore (1934: 196) reported that Aboriginal people of inland New South Wales blocked off the upper sections of creeks and gullies during floods to impound fish, a major food source. In addition, where bodies of water without fish formed after rain, these waterholes would be stocked with fish caught elsewhere and transported 'in coolamons [large wooden dishes], water-filled hollow logs, and in baskets' (Gilmore 1934: 196). As introduced stock comprised 'ova, or small fish', it is clear that the introduced stocks were intended to breed and create new generations of stock (Gilmore 1933: 14). This conclusion is supported further, given that both 'male and female' fish were used to stock these waterholes (Gilmore 1934: 196–197). Will Trueman (2011: 24-11–24-12) similarly concluded that Gilmore's (1934) descriptions of various forms of active fish management in the Murray-Darling Basin conform to aquaculture. Indeed, Trueman (2011: 24-12–24-13) reported that contemporary Yorta Yorta people of the central Murray River region continue to practise artificial seeding of waterways with Murray cod eggs, which they also had artificially fertilized. Yorta Yorta Elder Donald Briggs stated:

> In those days they would get the female cod in the breeding season and if they had the eggs, they would squirt the eggs out of the female into some logs and get the milt out of the males and put it on the eggs. They'd make up a yard out of the logs; protect it with branches, in a foot or so of water, only if the temperature was right. After 28 days the eggs and young cod would be gone. The old people did that for years. That was before any of the inspectors were doing it, in the 20's, dad told me about it. It had to be done at the right time during the floods, the fish used to go out there and do it themselves.
>
> (Cited in Trueman 2011: 24-12–24-13)

The best evidence for the deliberate alteration of the environment to extend the range of freshwater fauna comes from Toolondo, in southwest Victoria, where Aboriginal people excavated a 3 km-long channel system to connect Budgeongutte Swamp (within the natural range of eels) with Clear Swamp (located to the northwest and outside the natural range of eels). Lourandos (1980: 254) argues that 'the size and construction of these drains points to their operation as more than mere eel harvesting devices'. The main channel is 2.5 m wide and 1 m deep but would have been deeper except for eroded infill. It most probably functioned to allow migrating eels to extend their range into a new and previously inaccessible swamp. Lourandos (1980: 254) concluded that 'an extension of eel range, by providing access to further inland swamps and waterways, would have led to an increase in the annual production of eels'. Furthermore, Lourandos (1980: 263–254) argues that a system of side channels functioned as traps to capture the downstream migrating eels. Heather Builth (2014: 165) points out that since it is elvers that migrate upstream, the artificial channel at Toolondo would have provided a new place for young eels to grow up before they migrated downstream (first through the artificial channel) as adults. Lourandos (1980: 253) obtained a radiocarbon date of 210±120 BP for the base of the channel infill, which suggests that the infill is recent, and most likely immediately precontact. The date for the initial excavation of the channel has yet to be determined, but the evidence indicates that this practice is clearly part of Aboriginal tradition prior to European arrival, and is not of European influence.

Protected Rearing

Gilmore (1934: 169, 194–195, 199) noted that along the Darling, Murrumbidgee, and Lachlan Rivers of southern central New South Wales, Aboriginal people constructed stone and timber barrier dam fish traps across streams to hold back larger fish (some >30 kg) and to allow small fish to pass through unimpeded. She noted that without the barrier traps, 'the great fish would devour the smaller varieties and the end would be loss' of fish stocks; 'a loss that the years since [European settlement] have proved fact . . . When the blacks went, the fish went' (see also Humphries 2007: 110). Many dams were constructed from a large tree of appropriate size and form that had been deliberately felled (by undermining the tree's root system near the edge of a creek bank during floods) and carefully manoeuvered into place by numerous men working with flood water currents (Gilmore 1934: 199–204).

Gilmore (1934: 191–205) indicated that barrier dam fish traps were numerous across the inland waterways of New South Wales. For example, she noted that 'on creeks that were not constant, and in little gullies that only ran sometimes, I have seen scores of timber balks or traps' (Gilmore 1934: 194). The pervasiveness of these facilities is revealed further by the comment that back 'in a day when every gully had its tiny balk of bush and wood, and every gully had its tiny balk of stones and logs' (Gilmore 1934: 197). Log barrier dams occurred across a large area between the upper Murray River and the Lachlan River, centring on the Murrumbidgee River, with specific examples at Wagga Wagga, Deniliquin, Narrandera, Ardlethan, and Bland Creek seen in the 1870s and 1880s (Gilmore 1934: 195, 204). Following a survey of historical records, Trueman (2011: 24-1) concluded that 'The historical evidence suggests that wooden weir fish traps on anabranches of the main rivers and in creeks was a technology that was widely used by [A]boriginal people in the southern Murray-Darling Basin'.

In the Channel Country of arid southwest Queensland, Alice Duncan-Kemp (1968: 274–275) reported that Aboriginal people: 'went to a great deal of trouble to trap game and fish. In the streams and watercourses, especially in the deeper permanent holes, they constructed traps; some were huge affairs built of stone or stiffly staked, woven reeds, resembling small pens. In these pens were mustered fish by the hundreds in good seasons, and here they were kept alive—and fat—until required for a feast'.

As with the evidence for translocation, there are not many tangible examples of protected rearing in the archaeological record. Once again, southwest Victoria provides the best-known example with significant time depth.

The Lake Condah-Darlot Creek fish trapping system in southwest Victoria incorporated features that have been interpreted as fish holding ponds created by the local

Gunditjmara people. The implications of these features are significant, given that they have been used as a key indicator for attributing the practice of aquaculture to precontact Aboriginal peoples of southwest Victoria. Arguments for the existence of these holding ponds commenced with an interesting observation by Peter Coutts, Rudy Frank, and Phillip Hughes (1978: 28) as lake levels gradually fell following heavy rains at Lake Condah in June 1977: 'As the lake level dropped, water was trapped in pools, some of which were very deep (3–4 m) and extensive (50 m across). These pools were connected by now dry or damp stone races and canals or by a series of minor pools. In prehistoric times, fish could have been captured in these ponds and eels could have been taken in traps if they attempted to escape overland along the artificial structures towards the main body of the lake'.

Builth (2004: 175, 2014: 436) also reports on an area possibly 'used to hold or "grow" eels' near Homerton along Darlot Creek. A little further south along Darlot Creek, at Tyrendarra, Builth (2004: 175, 2014: 392–396) noted that the form of certain eel trapping devices was more consistent with penning of eels than simply trapping eels. That is, channels were constructed to divert water from Darlot Creek into adjacent complexes of depressions/swamps augmented by dams and linked through further channels. Based on hydrological modelling, it was hypothesized that these 'pens' were used to hold young eels (elvers) swimming upstream during spring and to provide favourable long-term conditions for subsequent growth into adulthood. Following in-situ maturation, adult eels would, after their normal 7–20-year 'terrestrial' life cycle, begin their autumn migration downstream where many were trapped and killed for consumption (Builth 2014: 410). Elvers were kept in pens separate from adults to protect them from adult predation (Builth 2014: 411).

Penning evidence ('growing ponds') indicates the inadequacy of the term 'fish trap' to accommodate the broad range of functions associated with Aboriginal eeling in the Condah district. It is for this reason that Builth (2014) uses the term 'eel aquaculture'. Butlin (1983: 126) also thought it appropriate to refer to Gunditjmara eel management as 'eel farming'. Lourandos (1987: 307), too, concluded that Toolondo and other similar sites such as Mt William (see later) located immediately east of Gariwerd (The Grampians) 'could be viewed, in effect, as eel "farms", or at least managed eel habitats'.

As discussed earlier, archaeological dating for the commencement of the Toolondo eel aquaculture system is still to be determined, but recent research on the archaeology of the World Heritage Budj Bim site, which encompasses the Lake Condah systems described ethnohistorically, has revealed that the stone-walled eel management system there dates back to at least 6600 years (McNiven et al. 2012), with evidence for later rebuilding of walls to maintain the structures over time.

Other freshwater aquaculture systems exist elsewhere in Victoria. In 1841, George Augustus Robinson recorded a landscape-scale eel fishing facility constructed in low-lying marshy country near Mt William. The site covered an area of 'at least 15 acres [6 ha]' and featured a complex of excavated channels up to 500 m in length across which weirs with eeling baskets were put into place. He noted that 'In single measurement there must have been some thousands of yards of this trenching and banking' (Clark 1998: 308). This structure 'remains the largest earthen construction of pre-contact Aboriginal people recorded by Europeans for any part of Australia' (McNiven & Bell 2010: 95). It is also one of the largest documented hunter-gatherer fish trapping complexes in the world. The archaeological existence of this site remains unknown, but preliminary investigations indicate that some of the complex may have escaped destruction from ploughing and gold mining activity (van der Walt in prep.). Campbell (1965: 207) suggests that the extensive channel trenching documented by Robinson near Mt William not only functioned as eel traps but also 'is likely to have provided a suitable irrigated environment for the growth of eels, fish, bird and plant life especially during the dry Victorian summer'.

There are further examples of artificial management of waterways by Aboriginal peoples to promote resource increase. Campbell (1965: 206–207) reports how Aboriginal people in the Roper River region of the Northern Territory artificially maintained wet season high water levels in Waggon Lagoon during the dry season by constructing dams of felled trees with stakes, paperbark, and clay across streams and channels to divert water into the lagoon. More recent research in this area by Marcus Barber and Sue Jackson (2011, 2015) confirms Campbell's findings. Barber & Jackson record that the area around Waggon Lagoon, and Elsey Station generally, is of high cultural significance to local Aboriginal communities, with Dreaming stories associated with the water area and many of their associated landscapes and faunal resources. Aboriginal lore (stories) and Law (rules for living) require the active management of water for both human and animal use. Barber & Jackson (2015) document traditional water management activities as including the construction of weirs, recognized in a legal judgement from 1946 as having been in existence 'from time immemorial' (2015: 294). Barber & Jackson cite the classic book *We of the Never-Never* by Aeneas Gunn (1908: 276): 'Being so shallow and wide-spreading, the lagoons would dry up early in the "dry" were it not that the blacks are able to refill them at will from the river; for here the Roper indulges in a third "duck-under," so curious that with a few logs and sheets of bark the blacks can block the way of its waters and overflow them into the lagoons, *thereby ensuring a plentiful larder to hosts of wild fowl, and, incidentally, to themselves*' (emphasis added).

From Central Australia, Williams (1998: 78 citing Reuther 1981) reports that 'areas of stream channels were dammed to increase stocks of fish' by the Diyari (Diari) desert people of northeast South Australia. Various Aboriginal groups along the Murray River of South Australia constructed 'fish pounds' with stake fences as a form of live storage and projected rearing to help regulate seasonal variations in the availability of fish (Clarke 2002: 156, 160).

Stone-walled fish traps that also acted as temporary holding pens for fish are known from Brewarrina in New South Wales (Maclean, Bark, Moggridge, Jackson, & Pollino 2012). The Brewarrina fish traps (known to local Ngyampa people as *Biame's Ngunnhu*) are regarded as highly significant to Ngyampa Traditional Owners, and to the other Aboriginal groups who used, and still have a connection to, the stone-walled traps. The heritage listing for the traps recognizes their antiquity, although no scientific dating of the structures has been possible: 'The traps demonstrate the development of a highly skilled fishing technique involving a thorough understanding of the engineering works

[sic] (dry stone walls), river hydrology and fish biology, as well as a distinctive way of life no longer practised and of exceptional interest' (cited in Maclean et al. 2012: 11).

Although primarily a trap, rather than a locale for the artificial increase in fish stocks, the Brewarrina traps do demonstrate the practice of damming a large river for the purposes of storing fish for long periods of time to allow for major feasting events at major ceremonial gatherings.

Summary

As with terrestrial fauna, Aboriginal people from different ecosystems across Australia artificially enhanced the abundance and distribution of freshwater food species using a variety of water management techniques, including translocation of species and the deliberate protection of significant species to ensure availability at times of need and/or large ceremonial gatherings. We see similar techniques in play in marine environments.

ENHANCED MARINE RESOURCES (FISH, CRAYFISH, AND SHELLFISH)

Indigenous coastal Australians procured and consumed a wide variety of marine animals, including shellfish, fish, crabs, turtles, dugongs, and whales. Nearly all recordings of Aboriginal and Torres Strait Islander use of marine resources discuss procurement of 'naturally' available marine animals. While for the most part this assumption of natural availability is correct, in various places around the Australian coastline there are ethnographic and archaeological examples of Indigenous peoples actively increasing the availability of selected marine resources.

Substrate Enhancement

Substrate enhancement is a form of habitat extension for the creation of artificial reefs for the establishment of new colonies of marine molluscs through emplacement within the intertidal zone of either a substrate (e.g., rocks, old shells, etc.) upon which juvenile oysters attach, or pieces of wood for teredo worms to burrow into and nest.

Perhaps the most common form of artificial reef creation for establishment of new oyster colonies is associated with the construction of stone-walled tidal fish traps. Examples of this process have been hypothezised for fish traps at Hinchinbrook Island in north Queensland (Campbell 1982: 102) and documented amongst the Lardil, Yangkaal, and Kaiadilt peoples of the Wellesley Islands in the Gulf of Carpentaria in Queensland

(Memmott, Robins, & Stock 2008: 82) and the Bardi people of north Western Australia (Smith 1983: 34).

The wood-boring marine mollusc, teredo worm (Teredinidae), was eaten by many different Aboriginal groups along Australia's coastline (e.g., Gardner 2013; Isaacs 1989: 175–176). While most observations of teredo worm consumption refer to procurement from naturally available sources of decaying wood within the intertidal zone, a rare instance of teredo farming comes from coastal southeast Queensland. Early colonial settler Tom Petrie (1904: 75), who lived with various southeast Queensland Aboriginal peoples during the 1830s and 1840s, recorded his observations of teredo worm (known locally as *cobra*) farming along the lower tidal and salt water reaches of southeast Queensland rivers and creeks. Along these waterways, Aboriginal people constructed piles of wood as extra habitats for *cobra*. According to Petrie: 'They all took care to have plenty coming on by cutting swamp oak saplings and carrying these on to a mud bank dry at low water, and piling them up there'. Swamp oak (*Casuarina glauca*) wood was purposefully selected as *cobra* obtained from this wood 'were considered the largest and best'. The wood pile *cobra* farms 'would be dry at low water always, and covered at high, and the natives would visit them in about a year's time, making fresh ones then to take their place'.

In Moreton Bay, southeast Queensland, the Aboriginal people of North Stradbroke Island continue the tradition of 'oyster farming . . . handed down from their ancestors' (Ross with members of the Quandamooka Aboriginal Land Council 1996: 108–109). Strategies include encouraging oyster growth and fat content by moving small oysters into optimal growth conditions in deeper water, restocking depleted oyster beds, and extending oyster habitats through construction of artificial reefs ('islands') on top of natural high points under the sea using old oyster shells at just the right depth to maximize uptake of oyster spat. The existence of this practice for well over 1000 years has been documented in the excavation of the Peel Island shell midden, which demonstrates evidence for regular restocking of depleted reefs following long periods of harvesting (Ross, Coghill, & Coghill 2015). Variation in the discard rates of oyster shells onto the midden is interpreted as being a result of alternating periods of shellfish abundance—when remains are discarded onto the site—and reef decline—when spent shells are taken back to the reefs and deposited under the sea to rebuild the reef.

In many ways, the oyster farming practices of Moreton Bay incorporate, in one single example, all the elements of resource husbandry discussed in this chapter: shelter construction in the provision of artificial reefs to provide habitat for oyster spat growth; translocation in the bay-wide mobilization of oysters to populate the reefs; restocking of depleted reefs by the manual movement of oysters from neighbouring reefs when one reef has been fully exploited; and protected rearing by the movement of oysters on a reef from shallow water to deep water to ensure maximum growth opportunities. There are many other examples of these husbandry techniques relating to marine resources management in Australia. We begin by considering another example of shelter construction.

Shelter Creation

Torres Strait Islanders constructed artificial shelters for crayfish and fish. For example, people of the island of Mer in eastern Torres Strait construct *keiar meta* (crayfish houses) on the fringing reef. As recorded by Robert Johannes and Wallace MacFarlane (1984: 257), 'these are spots where crayfish sought shelter in holes and crevices. The spots were sometimes enlarged by piling coral and coral rock loosely on top to create additional shelter. Overgrowth of corals and coralline algae would gradually cement the fragments together, creating a physically stable habitat and a readily accessible source of crayfish'. In central Torres Strait, after harvesting meat from clam shells, the opened bivalve shells were placed, interior surface down, onto the reef surface as 'that makes more clam shells come up' (Kebisu 2008: 10). Kris Billy (2008: 93) of the island of Warraber in central Torres Strait noted that clam shells were placed 'back onto the reef to make a home for the fish'.

Translocation

In 1865, geologist Norman Taylor recorded that Snowy River Aboriginal people of east Gippsland in Victoria translocated teredo mollusc borers within wood from the Genoa River estuary to the Snowy River estuary via the coast over a distance of 120 km to establish a new source of food. He noted:

> Genoa Jack, an aboriginal [sic], says that formerly there were no Warragárá (a species of Teredo, living in rotten logs lying in the half-saltwater of the Genoa and tributaries) in the Snowy River, till the Dora or Snowy River blacks, who used to come periodically to the Genoa, discovered it, cut up the logs into billets, and carried them along the coast to the Snowy River, where they split them and planted them upright in the mud. He says they are plentiful there now.
>
> (Taylor 1866, cited in Turner 1971: 140)

The placement of wood to attract teredo molluscs required nuanced ecological knowledge, as these invertebrates have quite specific estuarine habitat requirements in terms of salinity levels, location within the water profile, and water silt content (Ivezich, Hardie, & Candy 2012).

Protected Rearing

Torres Strait Islanders collect isolated clams from reefs and place these into clusters or colonies for protected rearing and restricted use. For example, on Mer, people 'gather giant clams of the genera *Tridacna* and *Hippopus* and place them on the family reef as a food reserve. Such "clam gardens," . . . are sometimes marked by a low rock enclosure'

FIGURE 12.2. Falen Passi at his clam (*terpar, Tridacna crocea*) garden established on the fringing reef at Akitir, Mer (Murray Island), eastern Torres Strait, June 2021.

(Photograph: Garrick Hitchcock).

(Johannes & MacFarlane 1984: 257–258) (Figure 12.2). Clam gardens are owned by specific families (with restricted ownership and access publically indicated by stone markers) as a 'risk reducing strategy' (Kinch, 2008: 183); in short, an insurance policy for food security. Daisy Kabay (2008: 56) of Masig in central Torres Strait stated: 'We sometimes make a garden with clam shells by putting the shells together on the reef and make a ring of stones around it. The rule is that once you have done that, other people are not allowed to take those clams'. Furthermore, 'when you are short on meat you go there and get your meat' (Kabay 2008: 45). On the island of Poruma, also in central Torres Strait, Rev. William MacFarlane (1917–1956: Item 13) was informed in 1929 that clam gardens were used 'when hard up for tucker [food]' (see also Lui 2008a: 49). Similar practices are documented for Iama in central Torres Strait (Lui 2008b: 61), with Mareko Kebisu (2008: 50) adding that people 'sometimes they only eat the [clam garden] meat because the weather is no good and they can't go fishing and hunting'. Similar clam garden practices, including territorial demarcation with stone enclosures, to create bad-weather food reserves have been documented ethnographically in Papua New Guinea (e.g., Kinch 2008: 183; Maclean 1978). In both Torres Strait and Papua New Guinea, clam gardens were established by residential island communities that were sedentary to semisedentary and relied heavily on horticultural plant foods.

Summary

Coastal Australia provides hundreds of examples of Aboriginal marine resource husbandry: from the construction of fish traps and the development of specific substrate habitat for faunal shelter to translocation and management of specific species. Here we have provided only a few brief examples, but they are by no means rarities or oddities. It is clear that marine resource management was a vital activity for Aboriginal people along the entire Australian coastline.

CONCLUSION

All of the practices discussed in this chapter, which increase the abundance of animal food resources, both terrestrial and aquatic, concern enhancement of existing ecologies. Because these enhancement practices work with local ecological processes and ecosystems, they are invariably sustainable and reversible. Campbell (1965: 210–211) noted that a 'striking feature about most of the food producing activities was its short duration, natural conditions being allowed to complete the process. This permitted the Aborigines to leave the region and still obtain the benefit of their actions on their return. Thus, food production supplemented but did not hinder food gathering and hunting.' In a sense, many of the strategies developed by Aboriginal people to increase the abundance of animal resources artificially were tailored for a mobile lifeway. Indeed, 'in an environment where fire, flood, and drought are natural events, this ability to retain independence and freedom of movement is perhaps the key to their success and long-term survival' (Philip & Garden 2016: 59). It is for this reason that Bill Gammage (2011: 281) states that Aboriginal people 'farmed' the landscape but 'were not farmers'; the former 'an activity' and the latter 'a lifestyle' (see also Pascoe 2014; Ross et al. 2011). Yet in some circumstances it is evident that resource enhancement was geared to 'regulate the availability' of food resources in regions to support decreased mobility and more sedentary and geographically restricted settlement patterns (Lourandos 1976: 187).

An important implication of the enhanced ecologies approach detailed here is that subsistence practices of many Aboriginal groups across Australia were structured not by the 'natural' environment but by a humanly 'constructed' environment. Roy Ellen (1982: 14) made the astute observation that 'what are often described as environmental correlations are, in fact, correlations between behaviour and products of that behaviour, in the form of a modified landscape'. Furthermore, 'what are often described as determining relationships between environment and behaviour are, in fact, determining relations between modes of subsistence and other aspects of social behaviour' (Ellen 1982: 14). Such a view turns the romanticized and primitivist notion of Aboriginal people 'living in harmony' on its head; clearly it is a case of living with a nature constructed by people.

Of relevance in the Australian context is the ethnographically documented relationship between the development of enhanced fish resources and large-scale interregional social/ceremonial gatherings. In this instance, abundance of a specific food resource (freshwater fish) was related to the demands to provision hundreds, and even thousands, of people attending the gatherings (see McNiven & Lambrides, this volume). Here, Aboriginal people were adapting and modifying the environment to suit the demands of society and not the other way around, as assumed in many environmentally deterministic models. As pointed out by Lourandos (1976, 1980, 1988), as the development of social gatherings has a history, by extension the concomitant development of resource enhancement practices can similarly be historicized.

Ethnographic evidence for resource enhancement practices is patchy across Australia, suggesting strongly that they cannot be considered pan-continental but as regionally specific practices undertaken for regionally specific purposes. We argue that while enhanced ecologies and ecosystem engineering were environmental management strategies employed by most—if not all—Indigenous communities in Australia and New Guinea, the specific nature of those strategies in terms of scope and intensity was regionally diverse and historically contingent.

Ideas presented in this chapter are in many respects not new for Australian archaeology as they have been foundational to the work of Lourandos for over 40 years (see Lourandos & Ross, this volume). While many Australian archaeologists have seen the possibilities presented by Lourandos's work, it is clear from the continued explicit or implicit reference to 'natural' resource availability in the literature that much work remains to be done. In this sense, understanding the role of Aboriginal peoples in constructing food resource availability has yet to be fully realized and continues to present an important ongoing theoretical and empirical challenge for Australian archaeology. Identifying such nuanced practices in the archaeological record is not straightforward. Although some practices will inevitably remain invisible, innovative approaches coupled with improved analytical methods promise to shed light on these and other practices from beyond the historical past. However, far from being simply an academic issue, recognition of Aboriginal agency in the construction, elaboration, and management of their environmental and ecological world has important ethical concerns, as ignoring the potential of such agency, or indeed denying such potential agency, is an extension of colonial silencing and marginalization.

ACKNOWLEDGEMENTS

Garrick Hitchcock kindly provided unpublished sources of information on Torres Strait Islander use of marine resources. For archaeological information on excavated earthen channels for eeling in western Victoria, we thank Ané van der Walt. John Bradley and Bruno David made helpful and stimulating comments on an earlier draft of this chapter.

References

Adams, W. Y. (1998). *The philosophical roots of anthropology*. Stanford, CA: CSLI.

Ash, J., & David, B. (2008). Mua 22: Archaeology at the old village site of Totalai. *Memoirs of the Queensland Museum, Cultural Heritage Series, 4*(2), 327–348.

Baker, R. (1993). Traditional Aboriginal land use in the Borroloola region. In N. M. Williams & G. Baines (Eds.), *Traditional ecological knowledge: Wisdom for sustainable development* (pp. 126–143). Canberra: Centre for Resource and Environmental Studies, Australian National University.

Barber, M., & Jackson, S. (2011). *Indigenous water values and water planning in the upper Roper River, Northern Territory*. Canberra: CSIRO Water for Healthy Country National Research Flagship.

Barber, M., & Jackson, S. (2015). Remembering 'the blackfellows' dam': Australian Aboriginal water management and settler colonial riparian law in the upper Roper River, Northern Territory. *Settler Colonial Studies, 5*(4), 282–301.

Bayly, I. A. E. (1999). Review of how indigenous people managed for water in desert regions of Australia. *Journal of the Royal Society of Western Australia, 82*, 17–25.

Billy, K. (2008). Affidavit of Kris Lui Billy. Sworn on October 2008. Torres Strait Regional Seas Native Title Claim, Q6040 of 2001. Native Title Office, Torres Strait Regional Authority, Thursday Island, Queensland, Australia.

Bindon, P. R. (1997). Aboriginal people and granite domes. *Journal of the Royal Society of Western Australia, 80*, 173–179.

Bindon, P., & Lofgren, M. (1982). Walled rock shelters and a cached spear in the Pilbara region, Western Australia. *Records of the Western Australian Museum, 10*(2), 111–126.

Bird, D. W., Bliege Bird, R., & Parker, C. H. (2005). Aboriginal burning regimes and hunting strategies in Australia's Western Desert. *Human Ecology, 33*(4), 443–464.

Birdsell, J. B. (1953). Some environmental and cultural factors influencing the structuring of Australian Aboriginal populations. *American Naturalist, 87*, 171–207.

Bliege Bird, R., Bird, D. W., Codding, B. F., Parker, C. H., & Jones, J. H. (2008). The 'fire stick farming' hypothesis: Australian Aboriginal foraging strategies, biodiversity, and anthropogenic fire mosaics. *Proceedings of the National Academy of Sciences, 105*(39), 14796–14801.

Bliege Bird, R., Tayor, N., Codding, B. F., & Bird, D. W. (2013). Niche construction and Dreaming logic: Aboriginal patch mosaic burning and varanid lizards (*Varanus gouldii*) in Australia. *Proceedings of the Royal Society B: Biological Sciences, 280*(1772), 20132297.

Bliege Bird, R., Bird, D. W., & Codding, B. F. (2016). People, El Niño southern oscillation and fire in Australia: Fire regimes and climate controls in hummock grasslands. *Philosophical Transactions of the Royal Society B: Biological Sciences, 371*(1696), 20150343.

Bolton, B. L., & Latz, P. K. (1978). The western Hare-Wallaby, *Lagorchestes hirsutus* (Gould) (Macropdidae) in the Tanami desert. *Australian Wildlife Research, 5*(3), 285–293.

Bowman, D. (1998). The impact of Aboriginal landscape burning on the Australian biota. *New Phytologist, 140*, 385–410.

Bowman, D., Walsh, A., & Prior, L. D. (2004). Landscape analysis of Aboriginal fire management in central Arnhem Land, north Australia. *Journal of Biogeography, 31*, 207–223.

Bradley, J. (2006). The social, economic and historical construction of cycad palms among the Yanyuwa. In B. David, B. Barker, & I. J. McNiven (Eds.), *The social archaeology of Australian Indigenous societies* (pp. 161–181). Canberra: Aboriginal Studies Press.

Brumm, A. (2021). Dingoes and domestication. *Archaeology in Oceania, 56*, 17–31.

Builth, H. (2004). Mt Eccles lava flow and the Gunditjmara connection: A landform for all seasons. *Proceedings of the Royal Society of Victoria, 116*(1), 163–182.

Builth, H. (2014). *Ancient Aboriginal aquaculture rediscovered: The archaeology of an Australian cultural landscape.* Saarbrücken: Lambert Academic.

Burbidge, A., & McKenzie, N. L. (1989). Patterns in the decline of Western Australian vertebrate fauna: Causes and conservation implications. *Biological Conservation, 50*, 143–198.

Butlin, N. G. (1983). *Our original aggression: Aboriginal populations of southeastern Australia 1788–1850.* Sydney: George Allen & Unwin.

Cameron, E., Cogger, H., & Heatwolf, H. (1984). Torres Strait: A natural laboratory. In M. Archer & G. Clayton (Eds.), *Vertebrate zoogeography and evolution in Australasia: Animals in space and time* (pp. 1151–1155). Carlisle, Western Australia: Hesperian Press.

Campbell, A. H. (1965). Elementary food production by the Australian Aborigines. *Mankind, 6*(5), 206–211, 6(6), 288.

Campbell, J. B. (1982). Automatic seafood retrieval systems: The evidence from Hinchinbrook Island and its implications. In S. Bowdler (Ed.), *Coastal archaeology in eastern Australia* (pp. 96–107). Canberra: Research School of Pacific Studies, Australian National University Press.

Clark, I. D. (Ed.) (1998). *The journals of George Augustus Robinson, Chief Protector, Port Phillip Aboriginal Protectorate, Volume Two: 1 October 1840–31 August 1841.* Melbourne: Heritage Matters.

Clarke, P. A. (2002). Early Aboriginal fishing technology in the Lower Murray, South Australia. *Records of the South Australian Museum, 35*(2), 147–167.

Coutts, P. J. F., Frank, R. K., & Hughes, P. 1978. *Aboriginal Engineers of the Western District, Victoria.* Records of the Victorian Archaeological Survey 7. Melbourne: VAS.

David, B., & Denham, T. (2006). Unpacking Australian prehistory.. In B. David, B. Barker, & I. J. McNiven (Eds.), *The social archaeology of Australian Indigenous societies* (pp. 52–71). Canberra: Aboriginal Studies Press.

David, B., McNiven, I., Manas, L., Manas, J., Savage, S., Crouch, J., Neliman, G., & Brady, L. (2004). Goba of Mua: Archaeology working with oral tradition. *Antiquity, 78*, 158–172.

David, B., McNiven, I. J., & Weisler, M. I. (2008). Archaeological excavations at Gerain and Urakaraltam. *Memoirs of the Queensland Museum, Cultural Heritage Series, 4*(2), 401–428.

Denevan, W. M. (1992). The pristine myth: The landscape of the Americas in 1492. *Annals of the Association of American Geographers, 82*(3), 369–385.

Duncan-Kemp, A. M. (1961). *Our Channel Country: Man and nature in south-west Queensland.* Sydney: Angus & Robertson.

Duncan-Kemp, A. M. (1968). *Where strange gods call.* Fortitude Valley, Brisbane: W. R. Smith & Paterson.

Ellen, R. (1982). *Environment, subsistence and system: The ecology of small-scale social formations.* Cambridge: Cambridge University Press.

Erickson, C. L. (2006). The domesticated landscapes of the Bolivian Amazon. In W. Balée & C. L. Erickson (Eds.), *Time and complexity in historical ecology: Studies in the neotropical lowlands* (pp. 235–278). New York: Columbia University Press.

Field, J. H., Kealhofer, L., Cosgrove, R., & Coster, A. C. F. (2016). Human-environment dynamics during the Holocene in the Australian Wet Tropics of NE Queensland: A starch and phytolith study. *Journal of Anthropological Archaeology, 44*(B), 216–234.

Flannery, T. (1990). Pleistocene faunal loss: Implications of the aftershock for Australia's past and future. *Archaeology in Oceania, 25*, 25–67.

Flannery, T. F., & White, J. P. (1991). Animal translocations: Zoogeography of New Ireland mammals. *National Geographic Research & Exploration, 7*(1), 96–113.

Fowler, C. S. (1986). Subsistence. In W. L. d'Azevedo (Ed.), *Handbook of North American Indians. Vol. II. Great Basin* (pp. 64–97). Washington, DC: Smithsonian Institution.

Frankel, D. (1982). An account of Aboriginal use of the Yam-Daisy. *The Artefact 7* (1–2), 43–45.

Gammage, B. (2011). *The biggest estate on Earth: How Aborigines made Australia.* Sydney: Allen & Unwin.

Gardner, M. (2013). A short historical investigation into cross-cultural Australian ideas about the marine animal group Teredinidae, their socioecological consequences and some opinions. *Coolabah, 11,* 266–279.

Gerritsen, R. (2008). *Australia and the origins of agriculture.* BAR International series 1874. Oxford: Archaeopress.

Gilmore, M. (1933). Aboriginal science. Fish-traps and fish-balks. *Sydney Morning Herald,* 8 November, p. 14.

Gilmore, M. (1934). *Old days: Old ways. A book of recollections.* Sydney: Angus & Robertson.

Gilmore, M. (1935). *More Recollections.* Sydney: Angus and Robertson.

Golson, J. (1977). The ladder of social evolution: Archaeology and the bottom rungs. *Australian Academy of the Humanities, Proceedings, 8,* 41–56.

Gott, B. (1982). Ecology of root use by the Aborigines of southern Australia. *Archaeology in Oceania, 17*(1), 59–67.

Gott, B. (1983). Murnong–*Microseris scapigera*: A study of a staple food of Victorian Aborigines. *Australian Aboriginal Studies, 1983*(1), 2–18.

Gottesfeld, L. M. J. (1994). Aboriginal burning for vegetation management in northwest British Columbia. *Human Ecology, 22*(2), 171–188.

Grey, G. (1841). *Journals of two expeditions of discovery in north-west and Western Australia, during the years 1837, 38, and 39.* 2 vols. London: T. & W. Boone.

Guislain, L., Knapp, L., Lullfitz, & Speldewinde, P. (2020). Are Karda (*Varanus rosenbergii*) more abundant around traditional Noongar lizard traps? *Journal of the Royal Society of Western Australia, 103,* 43–47.

Gunn, J. (1908). *We of the Never-Never.* New York: Macmillan.

Gunn, R. G. (2006). Mulka's Cave Aboriginal rock art site: Its context and content. *Records of the Western Australian Museum, 23,* 19–41.

Hallam, S. J. (1975). *Fire and hearth: A study of Aboriginal usage and European usurpation in south-western Australia.* Canberra: Australian Institute of Aboriginal Studies.

Hallam, S. J. (1989). Plant usage and management in south-west Australian Aboriginal societies. In D. R. Harris & G. C. Hillman (Eds.), *Foraging and farming: The evolution of plant exploitation* (pp. 136–151). London: Unwin & Hyman.

Hames, R. (2007). The ecologically noble savage debate. *Annual Review of Anthropology, 36,* 177–190.

Harris, D. R. (1977). Subsistence strategies across Torres Strait. In J. Allen, J. Golson, & R. Jones (Eds.), *Sunda and Sahul: Prehistoric studies in Southeast Asia, Melanesia and Australia* (pp. 421–463). London: Academic Press.

Harris, D. R. (1989). An evolutionary continuum of people-plant interaction. In D. R. Harris & G. C. Hillman (Eds.), *Foraging and farming: The evolution of plant domestication* (pp. 11–26). One World Archaeology 13. London: Unwin Hyman.

Harris, D. R., Barham, A. J., & Ghaleb, B. (1985). Archaeology and recent palaeoenvironmental history of Torres Strait, northern Australia. Preliminary report to the Research and

Exploration Committee of the National Geographic Society on 'Part IIA of The Torres Strait Research Project July-October 1984'. University College London. (Unpubl.).

Head, L. (2000). *Second nature: The history and implications of Australia as Aboriginal landscape.* Syracuse, NY: Syracuse University Press.

Head, L. (2008). Is the concept of human impacts past its use-by date? *The Holocene, 18*(3), 373–377.

Heinsohn, T. E. (2001). Human influences on vertebrate zoogeography: Animal translocation and biological invasions across and to the east of Wallace's Line. In I. Metcalfe, J. M. B. Smith, M. Morwood, & I. Davidson (Eds.), *Faunal and floral migrations and evolution in SE Asia-Australasia* (pp. 153–170). Lisse: A.A. Balkema.

Heinsohn, T. E. (2010). Marsupials as introduced species: Long-term anthropogenic expansion of the marsupial frontier and its implications for zoogeographic interpretation. In S. Haberle, J. Stevenson, & M. Prebble (Eds.), *Altered ecologies: Fire, climate and human influence on terrestrial landscapes* (pp. 133–176). Terra Australis 32. Canberra: ANU E-Press.

Hercus, L., & Clarke, P. (1986). Nine Simpson Desert wells. *Archaeology in Oceania, 21*(1), 51–62.

Hiscock, P. (1994). Technological responses to risk in Holocene Australia. *Journal of World Prehistory, 8*(3), 267–292.

Horton, D. (1982). The burning question: Aborigines, fire and Australian ecosystems. *Mankind, 13*(3), 237–251.

Humphries, P. (2007). Historical Indigenous use of aquatic resources in Australia's Murray-Darling Basin, and its implications for river management. *Ecological Management & Restoration, 8*(2), 106–113.

Hunn, E. S., & Williams, N. M. (1982). Introduction. In N. M. Williams & E. S. Hunn (Eds.), *Resource managers: North American and Australian hunter-gatherers* (pp. 1–16). Canberra: Australian Institute of Aboriginal Studies.

Hynes, R. A., & Chase, A. K. (1982). Plants, sites and domiculture: Aboriginal influence upon plant communities in Cape York Peninsula. *Archaeology in Oceania, 17*(1), 38–50.

Irvine, F. R. (1970). Evidence of change in the vegetable diet of Australian Aborigines. In A. R. Pilling & R. A. Waterman (Eds.), *Diprotodon to detribalization: Studies of change among Australian Aborigines* (pp. 278–284). East Lansing: Michigan State University Press.

Isaacs, J. (1989). *Bush food: Aboriginal food and herbal medicine.* Sydney: Weldon.

Ivezich, M., Hardie, R., & Candy, R. (2012). Optimising the design life and ecological benefit of large wood installations in estuarine reaches. In J. R. Grove & I. D. Rutherford (Eds.), *Proceedings of the 6th Australian Stream Management Conference, Managing for extremes, February, 2012, Canberra, Australia* (pp. 1–9). The River Basin Management Society.

Jackson, S., & Barber, M. (2016). Historical and contemporary waterscapes of North Australia: Indigenous attitudes to dams and water diversions. *Water History, 8*(4), 385–404.

Johannes, R. E., & MacFarlane, J. W. (1984). Traditional sea rights in the Torres Strait Islands. In K. Ruddle & T. Akimichi (Eds.), *Maritime institutions of the western Pacific* (pp. 253–266). Senri Ethnological Studies No. 17. Osaka: National Museum of Ethnology.

Jones, R. (1969). Fire-stick farming. *Australian Natural History, 16*, 224–228.

Jones, R. (1977). Man as an element of a continental fauna: The case of the sundering of the Bassian bridge. In J. Allen, J. Golson, & R. Jones (Eds.), *Sunda and Sahul: Prehistoric studies in Southeast Asia, Melanesia and Australia* (pp. 317–386). London: Academic Press.

Jones, R. (1992). Philosophical time travellers. *Antiquity, 66*, 744–757.

Kabay, D. (2008). Affidavit of Daisy Kabay. Sworn on October 2008. Torres Strait Regional Seas Native Title Claim, Q6040 of 2001. Native Title Office, Torres Strait Regional Authority, Thursday Island, Queensland, Australia.

Kearney, A., Bradley, J., & Brady, L. M. (2019). Kincentric ecology, species maintenance and the relational power of place in northern Australia. *Oceania, 89*(3), 316–335.

Kebisu, M. (2008). Affidavit of Mareko Kebisu. Sworn on 2008. Torres Strait Regional Seas Native Title Claim, Q6040 of 2001. Native Title Office, Torres Strait Regional Authority, Thursday Island, Queensland, Australia.

Keeley, L. H. (1995). Protoagricultural practices among hunter-gatherers: A cross-cultural survey. In T. D. Price & A. B. Gebauer (Eds.), *Last hunters–first farmers: New perspectives on the prehistoric transition to agriculture* (pp. 243–272). Santa Fe, NM: School of American Research Press.

Keen, I. (2004). *Aboriginal economy and society: Australia at the threshold of colonialism*. South Melbourne: Oxford University Press.

Keen, I. (2021). Foragers or farmers: *Dark Emu* and the controversy over Aboriginal agriculture. *Anthropological Forum, 31*(1),106–128.

Kerwin, B., & Breen, J. G. (1981). The land of stone chips. *Oceania, 51*(4), 286–311.

Kimber, R. G. (1984). Resource use and management in central Australia. *Australian Aboriginal Studies, 1984*(2), 12–23.

Kinch, J. (2008). From prehistoric to present: Giant clam (Tridacnidae) use in Papua New Guinea. In A. Antczak & R. Cipriani (Eds.), *Early human impact on megamolluscs* (pp. 179–188). BAR International Series 1865. Oxford: Archaeopress.

Krech, S. (1999). *The ecological Indian: Myth and history*. New York: Norton.

Latz, P. K. (1995). *Bushfires and bushtucker: Aboriginal plant use in Central Australia*. Alice Springs, NT: IAD Press.

Lawton, H. W., Wilke, P. J., DeDecker, M., & Mason, W. M. (1976). Agriculture among the Paiute of Owens Valley. *Journal of California Anthropology, 3*, 13–50.

Leavesley, M. (2005). Prehistoric hunting strategies in New Ireland, Papua New Guinea: The evidence of the cuscus (*Phalanger orientalis*) remains from Buang Merabak cave. *Asian Perspectives, 44*(1), 207–218.

Leavesley, M. (2006). Late Pleistocene complexities in the Bismarck Archipelago. In I. Lilley (Ed.), *Archaeology of Oceania: Australia and the Pacific Islands* (pp. 189–204). Malden, MA: Blackwell.

Lepofsky, D., & Lertzman, K. (2008). Documenting ancient plant management in the northwest of North America. *Botany, 86*(2), 129–145.

Lewis, H. T. (1982). Fire technology and resource management in Aboriginal North America and Australia. In N. M. Williams & E. S. Hunn (Eds.), *Resource managers: North American and Australian hunter-gatherers* (pp. 45–67). Canberra: Australian Institute of Aboriginal Studies.

Lightfoot, K. G., Cuthrell, R. Q., Striplen, C. J., & Hyljema, M. G. (2013). Rethinking the study of landscape management practices among hunter-gatherers in North America. *American Antiquity, 78*(2), 285–301.

Liljeblad, S., & Fowler, C. S. (1986). Owens Valley Paiute. In W. L. d'Azevedo (Ed.), *Handbook of North American Indians. Vol. II. Great Basin* (pp. 412–434). Washington, DC: Smithsonian Institution.

Lourandos, H. (1976). Aboriginal settlement and land use in south western Victoria: A report on current field work. *The Artefact, 1*(4), 174–193.

Lourandos, H. (1980). Change or stability? Hydraulics, hunter-gatherers and population in temperate Australia. *World Archaeology, 11*(3), 245–266.

Lourandos, H. (1987). Swamp managers of southwestern Victoria. In D. J. Mulvaney & J. P. White (Eds.), *Australians to 1788* (pp. 293–307). Broadway, NSW: Fairfax, Syme & Weldon Associates.

Lourandos, H. (1988). Palaeopolitics: Resource intensification in Aboriginal Australia and Papua New Guinea. In T. Ingold, D. Riches, & J. Woodburn (Eds.), *Hunters and gatherers: History, evolution and social change* (pp. 148–160). Oxford: Berg.

Lourandos, H. (1997). *Continent of hunter-gatherers: New perspectives in Australian prehistory.* Cambridge: Cambridge University Press.

Lourandos, H. (2008). Constructing 'hunter-gatherers', constructing 'prehistory'. *Australian Archaeology, 67,* 69–78.

Lourandos, H. (2021). Tragedy or transformation: Australian archaeology at the crossroads (again). Comment on Porr and Vivian-Williams 'The tragedy of Bruce Pascoe's *Dark Emu*'. *Australian Archaeology, 87*(3), 311–312.

Luer, G. M. (1998). The Naples canal: A deep Indian canoe trail in southwestern Florida. *The Florida Anthropologist, 51*(1), 25–36.

Lui, G. (2008a). Affidavit of George Lui. Sworn on October 2008. Torres Strait Regional Seas Native Title Claim, Q6040 of 2001. Native Title Office, Torres Strait Regional Authority, Thursday Island, Queensland, Australia.

Lui, L. (2008b). Affidavit of Alice-Maria Lizzie Lui. Sworn on October 2008. Torres Strait Regional Seas Native Title Claim, Q6040 of 2001. Native Title Office, Torres Strait Regional Authority, Thursday Island, Queensland, Australia.

Maclean, J. L. (1978). The clam gardens of Manus. *Harvest, 4,* 87–92.

Maclean, K., Bark, R. H., Moggridge, B., Jackson S., & Pollino C. (2012). *Ngemba water values and interests: Ngemba old mission billabong and Brewarrina Aboriginal fish traps (Baiame's Nguunhu).* Australia: CSIRO.

McNiven, I. J. (2008). Inclusions, exclusions, transitions: Torres Strait Islander constructed landscapes over the past 4000 years. *The Holocene, 18*(3), 449–462.

McNiven, I. J. (2016). Increase rituals and environmental variability on small residential islands of Torres Strait. *Journal of Island and Coastal Archaeology, 11,* 195–210.

McNiven, I. J. (2021). Bandwagons and bathwater. Comment on Porr and Vivian-Williams 'The tragedy of Bruce Pascoe's *Dark Emu*'. *Australian Archaeology, 87*(3), 316–317.

McNiven, I. J., & Bell, D. (2010). Fishers and farmers: Historicising the Gunditjmara freshwater fishery, western Victoria. *The La Trobe Journal, 85,* 160–163.

McNiven, I. J., & Hitchcock, G. (2004). Torres Strait Islander marine subsistence specialisation and terrestrial animal translocation. *Memoirs of the Queensland Museum, Cultural Heritage Series, 3*(1), 105–162.

McNiven, I. J., & Russell, L. (1995). Place with a past: Reconciling wilderness and the Aboriginal past in World Heritage areas. *Royal Historical Society of Queensland Journal, 15,* 505–519.

McNiven, I. J., & Russell, L. (2005). *Appropriated pasts: Indigenous peoples and the colonial culture of archaeology.* Walnut Creek, CA: AltaMira Press.

McNiven, I. J., Crouch, J., Richards, T., Gunditj Mirring Traditional Owners Aboriginal Corporation, Dolby, N., & Jacobsen, G. (2012). Dating Aboriginal stone-walled fishtraps at Lake Condah, southeast Australia. *Journal of Archaeological Science, 39*(2), 268–286.

Memmott, P., Robins, R., & Stock, E. (2008). What exactly is a fish trap?: Methodological issues for the study of Aboriginal intertidal rock wall fish traps, Wellesley Islands region,

Gulf of Carpentaria, Australia. In J. Connolly & M. Campbell (Eds.), *Comparative island archaeologies* (pp. 73–96). British International Series S1829. Oxford: Archaeopress.

Mitchell, M. B. (2016). *The Esperance Nyungars, at the frontier: An archaeological investigation of mobility, aggregation and identity in late-Holocene Aboriginal society, Western Australia* (PhD thesis). Australian National University, Canberra.

Mooney, S. D., Harrison, S. P., Bartlein, P. J., Daniau, A.-L., Stevenson, J., Brownlie, K. C., . . . Williams, N. (2011). Late Quaternary fire regimes of Australasia. *Quaternary Science Reviews, 30*, 28–46.

O'Connell J. F., & Hawkes, K. (1981). Alyawara plant use and optimal foraging theory. In B. Winterhalder & E. A. Smith (Eds.), *Hunter-gatherer foraging strategies: Ethnographic and archaeological analyses* (pp. 99–125). Chicago: University of Chicago Press.

Panter-Brick, C., Layton, R. H., & Rowley-Conwy, P. (2001). Lines of inquiry. In C. Panter-Brick, R. H. Layton, & P. Rowley-Conwy (Eds.), *Hunter-gatherers: An interdisciplinary perspective* (pp. 1–11). Cambridge: Cambridge University Press.

Pascoe, B. (2014). *Dark emu black seeds: Agriculture or accident?* Broome, WA: Magabala Books.

Peterson, N. (1976). The natural and cultural areas of Aboriginal Australia: A preliminary analysis of population groupings with adaptive significance. In N. Peterson (Ed.), *Tribes and boundaries in Australia* (pp. 50–71). Canberra: Australian Institute of Aboriginal Studies.

Petrie, C. C. (1980) [1904]. *Tom Petrie's reminiscences of early Queensland.* Windsor, Victoria: Curry O'Neil.

Petty, A. M. (2012). Introduction to *Fire-Stick Farming. Fire Ecology, 8*(3), 1–2.

Philip, J., & Garden, D. (2016). Walking the Thylacine: Records of Indigenous companion animals in Australian narrative and photographic history. *Society & Animals, 24*, 34–62.

Porr, M., & Vivian-Williams, E. (2021). The tragedy of Bruce Pascoe's *Dark Emu*. Forum piece. *Australian Archaeology, 87*(3), 300–304.

Preece, N. D. (2013). Tangible evidence of historic Australian indigenous savanna management. *Australian Ecology, 38*(3), 241–250.

Price, T. D., & Brown, J. A. (Eds.) (1985). *Prehistoric hunter-gatherers: The emergence of cultural complexity.* Orlando, FL: Academic Press.

Pyke, M. L., Close, P. G., Dobbs, R. J., Toussaint, S., Smith, B., Cox, Z., . . . Clifton, J. (2021). 'Clean him up . . . make him look like he was before': Australian Aboriginal management of wetlands with implications for conservation, restoration and multiple evidence base negotiations. *Wetlands, 41*(2), 1–16.

Reuther, J. G. (1981). *The Diari.* Vols. 1–13. Manuscript. Translated by the Rev. P. A. Scherer. Canberra: Australian Institute of Aboriginal and Torres Strait Islander Studies.

Roscoe, P. (2002). The hunters and gatherers of New Guinea. *Current Anthropology, 43*, 153–162.

Ross, A. with members of the Quandamooka Aboriginal Land Council (1996). Aboriginal approaches to cultural heritage management: A Quandamooka case study. In S. Ulm, I. Lilley, & A. Ross (Eds.), *Australian Archaeology '95: Proceedings of the 1995 Australian Archaeological Association annual conference* (pp. 107–112). Tempus 6. St Lucia: Anthropology Museum, University of Queensland.

Ross, A., Coghill, S., & Coghill, B. (2015). Discarding the evidence: The place of natural resources stewardship in the creation of the Peel Island Lazaret Midden, Moreton Bay, southeast Queensland. *Quaternary International, 385*, 177–190.

Ross, A., Pickering-Sherman, K., Snodgrass, J. G., Delcore, H. D., & Sherman, R. (2011). *Indigenous peoples and the collaborative stewardship of nature: Knowledge binds and institutional conflicts.* Walnut Creek, CA: Left Coast Press.

Rowlands, R. J., & Rowlands, J. M. (1969). An Aboriginal dam in northwestern New South Wales. *Mankind, 7*(2), 132–136.

Russell-Smith, J., Lucas, D., Gapindi, M., Gunbunuka, B., Kapirigi, N., Namingum, G., . . . Chaloupka, G. (1997). Aboriginal resource utilization and fire management practice in western Arnhem Land, monsoonal northern Australia: Notes for prehistory, lessons for the future. *Human Ecology, 25*(2), 159–195.

Russell-Smith, J., Whitehead, P., & Cooke, P. (Eds.) (2010). *Culture, ecology and economy of fire management in North Australian savannas: Rekindling the Wurrk tradition.* Collingwood, Victoria: CSIRO.

Shipek, F. (1989). An example of intensive plant husbandry: The Kumeyaay of southern California. In D. R. Harris & G. C. Hillman (Eds.), *Foraging and farming: The evolution of plant exploitation* (pp. 159–170). London: Unwin Hyman.

Smith, B. D. (1998). Between foraging and farming. *Science, 279,* 1651–1652.

Smith, B. D. (2001). Low-level food production. *Journal of Archaeological Research, 9*(1), 1–43.

Smith, E. A., & Wishnie, M. (2000). Conservation and subsistence in small-scale societies. *Annual Review of Anthropology, 29,* 493–524.

Smith, M. (1983). Joules from pools: Social and techno-economic aspects of Bardi fish traps. In M. Smith (Ed.), *Archaeology at ANZAAS 1983* (pp. 29–45). Perth: Western Australian Museum.

Spriggs, M. (1997). *The island Melanesians.* Cambridge, MA: Blackwell.

Steward, J. H. (1930). Irrigation without agriculture. *Papers of the Michigan Academy of Sciences, Arts, and Letters, 12,* 149–156.

Sutton, P., & Walshe, K. (2021). *Farmers or hunter-gatherers? The Dark Emu debate.* Melbourne, Victoria: Melbourne University Press.

Taylor, N. (1866). Appendix D. *Reports relative to the Geological Survey of Victoria, 1865* Mebourne: Government Printer.

Taylor, S. G. (1990). Naturalness: The concept and its application to Australian ecosystems. *Proceedings of the Ecological Society of Australia, 16,* 411–418.

Terrell, J. E., Hart, J. P., Barut, S., Cellinese, N., Curet, A., Denham, T., . . . Staller, J. E. (2003). Domesticated landscapes: The subsistence ecology of plant and animal domestication. *Journal of Archaeological Method and Theory, 10*(4), 323–368.

Terry, M. (1974). *War of the Warramullas.* Sydney: Rigby.

Thomson, D. F. (1939). The seasonal factor in human culture illustrated from the life of a contemporary nomadic group. *Proceedings of the Prehistoric Society, 5*(2), 209–221.

Tindale, N. B. (1974). *Aboriginal tribes of Australia.* Berkeley: University of California Press.

Tindale, N. B., & Lindsay, H. A. (1963). *Aboriginal Australians.* Brisbane: The Jacaranda Press.

Trueman, W. (2011). *True tails of the trout cod: River histories of the Marry-Darling Basin.* Canberra: Murray-Darling Basin Authority.

Turner, R. D. (1971). Australian shipworms. *Australian Natural History, 17*(4), 139–145.

Turney, C. S. M., Kershaw, A. P., Moss, P., Bird, M. I., Fifield, L. K., Cresswell, R. G., . . . Zhou, Y. (2001). Redating the onset of burning at Lynch's Crater (North Queensland): Implications for human settlement in Australia. *Journal of Quaternary Science, 16*(8), 767–771.

Van der Walt, A. (in prep.). *The Narrative Atlas: Creativity and multivocality in Indigenous archaeology* (PhD thesis). Monash University, Melbourne.

Veth, P., O'Connor, S., & Wallis, L. A. (2000). Perspectives on ecological approaches in Australian archaeology. *Australian Archaeology, 50,* 54–66.

Wallis, L. A., & Matthews, J. (2016). Built structures in rockshelters of the Pilbara, Western Australia. *Records of the Western Australian Museum, 31*, 1–26.

Warren, G. (2021). Is there such a thing as hunter-gatherer archaeology? *Heritage, 4*, 794–810.

Wheeler, R. J. (1995). The Ortona canals: Aboriginal canal hydraulics and engineering. *The Florida Anthropologist, 48*(4), 265–281.

White, J. P., & O'Connell, J. F. (1982). *A prehistory of Australia, New Guinea and Sahul.* Sydney: Academic Press.

Widmer, R. J. (1988). *The evolution of the Calusa: A nonagricultural chiefdom on the southwest Florida coast.* Tuscaloosa: The University of Alabama Press.

Williams, A. N., Mooney, S. D., Sisson S. A., & Marlon, J. (2015). Exploring the relationship between Aboriginal population indices and fire in Australia over the last 20,000 years. *Palaeogeography, Palaeoclimatology, Palaeoecology, 432*, 49–57.

Williams, E. (1998). The archaeology of lake systems in the middle Copper Basin, north-eastern South Australia. *Records of the South Australian Museum, 30*(2), 69–91.

Yasuoka, H. (2013). Dense wild yam patches established by hunter-gatherer camps: Beyond the wild yam question: Toward the historical ecology of rainforests. *Human Ecology, 41*, 465–475.

Yen, D. E. (1989). The domestication of environment. In D. R. Harris & G. C. Hillman (Eds.), *Foraging and farming: The evolution of plant domestication* (pp. 55–75). One World Archaeology 13. London: Unwin Hyman.

Zeanah, D. W., Codding, B. F., Bliege Bird, R., & Bird, D. W. (2017). Mosaics of fire and water: The co-emergence of anthropogenic landscapes and intensive seed exploitation in the Australian arid zone. *Australian Archaeology, 83*(1–2), 2–19.

CHAPTER 13

THE COMING OF THE DINGO

JANE BALME AND SUE O'CONNOR

INTRODUCING THE DINGO

THE dingo, or Australian 'native' dog (Figure 13.1), is a placental mammal and, apart from some rats and bats, is the only terrestrial placental to have been present in Australia before European colonization. The dingo's taxonomic classification is a subject of some debate. It is usually classified as *Canis lupus dingo* or *Canis familiaris dingo,* but Crowther, Fillios, Colman, and Letnic (2014) and Smith et al. (2019) have suggested that dingoes are sufficiently morphologically distinct from *C. familiaris* to warrant a separate species name and that the taxonomic name *Canis dingo* should be used. Not all researchers support this suggestion. Jackson et al. (2017, 2019), for example, have argued that dingoes should be considered a variety or breed of *C. familiaris.* This conclusion is based on a diversity of biological, ecological, and genetic evidence, in addition to morphology. Their argument for classification as *C. familiaris* reflects interpretations of genetic evidence that dingoes are a feral derivative of one of the lineages of domestic dogs (e.g., Oskarsson et al. 2012; Skoglund, Ersmark, Palkopoulou, & Dalén 2015)—although this interpretation is still unresolved (Ballard & Wilson 2019).

Some late nineteenth- and early twentieth-century researchers (e.g., Etheridge 1916; Krefft 1870; McCoy 1882) suggested that dingoes might be native to Australia, on the basis of dingo bones being in apparent association with the fossils of extinct species. It is now generally accepted, however, that these associations are spurious and that the dingo is a recent arrival. The arrival time, based on mtDNA research, has been suggested to be as much as 18,000 years ago (Oskarsson et al. 2012), but other DNA studies have suggested diverse dates in the Early to Mid-Holocene range (see Koungoulos & Fillios 2020b: Table 1:2). However, molecular (DNA) dating is not an absolute dating method in itself, and the diverse dates no doubt arise from differences in the assumptions and divergent interpretations made by various researchers. A recent summary of these problems and their history is provided by Bromham (2019).

FIGURE 13.1. Adult dingo.

(Arco Images GmbH/Alamy Stock Photo.)

At present, the best estimates for the arrival of the dingo in Australia are provided by hard evidence, that is, absolute dates for the subfossils. There is no fossil evidence to suggest that dingoes arrived any earlier than the Late Holocene, but exactly when in the Late Holocene dingoes appeared is difficult to pinpoint. While dingo remains are found in both palaeontological and archaeological sites, many of these remains were excavated during the twentieth century when, because of the expense, few radiocarbon dates were obtained for each site. It was also common to excavate in thick excavation units so that associating dingo remains with the few available dates with any precision is difficult. Rodríguez-Rey et al. (2015) assess as reliable very few of the indirect dingo dates, and no dates older than 2200 years are listed on the FosSahul database of nonhuman vertebrate fossils from the Middle Pleistocene to the present in the Sahul region (Rodríguez-Rey et al. 2016). Their assessment criteria include consideration of the dating protocols and, particularly relevant for indirect dates, the quality of the association between dates and the bones.

The most precise dates are direct dates and few are available. The two oldest of these are from the Nullarbor Plain at the southern edge of Australia where a date of 3363–3211 cal BP[1] (3069±27 BP, SANU 54821) was received for the deepest dingo bones found in

Madura Cave (Balme, O'Connor, & Fallon 2018), and 3259–3022 cal BP (3031±34 BP, OxA-27532) for a specimen from surface deposits in Koonalda Cave (Walshe 2017). A date of 2381–1931 cal BP (2200±96 BP, NSW-30) was obtained from desiccated flesh from a dingo in Thylacine Hole, a palaeontological site also on the Nullarbor (Lowry & Merrilees, 1969). A direct date on dingo bone from excavations by Campbell (1988) on the coastal site of Moana, South Australia, provided a date of 2336–1299 cal BP (1850±240 BP, ETH 2732). Aside from these specimens, published radiometric dates that directly date dingo remains are younger than this and are mostly less than about 1000 years (Crowther et al., 2014: Table S2; Rodríguez-Rey et al. 2016). It should be noted that the direct date of 3570±100 BP on bone from Horseshoe Cave, which is on the Nullarbor and cited in Rodríguez-Rey et al. (2016) as being from dingo, is an error as the bone was not reported by Archer (1974) as deriving from dingo.

Despite the lack of direct dates older than about 3300 years, the most commonly quoted time estimate for the arrival of the dingo is 5000–4000 years ago. This estimate is largely based on the fact that, before the direct date on the Madura Cave dingo was obtained, many researchers relied on Milham and Thompson's (1976) interpretation that the dingo bones at the site were in good association with a radiocarbon date of 3931–3478 cal BP (3450±95 BP, ANU807). Because Madura Cave is on the southern edge of Australia, researchers have added some extra years onto this date to allow for the dingo's dispersal to this southern area. The suggested 500 years is possibly based on Gollan's (1984: 924) proposal that it is hard to see a lag time of greater than 500 years for dingoes to reach the area from their northern entry point. However, we have previously argued (Balme et al. 2018) that there is no reason to suggest such a slow dispersal of dingoes, especially if it was aided by people (see below). Current evidence suggests that the earliest direct date for dingoes—that from Madura Cave—is probably close to the time that dingoes originally arrived in Australia. Because they arrived after the sea-level rise in Bass Strait, which separated mainland Australia from Tasmania about 11,000 years ago (Lambeck & Chappell 2001), dingoes did not reach Tasmania.

Koungoulos and Fillios (2020b: 3) suggest that the lack of older dingo fossils is due to poor preservation in hot, humid, northern sites. It is true that some of the northern sites do not preserve bone well. However, bone spanning the Holocene is extremely well preserved in sandstone sites containing midden material that contribute to the alkalinity of the deposits, and in the limestone sites of the southern Kimberley. Madjedbebe, a sandstone rock shelter on the western edge of the Arnhem Land Plateau, has very well-preserved bone in its upper midden deposits dating to the past 8000 years (Clarkson et al. 2017), yet no dingo bones have been identified (Tiina Manne personal communication, 8 May 2020). Nawamoyn, another west Arnhem Land coastal plain site with both marine and land mammal fauna, dates from about 8000 years ago, but this site only has dingo bones in the uppermost spit (Schrire 1982: 123). Further south, in the limestone caves of the southern Kimberley, the site of Riwi contains a faunal sequence representing about 46,000 years, but dingo bones are only present in the Late Holocene levels (Balme et al. 2019). At Widgingarri Shelter 1 in the west Kimberley, which has bone preserved throughout its >28,000 years of deposits, the dingo is represented only in the uppermost spit (O'Connor 1999: 59). Mordor Cave on the Cape York Peninsula has dingo remains in Stratigraphic Unit 2 but not in Stratigraphic Unit 3, which dates from 1580±70 BP (1565–1305 cal BP) (David & Dagg 1993).

The suggestion that dingoes were brought to Australia by people *after*, rather than before, 3500 years ago is also consistent with evidence from New Guinea and islands to Australia's north where dog bones are not found in contexts older than 3300 years ago. The earliest evidence for dogs in New Ireland (Papua New Guinea) is from the Kamgot site on Anir Island where dog bones are in the Early Lapita layer dated to between c. 3300 and 3000 cal BP (Summerhayes, Szabó, Leavesley, & Gaffney 2019; Summerhayes, Szabo, Fairbairn et al. 2019; Manne et al. 2020). On mainland Papua New Guinea, the oldest dog date is for a mandible from Late Lapita deposits with good stratigraphic integrity in the Moiapu 1 site at Caution Bay, where it is associated with a date of between 2573 and 2702 cal BP (Manne et al. 2020). In Southeast Asia, the oldest evidence for dogs is a burial from Matja Kuru 2 Cave in East Timor, at ~3000 cal BP (Gonzales, Clark, O'Connor, & Matisoo-Smith 2013). Stable isotope analyses indicate that in life this Timor dog ate a diet dominated by terrestrial plant foods rather than meat and thus was living in an agricultural community (Gonzales et al. 2013: 14).

Fillios and Taçon (2016) argue against the scenario that the dingo was introduced to Australia as a domestic commensal on the basis that pottery and other Neolithic cultural traits do not appear in the Australian archaeological record at the time of the dingo's arrival. However, this is a nonsequitur as prehistory presents numerous examples of the resident population's rejection of introduced cultural items and practices. For example, we know that when Macassans from the island of Sulawesi arrived on the Arnhem Land coast about 400 years ago (Taçon et al. 2010), they brought pottery and a knowledge of agricultural practices (e.g., Macknight 1976), but despite extensive interaction and exchange, the Indigenous Australians adopted neither pottery manufacture nor agriculture.

As dingoes arrived in Australia after the sea-level rise, they must have come by watercraft, as travel to Australia from Wallacea involves a water crossing of at least 150 km. It can therefore be assumed that dingoes came with people and that they arrived as tamed animals. It is unlikely that the dingo was present on watercraft as food, as the Wallacean waters are some of the richest fishing grounds in the world and carrying extra load would have been both unnecessary and hazardous.

Where Did Dingoes Come From?

The origin of the dingo remains unresolved, but much of the recent debate has been based on findings from research on genetics, albeit with variable results. Savolainen Leitner, Wilton, Matisoo-Smith, & Lundeberg (2004) analysed modern mtDNA from dingoes, Eurasian wolves, and dogs from across the globe, as well as archaeological dog samples from Polynesia. They identified a distinctive substitution in dingo mtDNA

(A29). From this study, they suggest that the dingo lineage originated from a domestic population in east Asia ~5000 years ago, and spread with people through Taiwan, the Philippines, and into Island Southeast Asia (ISEA) after 4000 BP as part of a widespread and rapid Austronesian expansion.

A contrasting interpretation is Oskarsson et al.'s (2012) comparison of the frequency and distribution of modern dog haplotypes in Mainland Southeast Asia (MSEA) and ISEA, including samples from Taiwan and the Philippines, with dingoes (A29) and ancient Polynesian dogs (Arc1 and Arc2). They found that all three haplotypes were present in South China, MSEA, and Indonesia, but absent in Taiwan and the Philippines. These results indicate that Australian dingoes were introduced from South China/MSEA rather than via a northern route through Taiwan and the Philippines. Oskarsson et al.'s results also differ from Savolainen and colleagues (2004) in suggesting that the separation of the dingo lineage occurred before the Neolithic. The study of Sacks et al. (2013), based on Y chromosome analysis, largely supports the findings of Oskarsson et al. (2012) that dingoes more likely originated in MSEA rather than Taiwan, although they suggest that a Taiwan origin remains a possibility. The presence of a unique haplogroup in dingoes that was not seen in ISEA dog populations was argued to indicate direct translocation from the Mainland (or Taiwan) to Australia, with mutations interpreted as indicating that the separation occurred between 5000 and 4000 years ago. Freedman et al. (2014) also propose an origin for the dingo in MSEA and a pre-Neolithic translocation. They found that dingoes have only two copies of the starch digestion gene; they therefore reason that its separation must have occurred before dogs were domesticated and were eating a diet rich in cereals.

Recent complete DNA sequencing of modern wild populations of dingoes (Cairns, Brown, Sacks, & Ballard 2017; Cairns, Shannon, Koler-Matznick, Ballard, & Boyko 2018; Cairns & Wilton 2016; Zhang et al. 2020), together with morphological analysis (Koungoulos 2020), have suggested that there are two distinct populations with divergent evolutionary histories in Australia today: a northwest lineage and a southeast lineage. Cairns and colleagues (2018) suggest that the Fraser Island dingoes represent a third genetically identifiable group and are most closely related to the northwest dingoes. These researchers believe that this diversity supports at least two separate dingo immigrations into Australia, probably from different ancestral populations, with the southeastern dingoes sharing ancestry with Southeast Asian dogs. While no clear ancestral relationship is proposed for the northwest/Fraser Island lineages, they may have a separate evolutionary origin in an as yet unsampled area of Asia.

Cairns and colleagues (2018) also explored the phylogenetic relationship between dingoes and New Guinea singing dogs (NGSDs). Their analyses confirmed that NGSDs form a separate lineage, distinct from but related to all the dingo lineages; this suggests that the NGSDs diverged before the differentiation of the dingo lineages occurred. While this hypothesis is plausible, the suggestion by Cairns and Wilton (2016) that dingoes most likely immigrated from New Guinea via the land bridge that connected it to Australia until ~8000 years ago cannot be sustained due to the absence of dogs anywhere in New Guinea before ~3300 years ago, coupled with the most recent assessment of the arrival time for the dingo in Australia discussed above. Nevertheless, it is possible that dogs may have reached Australia from New Guinea travelling with people on boats through the Torres Strait Islands and down the northeastern coast of Queensland in the Late Holocene (McNiven & Hitchcock 2004: 121). This view receives some support from geometric morphometric studies that show affinities between the southeast dingo population and NGSDs (Koungoulos 2020). However, Koungoulos' study is at odds with a recent study by Manne et al. (2020: Fig. 10) based on M1 teeth measurements on NGSDs and other New Guinea dog specimens, including Moiapu 1 from Caution Bay, and Australian dingoes. Their work supports a separate origin for the dingo from all the Melanesian dogs and indicates that the dog was introduced into New Guinea more than once. They suggest that the absence of dogs in mainland New Guinea sites prior to late Lapita times demonstrates that they are not descended from an earlier Melanesian population (as represented by the Kamgot dog in New Ireland), but rather result from a separate introduction of the dog into New Guinea from Island Southeast Asia after ~2700 cal BP. If they are correct, then the Australian dingo cannot have derived from New Guinea, for it was already widely spread throughout mainland Australia by this time. While it remains a possibility that the southeast Australian dingo lineage may be derived from the initial Melanesian dog dispersal indicated by Kamgot, it seems unlikely that this could have occurred without leaving a trace in either mainland New Guinea or the Torres Strait Islands. As Manne et al. (2020: 10) point out, the fact that the 'Early Lapita Kamgot remains of New Ireland are the only known dog remains of that age east of Island Southeast Asia and north of Australia suggests that it probably represents an early dog arrival that did not survive into later times, probably due to limited (unviable) founder population(s).' There is no doubt that dogs resembling dingoes were present on the Torres Strait Islands at the time of early European contact (McNiven & Hitchcock 2004), but they may have reached these islands as the companions of people boating north from the Australian mainland. The Torres Strait was not a barrier to movement, with objects, ideas, and people moving fluidly south from New Guinea and north from Australia into the islands in the Late Holocene (see McNiven, 'Coral Sea', this volume).

Another view about the origin of the dingo comes from a recent human genetics study that found evidence of substantial gene flow between Indian populations and Australian populations estimated to have occurred ~4200 years ago (Pugach, Delfin, Gunnarsdóttir, Kayser, & Stoneking 2013). On this basis, the authors proposed an Indian origin for the dingo. An early morphometric study by Gollan (1982, 1984) also argued for an Indian origin for the dingo based on similarities between the crania of dingoes and Indian pariah dogs. However, Pugach and colleagues' interpretations have now been challenged as other studies have identified the genome of Australian Indigenous people as unique and of greater antiquity (e.g., Bergström et al. 2016; Nagle et al. 2017). In addition, dingo genetic studies (e.g., Cairns & Wilton 2016; Price & Bird 2013) have found that dingoes are more closely related to Southeast Asian dogs than European dogs.

The Dingo in a New Environment

The arrival of a large predator in a new continent clearly had the potential for initiating dramatic environmental changes, and dingoes have been suggested to have caused, or contributed to, declines of other animals across mainland Australia (Johnson & Wroe 2003). In particular, they have been implicated in the extinction of the thylacine (*Thylacinus cynocephalus*) (also known as the Tasmanian tiger) and the Tasmanian devil (*Sarcophilus* sp.). The dingo's proposed role in these extinctions varies. As a major contributor, it has been suggested that dingoes outcompeted these other large predators (e.g., Fillios, Crowther, & Letnic 2012; McNab 2005; Wroe, Clausen, McHenry, Moreno, & Cunningham 2007) or even reduced their populations by direct killing (Letnic, Fillios, & Crowther 2012). Other researchers have argued that such factors as Late Holocene climate change, changes in people's technology, human population increases, or a combination of these factors, acted in conjunction with the introduction of the dingo to cause the extinctions (Brown 2006; Johnson & Wroe 2003; Prowse, Johnson, Bradshaw, & Brook 2014; White, Mitchell, & Austin 2018). However, for the reasons we have discussed, most of these arguments have rested on the imprecise co-occurrence of the various factors. Recently, White, Saltré, Bradshaw, and Austin (2018) have used direct dates on mainland thylacine and Tasmanian devil subfossils, as well as dates that Rodríguez-Rey et al. (2015) have assessed as reliable for these species from the FosSahul database (Rodríguez-Rey et al. 2016), to model the likely mainland extirpation time for thylacine and the Tasmanian devil. White et al. conclude that the extinctions of the two species are likely to be synchronous, with the suggested extinction date being 3227 cal BP (CI: 3170–3281) for thylacines and 3179 cal BP (CI: 3131–3224) for Tasmanian devils. These dates are very close to our suggested dingo arrival date of 3363–3211 cal BP, which seemingly provides support for the dingoes' contribution to their extinctions. However, this hypothesis requires further investigation, and there remains a need for a greater number of direct dingo dates from different parts of the continent.

The Arrival of the Dingo and Indigenous People

Significantly, the arrival of the dingo in Australia would have had a tumultuous impact on the lifeways of Indigenous people. The close bond between dingoes and Indigenous Australians has been recorded by numerous observers (for summaries, see Balme & O'Connor 2016; Koungoulos & Fillios 2020a, 2020b; Smith 2015). Observations by early European settlers, anthropologists, and other written and visual sources suggest that dingoes were thoroughly incorporated into Indigenous people's kinship systems and

FIGURE 13.2. Modborronggo, one of the Lightning Brothers' dingoes at Yiwarlarlay in Wardaman Country, Northern Territory (Kelly, David, & Flood 2021). Information from Bruno David, as obtained on-site from Wardaman Elders Elsie Raymond and Tarpot Ngamunagami in 1989.

(Image courtesy of Bruno David and with permission from Wardaman people.)

cosmologies, holding important positions in stories, songlines, and ceremonies across vast areas of the continent (e.g., Berndt & Berndt 1942; Hamilton 1972; Meehan, Jones, & Vincent 1999; Rose 1992). Dingoes and dingo tracks also appear as rock art motifs (Figure 13.2), especially in northern Australia (e.g., Welch 1993; Wright 1968). Dingoes with especially close bonds to individuals were afforded burial rites similar to those of humans (see Gunn, Whear, & Douglas 2010; Meehan et al. 1999). In daily life, dingoes were used for a variety of purposes, such as for personal protection, warmth, companionship, and as 'living technology' for hunting.

One of the most contested issues pertaining to dingoes in the anthropological literature concerns their role in hunting. Gould (1967: 46), Hamilton (1972: 290), and White (1972: 204) state that in the groups with whom they worked in the desert region, dingoes were rarely employed as hunting aids. They note that it was only with the introduction of European dogs that hunting methods changed. In contrast, Hayden (1975) argued that dingoes had major economic benefits as hunting aids in arid and semiarid regions of Australia. It is often difficult to know whether ethnographic accounts refer to dingoes or dogs, as European dogs were introduced as working animals and spread rapidly with the European frontier across the continent. However, some early observations by European explorers, settlers, and anthropologists indicate that Aboriginal people may not have seen European dogs until the 1940s, and in some more remote areas of the desert, dogs did not replace dingoes in camps until the 1960s (Kästner 2012: 266). As such, accounts that predate this time probably refer to dingoes. Even today, there is surprisingly little hybridization in wild canids (Cairns, Nesbitt, Laffan, Letnic, & Crowther 2020).

Accounts of dingoes being used as a hunting aid suggest that their utility varied regionally or even locally depending on the terrain. In the deserts and semiarid regions with open vegetation associations that typify much of the country, dingoes are often reported as not being useful for hunting large game. For example, Hayden (1975) summarizes observations of hunting with dingoes in central Australia and frequently identifies kangaroos as the prey hunted. He concludes, however, that capture using dingoes as hunting aids was possibly less routine than when hunters were using other methods. Hamilton (1972: 291) records that dogs were a liability on men's hunting expeditions in the arid centre where stealth was the strategy used to capture prey, although she does report that dogs can be useful in herding kangaroos into blind gullies in the mountain range country (Hamilton 1972: 291). Gould (1969: 263) records a similar observation for the Western Desert region, an observation shared by Kolig (1978) for the Kimberley region and by White (1972) for people living in Yalata, South Australia. Presumably in these open areas, large game would have easily detected the presence of dingoes and have been scared off.

It is also possible that kangaroos were too fast for dogs to hunt down in open areas, as Nind (1831: 29) reports for southwestern Australia. However, Nind also reports that in this same region dogs were used to flush out game when 'numerous' hunters were available (1831: 30). In the tropical forests of northeastern Australia, there are records of dingoes being used to flush out and direct game into more open areas where they were ambushed by hunters (e.g., Lumholtz 1889: 196). Similar observations were made by Ward in his journals, which were published by Fountain (1907: 291). Ward's records are for northeastern Australia and almost certainly refer to forested environments as he remarks upon the absence of kangaroos away from the forest (Fountain 1907: 260). Thomson (1949: 65–66) records successful use of this same technique in Arnhem Land in northern Australia.

The utility of dingoes for men's hunting of large game, or indeed women's hunting as recorded by Kaberry (1939: 22) in the Kimberley and by Eylmann (1908: 276) for central Australia, appears to vary across the continent. However, dogs regularly accompanying women on their daily foraging trips are frequently remarked upon (e.g., Hamilton 1972; Gould 1969; Meehan et al. 1999). In the course of these foraging trips with dingoes, women's encounters with game would have dramatically increased. The game encountered were primarily a variety of small- to medium-sized animals—less than 10 kg (e.g., Hamilton 1972; Hayden 1975, Kästner 2012: 266; Meehan et al. 1999), such as bandicoots, brush kangaroo, and possums in southwest Australia (Nind 1831: 29) and snakes, rats, and lizards in western New South Wales (Curr 1886: 47). These sources indicate that when women used dingoes for hunting small- to medium-sized game, whether in the course of foraging for other foods or in expeditions specifically to target such game (e.g., Hamilton 1972; Meehan et al. 1999), they were highly successful. The varied prey of dingoes engaged in Aboriginal hunting expeditions is also consistent with current observations about the diets of dingoes/wild dogs, which shows them to be opportunistic hunters concentrating on abundant vertebrates (Corbett 1995) that are easy to access and catch (Corbett & Newsome 1987).

How Quickly Did Relationships between People and Dingoes Develop?

The oldest dated direct evidence of bonds between Aboriginal people and dingoes is a dingo burial found at Captain Stephensons Point at Mallacoota on the southeast coast of Australia. The shallow pit in which this dingo was buried was about 5 cm below a date on charcoal of 890±90BP (933–658 cal BP) (Gollan 1984: 340). It is unclear how long before this time that close relationships between dingoes and people may have formed. However, Balme and O'Connor (2016: 778) have suggested that it may have been very soon after the dingo's arrival on the continent. Their suggestion is based largely on the history of the introduction of European dogs in Tasmania where dingoes were not present. European dogs, such as Irish wolfhounds and deerhounds, were introduced specifically to help Europeans catch kangaroos until their own attempts at food production could be more successful (Boyce 2006: 106). Within the space of 20 years, dogs were incorporated into Tasmanian Aboriginal life. They were used for hunting, but even in areas such as the rugged west coast where large hunting dogs were of little use (Boyce 2006: 115), dogs were used as blankets and sentries, entered traditional trade and exchange systems (Jones 1970), and were incorporated into ritual life (e.g., Robinson November 1830: 278 in Plomley 1966).

The dingo was brought to Australia presumably as a commensal animal, and once the dingoes arrived, they became 'wild'. While the situation in Tasmania is different, in that there was no gap between domestication and adoption, it does illustrate the rapid incorporation of dogs into people's lives.

Interpreting Changes in the Holocene Archaeological Record and the Role of Dingoes

It is difficult to document the development of the relationship between dingoes and Indigenous people. While we have suggested that the relationship may have developed very quickly, identifying the uptake in the archaeological record is not easy. Whereas elsewhere in the world, early relationships between people and dogs are identified from morphological changes resulting from selective breeding of dogs, there is little morphological evidence for such selection registered in fossil dingo bones, including those recovered from archaeological sites. This absence suggests that new genetic stock was constantly being added to Aboriginal camp dogs (Gollan 1982), and for this reason, camp dingoes have to be thought of as commensal rather than as domesticated animals.

Direct archaeological evidence for a close bond between people and dingoes, such as in rock art and burials, is not very useful, as rock art is very difficult to date and evidence from burials relies on excellent preservation and is rarely found. Direct evidence for the use of dogs as a hunting technology (e.g., Perri 2020; Shipman 2010) similarly relies on preservation of fragile bones and/or materials, such as dog shelters and collars, not usually associated with hunter-gatherer societies. Thus, archaeological evidence has to be derived from indirect evidence.

If dingoes were incorporated quickly into Aboriginal culture, we should be able to see evidence for changes in subsistence and concomitant evidence for higher population densities and increased sedentism. This is, in fact, exactly what we see in the Australian archaeological record in the Late Holocene.

In the late 1970s and 1980s, a number of Australian archaeologists (see papers in David, Barker, & McNiven 2006; Lourandos 1980, 1985; Morwood 1987) recognized changes in the archaeological record, including resource diversification, novel stone tool and plant processing technologies, and, in some cases, increased sedentism beginning about 4000 years ago. These changes were seen as reflecting 'intensification' or increased investment in resource extraction across a range of environments using novel technologies and as being largely internally driven by changes in social complexity. Over the last few years, it has been increasingly recognized that many of the changes identified in these early papers had their antecedents earlier in the Holocene and that what we see in the Late Holocene is their efflorescence. It has also been recognized that the nature and distribution of these changes varied regionally (see Ulm 2013 for a summary). Despite this recognition, it is widely acknowledged that the Australian archaeological record has seen a net increase in number of sites, density of nonorganic assemblages, as well as great varieties of technologies and site types in the Late Holocene. For example, Williams and colleagues (Williams, Ulm, Turney, Rohde, & White 2015; Williams, Veth, Steffen et al. 2015) have used time-series modelling of radiocarbon dates from sites across Australia to hypothesize population changes over time. Most significantly, they note that after about 4000 cal BP, for the first time there was a decoupling of population and environmental change. Instead of declining in the face of a climatic downturn resulting from El Niño Southern Oscillation (ENSO), populations increased exponentially until the arrival of Europeans. They suggest that the efflorescence of technologies previously developed is explained by their more widespread use to sustain these populations (Williams, Ulm, Turney et al. 2015). We propose an alternative (or additional) interpretation of this data—that changes in women's hunting with the uptake of dingoes as hunting partners explain the increase in the number of sites and more intensive occupation of sites after 3500 years ago.

Balme and O'Connor (2016) have argued that the partnership of women and dingoes would have had significant effects on the social and economic lifeways of Indigenous people. Dingoes effectively increased women's prey encounter rate and probably broadened women's prey selection and their contribution of meat to the diet. Not only were economic lives changed, but there would have been a substantial reorganization of gender roles in the food quest. Increasing the amount of protein in women's diets is also likely to have improved women's fecundity (Marlowe 2001) and undoubtedly the health of the children accompanying them. This, in turn, is likely to have resulted in shorter spacing between births and lowered infant/child mortality. More reliable nutrition would also have allowed longer patch residence times (freshwater permitting). The sum outcome of these changes would be predicted to be seen in increases in sedentism of local groups in the better-watered parts of Australia and an increase in population size over the Late Holocene. As we discuss below, this is precisely what we see in the Australian archaeological record.

Women's changing role in the food quest may have given rise to other changes in Indigenous societies associated with the Late Holocene, for example, 'prestige hunting' by men. Ethnographic accounts of large-game hunting in traditional hunter-gatherer societies indicate that it was usually the focus of men. However, despite the time and effort devoted to it, large-game hunting was frequently unsuccessful. Anthropologists have seen this as a type of 'costly signalling', alerting other members of the group to the qualities or prowess of the hunter (e.g., Bliege-Bird, Smith, & Bird 2001; Hawkes 1991; Speth 2010). One might interpret some men's hunting tools, such as Kimberley points, which began to be manufactured or had an efflorescence in the Late Holocene, as a technological extension of this competitive male signalling (e.g., Moore 2013) and as a response to women's greater success at hunting.

These changes in subsistence organization should be evident in Late Holocene faunal assemblages from archaeological sites. The changes might vary depending on the environment, but, in most sites, assemblages would show an increase in the proportion and number of small and mid-sized animal species in comparison to assemblages from palaeontological sites. Of course, this might be complicated by the nature of the commensal relationship between dingoes and people. If dingoes are sharing the same camp as people, they may remove and eat the bones discarded by people, thus decreasing the likelihood that such changes, if they occurred, could be elucidated from the archaeological record.

Changes in the diversity of the fauna and a reduction in their size from the Late Holocene in a few archaeological sites have been noted by several researchers. Explanations include economic intensification in southwestern Victoria (Lourandos 1985) and southeastern Queensland (Morwood 1987); changes in technology, particularly axes, that are relevant to the capture of small nocturnal animals in the northern tablelands of New South Wales (McBryde 1985); and the overpredation of large mammals by dingoes (Fillios et al. 2012; Fillios, Gordon, Koch, & Letnic 2010) or by a combination of overpredation by dingoes of large animals and human selection of 'less risky' smaller animals (Koungoulos 2017).

This evidence for changes in the faunal composition toward smaller animals in the Late Holocene archaeological record is tantalizing and has been also presented as possibly related to the arrival of the dingo (Balme & O'Connor 2016; Koungoulos & Fillios 2020b; Fillios et al. 2010; Letnic, Fillios, & Crowther 2014). However, the inadequacy of the time resolution and small sample sizes in these sites makes it difficult to disentangle the changes from other possible causes, such as climate change. For example, the sequence in Tunnel Cave in southwest Australia, which is mentioned in all four papers listed above, has higher proportions of smaller animals in stratigraphic layers 1 and 2 which occur above a date of 4280±60 (4894–4574 cal BP) obtained for stratigraphic layer 3 (Dortch 2004: 77). Precisely when the changes occurred after that date is not clear, as the only available date above it is 1370±40 (1309–1176 cal BP) from stratigraphic layer 1. Because radiocarbon dates for the site suggest that deposition was uneven (Dortch 2004: 77), averaging the two dates to obtain a date for layer 2 is not appropriate. In addition, as many of the other sites discussed by these authors were analysed in the 1970s when it was common to identify only a few anatomical elements and fewer radiocarbon dates were obtained, none of the analyses are in sufficient detail or with adequate time resolution to resolve the timing and causes of these changes, or indeed, to ascertain whether the changes did in fact occur. Evaluating this evidence will have to wait until new analyses are available. Nevertheless, it is worth mentioning that not all Australian sites follow this pattern. For example, at Carpenters Gap 1 in northwest Australia, there is an increase in medium- and large-sized macropods in the Holocene (Maloney, O'Connor, Wood, Aplin, & Balme 2018: 222). At Riwi, also in the northwest but closer to the desert than Carpenters Gap 1, an increase in the abundance and proportions of medium- and large-sized macropods begins 34,000 years ago and continues throughout the Holocene (Balme et al. 2019).

DISCUSSION AND CONCLUSION

The development of a close relationship between people and canids, which in some places led to dog domestication (e.g., Clutton Brock 1995; Shipman 2015), is usually linked to their use as cooperative hunters. However, in the course of the development of this relationship, dogs undoubtedly took on many other roles such as companions, guards, blankets. The utility of dogs as hunting aids depends on many factors, including environment, prey type, and other technology (see Lupo 2017; Perri 2020). Whatever the case, their use as hunters may have had a profound effect on other aspects of society. We have argued that the arrival of dingoes on the Australian continent in the Late Holocene had a dramatic influence on Indigenous societies. In the open Australian environments, dingoes served as living hunting technology, primarily for women, and the consequences of the increased contribution of meat to the diet would have improved fecundity, leading to larger populations. The greater meat contribution of women would have had follow-on effects, such as the development of men's prestige hunting and associated technologies, ceremonies and songlines associated with hunting, and the myriad other roles dingoes played in society. Because of the varying utility of dogs in hunting, elsewhere in the world newly formed relationships between people and canids may not have had the same consequences, but, as labour is gender-divided in all human societies, it is worth considering the wider effects of dogs as hunting aids.

Note

1. All calibration of radiocarbon dating was done using OxCal to 2 sigma using the SHCal13 calibration curve (Bronk Ramsey 2009).

References

Archer, M. (1974). New information about the Quaternary distribution of the thylacine (Marsupialia, Thylacinidae) in Australia. *Journal of the Royal Society of Western Australia, 57* (2), 43–50.

Ballard, J., & Wilson, L. (2019). The Australian dingo: Untamed or feral? *Frontiers in Zoology, 16* , 2, doi.org/10.1186/s12983-019-0300-6.

Balme, J., & O'Connor, S. (2016). Dingoes and Aboriginal social organisation in Holocene Australia. *Journal of Archaeological Science: Reports, 7* , 775–781.

Balme, J., O'Connor, S., & Fallon, S. (2018). New dates on dingo bones from Madura Cave provide oldest firm evidence for arrival of the species in Australia. *Scientific Reports, 8* , doi:10.1038/s41598–018-28324-X 1.

Balme, J., O'Connor, S., Maloney, T., Vannieuwenhuyse, D., Aplin, K., & Dilkes-Hall, I. E. (2019). Long-term occupation on the edge of the desert: Riwi Cave in the southern Kimberley, Western Australia. *Archaeology in Oceania, 54* , 35–52.

Bergström, A., Nagle, N., Chen, Y., McCarthy, S., Pollard, M. O., Ayub, Q., . . . Mitchell, J. (2016). Deep roots for Aboriginal Australian Y chromosomes. *Current Biology, 26*, doi: org/10.1016/j.cub.2016.01.028.

Berndt, R. M., & Berndt, C. H. (1942). A preliminary report of fieldwork in the Ooldea region, western South Australia. *Oceania, 13*(2), 143–169.

Bliege Bird, R., Smith, E., & Bird, D. (2001). The hunting handicap: Costly signaling in human foraging strategies. *Behavioural Ecology and Sociobiology, 50* , 9–19.

Boyce, J. (2006). Canine revolution: The social and environmental impact of the introduction of the dog to Tasmania. *Environmental History, 11* , 102–129.

Bromham, L. (2019). Six impossible things to do before breakfast: Assumptions, models, and belief in molecular dating. *Trends in Ecology and Evolution, 35* (5), 474–486.

Bronk Ramsey, C. (2009). Bayesian analysis of radiocarbon dates. *Radiocarbon, 51* (1), 337–360.

Brown, O. J. F. (2006). Tasmanian devil (*Sarcophilus harrisii*) extinction on the Australian mainland in the mid-Holocene: Multicausality and ENSO intensification. *Alcheringa, 30* (Supplement 1), 49–57.

Cairns, K. M., Brown, S. K., Sacks, B. N., & Ballard, J. W. O. (2017). Conservation implications for dingoes from the maternal and paternal genome: Multiple populations, dog introgression, and demography. *Ecology and Evolution, 7* , 9787–9807.

Cairns, K. M., Nesbitt, B. J., Laffan, S. W., Letnic, M., & Crowther, M. S. (2020). Geographic hot spots of dingo genetic ancestry in southeastern Australia despite hybridisation with domestic dogs. *Conservation Genetics, 21* , 77–90.

Cairns, K. M., Shannon, L. M., Koler-Matznick, J., Ballard, J. W. O., & Boyko, A. R. (2018). Elucidating biogeographical patterns in Australian native canids using genome wide SNPs. *PLoS ONE 13* (6), e0198754, doi.org/10.1371/journal.pone.0198754.

Cairns, K. M., & Wilton, A. N. (2016). New insights on the history of canids in Oceania based on mitochondrial and nuclear data. *Genetica, 144*, 553–565.

Campbell, V. A. (1988). *The coastal archaeology of the Fleurieu Peninsula: Preliminary investigations* (Unpublished MA thesis). Flinders University, South Australia.

Clarkson, C., Jacobs, Z., Marwick, B., Fullagar, R., Wallis, L., Smith, M., . . . Pardoe, C. (2017). Human occupation of northern Australia by 65,000 years ago. *Nature, 547*, 306–310.

Clutton-Brock, J. (1995). Origins of the dog: Domestication and early history. In J. Serpell (Ed.), *The domestic dog: Its evolution, behaviour, and interactions with people* (pp. 7–20). Cambridge: Cambridge University Press.

Corbett, L. K. (1995). *The dingo in Australia and Asia*. Sydney: UNSW Press.

Corbett, L. K., & Newsome, A. E. (1987). The feeding ecology of the dingo. III. Dietary relationships with widely fluctuating prey populations in arid Australia: An hypothesis of alternation of predation. *Oecologia, 74*, 215–227.

Crowther, M., Fillios, M., Colman, N., & Letnic, M. (2014). An updated description of the Australian dingo (*Canis dingo* Meyer, 1793). *Journal of Zoology, 293* (3), 192–203.

Curr, E. M. (1886). *The Australian race*, Vol. 2. Melbourne: John Ferres, Government Printer.

David, B., Barker, B., & McNiven, I. J. (Eds.) (2006). *The social archaeology of Australian Indigenous societies*. Canberra: Aboriginal Studies Press.

David, B., & Dagg, L. (1993). Two caves. *Memoirs of the Queensland Museum, 33* (1), 143–162.

Dortch, J. (2004). *Palaeo-environmental change and the persistence of human occupation in south-western Australian forests*. BAR International Series 1288. Oxford: Archaeopress.

Etheridge, R., Jr. (1916). The cylindro-conical and cornute stone implements of western New South Wales: The warrigal, or 'dingo' introduced or indigenous? *Memoirs of the Geological Survey of New South Wales, Ethnological Series, 2*, 1–70.

Eylmann, E. (1908). *Die eingeborenen der colonie Südaustralien* (*The Natives of the Colony of South Australia*). Berlin: Reiner.

Fillios, M., Crowther, M., & Lentic, M. (2012). The impact of the dingo on the thylacine in Holocene Australia. *World Archaeology, 44*(1),118–134.

Fillios, M., Gordon, C., Koch, F., & Letnic, M. (2010). The effect of a top predator on kangaroo abundance in arid Australia and its implications for archaeological faunal assemblages. *Journal of Archaeological Science, 37*, 986–993.

Fillios, M., & Taçon, P. (2016). Who let the dogs in? A review of the recent genetic evidence for the introduction of the dingo to Australia and implications for the movement of people. *Journal of Archaeological Science: Reports, 7*, 782–792.

Fountain, P. (1907). *Rambles of an Australian naturalist*. London: John Murray.

Freedman, A. H., Gronau, I., Schweizer, R. M., Ortega-Del Vecchyo, D., Han, E., Silva, P. M., . . . Novembre, J. (2014). Genome sequencing highlights the dynamic early history of dogs. *PLOS Genetics, 10* (8), e1004016.

Gollan, K. (1982). *Prehistoric dingo* (PhD thesis). Australian National University, Canberra.

Gollan, K. (1984). The Australian dingo: In the shadow of man. In M. Archer & G. Clayton (Eds.), *Vertebrate zoogeography and evolution in Australia: Animals in space and time* (pp. 921–927). Carlisle: Hesperian Press.

Gonzales, A., Clark, G., O'Connor, S., & Matisoo-Smith, L. (2013). A 3000 year old dog burial in Timor-Leste. *Australian Archaeology, 76*, 13–20.

Gould, R. (1967). Notes on hunting, butchering, and sharing of game among the Ngatatjara and their neighbors in the West Australian desert. *Kroeber Anthropological Society Papers, 36*, 41–66.

Gould, R. (1969). Subsistence behaviour among the Western Desert Aborigines of Australia. *Oceania, 39*, 253–274.

Gunn, R. G., Whear, R. L., & Douglas, L. C. (2010). A dingo burial from Arnhem Land plateau. *Australian Archaeology, 71*, 11–16.

Hamilton, A. (1972). Aboriginal man's best friend? *Mankind, 82*, 87–295.

Hawkes, K. (1991). Showing off: Tests of a hypothesis about men's foraging goals. *Ethology and Sociobiology, 12*, 29–54.

Hayden, B. (1975). Dingoes: Pets or producers? *Mankind, 10*, 1–15.

Jackson, S., Fleming, P., Eldridge, M., Ingleby, S., Flannery, T., Johnson, R., ... Helgen, K. (2019). The dogma of dingoes—Taxonomic status of the dingo: A reply to Smith et al. *Zootaxa, 4564*(1), 198.

Jackson, S., Groves, C. P., Fleming, P. J. S., Aplin, K. P., Eldridge, M. D. G., Gonzalez, A., & Helgen, K. M. (2017). The wayward dog: Is the Australian native dog or dingo a distinct species? *Zootaxa, 4317*(2), 201–224.

Johnson, C., & Wroe, S. (2003). Causes of extinction of vertebrates during the Holocene of mainland Australia: Arrival of the dingo or human impact? *The Holocene, 13*, 941–948.

Jones, R. (1970). Tasmanian Aborigines and dogs. *Mankind, 7*, 256–271.

Kaberry, P. M. (1939). *Aboriginal woman sacred and profane*. London: Routledge. (Second edition Taylor and Francis [2003]).

Kästner, S. (2012). *Jagende sammlerinnen und sammelnde jägerinnen. Wie Australische Aborigines-frauen tiere erbeuten* (Hunting gatheresses and gathering huntresses: How Australian Aboriginal women hunt animals). Ethnologie Band 42. Berlin: Lit Verlag.

Kelly, M., David, B., & Flood, J. (2021). Scene but not heard: Seeing scenes in a northern Australian Aboriginal site. In I. Davidson & A. Nowell (Eds.), *Making scenes: Global perspectives on scenes in rock art*. New York: Berghahn Books.

Kolig, E. (1978). Aboriginal dogmatics: Canines in theory, myth and dogma. *Bijdragen tot de Taal-, Land- en Volkenkunde, 134*(1), 84–115.

Koungoulos, L. (2017). *Canis dingo* and the Australian fauna trend: A new explanatory model integrating ecological data. *Journal of Archaeological Science: Reports, 14*, 38–45.

Koungoulos, L. (2020). Old dogs, new tricks: 3D geometric analysis of cranial morphology supports ancient population substructure in the Australian dingo. *Zoomorphology, 139*, 263–275.

Koungoulos, L., & Fillios, M. (2020a). Between ethnography and prehistory: The case of the Australian dingo. In B. Bethke & A. Burtt (Eds.), *Dogs: Archaeology of the human-canine connection beyond domestication* (pp. 206–231). Gainesville: University Press of Florida.

Koungoulos, L., & Fillios, M. (2020b). Hunting dogs down under? On the Aboriginal use of tame dingoes in dietary game acquisition and its relevance to Australian prehistory. *Journal of Anthropological Archaeology, 58*, doi.org/10–1016/j.jaa.2020.101146.

Krefft, G. (1870). *Guide to Australian fossil remains exhibited by the trustees of the Australian Museum and arranged and named by Gerard Krefft, F.L.S., curator and secretary*. Sydney: F. White.

Lambeck, K., & Chappell, J. (2001). Sea level change through the last glacial cycle. *Science, 27*, 679–686.

Letnic, M., Fillios, M., & Crowther, M. (2012). Could direct killing by larger dingoes have caused the extinction of the thylacine from mainland Australia? *PLoS One, 7*(5), e34877.

Letnic, M., Fillios, M., & Crowther, M. S. (2014). The arrival and impacts of the dingo. In A. S. Glen & C. R. Dickman (Eds.), *Carnivores of Australia: Past, present and future* (pp. 55–69). Melbourne: CSIRO Publishing.

Lourandos, H. (1980). Change or stability? Hydraulics, hunter-gatherers and population in temperate Australia. *World Archaeology, 11*, 245–266.

Lourandos, H. (1985). Intensification and Australian prehistory. In T. D. Price & J. A. Brown (Eds.), *Prehistoric hunter–gatherers: The emergence of cultural complexity* (pp. 385–423). Orlando, FL: Academic Press.

Lowry, J., & Merrilees, D. (1969). Age of the desiccated carcase of a thylacine (Marsupialia, Dasyuroidea) from Thylacine Hole, Nullarbor region, Australia. *Helictite, 7* (1), 15–16.

Lumholtz, C. (1889). *Among cannibals: Account of four years travels in Australia, and camp life with the Aborigines of Queensland.* (Facsimile of 1st edition [1980]). Canberra: Australian National University Press.

Lupo, K. D. (2017). When and where do dogs improve hunting productivity? The empirical record and some implications for early Upper Paleolithic prey acquisition. *Journal of Anthropological Archaeology, 47*, 139–151.

MacKnight, C. C. (1976). *The Voyage to Marege': Macassan trepangers in northern Australia.* Carlton: Melbourne University Press.

Maloney, T., O'Connor, S., Wood, R., Aplin, K., & Balme, J. (2018). Carpenters Gap 1: A 47,000 year old record of indigenous adaptation and innovation. *Quaternary Science Reviews, 191*, 204–228.

Manne, T., David, B., Petchey, F., Leavesley, M., Roberts, G., Szabo, K., . . . Richards, T. (2020). How long have dogs been in Melanesia? New evidence from Caution Bay, south coast of Papua New Guinea. *Journal of Archaeological Science: Reports, 30*, doi.org/10–1016/j.jasrep.2020.102255.

Marlowe, F. (2001). Male contribution to diet and female reproductive success among foragers. *Current Anthropology, 42*, 755–760.

McBryde, I. (1985). Backed blade industries from the Graman rock shelters, NSW: Some evidence on function. In P. Bellwood & V. N. Misra (Eds.), *New advances in Indo-Pacific prehistory* (pp. 231–248). New Delhi: Oxford and IBH Publishing Co.

McCoy, F. (1882). The dingo, prodromus of the palaeontology of Victoria. *Geological Survey of Victoria, 7*, 7–10.

McNab, B. K. (2005). Uniformity in the basal metabolic rate of marsupials its causes and consequences. *Revista Chilena de Historia Natural, 78*, 183–198.

McNiven, I. J., & Hitchcock, G. (2004). Torres Strait Islander marine subsistence specialisation and terrestrial animal translocation. *Memoirs of the Queensland Museum Cultural Heritage Series, 3* (1), 105–162.

Meehan, B., Jones, R., & Vincent, A. (1999). Gulu-kula: Dogs in Anbarra society, Arnhem Land. *Aboriginal History, 23*, 83–106.

Milham, P., & Thompson, P. (1976). Relative antiquity of human occupation and extinct fauna at Madura Cave, southeastern Western Australia. *Mankind, 10* (3), 175–180.

Moore, M. (2013). Simple stone flaking in Australasia: Patterns and implications. *Quaternary International, 285*, 140–149.

Morwood, M. (1987). The archaeology of social complexity in south-east Queensland. *Proceedings of the Prehistoric Society, 53*, 337–350.

Nagle, N., van Oven, M., Wilcox, S., van Holst Pellekaan, S., Tyler-Smith, C., Xue, Y., . . . Mitchell, R. J. (2017). Aboriginal Australian mitochondrial genome variation—an increased understanding of population antiquity and diversity. *Scientific Reports, 7* , 43041, doi.org/10.1038/srep43041.

Nind, S. (1831). Description of the natives of King George's Sound (Swan River Colony) and adjoining country. *Royal Geographic Society Journal, 1* , 21–51.

O'Connor, S. (1999). *30,000 years of Aboriginal occupation: Kimberley, north west Australia.* Terra Australis 14. Canberra: ANU E Press.

Oskarsson, M. C. R., Klütsch, C. F. C., Boonyaprakob, U., Wilton, A., Tanabe, Y., & Savolainen, P. (2012). Mitochondrial DNA data indicate an introduction through Mainland Southeast Asia for Australian dingoes and Polynesian domestic dogs. *Proceedings of the Royal Society B. Biological Sciences, 279* , 967–974.

Perri, A. (2020). Prehistoric dogs as hunting tools: The advent of animal biotechnology. In B. Bethke & A. Burtt (Eds.), *Dogs: Archaeology of the human-canine connection beyond domestication* (pp. 7–44). Gainesville: University Press of Florida.

Plomley, N. J. B. (1966). *Friendly mission, the Tasmanian journals and papers of George Augustus Robinson, 1829–34.* Hobart: Tasmanian Historical Research Association.

Price, M. H., & Bird, D. W. (2013). Interpreting the evidence for middle Holocene gene flow from India to Australia. *Proceedings of the National Academy of Sciences of the United States of America, 110*(32), 2948.

Prowse, T. A. A., Johnson, C. N., Bradshaw, C. J. A., & Brook, B. W. (2014). An ecological regime shift resulting from disrupted predator-prey interactions in Holocene Australia. *Ecology, 95* (3), 693–702.

Pugach, I., Delfin, F., Gunnarsdóttir, E., Kayser, M., & Stoneking, M. (2013). Genome-wide data substantiate Holocene gene flow from India to Australia. *Proceedings of the National Academy of Sciences of the United States of America, 110* (5), 1803–1808.

Rodríguez-Rey, M., Herrando-Pérez, S., Brook, B. W., Saltré, F., Alroy, J., Beeton, N., . . . Bradshaw, C. J. A. (2016). FosSahul database, Version 1. ÆKOS Data Portal, rights owned by University of Adelaide, http://doi.org/10.4227/05/56F077B3054E9.

Rodríguez-Rey, M., Herrando-Pérez, S., Gillespie, R., Jacobs, Z., Saltré, F., Brook, B. W., . . . Bradshaw, C. J. A. (2015). Criteria for assessing the quality of Middle Pleistocene to Holocene vertebrate fossil ages. *Quaternary Geochronology, 30* , 69–79.

Rose, D. B. (1992). *Dingo makes us human: Life and land in an Aboriginal Australian culture.* Cambridge: Cambridge University Press.

Sacks, B. N., Brown, S. K., Stephens, D., Pedersen, N. C., Wu, J.-T., & Berry, O. (2013). Y chromosome analysis of dingoes and Southeast Asian village dogs suggests a neolithic continental expansion from Southeast Asia followed by multiple Austronesian dispersals. *Molecular Biology and Evolution, 30* (5), 1103–1118.

Savolainen, P., Leitner, T., Wilton, A., Matisoo-Smith, E., & Lundeberg, J. (2004). A detailed picture of the origin of the Australian dingo, obtained from the study of mitochondrial DNA. *Proceedings of the National Academy of Sciences of the United States of America, 101*(33), 12387–12390.

Schrire, C. (1982). *The Alligator Rivers: Prehistory and ecology in western Arnhem Land.* Canberra: Department of Prehistory, Research School of Pacific Studies, Australian National University.

Shipman, P. (2010). The animal connection and human evolution. *Current Anthropology, 51* (4), 519–538.

Shipman, P. (2015). *The invaders: How humans and their dogs drove Neanderthals to extinction.* Cambridge, MA: Harvard University Press.

Skoglund, P., Ersmark, E., Palkopoulou, E., & Dalén, L. (2015). Ancient wolf genome reveals an early divergence of domestic dog ancestors and admixture into high-latitude breeds. *Current Biology, 25* (11), 1515–1519.

Smith, B. (2015). The role of dingoes in Indigenous Australian lifestyle, culture, and spirituality. In B. Smith (Ed.), *The dingo debate: Origins, behaviour and conservation* (pp. 81–101). Melbourne: CSIRO Publishing.

Smith, B. P., Cairns, K. M., Adams, J. W., Newsome, T. M., Fillios, M., Déaux, E. C., . . . Crowther, M. S. (2019). Taxonomic status of the Australian dingo: The case for *Canis dingo* Meyer, 1793. *Zootaxa, 4564* (1), 173–197.

Speth, J. D. (2010). *The paleoanthropology and archaeology of big-game hunting: Protein, fat or politics?* New York: Springer.

Summerhayes, G. R., Szabó, K., Fairbairn, A., Horrocks, M., McPherson, S., & Crowther, A. (2019). Early Lapita subsistence: Evidence from Kamgot, Anir Islands, New Ireland Province, Papua New Guinea. In S. Bedford & M. Spriggs (Eds.), *Debating Lapita: Chronology, society and subsistence* (pp. 380–402). Terra Australis 52. Canberra: Australian National University Press.

Summerhayes, G. R., Szabó, K., Leavesley, M., & Gaffney, D. (2019). Kamgot at the lagoon's edge: Site position and resource use of an Early Lapita site in Near Oceania. In S. Bedford & M. Spriggs (Eds.), *Debating Lapita: Chronology, society and subsistence* (pp. 89–103). Terra Australis 52. Canberra: Australian National University Press.

Taçon, P. S. C., May, S. K., Fallon, S. J., Travers, M., Wesley, D., & Lamilami, R. (2010). A minimum age for the early depictions of Southeast Asian praus in the rock art of Arnhem Land, Northern Territory. *Australian Archaeology, 71* , 1–10.

Thomson, D. F. (1949). Arnhem Land: Explorations among an unknown people part III. On foot across Arnhem Land. *The Geographic Journal, 114* , 53–67.

Ulm, S. (2013). 'Complexity' and the Australian continental narrative: Themes in the archaeology of Holocene Australia. *Quaternary International, 285* , 182–192.

Walshe, K. (2017). Koonalda Cave, Nullarbor Plain, South Australia—Issues in optical and radiometric dating of deep karst caves. *Geochronometria, 44* , 366–373.

Welch, D. (1993). The early rock art of the Kimberley, Australia: Developing a chronology. In I. Steinbring & A. Watchman (Eds.), *Time and space: Dating and spatial considerations in rock art research papers of Symposia F and E, Second AURA Congress, Cairns 1992* (pp. 13–21). Occasional AURA Publication 8. Melbourne: Australian Rock Art Research Association.

White, I. (1972). Hunting dogs at Yalata. *Mankind, 8* (3), 201–205.

White, L. C., Mitchell, K. J., & Austin, J. J. (2018). Ancient mitochondrial genomes reveal the demographic history and phylogeography of the extinct, enigmatic thylacine (*Thylacinus cynocephalus*). *Journal of Biogeography, 45* (1), 1–13.

White L. C., Saltré, F., Bradshaw, C. J. A., & Austin, J. J. (2018). High-quality fossil dates support a synchronous, Late Holocene extinction of devils and thylacines in mainland Australia. *Biology Letters, 14* (1), 20170642, http://dx.doi.org/10.1098/rsbl.2017.0642.

Williams, A. N., Ulm, S., Turney, C. S. M., Rohde, D., & White, G. (2015). Holocene demographic changes and the emergence of complex societies in prehistoric Australia. *PLoS ONE, 10* (6), e0128661, doi:10.1371/journal.pone.0128661.

Williams, A. N., Veth, P., Steffen, W., Ulm, S., Turney, C. S. M., Reeves, J., . . . Smith, M. (2015). A continental narrative: Human settlement patterns and Australian climate change over the last 35,000 years. *Quaternary Science Reviews, 123* , 91–112.

Wright, B. (1968). *Rock art of the Pilbara region, north-west Western Australia*. Canberra: Australian Institute of Aboriginal Studies.

Wroe, S., Clausen, P., McHenry, C., Moreno, K., & Cunningham, E. (2007). Computer simulation of feeding behaviour in the thylacine and dingo as a novel test for niche overlap. *Proceedings of the Royal Society B, 274* (1627), 2819–2828.

Zhang, S.-j., Wang, G.-D., Ma, P., Zhang, L.-l., Yin, T.-T., Liu, Y.-h., . . . Savolainen, P. (2020). Genomic regions under selection in the feralization of the dingoes. *Nature Communications*, 11, 671, doi.org/10.1038/s41467-020-14515-6.

CHAPTER 14

FIRE AND THE TRANSFORMATION OF LANDSCAPES

CASSANDRA ROWE, JANELLE STEVENSON,
SIMON CONNOR, AND MATTHEW ADELEYE

INTRODUCTION

FIRE has an ancient, geological history and appeared on Earth approximately 350–400 million years ago in the Late Devonian period (Bowman et al. 2011). It evolved under the direct influence of climate (e.g., drought, wind, fuel moisture content) and the build-up of burnable biomass at various temporal and spatial scales. Once established, fire affected atmospheric chemistry and the carbon cycle to become a key physical environmental agent (Conedera et al. 2009; Scott 2000).

In fire's biological and ecological history, its role is demonstrated not only as a mechanism that consumed biomass, but one which exerted major evolutionary force to create environmental heterogeneity and drive biodiversity in fire-prone ecosystems. Fire also promotes and maintains biodiversity by serving as an agent of natural selection: sustained coexistence within fire-prone ecosystems has enabled the evolution of distinctive fire-response traits in both flora and fauna (He, Lamont, & Pausas 2019).

Fire also has a long human history. The 'capture' of fire by *Homo erectus* after 1.7 million years ago represents a significant step in human evolution. Fire is seen as one component promoting changes in hominin development, both biologically-physiologically (e.g., larger brain sizes via higher quality diets: Twomey 2013) and sociality (social organization focused on the hearth: Gowlett 2016). Humans progressively learned how to preserve, transport, and light fire, until the eventual 'domestication' of fire (Conedera et al. 2009; Coughlan & Petty 2012). Archaeological deposits provide evidence for routine and controlled use of fire by the Middle Pleistocene, 790–690,000 years ago, enabling human occupation of harsh climates, cooking of foods, processing of tool materials, and manipulation of habitat (Coughlan & Petty 2012; Kull 2008). Fire served a leading role in how humans and the environment have interacted through time (Dearing 2006). Bowman et al. (2011) detail the historical development of humanity's deep interrelationship with fire and suggest that even today it continues to undergo changes in expression.

Landscape fires occur as single events. Each event has a beginning and an end, and as they burn, they have individual measurable properties (Williams et al. 2009). Fires, however, also recur in the environment, formulating a fire regime. Put simply, a fire regime is the history of fires across an environment: a sequence of burn events of characteristic frequency, extent, and severity in relation to a series of governing factors (cultural, biotic, abiotic, and/or climatic) at any one place on the ground (Guyette, Muzika, & Dey 2002; Williams et al. 2009).

The environmental and human interactions of fire cannot be solely or sufficiently understood by treating fires as discrete events. In terms of any ecological 'transformation', it is the spatial and temporal patterning of fire recurrence that is important, not just biological responses to individual fires. While the effects of a single fire event are pertinent to populations of plants (see Gill 1999), and to the physical structure of vegetation (see Vigilante & Bowman 2004), it follows that plant species are not 'fire adapted' or 'adapted to fire' per se; rather they are adapted to a particular fire regime and its components (Conedera et al. 2009; Williams et al. 2009). The fire regime concept is important because it is the framework through which long-term variation in climate and/or changes in human activity are investigated regarding their influence on fire properties, a regime's space-time window, and the impacts of fire on landscapes and biodiversity. It is fire regimes, and notably changes between regimes, that are recorded in palaeoecology and are of relevance to archaeology. From an archaeological viewpoint, fire regimes may be studied for insight into their human creator (particularly in terms of resource use, technological application of fire, and how they have applied it to the landscape). Palaeoecological perspectives seek insights into when and where different regimes occurred (intensity, size, frequency, seasonality), why they occurred (climatic and/or anthropogenic ignition), and what was their outcome (ecosystem shifts; changes in the composition, structure, and function of plant assemblages).

Australia is a fire-prone continent (Williams et al. 2009), and as Kull (2008: 426) describes, 'the most famous home of fire'. Evidence of fire exists in the Greater Australian region at least as far back as the Late Oligocene to Mid-Miocene (25–13 million years ago: Sluiter, Blackburn, & Holdgate 2017). Human colonization subsequently occurred in the Late Pleistocene (Clarkson et al. this volume; Norman et al. 2018, this volume). Therefore, for as long as humans have occupied the wider region, there has been an interaction between unplanned fires, consciously lit anthropogenic fires, landscapes, and biodiversity. Cultural burning is an ancient and important spiritual and customary practice for Indigenous Australians, as well as a means to increase resource availability, to suppress woody species in favour of grassland diversity, and to mitigate uncontrolled fires (Foreman 2016).

In contemporary Australia, the diversity of fire regimes is high (Murphy et al. 2013). Fire regimes vary geographically, their components vary widely, and their effects vary substantially (Archibald, Lehmann, Gómez-Dans, & Bradstock 2013). The elements of a fire regime are interrelated and not easily separated (Johnson 2016). Fire regimes, whether past, present, or future, are a contentious topic. Much disagreement arises from differing disciplinary perspectives, methods, and spatiotemporal scales of analysis (Foreman 2016). Knowledge of climatic fire regimes and natural regime diversity (and outcome) in time remains patchy. Understandings of the diversity and outcome within human fire regimes in the past also remains limited. Underdeveloped relationships and/ or challenges in communication between palaeoecology and archaeology, conservation biology, and land management are apparent (Birks 2012). These challenges are compli- cated by discussion and debate in the public sphere regarding cultural landscapes (e.g., the debate sparked by the publications of Gammage 2012 and Pascoe 2014; see Hiscock 2014; Sutton & Walshe 2021).

To understand environmental 'transformation' in Australia requires greater interdisciplinarity to link not only past to present and future, but the social and physical aspects of fire regimes in Australia and its surrounds (Bliege Bird & Nimmo 2018; Head 1994a, 1994b; see also Larson, Kipfmueller, & Johnson 2021). Conedera et al. (2009) con- clude that a broad and rigorous use of palaeoenvironmental charcoal proxies will allow a better understanding of the long-term climate–fire–vegetation interactions at different spatial and temporal scales and the role of human activities in present and ancient fire- regime histories. This chapter echoes such statements.

This chapter brings together discussions on the biogeography of fire in Greater Australia and of fire regimes through time. Emphasis is placed on the Holocene, which offers insight into current methodological approaches for palaeoecological charcoal analysis, as well as recommended future directions of charcoal-fire research (both tech- nical and conceptual). Case studies have been included throughout. These serve as key examples of integrated research, and of explorations in combining this regions' geo- logical, ecological, and human history of fire and fire's effect. In this sense, our chapter complements a range of prominent publications on the subjects of fire regimes and bio- diversity (e.g., Bradstock, Gill, & Williams 2012; Gill, Woinarski, & York 1999; Miller & Murphy 2017), fire ecology, policy, and management issues (e.g., Carym, Lindenmayer, & Dovers 2003), and explorations of the relationship between cultural practices, ecosystems, and fire regimes (e.g., Fletcher, Hall, & Alexandra 2020; Mooney, Webb, & Attenbrow 2007).

Constructing Records of Fire

The use of charcoal in lake and swamp settings to reconstruct fire regimes began with the pioneering study of Iversen (1944), revealing that Neolithic people had cleared European forests with fire. While it took considerable time for the acceptance of charcoal quantification in conjunction with pollen analysis as a standard protocol, it has been part of Australian palaeoenvironmental science since the late 1970s, with Robyn Clark developing the much adopted 'point-count' method for Australian conditions (Clark 1982). It has been a curious process for those working in flammable environments such as Australia, to see other parts of the world, especially Northern Hemisphere temperate zones, coming to terms with the significant role fire has played in transforming landscapes, especially in the hands of people (Roos, Williamson, & Bowman 2019; Vannière et al. 2016; Whitlock, Higuera, McWethy, & Briles 2010).

The extraction of charcoal from sedimentary sequences differs from the methodological approach used for an archaeological sequence. While the taxonomic identification of hearth and other charcoal fragments is the goal of anthracology (e.g., Whitau, Vannieuwenhuyse, Dotte-Sarout, Balme, & O'Connor 2018), for lake and sedimentary sequences it is the changes in the quantity of charcoal that is the primary focus; peaks of charcoal abundance being related to fire events or periods of greater fire activity in the landscape (Figure 14.1).

There have been attempts to standardize the terminology and taphonomic pathways of the charcoal recovered from sedimentary sequences (e.g., Jones, Chaloner, & Kuhlbusch 1997), with the two main fractions currently quantified being:

- Micro-charcoal—particles viewed under a compound microscope, usually on pollen slides, and generally between 10 and 125 µm in size (Figure 14.1). Experimental studies suggest that this fraction is from a local to extraregional origin and transported by wind and water (Clark 1988; Clark & Patterson 1997; Whitlock & Larsen 2001).
- Macro-charcoal—particles viewed under a stereo microscope (Figure 14.1) and generally larger than 125 µm in size. This fraction has a local origin, usually from within the catchment, and is dispersed by wind and water (Clark & Patterson 1997; Whitlock & Larsen 2001).

There are several review papers on the methodology and other aspects of charcoal data analysis (e.g., Conedera et al. 2009; Mooney & Tinner 2011; Whitlock & Larsen 2001), but in essence it is relatively straightforward. Charcoal data up until the 1990s were primarily collected from pollen microscope slides and so these data are based on discontinuous sampling, with decades or centuries between data points (Figure 14.1). The more recent and now standard approach is to sample continuously down a core for macro-charcoal, resulting in a continuous time series—that is, no missing time intervals (see Stevenson & Haberle 2018). This is more appropriate as major fire events are periodic and can easily be missed with discontinuous sampling. Continuous sampling also provides an excellent record of background fire in the landscape.

Several researchers have drawn attention to the idea that charcoal particle size should not be viewed as a function of distance alone, and that some thought needs to be given to fuel type in our interpretations of past fire, especially in the Australian landscape (e.g., Fletcher et al. 2014; Fletcher, Bowman, Whitlock, Mariani, & Stahle 2018). However,

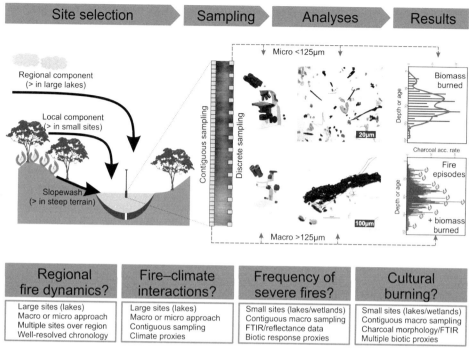

FIGURE 14.1. Illustration of the palaeofire research process (top panels) and its application to selected research agendas (lower panels). Site selection influences the spatial scale represented in palaeofire reconstructions. Sampling/analytical strategy determines which aspects of past fire regimes can be reconstructed (e.g., fire episode frequency requires high-resolution contiguous records). All research agendas require excellent chronologies. FTIR = Fourier Transformed Infrared Spectroscopy.

these interpretations remain to be validated empirically. Until we carry out experimental or better observational studies in Australian settings, we will continue to rely on the Northern Hemisphere models of charcoal transport.

For any one site, compiled charcoal data when paired with a robust chronology can be presented as an influx rate to the basin (expressed as most commonly as particles/cm^2 per year). But for contiguously sampled sites we can do more through the statistical decomposition of the data to pull out 'peaks' of fire activity; influx values that sit at a confidence interval of >95% of the running mean. These peaks provide a picture of fire return interval and fire frequency, with the magnitude of the peaks taken as an estimate of fire magnitude. The development of the approach as well as the various time-series analysis tools has largely been a North American endeavour, and the interested reader is encouraged to engage with the following papers for more technical detail: Carcaillet, Bouvier, Frechette, Larouche, and Richard (2001); Clark and Royall (1996); Gavin, Brubaker, & Lertzman (2003); Higuera, Gavin, Bartlein, and Hallett (2010); Kelly, Higuera, Barrett, and Hu (2011); and Long, Whitlock, Bartlein, and Millspaugh (1998).

The other form of analyses encountered in the literature are the big syntheses of charcoal data to reconstruct regional or global fire histories. These are based on both discontinuous (micro-charcoal) and contiguously sampled (primarily macro-charcoal) records. These syntheses are large smoothing or averaging exercises and reflect the background signal of charcoal through time. As such, they are often criticized for merging unrelated biogeographies and biomes of fire. Even so, syntheses serve to illustrate the relative amount of fire activity over time. Recent examples include Mooney et al. (2011) and Mooney, Harrison, Bartlein, and Stevenson (2012) for Australia, as well as Marlon et al. (2008) and Power et al. (2008) for a more global perspective.

Time-series analysis, while revealing episodes when there was a greater amount of fire and hence biomass consumed in the landscape, cannot answer some of the other challenging questions that need answers, such as the temperature or intensity of the fire or the type of vegetation burnt. Temperature and intensity are fundamental for disentangling 'wildfire' events from the more nuanced cultural burning practices captured in sedimentary records. Currently, there are teams in Australia and elsewhere exploring a number of different methodological approaches to studying the long-term interactions between climate-driven and cultural fire. Fields of analysis include Fourier transformed infrared spectroscopy (FTIR) (e.g., Gosling, Cornelissen, & McMichael 2019), the reflectance properties of charcoal (e.g., Belcher et al. 2018), hydrogen pyrolosis (e.g., Rehn, Rehn, & Possemiers 2019), and biomarkers such as levoglucosan (Zennaro et al. 2015). Charcoal morphology is not often employed given the time-consuming nature of this type of analysis, but it does have the power to distinguish between herbaceous and woody vegetation as the fuel source, an important distinction, for example, around questions of whether cultural burning was associated with grasslands in the past (Umbanhowar & Mcgrath 1998; Umbanhowar & Umbanhowar 2021). More intense fires will also produce more woody charcoal. In Australia, work done by Rehn et al. (2019) on the application of neural networks to charcoal assemblage images may be the way forward, with preliminary analyses recording a 75% success rate for charcoal classification. New research to answer the question 'What was burning in the past?' has used scanning electron microscopy (SEM) on charcoal particles between 180 and 250 μm in size (Marguerie, Krause, & Whitlock 2020), providing a fine-grained landscape reconstruction when coupled with the pollen record, as records of burning on their own cannot reveal the full story of landscape transformation.

A summary of some common questions around the fire in the archaeology–palaeoecology research space is listed in Figure 14.1 along with the most appropriate methodological approaches.

The Biogeography of Fire

Australia is a flammable landscape and three 'great ages' of fire in Australia are spoken of: the pre-human, Aboriginal Australian, and European settlement (Bowman 2003a).

Charcoal records that extend pre-Quaternary (i.e., pre-2.6 million years ago) (e.g., see overview from Kershaw Clark, Gill, & D'Costa 2002 and Macphail, Pillans, Hope, & Clark 2020) are important because they reveal the long biogeographical legacy of burning; how fire was already a component of Australian landscape dynamics before human arrival. Fires helped drive the evolution of Australian fire-adapted plants that came to use fire as a mode of interspecific competition (He et al. 2019; Pausas & Lamont 2018). Flammable vegetation gradually replaced less fire-adapted flora in all but the most fire-protected sites. Pre-human fires are suggested to have had very large spatial scales guided by climate and to have created a 'coarse-scale' mosaic of vegetation in different stages of broad recovery (Bowman 2003b; Weston & Jordan 2017). People actively influenced fire regimes via changes to fuel types, modifying fuel structure and continuity, and igniting few or many fires in different seasons under various climatic conditions (Perry, Wilmshurst, McGlone, McWethy, & Whitlock 2012). Aboriginal-anthropogenic fire is considered 'pyrodiverse' (Bliege Bird et al. 2018—see also 'Arid Zone' section later). Higher frequency, lower intensity Aboriginal fire is associated with shifts in the pre-human fire-adapted vegetation structure from dense to open understories. This change initiated a finer plant-habitat mosaic than that caused by natural ignitions. In turn, European fire regimes appear to have removed the finer-grained habitat mosaic. Vegetation adapted to frequent Aboriginal low-level fire became degraded following European settlement. European-anthropogenic fires were often geographically larger and more intense because of altered fuel loads and shifts in seasonal timing and frequency (Marsden-Smedley 1998). This caused the range and abundance of many plant species to change (Bowman 2003a, 2003b). Human contributions to fire regimes incorporate both ignitions and active fire suppression, and these represent the signals to look for in palaeoecological-archaeological research (McWethy et al. 2013).

Long Quaternary records, including both terrestrial (e.g., Lynch's Crater, Lake George, Caledonia Fen, Lake Wangoom, and Lake Selina) and marine (e.g., ODP 820, ODP 765, and MD03-2611) cores, have demonstrated climate's prevailing influence over the tempo and direction of biomass burning trends in Greater Australia over glacial–interglacial timescales (see De Deckker et al., 2020; Gallagher & Wagstaff, 2021; Kershaw, Bretherton, & van der Kaars 2007; Kershaw et al. 2002; Lynch, Abramson, Görgen, Beringer, & Uotila 2007; Moss & Kershaw 2007). Despite the allure of long-term palaeorecords, their geographic representation is sparse and not necessarily optimal for comparison with the archaeological record, which is often more highly resolved temporally and spatially than palaeofire records. The Holocene emerges as the most promising arena for exploring the archaeology–palaeoecology nexus. Even so, unequivocal signals of anthropogenic fire have been difficult to find in Holocene records and have gone undetected in continental-scale compilations of Holocene fire history from multiple palaeofire records (Mooney et al. 2012; Williams, Mooney, Sisson, & Marlon 2015).

Absence of evidence, however, is not evidence of absence. Targeted, local-scale investigations demonstrate compelling links between occupation dates and fire frequency. These include a carefully designed study of Holocene archaeological sites and palaeoecological archives in the Namadgi National Park, Australian Capital Territory (Theden-Ringl 2018), paired records of coastal occupation and fire-regime change in northwest Tasmania (Romano & Fletcher 2018), and the multisite study of Bass Strait islands (Adeleye et al. 2020—see 'Islands' section later). Theden-Ringl (2018) showed that past fire frequency within a catchment was often positively related to the catchment's occupation density (revealed through archaeological investigation), and that the timing of this peak occupation differed between neighbouring catchments. This fine-scale spatiotemporal variation likely explains why coarse-scale regional compilations have failed to find clear signals of anthropogenic burning. The temporal and spatial resolution of most studies biases them toward recording only very large-scale fire-driven changes and toward climate-driven fires. The aforementioned studies also remind us that past fire regimes were multifaceted, not confined solely to the overall amount of biomass burned. With methodological development, palaeofire frequency and intensity may emerge as the hallmarks of past anthropogenic fire.

A compilation of biomass burned during the Holocene across the broadly defined bioclimatic zones of Australia into New Guinea is illustrated in Figure 14.2. This compilation considers variations in the overall amount of charcoal accumulated in each record. In this respect it differs from previous compilations where each record received equal weight (Kershaw et al. 2002; Mooney et al. 2012; Williams et al. 2015). The presentation in Figure 14.2 allows the overall amount of burning, as well as its variability, to be compared between different biomes.

The Dry Temperate zone, encompassing the southern and eastern Australian mainland, had the greatest levels of Holocene biomass burned (mean charcoal score, $\mu = 0.11$). This was followed by the Wet Temperate zone of Tasmania ($\mu = 0.09$) and then by the Dry Tropics of Australia's Top End ($\mu = 0.07$). The lowest Holocene levels of biomass burned were in the Wet Tropics and Arid zones ($\mu = 0.05$). These zones are found at the extreme limits of the aridity–productivity gradient (Pausas & Bradstock 2007). Tropical rainforests are usually too wet to burn, even in drought years, while deserts have too little fuel continuity for fires to spread, despite flammable conditions.

The biogeography of fire in Greater Australia was dynamic through time. Figure 14.2 shows several distinct waves of burning that expressed themselves at different times in different biomes. The strong wave of burning in the Dry Tropics from 10.5 to 6 ka suggests a very different fire regime at that time compared to later in the Holocene. Perhaps only recent burning levels (since 1950 CE) are comparable to that first wave. Mid-Holocene burning was concentrated in the Dry Temperate zone, both in terms of overall biomass burned and its variability. Late Holocene burning levels were low in all but the Wet Temperate zone. European colonization and subsequent changes in fire regimes had a stark effect on biomass burned in all biomes (Figure 14.2). Levels of burning in recent decades sit far outside the Holocene envelope, apart from the fuel-limited Arid zone.

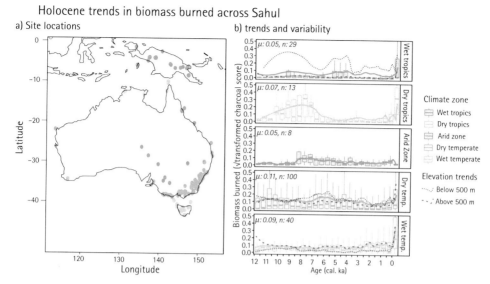

FIGURE 14.2. Holocene biomass-burned trends in the major biomes of Sahul. (a) Location of the sedimentary charcoal records used in the palaeofire compilation; (b) Holocene trends and variability in biomass burned from 12 cal. ka to today. Data were compiled from the Global Paleofire Database and Neotoma Paleoecology Database, with the addition of three sites from Northern Australia (Dry Tropics zone) and eleven sites from Bass Strait (Wet Temperate zone). Data were converted to charcoal accumulation rates using the available age-depth models. A min-max transformation was applied to each group of records with the same quantification technique (e.g., charcoal point count, macroscopic particle count). This results in the sample with the highest charcoal accumulation rate for each technique receiving a score of 1. Scores were square-root transformed to emphasize trends. See Mariani et al. (2022) for further details.

If nothing else, these reconstructions (Figure 14.2) show that fire's role as a biomass consumer has not always been as strong as in recent decades. This means that fire ecology in the Australian region has based its observations on an unusual period of fire-regime transformation. How fire regimes were before European colonization and what role they played in the different ecosystems are questions that cannot be addressed by fire ecology or indeed from palaeofire reconstructions of biomass alone. Along with the deep knowledge of cultural burning embedded in Indigenous cultural practices, archaeology and palaeoecology have a key role to play in analysing the fire-vegetation-culture nexus in times past. This kind of information will become increasingly important for embedding cultural practices in the resolution of contemporary landscape-management problems.

In the following sections, we depart from earlier attempts to synthesize environmental transformations based on regional-scale charcoal compilations and instead attempt to bring together pollen-based vegetation change and fire history for key sites within each biome. The result is a series of 'fire moments' that explore fire's role as an environmental transformer, an artefact of climate, vegetation, and culture.

TROPICS

Wet Tropics

The Wet Tropics refers to the zones of New Guinea and northeastern Australia where rainforests prevail under a humid, aseasonal climate. The abundance of natural lakes and wetlands in this perennially wet zone have facilitated a long program of palaeoecological research. Perhaps the best example of landscape 'transformation' on the Australian continent comes from Lynch's Crater on the Atherton Tablelands of northeast Australia. Dung-inhabiting fungi declined in the sediments around 41,000 cal BP, linked to megafaunal extinction (Rule et al. 2012). This decline was followed by increases in grassland and sclerophyll trees and shrubs as the vegetation shifted into a new and more fire-prone ecological state. This sounded the death knell for various fire-sensitive conifers in the region (Rule et al. 2012). The degree to which Aboriginal people were involved in this ecological transition is debated, but there is strong evidence that patches of grassland and sclerophyll woodland were maintained within the rainforest matrix by frequent cultural burning (Field, Kealhofer, Cosgrove, & Coster 2016; Lynch et al. 2020).

In New Guinea, fire is one of the principal means through which rainforests are opened up and converted into other vegetation types, including agricultural and garden plots. Evidence for these conversions in the past occurs frequently in the Holocene palaeoecological record, often indicated by rapid vegetation change and increased charcoal density (Haberle 2003, 2007). These local-scale changes were time-transgressive, occurring at different sites at different times, and were usually consistent with occupation patterns revealed through archaeology. While climate governed past fire activity on regional scales in New Guinea (Haberle, Hope, & van der Kaars 2001), the clarity of human-induced transformations at the local scale raised hope that similarly obvious signals of human activity might be identified in Australian environments (Head 1994b). Such signals have remained elusive, even when the most detailed palaeoecological analyses have been applied in the Australian Wet Tropics (Haberle 2005) or to analysing the impacts of megafaunal extinction in southern Australia (Johnson 2016). As the following sections illustrate, the search for cultural burning's signal in past Australian landscapes has called for a diversity of approaches that integrate fire ecology, palaeoecology, and archaeology.

Dry Tropics

Tropical savannas dominate the northern quarter of the Australia continent (Beringer et al. 2015; mapped in Fox, Neldner, Wilson, & Bannink 2001). Three isolated areas of savanna occur in eastern New Guinea (Joseph et al. 2019; mapped by Blake, Saunders,

McAlpine, & Paijmans 2010), within the lowland Western, and Central and Oro Provinces of Papua New Guinea (PNG).

Australian and New Guinean savannas comprise variable tree cover over a largely continuous grassy understory (Scholes & Archer 1997). Fires are a pervasive feature (Williams, Muller, Wahren, Setterfield, & Cusack 2003). High temperatures and substantial rainfall during monsoonal wet seasons are conducive to plant growth. Fuel (and particularly grass fuel) then cures during the subsequent dry season and is available to burn. Dry season weather conditions also promote fire spread. This annual wet-dry cycle, of abundant growth and curing, means fire probability is high (potentially annual) and burning of grass biomass extensive. Within this cycle the limiting factor for tropical savanna fire regimes is ignition, from lightning and anthropogenic sources (Williams et al. 2009; Woinarski, Mackey, Nix, & Traill 2007).

Palaeoecological research is less established in tropical savannas compared to temperate southeastern environments and the mountainous regions of Australia and New Guinea, respectively (see review in Reeves et al. 2013, and methodologies in study site options from Field, McGowan, Moss, & Marx 2017). Initially, questions emerged as to how perceptible temporal and/or spatial changes in savanna fire activity and associated vegetation impacts may be in palaeoecology. The predominant grassy-herbaceous fuels can produce low charcoal values, for example. Furthermore, Clark (1983) highlighted how savannas are fire-tolerant, that woody-sclerophyll taxa of the seasonal tropics are well adapted to burning, and debated whether potentially subtle vegetation changes may be missed at the level of resolution of pollen-charcoal analysis. Since Clark (1983), palaeoecology has been able to take advantage of developments in observational studies dedicated to climate–fuel–fire relationships, most particularly where manipulative fire-plot experiments have become a feature of fire research in north Australia savannas (see Russell-Smith, Price, & Murphy 2010; Russell-Smith, Whitehead, Cook, & Hoare 2003; Williams et al. 2003). Such experiments indicate fire regimes act as an important modifier of savanna tree-grass biomass and woody-type relationships at local and site-specific scales. Expansion in scale and water availability strongly influences savanna structure and composition (Russell-Smith et al. 2010; Scholes & Archer 1997). Modern observations increasingly provide the interpretative cues from which savanna palaeoecology can draw.

Next we explore the Dry Tropic biome using three examples: Girraween in the Northern Territory (Rowe et al. 2019a), Weipa in north Queensland (Stevenson, Brockwell, Rowe, Proske, & Shiner 2015), and Caution Bay on the south coast of PNG (Rowe et al. 2019b). We use these examples as representative of two Australian and one PNG savanna bioregions, and we discuss two points pertinent to palaeoecology within the tropical savanna biome: What vegetation transformation can we detect via pollen and charcoal analysis? How can we understand fire ignition in terms of climate and/or people?

Under savanna fire regimes dominated by regular, high-severity burning, grasses are promoted and woody biomass declines. Fire-sensitive pan-tropical, deciduous tree-shrub species are at higher risk in comparison to sclerophyll vegetative resprouters

(Lawes, Murphy, Midgley, & Russell-Smith 2011; Williams et al. 2009). Repeated grass-led fires of an intensity able to maintain open canopy cover are evident earlier in the Holocene at Girraween and Caution Bay. A pronounced increase in burning ~1000 BP demonstrates the impact of large multiple burning events at Weipa, altering tree presence and instigating ecosystem variability. Under frequent but low- to moderate-intensity burning regimes, grasses may remain, but woody vegetation becomes structurally stable (Russell-Smith et al. 2010). This fire regime—showing support rather than destruction of woody cover—is consistent at Weipa and maintained for much of the Holocene. The sites of Girraween and Caution Bay demonstrate a more recent regime switch; eucalypts (Girraween) and *Pandanus* (Caution Bay) increased in relative abundance from the Mid- into Late Holocene, as grasses and the more fire-sensitive undergrowth were suppressed. In the absence of burning, fire-sensitive woody forest recruitment occurs, and grasses are outcompeted (Lawes et al. 2011; Russell-Smith et al. 2010). At no stage in our three savanna records were Holocene burning patterns low enough to permit competitive bioclimatic advantage and widespread expansion of fire-sensitive woody taxa. Modern-day assessments implicate early-season fires as having adverse effects on long-term woody presence and diversity (Russell-Smith et al. 2010; Williams et al. 2009).

What continues for the Australian–New Guinean savanna is the palaeoecological question of distinguishing ignition and long-term drivers of fire, made difficult in the region given relatively low human population densities and/or high lightning strike densities that provide plentiful natural ignition (Bowman et al. 2011; Williams et al. 2009). Bowman et al. (2011) and Roos et al. (2014) discuss the disagreements, including degrees to which humans overrode otherwise natural fire ignitions, spatial extent, and whether savanna effects were intentional or unintentional. Bowman et al. (2011) suggest as key the study of known transitions from one fire source to another or one style of human fire management to another, with a call for greater methodological integration between the natural and social sciences (see also Roos et al. 2014).

Aboriginal arrival influenced savanna fire regimes by changing their timing and locations, as well as by altering fuel structure and abundance (as mentioned earlier; see also Bowman et al. 2011). Vegetation changes associated with low- to moderate-intensity burning coincided in space and time with human changes known from archaeology, anthropology, and historical sources at Weipa, Caution Bay, and Girraween. A further clear example is provided by Mackenzie, Moss, and Ulm (2020), linking multidisciplinary records to track Indigenous fire management across the Southern Wellesley Archipelago (Gulf of Carpentaria savanna region). Research today among Indigenous communities in northern Australia demonstrates that lower intensity burning is simultaneously patchy and designed to manipulate habitat for a wide variety of food resources (Trauernicht, Muller, Wahren, Setterfield, & Cusack 2016). These burning practices are initiated early in the monsoonal dry season and continued through the dry season, to create a fine-scale mosaic of burnt and unburnt areas, often resulting in a savanna embedded with other important ecosystems types (e.g., grasslands, vine thickets, and/or monsoonal forests) (Williams et al. 2009). In palaeoecology, ubiquitous charcoal-fire records and lower fuel load indicators (such as grasses) are linked with structural woody complexity and plant diversity.

Displacement of Indigenous management across the tropical savannas within the past century has seen associated fire regimes replaced with either the removal of fire, or very large infrequent fires in many areas under European management, and/or the domination of large severe-intensity fires set by lightning in the late dry season (Bowman et al. 2011; Trauernicht et al. 2016). This change is what Mackenzie et al. (2020) show: a disruption of an earlier anthropogenic fire regime characterized by low fire activity and spatial variability. In short, the removal of Traditional Owners from South Wellesley increased fire activity and area burnt as large fires occurred outside the early dry season. Vegetation thickening is a considered consequence of the disruption of Indigenous fire management in the savanna region. In composition, change in savanna fire type is simultaneously implicated in declines of specific taxa, including widespread mortality in one of the savanna's few non-eucalypt overstory trees, the fire-sensitive conifer *Callitris intratropica* (Bowman et al. 2011; Trauernicht et al. 2016). Lowest plant diversity and highest record of burning occur in the most recent part of the pollen records at Weipa and Caution Bay. At Girraween, the period of contact between European and Indigenous people is also reflected in lower ecosystem diversity, but with the removal of fire.

ARID ZONE

The vast arid interior of Australia provides scant vegetation cover for fire to spread, yet it is in these arid environments that the grain of the landscape mosaic is most obviously tied to cultural fire. Research in the Western Desert shows that lightning-strike fires produce coarse-grained landscapes with low pyrodiversity at the local scale, contrasting with the fine mosaics of multistage vegetation found where cultural burning is practiced intensively (Bliege Bird et al. 2018).

Pyrodiversity is a significant habitat cue for native animals, such as monitor lizards and dingoes (Bliege Bird, Bird, Codding, Parker, & Jones 2008). Martu people use fire in ways that create pyrodiversity, which in turn increases food availability (Bliege Bird et al. 2008; Bliege Bird et al. 2018). Detection of the fine-scale mosaics in pyrodiverse landscapes remains challenging for palaeoecological methods that tend to be inconclusive at very fine spatial and temporal scales. Significantly for archaeological and palaeoecological interpretation, cultural burning in these landscapes can counteract the effects of climatic variability by reducing ignitions in years when the climate would otherwise cause ignitions to increase (Bliege Bird, Bird, & Codding 2016). Current palaeoecological research approaches are ill-equipped to detect these nuanced impacts of cultural burning and may never succeed in doing so. A more holistic and inclusive approach, combining Indigenous and Western knowledge systems, is required to understand the profound legacy of cultural burning in today's ecosystems and landscapes.

Arid zone palaeoecology is hampered by the scarcity of wetlands and lakes, the traditional ('conventional') study sites used as sedimentary archives. Arid climates are unfavourable for the preservation of organic materials, including pollen and charcoal, and as such Australian (semi)arid regions are poorly represented in late Quaternary ecological reconstructions (Boyd 1990; Fitzsimmons et al. 2013; Matley, Sniderman, Drinnan, & Hellstrom 2020). In most cases reconstructions rely on geomorphic archives such as dunes (e.g., Hesse 2011), playas (e.g., Singh & Luly 1991), and fluvial systems (e.g., Nanson et al. 2008)—records inclined to preserve responses to climatic change (Fitzsimmons et al. 2013). In response, it is the arid zone from which experimentations in sourcing 'novel archives' (Matley et al. 2020: 672) are arising. Mound Springs (e.g., Boyd 1990), stick-nest rat middens (e.g., McCarthy, Head, & Quade 1996; Pearson & Dodson 1993), and speleothems (e.g., Matley et al. 2020) have all been shown to entrap fossil pollen and charcoal, their refinement representative of future directions in research. Where sequences are currently discontinuous, and at this stage not able to tease out patterns in fire recurrence, they are able to identify plant–fire relationships at points in time. Expansions of forbs and grasses, for example, resulted from increased Late Holocene fire occurrences on the Nullarbor Plain of southwestern Australia (Matley et al. 2020).

In arid zones where conditions are less than ideal for fossil preservation, indicator pollen approaches could help circumvent some of these methodological challenges. Studies from Salt Lake (Thomas, Enright, & Kenyon 2001), Lake Tyrrell (Luly 1993), and lake formations in the Darling Anabranch dunefields (Cupper 2005; Cupper, Drinnan, & Thomas 2000) show Early-to-Mid-Holocene moist conditions in the Australian interior gave way to regional aridity during the Late Holocene, and that fire incidence increased with desiccation of the landscape (Cupper 2005). Mid-Holocene declines in *Callitris* and *Allocasuarina* from Australian interior landscapes are attributed to this fire activity, while heath, composed of fire-tolerant taxa *Banksia*, *Hakea*, and *Grevillea*, expanded. In turn, reduced incidences of Late Holocene burning have been related to predominance of Amaranthaceae. Amaranthaceae are low open shrublands that are less flammable, and Holocene interior ecosystems with understoreys of Amaranthaceae were less likely to burn than vegetation with a grassy understorey (Cupper 2005; Luly 1993). Given limited biological preservation and associated small assemblages of pollen, researchers such as Boyd (1990); Cupper (2005); Luly (1993); Matley et al. (2020); and Thomas et al. (2001) all make use of keystone pollen indicator species (*Callitris*, Amaranthaceae), capable of helping to define a broader ecosystem, while linked to a particular fire regime. Fire-sensitive *Callitris* is similarly used within dry tropical savanna palaeoecological research. The indicator-species approach can be seen in the early foundational palynological works of Iversen (1944, and as earlier). Conceptually, pollen-plant-fire profiling may serve in tracing one of the linked landscape effects of Western Desert Martu burning for food procurement; that pyrodiversity promotes greater accessibility of dietary staple plants such as *Solanum* (Zeanah, Codding, Bliege Bird, & Bird 2017). Temporal stability of *Solanum* pollen, in combination with charcoal, may provide a valuable signal for the prevalence and/or intensity of cultural burning in the Western Desert in the past.

Temperate Environments

Dry Temperate (Mainland Australia)

Southeastern Australia's temperate zone is synonymous with fire, particularly the large and intense bushfires that periodically sweep through the sclerophyll forests of this region. *Eucalyptus* species dominate the wet tall forests, dry forests, and woodlands of this region, with the openness and height of the canopy determined by environmental variables such as precipitation and soil nutrition (Tozer et al. 2010). These factors also influence the complexity of the understory, but so does fire, a scenario reflected in the analysis presented in Figure 14.2, with this 'dry temperate' landscape recording overall the greatest levels of biomass burned during the Holocene. Patches of temperate rainforest exist in SE Mainland Australia with strong floristic affinities with Tasmanian rainforests (see next section). There are few rainforest palaeoecological records from the SE Mainland (see McKenzie & Kershaw 2000) compared to records from the fire-prone sclerophyll, shrubland, and grassland environments that are the focus of this section.

Palaeoecological sites from around the Sydney basin record the highest levels of charcoal accumulation during the Mid-Holocene, in association with decreases in *Eucalyptus* and other woody canopy species (e.g., Black & Mooney 2007; Black, Mooney, & Attenbrow 2008; Black, Mooney, & Haberle 2007; Chalson 1983; Kodela & Dodson 1988; Mooney et al. 2007). Increased fire activity and/or intensity (an unresolved factor) is considered by these researchers as a combined signal of climate (increasing El Niño intensity and variability) and human activity. However, the much lower accumulation rates of charcoal in the Late Holocene, alongside a shift to more grassy understories, align with archaeological evidence for more intensive occupation of the region (Black et al. 2008; Mooney et al. 2011). This no doubt reflects what we know about Indigenous fire use in the historic past: low-intensity fires leading to 'cleaner' and more open understories (see, e.g., Foreman 2016, 2020; Gott 2005).

One of southeastern Australia's most researched cultural landscapes is found on the volcanic plains stretching between Melbourne and Mt Gambier. The region is home to some of the world's longest oral histories and earliest freshwater fishing structures (Matchan, Phillips, Jourdan, & Oostingh 2020; McNiven et al. 2012, 2015). The volcanic plains are scattered with dozens of maar craters, many containing lakes and swamps. Pollen and macrofossil assemblages in sediment cores from these lakes and swamps have provided an unparalleled picture of past environmental change (e.g., Builth et al. 2008; Kershaw et al. 2004; Lewis 2012). Integration of archaeological and palaeoecological data has revealed, among other things, that eel traps around Lake Condah were constructed between 6600 and 5400 cal BP to take advantage of periods of higher streamflow (McNiven et al. 2015). The same period marks the establishment of eucalypt-wooded grasslands as the predominant vegetation of the volcanic plains (Builth et al. 2008; D'Costa, Edney, Kershaw, & De Deckker 1989). For southeastern

Australia as a whole, the Mid-Holocene represents a peak in biomass burning (Figure 14.2; Adeleye, Haberle, Connor, Stevenson, & Bowman 2021a) and a period of increasing plant biodiversity (Adeleye et al. 2020). At the same time as eel trapping was being developed, if not before, there is an intriguing possibility that the entire plains landscape was being deliberately modified using fire to promote a diversity of plant resources and forestall forest encroachment. Investigation of this question would require reanalysis of existing sediment cores to reconstruct Holocene fire frequency and its interactions with local plant diversity on the volcanic plains. Quantitative methods of past land-cover reconstruction have highlighted how Indigenous people in Tasmania used fire to maintain open vegetation from the glacial period into the Holocene (Mariani et al. 2019). Application of the same techniques to SE Mainland Australia is likely to further support Indigenous narratives about the antiquity and prevalence of cultural burning across this landscape.

Wet Temperate (Tasmania)

Fire has long been considered the driving force behind Tasmanian vegetation change (Bowman & Jackson 1981; Jackson 1968). In particular, changes in fire frequency can cause vegetation to shift from one type to another, establishing a new metastable ecological state with a new fire regime. Numerous examples of forest-to-moorland transitions have been revealed by palaeoecological records, including in the Gog Range (Fletcher, Wood, & Haberle 2014) and contrasting forest trajectories in Tasmania's subalpine zone (Mariani et al. 2019).

Tasmania's abundance of glacial lakes compared to other parts of Sahul has meant that its vegetation and fire history is well established. Its vegetation also lends itself to palaeoecological reconstruction, with each of its dominant species producing a distinct pollen type. On the mainland, it is very difficult to distinguish among the great diversity of *Eucalyptus*-dominated vegetation types, while in Tasmania it is a relatively simple task to distinguish among various rainforest, sclerophyll forest, heathland, and moorland communities. Perhaps because of this pollen identification advantage, Tasmanian records have been able to more conclusively interrogate the relative contributions of climatic, ecological, and anthropogenic factors that have shaped past fire regimes.

An important problem in palaeoecological data generally is the 'swamping' of pollen assemblages by the pollen of wind-pollinated species. The impact of this swamping on interpretation should not be underestimated. Tasmanian pollen records from the highlands are dominated by *Nothofagus*, leading to the impression of rainforest dominance through the Holocene. This impression seemed at odds with the rich archaeological record and the region's contemporary vegetation, which is dominated by buttongrass moorland. Analysis of the pollen records using analogue matching showed that buttongrass had been a permanent feature of highland landscapes for the entire Holocene, reflecting a cultural landscape maintained through frequent and deliberate use of fire (Fletcher & Thomas 2010). More recently, the vast extent of this cultural landscape was estimated by converting pollen data into vegetation cover estimates (Mariani et al. 2017, 2019). In the area around Cradle Mountain, rainforest vegetation never exceeded 40% of the landscape, despite rainforest pollen contributing to 80% of the pollen assemblages. Most of the landscape was heathland and moorland—both maintained through cultural burning (Mariani et al. 2017). This type of modelling, by converting pollen data into vegetation estimates, promises to provide more realistic landscape scenarios to contextualize the archaeological record.

Northern Tasmania has yielded unique insights into the cultural use of fire in the past. The strong correspondence between changes in fire frequency, human occupation, and heathland development at Waterhouse Marsh, northeast Tasmania, implicated human manipulation of fire frequency in driving vegetation change (Thomas & Kirkpatrick 1996). This single-site approach was extended to an intersite comparison between two coastal wetlands in northwest Tasmania—one adjacent to a high-intensity occupation site and another remote from occupation sites (Romano & Fletcher 2018). At the intensively occupied site, manipulation of fire frequency was used to confer stability on the vegetation during a period of environmental upheaval (Romano & Fletcher 2018). The results point to a spatially targeted use of fire in particular habitats and not in others, highlighting the critical importance of linking catchment-scale palaeoecological records to archaeological records within the same catchments.

Another example of the fire-vegetation-culture nexus comes from northern Tasmania's Surrey Hills, presently covered in rainforest but dominated by grasslands and savannas at the time of European colonization. Analysis of sediment profiles and tree rings revealed the present-day forests to be regrowth following the cessation of Indigenous burning regimes (Fletcher et al. 2020). This pattern is replicated throughout the Sahul forest zone, according to Indigenous knowledge, historical reports, and emerging palaeoecological reconstructions (Mariani et al. 2022). Much more evidence for past cultural burning is likely to be hiding in plain sight, obscured only by scientific orthodoxies that have tended to overlook or undervalue the cultural aspects of fire.

ISLAND ENVIRONMENTS

By their very nature, islands are isolated, confined geographical spaces and in most cases incorporate shallower time-depths of human settlement. As such, islands are often seen as ideal arenas or 'laboratories' for studies of interactions between human and environmental processes (Kirch & Hunt 1997; MacArthur & Wilson 1967; Veth, O'Connor, & Wallis 2000). The buffering effects of great size and diversity evident on continental lands are lacking on islands; their limited size makes small changes capable of general effects, providing a relatively clear record of the role of people in environmental change. As bounded systems, the scale of landscapes and the scale of archaeological evidence are typically more compatible, permitting closer integrations of palaeoecological and archaeological data. Palaeoecological studies can help extrapolate baseline (pre-human impact) levels of environmental change and examine biotic changes brought about by human settlement, in particular habitat modification (Kirch 1997; Sadler 1999; Veth et al. 2000). Islands as model systems also allow for reflection back onto continental situations. In this way, Kirch (1997) refers to an island as a microcosm of greater change. In the Australian region, these features reach their fullest development in the island regions of the Torres Strait and Bass Strait. Supportive illustration is provided in Figure 14.3.

Torres Strait: An Example of Paired and Comparative Palynological Studies

Rowe (2007a, 2015) presents palaeoecological analyses from Torres Strait's western-group islands. A multisite approach, combining inland and coastal swamp investigations, permitted two scales of environmental observation—the local-island and more regional Torres Strait scale. Methodologically, an archaeological rock-shelter pollen-charcoal sequence (Badu 15; Rowe 2007b) was incorporated, in recognition of the interpretative difficulties of separating human from naturally influenced fire regimes and vegetation change. Knowing that the upper section of David et al.'s (2004) excavation incorporated a differentiated period of permanent occupation, deeper (periodically occupied) strata were examined for evidence of similar palaeoecological trends. Badu 15's lowest layers predated occupation altogether, permitting insight into vegetation and fire response to climatic and sea-level activity in the absence of humans. This approach is especially important for 'scaling' changes in charcoal and pollen (Pearsall 2000). Reconstruction at Badu 15 spanned a period from before 8000 years ago and provided information concerning environments older than any of the island's swamp-based palaeoecological studies, allowing for a paired off-site record comparison (cf. Pearsall 2000).

Both rock shelter and swamp charcoal counts signal fire has been present within Torres Strait ecosystems since at least the Early to Mid-Holocene. At this time, widespread eucalypt forest was maintained. Swamp records initially contain low charcoal concentrations, followed by two-step increases peaking in the Late Holocene. Such data revealed a shift from landscapes with occasional fire activity to islands where fire disturbance was common. Frequent fire facilitated eucalypt forest fragmentation, the opening of woody canopy cover, encouraged understory growth, and likely created varied mixed-plant components at different successional stages.

Badu 15's post-3500 BP sediments presented a number of important features that, in combination, confirms an anthropogenic explanation for this Late Holocene landscape transformation. Artefact recovery, degree of eucalypt decline, and rate of sedimentation increase were unparalleled in earlier parts of the record. Eucalypts demonstrated a fourfold decrease from that time; charcoal exhibits an even larger order of magnitude increase. In utilizing the Badu 15 evidence, it is unlikely that naturally occurring fires had such a marked and sustained island impact as in the period beginning 3500–3000 BP. Fire is a strong component of modern Islander–environment interaction, and historical ethnographic texts describe burning (clearing) as one means to assist wild-food collection and preparation in plant cultivation (Haddon 1912: 148).

Bass Strait

The more than one hundred islands of Bass Strait in southeast Australia have a unique history of formation and human occupation. The islands were formed in the Holocene (the last 11,700 years) between 8000 and 6000 years ago when sea level rose to its maximum (Sloss, Murray-Wallace, & Jones 2007; Williams, Ulm, Sapienza, Lewis, & Turney 2018). Previous palaeoecological studies from Bass Strait islands suggest the Bassian Plain was dominated by treeless vegetation at the height of the last glacial period (D'Costa, Grindrod, & Ogden 1993; Hope 1978). Woodland expanded and fire activity increased as climates became warmer and wetter from the Early Holocene, but then declined in favour of heathlands and scrub as sea levels rose after 8000 cal BP (Adeleye et al. 2021b; Ladd, Orchiston, & Joyce 1992; McWethy, Haberle, Hopf, & Bowman 2017). Archaeological investigations by Sim (1998) suggest the islands, especially on the eastern side (Furneaux Group Islands: FGI), experienced intense human occupation during the Early Holocene, but this reduced after 5000 years ago due to sea-level inundation, reductions in island size, and depletion of resources. Because their occupation history differs from Tasmania and mainland Australia, the FGI provide a 'natural laboratory' to investigate the different roles of climate and humans on the Australian landscape in the past.

In order to gain insight into Indigenous land use/fire usage on the FGI during the Holocene, Adeleye et al. (2021a) used multiple sedimentary charcoal records (eleven sites) to reconstruct the amount of vegetation biomass burned and changes in fire frequency (Figure 14.3). These reconstructions were also compared to archaeological records of human occupation of the FGI and to other climatic variables. It was found that human fire usage is reflected in fire frequency and climate-driven fire is reflected in the amount of biomass burned during the Holocene. Adeleye et al. (2021a) confirmed that Indigenous people used frequent fires to maintain open woodland on the FGI during the period of intense occupation in the Early Holocene. This Early Holocene cultural burning practice reduced fuel load and connectivity in woodlands, which in turn reduced the amount of biomass burning linked to climate (Figure 14.3). The subsequent reduction of Indigenous frequent fire usage in woodlands and other dense vegetation in the Mid-Holocene led to an increase in woody fuel and biomass burned on the FGI.

This type of comparative palaeoecological study not only helps us to understand the different roles of climate and Indigenous people in transforming Australian landscapes in the past but also provides a deeper insight into how ecosystem health was maintained by the constant dialogue between Indigenous cultural burning and past climate. Such

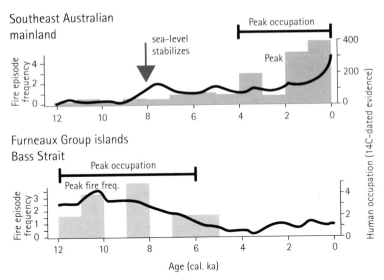

FIGURE 14.3. Contrasting histories of fire–human interactions in Southeast Australia and the Bass Strait islands. In each region, the highest frequency of fire episodes is associated with peak occupation periods and changes in land use. Vertical bars represent 14C-dated archaeological evidence in each region; the thick line is a reconstruction of fire episode frequency from multiple high-resolution contiguous charcoal records; see Adeleye et al. (2021a).

knowledge is vital to developing management plans to preserve biocultural heritage and to help minimize the occurrence of destructive fires in Australia in the future.

STATEMENT IN CONCLUSION

More than twenty-five years ago, Lesley Head reflected on the progress made in understanding human imprints on the Australian landscape in deep time (Head 1994b). She advocated a research agenda centred on the data-rich Holocene, integrating archaeological and palaeoecological approaches at complementary spatial scales. This research agenda remains as relevant now as it did in 1994. In addition, methodological advances have launched possibilities that would have been inconceivable two decades ago. It is now possible to interrogate palaeoecological records to estimate past fire frequencies, to determine what plants were burnt and at what temperature, and to reconstruct the past abundance of plant species in the landscape. All of these developments open pathways to more realistic scenarios of how Greater Australia's cultural landscapes came into being. Such scenarios are critical to firing public imagination and contributing to a more informed, curious populace (Head 1994b).

Perhaps the greatest advance in the past two decades has not been methodological, but conceptual. This conceptual shift has occurred on two levels. The first is the search for a continental-scale 'transformation' event has been abandoned in favour of more nuanced studies of the fire-vegetation-culture nexus at the catchment scale. Australia has a vast array of ecosystems, from fire-prone to fire-sensitive. There is growing recognition that each ecosystem is likely to exhibit unique responses to fire-regime changes as subtle, adaptive, and finely patterned as those imposed by cultural burning. The second conceptual shift is in the acknowledgement that Western science cannot tell the whole story when it comes to ancient, culturally constructed landscapes. Accurate and nuanced understanding of the diversity and complexity of Australian landscapes will only come through Western science partnering respectfully and ethically with Indigenous knowledge.

Acknowledgments

The authors are grateful to Rebecca Bliege Bird, Patrick Moss, and Michael-Shawn Fletcher for their detailed and constructive reviews, and to Ian McNiven for his editorial guidance. We also thank all contributors to the Global Palaeofire Database (paleofire.org) and Michela Mariani (University of Nottingham) for making their data available for this analysis, and Boris Vannière (CNRS, Université Bourgogne Franche-Comté) for encouraging new approaches to palaeofire synthesis. We further acknowledge and thank our Aboriginal partner communities where it has been our pleasure and education to collaborate on Country.

References

Adeleye, M. A., Haberle, S. G., Connor, S. E., Stevenson, J., & Bowman, D. M. J. S. (2021a). Indigenous fire-managed landscapes in Southeast Australia during the Holocene—New insights from the Furneaux Group Islands, Bass Strait. *Fire, 4*, 1–17.

Adeleye, M. A., Haberle, S. G., Harris, S., Hopf, F. V.-L., Connor, S., & Stevenson, J. (2021b). Holocene heathland development in temperate oceanic Southern Hemisphere: Key drivers in a global context. *Journal of Biogeography, 48*(5), 1048–1062.

Adeleye, M. A., Mariani, M., Connor, S., Haberle, S. G., Herbert, A., Hopf, F., & Stevenson, J. (2020). Long-term drivers of vegetation turnover in Southern Hemisphere temperate ecosystems. *Global Ecology and Biogeography, 30*, 557–571.

Archibald, S., Lehmann, C. E., Gómez-Dans, J. L., & Bradstock, R. A. (2013). Defining pyromes and global syndromes of fire regimes. *Proceedings of the National Academy of Sciences, 110*, 6442–6447.

Belcher, C. M., New, S. L., Santín, C., Doerr, S. H., Dewhirst, R. A., Grosvenor, M. J., & Hudspith, V. A. (2018). What can charcoal reflectance tell us about energy release in wildfires and the properties of pyrogenic carbon? *Frontiers in Earth Science, 6*, 169. DOI=10.3389/feart.2018.00169.

Beringer, J., Hutley, L. B., Abramson, D., Arndt, S. K., Briggs, P., Bristow, M., . . . Evans, B. J. (2015). Fire in Australian savannas: From leaf to landscape. *Global Change Biology, 21*, 62–81.

Birks, H. J. B. (2012). Ecological palaeoecology and conservation biology: Controversies, challenges, and compromises. *International Journal of Biodiversity Science, Ecosystem Services & Management, 8*, 292–304.

Black, M. P., & Mooney, S. D. (2007). The response of Aboriginal burning practices to population levels and El Niño–Southern Oscillation Events during the Mid- to Late Holocene: A case study from the Sydney Basin using charcoal and pollen analysis. *Australian Geographer*, 38(1), 37–52.

Black, M. P., Mooney, S. D., & Attenbrow, V. (2008). Implications of a 14,200 year contiguous fire record for understanding human–climate relationships at Goochs Swamp, New South Wales, Australia. *The Holocene*, 18(3), 437–447.

Black, M. P., Mooney, S. D., & Haberle, S. G. (2007). The fire, human and climate nexus in the Sydney Basin, eastern Australia. *The Holocene*, 17(4), 469–480.

Blake, D. H., Saunders, J. C., McAlpine, J. R., & Paijmans, K. (2010). No. 32 Land-form types and vegetation of eastern Papua. In *CSIRO land research surveys* (pp. 1–64). Melbourne: CSIRO.

Bliege Bird, R., Bird, D. W., & Codding, B. F. (2016). People, El Niño southern oscillation and fire in Australia: fire regimes and climate controls in hummock grasslands. *Philosophical Transactions of the Royal Society B*, 371, 20150343.

Bliege Bird, R., Bird, D. W., Codding, B. F., Parker, C. H., & Jones, J. H. (2008). The 'fire stick farming' hypothesis: Australian Aboriginal foraging strategies, biodiversity, and anthropogenic fire mosaics. *Proceedings of the National Academy of the Sciences*, 105(39), 14796–14801.

Bliege Bird, R., Bird, D. W., Fernandez, L. E., Taylor, N., Taylor, W., & Nimmo, D. (2018). Aboriginal burning promotes fine-scale pyrodiversity and native predators in Australia's Western Desert. *Biological Conservation*, 219, 110–118.

Bliege Bird, R. B., & Nimmo, D. (2018). Restore the lost ecological functions of people. *Nature Ecology & Evolution*, 2, 1050–1052.

Bowman, D. (2003a). Bushfires: A Darwinian perspective. In G. Carym, D. Lindenmayer, & S. Dovers (Eds.), *Australian burning: Fire ecology, policy and management issues* (pp. 3–15). Canberra: CSIRO.

Bowman, D. (2003b). Australian landscape burning: A continental and evolutionary perspective. In I. Abbott & N. Burrows (Eds.), *Fire in ecosystems of south-western Australia: Impacts and management* (pp. 107–118). Kerkwerve, The Netherlands: Backhuys.

Bowman, D., & Jackson, W. (1981). Vegetation succession in southwest Tasmania. *Search*, 12, 358–362.

Bowman, D. M., Balch, J., Artaxo, P., Bond, W. J., Cochrane, M. A., D'antonio, C. M.,Kull, C. A. (2011). The human dimension of fire regimes on Earth. *Journal of Biogeography*, 38, 2223–2236.

Boyd, W. E. (1990) Quaternary pollen analysis in the arid zone of Australia: Dalhousie Springs, Central Australia. *Review of Palaeobotany and Palynology*, 64, 331–341.

Bradstock, R. A., Gill, M. A., & Williams, R. J. (Eds.) (2012). *Flammable Australia: Fire regimes, biodiversity and ecosystems in a changing world*. Melbourne: CSIRO.

Builth, H., Kershaw, A. P., White, C., Roach, A., Hartney, L., McKenzie, M., . . . Jacobsen, G. (2008). Environmental and cultural change on the Mt Eccles lava-flow landscapes of southwest Victoria, Australia. *The Holocene*, 18, 413–424.

Carcaillet, C., Bouvier, M., Frechette, B., Larouche, A., & Richard, P. (2001). Comparison of pollen slide and sieving methods in lacustrine charcoal analyses for local and regional fire history. *The Holocene*, 11(4), 467–476.

Carym, G., Lindenmayer, D., & Dovers, S. (Eds.) (2003). *Australian burning: Fire ecology, policy and management issues*. Canberra: CSIRO.

Chalson, J. (1983). *Palynology and palaeoecology of Jibbon Swamp, Royal National Park, New South Wales* (Honours thesis). University of New South Wales, Kensington.

Clark, J. S. (1988). Particle motion and the theory of charcoal analysis—source area, transport, deposition, and sampling. *Quaternary Research, 30*, 67–80.

Clark, J. S., & Patterson, W. A. (1997). Background and local charcoal in sediments: Scales of fire evidence in the palaeorecord. In J. S. Clark, H. Cashier, J. W. Goldammer, & B. Stocks (Eds.), *Sediments of biomass burning and global change* (pp. 23–48). Berlin: Springer-Verlag.

Clark, J. S., & Royall, P. D. (1996). Local and regional sediment charcoal evidence for fire regimes in presettlement north-eastern North America. *Journal of Ecology, 84*, 365–382.

Clark, R. L. (1982). Point count estimation of charcoal in pollen preparations and thin sections of sediments. *Pollen et Spores, 24*(3–4), 523–535.

Clark, R. L. (1983). Pollen and charcoal evidence for the effects of Aboriginal burning on the vegetation of Australia. *Archaeology in Oceania, 18*(1), 32–37.

Conedera, M., Tinner, W., Neff, C., Meurer, M., Dickens, A. F., & Krebs, P. (2009). Reconstructing past fire regimes: Methods, applications, and relevance to fire management and conservation. *Quaternary Science Reviews, 28*, 555–576.

Coughlan, M. R., & Petty, A. M. (2012). Linking humans and fire: A proposal for a transdisciplinary fire ecology. *International Journal of Wildland Fire, 21*, 477–487.

Cupper, M. L. (2005). Last glacial to Holocene evolution of semi-arid rangelands in south-eastern Australia. *The Holocene, 15*, 541–553.

Cupper, M. L., Drinnan, A. N., & Thomas, I. (2000). Holocene palaeoenvironments of salt lakes in the Darling Anabranch region, south-western New South Wales, Australia. *Journal of Biogeography, 27*, 1079–1094.

David, B., McNiven, I. J., Mitchell, R., Orr, M., Haberle, S., Brady, L., & Crouch, J. (2004). Badu 15 and the Papuan-Austronesian settlement of Torres Strait. *Archaeology in Oceania, 39*, 65–78.

D'Costa, D. M., Edney, P., Kershaw, A. P., & De Deckker, P. (1989). Late Quaternary palaeoecology of Tower Hill, Victoria, Australia. *Journal of Biogeography, 16*, 461–482.

D'Costa, D. M., Grindrod, J., & Ogden, R. (1993). Preliminary environmental reconstructions from late Quaternary pollen and mollusc assemblages at Egg Lagoon, King Island, Bass Strait. *Australian Journal of Ecology, 18*, 351–366.

Dearing, J. A. (2006) Climate human environment interactions: Resolving our past. *Climate of the Past Discussions, 2*, 563–604.

De Deckker, P., Moros, M., Perner, K., Blanz, T., Wacker, L., Schneider, R., . . . Jansen, E. (2020). Climatic evolution in the Australian region over the last 94 ka-spanning human occupancy and unveiling the Last Glacial Maximum. *Quaternary Science Reviews, 249*, 106593.

Field, E., McGowan, H. A., Moss, P. T., & Marx, S. K. (2017). A late Quaternary record of monsoon variability in the northwest Kimberley, Australia. *Quaternary International, 449*, 119–135.

Field, J., Kealhofer, L., Cosgrove, R., & Coster, A. (2016). Human-environment dynamics during the Holocene in the Australian Wet Tropics of NE Queensland: A starch and phytolith study. *Journal of Anthropological Archaeology, 44*, B, 216–234.

Fitzsimmons, K. E., Cohen, T. J., Hesse, P. P., Jansen, J., Nanson, G. C., May, J. H., . . . Larsen, J. (2013). Late Quaternary palaeoenvironmental change in the Australian drylands. *Quaternary Science Reviews, 74*, 78–96.

Fletcher, M-S., Bowman, D. M. J. S., Whitlock, C., Mariani, M., & Stahle, L. (2018). The changing role of fire in conifer-dominated temperate rainforest through the last 14,000 years. *Quaternary Science Reviews, 182*, 37–47.

Fletcher, M.-S., Hall, T., & Alexandra, A. N. (2020). The loss of an indigenous constructed landscape following British invasion of Australia: An insight into the deep human imprint on the Australian landscape. *Ambio, 50*, 138–149.

Fletcher, M.-S., & Thomas, I. (2010). The origin and temporal development of an ancient cultural landscape. *Journal of Biogeography, 37*, 2183–2196.

Fletcher, M.-S., Wolfe, B. B., Whitlock, C., Pompeani, D. P., Heijnis, H., Haberle, S. G., . . . Bowman, D. M. (2014). The legacy of mid-Holocene fire on a Tasmanian montane landscape. *Journal of Biogeography, 41*(3), 476–488.

Fletcher, M.-S., Wood, S., & Haberle, S. (2014). A fire-driven shift from forest to non-forest: Evidence for alternative stable states? *Ecology, 95*, 2504–2513.

Foreman, P. (2020). The 1840 Western Port journey and Aboriginal fire history in the grassy ecosystems of lowland, mesic south-eastern Australia. *Australian Journal of Botany, 68*(4), 320–332.

Foreman, P. W. (2016). A framework for testing the influence of Aboriginal burning on grassy ecosystems in lowland, mesic south–eastern Australia. *Australian Journal of Botany, 64*, 626–642.

Fox, I. D., Neldner, V. J., Wilson, G. W., & Bannink, P. J. (2001). *Vegetation of the Australian tropical savannas*. Brisbane: Queensland Government, Environmental Protection Agency.

Gallagher, S. J., & Wagstaff, B. E. (2021). Quaternary environments and monsoonal climate off northwest Australia: Palynological evidence from Ocean Drilling Program Site 765. *Quaternary Science Reviews, 259*, 106917.

Gammage, B. (2012). *The biggest estate on Earth: How Aborigines made Australia*. Sydney: Allen & Unwin.

Gavin, D. G., Brubaker, L. B., & Lertzman, K. P. (2003). Holocene fire history of a coastal temperate rainforest based on soil charcoal radiocarbon dates. *Ecology, 84*, 186–201.

Gill, A. M. (1999). Biodiversity and bushfires: an Australia-wide perspective on plant-species changes after a fire event. In A. M. Gill, J. C. Woinarski, & A. York (Eds.), *Australia's biodiversity—Responses to fire: Plants, birds and invertebrates* (pp. 9–53). Environment Australia Biodiversity Technical Paper: 1. Canberra.

Gill, A. M., Woinarski, J. C., & York, A. (1999). *Australia's biodiversity—Responses to fire: Plants, birds and invertebrates*. Environment Australia Biodiversity Technical Paper: 1. Canberra.

Gosling, W. D., Cornelissen, H. L., & McMichael, C. N. H. (2019). Reconstructing past fire temperatures from ancient charcoal material. *Palaeogeography, Palaeoclimatology, Palaeoecology, 520*, 128–137.

Gott, B. (2005) Aboriginal fire use in south-eastern Australia: Aims and frequency. *Journal of Biogeography, 32*, 1203–1208.

Gowlett, J. A. (2016). The discovery of fire by humans: A long and convoluted process. *Philosophical Transactions of the Royal Society B: Biological Sciences, 371*, 20150164.

Guyette, R. P., Muzika, R. M., & Dey, D. C. (2002). Dynamics of an anthropogenic fire regime. *Ecosystems, 5*, 472–486.

Haberle, S. (2003). The emergence of an agricultural landscape in the highlands of New Guinea. *Archaeology in Oceania, 38*, 149–158.

Haberle, S. (2005). A 23,000-yr pollen record from Lake Euramoo, Wet Tropics of NE Queensland, Australia. *Quaternary Research, 64*, 343–356.

Haberle, S. (2007). Prehistoric human impact on rainforest biodiversity in highland New Guinea. *Phil. Trans. R. Soc. B, 362*, 219–228.

Haberle, S., Hope, G., & van der Kaars, S. (2001). Biomass burning in Indonesia and Papua New Guinea: Natural and human-induced fire events in the fossil record. *Palaeogeography, Palaeoclimatology, Palaeoecology, 171*, 259–268.

Haddon, A. C. (1912). *Reports on the Cambridge Anthropological Expedition to Torres Straits.* Vol. 4. Cambridge: Cambridge University Press.

Head, L. (1994a). Landscapes socialised by fire: Post-contact changes in Aboriginal fire use in northern Australia, and implications for prehistory. *Archaeology in Oceania, 29*, 172–181.

Head, L. (1994b). Both ends of the candle? Discerning human impact on the vegetation. *Australian Archaeology, 39*, 82–86.

He, T., Lamont, B. B., & Pausas, J. G. (2019). Fire as a key driver of Earth's biodiversity. *Biological Reviews, 94*, 1983–2010.

Hesse, P. (2011). Sticky dunes in a wet desert: Formation, stabilisation and modification of the Australian desert dunefields. *Geomorphology, 134*, 309–325.

Higuera, P. E., Gavin, D. G., Bartlein, P. J., & Hallett, D. J. (2010). Peak detection in sediment–charcoal records: Impacts of alternative data analysis methods on fire-history interpretations. *International Journal of Wildland Fire, 19*, 996–1014.

Hiscock, P. (2014). Creators or destroyers? The burning questions of human impact in ancient Aboriginal Australia. *Humanities Australia, 5*, 40–52.

Hope, G. S. (1978). The Late Pleistocene and Holocene vegetational history of Hunter Island, north-western Tasmania. *Australian Journal of Botany, 26*, 493–514.

Iversen, J. (1944). *Viscum, Hedera* and *Ilex* as climate indicators: A contribution to the study of the post-glacial temperature climate. *Geologiska Föreningen i Stockholm Förhandlingar, 66*, 463–483.

Jackson, W. (1968). Fire, air, water and earth—An elemental ecology of Tasmania. *Proceedings of the Ecological Society of Australia, 3*, 9–16.

Johnson, C. N. (2016). Fire, people and ecosystem change in Pleistocene Australia. *Australian Journal of Botany, 64*, 643–651.

Jones, T. P., Chaloner, W. G., & Kuhlbusch, T. A. J. (1997). Proposed bio-geological and chemical based terminology for fire-altered plant matter. In J. S. Clark, H. Cachier, J. G. Goldammer, & B. Stocks (Eds.), *Sediment records of biomass burning and global change* (pp. 9–22). Berlin: Springer-Verlag.

Joseph, L., Bishop, K. D., Wilson, C. A., Edwards, S. A., Lova, B., Campbell, C. D., . . . Drew, A. (2019). A review of evolutionary research on birds of the New Guinean savannas and closely associated habitats of riparian rainforests, mangroves and grasslands. *Austral Ornithology, 119*, 317–330.

Kelly, R. F., Higuera, P. E., Barrett, C. M., & Hu, F. S. (2011). A signal-to-noise index to quantify the potential for peak detection in sediment-charcoal records. *Quaternary Research, 75*, 11–17.

Kershaw, A. P., Bretherton, S. C., & van der Kaars, S. (2007). A complete pollen record of the last 230 ka from Lynch's Crater, north-eastern Australia. *Palaeogeography, Palaeoclimatology, Palaeoecology, 251*, 23–45.

Kershaw, A. P., Tibby, J., Penny, D., Yezdani, H., Walkley, R., Cook, E., & Johnston, R. (2004). Latest Pleistocene and Holocene vegetation and environmental history of the Western Plains of Victoria. *Proceedings of the Royal Society of Victoria, 116*, 141–163.

Kershaw, P., Clark, J. S., Gill, A. M., & D'Costa, D. (2002). A history of fire in Australia. In R. A. Bradstock, R. J. Williams, & M. A. Gill (Eds.), *Flammable Australia: Fire regimes, biodiversity and ecosystems in a changing world* (pp. 3–25). Canberra: CSIRO.

Kirch, P. V. (1997). Introduction: The environmental history of Oceanic Islands. In P. V. Kirch & T. L. Hunt (Eds.), *Historical ecology in the Pacific Islands. Prehistoric environmental and landscape change* (pp. 1–21). New Haven, CT: Yale University Press.

Kirch, P. V., & Hunt, T. L. (1997). *Historical ecology in the Pacific Islands.* New Haven, CT: Yale University Press.

Kodela, P. G., & Dodson, J. R. (1988). A Late Holocene vegetation and fire record from Kuring-gai Chase National Park, New South Wales. *Proceedings of the Linnean Society of New South Wales, 110,* 317–326.

Kull, C. A. (2008). Landscapes of fire: Origins, politics and questions. In B. David & J. Thomas (Eds.), *Handbook of landscape archaeology* (pp. 424–429). Walnut Creek, CA: Left Coast Press.

Ladd, P. G., Orchiston, D. W., & Joyce, E. B. (1992). Holocene vegetation history of Flinders Island. *New Phytologist, 122,* 757–767.

Larson, E. R., Kipfmueller, K., & Johnson, L. (2021). People, fire, and pine: Linking human agency and landscape in the Boundary Waters Canoe Area Wilderness and beyond. *Annals of the American Association of Geographers, 111,* 1–25.

Lawes, M. J., Murphy, B. P., Midgley, J. J., & Russell-Smith, J. (2011) Are the eucalypt and non-eucalypt components of Australian tropical savannas independent? *Oecologia, 166,* 229–239.

Lewis, T. M. (2012). A plant macrofossil identification tool for south-western Victoria. *The Artefact, 35,* 88–98.

Long, C. J., Whitlock, C., Bartlein, P. J., & Millspaugh, S. H. (1998). A 9000-year fire history from the Oregon Coast Range, based on a high-resolution charcoal study. *Canadian Journal of Forestry Research, 28,* 774–787.

Luly, J. G. (1993). Holocene palaeoenvironments near Lake Tyrrell, semi-arid northwestern Victoria, Australia. *Journal of Biogeography, 20,* 587–598.

Lynch, A., Ferrier, Å., Ford, A., Haberle, S., Rule, S., Schneider, L., . . . Metcalfe, D. (2020). Rainforest, woodland or swampland? Integrating time, space and culture to manage an endangered ecosystem complex in the Australian Wet Tropics. *Landscape Ecology, 35,* 83–99.

Lynch, A. H., Abramson, D., Görgen, K., Beringer, J., & Uotila, P. (2007). Influence of savanna fire on Australian monsoon season precipitation and circulation as simulated using a distributed computing environment. *Geophysical Research Letters, 34,* 20.

MacArthur, R. H., & Wilson, E. O. (1967). *The theory of island biogeography.* Princeton, NJ: Princeton University Press.

Mackenzie, L., Moss, P., & Ulm, S. (2020). A late-Holocene record of coastal wetland development and fire regimes in tropical northern Australia. *The Holocene, 30,* 1379–1390.

Macphail, M., Pillans, B., Hope, G., & Clark, D. (2020). Extirpations and extinctions: A plant microfossil-based history of the demise of rainforest and wet sclerophyll communities in the Lake George basin, Southern Tablelands of NSW, south-east Australia. *Australian Journal of Botany, 68,* 208–228.

Marguerie, D., Krause, T. R., & Whitlock, C. (2020). What was burning in the past? Charcoal identifications supplement an Early-Holocene fire-history reconstruction in Yellowstone National Park, USA. *Quaternary International, 593–594,* 256–269. doi.org/10.1016/j.quaint.2020.09.033.

Mariani, M., Connor, S., Theuerkauf, M., Herbert, A., Kunes, P., Bowman, D., . . . Briles, C. (2022). Disruption of cultural burning promotes shrub encroachment and unprecedented wildfires. *Frontiers in Ecology and the Environment, 20*(5), 292–300.

Mariani, M., Connor, S. E., Fletcher, M. S., Theuerkauf, M., Kuneš, P., Jacobsen, G., . . . Zawadzki, A. (2017). How old is the Tasmanian cultural landscape? A test of landscape openness using quantitative land-cover reconstructions. *Journal of Biogeography, 44*, 2410–2420.

Mariani, M., Fletcher, M.-S., Haberle, S., Chin, H., Zawadzki, A., & Jacobsen, G. (2019). Climate change reduces resilience to fire in subalpine rainforests. *Global Change Biology, 25*, 2030–2042.

Marlon, J. R., Bartlein P. J., Carcaillet C., Gavin D. G., Harrison S. P., Higuera P. E., . . . Prentice I. C. (2008). Climate and human influences on global biomass burning over the past two millennia. *Nature Geoscience, 1*(10), 697–702.

Marsden-Smedley, J. B. (1998). Changes in southwestern Tasmanian fire regimes since the early 1800s. *Papers and Proceedings of the Royal Society of Tasmania, 132*, 15–29.

Matchan, E. L., Phillips, D., Jourdan, F., & Oostingh, K. (2020). Early human occupation of southeastern Australia: New insights from 40Ar/39Ar dating of young volcanoes. *Geology, 48*, 390–394.

Matley, K. A., Sniderman, J. K., Drinnan, A. N., & Hellstrom, J. C. (2020). Late-Holocene environmental change on the Nullarbor Plain, southwest Australia, based on speleothem pollen records. *The Holocene, 30*, 672–681.

McCarthy, L., Head, L., & Quade, J. (1996). Holocene palaeoecology of the northern Flinders Ranges, South Australia, based on stick-nest rat (*Leporillus* spp.) middens: A preliminary overview. *Palaeogeography, Palaeoclimatology, Palaeoecology, 123*, 205–218.

McKenzie, G. M., & Kershaw, A. P. (2000). The last glacial cycle from Wyelangta, the Otway region of Victoria, Australia. *Palaeogeography, Palaeoclimatology, Palaeoecology, 155*, 177–193.

McNiven, I. J., Crouch, J., Richards, T., Dolby, N., Jacobsen, G., & Gunditj Mirring (2012). Dating Aboriginal stone-walled fishtraps at Lake Condah, southeast Australia. *Journal of Archaeological Science, 39*, 268–286

McNiven, I. J., Crouch, J., Richards, T., Sniderman, K., Dolby, N., & Gunditj Mirring (2015). Phased redevelopment of an ancient Gunditjmara fish trap over the past 800 years: Muldoons Trap Complex, Lake Condah, southwestern Victoria. *Australian Archaeology, 81*, 44–58.

McWethy, D. B., Haberle, S. G., Hopf, F., & Bowman, D. M. J. S. (2017). Aboriginal impacts on fire and vegetation on a Tasmanian Island. *Journal of Biogeography, 44*, 1319–1330.

McWethy, D. B., Higuera, P. E., Whitlock, C., Veblen, T. T., Bowman, D. M. J. S., Cary, G. J., ... Perry, G. L. W. (2013). A conceptual framework for predicting temperate ecosystem sensitivity to human impacts on fire regimes. *Global Ecology and Biogeography, 22*, 900–912.

Miller, B. P., & Murphy, B. P. (2017). Fire and Australian vegetation. In D. A. Keith (Ed.), *Australian vegetation* (pp. 113–135). Cambridge: Cambridge University Press.

Mooney, S. D., Harrison, S. P., Bartlein, P. J., Daniau A.-L., Stevenson, J., Brownlie, K. C., ... Williams, N. (2011). Late Quaternary fire regimes of Australasia. *Quaternary Science Reviews, 30*(1–2), 28–46.

Mooney, S. D., Harrison, S. P., Bartlein, P. J., & Stevenson, J. (2012). The prehistory of fire in Australasia. In R. A. Bradstock, M. A. Gill, & R. J. Williams (Eds.), *Flammable Australia: Fire regimes, biodiversity and ecosystems in a changing world* (2nd ed., pp. 3–25). Canberra: CSIRO.

Mooney, S. D., & Tinner, W. (2011). The analysis of charcoal in peat and organic sediments. *Mires and Peat, 7*, Art. 9.

Mooney, S. D., Webb, M., & Attenbrow, V. (2007). A comparison of charcoal and archaeological information to address the influences on Holocene fire activity in the Sydney Basin. *Australian Geographer, 38*(2), 177–194.

Moss, P. T., & Kershaw, A. P. (2007). A late Quaternary marine palynological record (oxygen isotope stages 1 to 7) for the humid tropics of northeastern Australia based on ODP Site 820. *Palaeogeography, Palaeoclimatology, Palaeoecology, 251*(1), 4–22.

Murphy, B. P., Bradstock, R. A., Boer, M. M., Carter, J., Cary, G. J., Cochrane, M. A., . . . Bowman, D. M. (2013). Fire regimes of Australia: A pyrogeographic model system. *Journal of Biogeography, 40*, 1048–1058.

Nanson, G. C., Price, D. M., Jones, B. G., Maroulis, J. C., Coleman, M., Bowman, H., . . . Larsen, J. R. (2008). Alluvial evidence for major climate and flow regime changes during the middle and late Quaternary in eastern central Australia. *Geomorphology, 101*, 109–129.

Norman, K., Inglis, J., Clarkson, C., Faith, J. T., Shulmeister, J., & Harris, D. (2018). An early colonisation pathway into northwest Australia 70–60,000 years ago. *Quaternary Science Reviews, 180*, 229–239.

Pascoe, B. (2014). *Dark emu black seeds: Agriculture or accident?* Broome: Magabala Books.

Pausas, J. G., & Bradstock, R. A. (2007). Fire persistence traits of plants along a productivity and disturbance gradient in Mediterranean shrublands of south-east Australia. *Global Ecology and Biogeography, 16*, 330–340

Pausas, J. G., Lamont, B. B. (2018). Ecology and biogeography in 3D: The case of the Australian Proteaceae. *Journal of Biogeography, 45*, 1469–1477.

Pearsall, D. M. (2000). *Paleoethnobotany. A handbook of procedures.* San Diego, CA: Academic Press.

Pearson, S., & Dodson, J. R. (1993). Stick-nest rat middens as sources of paleoecological data in Australian deserts. *Quaternary Research, 39*, 347–354.

Perry, G. L., Wilmshurst, J. M., McGlone, M. S., McWethy, D. B., & Whitlock, C. (2012). Explaining fire-driven landscape transformation during the initial burning period of New Zealand's prehistory. *Global Change Biology, 18*, 1609–1621.

Power, M. J., Marlon, J., Ortiz, N., Bartlein, P. J., Harrison, S. P., Mayle, F. E., . . . Zhang, J. H. (2008). Changes in fire regimes since the Last Glacial Maximum: An assessment based on a global synthesis and analysis of charcoal data. *Climate Dynamics, 30*, 887–907.

Reeves, J. M., Bostock, H. C., Ayliffe, L. K., Barrows, T. T., De Deckker, P., Devriendt, L. S., . . . Griffiths, M. L. (2013). Palaeoenvironmental change in tropical Australasia over the last 30,000 years—A synthesis by the OZ-INTIMATE group. *Quaternary Science Reviews, 74*, 97–114.

Rehn, E., Rehn, A., & Possemiers, A. (2019). Fossil charcoal particle identification and classification by two convolutional neural networks. *Quaternary Science Reviews, 226*, 106038.

Romano, A., & Fletcher, M. S. (2018). Evidence for reduced environmental variability in response to increasing human population growth during the late Holocene in northwest Tasmania, Australia. *Quaternary Science Reviews, 197*, 93–208.

Roos, C. I., Bowman, D. M., Balch, J. K., Artaxo, P., Bond, W. J., Cochrane, M., . . . Krawchuk, M. A. (2014). Pyrogeography, historical ecology, and the human dimensions of fire regimes. *Journal of Biogeography, 41*, 833–836.

Roos, C. I., Williamson, G. J., & Bowman, D. M. J. S. (2019). Is anthropogenic pyrodiversity invisible in paleofire records? *Fire, 2*, 42.

Rowe, C. (2007a). A palynological investigation of Holocene vegetation change in Torres Strait, seasonal tropics of northern Australia. *Palaeogeography, Palaeoclimatology, Palaeoecology, 251*, 83–103.

Rowe, C. (2007b). Landscapes in Torres Strait history. In B. David, B. Barker, & I. J. McNiven (Eds.), *The social archaeology of Australian Indigenous societies* (pp. 270–287). Canberra: Aboriginal Studies Press.

Rowe, C. (2015). Late Holocene swamp transition in the Torres Strait, northern tropical Australia. *Quaternary International, 385,* 56–68.

Rowe, C., Brand, M., Hutley, L. B., Wurster, C., Zwart, C., Levchenko, V., & Bird, M., (2019a). Holocene savanna dynamics in the seasonal tropics of northern Australia. *Review of Palaeobotany and Palynology, 267,* 17–31.

Rowe, C., David, B., Mialanes, J., Ulm, S., Petchey, F., Aird, S., . . . Richards. T. (2019b). A Holocene record of savanna vegetation dynamics in southern lowland Papua New Guinea. *Vegetation History and Archaeobotany, 29,* 1–14.

Rule, S., Brook, B., Haberle, S., Turney, C., Kershaw, A. P., & Johnson, C. (2012). The aftermath of megafaunal extinction: Ecosystem transformation in Pleistocene Australia. *Science, 335,* 1483–1486.

Russell-Smith, J., Price, O. F., & Murphy, B. P. (2010). Managing the matrix: Decadal responses of eucalypt-dominated savanna to ambient fire regimes. *Ecological Applications, 20,* 1615–1632.

Russell-Smith, J., Whitehead, P. J., Cook, G. D., & Hoare, J. L. (2003). Response of *Eucalyptus*-dominated savanna to frequent fires: Lessons from Munmarlary, 1973–1996. *Ecological Monographs, 73,* 349–375.

Sadler, J. P. (1999). Biodiversity on oceanic islands: A palaeoecological assessment. *Journal of Biogeography, 26,* 75–87.

Scholes, R. J., & Archer, S. R. (1997). Tree-grass interactions in savannas. *Annual Review of Ecology and Systematics, 28,* 517–544.

Scott, A. C. (2000). The pre-Quaternary history of fire. *Palaeogeography, Palaeoclimatology, Palaeoecology, 164,* 281–329.

Sim, R. (1998). *The archaeology of isolation? Prehistoric occupation in the Furneaux Group of islands, Bass Strait, Tasmania* (PhD thesis). Australian National University, Canberra.

Singh, G., & Luly, J. (1991). Changes in vegetation and seasonal climate since the last full glacial at Lake Frome, South Australia. *Palaeogeography, Palaeoclimatology, Palaeoecology, 84,* 75–86.

Sloss, C. R., Murray-Wallace, C. V., & Jones, B. G. (2007). Holocene sea level change on the southeast coast of Australia: A review. *The Holocene, 17,* 999–1014.

Sluiter, I. R., Blackburn, D. T., & Holdgate, G. R. (2017). Fire and Late Oligocene to Mid-Miocene peat mega-swamps of south-eastern Australia: A floristic and palaeoclimatic interpretation. *Australian Journal of Botany, 64,* 609–625.

Stevenson, J., Brockwell, S., Rowe, C., Proske, U., & Shiner, J. (2015). The palaeo-environmental history of Big Willum Swamp, Weipa: An environmental context for the archaeological record. *Australian Archaeology, 80,* 17–31.

Stevenson, J., & Haberle, S. (2018). *Macro charcoal analysis: A modified technique used by the Department of Archaeology and Natural History.* PalaeoWorks Technical Report: No. 5. ANU Open Research. http://hdl.handle.net/1885/144170.

Sutton, P., & Walshe, K. (2021). *Farmers or hunter-gatherers? The Dark Emu debate.* Melbourne: Melbourne University Press.

Theden-Ringl, F. (2018). *Common cores in the high country. The archaeology and environmental history of the Namadgi Ranges* (PhD thesis). Australian National University, Canberra.

Thomas, I., Enright, N. J., & Kenyon, C. E. (2001). The Holocene history of Mediterranean type plant communities, Little Desert National Park, Victoria, Australia. *The Holocene, 11,* 691–697.

Thomas, I., & Kirkpatrick, J. B. (1996). The roles of coastlines, people and fire in the development of heathlands in northeast Tasmania. *Journal of Biogeography, 23*, 717–728.

Tozer, M. G., Turner, K., Keith, D. A., Tindall, D., Pennay C., Simpson, C., ... Cox, S. (2010). Native vegetation of southeast NSW: A revised classification and map for the coast and eastern tablelands. *Cunninghamia, 11*(3), 359–406.

Trauernicht, C., Murphy, B. P., Prior, L. D., Lawes, M. J., & Bowman, D. M. (2016). Human-imposed, fine-grained patch burning explains the population stability of a fire-sensitive conifer in a frequently burnt northern Australia savanna. *Ecosystems, 19*, 896–909.

Twomey, T. (2013). The cognitive implications of controlled fire use by early humans. *Cambridge Archaeological Journal, 23*, 113–128.

Umbanhowar, C. E., & Mcgrath, M. J. (1998). Experimental production and analysis of microscopic charcoal from wood, leaves and grasses. *The Holocene, 8*(3), 341–346.

Umbanhowar, C. E., & Umbanhowar, J. A. (2021). Improving the efficiency of sediment charcoal image analysis. *The Holocene, 31*(7), 1229–1233. doi:10.1177/09596836211003226.

Vannière, B., Blarquez, O., Rius, D., Doyen, E., Brücher, T., Colombaroli, D., ... Olofsson, J. (2016). 7000-year human legacy of elevation-dependent European fire regimes. *Quaternary Science Reviews, 132*, 206–212.

Veth, P., O'Connor, S., & Wallis, L. A. (2000). Perspectives on ecological approaches in Australian archaeology. *Australian Archaeology, 50*, 54–66.

Vigilante, T., & Bowman, D. M. (2004). Effects of fire history on the structure and floristic composition of woody vegetation around Kalumburu, North Kimberley, Australia: A landscape-scale natural experiment. *Australian Journal of Botany, 52*, 381–404.

Weston, P. H., & Jordan, G. J. (2017). Evolutionary biogeography of the Australian flora in the Cenozoic era. In D. A. Keith (Ed.), *Australian vegetation* (3rd ed., pp. 40–63). Cambridge: Cambridge University Press.

Whitau, R., Vannieuwenhuyse, D., Dotte-Sarout, E., Balme, J., & O'Connor, S. (2018). Home is where the hearth is: Anthracological and microstratigraphic analyses of Pleistocene and Holocene combustion features, Riwi Cave (Kimberley, Western Australia). *Journal of Archaeological Method and Theory, 25*, 739–776.

Whitlock, C., Higuera, P. E., McWethy, D. B., & Briles, C. E. (2010). Paleoecological perspectives on fire ecology: Revisiting the fire-regime concept. *The Open Ecology Journal, 3*, 6–23.

Whitlock, C., & Larsen, C. P. S (2001). Charcoal as a fire proxy. In J. P. Smol, H. J. B. Birks, & W. M. Last (Eds.), *Tracking environmental change using lake sediments: Terrestrial, algal, and siliceous indicators* (Vol. 3, pp. 75–97). Dordrecht: Kluwer.

Williams, A. N., Mooney, S. D., Sisson, S. A., & Marlon, J. (2015). Exploring the relationship between Aboriginal population indices and fire in Australia over the last 20,000 years. *Palaeogeography, Palaeoclimatology, Palaeoecology, 432*, 49–57. doi:10.1016/j.palaeo.2015.04.030.

Williams, A. N., Ulm, S., Sapienza, T., Lewis, S., & Turney, C. M. S. (2018). Sea-level change and demography during the last glacial termination and early Holocene across the Australian continent. *Quaternary Science Reviews, 182*, 44–154.

Williams, R. J., Bradstock, R. A., Cary, G. J., Enright, N. J., Gill, A. M., Liedloff, A. C. ... York, A. (2009). *Interactions between climate change, fire regimes and biodiversity in Australia—A preliminary assessment*. Report to the Department of Climate Change and Department of the Environment, Water, Heritage and the Arts, Canberra.

Williams, R. J., Muller, W. J., Wahren, C. H., Setterfield, S. A., & Cusack, J. (2003). Vegetation. In A. N. Andersen, G. D. Cook, & R. J. Williams (Eds.), *Fire in tropical savannas. The Kapalga experiment* (pp. 79–106). New York: Springer-Verlag.

Woinarski, J., Mackey, B., Nix, H., & Traill, B. (2007). *The nature of northern Australia: Its natural values, ecological processes and future prospects.* Canberra: ANU e-Press.

Zeanah, D. W., Codding, B. F., Bliege Bird, R., & Bird, D. W. (2017). Mosaics of fire and water: The co-emergence of anthropogenic landscapes and intensive seed exploitation in the Australian arid zone. *Australian Archaeology, 83,* 2–19.

Zennaro, P., Kehrwald, N., Marlon, J., Ruddiman, W. F., Brücher, T., Agostinelli, C., . . . Barbante, C. (2015). Europe on fire three thousand years ago: Arson or climate? *Geophysical Research Letters, 42,* 5023–5033. doi:10.1002/ 2015GL064259.

CHAPTER 15

STONE-WALLED FISH TRAPS OF AUSTRALIA AND NEW GUINEA AS EXPRESSIONS OF ENHANCED SOCIALITY

IAN J. MCNIVEN AND ARIANA B. J. LAMBRIDES

INTRODUCTION

FOR thousands of years, many Indigenous communities of Australia and New Guinea have fished their rivers and seas to obtain fish as an important source of protein. Importantly, this resource selection was mediated by sophisticated ecological knowledge and cultural preference for certain species and capture technologies. As with other parts of the globe, the archaeology of marine and freshwater fishing in this broad and diverse region has been confined largely to analyses of fish bones in occupation deposits (e.g., Allen 2017; Lambrides, McNiven, & Ulm 2019). Indeed, the region reveals key high-resolution examples for Late Pleistocene fishing in a global context, with freshwater fish bones at Lakes Mungo and Tandou in western New South Wales (Australia) dated to ~30,000–20,000 years ago (Balme 1995; Long et al. 2014), and marine fish bones at New Ireland (Papua New Guinea) dated to ~35,000 years ago (Allen, Gosden, & White 1989: 552). In Timor-Leste, on Australia's doorstep, the earliest evidence for fishing dates to ~44,000–42,000 years ago, and here some of the oldest known examples of shell fish hook manufacture are recorded at 23,000–16,000 years ago (Hawkins et al. 2017; O'Connor, Ono, & Clarkson 2011). The earliest known example of shell fish hooks recovered in association with mortuary practices comes from the nearby Alor Island (Indonesia), which demonstrates the cosmological and ritual dimension of fishing and the sea to this community from a minimum of 12,000 years ago (O'Connor et al. 2017). In terms of nonportable fishing technology, the world's oldest known stone-walled fish trap, dated to at least 6600 years ago, is at Lake Condah in southwest Victoria in southeastern Australia. This fish trap provides evidence for deliberate manipulation and management of waterways to harvest short-finned eels (McNiven et al. 2012).

This chapter concerns the archaeology of Indigenous fishing practices in Australia and New Guinea, focusing on trapping facilities and especially stone-walled fish traps in freshwater and marine contexts. It is organized around four central themes: (1) the archaeology of stone-walled fish traps in terms of technical and social dimensions to explore current and emerging research topics; (2 and 3) surveys of ethnographic and archaeological records on Indigenous fishing methods in freshwater and marine contexts to reveal the diversity of fishing practices used across the region; and (4) the ongoing archaeological challenges associated with investigating links between changes in social organization and the establishment of stone-walled fish traps as fixed-in-place facilities in land- and seascapes.

ARCHAEOLOGY OF STONE-WALLED FISH TRAPS

Nearly all archaeological research on fish traps across Australia and New Guinea has taken place in Australia. Most of this research has concerned stone-walled fish traps in freshwater and marine contexts, with archaeological evidence for organic fish traps extremely rare. Archaeological research on coral/stone-walled fish traps in Australia and New Guinea has technical (e.g., preservation and visibility, mapping and recording, form and classification, chronology and dating) and social (e.g., ownership, territoriality, organization) dimensions.

Technical Dimensions

Our capacity to document archaeologically the material dimensions of fishing practices (e.g., faunal remains and fishing technology) are mediated by variable preservation and visibility. Beyond recovered shell fish hooks, to date little archaeological evidence of organic fishing technologies (e.g., basket traps, stake fence weirs) have been recorded in either Australia or New Guinea, as wetland archaeology is poorly developed across the region. Nonportable trapping facilities are often the only available archaeological evidence for fish-capture techniques, and as such research has focused on fixed-in-place structures such as coral-walled (marine) fish traps in Papua New Guinea and stone-walled (freshwater and marine) fish traps in Australia. The identification of fish traps in the region has been achieved primarily through pedestrian surveys, which are often guided by historical records and oral histories (e.g., Carter et al. 2004; Roberts et al. 2016), and less frequently, by aerial survey in order to facilitate large-scale surveys (e.g., Memmott, Robins, & Stock 2008).

These seemingly robust structures have undergone cultural and natural modification in shape and form through time. For example, McEldowney (1995: 275) found that only 49% of coral-walled fish traps at Andra Island (Papua New Guinea) visible in 1943 remained in 1987. The long-term preservation of stone/coral-walled fish traps is likely to be reduced along wave-active coastlines compared to the calmer waters of protected inlets (Rowland & Ulm 2011: 37). Curation of walled traps directly influences their preservation and visibility. Ethnographic observations note the deliberate curatorial dismantling of stone-walled tidal traps in marine contexts to ensure that fish were not caught in traps while people were not around to collect the catch. In some cases, the 'entire length' of the stone-walled trap was 'dismantled' (Smith 1983: 31–32), and in other situations a short section of wall was left open to allow fish to escape. Seasonal curatorial dismantling is known also for freshwater organic fish traps. Gibbs (2011: 8) noted that the Barragup mungah brush-walled weir on the Serpentine River in southwest Western Australia required annual maintenance as it was 'partially demolished each year, or washed away by winter flooding'.

Walled trap destructive processes may be ameliorated where building blocks are cemented together by coralline algae (McEldowney 1995: 275, 276, 319) or oysters (e.g., Memmott, Robins, & Stock 2008: 89, 91; Roth 1901: 23). Similarly, burial of coral/stone-walled fish traps in sediments will aid preservation but at the possible cost of visibility and accessibility (e.g., Memmott, Robins, & Stock 2008: 79). Despite these preservation issues, stone-walled fish traps have greater potential for preservation compared to many other fishing technologies such as organic weirs, baskets, and nets. In this sense, stone-walled traps are likely to be overrepresented in the archaeological record compared to other fishing practices. This highlights the important role of ethnographic records and oral histories for documenting the possible range of fishing techniques used in the past.

The mapping and recording approach utilized can impact assessments of trap construction and function, which emphasizes the importance of comprehensive and systematic methods that move beyond basic sketch maps and limited photography (e.g., Dortch, Dortch, & Reynolds 2006; Kreij, Scriffignano, Rosendahl, Nagel, & Ulm 2018; McNiven et al. 2015; Roberts et al. 2016). Mapping of freshwater stone-walled traps has concentrated on ground surveys using grids (to allow drawing of individual rocks) (e.g., Coutts, Frank, & Hughes 1978; McNiven et al. 2012) or Total Station surveying instruments for the creation of Digital Elevation Models (DEMs) to analyse functionality at different water levels (e.g., Builth 2014; Richards 2013). In contrast, nearly all mapping of marine (tidal) coral/stone-walled fish traps, especially fish trap complexes, in Australia (e.g., Barham 2000; Campbell 1982; Dortch 1997; McNiven 1994; Memmott, Robins, & Stock 2008) and New Guinea (e.g., McEldowney 1995) has entailed tracings of aerial photographs. Aerial mapping has increasingly turned to plane- and drone-based photogrammetry to produce detailed DEMs and 3D contour topographic models amenable for GIS (Geographic Information System) analysis of water-flow patterns and trap function in response to short-term tidal fluctuations and long-term sea-level change (e.g., Kreij et al. 2018; Van Waarden & Wilson 1994).

Archaeologists have developed a wide range of terms to describe the form of marine (tidal) walled fish traps, focusing on descriptions of shape (e.g., Dix & Meagher 1976), function (e.g., Campbell 1982), and structural composition (e.g., Dortch et al. 2006). It is well recognized that designations are often arbitrary and subjective, with little scope for consistency and replicability, which can influence our ability to undertake regional assessments of trap construction and function (Kreij et al. 2018: 149; Memmott, Robins, & Stock 2008; Rowland & Ulm 2011). Godwin (1988: 52) identified three major morphological types of stone-walled fish traps in freshwater and marine contexts in Australia: horseshoe or semicircular, maze-like, and V-shaped. Rowland and Ulm's (2011: 3) authoritative survey identified five basic types: U-shaped, V-shaped, O-shaped, straight, and rectangular. The wide range of terms developed over the past four decades to describe freshwater stone-walled structures in southwest Victoria (e.g., Builth 2014; Clark 1991; Coutts et al. 1978) can be simplified down to three broad structure types: channels, weirs, and dams (Brown, Rose, McNiven, & Crocker 2017: 15). Most recently, Kreij et al. (2018: 159) suggested that a classification system based on geometric features derived from measures of length, height, and elevation, obtained through photogrammetric mapping, can offer 'a less subjective interpretation of fish trap construction and function.'

Archaeological approaches to absolute and relative dating of coral/stone-walled fish traps include association with the age of fish bones in adjacent middens (e.g., Bowen 1998; Walters 1985b; cf. Godwin 1988: 52–54; Memmott, Robins, & Stock 2008: 92), functionality linked to chronological changes in nearby lake/sea levels (e.g., Builth et al. 2008; Campbell 1982; Dortch 1997; Head 1989; Kreij et al. 2018; Memmott, Robins, & Stock 2008: 91; Roberts et al. 2016), degrees of coralline cementation (e.g., McEldowney 1995: 319–320), and radiocarbon dating of sedimentary infill matrices (e.g., Lourandos 1980; McNiven et al. 2012). No attempt has been made to radiocarbon-date the archaeological remains of organic fish traps in Australia and New Guinea. Attempts to date stone-walled tidal fish traps have been unsuccessful due to failure to recover datable materials within secure stratigraphic contexts (Dortch 1997: 21; Dortch et al. 2006; McNiven 1994).

In one of the only examples in Australia (and New Guinea) of chronometric dating of a stone-walled fish trap structure, McNiven et al. (2012, 2015) found that, after initial construction at least 6600 years ago, Muldoons Trap Complex at Lake Condah (western Victoria) witnessed a major expansion in building activity starting around 800 years ago. Kreij et al. (2018), using inundation modelling, showed that Kaiadilt Aboriginal stone-walled fish traps of Sweers Island (southern Gulf of Carpentaria) were constructed in the past 3500 years. These examples provide the first temporally constrained evidence for stone-walled fish trap construction and expansion, which directly enhances our capacity to explore the broader social (e.g., gender, organizational, ownership) contexts and relationships that underpin the installation of these fixed-in-place facilities.

Social Dimensions

Fish traps are expressions of fundamentally social phenomena whereby communities decide who constructs, maintains, and uses these facilities, and determine the protocols for catch distribution. The notion of community includes ancestors and other spiritual beings and forces associated with the cosmological dimensions of fish traps, which relates to the ontology of site origins and ownership, and rituals of site engagement, resource access, and enhancement.

Explorations of the sociality of fish traps and fishing more broadly were at the forefront of theoretical thinking in Australian archaeology in the 1970s and 1980s. Examples include food taboos and the apparent cessation of fishing in Tasmania around 3500 years ago (Jones 1978; see also Bassett 2004; Sim 1999), gender roles and the uptake of shell fish hooks in New South Wales within the past 1000 years (Bowdler 1976; see also Walters 1988), and social complexity and elaboration of eel traps and eel farming in southwest Victoria over the past 3000 years (Lourandos 1980, 1983; see also McNiven et al. 2015). Only recently have archaeologists returned to theoretical issues of fish trap sociality in terms of gender (Lamb, David, Barker, Pivoru, & Alex 2019), social complexity (Builth 2014; Richards 2013), and cosmology and ritual (Bradley & McNiven 2019).

Coral/stone-walled fish traps, being among the largest engineered structures created by Indigenous peoples of Australia and New Guinea, are monumental and fixed-in-place expressions of resource extraction and sociality. Their physical scale, visibility, and durability place these sites as significant landscape and seascape features. Furthermore, the high social demands of coral/stone-walled fish traps in terms of histories of construction, maintenance, and use ensures that they contribute to the complex ways that freshwater and marine fishers conceptualize, temporalize, and inhabit their worlds. In this sense, coral/stone-walled fish traps are enduring and inherent features of inhabited waterscapes. That is, through the processes of continued visitation and use, coral/stone-walled fish traps constantly accumulate emplaced meaning and significance for fishers whose actions build on the inherited knowledge and labours of past generations and the enabling authority of the ancestors. Importantly, inhabited waterscapes involve people not living *off* aquatic resources but *with* aquatic worlds.

Although inhabited waterscapes concern inland and coastal peoples, the division between freshwater and saltwater can be arbitrary, especially along the lower estuarine reaches of waterways where the inland extent of tidal and saltwater influences can extend for many kilometres and vary seasonally. For many coastal communities, freshwater and saltwater differ ontologically, such that aquatic resource use encompasses the cosmological and spiritual realms (Gibson 2012; Jackson 2005; McNiven 2004; Morphy & Morphy 2006; Strang 2009; Toussaint, Sullivan, & Yu 2005). For example, the Yolngu of northeast Arnhem Land (northern Australia) describe the interactions between rivers and the sea as expressions of differing spiritual forces and agentive qualities between freshwater and saltwater (e.g., Morphy & Morphy 2006).

Beyond such ontological concerns, Indigenous fisheries of New Guinea and Australia can be considered in terms of freshwater and marine capture practices, with an acknowledgment that such a separation can be difficult and somewhat arbitrary in estuarine contexts. As seen in the following two sections, such a separation is heuristically instructive in revealing not only the diversity and complexity of differing fishing practices recorded ethnographically, but also the current limitations of archaeological research to appreciate this diversity and complexity. Although stone-walled fish traps have high archaeological visibility, ethnographic records indicate that such facilities represent one of many different types of fishing methods recorded over the past two centuries.

The following survey of fishing practices belies the complexities of social arrangements associated with the construction and production of different fishing technologies, and also the organization and undertaking of each method and associated differences in catch process—for instance, specialist versus nonspecialist operators, solitary versus cooperative pursuit, immediate versus delayed returns, small-scale versus large-scale harvesting, selective versus indiscriminate species capture, and live versus dead recovery. In most cases, available records do not provide such details.

Freshwater Fishing Practices and Fish Traps

Tropical New Guinea

Broad-scale ethnographic surveys of Indigenous freshwater fishing practices in New Guinea are rare (e.g., Mys & van Zwieten 1990; Quinn 2009; van der Heijden 2002). Regional ethnographic recordings indicate that freshwater (streams, rivers, and lakes) fishing in eastern New Guinea (Papua New Guinea) and western New Guinea (Indonesia) ranges from coastal lowlands through to highland valleys. A broad range of freshwater fishing methods is employed across New Guinea (Table 15.1). While both men and women use some fishing methods, in most cases methods are used primarily by either men (e.g., spears, bows and arrows) or women (e.g., hand-held nets). In marked contrast to Australia (see below), ethnographic references to freshwater stone-walled traps in New Guinea are rare. Use of organic/mud weirs was a 'communal activity' (Mys & van Zwieten 1990: 7). Little ethnographic information has been published on Indigenous freshwater fishing rituals in New Guinea (e.g., Lamb et al. 2019: 51; Landtman 1927: 144, 1933: 30).

In New Guinea, freshwater fish bones have been recovered from archaeological sites (e.g., McNiven et al. 2010) but no associated fishing technology has been documented. The lack of archaeologically recorded stone-walled freshwater traps reflects their apparent ethnographic rarity. Such rarity may also reflect poor preservation due to erosion associated with high rainfall (up to 8 m per year in some locations) across tropical

Table 15.1. Ethnographic examples of freshwater fishing methods in New Guinea.

Technique	Location	Gender	Reference
hook/gorge & line	Lake Sentani (WNG)	men	Boeseman (1963: 229)
	Lower Fly River (PNG)		Landtman (1927: 142, 1933: 29)
	Papuan Gulf (PNG)	men	Williamson (1913)
poison	Humboldt Bay region (WNG)		van der Sande (1907: 170)
	Marind (WNG)		Kooijman, Dorren, Veeger, Verschueren, & Luyken (1958: 5)
	Torassi River (PNG)	men & women	Hitchcock (2004: 171)
	Lower Fly River (PNG)		Landtman (1927: 144, 1933: 30)
	Lake Murray (PNG)		Busse (1991)
	Papuan Gulf (PNG)		Williamson (1913)
	Ok Tedi River (PNG)		Austen (1923: 345)
	Mt Hagen (PNG)		Ross (1936: 349)
	May River (PNG)	men	Swadling et al. (1988: fig. 133)
spear	Ajamaroe Lakes region (WNG)		Boeseman (1956: 25)
	Lake Sentani (WNG)	men	Boeseman (1963: 229)
	Torassi River (PNG)	men	Hitchcock (2004: 171)
	Turama River (PNG)	men	Austen (1946)
	Upper Strickland River (PNG)	men	Minnegal (1994: 151)
	Lower Ramu River (PNG)	men	Swadling et al. (1988: fig. 135)
	Lake Kutubu (PNG)	men	Williams (1940: 156)
	Aramia River (PNG)	men	Crawford (1981: 92)
bow & arrow	Muyu River (WNG)		Schoorl (1993: 72)
	Binaturi River (PNG)	men	Gumoi (2010: 309)
	Lower Fly River (PNG)		Landtman (1927: 144, 1933: 30)
	Aramia River (PNG)	men	Lyons (1926: 340)
	Upper Strickland River (PNG)	men	Minnegal (1994: 154)
	Papuan Gulf (PNG)		Williamson (1913)
	Ok Tedi River (PNG)		Austen (1923: 345)
	Mt Hagen (PNG)		Ross (1936: 346, 349)

(*continued*)

Table 15.1. Continued

Technique	Location	Gender	Reference
woven basket trap	Marind (WNG)		Kooijman et al. (1958: 5)
	Binaturi River (PNG)	women	Gumoi (2010: 316)
	Lower Fly River (PNG)	men & women	Landtman (1927: 145)
	Aramia River (PNG)	women	Crawford (1981: 91), Lyons (1926: 341)
	Turama River (PNG)	women	Austen (1946)
	Arafundi River (PNG)	women	Roscoe & Telban (2004: 101)
	Chambri Lakes (PNG)	women	Mead (1963: 240)
	Mt Hagen (PNG)		Ross (1936: 349)
	Mubi River (PNG)		Williams (1940: 157)
hand-held net	Lake Sentani (WNG)	women	Cheesman (1938: 29)
	Binaturi River (PNG)	women	Gumoi (2010: 313)
	Torassi River (PNG)	women	Hitchcock (2004: 171)
	Aramia River (PNG)	women	Crawford (1981: 92), Lyons (1926: 341)
	Papuan Gulf (PNG)	men & women	Williamson (1913)
	Sepik River (PNG)	women	Swadling et al. (1988: fig. 134)
	Goodenough Island (PNG)		Jenness & Ballantyne (1920: 1921)
	Mubi River (PNG)		Williams (1940: 157)
stick/fence trap	Lake Sentani (WNG)	women	Boeseman (1963: 227, 229)
	Mubi River (PNG)		Williams (1940: 157)
staked net	Lake Sentani (WNG)	women	Cheesman (1938: 29)
organic/mud weir	Ajamaroe & Aitinjo Lakes (WNG)		Boeseman (1956: 25, 1963: 235)
	Marind (WNG)		Kooijman et al. (1958: 5)
	Torassi River (PNG)	men & women	Hitchcock (2004: 171)
	Binaturi River (PNG)	men	Gumoi (2010: 314–316)
	Lower Fly River (PNG)		Landtman (1927: 144, 1933: 30)
	Aramia River (PNG)	women	Crawford (1981: 92), Lyons (1926: 341)
	Kikori River (PNG)	women	Lamb et al. (2019)

Table 15.1. Continued

Technique	Location	Gender	Reference
	Papuan Gulf (PNG)	men & women	Williamson (1913)
	Arafundi River (PNG)	men	Roscoe & Telban (2004: 101)
	Goodenough Island (PNG)		Jenness & Ballantyne (1920: 191)
stone weir	Upper Watut River (PNG)	men	Blackwood (1978: 36)

WNG=western New Guinea (Indonesia), PNG=Papua New Guinea

New Guinea. While there is limited ethnographic information on freshwater fishing practices in New Guinea (Table 15.1), available records do indicate a more focused use of organic fishing technologies (e.g., basket traps, stick/fence traps, nets, poison). Importantly, Lamb et al. (2019) provide an informative investigation of the poor archaeological preservation potential of aquatic resources obtained from organic/mud weirs by Rumu women in the Kikori River region of Papua New Guinea (Figure 15.1), and as such, they emphasize the importance of ethnography to expand our understanding of past subsistence regimes, utilized capture technologies, and gendered division of labour.

Tropical to Temperate Australia

Few ethnographic surveys have been made of the freshwater fishing practices of Indigenous Australians (e.g., Lawrence 1969; Rowland & Ulm 2011: 32–36). Numerous regional ethnographies indicate that the broad range of freshwater fishing methods employed is similar to that documented for New Guinea (Table 15.2). Again, some methods are used together, such as weirs used with woven basket traps (e.g., Altman 1983) and spears (e.g., Mathews 1903). Poisons are used to stupefy or kill fish, and in one practice waters are deliberately muddied to drive freshwater fish, seeking oxygen, to the surface (e.g., Hamlyn-Harris 1916: 14; Roth 1901: 19–20; Walters 1985a: 50). Freshwater weirs in Australia operate mostly with flood waters (e.g., Bates 1985: 251; Mathews 1903; Richards 2011). There is ethnographic evidence for trap complexes with features constructed at different elevations to allow operation at differing flood levels (e.g., Brewarrina fishery, New South Wales—Mathews 1903: 152). As with New Guinea, ethnographic recordings of Australian Indigenous freshwater fishing rituals are rare (e.g., Gibbs 2011: 10).

Although many published references on Indigenous Australian fishing do not mention gender, it is apparent that both men and women were fishers, but there was considerable regional variability in male-only and female-only activities. Frequently, these gender roles are complex, such as with the Gunditjmara of southwest Victoria where woven fishing baskets are made by women but used by men to fish (Gunditjmara People & Wettenhall 2010).

FIGURE 15.1. Top: Rumu women freshwater fishing with mud and brush weir on Epe Creek, Kikori River region, Papua New Guinea, February 2009.

(Photograph by Lara Lamb.)

Bottom: Gunditjmara stone-walled freshwater fish trap at Lake Condah, southwest Victoria, Australia, April 2008. Archaeological excavations revealed a buried channel dated to at least 6600 years ago.

(Photograph by Ian J. McNiven.)

STONE-WALLED FISH TRAPS OF AUSTRALIA AND NEW GUINEA 423

Table 15.2. Ethnographic examples of freshwater fishing methods in Australia.

Technique	Location	Gender	Reference
hook/gorge & line	Daly River (NT)		Massola (1956: 13), Spencer & Gillen (1904: 677)
	Alligator River (NT)		Spencer & Gillen (1904: 678)
	Central Darling River (NSW)		Dunbar (1944: 176)
	Gippsland Lakes (VIC)	women	Massola (1956: 6), Gerritsen (2001)
	Lower Murray River (SA)	men	Massola (1956: 4), Berndt et al. (1993: 562)
poison	Cape York Peninsula (QLD)		Thomson (1939: 215)
	Middle Palmer River (QLD)		Roth (1901: 19)
	Tully River (QLD)		Roth (1901: 19–20)
	Marlborough Creek (QLD)		Hamlyn-Harris (1916: 19)
	Upper Burnett River (QLD)		Hamlyn-Harris (1916: 20)
	Moreton Bay region (QLD)	men	Petrie (1992: 74)
	Katherine River (NT)		Hamlyn-Harris (1916: 21)
spear	Central Australia (NT)		Spencer & Gillen (1904: 676)
	Lower Tully River (QLD)	men	Roth (1901: 24)
	Moreton region (QLD)	men	Petrie (1992: 74)
	Central Darling River (NSW)		Dunbar (1944: 172)
	Gippsland Lakes (VIC)		Massola (1964: 6)
	Lower Murray River (SA)	men	Berndt et al. (1993: 562), Clarke (2002: 153)
	Koombana Bay (WA)		Roth (1903: 47)
woven basket trap	Tully River (QLD)	women	Roth (1901: 21)
	Western District (VIC)	men & women	Dawson (1881: 94), Gunditjmara People & Wettenhall (2010)
	Arnhem Land (NT)	men	Altman (1983)
hand-held net	Boulia district (QLD)		Roth (1901: 22)
	Pennefather River (QLD)	women	Roth (1901: 22)
	North Pine River (QLD)	men	Petrie (1992: 73), Walters (1985a: 53)
	Gippsland Lakes (VIC)	women	Smyth (1878, I: 389–390)
	West Kimberley (WA)	men	Bates (1985: 257)
	Fish Creek (NT)	men	McCarthy & McArthur (1960: 152)

(continued)

Table 15.2. Continued

Technique	Location	Gender	Reference
staked net	Lower Tully River (QLD)	men	Roth (1901: 22)
	Richmond River (NSW)		Bundock (1978: 264)
	Central Murray River (NSW)	men	Beveridge (1884: 48)
	Lake Eyre region (SA)		Horne & Aiston (1924: 63–64)
seine net	Central Murray River (NSW)	men	Beveridge (1884: 46–47)
	Lake Tyers (VIC)		Smyth (1878, I: 389)
organic/mud weir	Birthday Creek (QLD)		Roth (1901: 23)
	North Pine River (QLD)	men	Petrie (1992: 73)
	Central Murray River (NSW)		Beveridge (1884: 48)
	Western District (VIC)		Dawson (1881: 94)
	Koombana Bay (WA)		Roth (1903: 47)
	Serpentine River (WA)	men & women	Gibbs (2011), Hammond (1933: 46–47)
	West Kimberley (WA)		Bates (1985: 254)
	Bulgai Creek (NT)		Altman (1983)
stone weir	Nepean River (NSW)		Campbell (1978: 122)
	Brewarrina (NSW)		Dargin (1976), Mathews (1903)
	Western District (VIC)		McNiven & Bell (2010)
	Lake Colongulac (VIC)	women	Dawson (1881: 94)
	Salt Creek (VIC)	men & women	Dawson (1881: 94)
	Lake Condah (VIC)		Richards (2011)
	Lake Eyre region (SA)		Horne & Aiston (1924: 63–64)
	Coorong (SA)		Clarke (2002: 155)

NT=Northern Territory, QLD=Queensland, NSW=New South Wales, VIC=Victoria, SA=South Australia, WA=Western Australia

Freshwater fishing produced some of the largest items of portable and fixed-in-place traditional technology created by Indigenous Australians. For example, fishing nets made by Aboriginal peoples of the central Murray River region (New South Wales) measured 90 m x 1.2 m (Beveridge 1884: 45). Balme (1995: 17) points out that such fishing nets 'must have' had major social organizational implications given the investment in net manufacture. This point is reinforced by reference to Satterthwait's (1987: 615) estimate of 97–112 person days to manufacture an ethnographically recorded plant fibre net from western New South Wales measuring c. 18 x 12 m, with a 5 cm mesh gauge and 7.5–9 km of cord. Based on these estimates, the large fishing net recorded by Beveridge (1884: 45) would have required over 200 person days to manufacture.

The eel farm near Mt William (Victoria) covered an area of at least 6 ha and comprised a maze of excavated channels into which woven basket traps were placed at various intervals (Lourandos 1980, 1987). Dawson (1881: 94) recorded Aboriginal people of southwest Victoria constructing 1-m-high 'clay embankments' up to 370 m long to trap fish.

Little archaeological evidence of portable freshwater fishing technologies has been recovered in Australia. For example, none exists for ethnographically recorded stone sinkers used on fishing lines and fishing nets on the Lower Murray River in South Australia and at Lake Tyers in Victoria (Berndt, Berndt, & Stanton 1993: 96; Smyth 1878, I: 389–390). In the central Murray River region, neither ethnographically recorded baked clay sinkers used on fishing nets (Beveridge 1884: 47) nor 'ground flat and polished' stones banged together underwater to frighten fish into fishing nets (Anonymous 1878: 28–29) have been identified archaeologically. However, two apparent fish hooks made of bone have been excavated from a grave on the central Murray River (Gallus & Gill 1973). Fish bones provide an indirect means of inferring freshwater fishing methods in the past, with Balme (1983, 1995) associating the size-range characteristics of golden perch otoliths recovered from 22,000–27,000 BP sites in the lower Darling River region of western New South Wales with capture by gill nets.

The most well-documented archaeological expressions of freshwater fishing in Australia are stone-walled traps associated with lakes (e.g., Lake Condah, Victoria—Coutts et al. 1978) and waterways (e.g., Great Basalt Wall, Queensland—Flecker 1951; Manu Manu Creek, Queensland—Rowland & Ulm 2011: 34–36; Darlot Creek, Victoria—Builth 2014; and Kalgan River, Western Australia—Dix & Meagher 1976: 182) (Figure 15.1). A rare archaeological example of an organic (wooden stake) weir was recorded at Blackwater Creek in southwest Western Australia, comprising 'over 20 wooden stakes . . . and a single horizontal timber' with steel axe cut marks (Dortch & Gardner 1976: 275). Ethnographic information in Table 15.2 suggests strongly that stone-walled fish traps are overrepresented in archaeological evidence compared to other freshwater fishing methods such as nets. Despite this issue, archaeological analyses have provided the profound insight of the association of stone-walled fish traps in southwest Victoria with aquaculture (Builth 2014).

MARINE FISHING PRACTICES AND FISH TRAPS

Tropical New Guinea

Ethnographic surveys of Indigenous marine fishing practices for New Guinea (e.g., Anell 1955; Pernetta & Hill 1981; Quinn 2009; Reinman 1967) contextualize a wide range of marine fishing methods (Table 15.3). As is true of freshwater fishing, some marine

Table 15.3. Ethnographic examples of marine fishing methods in New Guinea.

Technique	Location	Gender	Reference
hook/gorge & line	MacCluer Gulf (WNG)		Anell (1955: 88)
	Mimika (WNG)	men	Wollaston (1912: 121)
	Lower Fly River (PNG)		Landtman (1933: 29)
	Dobu Island (PNG)		Jenness & Ballantyne (1920: 193)
	East New Britain (PNG)		Powell (1883: 177)
	Huon Gulf (PNG)		Maaz, Picasso, & Meyer (2012: 55)
	Ponam Island (PNG)	men & women	Carrier (1982)
poison	Andra Island (PNG)	men & women	McEldowney (1995: 342, 358)
	East New Britain (PNG)		Powell (1883: 177)
	Tanga Islands (PNG)	men	Bell (1947: 317)
	Mailu Island (PNG)		Specht & Fields (1984: 50)
spear	Mimika (WNG)	men	Wollaston (1912: 121)
	Lower Fly River (PNG)	men	Landtman (1927: 143, 1933: 29)
	East New Britain (PNG)		Powell (1883: 177)
	Tanga Islands (PNG)	men	Bell (1947: 317)
	Andra Island (PNG)	men & women	McEldowney (1995: 343, 358)
bow & arrow	Marind (WNG)	men	Kooijman et al. (1958: 46)
	Purari Delta (PNG)		Haines (1979)
	Manus Island (PNG)		Mitton (1979: 29)
harpoon	Mimika (WNG)	men	Wollaston (1912: 122)
	Asmat (WNG)		Schneebaum (1985: 154, 156)
	Andra Island (PNG)	men	McEldowney (1995: 342–343, 358)
woven basket trap	Cenderawasih Bay (WNG)		van der Sande (1907: 169)
	Marind (WNG)	women	McNiven (2010)
	Lower Fly River (PNG)	men & women	Landtman (1927: 145, 1933: 30)
	Purari Delta (PNG)	women	Haines (1979: 85)
	Papuan Gulf (PNG)	women	Frusher & Subam (1981)
	Ponam Island (PNG)	men & women	Carrier (1982: 913–914)

Table 15.3. Continued

Technique	Location	Gender	Reference
	New Britain (PNG)	men	Martin (2006)
	Tanga Islands (PNG)	women	Bell (1947:318)
	Goodenough Island (PNG)	men	Jenness & Ballantyne (1920:190–192)
	Manam Island (PNG)	men	Swadling et al. (1988: fig. 125)
hand-held net	Marind (WNG)	women	Kooijman et al. (1958:46)
	Ponam Island (PNG)	men & women	Carrier (1982:906–907)
	Andra Island (PNG)	men & women	McEldowney (1995:336–341)
	Kaiep village (PNG)	women	Swadling et al. (1988: fig. 126)
	Tanga Islands (PNG)	men	Bell (1947:317)
staked net	Papuan Gulf (PNG)		Frusher & Subam (1981)
	Port Moresby (PNG)	men	Pulsford (1975)
net set by canoe	Goodenough Island (PNG)	men	Jenness & Ballantyne (1920:190)
	New Britain (PNG)	men	Quinn (2009:144)
	Ponam Island (PNG)	men	Carrier (1982:906)
	Andra Island (PNG)	men	McEldowney (1995:336)
organic/mud weir	Lower Fly River (PNG)		Chalmers (1903:117–118), Landtman (1927:144)
stone/coral weir	Ponam Island (PNG)	men & women	Carrier (1982:913)
	Andra Island (PNG)	men & women	McEldowney (1995)
	Rossel Island (PNG)		Levinson (2008)

WNG=western New Guinea (Indonesia), PNG=Papua New Guinea

fishing techniques are used in conjunction, such as organic weirs and woven basket traps. The largest fishing nets include those from West New Britain Province, which measure over 100 m in length, take 1–2 months to manufacture, and require seven to eight men to operate (Quinn 2009: 144). In terms of illustrating the potential overrepresentation of tidal traps in the archaeological record, McEldowney (1995: 327) points out that for the Andra people of the Admiralty Islands of northern Papua New Guinea, 'walled traps are only one of 28 fishing methods' recognized. Curiously, and in contrast to Australia (see below), few examples of coral/stone-walled tidal traps in marine contexts have been recorded in New Guinea beyond the Admiralty Islands (Carrier 1982; McEldowney 1995). Rituals to increase marine fish catches have been recorded for some parts of Papua New Guinea—for example, to 'raise the likelihood of successful catches' in coral-walled tidal traps (McEldowney 1995: 365) and to 'induce' or 'invite' fish to enter woven basket traps (Landtman 1927: 144–145).

Schoeffel (1985: 164) suggests that '[i]n those Pacific island communities where fishing is a major part of the local subsistence and cash economy, there is typically a division of labour between men and women in which men fish from canoes and boats in deep water, or from the reefs at night using flares and handnets, and women glean the reefs, soft shores and swamps for a variety of edible species and, in many communities, also use fish traps, nets and hand lines to catch fish in lagoons and tidal pools' (see also Chapman 1987; Pernetta & Hill 1981: 185–186). Indeed, 'in Pacific communities where fishing is done, the contribution of women's fishing to the daily diet is at least as significant as that of men' (Schoeffel 1985: 160) (Figure 15.2).

Direct archaeological evidence of marine fishing technology in New Guinea includes shell net weights (e.g., Allen 2017; Shaw & Langley 2017), fish hooks (e.g., Szabó 2007), and walled traps (e.g., McEldowney 1995). In terms of walled traps, McEldowney's (1995) investigation of intertidal fish traps constructed of coral rubble on Andra and Ponam Islands (Admiralty Islands group, northern Papua New Guinea) is unique for New Guinea and is one of the most comprehensive archaeological analysis of marine tidal trap use for Australia and New Guinea (Figure 15.3). McEldowney's (1995) insights were enhanced by ethnographic information provided by local people who continue to use some of these facilities. Over 400 traps were recorded (using aerial photographs), with most comprising walls forming a V-shaped corridor to channel fish into a heart-shaped enclosure (McEldowney 1995: 250). On Ponam Island, over 100 traps link to form a continuous feature stretching over 3 km along the intertidal zone (McEldowney 1995: fig. 45). Most of the traps required annual rebuilding as they were constructed on the windward extent of the reef, which is exposed to seasonally destructive waves (McEldowney 1995: 235–250).

Tropical to Temperate Australia

Ethnographic overviews of Australian Indigenous marine fishing practices are limited (e.g., Lawrence 1969), as are overviews of specific fishing technologies (e.g., fish hooks— Attenbrow 2010; Gerritsen 2001; Massola 1956). The range of ethnographically known marine fishing methods shares many similarities with those methods used in New Guinea (Table 15.4). As with freshwater fishing, the range of utilized methods expands when fish drives are included, which refers to the corralling of fish by groups into cul-de-sacs or shallows for spearing or clubbing (e.g., Bates 1985: 252; Dortch 1997; Martin 1988: 47; Rouja 1998). Marine fish drives can also include the 'singing' (ritual calling up) of dolphins in Moreton Bay (southeast Queensland) and the Eyre and Yorke Peninsulas (South Australia) to corral fish into shallows for netting and spearing (Hall 1984; Martin

FIGURE 15.2. Top: Elema women marine fishing with hand nets (*keve*) on the shore of Orokolo Bay, Papuan Gulf, Papua New Guinea, January 1935.

(Photograph by F. E. Williams (from the collection of the National Archives of Australia. NAA: A6510, 239).)

Bottom: Butchulla men marine fishing with hand nets near Sandy Cape, northern K'gari, Queensland, Australia, December 1843.

(Lithograph based on drawing by Harden S. Melville (Melville 1849: pl. 5.).)

1988: 36, 41, 83; Roberts et al. 2016: 5). There are not always clear distinctions between organic and nonorganic fish trap constructions. Some walled traps are 'composite' structures with organic (stake and brush) walls and stone foundations (e.g., Dortch 1997: 16). Furthermore, fish constrained within tidal weirs can be picked up (if the trap is high and dry at low tide), netted (e.g., Memmott, Robins, & Stock 2008: 83–84; Petrie

Table 15.4. Ethnographic examples of marine fishing methods in Australia.

Technique	Location	Gender	Reference
hook/gorge & line	Torres Strait (QLD)	men & women	Haddon (1912: 155)
	Dunk Island (QLD)		Banfield (1908: 18)
	Keppel Islands (QLD)		Roth (1901: 21, 1904: 33)
	Sydney region (NSW)	women	Bowdler (1976: 253)
poison	Torres Strait (QLD)		Haddon (1912: 159)
	Dunk Island (QLD)		Hamlyn-Harris (1916: 4)
	Burdekin (QLD)		Roth (1901: 19)
	One Arm Point (WA)	men	Rouja (1998: 163–164)
spear	Torres Strait (QLD)	men & women	Haddon (1912: 155–158)
	Wellesley Islands (QLD)	men	Memmott, Robins, & Stock (2008: 82)
	Moreton region (QLD)	men	Petrie (1992: 72)
	Sydney region (NSW)	men	Bowdler (1976)
	Eyre Peninsula (SA)		Martin (1988: 45)
	Leschenault (WA)		Bunbury & Morrell (1930: 76)
	One Arm Point (WA)		Rouja (1998: 165–168)
	West Kimberley (WA)		Bates (1985: 255)
	Hemple Bay (NT)	men	McCarthy & McArthur (1960: 170)
harpoon	Tully River mouth (QLD)		Roth (1901: 23–24)
woven basket trap	Cape Stewart (NT)	men	Peterson (2003: 146–147)
hand-held scoop net	Torres Strait (QLD)	men	Haddon (1912: 155–156)
	K'gari (QLD)	men	Roth (1901: 23)
	Moreton region (QLD)	men	Petrie (1992: 72), Walters (1985a)
staked net	Moreton Bay (QLD)		Steele (1972: 19)
seine net	Rapid Bay (SA)	men	Worsnop (1897: 90)
	Encounter Bay (SA)	men	Worsnop (1897: 90)
organic/mud weir	Mapoon (QLD)		Roth (1901: 23)
	Saltwater Creek (QLD)	women	Rowland & Ulm (2011: 22)

STONE-WALLED FISH TRAPS OF AUSTRALIA AND NEW GUINEA   431

Table 15.4. Continued

Technique	Location	Gender	Reference
	Moreton region (QLD)	men	Petrie (1992:73–74), Walters (1985a: 51)
	Eyre Peninsula (SA)		Martin (1988: 37), Mountford (1939)
	Oyster Harbour (WA)		Dortch (1997: 21)
	West Kimberley (WA)		Bates (1985: 254)
	Cape Stewart (NT)	men	Peterson (2003: 146–147)
	Glyde River (NT)	men	Thomson (1938)
	Wessel Islands (NT)	men	Peterson (2003: 149)
stone/coral weir	Torres Strait (QLD)	men & women	Haddon (1912: 158–159), Lawrie (1970: 343)
	Wellesley Islands (QLD)	men & women	Memmott, Robins, & Stock (2008: 82), Roth (1901: 23)
	Mt. Dutton Bay (SA)		Mountford (1939)
	West Kimberley (WA)		Bates (1985: 255)
	Dampierland Peninsula (WA)	men & women	Akerman (1976), Smith (1983)
	Oyster Harbour (WA)	men	Dortch (1997: 21)
	Hyland Bay (NT)		Basedow (1907: 23)

QLD=Queensland, NSW=New South Wales, NT=Northern Territory, SA=South Australia, WA=Western Australia

1992: 73; Roth 1901: 23), or speared (e.g., Akerman 1976; Campbell 1978: 123; Johannes & MacFarlane 1991: 99; Memmott, Robins, & Stock 2008: 82) if water remained in the trap. In the latter case, walled traps can also function as holding or storage ponds for fish (e.g., Akerman 1976; Smith 1983: 33). The size of fish nets is variable, ranging from smaller single-person hand-held nets (Melville 1849) to large examples, like the plant fibre seine net collected by Flinders measuring 26 m x 1 m from Moreton Bay Aboriginal people in southeast Queensland in 1799 (Steele 1972: 19) (Figure 15.2).

Rituals associated with increasing marine fish catches, recorded in various parts of Australia (e.g., Haddon 1908: 217; Thomson 1938: 197), are used to draw fish into natural rock pools and stone-walled tidal traps (e.g., Haddon 1935: 197; Roberts et al. 2016: 5; Sullivan 1998: 101). In many cases, rituals aim to engage ancestral spirits who exercise power over fishing success. For example, Aboriginal men at Cape Stewart in Arnhem Land (northern Australia) would place a large baler shell at the apex of a V-shaped organic fence tidal weir in the hope of 'warding off ancestral ghosts who might interfere with its workings' (Peterson 2003: 146–147). In the Glyde River area of Arnhem Land,

Thomson (1938: 197–198) recorded that only senior landowners had the knowledge to undertake rituals 'to propitiate the [guardian] spirits of the totemic ancestors' to 'let go' of fish such that they could be trapped.

Ethnographic information indicates that marine fishing by Indigenous Australians was highly variable in terms of gender roles (Table 15.4). In some communities, particular fishing technologies were used by both men and women, but in other communities equivalent technologies may be used by only men or women (Table 15.4). Bowdler (1976: 249–250) noted that across Australia, nets and hooks/lines were used by men and/or women, whereas use of spears and poisons tended to be male activities. Overall, 'most of the fishing in Australia was done by men' (Bowdler 1976: 250).

Direct archaeological evidence of portable marine fishing technology in Australia includes shell fish hooks (e.g., Attenbrow 2010; Bowdler 1976) and bone barbs from fishing spears (e.g., Lampert 1966). The rarity of archaeologically recorded stone sinkers in Australian marine contexts (e.g., Carter 2001: 52) parallels the rarity of such objects in ethnographic recordings (e.g., Torres Strait—Haddon 1912: 155; Western Australia—Bates 1985: 250–251). Some studies have used archaeological fish bones to infer capture techniques based on the feeding behaviour of specific fish taxa (e.g., omnivorous fish are more likely taken by netting, spearing, and poisoning, while baited hooks are more suited to carnivorous fish—Butler 1994), fish behaviour (e.g., certain species avoid some capture techniques but not others—Colley & Jones 1987), and fish size (e.g., small fish are more likely caught using mass harvesting techniques such as tidal traps and nets—Attenbrow & Steele 1995). In Australia, rock art has provided unique (albeit very rare) graphic representations of marine fishing technology and practices (e.g., Chasm Island (Burrabarra), Gulf of Carpentaria—Mountford 1956: 102–104).

Stone-walled tidal traps provide the best documented and most extensive archaeological evidence of Australian Indigenous marine fishing technology. These traps have been recorded in Queensland (e.g., Barham 2000; Campbell 1982; Kreij et al. 2018; McNiven 1994; Memmott, Robins, & Stock 2008; Rowland & Ulm 2011; Walters 1985b), New South Wales (e.g., Godwin 1988), South Australia (e.g., Martin 1988; Roberts et al. 2016), Western Australia (e.g., Dix & Meagher 1976; Dortch 1997; Dortch et al. 2006; Smith 1983), and the Northern Territory (e.g., Bradley & McNiven 2019). It is difficult to know to what extent the absence of recorded stone-walled tidal fish traps of unambiguous Aboriginal origin in temperate Tasmania and Victoria relates to lack of use of such facilities (a view consistent with ethnographic records) or poor preservation (a view consistent with the rough seas of southeastern Australia). Rowland and Ulm's (2011) survey of Queensland fish traps is the single most detailed and comprehensive study of fish traps in Australia. The largest concentration of marine stone-walled fish traps in Australia is the Wellesley Islands and adjacent mainland in the Gulf of Carpentaria of Queensland where '108 trap sites containing at least 334 traps' have been recorded (Memmott, Robins, & Stock 2008: 77). Johannes and MacFarlane (1991: 99) calculated that Mer (Murray Island) in eastern Torres Strait has 7 km of tidal fish trap walls amounting to around 3500 tonnes of rock (Figure 15.3). It is unknown why the number of tidal traps is highest along northern tropical coasts compared to subtropical coasts of Australia.

FIGURE 15.3. Top: Coral-walled tidal fish trap (GMG-D) exposed at low tide on the reef edge on the north side of Andra Island, Admiralty Islands Group, northern Papua New Guinea, looking south.

(Photograph by Holly McEldowney (McEldowney 1995: Plate 10.).)

Bottom: Oblique aerial view of stone-walled fish traps (*sai*) exposed at low tide on the north side of Ugar (Stephen Island), eastern Torres Strait, Australia, looking northeast, May 2002.

(Photograph by Garrick Hitchcock.)

Archaeological evidence of organic (wooden stake) tidal marine traps is rare and is currently limited to the Eyre Peninsula of South Australia (Martin 1988: 61–63, 70–71). Porter Bay Site 1 revealed at least one hundred stakes (some with interwoven branches) over 50 m (Martin 1988: 61). Whereas techniques to date stone-walled tidal traps remain elusive beyond written and oral histories, the potential to radiocarbon date organic traps has not been realized.

SOCIALITY OF WALLED FISH TRAPS: ONGOING ARCHAEOLOGICAL CHALLENGES

The above surveys of fishing practices and trap use recorded ethnographically and archaeologically make it clear that the diverse freshwater and marine fishing methods utilized across New Guinea and Australia were underpinned by ecological knowledge, social arrangements, and cultural preference for certain species and capture strategies. Social arrangements operate at multiple levels, with decision making encompassing the manufacture, use, and maintenance of fishing technologies, considerations of ownership, access, and use of aquatic resources, and protocols associated with the distribution and consumption of the catch. In regards to fixed-in-place fishing facilities, such as stone-walled fish traps, the social and ecological landscape is uniquely transformed in such a way that could be considered distinct from other fishing practices. Stone-walled fish traps have the capacity to artificially increase the 'abundance' of aquatic resources and to 'regularize (stabilize)' this availability and increase its 'reliability' by enhancement of fish habitats and stocks through aquaculture (Lourandos 1976: 178, 1980: 246). This multidimensionality presents a series of research challenges for archaeology to investigate and elucidate in terms of the organizational aspects of stone-walled fish trap construction and the socioeconomic and sociopolitical implications associated with trap establishment, maintenance, and use in the past.

Structuring Structures

Construction of a stone-walled fish trap establishes a fixed-in-place facility in a land-/seascape with ongoing social commitments to, and implications for, ownership, maintenance, and use. It should also be noted that while these facilities are considered fixed-in-place, the persistence of these features on the landscape is both ecologically (e.g., sea-level changes, storm activity) and socially determined, with the latter influencing whether these traps are maintained, disused, or dismantled (see Bradley & McNiven 2019). Following Ingold's (1993: 152) notion of 'taskscape', construction of a stone-walled fish trap added a monumentalized structure to a 'landscape' as 'an enduring record of—and testimony to—the lives and works of past generations who have dwelt within it, and in doing so, have left there something of themselves'. As highly visual and fixed-in-place facilities, stone-walled fish traps redefine the social geometry of land- and seascapes, not just spatially but also temporally. For instance, these facilities signal past investments of labour, patterns of ownership (see below), and future investments in fishing activities, which are associated with social relationships and obligations by specific groups of people. Thus, while stone-walled fish traps function intermittently as fish-capture facilities, they function permanently as material dimensions of social relationships that implicate affiliation and exclusion. More specifically, such material dimensions are generative in terms of 'structuring future social acts and interactions' as 'structuring structures' (McNiven 2013: 576). In this sense, the timing of trap construction (and phased elaboration as documented at Lake Condah—McNiven et al. 2015) may be matched by concomitant changes in cultural practices registered archaeologically at other sites in the region that stem from interregional gatherings, resource enhancement, and ownership exclusivity.

Interregional Gatherings

Ethnographic records indicate that a number of Aboriginal groups across Australia participated in interregional gatherings supported by seasonal superabundances of fish. Some of these gatherings were marine fish based, such as at King George Sound in Western Australia (Dortch 1997: 30). Most ethnographic examples concern freshwater fish, such as at Brewarrina in central northern New South Wales (Mathews 1903: 153), Lake Bolac in southwest Victoria (Dawson 1881; Kenyon 1928: 146), and Serpentine River in southwest Western Australia (Gibbs 2011; Hammond 1933: 46–48; Paterson 1896: 289). Duncan-Kemp (1968: 274–275) noted that in the Channel Country of arid southwest Queensland, 'pens' constructed of 'stone or stiffly staked, woven reeds' held 'hundreds' of fish taken in 'good seasons, and . . . kept alive–and fat–until required for a feast', presumably associated with gatherings. Gilmore (1934: 191) recorded that 'larger fish traps' across inland New South Wales 'were for the purpose of fencing back the big fish in the streams of the greater rivers, so that, when on the upper reaches great tribal gatherings took place, there would be plenty of food easily obtained, and at hand'. Furthermore, 'it was said that for at least two or three years before such gatherings the waters would be examined for the quantity and size of the fish; and at least a year beforehand the trap, weir or barrier, would be closed by its key stones so that only the small fish could go through' (Gilmore 1934: 197).

Large-scale gatherings were undertaken for a broad range of social, political, economic (including trade and exchange), and ceremonial reasons, with attendees numbering from the 'hundreds' (Hammond 1933: 46), up to 'one thousand' (Kenyon 1928: 146) and even 'five thousand' (Gilmore 1934: 192), and staying for up to 'two or three months' (Bates 1985: 251). All of these large-scale gatherings were associated with weir-based fishing during annual flooding of waterways. In the absence of these fisheries management facilities, 'you could not suddenly put five thousand people down on any river in Australia now and expect them to live, not even for a week' (Gilmore 1934: 195).

Lourandos (1980, 1988: 159) argued that food surpluses from large-scale fishing facilities in southwest Victoria set the scene for positive feedback processes and a 'self-amplifying system' that produced increased carrying capacity, population, social relations, social complexity, and interregional gatherings over the past 3000 years. Other Australian archaeologists making the link between large-scale fish-trapping structures and large-scale interregional gatherings associated with attendance at nearby ceremonial sites have followed Lourandos's approach (e.g., Toorbul Point marine trap in Queensland—Walters 1985b; Eyre Peninsula marine traps in South Australia—Martin 1988: 83, and Oyster Harbour marine traps in Western Australia—Dortch 1997: 30). In particular, Walters (1985b: 41) associated the Toorbul Point stone-walled fish trap with interregional gatherings by relating the trap to broader landscape features, including a ceremonial 'bora' site located 5 km inland and a large residential site marked by a 'huge midden complex' (with high densities of fish bones) located 3 km away at Sandstone Point.

Despite the plausibility of these links, it needs to be kept in mind that ethnographic records indicate that many stone-walled traps have no association with gatherings and were used only by local clan groups (e.g., Campbell 1978: 129–130; McNiven & Bell 2010). In some cases, walled fish traps had only limited capacity for food production. McEldowney (1995) found that the Andra Islanders of northern Papua New Guinea could not 'intensify fish production' through construction of walled traps on reefs, as functionality was restricted to about two weeks per year due to narrow windows of appropriate tides and weather patterns for maintenance and use (McEldowney 1995: 314, 325). As such, Andra Islanders relied on netted fish for 'ceremonial exchanges and feasts' (McEldowney 1995: 368, 445–448). These ethnographic examples suggest that it does not necessarily follow that all archaeologically known stone-walled traps should be linked to interregional gatherings and, by extension, social complexity (Godwin 1988). Documenting such links archaeologically remains conceptually and methodologically challenging, and limited to contextual evidence such as temporally coincident increases in site numbers, occupational intensities, and use of exotic raw materials. Walters (1985b) noted that the scale of such changes needs to be investigated at a district level, with relevant sites located up to 3–5 km from fish traps. Lourandos (1980, 1983, 1987, 1988) made the important point that interregional gatherings do not take place in isolation and represent reorganizations in society at regional and indeed interregional scales.

Resource Enhancement

Whether associated with interregional gatherings and/or use by local owners/residents, stone-walled fish traps can also enhance fish stocks, such as through aquaculture practices. Lourandos (1987: 307) argued that some stone-walled fish traps in southwest Victoria were associated with fish 'farms' and what Builth (2014) termed fish 'aquaculture'. Central to this aquaculture was construction of stone-walled traps in conjunction with artificially constructed channels to feed water and eels into growing/containment ponds (Builth 2014). These ponds were both natural depressions and low-lying areas that were dammed off with rock walls to artificially hold water (and eels) (Builth 2014). The eel aquaculture and trapping system at Toolondo in western Victoria features 3 km of excavated earthen channels to artificially feed water and eels into a natural (small lake) depression (Lourandos 1980). Similar large-scale manipulation of waterways through excavation of channels to feed flood waters into low-lying areas to create growing/containment ponds for freshwater fish was recorded ethnographically in the Murray-Darling Basin of New South Wales (Humphries 2007). Lourandos (1980) argued that such aquaculture facilities (including stone-walled traps) provided opportunities for local groups to override the *natural* (seasonal) availability of fish, such that they became a *culturally* (perennially) available resource. In this context, Lourandos (1980: 246) stated that '[t]hese environmental manipulations are not seen as attempts to increase environmental productivity, but to regularize (stabilize) the availability of resources'.

Regularized enhancement of fish resources provided opportunities for areas to permanently support groups throughout the year instead of seasonal occupation (Builth 2004; Lourandos 1980). The result of this 'artificial niche expansion', at least in southwest Victoria, was the establishment of more clan groups with relatively higher population densities and greater sedentism and social complexity compared to many other parts of Australia (Lourandos 1980: 258). Lourandos's model has been supported by McNiven et al. (2015: 55), who noted that major elaborations of stone-walled fish traps and associated aquaculture facilities at Lake Condah over the past 800 years correlate with broader regional increases in site establishment and occupation intensity within the past 1000 years.

In some marine contexts across Australia and New Guinea, it is clear that construction of tidal fish traps increased production not only of fish but also of other marine resources. For example, the Lardil, Yangkaal, and Kaiadilt peoples of the Wellesley Islands in the Gulf of Carpentaria reported that in addition to fish, stone-walled tidal traps also supplied turtles, dugongs, crabs, and molluscs (Memmott, Robins, & Stock 2008: 75). Indeed, construction of traps created new habits for foods such as crabs (crevices within rock walls), oysters (rock wall substrates), and other molluscs (soft sediments accumulating within traps) (Campbell 1982: 102; Memmott, Robins, & Stock 2008: 82). For the Bardi people of Western Australia, stone walls of tidal traps provided a culturally constructed substrate for oyster colonies, which were used as a food source (Smith 1983: 34). On Iama in central Torres Strait, clam gardens were established within the confines of stone-walled tidal fish traps (Lui 2008: 57).

More broadly, stone-walled tidal fish traps can also reduce inshore water movement, resulting in increased sedimentation of reef flats and expansion of mangroves and associated marine resources such as molluscan communities (e.g., Saenger & Hopkins 1975). Although attempts have been made to determine the age of stone-walled tidal fish traps indirectly by association with dated fish bones in nearby middens in Australia (e.g., Bowen 1998), opportunities exist to expand such links based on nonfish resources obtained from fish traps (see Kemp 2006).

Ownership Exclusivity

Ethnographic accounts of freshwater and marine fish traps in Australia and New Guinea often mention the importance of ownership in terms of who can use traps and what happens with the fish catch (e.g., Crawford 1981: 91; Gibbs 2011: 10; Mathews 1903: 151–153). For example, the Malagun stone-walled tidal trap of the Bardi people of northern Western Australia was reconstructed by people with 'traditional rights of access to, and ownership of the area' (Smith 1983: 30). Furthermore, distribution of the trap's catch was based on kinship relationships and a moral economy of 'obligation' and 'reciprocity' augmented by friendship and political alliances (Smith 1983: 34; cf. Rouja 1998: 249–250). On Erub in eastern Torres Strait, stone-walled tidal traps were exclusively owned and used by particular clans, but the fish catch was shared (Scott & Mulrennan 1999: 159). On Erub, as in many places, fishing practices that produced fish surpluses were embedded in broader social relations and kin-based networks of reciprocity (see Martin 2006).

Andra Island coral-walled tidal fish traps of northern Papua New Guinea were owned by specific families through patrilineal inheritance (McEldowney 1995: 314, 440). Ownership provided privileged access to fish and other marine resources such as molluscs obtained from within these fish traps (McEldowney 1995: 315). Indeed, some fish traps were maintained and even constructed purely to assert reef ownership and associated resource access rights (McEldowney 1995: 315, 449). The process of maintaining and reconstructing a walled trap after damage was central to the process of demonstrating and asserting ownership. It was 'stressed' to McEldowney 'that the repeated performance of this [maintenance] task was crucial for demonstrating and reaffirming ownership of a trap or set of traps by a lineage' (1995: 249).

In eastern Torres Strait, large stone-walled fish traps (*sai*) and the associated reef enclosed within the traps and to their seaward side are collectively owned by specific clans and families. Reef ownership was usually a seaward extension of land ownership and vice versa (Scott 2008: 240). For example, on Erub, the landward extension of reef ownership was 'often aligned with the *teter pim* (the beachward ends of *sai* walls, literally the *sai's* "toehold")' (Scott 2008: 242). In some cases, extension of fish trap and reef ownership to adjacent sections of land also manifested establishment of residential bases as an assertion of land, trap, and reef ownership. Such an association provides opportunities to examine archaeologically the extent to which establishment dates of residential sites and adjacent fish traps coincide. Beyond this basic association, direct and indirect material markers of stone-walled fish trap ownership are poorly known and represent a challenge for future archaeological research.

Conclusion

Freshwater and marine fishing by Indigenous peoples of Australia and New Guinea involved a wide range of methods of which stone-walled traps were used by a minority of groups in selected regions. This trend may relate partially to geographically patchy ethnographic and archaeological records. Yet such fixed-in-place facilities have high archaeological visibility and indeed represent some of the largest engineered structures constructed by Indigenous peoples in both regions. Although the 6600-year-old fish trap at Lake Condah in southwest Victoria is the earliest known stone-walled fish trap in the world, attempts to date these facilities in other parts of Australia and New Guinea have been less successful and represent a methodological challenge for archaeology. Archaeological research in the Lake Condah region has also enhanced understandings of local Gunditjmara elaboration of stone-walled fish trap technologies for aquaculture and fish-resource enhancement in terms of abundance, regularization, and reliability. Such archaeological insights have not only challenged conventional understandings of Aboriginal Australians as hunter-gatherers, but have also laid the foundations for paradigmatic shifts in Australian archaeology that are underpinned by sociodemographic models of social complexity (see Lourandos & Ross, this volume). It is understanding the social dimensions of stone-walled fish traps in terms of the restructuring of intergroup dynamics, and land and resource ownership and control, which presents major conceptual challenges for archaeologists into the future. Key to meeting such challenges is developing understandings of the material correlates of these social dimensions that are amenable to archaeological enquiry. In this sense, Australia and New Guinea provide rare opportunities to advance understandings of stone-walled fish traps, given that they are still maintained and used by numerous Indigenous communities in both regions today. These new understandings will continue to provide insights into the dynamic role of these fixed-in-place facilities in transforming land- and seascapes across spatial and temporal scales.

Acknowledgments

This chapter was improved by helpful comments and contributions by Bruno David, Garrick Hitchcock, Lara Lamb, Holly McEldowney, Monica Minnegal, and Chris Urwin.

References

Akerman, K. (1976). Fishing with stone traps on the Dampierland Peninsula, Western Australia. *Mankind*, 10(3), 182.

Allen, J. (2017). *Excavations at Motupore Island, Central District, Papua New Guinea*. Vols. 1 & 2. University of Otago, Working Papers in Anthropology No. 4. Dunedin: Department of Anthropology & Sociology, University of Otago.

Allen, J., Gosden, C., & White, J. P. (1989). Human Pleistocene adaptations in the tropical island Pacific: Recent evidence from New Ireland, a Greater Australian outlier. *Antiquity*, *63*(240), 548–561.

Altman, J. (1983). Eastern Gunwinggu fish trapping at Gunbatgarri. *The Beagle*, *1*(7), 59–71.

Anell, B. (1955). *Contribution to the history of fishing in the Southern Seas*. Studia Ethnographica Upsaliensia IX.

Anonymous. (1878). *Catalogue of the objects of ethnographic art in the National Gallery, published by the direction of the Trustees of the Public Library and Museums of Victoria*. Melbourne: Mason, Firth & M'Cutcheon.

Attenbrow, V. (2010). Aboriginal fishing in Port Jackson, and the introduction of shell fish-hooks to coastal New South Wales, Australia. In D. Lunney, P. Hutchings, & D. Hochuli (Eds.), *The natural history of Sydney* (pp. 16–34). Mosman: Royal Zoological Society of NSW.

Attenbrow, V., & Steele, D. (1995). Fishing in Port Jackson, New South Wales—more than met the eye. *Antiquity*, *69*(262), 47–60.

Austen, L. (1923). The Tedi River District of Papua. *The Geographical Journal*, *62*(5), 335–349.

Austen, L. (1946). Notes on the food supply of the Turamarubi of western Papua. *Mankind*, *3*(8), 227–230.

Balme, J. (1983). Prehistoric fishing in the lower Darling, western New South Wales. In C. Grigson & J. Clutton-Brock (Eds.), *Animals and archaeology: 2. Middens, fishes and birds* (pp. 19–32). British Archaeological Reports, International Series S183: Oxford: BAR.

Balme, J. (1995). 30,000 years of fishery in western New South Wales. *Archaeology in Oceania*, *30*(1), 1–21.

Banfield, E. J. (1908). *The confessions of a beachcomber*. Unwin: London.

Barham, A. J. (2000). Late Holocene maritime societies in the Torres Strait Islands, northern Australia—cultural arrival or cultural emergence? In S. O'Connor & P. Veth (Eds.), *East of Wallace's Line* (pp. 223–314). Rotterdam: A. A. Balkema.

Basedow, H. (1907). Anthropological notes on the western coastal tribes of the Northern Territory of South Australia. *Transactions of the Royal Society of South Australia*, *31*, 1–62.

Bassett, E. (2004). Reconsidering evidence of Tasmanian fishing. *Environmental Archaeology*, *9*(2), 135–142.

Bates, D. (1985). *The native tribes of Western Australia*. I. White (Ed.). Canberra: National Library of Australia.

Bell, F. L. S. (1947). The place of food in the social life of the Tanga. *Oceania*, *17*(2), 310–326.

Berndt, R. M., Berndt, C. H., & Stanton, J. (1993). *A world that was: The Yaraldi of the Murray River and lakes, South Australia*. Carlton: Melbourne University Press.

Beveridge, P. (1884). Of the Aborigines inhabiting the great lacustrine and riverine depression of the lower Murray, lower Murrumbidgee, lower Lachlan, and lower Darling. *Journal and Proceedings of the Royal Society of New South Wales*, *17*, 19–74.

Blackwood, B. (1978). *The Kukukuku of the upper Watut*. C. R. Hallpike (Ed.). Monograph Series No. 2. Oxford: Pitt Rivers Museum.

Boeseman, M. (1956). The lake resources of Netherlands New Guinea. *Quarterly Bulletin of the South Pacific Commission 1956*, 23–25.

Boeseman, M. (1963). Notes on the fishes of Western New Guinea I. *Zoologische Mededelingen*, *38*(14), 221–242.

Bowdler, S. (1976). Hook, line and dilly bag: An interpretation of an Australian coastal shell midden. *Mankind*, *10*(4), 248–258.

Bowen, G. (1998). Towards a generic technique for dating stone fish traps and weirs. *Australian Archaeology*, 47, 39–43.

Bradley, J., & McNiven, I. J. (2019). 'Why those old fellas stopped using them?': Socio-religious and socio-political dimensions of stone-walled tidal fish trap use and dis-use amongst the Yanyuwa of northern Australia. *Journal of Island and Coastal Archaeology*, 14(3), 337–355.

Brown, S., Rose, D., McNiven, I., & Crocker, S. (2017). *Australia's nomination of Budj Bim Cultural Landscape. World Heritage nomination for inscription in the UNESCO World Heritage List*. Canberra: Department of Environment and Energy.

Builth, H. (2004). Mt Eccles lava flow and the Gunditjmara connection: A landform for all seasons. *Proceedings of the Royal Society of Victoria*, 116(1), 163–182.

Builth, H. (2014). *Ancient Aboriginal aquaculture rediscovered*. Saarbrucken, Germany: LAP Lambert Academic Publishing.

Builth, H., Kershaw, A. P., White, C., Roach, A., Hartney, L., McKenzie, M., . . . Jacobsen, G. (2008). Environmental and cultural change on the Mt Eccles lava-flow landscapes of south-west Victoria, Australia. *The Holocene*, 18(3), 413–424.

Bunbury, W., & Morrell, W. P. (Eds.) (1930). *Early days in Western Australia*. Oxford: Oxford University Press.

Bundock, M. (1978). Notes on the Richmond blacks. In I. McBryde (Ed.), *Records of times past: Ethnohistorical essays on the culture and ecology of the New England tribes* (pp. 261–266). Canberra: Australian Institute of Aboriginal Studies.

Busse, M. (1991). Environment and human ecology in the Lake Murray-Middle Fly area. In D. Lawrence & T. Cansfield-Smith (Eds.), *Sustainable development for traditional inhabitants of the Torres Strait region* (pp. 441–449). Cairns: Great Barrier Reef Marine Park Authority.

Butler, V. (1994). Fish feeding behaviour and fish capture: The case for variation in Lapita fishing Strategies. *Archaeology in Oceania*, 29(2), 81–90.

Campbell, J. B. (1982). Automatic seafood retrieval systems: The evidence from Hinchinbrook Island and its implications. In S. Bowdler (Ed.), *Coastal archaeology in eastern Australia* (pp. 96–107). Canberra: Research School of Pacific Studies, Australian National University Press.

Campbell, V. (1978). Two fish traps located on the mid-north coast of New South Wales. In I. McBryde (Ed.), *Records of times past: Ethnohistorical essays on the culture and ecology of the New England tribes* (pp. 122–134). Canberra: Australian Institute of Aboriginal Studies.

Carrier, J. G. (1982). Fishing practices on Ponam Island (Manus Province, Papua New Guinea). *Anthropos*, 77(5/6), 904–915.

Carter, M. (2001). New evidence for the earliest human occupation in Torres Strait, north-eastern Australia. *Australian Archaeology*, 52, 50–52.

Carter, M., Barham A. J., Veth, P., Bird, D. W., O'Connor, S., & Bliege Bird, R. (2004). The Murray Islands Archaeological Project: Excavations on Mer and Dauar, eastern Torres Strait. *Memoirs of the Queensland Museum, Cultural Heritage Series*, 3, 163–182.

Chalmers, J. (1903). Notes on the natives of Kiwai Island, Fly River, British New Guinea. *The Journal of the Anthropological Institute of Great Britain and Ireland*, 33, 117–124.

Chapman, M. D. (1987). Women's fishing in Oceania. *Human Ecology*, 15(3), 267–288.

Cheesman, L. E. (1938). The Cyclops Mountains of Dutch New Guinea. *The Geographical Journal*, 91(1), 21–30.

Clarke, A. (1991). *Lake Condah project Aboriginal archaeology resource inventory*. Occasional Report 36, Victoria Archaeological Survey. Melbourne: Department of Conservation & Environment.

Clarke, P. A. (2002). Early Aboriginal fishing technology in the Lower Murray, South Australia. *Records of the South Australian Museum*, 35(2), 147–167.

Colley, S. M., & Jones, R. (1987). New fish bone data from Rocky Cape, north west Tasmania. *Archaeology in Oceania*, 22(2), 67–71.

Coutts, P. J. F., Frank, R. K., & Hughes, P. (1978). *Aboriginal engineers of the Western District, Victoria*. Records of the Victorian Archaeological Survey 7.

Crawford, A. L. (1981). *Life and ceremony of the Gogodala*. Bathurst: The National Cultural Council of Papua New Guinea in association with Robert Brown and Associates.

Dargin, P. (1976). *Aboriginal fisheries of the Darling-Barwon Rivers*. Brewarrina: Brewarrina Historical Society.

Dawson, J. (1881). *Australian Aborigines. The languages and customs of several tribes of Aborigines of the Western District of Victoria, Australia*. Melbourne: George Robertson.

Dix, W. C., & Meagher, S. J. (1976). Fish traps in the south-west of Western Australia. *Records of the Western Australian Museum*, 4(2), 171–187.

Dortch, C. E. (1997). New perceptions of the chronology and development of Aboriginal fishing in south-western Australia. *World Archaeology*, 29(1), 15–35.

Dortch, C. E., & Gardner, G. (1976). Archaeological investigations in the Northcliffe district, Western Australia. *Records of the Western Australian Museum*, 4(3), 257–293.

Dortch, J., Dortch, C., & Reynolds, R. (2006). Test excavation at the Oyster Harbour stone fish traps, King George Sound, Western Australia: An investigation aimed at determining the construction method and maximum age of the structures. *Australian Archaeology*, 62(1), 38–43.

Dunbar, G. K. (1944). Notes on the Ngemba tribe of the Central Darling River, Western New South Wales. *Mankind*, 3(6), 172–180.

Duncan-Kemp, A. M. (1968). *Where strange gods call*. Kemp Place: W. R. Smith & Paterson Pty Ltd.

Flecker, P. O. (1951). Remains of Aboriginal habitation on the Great Barrier Wall. *The North Queensland Naturalist*, 19(97), 1–2.

Frusher, S. D., & Subam, S. (1981). Traditional fishing methods and practices in the northern Gulf of Papua. *Harvest*, 7(4), 150–158.

Gallus, A., & Gill, E. D. (1973). Aboriginal bone fish-hooks with Aboriginal skeletons at Wallpolla Creek, west of Mildura, Victoria, Australia. *Memoirs of the National Museum of Victoria*, 34, 215–216.

Gerritsen, R. (2001). Aboriginal fish hooks in southern Australia: Evidence, arguments and implications. *Australian Archaeology*, 52, 18–28.

Gibbs, M. (2011). An Aboriginal fish trap on the Swan Coastal Plain: The Barragup mungah. *Records of the Western Australian Museum*, 79, 4–15.

Gibson, L. (2012). 'We are the river': Place, wellbeing and Aboriginal identity. In S. Atkinson, S. Fuller, & J. Painter (Eds.), *Wellbeing and place* (pp. 201–215). Surrey: Ashgate Publishing Ltd.

Gilmore, M. (1934). *Old days: Old ways. A book of recollections*. Sydney: Angus & Robertson Ltd.

Godwin, L. (1988). Around the traps: A reappraisal of stone fishing weirs in northern New South Wales. *Archaeology in Oceania*, 3(2), 49–59.

Gumoi, M. T. (2010). *Towards a holistic understanding of rural livelihood systems: The case of the Bine, Western Province, Papua New Guinea* (PhD thesis). Lincoln University, Canterbury, New Zealand.

Gunditjmara People, & Wettenhall, G. (2010). *The people of Budj Bim: Engineers of aquaculture, builders of stone house settlements and warriors defending Country*. Ballarat: PRESS Publishing.

Haddon, A. C. (Ed.). (1908). *Reports of the Cambridge Anthropological Expedition to Torres Straits. Vol. VI. Sociology, magic and religion of the Eastern Islanders*. Cambridge: Cambridge University Press.

Haddon, A. C. (1912). Hunting and fishing. In A. C. Haddon (Ed.), *Reports of the Cambridge Anthropological Expedition to Torres Straits. Vol. IV. Arts and crafts* (pp. 152–171). Cambridge: Cambridge University Press.

Haddon, A. C. (1935). *Reports of the Cambridge Anthropological Expedition to Torres Straits. Vol. I. General ethnography*. Cambridge: Cambridge University Press.

Haines, A. K. (1979). The subsistence fishery of the Purari Delta. *Science in New Guinea, 6*(2), 80–95.

Hall, J. (1984). Fishing with dolphins?: Affirming a traditional Aboriginal fishing story in Moreton Bay, S.E. Queensland. In R. J. Coleman, J. Covacevich, & P. Davie (Eds.), *Focus on Stradbroke* (pp. 16–22). Brisbane: Boolarong Publications.

Hamlyn-Harris, R. (1916). On fish poisoning and poisons employed among the Aborigines of Queensland. *Memoirs of the Queensland Museum, 5*, 1–22.

Hammond, J. E. (1933). *Winjan's people: The story of the south-west Australian Aborigines*. Perth: Imperial Printing Co. Ltd.

Hawkins, S., O'Connor, S., Maloney, T. R., Litster, M., Kealy, S., Fenner, J. N., . . . Louys, K. (2017). Oldest human occupation of Wallacea at Laili Cave, Timor-Leste, shows broad-spectrum foraging responses to late Pleistocene environments. *Quaternary Science Reviews, 171*, 58–72.

Head, L. (1989). Using palaeoecology to date Aboriginal fishtraps at Lake Condah, Victoria. *Archaeology in Oceania, 24*(3), 110–115.

Hitchcock, G. (2004). *Wildlife is our gold: Political ecology of the Torassi River borderland, south-west Papua New Guinea* (PhD thesis). University of Queensland, Brisbane.

Horne, G., & Aiston, G. (1924). *Savage life in central Australia*. London: Macmillan.

Humphries, P. (2007). Historical Indigenous use of aquatic resources in Australia's Murray-Darling Basin, and its implications for river management. *Ecological Management and Restoration, 8*(2), 106–113.

Ingold, T. (1993). The temporality of the landscape. *World Archaeology, 25*(2), 152–174.

Jackson, S. (2005). Indigenous values and water resource management: A case study from the Northern Territory. *Australasian Journal of Environmental Management, 12*(3), 136–146.

Jenness, D., & Ballantyne, A. (1920). *The North D'Entrecasteaux*. Oxford: Clarendon Press.

Johannes, R. E., & MacFarlane, J. W. (1991). *Traditional fishing in the Torres Strait Islands*. Hobart: CSIRO Division of Fisheries.

Jones, R. (1978). Why did the Tasmanians stop eating fish? In R. A. Gould (Ed.), *Explorations in ethno-archaeology* (pp. 11–47). Albuquerque: University of New Mexico Press.

Kemp, L. V. (2006). *Ancient stonewall fish traps on the south coast of South Africa: Documentation, current use, ecological effects and management implications* (MSc thesis). University of Cape Town, Cape Town.

Kenyon, A. S. (1928). The Aboriginal Protectorate of Port Phillip: Report of an expedition to the Aboriginal tribes of the western interior by the Chief Protector, George Augustus Robinson. *The Victorian Historical Magazine, 12*(3), 134–171.

Kooijman, S., Dorren, M., Veeger, L., Verschueren, J., & Luyken, R. (1958). *Report of the investigation into the problem of depopulation amongst the Marind-anim of Netherlands New Guinea.* South Pacific Commission Population Studies S.18 Project. Noumea, New Caledonia.

Kreij, A., Scriffignano, J., Rosendahl, D., Nagel, T., & Ulm, S. (2018). Aboriginal stone-walled intertidal fishtrap morphology, function and chronology investigated with high-resolution close-range Unmanned Aerial Vehicle photogrammetry. *Journal of Archaeological Science, 96*, 148–161.

Lamb, L., David, B., Barker, B., Pivoru, R., & Alex, C. (2019). Female weir fishers of the southern lowlands of Papua New Guinea: Implications for an archaeology of gendered activities. *Australian Archaeology, 85*(1), 48–56.

Lambrides, A. B. J., McNiven, I. J., & Ulm, S. (2019). Meta-analysis of Queensland's coastal Indigenous fisheries: Examining the archaeological evidence for geographic and temporal patterning. *Journal of Archaeological Science: Reports, 28*, 102057.

Lampert, R. J. (1966). An excavation at Durras North, New South Wales. *Archaeology and Physical Anthropology in Oceania, 1*(2), 83–118.

Landtman, G. (1927). *The Kiwai Papuans of British New Guinea.* London: Macmillan.

Landtman, G. (1933). *Ethnographical collection from the Kiwai District of British New Guinea.* Helsinki: Commission of the Antell Collection.

Lawrence, R. (1969). *Aboriginal habitat and economy.* Occasional Papers No. 6. Canberra: Department of Geography, Australian National University.

Lawrie, M. (1970). *Myths and legends of Torres Strait.* St. Lucia: University of Queensland Press.

Levinson, S. (2008). Landscape, seascape and the ontology of places on Rossel island, Papua New Guinea. *Language Sciences, 30*, 256–290.

Long, K., Stern, N., Williams, I. S., Kinsley, L., Wood, R., Sporcic, K., . . . Grün, R. (2014). Fish otolith geochemistry, environmental conditions and human occupation at Lake Mungo, Australia. *Quaternary Science Reviews, 88*, 82–95.

Lourandos, H. (1976). Aboriginal settlement and land use in south western Victoria: A report on current field work. *The Artefact, 1*(4), 174–193.

Lourandos, H. (1980). Change or stability? Hydraulics, hunter-gatherers and population in temperate Australia. *World Archaeology, 11*(3), 245–266.

Lourandos, H. (1983). Intensification: A late Pleistocene-Holocene archaeological sequence from southwestern Victoria. *Archaeology in Oceania, 18*(2), 81–94.

Lourandos, H. (1988). Palaeopolitics: Resource intensification in Aboriginal Australia and Papua New Guinea. In T. Ingold, D. Riches, & J. Woodburn (Eds.), *Hunters and gatherers: History, evolution and social change* (pp. 148–160). Oxford: Berg.

Lourandos, H. (1987). Swamp managers of southwestern Victoria. In D. J. Mulvaney & J. P. White (Eds.), *Australians to 1788* (pp. 292–307). Broadway, NSW: Fairfax, Syme & Weldon.

Lui, L. (2008). Affidavit of Alice-Maria Lizzie Lui. Sworn on October 2008. Torres Strait Regional Seas Native Title Claim, Q6040 of 2001. Native Title Office, Torres Strait Regional Authority, Thursday Island, Queensland, Australia.

Lyons, A. P. (1926). Notes on the Gogodara tribe of western Papua. *The Journal of the Royal Anthropological Institute of Great Britain and Ireland, 56*, 329–359.

Maaz, K., Picasso, S., & Meyer, A. J. P. (2012). *Fish hooks of the Pacific Islands.* Munich: Hirmer Publishers.

Martin, K. (2006). A fish trap for custom: How nets work at Matupit. *Paideuma: Mitteilungen zur Kulturkunde 52* , 73–90.

Martin, S. (1988). *Eyre Peninsula and west coast Aboriginal fish trap survey*. Unpublished report. Adelaide: South Australian Department of Environment and Planning.

Massola, A. (1956). Australian fish hooks and their distribution. *National Museum of Victoria Memoirs*, 22(1), 1–16.

Massola, A. (1964). Queensland harpoons and their distribution. *National Museum of Victoria Memoirs*, 26, 201–207.

Mathews, R. H. (1903). The Aboriginal fisheries at Brewarrina. *Journal and Proceedings of the Royal Society of New South Wales*, 37, 146–156.

McCarthy, F. D., & McArthur, M. (1960). The food quest and the time factor in Aboriginal economic life. In C. P. Mountford (Ed.), *Records of the American-Australian Scientific Expedition to Arnhem Land. 2. Anthropology and nutrition* (pp. 145–194). Parkville: Melbourne University Press.

McEldowney, P. H. (1995). *Subsistence intensification in the late prehistory of Manus* (PhD thesis). Australian National University, Canberra.

McNiven, I. J. (1994). *Booral: Cultural heritage management plan*. Unpublished report. Maryborough: Queensland Department of Environment & Heritage.

McNiven, I. J. (2004). Saltwater people: Spiritscapes, maritime rituals and the archaeology of Australian Indigenous seascapes. *World Archaeology*, 35(3), 329–349.

McNiven, I. J. (2010). 'Oh wonderful beach': The Marind-anim of Papua and ethnographic foundations for an archaeology of a littoral sea people. *The Artefact*, 33, 91–108.

McNiven, I. J. (2013). Ritualized middening practices. *Journal of Archaeological Method and Theory*, 20(4), 552–587.

McNiven, I. J., & Bell, D. (2010). Fishers and farmers: Historicising the Gunditjmara freshwater fishery, western Victoria. *The La Trobe Journal*, 85, 83–105.

McNiven, I. J., Crouch, J., Richards, T., Gunditj Mirring Traditional Owners Aboriginal Corporation, Dolby, N., & Jacobsen, G. (2012). Dating Aboriginal stone-walled fishtraps at Lake Condah, southeast Australia. *Journal of Archaeological Science*, 39(2), 268–286.

McNiven, I. J., Crouch, J., Richards, T., Sniderman, K., Dolby, N., & Gunditj Mirring Traditional Owners Aboriginal Corporation. (2015). Phased redevelopment of an ancient Gunditjmara fish trap over the past 800 years: Muldoons Trap Complex, Lake Condah, southwestern Victoria. *Australian Archaeology*, 81, 44–58.

McNiven, I. J., David, B., Aplin, K., Pivoru, M., Pivoru, W., Sexton, A., . . . Kemp, N. (2010). Historicising the present: Late Holocene emergence of a rainforest hunting camp, Gulf Province, Papua New Guinea. *Australian Archaeology*, 71, 41–56.

Mead, M. (1963). *Sex and temperament in three primitive societies*. London: Routledge & Kegan Paul.

Melville, H. S. [1849]. *Sketches in Australia and the adjacent islands, selected from a number taken during the surveying voyage of H.M.S. 'Fly' and 'Bramble' under the command of Capt. F.P. Blackwood, R.N. during the years 1842–46*. London: Dickinson.

Memmott, P., Robins, R., & Stock, E. (2008). What exactly is a fish trap?: Methodological issues for the study of Aboriginal intertidal rock wall fish traps, Wellesley Islands region, Gulf of Carpentaria, Australia. In J. Connolly & M. Campbell (Eds.), *Comparative island archaeologies* (pp. 73–96). British Archaeological Reports International Series S1829. Oxford: Archaeopress.

Minnegal, M. (1994). *Fishing at Gwaimasi: The interaction of social and ecological factors in influencing subsistence behaviour* (PhD thesis). Department of Anthropology and Sociology, University of Queensland, Brisbane.

Mitton, R. D. (1979). *The people of Manus*. Records of the National Museum and Art Gallery, No. 6. Boroko: Papua New Guinea National Museum and Art Gallery.

Morphy, H., & Morphy, F. (2006). Tasting the waters: Discriminating identities in the waters of Blue Mud Bay. *Journal of Material Culture*, 11(1/2), 67–85.

Mountford, C. P. (1939). Aboriginal methods of fishing and cooking as used on the southern coast of Eyre's Peninsula, South Australia. *Mankind*, 2(7), 196–200.

Mountford, C. P. (1956). *Records of the American-Australian Scientific Expedition to Arnhem Land 1: Art, myth and symbolism*. Carlton: Melbourne University Press.

Mys, B. M. F., & van Zwieten, P. (1990). *Subsistence fisheries in lower order streams: Notes on species preference, fishing methods, catch composition, yield and dietary importance of fish.* Report prepared for Sepik River Fish Stock Enhancement Project PNG/85/001. Field Document No. 11. Rome: Food & Agriculture Organisation of the United Nations.

O'Connor, S., Mahirta., Samper Carro, S. C., Hawkins, S., Kealy, S., Louts, J., & Wood, R. (2017). Fishing in life and death: Pleistocene fish-hooks from a burial context on Alor Island, Indonesia. *Antiquity*, 91(360), 1451–1468.

O'Connor, S., Ono, R., & Clarkson, C. (2011). Pelagic fishing at 42,000 years before the present and the maritime skills of modern humans. *Science*, 334(6059), 1117–1121.

Paterson, C. A. (1896). Notes about the tribes inhabiting the coastal districts from Geraldton to Albany, and those of territories nearest adjoining them. *Transactions of the Royal Society of South Australia*, 16, 288–291.

Pernetta, J. C., & Hill, L. (1981). A review of marine resource use in coastal Papua. *Journal de la Société des Océanistes*, 37(72), 175–191.

Peterson, N. (2003). *Donald Thomson in Arnhem Land*. Carlton: Miegunyah Press.

Petrie, C. C. (1992/1904). *Tom Petrie's reminiscences of early Queensland*. St. Lucia: University of Queensland Press.

Powell, W. (1883). *Wanderings in a wild country, or, three years amongst the cannibals of New Britain*. London: Sampson Low, Marston, Searle, & Rivington.

Pulsford, R. L. (1975). Ceremonial fishing for tuna by the Motu of Pari. *Oceania*, 46(2), 107–113.

Quinn, N. J. (2009). Traditional methods of fishing (Southwest Pacific). In V. R. Squires (Ed.), *The role of food, agriculture, forestry and fisheries in human nutrition, Vol. 2* (pp. 140–161). Paris: EOLSS Publications.

Reinman, F. M. (1967). Fishing: An aspect of oceanic economy: An archaeological approach. *Fieldiana Anthropology*, 56(2), 95–208.

Richards, T. (2011). A late nineteenth-century map of an Australian Aboriginal fishery at Lake Condah. *Australian Aboriginal Studies 2011 / 2*, 64–87.

Richards, T. (2013). *Transegalitarian hunter-gatherers of Southwest Victoria, Australia* (PhD thesis). Monash University, Melbourne.

Roberts, A., Mollenmans, A., Agius, Q., Graham, F., Newchurch, J., Rigney, L. I., … Wanganeen, K. (2016). 'They planned their calendar . . . they set up ready for what they wanted to feed the tribe': A first-stage analysis of Narungga fish traps on Yorke Peninsula, South Australia. *The Journal of Island and Coastal Archaeology*, 11(1), 1–25.

Roscoe, P., & Telban, B. (2004). The people of the Lower Arafundi: Tropical foragers of the New Guinea rainforest. *Ethnology*, 43(2), 93–115.

Ross, W. (1936). Ethnological notes on Mt Hagen tribes (Mandated Territory of New Guinea). *Anthropos*, 31(3/4), 341–363.

Roth, W. E. (1904). *Domestic implements, arts, and manufactures*. North Queensland Ethnography: Bulletin No. 7. Brisbane: Government Printer.

Roth, W. E. (1901). *Food: Its search, capture, and preparation*. North Queensland Ethnography: Bulletin No. 3. Brisbane: Government Printer.

Roth, W. E. (1903). Notes of savage life in the early days of Western Australian settlement. *Proceedings of the Royal Society of Queensland, 17,* 45–69.

Rouja, P. M. (1998). *Fishing for culture: Toward an Aboriginal theory of marine resource use among the Bardi Aborigines of One Arm Point, Western Australia* (PhD thesis). University of Durham, Durham.

Rowland, M. J., & Ulm, S. (2011). Indigenous fish traps and weirs of Queensland. *Queensland Archaeological Research, 14,* 1–58.

Saenger, P., & Hopkins, M. S. (1975). Observations on the mangroves of the southeastern Gulf of Carpentaria, Australia. In G. Walsh, S. Saedahert, & H. Teas (Eds.), *Proceedings of the International Symposium on the Biology and Management of Mangroves* (pp. 126–136). Gainesville, FL: Institute of Food and Agricultural Sciences, University of Florida.

Satterthwait, L. (1987). Socioeconomic implications of Australian Aboriginal net hunting. *Man, 22*(4), 613–636.

Schneebaum, T. (1985). *Asmat images from the collection of the Asmat Museum of Culture and Progress*. Asmat Museum of Culture and Progress.

Schoeffel, P. (1985). Women in the fisheries of the South Pacific. In *Women in development in the South Pacific: Barriers and opportunities* (pp. 156–175). Canberra: Development Studies Centre, The Australian National University.

Schoorl, J. W. (1993). *Culture and change among the Muyu*. Leiden: KITLV Press.

Scott, C. (2008). Torres Strait regional sea claim. Statement and report of Colin Scott, anthropologist, September 2008. Unpublished report, Torres Strait Regional Authority, Thursday Island, Queensland.

Scott, C., & Mulrennan, M. (1999). Land and sea tenure at Erub, Torres Strait: Property, sovereignty and the adjudication of cultural continuity. *Oceania, 70,* 146–176.

Shaw, B., & Langley, M. C. (2017). Investigating the development of prehistoric cultural practices in the Massim region of eastern Papua New Guinea: Insights from the manufacture and use of shell objects in the Louisiade Archipelago. *Journal of Anthropological Archaeology, 48,* 149–165.

Sim, R. (1999). Why the Tasmanians stopped eating fish: Evidence for late Holocene expansion in resource exploitation strategies. In J. Hall & I. J. McNiven (Eds.), *Australian coastal archaeology* (pp. 263–270). Canberra: Australian National University.

Smith, M. (1983). Joules from pools: Social and techno-economic aspects of Bardi fish traps. In M. Smith (Ed.), *Archaeology at ANZAAS 1983* (pp. 29–45). Perth: Western Australian Museum.

Smyth, R. B. (1878). *The Aborigines of Victoria: With notes relating to the habits of the natives of other parts of Australia and Tasmania*. Vols. 1 & 2. Melbourne: Government Printer.

Specht, J., & Fields, J. (1984). *Frank Hurley in Papua: Photographs of the 1920–1923 expeditions*. Bathurst: Robert Brown and Associates in association with the Australian Museum.

Spencer, B., & Gillen, F, J. (1904). *The northern tribes of Central Australia*. London: Macmillan.

Steele, J. G. (1972). *The explorers of the Moreton Bay district 1770–1830*. St Lucia: University of Queensland Press.

Strang, V. (2009). *Gardening the world: Agency, identity and the ownership of water*. New York: Berghahn.

Sullivan, P. (1998). Salt water, fresh water and Yawuru social organization. In N. Peterson & B. Rigsby (Eds.), *Customary marine tenure in Australia* (pp. 96–108). Sydney: University of Sydney Oceania Publications.

Swadling, P., Schäublin, B. H., Goreck, P., & Tiesler, F. (1988). *The Sepik-Ramu: An introduction*. Boroko: PNG National Museum.

Szabó, K. (2007). An assessment of shell fishhooks of the Lapita cultural complex. In A. Anderson, K. Green, & F. Leach (Eds.), *Vastly ingenious: The archaeology of Pacific material culture in honour of Janet Davidson* (pp. 227–241). Dunedin: Otago University Press.

Thomson, D. F. (1938). A new type of fish trap from Arnhem Land, Northern Territory of Australia. *Man, 38*, 193–198.

Thomson, D. F. (1939). The seasonal factor in human culture illustrated from the life of a contemporary nomadic group. *Proceedings of the Prehistoric Society, 5*(2), 209–221.

Toussaint, S., Sullivan, P., & Yu, S. (2005). Waterways in Aboriginal Australia: An interconnected analysis. *Anthropological Forum, 15*, 61–74.

Van der Heijden, P. G. M. (2002). The artisanal fishery in the Sepik-Ramu catchment area, Papua New Guinea. *Science in New Guinea, 27*(1–3), 101–119.

Van der Sande, G. A. J. (1907). *Ethnography and anthropology*. Nova Guinea, Vol. 3. Leyden: E. J. Brill.

Van Waarden, N., & Wilson, B. (1994). Developing a hydrological model of the Lake Condah fish traps in western Victoria using GIS. In I. Johnson (Ed.), *Methods in the mountains* (pp. 81–90). Sydney University Archaeological Methods Series 2. Sydney: Archaeological Computing Laboratory, Department of Prehistoric and Historical Archaeology, The University of Sydney.

Walters, I. (1988). Fish hooks: Evidence for dual social systems in Southeastern Australia? *Australian Archaeology, 27*, 98–114.

Walters, I. (1985a). Some observations on the material culture of Aboriginal fishing in the Moreton Bay area: Implications for archaeology. *Queensland Archaeological Research, 2*, 50–57.

Walters, I. (1985b). The Toorbul Point Aboriginal fish trap. *Queensland Archaeological Research, 2*, 38–49.

Williams, F. E. (1940). Natives of Lake Kutubu. *Oceania, 11*(2), 121–157.

Williamson, R. W. (1913). Some unrecorded customs of the Mekeo people of British New Guinea. *The Journal of the Royal Anthropological Institute of Great Britain and Ireland, 43*, 268–290.

Wollaston, A. F. R. (1912). *Pygmies and Papuans: The Stone Age to-day in Dutch New Guinea*. London: John Murray.

Worsnop, T. (1897). *The prehistoric arts, manufactures, works, weapons, etc., of the Aborigines of Australia*. Adelaide: Government Printer.

CHAPTER 16

THE MEANING OF DITCHES

An Ethnography of Field Systems and Other Networks in a New Guinea Landscape

CHRIS BALLARD

THE IDEA OF THE DITCH

WHEN is a ditch not—or not simply—a ditch? Archaeologists, as prodigious diggers themselves, have given more thought than most to the idea of the ditch. Ditches are excavated, drawn in profile, mapped as field systems, and surveyed for their hydraulic efficiency. But they are less commonly subjected to sustained enquiry into questions about their immaterial as well as material properties, and the various ways in which they condition and constrain action and thought, and reflect structuring principles. How do we map the environmental conditions, reconstruct technologies, conceive of fields of intentionality, and identify the unspoken habitual practices that combine to produce ditches in the archaeological record? And how might we draw on and integrate the insights from ethnography and history, and from the self-accounts of ditch-digging communities, to enhance our understanding of the wider contexts of meaning within which ditches are dug?

To explore these questions, I draw largely on archaeological, ethnographic, and agronomic sources on ditches from the New Guinea Highlands, for several reasons. First, elaborate ditched field systems are found in most of the large inter-montane valleys of the Highlands region, along the length of the island of New Guinea (Ballard 2017: Figures 5.1, 5.3; see Ballard, Denham, & Haberle 2013 for additional coverage of lowland field systems). Second, the relative recency of contact between the Highlands and the outside world, a process which unfolded between the late 1920s and the 1960s, has made it possible not only to document traditional agricultural systems operating with minimal changes but also to ask those who had been alive before contact about the broader cultural contexts for agricultural practices, including ditching. Third, archaeological

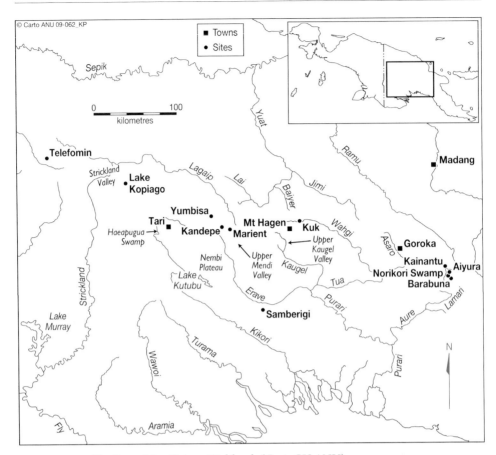

FIGURE 16.1. The Papua New Guinea Highlands (CartoGIS ANU).

investigation of Highland ditch systems, which began in the late 1960s, has revealed a spectacular history of swampland drainage centred on the Kuk Early Agricultural Site (Figure 16.1), with an antiquity in excess of 4000 years, although it was abandoned by the time of colonial contact in the 1930s (Golson, Denham, Hughes, Swadling, & Muke 2017; Gaffney & Denham this volume). Finally, my own research has addressed a living swampland drainage network developed by Huli speakers in the Southern Highlands, providing access to agricultural practices still substantially set within enduring webs of cultural meaning and significance. What follows is essentially an ethnography of ditches and drains, focused largely on Huli self-accounts rather than the historical or archaeological analyses of outsiders.

First, some precepts, simple enough but significant for the way we approach the meaning of ditches. Like fences, hedges, walls, and other boundary-marking or containing structures, ditches are both physical and symbolic acts of enclosure, which can be extended and linked to each other to form networks or systems extending over vast areas. But ditches also endure in ways that most other structures do not: unlike fences and walls, they cannot be disassembled and transported elsewhere; neither are they easily effaced—even when infilled, the trace of the ditch can be detected in the relative compactness of the soil or the movement of subsurface water. The relationship between ditches and water is another critical distinction, because ditches intersect not just the physical and social topography of the land but also the flow of surface water (which is often the basis for the selection of a ditch over another form of boundary). The flow within and between ditches then demands a particular kind of network or gravitational grid which ensures that water is removed or retained at a desired rate, through networks of drainage or reticulation, respectively, usually requiring an outlet or articulation with the natural drainage system. Thinking about ditches thus necessarily requires an understanding of the properties of water within a specific ecology and within a particular symbolic logic.

The title of this chapter is taken from two different papers by geographer Tim Bayliss-Smith (Bayliss-Smith 2007; Bayliss-Smith & Golson 1999), both addressing the problem of finding meaning for ditches in the Papua New Guinea Highlands. The repetition is deliberate, acknowledging the prior work of Bayliss-Smith, Golson, and others, while flagging the intractable and iterative nature of the challenge. Following a brief overview of the literature on ditches and field systems from the New Guinea Highlands, I turn to the case of Huli ditches to show how the perspectives and tools of archaeology, history, and ethnography, used in combination, can supply a richer understanding of—or more probing questions about—the meaning of ditches. In its understanding of field systems, this work builds in particular upon the detailed analyses of field systems by Andrew Fleming (1988), Tom Williamson (1987), Helen Wickstead (2008), Stephen Rippon (2012) and others in the United Kingdom, and by Leigh Johnson (1986), Ian Barber (2001), and Alexander Bell (2013) and others in Aotearoa/New Zealand. What can be recognized as ethnographic and historic insights are woven into all of their accounts, but their focus is largely on the formal description and analysis of networks of archaeological or relic field systems. In this chapter, the ethnography of the ditch is the central concern, and I would argue that the value of such an account lies not in its contested potential as a Pacific source of direct analogies for archaeological or historical ditch networks in Europe or elsewhere (Roscoe 2009; Spriggs 2008), but rather to recall to anyone confronted with evidence for a ditch that its meanings are multiple and layered.

DITCHED FIELD SYSTEMS OF THE NEW GUINEA HIGHLANDS

The ditched field systems of the central highlands of New Guinea first drew the attention of outsiders through a series of pioneering flights over the region during the 1930s. The Wahgi Valley, where Kuk Swamp is located, presented 'a continuous patchwork of gardens, laid off in neat squares like chess-boards' to prospector Mick Leahy on his first flight over the valley in 1933 (Leahy & Crain 1937: 162; see the aerial photograph in Leahy 1994: 93). Above Huli territory in 1936, anthropologist F. E. Williams wrote of 'a closely and permanently cultivated agricultural district. Indeed, from our very elevated view point it *looked curiously European*' (Anon. 1936–1937: 121, emphasis in original). In West New Guinea, pilot Frits Wissel had seen 'what looked like irrigation ditches' on the margins of the Paniai Lakes in 1936 (Wissel n.d.), and the Archbold expedition, which first overflew the vast Grand Valley of the Baliem River in 1938, described 'beautifully patterned gardens laid out in rich alluvial flats. Broad ditches in these gardens were in many cases full of water, for much of the valley was low-lying and swampy' (Archbold, Rand, & Brass 1942: 208). A series of ground studies based on fieldwork by geographers and anthropologists between the 1950s and 1980s were able to situate the roles of these ditches and ditch networks within active agricultural systems (e.g., Bayliss-Smith 1985; Brookfield & Brown 1963; Pospisil 1963).

But it was the reports from the 1970s of the discovery by Jack Golson and his colleagues of some of the earliest ditched field systems in the world, at Kuk Swamp and other sites in the Wahgi Valley, which established the New Guinea Highlands as a locus for the archaeological study of drainage networks (Denham 2018; Golson et al. 2017). The sequence of six major phases of swampland use and abandonment at Kuk begins at 10,000 BP with a single, substantial but ambiguous palaeochannel and features on a palaeosurface, accompanied by elevated charcoal densities and starch grains of *Colocasia* taro. Similarly ambiguous curvilinear channels with more clearly artificial 'island-bed' surfaces characterize Phase 2 (6950–6440 BP), but Phase 3 provides definite evidence for rectilinear ditch networks from about 4400 BP to 2500 BP. Phase 4 runs from about 2000 BP to a clear end at 1100 BP associated with the fall of a volcanic ash, Olgaboli tephra. Identified in the walls of new drains dug for the Kuk Tea Research Station from 1969, this Phase 4 ditch network can be reconstructed as a dense rectilinear grid of gardens, assumed to be for *Colocasia* taro, each some 10–20 m in width. Phase 5 (c. 700–300 BP) and Phase 6 (300–50 BP) are essentially continuous at Kuk, separated at most by a brief hiatus marked by another ashfall, the Tibito tephra. Both phases represent a more intensive use of the swamp, possibly with a more diverse register of crops, including banana, yam, and winged bean, and from the start of Phase 6 the introduction of the new dominant staple for the Highlands, the sweet potato (*Ipomoea batatas*). By the time of first contact in the Wahgi Valley in 1933, the valley floor and its field systems had been largely abandoned, with explanations including malaria epidemics, warfare, excessive moisture, or all three in combination (Gorecki 1979: 101–102). Paul Gorecki (1985) was able to document and reconstruct the process of resettlement of the valley floor from about 1960, and the excavation of a '7th Phase' network of drains in the Kuk swamp, 54 km in length, over a period of seventeen years by a mixed community of local landowners and immigrants from other valleys.

The investigation of the field systems at Kuk followed two broad strategies: inspection of earlier drains exposed in profile in the walls of the modern grid of tea plantation drains, which allowed for extrapolation of the network between drains; and open-area excavations designed to uncover the stratigraphic layering in plan of drains from the different phases. Across the fifty-year life of the Kuk research project, interpretations of the drains and their articulation as field systems have transformed, from a primary focus on their hydraulic properties to the realization that 'cultural norms' have always played a critical role in determining the form of both drains and their networks and the constitution of fundamentally social landscapes (Bayliss-Smith & Golson 1999). In place of a simple swampland/dryland distinction, we now have a more graduated set of zones from swamp centres, through an intermediate zone, to drier swamp margins (Bayliss-Smith, Golson, Hughes, Blong, & Ambrose 2005: 119–120), and a refined sense of the relative weight of social and environmental causes of field system decline and abandonment in each of these different zones, particularly following the adoption of sweet potato in Phase 6 at Kuk (Bayliss-Smith, Golson, & Hughes 2017b). A wider range of drivers of agricultural change at Kuk has been explored through a series of six 'ethnographic models'; however, the models (economic rationality, social inequality, population crisis, future security, property symbolism, and climate change adaptation) appear more sociological than ethnographic in inspiration, and explanations grounded in 'sacred geography' or cosmology are specifically excluded (Bayliss-Smith 2007).

Beyond the Wahgi Valley, two notable studies of high-altitude ditched field systems illustrated regional variants. Tim Bayliss-Smith (1985) documented the re-excavation of drained field systems for taro above 2000 m in the Tambul area, also the find-spot for a 4000-year-old wooden digging spade, but a marginal environment for settlement prior to the adoption of sweet potato during the past 300–400 years. At an even higher altitude of 2550 m, which marks the limit of human settlement even with sweet potato, anthropologist Paul Wohlt (1978) mapped drains along the wetland margins at Yumbisa, proposing a detailed historical reconstruction of the expansion of the field system based on oral traditions.

Further afield, in Papua New Guinea's Southern Highlands, archaeological investigation of field systems had been cursory but promising (Ballard 1995, I: 193–195). Peter White conducted an aerial reconnaissance of the drainage network at Lake Kopiago, amongst Duna-speaking neighbours of the Huli, and generated a date of 500 BP from a ditch feature exposed in a road cutting; and Ron Lampert and Jack Golson surveyed the Haeapugua and other Huli swamps from the air in 1972, with Golson returning to the Mogoropugua Valley in 1980, where he investigated ditch features freshly exposed by drainage of the swamp for a coffee project. Radiocarbon results from charcoal samples and the presence of Tibito tephra in these exposed sections at Mogoropugua and Kopiago suggested that these field systems corresponded to Phases 5 and 6 of the Kuk sequence; subsequent archaeological and palaeo-ecological work has identified a sequence of wetland use in the Tari region equivalent to Late Phase 3 through to Phase 6 (and Phase 7) at Kuk (Ballard 1995; Haberle 1993). Unlike Kuk and the Wahgi Valley swamps, the Huli ditched field systems in the Tari region appeared not to have suffered any interruption in use over the past few centuries, and thus presented an opportunity to investigate an agricultural system similar to Kuk Swamp, but with a continuous and continuing tradition of wetland drainage.

Huli speakers of the Tari region in Hela (formerly Southern Highlands) Province, Papua New Guinea, probably numbered about 50,000 at first contact in the 1930s, and approximately 70,000 by 1990. Huli territory is centred on eight or more contiguous inter-montane basins, most with a swampy core and separated from each other by limestone ridges, at altitudes between 1600 and 2250 m (though Huli settlements are found down to 1200 m and as high as 2750 m). The Haeapugua swamp, as the largest of the Huli wetlands but removed from the urban developments around the township of Tari, presented an obvious focus for more intensive enquiry. Over some twenty months between 1989 and 1992, equipped with low-level vertical and oblique aerial photographs, I visited and mapped approximately 3000 gardens marked out by deep ditches and set within a single contiguous field system (Figure 16.2). The landowners who accompanied me through their gardens were able to provide detailed histories of land use, including sequences of enclosure and drainage, and of conflict over land.

But living systems are not available for archaeological excavation in the way that the Kuk tea research station, situated on land alienated during the colonial period, gave access to the abandoned networks of the Wahgi Valley. The same Huli landowners who were quite willing to confide in me either sacred knowledge or the genealogical

FIGURE 16.2. The Haeapugua Basin field system (CartoGIS ANU).

knowledge critical to the maintenance of their rights to land were not to be moved when I asked for permission to excavate in their richest and most productive gardens; these were areas which, by no coincidence, were also those where the most complex sequences of use were exposed in modern ditch sections. Elsewhere, what turned out to be strong continuities in the use and reuse of the existing ditch system meant that there were fewer older ditches exposed in ditch walls; the conservatism of the existing ditch networks in the region both obscures their own histories of development and, through a combination of dryland vegetation regrowth and rise in wetland water tables, offers very limited access to earlier, nonaligned networks. While I was allowed to excavate small open areas within strips of land allocated to pig droveways, I turned my attention increasingly towards a more immediately threatened resource than buried ditches: the detailed historical and ritual traditions rapidly being lost with the death of older men and women who had learned and practiced these traditions prior to colonial contact. A focus on the Haeapugua wetlands also finds a parallel in Huli thought, in which wetlands figure prominently as centres of fertility and fertile substance within a sacred and moral geography. The history of Huli use of the wetlands is thus sensitive not only to broader economic conditions but also to changes in the fundamental structure of Huli engagement with their cosmos.

FLUID ONTOLOGIES

Huli are renowned diggers of ditches. In the Tari region, ditches effectively fill the function served elsewhere in New Guinea by fences. A dense network of ditches and drains, commonly 2–3 m but sometimes up to 5 m deep, covers each of the central basin floors, forming a fine mesh or grid scored into the landscape (Figure 16.3). Only around swidden gardens in forest frontier zones that have not previously been enclosed by ditches, or in areas with shallow soils or large stones, such as the steep inter-basin limestone ridges or the boulder-strewn slopes of the larger mountains, are ditches replaced by fences. Ditches mark the boundaries of individual gardens, house areas, and sacred sites but also provide trackways for pigs and humans within and beyond local parish areas, and serve in times of war as defensive networks. Visible from the air as a grid, with trees planted along the upcast walls, the ditches extend into the heart of most of the swamps as wetland drains, and deep into the surrounding forests, where ditches up to 2.5 m in depth are dug into slopes at altitudes of up to 2100 m.

The first Europeans to meet Huli people, the mining prospectors Jack and Tom Fox, were astonished to find themselves travelling almost continuously along 'sunken roads' for more than a week as they crossed Huli territory in November 1934 (Fox n.d.). Colonial officials and missionaries who established the first stations in the region during the 1950s were quick to speculate over the origins and functions of these remarkable ditches, as French filmmaker and adventurer Pierre-Dominique Gaisseau recounted during a brief visit just as the area was first being opened up to outsiders (1957: 123): 'We

FIGURE 16.3. Huli ditches and drains, from top left, clockwise: (a) view over Haeapugua Basin; (b) clearing an ancestral *iba puni* drain; (c) a modern grave by the roadside; (d) a dryland *gana* ditch; and (e) a wetland *gana* drain with upcast walls.

(Photos by Chris Ballard.)

had already discussed these ditches with the Europeans stationed here, and each had produced a different explanation. They were territorial boundaries, to prevent the pigs wandering away from one clan to the next; or they were a system of defence; or drainage canals; or simply means of communication that could be kept open more easily than if they were built on level ground among the undergrowth. All the explanations seemed equally plausible to us, and perhaps the truth is a combination of the lot'.

One answer to the question of why Huli dig such deep and extensive networks of ditches is because they can and sometimes must—the soil, the landscape, and the exigencies of local hydrology allow for and even encourage such a response. The deep, weathered volcanic soils of the Huli valleys, and the peaty soils of the swampy centres, require drainage to maintain moisture balance but also hold their shape well when excavated for ditches. High year-round rainfall, in common with much of interior New Guinea, of about 2500 mm (Wood 1984: 37) poses a flood risk for the swampy valley floors, and the management of water is thus a key concern, especially when populations and demand for land are expanding. But water management is much more than a simple hydraulic exercise for Huli, and the central role of water in Huli lives and landscapes finds deep echoes in pre-Christian cosmology and ritual.

Water is the core element in a Huli register of potent fluids, including menstrual blood, semen, and mineral oil; the term for water (*iba*) is the root for the generic term for fertile substances more generally (*ibane*), such as grease, sap, or juice. These fluids are all potentially fertile if their flow is correctly managed, but highly dangerous if allowed to diffuse inappropriately. In the most widely recounted cosmogonic myth, pure water contained in a gourd is rejected by the first woman in favour of mortal breastmilk for her infant; the breastmilk introduces death to humans while a snake drinks the spilt water, gaining immortality (Goldman 1983: 93; Wardlow 2006: 63–66). Any loss of water in the human body or the landscape is a critical sign of an inexorable tendency in the Huli world towards entropy or decline, and actions designed to restore fertility and vitality to the body and the land were the primary focus of both personal and communal pre-Christian ritual. In Huli eschatology, the final demise of the world will be signalled by the conversion of swamps (*pugua*) to dry land (*dindi kui* or 'real land') and a diminution in the roar of waterfalls as the rivers slow to a trickle. The permanently moist swamps, which appear to resist even the harshest droughts, are thus both centres of fertility and a focus formerly for regenerative rituals, as a senior ritual leader describes: 'We try to stop the land from drying out, but now all the waters have left. Only the Piwa, Hulia, and Alua rivers are left to us, and we look after them. If these are lost, and the Tagali River slows to a trickle, fire will destroy us all' (Hubi-Morali, interview, 4 November 1992).

The spectre of an overabundance of water is viewed as a comparable, though not equal, threat. Regular floods in most of the basins are a constant hazard, often the result of tributaries back-flooding from junctions with larger rivers. This is held to be caused by blockages of flotsam at gorges or bends near such confluences, which are cleared by *iba tiri* ('water fool') spirits (Goldman 1998). *Iba tiri* were formerly encouraged and sustained in this work through the performance of rituals above river junctions, in which ritual leaders would throw bundles of pork tied around an axe into the river, to assist in the work of cutting up the flotsam.

Rivers structure Huli sacred geography at the global level: regional drainage provides the basis for one of the fundamental axes of Huli orientation, the distinction between *mane*, upriver or headwaters, and *wabi*, downriver or the lower reaches of any given river. For most Huli this represents a broad flow from north to south and is associated with the course of human life. The spirits of Huli dead (*dinini*) are thought to travel down smaller tributaries to the Tagali River, and ultimately to a location beyond the known universe, identified as Humbirini Andaga.

Both beneath and within the visible rivers, other invisible flows of fertile substance constitute a regenerative cycle that guarantees the survival of the cosmos. Mineral oil, as the most condensed (and thus dangerous) form of fertile substance is known to emanate from the underground at seeps and is understood to be the sun in its nocturnal, fluid form, travelling as an immortal snake from southwest to northeast before bursting into flame at dawn (Ballard 1998). This flow of fertile substance surfaces at numerous locations in the Huli landscape, each of them consecrated as a major ritual site at which region-wide rituals were coordinated to monitor and replenish the earth's fertility (Frankel 1986: 16–26; Goldman 1983: 113–120). Flowing broadly from southwest to northeast, against the slope of the land, this fertile substance moves like water within certain rivers and streams, but travels upstream, against the visible flow. Interrupting this flow, or failing to ritually replenish the cycle of fertile substance, can provoke apocalypse, the end of all life on earth until a new cycle or epoch is initiated (Ballard 1998). Water itself is imbued with life and agency, and individual bodies of water such as rivers and ponds are also identified as the embodiment of named ancestral and preancestral spirits, with whom relationships are constantly maintained through offerings and a posture of respect. In a striking confirmation of the intimacy of this association, clans that had been completely routed in war and forced to move from their ancestral lands describe their pools and streams moving with them, resurfacing in their new territories.

These cosmological understandings of water also govern relationships at the personal level, and most markedly in relationships between men and women (Frankel 1986; Goldman 1983; Wardlow 2006). Although the valence of different bodily fluids is often expressed in terms of male-female antagonism and a general fear of female pollution among men (e.g., Goldman 1983: 94–96), it is probably more accurate to insist that male and female fluids all share a bivalence in potency, as either fertile or destructive. Male semen, incorrectly managed, can damage both women and children. Menstrual blood can be a source of poison, capable of desiccating male bodies but, correctly controlled and ritually encased in a bamboo tube, it is also the most fertile of human fluids, formerly planted in swamps to enhance the fertility of the land. What makes fluid fertile is its transfer in a managed way, through controlled interactions between men and women. If the *iba tiri* water fool spirits are thought of as 'cosmic plumbers' (Goldman 1998: 97), Huli men, in particular, see themselves as fluid managers, controlling flows between men and women, between social groups, and between the seen and unseen worlds. Historically, success in an escalating series of ritual actions, ranging from household ceremonies to communal initiations, and culminating in major regional ritual performances, revolved around the manner in which fluids were generated, contained, and deposited or transferred. At the level of the landscape, ditches and drains are thus the primary means through which Huli seek to manage and control the fertility of the land, and to assert their own identities at successively more inclusive scales.

HULI DITCHES AND DRAINS

The Technology of Digging

The technology of Huli ditch-digging prior to the introduction of steel tools depended on a small suite of tools, all produced in wood: a long-handled spade (*keba*) with a flattened paddle at one end (or more rarely, both ends), used almost exclusively by men to excavate ditches; and an even longer hooked pole (*iba wango*) used to drag weeds out of wetland drains (Figure 16.3). Various digging sticks were then used to prepare and manage garden beds, the larger and heavier types (*habono*, *homabu*) being reserved for men, while both men and women used shorter digging sticks (*nama*). When not in use, tools were often kept submerged in drains to maintain suppleness and density; archaeological finds of spades and other wooden tools, retrieved from infilled drains and dating to over 4000 BP, suggest that this essential technology has changed little over time and across the Highlands region (Denham 2018: 137–139; Powell 1974; Powell & Harrison 1982: 54–56).

Types of Ditches

The basic Huli term for ditches of any size or function is *gana*. Given the importance, wide distribution, and range of functions of *gana*, the taxonomy for different *gana* forms is surprisingly shallow. A number of further distinctions are drawn to identify: *iba puni* drains (literally 'water drain'), which are found largely in wetlands, but can vary in size from small conduits through to the largest artificial channels; *mabu gana* ('garden ditch'), which are the ditches that enclose garden blocks; and *de gana*, the small ditches dug within a garden block to mark off plots belonging to individual men or women, which contribute only marginally to drainage of the garden surface in wetlands. In a network of wetland drains, these three terms form a hierarchy, with *iba puni* serving as the major drains articulating with the natural drainage system, *mabu gana* marking off garden blocks alongside *iba puni*, and *de gana* found only with garden blocks (see Ballard 2017: Figure 5.6). Where major and minor *iba puni* generally respect hydraulic gradients, running perpendicular to the dryland margin, *gana* drains run both parallel and perpendicular to the *iba puni*.

As dryland ditches are generally deeper and wider than wetland drains, the volume of soil excavated is greater, much of the upcast being heaped immediately above either side of the ditch as mud walls (*gana nene*), further increasing the apparent depth of the ditch. Two further contrasts between wetland drains and dryland ditches should be mentioned: first, dryland ditches need only encompass a single block to render an area available for gardening, whereas wetland blocks require the presence of an extensive network of larger drains to be viable; and second, while dryland ditches in deep volcanic soils are relatively stable, the requirements of wetland drain maintenance may actually require more labour over time than their initial excavation.

More important than category terms for different types of ditch are the specific identities of individual ditches, which are named for the historic ancestors who first dug them. A *gana* dug by Hege will be referred to in conversation as Hege *gana*; consequently, the names of ditches are themselves the subject of dispute in competing claims to land. It is this historic knowledge, so vital in claims to the land encompassed by ditches, rather than distinctions founded on *gana* form or size, that is of critical importance to Huli.

Ditches for Gardens

Wetland and dryland garden blocks or *mabu* are defined through their enclosure by drains and ditches. Garden blocks vary considerably in size and shape according to the antiquity of local settlement and the corresponding history of the subdivision of blocks. At Haeapugua, blocks are commonly about one acre (0.4 ha) in area and more or less rectangular in shape. *Mabu* blocks are then divided internally into smaller garden areas—either temporarily, through the use of *de gana*, to distinguish areas with different users, or permanently, through physical subdivision by additional *gana*, to denote separate ownership or a new function for the enclosed land.

Three types of block other than the basic *mabu* garden were distinguished prior to contact, defined in each case by the excavation of encircling *gana*: ritual enclosures, such as *gebeanda* or *liruanda* ritual sites, or *haroli tayanda* bachelor groves; *mabu* garden blocks that had been converted into residential blocks with their associated *gama* kitchen gardens; and *mabu* garden blocks subdivided to create *nogo dugudugu* ('pig-lead') thoroughfares to permit the movement of pigs without the danger of their intruding on garden areas (see later discussion).

Major garden projects, such as coordinated wetland drainage or the enclosure of cleared forest with ditches, require labour groups larger than individual family units. Commonly, major ditching or drainage works draw on the labour of a fairly closely related group of eight to ten men, a project group formed around one or more individuals as the 'source' or *tene* of the particular project: the *mabu tene* ('garden source') or *mabu anduane* ('garden owner') then coordinates garden projects involving the labour team and their wider families (for details of Huli garden production in wetlands, see Ballard 2001; Powell & Harrison 1982; Wood 1984). Clearance or re-excavation of the largest drainage channels can involve a wide cross-section of the basin's community who, by contributing to the drainage of a large portion of the swamp, establish their claim to the use of a significant area of land. In one documented instance, this involved a labour pool of thirty-two men from three different clan parishes, mostly aged between sixteen and thirty, of whom only ten to twelve worked on the project at any one time (Ballard 1995). The key factor determining the sustainability of wetland gardens is the ability of the gardeners to maintain the drainage network. Wood (1984: 168) has demonstrated that sweet potato yields from wetland gardens at Haeapugua, after peaking within the first ten years of garden use, decline only very slowly thereafter; wetland gardens created on the alluvial levees around the major drains flowing through Haeapugua have remained the most productive gardens in the basin, despite near-continuous use over more than a century.

The variation in size of the garden blocks defined by ditches and drains is often a good indication of the nature of the hydrological environment. As a general rule, the larger the block at Haeapugua, the wetter the soil conditions. Block shape also appears to vary according to environment. Almost all of the wetland blocks are rectilinear and generally symmetrical in form, with angled rather than curved corners. This is in contrast with dryland blocks, which take a much wider variety of forms, being generally asymmetrical and often curvilinear. Blocks in the most densely infilled dryland areas appear as an amalgam of rectangular and 'lobate' shapes forming clusters of truncated ovals. Evidently, the shape of individual blocks is closely related to the overall alignment of the respective wetland and dryland field systems. The layout of the dryland blocks is essentially random, with no easily identifiable focus in their alignment. In contrast, the wetland blocks are clearly oriented along common axes in a formation identified by Fleming (1988) in his analysis of the Dartmoor reave field systems as 'coaxial'. In the Haeapugua wetlands, the common axes of orientation are the major *iba puni* drainage channels.

Figure 16.2 shows the field system of garden ditches and drains on the eastern side of the Haeapugua Basin, with the Tagali River running from north to south on the western margin. The full extent of the network in use during the twentieth century is visible, along with elements of earlier 'covert' systems. The only new ditches added to the network between 1959 and 1989 were those associated with the division or partition of existing blocks to accommodate vehicular roads and church, clinic, and school buildings. The structure of the field system can be analysed for information about its likely genesis and sequence of development. There is some evidence of a tendency for block sizes to decrease over time, insofar as older blocks under continuous use are progressively reduced in size through subdivision. This is suggested, in part, by the distinction between the small, heavily subdivided blocks on the long-settled dryland areas and the larger, and presumably more recently delineated, wetland blocks. It is possible that this is simply a function of the differences between wetland and dryland conditions and technologies: houses are more likely to be constructed on well-drained soils, and dryland subdivision may thus reflect the restricted distribution of settlement. But if these putative earlier, larger dryland blocks are reconstructed, an interesting relationship emerges between size and shape.

There is a pattern evident in dryland field form in which earlier and larger lobate or curvilinear fields (shown as bold lines in Ballard 2017: Figure 5.12) appear to have been subdivided into or transected by progressively smaller and more rectilinear field forms. In almost all wetland areas, considerably larger, rectilinear field forms are the norm. Although topography clearly plays a role in allowing for construction of the large rectilinear forms on the more level wetlands, the distinction between rectilinear and curvilinear forms also marks a historical division. Within the wetland area, there are also hints of an earlier phase of the rectilinear field system, with anomalous blocks laid out on a different coaxial alignment (shown as dashed lines in Ballard 2017: Figure 5.12).

Walkways and Droveways

In addition to ditches dug to demarcate gardens or residential spaces, there are also areas set aside for the movement of people and pigs across the landscape. In most dryland areas, the deep *gana* ditches are themselves the paths along which both people and pigs travel in their daily circuits, which can be hazardous in wet weather and almost invariably involve much wading through mud. But, in certain areas, parallel ditches were dug at a distance of at least 5 m from each other, excising land from the surrounding garden blocks to create dedicated walkways for people (*hariga*) and droveways for pigs. Ancient walkways, or *bambali hariga*, sunk into the landscape and with very large trees along their walls, provided access between different basins, allowing people (and their pigs) to travel longer distances without negotiating passage with individual landowners. Many of the major trackways were later extended to serve as vehicle roads by the colonial administration.

Along the fertile swamp margins at Haeapugua, shorter lengths of walkway were created to channel people and pigs from dryland residential blocks out into the swamp, to garden and forage for worms, respectively. The primary function of these raised passages was to allow small herds of pigs to be driven out to the swampy centre of the basin each morning, before enticing them back to their pens each evening with sweet potato; this primacy of function is reflected in the term most commonly used to refer to them, as *nogo dugudugu* ('pig lead'). Where *hariga* tracks for people usually ran perpendicular to the drainage pattern, crossing from one clan territory to the next, pig droveways followed the drains down into the swamp, safely within the bounds of a single clan territory (for maps of all trackways and droveways in the Haeapugua Basin, see Ballard 1995, I: Figures C7 & C8).

Ditches and Warfare

The mining prospectors who were the first Europeans to enter Huli territory in 1934, twin brothers Tom and Jack Fox, were both survivors of World War I trench warfare in Flanders, and the shocking violence of their passage may have been a response on their part to finding themselves again in networks of deep ditches, designed deliberately to frustrate attackers. Amongst their many functions, certain Huli *gana* were also excavated to act or double as defences or war ditches (*wai gana*), channelling and blocking movement strategically, and confusing attackers caught in mazes sunk beneath the level of the land. Fences (*pabe*), gateways (*panga*), and garrisoned blockhouses (*wai pabeanda*) further contributed to the defence of clan territories.

The destruction of ditches on enemy land was thus a marker of success in warfare. When the first government patrol post was established in Huli territory in 1951, at what would later become the township of Tari, a war raging across the Haeapugua Basin between the Tani and Tigua clans was initially monitored and then brought to an end by patrol officers and police armed with rifles. Patrol Officer Arthur Carey describes the aftermath of battle: 'For about four miles at a width of two hundred to three hundred yards, every living thing had been destroyed. The pit-pit [grass] was flattened as if by a roller, trees were either cut down or ringed, gardens were uprooted, houses burnt to the ground, and the big ditches broken or filled in. It left one with a feeling akin to awe at the savage force behind it all' (Carey 1952). The Tani clan prisoners taken by Carey served out their sentences constructing the airstrip at Tari, which became known amongst other clans, rather derisively, as the 'Tani ditch' (*Tani gana*).

The Aesthetics of Ditches

Across a few flickering frames of black-and-white footage, a number of older Huli men can be seen showing to an audience of youthful initiates an intricate model landscape, delicately sculpted in miniature out of the muddy ground at their feet to illustrate the ideal forms of houses and deep ditch networks, and their disposition across the landscape. The footage, shot in 1957 by the French filmmaker Gaisseau, is all that remains to document this fascinating practice, a minor component of an elaborate week-long initiation ceremony, known as *tege pulu* and now abandoned. These idealized miniatures point both to the centrality of ditches in the way Huli fashion their landscape, and to questions around the aesthetics of the ditch and its association with Huli understandings of identity and tradition.

Much as Huli bodies are scrutinized for qualities such as the sheen and gloss of skin, which can radiate an aura of health, success, and efficacy (Frankel 1986: 56), so, too, Huli ditches are subject to aesthetic evaluation. Comment is frequently passed on the straight lines and uniform smoothness of the mud finish of ditch walls, the moulded corners (*gana gembone*) of ditch intersections, or the care with which different cordyline or tree species have been planted and spaced along the crest of the *gana nene* wall (see Ballard 1995, II: Figure B18). Older men and women deplore the collapse of standards evident in the appearance and upkeep of modem ditches. Perhaps, the one context in which these standards are considered still to be upheld is where compensation for a death is being sought and large groups of kin and affines construct immaculate *gana* alongside roads to contain the newly erected grave (*homalianda*) (Figure 16.3).

Ditches as Boundaries

Underpinning all of the material functions of ditches and drains—their role in creating garden spaces, and in managing the movement of water, people, pigs, and enemies—is their central importance as the primary means of the human inscription of space, of the creation of meaningful distinction within the Huli landscape. The act of ditching is constitutive of Huli identity and of claims to land; clan origin narratives all refer to the initial creation of ditches, the 'cutting of the land' by ancestors, as their foundational claim to parish territories. 'His ditch is there' is the definitive statement of current or past possession by an individual, and of the assumption that ditches endure beyond the lives of their creators. If the initiation of a new *gana* is an open declaration of a claim to the enclosed land, the re-excavation of an existing *gana* is a historically conscious act, the reaffirmation of an ancestral claim to that land; hence the significance of the boast, 'I made my gardens there along the ancient marks'. In swamplands such as Haeapugua, the act of digging *gana* is sufficient in itself to serve as the basis for rights to produce from the enclosed land. Along with planted trees, excavated ditches serve as evidence in customary disputes of rights developed through use of the land (e.g., Goldman 1983: 139–140).

Generally, the outer boundaries of Huli parishes or clan territories are aligned with named water features, such as lakes, ponds, rivers, and streams, which are then channelled and managed to some extent once they reach the flat wetlands, as major *iba puni* drains. Within clan territories, internal subdivision of ditched and drained areas descends through a hierarchy of social units and size of ditch, from major ditches along subclan boundaries through to the shallower ditches that surround individual garden or residential blocks, and down to the smallest *de gana* ditches which mark ownership of subplots by individuals or areas gardened by different women within a single family.

Ditches signal at least three core aspects of Huli cultural identity: maleness, in that only men are said to ditch and fence, either literally or metaphorically; Huli-ness, as an explicit marker of ethnic identity; and fully 'modern' humanness, as an integral component in the historic emergence of *mabu* gardens (addressed later). The digging of ditches, along with building fences, is said to be an exclusively male activity, and one of many practices that distinguish male from female lives, activities, and spaces. Formerly, ditches also physically demarcated male and female space: men and women slept separately in men's (*agandia* or *balamanda*) and women's (*wandia*) houses, respectively, within discrete residential blocks. The movement of women, in particular, was circumscribed by restrictions on entering men's gardens or houses, ritual sites, and bachelor cult groves. Formal adages (*pureremo*) inculcated these social norms, much as the miniature landscapes demonstrated them to the eye:

> There are women's houses and men's houses.
> Don't sleep in the women's house, sleep in the men's house.
> Clear swidden gardens outside, dig ditches and make real gardens inside [the ditch boundaries].
> Outside is for pigs, gardens are for people.
> Women's houses are for women, men's houses are for men. It is said thus.
> (Duliya, interview, 17 August 1991)

Since the 1950s and with the active encouragement of the missions, the proscriptions on male and female cohabitation have relaxed considerably, and houses in which married couples live and sleep together are common (Wardlow 2006: 53–54).

Huli ditches are also markers of ethnic identity on a regional scale: along the Highlands Highway, between the small towns of Margarima and Nipa, an obvious boundary between ditched and unditched gardens coincides neatly with the boundary between Huli- and Wola-speaking communities; the deep drains and upcast walls seen by Paul Gorecki at Kuk Swamp during the 1970s were dug by Huli immigrants to the

Wahgi Valley (Gorecki 1982: Plate 21); and Huli migrants moving south and east towards the oilfield developments around Lake Kutubu have stamped their presence on the ground of their Foi and Fasu hosts by digging their distinctive ditches.

Ditches as History

Ditches are also read—by Huli as well as archaeologists—as signs of the past. If the accumulation of networks of *gana* ditches forms a dense grid that covers much of the occupied Huli landscape, there is a corresponding grid of genealogies that ties the ditch networks to known individuals, named as ancestors in genealogies that ostensibly extend between twelve and twenty generations. Typically, disputes over land draw on the intersection of these two fine meshes of proof: Who was the first ancestor to 'cut' the land with a ditch or drain? Who is the ditch named for? Who has recut or cleaned the ditch since? For at least the last two centuries, this exceptional detail in the recall of human and landscape history allows for a close reconstruction of sequences—if not absolute chronologies—of land use, at a much finer resolution than archaeological excavation or radiocarbon dating might permit.

But Huli oral traditions also speak to much deeper pasts, organized around a series of epochs, each one characterized by a particular staple food. In a mythical, pre-human epoch peopled by spirit ancestors, referred to as 'the time when rotten wood was eaten' (*ira goba naga*), only wild foods and wild pandanus nuts were consumed. Following this epoch was a second, 'the time when taro was eaten' (*ma naga*), in which people now recognized as fully human domesticated and ate taro (*ma*; *Colocasia esculenta*), cucumber (*bambo*; *Cucumis sativus*), bottle gourd (*mbagua*; *Lagenaria siceraria*), and yam (*nandi*; *Dioscorea alata*). The third and current epoch is the time of sweet potato (*hina naga*), and Huli and scientific histories are broadly in accord in timing the local adoption of this South American crop shortly before the fall of Tibito tephra from the Long Island eruption of c. 1665–1668 CE (Blong & Kurbatov 2020).

For Huli people, these epochs have left distinctive material residues in the landscape. The first epoch of wild foods involved no domestication and required no gardens (or ditches). Gardens were an invention of the time of taro—first as swidden plots for taro (*e ma*) and then, as the numbers of domesticated pigs grew, proper gardens (*mabu*) enclosed by ditches (note the presence in both garden terms of taro or *ma* as the primary or most prestigious staple). But as Huli men dig deep drains within the swamps today, they unearth traces of these earlier epochs. Thick, black, organic-rich layers of preserved swamp forest are uncovered, containing the seeds and leaves of wild pandanus species (*mundiya* and *tawa*; *Pandanus antaresensis*), the direct remains of the time of rotten wood, said to have ended with a cataclysmic flood. Closer to the surface, thin lenses of a green, sandy tephra are also found, often within the fill of ancient ditches exposed in profile; this soil is known to Huli as *mbi mu* ('darkness sand'), and features in oral traditions about named ancestors alive at the time the ash fell (the 'time of darkness' or *mbingi*)

(Ballard 1998; Blong 1982); the tephra is clearly identifiable as Tibito and serves as a useful temporal marker for Huli and archaeologists alike. Two further developments in the landscape of ditches are linked to the adoption of sweet potato, which is widely held to have triggered an explosion in human and pig populations: the deepening of existing dryland *gana* ditches in the central basins to form war ditches (*wai gana*), regarded as a historic response to the rise in the frequency and intensity of warfare; and the excavation of parallel sets of ditches to create pig droveways (*nogo dugudugu*) as pig herds grew and forage areas in the major swamps contracted.

Ditches in the Cosmos

One final but critical aspect of Huli ditches to consider is their position within local cosmology. Huli men model their actions as drain diggers and water managers on the *iba tiri* water spirits, controlling fertility and production at the micro scales of the family or clan. On the larger stage of Huli cosmology, ditches play a number of roles in the management and control of fertility. The core of fertile substance, the mineral oil that runs beneath the earth in the form of a python, or the sun by night, surfaces at various locations in the Huli landscape (Ballard 1998; Frankel 1986). The most important of these locations were marked by caves within which senior ritual leaders replenished the snake with offerings of mineral oil, ochre, and blood. Access to these caves involved passage through a carefully cleared avenue through a grove of towering hoop pines (*guraya*, *Araucaria cunninghamii*), which can grow up to 60 m in height and last for as long as 450 years, crossing a series of ditches and gateways that marked the boundaries of successively more ancient epochs. As they crossed each ditch, ritual performers would travel back in time, shedding their clothes, and consuming only those foods appropriate to the epochal space they were entering.

But the elaborate tracks of the python between these major ritual centres or *gebeanda*, passing deep beneath mountain ranges and upstream through visible rivers, and occasionally manifesting as rocky outcrops, also imposed profound restrictions on where Huli could or could not dig their ditches. One of the two most important Huli ritual sites, the cave at Gelote, lies in the Haeapugua Valley, on the western banks of the Tagali River (just outside the area shown on Figure 16.2); but at various specific points within the Haeapugua field system, anomalous gaps in the network mark points where it was regarded as simply too dangerous to risk digging into the earth's surface, or even building a house: 'It is said that if you cut where the python goes, blood will come out. Women are not to make mounded gardens, men are not to dig ditches or to clear swidden gardens [in these places] . . . or the good things [that flow from the python] would be cut' (Timothy Meria, interview, 17 April 1991). Disrupting the passage of the sun in this way, and thus the flow of the complex of nutritive substances associated with the python, risked bringing the present epoch to a fiery, apocalyptic end (Ballard 1998).

Reclamation and Abandonment

When ditches and drains fail, fall into disuse, or are abandoned, they do so for social, hydrological, and cosmological reasons, often in combination. Ditches and drains can be deliberately infilled by an enemy in war, but more commonly they simply fall into disrepair. The processes of mobilization required to initiate large-scale garden projects, particularly in wetlands, are themselves subject to entropic forces, as the labour teams age, or fall apart through dispute, or cease to acknowledge the leadership of the project owner. Wetland garden blocks, reclaimed for periods of about a decade, are allowed to revert to swamp either individually or in clusters of contiguous blocks if the major outlet drains fail. Major floods can also overwhelm a drainage network in the swamp, scouring garden surfaces, destroying crops, and infilling drains with sediment. And pigs, often cited as the historical reason why Huli turned to ditches to protect their gardens, present a constant threat to the integrity of ditch form and the viability of gardens.

Huli explanations for the abandonment of wetland gardens constitute a refrain built around this triad of pigs, water, and labour: 'swamp gardens are abandoned because of water, pigs, and laziness. Truly, water is the cause, because when water fills the ditches, pigs swim across and destroy the gardens' (Tumbu, interview, 2 January 1991). Pigs, and the caprice of water, are especially singled out for blame:

> Other people's pigs forage in the swamps for worms. But they are really hungry for sweet potato and they come up to the edges of the drains. When they find one that has collapsed a bit, one of the pigs will see this and force its way across the drain. A second will see the tracks of the first and follow it into the garden. Then a third, and they'll eat up everything. Pigs know that all of the good food is in the gardens. Then the water follows the pigs in and people say, 'Now it's too hard,' and they go back to the dry land.
>
> (Kamiali, interview, 26 August 1991)

The third cause, 'laziness', perhaps speaks to the deeper problem behind the failure of ditches. In some respects, the only real limit on the longevity of wetland gardens is the ability of the gardens' owners and users to maintain their drains (though see later on the general fate of drained swamps). There is no doubt that this becomes increasingly difficult over the lifetime of a wetland garden, largely because unconsolidated sediments are not necessarily easier to excavate than compact peat turves. The tendency for wetland gardens to last for approximately ten years may thus date the point at which drain-wall slumping and sediment accumulation in the surrounding drains defeat casual attempts at maintenance.

At the heart of the Huli cosmic process of entropy is the sense that humans and human projects are ultimately set up to fail. The drainage of peat swamps leads to shrinkage of the surface peats and a consequent decline in the height of the swamp surface. Recorded shrinkage rates at the experimental tea plantations at Kuk and Olgaboli in the Wahgi Valley showed dramatic declines in swamp surfaces of 60–70 cm within 3–12 months, stabilizing at an average total loss in height of about 90 cm after seven years (McGrigor 1973: 34); near to the drains themselves, losses of up to 120 cm were recorded (Hartley 1967: 33). When combined with the possibility of an increase in the elevation of the main river channels as their levees develop, the scope for flooding of the swamp after the inception of a reclamation process is considerable. To some extent, peat swamp drainage is always doomed to cyclical failure.

Ditches and drains are woven into the fabric of Huli life and thought. Articulated with each other within networks or field systems, they give material expression to other kinds of networks—of kinship, genealogy and ethnicity, production and consumption, and ritual and ceremonial performance. Through this process of assemblage, Huli ditches and drains achieve a kind of collective monumentality that far exceeds their individual scale, constituting an entire landscape of memory and practice that becomes visible not from the land's surface, but from the contrasting perspectives either of walking within the ditch, or of an aerial gaze.

Some Conclusions

What might this account of Huli ditches tell us about ditches either in earlier periods or elsewhere in the New Guinea Highlands? As an ethnography, this chapter documents a particular moment set within a much longer history of use that extends both before the period of my field observations and since. It speaks to a time when sweet potato was overwhelmingly the dominant crop in both dryland and wetland gardens, and may thus be generalizable only to the period of the past three or four centuries, such as Phase 6 at Kuk (Bayliss-Smith et al. 2017b). Bayliss-Smith, Golson, and Hughes (2017a: 241–243) point out, for example, that taro beetle infestation would have required fallows between each crop of taro from pre–sweet potato gardens, considerably reducing the returns from investment in swamp drainage; and, as James Watson (1977) observed long ago, sweet potato's qualities as a fodder for pigs presumably transformed the cycle of intensification between sweet potato and pig production, and the role of wetland gardens as centres for the production of fodder (Ballard 2001). The visible drain network and the practices observed at Haeapugua are thus the product of a specific phase in the agricultural history of the New Guinea Highlands.

Can we extrapolate from Huli experience to that of other communities in New Guinea's famously diverse cultural landscape? Certain elements of Huli culture do appear exceptional, including the emphasis on genealogy and historical recall, which places a particular kind of weight on ditches as material proofs of the past. Huli cosmological elaboration is matched elsewhere in the Highlands (for instance, amongst the Telefol or Iqwaye), but it is unusual both for a society practicing intensive valley floor agriculture (such as the Grand Valley Dani or the Wahgi Valley communities around the Kuk site), and because Huli placed such importance on extending their vision of the universe, and their central role in sustaining it, to their neighbours in all directions (Frankel 1986: 16–26; Ballard 1994). But the ways in which ditches and drains are obviously implicated in Huli cosmology and sacred geography suggest that the possibility of something more than hydraulic, agronomic, or social significance needs to be conceived as playing a part in the structuring of field systems. This holds true for all other societies of the New Guinea Highlands that have left traces of their shaping of landscapes in the form of ditched field systems, even if those forms and the cosmologies that underpin them are radically different in nature from those of the Huli.

ACKNOWLEDGMENTS

I thank Laurence Goldman, Tim Bayliss-Smith, and Ian McNiven for their careful reading and comments on a draft of this chapter. I also acknowledge the many hundreds of Huli women and men who walked with me over their landscape, trying to teach me to see and understand it properly.

REFERENCES

Anon. [Williams, F. E.] (1936–1937). Aerial reconnaissance of the Hides-O'Malley area in the interior of Papua, visited by them on foot in the early half of 1936 and to be patrolled later by Mr. Champion. *Tijdschrift Nieuw Guinea*, 1, 62–68, 117–127.

Archbold, R., Rand, A. L., & Brass, L. J. (1942). Results of the Archbold Expeditions. No.41: Summary of the 1938–39 New Guinea Expedition. *Bulletin of the American Museum of Natural History*, 79(3), 197–288.

Ballard, C. (1994). The centre cannot hold: Trade networks and sacred geography in the Papua New Guinea Highlands. *Archaeology in Oceania*, 29(3), 130–148.

Ballard, C. (1995). *The death of a great land: Ritual, history and subsistence revolution in the Southern Highlands of Papua New Guinea* (PhD thesis). 2 vols. Australian National University, Canberra. http://hdl.handle.net/1885/7510

Ballard, C. (1998). The sun by night: Huli moral topography and myths of a time of darkness. In L. R. Goldman & C. Ballard (Eds.), *Fluid ontologies: Myth, ritual and philosophy in the Highlands of Papua New Guinea* (pp. 67–85). Westport, CT: Bergin & Garvey.

Ballard, C. (2001). Wetland drainage and agricultural transformations in the Southern Highlands of Papua New Guinea. *Asia-Pacific Viewpoint*, 42(2/3), 287–304.

Ballard, C. (2017). The wetland field systems of the New Guinea Highlands. In J. Golson, T. Denham, P. Hughes, P. Swadling, & J. Muke (Eds.), *Ten thousand years of cultivation at Kuk Swamp in the Highlands of Papua New Guinea* (pp. 65–83). Terra Australis 46. Canberra: ANU Press.

Ballard, C., Denham, T., & Haberle, S. (2013). Wetland archaeology in the highlands of New Guinea. In F. Menotti & A. O'Sullivan (Eds.), *The Oxford handbook of wetland archaeology* (pp. 231–248). Oxford: Oxford University Press.

Barber, I. (2001). Wet or dry: An evaluation of extensive archaeological ditch systems from far northern New Zealand. In C. M. Stevenson, G. Lee, & F. J. Morin (Eds.), *Pacific 2000:*

Proceedings of the Fifth International Conference on Easter Island and the Pacific (pp. 41–50). Los Osos, CA: Bearsville Press.

Bayliss-Smith, T. (1985). Pre-ipomoean agriculture in the New Guinea Highlands above 2000 metres: Some experimental data on taro cultivation. In I. S. Farrington (Ed.), *Prehistoric intensive agriculture in the tropics* (pp. 285–320). BAR International Series 232. Oxford: British Archaeological Reports.

Bayliss-Smith, T. (2007). The meaning of ditches: Interpreting the archaeological record from New Guinea using insights from ethnography. In T. P. Denham, J. Iriarte, & L. Vrydaghs (Eds.), *Rethinking agriculture: Archaeological and ethnoarchaeological perspectives* (pp. 126–148). Walnut Creek, CA: Left Coast Press.

Bayliss-Smith, T., & Golson, J. (1999). The meaning of ditches: Deconstructing the social landscapes of drainage in New Guinea, Kuk, Phase 4. In C. Gosden & J. Hather (Eds.), *The prehistory of food: Appetites for change* (pp. 199–231). London: Routledge.

Bayliss-Smith, T., Golson, J., & Hughes, P. (2017a). Phase 4: Major disposal channels, slot-like ditches and grid-patterned fields. In J. Golson, T. Denham, P. Hughes, P. Swadling, & J. Muke (Eds.), *Ten thousand years of cultivation at Kuk Swamp in the Highlands of Papua New Guinea* (pp. 239–268). Terra Australis 4. Canberra: ANU Press.

Bayliss-Smith, T., Golson, J., & Hughes, P. (2017b). Phase 6: Impact of the sweet potato on swamp landuse, pig rearing and exchange relations. In J. Golson, T. Denham, P. Hughes, P. Swadling, & J. Muke (Eds.), *Ten thousand years of cultivation at Kuk Swamp in the Highlands of Papua New Guinea* (pp. 297–324). Terra Australis 4. Canberra: ANU Press.

Bayliss-Smith, T., Golson, J., Hughes, P., Blong, R., & Ambrose, W. (2005). Archaeological evidence for the Ipomoean Revolution at Kuk Swamp, upper Wahgi valley, Papua New Guinea. In C. Ballard, P. Brown, R. Bourke, & T. Harwood (Eds.), *The sweet potato in Oceania: A reappraisal* (pp. 109–120). Sydney: University of Pittsburgh & University of Sydney.

Bell, A. C. (2013). *The sweet potato factory: An archaeological investigation of the Pouerua cultivation landscape* (PhD thesis). University of Otago, Dunedin.

Blong, R. J. (1982). *The time of darkness: Local legends and volcanic reality in Papua New Guinea.* Canberra: ANU Press.

Blong, R. J., & Kurbatov, A. V. (2020). Steps and missteps on the path to a 1665–1668 CE date for the VEI 6 eruption of Long Island, Papua New Guinea. *Journal of Volcanology and Geothermal Research, 395,* 106828.

Brookfield, H. C., & Brown, P. (1963). *Struggle for land: Agriculture and group territories among the Chimbu of the New Guinea Highlands.* Melbourne: Oxford University Press.

Carey, A. T. (1952). Tari River basin, north western Papua. Lake Kutubu Patrol Report No.6 for 1952 / Tari Patrol Report No.1 for 1952. National Archives of Papua New Guinea, Waigani.

Denham, T. (2018). *Tracing early agriculture in the Highlands of New Guinea: Plot, mound and ditch.* London: Routledge.

Fleming, A. (1988). *The Dartmoor reaves: Investigating prehistoric land divisions.* London: Batsford.

Fox, J. (n.d.). Fox Bros 1934, 1935 prospecting trips. Unpublished manuscript. Photocopy held at the New Guinea Collection, Michael Somare Library, University of Papua New Guinea, AL-101/5.

Frankel, S. (1986). *The Huli response to illness.* Cambridge: Cambridge University Press.

Gaisseau, P. D. (1957). *Visa to the prehistoric world.* London: Frederick Muller.

Goldman, L. R. (1983). *Talk never dies: The language of Huli disputes.* London: Tavistock.

Goldman, L. R. (1988). A trickster for all seasons: The Huli iba tiri. In L. R. Goldman & C. Ballard (Eds.), *Fluid ontologies: Myth, ritual and philosophy in the Highlands of Papua New Guinea* (pp. 87–124). Westport, CT: Bergin & Garvey.

Golson, J., Denham, T., Hughes, P., Swadling, P., & Muke, J. (Eds.) (2017). *Ten thousand years of cultivation at Kuk Swamp in the Highlands of Papua New Guinea.* Terra Australis 4. Canberra: ANU Press.

Gorecki, P. P. (1979). Population growth and abandonment of swamplands: A New Guinea Highlands example. *Journal de la Société des Océanistes, 35*(63), 97–107.

Gorecki, P. P. (1982). *Ethnoarchaeology at Kuk: Problems in site formation processes* (PhD thesis). University of Sydney, Sydney.

Gorecki, P. P. (1985). The conquest of a new 'wet and dry' territory: Its mechanism and its archaeological consequence. In I. S. Farrington (Ed.), *Prehistoric intensive agriculture in the tropics* (pp. 321–345). British Archaeological Reports International Series 232. Oxford: British Archaeological Reports.

Haberle, S. G. (1993). *Late Quaternary environmental history of the Tari Basin, Papua New Guinea* (PhD thesis). Australian National University, Canberra.

Hartley, A. C. (1967). Wahgi Swamp. Report on reclamation of phragmites peat swamp in the Western Highlands. Unpublished report to the Department of Agriculture, Stock and Fisheries, Port Moresby.

Johnson, L. (1986). *Aspects of the prehistory of the far northern valley systems* (MA thesis). University of Auckland, Auckland.

Leahy, M. J. (1994). *Explorations into Highland New Guinea.* Bathurst: Crawford House Press.

Leahy, M. J., & Crain, M. (1937). *The land that time forgot: Adventures and discoveries in New Guinea.* London: Funk & Wagnalls.

McGrigor, A. (1973). *Comments on drainage in the Highlands of Papua New Guinea.* Research Bulletin No.9. Port Moresby: Department of Agriculture, Stock and Fisheries.

Pospisil, L. (1963). *Kapauku Papuan economy.* Yale University Publications in Anthropology No.67. New Haven, CT: Department of Anthropology, Yale University.

Powell, J. M. (1974). A note on wooden gardening implements of the Mt. Hagen region, New Guinea. *Records of the Papua New Guinea Museum, 4,* 21–28.

Powell, J. M., & Harrison, S. (1982). *Haiyapugwa: Aspects of Huli subsistence and swamp cultivation.* Occasional Paper (New Series) No.1. Waigani: Geography Department, University of Papua New Guinea.

Rippon, S. (2012). *Making sense of an historic landscape.* Oxford: Oxford University Press.

Roscoe, P. (2009). On the 'pacification' of the European Neolithic: Ethnographic analogy and the neglect of history. *World Archaeology, 41*(4), 578–588.

Spriggs, M. (2008). Ethnographic parallels and the denial of history. *World Archaeology, 40*(4), 538–552.

Wardlow, H. (2006). *Wayward women: Sexuality and agency in a New Guinea society.* Berkeley: University of California Press.

Watson, J. B. (1977). Pigs, fodder and the Jones Effect in postipomoean New Guinea. *Ethnology, 16*(1), 57–70.

Wickstead, H. (2008). *Theorizing tenure: Land division and identity in later prehistoric Dartmoor, south-west Britain.* British Archaeological Reports, British Series, BAR 465. Oxford: Archaeopress.

Williamson, T. (1987). Early co-axial field systems on the East Anglian boulder clays. *Proceedings of the Prehistoric Society, 53,* 419–431.

Wissel, F. J. (n.d.). *Kapal udara: An aviator's reminiscences of the Far East, 1934–1948*. Unpublished manuscript.

Wohlt, P. B. (1978). *Ecology, agriculture and social organization: The dynamics of group composition in the Highlands of Papua New Guinea* (PhD thesis). University of Minnesota. Ann Arbor: University Microfilms International.

Wood, A. W. (1984). *Land for tomorrow: Subsistence agriculture, soil fertility and ecosystem stability in the New Guinea highlands* (PhD thesis). University of Papua New Guinea, Port Moresby.

CHAPTER 17

ENGAGING AND DESIGNING PLACE

Furnishings and the Architecture of Archaeological Sites in Aboriginal Australia

BRUNO DAVID, JEAN-JACQUES DELANNOY,
CHRIS URWIN, JOANNA FRESLØV,
RUSSELL MULLETT, AND CHRISTINE PHILLIPS

INTRODUCTION

IT is commonplace in Australian Indigenous archaeology to search for, map, quantify, and investigate the contents of a site as a way to accumulate evidence of its past occupation, and as a means by which to tell the (hi)story of a place. Less common is the study of how sites and landscapes themselves have been constructed through deliberate design, 'adaptation' (we prefer the term 'bricolage'), and social engagement. These latter matters relate more to 'building', traditionally the province of engineers and architects, subjects that have rarely been broached in Australian archaeology. This is despite their considerable archaeological interest elsewhere in the world, especially in relation to permanent towns and villages and state-based societies. One of us (CP) clearly remembers the shock of commencing a first-year undergraduate architecture course at a prestigious Australian university in 1993, wondering why the survey of Australian architecture began with European settlement. Were the building works of Aboriginal peoples prior to settlement not architecture? Many years on, and now a professional architect, the bewilderment has not shaken, while the conviction that Aboriginal constructions are nothing but architectural expressions remains stronger than ever.

Often local Aboriginal and Torres Strait Islander community members will hold cultural knowledge about how places are, or were, constructed (note that *all* places have contemporary significance steeped in local cosmologies to community members; the aim of our analyses is to determine *how* such places were created as physical places by examining what people did: the places themselves). Sometimes knowledge of construction methods will be known by contemporary community members themselves (or recorded in archives), but sometimes it will not, either because the activities in question took place a long time ago and have been forgotten, or because the place itself was only recently rediscovered. Irrespective of the cause, archaeological methods enable the study of the physical places to shed light on how their shapes changed through time and the methods used to do so. The sites discussed in this chapter in each case underwent construction thousands of years ago (and in at least two cases, more than c. 10,000 years ago). Our aim is to determine what happened at each place at the time of their construction. In each case, the archaeological investigations were overseen by local Elders (sometimes involving younger community members also) at the request of the local Aboriginal representative organization. In each case also, the nature and methods of the site's construction were not previously known by the local community (nor did the language names of the sites, where known, reveal anything about their construction), as communicated back to the authors during the reporting of results. Researching together, it is through archaeology working closely with geomorphology that the sites' changing shape and methods of construction came to be known.

In this chapter, we show that 'the action or process of building' or 'constructing edifices of any kind for human use'—'architecture' following the Oxford English Dictionary Online (2020)—is as relevant to Indigenous Australia as it is elsewhere. Australian Indigenous archaeology, as a discipline aiming to understand the Aboriginal and Torres Strait Islander past, would thus benefit greatly from better incorporating in its intellectual reach how structures, sites, and landscapes were built for use through skilful planning and cultural design.

SITES AS ARCHITECTURE IN AUSTRALIAN ABORIGINAL ARCHAEOLOGY

Early colonial observers on many occasions commented on how Aboriginal peoples across Australia designed and purpose-built varied kinds of facilities (e.g., fish traps, dwellings) across the landscape, such as in the Reverend Peter MacPherson's (1884) 'The oven-mounds of the aborigines in Victoria'; E. J. Statham's (1892) 'Observations on shell-heaps and shell-beds' of Ballina and other parts of northeastern New South Wales, where massive and well-stratified shell mounds were described; and explorer A. C. Gregory's (1858) discovery of 'many small stone huts' (subsequently found to be Aboriginal hawk and eagle-hunting hides; see Browne 1895; Lewis 1988a) in the Victoria River District of the Northern Territory. Such sites were often commented upon for how they were designed with forethought that took account of their surroundings—how they functioned *with* the landscapes in which they were set—such as in the raised wooden platforms of Arnhem Land, beneath which smoky fires could be lit to keep mosquitoes away at night, for example (Memmott & Fantin 2005). While the notion of articulating 'engineered landscapes' (see David & Hamacher 2018; McNiven 2017; McNiven et al. 2012) thus focuses on how constructions *work* by considering their functioning parts (e.g., Campbell 1979, 1982), the idea of sites as architecture is concerned more with how sites were *built*, both through design and cumulative growth, much like working out the technological characteristics of stone artefacts, but at a landscape scale. This concept of construction has rarely been adequately addressed for Australian Aboriginal sites (but see, e.g., McNiven's [2013: 575–577] notion of 'ritualised middening', which refers to the deliberate construction of midden deposits as forms of 'living architecture'). We often think of individual places, whether they be open-air sites, rock shelters, or caves, as essentially 'natural' features of the landscape onto which people carried out activities, in the process arranging things, modifying their surroundings, and accumulating layers of discarded refuse and artefacts. In this conception, the sites appear to have simply, or 'naturally', grown, rather than having been actively built. Yet, like all architecture, those sites are themselves products of social and cultural planning, improvisation or bricolage, and activities, and through cultural understandings they are thereby progressively constructed both *for* specific purposes and *through* the ways they are engaged.

The notion of 'engagement' is a useful one that allows a consideration of environmental properties to be imbued with social and cultural mores. We engage *in* rather than *with* things (in the sense that the meaningfulness, and thus usability, of things is already relational or at one). It enables us to go beyond asking if a component of the lived and experienced landscape is 'natural' (as distinct from, and mutually exclusive of, 'cultural'), so common in Western philosophical and linguistic discourse. Engagement is at key in Heidegger's (e.g., 1993) and, later, Ingold's (e.g., 1995) and Thomas's (e.g., 2007) 'dwelling' and 'inhabitation', Casey's (e.g., 1993) 'placial', and Deleuze and Guattari's (1994) 'striated' or territorialized space. It focuses not on features of the landscape as detached and separate, but as socially and ontologically embedded, and therefore socially meaningful. Through the ways they are conceptually and physically engaged, places are subject to social and cultural responsibility and compliance (see also Backhaus 2002; for anthropological perspectives, see Feld & Basso 1996). Such a territorialization of space sees social actions shape places as culturally meaningful locales: Social activities build surroundings through the ways they are culturally inhabited, and the physical edifices that are constructed in the process are shaped through such engagements (which involves both design and bricolage, see Conkey & Fisher 2020). For Memmott (2007: 4), 'there is now an abundance of documentation to indicate Aboriginal vernacular architecture is an expression of a complex set of relationships between the physical environment and the social environment'.

Individuals and groups may thus take advantage of preexisting features of the environment, such as overhangs as protection from rain, or a rock wall to shelter from the wind, but in making places home, individual features are created, arranged, modified, and built upon. Sites are at least in part planned structures designed for the occasion. Whether they are open-air sites or rock shelters and caves, they are planned purposefully for use (which is not to say they were used as originally intended) and built upon as activities literally *take* place. Archaeological sites are constructions that were socially built following the traditions, understandings, and situations of the day. As an example, the forked posts and ridge-poles used in Yolngu ceremonial architecture are not simply wooden frames, but 'esteemed [. . .] religious objects, rich in meaning, and are used across both the profane and sacred spectrum of Yolngu life' (Fantin & Memmott 2005: 1787):

> They are employed in a variety of ways depending on the nature and ancestral origin of the ceremony. Traditionally they were often used as a storage place for the deceased's bones (wrapped in bark) as well [as] having a role in ritual dance. Their significance originates in the mythology of the Wagilag sisters who built the first dwelling in the region. In the Wagilag sacred history for Yolngu of the mainland in northeast Arnhem Land, a vaulted shelter supported on forked posts is built by two sisters as they camp beside a sacred waterhole where an Olive Python Ancestor resides. In this story, which is regularly depicted in Yolngu paintings, the shelter plays an important role in the protection of the women from both the Python and the environment.

Sometimes knowledge of how places were constructed, why, and how those acts of construction were meaningful at the time the activities took place can be revealed by contemporary Indigenous knowledge. But sometimes such knowledge from ancestral times will not be available (e.g., where the activities took place so long ago that they have been forgotten). In the latter case, researchers will not usually be able to determine cosmological dimensions of architectural features, because they will not have access to the worldviews and cultural details of the builders, those fundamental dimensions that reveal how and why things are meaningful. The structural principles of construction can, nevertheless, be worked out by determining the *chaînes opératoires* or sequences of action employed in the making, modifying, and positioning of elements and features. Such a perspective enables archaeologists to enquire both into the cultural practices of building at particular times and places, and to better understand individual activities in broader contexts of site use. In short, the site, not just its contents, needs to be treated as an artefact and as a cultural expression. Here we present three examples to illustrate the point.

Nawarla Gabarnmang, Arnhem Land

The hard quartzite rock shelter of Nawarla Gabarnmang is found near the centre of the Arnhem Land plateau, towards the northern end of Jawoyn Country in the Northern Territory. The site has two entrances, a northern one perched above a shallow open valley, and a southern one that gives way to an elongated 'courtyard' which stretches to a low rock plateau. The rock shelter has a flat, ashy floor well protected from the elements by a multilayered horizontal ceiling held aloft by more than fifty pillars. Much of the ceiling and thirty-six of the pillars are covered with rock art, often in densely painted panels (Gunn 2018). On the floor isolated blocks known as 'pillows' by local Jawoyn and visiting Elders are interspersed across the site, evidence of their positioning and use as places to rest by the Old People. The site was mapped in detail and archaeologically excavated from 2010 to 2012. The earliest archaeological evidence of people at the site dates to sometime before 45,610–52,160 cal BP (David et al. 2011, 2019a), continuing almost unabated (at an archaeological timescale) to the 1930s. Archaeological investigations revealed numerous finds, such as evidence of an edge-ground axe dating back to c. 35,500 cal BP (Geneste, David, Plisson, Delannoy, & Petchey 2012), the emergence of densely painted ceiling surfaces during the Late Holocene (e.g., Castets 2017; David et al. 2017; Gunn 2018), and a buried painted stone dated to between 27,000 and 28,000 cal BP (David et al. 2013). However, the most detailed findings did not relate to individual portable artefacts, but rather to the way the site was artificially shaped over an extended period of time, as explained later in this chapter.

The evidence of social construction, design, and of a growing living space comes in the first instance not from the buried deposits, but through a detailed geomorphological-archaeological ('archaeomorphological') mapping of the rock pillars, ceiling, and individual blocks found on the current surface (for a discussion of 'archaeomorphology' and 'archaeomorphological' mapping, see Delannoy et al. 2017; Delannoy, David, Gunn, Geneste, & Jaillet 2018). Through such mapping, the physical characteristics of rock surfaces and individual blocks can be identified, and formation processes, including transport mechanisms for the blocks, investigated. Archaeomorphological mapping aims to understand the history of a site by investigating the technological and taphonomic sequence of events that have led to its current state. The characteristics of each physical object, including rock walls and ceilings, are mapped to enable a *chaîne opératoire* approach to sites and landscapes, to understand the processes that caused them to be how they are today.

The Nawarla Gabarnmang quartzite formed some 1700 million years ago when sand was laid down in a shallow marine environment. Over long geological timeframes, the sand was converted to rock through strong subterranean compaction. Under its own weight, vertical hairline fractures developed through the rock, and through time penetrating water weathered away the rock matrix surrounding the fissures (a weathering process known as 'ghost rock' formation or 'phantomization', first described by Erhard [1967] and subsequently elaborated by Quinif [2010]). Eventually the weathered products were evacuated through water action, leaving behind the remnant pillars on each side of what had once been thin fissures (for a detailed description, see Delannoy et al. 2017). The pillared structure thus precedes the arrival of people by many millions of years. However, the archaeological site that we see today is not the same as the geological site described in this paragraph, for it has been actively worked on and engaged by the Old People over the past c. 50,000 years and possibly more (the basal cultural levels remain undated).

A particularly instructive area of the site to understand those cultural workings is its southwestern corner. Here the upper levels of some pillars have been flaked away by people, and the tops of other pillars have been vertically sectioned by flaking and removed, in each case resulting in a wide space of a few tens of centimetres between the top of the pillar and the quartzite ceiling above it (Figure 17.1C). Individual pillars could, and were, then toppled, the smaller blocks carried away either to the southern or northern entrances of the rock shelter (Figure 17.1A). The larger toppled blocks were further flaked into smaller pieces and similarly removed. We know this because in the southwestern corner of the site, the last area to have thus been worked, a number of pillars were only partially removed, the flaking and sectioning of their upper sections followed by fragmentation and removal of toppled blocks to outer parts of the site being left unfinished (Figure 17.2). The northern entrance to the site is made up of hundreds and possibly thousands of anthropically shaped and accumulated slabs of rock of consistent size and shape, typically a few tens of centimetres long and wide. The slabs came from different parts of the site and were placed outside the rock shelter, presumably to clear the internal space of debris. The removal of pillars in this way created wide spaces within the shelter; before their removal, the space between the pillars formed 1–2 m-wide intersecting corridors (weathered and evacuated fissure lines). After the pillar removals, the central and central-eastern parts of the site expanded to up to 8 m-wide open spaces between retained pillars. Throughout these changes, the site continued to be protected from the elements by a protective roof overhead, although the ceiling rock became thinner (the distance from bedrock to ceiling thereby increasing) as individual quartzite layers became detached overhead. It is not known whether the ceiling layers were purposefully removed, or whether they simply collapsed after the supporting pillars were removed by people, but either way, the fallen ceiling rock was also fragmented into smaller pieces by flaking and carried away to the northern and southern entrances. We know this because of the flaked edges they exhibit in their 'discarded' (or storage?) locations on the talus slopes.

The antiquity of such rock workings was revealed during the archaeological excavations in the rock shelter. The removal of the pillars and fallen ceiling rock began 35,000–23,000 cal BP and ended c. 11,000 cal BP, even though the site continued to be used to recent times (Delannoy et al. 2017: 238; see also David et al. 2018).

The social shaping of Nawarla Gabarnmang through the removal of pillars, ceiling rock layers, and 'disposal' of fallen rocks to the site's two entrance taluses puts into question the notion of occupied caves and rock shelters as 'natural' features of the landscape. Rather, people shaped their living spaces through a combination of purposeful rock working and incidental effects of landscape engagements. Nawarla Gabarnmang is not simply a double-ended rock shelter, but an actively designed, modified, and curated cultural site, each act of pillar removal and rock clearance progressively shaping the rock as an architectural construct. Understanding Nawarla Gabarnmang as a cultural construct is not simply about asking whether it was 'naturally' versus 'culturally' formed, but, rather, about understanding the specific steps of the *chaîne opératoire* or socially mediated operational sequence that through time shaped the site (David et al. 2018). Such an approach is less concerned with the finished product or its functional outcomes as with the systematic, progressive steps followed during construction, each step, and

FIGURE 17.1. Nawarla Gabarnmang. A: Northern entrance. B: 3D laser model from the northern entrance looking south. The wide voids between pillars on the left-hand side of the image were caused by the removal of pillars by people during the Late Pleistocene. C: Initial stages of pillar removal in the southwestern sector of the site. In the two upper photos, the pillar's top rock stratum was vertically sectioned. In the two bottom photos, the upper part was flaked away. Removal of the upper parts of pillars enabled them to then be toppled.

(Photos A & C by Bruno David; image B by Jean-Jacques Delannoy.)

FIGURE 17.2. Nawarla Gabarnmang, stages of pillar reduction in southwest sector of site. The layers of rock that originally stood on the remnant base can be seen strewn on both sides. These removed strata contain flaking marks. In some cases, large conjoining pieces are found far apart. Some fragments have been inverted on the ground. Pieces have been removed towards the talus at the southern entrance. 'A3' = Art Panel 3. 'D-7', 'D-8', and 'D-9' refer to the progressively numbered rock strata of the site's pillars (D-7 stood higher than D-8 and D-9).

(Photo and artwork by Jean-Jacques Delannoy.)

the whole, marking the particular sociocultural sequence of actions employed (Leroi-Gourhan 1964; see also McFadyen 2008; Renfrew & Bahn 2000: 388). Applying a *chaîne opératoire* approach to the construction and transformation of occupied or otherwise-used places is thus a way of investigating the culture of dwelling (Heidegger 1993; Ingold 1995) and inhabitation (Thomas 2007), as emplaced social engagements. To properly understand this material becoming, the role of people as architectural agents, and in varied ways as shapers of their lived worlds, needs to be worked out and recognized. This includes the shaping of sites both as one-off constructions and their gradual elaboration for multiple purposes and over long periods of time. Despite notable exceptions (such as where Aboriginal knowledge has been available, e.g., the Brewarrina fish traps, see Hope & Vines 1994; Mathews 1903; for an archaeological exception, see McNiven et al. 2012), this is a dimension of archaeology that has not been well understood, or applied, in Australian Indigenous archaeology so far.

Borologa 1, Kimberley

Nawarla Gabarnmang may be a remarkable site, both for its structural features and its rock art, but it is not alone in its social construction. Like Arnhem Land, the Kimberley region of northwestern Australia is also renowned for its rich rock art imagery whose geographical reach changed through time. In recent years, research has focused on a wide range of topics (see, e.g., O'Connor, Veth, & Barham 1999), including the region's rock art, both its antiquity (e.g., Finch et al. 2020; O'Connor & Fankhauser 2001; Ross, Westaway, Travers, Morwood, & Hayward 2016) and its changing spatial distribution implicating changing social and territorial relations (e.g., Harper, Veth, & Ouzman 2020; Lewis 1988b). New research has also begun to investigate how people actively constructed sites in the past, again instances of architectural design. Here we illustrate the point through one extensively painted site near the Drysdale River in Balanggarra Country: Borologa 1 (for further details, see Delannoy et al. 2020a).

Borologa 1 is a slanted quartzite boulder that sits slightly above an ancient alluvial terrace at the base of a hill (Figure 17.3A). The multilayered boulder had detached from a cliff-line further up the hill and slid down, coming to rest in its current position tens of thousands of years ago (Genuite 2019; Genuite et al. 2021). Gwion Gwion paintings at the site have not been dated, but similar motifs in other nearby sites have been, and they date to c. 11,520–12,680 cal BP (Finch et al. 2020). The Borologa 1 Gwion Gwion paintings are thus likely to also be terminal Pleistocene in age. Around 2500–2700 cal BP, aeolian sands began accumulating along the boulder's southern side, continuing to do so today, covering archaeological deposits under its major overhang in the process.

A detailed archaeomorphological mapping of the site revealed that the boulder's rock walls had been worked not only for the making of stone tools but also to hollow out alcoves in at least two major areas, its southeastern corner and SSW side. The southern side had parts of the rock wall artificially removed, creating a deep alcove whose original rock fill was removed to the outer edges of the overhang and beyond (Figure 17.3B). The walls of the alcove's cavity were then painted, and further constructions ensued (Delannoy et al. 2020a). Two massive slabs of quartzite weighing c. 600 kg each were shaped and positioned one on top of the other in the northwestern side of the artificially created SSW alcove, closing it off from the outside (Figures 17.3D, 3F, and 3G).

Further away, at the eastern edge of the site just outside the southeastern alcove, a 1.7 m-long × 1.0 m-wide × 20 cm-thick, flat quartzite slab was carefully positioned horizontally, probably to give higher and better access to the now-painted adjacent rock wall and overhanging ceiling (Figures 17.3A and 3C). The slab was supported and balanced horizontally by small, flaked rocks, creating a tabletop-like surface (Delannoy et al. 2020a). Additionally, between 2110 and 2370 cal BP, a 186 kg, 60 cm-long × 55 cm-wide × 27 cm-thick rock slab was removed from the southwestern corner of the boulder and carried or dragged 3 m to the east and permanently positioned into place by wedging three chock-blocks under one of its corners to create a flat working surface (Figure 17.3E): The slab was purpose-designed into a massive grinding stone for the crushing and grinding

FIGURE 17.3. Borologa 1, Balanggarra Country, Kimberley. A: South side of rock shelter. B: 270 kg block extracted from the ceiling of the SSW alcove and repositioned near its outer edge. C: 1.7 m-long × 1.0 m-wide × 20 cm-thick ceiling slab anthropically positioned horizontally at base of southeastern alcove. D, F, G: The two massive quartzite blocks positioned into place to seal the northwestern corner of the artificial SSW alcove. Photo G shows the sinuous gap between the ceiling and the top of the uppermost block to be 1 cm thick. E: The 186 kg buried grinding stone revealed through archaeological excavation. Between 2110 and 2370 cal BP, the large quartzite block was removed from the southwestern corner of the rock outcrop, moved 3 m to its current position, had a corner wedged with three chock blocks to create a horizontal upper surface, and was repeatedly used as a grinding stone over a period close to 2000 years.

(Photo A by Jean-Jacques Delannoy; photos B–G by Bruno David.)

of pigments to make paint. Both the grinding stone and horizontal slab could well be thought of as furniture. The nearby wall and artificially hollowed out alcove were then extensively, and repeatedly, painted in a sequence of painting events. These events could be differentiated by dating charcoal associated with the pigment micro-debitage that fell along the edges of the grindstone after each incidence of use; as they fell to the ground, the small particles of crushed and ground pigment accumulated along the edge of the grinding stone, rapidly becoming buried by fast-accumulating aeolian sands. This part of the site saw a sequence of occupational events dating within 2110–2370 cal BP, 1160–2080 cal BP, 760–1110 cal BP, 500–630 cal BP, and 120–480 cal BP. Each occupational phase was followed by a hiatus variably lasting between 110 and 660 years. The past 500–630 years saw much shorter spacing between occupations, within an archaeological timescale at times giving the appearance of near-continuous occupation (David et al. 2019b: 68–74).

In total more than 3.5 tonnes of rock were manually extracted from the artificial alcoves at Borologa 1, and some of these blocks were then repositioned for specific uses, such as the horizontal slab and grinding stone mentioned earlier. A calibrated radiocarbon age of 9303–9530 cal BP on a wasp nest from the southeastern alcove's ceiling indicates that it must have already existed by that time; therefore, it dates the creation of the alcove to an earlier time. In the SSW alcove, the rock was also likely to have been hollowed out during the Late Pleistocene or Early Holocene, as both Elegant Action and Kimberley Stout figures were painted in the hollowed-out cavity, art styles that are thought to date to such times (the alcove must already have existed when the paintings were made within its depths) (Gunn et al. 2019). As was the case at Nawarla Gabarnmang 700 km to the east, Borologa 1 is not just an overhang under a massive quartzite boulder, but an actively constructed space that, in its planning and construction, deserves to be thought of as actively built *architecture*, just as the term is used elsewhere in the world.

Cloggs Cave, Southeast Australia

Cloggs Cave is a limestone site located in the foothills of the Australian Alps (southeast Australia). The site is perched at 72.3 m above sea level (a.s.l.), 17 m above a palaeochannel and current flood plain of the Buchan River (for details, see Delannoy et al. 2020b). As a result of Josephine Flood's (1973a, 1973b, 1974, 1980) doctoral research, the site has been well-known in Australian archaeology since the early 1970s. Flood's excavations inside the cave uncovered a long, 2.4 m-deep sequence, with the remains of megafauna and large extant fauna occurring in the deepest excavated strata. Sitting atop the megafauna levels are dense deposits of microfauna bones (mostly derived from owl roosts), some also containing small quantities of stone artefacts. In much of the area excavated by Flood, the deepest anthropic deposits occur adjacent to, rather than neatly above, the layers with the megafauna remains; a vertical disconformity separates these discrete deposits. Thin, ashy strata cap much of the entire excavated deposit. However, uncertainties long surrounded the relative chronology and depositional sequence of the megafaunal and anthropic deposits, causing Cloggs Cave's megafaunal deposits to play a disputed role in debates concerning the timing and drivers of Australian megafaunal extinctions (e.g., see Wroe et al. 2013).

A new programme of archaeomorphological research, including small-scale excavations within the cave, was initiated by the GunaiKurnai Land and Waters Aboriginal Corporation in 2019 (see David et al. 2021a, 2021b). The new investigations showed that the megafaunal deposits date to c. 52,000 years ago and that Aboriginal people first used the cave c. 23,000 years ago (David et al. 2021a, 2021c). The cave saw intensive human activity at various times in the past, including between c. 4400 and 1600 cal BP, with earlier hearths and wooden artefacts dating back to the Pleistocene–Holocene boundary and beyond having also remained in excellent states of preservation (David et al. 2021a, 2021b; Delannoy et al. 2020b). The more recent, Late Holocene period of use has an unusual material signature: Very few stone artefacts and little to no food remains were deposited within the cave at this time. But a standing stone was erected c. 1600–2100, and repeated burning events within the cave caused layers of ash to accumulate. This signature, when combined with current GunaiKurnai cosmological knowledge together with the available ethnographic evidence for GunaiKurnai cave use, suggests that recurring ritual activity relating to the actions of *mulla-mullung* ('magic men') took place within the cave over the past c. 2100 years (David et al. 2021a, 2021b).

As part of the new phase of research, Delannoy et al. (2020b) analysed the spatial history of Cloggs Cave using high-resolution LiDAR 3D mapping. The site can be divided into several key zones according to its geomorphology (Figure 17.4). Immediately outside the cave are overhanging Rock shelter and Porch areas and a steep talus slope that leads to the floodplain below; inside the cave are the Main and Upper Chambers connected by an Upper Gallery. Mapping of the site has enabled (1) reconstruction of how the cave was initially formed by geological processes over c. 400 million years; and (2) a detailed assessment of the ways in which people furnished the cave over time, modifying it in the process.

Cloggs Cave initially formed some 400 million years ago, as part of the Buchan Group carbonate formation (VandenBerg et al. 1996). During the most recent 350 million years, regional limestone underwent karst dissolution, causing the planation of ridge-lines and phantomization of the substrate. Within the past five million years, circulating underground water caused Cloggs Cave's karstic structure to form. In more recent times, ongoing dissolution of the rock caused successive rock-fall and sediment evacuation (see Delannoy et al. 2020b). Rock-fall enlarged the Upper Gallery and Main Chamber cavities, dramatically changing the morphology of the Rock shelter and Porch (Figure 17.4).

Cloggs Cave is not only a remarkable karst formation; it is also a classic example of how the Old People modified the site while engaging with it, turning it into an architectural space. We say 'classic' because the cave is not large, nor does it feature immediately noticeable evidence of human use and impacts. Rather, it is by careful mapping of the site's three-dimensional space that the evidence for its working by the Old

ENGAGING AND DESIGNING PLACE 485

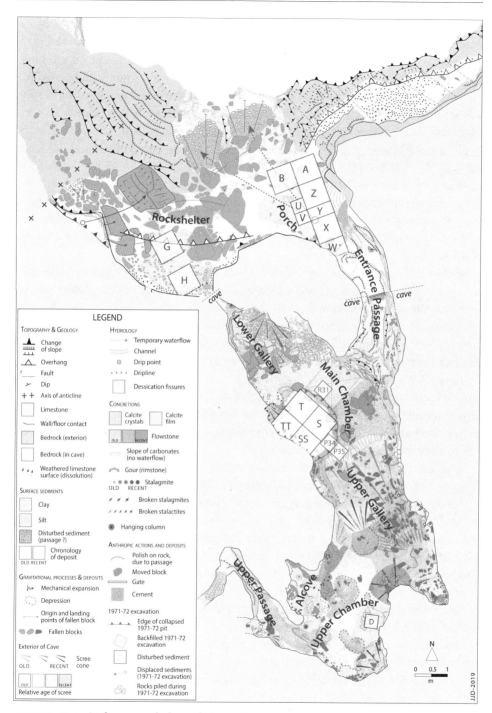

FIGURE 17.4. Archaeomorphology of Cloggs Cave.
(Cartography by Jean-Jacques Delannoy; artwork by Jean-Jacques Delannoy and Bruno David.)

People has been revealed. The anthropic arrangements are perhaps most evident in the Alcove, located in the northwest corner of the Upper Chamber (Figures 17.4 and 17.5). The Alcove, formed through rock collapse, has a low-hanging ceiling some 0.7 m high. The remains of some of the fallen blocks can be seen on (and slightly embedded in) the floor's soft sediments. On the Alcove's floor several shallow depressions and a subsidence hollow measuring c. 40 cm in diameter can also be seen. A rounded stone artefact was found in this hollow, and nearby is a stone arrangement consisting of eight small blocks (Delannoy et al. 2020b; Figure 17.5D). The arranged blocks did not form through rock-fall from the adjacent wall or ceiling; and today the ceiling overhead is covered with stalactites. Rather, the blocks on the ground are morphologically similar to the rock strata on the lower part of the wall in the Upper Chamber 3.8 m away (Figure 17.4). The arranged stones almost certainly originate from a scree of fallen blocks beneath the Upper Chamber wall (a space between blocks on the floor signals missing, removed blocks).

Further anthropic engagements with this part of the cave are also evident: Stalactites were broken from the ceiling, and a localized patch of whitish calcite powder can be seen near the stone arrangement in the Alcove (Figure 17.5D). The stalactites (Figures 17.5A and 5B) could not have been broken by animals (as no animal of sufficient size could enter the cave through its narrow, elevated entrance), nor could they have broken through earthquakes (the effects of seismic activity on stalactites has been studied by a number of authors (see Becker et al. 2006; Lacave, Koller, & Egozcue 2004); earthquakes tend to break stalactites closer to the tip rather than near their bases, following the pattern of seismic waves, unlike the case in the Alcove). Here, only stalactites within and immediately adjacent to the Alcove were broken, and only to a height within human reach; higher stalactites were not broken.

To determine when people broke the stalactites, U-series dating was undertaken on a number of stalactite regrowths ('soda straws'). The oldest soda straw regrowth over a broken stalactite stump began 23,230 ± 300 years ago; therefore, the first breakage events took place sometime prior to c. 23,000 years ago (there is no guarantee that soda straws began regrowing straight after the parent stalactites were broken, hence the *minimum* age for the earliest breakage event). More recent phases of regrowth have also been identified, which means that some breakage events may have occurred more recently. The presence of crushed calcite on the floor indicates that people were processing speleothems into powder, but whether they were reducing broken stalactites, flowstone, or other calcite formations remains unknown (analysis of the crushed calcite to better determine the original speleothem(s) is in progress). This aspect of cave use is the subject of ongoing investigation, and it is worth noting that a portable grindstone with residues of crushed crystalline mineral was found 8 m away, from excavation levels dating to c. 1600–2100 cal BP (Stephenson et al. 2020).

As well as extensive remodelling of the Alcove by the Old People, large blocks of limestone were rearranged near the entrance of the cave. Two large limestone blocks were prised from the floor of the Entrance Passage and placed on the floor of the access point to the Main Chamber some 1.5 m away (Figure 17.4). The larger of the two blocks weighs

ENGAGING AND DESIGNING PLACE 487

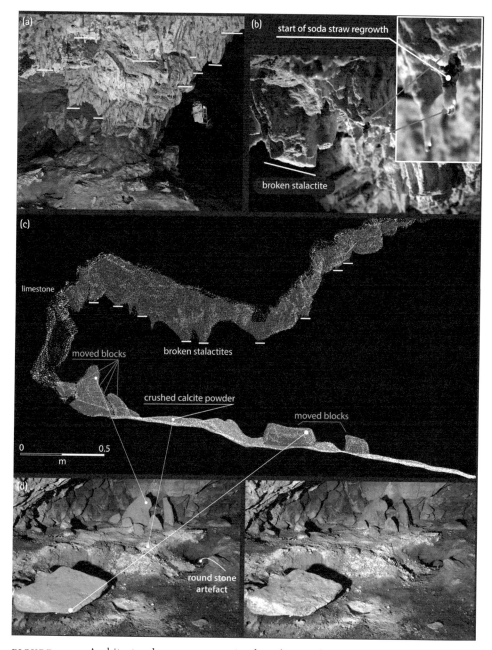

FIGURE 17.5. Architectural arrangements in the Alcove of Cloggs Cave (see Figure 17.4 for location). Yellow lines on images A, B, and C show areas where the Old People removed stalactites. Image C is a cross-section view of the Alcove showing the location of moved blocks purposefully constructed into a stone arrangement, crushed calcite on the floor, and soda straw regrowths on the ceiling.

(3D acquisition by Johan Berthet; photos and artwork by Jean-Jacques Delannoy.)

315 kg. Given that these blocks are barely buried in the sediments of the cave floor, they were probably positioned there during Late Holocene times (Delannoy et al. 2020b). In their current position, the blocks make it easier to step down the 1 m drop from the Entrance Passage into the Main Chamber, especially keeping in mind the subdued light and thus reduced visibility in the cave. These blocks were almost certainly positioned by the Old People to improve *access to* and *use of* the cave, key functional considerations of more commonly recognized architectural projects and features today.

DISCUSSION

Australian Aboriginal sites such as rock shelters and caves are not simply physical places that have accumulated cultural deposits more or less rich in stone artefacts, food refuse, and the like (for stone-walled structures in the Pilbara, see, e.g., Bindon & Lofgren 1982; Wallis & Matthews 2016; for stone houses in southwestern Victoria, the Kimberley, and southwest Queensland, see, e.g., McNiven, Dunn, Crouch, & Gunditj Mirring Traditional Owners Aboriginal Corporation 2017; O'Connor 1987; Wallis et al. 2017; Wesson 1981). They are themselves social structures built of cultural knowledge amenable to archaeological investigation. As artefacts in their own right, sites, and the technological steps used to construct them as living or otherwise-used places, can be unpacked. Identifying *chaînes opératoires*, or 'reverse-engineering' constructions step by step to determine both how they were built and their operational logic, is a key dimension of archaeomorphology. How such sites were *constructed*, and not just their use as site-scale functional artefact *types*, is itself a cultural signature worthy of investigation. Here we have focused on caves and rock shelters, but the principles that (1) sites were constructed in design and engagement; (2) the ways they were built can be worked out through careful, fine-grained investigation (both archaeomorphological and through local knowledge from Aboriginal Traditional Owners); and (3) transdisciplinary investigations (including excavation) will enable more details and perspectives to be revealed. This applies to all kinds of sites, including open sites such as shell accumulations (e.g., McNiven 2013), earth mounds, fish traps (e.g., McNiven et al. 2012), stone artefact scatters, and so forth (e.g., Memmott, Robins, & Stock 2008).

Sites are built in cultural practices that have their own histories, and how we think of those sites through the terms we use helps consciously clarify and subliminally structure in our minds both how places and their cultural practices fit in a broader social world. Many of the sites and site types discussed in this chapter have been known about by archaeologists for a long time. It is not only what we are seeing as physical places that we are concerned with here but also *how* we think of places and, thereby, how we investigate them. Thinking of Nawarla Gabarnmang, Borologa 1, Cloggs Cave, and countless other Aboriginal sites in the language of engineered landscapes (e.g., among fish traps, Baiame's Ngunnhu at Brewarrina, Budj Bim in southwestern Victoria) and purpose-designed architecture makes us question the conceptual limitations that are often linguistically and cognitively imposed on Aboriginal sites in Australia (see also Memmott 2007). While concepts such as calculated or 'engineered' constructions, designed 'architectural' sites and features, and positioned 'furniture' and 'furnishings' within sites are commonly applied to cultural practices across much of the world, they are less so for Aboriginal Australia. This is not because such sites, features, and construction processes do not apply, but rather because of the failure of such language to be more broadly used. The way language frames understandings of the Aboriginal past also exposes the limitations of what is a long-standing, albeit subliminal, Primitivist Project that commonly prevents or inhibits transcending preconceptions about Aboriginality as the 'other' (see Barkan & Bush 1995; Fabian 1983; Torgovnick, 1990; see also David, Langton, & McNiven 2002; McNiven & Russell 2005). Those limitations concern more than archaeological descriptions, for they have much deeper and wider social implications that limit how Aboriginal practices are considered and achievements recognized. Rhys Jones's (1969) notion of 'firestick farming' and the concepts underlying Bill Gammage's (2012) *The Biggest Estate on Earth*, for instance, quickly remind of the power to ponder, and reason, in ways other than those more conventional ones that much of the world has been more accustomed to apply to Aboriginal achievements. Reframing how 'archaeological sites' are thought about as Aboriginal cultural designs and architectural constructs, and their working in broader settings as engineered landscapes, is entirely in step with how such past and contemporary sites and landscapes operated and how they are aptly also considered in many other parts of the world.

ACKNOWLEDGEMENTS

For the research at Cloggs Cave, we thank the GunaiKurnai Elders Council and the GunaiKurnai Land and Waters Aboriginal Corporation, and Martin and Vicky Hanman of Buchan for all your help. At Nawarla Gabarnmang, thank you to the late Margaret Katherine and the Jawoyn Association Aboriginal Corporation for the 2010–2012 research presented here. At Borologa 1, thank you to Augustine Unghango and Balanggarra Traditional Owners, the Balanggarra Aboriginal Corporation, Sven Ouzman, Peter Veth, Sam Harper, Maria Myers, Cecilia Myers, Susan Bradley, and the staff at Theda and Doongan Stations, Kimberley Foundation Australia, Dunkeld Pastoral Co. Pty. Ltd., and the Australian Research Council 'Kimberley Visions: Rock Art Style Provinces of North Australia' project LP150100490 for funding and support. Thank you also to the field team: Isaac Barney, Frank Boulden, Leigh Douglas, Adrian French, Ben Gunn, Paul Hartley, Brigid Hill, Lucas Karadada, Madeleine Kelly, Lorraine Lee, Robin Maher, William Maraltidj, Michael Morlumbin, Ken Mulvaney, Nick Sundblom, Patrick Tataya, Gareth Unghango, Jeremy Unghango, Scott Unghango, Ian Waina, Rowan Waina, and Uriah Waina. Thank you to the Australian Research Council Centre of Excellence for Australian Biodiversity and Heritage project CE170100015 for funding this research, and the Monash Indigenous Studies Centre at Monash University and EDYTEM at the Université Savoie Mont Blanc for research support. We thank Paul Memmott and Ian McNiven for much-appreciated comments on an earlier draft.

REFERENCES

Backhaus, G. (2002). Auto-mobility and the route-scape. In G. Backhaus & J. Murungi (Eds.), *Transformations of urban and suburban landscapes: Perspectives from philosophy, geography, and architecture* (pp. 97–124). Terra Australis 47. Lanham, MD: Lexington Books.

Barkan, E., & Bush, R. (Eds.) (1995). *Prehistories of the future: The primitivist project and the culture of modernism.* Stanford, CA: Stanford University Press.

Becker, A., Davenport, C. A., Eichenberger, U., Gilli, E., Jeanin, P.-Y., & Lacave, C. (2006). Speleoseismology: A critical perspective. *Journal of Seismology, 10,* 371–388.

Bindon, P., & Lofgren, M. (1982). Walled rock shelters and a cached spear in the Pilbara region, Western Australia. *Records of the Western Australian Museum, 10,* 111–126.

Browne, H. Y. L. (1895). Government geologist's report on explorations in the Northern Territory. *South Australian Parliamentary Papers, 82,* 3–13.

Campbell, J. B. (1979). Settlement patterns on offshore islands in north-eastern Queensland. *Australian Archaeology, 9,* 18–32.

Campbell, J. B. (1982). Automatic seafood retrieval systems: The evidence from Hinchinbrook Island and its implications. In S. Bowdler (Ed.), *Coastal archaeology in eastern Australia* (pp. 96–107). Canberra: Research School of Pacific Studies, Australian National University Press.

Casey, E. S. (1993). *Getting back into place: Toward a renewed understanding of the place-world.* Bloomington: Indiana University Press.

Castets, G. (2017). *Apports de l'analyse des matières colorantes et colorées dand l'étude intégrée d'un site orné* (PhD thesis). Université Grenoble Alpes, Grenoble.

Conkey, M. W., & Fisher, R. A. (2020). The return of the bricoleur? Emplotment, intentionality, and tradition in Paleolithic art. *Journal of Archaeological Method and Theory 27,* 511–525. https://doi.org/10.1007/s10816-020-09466-7

David, B., Barker, B., Petchey, F., Delannoy, J.-J., Geneste, J.-M., Rowe, C., . . . Whear, R. (2013). A 28,000 year old excavated painted rock from Nawarla Gabarnmang, northern Australia. *Journal of Archaeological Science, 40,* 2493–2501.

David, B., Delannoy J.-J., Gunn, R., Chalmin, E., Castets, G., Petchey, F., . . . Pietrzak, U. (2017). Dating painted Panel E1 at Nawarla Gabarnmang, southern Arnhem Land plateau. In B. David., P. S. C. Taçon, J.-J. Delannoy, & J.-M. Geneste (Eds.), *The archaeology of rock art in western Arnhem Land, Australia* (pp. 245–302). Terra Australis 47. Canberra: ANU Press.

David, B., Delannoy, J.-J., Katherine, M., Whear, R., Geneste, J.-M., & Gollings, J. (2018). Nawarla Gabarnmang: A spectacular rock-shelter in Arnhem Land, in Australia's far north, questions assumptions about the nature of design, provoking reflection on the boundaries between the natural and the built. *Landscape Architecture Australia, 158,* 52–58.

David, B., Delannoy, J.-J., Mialanes, J., Clarkson, C., Petchey, F., Geneste, J.-M., . . . Castets, G. (2019a). 45,610–52,160 years of site and landscape occupation at Nawarla Gabarnmang, Arnhem Land plateau (northern Australia). *Quaternary Science Reviews, 215,* 64–85.

David, B., Delannoy, J.-J., Petchey, F., Gunn, R. G., Huntley, J., Veth, P., . . . Wong, V. (2019b). Dating painting events through by-products of ochre grinding: Borologa, Kimberley, Australia. *Australian Archaeology, 85*(1), 57–94.

David, B., Fresløv, J., Mullett, R., Delannoy, J.-J., Petchey, F., GunaiKurnai Land and Waters Aboriginal Corporation, . . . Ash, J. (2021a). Paradigm shifts and ontological turns at Cloggs Cave, Gunaikurnai Country, Australia. In O. M. Abadía & M. Porr (Eds.), *Ontologies of rock art: Images, relational approaches and Indigenous knowledge* (pp. 135–160). London: Routledge.

David, B., Fresløv, J., Mullett, R., GunaiKurnai Land and Waters Aboriginal Corporation, Delannoy, J.-J., McDowell, M., . . . Green, H. (2021b). 50 years and worlds apart: Rethinking the Holocene occupation of Cloggs Cave (East Gippsland, SE Australia) five decades after its initial archaeological excavation and in light of GunaiKurnai world views. *Australian Archaeology, 87*, 1–20. https://doi.org/10.1080/03122417.2020.1859963

David, B., Arnold, L. J., Delannoy, J.-J., Fresløv, J., Urwin, C., Petchey, F., . . . Hellstrom, J. (2021c). Late survival of megafauna refuted for Cloggs Cave, SE Australia: Implications for the Australian Late Pleistocene megafauna extinction debate. Quaternary Science Reviews 253, 106781. https://doi.org/10.1016/j.quascirev.2020.106781

David, B., Geneste, J.-M., Whear, R. L., Delannoy, J.-J., Katherine, M., Gunn, R. G., . . . Matthews, J. (2011). Nawarla Gabarnmang, a 45,180 ± 910 cal BP site in Jawoyn country, south-west Arnhem Land plateau. *Australian Archaeology, 73*, 73–77.

David, B., & Hamacher, D. W. (2018). Environment and landscape. In S. L. López Varela (Ed.), *The encyclopedia of archaeological sciences*. New York: John Wiley & Sons. https://doi.org/10.1002/9781119188230.saseas0215

David, B., Langton, M., & McNiven, I. J. (2002). Re-inventing the wheel: Indigenous peoples and the master race in Philip Ruddock's "wheel" comments. *PAN—Philosophy, Activism, Nature, 2*, 31–46.

Delannoy, J.-J., David, B., Fresløv, J., Mullett R., GunaiKurnai Land and Waters Aboriginal Corporation, Green, H., . . . Wong, V. N. L. (2020b). Geomorphological context and formation history of Cloggs Cave: What was the cave like when people inhabited it? *Journal of Archaeological Science: Reports 33*, 102461. https://doi.org/10.1016/j.jasrep.2020.102461

Delannoy, J.-J., David, B., Geneste, J.-M., Katherine, M., Sadier, B., & Gunn, R. (2017). Engineers of the Arnhem Land plateau: Evidence for the origins and transformation of sheltered spaces at Nawarla Gabarnmang. In B. David, P. S. C. Taçon, J.-J. Delannoy, & J.-M. Geneste (Eds.), *The archaeology of rock art in western Arnhem Land, Australia* (pp. 197–243). Terra Australis 47. Canberra: ANU Press.

Delannoy, J.-J., David, B., Genuite, K., Gunn, R., Finch, D., Ouzman, S., . . . Skelly, R. J. (2020a). Investigating the anthropic construction of rock art sites through archaeomorphology: The case of Borologa, Kimberley, Australia. *Journal of Archaeological Method and Theory 27*, 631–669. https://doi.org/10.1007/s10816-020-09477-4

Delannoy J.-J., David, B., Gunn, R., Geneste, J.-M., & Jaillet, S. (2018). Archaeomorphological mapping: Rock art and the architecture of place. In B. David & I. J. McNiven (Eds.), *The Oxford handbook of the archaeology and anthropology of rock art* (pp. 833–856). Oxford: Oxford University Press.

Deleuze, G., & Guattari, F. (1994). *What is philosophy?* New York: Columbia University Press.

Erhard, H. (1967). *La genèse des sols en tant que phénomènes géologique.* Paris: Masson.

Fabian, J. (1983). *Time and the other: How anthropology makes its object.* New York: Colombia University Press.

Fantin, S., & Memmott, P. (2005). Yolngu ceremonial architecture (Australia). In B. Taylor (Ed.), *Encyclopedia of religion and nature 1* (pp. 1786–1787). London: Continuum.

Feld, S., & Basso, K. H. (1996). *Senses of place.* Santa Fe, NM: School of American Research Press.

Finch, D., Gleadow, A., Hergt, J., Levchenko, V. A., Heaney, P., Veth, P., . . . Green, H. (2020). 12,000-year-old Aboriginal rock art from the Kimberley region, Western Australia. *Science Advances, 6*(6), eaay3922. https://doi.org/10.1126/sciadv.aay3922

Flood, J. (1973a). *The moth hunters: Investigations towards a prehistory of the south-eastern highlands of Australia* (PhD thesis). Australian National University, Canberra.

Flood, J. (1973b). Pleistocene human occupation and extinct fauna in Cloggs Cave, Buchan, south-east Australia. *Nature, 246,* 303.

Flood, J. (1974). Pleistocene man at Cloggs Cave: His tool kit and environment. *Mankind, 9,* 175–188.

Flood, J. (1980). *The moth hunters: Aboriginal prehistory of the Australian Alps.* Canberra: Australian Institute of Aboriginal Studies.

Gammage, B. (2012). *The biggest estate on earth: How Aborigines made Australia.* St Leonards: Allen & Unwin.

Geneste, J.-M., David, B., Plisson, H., Delannoy, J.-J., & Petchey, F. (2012). The origins of ground-edge axes: New findings from Nawarla Gabarnmang, Arnhem Land (Australia) and global implications for the evolution of fully modern humans. *Cambridge Archaeological Journal, 22,* 1–17.

Genuite, K. (2019). *Paléogéographies et reconstitution géomorphologique 3D: Application aux environnements de sites ornés* (PhD thesis). Université Grenoble Alpes, Grenoble.

Genuite, K., Delannoy, J.-J., David, B., Unghango, A., Balanggarra Aboriginal Corporation, Cazes, G., . . . Urwin, C. (2021). Determining the origin and changing shape of landscape-scale rock formations with three-dimensional modelling: The Borologa rock shelters, Kimberley region, Australia. *Geoarchaeology 36,* 662–680. DOI: 10.1002/gea.21863

Gregory, A. C. (1858). Journal of the North Australian Exploring Expedition, under the command of Augustus C. Gregory, Esq. (Gold Medallist R. G. S.); with report by Mr. Elsey on the health of the party. *The Journal of the Royal Geographical Society of London, 28,* 1–137.

Gunn, R. G. (2018). *Art of the ancestors: Spatial and temporal patterning in the ceiling rock art of Nawarla Gabarnmang, Arnhem Land, Australia.* Oxford: Archaeopress Archaeology. https://www.archaeopress.com/Archaeopress/download/9781789690705

Gunn, R., David, B., Douglas, L., Delannoy, J.-J., Harper, S., Heaney, P., . . . Veth, P. (2019). 'Kimberley Stout figures': A new rock art style for Kimberley rock art, north-western Australia. *Australian Archaeology, 85,* 151–169.

Harper, S., Veth, P., & Ouzman, S. (2020). Kimberley rock art. In C. Smith (Ed.), *Encyclopedia of global archaeology.* New York: Springer-Verlag. https://doi.org/10.1007/978-3-319-51726-1

Heidegger, M. (1993). Building, dwelling, thinking. In D. F. Krell (Ed.), *Martin Heidegger: Basic writings* (pp. 423–440). London: Routledge.

Hope, J., & Vines, G. (1994). Brewarrina Aboriginal fisheries conservation plan. Unpublished report to the Brewarrina Aboriginal Cultural Museum, Brewarrina.

Ingold, T. (1995). Building, dwelling, living: How animals and people make themselves at home in the world. In M. Strathern (Ed.), *Shifting contexts: Transformations in anthropological knowledge* (pp. 57–80). London: Routledge.

Jones, R. (1969). Fire-stick farming. *Australian Natural History, 16*(7), 224–228.

Lacave, C., Koller, M. G., & Egozcue, J. J. (2004). What can be concluded about seismic history from broken and unbroken speleothems? *Journal of Earthquake Engineering, 8,* 431–455.

Leroi-Gourhan, A. (1964). *Le geste et la parole 1: Technique et language.* Paris: Albin Michel.

Lewis, D. (1988a). Hawk hunting hides in the Victoria River District. *Australian Aboriginal Studies, 2,* 74–78.

Lewis, D. (1988b). *The rock paintings of Arnhem Land, Australia: Social, ecological, and material culture change in the post-glacial period.* BAR International Series 415. Oxford: British Archaeological Reports.

MacPherson, P. (1884). The oven-mounds of the aborigines in Victoria. *Journal and Proceedings of the Royal Society of New South Wales, 18,* 49–59.

Mathews, R. H. (1903). The aboriginal fisheries at Brewarrina. *Journal and Proceedings of the Royal Society of New South Wales, 37,* 146–156.

McFadyen, L. (2008). Building and architecture as landscape practice. In B. David & J. Thomas (Eds.), *Handbook of landscape archaeology* (pp. 307–314). Walnut Creek, CA: Left Coast Press.

McNiven, I. J. (2013). Ritualized maddening practices. *Journal of Archaeological Method and Theory, 20,* 552–587. DOI 10.1007/s10816-012-9130-y

McNiven, I. J. (2017). The detective work behind the Budj Bim eel traps World Heritage bid. *The Conversation.* https://theconversation.com/the-detective-work-behind-the-budj-bim-eel-traps-world-heritage-bid-71800

McNiven, I. J., Crouch, J., Richards, T., Dolby, N., Jacobsen, G., Gunditj Mirring Traditional Owners Aboriginal Corporation. (2012). Dating Aboriginal stone-walled fishtraps at Lake Condah, southeast Australia. *Journal of Archaeological Science, 39,* 268–286.

McNiven, I. J., Dunn, J. E, Crouch, J., & Gunditj Mirring Traditional Owners Aboriginal Corporation. (2017). Kurtonitj stone house: Excavation of a mid-nineteenth century Aboriginal frontier site from Gunditjmara country, southwest Victoria. *Archaeology in Oceania, 52*(3), 171–197.

McNiven, I. J., & Russell, L. (2005). *Appropriated pasts: Indigenous peoples and the colonial culture of archaeology.* Lanham, MD: AltaMira Press.

Memmott, P. (2007). *Gunyah, goondie and wurley: The Aboriginal architecture of Australia.* St Lucia: University of Queensland Press.

Memmott, P., & Fantin, S. (2005). The study of Indigenous ethno-architecture in Australia. In B. Rigsby & N. Peterson (Eds.), *Donald Thomson: The man and scholar* (pp. 185–210). Canberra: Academy of the Social Sciences.

Memmott, P., Robins, R., & Stock, E. (2008). What exactly is a fish trap? Methodological issues for the study of Aboriginal intertidal rock wall fish traps, Wellesley Islands region, Gulf of Carpentaria, Australia. In J. Connolly & M. Campbell (Eds.), *Comparative island archaeologies* (pp. 73–96). British International Series S1829. Oxford: Archaeopress.

O'Connor, S. (1987). The stone house structures of High Cliffy Island, north-west Kimberley, Western Australia. *Australian Archaeology, 25,* 30–39.

O'Connor, S., & Fankhauser, B. L. (2001). Art at 40,000 BP? One step closer: An ochre covered rock from Carpenter's Gap Shelter 1, Kimberley region, Western Australia. In A. Anderson, R. Jones, I. Lilley, & S. O'Connor (Eds.), *Histories of old ages: Essays in honour of Rhys Jones* (pp. 287–300). Canberra: Pandanus Books.

O'Connor, S., Veth, P., & Barham, A. (1999). Cultural versus natural explanations for lacunae in Aboriginal occupation deposits in northern Australia. *Quaternary International, 59*(1), 61–70.

Oxford English Dictionary Online. (2020). Oxford: Oxford University Press. https://doi.org/10.1093/acref/9780199571123.001.0001.

Quinif, Y. 2010. *Fantômes de roche et fantômisation. Essai sur un nouveau paradigme de karstogénèse.* Karstologia Mémoires 18. Mons: Association Française de Karstologie.

Renfrew, C., & Bahn, P. G. (2000). *Archaeology: Theories, methods and practice.* London: Thames & Hudson.

Ross, J., Westaway, K., Travers, M., Morwood, M., & Hayward, J. (2016). Into the past: A step towards a robust Kimberley rock art chronology. *PLoS One, 11*(8), e0161726.

Stephenson, B., David, B., Fresløv, J., Arnold, L. J., GunaiKurnai Land and Waters Aboriginal Corporation, Delannoy, J.-J., . . . Hellstrom, J. (2020). 2000 year-old Bogong moth (*Agrotis infusa*) Aboriginal food remains, Australia. *Scientific Reports 10*, 22151. https://doi.org/10.1038/s41598-020-79307-w

Statham, E. J. (1892). Observations on shell-heaps and shell-beds: Significance and importance of the record they afford. *Journal and Proceedings of the Royal Society of New South Wales, 26*, 304–314.

Thomas, J. (2007). Mesolithic-Neolithic transitions in Britain: From essence to inhabitation. *Proceedings of the British Academy, 144*, 423–439.

Torgovnick, M. (1990). *Gone primitive: Savage intellects, modern lives*. Chicago: The University of Chicago Press.

VandenBerg, A. H. M., Henrdickx, M. A., Willman, C. E., Magart, A. P. M., Oranskaia, A., Rooney, S., & White, A. J. R. (1996). *The geology and prospectivity of the Orbost 1:100,000 map area, eastern Victoria*. Victorian Initiative for Minerals and Petroleum Report 25. Fitzroy: Department of Natural Resources and Environment.

Wallis, A. L., Davidson, I., Burke, H., Mitchell, S., Barker, B., Hatte, E., Cole, N., & Lowe, K. (2017). Aboriginal stone huts along the Georgina River, southwest Queensland. *Queensland Archaeological Research, 20*. https://doi.org/10.25120/qar.20.2017.3584.

Wallis, A. L., & Matthews, J. (2016). Built structures in rockshelters of the Pilbara, Western Australia. *Records of the Western Australian Museum, 31(1)*, 1–26. https://doi.org/10.18195/issn.0312-3162.31(1).2016.001-026.

Wesson, J. (1981). Excavations of stone structures in the Condah area, western Victoria. Unpublished MA preliminary thesis. Bundoora: La Trobe University.

Wroe, S. W., Field, J. H., Archer, M., Grayson, D. K., Price, G. J., Louys, J., . . . Mooney, S. D. (2013). Climate change frames debate over the extinction of megafauna in Sahul (Pleistocene Australia–New Guinea). *Proceedings of the National Academy of Sciences of the United States of America, 110*, 8777–8781.

PART IV

LONG-TERM CHRONOLOGICAL TRENDS AND CULTURAL CHANGE

CHAPTER 18

PERSISTENCE OF COMPLEXITY

Continuation of Intensification, Population Change, and Sociostructural Change in Current Debates in Australian Archaeology

HARRY LOURANDOS AND ANNIE ROSS

INTRODUCTION

CHANGE and dynamics in past hunter-gatherer societies were the focus of the Intensification debate, which began in the late 1970s, a critical time for world archaeology. Intensification models challenged conventional theories that focused on environmental explanations for human behaviour (Lourandos & Ross 1994; see also Brian 2006). Globally, research based on Intensification theory was directed at questions of resource use and economy, demography, and sociostructural change. The debate was a reaction to static and functionalist perspectives, such as environmental determinism and optimal foraging theory (e.g., Smith et al. 1983; Winterhalder & Smith 2000), which emphasized the passive nature of hunter-gatherer societies largely under the control of environmental/ecological conditions. Intensification also questioned the accepted anthropological paradigm that contrasted hunter-gatherers with other societies such as horticulturalists and agriculturalists. Instead, examples were presented to demonstrate the *similarities* between these societies as regards resource use and management, demography, and socioeconomic structure. These examples also examined change in both the long- and short-term via the archaeological record.

The Australian Intensification debate contributed significantly to these global discourses. Australian ethnographic and ethnohistorical material was reevaluated and explored in light of more expansive and complex models of hunter-gatherers. At first, the Australian debate emphasized the Mid- to Late Holocene period, a source of plentiful archaeological information, and many predictions made in earlier stages of the debate were supported by later information. In time, the debate broadened to include earlier phases of Australian archaeology, including the Pleistocene, along with newer research and evidence (e.g., Lourandos & David 1998, 2002). The issues at hand were long- and short-term hunter-gatherer cultural dynamics, and the ways, models, and perspectives by which these were examined.

In this chapter, we review the Intensification debate, especially its historical and theoretical foundations and development (often overlooked in recent commentaries), and discuss the results of past and recent research, including questions of resource use, demography, and sociostructural change. We give thought to the debate's lasting influences on Australian archaeology, on changing perceptions of hunter-gatherers, and on the construction of prehistory. Finally, we consider how the Intensification debate has evolved into a broader postmodern discourse that continues to challenge narrow behavioural ecology paradigms and incorporates new models of human behavioural analyses that emphasize sociocultural and identity relationships between people and place, cultural and natural heritage, and the role of multivocality in narrating the past.

Early Explanatory Models: Deterministic Approaches

Early explanatory models and paradigms in Australian archaeology can be traced back to the work of Birdsell (e.g., 1953, 1957, 1977), an American geneticist who worked with Aboriginal communities beginning in 1938–1939. Basing his observations on ethnographic information, Birdsell argued that Aboriginal population levels were largely controlled by climate as measured by rainfall, demonstrating a close relationship sustained through time. Birdsell saw the Australian continent as filled to saturation point by founding Aboriginal populations, a rapid process of a few thousand years, followed by stabilization of the population, which was closely tied to environmental fluctuations (Birdsell 1977). Sociocultural factors, including human modification of natural resources, played only a minor role in altering these conditions.

Birdsell's model was set in the dominant North American paradigm in the anthropology–archaeology of the time: cultural ecology (Steward 1968). From these origins, Birdsell's model viewed both the natural environment and society as largely self-regulating systems, and in this way, Australian Aboriginal demography as homeostatically regulated.

Therefore, Australian archaeology, right from its modern beginnings, inherited both the dominant North American paradigm of cultural ecology and the stability model, set firmly within ecological theory. In many ways, these paradigms and their accompanying models continue to influence Australian archaeology, particularly in their modern form of evolutionary ecology–behavioural ecology. As such, they can be viewed as the traditional paradigm and model for understanding Aboriginal economic and settlement behaviour and their archaeological evidence.

The Intensification Debate

The Intensification debate emerged out of the classic *ecological* versus *structural* debate. The heightened tensions that developed between these two approaches in archaeology were best represented by the *ecologically* oriented processual archaeologists of North America versus the *social* or structural school of Great Britain.

North American processualism centred on cultural ecology or optimal foraging theory, both of which were influenced by evolutionary ecology (Steward 1968) and sociobiology (Wilson 1975). In contrast, British structuralists (e.g., Bender 1978, 1981; Friedman 1979) were influenced in part by contemporary French neo-Marxist anthropological thought (e.g., Godelier 1975). The debating ground between these two dominant schools of thought centred on the extent to which society, economy, and demography were shaped by environmental-biological factors, as opposed to sociocultural conditions.

Intensification approaches resulted in a critique of the environmental paradigm (Huchet 1991; Thomas 1981; Williams 1987). Research focused on issues such as economic intensification of resource production and its ecological and socio-cultural setting, drawing upon data from a wide range of world anthropological study areas. In highland New Guinea, for example, explanations for increases in garden production and domestic pig numbers—when built on Intensification modelling—included ecologically oriented models (Golson 1977), or diet and demography (Morren 1984), through to sociopolitics (Modjeska 1982). This explanatory sequence and range of explanatory options in many ways found parallels in the Australian Intensification debate of this time (Lourandos 1988). Similar processes of economic Intensification, in the form of resource storage, plant management, water control systems, and sedentism, were seen to occur in both horticultural (e.g., New Guinean) and hunter-gatherer (e.g., Australian) societies, thus blurring the distinction between these two socioeconomic categories (Lourandos 1997), and challenging the grand evolutionary narratives of the superiority of postagrarian societies over hunter-gatherers (Porr & Matthews 2016; Richards 2013; Ross 2020).

The world anthropological debate was extended in the 1980s to include archaeological data as the *historical* dimension of the processes concerned. International archaeological interest in these hunter-gatherer issues stimulated the ways in which they could be resolved both theoretically and methodologically (e.g., Gamble 1986; Price & Brown 1985; Woodburn 1980). In so doing, the conventional, narrow models of hunter-gatherers began to be supplanted by more dynamic, expansive alternatives. These new archaeological studies and approaches also contributed to sociocultural anthropology, expanding its traditionally more *ahistorical* emphasis (Ingold 1988, 2013; Schrire 1984).

The Intensification Debate in Australian Archaeology

The Australian Intensification debate was intertwined with this international hunter-gatherer discourse and literature. The broadening of archaeological perspectives in Australia at the time can also be associated with the British postprocessual movement in archaeology, which emerged in the mid-1980s, and which expanded contemporary theoretical frameworks, deconstructed prior approaches, and stimulated interdisciplinary studies (e.g., Hodder 1989; Shanks & Tilley 1987; Wylie 2002). The deep roots of the debate in Australia, therefore, enabled archaeology to expand upon and question established approaches and their relevance in the changing world of the time.

As with the international debate, the Australian Intensification debate was largely a reaction to traditional archaeological and anthropological paradigms that viewed Australian Aboriginal people and their prehistory as essentially static, with socioeconomic and demographic changes viewed as largely insignificant and under environmental control. Despite the critique of such models (e.g., Lourandos 1980a), Birdsell's influence is clearly evident in the pioneering work of Jones (1977), for example, who discounted the idea that Aboriginal technology could have altered the steady-state relationship between Aboriginal population levels and environment throughout Australia's lengthy prehistory. Lourandos countered with comparisons between southwestern Victorian and Tasmanian population estimates that suggested Aboriginal populations had increased through time and that Aboriginal technological and sociocultural practices were involved in this change (Lourandos 1977, 1980a, 1980b). The overall assessment, based on ethnohistorical evidence from these two *contrasting* regions, when applied to archaeological data, suggested that demographic as well as sociocultural changes had to be considered in explaining and modelling long-term historical processes, especially during the Mid- to Late Holocene period on the Australian mainland. This exchange between Jones and Lourandos sat at the core of the Australian debate and, by focusing on demographic and sociocultural factors and changes, allowed these issues to be discussed widely in regard to Australian prehistory.

Mid- to Late Holocene Spatiotemporal Trends

One of the main archaeological observations underscoring the Intensification debate concerned temporal and spatial trends in the patterning of archaeological sites, based on a broad range of methods and approaches. Many researchers independently observed increases in both the number and use of archaeological sites, especially in the Late Holocene period, in a broad range of environments across mainland Australia (Lourandos 1997; Lourandos & Ross 1994; see Williams 2013 for a recent reassessment). Of particular relevance to the debate concerning environment as a determinant of population change and resource intensification is recent work from the arid Roxby Downs region of South Australia. Hughes, Sullivan and Hiscock (2017; see also Hughes, Way and Sullivan 2021) have demonstrated a significant increase in artefact discard rates at sites in this area dating to the Mid- to Late Holocene. Using in-depth geomorphological analyses to argue that increased discard cannot be explained simply as 'a reflection of the surface visibility and survival of sites of this age' (Hughes et al. 2017:81), Hughes et al. (2017:81) conclude that:

> water availability was not a simple determinant of initial colonisation of the deserts, rather our results illustrate that the technological, social and ideological characteristics of forager groups were significant factors in determining their preparedness and capacity to move away from locations of reliable and abundant water and to exploit more risky landscapes
>
> (see also Hughes et al. 2021 for further discussion of this result and interpretation).

These phenomena of increases in site numbers and artefact discard rates were so widespread in southeastern Australia that they became synonymous with the debate, and population increase came to be regularly confused with the term *Intensification*.

Apart from spatiotemporal trends, general archaeological observations regarding the Mid- to Late Holocene period included a range of other patterns relating to Aboriginal settlement and land use, which occurred across a variety of environments ranging from arid and semiarid areas to wetlands and from rainforests to highlands and islands. Other trends seen in the Holocene archaeological record related to demographic and sociostructural change, including shifts in resource use and stone technologies, rock art, aspects of exchange, cemeteries, and skeletal data. Here we summarize these trends (for a detailed summary, see Lourandos & Ross 1994).

1. *Intensification of resource use* is observed in grass seed exploitation and use in arid Australia (Allen 1974; O'Connell & Hawkes 1984; Smith 1986, 2013); eel fishing in southwestern Victoria (water controls, fish traps) (Builth 2004, 2014; Builth et al. 2008; McNiven, Crouch, Richards, Dolby, & Jacobsen 2012; Richards 2013); new fishing technology in the Whitsunday Islands (Barker 2004) and south coast New South Wales (Attenbrow 2010); oyster farming (Ross, Coghill, & Coghill 2015) and fishing (Ulm 2006; Walters 1989) in Moreton Bay, Queensland; and toxic cycad exploitation in north Queensland (David & Lourandos 1997; Ferrier & Cosgrove 2012). Eel fishing and grass seed harvesting are both associated with signs of demographic change and, ethnohistorically, with large-scale ceremonial occasions and storage (Lourandos 1980a, 1980b, 1988; Smith 1986, 2013). Cycads are also linked, ethnohistorically, to large-scale ceremonial occasions (Beaton 1985; Bradley 2006).
2. *Demographic change and territoriality* (including larger, denser populations) are suggested by evidence across a number of regions and from a range of archaeological data, such as in the recent regionalized rock art of Cape York Peninsula

(David & Lourandos 1998) and in skeletal data and cemeteries from the Murray River Valley and wider southeastern Australia (Pardoe 1988, 1995; Webb 1984; see Littleton, Karsten, & Allen, this volume). These processes peaked in the Mid- to Late Holocene but, in some cases, began in the Late Pleistocene and Early Holocene.

3. *Demographic expansion* into more peripheral and marginal areas can be seen in the arid environs of central Australia (Ross, Donnelly, & Wasson 1992) and the Mallee of northwestern Victoria (Ross 1985); in the recent establishment of earth mounds in the wetlands of southwestern Victoria and other wetland areas of southeastern Australia (Balme & Beck 1996); as well as in the more intensive use of islands in northern and eastern Australia (Barker 1991, 2004; McNiven, De Maria, Weisler, & Lewis 2014; O'Connor 1992; Rowland, Wright, & Baker 2015) and rainforests in northeastern (Cosgrove, Field, & Ferrier 2007; Ferrier 2015; Ferrier & Cosgrove 2012; Horsfall 1987) and southeastern (Morwood 1987) Australia.

4. *Extensive and geographically complex exchange systems and social networks* are clearly visible in Victoria and wider southeastern Australia in the past 1000–2000 years and are supported strongly by ethnohistorical evidence (Lourandos 1988; Lourandos & Ross 1994; McBryde 1978, 1984). The recent spread of one language family throughout the arid zone (McConvell & Evans 1997; see McConvell & Evans, this volume) reinforces ethnohistorical evidence of extensive exchange and trade networks (Gould 1980; McCarthy 1939; Mulvaney 1976) throughout this vast region.

In short, in all the above examples, the sociodemographic dynamic can clearly be seen at play, along with the social dynamic, linked to resource intensification and large-scale intergroup gatherings. Environmental change and unpredictability may have served as a backdrop in these examples (Hughes et al. 2017), but decisions and reactions emerged out of the social context.

Changing Perceptions of Hunter-Gatherers

Throughout the 1980s, the renewed examination of hunter-gatherer societies of both the past and the present led to a change in perceptions of hunter-gatherers generally—extending beyond environmental paradigms—and the appreciation of the much wider range of traditional societies that could be classed as hunter-gatherers. As the key yardstick effectively distinguishing hunter-gatherers from other societies was their reliance on wild resources rather than domesticates, the range was vast. This variability extended from low-population density, mobile, egalitarian groups, on the one hand, to socially hierarchical, populous, sedentary societies, including those of the northwest coast of North America, on the other (Ames 1985; Suttles 1968). For example, the Calusa of South Florida, North America, had all the latter characteristics plus centralized political authority (a king and a state formation) and a standing army but avoided farming, instead depending on wild foods (Marquardt 1988). Therefore, varying levels of sociocultural complexity as regards economy, society, demography, and the like could be seen to characterize these societies, and the resulting *cline* or *continuum* in social variation through time (that this range suggested) was observable via the archaeological record. Hunter-gatherers also could now be seen as having dynamic histories as active rather than passive agents, living in changing landscapes both natural and cultural (Lourandos 1997).

Intensification frameworks, therefore, allow for the recognition of a large range of economic, social, and population variation within and between groups. Some critics have argued that Intensification suggests a relatively uniform, reductionist, and unilinear chronological trajectory (e.g., Allen & Ballard 2001; Brookfield 2001; Ulm 2013). We would argue very differently. The concept of Intensification allows a comparison of a range of different societies, based on the degree of intensification of production practised and the consequent population, along with the social and political systems generated. Using Intensification as an explanatory model, previously anomalous examples of hunter-gatherers can be accommodated, theorized, and tracked through time via the archaeological record.

In these ways, Australian archaeologists, comparing population size based on economic production, showed that some Australian hunter-gatherer societies supported population numbers that overlap with hunter-horticulturalists in New Guinea (Lourandos 1977, 1980a), suggesting comparable energy-harnessing strategies. Similarities were also noticed in sociopolitical structures between certain Australian and New Guinea societies (Lourandos 1988).

All the examples we have given indicate that hunter-gatherers did not necessarily need the arrival of agriculture or horticulture to be freed from environmental constraints and thus be transformed. This process also could take place within a wild food context and be stimulated by sociocultural practices outside the supposed limitations of the environment. That is, the sociocultural complexity of hunter-gatherers did not necessarily *follow* agriculture, as traditional models would have it, and indeed may have preceded it (as seen above) and thus may have stimulated its beginnings.

Social Dynamics

For hunter-gatherers, an inherent *dynamic* exists in alliance formation and the expansion of social networks, as argued by Bender (1978, 1981, 1985). The *intensification* of resource use, she argued, was linked to these competitive sociopolitical events and was expressed in ritual, feasting, trade, and exchange, much as is acknowledged for farmers and more complex societies. While these issues relate to the question of agriculture and its expansion, as seen in New Guinea and elsewhere, they can also be applied to transformations *within* hunter-gatherer societies.

Examples in Australian societies, such as the Mount William and Toolondo earth works and water controls associated with eel fishing and management in southwestern

Victoria, have been viewed in such contexts: nested in a complex, competitive, and populous web of sociopolitical interaction, expressed through large-scale intergroup gatherings, ceremony, feasting, and exchange. The ethnohistorical Mount William complex covered some 6 hectares of elaborate drainage, which was quite beyond the needs of the local group: it served as an enormous holding tank whereby eels could subsist year round, to be tapped and harvested in large numbers when they migrated following the autumn rains (Builth 2004, 2006, 2014; Builth et al. 2008; McNiven & Bell 2010; Williams 1987; see also Richards 2013). Generally, the same applied to the well over 3 km of drainage channels at Toolondo that artificially connected local swamps, expanding the range of eels (Lourandos 1980a, 1983, 1987).

There are many other similar examples of intensive resource management and/or production for social requirements. Bradley (2006: 161), for example, assessed the ways in which the Yanyuwa of the southwestern Gulf of Carpentaria have intensified production of cycads to meet social and ceremonial obligations:

> [C]ycad use among the Yanyuwa provides first-hand evidence for Lourandos' notions of intensive resource use, given that, among the Yanyuwa, intense religious and practical use of cycad seeds ... is not just about food, but at its core also concerns worldviews and how people organize themselves, among themselves and on the ground.

Other Australian examples of *intensified resource production* in competitive, sociopolitical contexts like the above include grass seeds and storage (Allen 1974; O'Connell & Hawkes 1984); cycad management (Beaton 1985); bunya nut production (Morwood 1987; Whincop, Sheppard, Ross, & Sneddon 2012); fish traps (Godwin 1988; Rowland & Ulm 2011); the development of marine fisheries (Humphries 2007; Ross et al. 2015; Richards 2013; Walters 1989); and production of moth 'cakes' to sustain long-term ceremonies and settlements in the southeastern highlands (Flood 1980).

These examples of *intensified* production linked to intergroup—macro-group—contexts point to heightened activity *beyond* the band level of socioeconomic production that is the unit of analysis of most hunter-gatherer research, such as occurs in optimal foraging theory (Winterhalder & Smith 2000). Incentives exist at the intergroup socioeconomic level; therefore, as in agricultural societies, the goal is to *increase* resource production beyond the band level and to develop techniques, strategies, and practices to accomplish this increase. In this way, *surplus* production can be drawn upon to cover future needs, such as supporting large-scale, populous intergroup events and gatherings that may run for lengthy periods of time (months in some cases) (Lourandos 1988). Use and *intensified* use of grass seeds, eel fishing, bunya nuts, oysters, and the like are clear examples of these practices in Australia.

Complex alliance formations in Aboriginal Australia have also been explained as providing a social insurance against fluctuating climate and environment (Gibbs & Veth 2002; Veth 2006), while Peterson (1976) looked to natural regional drainage basins as the clue to Australian Aboriginal demography, following demographic models reminiscent of Birdsell (1953, 1977). Based on ethnographic evidence (as from southwestern

Victoria), it could also be argued that these basin environs were strongly contested territorially. This suggests complex sociopolitical interactions beyond purely environmental dictates (Lourandos 1977, 1980a, 1980b, 1985; Richards 2013). These and similar examples, comparing world hunter-gatherer societies with those in Australia, were a challenge to more environmentally deterministic scenarios and pointed to the rich complexity of sociocultural dynamics (Bender 1985; Price & Brown 1985; Ingold 1988; Lourandos 1997). These fresh approaches also pulled us well away from earlier, narrower social models of hunter-gatherers.

LANDSCAPES MANAGED AND WILD

Once the boundaries around the traditional hunter-farmer debates were breached, there was room to explore the grey areas in between. These included distinctions between wild and managed resources and landscapes that blurred ecological/biological and sociocultural differences (Ross, Sherman, Snodgrass, Delcore, & Sherman 2011). Jones's (1969) examination of Indigenous Australian (including Tasmanian) use of fire, which he termed *firestick farming*, reopened the debate on the extent of Aboriginal ecological manipulation (see also Horton 1982). Kimber (1984) explored the impact of Aboriginal fire practices on arid zone flora and fauna, arguing that these activities are akin to horticulture (see also Bird, Bird, & Parker 2005), while Hynes and Chase (1982) developed concepts of domiculture to explain the more complex *socio-ecological* relationships between people and plants in Cape York Peninsula, northeastern Australia. Yen (1989) conceptualized such grey areas as domesticated landscapes.

It was Harris (1977), however, who modelled an ethnographic subsistence continuum from Cape York Peninsula (Australia) across Torres Strait and into southern New Guinea, thereby demonstrating that there is no clear division—economically, socially, and culturally—between hunting-gathering and farming. The relationships here among plants, people, and practices were *clinal*, not dichotomous. Manipulation or management of plants, commonly used in almost all regions of Australia and New Guinea, further complicated any previously held tidy divisions between resource users and managers (Golson 1971; Lourandos 1997; Ross et al. 2011). On the New Guinea side of the divide, ethnographic examples of hunter-horticulturalists (Lourandos 1980a) and intensive wild sago producers (Ohtsuka 1977; Urwin, Rhoads, & Bell, this volume) further blurred traditional hunter-farmer boundaries (see also Florin & Carah 2018; Roscoe 2002).

EVIDENCE FOR COMPLEXITY

Based on the above discussion of Australian archaeological data, it is clear that a combination of interrelated factors would best explain the changes and trends observed, including: environmental/ecological, sociodemographic, and postdepositional. The *complexity* of the trends indicates that single *prime mover* models cannot be sustained (Lourandos 1997). Demography, for example, is enmeshed with environmental, economic, political, and other sociocultural factors (Pardoe 1995; David & Lourandos 1998). The impacts of environmental changes and fluctuations are themselves mitigated by a wide range of sociocultural responses (Huchet 1991; Ross et al. 2011).

Richards (2013) has taken up this latter point. His reanalysis of old and new data from southwestern Victoria has demonstrated that the patterns of resource use and intensification of resource use, including the development of aquaculture systems and population change, are not linked solely to environmental variation:

> [C]limatic change, including higher, lower and variable effective precipitation regimes (as reflected in lake-levels) has not precipitated or negatively affected the development and proliferation of eel trapping and aquacultural infrastructure— people started trapping eels on a large scale well into a much wetter period than at present and continued doing so through periods that were still wet, but fluctuated from somewhat wetter than present to slightly less wet than present conditions, placing and adjusting their constructs in accord with local and variable conditions.
>
> (Richards 2013: 222)

Richards does not suggest that environmental factors are irrelevant to such changes; rather, he argues that many factors are linked to the intensification of modes of economic production and associated social, political, and cultural changes. Ross et al. (2015) make a similar observation, demonstrating that intensive oyster management in Moreton Bay, southeastern Queensland, was not linked solely to climatic variation, but rather incorporated a range of economic and sociocultural instigating factors. Clearly, a focus on a single causal factor for intensification and social change is folly.

Other more recent studies have similarly focused on investigating regional long-term spatiotemporal trends in a number of Australian environments. In a series of papers, David and Lourandos (1997, 1998; Lourandos & David 1998, 2002) explored the archaeological trends and rock art changes in Cape York Peninsula and explained them through models combining environmental, demographic, and sociostructural changes over time. They employed the same method as Bird and Frankel (1991) and Holdaway and Porch (1995), using the regional spread of radiocarbon dates to produce long-term demographic trends. Using a large number of dates from rock shelter sites in Cape York Peninsula, they showed that demography (as measured by site use) appears to track, in a broad general way, environmental trends until the Mid- to Late Holocene period, when the two temporal trends are *reversed*.

David and Lourandos (1998) explained the archaeological changes in rock art indicating shifts from more uniform engravings to regionalized painted styles during the Late Holocene as changes from more homogeneous *open* systems to more *closed*, compartmentalized local systems. They saw these systems as a trend from more open sociopolitical networks (stretching over very broad geographical areas) to more territorially bounded sociopolitical units. They interpreted this temporal trend and pattern as being due to increases in population sizes and densities: shifts from a more dispersed, lower-density demographic pattern to one of higher population density requiring management of a range of resources via territorially bounded sociopolitical units.

Lourandos and David (2002) extended these site-trend methods to a number of regional Australian study areas in contrasting environments across the continent, drawing upon large numbers of radiocarbon dates from archaeological sites. Their results produced trends that were broadly similar to those from Cape York Peninsula in all regions investigated, which they explained in similar ways (Lourandos & David 2002).

In all, these studies allowed long-term archaeological and environmental temporal trends to be compared and connected by inference to demographic and sociostructural factors, and in so doing, to demonstrate the *entanglement* of the processes involved. The general results indicated that:

1. before the Mid- to Late Holocene period, archaeological trends are more closely tied to general environmental trends;
2. in contrast, during the Mid- to Late Holocene period, in general the archaeological trends appear as a *reversal* of the environmental trends, a phenomenon found in most Australian environments; and
3. the sociodemographic dynamic is at play in all examples.

CRITIQUING THE INTENSIFICATION MODEL

In Australian archaeology the turnover of explanatory models is commonplace, with models replaced in the wake of subsequent research and critique. For example, Gould's (1980) view of arid Australia's prehistory as largely "unchanging" has been redefined with more recent data and the application of dynamic, complex models including environmental determinism, behavioural ecology, social archaeology, Indigenous methodologies, and sociocultural/ceremonial adaptations (Smith 2013; Veth 2006; Veth, Smith, & Hiscock 2008; see also Gibbs & Veth 2002; Veth, O'Connor, & Wallis 2000; Veth et al., this volume).

There have also been many critiques of Intensification. Bird and Frankel (1991), for example, argued against a sociocultural explanation for the 11,000 year sequence from southwestern Victoria (Lourandos 1983; Williams 1987), preferring various environmental interpretations and offering no critique of prior interpretations that were based on a combination of sociocultural and ecological elements firmly set within a detailed ethnohistorical context (Lourandos 1977, 1980a, 1980b, 1983, 1985). When reconfigured, however, their trends generally matched those of the original models and were, in fact, the *reverse* of the general climatic temporal trend (Lourandos & Ross 1994; Richards 2013; see also McNiven, David, & Lourandos 1999).

Using comparable techniques, Holdaway and Porch (1995) modelled the rich 26,000-year Pleistocene archaeological sequence from southwestern Tasmania. They interpreted the fluctuations in site use through time as largely due to adjustments to climatic fluctuations over this very long period. A similar overview of data from this Tasmanian region by Cosgrove, Allen, and Marshall (1990) was also largely environmentally framed. Critique focused on the 26,000 year time span of the purported semi-sedentary occupation as compared with an alternative more seasonally mobile subsistence pattern across this vast, open glacial environment (David & Lourandos 1997; Lourandos 1993, 1997: 247–254; Lourandos & David 1998, 2002).

Others have taken a middle-range approach to the Australian Holocene and earlier time periods. Hiscock (2008), for example, argues that emphasis should be placed on regional approaches and sequences. He contextualizes regional histories within nuanced ecological and social environments, and he sees dynamism and change as key explanatory variables. Rather than contrasting the Holocene and Pleistocene time periods, Hiscock also considers the similarities between their archaeological patterns.

In contrast, Allen and O'Connell (1995), by focusing almost exclusively on the terminal Pleistocene-Holocene boundary and highlighting environmental change, have largely ignored the numerous and complex aspects of archaeological change of the more recent Mid- to Late Holocene period in both New Guinea and northern Australia. This serves to reinforce the traditional worldwide 'towards agriculture and horticulture' model that privileges environmental explanations centred on environmental change at the Pleistocene-Holocene boundary. Only here, in Australia, the archaeological details do not really fit, as most evidence occurs much more recently, in the Mid- to Late Holocene period (Lourandos 1997: 330–335; Lourandos 2008).

Like all explanatory models, the Intensification Model has also been challenged by a massive increase in data, due to expanded archaeological and cultural heritage investigations of the past three decades. Many of the gaps in the archaeological record existing in the 1980s and 1990s, when Intensification peaked as an effective explanatory tool, have now been filled, but not always in accordance with hypotheses generated by the Intensification debate. Details of how these new data have challenged Intensification have been presented by others, and it is beyond the scope of this chapter to address every example. Here we review three recently published major critiques, their key elements, and their impact on Intensification as an explanatory tool.

Williams, Ulm, Goodwin, and Smith (2010) have provided one of the most detailed reviews of the archaeological database for Holocene sites in central and northern Australia. Assessing over 1000 radiometric dates from over 600 archaeological sites, they demonstrated a highly varied pattern of site use across northern and central Australia in the past 2000 years. They explained the patterns, including resource availability and exploitation, and technological change, largely in environmental terms as responses to fluctuations in the El Niño Southern Oscillation (ENSO) index across this period. They argued that 'hunter-gatherers developed systems of mobility and technology to stabilize fluctuations in resource availability' and that there existed 'significant periods of population collapse and recovery during periods of environmental instability' (Williams et al., 2010: 831).

More recently, Williams (2013), using an expansive Australia-wide database of 5041 radiocarbon dates from 1750 archaeological sites, produced chronological trends and interpretations broadly similar to those of Lourandos and David (2002), stating that '[t]hese data give no support for an early saturation of the continent. . . . The greatest increase in population occurred in the Late Holocene, but in contrast to existing intensification models, changes in demography and diversification of economic activity began much earlier' (Williams 2013: 1). Despite inaccuracies regarding Intensification Models, these findings also broadly support those of Lourandos and David (2002), as does Williams's statement that '[a]lthough there is evidence of exponential growth in the Late Holocene along the lines proposed by Beaton and Lourandos—the data here suggest it forms part of a longer process beginning in the terminal Pleistocene' (Williams 2013: 8). Also in support is the finding that '[s]ome demographic changes appear to be in response to major climatic events, most notably during the last glacial maximum' (Williams 2013: 1).

Ulm (2013) also observed considerable variation in the Australian Holocene archaeological record regarding site occupation rates, technological change, natural resource exploitation, and demographic growth and decline. This evidence, he argues, most strongly challenges the pan-continental model proposed by Intensification approaches for the Mid- to Late Holocene period. 'Instead, variability . . . can be understood as a product of local adaptations reflecting the operation of historically situated systems of social organization in diverse environmental settings' (Ulm 2013: 182).

Continent-wide explanations, Ulm maintains, are problematic because they 'homogenise significant regional variability' (Ulm 2013: 184). Based on new dates for the introduction of various changes, Ulm argues that examples of technological change (backed artefacts), resource use (seed grinding), increased site use (occupation dates), and sociopolitical changes (cemeteries and certain art styles) do not date neatly to the Mid- to Late Holocene. Instead, he argues, such changes were introduced much earlier in the Holocene (and in some cases in the Late Pleistocene), only achieving efflorescence in the Late Holocene. Ulm concludes that 'these findings run counter to orthodox [Intensification] accounts of Late Holocene culture change which emphasise undifferentiated cumulative trajectories towards increased occupation' (Ulm 2013: 186).

But as McNiven et al. (2012) explain, the earlier appearance of fish traps and artificial ponds in southwestern Victoria does not preclude the *intensification* of fisheries or eeling in more recent contexts, a general argument that applies to all these early examples. For example, at Lake Condah (southwestern Victoria), large-scale fish traps were initiated c. 6600 cal BP during high lake-level stands, were abandoned during subsequent periods of seasonally fluctuating water levels, and were then reestablished c.1370 cal BP when lake levels were relatively low (Head 1989; Richards 2013). When these data are connected to other data from southwestern Victoria, such as results from recent new shell midden and mound analyses undertaken by Richards (2013), the lack of 'fit' between environmental data and archaeological evidence for resource intensification and social change is further emphasized:

> Further consideration of transegalitarian [complex hunter-gatherer societies] indicators such as the focal coastal seasonal settlements from c. 4,000 cal BP, the appearance and proliferation of earth mounds from c. 2,350 cal BP, etc., reveals that they are not obviously trending with or against environmental changes. . . . Instead, new features were added regardless of whether it was a wetter or drier interval, so that transegalitarian indicators cumulatively increased over time, without any being discarded. It is evident that social factors, not environmental ones, were the drivers of change in SW Victorian Aboriginal societies, a conclusion in accord with the work of Lourandos and Williams and contrary to adaptationist-cum-environmental-deterministic slanted statements by Builth et al. (2008: 423), Bird and Frankel (1991a: 10) and Hiscock (2008: 189).
>
> (Richards 2013: 222)

Similarly, use of grass seeds in arid areas is seen to have shifted in time from a 'lean season' food to a resource supporting large-scale intergroup occasions (Smith 1986). More recent Intensification approaches (David & Lourandos 1998; Lourandos 1997, 2008) also acknowledge more nuanced trajectories of change scaled at varying levels of visibility (large-scale, middle range).

In all, however, while abundant quantities of new data have been amassed over the past three decades (much of it from northern Australia), new regional models are few and far between; and the Mid- to Late Holocene period remains, as before, prominently overrepresented in our databases (Ulm 2013). And despite Ulm's arguments (above), he does acknowledge that 'there *is* a clear disjunction in the archaeological trajectories of many regions between 5000 and 1000 years ago', and that a 'continental narrative *is* important in providing a general heuristic framework' (Ulm 2013: 188—emphasis added). 'Regions do not somehow exist as autonomous entities unrelated to other groups, historical trajectories or traditions. . . . [S]ocial networks connected Aboriginal people from one side of the vast Australian continent to the other and to New Guinea across Torres Strait' (Ulm 2013: 189). In short, Ulm agrees that regional variability *does* exist within a continent-wide sociocultural framework; this explanation lies at the heart of Intensification modelling, especially in its twenty-first century construction.

DISCUSSION: INTENSIFICATION AND SOCIOSTRUCTURAL CHANGE PARADIGMS

Hunter-gatherer studies continue to undergo transformation. Changing views of hunter-gatherers defined the World Hunter-Gatherer Conferences from the mid-1960s through to the mid-1980s. This period can be seen as the golden age of recent hunter-gatherer studies. Here Bender and Morris (1988) saw a trend over time from more ecologically oriented approaches and attempts to fit hunter-gatherers into one unitary category to increasingly more varied approaches and definitions, including the sociopolitical. This theoretical trend continues today and closely resembles that observed throughout Australian archaeology. But with the ever-widening number of participants in archaeology, including those of the Third World, beginning around the mid-1980s (see also Bender 2006), together with emerging Indigenous perspectives, the very usefulness of the term *hunter-gatherer* has begun to be questioned.

In Australian archaeology, as regards both the remote and recent past, there has been an increasing destabilization of hunter-gatherer as a widely used term for Aboriginal Australians' economy and way of life (David & Denham 2006; Lourandos, David, Barker, & McNiven 2006; McNiven & Russell 2005: 38–41; Richards 2013). Challenges to the term closely identify it with postcolonial constructions of Australia's Indigenous peoples and their histories. For example, anthropological unilinear evolutionary models from generations ago *begin* with hunter-gatherers, thereby underscoring their subservience to more modern societies. Today, the politics of constructing the identities of Indigenous peoples, and the role of historical construction in these events, is well demonstrated by more recent postcolonial studies (e.g., McNiven & Russell 2005). These important issues are also of concern to archaeologists operating in postcolonial paradigms and raise questions about the ways they construct the past.

New directions, including the phenomenological, are beginning to leave behind the old division between nature and culture (Meskell 2012; Ross et al. 2011); a division that is itself wrapped in the folds of early colonialism. In addition, more reflexive attitudes take into consideration the roles of the researcher and the researched and their broader influences. In these ways, many of the prior problems and limitations faced by hunter-gatherer studies can be overcome. The underlying historical dimension of these new, contemporary approaches has renewed and reinvigorated prior debates, at the same time accommodating present concerns, including the Indigenous. In these ways, too, the present and the past are intertwined and are created together (Bender 2006; Hodder 2012).

In many ways, Intensification has now metamorphosed into the new phenomenological archaeology—social archaeology or Indigenous Archaeologies methodologies (e.g., Atalay 2008). The application of Intensification to archaeological explanation is still, we argue, valid. Understanding the sociocultural elements of past human behaviour and their reification through the visibility of the archaeological record is a vital component of explanatory devices in archaeological discourse. But like all good theoretical models, Intensification has changed. Early versions have now proven overly simplistic. The Holocene is indeed a more complex and diverse space than was recognized in the 1980s and 1990s. And the Pleistocene era accommodated far more complex human–environment relationships than the dichotomous approaches of early versions of Intensification allowed. But we must be careful not to throw out the epistemological baby with the empirical bath water.

Today Intensification as a theoretical trope can still inform current explanatory debates. We argue that modern Intensification modelling contrasts with evolutionary ecology, which is still largely a deterministic paradigm in which hunter-gatherer behaviour (e.g., economic, social, political, and cultural) is governed almost 'blindly' by the vagaries of climate. Evolutionary ecology varies little from optimal foraging theory (Ross et al. 2015), often failing to explain the numerous case studies in which human behaviour does not accord with data on environmental change (Lupo 2007; contra Porr & Matthews 2016). With regard to relationships between people and environment, Porr and Matthews (2016: 254) maintain that 'such approaches also ignore fundamental questions such as, what exactly is the natural environment in this case and how are the respective relationships conceptualised?' This is particularly the case in Australian Aboriginal archaeology, where many researchers recognize that Indigenous knowledge and narratives of both place and object are grounded in the sociocultural narratives of people, place, and environment (e.g., Brady & Kearney 2016; McDonald & Veth 2013; Ross 2020; Ross et al. 2015). In many ways, Intensification is now the face of social change in archaeological explanation; social archaeology is very much based in the epistemologies and paradigms of Intensification.

The rise of the Indigenous Archaeologies methodology (e.g., Atalay 2008; Colwell-Chanthaphonh & Ferguson 2006; Nicholas & Markey 2015) was specifically designed to merge Western and Indigenous ways of knowing into a multivocal explanation of the past (Atalay 2008; Brady & Kearney 2016; Byrne 2005). In many ways, this is what Intensification also sought to do. By acknowledging the role of social change in the Aboriginal past—and its present—Intensification was decades ahead of the theoretical and methodological 'game' of archaeology. With the rise of postprocessualism and the increasing acceptance of incorporating the views and beliefs of First Nations peoples into explanations of archaeological data, the 'normative' paradigm of human behaviour—guiding the metanarratives of behaviourist theories like optimal foraging, evolutionary ecology, and environmental determinism—is being challenged (Ross 2020). As philosophers of science acknowledge, we must take seriously the *context* of science, which includes the social dynamics, political economy, and institutional settings that constitute scientific practice (Hodder 2012; Wylie 2002). Although in the 1980s and 1990s practitioners rarely acknowledged Indigenous knowledge (Langford 1986), those following an Intensification approach recognized the role of the present in the past and the place of ethnography in developing explanatory models; they were well placed to adopt an Indigenous Archaeologies methodological approach to their practice.

Conclusion

The Australian Intensification debate was largely a reaction to earlier paradigms and narratives framed in terms of long-term cultural stability and resulted in genuine paradigm change and counternarrative (Brian 2006). The debate reoriented archaeology away from largely environmentally deterministic approaches towards more inclusive, nuanced socio-ecological frameworks that invited diversity, including Indigenous and minority opinion. The image of Australian hunter-gatherers also underwent a transformation from passive societies, largely controlled by environmental forces, to active agents within both natural and sociocultural environments.

The general debate has widened to include earlier time periods, and while Mid- to Late Holocene changes continue to be discussed, today ecologically informed approaches sit alongside wider ecological/social frameworks and more middle-range emphases. Middle-range approaches question the general continental narrative and accentuate regional and local archaeologies. New directions are opening up and are challenging us to employ a range of innovative strategies and models beyond the traditional spatiotemporal and environmental/ecological frameworks, although these, too, can be reworked and reimagined to meet the more nuanced needs of today that include Indigenous, legislative, public archaeological, and wider private enterprise concerns.

As regards Intensification, population change, and sociostructural change, the following can be said: resource intensification is clearly evident in the ethnographic and ethnohistorical examples of a range of natural resources modified by Aboriginal people, many of which were used to underwrite large-scale intergroup events and ceremonies, beyond the level of the local group or band. The archaeological signatures of these examples emphasize the Mid- to Late Holocene period, although they may have begun earlier.

Evidence for the existence of higher Aboriginal population numbers than previously recognized is supported by reevaluations of ethnohistorical data. Archaeological temporal trends (radiocarbon dates), as well as skeletal, cemetery, and rock art data, all suggest increasing population in the Late Pleistocene, continuing throughout the Early Holocene, and peaking in the Mid- to Late Holocene.

Sociostructural complexity is clearly evident in ethnographic and ethnohistorical examples from Aboriginal Australia, including social hierarchies (based on seniority) controlling large-scale intergroup ceremonial events and gatherings related to vast exchange (and trading) networks. These social structures were operating throughout southeastern Australia, especially in southwestern Victoria, linked to powerful and socially connected polygynous leaders (Lourandos 1988; Richards 2013), and in other Australian regions as well. Archaeological examples of resource intensification, extensive exchange and trade networks, semi-sedentary settlement patterns, and larger, denser populations are all indications of more complex sociocultural structures and their dynamic potential.

As the Intensification debate has changed perceptions of hunter-gatherers, destabilization of the term also is now leading to new narratives regarding hunter-gatherers. As the narrative and paradigm have shifted, so, too, has the framing of prehistory from stability to change, focusing on regional histories or prehistories. Both prehistory and hunter-gatherer are, in these ways, social constructions within particular frameworks, approaches, or paradigms that were current in their day and in time will shift and be destabilized. Knowing from where the debate has come can point us to where it is heading.

ACKNOWLEDGEMENTS

Many thanks to the editors for asking us to contribute this chapter, which is an updated and expanded version of earlier papers: Lourandos and Ross (1994) and Lourandos (2008).

REFERENCES

Allen, B. J., & Ballard, C. (2001). Beyond intensification? Reconsidering agricultural transformations. *Asia Pacific Viewpoint, 42*(2/3), 157–162.

Allen, H. (1974). The Bagundji of the Darling Basin: Cereal gatherers in an uncertain environment. *World Archaeology, 5*(3), 309–322.

Allen, J., & O'Connell J. F. (Eds.). (1995). Transitions: Pleistocene to Holocene in Australia and Papua New Guinea. *Antiquity*, 69.

Ames, K. M. (1985). Hierarchies, stress, and logistical strategies among hunter-gatherers in northwestern North America. In T. D. Price & J. A. Brown (Eds.), *Prehistoric hunter-gatherers: The emergence of cultural complexity* (pp. 155–180). Orlando, FL: Academic Press.

Atalay, S. (2008). Multivocality and Indigenous Archaeologies. In J. Habu, C. Fawcett, & J. M. Matsunaga (Eds.), *Evaluating multiple narratives: Beyond nationalist, colonialist, imperialist archaeologies* (pp. 29–44). New York: Springer Science & Business Media.

Attenbrow, V. J. F. (2010). Aboriginal fishing in Port Jackson, and the introduction of shell fish-hooks to coastal New South Wales, Australia. In D. Lunney, P. Hutchings, & D. Hochuli (Eds.), *The natural history of Sydney* (pp. 16–34). Mosman: Royal Zoological Society of NSW.

Balme, J., & Beck, W. (1996). Earth mounds in southeastern Australia. *Australian Archaeology, 42*(1), 39–51.

Barker, B. C. (1991). Nara Inlet 1: Coastal resource use and the Holocene marine transgression in the Whitsunday Islands, central Queensland. *Archaeology in Oceania, 26*(3), 102–109.

Barker, B. (2004). *The sea people: Late Holocene maritime specialisation in the Whitsunday Islands, central Queensland.* Terra Australis 20. Canberra: Pandanus Books, Research School of Pacific and Asian Studies, The Australian National University.

Beaton, J. (1985). Evidence for a coastal occupation time-lag at Princess Charlotte Bay (north Queensland) and implications for coastal colonisation and population growth theories for Aboriginal Australia. *Archaeology in Oceania, 20*(1), 1–20.

Bender, B. (1978). Gatherer-hunter to farmer: A social perspective. *World Archaeology, 10*(2), 204–222.

Bender, B. (1981). Gatherer-hunter intensification. In A. Sheridan & G. N. Bailey (Eds.), *Economic archaeology: Towards an integration of ecological and social approaches* (pp. 149–157). British Archaeological Reports International Series 96. Oxford: BAR.

Bender, B. (1985). Prehistoric developments in the American midcontinent and in Brittany, northwest France. In T. D. Price & J. A. Brown (Eds.), *Prehistoric hunter-gatherers: The emergence of cultural complexity* (pp. 21–57). Orlando, FL: Academic Press.

Bender, B. (2006). Destabilising how we view the past: Harry Lourandos and the archaeology of Bodmin Moor, south-west England. In B. David, B. Barker, & I. J. McNiven (Eds.), *The social archaeology of Australian Indigenous societies* (pp. 306–316). Canberra: Aboriginal Studies Press.

Bender, B., & Morris, B. (1988). Twenty years of history, evolution and social change in gatherer-hunter studies. In T. Ingold, D. Riches, & J. Woodburn (Eds.), *Hunters and gatherers: History, evolution and social change* (pp. 4–14). New York: Berg.

Bird, C. F., & Frankel, D. (1991). Chronology and explanation in western Victoria and south-east South Australia. *Archaeology in Oceania, 26*(1), 1–16.

Bird, D. W., Bird, R. B., & Parker, C. H. (2005). Aboriginal burning regimes and hunting strategies in Australia's Western Desert. *Human Ecology, 33*(4), 443–464.

Birdsell, J. B. (1953). Some environmental and cultural factors influencing the structuring of Australian Aboriginal populations. *The American Naturalist, 87*(834), 171–207.

Birdsell, J. B. (1957). Some population problems involving Pleistocene man. *Cold Spring Harbor Symposia on Quantitative Biology, 22,* 47–69.

Birdsell, J. B. (1977). The recalibration of a paradigm for the first peopling of Greater Australia. In F. J. Allen, J. Golson, & R. M. Jones (Eds.), *Sunda and Sahul: Prehistoric studies in Southeast Asia, Melanesia, and Australia* (pp. 113–167). London: Academic Press.

Bradley, J. J. (2006). The social, economic and historical construction of cycad palms among the Yanyuwa. In B. David, B. Baker, & I. J. McNiven (Eds.), *The social archaeology of Australian Indigenous societies* (pp. 161–181). Canberra: Aboriginal Studies Press.

Brady, L. M., & Kearney, A. (2016). Sitting in the gap: Ethnoarchaeology, rock art and methodological openness. *World Archaeology, 48*(5), 642–655.

Brian, D. (2006). Harry Lourandos, the 'Great Intensification Debate', and the representation of Indigenous pasts. In B. David, B. Barker, & I. J. McNiven (Eds.), *The social archaeology of Australian Indigenous societies* (pp. 107–122). Canberra: Aboriginal Studies Press.

Brookfield, H. (2001). Intensification, and alternative approaches to agricultural change. *Asia Pacific Viewpoint, 42*(2/3), 181–192.

Builth, H. (2004). Mt Eccles lava flow and the Gunditjmara connection: A landform for all seasons. *Proceedings of the Royal Society of Victoria, 116*(1), 163–182.

Builth, H. (2006). Gunditjmara environmental management: The development of a fisher-gatherer-hunter society in temperate Australia. In J. Kim, C. Grier, & J. Uchiyama (Eds.), *Beyond affluent foragers* (pp. 4–23) Oxford: Oxbow Books.

Builth, H. (2014). *Ancient Aboriginal aquaculture rediscovered.* Saarbrucken, Germany: LAP Lambert Academic Publishing.

Builth, H., Kershaw, A. P., White, C., Roach, A., Hartney, L., McKenzie, M., . . . Jacobsen, G. (2008). Environmental and cultural change on the Mt Eccles lava-flow landscapes of south-west Victoria, Australia. *The Holocene, 18*(3), 413–424.

Byrne, D. (2005). Messages to Manilla. In R. Paton, I. Macfarlane, & M.-J. Mountain (Eds.), *Many exchanges: Archaeology, history, community and the work of Isabel McBryde* (pp. 53–62). Canberra: Aboriginal History.

Colwell-Chanthaphonh, C., & Ferguson, T. J. (2006). Memory pieces and footprints: Multivocality and the meanings of ancient times and ancestral places among the Zuni and Hopi. *American Anthropologist, 108*(1), 148–162.

Cosgrove, R., Allen, J., & Marshall B. (1990). Palaeo-ecology and Pleistocene human occupation in south central Tasmania. *Antiquity, 64*(242), 59–78.

Cosgrove, R., Field, J., & Ferrier, Å. (2007). The archaeology of Australia's tropical rainforests. *Palaeogeography, Palaeoclimatology, Palaeoecology, 251*(1), 150–173.

David, B., & Denham, T. (2006). Unpacking Australian prehistory. In B. David, B. Barker, & I. J. McNiven (Eds.), *The social archaeology of Australian Indigenous societies* (pp. 52–71). Canberra: Aboriginal Studies Press.

David, B., & Lourandos, H. (1997). 37,000 years and more in tropical Australia: Investigating long-term archaeological trends in Cape York Peninsula. *Proceedings of the Prehistoric Society, 63*, 1–23.

David, B., & Lourandos, H. (1998). Rock art and socio-demography in northeastern Australian prehistory. *World Archaeology, 30*(2), 193–219.

Ferrier, Å. (2015). *Journeys into the rainforest: Archaeology of culture change and continuity on the Evelyn Tableland, North Queensland.* Terra Australis 43. Canberra: Australian National University Press.

Ferrier, Å., & Cosgrove, R. (2012). Aboriginal exploitation of toxic nuts as a late-Holocene subsistence strategy in Australia's tropical rainforests. In S. G. Haberle & B. David (Eds.), *Peopled landscapes: Archaeological and biogeographic approaches to landscapes* (pp. 103–120). Terra Australis 34. Canberra: Australian National University E Press.

Flood, J. (1980). *The moth hunters: Aboriginal prehistory of the Australian Alps.* Canberra: Australian Institute of Aboriginal and Torres Strait Islander Studies.

Florin, S. A., & Carah, X. (2018). Moving past the 'Neolithic problem': The development and interaction of subsistence systems across northern Sahul. *Quaternary International, 489*, 46–62.

Friedman, J. (1979). System, structure and contradiction in the evolution of 'Asiatic' social formations. *Social studies in Oceania and Southeast Asia,* 2. Copenhagen: National Museum of Denmark.

Gamble, C. (1986). *The palaeolithic settlement of Europe.* Cambridge: Cambridge University Press.

Gibbs, M., & Veth, P. (2002). Ritual engines and the archaeology of territorial ascendancy. In S. Ulm, C. Westcott, J. Reid, A. Ross, I. Lilley, J. Prangnell, and L. Kirkwood (Eds.), *Barriers, borders, boundaries: Proceedings of the 2001 Australian Archaeological Association Annual Conference* (pp. 11–19). Tempus 7. Brisbane: Anthropology Museum, University of Queensland.

Godelier, M. (1975). Modes of production, kinship, and demographic structures. *Marxist Analyses and Social Anthropology, 2*, 3–27.

Godwin, L. (1988). Around the traps: A reappraisal of stone fishing weirs in northern New South Wales. *Archaeology in Oceania, 23*(2), 49–59.

Golson, J. (1971). Both sides of the Wallace Line: Australia, New Guinea, and Asian prehistory. *Archaeology and Physical Anthropology in Oceania, 6*(2), 124–144.

Golson, J. (1977). No room at the top: Agricultural intensification in the New Guinea Highlands. In F. J. Allen, J. Golson, & R. M. Jones (Eds.), *Sunda and Sahul: Prehistoric studies in Southeast Asia, Melanesia, and Australia* (pp. 601–638). London: Academic Press.

Gould, R. A. (1980). *Living archaeology.* Cambridge: Cambridge University Press.

Harris, D. R. (1977). Subsistence strategies across Torres Strait. In F. J. Allen, J. Golson, & R. M. Jones (Eds.), *Sunda and Sahul: Prehistoric studies in Southeast Asia, Melanesia, and Australia* (pp. 421–463). London: Academic Press.

Head, L. (1989). Using palaeoecology to date Aboriginal fishtraps at Lake Condah, Victoria. *Archaeology in Oceania, 24*, 110–115.

Hiscock, P. (2008). *Archaeology of ancient Australia*. London: Routledge.

Hodder, I. (1989). Post-modernism, post-structuralism and post-processual archaeology. In I. Hodder (Ed.), *The meaning of things: Material culture and symbolic expression* (pp. 64–78). London: Unwin Hyman.

Hodder, I. (2012). *The present past: An introduction to anthropology for archaeologists*. Barnsley, UK: Pen and Sword Books.

Holdaway, S., & Porch, N. (1995). Cyclical patterns in the Pleistocene human occupation of southwest Tasmania. *Archaeology in Oceania, 30*(2), 74–82.

Horsfall, N. (1987). *Living in rainforest: The prehistoric occupation of north Queensland's humid tropics* (PhD thesis). James Cook University, Townsville.

Horton, D. R. (1982). The burning question: Aborigines, fire and Australian ecosystems. *Mankind, 13*(3), 237–252.

Huchet, B. (1991). Theories and Australian prehistory: The last three decades. *Australian Archaeology, 33* (1), 44–51.

Hughes, P., Sullivan, M., & Hiscock, H. (2017) Palaeoclimate and human occupation in south-eastern arid Australia. *Quaternary Science Reviews, 163*, 72–83.

Hughes, P., Way, A. & Sullivan, M. (2021) Are the widespread scatters of stone artefacts on dune surfaces in southeastern arid Australia really late Holocene in age? *Australian Archaeology, 87*(1).

Humphries, P. (2007). Historical Indigenous use of aquatic resources in Australia's Murray-Darling Basin, and its implications for river management. *Ecological Management and Restoration, 8*(2), 106–113.

Hynes, R. A., & Chase, A. K. (1982). Plants, sites and domiculture: Aboriginal influence upon plant communities in Cape York Peninsula. *Archaeology in Oceania, 17*(1), 38–50.

Ingold, T. (1988). Notes on the foraging mode of production. In T. Ingold, D. Riches, & J. Woodburn (Eds.), *Hunters and gatherers: History, evolution and social change* (pp. 269–285). New York: Berg.

Ingold, T. (2013). Dreaming of dragons: On the imagination of real life. *Journal of the Royal Anthropological Institute, 19*(4), 734–752.

Jones, R. (1969). Fire-stick farming. *Australian Natural History, 16*(7), 224–228.

Jones, R. (1977). Man as an element of a continental fauna: The case of the sundering of the Bassian bridge. In F. J. Allen, J. Golson, & R. M. Jones (Eds.), *Sunda and Sahul: Prehistoric studies in Southeast Asia, Melanesia, and Australia* (pp. 317–386). London: Academic Press.

Kimber, R. G. (1984). Resource use and management in central Australia. *Australian Aboriginal Studies, 2*, 12–23.

Langford, R. F. (1986). Our heritage-your playground. *Australian Archaeology, 16*, 1–6.

Lourandos, H. (1977). Aboriginal spatial organization and population: South-western Victoria re-considered. *Archaeology and Physical Anthropology in Oceania, 12*, 202–225.

Lourandos, H. (1980a). Change or stability?: Hydraulics, hunter-gatherers and population in temperate Australia. *World Archaeology, 11*, 245–266.

Lourandos, H. (1980b). *Forces of change: Aboriginal technology and population in southwestern Victoria* (PhD thesis). University of Sydney, Sydney.

Lourandos, H. (1983). Intensification: A late Pleistocene-Holocene archaeological sequence from southwestern Victoria. *Archaeology in Oceania, 18*, 81–94.

Lourandos, H. (1985). Intensification and Australian prehistory. In T. D. Price & J. A. Brown (Eds.), *Prehistoric hunter-gatherers: The emergence of cultural complexity* (pp. 385–423). Orlando, FL: Academic Press.

Lourandos, H. (1987). Swamp managers of southwestern Victoria. In D. J. Mulvaney & J. P. White (Eds.), *Australians to 1788* (pp. 292–307). Broadway, NSW: Fairfax, Syme & Weldon.

Lourandos, H. (1988). Palaeopolitics: Resource intensification in Aboriginal Australia and Papua New Guinea. In T. Ingold, D. Riches, & J. Woodburn (Eds.), *Hunters and gatherers: History, evolution and social change* (pp. 148–160). Oxford: Berg.

Lourandos, H. (1993). Hunter-gatherer cultural dynamics: Long- and short-term trends in Australian prehistory. *Journal of Archaeological Research, 1*(1), 67–88.

Lourandos, H. (1997). *Continent of hunter-gatherers: New perspectives in Australian prehistory.* Cambridge: Cambridge University Press.

Lourandos, H. (2008). Constructing 'hunter-gatherers', constructing 'prehistory': Australia and New Guinea. *Australian Archaeology, 67,* 69–78.

Lourandos, H., & David, B. (1998). Comparing long-term archaeological and environmental trends: North Queensland, arid and semi-arid Australia. *The Artefact, 21,* 105–114.

Lourandos, H., & David, B. (2002). Long-term archaeological and environmental trends: A comparison from late Pleistocene-Holocene Australia. In P. Kershaw, B. David, N. Tapper, D. Penny, J. Brown, & J. Smith (Eds.), *Bridging Wallace's Line: The environmental and cultural history and dynamics of the SE-Asian-Australian region* (pp. 307–338). Edition: Advances in GeoEcology 34. Reiskirchen: Catena Verlag.

Lourandos, H., David, B., Barker, B., & McNiven, I. J. (2006). An interview with Harry Lourandos. In B. David, B. Barker, & I. J. McNiven (Eds.), *The social archaeology of Australian Indigenous societies* (pp. 20–39). Canberra: Aboriginal Studies Press.

Lourandos, H., & Ross, A. (1994). The great 'intensification debate': Its history and place in Australian archaeology. *Australian Archaeology, 39,* 54–63.

Lupo K. D. (2007). Evolutionary foraging models in zooarchaeological analysis: Recent applications and future challenges. *Journal of Archaeological Research, 15*(2), 143–189.

Marquardt, W. H. (1988). Politics and production among the Calusa of South Florida. In T. Ingold, D. Riches, & J. Woodburn (Eds.), *Hunters and gatherers: History, evolution and social change* (pp. 161–188). New York: Berg.

McBryde, I. (1978). Wil-im-ee Moor-ring: or, where do axes come from? Stone axe distribution and exchange patterns in Victoria. *Mankind, 11*(3), 354–382.

McBryde, I. (1984). Kulin greenstone quarries: The social contexts of production and distribution for the Mt William site. *World Archaeology, 16,* 267–285.

McCarthy, F. D. (1939). 'Trade' in Aboriginal Australia, and 'trade' relationships with Torres Strait, New Guinea and Malaya. *Oceania, 9* (4), 405–439, *10*(1), 80–104, *10*(2), 171–195.

McConvell, P., & Evans, N. (Eds.). (1997). *Archaeology and linguistics: Aboriginal Australia in global perspective.* Melbourne: Oxford University Press.

McDonald, J., & Veth, P. (2013). The archaeology of memory: The recursive relationship of Martu rock art and place. *Anthropological Forum, 23*(4), 367–386.

McNiven, I. J., & Bell, D. (2010). Fishers and farmers: Historicising the Gunditjmara freshwater fishery, western Victoria. *The La Trobe Journal, 85,* 83–105.

McNiven, I. J., Crouch, J., Richards, T., Dolby, N., & Jacobsen, G. (2012). Dating Aboriginal stone-walled fishtraps at Lake Condah, southeast Australia. *Journal of Archaeological Science, 39*(2), 268–286.

McNiven, I. J., David, B., & Lourandos, H. (1999). Long-term Aboriginal use of western Victoria: Reconsidering the significance of recent Pleistocene dates for the Grampians-Gariwerd region. *Archaeology in Oceania, 34*(2), 83–85.

McNiven, I. J., De Maria, N., Weisler, M., & Lewis, T. (2014). Darumbal voyaging: Intensifying use of central Queensland's Shoalwater Bay islands over the past 5000 years. *Archaeology in Oceania, 49*(1), 2–42.

McNiven, I. J., & Russell, L. (2005). *Appropriated pasts: Indigenous peoples and the colonial culture of archaeology*. Walnut Creek, CA: Altamira Press.

Meskell, L. (2012). *The nature of heritage: The new South Africa*. Chichester, West Sussex: John Wiley & Sons.

Modjeska, N. (1982). Production and inequality: Perspectives from central New Guinea. In A. Strathern (Ed.), *Inequality in New Guinea highlands societies* (pp. 50–108). Cambridge: Cambridge University Press.

Morren, G. E. B. J. (1984). Warfare on the highland fringe of New Guinea: The case of the mountain Ok. In R. B. Ferguson (Ed.), *Warfare, culture, and environment* (pp. 169–207). Orlando, FL: Academic Press.

Morwood, M. J. (1987). The archaeology of social complexity in south-east Queensland. *Proceedings of the Prehistoric Society, 53*, 337–350.

Mulvaney, D. J. (1976). 'The chain of connection': The material evidence. In N. Peterson (Ed.), *Tribes and boundaries in Australia* (pp. 121–132). Canberra: Australian Institute of Aboriginal Studies.

Nicholas, G., & Markey, N. (2015). Traditional knowledge, archaeological evidence, and other ways of knowing. In R. Chapman & A. Wylie (Eds.), *Material culture as evidence: Best practices and exemplary cases in archaeology* (pp. 287–307). New York: Routledge.

O'Connell, J. F., & Hawkes, K. (1984). Food choice and foraging sites among the Alyawara. *Journal of Anthropological Research, 40*(4), 504–535.

O'Connor, S. (1992). The timing and nature of prehistoric island use in northern Australia. *Archaeology in Oceania, 27*, 49–60.

Ohtsuka, R. (1977). The sago eaters: An ecological discussion with special reference to the Oriomo Papuans. In F. J. Allen, J. Golson, & R. M. Jones (Eds.), *Sunda and Sahul: Prehistoric studies in Southeast Asia, Melanesia, and Australia* (pp. 465–492). London: Academic Press.

Pardoe, C. (1988). The cemetery as symbol. The distribution of prehistoric Aboriginal burial grounds in southeastern Australia. *Archaeology in Oceania, 23*, 1–16.

Pardoe, C. (1995). Riverine, biological and cultural evolution in southeastern Australia. *Antiquity, 69* (265), 696–713.

Peterson, N. (Ed.). (1976). *Tribes and boundaries in Australia*. Canberra: Australian Institute of Aboriginal Studies.

Porr, M., & Matthews, J. (2016). Thinking through story: Archaeology and narratives. *Hunter Gatherer Research, 2*(3), 249–274.

Price, T. D., & Brown, J. A. (Eds.). (1985). *Prehistoric hunter–gatherers: The emergence of cultural complexity*. New York: Academic Press.

Richards, T. (2013). *Transegalitarian hunter-gatherers of southwest Victoria, Australia* (PhD thesis). Monash University, Melbourne.

Roscoe, P. (2002). Hunters and gatherers of New Guinea. *Current Anthropology, 43* (1), 153–162.

Ross, A. (1985). Archaeological evidence for population change in the Middle to Late Holocene in southeastern Australia. *Archaeology in Oceania, 20*(3), 81–89.

Ross, A. (2020). Challenging metanarratives: The past lives in the present. *Archaeology in Oceania, 55*(2), 65–71.

Ross, A., Coghill, S., & Coghill, B. (2015). Discarding the evidence: The place of natural resources stewardship in the creation of the Peel Island Lazaret Midden, Moreton Bay, southeast Queensland. *Quaternary International, 385,* 177–190.

Ross, A., Donnelly, T. H., & Wasson, R. J. (1992). The peopling of the arid zone: Human-environment interactions. In J. Dodson (Ed.), *The naive lands: Prehistory and environmental change in Australia and the south-west Pacific* (pp. 76–114). Melbourne: Longman Cheshire.

Ross, A., Sherman, K. P., Snodgrass, J. G., Delcore, H. D., & Sherman, R. (2011). *Indigenous peoples and the collaborative stewardship of nature: Knowledge binds and institutional conflicts.* Walnut Creek, CA: Left Coast Press.

Rowland, M. J., & Ulm, S. (2011). Indigenous fish traps and weirs of Queensland. *Queensland Archaeological Research, 14,* 1–58.

Rowland, M. J., Wright, S., & Baker, R. (2015). The timing and use of offshore islands in the Great Barrier Reef Marine Province, Queensland. *Quaternary International, 385,* 154–165.

Schrire, C. (Ed.). (1984). *Past and present in hunter-gatherer studies.* Orlando, FL: Academic Press.

Shanks, M., & Tilley, C. (1987). *Social theory and archaeology.* Cambridge: Polity Press.

Smith, E. A., Bettinger, R. L., Bishop, C. A., Blundell, V., Cashdan, E., Casimir, M. J., . . . Richerson, P. J. (1983). Anthropological applications of optimal foraging theory: A critical review [and comments and reply]. *Current Anthropology, 24* (5), 625–651.

Smith, M. A. (1986). The antiquity of seedgrinding in arid Australia. *Archaeology in Oceania, 21*(1), 29–39.

Smith, M. A. (2013). *The archaeology of Australia's deserts.* Cambridge: Cambridge University Press.

Steward, J. (1968). Cultural ecology. In D. L. Sills (Ed.), *International Encyclopedia of the Social Sciences* (pp. 337–344). New York: Macmillan.

Suttles, W. (1968). Coping with abundance: Subsistence on the northwest coast. In R. B. Lee & I. DeVore (Eds.), *Man the hunter* (pp. 56–68). Chicago: Aldine.

Thomas, N. (1981). Social theory, ecology and epistemology: Theoretical issues in Australian prehistory. *Mankind, 13,* 165–177.

Ulm, S. (2006). *Coastal themes: An archaeology of the southern Curtis coast, Queensland.* Terra Australis 24. Canberra: Australian National University E Press.

Ulm, S. (2013). 'Complexity' and the Australian continental narrative: Themes in the archaeology of Holocene Australia. *Quaternary International, 285,* 182–192.

Veth, P. (2006). Social dynamism in the archaeology of the Western Desert. In B. David, B. Barker, & I. J. McNiven (Eds.), *The social archaeology of Australian Indigenous societies* (pp. 242–253). Canberra: Aboriginal Studies Press.

Veth, P., O'Connor, S., & Wallis, L. A. (2000). Perspectives on ecological approaches in Australian archaeology. *Australian Archaeology, 50*(1), 54–66.

Veth, P., Smith, M., & Hiscock, P. (Eds.). (2008). *Desert peoples: Archaeological perspectives.* Malden, MA: Blackwell.

Walters, I. (1989). Intensified fishery production at Moreton Bay, southeast Queensland, in the late Holocene. *Antiquity, 63,* 215–224.

Webb, S. (1984). Intensification, population and social change in southeastern Australia: The skeletal evidence. *Aboriginal History, 8*(1/2), 154–172.

Whincop, M., Sheppard, L., Ross, A., & Sneddon, A. (2012). *Bunya Mountains, Queensland–Identification, assessment and management of Indigenous cultural heritage values.* Report prepared for Burnett Mary Regional Group. UniQuest Project (C00351), The University of Queensland.

Williams, A. N. (2013). A new population curve for prehistoric Australia. *Proceedings of the Royal Society B: Biological Sciences, 280*(1761), 1–9.

Williams, A. N., Ulm, S., Goodwin, I. D., & Smith, M. (2010). Hunter-gatherer response to late Holocene climatic variability in northern and central Australia. *Journal of Quaternary Science, 25*(6), 831–838.

Williams, E. (1987). Complex hunter-gatherers: A view from Australia. *Antiquity, 61* (232), 310–321.

Wilson, E. O. (1975). *Sociobiology: The new synthesis.* Cambridge, MA: Harvard University Press.

Winterhalder, B., & Smith, E. A. (2000). Analyzing adaptive strategies: Human behavioral ecology at twenty-five. *Evolutionary Anthropology: Issues, News, and Reviews, 9*(2), 51–72.

Woodburn, J. (1980). Hunters and gatherers today and reconstruction of the past. In E. Gellner (Ed.), *Soviet and Western anthropology* (pp. 95–117). New York: Columbia University Press.

Wylie, A. (2002). *Thinking from things: Essays in the philosophy of archaeology.* Berkeley: University of California Press.

Yen, D. E. (1989). The domestication of environment. In D. R. Harris & G. C. Hillman (Eds.), *Foraging and farming: The evolution of plant domestication* (pp. 55–75). London: Unwin Hyman.

CHAPTER 19

PAST ABORIGINAL POPULATIONS AND DEMOGRAPHIC CHANGE USING RADIOCARBON DATA AND TIME-SERIES ANALYSIS

ALAN N. WILLIAMS, SEAN ULM, AND MIKE SMITH

INTRODUCTION

UNDERSTANDING population changes over the entire 50,000 years+ (50 ka) of human history of Sahul is central to several long-standing debates in Australian archaeology. These include the rapidity of the initial peopling of Sahul (Beaton 1983; Birdsell 1957; O'Connell & Allen 2012; Smith 1980); the general size and structure of populations through the Pleistocene, and especially during the dramatic environmental changes associated with the Last Glacial Maximum (LGM) (e.g., Davidson 1990; O'Connor, Veth, & Hubbard 1993; Smith 1989, 2013; Veth 1989); the intensification and rapid growth of societies in the Late Holocene (Lourandos 1983, 1997; Smith & Ross 2008); and how these populations were influenced by and/or were active agents in past climatic and vegetation change (e.g., Flood 1980; Gould 1977; Head 1989, 2000; Horton 2000; Kohen 1995; McBryde 1974; Smith 1988, 1993, 2013; Veth 1989, 1993). Exploration has included both qualitative and quantitative changes in populations, especially focussing on the composition and absolute population sizes at the time of European contact some 230 years ago (Mulvaney & White 1987).

These debates have developed, at least in part, in the absence of robust data. For example, in the case of the initial peopling of Australia, there remains a lack of archaeological sites dating to Marine Isotope Stages 3 and 4 (~70–40 ka) to test hypotheses about the distribution and movement of past populations. Even the timing of the arrival of people on the continent remains disputed, with findings from a single site, Madjedbebe rock shelter in northern Australia, suggesting an age of ≥65 ka for arrival (Clarkson et al. 2017), compared with those arguing for an age closer to 50 ka based on the broader archaeological record (O'Connell et al. 2018; see also Allen & O'Connell 2020, for detailed discussion). Estimates for the number of original arrivals range from a small hunting group up to a few hundred individuals (Birdsell 1957; Davidson 1990; Smith 1980), with little scientific basis for either. Population estimates at the time of European invasion in the late eighteenth century are widely divergent, due to the uncertainty around how many people died through disease, notably smallpox, and during the frontier wars prior to detailed census or documentation. Values range from as low as 300,000 based on nineteenth-century census data (Radcliffe-Brown 1930) up to ~1.2 million when correcting for estimated losses (Butlin 1983; Campbell 2002). Between these two uncertain points, there are variable data due to the inherent nature of discontinuous archaeological records and paucity of sites from across Australia, each providing a short window into the activities of past Aboriginal societies.

The compilation of discontinuous archaeological records into a single regional or continental dataset is proving increasingly important to progress these unresolved questions, allowing statistical interrogation of data gaps and correlation with other indices, such as palaeoclimatic records and indices of fire frequency. Early attempts to address this have been made, including artefact discard rates (e.g., Attenbrow, Robertson, & Hiscock 2009), midden deposits (e.g., Beaton 1983), regional site histories (e.g., Smith & Ross 2008), ethnographic records (e.g., Keen 2004), and rock art distribution (e.g., McDonald 2008). One of the more comprehensive approaches has been in the application of time-series methods to archaeological radiocarbon ages. By combining large datasets of radiocarbon ages—and inferring that these data reflect human activity—from a given locale or region using calibration and statistical approaches, a continuous temporal curve of human behaviour can be developed. The data produced by this approach is quantitative and allows statistically rigorous correlations to be undertaken where necessary.

While initially developed in the 1980s (Geyh 1980; Rick 1987), the use of radiocarbon data as a proxy for human activity has grown exponentially in recent years as the numbers of radiocarbon determinations increase and access to radiocarbon calibration programs becomes readily available (such as OxCal, Bacon, or CALIB). The proliferation of the technique probably began with Gamble, Davies, Pettitt, Hazelwood, and Richards (2005), who first identified 'population events' across Europe through the LGM using a large radiocarbon dataset from Europe. This paved the way for a large number of other studies around the world, most notably works on population histories through the Terminal Pleistocene and Holocene in Europe, North America, South America, and Japan (e.g., Barbarena, Mendez, & Eugina de Porras 2016; Barbarena, Prates, & Eugenia de Porras 2015; Buchannan, Collard, & Edinborough 2008; Buchanan, Hamilton, Edinborough, O'Brien, & Collard 2011; Collard, Buchanan, Hamilton, & O'Brien 2010; Collard, Edinborough, Shennan, & Thomas 2010; Crema, Habu, Kobayashi, & Madella

2016; Downey, Randall Hass, & Shennan 2016; Gayo, Latorre, & Santoro 2015; Robinson, Zahid, Codding, Hass, & Kelly 2019; Shennan & Edinborough 2007; Shennan et al. 2013) and revolutionary work to develop a technique to correct radiocarbon data for taphonomic loss through time (e.g., Johnson & Brook 2011; Surovell & Brantingham 2007; Surovell, Byrd Finley, Smith, Brantingham, & Kelly 2009; Timpson et al. 2014) and/or spatial bias (Crema, Bevan, & Shennan 2017). Similar to other geochronological fields, in recent years, researchers are continuing to refine the technique with increasingly complex exploration of Bayesian modelling and kernel density estimates (see Crema & Shoda 2021, for discussion and review).

In Australia, the use of radiocarbon data was taken up shortly after its initial application, with a plethora of studies in the 1990s (Allen & Holdaway 1995; Allen & O'Connell 1995; Bird & Frankel 1991; David & Lourandos 1997; Holdaway & Porch 1995, 1996; Lourandos 1993; Lourandos & David 1998; Smith & Sharp 1993; Ulm & Hall 1996). All of these studies were based on the exploration of trends in radiocarbon ages within regions or specific time periods, rather than undertaken at a continental scale and usually without access to radiocarbon calibration. In 2008, one of the authors (AW) initiated a long-term research program focussing on the use of the radiocarbon data to provide regional and continental models to explore and correlate population change at qualitative and quantitative scales with palaeoclimatic records.

Here we present a summary of the research outcomes and models developed by the research group to provide an authoritative view on past Australian populations. We further explore and respond to some of the criticism directed towards the approach and provide a guide to future research directions for Australian archaeology.

DATA AND METHODS

The models developed by Williams and co-authors are based on 5044 radiocarbon ages from 1748 archaeological sites across Australia, harvested from results presented in over 1000 publications (Williams, Ulm, Smith, & Reid 2014) (Figure 19.1). Radiocarbon ages were compiled between 2008 and 2014 and released as three discrete databases aligned with major environmental regions—arid zone (Williams, Smith, Turney, & Cupper 2008), tropics (Williams & Smith 2012), and southern latitudes (Williams & Smith 2013), with specific analytical publications relating to each. A further previously developed dataset for Queensland (IDASQ) (Ulm & Reid 2000) was added to provide complete coverage of the modern Australian continent.

The methods used in the exploration of these data were variable and are outlined in detail in each of the publications. However, at a general level, temporal analysis included two main approaches: (1) combining the calibrated probability ranges of multiple radiocarbon ages using a calibration program (e.g., OxCal) into a single 'sum probability distribution' (also known as a 'probability distribution function' and 'temporal

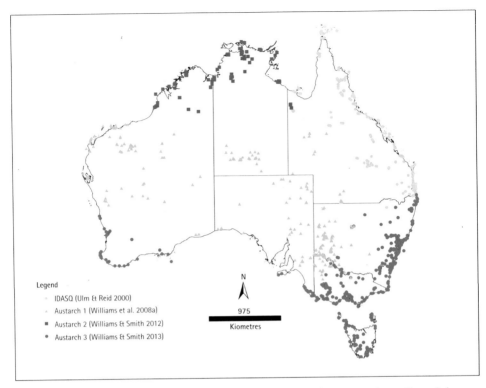

FIGURE 19.1. Map showing the distribution of radiocarbon data across Australia and the various AustArch datasets broken down by their regional development. Each dot represents a site containing archaeological radiocarbon data and recorded in the datasets.

frequency distribution'), and thereby providing a continuous time series plot; and/or (2) calibration of radiocarbon dates to provide calendar ages and their division into temporal intervals/slices/bins to produce a histogram of changing numbers of samples through time. The former approach allowed for direct statistical comparison with other times-series records using methods such as ARIMA (auto-regressive integrated moving average) models (e.g., Williams, Mooney, Sisson, & Marlon 2015). The latter approach allowed for the further statistical manipulation of the data to 'correct' for taphonomic loss using methods outlined by Surovell and colleagues (2009) and modified by Williams (2012). This required the realignment of the data with a quasi-exponential decay curve based on geological samples to increase the representation of deep-time data, while reducing the influence of more recent ages. It also allowed for the application of methods outlined in Peros, Munoz, Gajewski, and Viau (2010) through which exploration of percentage change between time intervals allowed for population rates to be determined at an annual scale (labelled as Gr_{Ann} in subsequent sections). By then applying compound equations to population estimates, these methods allowed quantitative numbers of people through time to be developed. Further details of these methods can be found in Williams (2012, 2013).

Changes Through Time

Overall, the data show a positive curvilinear shape over the last 50 ka, beginning with an initial seeding population and growing up to the time of European invasion (Figure 19.2). At a general level, population densities remained low throughout the Pleistocene, before an increase beginning at ~12 ka and peaking in the last 1000 years. Notable features include low numbers between 50 and 20 ka; a significant increase between 20 and 18 ka, before a decline to some of its lowest values between 16 and 12 ka; and then a constant increase from 12 to 0.4 ka. From 12 ka, the curve begins initially as a steady increase, within which there are a series of pulses (at ~8.3–6.6 ka, 4.4–3.7 ka, and 1.6–0.4 ka). While not as clear, several declines or plateaus are also evident through the Holocene (at ~5.6–4.8 ka, 2.6–2.2 ka, and 0.4–0 ka). The taphonomically corrected data (Figure 19.2) effectively exaggerates or subdues the numbers of dates in any given time interval, but in general it provides broadly similar trends, including the decline in values after 18 ka and the stepwise increase through the Holocene. Perhaps the most significant difference is that the corrected data suggests that for the period before the LGM (21 ± 3 ka), Pleistocene values were broadly comparable with those during the Early Holocene until ~8 ka, which may align more closely with the high populations proposed by Bradshaw et al. (2021). Overall, current data suggests that except for the consequences of major climatic shifts and the effects of significant technological change in the Holocene, a relatively low level of population, probably well below ecological carrying capacity, was maintained for much of the peopling of Australia.

Many of the key features of the trends in the population appear to be associated with major climatic changes, most notably the LGM and Meltwater Pulse 1A (~14 ka). The former sees an increase in data, but further interrogation shows that this increase reflects a dating focus of researchers on the Willandra Lakes region—a known ecological refuge during this period—which artificially inflates this part of the curve. On removing the Murray Darling data, results show a decline in populations through the peak of the LGM, with a nadir immediately after the event (between ~18 and 16 ka), which aligns closely with the end of the climate disruption based on new research by Cadd et al. (2021). This late collapse may reflect the disjunction between moisture and thermal regimes as climate warmed, creating more difficult physiological conditions for human populations following the LGM when evapotranspiration from increasing temperatures outpaced the availability of water in the landscape (Reeves et al. 2013). Quantitatively, the difference between pre- and immediately post-LGM populations is a decline of ~60%, and values do not recover until the Holocene.

Populations remained low throughout the terminal Pleistocene, with some archaeological evidence suggesting that LGM behaviours and site use remained unchanged (AAJV, 2017; Barry et al. 2021; Williams, Atkinson et al. 2014), perhaps reflecting significant long-term disruption of Aboriginal societies during the LGM. Specific information about palaeoclimate on the shoulder of the LGM is relatively limited to date.

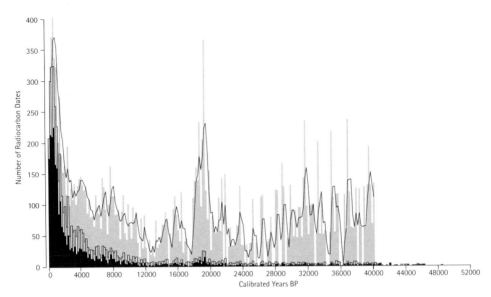

FIGURE 19.2. The entire dataset ($n = 4575$; $\Delta T = 155$) calibrated and data-binned into 200-year time intervals, uncorrected for taphonomic loss and presented as a stacked bar chart (white bars = rock shelter data; black bars = open site data). Grey bars present the same data-bins with open site data taphonomically corrected and combined with uncorrected rock shelter site data; a 600-year moving average (black) line is presented through the taphonomic data. Note that although the dataset extends to 50 ka, adjustments for taphonomic loss reduce coverage to the last 40 ka due to the intrinsic limitations of the method (see Williams 2013, for further discussion).

Further understanding of this period is essential in future research. Williams, Ulm, Sapienza, Lewis, & Turney (2018) hypothesized that changes observed in the Early Holocene were the result of rapidly rising sea-level following Meltwater Pulse 1A at 14.6–8 ka, providing a driver for aggregation of populations and re-expansion into previously abandoned or marginal post-LGM landscapes (see also Barry et al. 2021). The reduction of the continental landmass by some 21.6% (2.12 million km²) due to sea-level rise, in combination with ameliorating climate—the Holocene climatic optimum—probably resulted in packing and strong growth of populations between ~12 and 6 ka. During this time, there is evidence of activation of new sites (e.g., Ulm 2013); dense occupation deposits (e.g., Lourandos 1997; Smith 2006; Smith, Williams, & Ross 2017) and increasing rock engravings (Smith 2013); and appearance of complex technology (e.g., fish traps) and food processing techniques (e.g., *Macrozamia* plants and grass seeds) (McNiven et al. 2012; Smith 2013). Previously we have suggested that many of these changes converge on traits more characteristic of agricultural societies (Williams, Ulm, Turney, Rodhe, & White 2015). We suggest that the manipulation of the natural environment by Aboriginal societies in order to stabilize returns from bush foods constitutes a form of 'low level food production' (see also Keen 2021), which in Australia reflects a long trajectory of expansion and elaboration of foraging economies.

The Late Holocene sees a decoupling of the population-climate relationship observed previously. While responses are still evident, notably a short decline and disaggregation with the onset of aridification from El Nino Southern Oscillation (ENSO) at 4–2 ka, populations consistently increase until the invasion of Europeans at ~0.2 ka. This decoupling is in large part the end result of packing thresholds from the Early and Mid-Holocene that would have presumably restricted the availability of movement into new habitats and patches (environmental infilling), thereby leading to technological and behavioural investments to maintain calorific returns, which ultimately buffers populations from future climate variability. Archaeologically, these investments are evident through the appearance and widespread use of seed-grindstones (Smith 2013); the diversification of a wooden toolkit (Smith 2013; Veth, Hiscock, & Williams 2011); advanced elaborate food processing techniques; and greater reliance on marine resources including migration and exploitation of off-shore islands previously too unproductive for use (Ulm 2011). Mosaic patch burning to encourage small game may also be part of these behaviours (e.g., Bliege-Bird, Bird, Codding, Parker, & Jones 2008; Bliege-Bird, Tayor, Codding, & Bird 2013), but currently our knowledge of this is temporally poor. Highest populations were reached in the last 2000 years, with some 50% of radiocarbon data within this period, and extending across all parts of Australia. This expansion aligns with the well-documented spread of *Wati* language across the western deserts as one ground-truth example of this model (Smith 2005). There is also increasing regional differentiation of art styles and formalization of exchange networks, all suggesting the formation of stronger territorial boundaries resulting from environmental demographic packing (David 2002; Lourandos 1997; Ross 2013; Smith 2013). Along with others (e.g., David 2002), we hypothesize that these conditions would have been conducive to the formation of the social (e.g., classificatory kin system) and religious (the 'Dreaming') systems documented in the ethnographic period (Smith 2021).

The data declines in the most recent 500 years. In part, this is the result of dating strategies where many researchers avoid directly dating recent stratigraphic units that contain historical materials (e.g., glass, metal, etc.), and probably also reflects the impact since 1700 of introduced smallpox and other diseases to the Aboriginal population. Frontier violence also likely played a significant role, as is becoming apparent in the work of Wallis, Burke, and Dardengo (2022). Importantly however, there is still data present into the twentieth century, suggesting that at least in some areas, traditional use and custom continued to near present day. A tangible reminder of this continuity is the recent documentation of a mid-twentieth-century culturally modified tree in western New South Wales (Spry et al. 2020; see also Morrison & Shepard 2013).

The GR_{Ann} analysis of the uncorrected dataset indicates an average annual population growth rate of 0.01% over the last 50 ka, with a range of between 0.07 and −0.03%. These values are consistent with observed contemporary hunter-gatherer populations (Pennington 2001). The GR_{Ann} values broadly align with the trends outlined above, including significant decline during the LGM before a fluctuating but stepwise increase through the Holocene (Figure 19.3). When applying quantitative values to these birth/death rates, we find that >1000 and <3000 people would have been needed at 50 ka to

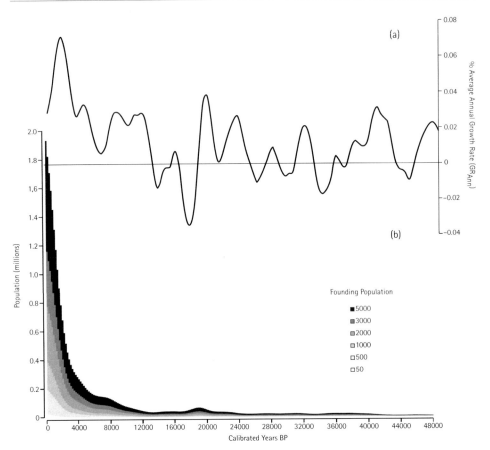

FIGURE 19.3. A: The GR$_{Ann}$ (average annual growth rate) developed using data in Figure 19.2 and showing the growth and/or decline of the population as a percentage (df = 25; see Williams 2013, for further details). B: The population of Australia when applying various founding populations at 50 ka and applying growth or decline in accordance with the GR$_{Ann}$ values. Williams (2013) considered that a founding population of between 1000 and 3000 people was required to reach values observed at time of European invasion.

result in values of between ~380,000 and 1.15 million Aboriginal people at the time of European invasion. While these initial seeding values may appear high, they conform closely with genomic studies (Tobler et al. 2017). More recent research by Bradshaw et al. (2019) undertaking complex stochastic modelling of the minimum founding populations reached a similar conclusion, suggesting that 1300–1550 people would have been required over a short period of time to avoid long-term extinction.

Between the initial peopling of Sahul and European invasion, Williams (2013) provided a range of quantitative population values. At a general level, these suggest that for much of the Pleistocene, populations were likely <50,000 (~1 person/385 km^2), values that allowed exploration of much of the continent, but unlikely to support establishment of permanent regionalism. It was not until the Early Holocene that values exceed this, with a steady increase from ~100,000 at 6 ka (1 person/70–80 km^2) to ~250,000 (1 person/30 km^2) at 2.5 ka and culminating at ~1.15 million (1 person/7 km^2) at 0.5 ka. In contrast, genomic research suggests long-term continuity in distinct regional populations from 42 ka (Tobler et al. 2017). Some modelling also indicate potentially early populations at saturation levels could have been up to 6.5 million across Sahul shortly after arrival (Bradshaw et al. 2021). Currently, there is no archaeological evidence in support of these estimates and these figures are discrepant with the radiocarbon data. Neither of these recent studies have been robustly tested against current archaeological data, which does not easily correlate with the numbers of people being proposed.

Discussion and Conclusions

The use of radiocarbon data as a proxy for human activity forms an important tool for understanding the past. While first explored in the 1980s, it has become a prolific technique globally in the last decade and has resulted in innovative and new ways to look at past behaviour, especially past demography. In Australia, we have applied the technique to explore qualitative and quantitative changes of past populations over the last 50,000 years; and to try and resolve long-standing questions in relation to the initial peopling of the continent, survival through the LGM, and intensification of production in the last 5000 years. Our aim has been to provide overarching continent- and regional-scale frameworks for researchers to cross-correlate, test, and compare with on-ground data. Our findings both supplement existing ideas and concepts, as well as shed new light on population trends in the past.

Specifically, our data suggests that initial peopling would have needed at least a thousand people to succeed and was likely a deliberate, rather than accidental, act. These findings have been validated by other studies (e.g., Allen & O'Connell 2020; Bird et al. 2019; Bradshaw et al. 2019; Kealy, Louys, & O'Connor 2018) and robustly resolve many debates about the nature and mechanism of arrival in Sahul. Populations remained low throughout the Pleistocene and were severely disrupted by the LGM. Recent modelling by Bradshaw et al. (2021) has begun to question these low populations, but their suggestion of millions of people across the continent remains at odds with the sparse archaeological record, and further work is required to cross-correlate the two datasets. Demographic recovery from the LGM appears to have been delayed during the Terminal Pleistocene as a result of both climatic disruption and rapid sea-level change— the latter resulting in the loss of ~25% of the continent. These results align well with an archaeological record characterized by an austere material culture through this period, with frequent site abandonment and a pattern of reduced activity outside of high resource ecological refuges or what Smith (2013: 116) refers to as 'cryptic refugia'. In the Sydney Basin, Williams, Atkinson and colleagues (2014) showed that an LGM refuge on the banks of the Hawkesbury-Nepean River continued unchanged until the Early

Holocene. More recently, a campsite in Parramatta identified by Barry et al. (2021) is interpreted by them as the first evidence of people expanding from LGM refuges at ~14 ka, several thousand years after the LGM ended (see also Smith, Williams, & Wasson 1991 for comparable ideas about sites in the Strzelecki dune field located mostly in northeast South Australia). The last 10,000 years show a significant increase in population across Australia, both as a result of packing due to loss of landmass following Meltwater Pulse 1A and socioeconomic evolution during a period of increasingly stable climatic conditions. From this time onwards, there is increasing archaeological evidence of growing populations, technological innovation, diversification of language, establishment of landesque capital, and complex art systems.

While trends in radiocarbon dating frequencies match other archaeological indices, the technique is criticized by some scholars, who highlight three main concerns (e.g., Attenbrow & Hiscock 2015; Becerra-Valdivia, Leal-Cervantes, Wood, & Higham 2020; Carleton & Groucutt 2020; Torfing 2015): (1) the reliability of individual radiocarbon assays and concern that radiocarbon datasets may contain a significant number of age-determinations that are inaccurate; (2) the need to demonstrate that at a *site* or in a specific layer that the material actually dated (charcoal, shell or animal bone, etc.) is associated with past human activity, and how this therefore affects larger datasets; and (3) the interpretation of the data as a proxy for demographic trends rather than changes in residential mobility. The first issue is mostly applicable to radiocarbon data undertaken prior to 2000, when methods and approaches were still developing. However, the majority of Australian radiocarbon data was determined after this period (Williams, Ulm, Smith, & Reid 2014), and in any case the radiocarbon technique has underpinned archaeological research in Australia for more than fifty years. By far the most persistent criticisms have been based on (2), which is fundamental to the rationale for radiocarbon dating in archaeological contexts. A coherent regional signal in radiocarbon data frequencies can usually be delineated once a sufficient sample size has been achieved—usually in the order of a few hundred dates for a region. An increasing sample size tends to swamp sampling issues at individual sites and highly repeatable plots can be obtained. This concern has been explored and demonstrated in a range of studies, notably Timpson et al. (2014) and Holland-Lulewicz and Ritchison (2021), as well as an initial exploration of the technique by Williams (2012). It is relevant that initial results produced nearly a decade ago using this technique have proved to be remarkably robust despite the addition of much new data. Finally (3), this issue was tested by Williams, Ulm and colleagues (2015) by comparing radiocarbon data with other archaeological indices, which demonstrated similar trends in different environmental regions, indicative of widespread changes in demography rather than more localized changes in residential mobility (see also Williams & Ulm 2016, and Smith 2016). It is notable that Hughes, Sullivan, and Hiscock (2017), who criticized the analyses presented here, produced closely similar results in their own analysis, showing sparse use and visitation of the Roxburgh Downs area in the LGM and terminal Pleistocene, then increasing activity in the Holocene—inadvertently confirming the utility and robustness of radiocarbon data frequency data. We highlight, however, that such debates and criticism of the use of radiocarbon data as a proxy are not exclusive to Australia, with researchers internationally exploring the methods and application of the technique. Beyond Australia, Crema and Shoda (2021) and Carleton and Groucott (2020) provide two of the most recent publications detailing alternate views and some of the methodological issues to be aware of when considering the use of the technique.

Our research identifies several areas for future research, most notably the need to fill a number of spatial and temporal gaps in the archaeological record. These include a greater focus on the Terminal Pleistocene and Early Holocene, a long period of rapid postglacial environmental change that has been overlooked during the major debates of the last few decades (except for Allen & O'Connell 1995), and where most attention has been given to LGM survival and Late Holocene intensification. This postglacial transition provides a critical link between these two foci events. Spatially, there are a significant number of regions where little archaeological data has been recovered—many of which are central to recent modelling of initial peopling pathways of the continent (e.g., Bradshaw et al. 2019, 2021; Crabtree et al. 2021). These include the Kimberley where Terminal Pleistocene sea-level inundation of ~1 million km^2 should have resulted in widespread migration of people into the northwest. Attention needs to be directed to the Tanami Desert, Sturt Plateau, Mitchell Grass Downs, and Davenport Murchison Ranges to explore interactions between the tropics and the arid core; and in the southwest, Murchison, Coolgardie, and Avon Wheatbelt, to further understand the interactions between the Western Deserts and surrounding coastal fringe. Other key areas include the eastern fringes of the arid zone in the Simpson-Strzelecki Desert and Channel Country, marginal country where boom and bust stresses on populations should be readily discernible in the archaeological record.

Overall, these radiocarbon-informed models have reframed archaeological research towards 'big data', allowing a macro-scale or big-picture understanding of past activity and population trends—something that has become increasing rare in the last two decades of Australian research. While criticism of such research and approaches remains, it nonetheless provides an important facet of archaeological research to further understand the past and acts as a useful framework for researchers to place their works into a broader context.

REFERENCES

AAJV (Austral–Extent Heritage Joint Venture). (2017). Windsor Bridge Replacement Project—Aboriginal Archaeological Excavation Report. Unpublished Report to NSW Roads and Maritime Services. http://www.rms.nsw.gov.au/projects/sydney-west/windsor-bridge-replacement/project-documents.html.

Allen, J., & Holdaway, S. (1995). The contamination of Pleistocene radiocarbon determination in Australia. *Antiquity*, 69(1), 101–112.

Allen, J., & O'Connell, J. F. (Eds.) (1995). *Transitions: Pleistocene to Holocene in Australia and Papua New Guinea*, Oxford: Oxford University Press.

Allen, J., & O'Connell, J. F. (2020). A different paradigm for the initial colonisation of Sahul. *Archaeology in Oceania, 55*(1), 1–14.

Attenbrow, V., & Hiscock, P. (2015). Dates and demography: Are radiometric dates a robust proxy for long-term prehistoric demographic change? *Archaeology in Oceania, 50*(Supplement), 29–35.

Attenbrow, V., Robertson, G., & Hiscock, P. (2009). The changing abundance of backed artefacts in south-eastern Australia: A response to Holocene climate change? *Journal of Archaeological Science, 36*, 2765–2770.

Barbarena, R., Mendez, C., & Eugina de Porras, M. (2016). Zooming out from archaeological discontinuities: The meaning of mid-Holocene temporal troughs in South American deserts. *Journal of Anthropological Archaeology, 46*, 68–81.

Barberena, R., Prates, L., & Eugenia de Porras, M. (2015). The human occupation of north-western Patagonia (Argentina): Palaeoecological and chronological trends. *Quaternary International, 356*, 111–126.

Barry, L., Graham, I., Mooney, S. D., Toms, P. S., Wood, J. C., & Williams, A. N. (2021). Tracking an exotic raw material: Aboriginal movement through the Blue Mountains, Sydney, NSW during the Terminal Pleistocene. *Australian Archaeology, 87*(1), 63–74. https://doi.org/10.1080/03122417.2020.1823086

Beaton, J. M. (1983). Does intensification account for changes in the Australian Holocene archaeological record. *Archaeology in Oceania, 18*, 94–97.

Becerra-Valdivia, L., Leal-Cervantes, R., Wood, R., & Higham, T. (2020). Challenges in sample processing within radiocarbon dating and their impact in 14C-dates-as-data studies. *Journal of Archaeological Science, 113*, 105043.

Bird, C. F. M., & Frankel, D. (1991). Chronology and explanation in western Victoria and south-east South Australia. *Archaeology in Oceania, 26*(1), 1–16.

Bird, M., Condie, S. A., O'Connor, S., O'Grady, D., Reepmeyer, C., Ulm, S., Zega, M., . . . Bradshaw, C. J. A. (2019). Early human settlement of Sahul was not an accident. *Scientific Reports, 9*, 8220. https://doi.org/10.1038/s41598-019-42946-9

Birdsell, J. (1957). Some population problems involving Pleistocene man. *Cold Spring Harbor Symposium, 22*, 47–69.

Bliege-Bird, R., Bird, D. W., Codding, B. F., Parker, C. H., & Jones, J. H. (2008). The 'fire-stick farming' hypothesis: Australian Aboriginal foraging strategies, biodiversity and anthropogenic fire mosaics. *Proceedings of the National Academy of Sciences, 105*(39), 14796–14801.

Bliege-Bird, R., Tayor, N., Codding, B. F., & Bird, D. W. (2013). Niche construction and Dreaming logic: Aboriginal patch mosaic burning and varanid lizards (*Varanus gouldii*) in Australia. *Proceedings of the Royal Society B, 280*, 20132297.

Bradshaw, C. J. A., Norman, K., Ulm, S., Williams, A. N., Clarkson, C., Chadoeuf, J., . . . Saltré, F. (2021). Stochastic models support rapid peopling of Late Pleistocene Sahul. *Nature Communications, 12*, 2440. https://doi.org/10.1038/s41467-021-21551-3

Bradshaw, C. J. A., Ulm, S., Williams, A. N., Bird, M. I., Roberts, R. G., Jacobs, Z., & Saltré, F. (2019). Minimum founding populations for the first peopling of Sahul. *Nature Ecology & Evolution, 3*, 1057–1063. https://doi.org/10.1038/s41559-019-0902-6

Buchanan, B., Collard, M., & Edinborough, K. (2008). Paleoindian demography and the extraterrestrial impact hypothesis. *Proceedings of the National Academy of Sciences of the United States of America, 105*, 11651–11654.

Buchanan, B., Hamilton, M. J., Edinborough, K., O'Brien, M. J., & Collard, M. (2011). A comment on Steele's (2010) 'Radiocarbon dates as data: Quantitative strategies for estimating colonization front speeds and event densities'. *Journal of Archaeological Science, 38*, 2116–2122.

Butlin, N. G. (1983). *Our original aggression: Aboriginal populations of southeastern Australia 1788–1850*. Sydney: Allen & Unwin.

Cadd, H., Petherick, L., Tyler, J., Herbert, A., Cohen, T. J., Sniderman, K., . . . Harris, M. R. P. (2021). A continental perspective on the timing of environmental change during the last glacial stage in Australia. *Quaternary Research, 102*, 5–23. https://doi.org/10.1017/qua.2021.16

Campbell, V. (2002). *Invisible invaders: Smallpox and other diseases in Aboriginal Australia 1780–1880*. Carlton: Melbourne University Press.

Carleton, W. C., & Groucutt, H. S. (2020). Sum things are not what they seem: Problems with point-wise interpretations and quantitative analyses of proxies based on aggregated radiocarbon dates. *The Holocene, 31*(4), 630–643.

Clarkson, C., Jacobs, Z., Marwick, B., Fullagar, R., Wallis, L., Smith, M., . . . Florin, S. A. (2017). Human occupation of northern Australia by 65,000 years ago. *Nature, 547*(7663), 306–310.

Collard, M., Buchanan, B., Hamilton, M., & O'Brien, M. J. (2010). Spatiotemporal dynamics and causes of the Clovis-Folsom transition. *Journal of Archaeological Science, 37*, 2513–2519.

Collard, M., Edinborough, K., Shennan, S., & Thomas, M. G. (2010). Radiocarbon evidence indicates that migrants introduced farming to Britain. *Journal of Archaeological Science, 37*, 866–870.

Crabtree, S. A., White, D. A., Bradshaw, C. J. A., Saltré, F., Williams, A. N., Beaman, R. J., . . . Ulm, S. (2021). Landscape rules predict optimal superhighways for the first peopling of Sahul. *Nature Human Behaviour, 5*, 1303–1313. https://doi.org/10.1038/s41562-021-01106-8

Crema, E. R., Bevan, A., & Shennan, S. (2017). Spatio-temporal approaches to archaeological radiocarbon dates. *Journal of Archaeological Science, 87*, 1–9.

Crema, E. R., Habu, J., Kobayashi, K., & Madella, M. (2016). Summed probability distribution of 14 C dates suggests regional divergences in the population dynamics of the Jomon period in eastern Japan. *Plos One, 11*, e0154809.

Crema, E. R., & Shoda, S. (2021). A Bayesian approach for fitting and comparing demographic growth models of radiocarbon dates: A case study on the Jomon-Yayoi transition in Kyushu (Japan). *Plos One, 16*(5), e0251695.

David, B. (2002). *Landscapes, rock-art and the Dreaming: An archaeology of preunderstanding*. London: Leicester University Press.

David, B., & Lourandos, H. (1997). 37,000 years and more in tropical Australia: Investigating long-term archaeological trends in Cape York Peninsula. *Proceedings of the Prehistoric Society, 63*, 1–23.

Davidson, I. (1990). Prehistoric Australian demography. In B. Meehan & N. White (Eds.), *Hunter-gatherer demography: Past and present* (pp. 41–58). Oceania Monograph 39. Sydney: University of Sydney.

Downey, S. S., Randall Hass Jr, W., & Shennan, S. J. (2016). European Neolithic societies showed early warning signals of population collapse. *Proceedings of the National Academy of Sciences of the United States of America, 113*(35), 9751–9756.

Flood, J. (1980). *The moth hunters. Aboriginal prehistory of the Australian Alps*. Canberra: Australian Institute of Aboriginal Studies.

Gamble, C., Davies, W., Pettitt, P., Hazelwood, L., & Richards, M. (2005). The archaeological and genetic foundations of the European population during the Late Glacial implications for 'agricultural thinking'. *Cambridge Archaeological Journal, 15*, 193–223.

Gayo, E. M., Latorre, C., & Santoro, C. M. (2015). Timing of occupation and regional settlement patterns revealed by time-series analyses of an archaeological radiocarbon database for the South-Central Andes (16°–25°S). *Quaternary International, 356*, 4–14.

Geyh, M. A. (1980). Holocene sea-level history: Case study of the statistical evaluation of 14C dates. *Radiocarbon, 22*(3), 695–704.

Gould, R. A. (1977). Puntutjarpa Rockshelter and the Australian desert culture. *Anthropological Papers of the American Museum of Natural History, 54*, 1–187.

Head, L. (1989). Prehistoric Aboriginal impacts on the Australian vegetation: An assessment of the evidence. *Australian Geographer, 20*, 37–45.

Head, L. (2000). *Second nature. The history and implications of Australia as Aboriginal landscape.* New York: Syracuse University Press.

Holdaway, S., & Porch, N. (1995). Cyclical patterns in the Pleistocene human occupation of southwest Tasmania. *Archaeology in Oceania, 30*, 74–82.

Holdaway, S., & Porch, N. (1996). Dates as data. In J. Allen (Ed.), *Report of the Southern Forests Archaeological Project. Volume 1—Site descriptions, stratigraphies and chronologies* (pp. 251–275). Bundoora: La Trobe University.

Holland-Lulewicz, J., & Ritchison, B. T. (2021). How many dates do I need? *Advances in Archaeological Practice, 2021*, 1–16

Horton, D. (2000). *The pure state of nature: Sacred cows, destructive myths and the environment.* St Leonards, NSW: Allen & Unwin.

Hughes, P. J., Sullivan, M. E., & Hiscock, P. (2017). Palaeoclimate and human occupation in southeastern arid Australia. *Quaternary Science Reviews, 163*, 72–83.

Johnson, C. N., & Brook, B. W. (2011). Reconstructing the dynamics of ancient human populations from radiocarbon dates: 10 000 years of population growth in Australia. *Proceedings of the Royal Society B, 278*, 3748–3754.

Kealy, S., Louys, J., & O'Connor, S. (2018). Least-cost pathway model indicate northern human dispersal from Sunda to Sahul. *Journal of Human Evolution, 125*, 59–70.

Keen, I. (2004). *Aboriginal economy and society: Australia at the threshold of colonisation.* South Melbourne: Oxford University Press.

Keen, I. (2021). Foragers or farmers: Dark Emu and the controversy over Aboriginal agriculture. *Anthropological Forum, 31*(1), 106–128.

Kohen, J. L. (1995). *Aboriginal environmental impacts.* Sydney: UNSW Press.

Lourandos, H. (1983). Intensification: A late Pleistocene-Holocene archaeological sequence from southwestern Victoria. *Archaeology in Oceania, 11*, 245–266.

Lourandos, H. (1993). Hunter-gatherer cultural dynamics: Long-and short-term trends in Australian prehistory. *Journal of Archaeological Research, 1*(1), 67–88.

Lourandos, H. (1997). *Continent of hunter-gatherers: New perspectives in Australian prehistory.* Cambridge: Cambridge University Press.

Lourandos, H., & David B. (1998). Comparing long-term archaeological and environmental trends: North Queensland, arid and semi-arid Australia. *The Artefact, 21*, 105–114.

McBryde, I. (1974). *Aboriginal prehistory in New England: An archaeological survey of north-eastern New South Wales.* Sydney: Sydney University Press.

McDonald, J. (2008). *Dreamtime superhighway: An analysis of Sydney Basin rock art and prehistoric information exchange.* Terra Australis 27. Canberra: ANU E-Press.

McNiven, I. J., Crouch, J., Richards, T., Dolby, N., Jacobsen, G., & Gunditj Mirring Traditional Owners Aboriginal Corporation. (2012). Dating Aboriginal stone-walled fishtraps at Lake Condah, southeast Australia. *Journal of Archaeological Science, 39*, 268–286.

Morrison, M., & Shepard, E. (2013). The archaeology of culturally modified trees: Indigenous economic diversification within colonial intercultural settings in Cape York Peninsula, northeastern Australia. *Journal of Field Archaeology, 38*(2), 143–160.

Mulvaney, D. J., & White, J. P. (1987) How many people? In D. J. Mulvaney & J. P. White (Eds.), *Australians to 1788* (pp. 114–119). Sydney: Fairfax, Syme & Weldon Associates.

O'Connell, J. F., & Allen, J. (2012). The restaurant at the end of the universe: Modelling the colonisation of Sahul. *Australian Archaeology, 74*, 5–17.

O'Connell, J. F., Allen, J., Williams, M. A. J., Cooper, A., Williams, A. N., Turney, C. S. M., . . . Brown, G. (2018). When did *Homo sapiens* first reach Southeast Asia and Sahul? *Proceedings of the National Academy of Sciences of the United States of America, 115*(34), 8482–8490. https://doi.org/10.1073/pnas.1808385115

O'Connor, S., Veth, P., & Hubbard, N. (1993). Changing interpretation of postglacial human subsistence and demography in Sahul. In M. A. Smith, M. Spriggs, & B. Fankhauser (Eds.), *Sahul in review* (pp. 95–108). Occasional Papers in Prehistory No. 24. Canberra: Department of Prehistory, Research School of Pacific Studies, The Australian National University.

Pennington, R. (2001). Hunter-gatherer demography. In C. Panter-Brick, R. H. Layton, & P. Rowley-Conwy (Eds.), *Hunter-gatherers: An interdisciplinary perspective* (pp. 170–204). Cambridge: Cambridge University Press.

Peros, M. C., Munoz, S. E., Gajewski, K., & Viau, A. E. (2010). Prehistoric demography of North America inferred from radiocarbon data. *Journal of Archaeological Science, 37*, 656–664.

Radcliffe-Brown, A. R. (1930). Former numbers and distribution of the Australian Aborigines. *Official Year Book, 23*, 688–696.

Reeves, J. M., Barrows, T. T., Cohen, T. J., Kiem, A. S., Bostock, H. C., Fitzsimmons, K. E., . . . OZ-INTIMATE Members (2013). Climate variability over the last 35,000 years recorded in marine and terrestrial archives in the Australian region: An OZ-INTIMATE compilation. *Quaternary Science Reviews, 74*, 21–34.

Rick, J. W. (1987). Dates as data: An examination of the Peruvian pre-ceramic radiocarbon record. *American Antiquity, 52*(1), 55–73.

Robinson, E., Zahid, H. J., Codding, B. F., Hass, R., & Kelly, R. L. (2019). Spatiotemporal dynamics of prehistoric human population growth: Radiocarbon 'dates as data' and population ecology models. *Journal of Archaeological Science, 101*, 63–71.

Ross, J. (2013). A continent of nations: The emergence of new regionally distinct rock art styles across Australia. *Quaternary International, 285*, 161–171.

Shennan, S., Downey, S. D., Timpson, A., Edinborough, K., Colledge, S., Kerig, T., . . . Thomas, M. G. (2013). Regional population collapse followed initial agricultural booms in mid-Holocene Europe. *Nature Communications, 4*, 2486. https://doi.org/10.1038/ncomms3486

Shennan, S., & Edinborough, K. (2007). Prehistoric population history: From the Late Glacial to the late Neolithic in central and northern Europe. *Journal of Archaeological Science, 34*, 1339–1345.

Smith, L. R. (1980) *The Aboriginal population of Australia*. Canberra: The Australian National University.

Smith, M. A. (1988). *The pattern and timing of prehistoric settlement in Central Australia* (PhD thesis). University of New England, Armidale.

Smith, M. A. (1989). The case for a resident human population in the Central Australian Ranges during full glacial aridity. *Archaeology in Oceania, 24*, 93–105.

Smith, M. A. (1993). Biogeography, human ecology and prehistory in the sandridge deserts. *Australian Archaeology, 37*, 35–50.

Smith M. A. (2005). Desert archaeology, linguistic stratigraphy and the spread of the Western Desert language. In P. Veth, M. Smith, & P. Hiscock (Eds.), *Desert peoples: Archaeological perspectives* (pp. 222–242). Oxford: Blackwell.

Smith, M. A. (2006). Characterising late Pleistocene and Holocene stone artefact assemblages from Puritjarra rock shelter: A long sequence from the Australian desert. *Records of the Australian Museum, 58*, 371–410.

Smith, M. A. (2013). *The archaeology of Australia's deserts.* New York: Cambridge University Press.

Smith, M. A. (2016). The use of summed-probability plots of radiocarbon data in archaeology. *Archaeology in Oceania, 51*(3), 214–215.

Smith, M. A. (2021). Historisizing the 'Dreaming': An archaeological perspective from arid Australia. In I. J. McNiven & B. David (Eds.), *The Oxford handbook of the archaeology of Indigenous Australia and New Guinea.* Oxford: Oxford University Press. https://doi.org/10.1093/oxfordhb/9780190095611.013.35

Smith, M. A., & Ross, J. (2008). What happened at 1500–1000 BP in central Australia? Timing, impact and archaeological signatures. *The Holocene, 18*(3), 387–396.

Smith, M. A., & Sharp, N. D. (1993). Pleistocene sites in Australia, New Guinea, and Island Melanesia: Geographic and temporal structure of the archaeological record. In M. A. Smith, M. Spriggs, & B. Fankhauser (Eds.), *Sahul in review* (pp. 37–59). Occasional Papers in Prehistory No. 24. Canberra: Department of Prehistory, Research School of Pacific Studies, The Australian National University.

Smith, M., Williams, A., & Ross, J. (2017). Puntutjarpa rock shelter revisited: A chronological and stratigraphic reappraisal of a key archaeological sequence for the Western Desert, Australia. *Australian Archaeology, 83*, 20–31.

Smith M. A., Williams, E., & Wasson, R. J. (1991). The archaeology of the JSN site: Some implications for the dynamics of human occupation in the Strzelecki Desert during the late Pleistocene. *Records of the South Australian Museum, 25*(2), 175–92.

Spry, C., Hayes, E., Allen, K., Long, A., Paton, L., Hua, Q., . . . Orange Local Aboriginal Land Council. (2020). Wala-gaay Guwingal: A twentieth century Aboriginal culturally modified tree with an embedded stone tool. *Australian Archaeology, 86*(1), 3–20.

Surovell, T. A., & Brantingham, P. J. (2007). A note on the use of temporal frequency distributions in studies of prehistoric demography. *Journal of Archaeological Science, 34*, 1868–1877.

Surovell, T. A., Byrd Finley, J., Smith, G. M., Brantingham, P. J., & Kelly, R. (2009). Correcting temporal frequency distributions for taphonomic bias. *Journal of Archaeological Science, 36*, 1715–1724.

Timpson, A., Collegde, S., Crema, E., Edinborough, K., Kerig, T., Manning, K., . . . Shennan, S. (2014). Reconstructing regional population fluctuations in the European Neolithic using radiocarbon dates: A new case-study using an improved method. *Journal of Archaeological Science, 52*, 549–557.

Tobler, R., Rohrlach, A., Soubrier, J., Bover, P., Llamas, B., Tuke, J., . . . Cooper, A. (2017). Aboriginal mitogenomes reveal 50,000 years of regionalism in Australia. *Nature, 544*, 180–184.

Torfing, T. (2015). Neolithic population and summed probability distribution of 14C-dates. *Journal of Archaeological Science, 63*, 193–198.

Ulm, S. (2011). Coastal foragers on southern shores: Marine resource use in northeast Australia since the late Pleistocene. In N. F. Bicho, J. A. Haws, & L. G. Davis (Eds.), *Trekking the shore: Changing coastlines and the antiquity of coastal settlement* (pp. 441–461). New York: Springer.

Ulm, S. (2013). 'Complexity' and the Australian continental narrative: Themes in the archaeology of Holocene Australia. *Quaternary International, 285*, 182–192.

Ulm, S., & Hall, J. (1996). Radiocarbon and cultural chronologies in southeast Queensland prehistory. In S. Ulm, I. Lilley, & A. Ross (Eds.), *Australian archaeology '95: Proceedings of the 1995 Australian Archaeological Association Annual Conference* (pp. 45–62). St. Lucia: University of Queensland.

Ulm, S., & Reid, J. (2000). Index of dates from archaeological sites in Queensland. *Queensland Archaeological Research, 12*, 1–129.

Veth, P. M. (1989). Islands in the interior: A model for the colonisation of Australia's arid zone. *Archaeology in Oceania, 24*, 81–92.

Veth, P. M. (1993). *Islands in the interior: The dynamics of prehistoric adaptations within the arid zone of Australia*. International Monographs in Prehistory. Ann Arbor, Michigan.

Veth, P. M., Hiscock, P., & Williams, A. N. (2011). Why the appearance of tulas in Australia is linked to ENSO. *Australian Archaeology, 72*, 7–14.

Wallis, L. A., Burke, H., & Dardengo, M. (2022). A comprehensive online database about the Native Mounted Police and frontier conflict in Queensland. *Journal of Genocide Research, 24*(3), 402–418. https://doi.org/10.1080/14623528.2020.1862489

Williams, A. N. (2012). The use of summed radiocarbon probability distributions in archaeology: A review of methods. *Journal of Archaeological Science, 39*, 578–589.

Williams, A. N. (2013). A new population curve for prehistoric Australia. *Proceedings of the Royal Society B, 280*, 20130486.

Williams, A. N., Atkinson, F., Lau, M., & Toms, P. (2014). A Glacial cryptic refuge in southeast Australia: Human occupation and mobility from 36,000 years ago in the Sydney Basin, New South Wales. *Journal of Quaternary Science, 29*(8), 735–748.

Williams, A. N., Mooney, S., Sisson, S., & Marlon, J. (2015). Exploration of the human-fire relationship of in Australia over the last 20,000 years. *Palaeogeography, Palaeoclimatology, Palaeoecology, 432*, 49–57.

Williams, A. N., & Smith, M. A. (2012). AustArch 2: A database of ^{14}C and luminescence ages from archaeological sites in the Top End. *Australian Archaeology, 74*, 146.

Williams A. N., & Smith, M. A. (2013). AustArch3: A database of ^{14}C and luminescence ages from archaeological sites in southern Australia. *Australian Archaeology, 76*, 102.

Williams, A. N., Smith, M. A., Turney, C. S. M., & Cupper, M. L. (2008). AustArch 1: A database of 14C and luminescence ages from archaeological sites in the Australian arid zone. *Australian Archaeology, 66*, 99.

Williams, A. N., & Ulm, S. (2016). Radiometric dates are a robust proxy for long-term demographic change: A comment on Attenbrow and Hiscock (2015). *Archaeology in Oceania, 51*(3), 216–217.

Williams, A. N., Ulm, S., Sapienza, T., Lewis, S., & Turney, C. S. M. (2018). Sea-level change and demography during the Last Glacial Termination and Early Holocene across the Australian continent. *Quaternary Science Reviews, 182*, 144–154.

Williams, A. N., Ulm, S., Smith, M. A., & Reid, J. (2014). AustArch: A database of ^{14}C and non-^{14}C ages from archaeological sites in Australia—Composition, compilation and review (Data Paper). *Internet Archaeology, 36*. https://doi.org/10.11141/ia.36.6

Williams, A. N., Ulm, S., Turney, C. S. M., Rodhe, D., & White, G. (2015). The establishment of complex society in prehistoric Australia: Demographic and mobility changes in the Late Holocene. *Plos One, 10*(6), e0128661

Williams, A. N., Veth, P. M., Steffen, W., Ulm, S., Turney, C. S. M., . . . Smith, M. (2015). A continental narrative: Human settlement patterns and Australian climate change over the last 35,000 Years. *Quaternary Science Reviews, 123*, 91–112.

CHAPTER 20

THE BIG FLOOD

*Responding to Sea-Level Rise and
the Inundated Continental Shelf*

JONATHAN BENJAMIN AND SEAN ULM

INTRODUCTION

FOR most of the human history of the continent, mainland Australia was joined to both New Guinea and Tasmania to form the supercontinent of Sahul (Figure 20.1). Given the scale and duration of low sea-level periods, the known onshore archaeological records dating to the Late Pleistocene and Early Holocene can only be considered to represent the inland components of past settlement. The lack of knowledge of the now submerged archaeological record is problematic because coastal occupation is considered central to understanding hominin dispersal and adaptation across the globe (Bailey et al. 2015; Clarkson et al. 2017; Dillehay, 2000; Williams, Ulm, Sapienza, Lewis, & Turney 2018).

A continental archaeological record that ignores the submerged coastal regions lost from view with rising sea levels can only be considered partial and should be viewed with scepticism since coastal populations and landscapes would have been important culturally and environmentally. The exposure of these coastal regions and subsequent inundation by postglacial sea-level rise must have dramatically impacted human lives, cultural traditions and interactions, population densities and dispersals, and social and economic conditions. More data, especially relative to coastal occupation, migration, and cultural adaptation, as well as responses to sea-level changes and lost landmasses, are available to archaeologists who are 'willing to get wet' and continue the archaeological search for the human past in what is the next frontier for world archaeology: the marine environment.

It was during the Late and Terminal Pleistocene and Early Holocene when sea levels fluctuated significantly that some of the major transformations of early human history took place. These include large and long-standing questions concerning

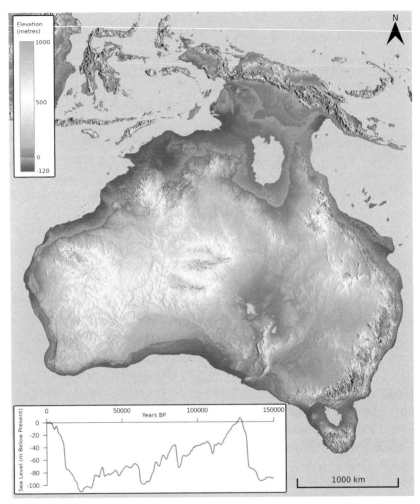

FIGURE 20.1. Continent of Sahul with darker shaded areas showing 2 million square kilometres of land inundated by Late Pleistocene and Early Holocene sea-level rise. Inset shows global sea-level change based on Red Sea deep sea oxygen isotope record (Grant et al. 2012).

human dispersals and routes out of Africa into Europe and Asia, and eventually Australia. The development of seafaring technology and diversification and intensification of palaeoeconomies (including marine resources) all took place during these periods (Bird et al. 2019; Fredericksen, Spriggs, & Ambrose 1993; Hawkins et al. 2017; Leavesley & Allen 1998; O'Connor, Ono, & Clarkson 2011; Veth et al. 2017). The exposed landmasses likely included favourable locations for hunter-gatherer settlement and dispersal, and included ample freshwater, desirable microclimates, ecological diversity, and the added value for marine resource exploitation and seaborne travel afforded by these rich palaeocoastlines (Bailey & Flemming 2008; Bailey, Galanidou, Peeters, Jöns, & Mennenga 2020; Bird, Taylor, & Hunt 2005; Faure, Walter,

& Grant 2002). These conditions could have supported relatively high population densities and, therefore, high concentrations of archaeological sites as compared to hinterlands. Yet, despite some scepticism about these possibilities (Mellars, Gori, Carr, Soares, & Richards 2013; Petraglia, Breeze, & Groucutt 2019), relatively little is known about the environments of these now-submerged landscapes, the lifeways of their human occupants, their role in patterns of human dispersal and development, or the impact of a sustained sea-level rise from a Last Glacial Maximum low of –130 m at c. 20 ka to reach the present level at c. 7000 cal BP. This dearth of knowledge is now set to change in Australia and, indeed, world archaeology in the twenty-first century (Bailey et al. 2020).

SUBMERGED LANDSCAPE ARCHAEOLOGY: INTERNATIONAL CONTEXT

Finding and investigating underwater environments, previously considered to be lost to the world of archaeology, is of global significance and represents a worldwide challenge. In Europe, Western Asia, and North America, thousands of submerged ancient sites have been documented, representing drowned cultural landscapes across a range of chronological periods and in various physical environments and depths below modern sea level.

The existence of submerged archaeology, in many cases strikingly well-preserved, clearly demonstrates the potential for survival and recovery of material from under water (Bailey et al. 2020; Benjamin, Bonsall, Pickard, & Fischer 2011; Evans, Flatman, & Flemming 2014; Masters & Flemming 1983) and in some cases can reshape the archaeological record or demonstrate early examples of human response to sea-level change (e.g., Galili et al. 2019). Interest in submerged landscape studies was recognized over a century ago. Early works included Boyd Dawkins (1870) and then Reid's (1913) seminal publication on *Submerged Forests*. These were amongst the earliest to insist that attention must be paid to submerged deposits as an archaeological resource. Grahame Clark's (1936) work on the *Mesolithic of Northern Europe* was influenced by the find of a barbed point (the Leman and Ower Harpoon) four years earlier by the crew of the English fishing trawler *Colinda*.

Throughout the second half of the twentieth century, underwater archaeologists mostly worked locally and in relative isolation, particularly in 'hot spot' regions of the southwest Baltic (Denmark) and Mediterranean Levant (Israel) from the 1970s onwards. In these latter regions, diving archaeologists identified known archaeological sites that were visible and accessible in shallow-water conditions. Significant underwater archaeological sites included Tybrind Vig (Andersen 1985) and Atlit Yam (Galili et al. 1993). The work undertaken by archaeologists diving in the Black Sea, particularly the Bulgarian coast, has been perhaps the most overlooked by the international community of scholars and is itself a significant 'hot spot' that was described by Draganov (1995) and more recently summarized by Peev et al. (2020), with work spanning over four decades.

In North America, submerged sites first began to be discussed amongst the archaeological community in the late 1950s (Goggin 1960), with serious scholarship ensuing in the 1960s and 1970s in the Gulf of Mexico and particularly off the coast of northwest Florida (see Garrison and Cook Hale 2021 for a recent review on the history of submerged landscape studies in North America). The Gulf of Mexico work, such as that highlighted by Anuskiewicz and Dunbar (1993) and Faught and Donoghue (1997), has given rise to serious consideration by the research and heritage management community in North America, which has led to other major projects funded and more community-focused work, such as that undertaken by Robinson, Gibson, Caccioppoli, & King (2020) and King, Robinson, Gibson, & Caccioppoli (2020).

The work in Europe and North America has led to the acknowledgement of the potential for significant submerged sites to make a qualitative impact on the regional archaeological record. This research has highlighted that the preservation conditions of underwater sites is sometimes better than that of terrestrial sites due to relatively stable, cool, and low-oxygen environmental conditions. These regions have also produced local 'models' for site prospection (Fischer 1995; Galili, Kolska Horwitz, & Rosen 2018) which articulate the process and theory behind the archaeological search for submerged sites and in situ deposits. Models for site prospection have been critiqued (Grøn 2018) and evaluated for further, wider international adaptation (Benjamin 2010). In Australia, a national model is not possible, owing to the scale of the issue and the variety of regional challenges and opportunities in the various environmental and cultural landscapes. However, regional models are now coming to light, with lessons learned from overseas and domestic experience (Wiseman et al. 2021).

Sahul Archaeology: Coastal and Submerged Cultural Landscapes

Coasts have long been considered as central to the earliest peopling of the Australian and New Guinea continent. Sahul has never been connected to Sunda, with multiple crossings of up to 100 km required to travel between islands across Wallacea to reach the Australian mainland (Bird et al. 2018, 2019; Kealy, Louys, & O'Connor 2018; Norman et al. 2018). Multiple colonization events with multiple entry points are likely, with the northwest Australian shelf modelled as the most likely route followed closely by the Bird's Head of west New Guinea (Bird et al. 2019; Bradshaw et al. 2019, 2021). Voyaging to Sahul was purposeful with large groups required for successful colonization, in the order of 1300 to 1550 people (Bradshaw et al. 2019). The earliest landfalls and settlements on the continent are now up to 130 m under water.

Early archaeological sites on precipitous shorelines or on islands close to the edge of the continental shelf indicate that the seafaring people who peopled Sahul continued to use coastal resources (Allen, Gosden, & White 1989; Codding, O'Connell, & Bird 2014; Fredericksen et al. 1993; Leavesley et al. 2002; Ulm 2011; Veth et al. 2017). For example, marine resources are well represented in faunal assemblages from Boodie Cave on Barrow Island off northwest Australia before 42,000 cal BP, with transport distances to the contemporary coastline up to 20 km (Veth et al. 2017). Similarly, in New Ireland in eastern Papua New Guinea, people used a range of coastal resources at the sites of Buang Merabek from 44,000 cal BP and at Matenkupkum from 41,000 cal BP (Leavesley & Allen 1998; Leavesley et al. 2002). All of these data point to the now submerged continental shelves around Australia hosting people over millennia.

Coasts are also considered important in the peopling of the rest of the Sahul continent. Bowdler (1977) argued that the earliest peopling would have been coastally oriented before moving to inland areas. These ideas are given support by recent genetic studies that suggest that people moved rapidly around the east and west coasts of Australia before meeting up in the south of the continent (Tobler et al. 2017). Recent modelling of the movement of people throughout Sahul show the now-submerged continental shelves as important conduits of movement and connectivity, including across the broad plains which once connected northern Australia to New Guinea (Crabtree et al. 2021). Some Australian Indigenous oral traditions retain detailed knowledge of drowned cultural landscapes (Nunn & Reid 2016).

With the recent discoveries of submerged sites confirmed along the west coast of Australia (Benjamin et al. 2018, 2020; Wiseman et al. 2021), it is reasonable to conclude that they also exist on the continental shelf around the entire continent and should be a focus for future research. These landscapes include important areas which previously connected now isolated environments, such as the submerged landmass between Australia and New Guinea, as well as the Bass Strait, separating mainland Australia from Tasmania. Further, there are countless smaller islands which were part of the mainland at various periods of human history on the continent. These and the submerged areas that now separate them are currently attracting greater consideration and integrated study through archaeological and marine scientific methods.

SUBMERGED LANDSCAPE ARCHAEOLOGY: EVIDENCE FROM AUSTRALIA

Historically, there have been relatively few submerged landscape archaeological studies in Australia, and maritime archaeology has focused almost entirely on the archaeology of recent historic periods, especially shipwrecks and maritime infrastructure of colonial and postcolonial eras. The pioneering Cootamundra Shoals survey (Flemming 1982) represented an early attempt to prospect for submerged sites in Australia, some

240 km northwest of Darwin. Flemming's team understood that the shoals represented high ground during periods of lower sea level and were a potential area of interest to investigate the entry by people into Australia. During a month of diving and marine survey, Flemming acknowledged the difficulties and challenges of marine scientific and archaeological work offshore. While greater emphasis on marine and diver-based scientific research has meant more understanding of potential offshore site locations, so, too, are there more constraints in place today as compared with a generation ago during Flemming's pioneering work. Modern considerations now include greater emphasis on health and safety risks and the increased cost implications, and specialist training and qualifications required by researchers and technical staff. While the archipelago and Cootamundra Shoals would have certainly been home to both fauna and flora that would have provided a pathway to Australia (Bird et al. 2018), no submerged cultural sites were encountered and no artefacts were recorded by Flemming's team. Instead, emphasis was placed on the importance of past landscape reconstruction to inform the survey plan. Nevertheless, this important early attempt to study the submerged landscape highlighted the potential for future studies.

Like Flemming before him, Dortch (1997, 2002) argued the case for investigating the potential for submerged material to be found in both freshwater and marine environments. Dortch (2002) undertook a pilot project in the Dampier Archipelago in Western Australia to locate rock art, specifically petroglyphs, on granophyre outcrops on what is now the seabed. Based on the extensive rock art assemblages found onshore at similar outcrops, Dortch (2002) established a basic model of where material existed and in locations that he thought would be conducive to the survival of sea-level transgressions. Dortch also considered the potential archaeology of the local area: lithic scatters, quarry sites, and material embedded in indurated carbonate deposits. Unlike Flemming's work, Dortch concluded that future surveys should deploy a comparatively modest, shore-based approach. His concerns, that locating rock art in the marine environment did not warrant the expenditure of a large seagoing expedition, are understandable. Marine work, particularly in the offshore environment can be costly. As Bailey (2014) noted, archaeologists should take some care to avoid repeated failure that could lead to disinterest or dismissal by the wider community. The possibility of chance finds in the archipelago, frequented by sports divers, was also emphasized by Dortch, which is in line with many of the international models, such as those practiced in the hotspots of Denmark and Israel (see Benjamin 2010; Fischer 1995; Galili et al. 2019).

Nutley has undertaken multiple reviews of the state of research in studies of inundated Indigenous sites in Australia, first as part of his graduate studies (Nutley 2005) and later to assess the preservation scenarios for various types of material culture frequently encountered in Australia, including shell middens, carved trees, bora rings, fish traps, stone artefacts, rock outcrops, rock shelters, and rock art (Nutley 2014). Nutley noted that fish traps, rocky outcrops, and caves or rock shelters remain relatively stable and are less likely to be impacted by marine transgressions than exposed, open-air sites, such as those found in Denmark. He therefore highlighted these as higher potential features for prospection (Nutley, Coroneos, & Wheeler 2016). Nutley (2014) also noted a previous lack of engagement and future need for Australian archaeology to continue submerged landscape research despite previous attempts and, until that point, a lack of positive results. The criteria outlined by Nutley (2014) represent an important phase of identifying preservation conditions in known examples to move towards the unknown since little work had been undertaken, and no confirmed offshore underwater sites had been discovered.

Other surveys, generally working in the intertidal zone, such as the studies in Cygnet Bay Tasmania (Lewczak & Wilby 2010), Flying Foam Passage (Dortch, Beckett, Paterson, & McDonald 2021) and North Gidley Island (Leach et al. 2021) Western Australia, McNiven (2004) in northeastern Australia, and Ulm (2006) in central Queensland, have documented archaeological material on coastal fringes within the intertidal zone. These sites demonstrate the importance of the intertidal zones. These are areas where material encountered may be indicative of further, deeper water sites, formed prior to relative stabilization (usually between c. 7000 and 5500 years ago, with other considerations for isostatic and tectonic adjustment). The intertidal zones in micro-tidal environments are smaller, whereas areas with larger tidal movements can provide other challenges in preservation and operational considerations for diver or snorkel survey. These intertidal zones, noted by Dortch (2002), should be the starting point for archaeological surveys, particularly those operating on smaller budgets, prior to pushing the archaeological boundaries offshore.

During the Deep History of Sea Country (DHSC) project, undertaken in collaboration with the Murujuga Aboriginal Corporation, submerged archaeological material was discovered through an iterative program of fieldwork in the Dampier Archipelago, Murujuga, Western Australia (Benjamin et al. 2020; Veth et al. 2020) (Figure 20.2). The DHSC team built on domestic and international work, by developing an iterative process and predictive model for site location that considered the onshore archaeological record, satellite and aerial data collection and interpretation, and geophysical surveys of seabed in search for conducive conditions for site visibility and preservation. Hot spots and high potential areas were then targeting and tested through snorkeller and diver investigations, with two new sites recorded below the low watermark and various other intertidal finds located around the archipelago. These new submerged sites include in situ lithic assemblages associated with submerged palaeochannels and freshwater billabongs, clearly demonstrating past human presence on a now drowned land surface. These discoveries demonstrate the potential and viability of underwater archaeological research in Australia and resulted in recommendations for a long-term strategy and the growth of a new research community to tackle the large and diverse coastal and marine environments flanking the Australian continent (Figure 20.3).

Methodologically, the DHSC project showed that through interdisciplinary marine/ geoarchaeological methods and a suite of regional and site-scale methods, it is possible to identify high-priority areas for diver-based investigation to produce archaeologically positive findspots and confirm the presence of underwater sites. While the Dampier Archipelago (Murujuga) was selected for its archaeologically rich cultural

FIGURE 20.2. Divers investigate the seabed and record lithic artefacts at Cape Bruguieres during the DHSC Project fieldwork.

(Photographs: S. Wright; see Benjamin et al. 2020.)

landscape, there is a strong likelihood of encountering archaeology offshore in a variety of conditions represented by Australia's continental shelf.

Discussion and Future Directions

In the past decade archaeological interest has increasingly focused on the 20 million km² of land that would have been available, even favourable, for human occupation during the low sea level of the Last Glacial Period across the globe. Exposure of this enormous scale of prior cultural landscapes and subsequent drowning by postglacial sea-level rise would have dramatically impacted global patterns of human population dispersal, cultural change and adaptations, and socioeconomic development. Archaeological evidence from underwater sites is critical to understanding these important processes that have helped define human history. The discovery of in situ lithic assemblages on Western Australia's continental shelf demonstrates past human use of a now-drowned land surface—it is a proof of concept that should change the face of archaeological practice as it represents the offshore extension of the terrestrial archaeological record. In New Guinea, the uplifted Bobongara terraces with archaeological

THE BIG FLOOD   549

FIGURE 20.3. Marine geophysical work can be complex and time consuming, but invaluable to underpin locations for diving prospection.

(Photograph: J. Benjamin.)

material dating to at least 40,000 and perhaps as early as 60,000 years ago provide additional contexts for investigating areas of the seabed that are now dry land (Groube, Chappell, Muke, & Price 1986). Investigating and understanding this record in partnership with Indigenous traditional owners and custodians present one of the last frontiers in the archaeology of Australia and New Guinea and one with enormous potential. The findings reported by the DHSC project, building on past work, demonstrate that underwater cultural material can survive inundation by sea-level rise in an Australian context, and that it can be located and studied using a combination of predictive modelling and an appropriate suite of underwater and remote-sensing techniques. The ambiguities over the depositional status of artefacts found in shallow water close to the present-day shoreline can be resolved through conventional archaeological and geoarchaeological analysis. In addition, evaluation of site formation hypotheses taking account of known and identifiable processes of coastal disturbance and change can help chronologically constrain seabed sites, as was the case at Cape Bruguieres, where a limiting date of preinundation (c. 7000 cal BP) was ascribed (Benjamin et al. 2020). However, the sites found in the Dampier Archipelago could be older, and further study is required to better reconcile the ages of those findings.

While Holocene material is only likely to be found in shallow waters (i.e., <20 m below mean sea level [MSL]), Pleistocene material is likely to be present in both shallow and deeper water as well as further offshore. Material from the Last Glacial Maximum may be located as deep as 130 m below current MSL. The combination of techniques and evidence trialled by the various projects cited earlier provides a baseline for features that could be preserved and identified through marine survey techniques. As such, we encourage future scholars working in Indigenous Archaeology to push the boundaries of coastal archaeology and to integrate offshore areas. Similarly, or perhaps conversely, we encourage those working in the more traditional field of maritime archaeology to train in and prepare for archaeological encounters and discoveries of all types and periods. This preparation may require greater understanding of flaked stone technology, or more consideration for the archaeological signature of older or more ephemeral features beyond shipwrecks or maritime installations. The recent results by the DHSC project represent a first step, and only by continuing along these lines will archaeology in Australia realize the potential of the vast and formerly productive continental shelves. Notably, the initial discovery of lithics on the now-submerged Pleistocene land surface of Cape Bruguieres channel was by John McCarthy and Chelsea Wiseman, two doctoral candidates from Flinders University who had been trained in submerged sites in Europe and the Middle East. That is, both archaeologists had previously encountered lithics in the marine environment and were able to transfer that skill set to an Australian context. However, there is now greater potential for training in Australia as submerged archaeology is no longer hypothetical. There is also a current need to consider these recent findings and their impact on the management and protection of submerged Indigenous heritage in subtidal jurisdictions. As we move from 'potential' to the 'confirmed' presence of submerged underwater cultural heritage in Australia, a much more robust discourse, involving government, industry, researchers, and Traditional Owners and custodians, becomes increasingly inevitable (McCarthy et al. 2021).

Archaeology of submerged environments spanning from the intertidal zone to deep water down to –130 m below modern sea levels will contribute to the archaeology of Australia and New Guinea in two main ways. Firstly, these data will fill in some of the nearshore gaps where coastal sites seem to end at the waterline. It is highly probable that nearshore shallow water sites will be found if appropriate investigations are undertaken as part of research projects or development-led archaeological investigations. Second, deeper water sites, particularly those encountered further offshore with continental shelves extending hundreds of kilometres, will provide evidence about large regions of the continent that remain entirely unknown. Knowledge of these areas will be vital for characterizing the diversity of lifeways of people across vast swathes of space and time in Sahul.

In the wake of international and recent studies, there is an opportunity to create a community of practice for submerged landscape archaeology in Australia. However, a single Australian model is unrealistic, unlike in Denmark and Israel. The continental scope and scale, variety and complexity of Sahul is diverse and complex. Models may develop, though they will be most useful at the regional or local scale. The size of the continent and its associated environmental diversity mean that there are too many variables for a single approach beyond the coarsest detail that relates to the two simple facts for all submerged archaeology: site formation and site preservation. Add to the equation the requirement for archaeological visibility and recognizability by archaeologists (or someone willing to inform a local archaeologist) and a generalized, coarse-scale model can be considered at a national level; though this model is but a mere starting point for more precise regional or local investigations and methodologies. The methods tested in the Dampier Archipelago may be relevant to the Pilbara coast, but only partially helpful in assessing areas that differ considerably in terms of environmental conditions. At a minimum, methods applied in Western Australia would require some level of adaptation. As an example, a sub-bottom profiler was not used on the sediment-starved shelf, as stratified sedimentary deposits in the Dampier Archipelago are rare, and this type of seismic survey would likely contribute little useful information. However, in other seabed contexts of Australia where previously terrestrial land surfaces (palaeosols) might be preserved, the application of sub-bottom profiler systems would be useful, particularly when coupled with other techniques such as a multibeam echosounder and geotechnical coring (see Astrup et al. 2020; Garriso 1992; Missiaen et al. 2017; Tizzard, Bicket, Benjamin, & De Loecker 2014). A combined approach to reconstruct past coastal environments and establish priority locations, as applied overseas, will support higher probability for archaeological material to be encountered by diver or drop-camera surveys.

Conclusion

We can now draw on both domestic and international experience to underpin the next generation of underwater cultural heritage management and submerged archaeological research practice in Australia and New Guinea. However, allowing a mature submerged landscape subdiscipline of archaeology to form and realize its full potential will require a new generation of scholars, students, practitioners, and interested and engaged community members who can work with industry, policymakers, and Traditional Owners and custodians. Results from remote sensing during the DHSC project have numerous methodological implications. The evaluation of how effective the terrestrial analogy can be in determining priority study areas for submerged landscape archaeology has both pros and cons. While known terrestrial sites on land and in intertidal zones will likely lead to more discoveries, it is also important to remember that models can generate a self-fulfilling prophecy; finding sites you expect to be there can perpetuate research bias. Rather, there is also a need for exploratory, blue-skies surveys, in areas where evidence is likely to produce new and possibly exciting data that are unpredictable, and which vary from the terrestrial record. Such research is potentially costly, which is why underwater cultural heritage management needs to collaborate with industry which collects seabed data for other purposes. Indeed, industry undertaking environmental predisturbance seabed surveys or monitoring will undoubtedly be important in the coming century of research in the marine environment.

The search from onshore to offshore should be continued. This strategy was demonstrably effective at Cape Bruguieres Channel, where archaeological material could be found in the intertidal zone, and dive teams were able to confirm a sub-tidal archaeological site. Terrestrial analogy as applied here is a useful contributing framework to identify prospective areas, and in the case of Cape Bruguieres Channel, has proved effective in locating archaeological material. However, preservation characteristics and postdepositional processes remain a significant factor. The combination of remote sensing, ground-truthing, and geological sampling is particularly important in determining the impact of formation and erosional processes over time, in conjunction with the application of terrestrial analogues. Thus, a multipronged, multiscalar approach to survey in both the nearshore shallows and deeper offshore environments which considers environmental and cultural variables must be encouraged for the potential of submerged landscape archaeology to be realized in the twenty-first century.

ACKNOWLEDGEMENTS

The authors thank Professor Geoff Bailey for his feedback on an earlier version of this chapter. We acknowledge the Deep History of Sea Country (DHSC) project team, and the various contributors, partners, and sponsors of the DHSC project as well as the ARC Centre of Excellence for Australian Biodiversity and Heritage (CABAH). The authors acknowledge the Australian Research Council for supporting the DHSC project through its Discovery Projects funding scheme (DP170100812), and CABAH through its Centre of Excellence scheme (CE170100015). Thanks to Damien O'Grady (James Cook University) for preparing Figure 20.1. The authors recognize Traditional Owner groups around Australia and respect their relationship with their ancestral lands and sea country.

REFERENCES

Allen, J., Gosden, C., & White, J. P. (1989). Human Pleistocene adaptations in the tropical island Pacific: Recent evidence from New Ireland, a Greater Australian outlier. *Antiquity, 63*(240), 548–561. https://doi.org/10.1017/S0003598X00076547

Andersen, S. H. (1985). Tybrind Vig: A preliminary report on a submerged Ertebølle settlement on the west coast of Fyn. *Journal of Danish Archaeology, 4*(1), 52–69. https://doi.org/10.1080/0108464X.1985.10589935

Anuskiewicz, R. J., & Dunbar, J. S. (1993). Evidence of prehistoric man at Ray Hole Springs: A drowned sinkhole located 32 km offshore on the continental shelf in 12 m seawater. In J. N. Heine & N. L. Crane (Eds.), *Diving for science . . . 1993: Proceedings of the American Academy of Underwater Sciences thirteenth annual scientific diving symposium* (pp. 1–11). Nahant, MA: American Academy of Underwater Sciences.

Astrup, P., Skriver, C., Benjamin, J., Stankiewicz, F., Ward, I., McCarthy, J., . . . Bailey, G. (2020). Underwater shell middens: Excavation and remote sensing of a submerged Mesolithic site at Hjarnø, Denmark. *The Journal of Island and Coastal Archaeology*, 15(5), 457–476. https://doi.org/10.1080/15564894.2019.1584135

Bailey, G. (2014). New developments in submerged prehistoric archaeology: An overview. In A. Evans, J. Flatman, & N. Flemming (Eds.), *Prehistoric archaeology on the continental shelf: A global review* (pp. 291–300). New York: Springer. https://doi.org/10.1007/978-1-4614-9635-9_16

Bailey, G. N., Devès, M. H., Inglis, R. H., Meredith-Williams, M. G., Momber, G., Sakellariou, D., . . . Alsharekh, A. M. (2015). Blue Arabia: Palaeolithic and underwater survey in SW Saudi Arabia and the role of coasts in Pleistocene dispersals. *Quaternary International*, 382, 42–57. https://doi.org/10.1016/j.quaint.2015.01.002

Bailey, G. N., & Flemming, N. C. (2008). Archaeology of the continental shelf: Marine resources, submerged landscapes and underwater archaeology. *Quaternary Science Reviews*, 27(23-24), 2153–2165. https://doi.org/10.1016/j.quascirev.2008.08.012

Bailey, G., Galanidou, N., Peeters, H., Jöns, H., & Mennenga, M. (Eds.) (2020). *The archaeology of Europe's drowned landscapes.* New York: Springer. https://doi.org/10.1007/978-3-030-37367-2

Benjamin, J. (2010). Submerged prehistoric landscapes and underwater site discovery: Reevaluating the 'Danish Model' for international practice. *The Journal of Island and Coastal Archaeology*, 5(2), 253–270. https://doi.org/10.1080/15564894.2010.506623

Benjamin, J., O'Leary, M., Ward, I., Hacker, J., Ulm, S., Veth, P., . . . Bailey, G. (2018). Underwater archaeology and submerged landscapes in Western Australia. *Antiquity*, 92(363), 1–9. https://doi.org/10.15184/aqy.2018.103

Benjamin, J., O'Leary, M., McDonald, J., Wiseman, C., McCarthy, J., Beckett, E., . . . Bailey, G. (2020). Aboriginal artefacts on the continental shelf reveal ancient drowned cultural landscapes in northwest Australia. *PLoS ONE*, 15(7), e0233912. https://doi.org/10.1371/journal.pone.0233912

Benjamin, J., Bonsall, C., Pickard, C., & Fischer, A. (2011). *Submerged prehistory*. Oxford: Oxbow Books.

Bird, M. I., Taylor, D., & Hunt, C. (2005). Palaeoenvironments of insular Southeast Asia during the Last Glacial Period: A savanna corridor in Sundaland? *Quaternary Science Reviews*, 24(20-21), 2228–2242. https://doi.org/10.1016/j.quascirev.2005.04.004

Bird, M. I., Beaman, R. J., Condie, S. A., Cooper, A., Ulm, S., & Veth, P. (2018). Palaeogeography and voyage modeling indicates early human colonization of Australia was likely from Timor-Roti. *Quaternary Science Reviews*, 191, 431–439. https://doi.org/10.1016/j.quascirev.2018.04.027

Bird, M. I., Condie, S. A., O'Connor, S., O'Grady, D., Reepmeyer, C., Ulm, S., & Bradshaw, C. J. A. (2019). Early human settlement of Sahul was not an accident. *Scientific Reports*, 9, 8220. https://doi.org/10.1038/s41598-019-42946-9

Bowdler, S. (1977). The coastal colonization of Australia. In J. Allen, J. Golson, & R. Jones (Eds.), *Sunda and Sahul: Prehistoric studies in South East Asia, Melanesia and Australia* (pp. 205–246). London: Academic Press.

Boyd Dawkins, W. 1870 On the discovery of flint and chert under a submerged forest in West Somerset. *The Journal of Ethnological Society of London* 2(2), 141-146.

Bradshaw, C. J. A., Norman, K., Ulm, S., Williams, A. N., Clarkson, C., Chadoeuf, J., . . . Saltré, F. (2021). Stochastic models support rapid peopling of Late Pleistocene Sahul. *Nature Communications, 12*, 2440. https://doi.org/10.1038/s41467-021-21551-3

Bradshaw, C. J. A., Ulm, S., Williams, A. N., Bird, M. I., Roberts, R. G., Jacobs, Z., & Saltré, F. (2019). Minimum founding populations for the first peopling of Sahul. *Nature Ecology & Evolution, 3*, 1057–1063. https://doi.org/10.1038/s41559-019-0902-6

Clark, J. G. D. (1936). *The Mesolithic settlement of Northern Europe: A study of the food-gathering peoples of Northern Europe during the early post-glacial period.* Cambridge: Cambridge University Press.

Clarkson, C., Jacobs, Z., Marwick, B., Fullagar, R., Wallis, L., Smith, M., . . . Pardoe, C. (2017). Human occupation of northern Australia by 65,000 years ago. *Nature, 547*, 306–310. https://doi.org/10.1038/nature22968

Codding, B. F., O'Connell, J. F., & Bird, D. W. (2014). Shellfishing and the colonization of Sahul: A multivariate model evaluating the dynamic effects of prey utility, transport considerations and life-history on foraging patterns and midden composition. *Journal of Island and Coastal Archaeology, 9*, 238–252. https://doi.org/10.1080/15564894.2013.848958

Crabtree, S. A., White, D. A., Bradshaw, C. J. A., Saltré, F., Williams, A. N., Beaman, R. J., . . . Ulm, S. (2021). Landscape rules predict optimal superhighways for the first peopling of Sahul. *Nature Human Behaviour, 5*, 1303–1313. https://doi.org/10.1038/s41562-021-01106-8

Dillehay, T. D. (2000). *The settlement of the Americas: A new prehistory.* New York: Basic Books.

Dortch, C. (1997). Prehistory down under: Archaeological investigations of submerged Aboriginal sites at Lake Jasper, Western Australia. *Antiquity, 71*(271), 116–123. https://doi.org/10.1017/S0003598X0008460X

Dortch, C. E. (2002). Preliminary underwater survey for rock engravings and other sea floor sites in the Dampier Archipelago, Pilbara region, Western Australia. *Australian Archaeology, 54*, 37–42. https://doi.org/10.1080/03122417.2002.11681739

Dortch, J., Beckett, E., Paterson, A., & McDonald, J. (2021). Stone artifacts in the intertidal zone, Dampier Archipelago: Evidence for a submerged coastal site in northwest Australia. *The Journal of Island and Coastal Archaeology, 16*(2–4), 509–523. https://doi.org/10.1080/15564894.2019.1666941

Draganov, V. (1995). Submerged coastal settlements from the Final Eneolithic and the Early Bronze Age in the sea around Sozopol and Urdoviza Bay near Kiten. In D. Bailey & I. Panayotov (Eds.), *Prehistoric Bulgaria* (pp. 225–241). Madison, WI: Prehistory Press.

Evans, A. M., Flatman, J. C., & Flemming, N. (2014). *Prehistoric archaeology on the continental shelf.* New York: Springer. https://doi.org/10.1007/978-1-4614-9635-9

Faught, M. K., & Donoghue, J. F. (1997). Marine inundated archaeological sites and paleofluvial systems: Examples from a karst-controlled continental shelf setting in Apalachee Bay, northeastern Gulf of Mexico. *Geoarchaeology, 12*(5), 417–458. https://doi.org/10.1002/(SICI)1520-6548(199708)12:5%3C417::AID-GEA1%3E3.0.CO;2-2

Faure, H., Walter, R. C., & Grant, D. R. (2002). The coastal Ice Age springs on emerged continental shelves. *Global Planetary Changes, 33*(1-2), 47–56. https://doi.org/10.1016/S0921-8181(02)00060-7

Fischer, A. (1995). An entrance to the Mesolithic world below the ocean: Status of ten years' work on the Danish sea floor. In A. Fischer (Ed.), *Man and sea in the Mesolithic: Coastal settlement above and below present sea level* (pp. 371–384). Oxford: Oxbow.

Flemming, N. C. (1982). Sirius expedition. Cootamundra Shoals Survey 1982. Expedition Report.

Fredericksen, C., Spriggs, M., & Ambrose, W. (1993). Pamwak rockshelter: A Pleistocene site on Manus Island, Papua New Guinea. In M. A. Smith, M. Spriggs, & B. Fankhauser (Eds.), *Sahul in review: Pleistocene archaeology in Australia, New Guinea and Island Melanesia* (pp. 144–152). Canberra: Australian National University.

Galili, E., Benjamin, J., Eshed, V., Rosen, B., McCarthy, J., & Kolska Horwitz, L. (2019). A submerged 7000-year-old village and seawall demonstrate earliest known coastal defence against sea-level rise. *PLoS ONE, 14*(12), e0222560. https://doi.org/10.1371/journal.pone.0222560

Galili, E., Kolska Horwitz, L., & Rosen, B. (2018). 'The Israeli Model' for the detection, excavation and research of submerged prehistory. *Turkish Institute for Nautical Archaeology (TINA) Maritime Archaeology Periodical, 10*.

Galili, E., Weinstein-Evron, M., Hershkovitz, I., Gopher, A., Kislev, M., Lernau, O., . . . Lernaut, H. (1993). Atlit-Yam: A prehistoric site on the sea floor off the Israeli coast. *Journal of Field Archaeology, 20*(2), 133–157. https://doi.org/10.1179/jfa.1993.20.2.133

Garrison, E. G. (1992). Recent archaeogeophysical studies of palaeoshorelines of the Gulf of Mexico. In L. L. Johnson & M. J. Stright (Eds.), *Paleoshorelines and prehistory: An investigation of method* (pp. 103–116). Boca Raton, FL: CRC Press.

Garrison, E. G., & Cook Hale, J. W. (2021). "The early days" – Underwater prehistoric archaeology in the USA and Canada. *The Journal of Island and Coastal Archaeology, 16*(1), 27–45. https://doi.org/10.1080/15564894.2020.1783399

Goggin, J. M. (1960). Underwater archaeology: Its nature and limitations. *American Antiquity, 25*(3), 348–354. https://doi.org/10.2307/277518

Grant, K. M., Rohling, E. J., Bar-Matthews, M., Ayalon, A., Medina-Elizalde, M., Bronk Ramsey, C., . . . Roberts, A. P. 2012 Rapid coupling between ice volume and polar temperature over the past 150,000 years. *Nature, 491*, 744–747.

Grøn, O. (2018). Some problems with modelling the positions of prehistoric hunter-gatherer settlements on the basis of landscape topography. *Journal of Archaeological Science: Reports, 20*, 192–199. https://doi.org/10.1016/j.jasrep.2018.04.034

Groube, L., Chappell, J., Muke, J., & Price, D. (1986). A 40,000 year-old human occupation site at Huon Peninsula, Papua New Guinea. *Nature, 324*, 453–455. https://doi.org/10.1038/324453a0

Hawkins, S., O'Connor, S., Maloney, T., Litster, M., Kealy, S., Fenner, J. N., & Louys, J. (2017). Oldest human occupation of Wallacea at Laili Cave, Timor-Leste, shows broad-spectrum foraging responses to Late Pleistocene environments. *Quaternary Science Reviews, 171*, 58–72. https://doi.org/10.1016/j.quascirev.2017.07.008

Kealy, S., Louys, J., & O'Connor, S. (2018). Least-cost pathway models indicate northern human dispersal from Sunda to Sahul. *Journal of Human Evolution, 125*, 59–70. https://doi.org/10.1016/j.jhevol.2018.10.003

King, J. W., Robinson, D. S., Gibson, C. L., & Caccioppoli, B. J. (2020). *Developing protocols for reconstructing submerged paleocultural landscapes and identifying ancient Native American archaeological sites in submerged environments: Final report*. Sterling, VA: US Department of the Interior, Bureau of Ocean Energy Management, Office of Renewable Energy. OCS Study BOEM 2020-023.

Leach, J., Wiseman, C., O'Leary, M., McDonald, J., McCarthy, J., Morrison, P., . . . Benjamin, J. (2021). The integrated cultural landscape of North Gidley Island: Coastal, intertidal and nearshore archaeology in Murujuga (Dampier Archipelago), Western Australia. *Australian Archaeology, 87*(3), 251–267. https://doi.org/10.1080/03122417.2021.1949085

Leavesley, M., & Allen, J. (1998). Dates, disturbance and artefact distributions: Another analysis of Buang Merabak, a Pleistocene site on New Ireland, Papua New Guinea. *Archaeology in Oceania, 33*(2), 63–82. https://doi.org/10.1002/j.1834-4453.1998.tb00405.x

Leavesley, M. G., Bird, M. I., Fifield, L. K., Hausladen, Santos, G. M., & di Tada, M. L. (2002). Buang Merabak: Early evidence for human occupation in the Bismarck Archipelago, Papua New Guinea. *Australian Archaeology, 54,* 55–57. https://doi.org/10.1080/03122 417.2002.11682070

Lewczak, C., & Wilby, C. (2010). *Aboriginal quarry site, Rocky Point, Port Cygnet: Maritime archaeological investigation.* Report for Southeast Tasmania Aboriginal Corporation. Cosmos Archaeology.

Masters, P. M., & Flemming, N. C. (Eds.) (1983). *Quaternary coastlines and marine archaeology: Towards the prehistory of land bridges and continental shelves.* London: Academic Press.

McCarthy, J., Wiseman, C., Woo, K., Steinberg, D., O'Leary, M., Wesley, D., . . . Benjamin, J. (2021). Beneath the Top End: a regional assessment of submerged archaeological potential in the Northern Territory, Australia. *Australian Archaeology, 88*(1), 65–83 https://doi.org/10.1080/0 3122417.2021.1960248

McNiven, I. J. (2004). Saltwater people: Spiritscapes, maritime rituals and the archaeology of Australian Indigenous seascapes. *World Archaeology, 35*(3), 329–349. https://doi.org/ 10.1080/0043824042000185757

Mellars, P., Gori, K. C., Carr, M., Soares, P. A., & Richards, M. B. (2013). Genetic and archaeological perspectives on the initial modern human colonization of southern Asia. *Proceedings of the National Academy of Sciences of the United States of America, 110*(26), 10699–10704. https://doi.org/10.1073/pnas.1306043110

Missiaen, T., Pieters, M., Maes, F., Kruiver, P., De Maeyer, P., & Seys, J. (2017). The SeArch Project: Towards an assessment methodology and sustainable management policy for the archaeological heritage of the North Sea in Belgium. In G. Bailey, J. Harff, & D. Sakellariou (Eds.), *Under the sea: Archaeology and palaeolandscapes of the continental shelf* (pp. 415–424). Cham: Springer. https://doi.org/10.1007/978-3-319-53160-1_27

Norman, K., Inglis, J., Clarkson, C., Faith, J. T., Shulmeister, J., & Harris, D. (2018). An early colonisation pathway into northwest Australia 70–60,000 years ago. *Quaternary Science Reviews, 180,* 229–239. https://doi.org/10.1016/j.quascirev.2017.11.023

Nunn, P. D., & Reid, N. J. (2016). Aboriginal memories of inundation of the Australian coast dating from more than 7000 years ago. *Australian Geographer, 47*(1), 11–47. https://doi.org/ 10.1080/00049182.2015.1077539

Nutley, D. (2005). *Surviving inundation: An examination of environmental factors influencing the survival of inundated Indigenous sites in Australia within defined hydrodynamic and geological settings* (Unpublished MMA thesis). Flinders University, Adelaide.

Nutley, D. (2014). *Inundated site studies in Australia.* In A. Evans, J. Flatman, & N. Flemming (Eds.), *Prehistoric archaeology on the continental shelf: A global review* (pp. 255–273). New York: Springer. https://doi.org/10.1007/978-1-4614-9635-9_14

Nutley, D. M., Coroneos, C., & Wheeler, J. (2016). Potential submerged Aboriginal archaeological sites in South West Arm, Port Hacking, New South Wales, Australia. In J. Harff, G. Bailey, & F. Lüth (Eds.), *Geology and archaeology: Submerged landscapes of the continental shelf* (pp. 265–285). London: Geological Society of London. https://doi.org/10.1144/SP411.3

Peev, P., Farr, R. H., Slavchev, V., Grant, M. J., Adams, J., & Bailey, G. (2020). Bulgaria: Sea-level change and submerged settlements on the Black Sea. In G. Bailey, N. Galanidou, H. Peeters, H. Jöns, & M. Mennenga (Eds.), *The archaeology of Europe's drowned landscapes* (pp. 393–412). Cham: Springer. https://doi.org/10.1007/978-3-030-37367-2_20

Petraglia, M. D., Breeze, P. S., & Groucutt, H. S. (2019). Blue Arabia, green Arabia: Examining human colonisation and dispersal models. In N. Rasul & I. Stewart (Eds.), *Geological setting, palaeoenvironment and archaeology of the Red Sea* (pp. 675–683). Cham: Springer. https://doi.org/10.1007/978-3-319-99408-6_30

O'Connor, S., Ono, R., & Clarkson, C. (2011). Pelagic fishing at 42,000 years before the present and the maritime skills of modern humans. *Science, 334,* 1117–1121. https://doi.org/10.1126/science.1207703

Reid, C. (1913). *Submerged forests.* London: Cambridge University Press.

Robinson, D. S., Gibson, C. L., Caccioppoli, B. J., & King, J. W. (2020). *Developing protocols for reconstructing submerged paleocultural landscapes and identifying ancient Native American archaeological sites in submerged environments: Geoarchaeological modeling.* Sterling, VA: US Department of the Interior, Bureau of Ocean Energy Management. OCS Study BOEM 2020-024.

Tizzard, L., Bicket, A. R., Benjamin, J., & De Loecker, D. (2014). A Middle Palaeolithic site in the southern North Sea: Investigating the archaeology and palaeogeography of Area 240. *Journal of Quaternary Science, 29*(7), 698–710. https://doi.org/10.1002/jqs.2743

Tobler, R., Rohrlach, A., Soubrier, J., Bover, P., Llamas, B., Tuke, J., . . . Cooper, A. (2017). Aboriginal mitogenomes reveal 50,000 years of regionalism in Australia. *Nature, 544,* 180–184. https://doi.org/10.1038/nature21416.

Ulm, S. (2006). *Coastal themes: An archaeology of the Southern Curtis Coast, Queensland.* Canberra: ANUE Press.

Ulm, S. (2011). Coastal foragers on southern shores: Marine resource use in northeast Australia since the Late Pleistocene. In N. F. Bicho, J. A. Haws, & L. G. Davis (Eds.), *Trekking the shore: Changing coastlines and the antiquity of coastal settlement* (pp. 441–461). New York: Springer. https://doi.org/10.1007/978-1-4419-8219-3_19

Veth, P., McDonald, J., Ward, I., O'Leary, M., Beckett, E., Benjamin, J., . . . Bailey, G. (2020). A strategy for assessing continuity in terrestrial and maritime landscapes from Murujuga (Dampier Archipelago), North West Shelf, Australia. *The Journal of Island and Coastal Archaeology, 15*(4), 477–503. https://doi.org/10.1080/15564894.2019.1572677

Veth, P., Ward, I., Manne, T., Ulm, S., Ditchfield, K., Dortch, J., . . . Kendrick, P. (2017). Early human occupation of a maritime desert, Barrow Island, north-west Australia. *Quaternary Science Reviews, 168,* 19–29. https://doi.org/10.1016/j.quascirev.2017.05.002

Williams, A. N., Ulm, S., Sapienza, T., Lewis, S., & Turney, C. S. (2018). Sea-level change and demography during the last glacial termination and early Holocene across the Australian continent. *Quaternary Science Reviews, 182,* 144–154. https://doi.org/10.1016/j.quascirev.2017.11.030

Wiseman, C., O'Leary, M., Hacker, J., Stankiewicz, F., McCarthy, J., Beckett, E., . . . Benjamin, J. (2021). A multi-scalar approach to marine survey and underwater archaeological site prospection in Murujuga, Western Australia. *Quaternary International, 584,* 152–170. https://doi.org/10.1016/j.quaint.2020.09.005

CHAPTER 21

DATING ROCK ART

A Kimberley Perspective

HELEN GREEN, DAMIEN FINCH,
ANDREW GLEADOW, RÉKA-H. FÜLÖP,
AND ZENOBIA JACOBS

INTRODUCTION

ROCK art provides an insight into the past in a way that no other archive can, representing the world's most widespread and enduring record of human symbolic activity. Rock art records evidence for the emergence of modern human cognition, complex abstract reasoning, and symbolic behaviour, potentially from premodern human species or subspecies that no longer exist (Hoffman et al. 2018). The durable landscapes in which rock art is often found offer a means by which important human experiences and events were transferred between different groups and across generations. However, it is only by reliably and accurately dating rock art across varied spatial scales extending to the global that we can better understand its spatial history and the development of cognitive abilities within our species. Dating rock art also allows us to correlate subjects depicted in the art with occupation deposits, ethnographic information, and records of past events, including changes in social relations, population, climate, and sea level, helping to build a global picture of how and when we came to be who we are today.

In some regions of the world, rock art has been dated with great success, positioning the history of important cultural sites on absolute timescales and facilitating the integration of rock art within a broader archaeological context (e.g., Quiles et al. 2016). Direct dating of components of rock art 'paints' (pigments made of potentially multiple constituents such as colourants and fixatives, the total composition of which are often called 'paint pots' in Europe) usually provides ages as close to the timing of the art as possible, although the 'old charcoal' problem (reuse of charcoal found on or in the ground) remains. However, dating the art directly by dating the pigment is only achievable in areas where charcoal has been used as the rock marking medium (e.g., Quiles et al. 2016; Valladas et al. 2001) or where organic particles have been preserved in the painting, such as paint-fibres or other kinds of organic binders (e.g., Watchman & Cole 1993). In regions where ochres (mostly iron oxide minerals) are the preferred pigment choice, insufficient organic material usually means that the direct dating of rock art is not possible (Ward, Watchman, Cole, & Morwood 2001). In regions lacking organic pigments, research has instead focused on the dating of associated materials with the potential to provide indirect, bracketing ages for the rock art, in particular accreted deposits below and/or above the art. Methods which date geomorphological 'events' related to cave and rock shelter formation and evolution can provide age constraints for any art found on the walls and ceilings (e.g., Genuite et al. 2021; Sadier et al. 2012), whilst techniques applied to rock surface coatings and fossilized insect nests provide constraints for the under or overlying motif (e.g., Finch et al. 2020, 2021; Jones et al. 2017; Roberts et al. 1997).

Some rock art dating campaigns have challenged conventional ideas about the origin of modern human cognition and symbolic expression. Radiocarbon ages from Chauvet Cave in France significantly impacted commonly accepted theories of the evolution of prehistoric art (Valladas et al. 2001). Such theories have long positioned Europe as the 'cradle' of modern human symbolic evolution, simply because since the late 1800s, academic rock art research and the discovery of demonstrably ancient rock art well-preserved in deep caves had come from Europe. However, 100,000-year-old findings in South Africa identified the symbolic use of substances with evidence of paint mixing (Henshilwood et al. 2011) and abstract art in the form of engraved ochre and ostrich eggshell fragments (Tylén et al. 2020), suggesting the capacity for rock art by the first fully modern humans.

Dating of rock art in Southeast Asia has demonstrated the presence of some of the world's earliest known rock art outside of Europe. In 2014, the Uranium-Thorium (U-Th) dating of speleothems overlying rock art in Sulawesi implied that humans were engaging in symbolic practices by 40 thousand years (ka) ago, at opposite ends of the Pleistocene Eurasian world where the origins of art were supposed to have taken place (Aubert et al. 2014). More recently again, painted art in Spain has been dated to at least 64.8 ka (Hoffman et al. 2018), making it the world's oldest dated rock art by a significant margin, and signaling that late Neanderthals had the cognitive abilities to make and use abstract visual symbols (Appenzeller 2018).

In Europe the earliest known modern humans date to c. 44,000 cal BP (Fewlass et al. 2020; Hublin et al. 2020). However, modern humans have been in Australia since at least 48,000 cal BP (Tobler et al. 2017), with widespread agreement for an even earlier date between 50,000 and 65,000 years ago (Clarkson et al. 2017), suggesting great potential to explore long sequences of modern human art. Some of the world's richest and most complex repertoires of rock art are found in northern Australia, with sequences of stylistic changes suggesting an extensive depth in time (Morwood, Walsh, & Watchman 1994; Watchman & Jones 1998). Australian rock art represents a fundamental part of a cultural landscape created by the ancestors of those who remain on Country, with rock art paintings continuing to be created to the present day (Chalarimeri 2001). Until recently, difficulties in dating Australian rock art have resulted in very few quantitative ages for or relating to rock art, and until the mid- to late 1980s a marginalization of the study of rock art across much of the world. Due to these dating difficulties, and despite aspirations to the contrary, rock art was poorly connected to archaeological understandings of the geography of our species' cognitive evolution. This chapter highlights recent advances in the dating of Australia's rock art, using the Kimberley region (NW Western Australia) as a case study to identify the requirements, challenges, and further potential of rock art dating.

Chronologies can be relative or absolute, and here we only address the dating of pictographs (pigment art) through absolute methods, rather than superimposition or interpretation of the subject matter depicted. Direct rock art dating requires that the archaeological item itself (i.e., pigment) is dated. However, a preference for ochre as the principal rock marking medium, and the unfavourable preservation conditions for charcoal on Kimberley rock surfaces, makes dating particularly difficult. Instead, much of the dating has been indirect, focused on the dating of materials that can provide minimum, maximum, or bracketing age constraints for associated motifs. Many rock art studies now employ interdisciplinary approaches when building chronological frameworks that reveal not only the age of the art but also periods of human occupation and how these relate to geomorphological transformations in the cultural sites in question. A range of dating techniques has been applied to Kimberley rock shelters to overcome the challenges presented by the environment in which the art is found. The adaptation of current techniques and approaches applied to sites in the Kimberley are relevant to the global rock art research community.

Rock Shelter Formation

The great majority of Kimberley rock art is found in sandstone terranes of the Paleoproterozoic Kimberley Basin, especially in two of its stratigraphic units: the Wumaamin Miliwundi (formerly King Leopold) Sandstone and the Warton Sandstone (Donaldson 2012). Across most of the basin, these sandstone formations are essentially flat-lying and undeformed, although they are heavily jointed on a regional scale and locally fractured. Massive quartz sandstone beds within these formations are typically 1–3 m thick and highly resistant to chemical weathering. They erode largely by mass wasting (Cazes et al. 2020), which creates, and eventually destroys, the rock shelters that host rock art. The landscape evolution processes involved are therefore important in providing control on the survival of rock art in the area.

Typical rock art shelters in the Kimberley Basin have a series of recurring characteristics which reflect their formation mechanisms. Most have rocky floors, and the deepest part of the shelters occur close to the base. The back walls of the shelters are fracture surfaces that are mostly oriented at high angles, generally sloping backwards towards the deepest recess and with a rounded (convex) lower edge and sharp upper junction at a bedding plane with a horizontal ceiling. These back walls and ceilings tend to be favoured locations for rock paintings. The floors of the shelters frequently contain fallen slabs or boulders representing sandstone strata that have fallen in one or more episodes of ceiling collapse.

The formation of these rock shelters can be understood in terms of a sequence that begins with deep erosion of weaker mudstone or shale interbeds near the shelter floor that progressively undermines the overlying sandstone beds. On occasion, such undermining may penetrate as much as 4–5 m inwards from the shelter opening to form a low bedding cave (i.e., one excavated by erosional removal of a particular bed) that is only about 0.5–1 m high. Subsequent ceiling collapse, often by intact slab falls, creates a new back wall and ceiling which may then be painted upon. The fallen slabs frequently remain intact but tend to slide outwards to greater or lesser degree, often leaving a gap or large cavity in front of the new back wall. In other cases, the fallen blocks may break up into smaller boulders, which disperse more widely downslope (Genuite et al. 2021).

Further enlargement of a rock shelter may then occur by additional overhanging slab falls that tend to step outwards towards the front of the shelter, creating a tiered sequence of stepped ceilings and a roughly triangular cross-section for the overall shelter. Eventually, such broadly overhanging rock shelters become unstable, especially with continued undermining, and eventually topple forwards to destroy the rock shelter, either completely or in part. This final collapse of the rock shelter is facilitated by the deeply penetrating joint planes that break up the continuity of the sandstone beds.

An important consequence of this developmental sequence for the rock shelters is that the back wall and ceiling rock surfaces which are the primary substrates for rock art are transitory features of the landscape. However, dating of the rock art (Finch et al. 2020, 2021) and accumulation of mineral accretions on rock surfaces (Green, Gleadow, Finch, Myers, & McGovern 2021; Green et al. 2021a) show that shelter-forming process rates are sufficiently slow that rock surfaces may survive for periods of up to tens of thousands of years.

Cosmogenic Nuclide Dating

Cosmogenic nuclides are produced by the interaction of high-energy cosmic particles with target nuclei in Earth's atmosphere (termed *meteoric* cosmogenic nuclides) and within the upper few metres of the Earth's surface (termed *in situ* cosmogenic nuclides) (Lal 1991). A number of these in-situ-produced cosmogenic nuclides, namely, ^{26}Al, ^{10}Be, ^{14}C, ^{36}Cl, ^{3}He, and ^{21}Ne, have been routinely used in the Earth Sciences for more than three decades (Blanckenburg & Willenbring 2014; Dunai 2010), making important contributions to the reconstruction of Quaternary glaciations (Ivy-Ochs & Briner 2014) and revolutionizing the field of quantitative geomorphology (Dixon & Riebe 2014; Granger & Schaller 2014). Applications to the field of archaeology have been more

DATING ROCK ART 563

limited (see review by Akçar, Ivy-Ochs, & Schlüchter 2008), but gaining traction, with a recent increased interest in applying the technique of burial dating to fossil-bearing sediments in both cave and open settings (e.g., Carbonell et al. 2008; Granger et al. 2015; Kuman et al. 2021; Luo et al. 2020; Partridge, Granger, Caffee, & Clarke 2003).

Method

The application of in-situ-produced cosmogenic nuclides to the study of sedimentary deposits is based on two principles: (a) the concentration of cosmogenic nuclides is proportional to the duration of exposure to cosmic radiation (i.e., concentration is proportional to 'age'); and (b) the ratio of two cosmogenic nuclides—where at least one nuclide is radioactive—will decrease from a set value (i.e., the production ratio) in proportion to the duration of shielding from cosmic radiation by burial (i.e., ratio is proportional to 'age'). The first principle is behind surface exposure dating (Anderson, Repka, & Dick 1996; Hidy, Gosse, Pederson, Mattern, & Finkel 2010; Repka, Anderson, & Finkel 1997), whereas the second principle is the basis of burial dating (Balco & Rovey 2008; Granger 2006).

Surface exposure dating is the simplest and most straightforward application of cosmogenic nuclide analysis and is also the most relevant to the dating of rock art shelters. The temporal evolution of the concentration of a cosmogenic nuclide in an exposed surface that is not eroding is described by the following equation (Lal 1991):

$$N(z,t) = N(z,0)e^{-\lambda t} + \frac{1-e^{-\lambda t}}{\lambda}\sum_{i=1}^{n}P(0)_{i}e^{-\rho z/\Lambda_{i}} \tag{1}$$

where $N(z, 0)$ is the initial (i.e., inherited) nuclide concentration, λ is the decay constant (for radionuclides), z is depth beneath the surface (cm)—zero for samples collected at the surface, t is exposure time (yr), ρ is density of the sampled material (g.cm^{-3}), and $P(0)$ and Λ_{i} are the surface cosmogenic nuclide production rate (atoms.g^{-1}yr^{-1}) and the mean cosmic ray attenuation length with depth [g.cm^{-2}] for a given production pathway, respectively (Granger & Smith 2000). Assuming no inherited nuclide concentration and neglecting muons that only account for a few percent of total production rate at the surface, the exposure age (T) is calculated from:

$$T = -\frac{1}{\lambda}ln\left[1-\frac{N(z,T)\lambda}{P(0)e^{-\rho z/\Lambda}}\right] \tag{2}$$

Although straightforward, there are two aspects of exposure dating that limit the applicability of the technique to dating archeological structures or artefacts (e.g., stone tools) directly (Akçar et al. 2008). First, the inherited concentration $N(z,0)$ cannot always be considered negligible. Second, the sample latitude and altitude values used to calculate the nuclide production rate $P(0)$ (Lifton, Sato, & Dunai 2014) might have changed over time, via sediment reworking for example. Despite these limitations, exposure dating of some artefacts can provide maximum limiting ages (e.g., Ivy-Ochs, Wüst, Kubik, Müller-Beck, & Schlüchter 2001) that in the absence of any other chronological data may still be valuable. Moreover, if chronological control is already available via other dating techniques, the complications related to inherited concentration and production rate may be exploited to provide additional, culturally important information (e.g., Verri et al. 2004, 2005).

Application to Rock Art

It is important to note that cosmogenic nuclide exposure dating cannot be applied to the dating of rock art directly. Instead, the method is used to date a geomorphological 'event' that either predates or postdates the art and therefore provides maximum or minimum ages, respectively. The first study to employ cosmogenic exposure dating to rock art was Phillips, Flinch, Elmore, and Sharma (1997), who used [36]Cl dating of schist panels with rock engravings in the Côa Valley (Portugal). Similarly, Pillans and Fifield (2013) used [10]Be to calculate long-term erosion rates for rock surfaces on Burrup Peninsula, Western Australia, suggesting that rock engravings found on these surfaces could survive for up to 60 ka based on the low rates of erosion and therefore lending support to the view that the engravings could be up to 30 ka old (e.g., Mulvaney 2011). Unlike Phillips et al. (1997) and Pillans and Fifield (2013) who provide maximum ages for the rock art, Sadier et al. (2012) used [36]Cl in samples from rock-fall scars at the entrance of Chauvet Cave in France to date a progressive sequence of cliff collapses and final closure of the cave to people and animals c. 22 ka, thus providing a minimum age for the art and fossils found in the cave.

The episodic nature of the processes that lead to the formation of rock shelters dotting the Kimberley landscape means that the principles behind Sadier et al. (2012) are readily applicable to Kimberley's rock art: dating the timing of rock shelter ceiling collapse by slab fall will provide a limiting age for the rock art found in the shelter. Depending on the geometry and dimensions of the rock shelter, the inherited nuclide concentration in the fallen slab may be substantial (i.e., $N(z_0,0) \gg 0$), and so the dating of ceiling collapse requires at least two measurements: one from a sample collected from the surface of the fallen slab, and one from a conjugate sample collected from the rock shelter ceiling (Figure 21.1). The age of ceiling collapse can thus be expressed as:

$$T \propto [N_{slab} - N_{ceiling}]/P(0)S_{slab} \tag{3}$$

where N_{slab} and $N_{ceiling}$ are the measured cosmogenic nuclide concentrations in the slab and conjugate ceiling sample, respectively, and S_{slab} is the topographic shielding correction factor for the slab sample (Dunne, Elmore, & Muzikar 1999). The latter is a key parameter that is difficult to estimate accurately for landforms with complicated geometries such as rock shelters (cf., Balco, Purvance, & Rood 2011) and so will likely dominate the uncertainty of the age that is calculated.

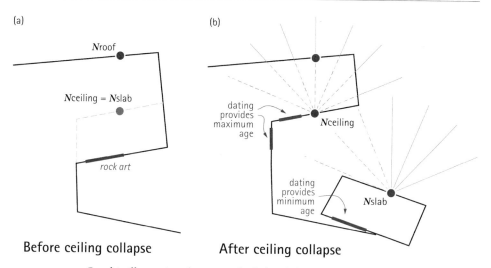

FIGURE 21.1. Graphic illustrating the principles behind the application of cosmogenic nuclide analysis for dating rock art. Green circles represent sampling locations, and blue lines depict the cosmic ray flux. Solid blue lines represent unobstructed cosmic rays, whereas dashed blue lines represent the proportion of the flux blocked because of topographic shielding. The obtained age is a maximum age for any art found on the freshly exposed ceiling and back panels and a minimum age for any art located on the underside of the fallen slab.

In addition to the slab and ceiling sample pair, collecting a third sample from the roof of the shelter, directly above the ceiling sample, is recommended as this will allow for estimating any nuclide accumulation in the ceiling sample that might have occurred following ceiling collapse. Accumulation of cosmogenic nuclides in the ceiling sample will result in a lower calculated age. For slabs that have a relatively unobstructed view of the sky, S_{slab} may be estimated in the field. However, where shielding geometry is more complex, a three-dimensional model of the shelter and surrounding topography is necessary to numerically calculate a shielding value (e.g., Balco et al. 2011).

Criticisms and Limitations

Both Phillips et al. (1997) and Pillans and Fifield (2013) received considerable criticism, mainly because the ages that their findings implied were too old and inconsistent with other evidence (e.g., Bednarik 1998; Watchman, Taçon, & Aubert 2014). However, it should be noted that both papers put forward a maximum age limit for the art based on the 'age' or preservation potential of the 'canvas' on which the engravings were made, rather than an age for the art itself. As noted earlier, cosmogenic nuclides may be used to date a geomorphic event—such as the collapse of a ceiling in a rock shelter—that will predate or postdate the art, and this will only provide a maximum or minimum age for the art. The usefulness of such ages will depend on many factors and needs to be considered on a case-by-case basis. The slow denudation rates reported for the Kimberley region by Cazes et al. (2020) imply that cosmogenic nuclide-derived maximum ages for rock art may in many instances substantially exceed the earliest timing for the peopling of the Australian continent but are nevertheless valid as maximum age estimates.

Future Directions

Given the geomorphic stability of the Kimberley landscape and the low rates of landscape lowering recorded (i.e., <<10 mm kyr^{-1}; Cazes et al. 2020), applying cosmogenic nuclides to dating rock shelter formation will be of most use where minimum ages may be obtained (e.g., rock art is present on the bottom of a fallen slab) or where the method is applied in conjunction with other techniques so that bracketing ages are obtained. Improvements will also be achieved from approaches that allow accurate calculation of S_{slab}, such as accurate and detailed three-dimensional reconstruction of rock shelters (e.g., Genuite et al. 2021).

RADIOCARBON DATING

Radiocarbon dating has been the primary source of chronometric dating in archaeological research since it was first developed in the 1940s (Bronk Ramsey 2008; Wood 2015). The ubiquity of carbon means that the technique can often be applied to material goods, food sources, shelters, and other evidence of past human activity. In Australia, the often-acidic soils cause much of this evidence to deteriorate rapidly. Charcoal, however, is often well preserved, and radiocarbon dating of charcoal within archaeological excavations is the source of a great deal of what we know about the chronology of early human activity in Australia. More recently, the practical limit of radiocarbon dating to material usually less than about 50,000 years old means that other techniques are required to date the very earliest human activity. Nonetheless, radiocarbon dating is still well suited to date much of the evidence of human activity in the last 50,000 years, and in ideal circumstances up to c. 60,000 years. Given the reliability of the method, and its widespread adoption for archaeological investigations, it is natural that it has been the focus of many attempts to date rock art.

Method

The radiocarbon dating method is based on the production of the unstable carbon isotope ^{14}C in the higher atmosphere where incoming cosmic particles interact with nitrogen atoms to produce ^{14}C. Such interactions are rare: the atmosphere contains about

10^{12} atoms of the stable carbon isotope, ^{12}C, for every atom of ^{14}C. The method relies on measuring the ratios of carbon isotopes in a once-living organism that has died and is no longer absorbing atmospheric ^{14}C. The half-life of ^{14}C is 5730 ± 40 years and carbon isotope ratios can be accurately measured, using accelerator mass spectrometry (AMS), for organisms that died up to about 50,000 years ago (Bronk Ramsey 2008). Pretreatment processes and AMS technology are under continuing scientific development with advances in the ability to reliably date smaller and older samples.

One complication is that the rate of ^{14}C production in the atmosphere changes over time as the level of incident cosmic radiation varies. So measured isotopic ratios need to be calibrated to account for this variation. There is ongoing scientific effort to improve the precision of the calibration curve, but the current curves allow for calibration of ages up to c. 55,000 years (with associated uncertainties) (Hogg et al. 2020; Reimer et al. 2020).

Application to Rock Art

The application of radiocarbon dating to rock art falls into two categories. One is the direct dating of the material used by the artist to make a motif; the other is the dating of carbon-bearing insect nests and mineral accretions found overlying or underlying the motif. In Australia, direct dating has been applied to motifs where the material used was beeswax, charcoal, or a paint that included an organic component such as paint-fibre binders. Radiocarbon dating has been applied to mineral accretions and mud wasp nests to provide minimum or maximum ages for overlying or underlying rock art, respectively.

Direct Dating of Motifs

Radiocarbon dating of the pigment material used to make the motif tells us when the organism providing the carbon-bearing component died. It is often assumed that this is the same as, or very close to, the time when the material was applied to the rock surface, but this is not always the case. A common exception arises when charcoal is made from old wood or when old charcoal is used (e.g., David, Armitage, Hyman, Rowe, & Lawson 1999). This risk is lower in northern Australia, where the action of termites and regular bushfires greatly reduces the volume of old wood and trees are relatively short-lived, at least in the time since people first arrived (Ogden 1981). When charcoal is used as a pigment, its porous nature makes it susceptible to contamination from younger carbon from microbial intrusion and biogenic processes as well as aeolian pyrogenic carbon. Contamination of pigments by old carbon is also a risk, particularly where the rock substrate contains ancient carbon, as in limestone regions. Pretreatment may remove some but not necessarily all this contamination, leaving a degree of uncertainty about the interpretation of the radiocarbon measurement. The age of charcoal rock art in the most intensively studied sites, such as Chauvet Cave in France, is still being debated after more than two decades of research (Jouve, Pettitt, & Bahn 2020; Quiles et al. 2016).

A notable example of direct dating of charcoal pigments in Australia is the large-scale program to date the rock paintings of the Western Desert. Plasma oxidation was used to extract carbon, which was then dated using accelerator mass spectrometry (McDonald et al. 2014). The ages determined for twenty-nine charcoal paintings ranged from modern to c. 3000 years ago with more than half being younger than c. 1000 years.

In Australia there is some limited evidence that charcoal pigments were used much earlier than the ages suggested by the motifs directly dated. A small rock (about 35 × 28 × 6 mm) fallen from the ceiling with two intersecting black lines, interpreted as part of a larger charcoal drawing or painting, was found in an archaeological excavation at Nawarla Gabarnmang in Arnhem Land in northern Australia (David et al. 2013a). A small scraping of ash adhering on the back of the rock suggested that the piece had been deposited in its final resting place c. 28,000 cal BP. The lack of evidence of *in situ*, charcoal-based art older than the Mid-Holocene is likely due to conditions in the often-open rock art shelters that do not favour preservation of older charcoal pigments.

One readily dated, but less common, type of rock art in northern Australia consists of beeswax figures where small pellets of wax from bee hives were used to form figures on rock shelter walls. Of the hundreds of figures dated, many are less than 500 years old, and most are less than 1500 years old, with the oldest motif dated to c. 5050 cal BP (4460 ± 80 BP) (Morwood, Walsh, & Watchman 2010; Nelson, Chaloupka, Chippindale, Alderson, & Southon 1995; Watchman & Jones 2002). Again, conditions rarely support preservation of these motifs beyond a few millennia.

In summary, direct radiocarbon dating of pigment is a technique that has been successfully applied to just a small fraction of more recent rock art made in the past few thousand years. Researchers must turn to other techniques to determine the age of older painted rock art, petroglyphs, and younger paintings with pigments that do not contain carbon.

Dating Mineral Accretions

Rock shelter surfaces commonly accumulate a range of coatings and accretions built up by the action of geochemical and biological processes, including nest construction by birds and insects such as mud wasps and termite tracks. Where such material is found overlying rock art, and the material can be radiometrically dated, then the measured age serves as a minimum age for the art. Similarly, the age of material underlying rock art will serve as a maximum age constraint for the motif. Attempts to reliably radiocarbon date such materials have been directed toward two main areas: dating of carbon-bearing components within mineral accretions associated with paintings; and dating of mud wasp nests.

Watchman pioneered the development of techniques to radiocarbon date mineral accretions in Australia (Watchman 1996, 2000, 2001; Watchman & Jones, 1998; Watchman, David, McNiven, & Flood 2000; Watchman, Walsh, Morwood, & Tuniz 1997). The accretions were found to contain the carbon-bearing calcium oxalate minerals whewellite and, less commonly, weddellite, as well as aeolian ash, charcoal, and organic material. Bulk samples of such accretions from sites across northern Australia were radiocarbon dated. Most of the ages reported, for identifiable rock art motifs, indicate the underlying art is older than Mid- to Late Holocene (David et al. 2013b; Watchman 2001). A common criticism of dating bulk samples is that, with multiple sources of carbon, it is not possible to confirm that the ages of the various fractions all coincide with the time when the accretion was formed (Aubert 2012; David et al. 2013a). Watchman et al. (1997) and Watchman et al. (2000) dated some samples where the oxalate minerals had been chemically isolated from the bulk accretion, but they, too, were of Mid- to Late Holocene age. Watchman et al. (1997: Table 2) forecast that some of these carbon ages for Kimberley rock art 'probably underestimate the age of the underlying paintings', and this has been borne out by recent results indicating a Pleistocene antiquity for paintings in the same styles (Finch et al. 2020, 2021). Some older ages were determined for layers bracketing pigment-rich layers, suggesting the presence of old rock art, but no identifiable motif was evident (Watchman 1993).

More recently, a similar technique has been used to date oxalate-rich accretions overlying and underlying rock paintings in Arnhem land in northern Australia (Jones, Levchenko, & Wesley 2017; Jones et al. 2017). Most of the samples were collected using a drill to grind off white mineral coatings overlying pigment. The resultant powder was then treated with hydrochloric acid with the aim of extracting just the calcium oxalate component. The acid-soluble oxalate fraction was dated as was the residual, acid-insoluble component. Radiocarbon ages for nine oxalate fractions ranged up to c. 9400 years ago. The authors concluded that the particular style of the motifs dated was in use from c. 9400 to 6000 cal BP. Some of the ages of the residue fractions were up to twice the age of the corresponding oxalate fraction, but others were very much younger (half the age). The reasons for these differences were not apparent to the authors, who concluded that further work is required to identify the mechanisms involved and to improve the robustness of the method.

The ubiquity of carbon is both the key to the success of radiocarbon dating and the reason for some of the most significant failures in its application. Anomalous results are often due to incorrect assumptions about the source and age of the carbon-bearing constituents in the sample being dated. The lessons from earlier decades of research suggest the following prerequisites if robust age constraints are to be derived from any form of accretion or material in contact with rock art. The key is to understand the extent to which the accretion acts as a closed system to carbon. The first step is to identify the sources and ages of the carbon in the accretion as it is formed. The next step is to determine if, over time, the accretion becomes impermeable to external sources of carbon contamination. This will vary with the underlying geology, local biogenic processes, and environmental conditions that may lead to expansion and contraction and weathering. Even after an accretion layer is sealed or closed the potential sources of further modern or ancient carbon contamination need to be identified. Sources of younger carbon such as soot, ash, microbes, or lichen are common, but ancient carbon may be transported across rock surfaces when carbonates in limestone dissolve in rain or pore water. Even in sandstone regions, it is possible that old, relatively insoluble rock coatings, including oxalates, may weather and mobilize across rock walls by colloidal transport.

Dating Mud Wasp Nests

Another form of accretion commonly found in the rock shelters of northern Australia are remnant nests built by mud dauber wasps (Figure 21.2). Pioneering research in the Kimberley region in the 1990s established that mineralized nests may survive for tens of thousands of years and that they could be dated both with optically stimulated luminescence (OSL) and radiocarbon techniques (Roberts et al. 1997; Yoshida, Roberts, & Olley 2003). However, the application of the OSL technique is greatly limited by the lack of suitably large nests in contact with rock art. The nests must be large enough that the inner quartz grains have always been shielded from sunlight from the time when the wasp applied mud to the rock surface. Initial attempts to use radiocarbon dating on wasp nests focused on dating pollen collected with the mud, but it was found that the older nests, in particular, often contained too little pollen (Roberts et al. 1997; Yoshida et al. 2003).

Recent work in the Kimberley region investigated newly constructed wasp nests to understand the relative abundance of the carbon-bearing constituents and the longevity of those components (Finch, Gleadow, Hergt, Levchenko, & Fink 2019). Charcoal was identified as the main source of carbon likely to last millennia in open rock shelters. The age of the charcoal, and other sources of carbon, in a range of modern nests was measured. These results, and other geochemical analyses, established that the inbuilt or

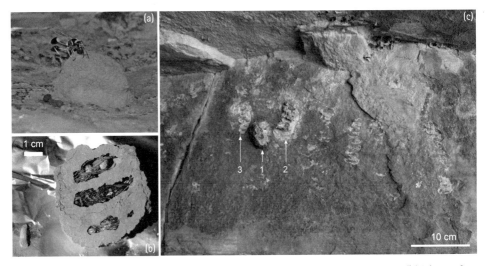

FIGURE 21.2. (a) Mud wasp adding a ball of mud to a nest under construction. (b) The underside of the same nest showing three cells each provisioned with spiders as food for the larvae (one shown in the lower left). The mud at the base of each cell, in an oval shape, often remains on the rock surface well after the outer surface has weathered away. (c) Rock shelter wall with numerous nests of different ages: (1) is the most recently constructed, (2) is older with most of the outer surface weathered away, and (3) is the oldest showing just the oval-shaped base of the nest cells.

(Photo credit to Damien Finch and Balanggarra Aboriginal Corporation.)

inherited age of charcoal in wasp nests is likely to have a mean value of about 260 years. While the inbuilt age introduces inaccuracy into the calculation of the age of underlying or overlying rock art, based on the radiocarbon age of the nest, it is relatively small in relation to the age of the art in most cases.

The research then addressed the question of the potential carbon contamination of the nest on rock shelter walls over many millennia. Two key conclusions were that mineralized wasp nests act as closed systems for carbon, and that any carbon in accretions that develop on old nests is extremely unlikely to be older than the nest in the sandstone-dominated geology of the region. Physical and chemical pretreatment protocols were then optimized to target the carbon in charcoal in the nest at time of construction for dating. The reported ages of seventy-five mud wasp nests varied from modern to just over 20 cal ka BP with half dating to more than 9400 years old. The median sample size of the old nests collected was just 247 mg, so this approach was applicable to the much more common, small, remnant nests that are too small for OSL dating (Finch et al. 2019).

The method of dating wasp nests was used to estimate the timing of the two oldest periods in the Kimberley rock art stylistic sequence. The radiocarbon ages of twenty-four mud wasp nests that were either under or over twenty-one different motifs, all belonging to the figurative Gwion style, were used to conclude that this style of painting proliferated around 12,000 years ago (Finch et al. 2020). For the oldest style of painted Kimberley rock art, the Naturalistic or Irregular Infill Animal period (IIAP), the age determinations on twenty-seven nests in contact with sixteen different motifs indicated that this period extended from 17,000 years ago to 13,000 years ago (Finch et al. 2021). Notably, the age of one painting of a kangaroo was determined to be between 17,500 and 17,100 years old, based on the ages of three overlying and three underlying wasp nests (Figure 21.3).

FIGURE 21.3. A kangaroo from the oldest modelled style of painted Kimberley rock art. (a) The yellow circles show the locations of four mud wasp nests overlying the motif. The ages of the four nests are c. 4300, 9400, 11,600, and 13,000 years old (median cal BP), so the underlying painting is more than 13,000 years old (Finch et al. 2021). (b) Same motif but with pigment digitally highlighted for clarity.

(Photo credit to Damien Finch, Pauline Heaney and Balanggarra Aboriginal Corporation.)

Future Directions

Recent research continues the development of methods to produce reliable age constraints by radiocarbon dating layers within mineral accretions (Green et al. 2021b). It is likely that the very oldest painted rock art in Australia no longer exists as identifiable, mostly complete, motifs, but old pigments may be preserved as layers within mineral accretions.

The application of radiocarbon dating to remnant mud wasp nests has produced useful initial insights into the chronological extent of the two oldest periods of painted rock art in the Kimberley region of Western Australia. More ages for wasp nests related to these and other Kimberley art styles will provide a more accurate and comprehensive chronology for rock art in this region. Mud wasp nests are common in other major rock art provinces of northern Australia, so there is the potential for the method to be applied more widely in Australia and elsewhere.

URANIUM-THORIUM (U-TH) DATING

U-Th dating was first proposed for dating corals and was subsequently used to date the formation of calcium carbonate cave deposits formed from groundwater. In archaeology, such age determinations may provide a chronology for artefacts embedded in the deposits or constrain ages for any associated rock art. The method is particularly useful for dating engravings or painted art made without radiocarbon-datable organic pigments or binders, and it has been used to produce the oldest known ages for rock art in the world (Aubert et al. 2019; Brumm et al. 2021; Hoffman et al. 2018).

Although some ages have been contested, U-Th dating of carbonates is widely considered well-established, mature, and typically precise, and it has been described as the most reliable chronometric technique currently available to date rock art (Pike, Hoffman, Pettitt, García-Diez, & Zilhão 2017). The datable age range spans from a few decades (Zhao, Yu, & Feng 2009) to 650–600 ka (Andersen et al. 2008; Cheng et al. 2013), making it an attractive alternative to ^{14}C dating by exceeding the limit for this method and requiring no calibration. Globally, most caves have developed in limestone terrains which provide a highly protected environment for any rock art they contain. However, in Australia, relatively little art occurs in deep limestone caves, and instead, the richest collections of rock art, found in the Kimberley, Arnhem Land, and Cape York Peninsula, all occur mainly in sandstone terrains and often in open shelters with minimal secondary calcite deposits. Consequently, rock art dating programs are focused on the development and adaptation of existing techniques for application to non-calcite materials (Green, Gleadow, Finch, Hergt, & Ouzman 2017).

Method

Uranium (U) is present as a trace element in many natural materials and occurs as six isotopes ranging in atomic weight from ^{233}U to ^{238}U. ^{238}U makes up 99.27% of natural uranium, with ^{235}U the next most abundant at only 0.72%. All the other isotopes occur at trace levels (Grenthe et al. 2011). U-Th dating is also known as a 'U-series' technique, as it utilizes intermediate isotopes in the U-series decay chain and is based on the radioactive decay series beginning with uranium isotopes and ending with a stable lead isotope. ^{238}U decays into daughter isotopes including ^{230}Th, and the different decay rates of the two isotopes result in an equilibrium being established where each isotope decays at exactly the rate at which it is produced. This equilibrium is disturbed when soluble uranium is present in groundwaters and insoluble thorium is not, resulting in minerals that precipitate out of groundwaters initially containing uranium but no thorium. This restarts the decay process, and the subsequent *in situ* decay of ^{234}U to ^{230}Th, with a half-life of 245,000 years, can be used to date the material by measuring the present levels of both isotopes (Bourdon, Henderson, Lundstrom, & Turner 2003).

The U-Th dating method is inherently suitable to carbonate material, such as coral and carbonate speleothems, as these develop from natural, U-bearing, Th-poor waters, resulting in secondary carbonate deposits with very large U/Th ratios. The extent to which the isotopes have reestablished equilibrium can consequently be used to date the speleothem formation.

Application to Rock Art

U-Th dating cannot be applied to pigments. Instead, the identification of thin calcite layers associated with rock art in limestone regions has been used to provide age constraints for associated motifs (Aubert et al. 2019; Brumm et al. 2021; Hoffman et al. 2018).

This approach is most effective when mineral accretions are found both underneath and overlying the paintings, providing a bracketing age constraint for the associated art (e.g., Brumm et al. 2021). Where calcite accretions have been identified overlying pigment, minimum age determinations have provided important information about the oldest examples of rock art across the globe. In Spain, a red scalariform design on a limestone cave wall is currently the world's oldest dated rock art, with a minimum age of 64.8 ka that, for many, implies Neanderthal authorship (Hoffman et al. 2018). Sulawesi hosts the world's oldest hunting scene, constrained by the U-Th dating of overlying calcite to 43.9 ka (Aubert et al. 2019), and the oldest known animal painting, with the depiction of a warty pig dated to at least 45.5 ka (Brumm et al. 2021). Rock engravings have also been dated using the same method, with a thin flowstone layer coating engravings at Creswell Crags used to date the oldest known rock art in Britain to 12,800 years ago (Pike et al. 2005).

In Australia, U-series dating methods have yet to be successfully applied to rock art sites. The paucity of art found in limestone environments makes U-Th difficult to apply in most Australian rock art provinces, as mineral accretions associated with rock art in non-limestone provinces very rarely contain calcium carbonate. In the Kimberley, where most rock art studies have taken place in sandstone environments, rock art–associated accretions are composed of a range of minerals, including sulphates, phosphates, and oxalates, to which U-series methods have never been applied (Green, Gleadow, Finch, Hergt et al. 2017; Green, Gleadow, & Finch 2017). Consequently, there are a range of challenges and limitations which must be overcome before any reliable ages might be achieved.

Criticisms and Limitations

Sampling Limitations

The foremost concern when sampling mineral accretions associated with rock art is that the preservation and conservation of the art is prioritized; that is, that the rock art is not damaged or that impacts are minimal and acceptable to all parties, especially Traditional Owners. As mineral accretions are generally not formed in singular 'events' as is more common with other rock art–associated materials such as fossilized mud wasp nests (Finch et al. 2020, 2021; Roberts et al. 1997) and shelter slab falls (Genuite et al. 2021), accurately identifying the stratigraphic relationship between the accretion layer and the art is crucial for reliable dating. Only the portion of the accretion with a direct relationship to the art is relevant, as the stratigraphic relationship of minerals accumulating around this point cannot be confirmed (however, an exception would be if the formation of a rock surface was being dated). This relationship can be particularly difficult to determine where mineral accretions largely obscure the art. Water flows and seepage responsible for accretion formation often also impact rock art panels with irregular hematite staining, in some instances obscuring the paintings and further complicating the interpretation of stratigraphic relationships, particularly where ochre is the rock-marking medium.

Issues associated with the inclusion of variable quantities of geological age substrate in the dated material plague rock art sampling in limestone environments (Aubert et al. 2018; Fontugne et al. 2013) and are avoided in the sandstone shelters more common in Australia. However, apparent stratigraphic relationships between rock art and accretionary layers can still be complicated by uneven 'canvas' surfaces resulting in preferential weathering of pigment from accretion protuberances.

The surest way to assess the stratigraphic relationship between the sampled geological material and the rock art motif is to remove intact fragments of mineral accretion to expose either substrate or underlying paint after removal of the accretion. Where this does not occur, the pigment is assumed to be sandwiched between accretion layers and may be assessed in cross-section.

In some settings (e.g., Hoffman, Pike, García-Diez, Pettitt, & Zilhão 2016; Pike et al. 2012), sampling is restricted to materials forming *over* (not under) art to reduce impacts to the associated motif. This limits the age constraint to minimum age estimates, precluding the production of bracketing age ranges. In rock art provinces that host multiple art styles or stylistic sequences (e.g., the Kimberley region in Australia), this is particularly restrictive, impeding any constraint on the absolute age intervals over which particular styles were produced. Such sampling restrictions also do not guarantee preservation of the underlying motif, with pigment often removed during sampling, which was adhered to the undersurface or sandwiched between layers of the removed accretion.

Timing of Mineral Deposition

The formation of secondary carbonates in caves is strongly dependent on climatic conditions, with similar conclusions made for mineral accretions forming in non-limestone environments (Green et al. 2021b). Consequently, as with most rock art–associated materials, although mineral accretions can provide useful constraints on the age of the associated rock art, they do not account for the potential lag time between the art's creation and the mineral precipitation. Any age produced for any single accretion has a relatively low probability of matching the age of the art which it underlies or overlies (Hellstrom 2012). The quantity and quality of ages required on each motif and style of art, to establish a robust chronology, is thus significant. This is particularly challenging when the number of available, suitable samples is already limited. Further, research has shown that layered mineral accretions in Kimberley rock art shelters can accumulate over intervals in excess of 25 ka (Green et al. 2021b). Consequently, although a bulk accretion age would be correct, its use would be limited.

Open System Behaviour of Mineral Accretions

A critical prerequisite for the successful application of U-Th dating to rock art–associated mineral accretions is that samples have behaved as a closed system with no loss or gain of U isotopes and are 'clean' of Th-bearing detritus.

$CaCO_3$ formations on the walls of deep limestone caves and mineral accretions forming in open sandstone shelters are commonly subject to water flow. Where the dated material is porous, open system behaviour of the mineral system may strongly impact the accuracy of any age determination, with such conditions favouring the leaching and redistribution of soluble uranium compounds (Hoffman, Pike, García-Diez, Pettitt, & Zilhão 2016), resulting in artificial age increases for any associated rock art (Plagnes et al. 2003; Scholz et al. 2014).

Where suitable material is available, sequential sampling along individual laminae and in stratigraphic order from the base to the outer surface of a layered accretion can be used to test for open system behaviour on the assumption that uranium leaching will not impact each layer uniformly but rather will result in incorrect ages which are not stratigraphically sequenced (Bajo et al. 2016; Hellstrom 2006; Hoffmann, Spötl, & Mangini 2009; Ludwig et al. 1992; Scholz & Hoffmann 2008; Scholz, Hoffmann, Hellstrom, & Bronk Ramsey 2012).

Detrital Thorium Contamination

Sequential sampling is also commonly used to correct for the inclusion of detrital ^{230}Th in the initial system. The detrital ^{230}Th correction value can be stratigraphically constrained based on the requirement that it must result in a sequence of ages which increase with depth from the accretion's outer surface (Hellstrom 2006).

Though largely insoluble, detrital ^{230}Th presents a significant challenge to reliable U-Th dating as it exists in detritus which can be incorporated into precipitating minerals, and if not corrected for, renders apparent U-Th ages erroneously old. In open rock art shelters such as those in Australia, exposed to prevailing weather systems and other external inputs, this is particularly significant.

Detrital ^{230}Th cannot be physically separated from radiogenic ^{230}Th prior to measurement but is generally accompanied by a larger amount of another Th isotope, ^{232}Th, at a known ratio (Wedepohl 1995). As ^{232}Th plays no part in the ^{238}U decay chain, it can be used to assess the contribution of detrital ^{230}Th to the calculated age. The ratio of total (radiogenic and detrital) ^{230}Th to ^{232}Th (^{230}Th/^{232}Th) can subsequently be used to identify 'clean' samples with low proportions of detrital Th.

Where samples are 'clean' and demonstrate high initial ^{230}Th/^{232}Th activity ratios (>300) and therefore low proportions of detrital ^{230}Th, this correction is less significant. However, where contamination is substantial, accurately constraining the correction value and the size of the assigned uncertainty greatly reduces the error associated with the final age. This approach to correcting for detrital contamination in speleothems is considered more appropriate than isochron determinations, as rather than assuming the detrital contaminant is homogenous, it addresses the 'geological scatter' of the detrital Th isotopic composition, both along layers and along growth axes, and attempts to determine and propagate that uncertainty through the age calculation (Hellstrom 2006).

In rock art dating, application of these correction techniques and closed system tests are difficult, requiring at least a triplet of sequential samples and multiple samples along coeval layers in material that is often restricted in size and may demonstrate no clear stratigraphy. Consequently, closed system behaviour is often assumed rather than tested for (Hoffman et al. 2018; Pike et al. 2012) and a mean bulk earth ^{230}Th/^{232}Th activity ratio value (0.825) with an arbitrarily assigned uncertainty of ±50% is often used to correct for contamination (Aubert et al. 2014, 2018; Hoffman et al. 2018).

Previous studies have found that the initial ^{230}Th/^{232}Th activity ratio value can vary between ~0.2 (Drysdale et al. 2006) and ~18 (Beck et al. 2001), highlighting the limitations in using just one bulk earth value to correct ages from disparate global locations and further, applying it to each layer within a sample that has formed over an extensive interval (Hellstrom 2006). A potentially incorrect initial (detrital) ^{230}Th correction could seriously affect the accuracy of the U-Th results.

Future Directions

The detailed characterization of rock art–associated mineral accretions in Kimberley rock shelters has identified multiple depositional systems which display detailed internal stratigraphies and well-crystallized mineral phases which contain enough uranium for radiometric dating (Green, Gleadow, Finch, Hergt, et al. 2017). Laser-ablation trace element mapping of such accretions has identified discrete layering of phosphates and identified important relationships between these layers and areas of elevated uranium concentrations. These key features of the Kimberley accretions offer clear opportunities to constrain initial thorium correction values and to test for open system behaviour when applying uranium-thorium methods. However, problems associated with the levels of initial thorium contamination in accretions collected from open rock shelters continue to limit attempts to produce precise ages for such materials.

OPTICAL DATING

Optical dating of sediments, first developed by Huntley, Godfrey-Smith, and Thewalt (1985), has been a key technique in establishing the timing of the earliest peopling of Australia (Bowler et al. 2003; Clarkson et al. 2017; Hamm et al. 2016; Roberts et al. 1994; Turney et al. 2001; Veth et al. 2017). The ubiquity of suitable quartz and feldspar grains in sedimentary deposits makes it a useful tool for estimating the timing of events dating back just a few years, or as far back as several tens or hundreds of thousands of years. It provides an alternative technique for deposits dating to beyond the effective limit of radiocarbon dating, ~50,000 years, or deposits that do not contain materials suitable for other dating methods. It also allows dating of complete sedimentary sequences, even when humans were absent, permitting the construction of temporal patterns of human presence and absence at a site. The application of optical dating to rock art is less well-known. In its simplest form, it can provide an age for the art or an artist's toolkit buried in sediments dated using optical dating (e.g., Henshilwood et al. 2002, 2011, 2018). Optical dating is generally not well-suited to the dating of art painted or engraved onto the surfaces of a rock shelter or cave wall, and its application in Australia has been limited. The most promising approach has been the dating of mud wasp nests that underlie or overlie rock paintings, providing maximum or minimum ages for the art, respectively. Optical dating of mud wasp nests was pioneered in Australia and was the first-ever published use of optical dating of single grains of quartz (Roberts et al. 1997).

Method

Optical dating is an umbrella term for a 'family' of techniques, including optically stimulated luminescence (OSL) and infrared stimulated luminescence (IRSL), that differentiate between the measurement of quartz and feldspar, respectively. Optical dating provides an estimate of the last time that sediment grains were exposed to sunlight or heat, so it can either be used to estimate the time of sediment deposition by natural processes or to estimate, by association, the age of objects of interest. Optical dating relies on a phenomenon characteristic of crystalline materials that allows a crystal (e.g., mineral) to trap and store energy from the environment and to release it as photons of light (luminescence) when stimulated. The energy that steadily builds up inside the mineral is sourced from the surrounding natural environment in the form of alpha- and beta-particles and gamma-ray radiation (derived from uranium, thorium—and the daughter products in their radioactive decay chains—and potassium) within about 30 cm of the sample. Additional contributions are due to the decay of these radioactive elements inside the mineral grains and to cosmic rays from outer space. The release of the stored energy can be triggered by exposure to sunlight or to intense heat. A prerequisite for optical dating is the complete release of all stored energy from the mineral before burial (i.e., to restart the optical dating 'clock'), so the calculated age would correspond to the last time the sample of grains were exposed to sunlight. The time since last release of stored energy is, therefore, proportional to the amount of energy stored in the mineral throughout the period of burial.

To calculate an optical age, two quantities need to be estimated: the energy stored during burial that is subsequently released and measured in the laboratory, termed the equivalent dose (D_e); and the rate of energy supplied, which is measured in the field and the laboratory, and referred to as the environmental dose rate (D_r). The age equation can, therefore, be written as follows:

$$Age\ estimate\ (ka) = \frac{Equivalent\ dose\ (D_e)(Gy)}{Environmental\ dose\ rate\ (D_r)\left(\dfrac{Gy}{ka}\right)}$$

D_e is reported in Gray (Gy), the Système International unit for absorbed dose, and D_r is reported in Gy/ka, where 'ka' is the conventional abbreviation for thousands of years. Ages are calculated directly in calendar years (or sidereal years) and are commonly reported in ka or, for young samples, in years. Reviews of optical dating for non-specialists include Aitken (1998), Jacobs and Roberts (2007), Duller (2008), and Roberts et al. (2015).

Application to Rock Art

Only a limited number of attempts have been made to constrain the age of rock paintings and engravings in Australia using optical dating. In northern Australia, circular engravings (pecked cupules) on the wall of Jinmium rock shelter were traced below ground level to a depth of about 1 m, where an engraved sandstone fragment was also recovered. Optical dating of single aliquots (composed of multiple grains) and single grains of quartz showed that the pecked cupules were buried by sediments within the last 10,000 years (Roberts et al. 1998).

Optical dating of mud wasp nests built on top of rock art in the Kimberley and Arnhem Land has also been tried. Three studies have so far reported experimental and dating results (Roberts et al. 1997; Ross, Westaway, Travers, Morwood, & Hayward 2016; Yoshida et al. 2003). The nests consist of sediment gathered by wasps from local streams and pools and then carried to rock shelters, where it is used to build their nests. It is assumed that the optical dating clock is sufficiently reset by sunlight when the grains are being transported to the rock shelter and/or on the surface of the nest during its construction; this assumption has been tested by direct dating of modern nests in each of these three studies. Once the nest is constructed, electron traps in the grains concealed within the nest (i.e., hidden from sunlight) start to steadily accrue energy. Grains embedded within the outer 1–3 mm rind of the nest are continuously exposed to sunlight, so their electron traps remain empty and are not useful for the purpose of dating. This places a limit on the minimum size of the nest suitable for optical dating. Samples amenable to dating must be many millimetres thick, so that grains can be extracted from the light-safe inner portions. Sufficiently large samples are rare, but it has been shown that, where they exist, they can survive for at least 30,000 years on the rock surface, suggesting that dating of Pleistocene rock art is within the temporal reach of this technique (Yoshida et al. 2003).

Several Late Holocene nests directly associated with rock art in the Kimberley were dated by Roberts et al. (1997) and Ross et al. (2016). The oldest minimum age estimates so far obtained include an age of 16,400 ± 1,800 years for an indurated nest overlying the headdress of a faded anthropomorphic painting (Roberts et al. 1997) and an age of 16,000 ± 1,000 years for a yam-like motif (Ross et al. 2016). While encouraging as proof of concept, to usefully constrain the ages of rock paintings requires a pattern of similarly old ages for many more paintings of similar styles, such as those recently obtained by radiocarbon dating of mud wasp nests (Finch et al. 2020, 2021). These optical dating studies nevertheless demonstrate the feasibility of using the method as an innovative complementary approach for the dating of mud wasp nests.

Issues/Criticisms

There are several issues related to optical dating of mud wasp nests. The stratigraphic relationship between the nest and art needs to be carefully demonstrated. Complexities of mud wasp nest construction, and any changes to the nest over time, need to be understood and considered. Not all nests represent a single building event; many are reused by wasps, sometimes over considerable time frames, and multiple generations of nest building can be superimposed. For nests overlying a rock painting, the light-safe grains associated most closely with the art will be those located nearest to the rock surface and immediately overlying the painting. Postdepositional changes to nests also need to be considered. Nests built recently are often poorly consolidated and easy to remove from the rock surface, whereas older nests can be as hard as cement. The cementation process, and how it may affect estimation of the environmental dose rate and/or changes in environmental dose rate through time, all need to be considered. It is also critically important to appreciate that a nest can only ever provide a minimum age for an underlying painting, or a maximum age for an overlying motif, and not an estimate of when the motif was painted. There may or may not be a significant time delay between the two events, requiring statistically meaningful numbers of nests to be dated to obtain a distribution of minimum or maximum age constraints.

Future Directions

Large-scale and systematic optical dating studies of nests, both off-art and associated with specific art styles, are required. Ideally, such studies would involve both optical and radiocarbon dating of the same nests for independent verification of the ages. Such comparisons may allay many of the issues described earlier, or at least highlight the most crucial aspects for further experimental investigation.

Optical dating can also be extended to the recently developed luminescence surface exposure dating techniques (e.g., Chapot, Sohbati, Murray, Pederson, & Rittenour 2012; Pederson et al. 2014; Sohbati et al. 2012; Sohbati, Murray, Porat, Jain, & Avner 2015), which operate on the premise that light can penetrate a rock, leaving a bleaching profile. In the case of rock engravings, material is removed from the natural rock surface during the process of engraving, thereby exposing a new surface and restarting the luminescence exposure clock. By measuring the microstratigraphic bleaching profile of the rock close to the surface, therefore, an estimate could be made of the time of the engraving. Although feasible in principle, several assumptions are involved in applying this method in practice. Several steps are required to validate the method for each lithology and site, making it a nonstandard application of optical dating, but one with exciting prospects.

CONCLUSION

The challenges associated with dating rock art are faced by researchers across the world. Each technique has associated problems and limitations, some of which are unique to particular environments, but all of which have implications for rock art dating programs worldwide. Increasingly, a multidisciplinary approach to rock art dating is required, with the strengths of one technique often alleviating the weaknesses of another. Methods which calibrate the rates of landscape processes and provide geomorphological context for the cultural site allow a first-order understanding of the potential for rock art survival in particular environments. In environments where opportunities for direct dating are limited, indirect dating techniques may be applied to a range of rock art–associated materials. However, the disparity between the age of these materials and the art itself necessitates that many samples are analysed to produce statistically significant results. Whilst all indirect dating techniques discussed here have the potential to provide bracketing ages for associated rock art, where they are applied in tandem, a broader set of more reliable results may be achieved.

In Australia's Kimberley region, careful adaptation of existing methodologies has produced the first substantial evidence to support a Pleistocene age for the rock art of this region (Finch et al. 2020, 2021; Roberts et al. 1997). Many more ages are required before the full chronological extent of the paintings still visible today can be determined. However, the robust results produced by multiple techniques have enhanced our understanding of the status, importance, and spread of Kimberley rock art traditions in a global context. The advances made in the Kimberley provide crucial information to inform the conservation and management strategies surrounding Australia's Indigenous cultural heritage and important insights for researchers working in similar environments around the world.

References

Aitken, M. J. (1998). *An introduction to optical dating*. Oxford: Oxford University Press.

Akçar, N., Ivy-Ochs, S., & Schlüchter, C. (2008). Application of in-situ produced terrestrial cosmogenic nuclides to archaeology: A schematic review. *E&G Quaternary Science Journal, 57*(1/2), 226–238.

Andersen, M. B., Stirling, C. H., Potter, E.-K., Halliday, A. N., Blake, S. G., McCulloch, M. T., . . . O'Leary, M. (2008). High-precision U-series measurements of more than 500,000 year old fossil corals. *Earth and Planetary Science Letters, 265*, 229–245.

Anderson, R. S., Repka, J., & Dick, G. (1996). Explicit treatment of inheritance in dating depositional surfaces using in situ Be-10 and Al-26. *Geology, 24*(1), 47–51.

Appenzeller, T. (2018). Europe's first artists were Neandertals. *Science, 359*, 852–853.

Aubert, M. (2012). A review of rock art dating in the Kimberley, Western Australia. *Journal of Archaeological Science, 39*(3), 573–577.

Aubert, M., Brumm, A., Ramli, M., Sutikna, T., Saptomo, E. W., Hakim, B., . . . Dosseto, A. (2014). Pleistocene cave art from Sulawesi, Indonesia. *Nature, 514*(7521), 223–237.

Aubert, M., Lebe, R., Oktaviana, A. A., Tang, M., Burhan, B., Hamrullah, . . . Brumm, A. (2019). Earliest hunting scene in prehistoric art. *Nature, 576*(7787), 442–445.

Aubert, M., Setiawan, P., Oktaviana, A. A., Brumm, A., Sulistyarto, P. H., Saptomo, E. W., . . . Brand, H. E. A. (2018). Palaeolithic cave art in Borneo. *Nature, 564*(7735), 254–257.

Bajo, P., Hellstrom, J., Frisia, S., Drysdale, R., Black, J., Woodhead, J., . . . Haese, R. (2016). "Cryptic" diagenesis and its implications for speleothem geochronologies. *Quaternary Science Reviews, 148*, 17–28.

Balco, G., Purvance, M. D., & Rood, D. H. (2011). Exposure dating of precariously balanced rocks. *Quaternary Geochronology, 6*(3–4), 295–303.

Balco, G., & Rovey, C. W. (2008). An isochron method for cosmogenic-nuclide dating of buried soils and sediments. *American Journal of Science, 308*(10), 1083–1114.

Beck, J. W., Richards, D. A., Edwards, R. L., Silverman, B. W., Smart, P. L., Donahue, D. J., . . . Biddulph, D. (2001). Extremely large variations of atmospheric C-14 concentration during the last glacial period. *Science, 292*, 2453–2458.

Bednarik, R. G. (1998). Cosmogenic radiation nuclides in archaeology: A response to Phillips et al. *Antiquity*, *72*(278), 811–815.

Blanckenburg, F. von, & Willenbring, J. K. (2014). Cosmogenic nuclides: Dates and rates of Earth-surface change. *Elements*, *10*(5), 341–346.

Bourdon, B, Henderson, G. M., Lundstrom, C. C., & Turner, S. P. (Eds.) (2003). *Uranium-series geochemistry*. Reviews in Mineralogy and Geochemistry, Vol. 52. Washington, DC: Mineralogical Society of America.

Bowler, J. M., Johnston, H., Olley, J. M., Prescott, J. R., Roberts, R. G., Shawcross, W., & Spooner, N. A. (2003). New ages for human occupation and climatic change at Lake Mungo, Australia. *Nature*, *421*, 837–840.

Bronk Ramsey, C. (2008). Radiocarbon dating: Revolutions in understanding. *Archaeometry*, *50*, 249–275.

Brumm, A., Oktaviana, A. A., Burhan, B., Hakim, B., Lebe, R., Zhao, J.-X., . . . Aubert, M. (2021). Oldest cave art found in Sulawesi. *Science Advances*, *7*(3), 1–12.

Carbonell, E., Castro, J. M. B. de, Parés, J. M., Pérez-González, A., Cuenca-Bescós, G., Ollé, A., . . . Arsuaga, J. L. (2008). The first hominin of Europe. *Nature*, *452*(7186), 465–469.

Cazes, G., Fink, D., Codilean, A. T., Fülöp, R., Fujioka, T., & Wilcken, K. M. (2020). 26Al/10Be ratios reveal the source of river sediments in the Kimberley, NW Australia. *Earth Surface Processes and Landforms*, *45*(2), 424–439.

Chalarimeri, A. M. (2001). *The man from the sunrise side*. Broome, WA: Magabala Books.

Chapot, M. S., Sohbati, R., Murray, A. S., Pederson, J. L., & Rittenour, T. M. (2012). Constraining the age of rock art by dating a rockfall event using sediment and rock surface luminescence dating techniques. *Quaternary Geochronology*, *13*, 18–25.

Cheng, H., Lawrence Edwards, R., Shen, C.C., Polyak, V.J., Asmerom, Y., Woodhead, J., . . . Calvin Alexander, E. (2013). Improvements in ^{230}Th dating, ^{230}Th and ^{234}U half-life values, and U-Th isotopic measurements by multi-collector inductively coupled plasma mass spectrometry. *Earth and Planetary Science Letters*, *371–372*, 82–91.

Clarkson, C., Jacobs, Z., Marwick, B., Fullagar, R., Wallis, L., Smith, M., . . . Pardoe, C. (2017). Human occupation of northern Australia by 65,000 years ago. *Nature*, *547*(7663), 306–310.

David, B., Armitage, R. A., Hyman, M., Rowe, M. W., & Lawson, E. (1999). How old is north Queensland's rock art? A review of the evidence, with new AMS determinations. *Archaeology in Oceania*, *34*(3), 103–120.

David, B., Barker, B., Petchey, F., Delannoy, J.-J., Geneste, J.-M., Rowe, C., . . . Whear, R. (2013a). A 28,000-year-old excavated painted rock from Nawarla Gabarnmang, northern Australia. *Journal of Archaeological Science*, *40*(5), 2493–2501.

David, B., Geneste, J.-M., Petchey, F., Delannoy, J.-J., Barker, B., & Eccleston, M. (2013b). How old are Australia's pictographs? A review of rock art dating. *Journal of Archaeological Science*, *40*(1), 3–10.

Dixon, J. L., & Riebe, C. S. (2014). Tracing and pacing soil across slopes. *Elements*, *10*(5), 363–368.

Donaldson, M. (2012). *Kimberley rock art*. Vols. 1–3. Mount Lawley, WA: Wildrocks.

Drysdale, R., Zanchetta, G., Hellstrom, J., Maas, R., Fallick, A., Pickett, M., . . . Piccini, L. (2006). Late Holocene drought responsible for the collapse of old world civilizations is recorded in an Italian cave flowstone. *Geology*, *34*, 101–104.

Duller, G. A. T. (2008). *Luminescence dating: Guidelines on using luminescence dating in archaeology*. Swindon: English Heritage.

Dunai, T. J. (2010). *Cosmogenic nuclides: Principles, concepts and applications in the Earth surface sciences.* Cambridge: Cambridge University Press.

Dunne, J., Elmore, D., & Muzikar, P. (1999). Scaling factors for the rates of production of cosmogenic nuclides for geometric shielding and attenuation at depth on sloped surfaces. *Geomorphology, 27*(1–2), 3–11.

Fewlass, H., Talamo, S., Wacker, L., Kromer, B., Tuna, T., Fagault, Y., . . . Hublin, J.-J. (2020). A ^{14}C chronology for the Middle to Upper Palaeolithic transition at Bacho Kiro Cave, Bulgaria. *Nature: Ecology & Evolution, 4,* 794–801.

Finch, D., Gleadow, A., Hergt, J., Levchenko, V. A., & Fink, D. (2019). New developments in the radiocarbon dating of mud wasp nests. *Quaternary Geochronology, 51,* 140–154.

Finch, D., Gleadow, A., Hergt, J., Levchencko, V. A., Heaney, P., Veth, P., . . . Green, H. (2020). 12,000-year-old Aboriginal rock art from the Kimberley region, Western Australia. *Science Advances, 6*(6) eaay3922, 1–9.

Finch, D., Gleadow, A., Hergt, J., Heaney, P., Green, H., Myers, C., . . . Levchenko, V. A. (2021). Ages for Australia's oldest rock paintings. *Nature Human Behaviour, 5*(3), 310–318.

Fontugne, M., Shao, Q., Frank, N., Thil, F., Guidon, N., & Boeda, E. (2013). Cross-dating (Th/U-14C) of calcite covering prehistoric paintings at Serra da Capivara National Park, Piaui, Brazil. *Radiocarbon, 55*(3), 1191–1198.

Genuite, K., Delannoy, J.-J., David, B., Unghango, A., Corporation, B. A., Cazes, G., . . . Urwin, C. (2021). Determining the origin and changing shape of landscape-scale rock formations with three-dimensional modelling: The Borologa rock shelters, Kimberley region, Australia. *Geoarchaeology.* 36 (4), 662–680.

Granger, D. E. (2006). A review of burial dating methods using ^{26}Al and ^{10}Be.. In L. L. Siame, D. L. Bourlès, and E. T. Brown (Eds.), In Situ-Produced Cosmogenic Nuclides and Quantification of Geological Processes. Special paper 415 (pp. 1–16). Boulder: Geological Society of America.

Granger, D. E., Gibbon, R. J., Kuman, K., Clarke, R. J., Bruxelles, L., & Caffee, M. W. (2015). New cosmogenic burial ages for Sterkfontein Member 2 Australopithecus and Member 5 Oldowan. *Nature, 522*(7554), 85–88.

Granger, D. E., & Schaller, M. (2014). Cosmogenic nuclides and erosion at the Watershed Scale. *Elements, 10*(5), 369–373.

Granger, D. E., & Smith, A. (2000). Dating buried sediments using radioactive decay and muogenic production of Al-26 and Be-10. *Nuclear Instruments & Methods in Physics Research Section B-Beam Interactions with Materials and Atoms, 172,* 822–826.

Green, H., Gleadow, A., & Finch, D. (2017) Characterisation of mineral deposition systems associated with rock art in the Kimberley region of northwest Australia. *Data in Brief, 14,* 813–835.

Green, H., Gleadow, A., Finch, D., Hergt, J., & Ouzman, S. (2017) Mineral deposition systems at rock art sites, Kimberley, Australia-field observations. *Journal of Archaeological Science: Reports, 14,* 340–352.

Green, H., Gleadow, A., Finch, D., Myers, C., & McGovern, J. (2021a). Micro-stromatolitic laminations and the origins of engraved, oxalate-rich accretions from Australian rock art shelters. *Geoarchaeology, 36*(6), 964–977.

Green, H., Gleadow, A., Levchenko, V. A., Finch, D., Myers, C., McGovern, J., . . . Pickering, R. (2021b). Dating correlated microlayers in oxalate accretions from rock art shelters: New archives of paleoenvironments and human activity. *Science Advances, 7*(33), 1–15.

Grenthe, I., Drożdżyński, J., Fujino, T., Buck, E. C., Albrecht-Schmitt, T. E., & Wolf, S. F., (2011). Uranium. In L. R. Morss, N. M. Edelstein, & J. Fuger (Eds.), *Chemistry of the actinide and transactinide elements* (Vol. 1., 4th ed., pp. 253–698). Dordrecht: Springer.

Hamm, G., Mitchell, P., Arnold, L. J., Prideaux, G. J., Questiaux, D., Spooner, N. A. . . . Johnston, D. (2016). Cultural innovation and megafauna interaction in the early settlement of arid Australia. *Nature*, *539*, 280–283.

Hellstrom, J. (2006). U–Th dating of speleothems with high initial Th using stratigraphical constraint. *Quaternary Geochronology*, *1*, 289–295.

Hellstrom, J. (2012). Absolute dating of cave art. *Science*, *336*, 1387–1388.

Henshilwood, C. S., d'Errico, F., Van Niekerk, K. L., Coquinot, Y., Jacobs, Z., Lauritzen, S.-E., . . . García-Moreno, R. (2011). A 100,000-year-old ochre-processing workshop at Blombos Cave, South Africa. *Science*, *334*(6053), 219–222.

Henshilwood, C. S., d'Errico, F., Van Niekerk, K. L., Dayet, L., Queffelec, A., & Pollarolo, L. (2018). An abstract drawing from the 73,000-year-old levels at Blombos Cave, South Africa. *Nature*, *562*(7725), 115–118.

Henshilwood, C. S., d'Errico, F., Yates, R., Jacobs, Z., Tribolo, C., Duller, G. A. T., . . . Wintle, A. G. (2002). Emergence of modern human behaviour: Middle stone age engravings from South Africa. *Science*, *295*(5558), 1278–1280.

Hidy, A. J., Gosse, J. C., Pederson, J. L., Mattern, J. P., & Finkel, R. C. (2010). A geologically constrained Monte Carlo approach to modelling exposure ages from profiles of cosmogenic nuclides: An example from Lees Ferry, Arizona. *Geochemistry, Geophysics, Geosystems*, *11*(9), Q0AA10.

Hoffmann, D. L., Pike, A. W. L., García-Diez, M., Pettitt, P. B., & Zilhão, J. (2016). Methods for U-series dating of $CaCO_3$ crusts associated with Palaeolithic cave art and application to Iberian sites. *Quaternary Geochronology*, *36*, 104–119.

Hoffmann, D. L., Spötl, C., & Mangini, A. (2009). Micromill and in situ laser ablation sampling techniques for high spatial resolution MC-ICPMS U-Th dating of carbonates. *Chemical Geology*, *259*, 253–261.

Hoffmann, D. L., Standish, C. D., García-Diez, M., Pettitt, P. B., Milton, J. A., Zilhéo, J., . . . Pike, A. W. G. (2018). U-Th dating of carbonate crusts reveals Neandertal origin of Iberian cave art. *Science*, *359*(6378), 912–915.

Hogg, A. G., Heaton, T. J., Hua, Q., Palmer, J. G., Turney, C. S. M., Southon, J., . . . Wacker, L. (2020). SHCal20 Southern Hemisphere calibration, 0–55,000 years cal BP. *Radiocarbon*, *62*(4), 759–778.

Hublin, J. J., Sirakov, N., Aldeias, V., Bailey, S., Bard, E., Delvigne, V., . . . Tsanova, T. (2020). Initial Upper Palaeolithic *Homo sapiens* from Bacho Kiro Cave, Bulgaria. *Nature*, *581*, 299–302.

Huntley, D. J., Godfrey-Smith, D. I., & Thewalt, M. L. W. (1985). Optical dating of sediments. *Nature*, *313*, 105–107.

Ivy-Ochs, S., & Briner, J. P. (2014). Dating disappearing ice with cosmogenic nuclides. *Elements*, *10*(5), 351–356.

Ivy-Ochs, S., Wüst, R., Kubik, P. W., Müller-Beck, H., & Schlüchter, C. (2001). Can we use cosmogenic isotopes to date stone artifacts? *Radiocarbon*, *43*(2B), 759–764.

Jacobs, Z., & Roberts, R. G. (2007). Advances in optically stimulated luminescence dating of individual grains of quartz from archaeological deposits. *Evolutionary Anthropology*, *16*, 210–223.

Jones, T., Levchenko, V., & Wesley, D. (2017). How old is X-ray art? Minimum age determinations for early X-ray rock art from the 'Red Lily' (Wulk) Lagoon rock art precinct, western Arnhem Land. In B. David, P. S. C. Taçon, J.-J. Delannoy, & M. Geneste (Eds.), *The archaeology of rock art in Western Arnhem Land, Australia* (pp. 129–143). Terra Australis 47. Canberra: ANU Press.

Jones, T., Levchenko, V. A., King, P. L., Troitzsch, U., Wesley, D., Williams, A. A., & Nayingull, A. (2017). Radiocarbon age constraints for a Pleistocene-Holocene transition rock art style: The Northern Running Figures of the East Alligator River region, western Arnhem Land, Australia. *Journal of Archaeological Science: Reports, 11*, 80–89.

Jouve, G., Pettitt, P., & Bahn, P. (2020). Chauvet Cave's art remains undated. *L'Anthropologie, 124*(3), 102765.

Kuman, K., Granger, D. E., Gibbon, R. J., Pickering, T. R., Caruana, M. V., Bruxelles, L., . . . Brain, C. K. (2021). A new absolute date from Swartkrans Cave for the oldest occurrences of *Paranthropus robustus* and Oldowan stone tools in South Africa. *Journal of Human Evolution, 156*, 103000, 1–12.

Lal, D. (1991). Cosmic-ray labeling of erosion surfaces: In situ nuclide production-rates and erosion models. *Earth and Planetary Science Letters, 104*(2–4), 424–439.

Lifton, N., Sato, T., & Dunai, T. J. (2014). Scaling in situ cosmogenic nuclide production rates using analytical approximations to atmospheric cosmic-ray fluxes. *Earth and Planetary Science Letters, 386*(C), 149–160.

Ludwig, K. R., Simmons, K. R., Szabo, B. J., Winograd, I. J., Landwehr, J. M., Riggs, A. C., & Hoffman, R. J. (1992). Mass-spectrometric ^{230}Th-^{234}U-^{238}U dating of the Devils Hole calcite vein. *Science, 258*, 284–287.

Luo, L., Granger, D. E., Tu, H., Lai, Z., Shen, G., Bae, C. J., . . . Liu, J. (2020). The first radiometric age by isochron 26Al/10Be burial dating for the Early Pleistocene Yuanmou hominin site, southern China. *Quaternary Geochronology, 55*, 101022, 1–7.

McDonald, J., Steelman, K. L., Veth, P., Mackey, J., Loewen, J., Thurber, C. R., & Guilderson, T. P. (2014). Results from the first intensive dating program for pigment art in the Australian arid zone: insights into recent social complexity. *Journal of Archaeological Science, 46*, 195–204.

Morwood, M., Walsh, G., & Watchman, A., (1994). The dating potential of rock art in the Kimberley, NW Australia. *Rock Art Research, 11*(2), 79–87.

Morwood, M. J., Walsh, G. L., & Watchman, A. (2010). AMS radiocarbon ages for beeswax and charcoal pigments in North Kimberley rock art. *Rock Art Research, 27*(1), 3–8.

Mulvaney, K. (2011). About time: Toward a sequencing of the Dampier Archipelago petroglyphs of the Pilbara region, Western Australia. *Records of the Western Australian Museum, Supplement, 79*(1), 30–49.

Nelson, D. E., Chaloupka, G., Chippindale, C., Alderson, M. S., & Southon, J. R. (1995). Radiocarbon dates for beeswax figures in the prehistoric rock art in northern Australia. *Archaeometry, 37*(1), 151–156.

Ogden, J. (1981). Dendrochronological studies and the determination of tree ages in the Australian tropics. *Journal of Biogeography, 8*(5), 405–420.

Partridge, T. C., Granger, D. E., Caffee, M. W., & Clarke, R. J. (2003). Lower Pliocene hominid remains from Sterkfontein. *Science, 300*(5619), 607–612.

Pederson, J. L., Chapot, M. S., Simms, S. R., Sohbati, R., Rittenour, T. M., Murray, A. S., & Cox, G. (2014). Age of Barrier Canyon–style rock art constrained by cross-cutting relations and luminescence dating techniques. *Proceedings of the National Academy of Sciences of the United States of America, 111*, 12986–12991.

Phillips, F. M., Flinsch, M., Elmore, D., & Sharma, P. (1997). Maximum ages of the Côa valley (Portugal) engravings measured with Chlorine-36. *Antiquity, 71*(271), 100–104.

Pike, A. W. G., Gilmour, M., Pettitt, P., Jacobi, R., Ripoll, S., Bahn, P., & Muñoz, F. (2005). Verification of the age of the Palaeolithic cave art at Creswell Crags, UK. *Journal of Archaeological Science, 32*(11), 1649–1655.

Pike, A. W. G., Hoffmann, D. L., Garcia-Diez, M., Pettitt, P. B., Alcolea, J., De Balbin, R., . . . Zilhao, J. (2012). U- series dating of Paleolithic art in 11 caves in Spain. *Science, 336*(6087), 1409–1413.

Pike, A. W. G., Hoffmann, D. L., Pettitt, P. B., García-Diez, M., & Zilhéo, J. (2017). Dating Palaeolithic cave art: Why U–Th is the way to go. *Quaternary International, 432*, 41–49

Pillans, B., & Fifield, L. K. (2013). Erosion rates and weathering history of rock surfaces associated with Aboriginal rock art engravings (petroglyphs) on Burrup Peninsula, Western Australia, from cosmogenic nuclide measurements. *Quaternary Science Reviews, 69*, 98–106.

Plagnes, V., Causse, C., Fontugne, M., Valladas, H., Chazine, J. M., & Fage, L. H. (2003). Cross dating (Th/U-14C) of calcite covering prehistoric paintings in Borneo. *Quaternary Research, 60*(2), 172–179.

Quiles, A., Valladas, H., Bocherens, H., Delquí-Količ, E., Kaltnecker, E., van der Plicht, J., . . . Geneste, J. M. (2016). A high-precision chronological model for the decorated Upper Paleolithic cave of Chauvet-Pont d'Arc, Ardèche, France. *Proceedings of the National Academy of Sciences of the United States of America, 113*(17), 4670–4675.

Reimer, P. J., Austin, W. E. N., Bard, E., Bayliss, A., Blackwell, P. G., Bronk Ramsey, C., . . . Talamo, S. (2020). The IntCal20 Northern Hemisphere radiocarbon age calibration curve (0–55 cal kBP). *Radiocarbon, 62*(4), 725–757.

Repka, J., Anderson, R. S., & Finkel, R. C. (1997). Cosmogenic dating of fluvial terraces, Fremont River, Utah. *Earth and Planetary Science Letters, 152*(1–4), 59–73.

Roberts, R., Bird, M., Olley, J., Galbraith, R., Lawson, E., Laslett, G., . . . Hua, Q. (1998). Optical and radiocarbon dating at Jinmium rock shelter in northern Australia. *Nature, 393*, 358–362.

Roberts, R. G., Jacobs, Z., Li, B., Jankowski, N. R., Cunningham, A. C., & Rosenfeld, A. B. (2015). Optical dating in archaeology: Thirty years in retrospect and grand challenges for the future. *Journal of Archaeological Science, 56*, 41–60.

Roberts, R., Jones, R., Spooner, N. A., Head, M. J., Murray, A. S., & Smith, M. A. (1994). The human colonisation of Australia: Optical dates of 53,000 and 60,000 years bracket human arrival at Deaf Adder Gorge, Northern Territory. *Quaternary Science Reviews, 13*(5–7), 575–583.

Roberts, R., Walsh, G., Murray, A., Olley, J., Jones, R., Morwood, M., . . . Naumann, I. (1997). Luminescence dating of rock art and past environments using mud-wasp nests in northern Australia. *Nature, 387*, 696–699.

Ross, J., Westaway, K., Travers, M., Morwood, M. J., & Hayward, J. (2016). Into the past: A step towards a robust Kimberley rock art chronology. *PLoS One, 11*, e0161726.

Sadier, B., Benedetti, L., Delannoy, J.-J., Bourlès, D., Jaillet, S., Arnaud, J., . . . Geneste, J.-M. (2012). Datations 36Cl de la fermeture de la grotte Chauvet, implications géomorphologiques et archéologiques. *Collection EDYTEM. Cahiers de Géographie, 13*(1), 63–78.

Scholz, D., & Hoffmann, D. (2008). 230Th/U-dating of fossil corals and speleothems. *E&G Quaternary Science Journal, 57*, 52–76.

Scholz, D., Hoffmann, D. L., Hellstrom, J., & Bronk Ramsey, C., (2012). A comparison of different methods for speleothem age modelling. *Quaternary Geochronology, 14*, 94–104.

Scholz, D., Tolzmann, J., Hoffmann, D. L., Jochum, K. P., Spötl, C., & Riechelmann, D. F. C. (2014). Diagenesis of speleothems and its effect on the accuracy of 230Th/U-ages. *Chemical Geology, 387,* 74–86.

Sohbati, R., Murray, A. S., Chapot, M. S., Jain, M., & Pederson, J. (2012). Optically stimulated luminescence (OSL) as a chronometer for surface exposure dating. *Journal of Geophysical Research, 117,* B09202, 1–7.

Sohbati, R., Murray, A. S., Porat, N., Jain, M., & Avner, U. (2015). Age of a prehistoric "Rodedian" cult site constrained by sediment and rock surface luminescence dating techniques. *Quaternary Geochronology, 30,* 90–99.

Tobler, R., Rohrlach, A., Soubrier, J. Bover, P., Llamas, B., Tuke, J., . . . Cooper, A. (2017). Aboriginal mitogenomes reveal 50,000 years of regionalism in Australia. *Nature, 544,* 180–184.

Turney, C. S. M., Bird, M. I., Fifield, L. K., Roberts, R. G., Smith, M., Dortch, C. E., . . . Creswell, R. G. (2001). Early human occupation at Devil's Lair, Southwestern Australia 50,000 years ago. *Quaternary Research, 55,* 3–13.

Tylén, K., Fusaroli, R., Rojo, S., Heimann, K., Fay, N., Johannsen, N. N., . . . Lombard, M. (2020). The evolution of early symbolic behavior in *Homo sapiens Proceedings of the National Academy of Sciences of the United States of America, 117*(9), 4578–4584.

Valladas, H., Tisnírat-Laborde, N., Cachier, H., Arnold, M., de Quiros, F. B., Cabrera-Valdes, V., . . . Moure-Romanillo, A. (2001). Radiocarbon AMS dates for Paleolithic cave paintings. *Radiocarbon, 43*(2B), 977–86.

Verri, G., Barkai, R., Bordeanu, C., Gopher, A., Hass, M., Kaufman, A., . . . Boaretto, E. (2004). Flint mining in prehistory recorded by in situ-produced cosmogenic 10Be. *Proceedings of the National Academy of Sciences of the United States of America, 101*(21), 7880–7884.

Verri, G., Barkai, R., Gopher, A., Hass, M., Kubik, P. W., Paul, M., . . . Boaretto, E. (2005). Flint procurement strategies in the Late Lower Palaeolithic recorded by in situ produced cosmogenic 10Be in Tabun and Qesem Caves (Israel). *Journal of Archaeological Science, 32*(2), 207–213.

Veth, P., Ward, U., Manne, T., Ulm, S., Ditchfield, K., Dortch, J., . . . Kendrick, P. (2017). Early human occupation of a maritime desert, Barrow Island, North-West Australia. *Quaternary Science Reviews, 168,* 19–29.

Ward, I., Watchman, A., Cole, N., & Morwood, M. (2001). Identification of minerals in pigments from Aboriginal rock art in the Laura and Kimberley regions, Australia. *Rock Art Research, 18,* 15–23.

Watchman, A. (1993). Evidence of a 25,000-year-old pictograph in northern Australia. *Geoarchaeology, 8*(6), 465–473.

Watchman, A. (1996). *Properties and dating of silica skins associated with rock art* (PhD thesis). University of Canberra, Canberra.

Watchman, A. (2000). A review of the history of dating rock varnishes. *Earth Science Reviews.* 49(1), 261–277.

Watchman, A. (2001). Dating oxalate minerals in rock surface deposits. In M. Jones & P. Sheppard (Eds.), *Australasian connections and new directions. Proceedings of the 7th Australasian Archaeometry Conference, Research in Anthropology and Linguistics 5* (pp. 401–411). Auckland: Department of Anthropology, University of Auckland.

Watchman, A., & Cole, N. (1993). Accelerator radiocarbon dating of plant-fibre binders in rock paintings from northeastern Australia. *Antiquity, 67,* 355–358.

Watchman, A., & Jones, R. (1998). Dating rock images in the tropical monsoon region of northern Australia. *Australian Aboriginal Studies, 1998/2*, 64–70.

Watchman, A. L., David, B., McNiven, I. J., & Flood, J. M. (2000). Micro-archaeology of engraved and painted rock surface crusts at Yiwarlarlay (the Lightning Brothers site), Northern Territory, Australia. *Journal of Archaeological Science, 27*(4), 315–325.

Watchman, A. L., & Jones, R. (2002). An independent confirmation of the 4 ka antiquity of a beeswax figure in Western Arnhem Land, northern Australia. *Archaeometry, 44*(1), 145–153.

Watchman, A., Taçon, P., & Aubert, M. (2014). Correspondence on 'Erosion rates and weathering history of rock surfaces associated with Aboriginal rock art engravings (petroglyphs) on Burrup Peninsula, Western Australia, from cosmogenic nuclide measurements' by B. Pillans & K. Fifield. *Quaternary Science Reviews, 69*, 98–106. *Quaternary Science Reviews, 91*, 70–73.

Watchman, A., Walsh, G., Morwood, M. J., & Tuniz, C. (1997). AMS radiocarbon age estimates for early rock paintings in the Kimberley, N.W. Australia: Preliminary results. *Rock Art Research, 14*(1), 18–26.

Wedepohl, K. H. (1995). The composition of the continental crust. *Geochimica et Cosmochimica Acta, 59*(7), 1217–1232.

Wood, R. (2015). From revolution to convention: The past, present and future of radiocarbon dating. *Journal of Archaeological Science, 56*, 61–72.

Yoshida, H., Roberts, R. G., & Olley, J. M. (2003). Progress towards single-grain optical dating of fossil mud-wasp nests and associated rock art in northern Australia. *Quaternary Science Reviews, 22*(10–13), 1273–1278.

Zhao, J. X., Yu, K. F., & Feng, Y. X. (2009). High-precision 238U-234U-230Th disequilibrium dating of the recent past: A review. *Quaternary Geochronology, 4*, 423–433.

PART V

CULTURAL DYNAMICS AND NETWORKS

CHAPTER 22

CORAL SEA CULTURAL INTERACTION SPHERE

IAN J. MCNIVEN

INTRODUCTION

THIS chapter focuses on ways of conceptualizing and exploring the long history of Indigenous cultural interactions and influences between southern New Guinea and northeastern Australia via Torres Strait. This topic is important for three reasons. First, colonialist assumptions and pejorative representations of Aboriginal Australians as passive recipients of advanced cultural traits from New Guineans infuse the history of Western scholarship on this topic. Such (mis)representations need to be questioned, understood, and expunged from modern scholarship. Second, the history of Australia extends well beyond the confines of European settlement and invasion, commencing in 1788. Australia has at least 65,000 years of human history, and for 85% of this time sea levels were lower and the landmasses of Australia (including Tasmania) and New Guinea joined to form the large island continent of Sahul (Clarkson et al. 2017). In this sense, the early colonization of Australia is also the early colonization of New Guinea. Shared geography and shared cultural origins inexorably link the histories of Australia and New Guinea (Lilley 2019; White & O'Connell 1982). Finally, a key dimension of interactions between Australia and New Guinea since sea-level rise at the end of the Ice Age and the formation of Torres Strait 8000–9000 years ago are long-distance exchange networks. As McNiven (2015a: 604) notes, 'Such connections represent key themes in the social and political histories of these regions, with complex alliance and ceremonial exchange systems expressing myriad inter-group cultural dynamics, adaptive strategies and the entrepreneurial desires of peoples to mutually construct their social worlds through inter-community networks'. In short, a history of long-distance exchange networks is a history of human agency and enterprise. All three points inform my development of the Coral Sea Cultural Interaction Sphere as a conceptual framework to investigate the historically dynamic nature of cultural interactions and influences between northeastern Australia and southern mainland Papua New Guinea over the past 3000 years.

THE CORAL SEA CULTURAL INTERACTION SPHERE

In 2004, I introduced the concept of the Coral Sea Cultural Interaction Sphere (CSCIS) as a heuristic to broaden anthropological and archaeological discussions of the movement of material culture traits between New Guinea and Australia away from an influential and often subliminal trope that largely reduced interaction to the diffusion of 'Papuan' cultural traits from New Guinea to Australia (McNiven, von Gnielinski, & Quinnell 2004: 284–285). This diffusionist approach developed during the second half of the nineteenth century as a tenet of social evolutionism and colonialist thinking whereby anthropologists constructed a view of Australian Aboriginal cultures as lowly, undeveloped, and passively receptive to higher-level and advanced cultural traits from overseas (see McNiven 2006a, 2020; McNiven & Russell 2005). During the first half of the twentieth century, the influence of 'Papuan' cultural traits on Cape York Peninsula Aboriginal societies became a focus for Australian anthropologists and the colonial diffusionism paradigm (McNiven 2006a; McNiven & Russell 2005). For example, Ronald Hamlyn-Harris (1915: 10) of the Queensland Museum in Brisbane noted that 'more writers than one have referred to presumed Papuan culture on Cape York Peninsula, and the list of objects illustrating it is now a formidable one'. Couched in a classic colonialist and pejorative trope, Hamlyn-Harris (1915: 10) added that 'the Queensland aboriginal was never an inventive genius, and his implements and weapons are remarkably constant, but that he is a born mimic and imitator is very apparent'. Anthropologist Daniel Davidson (1933: 266, 268) argued that geographical variations in different netting techniques used by Aboriginal Australians confirm that 'New Guinea [via Torres Strait] is the home of these techniques'. In characteristic derogatory language, Davidson added that 'it is a commonly-accepted belief that the influence of the Australians upon other ethnic areas has been practically nil' and that 'Australia, in its peripheral location, is marked by general backwardness' (Davidson 1933: 257, 266). Cambridge anthropologist Alfred Haddon (1904: 295) added, 'The miserable condition of the Australians precluded them from having much to offer to the Torres Straits Islanders in the way of exchange'.

Anthropologist/archaeologist Fred McCarthy (1940) of the Australian Museum in Sydney listed over fifty cultural traits (mostly different types of objects) forming part of Australian Aboriginal cultures, especially those in North Queensland, which he interpreted as being 'introduced' from 'New Guinea via Torres Strait'. These introduced traits included outrigger canoes, bows and arrows, fishhooks, stone axes, multipronged spears, and shell containers. As American anthropologist Herbert Noone (a colleague of McCarthy) quipped: 'So much evidence has been put forward to indicate that the Australian aboriginal has brought, or borrowed, many traits of his culture from overseas sources, that one is led to look for anything of his that is left' (Noone 1943: 279).

The CSCIS was also conceptualized in response to archaeological evidence that challenged McCarthy's (1940) belief that no archaeological examples existed of objects or cultural traits of Aboriginal origin moving from Australia into New Guinea via Torres Strait. McNiven et al. (2004: 273, 282, Table 1) document a 19.6-cm-long ground stone axe fashioned from gabbro and obtained on Daru Island (immediately northeast of Torres Strait) in the 1960s/1970s but probably found archaeologically on Kiwai Island (located 70 km to the northeast at the mouth of the Fly River) in southwest Papua New Guinea and taken to Daru. As Kiwai Island, like the entire southwest corner of mainland Papua New Guinea, features no exposures of gabbro, the Kiwai axe must have been imported. The nearest outcrops of gabbro are eastern Cape York Peninsula on mainland Australia and possibly the northern side of the central ranges of mainland Papua New Guinea. As McNiven et al. (2004: 284) state, 'This axe provides the first tentative evidence for prehistoric movement of material culture from mainland Australia to New Guinea'. Rejecting colonial diffusionist assumptions that 'cultural movements from New Guinea to Australia are much more probable than in the opposite direction' (Haddon 1935: 411), McNiven and colleagues (2004: 285) conclude that 'ideas and material culture generally move between groups through two-way trade and reciprocal exchanges'. Following archaeological research on the coast of central Queensland and possible external cultural influences, archaeologist Bryce Barker (2004: 148) similarly remarks that we must stop viewing Aboriginal peoples as 'being passive receivers of a diffusion of ideas and material culture from the north. Rather, their participation should be seen in the context of a greater degree of regional interaction, in which the flow of ideas and materials was probably mutual'. McNiven (1993: 27) notes that 'diffusionism is not a process per se, but the result of a complex set of interactive events'. In short, 'we must move beyond *diffusionism* and examine *interchanges*' (McNiven 2006a: 103).

Interregional interchanges form the basis of the CSCIS and centre on a series of ethnographically known, canoe-voyaging, and long-distance coastal exchange networks taking in the more than 2000 km of coast between southeast mainland Papua New Guinea and the east coast of Cape York Peninsula (Figure 22.1). It includes the 1200-km-long coast of southern mainland Papua New Guinea, the 150-km-wide Torres Strait, and the eastern coast of Cape York Peninsula, extending south for at least 600 km to Lizard Island. McCarthy (1939: 179–191, fig. 15) first detailed and linked these long-distance maritime exchange networks ('trunk trade routes') as the basis for the diffusion of cultural traits from New Guinea into northeast Australia via Torres Strait. These canoe-voyaging and maritime exchange networks provided the mechanism for the movement, sharing, and exchange of ideas and objects across southern New Guinea and northeastern Australia. Cultural choice informed by cultural beliefs and values provided the process for selective uptake of cultural traits and produced continuities and discontinuities in object distributions between New Guinea and Australia.

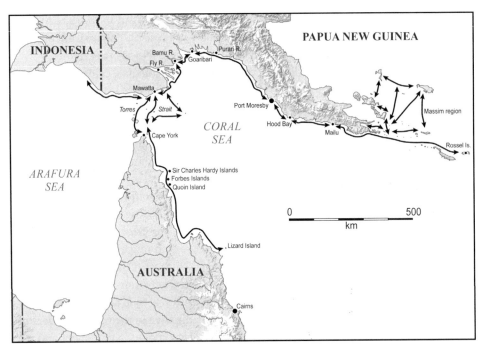

FIGURE 22.1. Ethnographically known maritime exchange networks along southern Papua New Guinea and northeastern Australia linking communities along more than 2000 km of coastline. Maritime exchange networks underpinned the Coral Sea Cultural Interaction Sphere over the past 3000 years.

Maritime Exchange Networks

Ethnographic research documents six major canoe-based voyaging exchange networks and numerous small-scale exchange networks that indirectly linked communities along the 2000 km of coast comprising the CSCIS (Figure 22.1). Five major exchange networks encompassed the southern coast of Papua New Guinea (see also Skelly & David 2017: chap. 17, and McNiven 2022 for overviews): the Massim, Mailu, Motu-Hood Bay, Motu-Papuan Gulf, and Torres Strait networks. The Massim network took in islands off the southeastern tip of mainland New Guinea (e.g., the Trobriand Islands) and centred on the famous *kula* exchange system (Leach 1983: Map 1; Malinowski 1922; Macintyre & Allen 1990: figs. 4–6). It connected with communities of the southeast coast of mainland Papua New Guinea (Mailu region) by inland and coastal exchange routes (Tueting 1935: 24–26). The Mailu network linked with the Massim region to the east (Irwin 1985), and extended westward for around 170 km to near Hood Bay and eastward for over 500 km to Rossel Island (Saville 1926: 152; see also Malinowski 1915; Seligmann 1910). The Motu-Hood Bay network centred on Motu peoples of the Port Moresby region and extended 140 km eastward to the Hood Bay region (Oram 1982: 9; Seligmann 1910: 92; Skelly et al. 2018). The Motu-Papuan Gulf network similarly centred on Motu peoples of Port

Moresby and encompassed coastal communities to the west along the Gulf of Papua through their famous *hiri* trade expeditions (Barton 1910; Dutton 1978, 1982; Skelly & David 2017; Seligmann 1910), which extended westward to the Purari River Delta (Oram 1982: 5) and perhaps to Goaribari Island (Chester 1878: 9; Stone 1880: 64, 188; see also Barker et al. 2012; Williams 1924: 125). Austin (cited in McCarthy 1939: 185–186) noted that Goaribari exchange relationships extended westward to the Bamu River and the Fly River mouth region opposite Torres Strait, adding that shells from Torres Strait have been traded eastward as far as Goaribari (see also Rhoads & MacKenzie 1991: 43). Thus, trading expeditions emanating from Port Moresby and Mailu linked villages across the Gulf and Central Provinces 'into a vast, articulating network of exchange that implicated much of the south coast and beyond' (Skelly et al. 2018: 184). The Torres Strait network linked island communities across the archipelago and communities of the adjacent mainland coasts of New Guinea to the north and Australia to the south (Haddon 1890, 1904; Landtman 1927; Lawrence 1994; Moore 1978; Vanderwal 2004). The northern peoples of Torres Strait also had exchange relationships with the Marind-anim of the southeast corner of Indonesian New Guinea (McNiven 1998: 107–109).

An eastern Cape York Peninsula network linked Torres Strait Islanders with Aboriginal communities along 600 km of mainland coast (McNiven 2015b; McCarthy 1939: 180–182; Mulvaney 1976). Anthropologist Alfred Howitt (1904: 11–12) was informed that Torres Strait Islanders would 'obtain wives from the Australian mainland' during their 'annual voyages . . . down the Cape York coast'. Peoples of central Torres Strait voyaged southward to 'islands off the east coast of Queensland, particularly the Sir Charles Hardy group and the Forbes Islands, whither they resorted every south-east season to live for a while and to barter' for objects such as stone for club heads, *zogo* ritual stones, and ochre (Haddon 1935: 88; McNiven & Russell-Cook 2020). The 'Koko Ya'o people of Lloyd Bay' informed anthropologist Donald Thomson (1939: 82) that Torres Strait Islanders 'came frequently in big canoes to Mitirindji (Quoin Island) off the mouth of the Pascoe River to obtain supplies of stone for their axes, and it is probable that tobacco was one of the important articles of exchange brought down during these voyages'. These islands are located around 200 km southeast of Cape York. In light of Torres Strait Islanders voyaging down the east coast of Cape York Peninsula, anthropologist Ursula McConnel (1953: 3) rightly noted that 'it is not surprising, therefore, to find cultural similarities existing also between the [Torres Strait] Islands and the Cape York mainland, particularly where direct contact by canoe has been made. . . . This external influence extends further south on the eastern coast than on the western Gulf coast, because the eastern coast is more accessible by canoe'. McCarthy (1958: 40–41) noted similarly that 'many of the introduced traits diffused from New Guinea via Torres Strait islands and Cape York by means of a long-established canoe trade; others came direct from the Torres Strait area'. Archaeologist Mike Rowland (1987: 42) also argued that 'the extent of canoe penetration from Papua New Guinea into Australia is of crucial importance since canoe transport may have provided the major mechanism for the introduction of other items of material culture' (see also Barham & Harris 1983: 538; Barham 2000: 233). All of this ethnographic information on exchange networks reinforces

Rowland's (1995: 9) comment that 'a chain of trade networks did link Papuans of the Gulf with the Aboriginal groups of Cape York'.

The interlinking of these six major exchange networks along the south coast of New Guinea and along the east coast of Cape York Peninsula indicates that it was theoretically possible for objects and cultural practices to exhibit shared uptake along the entire 2000 km length of the CSCIS (McNiven 2022). Two expressions of broad-scale interaction between southern New Guinea and northeastern Australia are shared biology (e.g., craniometrics and DNA) and shared material culture (e.g., double outrigger canoes).

SHARED BIOLOGY
(CRANIOMETRICS AND DNA)

During the nineteenth century, Torres Strait Islanders were included with New Guinea peoples as racially distinct ('Papuan', 'Melanesian', or 'Negroid') from Aboriginal peoples of mainland Australia to the south ('Australian' or 'Australioid') (e.g., Earl 1853: 189, 238; Haddon 1890: 388, 1935: 410; Howitt 1904: 3, 15, 28; Huxley 1870: 406; Keane 1896: 281, 283; Prichard 1847: 4; Topinard 1878: 495). Following the pejorative hierarchical social evolutionist thinking of the time, ethnologists/anthropologists saw the Australians as inferior to the Papuans (Anderson 2007; Ballard 2008; Douglas 2008, 2014; McNiven & Russell 2005). Yet anthropologists also commented that Cape York Aboriginal peoples possessed a Papuan appearance (e.g., frizzy hair) owing to immigration (Topinard 1878: 502), intrusion (McConnel 1930: 100), and infiltration (Thomson 1934a: 238) of New Guinea/Torres Strait peoples.

Anthropometric analyses of human skulls by physical anthropologists, all from museum collections and presumably of recent age, confirm gene flow between New Guinea and northeastern Australia. For example, Thomas's (1885: 328–329) analysis of Torres Strait Islander skulls revealed a complex picture of Melanesian, Australian/Australioid, and Polynesian racial 'admixture'. Macintosh and Larnach (1973: 1) found that 'Australian crania show their maximum resemblance to New Guinea crania in the region (Cape York) which is closest to New Guinea'. Furthermore, 'the contrast between Australian and New Guinea crania increases the further south we take the Australian sample' (Macintosh & Larnach 1973: 6). A similar cline was identified by Brace (1980: 146), who argued that increasing tooth size moving southward from Cape York across the Australian continent was 'caused by the introduction of genes for smaller teeth from the northeast [via Torres Strait]'. Pietrusewsky's (1979: 103, fig. 1) analysis of skulls found that 'the combined Cape York Peninsula and Torres Strait sample aligns with a sample from the Gulf District of Southern Papua New Guinea' and other New Guinea samples more than with other Australian samples (see also Giles 1976: 168).

Blood-group distribution studies have also revealed genetic mixing in the Torres Strait region. For example, Booth and Oraka (1968: 153) argued that relatively high frequencies of the *Rh^z* allele on the northern mainland coast of Torres Strait (compared to the south coast of New Guinea more broadly) 'probably resulted from some mingling with Australian Aborigines, who possess R_z [sic] in high frequency'. According to Kirk (1972: 373), the 'overall conclusion which emerges from the study of genetic markers amongst the immediate populations on both sides of Torres Strait is that they share, to an appreciable degree, a common genetic background'. While the craniometrics and genetic marker studies reveal gene flow between southern New Guinea and northeastern Australian peoples, it remains unknown if such interactions occurred before and/or after the formation of Torres Strait 8000–9000 years ago.

Recent analyses of nuclear DNA (nDNA) and mitochondrial DNA (mtDNA) genomes by geneticists reveal that Aboriginal Australians and Highland New Guinea peoples diverged around 37,000 years ago (with a 95% confidence interval of 25,000–40,000 years ago; Malaspinas et al. 2016: 210). Y chromosome data similarly suggest ancient divergence at least 48,000 years ago (with a 95% confidence interval of 42,800–54,900 years ago; Bergström et al. 2016: 810). Hudjashov et al. (2007: 8728) posit that mtDNA haplogroup Q subsequently entered Australia from New Guinea 30,400±9300 years ago, a conclusion challenged by the apparent use of Q haplogroup samples from peoples with recent Torres Strait Islander heritage (Nagle et al. 2017: 350). Malaspinas et al. (2016: 212) suggest that 'the best-fitting model for the Aboriginal Australian-Papuan data is one of continuous but modest gene flow, mostly unidirectional from Papuans to Aboriginal Australians, and geographically restricted to northeast Aboriginal Australians' within the past 10,000 years. Wright et al. (2018: 5) found that the nDNA of Aboriginal skeletal remains from the Mulgrave District of Cairns, located 800 km southeast of Cape York, revealed '~13% Papuan-related ancestry'. In terms of unidirectionality, Nagle et al. (2017: 351) point out that DNA studies concur that 'there is no evidence of back migration of females carrying Australian-specific mtDNA lineages into New Guinea after they arose within Australia'. Yet none of the DNA studies cited by Nagle et al. (2017) in support of this conclusion use DNA samples from relevant populations in North Queensland (McNiven et al. 2011: 5). DNA evidence for minimal gene flow between New Guinea and Australia (Nagle et al. 2017: 351; Tobler et al. 2017: 183) is inconsistent with historical, ethnographic, and anthropomorphic evidence for considerable connections. Indeed, some DNA analysts acknowledge that such patterns may be a sampling issue as current 'genetic data remains sparse' (Tobler et al. 2017: 180), necessitating 'acquisition of additional a[ncient] DNA samples from the eastern coastline of Cape York and New Guinea—and, ideally, the Torres Strait Islands too' (Collard et al. 2019: 613; see also Bergström 2017: 72).

SHARED MATERIAL CULTURE (DOUBLE OUTRIGGER CANOES)

Ethnographic records reveal complex patterns of object distributions between New Guinea and Australia via Torres Strait. Some objects occur across New Guinea and

Torres Strait but not Australia (e.g., dog-tooth body adornments, *Conus* armbands), some objects occur across northern Queensland and Torres Strait but not New Guinea (e.g., shell-handled spear throwers, *Nautilus* shell bead headbands), while other objects are shared across various parts of New Guinea, Torres Strait, and northern Queensland (e.g., bamboo smoking pipes, double outrigger canoes) (see McNiven 2022 for details). Ethnographic and archaeological details on double outrigger canoes are explored below.

Ethnographic Evidence

Across New Guinea and Australia, the two major areas of double outrigger canoe use 100–200 years ago were Torres Strait and the northern half of Cape York Peninsula (see also McNiven 2022) (Figure 22.2). In the Indonesian province of Papua, dugout canoes fitted with double outriggers occurred on Waigu Island and to the east around Cenderawasih (Geelvink) Bay (Haddon 1937: 324–330). In Papua New Guinea, double outrigger canoes had isolated occurrences on Nissan Island located east of New Ireland (Haddon 1937: 116) and in the Louisiade Archipelago in the southeast (Haddon 1937: 254; but see also Wood 2018: 220), as well as the mainland south coast opposite Torres Strait (Haddon 1900: 426). Double outrigger canoes were ubiquitous across Torres Strait (McNiven 2015c). On the east coast of Cape York Peninsula, Aboriginal communities as far south as the Stewart River made and used double outrigger canoes (Hale & Tindale 1934: 120–121; Roth 1910: 11; Thomson 1934a: 243–244, Pl. XXIX, 1952: 2, 1956: 36). On the west coast of Cape York Peninsula, double outrigger canoes occurred as far south as the Edward River (Haddon 1937: 186, fig. 113c; McConnel 1930: 104; 1953: 24–25; Roth 1910: 11–13, figs. 10, 11, Pl. VI.1), and to the Wellesley Islands in the southern Gulf of Carpentaria in postcontact times (Allen 1980: 97; Memmott 2010: 86, 91).

Observations by mid-nineteenth century European mariners document Torres Strait Islanders voyaging southward down the east coast of Cape York Peninsula (McNiven 2015b: 51). It is safe to assume that such observations are a proxy for the southern extent of double outrigger canoes because Torres Strait Islanders only voyaged in such vessels (McNiven 2015c). Naturalist John MacGillivray (1852, II: 15) observed double outrigger canoes extending from Cape York southward for a distance of nearly 900 km to Fitzroy Island near Cairns. Oral histories of Torres Strait Islanders also document voyaging up to 600 km south of Cape York to Lizard Island (Laade 1969: 39, 1973: 159).

Anthropologists (Davidson 1935: 12; Haddon 1937: 190–193; Hale & Tindale 1934: 121; McCarthy 1940: 268, 297; McConnel 1953: 9, 25; Spencer 1922: 73; Thomson 1934b: 233, 1952; Wood 2018: 214–215) and archaeologists (Beaton 1985: 18; Flood 1983: 223; Lourandos 1997: 47; Mulvaney & Kamminga 1999: 322; Rowland 1987, 2018) concur that double outrigger canoes entered Cape York Peninsula Aboriginal societies as a 'Papuan influence'. Ideas on the origin of double outrigger canoes in New Guinea range from westerly influences from Southeast Asia via the south coast of Indonesian New Guinea (Doran 1981: 92; Wood 2018) to easterly influences from Island Melanesia

(Haddon 1920: 122; Wood 2018). However, it is clear from Figure 22.2 that Australia (Torres Strait and Cape York Peninsula), at least in the recent past, was the key area for double outrigger canoes and not New Guinea (McNiven 2022). This geographical focus is consistent with an endogenous development, possibly focused on Torres Strait (Barham 2000: 249). Yet as Rowland (1995: 11) rightly notes, 'without chronological control it is difficult to determine whether out-riggers were invented in Papua New Guinea and the concept transferred to Australia or vice versa; or if out-riggers were independently invented in both areas'. At the very least it is clear that Torres Strait and the adjacent coast of Papua New Guinea to the immediate north and the adjacent coastline of Cape York Peninsula to the south shared a tradition of double outrigger canoe manufacture and use.

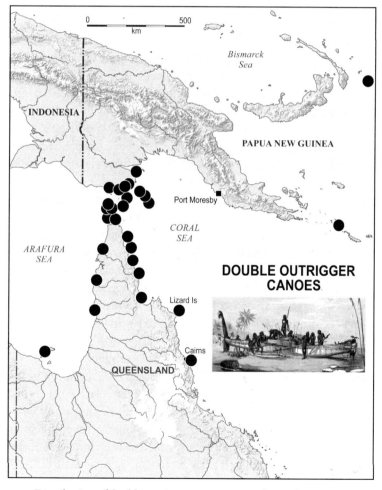

FIGURE 22.2. Distribution of double outrigger canoes across the study area.
(Inset: Torres Strait canoe from Melville 1849: pl. XIX.)

Archaeological Evidence

Direct archaeological evidence for double outrigger canoes is unknown for Torres Strait and North Queensland. The closest direct evidence is rock art, with red ochre paintings of over forty individual canoes on various rocky islands of western Torres Strait (Brady 2010: 429). Canoe paintings are unknown for Cape York Peninsula. The Torres Strait paintings usually reveal distinctive features of local canoes such as stern posts, central flags, central platform, and front sails. Interestingly, the only known possible example of a canoe painting with an outrigger is located at the site of Kabadul Kula on the island of Dauan in northwest Torres Strait (Brady 2010: 432). Associated dates for canoe rock art in Torres Strait come from archaeological excavation of sediments directly below the panel with the canoe and possible outrigger (which is located next to two other canoe paintings) at Kabadul Kula (McNiven, Brady, & Barham 2009). Accelerator mass spectrometry (AMS) radiocarbon dates on charcoal of c. 1200 to 1400 years ago are associated with a subsurface concentration of red ochre fragments (some with grinding facets) and provide insight into the age of the overlying rock art and canoe paintings (McNiven et al. 2009: 37). This dating casts doubt on the suggestion that the canoe with the possible outrigger also bears a crab-claw sail reminiscent of *lagatoi* canoes used in the *hiri* exchange network of the Gulf of Papua within the past 500 years (Brady 2010: 430–433; David et al. 2010: 40; McNiven et al. 2004: 244; Skelly & David 2017: 37).

Archaeological insights into the potential age of double outrigger canoes in the study area also focus on associated cultural practices. For example, archaeologist Jack Golson (1972: 396–397) associated the introduction of double outrigger canoes with the introduction of the pig to New Guinea from Southeast Asia dated at the time to 5000–6000 years ago (redated to within the past 3000 years—O'Connor et al. 2011). For single outrigger canoes, Golson linked introduction to New Guinea with 'the arrival of Austronesian speakers . . . within the last 2000–3000 years'. Archaeologist David Moore (1979: 310) connected the introduction of double outrigger canoes to Torres Strait with the arrival of pottery-making Austronesians on the south coast of Papua New Guinea, then dated to around 2000 years ago (e.g., Vanderwal 1973) and later redated to 2900 years ago with Lapita pottery finds at Caution Bay near Port Moresby (David et al. 2011; McNiven et al. 2011). McNiven (2015c) similarly linked the introduction of double outrigger canoes to Torres Strait with Austronesian influences, albeit with a slightly earlier date associated with the introduction of pottery to Torres Strait around 2500 years ago (e.g., McNiven et al. 2006). To the south in the Princess Charlotte Bay area of eastern Cape York Peninsula, Beaton (1985: 18) argued that 'the use of the islands 2500 years ago probably had to await the introduction of the outrigger canoe of Papua-Melanesian origin'. Archaeologist Anthony Barham (2000) also posited that double outrigger canoe use in Torres Strait and Cape York Peninsula dated to the past 2500 years, linking it to the development of what he called the 'Torres Strait Cultural Complex'. Other archaeologists concur that outrigger canoes diffused southward from Melanesia along the northeastern Australian coast down to central

CORAL SEA CULTURAL INTERACTION SPHERE   601

Queensland sometime in the Late Holocene (e.g., Barker 2004: 146; O'Connor & Veth 2000: 131; Rowland 1987: 42–43).

Archaeological Time Depth
of the CSCIS

The Coral Sea Cultural Interaction Sphere (CSCIS) was chronologically complex given that it comprised interregional exchange networks that, by definition, were socially and hence temporally dynamic. Furthermore, chronological insights into the age of interregional exchange networks and maritime mobility patterns more broadly across the area taken in by the CSCIS are incomplete owing to the patchiness of archaeological research. For example, no published archaeological excavation data is available for the 500 km of coastline on the east side of Cape York Peninsula from Jacky Jacky Creek (located 20 km south of Cape York) to just north of Princess Charlotte Bay. Similarly, no archaeological excavation data are available for the 500 km stretch of coastline westward of the Kikori River (western Gulf of Papua) through to the Fly River mouth and along the Trans-Fly coast to the international border of Papua New Guinea and Indonesia. The bulk of archaeological excavation information on the long-term history of the CSCIS concerns the south coast of mainland Papua New Guinea from the Kikori River eastward. For this region, archaeologist Bruno David (2008: 471) makes the point that 'occupational trends are best understood in terms of pulses rather than long-term trends, and these pulses appear to be associated with the operation of long-distance trade networks'. For purposes of analysis, the following discussion provides archaeological insights into the existence, or otherwise, of long-distance exchange relationships for three chronological periods: <1000 years, 1000–3000 years ago, and >3000 years ago. This discussion reveals that the CSCIS was historically dynamic with numerous reconfigurations over the past 3000 years.

<1000 Years Ago

Available evidence strongly indicates that the CSCIS, at least in its ethnographically defined form, dates to within the past 1000 years and particularly within the past 500 years. To date, archaeological information on the potential establishment dates for ethnographically known maritime exchange networks are limited to Papua New Guinea (see also Urwin, Rhoads, & Bell, this volume). For example, the island-based Massim (*kula*) exchange network began taking on its ethnographic form around 500 years ago (Egloff 1978; Shaw 2016: 119; Shaw & Langley 2017: 163–164). Between 500 and 1,000 years ago (termed the Expansion Phase by Egloff 1979), the island exchange network also incorporated pottery makers from the adjacent mainland (Collingwood Bay), indicating that 'the *kula* once extended outside its present boundaries' (Egloff 1978: 434). As such, the *kula* has seen 'increasing localization through time and a constriction of interaction in the north-western sector of the *kula* islands' (Egloff 1978: 434). Recent radiocarbon dating of engraved *Conus* shell valuables—found from the eastern Massim across to Collingwood Bay—to the Expansion Phase confirms that the spatial scale of the Massim exchange network was greater prior to the ethnographically known *kula* (Ambrose et al. 2012). The ethnographically known Mailu network emerged over the past 800 years (Irwin 1991: 508–509). Up to 300 years ago, it featured relatively high use of obsidian (compared to local chert) sourced to Fergusson Island in the Massim, imported through a well-developed exchange network requiring coastal voyaging trips over a distance of at least 250 km (Irwin 1978: 410, 413, 1985: 210–215; Irwin & Holdaway 1996; Irwin, Shaw, & Mcalister 2019: 11).

Archaeological insights into the history and antiquity of exchange relationships established by the Motu people of Port Moresby are well developed for the west (e.g., Papuan Gulf) and poor for the east (e.g., Hood Bay). Preliminary excavations at Hood Bay indicate a changing exchange relationship with the Motu over the past 500–600 years (Skelly et al. 2018). Insights into the development of the Motu-Papuan Gulf exchange network and the *hiri* rely on archaeological excavations at numerous sites along the Gulf of Papua. Relevant excavation data are available for Kerema (Frankel, Thompson, & Vanderwal 1994), the Vailala River area (David, Araho, Barker, Kuaso, & Moffat 2009; Skelly, David, Barker, Kuaso, & Araho 2010), Orokolo Bay (Allen & Duerden 1982: 56; Urwin, Hua, Skelly, & Arifeae 2018: 7; Rhoads 1982: 144, 1994), and the Kikori River (Barker, Lamb, David, Skelly, & Korokai 2015; David 2008: 469; Rhoads & MacKenzie 1991: 40, 42). These studies support archaeologist Jim Allen's (1977: 394) prediction that the 'archaeological solution to dating the *hiri* lies in excavating recipient villages to the west' of Port Moresby. All evidence converges on the conclusion that the *hiri* took its ethnographically known form around 500 years ago (Skelly & David 2017: 491–492). Although dates are not available for the antiquity of the Torres Strait exchange network, McNiven (2006b: 9) hypothesizes that it developed within the past 600–800 years as part of the broader emergence of ethnographically known social arrangements.

1000–3000 Years Ago

The period 1000–2000 years ago presents a complex and dynamic picture of changing intensities of long-distance exchange relationships involving southern New Guinea and Torres Strait. Obsidian and pottery sourcing studies reveal that the geographical reach of exchange relationships along the south coast of mainland Papua New Guinea and with Torres Strait during this time was similar in scale (albeit often of low intensity) to exchange networks recorded historically (Bickler 1997: 160). For example, use of obsidian at Mailu 1000–1600 years ago dropped to almost nothing (Irwin 1978: 408, 413, 1985: 210–215, 1991: 504–506; Irwin & Holdaway 1996: 232), while at Caution Bay near Port Moresby, use of imported Fergusson Island obsidian virtually ceased 1000–1900 years ago (Mialanes et al. 2016: 255). As such, the intensity of long-distance exchange networks along the southeast coast of mainland Papua New Guinea was less intense 1000–1600 years ago than in the past 1000 years and between 2000 and 3000 years ago (see below). Yet in the western Gulf and western Torres Strait, this period saw increased exchange activity. In the western Gulf in the mid-Kikori River region, 1000–1500 years ago marks a period of social dynamism associated with importation of pottery from Yule Island in the eastern Gulf and the Port Moresby region (Bickler 1997: 159; David 2008: 470; David et al. 2010; Marsaglia, Kramer, David, & Skelly 2016; see also Rhoads 1982: 140–141). This social dynamism extended to stone artefacts with stone axes dating to c. 1200–1900 years ago from the site of Kulupuari/Kikiniu on the mid-Kikori sourced to the Tapini region of the western Owen Stanley Ranges located 300 km to the east (Rhoads & MacKenzie 1991: 39).

In western Torres Strait, a pulse of production of locally made pottery with clear cultural links to New Guinea occurs on the islands of Pulu dating to 1500–1700 years ago (McNiven et al. 2006) and nearby Mabuyag dating to 1300–1600 years ago (Wright & Dickinson 2009). Archaeologist Duncan Wright and colleagues (2019) report on a single pottery sherd of possible New Guinea origin excavated from the island of Dauar in eastern Torres Strait dating to 1100–1500 years ago.

Between 1600 and 2000 years ago, Fergusson Island obsidian found in the Mailu region (e.g., Selai site at Amazon Bay on the mainland) and at the Oposisi site (Yule Island in the eastern Gulf) reveal sea-voyaging networks extending 250 km and 650 km, respectively (Allen, Summerhayes, Mandui, & Leavesley 2011; Irwin 1978, 1985, 1991). During this time, ceramics manufactured on Yule Island were traded to the Port Moresby district located over 100 km to the east (Summerhayes & Allen 2007: 113) and to the Kikori River region located 300 km to the west (Bickler 1997: 159). This period of activity matches a pulse of pottery use at the Ormi site on Dauar in eastern Torres Strait dated c. 1600–1900 years ago (Carter 2004: 266, 270; McNiven et al. 2006: 67). The Ormi sherds have been sourced to the Kikori River region and clearly were imported to Dauar through exchange with peoples from the western Gulf over a voyaging distance of at least 300 km (Carter 2004: 298, 304; Carter & Lilley 2008: 77).

The period 2000–3000 years ago is associated with the presence of late Lapita peoples (or at least late Lapita cultural influences—White 2018: 81) along the south coast of mainland Papua New Guinea. Arrival is dated to 2900 years ago (at Caution Bay, near Port Moresby—David et al. 2011; McNiven et al. 2011), with Lapita ceramics also found in the southern Massim on the islands of Wari (Negishi & Ono 2009) and Tubetube (Irwin et al. 2019), and at Hopo near the Vailala River in the Gulf of Papua (Skelly, David, Petchey, & Leavesley 2014). The Hopo ceramics, dated to around 2600 years ago, reveal Lapita-related activity extending westward along the south coast of mainland Papua New Guinea for a sea distance of over 700 km from the Massim. Obsidian artefacts from Hopo dating to 2600 years ago derive from Fergusson Island located 850 km to the east by sea (Skelly, Ford, Summerhayes, Mialanes, & David 2016). Archaeologist Robert Skelly and colleagues (2016: 135–136) rightly point out 'that obsidian exchange appears to have been part of social relationships that maintained links between people through time and across space' along the south coast of Papua New Guinea. Skelly et al. (2014: 470) conclude that 'the long-distance maritime networks linking the entire southern coast of Papua New Guinea in historical times may trace their origin to this [Lapita] period'. Furthermore, 'We hypothesise that this period of expansion witnessed heightened levels of seafaring by Austronesian-speaking terminal Lapita peoples expanding westward as emerging generations opened up their world towards new territorial and social opportunities in the face of increasing population levels' (Skelly et al. 2014: 485). If quantities of imported Fergusson Island obsidian are an indicator of intensity of exchange relationships, then the dramatic increase in the number of obsidian artefacts at the Bogi 1 site at Caution Bay in levels dated to c. 2000–2300 years ago point to intensified long-distance exchange relationships by post-Lapita residents (Mialanes et al. 2016: 253, 258–259).

An apparent lack of use of obsidian in the western Gulf 2000 to 2900 years ago points to minimal exchange relationships with obsidian-importing communities of the eastern Gulf (Skelly et al. 2016: 136). In contrast, pottery in eastern and western Torres Strait dating back to 2600 years ago suggests that peoples of the Gulf were extending their long-distance exchange networks westward (Carter 2004; McNiven et al. 2006). Specifically, McNiven et al. (2006) document an early phase of pottery use at Mask Cave on Pulu in western Torres Strait dating to 2400–2600 years ago. The deepest sherd at Mask Cave is associated with an AMS radiocarbon date of 2507±42 BP (charcoal), which calibrates to 2430–2740 cal BP (95.4%) (median probability = 2586 cal BP) with Calib 8.2 using the IntCal20 calibration dataset. Although of local manufacture, the Mask Cave pottery indicates 'influences from the Papua New Guinea mainland' (McNiven et al. 2011: 5). None of the Pulu sherds exhibit Lapita dentate-stamped designs, but the oldest sherd dated to 2586 cal BP just overlaps in time with the most recent Lapita ceramics at Caution Bay (dating to 2550 cal BP—David et al. 2019: 79). However, the early Pulu sherds correspond (at least in terms of age) with the Post-Lapita Transformative Tradition (c. 2150–2600 cal BP) of the south coast identified by David et al. (2012). Whether of terminal Lapita age (David et al. 2011: 586–597; Lilley 2019; Skelly et al. 2014: 471; Specht 2018: 100), and/or immediate post-Lapita age (McNiven et al. 2006: 75), the Pulu ceramics are linked to Lapita and its immediate aftermath along the south coast of mainland Papua New Guinea (Skelly & David 2017: 503). To what extent Torres Strait Islanders were connecting with pottery makers of the eastern Gulf or the as-yet undocumented 2400–2600-year-old pottery-making communities of the western Gulf to the Trans-Fly is a question for future research.

In terms of Cape York Peninsula, Rowland (1995: 11) makes the pertinent point that 'archaeological research has so far contributed little to defining areas of culture contact but may do so by establishing chronological controls on possible introduced items'. Unfortunately, little archaeological information is available on such 'chronological controls'. At present, insights are limited to the hypothesis that outrigger canoe introductions were linked to Austronesian influences along the south coast of Papua New Guinea (e.g., McNiven 2015c; Moore 1979; Rowland 1987), which have now been dated back to 2900 years ago with the arrival of Lapita peoples (e.g., David et al. 2011; McNiven et al. 2011).

>3000 Years Ago

Direct archaeological evidence for the CSCIS extending beyond 3000 years ago is weak. That is, excavated coastal sites with occupation deposits dating to more than 3000 years along the CSCIS are devoid of objects reflecting long-distance exchange. Relevant sites on the south coast of mainland Papua New Guinea include Bogi 1 at Caution Bay (McNiven et al. 2011) and Kukuba Cave near Yule Island (Vanderwal 1973). Torres Strait sites include Badu 15 (David et al. 2004), Berberass (Crouch, McNiven, David, Rowe, & Weisler 2007), Mask Cave (McNiven et al. 2006), Sarbi (Crouch 2015), and Dabangay (Wright 2011). Eastern Cape York Peninsula sites include Yindayin, Walaemini, and Alkaline Rock Shelters in the Princess Charlotte Bay area (Beaton 1985; Collard et al. 2019), and Sites 3 and 17 on Lizard Island (Lentfer, Felgate, Mills, & Specht 2013; Ulm, McNiven, Aird, & Lambrides 2019). For example, none of the pre-Lapita (pre-2900-year-old) sites at Caution Bay reveal obsidian (Mialanes et al. 2016). The absence of evidence for long-distance exchange relations prior to 3000 years ago does not negate the possibility of cultural interactions between North Queensland and southern New Guinea via Torres Strait. Indeed, DNA analyses by geneticist Anna-Sapfo Malaspinas and colleagues (2016: 212) indicated that gene flow between these regions has been 'continuous but modest' since the formation of Torres Strait 8000–9000 years ago (see also Collard et al. 2019). Furthermore, archaeologist Kat Szabó and colleagues (2020) detail how shell artefacts (e.g., *Conus* adze, *Nautilus* perforated disc bead, *Tectus niloticus* preform ring fragments, and ground *Conus* spires) dated 4000–4500 years ago at Caution Bay have parallels in the Bismarck Archipelago in northeastern Papua New Guinea and Southeast Asia, suggesting broad sharing of cultural practices via the sea between 3000 and 5000 years ago across what Heinsohn (2001, 2003) calls the Circum-New Guinea Archipelago.

DISCUSSION

The Coral Sea Cultural Interaction Sphere provides a useful framework to investigate the long-term history of social and cultural interactions between northeastern Australia and southern mainland Papua New Guinea. Explicitly maritime in focus, the CSCIS acknowledges the capacity of peoples with intimate seascape knowledge to undertake canoe voyages involving hundreds of kilometres of coastline to connect with myriad coastal communities. Torres Strait Islanders voyaging 600 km down the east coast of Cape York Peninsula to Lizard Island, Motu peoples of Port Moresby voyaging 300 km to the Purari River and perhaps 400 km to Goaribari Island, and Mailu seafarers voyaging 500 km to Rossel Island reveal the depth and scale of these maritime skills. The challenge for archaeology is to find material correlates of such voyaging to document long-distance connections independent of ethnography. In some cases, such connections involve direct voyaging. In other contexts, long-distance connections may reflect incremental movement of ideas (through diffusion) or objects (through down-the-line exchange).

One of the biggest challenges for the CSCIS framework is to undermine colonialist representations of the so-called inevitability of one-way (north-to-south) movement of ideas and objects from so-called more advanced southern New Guinea into less advanced northeastern Australia. Does linking development of the CSCIS with the movement of Austronesian and Lapita peoples along the south coast of Papua New Guinea towards northeastern Australia reaffirm the north-to-south focus of earlier scholarship? Importantly, my conceptualization of the CSCIS emphasizes *interchanges* and two-way movements of objects and ideas. A focus on interchanges also emphasizes that north-to-south movements of objects and ideas are no more inevitable than south-to-north movements of objects and ideas. Every directional movement of objects and ideas involves selectivity and agency by both provider and recipient. In some respects, Barham's notion of the Torres Strait Cultural Complex (TSCC) plays into this earlier mindset. Although Barham (2000) explicitly sees the Torres Strait Cultural Complex as encompassing two-way interactions, the extension of the label Torres Strait across 500 km of Aboriginal territorial seas of northern Cape York Peninsula is problematic.

More research is required to identify potential Aboriginal objects and traits that moved northward into Torres Strait and perhaps into southern New Guinea. Ethnographic information indicates that Torres Strait Islanders obtained objects such as shell-handled spear throwers, spears, and stone for club heads through exchange with Cape York Peninsula Aboriginal peoples (Haddon 1890: 331, 1935: 88; Moore 1979: 301–303). However, archaeologist Shelley Greer and colleagues (2015) draw our attention to considerable ethnographic information on the south-to-north movement of 'non-material' ritual and cult practices. Yet many of these ritual and cult practices have material dimensions. For example, Haddon (1935: 88) recorded that Central Islanders of Torres Strait voyaged southward to islands off the east coast of Cape York Peninsula to obtain ochre (for ceremonial body adornment), turtle grease (used to anoint ritual objects), and ritual stones though 'barter'. The Kaurareg of southwest Torres Strait imported red and white pigments from the Gudang of Cape York (Moore 1979: 224, 303). Geologist Friedrich von Gnielinski (2015: 76) identified Cape York Peninsula as a possible source of a ritual cobble installed at the ceremonial *kod* site on Pulu in western Torres Strait. These archaeological snippets indicate that we have barely scratched the surface when it comes to investigating the integration of Aboriginal cultural traits and Cape York Peninsula objects into the CSCIS.

Finally, northern movements of cultural traits and objects of Aboriginal Australian origin raise the question of pull factors and demands for such traits and objects by Torres Strait Islanders and their New Guinea neighbours. Archaeologist Ian Lilley (2019) takes up this question in a thought-provoking paper on the broader regional implications of Lapita marine specialists on the south coast of Papua New Guinea (David et al. 2011; McNiven et al. 2011) and pottery finds in Torres Strait (Carter & Lilley 2008; McNiven et al. 2006) and on Lizard Island (see Tochilin et al. 2012). He posits that Aboriginal peoples of northeastern Australia may have indirectly exercised agency in attracting Austronesian and Lapita peoples westward along the south coast of Papua New Guinea. That is, in addition to a broader Melanesian 'push' for such westward movements, Torres Strait Islanders exerted a 'pull' on Melanesian communities to the east in the wake of increased activity 3000–4000 years ago. Critically, such increased activity was an extension of broader demographic expansions across northeastern Australia (McNiven 2017; McNiven et al. 2006; see also David et al. 2004), where intensified use of islands off the coasts of northern and central Queensland after 3000 years ago was sustained by hypothesized increases in marine turtle resources (Lilley 2019: 109–110; McNiven, De Maria, Weisler, & Lewis 2014). These demographic changes 'may have reached a level of intensity that made it an attractive prospect for exploration by Austronesian populations seeking opportunities for trade and exchange' (Lilley 2019: 109). Building on Skelly and David (2017: 535), central to these opportunities may have been the rich shell resources of Torres Strait, especially for the manufacture of prestigious *Conus* armband exchange values. These opportunities may also have included an attraction to Torres Strait Islanders as like-minded maritime specialists inhabiting tropical seascapes rich in cosmological and ritual meaning (see Greer, Henry, & McIntyre-Tamwoy 2015: 75–76). In this sense, the long-term histories of northeastern Australia and southern New Guinea are intimately entwined, such that understanding the history of Torres Strait and the south coast of Papua New Guinea requires understanding the linked history of northern Queensland and vice versa. This new understanding 'allows us to remap our perceptions of the activities of Australian "hunter-gatherers" in Torres Strait and northeastern Australia from passive recipients of Melanesian enterprise to active players in processes that had impacts well beyond Australia's shores' (Lilley 2019: 111).

ACKNOWLEDGEMENTS

For helpful information on museum collections of New Guinea and Australian Indigenous material culture used in this chapter, I thank Rebecca Fisher and Kate Khan (Australian Museum), and Brit Asmussen and Dave Parkhill (Queensland Museum). For helpful information on New Guinea material culture, I thank Rob Skelly (Monash University), Barry Craig, Richard Aldridge, and Col Davidson, and on Cape York Peninsula Aboriginal material culture, I thank Lindy Allen. Special thanks to Bryce Barker, Bruno David, and Ian Lilley for helpful comments on earlier drafts of this chapter.

REFERENCES

Allen, J. (1977). Sea traffic, trade and expanding horizons. In J. Allen, J. Golson, & R. Jones (Eds.), *Sunda and Sahul: Prehistoric studies in Southeast Asia, Melanesia and Australia* (pp. 387–417). London: Academic Press.

Allen, J., & Duerden, P. (1982). Progressive results from the PIXE program for sourcing prehistoric Papuan pottery. In W. Ambrose & P. Duerden (Eds.), *Archaeometry: An Australian perspective* (pp. 45–59). Canberra: Research School of Pacific Studies, The Australian National University.

Allen, J., Summerhayes, G., Mandui, H., & Leavesley, M. (2011). New data from Oposisi: Implications for the Early Papuan pottery phase. *Journal of Pacific Archaeology, 2*(1), 69–81.

Allen, L. (1980). *An illustrated catalogue of Aboriginal artefacts from Queensland.* Cultural and Historical Records in Queensland No. 2. St Lucia: Anthropology Museum, University of Queensland.

Ambrose, W., Petchey, F., Swadling, P., Beran, H., Bonshek, E., Szabo, K., . . . Summerhayes, G. (2012). Engraved prehistoric *Conus* shell valuables from southeastern Papua New Guinea: Their antiquity, motifs and distribution. *Archaeology in Oceania, 47*(3), 113–132.

Anderson, K. (2007). *Race and the crisis of humanism.* London: Routledge.

Ballard, C. (2008). 'Oceanic negroes': British anthropology of Papuans, 1820–1869. In B. Douglas & C. Ballard (Eds.), *Foreign bodies: Oceania and the science of race 1750–1940* (pp. 157–201). Canberra: ANU E Press.

Barham, A. J., & Harris, D. R. (1983). Prehistory and palaeoecology of Torres Strait. In P. M. Masters & N. C. Flemming (Eds.), *Quaternary coastlines and marine archaeology* (pp. 529–557). London: Academic Press.

Barham, A. J. (2000). Late Holocene maritime societies in the Torres Strait Islands, northern Australia—cultural arrival or cultural emergence? In S. O'Connor & P. Veth (Eds.), *East of Wallace's Line* (pp. 223–314). Rotterdam: A. A. Balkema.

Barker, B. C. (2004). *The sea people: Late Holocene maritime specialisation in the Whitsunday Islands, Central Queensland.* Terra Australis 20. Canberra: Pandanus Books.

Barker, B., Lamb, L., David, B., Korokai, K., Kuaso, A., & Bowman, J. (2012). Otoia, ancestral village of the Kerewo: Modelling the historical emergence of Kerewo regional polities on the island of Goaribari, south coast of mainland Papua New Guinea. In B. David & S. G. Haberle (Eds.), *Peopled landscapes: Archaeological and biogeographic approaches to landscapes* (pp. 157–176). Terra Australis 34. Canberra: ANU E Press.

Barker, B., Lamb, L., David, B., Skelly, R., & Korokai, K. (2015). Dating of in situ longhouse (*dubu daima*) posts in the Kikori River delta: Refining chronologies of island village occupation in the lower Kikori River delta, Papua New Guinea. *Quaternary International, 385,* 27–38.

Barton, F. R. (1910). The annual trading expedition to the Papuan Gulf. In C. G. Seligmann (Ed.), *The Melanesians of British New Guinea* (pp. 96–120). Cambridge: Cambridge University Press.

Beaton, J. M. (1985). Evidence for a coastal occupation time-lag at Princess Charlotte Bay (North Queensland) and implications for coastal colonisation and population growth theories for Aboriginal Australia. *Archaeology in Oceania, 20*(1), 1–20.

Bergström, A., Nagle, N., Chen, Y., McCarthy, S., Pollard, M. O., Ayub, Q., . . . Tyler-Smith, C. (2016). Deep roots for Aboriginal Australian Y chromosomes. *Current Biology, 26*(6), 809–813.

Bergström, A. (2017). *Genomic insights into the human population history of Australia and New Guinea* (PhD thesis). Wellcome Trust Sanger Institute, Magdalene College, University of Cambridge, Cambridge.

Bickler, S. H. (1997). Early pottery exchange along the south coast of Papua New Guinea. *Archaeology in Oceania, 32*(2), 151–162.

Booth, P. B., & Oraka, R. E. (1968). Blood group frequencies along the south coast of Papua. *Archaeology and Physical Anthropology in Oceania, 3*(2), 146–155.

Brace, C. L. (1980). Australian tooth-size clines and the death of a stereotype. *Current Anthropology, 21*(2), 141–164.

Brady, L. M. (2010). *Pictures, patterns and objects: Rock-art of the Torres Strait Islands, north-eastern Australia.* North Melbourne: Australian Scholarly Publishing.

Carter, M. (2004). *North of the cape and south of the Fly: The archaeology of settlement and subsistence on the Murray Islands, eastern Torres Strait* (PhD thesis). James Cook University, Townsville.

Carter, M., & Lilley, I. (2008). Between the Australian and Melanesian realms: Archaeology of the Murray Islands and consideration of a settlement model for Torres Strait. In J. Connelly & M. Campbell (Eds.), *Comparative island archaeologies* (pp. 121–134). BAR International Series 1829. Oxford: Archaeopress.

Chester, H. M. (1878). *Narrative of expedition to New Guinea.* Brisbane: Government Printer.

Clarkson, C., Jacobs, Z., Marwick, B., Fullagar, R., Wallis, L., Smith, M., . . . Pardoe, C. (2017). Human occupation of northern Australia by 65,000 years ago. *Nature, 547*(7663), 306–310.

Collard, M., Wasef, S., Adams, S., Wright, K., Mitchell, R. J., Wright, J. L., . . . Westaway, M. C. (2019). Giving it a burl: Towards the integration of genetics, isotope chemistry, and osteoarchaeology in Cape York, tropical north Queensland, Australia. *World Archaeology, 51*(4), 602–619.

Crouch, J., McNiven, I. J., David, B., Rowe, C., & Weisler, M. (2007). Berberass: Marine resource specialisation and environmental change in Torres Strait over the past 4000 years. *Archaeology in Oceania, 42*(2), 49–64.

Crouch, J. (2015). Small island, 'big swamp', Kuiku Pad Reef: Sarbi 4200–3500 cal BP, western Torres Strait. *Quaternary International, 385*, 88–101.

David, B., McNiven, I. J., Mitchell, R., Orr, M., Haberle, S., Brady, L., & Crouch, J. (2004). Badu 15 and the Papuan-Austronesian settlement of Torres Strait. *Archaeology in Oceania, 39*(2), 65–78.

David, B. (2008). Rethinking cultural chronologies and past landscape engagement in the Kopi region, Gulf Province, Papua New Guinea. *The Holocene, 18*, 463–479.

David, B., Araho, N., Barker, B., Kuaso, A., & Moffat, I. (2009). Keveoki 1: Exploring the *hiri* ceramics trade at a short-lived village site near the Vailala River, Papua New Guinea. *Australian Archaeology, 68*, 11–23.

David, B., Geneste, J-M., Aplin, K., Delannoy, J-J., Araho, N., Clarkson, C., . . . Rowe, C. (2010). The Emo Site (OAC), Gulf Province, Papua New Guinea: Resolving long-standing questions of antiquity and implications for the history of the ancestral *hiri* maritime trade. *Australian Archaeology, 70*, 39–54.

David, B., McNiven, I. J., Richards, T., Connaughton, S., Leavesley, M., Barker, B., & Rowe, C. (2011). Lapita sites in the Central Province of mainland Papua New Guinea. *World Archaeology, 43*(4), 580–597.

David, B., McNiven, I. J., Leavesley, M., Barker, B., Mandui, H., Richards, T., & Skelly, R. (2012). A new ceramic assemblage from Caution Bay, south coast of mainland PNG: The linear shell end-impressed tradition from Bogi 1. *Journal of Pacific Archaeology, 3*, 73–89.

David, B., Aplin, K., Peck, H., Skelly, R., Leavesley, M., Mialanes, J., . . . Ford, A. (2019). Moiapu 3: Settlement on Moiapu Hill at the very end of Lapita, Caution Bay hinterland. In S. Bedford & M. Spriggs (Eds.), *Debating Lapita: Distribution, chronology, society and subsistence* (pp. 61–88). Terra Australis 52. Canberra: ANU Press.

Davidson, D. S. (1933). Australian netting and basketry techniques. *Journal of the Polynesian Society, 42*(4), 257–299.

Davidson, D. S. (1935). The chronology of Australian watercraft. *Journal of the Polynesian Society*, *44*(173), 1–16, *44*(174), 69–84, *44*(175), 137–152, *44*(176), 193–207.

Doran, E., Jr. (1981). *Wangka: Austronesian canoe origins*. College Station: Texas A & M University Press.

Douglas, B. (2008). Foreign bodies in Oceania. In B. Douglas & C. Ballard (Eds.), *Foreign bodies: Oceania and the science of race 1750–1940* (pp. 3–30). Canberra: ANU E Press.

Douglas, B. (2014). *Science, voyages, and encounters in Oceania, 1511–1850*. New York: Palgrave Macmillan.

Dutton, T. (1978). Language and trade in Central and South-East Papua. *Mankind*, *11*(3), 341–353.

Dutton, T. (Ed.). (1982). *The hiri in history: Further aspects of long distance Motu trade in Central Papua*. Pacific Research Monograph 8. Canberra: The Australian National University.

Earl, G. W. (1853). *The native races of the Indian Archipelago. Papuans*. London: Hippolyte Bailliere.

Egloff, B. J. (1978). The Kula before Malinowski: A changing configuration. *Mankind*, *11*(3), 429–435.

Egloff, B. J. (1979). *Recent prehistory in Southeast Papua*. Terra Australis 4. Canberra: Department of Prehistory, Research School of Pacific Studies, The Australian National University.

Flood, J. (1983). *Archaeology of the Dreamtime*. Sydney: Collins.

Frankel, D., Thompson, K., & Vanderwal, R. (1994). Kerema and Kinomere. In D. Frankel & J. W. Rhoads (Eds.), *Archaeology of a coastal exchange system: Sites and ceramics of the Papuan Gulf* (pp. 1–49). Research Papers in Archaeology and Natural History 25. Canberra: Division of Archaeology and Natural History, Research School of Pacific and Asian Studies, The Australian National University.

Giles, E. (1976). Cranial variation in Australia and neighbouring areas. In R. L. Kirk & A. G. Thorne (Eds.), *The origins of the Australians* (pp. 161–172). Human Biology Series No. 6. Canberra: Australian Institute of Aboriginal Studies.

Golson, J. (1972). Land connections, sea barriers and the relationship of Australian and New Guinea prehistory. In D. Walker (Ed.), *Bridge and barrier: The natural and cultural history of Torres Strait* (pp. 375–397). Canberra: Department of Biogeography & Geomorphology, Research School of Pacific Studies, The Australian National University Press.

Greer, S., Henry, R., & McIntyre-Tamwoy, S. (2015). Mainland magic: Interpreting cultural influences across Cape York–Torres Strait. *Quaternary International*, *385*, 69–78.

Haddon, A. C. (1890). The ethnography of the Western Tribe of Torres Strait. *Journal of the Anthropological Institute of Great Britain and Ireland*, *19*, 297–440.

Haddon, A. C. (1900). Studies in the anthropogeography of British New Guinea (Continued). *The Geographical Journal*, *16*(4), 414–440.

Haddon, A. C. (Ed.) (1904). *Reports of the Cambridge Anthropological Expedition to Torres Straits. Vol. 5: Sociology, magic and religion of the Western Islanders*. Cambridge: Cambridge University Press.

Haddon, A. C. (1920). Outriggers of Indonesian canoes. *Journal of the Royal Anthropological Institute of Great Britain and Ireland*, *50*, 69–134.

Haddon, A. C. (1935). *Reports of the Cambridge Anthropological Expedition to Torres Straits. Vol. 1: General ethnography*. Cambridge: Cambridge University Press.

Haddon, A. C. (1937). *Canoes of Oceania. Volume II. The canoes of Melanesia, Queensland, and New Guinea*. Bernice P. Bishop Museum Special Publication 28.

Hale, H. M., & Tindale, N. B. (1934). Aborigines of Princess Charlotte Bay, North Queensland. Part II. *Records of the South Australian Museum, 5*(2), 117–172.

Hamlyn-Harris, R. (1915). Some evidences of Papuan culture on Cape York Peninsula. *Memoirs of the Queensland Museum, 3*, 10–13.

Heinsohn, T. E. (2001). Human influences on vertebrate zoogeography: Animal translocation and biological invasions across and to the east of Wallace's Line. In I. Metcalfe, J. M. B. Smith, M. Morwood, & I. Davidson (Eds.), *Faunal and floral migrations and evolution in SE Asia-Australasia* (pp. 154–170). Lisse: A.A. Balkema.

Heinsohn, T. (2003). Animal translocation: Long-term human influences on the vertebrate zoogeography of Australasia (natural dispersal versus ethnophoresy). *Australian Zoologist, 32*(3), 351–376.

Howitt, A. W. (1904). *The native tribes of south-east Australia.* London: Macmillan.

Hudjashov, G., Kivisilda, T., Underhill, P. A., Endicott, P., Sanchez, J. J., Lin, A. A., . . . Forster, P. (2007). Revealing the prehistoric settlement of Australia by Y chromosome and mtDNA analysis. *Proceedings of the National Academy of Sciences of the United States of America, 104,* 8726–8730.

Huxley, T. H. (1870). On the geographical distribution of the chief modifications of mankind. *Journal of the Ethnological Society of London, 2*(4), 404–412.

Irwin, G. J. (1978). The development of Mailu as a specialized trading and manufacturing centre in Papuan prehistory: The causes and the implications. *Mankind, 11*(3), 406–415.

Irwin, G. (1985). *The emergence of Mailu as a central place in coastal Papuan prehistory.* Terra Australis 10. Canberra: Department of Prehistory, Research School of Pacific Studies, The Australian National University.

Irwin, G. (1991). Themes in the prehistory of coastal Papua and the Massim. In A. Pawley (Ed.), *Man and a half: Essays in Pacific anthropology and ethnobiology in honour of Ralph Bulmer* (pp. 503–510). Auckland: Polynesian Society.

Irwin, G., & Holdaway, S. J. (1996). Colonisation, trade and exchange: From Papua to Lapita. In J. Davidson, G. Irwin, B. F. Leach, A. Pawley, & D. Brown (Eds.), *Oceanic culture history: Essays in honour of Roger Green* (pp. 225–235). Dunedin: New Zealand Journal of Archaeology Special Publication.

Irwin, G., Shaw, B., & Mcalister, A. (2019). The origins of the Kula Ring: Archaeological and maritime perspectives from the southern Massim and Mailu areas of Papua New Guinea. *Archaeology in Oceania, 54*(1), 1–16.

Keane, A. H. (1896). *Ethnology.* Cambridge: Cambridge University Press.

Kirk, R. L. (1972). Torres Strait—Channel or barrier to human gene flow? In D. Walker (Ed.), *Bridge and barrier: The natural and cultural history of Torres Strait* (pp. 367–374). Canberra: Department of Biogeography & Geomorphology, Research School of Pacific Studies, The Australian National University Press.

Laade, W. (1969). Ethnographic notes on the Murray Islanders, Torres Strait. *Zeitschrift für Ethnologie, 94*(1), 33–46.

Laade, W. (1973). Notes on the clans, economy, trade and traditional law of the Murray Islanders, Torres Straits. *Journal de la Société des Oceanistes, 29*(30), 151–167.

Landtman, G. (1927). *The Kiwai Papuans of British New Guinea.* London: Macmillan.

Lawrence, D. (1994). Customary exchange across Torres Strait. *Memoirs of the Queensland Museum, 34*(1), 241–446.

Leach, J. (1983). Introduction. In J. W. Leach & E. Leach (Eds.), *The Kula: New perspectives on Massim exchange* (pp. 1–26). Cambridge: Cambridge University Press.

Lentfer, C. J., Felgate, M. W., Mills, R. A., & Specht, J. (2013). Human history and palaeoenvironmental change at site 17, Freshwater Beach, Lizard Island, northeast Queensland, Australia. *Queensland Archaeological Research, 16*, 141–164.

Lilley, I. (2019). Lapita: The Australian connection. In S. Bedford & M. Spriggs (Eds.), *Debating Lapita: Distribution, chronology, society and subsistence* (pp. 105–114). Terra Australis 52. Canberra: Australian National University Press.

Lourandos, H. (1997). *Continent of hunter-gatherers: New perspectives in Australian prehistory.* Cambridge: Cambridge University Press.

MacGillivray, J. (1852). *Narrative of the voyage of H.M.S. Rattlesnake.* 2 vols. London: T. & W. Boone.

Macintosh, N. W. G., & Larnach, S. L. (1973). A cranial study of the Aborigines of Queensland with a contrast between Australian and New Guinea crania. In R. L. Kirk (Ed.), *The human biology of Aborigines in Cape York* (pp. 1–12). Australian Aboriginal Studies No. 44. Human Biology Series No. 5. Canberra: Australian Institute of Aboriginal Studies.

Macintyre, M., & Allen, J. (1990). Trading for subsistence: The case from the southern Massim. In D. E. Yen & J. M. J. Mummery (Eds.), *Pacific production systems: Approaches to economic prehistory* (pp. 120–136). Occasional Papers in Prehistory No. 18. Canberra: Department of Prehistory, Research School of Pacific Studies, The Australian National University.

Malaspinas, A-S., Westaway, M. C., Muller, C., Soussa, V. C., Lao, O., Alves, I., . . . Willerslev, E. (2016). A genomic history of Aboriginal Australia. *Nature, 538*, 207–214.

Malinowski, B. (1915). The natives of Mailu: Preliminary results of Robert Mond research work in British New Guinea. *Transactions and Proceedings of the Royal Society of South Australia, 39*, 494–706.

Malinowski, B. (1922). *Argonauts of the western Pacific: An account of native enterprise and adventure in the archipelagoes of Melanesian New Guinea.* London: Routledge.

Marsaglia, K. M., Kramer, K. G., David, B., & Skelly, R. J. (2016). Petrographic analyses of sand temper/inclusions in ceramics of Kikiniu, Kikori River and modern sand samples from the Gulf Province (Papua New Guinea). *Archaeology in Oceania, 51*(2), 131–140.

McCarthy, F. D. (1939). 'Trade' in Aboriginal Australia, and 'trade' relationships with Torres Strait, New Guinea and Malaya. *Oceania, 9*(4), 405–439, *10*(1), 80–104, *10*(2), 171–195.

McCarthy, F. D. (1940). Aboriginal Australian material culture: Causative factors in its composition. *Mankind, 2*(8), 241–269, 2(9), 294–320.

McCarthy, F. D. (1958). Aborigines: Material culture. In A. H. Chisholm (Ed.), *The Australian encyclopaedia* (pp. 40–45). Sydney: Angus & Robertson.

McConnel, U. H. (1953). Native arts and industries on the Archer, Kendall and Holroyd Rivers, Cape York Peninsula, North Queensland. *Records of the South Australian Museum, 11*(1), 1–42.

McConnel, U. H. (1930). The Wik-Munkan tribe of Cape York Peninsula. *Oceania, 1*(1), 97–104.

McNiven, I. J. (1993). Tula adzes and bifacial points on the east coast of Australia. *Australian Archaeology, 36*, 22–33.

McNiven, I. J. (1998). Enmity and amity: Reconsidering stone-headed club (*gabagaba*) procurement and trade in Torres Strait. *Oceania, 69*, 94–115.

McNiven, I. J., von Gnielinski, F., & Quinnell, M. (2004). Torres Strait and the origin of large stone axes from Kiwai Island, Fly River estuary (Papua New Guinea). *Memoirs of the Queensland Museum / Cultural Heritage Series, 3*(1), 201–219.

McNiven, I. J., & Russell, L. (2005). *Appropriated pasts: Indigenous peoples and the colonial culture of archaeology.* Lanham: AltaMira Press.

McNiven, I. J., Dickinson, W. R., David, B., Weisler, M., von Gnielinski, F., Carter, M. & Zoppi, U. (2006). Mask Cave: Red-slipped pottery and the Australian-Papuan settlement of Zenadh Kes (Torres Strait). *Archaeology in Oceania, 41*(2), 49–81.

McNiven, I. J. (2006a). Colonial diffusionism and the archaeology of external influences on Aboriginal culture. In B. David, B. Barker, & I. J. McNiven (Eds.), *The social archaeology of Indigenous societies* (pp. 85–106). Canberra: Aboriginal Studies Press.

McNiven, I. J. (2006b). Dauan 4 and the emergence of ethnographically-known social arrangements across Torres Strait 600–800 years ago. *Australian Archaeology, 62,* 1–12.

McNiven, I. J., Brady, L. M., & Barham, A. J. (2009). Kabadul Kula and the antiquity of Torres Strait rock art. *Australian Archaeology, 69,* 29–40.

McNiven, I. J., David, B., Richards, T., Aplin, K., Asmussen, B., Mialanes, J., . . . Ulm, S. (2011). New direction in human colonisation of the Pacific: Lapita settlement of south coast New Guinea. *Australian Archaeology, 72,* 1–6.

McNiven, I. J., De Maria, N., Weisler, M., & Lewis, T. (2014). Darumbal voyaging: Intensifying use of central Queensland's Shoalwater Bay islands over the past 5000 years. *Archaeology in Oceania, 49*(1), 2–42.

McNiven, I. J. (2015a). Australasia and the Pacific. In C. Benjamin (Ed.), *A world with states, empires and networks, 1200 BCE–900 CE* (pp. 603–630). Cambridge History of the World, Volume 4/9. Cambridge: Cambridge University Press.

McNiven, I. J. (2015b). Precarious islands: Kulkalgal reef island settlement and high mobility across 700 km of seascape, central Torres Strait and northern Great Barrier Reef. *Quaternary International, 385,* 39–55.

McNiven, I. J. (2015c). Canoes of Mabuyag and Torres Strait. *Memoirs of the Queensland Museum / Culture, 8*(1), 127–207.

McNiven, I. J. (2017). Edges of worlds: Torres Strait Islander peripheral participation in ancient globalizations. In T. Hodos (Ed.), *The Routledge handbook of globalization and archaeology* (pp. 319–334). New York: Routledge.

McNiven, I. J. (2020). Primordialising Aboriginal Australians: Colonialist tropes and Eurocentric views on behavioural markers of modern humans. In M. Porr & J. Matthews (Eds.), *Interrogating human origins: Decolonisation and the deep human past* (pp. 96–111). New York: Routledge.

McNiven, I. J., & Russell-Cook, M. (2020). Seeing what they saw: Harden Sidney Melville's *Torres Strait Canoe and five men at the site of a wreck on the Sir Charles Hardy Islands, off Cape Grenville, North East Australia, 1874. NGV Magazine, 25,* 14–17.

McNiven, I. J. (2022). Beyond bridge and barrier: Reconceptualising Torres Strait as a co-constructed border zone in ethnographic object distributions between Queensland and New Guinea. *Queensland Archaeological Research, 25,* 25–46.

Melville, H. S. n.d. [1849]. *Sketches in Australia and the adjacent islands, selected from a number taken during the surveying voyage of H.M.S. 'Fly' and 'Bramble' under the command of Capt. F.P. Blackwood, R.N. during the Years 1842–46.* London: Dickinson.

Memmott, P. (2010). *Material culture of the Wellesley Islands.* Research Report Series 8. Brisbane: Aboriginal & Torres Strait Islander Studies Unit, The University of Queensland.

Mialanes, J., David, B., Ford, A., Richards, T., McNiven, I. J., Summerhayes, G. R., & Leavesley, M. (2016). Imported obsidian at Caution Bay, south coast of Papua New Guinea: Cessation of long distance procurement c. 1,900 cal BP. *Australian Archaeology, 82*(3), 248–262.

Moore, D. R. (1978). Cape York Aborigines: Fringe participants in the Torres Strait trading system. *Mankind, 11*(3), 319–325.

Moore, D. R. (1979). *Islanders and Aborigines at Cape York.* Canberra: Australian Institute of Aboriginal Studies.

Mulvaney, D. J. (1976). The chain of connection: The material evidence. In N. Peterson (Ed.), *Tribes and boundaries in Australia* (pp. 72–94). Social Anthropology Series No. 10. Canberra: Australian Institute of Aboriginal Studies.

Mulvaney, J., & Kamminga, J. (1999). *Prehistory of Australia.* Sydney: Allen & Unwin.

Nagle, N., Ballantyne, K. N., Van Oven, M., Tyler-Smith, C., Xue, Y., Taylor, D., . . . The Genographic Consortium (2017). Mitochondrial DNA diversity of present-day Aboriginal Australians and implications for human evolution in Oceania. *Journal of Human Genetics, 62*(3), 343–353.

Negishi, Y., & Ono, R. (2009). Kasasinabwana shell midden: The prehistoric ceramic sequence of Wari Island in the Massim, eastern Papua New Guinea. *People and Culture in Oceania, 25,* 23–52.

Noone, H. V. V. (1943). Some Aboriginal stone implements of Western Australia. *Records of the Australian Museum, 7*(3), 271–280.

O'Connor, S., & Veth, P. (2000). The world's first mariners: Savanah dwellers in an island continent. In S. O'Connor & P. Veth (Eds.), *East of Wallace's Line* (pp. 99–137). Rotterdam: A. A. Balkema.

O'Connor, S., Barham, A., Aplin, K., Dobney, K., Fairbairn, A., & Richards, M. (2011). The power of paradigms: Examining the evidential basis for early to mid-Holocene pigs and pottery in Melanesia. *Journal of Pacific Archaeology, 2,* 1–25.

Oram, N. (1982). Pots for sago: The hiri trading network. In T. Dutton (Ed.), *The hiri in history: Further aspects of long distance Motu trade in Central Papua* (pp. 1–34). Pacific Research Monograph 8. Canberra: The Australian National University.

Pietrusewsky, M. (1979). Craniometric variation in Pleistocene Australian and more recent Australian and New Guinean populations studied by multivariate procedures. *Occasional Papers in Human Biology, 2,* 83–123.

Prichard, J. C. (1847). *Researches into the physical history of mankind.* Vol. 5. London: Sherwood, Gilbert, & Piper.

Rhoads, J. W. (1982). Prehistoric Papuan exchange systems: The *hiri* and its antecedents. In T. Dutton (Ed.), *The hiri in history: Further aspects of long distance Motu trade in Central Papua* (pp. 131–151). Pacific Research Monograph 8. Canberra: The Australian National University.

Rhoads, J. W. (1994). The Popo site. In D. Frankel & J. W. Rhoads (Eds.), *Archaeology of a coastal exchange system: Sites and ceramics of the Papuan Gulf* (pp. 53–69). Research Papers in Archaeology & Natural History 25. Canberra: Division of Archaeology and Natural History, Research School of Pacific and Asian Studies, The Australian National University.

Rhoads, J. W., & MacKenzie, D. E. (1991). Stone axe trade in prehistoric Papua: The travels of python. *Proceedings of the Prehistoric Society, 57*(2), 35–49.

Roth, W. E. (1910). North Queensland ethnography. Bulletin No. 14. Transport and trade. *Records of the Australian Museum, 8*(1), 1–19.

Rowland, M. J. (1987). The distribution of Aboriginal watercraft on the east coast of Queensland: Implications for culture contact. *Australian Aboriginal Studies, 1987*(2), 38–45.

Rowland, M. J. (1995). Indigenous water-craft use in Australia. The 'big picture' and small experiments on the Queensland coast. *Bulletin of the Australian Institute for Maritime Archaeology, 19*(1), 5–18.

Rowland, M. J. (2018). 65,000 years of isolation in Aboriginal Australia or continuity and external contacts? An assessment of the evidence with an emphasis on the Queensland coast. *Journal of the Anthropological Society of South Australia, 42*, 211–240.

Saville, W. J. V. (1926). *In unknown New Guinea*. London: Seeley Service & Co.

Seligmann, C. G. (1910). *The Melanesians of British New Guinea*. Cambridge: Cambridge University Press.

Shaw, B. (2016). The Massim region of Papua New Guinea: A review and proposed chronology. *Journal of Pacific Archaeology, 7*, 106–125.

Shaw, B., & Langley, M. C. (2017). Investigating the development of prehistoric cultural practices in the Massim region of eastern Papua New Guinea: Insights from the manufacture and use of shell objects in the Louisiade Archipelago. *Journal of Anthropological Archaeology, 48*, 149–165.

Skelly, R., David, B., Barker, B., Kuaso, A., & Araho, N. (2010). Migration sites of the Miaro clan (Vailala River region, Papua New Guinea): Tracking Kouri settlement movements through oral tradition sites on ancient landscapes. *The Artefact, 33*, 16–29.

Skelly, R., David, B., Petchey, F., & Leavesley, M. (2014). Tracking ancient beach-lines inland: 2600-year-old dentate-stamped ceramics at Hopo, Vailala River region, Papua New Guinea. *Antiquity, 88*(340), 470–487.

Skelly, R., Ford, A., Summerhayes, G., Mialanes, J., & David, B. (2016). Chemical signatures & social interactions: Implications of West Fergusson Island obsidian at Hopo, east of the Vailala River (Gulf of Papua), Papua New Guinea. *Journal of Pacific Archaeology, 7*(1), 126–138.

Skelly, R., & David, B. (2017). *Hiri: Archaeology of long-distance maritime trade along the south coast of Papua New Guinea*. Honolulu: University of Hawai'i Press.

Skelly, R., David, B., Leavesley, M., Petchey, F., Guise, A., Tsang, R., . . . Richards, T. (2018). Changing ceramic traditions at Agila ancestral village, Hood Bay, Papua New Guinea. *Australian Archaeology, 84*(2), 181–195.

Specht, J. (2018). Research issues in the circum-New Guinea islands. In E. E. Cochrane & T. L. Hunt (Eds.), *The Oxford handbook of prehistoric Oceania* (pp. 90–111). Oxford: Oxford University Press.

Spencer, W. B. (1922). *Guide to the Australian ethnological collection exhibited in the National Museum of Victoria*. Melbourne: Government Printer.

Stone, O. C. (1880). *A few months in New Guinea*. London: Samson Low, Marston, Searle, & Rivington.

Summerhayes, G., & Allen, J. (2007). Lapita writ small? Revisiting the Austronesian colonisation of the Papuan south coast. In S. Bedford, C. Sand, & S. Connaughton (Eds.), *Oceanic explorations: Lapita and western Pacific settlement* (pp. 97–122). Terra Australis 26. Canberra: Australian National University E-Press.

Szabó, K., David, B., McNiven, I. J., & Leavesley, M. (2020). Preceramic shell-working, Caution Bay and the Circum-New Guinea Archipelago. In T. Thomas (Ed.), *Theory in the Pacific, the Pacific in theory: Archaeological perspectives* (pp. 123–144). London: Routledge.

Thomas, O. (1885). Account of a collection of human skulls from Torres Straits. *Journal of the Anthropological Institute of Great Britain and Ireland, 14*, 328–343.

Thomson, D. F. (1934a). The dugong hunters of Cape York. *Journal of the Royal Anthropological Institute of Great Britain and Ireland, 64*, 237–263.

Thomson, D. F. (1934b). Notes on a Hero Cult from the Gulf of Carpentaria, North Queensland. *Journal of the Royal Anthropological Institute of Great Britain and Ireland, 64*, 217–235.

Thomson, D. F. (1939). Notes on the smoking-pipes of North Queensland and the Northern Territory of Australia. *Man, 39*, 81–91.

Thomson, D. F. (1952). Notes on some primitive watercraft in northern Australia. *Man, 52*, 1–5.

Thomson, D. F. (1956). The fishermen and dugong hunters of Princess Charlotte Bay. *Walkabout, 2*(11), 33–36.

Tobler, R., Rohrlach, A., Soubrier, J., Bover, P., Llamas, B., Tuke, J., . . . Cooper, A. (2017). Aboriginal mitogenomes reveal 50,000 years of regionalism in Australia. *Nature, 544*, 180–184.

Tochilin, C., Dickinson, W. R., Felgate, M. W., Pecha, M., Sheppard, P., Damonc, F. H., . . . Gehrels, G. E. (2012). Sourcing temper sands in ancient ceramics with U-Pb ages of detrital zircons: A southwest Pacific test case. *Journal of Archaeological Science, 39*, 2583–2591.

Topinard, P. (1878). *Anthropology*. London: Chapman & Hall.

Tueting, L. T. (1935). *Native trade in southeast New Guinea*. Bernice P. Bishop Museum, Occasional Papers XI(15). Honolulu, Hawaii: The Museum.

Ulm, S., McNiven, I. J., Aird, S. J., & Lambrides, A. B. J. (2019). Sustainable harvesting of *Conomurex luhuanus* and *Rochia nilotica* by Indigenous Australians on the Great Barrier Reef over the past 2000 years. *Journal of Archaeological Science: Reports, 28*, 102017.

Urwin, C., Hua, Q., Skelly, R. J., & Arifeae, H. (2018). The chronology of Popo, an ancestral village site in Orokolo Bay, Gulf Province, Papua New Guinea. *Australian Archaeology, 84*(1), 90–97.

Vanderwal, R. L. (1973). *Prehistoric studies in central coastal Papua* (PhD thesis). Australian National University, Canberra.

Vanderwal, R. (2004). Early historical sources for the Top Western Islands in the western Torres Strait exchange network. *Memoirs of the Queensland Museum / Cultural Heritage Series, 3*(1), 257–270.

Von Gnielinski, F. (2015). The geology of the Mabuyag Island Group and its part in the geological evolution of Torres Strait. *Memoirs of the Queensland Museum / Culture, 8*(1), 55–78.

White, J. P., & O'Connell, J. F. (1982). *A prehistory of Australia, New Guinea and Sahul*. Sydney: Academic Press.

White, P. (2018). New Guinea. In E. E. Cochrane & T. L. Hunt (Eds.), *The Oxford handbook of prehistoric Oceania* (pp. 69–89). Oxford: Oxford University Press.

Williams, F. E. (1924). *The natives of the Purari Delta*. Anthropology Report No. 5. Territory of Papua. Port Moresby: Government Printer.

Wood, R. (2018). *Wangga*: The linguistic and typological evidence for the sources of the outrigger canoes of Torres Strait and Cape York Peninsula. *Oceania, 88*(2), 202–231.

Wright, D., & Dickinson, W. (2009). Movement of ideas not materials: Locally manufactured pottery on Mabuyag Island, Torres Strait. *Archaeology in Oceania, 44*, 38–41.

Wright, D. (2011). Mid Holocene maritime economy in the western Torres Strait. *Archaeology in Oceania, 46*(1), 23–27.

Wright, D., van der Kolk, G., & Dauareb community (2019). Ritual pathways and public memory: Archaeology of Waiet *zogo* in eastern Torres Strait, far north Australia. *Journal of Social Archaeology, 19*(1), 116–138.

Wright, J. L., Wasef, S., Heupink, T. H., Westaway. M. C., Rasmussen, S., Pardoe, C., . . . Lambert, D. M. (2018). Ancient nuclear genomes enable repatriation of Indigenous human remains. *Science Advances, 4*, 1–12.

CHAPTER 23

MORTARS AND PESTLES MAKE THE MID-HOLOCENE OCCUPATION OF NEW GUINEA AND THE BISMARCK ARCHIPELAGO VISIBLE

PAMELA SWADLING

INTRODUCTION

STONE mortars and pestles are distributed across New Guinea and the Bismarck Archipelago, but few have been found in Indonesian West Papua (Figures 23.1 and 23.2). The highest density of these artefacts is found in the highland valleys and basins of Papua New Guinea, located between 1500 and 2000 m above sea level. Today this same region has the highest human population density in New Guinea. This is not surprising as these valleys and basins are characterized by a generally reliable rainfall and well-drained soils enriched by volcanic ash.

Recent archaeological finds from highland sites in Papua New Guinea confirm that stone mortars and pestles date to the Mid-Holocene. Now that these distinctive stone artefacts are more securely dated, their distribution can be used as the basis for modelling Mid-Holocene population concentrations, and those artefacts with elaborate morphologies allow the modelling of social interaction.

Social interaction on the New Guinea mainland during the Mid-Holocene was primarily between the coast and the highlands rather than being trans-highland. There were two main coastal to highlands interaction spheres. These were between the Sepik-Ramu inland sea and the Central Highlands, and the Huon Gulf and the Eastern Highlands

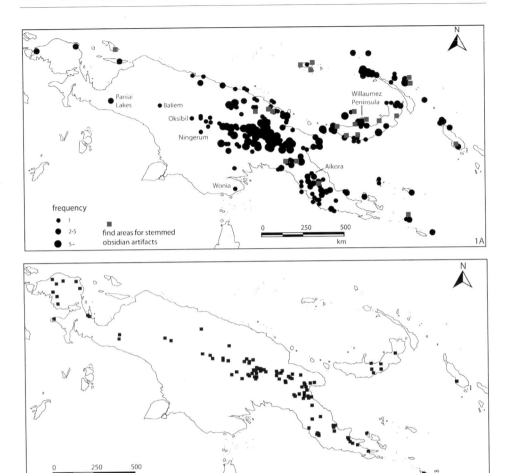

FIGURE 23.1. A. Distribution of stone mortars and pestles, and stemmed obsidian artefacts in New Guinea and the Bismarck Archipelago. B. Occurrence of *Castanopsis acuminatissima* in New Guinea and the Bismarck Archipelago following Barstow (2018) and Conn and Damas (no date).

(Figure 23.2). A third, smaller interaction sphere linked the Oro coast with the highlands in Oro and Central Provinces. It was through these interaction spheres that ideas about the production and use of stone mortars and pestles were spread.

Coastal communities also had spheres of interaction, the most important of which were the exchange networks that extended east and west of the Willaumez Peninsula of West New Britain. These in turn were linked to other down-the-line networks. This was how the stemmed obsidian artefacts of Mid-Holocene age from the Willaumez Peninsula were so widely dispersed. These networks also facilitated

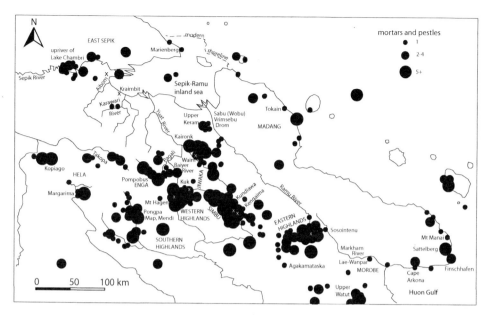

FIGURE 23.2. Mortar and pestle distribution from the Sepik-Ramu inland sea to the Huon Gulf, and inland to the Central and Eastern Highlands.

the spread of ideas about mortar and pestle production and use between coastal communities.

Antiquity

The only direct dates for mortars and pestles are from archaeological sites in the highlands; none has been found in any stratified archaeological site in the lowlands or on the coast. Mortars have been found in five highland sites, while pestles have been found in two sites, though these two sites are securely dated only at Waim in the Madang Highlands. The dates range from c. 7000–7500 cal BP at Kuk in the Western Highlands to c. 3500 cal BP at Noreikora Swamp in the Eastern Highlands (Table 23.1).

The antiquity of mortars and pestles in coastal and lowland regions is currently unknown. Since we have no radiocarbon-dated finds from coastal archaeological sites and they have not been found in Lapita sites, a Mid-Holocene age is implied on the basis of forms comparable to those found in the highlands (see Figures 23.3 and 23.4). This comparable age is no doubt true for the Mid-Holocene, but after pottery making spread, it is possible that wooden versions were more widely used in coastal and lowland regions. It should be noted that the scattered and isolated occurrence of stone mortars in eastern

Table 23.1. Mortars and pestles from archaeological sites in Papua New Guinea.

Site	Altitude m ASL	Artefact Type	Raw Material	Age	Reference
Noreikora Swamp (NFB) near Kainantu, Eastern Highlands	1625–1700	mortar fragment	unknown	between 3000–4000 cal BP	Watson & Cole (1977)
Joe's Garden, Ivane Valley, Papuan Highlands, Central Province	2000	mortar fragment	kaersutite basalt	4160–4410 cal BP	Field et al. (2020)
Nombe Rockshelter, Simbu	1720	mortar fragment	hornblende andesite	<4500 BP	Swadling (2005), White (1972)
Nombe Rockshelter, Simbu	1720	pestle	unknown	<4500 BP	Swadling (2005), White (1972)
Waim, Madang Highlands	2050–2100	pestle 1 base fragment	diorite	4200–5050 cal BP	Shaw et al. (2020)
Waim, Madang Highlands	2050–2100	pestle 2 base fragment	gabbro-diorite	4200–5050 cal BP	Shaw et al. (2020)
Western Highlands	>1500	mortar near complete	unknown	unknown	Golson (2000), Swadling (2005)
Kuk Swamp, Wahgi Valley, Western Highlands	1650	mortar rim fragment	tholeiitic basalt	7000–7500 BP Phase 1/ Phase 2 interface	Golson (2000), Fullagar & Golson (2017)

New Guinea implies complementary use of wooden mortars during the Mid-Holocene (Swadling 2017: 15).

FUNCTIONS

Highlands

In the highlands, prior to the advent of Christianity, mortars and pestles found on eroding landscapes or during land clearance were usually collected and placed in cult houses. As ritual objects, they were used to promote fertility, such as in garden 'magic', as well as in other male rituals (Berndt 1954). On the Huon Peninsula, nothing is known regarding their origins and use. There they are considered the work of spirits (Schuster 1946).

MORTARS AND PESTLES 621

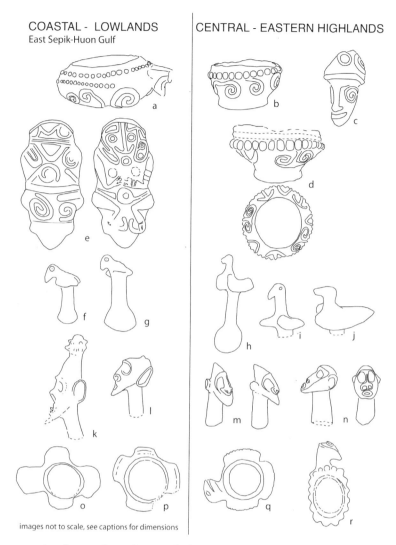

FIGURE 23.3. Artefacts with similar morphologies only found in the East Sepik and Huon Gulf coastal-lowlands and the central and Eastern Highlands.

    a. *Mortar with geometric designs:* near Raten, Middle Keram, East Sepik Province. Length 27 cm. JFA173, Jolika collection, de Young Museum (Swadling 2017: fig. 1.31).

    b. *Mortar with geometric designs:* Kengaima, near Kundiawa, Simbu Province. Height 13 cm. NS 45 194, Frankfurt Museum (Schmitz 1966: fig. 33; Newton 1979; Maier 2003).

    c. *Head with geometric designs:* Enga Province. Height 12.7 cm. JFA254, Jolika collection, de Young Museum (Swadling 2017: figs. 1.12, 1.32).

    d. *Mortar with geometric designs:* Mount Hagen area, Western Highlands Province. Length 20.3 cm. JFA209, Jolika collection, de Young Museum (Swadling 2017: 24, 33).

    e. *Figure with geometric designs:* Sabu, Keram foothills, Middle Ramu, Madang Province. Height 44 cm. E62594, Australian Museum (England 1946; Newton 1979; Höltker 1968; Specht 1988).

    f. *Bird pestle:* Marienberg area, lower Sepik, East Sepik Province. Height 14 cm. Vatican Ethnological Museum, Rome (Höltker 1951; Newton 1979; Swadling, Hauser Schäublin, Gorecki, & Tiesler 1988: fig. 58).

Recent residue studies on mortars and pestles from two highland archaeological sites have clarified their original use. The artefacts studied are the distal ends of two pestles from Waim in the Madang Highlands and a mortar from Joe's Garden in the Ivane Valley in the Central Province Highlands (Shaw et al. 2020; Field et al. 2020). The most common starch grains on pestle 1 from Waim are from *Castanopsis acuminatissima* (nut), followed by *Hydriastele* sp. (palm) and *Musa ingens* (banana), with a small contribution of *Saccharum officinarum* (sugarcane). *C. acuminatissima* was also the most prevalent plant taxa identified in soil samples taken adjacent to pestle 1, a finding consistent with on-site processing of this nut.

The starch grains on pestle 2 from Waim were mainly of *C. acuminatissima* (nut) and *Dioscorea alata* (greater yam), with lesser contributions from *Dioscorea pentaphylla* (five-leaf yam) and *Pueraria lobata* (Kudzu tuber). Waim is elevated at 2050–2100 m above sea level. *D. pentaphylla* might be a lower altitude import to Waim as its modern altitudinal range is 1550–1600 m asl. The same may be true of *D. alata*, as its extreme altitudinal limit is 2100 m asl (Shaw et al. 2020: 3, text S5; Bourke 2010).

The starch grains on the mortar fragment (Artefact F) from Joe's Garden in Ivane Valley were primarily from *C. acuminatissima*, with small quantities of *Pueraria lobata* and *Dioscorea bulbifera* (aerial yam). In addition, the starch on a water-worn metabasalt cobble (Artefact E) from Joe's Garden was primarily *C. acuminatissima*, with smaller

g. *Bird pestle:* Tokain, north mainland coast opposite Karkar Island, Madang Province. Height 17 cm. Anthropos Institute, St. Augustin, Germany (Höltker 1968; Newton 1979).

h. *Bird pestle:* fragment, Baiyer River area, Western Highlands Province. Height 14.5 cm. Linden Museum, Stuttgart.

i. *Bird pestle:* Baiyer River area, Western Highlands Province. Height 31.2 cm. Ethnologisches Museum, Berlin.

j. *Bird pestle:* fragment, Pongpa, Mendi area, Southern Highlands Province. Height 12 cm. 1980.030.001 PNG National Museum. Stolen from exhibition showcase during 2003 museum burglary (Swadling 1981: 55).

k. *Anthropomorphic head pestle:* fragment, Cape Arkona, Huon Gulf, Morobe Province. Height 21 cm. 105248, Field Museum, Chicago (Schuster 1946; Höltker 1951; Newton 1979).

l. *Anthropomorphic head pestle:* fragment, Finschhafen area, Yabem speakers, Huon Peninsula, Morobe Province. Height 12.5 cm. 605, Neuentdettelsau Mission Museum (Schmitz 1956; Newton 1979; Höltker 1968).

m. *Anthropomorphic head pestle:* fragment, Kopiago, Hela Province. Height 13.4 cm. 1989.18.1, PNG National Museum (Stewart & Strathern 1999).

n. *Anthropomorphic head pestle:* fragment, Pompobus, near Wapenamanda, Enga Province. Height 12.5 cm. Anthropos Institute, St. Augustin, Germany (Holtker 1968; Newton 1979).

o. *'Wing' mortar:* Mt Manai, Bobongara, where rainforest and grassland meet, Huon Peninsula, Morobe Province. Length c. 40 cm. PNG National Museum.

p. *'Wing' mortar:* Sattelberg Mission, Huon Peninsula, Morobe Province. Length c. 32 cm. (Neuhauss 1911; Newton 1979).

q. *Bird 'wing' mortar:* Agakamatasa, Okapa area, Eastern Highlands Province. Length c. 30 cm. E69130 Peabody Essex Museum, Salem.

r. *Bird mortar:* Sosointenu, Kainantu area, Eastern Highlands Province. Length 36 cm. 1979.034.001 PNG National Museum. Stolen from exhibition showcase during 2003 museum burglary (Bellwood 1978; Newton 1979).

MORTARS AND PESTLES 623

FIGURE 23.4. Artefacts with similar morphologies from New Guinea coastal areas and lowlands, and New Guinea highlands above 1000 m.

a. *Bossed bowl mortar:* upriver of Chambri Lake, East Sepik Province. Diameter c. 28 cm. National Gallery of Australia, 2008.116.

b. *Bossed bowl mortar:* near Moreguina, Central Province. Bowl mouth diameter 18 cm. PNG National Museum and Art Gallery, 1981.062.002 (Guise 1985: 13–14).

c. *Bossed bowl mortar:* Pagali, between Lai and Baiyer Rivers, Western Highlands Province. Bowl mouth diameter 23.5 cm. Australian Museum, E62491.

d. *Bossed bowl mortar:* Kundiawa, Simbu Province. Max. external diameter 27 cm. PNG National Museum and Art Gallery 010597 (Swadling 1981: 56).

e. *Pedestal bossed mortar:* Iniai, right tributary of Karawari River, East Sepik Province. Bowl mouth diameter c. 12 cm. John Friede collection (Meyer 1995: frontispiece).

f. *Pedestal bossed mortar:* Finschhafen, Morobe Province. Max. external diameter 20.3 cm. Current location unknown.

g. *Pedestal bossed mortar:* Kaironk, Madang Province. Max. external diameter 19 cm. PNG National Museum and Art Gallery, 010782 (Swadling 1981: 56).

(*continued*)

(continued)

h. *Pedestal bossed mortar:* Map, Mendi area, Southern Highlands Province. Max. external diameter c. 22 cm. Mendi Museum collection 1970s.

i. *Face mortar:* Vrimsebu, above Keram River, Middle Ramu, Madang Province. Max. external diameter 47 cm. PNG National Museum and Art Gallery, 016320 (Kasprus 1940–41; Newton 1979; Swadling 1981).

j. *Face mortar:* Drom near Wobu, Middle Ramu, Madang Province. Max. external diameter c. 35 cm. Current location unknown.

k. *Face mortar:* Margarima, Hela Province. Max external diameter c. 20 cm. Current location unknown.

l. *Face mortar:* Takopa, Paiela area, Enga Province. Max external diameter 34.7 cm. (Swadling 2017: 30).

m. *Face mortar:* near Moreguina, Central Province. Bowl mouth diameter 25 cm. PNG National Museum and Art Gallery, 1981.062.001 (Guise 1985: 13–14).

n. *Face mortar:* Upper Watut, Morobe Province. Max. external diameter c. 25 cm. Current location unknown.

o. *Face mortar:* Simbai area, Madang Province. Max external diameter c. 20 cm. Current location unknown.

p. *Raised wing bird pestle:* Wonia, upper Oriomo River, Trans Fly, Western Province. Height 30 cm. Australia Museum, E65762 (Barton 1908; Pretty 1965; Newton 1979; Specht 1988).

q. *Raised wing bird pestle:* Bige, Ningerum, Western Province. Height 30 cm. PNG National Museum and Art Gallery.

r. *Raised wing bird pestle:* fragment, Lae-Wampar, lower Markham River, Morobe Province. Height 12.6 cm. Private collection, Hamburg (Höltker 1951; Newton 1979).

s. *Raised wing, bird pestle:* Aikora River, north tributary of the Gira River, Morobe Province. Height 36 cm. British Museum, 1908.4-23.1 (Barton 1908; Höltker 1940/1941; Newton 1979).

t. *Raised wing bird pestle:* fragment, Wunin, Kecamatan Karubag, Baliem Valley, West Papua (Michael Gunn pers. comm. 2015). Estimated diameter 7 cm. Current location unknown.

u. *Raised wing bird pestle:* Oksibil, West Papua. Estimated diameter 6–7 cm. Current location unknown (Kusnowo & Nazif 1992).

v. *Bossed bowl mortar:* Willaumez Peninsula, West New Britain Province. Max. external diameter 30 cm. PNG National Museum and Art Gallery, FNK.04 (Goodenough 1952; Riesenfeld 1955).

w. *'Wing' mortar:* SagSag, bed of Gima River, West New Britain Province. Max. external diameter 30.5 cm, bowl mouth diameter 15.2 cm. Cambridge Museum of Archaeology and Anthropology, 1934.564 (Sherwin & Haddon 1933; Specht 1966: 380).

x. *Foot mortar:* Dami, Talasea, West New Britain Province. Bowl mouth diameter 24 cm. West New Britain Cultural Centre.

y. *Foot mortar:* Mt. Varzin, Gazelle Peninsula, East New Britain Province. Max. external diameter 25 cm. Ethnologisches Museum, Berlin (Parkinson 1999: 244; Specht 1966; Bühler 1946–1949: 239).

z. *Conical mortar with nipple-like base:* Wilaimbemki, Baining Mountains, East New Britain Province. Mouth opening ca. 30 cm. Current location unknown.

aa. *Foot mortar:* Batimolan, New Hanover, New Ireland. Height 29 cm. Museum der Kulturen, Basel, Vb 11055 (Bühler 1946–1949).

ab. *Foot mortar:* Soi Island, New Ireland. Height c. 30 cm. PNG National Museum and Art Gallery, 1980.028.051 (Swadling 1981: 57).

ac. *Conical mortar with nipple-like base:* Emo, Maledok Island, Tanga, New Ireland. Max. external diameter 24 cm. Current location unknown.

ad. *Wooden foot mortar:* modern. Lataul, Lihir Island, New Ireland. Height 16.5 cm. Used for crushing and smashing *galip* nuts (canarium), local name *apututut ame*. PNG National Museum and Art Gallery, 1984.065.040.

ae. *Wooden foot mortar:* modern. Siassi Islands, Morobe Province. Height c. 60 cm. PNG National Museum and Art Gallery, 1979.80.1 (Swadling 1981: 58).

amounts of *Pueraria lobata* and minor contributions from *Musa ingens* (banana), *Cyathea* sp. (tree fern), and *Psophocarpus tetragonolobus* (winged bean) (Field et al. 2020).

It is striking that *C. acuminatissima* is the common plant material on pestles and a mortar used in two widely separated highland regions, namely, the Madang and Central Highlands. These initial residue results indicate that *Castanopsis* was being pounded with available starch products such as yams, Kudzu tuber, and banana. Bulmer (1964) is correct in his prediction that *Castanopsis* will be found to be the main product to be pounded in mortars and pestles in the highlands. It is likely that plain forms were for domestic consumption, whereas elaborate forms (Figures 23.3 and 23.4) were for ceremonial occasions.

Castanopsis is one of the dominant tree species of the lower montane forest zone (1400–2000 m asl) of Papua New Guinea. Above this altitude, conifers and trees of the myrtle family become more common (Paijmans 1981: 92). Bourke (2010: 487) gives 700–2350 m as the usual mean altitudinal range for *Castanopsis* and 570–2440 m as its extreme range, noting that self-sown *Castanopsis* is more common above 1100 m. Figure 23.1B shows the occurrence of *Castanopsis* in New Guinea. Transplanted *Castanopsis* are characteristically found around long-established settlements, for example, the Nimai group in the Sinasina area of Simbu and Huli in Hela (Hide, Kimin, Kora, Kua, & Kua 1979: 5–6; Powell & Harrison 1982: 81).

The small, hazelnut-sized nuts of *Castanopsis* are seasonal, and there is some variability as to when they ripen. In Mendi in the Southern Highlands Province, a two-month season from August to September has been recorded (Harrison 1976: 33, 174), but generally it is from November to December (Bourke et al. 2002: 38). The nuts were once widely consumed in the highlands of Papua New Guinea. The Kalam (Madang Province) eat them raw or fire roasted and use their fingers to remove the cup and shell (Bulmer 1964: 148). Ankave-Anga (Gulf Province) women use a fruit bat bone to peel the nuts, followed by cooking and serving with specific leaves (Walter & Sam 2002: 135). The nuts are eaten raw or cooked in bamboo at Okapa, in the Eastern Highlands Province (Hamilton 1956, cited in Henty 1985). The Nimai in Simbu Province skin the nuts and cook them in a bamboo tube. Once the nuts are cooked, a stick is rammed down the tube to produce a paste for eating (Hide et al. 1979: 44). The nuts are boiled at Pomio in East New Britain Province. Children there are advised not to eat the nuts raw. Mouth ulcers, emaciation, and anaemia have been reported, probably due to the tannins that are common in the family Fagaceae (Baalen 1960, cited in Henty 1985). This ethnographic information suggests that in the Mid-Holocene the nuts were cooked before being processed with mortars and pestles.

The palaeo-pollen sequence for Kuk, an open archaeological site near Mount Hagen in the Wahgi Valley, shows that a mixed lower montane forest of *Castanopsis-Lithocarpus* persisted before, during, and after the Last Glacial Maximum around 20,000 years ago (Haberle, Lentfer, & Denham 2017: 157). Undisturbed, these mixed-oak forests are a favourable environment for procuring the following plant foods: *Castanopsis acuminatissima* trees that yield prolific quantities of small, highly nutritious, seasonal nuts; *Elaeocarpus, Sloanea, Finschia,* and *Sterculia* trees that produce other edible nuts and seeds; and fruits from vines, edible foliage from shrubs and ferns, edible fungi, and wild, edible, yam-like tubers. In addition, the upper montane *Nothofagus*-dominated forest could be visited to provide pandanus fruits (Bulmer 1964; Bulmer & Bulmer 1964; Clarke 1971; Denham 2018; Golson 1991).

During the Early Holocene, if not before, people of Papua New Guinea began managing starch-rich plants, including taro (*Colocasia esculenta*), yams (*Dioscorea* spp.), and bananas (*Musa* spp.); edible grasses such as sugarcane (*Saccharum* spp.) and pitpit (*Setaria* spp.); leafy vegetables; and protein and oil-rich palms (*Pandanus* spp.) and trees (*Castanopsis* sp.) (Denham 2018: 113). Encouraging and growing these crops required lower montane forests to be cleared. Because there are long fallow periods, there is time for secondary forest species to regenerate into mature forests. However, as the frequency of clearing and burning increases, secondary forest, including *Castanopsis*, is not able to regenerate and so montane forests degenerate into grasslands.

The lower parts of the major valleys in the highlands had been cleared and grasslands were established by 7000–6000 BP (Hope & Haberle 2005: 547). Bulmer (1964) predicted that, as forest was cleared, the extent of grasslands would increase and the supply of *Castanopsis* nuts would correspondingly decrease. Pollen studies have now demonstrated that there is a marked decrease in the levels of *Castanopsis* sp. pollen from Pleistocene levels to those in the Holocene (Denham, Haberle, & Lentfer 2004: 848). *Castanopsis* nuts continue to be eaten as a minor food in the Southern Highlands, Hela, and Enga Provinces (Bourke et al. 2002: 65, 67, 71, 77; Allen et al. 2002a: 51, 61, 65; Allen et al. 2002b: 67). Among the Huli, Enga, and Ipili peoples, *Castanopsis* is known as *pai* (Michael Bourke personal communication 2020). The survival status of *Castanopsis acuminatissima* is of such concern that it is now listed on the International Union for Conservation's threatened list (Barstow 2018). In some areas such as the Kaironk Valley in the Madang Highlands, at least one stand has conservation status (Field et al. 2020).

With a declining supply of *Castanopsis* nuts, the use of mortars and pestle would have declined. The highlands would also have become more regionally focussed when access to the coast ceased due to the infilling of the Sepik-Ramu inland sea. After c. 3000 BP, pigs brought to eastern New Guinea by the Austronesians, in due course, became a new source of ceremonial food in the highlands (David et al. 2019).

Lowlands-Coastal Areas

The altitudinal range for *Castanopsis* means that its nuts were not available to people living on the coast. Very different nuts are found in coastal-lowland regions, namely, coconuts and canarium. The altitudinal ranges for coconuts (*Cocos nucifera*) and canarium (*Canarium indicum*) are 0–950 m and 0–700 m, respectively (Bourke 2010: 487). Despite this altitude difference in nut resources, mortar and pestle use became widespread in both the highlands and coastal areas during the Mid-Holocene. Although we currently have no Mid-Holocene residue studies or radiocarbon dates for stone mortars and pestles from coastal-lowland areas, it is likely that pounding a nut and starchy food(s) into a paste-like pudding was the desired product in both regions at this time.

The difference in nut resources may therefore explain why the practice of pounding starch and nut products ceased in the highlands but continued into historical times in some coastal regions. In historical times, ceremonial puddings were once widely produced in northeast New Guinea, New Ireland, and Bougainville using mainly wooden mortars and pestles. Puddings include *harong* made from cooked bananas and taro pounded with canarium nuts at Bilibil Island, Madang Province (Mager 1952: 269). Another example is *pollom/porong* made from cooked taro pounded with coconut cream in the Siassi Islands, coastal Huon Peninsula, and Tami Island in Morobe Province (Harding 1967; Pomponio 1992; Coote 2007).

In Melanesia, stone mortars continue to be produced only on Gatokae Island in the western Solomon Islands. These islanders trade their stone mortars to other islands in the western Solomons where they are used with wooden pestles to make puddings consisting of root vegetables and roasted canarium nuts. The ingredients are pounded and then baked in stone ovens, and consumed mainly on special occasions (Hviding 1996).

After c. 3000 BP, ceramic pots become available for cooking tubers. When tubers are steam-cooked in pots, they are moister, softer, and more easily and quickly pounded (Narakobi 2002: 71–73), compared to those cooked in ash and embers, time-consuming earth ovens, and size-limited bamboo tubes. Once pots were available, stone mortars and pestles could be replaced by wooden versions. This would explain why stone mortars and pestles are absent from Lapita sites. In this way, the practice of pounding starch products and nuts to produce a paste (pudding) continued in some regions of coastal Papua New Guinea and in due course was taken out into the Pacific by Lapita colonists.

FORMER INLAND SEA (SEPIK-RAMU BASIN)

Formation

When Ian Hughes (1977) completed his study of Stone Age trade in New Guinea, he did not envisage that an inland sea once fronted the Central Highlands. Its existence was first proposed by Swadling at a Sepik Symposium in 1984 (Swadling 1984, 1990) and confirmed subsequently (Chappell 1993, 2005; Swadling 1997; Swadling, Hauser Schaublin, Gorecki, & Tiesler 1988; Swadling et al. 1989; Swadling & Hope 1992). This inland sea placed the north coast much closer to the large intermontane valleys and basins of the Central Highlands of Papua New Guinea. Such closeness would have allowed a more direct exchange of ideas and products between the coast and the highlands than the extensive swamps and floodplains allow today.

In the Pleistocene, the Sepik-Ramu Basin experienced episodes of flooding and infilling associated with the advances and retreats of the Ice Ages. The commencement of the last marine transgression and flooding of the continental shelf began after 20,000 years ago with the retreat of the last Ice Age. A shallow inland sea formed during the rapid postglacial rise in sea level. Its maximum extent was reached 6300–7500 BP, after which sea levels began to stabilize.

The Mid-Holocene shoreline shown in a schematic map by Chappell (2005) is reproduced in Figure 23.2. The extent of the Holocene inland sea was determined by radiocarbon-dated stratigraphic data and geomorphic mapping. Its western limit has not been determined. The alluvial deposits in the Ambunti area indicate that it did not extend so far west. Chambri Lake may be an unfilled inland sea embayment, but further fieldwork is required for this hypothesis to be confirmed.

Bosmun Island sat at the mouth of the inland sea. Discharge to the ocean had to pass either side of this island. The two channels were very different. To the west there was tidal inflow as Mid-Holocene coral and marine molluscs occur at Marienberg, whereas to the east the presence of microfauna indicates that the discharge was of freshwater.

Extensive floodplains and backswamps began forming in the inland sea after 6000 BP. Sediment carried by the two major rivers, the Sepik and Ramu, and others, such as the Yuat, probably flowed into the inland sea via elongated bird's foot deltas. In time, this sediment discharge formed deltaic plains, featuring beach ridges and sand barriers. Backswamps formed in the areas closed off by the prograding deltaic plains. Over time, the deltaic plains (now meander plains: see Chappell 2005: 535, fig. 5) would have protruded far into the inland sea. When the floodplains flooded in the wet season, it was probably possible to travel considerable distances by canoe. An estimate based on the present-day rate of sediment discharge by the Sepik and Ramu Rivers into the ocean indicates that it would have taken about 3000 years to infill the inland sea.

Radiocarbon dates show that the inland sea had infilled by about 4000 BP. The nonorganic sand and silty clay sediments found beneath 3–4 m of peat near Kraimbit village (Figure 23.2) may relate to infilling. Kraimbit at the south bank of the Blackwater Lakes is located to the east of Chambri Lake. Nonorganic fine sand was found lying at the base of one core site, whereas the other sites had a nonorganic silty clay sediment. There was a sharp and clear break at the base of the peat layer, which consists mainly of sago and grass remains, to sand or silty clay sediments. The lower and middle parts of the peat layer date to 3710–3560 cal BP, 3,620–3,440 cal BP, and 2,870–2,760 cal BP (Ono, Umemura, Ishida, & Takenaka 2015).

Contact between the north coast and Wañelek, located at 1710 m above sea level in the Madang Highlands, was maintained as the inland sea infilled. Pottery dating to 3000–2900 cal BP has been found in this site. Chemical and petrographic analysis reveals that the clay came from coastal Madang and near Chambri Lakes in the Middle Sepik (Gaffney et al. 2015; Summerhayes 2019: 255). Today, Aibom in the Chambri Lakes supplies pottery to much of the Middle Sepik (May & Tuckson 2000).

Mortars and Pestles in the Vicinity of the Inland Sea

Mortars and pestles are found on uplands adjacent to Mid-Holocene floodplains and deltas of the inland sea (Figure 23.2). Apart from three exceptions, they do not occur in the area of the former inland sea. The exceptions all come from the Middle Keram River area. It is possible that they come from former small islands in the inland sea, but it is more likely that they were acquired in the upper Keram River area, perhaps taken as ritual objects and taken to the Middle Keram as they were found near former villages. When the Ramu floodplain started to extend out into the inland sea, both Atemble and the upper Keram foothills would have been on or near the old Ramu River channel, which is now used by the Keram River (Yu, Chappell, & Flitchett 1991).

A tanged stone spade, found in the former Sepik Delta area of the inland sea near Ambunti, is comparable to similar finds from the highlands. The artefact was found by a woman when fishing in a lagoon near Brugnowi, some 15 km southwest of Ambunti (Swadling et al. 1988: 20; Swadling 1990: fig. 9). It probably dates to the Mid-Holocene. In the highlands, similar artefacts have been found at Wañelek in the Madang Highlands (Bulmer 1982: 196–197; 1973), at Wurup in the Wahgi Valley (Christensen 1975), plus another from the Western Highlands (Allen 1970).

PROCESSES LEADING TO THE DISTRIBUTION OF SIMILAR MORPHOLOGIES

Mortars and pestles with similar morphologies are found not only in different parts of New Guinea, but also in island regions, such as the Bismarck Archipelago. This distribution indicates that the people living in these different landscapes were linked by various networks. The widespread distribution of stemmed obsidian tools, another Mid-Holocene artefact, also confirms that extensive social links existed at this time (Figure 23.1). Most of these tools have been sourced to the Willaumez Peninsula in West New Britain. Using charcoal trapped in ash falls on this peninsula, the stemmed tools have been radiocarbon dated from before 6160–5740 cal BP to 3480–3160 cal BP (Torrence & Swadling 2008: 602).

Networks of trading partners were probably the process by which ideas about the use of mortars and pestles, as well as their distinctive morphologies, were exchanged between the inhabitants of different interaction spheres. This exchange would have been the case with the people of the inland sea and their contacts in the Central Highlands. Within each region further links would have extended the range of such ideas.

Clarifying whether it was just ideas that were exchanged or whether some of the artefacts were also traded can be determined by stone sourcing. The diorite and gabbro-diorite used to make the two Mid-Holocene pestles excavated at Waim are likely to have come from nearby sources (Shaw et al. 2020: Supplementary material). By contrast, the Early to Mid-Holocene mortar rim fragment from Kuk may be an import (Golson 2000).

The morphology of elaborate mortars and pestles allows us to model the social links that existed when these artefacts were being used in the Mid-Holocene (Figures 23.3 and 23.4). Coastal-highlands communities produced or adopted artefacts similar to those used by the other. There are two major coastal-highlands social interaction spheres, one from the shores of the inland sea into the valleys and basins of the Central Highlands, and the other from the Huon Gulf into the Eastern Highlands. A third, smaller coastal-highlands interaction sphere extended from the Oro coast into the highland valleys of Oro and Central Provinces. The three spheres also had maritime links and, via the Huon Gulf region, were articulated with the Willaumez Peninsula of West New Britain.

Mortar and pestle morphologies are different on either side of the Willaumez Peninsula (see Figure 23.4). This indicates that different trade networks extended to the east and west of this peninsula in the Mid-Holocene. The unique products of obsidian and certain pigments that are found on the Willaumez Peninsula ensured that this configuration continued into historic times (Chowning 1978; Specht 1981; Pengilley, Brand, Flexner, Specht, & Torrence 2019: fig. 3). To the west of the peninsula, network links extended from West New Britain and the Bali-Witu Islands to the north coast of New Guinea, the Sepik-Ramu inland sea, the Huon Gulf, and beyond to Oro, Milne Bay, and Central Provinces. Eastward from the Willaumez Peninsula, links went to East New Britain, Manus, New Ireland, and Bougainville.

Regional Variations in Form

The three coastal/lowlands-highlands social interaction spheres discussed above—(1) shores of the inland sea into the valleys and basins of the Central Highlands, (2) the Huon Gulf into the Eastern Highlands, and (3) the Oro coast into the highland valleys of Oro and Central Provinces—find expression in regional variations in mortar and pestle form.

Coastal-Lowlands (Sepik-Ramu Basin and Huon Gulf) and Central Highlands

Figure 23.3 shows the elaborate morphologies that are restricted to these interaction spheres.

Geometric decoration on mortars and figures (Figure 23.3a–e): Mortars and figures decorated with these designs seem to be concentrated in the upper Keram foothills of the Middle Ramu and the Central Highlands (Enga, Western Highlands, and Simbu Provinces).

Bird pestles with folded wings (Figure 23.3f–j): Bird pestles are found elsewhere, but such artefacts have raised wings or are just a bird head or recognizable species. Stylized birds with folded wings appear to be restricted to the inland sea and nearby coast (East Sepik and Madang Provinces) and the Central Highlands (mainly Western Highlands and Simbu Provinces). They are not found in the Eastern Highlands.

Bird and wing mortars (Figures 23.3o–r and 23.4w): These are characteristic of the Huon Gulf (Morobe Province), extending to West New Britain, and the Eastern Highlands (Eastern Highlands and Morobe Provinces). In the Central Highlands bird mortars are rare.

Anthropomorphic head pestles with pointed chins (Figure 23.3k–n): These have pointed chins, strong noses, eyes represented by depressions, and clearly shown ears. The most elaborate example comes from Cape Arkona on the Huon Gulf (Morobe Province), made distinctive by its top knot or stone club-like head covering. These pestles occur in both the Huon Gulf and Central Highlands (Hela and Enga Provinces).

Coastal-Lowlands (New Guinea) and Central Highlands

Figure 23.4 shows the elaborate mortar and pestle morphologies found in both of these regions.

Bossed bowls (Figure 23.4a and 4v): This morphology has the greatest geographic distribution. It is found in East Sepik, Madang, Morobe, West New Britain, Oro, Milne Bay, and Central Provinces and in the highlands in Enga, Yela, Southern Highlands, Western Highlands, Jiwaka, Madang, Simbu, Eastern Highlands, and Morobe Provinces.

Pedestal bossed bowls (Figure 23.4e–h): These occur in coastal/lowlands of the East Sepik and Morobe Provinces and in the highlands of the Enga, Hela, Southern Highlands, Western Highlands, Jiwaka, Madang, Simbu, Eastern Highlands, and Enga Provinces.

Anthropomorphic face mortars (Figure 23.4i–o): These are rare, the largest example coming from Vrimsebu, above the Keram River in the Middle Ramu, Madang Province. The upper Keram and Aiome area of the Middle Ramu have the highest density for these artefacts. In the highlands, they are found in the Southern Highlands, Enga, Western Highlands, Simbu, Eastern Highlands, and Morobe Provinces. The find from Moreguina in Central Province is an isolate.

Bird pestles with raised wings (Figure 23.4p–u): These pestles are all isolates and are widely dispersed. They are usually found along river systems and facilitate inland access. Sourcing the stone used to make these pestles, especially the Aikora, Wonia, and Ningerum examples, which are held in museums, will clarify whether they are made from near or distant sources. The only highland examples are from the Baliem Valley and Oksibil in Indonesian West Papua. Both areas were likely accessed by a route into the highlands via the Digul River from the south coast. Petrequin and Petrequin (2006:

159) mention an eastern trade route into the highlands for cowrie (*Cypraea moneta*) from the south coast.

Bismarck Archipelago

A distinct difference is found in the mortars found west and east of the Willaumez Peninsula of West New Britain. Those to the west of this peninsula show clear links with the New Guinea mainland (Figure 23.4v–w). Those to the east (East New Britain and New Ireland) lack these links and have distinctive morphologies.

Foot mortars (Figure 23.4x–y, aa): These are found from the Willaumez Peninsula of West New Britain east to East New Britain and New Ireland. Historic wooden examples of foot mortars were used in New Ireland and Bougainville, and interestingly in the Siassi and Tami Islands.

Mortars with nipple-like base (Figure 23.4z, ac): Examples have been found in East New Britain and New Ireland.

West Papua

Only a few mortars and pestles have been found in the highlands of Indonesian West Papua, whereas in Papua New Guinea (PNG) the highest density of finds comes from its highland valleys and basins. A combination of poor soils, limited *Castanopsis* habitat, and the importance of sago in lowland and coastal subsistence probably explains why fewer have been found in West Papua. With no volcanoes, the soils of West Papua are less fertile than those of PNG (Siebert et al. 2011). By comparison, PNG's soils are derived from volcanic ashes or have been enriched by ash falls originating from explosive eruptions (Hope & Hartemink 2007: 171). Moreover, the lower montane forest zone, the habitat of *Castanopsis*, only covers 2.1% of West Papua's total land area (Marshall 2007: 757), whereas in PNG it covers an extensive area (Paijmans 1981). Sago is the most important food for many West Papuan communities, and where this is also the case in PNG, for example, Manus (Hanson, Allen, Bourke, & McCarthy 2001: 243), few mortars and pestles are found.

Although the Mamberambo River and its tributaries drain the northern side of the West Papuan Highlands, a Mid-Holocene sea did not form along its river valleys as these valleys have a very different topography to the Sepik-Ramu Basin. Only one artefact, a bird pestle, has been found in the Baliem Valley in the Central Highlands of West Papua (Figure 23.4t). Most finds in the West Papuan Highlands come from the more readily accessed Paniai Lakes region.

Though few in number, the elaborate mortars and pestles found in West Papua are comparable to finds from eastern New Guinea. A Mid-Holocene stemmed obsidian tool from Biak Island in Cenderawasih Bay confirms that maritime links existed with eastern New Guinea (Torrence & Swadling 2008: 602). The low number of mortar and pestle finds indicates that West Papua was peripheral to the interaction spheres occurring in eastern New Guinea and the Bismarck Archipelago.

ART

The elaborate art of Mid-Holocene mortars and pestles, especially those artefacts with geometric designs, can be seen as the precursor to the rich artistic traditions of both the Sepik-Ramu and Lapita pottery. The latter dates from some centuries before 3000 cal BP.

This ancestry is evident when the characteristic features of Sepik-Ramu art and Lapita pottery are considered. Sepik art with its greatly elongated anthropomorphic noses, panels of tight geometric pattern, and use of a flowing line in the form of spirals and interlocking scrolls (A.W. 1971; Newton 1979) owes its origins to the art of the Mid-Holocene. Lapita pottery also has its antecedent. The characteristic features of this potting tradition, namely, anthropomorphic faces with long noses, geometric designs, especially repeating designs contained within horizontal bands, likewise owes much to the Mid-Holocene art of the Sepik-Ramu. This inheritance is not surprising, for by c. 3000–2900 cal BP, potters with Austronesian ancestry were trading their pottery (made from Aibom and Madang coast clay) via the infilling Sepik-Ramu inland sea to the Madang Highlands (Summerhayes 2019).

The artistic representation of birds on mortars and pestles is likely related to the distribution of birds of paradise. No species of birds of paradise occurs east of the New Guinea mainland apart from some islands in Milne Bay. Mortars and pestles decorated with bird features occur in the interaction spheres that link the Central Highlands with the inland sea, and the Eastern Highlands with the Huon Gulf and West New Britain. These finds, though primarily bird pestles with folded wings in the former and bird decoration on mortars in the latter, appear as clusters. The few bird pestles from West New Britain can be seen as related to links that the Willaumez Peninsula had with the inland sea and Huon Gulf. East of the Willaumez Peninsula, no mortars or pestles decorated with bird features have been recorded. The isolated, dispersed distribution of bird pestles with raised wings in New Guinea might be related to peoples penetrating inland areas to discover new varieties of birds of paradise (Figure 23.4p–u). The distribution of these pestles is curious, as they are all located on or near major river systems that facilitate inland access.

It needs to be kept in mind that many stone mortars and pestles are undecorated. These undecorated forms may have been communal artefacts used to process food for a group, with more elaborate (decorated) examples, such as the Vrimsebu mortar (Figure 23.4i), used for major ceremonial occasions. Some of the shallow mortars may have been used specifically to pound nuts, which were then consumed or mixed with another food.

CONCLUSION

Mortars and pestles provide important markers of population distribution and interaction in the Mid-Holocene of New Guinea and the Bismarck Archipelago. Comparable, distinctive Mid-Holocene artefacts are absent in the Nusa Tenggara archipelago of southern Wallacea. There the existence of a pre-Austronesian interaction sphere is currently based on the geographic distribution of unusual linguistic features attributed to a substrate language spoken before the arrival of the Austronesians (Shipton, O'Connor, Reepmeyer, Kealy, & Jankowski 2019).

The wide distribution of mortars and pestles, as well as stemmed obsidian artefacts, shows that extensive interaction spheres existed in New Guinea and the Bismarck Archipelago in the Mid-Holocene. These spheres linked coastal and inland areas and were also maritime in nature. Of the former, those linking the inland sea with the Central Highlands, and the Huon Gulf with the Eastern Highlands, were the most important. The main maritime interaction spheres extended to either side of the Willaumez Peninsula of West New Britain. To the west these linked with the Huon Gulf and the inland sea, and to the east they linked with East New Britain, New Ireland, and Bougainville. From the Huon Gulf, coastal networks extended to Oro, Milne Bay, and Central Provinces.

The declining availability of *Castanopsis*, the main nut pounded in the highlands due to land clearance, would have played a major role in the abandonment of mortars and pestles in the highlands. Decreasing coastal connectivity due to the infilling of the Sepik-Ramu inland sea may have also played a role in this abandonment. The continued availability of canarium and coconuts in coastal areas allowed the practice of pounding a nut and starch product to continue and in due course saw it taken to Oceania by Austronesians. Their pottery would have allowed tubers to be steam-cooked, and the softer result probably led to stone versions of mortars and pestles being abandoned in favour of wooden versions.

The elaborate art of the Mid-Holocene gave rise to some of the most distinctive and celebrated artistic traditions of Papua New Guinea. The long noses on representations of human faces, as well as the geometric and spiral features that characterize Mid-Holocene art, gave rise to Sepik-Ramu art. The latter also influenced the art of the Austronesians who arrived 3000 years ago. By 3000 years ago, pottery was being produced from Aibom clay in the Chambri Lakes as well as from clay located on the Madang north coast. This early pottery represents the antecedents of ethnographically known pottery-making traditions in this region. Increasingly, it is becoming evident that Papua New Guinea's cultural heritage is a legacy of Mid-Holocene artistic traditions of 3000–5000 years ago.

ACKNOWLEDGEMENTS

The author wishes to thank Michael Bourke, Robin Hide, and Ben Shaw for their helpful comments and information.

REFERENCES

Allen, B. J., Hide, R. L., Bourke, R. M., Ballard, C., Fritsch, D., Grau, R., . . . Kandasan, D. (2002a). *Enga Province: Text summaries, maps, code lists and village identification.* Agricultural Systems of Papua New Guinea. Working Paper No. 9. Revised edition. Canberra: Department of Human Geography, The Australian National University.

Allen, B. J., Hide, R. L., Bourke, R. M., Fritsch, D., Grau, R., Hobsbawn, P., ... Sem, G. (2002b). *Madang Province: Text summaries, maps, code lists and village identification.* Agricultural Systems of Papua New Guinea. Working Paper No. 7. Revised edition. Canberra: Department of Human Geography, The Australian National University.

Allen, J. (1970). Prehistoric agricultural systems in the Wahgi Valley: A further note. *Mankind, 7,* 177–183.

A.W. (1971). The art of the Sepik River. *Calendar of the Art Institute of Chicago, 65*(4) (September), 1–3.

Barstow, M. (2018). *Castanopsis acuminatissima. The IUCN Red List of Threatened Species* 2018:e.T62004491A62004494, https://dx.doi.org/10.2305/IUCN.UK.2018:1.RLTS.T620044 91A62004494.en.

Barton, F. R. (1908). Note on stone pestles from British New Guinea. *Man, 8,* 1–2.

Bellwood, P. (1978). *Man's conquest of the Pacific: The prehistory of Southeast Asia and Oceania.* Auckland: Collins.

Berndt, R. M. (1954). Contemporary significance of pre-historic stone objects in the Eastern Central Highlands of New Guinea. *Anthropos, 49,* 553–587.

Bourke, R. M. (2010). Altitudinal limits of 230 economic crop species in Papua New Guinea. In S. Haberle, J. Stevenson, & M. Prebble (Eds.), *Altered ecologies: Fire, climate and human influence on terrestrial landscapes* (pp. 473–512). Terra Australis 32. Canberra: ANU E Press.

Bourke, R. M., Allen, B. J., Hide, R. L., Fritsch, D., Grau, R., Hobsbawn, P., . . . Varvaliu, A. (2002). Southern Highlands Province: Text summaries, maps, code lists and village identification. *Agricultural systems of Papua New Guinea.* Working Paper No. 11. Revised edition. Canberra: Department of Human Geography, Australian National University.

Bühler, A. (1946–1949). Steingeräte, Steinskulpturen und Felszeichnungen aus Melanesien und Polynesien. *Anthropos, 41–44,* 225–274.

Bulmer, R. N. H. (1964). Edible seeds and prehistoric stone mortars in the highlands of East New Guinea. *Man, 64,* 147–150.

Bulmer, S. (1973). *Notes on 1972 excavations at Wanlek.* Working Papers in Anthropology, Archaeology, Linguistics and Maori Studies 29. University of Auckland, Department of Anthropology.

Bulmer, S. (1982). Human ecology and cultural variation in prehistoric New Guinea. *Monographiae Biologicae, 42,* 169–206.

Bulmer, S., & Bulmer, R. (1964). The prehistory of the Australian New Guinea Highlands. *American Anthropologist, 66*(4.2), 39–76.

Chappell, J. (1993). Contrasting Holocene sedimentary geologies of lower Daly River, northern Australia, and lower Sepik-Ramu, Papua New Guinea. *Sedimentary Geology, 83,* 339–358.

Chappell, J. (2005). Geographic changes of coastal lowlands in the Papuan past. In A. Pawley, R. Attenborough, J. Golson, & R. Hide (Eds.), *Papuan pasts: Cultural, linguistic and biological histories of Papuan-speaking peoples* (pp. 525–539). Canberra: Pacific Linguistics, Research School of Pacific and Asian Studies, The Australian National University.

Chowning, A. (1978). Changes in West New Britain trading systems in the twentieth century. *Mankind, 11,* 296–307.

Christensen, O. A. (1975). A tanged blade from the New Guinea highlands. *Mankind, 10,* 37–39.

Clarke, W. C. 1971. *Place and people: An ecology of a New Guinea community.* Berkeley: University of California Press.

Conn, B., & Damas, K. (no date). *Guide to trees of Papua New Guinea,* http://www.pngplants. org/PNGtrees/TreeDescriptions/Castanopsis_acuminatissima_Bl_A_DC.html.

Coote, E. (2007). An introduction to the Huon Gulf collection of the National Gallery of Australia. *OAS (Oceanic Art Society) Newsletter, 12*(5), 10–12.

David, B., Alpin, K., Peck, H., Skelly, R., Leavesley, M., Mialanes, J., ... Ford, A. (2019). Moiapu 3: Settlement on Moiapu Hill at the very end of Lapita, Caution Bay hinterland. In S. Bedford & M. Spriggs (Eds.), *Debating Lapita: Distribution, chronology, society and subsistence* (pp. 61–88). Terra Australis 52. Canberra; ANU E Press.

Denham, T. (2018). *Tracing early agriculture in the Highlands of New Guinea: Plot, mound and ditch*. Oxford: Routledge.

Denham, T. P., Haberle, S. G., & Lentfer, C. (2004). New evidence and revised interpretations of early agriculture in highland New Guinea. *Antiquity, 78*(302), 839–857.

England, P. (1946). The Ramu stones. *Mankind, 3*, 233–236.

Field, J. H., Summerhayes, G. R., Luu, S., Coster, A. C. F., Ford, A., Mandui, H., ... Kealhofer, L. (2020). Functional studies of a flaked and ground stone artefacts reveal starchy tree nut and root exploitation in mid-Holocene highland New Guinea. *The Holocene 30*(9) 1360–1374. DOI: 10.1177/0959683620919983

Fullagar, R., & Golson, J. (2017). Kuk stone artifacts: Technology, usewear and residues. In J. Golson, T. Denham, P. Hughes, P. Swadling, & J. Muke (Eds.), *Ten thousand years of cultivation at Kuk Swamp in the highlands of Papua New Guinea* (pp. 373–401). Terra Australis 46. Canberra: ANU E Press.

Gaffney, D., Summerhayes, G. R., Ford, A., Scott, J. M., Denham, T., Field, J., & Dickinson, W. (2015). Earliest pottery on New Guinea mainland reveals Austronesian influences in highland environments 3000 years ago. *PLosONE, 10*(9), e0134497.

Golson, J. (1991). The New Guinea Highlands on the eve of agriculture. *Bulletin of the Indo-Pacific Prehistory Association, 11*, 82–91.

Golson, J. (2000). A stone bowl fragment from the early middle Holocene of the upper Wahgi Valley, Western Highlands Province, Papua New Guinea. In A. Anderson & T. Murray (Eds.), *Australian archaeologist: Collected papers in honour of Jim Allen* (pp. 231–248). Canberra: Coombs Academic Publishing, The Australian National University.

Goodenough, W. H. (1952). Ethnological reconnaissance in New Guinea. *Pennsylvania University Museum, Bulletin, 17*(1), 5–37.

Guise, A. (1985). *Oral tradition and archaeological sites in the Eastern Central Province*. PNG National Museum Record No. 9, Port Moresby.

Haberle, S., Lentfer, C., & Denham, T. (2017). Palaeoecology. In J. Golson, T. Denham, P. Hughes, P. Swadling, & J. Muke (Eds.), *Ten thousand years of cultivation at Kuk Swamp in the highlands of Papua New Guinea* (pp. 145–161). Terra Australis 46. Canberra: ANU E Press.

Hanson, L. W., Allen, B. J., Bourke, R. M., & McCarthy, T. J. (2001). *Papua New Guinea rural development handbook*. Canberra: Land Management Group, Department of Human Geography, Research School of Pacific and Asian Studies, The Australian National University.

Harding, T. G. (1967). *Voyagers of the Vitiaz Strait: A study of a New Guinea trade system*. Seattle: University of Washington Press.

Harrison, S. (1976). A study of the diets of four families in the Mendi Sub-Province. Unpublished report.

Henty, E. E. (1985). Some nut-bearing plants in Papua New Guinea. *West Australian Nut and Tree Crop Association Yearbook, 10*, 19–27.

Hide, R., Kimin, M., Kora, A., Kua, G., & Kua, K. (1979). *A checklist of some plants in the territory of Sinasina Nimai (Simbu Province, Papua New Guinea), with notes on their uses.* Department of Anthropology Working Paper No. 54. Auckland: Auckland University.

Höltker, G. (1940–41). Einiges über Steinkeulenköpfe und Steinbeile in Neuguinea. Anthropos, 35–36: 681–736.

Höltker, G. (1951). Die Steinvögel in Melanesien. In *Südseestudien: Gedenkschrift zur Errinerung an Felix Speiser* (pp. 234–265). Basel: Museum für Völkerkunde und Schweizerischen Museum für Volkskunde.

Höltker, G. (1968). Altertümliche Steinartefäkte aus Neuguinea im Anthropos-Institut. *Ethnologica, 4*, 494–531.

Hope, G. S., & Haberle, S. G. (2005). The history of the human landscapes of New Guinea. In A. Pawley, R. Attenborough, J. Golson, & R. Hide (Eds.), *Papuan pasts: Cultural, linguistic and biological histories of Papuan-speaking peoples* (pp. 541–554). Canberra: Pacific Linguistics, Research School of Pacific and Asian Studies, The Australian National University.

Hope, G. S., & Hartemink, A. E. (2007). Soils of Papua. In A. J. Marshall & B. M. Beehler (Eds.), *The ecology of Papua. Part 1* (pp. 165–176). Singapore: Periplus Editions.

Hughes, I. M. (1977). *New Guinea Stone Age trade: The geography and ecology of traffic in the interior.* Terra Australis 3. Canberra: Department of Prehistory, Research School of Pacific Studies, The Australian National University.

Hviding, E. (1996). *Guardians of Marovo Lagoon: Practice, place, and politics in maritime Melanesia.* Honolulu: University of Hawai'i Press.

Kasprus, A. (1940–41). Der grosse 'prehistorische' Steinmörser in Atemble am mittleren Ramu-river in Neuguinea. Anthropos, 35–36: 647–654.

Kusnowo, A., & Nazif, A. H. (1992). *Yogotak hubuluk motok hanorogo.* Jakarta: Lembaga Ilmu Pengetahuan Indonesia.

Mager, J. F. (1952). *Gedaged-English dictionary.* Columbus, Ohio: American Lutheran Church.

Maier, O. (2003). Stone tool collection data sheets, Chimbu Province, PNG, 1958-196. Pacific Manuscripts Bureau, The Australian National University.

Marshall, A. J. (2007). The diversity and conservation of Papua's ecosystems. In A. J. Marshall & B. M. Beehler (Eds.), *The ecology of Papua. Part 2* (pp. 753–770). Singapore: Periplus Editions.

May, P., & Tuckson, M. (2000). *The traditional pottery of Papua New Guinea.* Adelaide: Crawford House.

Meyer, A. J. P. (1995). *Oceanic art.* Köln: Könemann.

Narakobi, B. (2002). *Two seasons.* Madang: Divine Word University Press.

Neuhauss, R. (1911). *Deutsch-Neu-Guinea.* 3 vols. Berlin: Dietrich Reimer.

Newton, D. (1979). Prehistoric and recent art styles in Papua New Guinea. In S. M. Mead (Ed.), *Exploring the visual art of Oceania* (pp. 32–57). Honolulu: University of Hawai'i Press.

Ono, E., Umemura, M., Ishida, T., & Takenaka, C. (2015). Preliminary investigation of the formation age and chemical characterization of the tropical peat in the middle Sepik Plain, northern Papua New Guinea. *Geoscience Letters, 2*(1): 6 pp.

Paijmans, K. (1981). Vegetation. In D. King & S. Ranck (Eds.), *Papua New Guinea atlas: A nation in transition* (pp. 92–93). Port Moresby: Robert Brown and Associates and University of Papua New Guinea.

Parkinson, R. (1999). *Thirty years in the South Seas.* Translation by John Dennison. Honolulu: University of Hawai'i Press.

Pengilley, A., Brand, C., Flexner, J., Specht, J., & Torrence, R. (2019). Detecting exchange networks in New Britain, Papua New Guinea: Geochemical comparisons between axe-adze blades and in situ volcanic rock sources. *Archaeology in Oceania, 54*, 200–213.

Petrequin, A.-M., & Petrequin, P. (2006). *Objets de pouvoir en Nouvelle-Guinée: Approche ethnoarchéologique d'un systeme de signes sociaux*. Paris: Éditions de la Réunion des Musées Nationaux.

Pomponio, A. (1992). *Seagulls don't fly into the bush: Cultural identity and development in Melanesia*. Belmont: Wadsworth.

Powell, J. M., & Harrison, S. (1982). *Haiyapugwa: Aspects of Huli subsistence and swamp cultivation*. Occasional Paper No.1. Port Moresby: Department of Geography, University of Papua New Guinea.

Pretty, G. (1965). Two stone pestles from Western Papua and their relationship to prehistoric pestles and mortars from New Guinea. *Records of the South Australian Museum, 15*, 119–130.

Riesenfeld, A. (1955). *Megalithic culture of Melanesia*. Leiden: Brill.

Schmitz, C. A. (1956). Two prehistoric stone objects from the Huon Peninsula. *Mankind, 3*, 127–128.

Schmitz, C. A. (1966). Steinerne Schalenmorser, pestille und vogelfiguren aus Zentral-Neuguinea. *Baessler-Archiv, 14*, 1–60.

Schuster, C. (1946). Prehistoric stone objects from New Guinea and the Solomons. *Mankind, 3*, 247–251.

Shaw, B., Field, J. H., Summerhayes, G. R., Coxe, S., Coster, A. C. F., Ford, A., . . . Kealhofer, L. (2020). Emergence of a Neolithic in highland New Guinea by 5000 to 4000 years ago. *Science Advances, 6* : eaay4573.

Sherwin, V. H., & Haddon, A. C. (1933). A stone bowl from New Britain. *Man, 33*, 160–162.

Shipton, C., O'Connor, S., Reepmeyer, C., Kealy, S., & Jankowski, N. (2019). Shell adzes, exotic obsidian, and inter-island voyaging in the Early and Middle Holocene of Wallacea. *The Journal of Island and Coastal Archaeology*. DOI:10.1080/15564894.2019.1581306

Siebert, L. et al. (2011). *Volcanoes of the world: A regional directory, gazetteer, and chronology of volcanism during the last 10,000 years* (second edition). New York: Hutchinson Ross Pub. Co.

Specht, J. (1966). Mortars and pestles in New Britain. *Journal of the Polynesian Society, 75*(3), 378–382.

Specht, J. (1981). Obsidian sources at Talasea, West New Britain, Papua New Guinea. *Journal of the Polynesian Society, 90*(3), 337–356.

Specht, J. (1988). *Pieces of paradise*. Sydney: Australian Museum Trust.

Stewart, P. J., & Strathern, A. (1999). Politics and poetics mirrored in indigenous stone objects from Papua New Guinea. *Journal of the Polynesian Society, 108*(1), 69–90.

Summerhayes, G. R. (2019). Austronesian expansions and the role of mainland New Guinea: A new perspective. *Asian Perspectives, 58*(2), 250–260.

Swadling, P. (1981; reprinted 1986). *Papua New Guinea's prehistory: An introduction*. Port Moresby: PNG National Museum and Art Gallery in association with Gordon & Gotch.

Swadling, P. (1984). Sepik prehistory. Paper prepared for Sepik Research Today, Wenner Gren Symposium No. 95, Basel, Switzerland.

Swadling, P. (1990). Sepik prehistory. In N. Lutkehaus, C. Kaufmann, W. E. Mitchell, D. Newton, L. Osmundsen, & M. Schuster (Eds.), *Sepik heritage: Tradition and change in Papua New Guinea* (pp. 71–86). Bathurst: Crawford House Press.

Swadling, P. (1997). Changing shorelines and cultural orientations in the Sepik-Ramu, Papua New Guinea: Implications for Pacific prehistory. *World Archaeology, 29*(1), 1–14.

Swadling, P. (2005). The Huon Gulf and its hinterlands: A long-term view of coastal-highlands interactions. In C. Gross, H. D. Lyons, & D. A. Counts (Eds.), *A polymath anthropologist: Essays in honour of Ann Chowning* (pp. 1–14). Research in Anthropology and Linguistics Monograph No. 6. Auckland: University of Auckland.

Swadling, P. (2017). Early art in New Guinea: Glimpses from prehistory. In J. Friede, T. Hays, & C. Hellmich (Eds.), *New Guinea Highlands: Art from the Jolika* Collection (pp. 12–55). Munich, London, & New York: Fine Arts Museums of San Francisco, de Young, DelMonico Books, & Prestel.

Swadling, P., Chappell, J., Francis, G., Araho, N., & Ivuyo, B. (1989). A late Quaternary inland sea and early pottery in Papua New Guinea. *Archaeology in Oceania, 24,* 106–109.

Swadling, P., Hauser Schäublin, B., Gorecki, P., & F. Tiesler, F. (1988). *The Sepik-Ramu: An Introduction.* Boroko: PNG National Museum.

Swadling, P., & Hope, G. (1992). Environmental change in New Guinea since human settlement. In J. Dodson (Ed.), *The naïve lands: Prehistory and environmental change in Australia and the Southwest Pacific* (pp. 13–42). Melbourne: Longman Cheshire.

Torrence, R., & Swadling, P. (2008). Social networks and the spread of Lapita. *Antiquity, 82,* 600–616.

Walter, A., & Sam, C. (2002). *Fruits of Oceania.* ACIAR Monograph No. 85. Translated P. Ferrar from Fruits d'Océanie. Canberra.

Watson, V., & Cole, J. D. (1977). *Prehistory of the Eastern Highlands of New Guinea.* Seattle: University of Washington Press.

White, J. P. (1972). *Ol Tumbuna: Archaeological excavations in the Eastern Highlands, Papua New Guinea.* Terra Australis 2. Canberra: Department of Prehistory, Research School of Pacific Studies, The Australian National University.

Yu, B., Chappell, J., & Flitchett, K. (1991). Natural diversions of the Ramu River in Papua New Guinea. *Australian Geographer, 22*(2), 161–167.

CHAPTER 24

AXE QUARRYING, PRODUCTION, AND EXCHANGE IN AUSTRALIA AND NEW GUINEA

ANNE FORD AND PETER HISCOCK

INTRODUCTION

GROUND-EDGE artefacts (GEAs), many of which have been called axes, are an innovative stone tool technology that became visible in the initial stages of colonization of Sahul—the continental landmass of Australia (including Tasmania) and New Guinea (Clarkson et al. 2017; Hiscock, O'Connor, Balme, & Maloney 2016). Nowhere else in the world were these tools developed so early; there is no evidence for their presence in earlier modern human sites in Africa or for any part of the Out-of-Africa migration towards Sahul. The advent of GEAs in Sahul is significant for a number of reasons; they were hafted, composite tools, as well as the earliest evidence globally of ground stone tools, typically associated elsewhere with Neolithic or agricultural communities of the past 10,000 years (Geneste, David, Plisson, Delannoy, & Petchey 2012). The development of this technology therefore highlights the innovation and flexibility of the first colonizers to Sahul and mirrors their success in adapting to a wide range of habitats soon after their first arrival. The ground stone axe may have played a prominent role as these tools are likely to have been multipurpose, being useful for a wide range of tasks as well as being highly portable and durable. Such qualities may be advantageous in a variety of contexts, since they reduce the need for a bulky, awkward tool kit and can enhance tool readiness. Ethnographically, axes were used in many tasks such as constructing shelters, chopping trees for firewood, removing wood and bark for the creation of shields, canoes, and other wooden implements, splitting tree trunks to access honey or grubs, creating notches to aid in tree climbing for hunting, butchering and skinning animals, and serving as weapons for fighting (Attenbrow & Kononenko 2019; Dickson 1981). In Papua New Guinea, axes are also essential in making gardens and creating long-distance voyaging canoes (McNiven, Von Gnielinksi, & Quinnell 2004; Rhoads & Mackenzie 1991).

Yet, over time, axes clearly evolved more than solely economic roles. Sahul's rich ethnographic records show that these artefacts were exchanged over long distances (Burton 1984a; McBryde 1984) and were employed in a range of social interactions. In Papua New Guinea, for example, axes were essential in the wealth and status economy, being used for bride-price transactions, war reparations, and mortuary feast ceremonies, as well as garden or canoe magic (Burton 1984a; Malinowski 1922). In Australia, axes were commonly used in economic and social exchanges in which maintenance of political relationships could involve reciprocal economic patterns, and they were sometimes incorporated into mythology. In these contexts, axes can be more than tools; they can also be symbols of the power, status, and ideology of those who possess them. This chapter will explore the development of this highly significant and evocative technology in Papua New Guinea and Australia, mapping changes in their roles and structures from initial colonization through to the Late Holocene and the precolonial period. Ethnographic overviews of stone axe/adze production and exchange in western New Guinea (Indonesian Papua) can be found in Pétrequin and Pétrequin (2002, 2006) and Hampton (1999).

WHAT IS AN AXE?

Axes are generally defined as tools used in chopping, splitting, or shaping wood, with an axe head/blade having symmetrical bevels and attached to a wooden haft or helve through a variety of measures that may include adhesives, ties, or sockets. However, within Australia and New Guinea, there is still considerable debate over the classification of these tools, which is complicated by different regional and temporal traditions. In Australia, descriptions of axes were the focus of work in the early 1970s by Dickson (1972, 1976, 1981), but morphology and technology have been little studied since then. Dickson initially labelled these implements as 'ground-edge axes' before rebadging them as 'hatchets', but as we discuss below the functional ascriptions are not as helpful or diagnostic as the presence of the ground edge.

No Australian axes are ground to a smooth surface all over (Figure 24.1A). Many are ground at only one end, whereas some are ground more extensively. All have areas with little or no grinding, such that earlier stages of production remain visible to allow reconstruction of the technological processes that shaped the specimen prior to grinding. While some specimens are made on carefully selected cobbles, without shaping, most are flaked and/or hammer-dressed into a roughly symmetrical shape with a cross-section suitable for grinding an edge. Shapes and sizes are variable. Often, specimens are long relative to width, and cross-sections range from flat to lenticular to almost circular.

Many specimens have flat or convex sides, but some have 'waisting' (concave margins) and others have a groove hammered or abraded around the circumference, perhaps to assist hafting. Sizes vary enormously across the Australian continent, ranging from less than 200 g to almost 4000 g. Raw material also varies greatly, largely reflecting geological patterns in each local area. Thus, while some axes are basaltic, others are hornfels, greywacke, quartzite, or other kinds of rock. Given the massive heterogeneity of specimens that Dickson labelled as axes or hatchets, their unifying characteristic is the ground edge. For this reason alone, recent researchers have begun labelling this class as ground-edge artefacts (GEAs).

Ethnographically, GEAs were typically attached to a wooden haft that was held as a handle. Virtually all ethnographic specimens in Australia have handles that wrap around the GEA. Commonly, the handle was a split stick or rattan wrapped around the stone artefact and bound with fibres below the stone head tightly enough to keep it in place. Often, an adhesive of some kind, such as resin, was packed around the junction of the handle and stone to anchor the head more securely to the handle. Variation in the details of hafting reflect not only the materials at hand but also the shape of the GEA.

Compared to Australia, New Guinea has an even more diverse range of axe technology, including types that are not mirrored in Australia (Figures 24.1B and 24.1C). This diversity includes the presence of large flaked axes during the Late Pleistocene, with no evidence of grinding, through to fully polished axes in the Mid- to Late Holocene, usually associated with the introduction of agriculture. In the Late Holocene, a further polished adze tradition is associated with Austronesian migrations. 'Axes' in New Guinea

FIGURE 24.1. Ground stone axes from Australia and New Guinea. A: GEA attributed to Mt William Axe Quarry, Victoria, Australia. B: Man holding Highland planilateral axe photographed near Kiowa rock shelter in 1960 by Susan Bulmer (from the Susan Bulmer collection at the University of Otago. Reproduced with permission with thanks to Glenn Summerhayes). C: Suloga axe shown to the author (AF) on Fergusson Island in the Massim region of Papua New Guinea.

range from flaked to ground edge to polished, and they include a wider range of hafting forms, including not only the wraparound type described above, but also footed (elbow-shaped) handles and sockets (Crosby 1977; Pétrequin & Pétrequin 2006). Defining axes in New Guinea is therefore even more difficult and challenges archaeologists to distinguish between these and other ground stone tools used for woodworking, such as adzes and chisels.

Traditionally, distinctions in axes and adzes focus on the symmetry of the bevels or refer to hafting style. However, in Papua New Guinea, with its rich ethnographic record of axe production and use, the definitions become blurred (Crosby 1977). For example, axes are usually hafted horizontally and adzes perpendicularly to their handles, and yet Papua New Guinea has examples of the same types of blades hafted in both manners (Bickler & Turner 2002; Malinowski 1934). Similarly, axes are usually considered to have symmetrical bevels and adzes asymmetrical, but in the Highlands, blades that are clearly hafted as axes sometimes have asymmetrical bevels (Burton 1984a). Relying on simplistic divisions of tools using modern definitions therefore obscures the diversity and flexibility of how these tools were used in the ethnographic and archaeological record. Because of this confusion, in the New Guinea literature there is continual switching between the terms *axe* and *adze*, with most archaeologists utilizing the term *axe-adze* as a way to bypass artificial distinctions.

Nor do archaeological investigations bear out the presumption that axes would necessarily be used solely to chop wood. Attenbrow and Kononenko (2019) studied the wear and residues on fifty-one GEAs from the east coast of Australia. Less than 10% were employed solely to chop wood, with approximately three quarters having multiple functions. These specimens were used on a wide variety of materials, not only on wood but also on soft, nonwoody plants, bone, nuts, skin, ochre, and other stones. It seems likely that chopping wood was the most common use of these tools, but they were also employed to pound and grind plants and seeds, as anvils for splitting nuts and powdering ochre, as hammers to break bone and knap rock, as well as an abrader on bone and a scraper of animal skins. These results give a sense of just how multipurpose GEAs are; thinking of these artefact forms as axes or hatchets not merely limits our insights into their function, but may simply be wrong for a significant portion of these tools. Hence, our thoughts about this category of lithic artefact should move beyond simple functional associations and explanations to something more multidimensional, reflecting the multifunctionality of the objects themselves.

SAHUL: THE FIRST AXE-MAKERS

The earliest evidence for GEAs comes from the north of the continent, with the oldest examples found at the site of Madjedbebe in Arnhem Land, Northern Territory (Figure 24.2A). Excavations in 1988–1989 produced flakes of Oenpelli dolerite and hornfels, with ground dorsal surfaces that dated to approximately 45 kya (Clarkson et al. 2015).

AXE QUARRYING, PRODUCTION, AND EXCHANGE 645

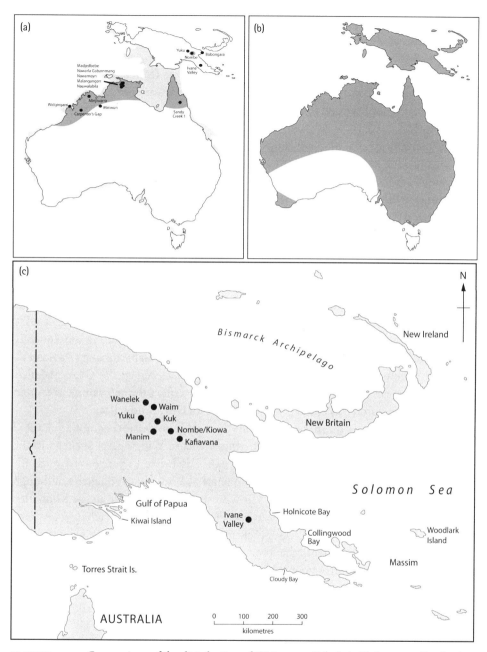

FIGURE 24.2. Comparison of the distribution of GEA across Sahul. A: Pleistocene distribution with archaeological sites mentioned in text featured. B: Late Holocene (data from Dickson 1981: 17). C: Locations and archaeological sites in Papua New Guinea discussed in text.

Subsequent excavations in 2012 and 2015 led by Chris Clarkson (Clarkson et al. 2017) have now placed the earliest clear occupation at the site between 68,690/61,260 and 55,090/50,380 cal BP[1] (Phase 2). In this phase, one GEA is reported from Square B1, ten axe flakes/fragments from Square B6, and three axe flakes from Square C4. Although the total number of axes from the 2012 and 2015 excavations are not reported, it is clear that there are numerous examples, making this the earliest site globally that shows GEA technology.

In northern Australia, Madjedbebe is not an isolated occurrence. Other early sites with GEA include Minjiwarra (Veth et al. 2019), Carpenters Gap 1 (CG1) (Hiscock et al. 2016), and Carpenters Gap 3 (CG3) (O'Connor, Maloney, Vannieuwenhuyse, Balme, & Wood 2014) in the Kimberley region of western Australia, and Nawarla Gabarnmang in Arnhem Land (Geneste et al. 2010, 2012). Minjiwarra has igneous GEA from 37.8 +/– 1.8 kya (Veth et al. 2019). CG1 has one basalt GEA flake that dates to between 43,941 and 48,875 cal BP (Hiscock et al. 2016) but no other specimens in the Pleistocene (Maloney, O'Connor, Wood, Aplin, & Balme 2018), and CG3 has two basaltic GEA flakes that date between 33,992 and 32,970 cal BP (O'Connor et al. 2014). The axe flakes from CG1 and CG3 are both from the initial stages of occupation, with little subsequent evidence for axe technology. Nawarla Gabarnmang has a similar record, with a single basalt GEA flake that dates to 35,400 +/– 410 cal BP (Geneste et al. 2010), but nothing subsequently until the Late Holocene (Geneste et al. 2012). Both Nawarla Gabarnmang (David et al. 2019) and Minjiwarra also have occupation records that predate the GEA evidence. However, these early intermittent records may partly reflect limited sample sizes and should not be interpreted as indicating the cessation of GEA production.

GEAs continue in northern Australia into the terminal Pleistocene but are limited in terms of numbers, and many sites lack complete axes. Widgingarri Shelter 1 in the Kimberley region (O'Connor 1999) has GEA flakes that date to 31,076–33,493 cal BP. Similar flakes are present throughout the sequence at Widgingarri Shelter 2, although the basal layers of this site are undated. Miriwun shelter, also located in the Kimberley region, has a single GEA flake that dates to Late Pleistocene levels (Dortch 1977). A complete GEA was found in Sandy Creek 1 rock shelter in Cape York Peninsula. Dating to older than 34,568–37,957 cal BP, this pink quartzite axe has hafting modifications in the form of waisting and grooving (Morwood & Trezise 1989). The two Arnhem Land rock shelters of Nawamoyn and Malangangerr, excavated by Carmel Schrire (1982), are particularly rich in GEA. Nawamoyn has a total of twenty-four axes, nine of which come from the earliest layer dated to 24,869–26,633 cal BP. Malangangerr has five complete axes that date to between 20,765 and 33,268 cal BP. The axes from both sites are largely made on porphyritic dolerite or hornfels, although quartz dolerite, hornblende schist, quartzite, and schist are also used. Nauwalabila, also in Arnhem Land, shares similarities to Nawamoyn and Malangangerr. Flakes made from porphyritic dolerite, schist, and hornfels, with grinding on the dorsal surface, were found to a depth of 1.5 metres and were dated to between 13.5 ± 0.9 kyr and 30.0 ± 2.4 kyr using OSL dating (Jones & Johnson 1985; Roberts, Jones, & Smith 1993). However, other volcanic material, including possible weathered axe/axe blanks, were found to a depth of 243 cm, dating to

53.4 ± 5.4 kyr; this finding suggests that GEA antiquity was perhaps at least as old here as at other Arnhem Land sites.

Early GEAs are found across northern Australia, but there are also axes in the northern part of Sahul, in what is today Papua New Guinea. Only one of these axes appears to be obviously similar to the Australian examples. It comes from Nombe rock shelter, located in Chimbu Province of the Highlands region, and is a single complete GEA from Stratum D1/5 (Mountain 1983) that dates to 25,550–19,600 cal BP (Denham & Mountain 2016). Similarities between the Nombe GEA and northern Australian specimens reveals that there are shared morphologies between the regions of northern Sahul, but the fact that so few GEAs look the same between the regions reinforces the impression of early and substantial differentiation on artefact forms across the continent.

In contrast, Late Pleistocene Papua New Guinea tends to have large hafted tools that have been termed *axes* or *waisted blades*, and that show modifications to produce stems, waisting, and grooving, but without a ground edge (see Golson 2001 for definitions of hafting modifications). These sites are mostly montane, including Yuku (Bulmer 2005), Nombe (Mountain 1983), and the Ivane Valley (Ford 2017). However, the most famous example is the coastal site of Bobongara on the Huon Peninsula, which consists of a series of raised coral reefs. More than one hundred large waisted tools, often called 'axes', were found on the surface of coral terrace IIIa, which has been dated to between 45,000 and 60,000 years old, using U-series dating (Chappell 2002). Excavations at the back of the terrace also found three waisted specimens *in situ*, one of which was grooved on both surfaces (Groube 1984; Groube, Chappell, Muke, & Price 1986). Specimens from Bobongara have been described as large, heavy, andesite flakes, detached from local boulders, and unifacially flaked into shape, with notches on both sides to create the distinctive waist. Based on their large size, robusticity, breakage patterns, and usewear traces, Groube (1989) proposed that the Bobongara waisted tools were used in forest clearance activities and therefore had similar uses to those for many GEAs. We do not offer a critique of Groube's interpretation (although see Ford 2017); we simply note that such specimens are not GEA and that this illustrates how many form–function relationships were in play.

A recurring theme in regions across northern Sahul (tropical Australia and New Guinea) is that the recovery of GEA from Late Pleistocene archaeological sites has been sporadic. Clearly, this technology is present from the first occupation of Sahul, but recovering specimens is difficult, with many sites only having axe flakes (flakes with grinding present on their dorsal surface that have been removed during either the use or recycling of an axe) rather than complete axes. Additionally, the recovery of both GEA and axe flakes varies between sites in a single region and laterally within a single site. This rarity is partly due to the utility of these items, which have long use-lives and are readily maintained. Consequently, all around the world, GEAs were often made from nonlocal raw materials and were reworked and recycled to the point where they might even become heirloom items. Because of this longevity, they are less likely to enter the archaeological record in great numbers. This explains their general rarity, and yet they are sometimes found in some sites but not in others of the same age. This pattern reflects differences in the rates of localized manufacture, caching, and disposal for reasons that are not well understood.

The small number of complete tools from these early sites and the lack of published information about them have meant that it is difficult both to determine the variation in shape of GEA and to show how their shapes and sizes relate to other hafted tools in the Pleistocene. For example, in Phase 3 of Madjedbebe, which dates to between 53,980/49,160 and 30,110/26,000 cal BP, a variety of GEA forms have been recovered, including shouldering/stemming, waisting, and grooving, which may indicate diverse hafting techniques (Clarkson et al. 2017). However, as we noted earlier, the unquantified data presented in the literature has provided strong reason to think there were regional differences in the kinds of GEA typically made during the Pleistocene. Regional differentiation is even more marked when we consider that adjacent regions did not manufacture axes.

In southern Australia, and in the islands of the Bismarck Archipelago, there is no evidence for any GEA technology in the Late Pleistocene. In the Bismarck Archipelago, fully ground axes appeared at the terminal Pleistocene (White, Flannery, O'Brien, Hancock, & Pavlish 1991), while GEAs appear in southern Australia only in the past 3000–3500 years, as shown in Figure 24.2B (Hiscock & Maloney 2017). These patterns reflect long-term regional limits to information flow, followed by changes in the transmission of norms, skills, and technology. For example, a number of the regions of tropical Australia in which there were Pleistocene GEAs were also regions that subsequently retained the non-Pama-Nyungan language (see McConvell & Evans, this volume) and did not have microliths, whereas the southern two-thirds of Australia in which no Pleistocene GEAs are found contains Pama-Nyungan languages and microliths. Geographic similarities in language and technological histories indicate that there were long-standing transmission networks and geographic boundaries to transmission (see Hiscock 2002; also Morwood & Hobbs 1995). Boundaries to the transmission of ideas and norms must have been strong, they were certainly very long lived. However, it is also clear that these boundaries eventually broke down, with Hiscock and Maloney (2017, 314) stating that there was 'significant upscaling in the magnitude of social transmissions and connectivity across mainland Australia 4000–2000 years ago'. Hence the patterns visible in ethnography and recent archaeological sites are not good proxies for the interactions and regionality that are apparent through the Pleistocene.

Golson (2001) has suggested that at least some of the early regional differentiation that is visible in archaeologically preserved technology may reflect phylogenetic connections, where cultural variation reflects distance from shared ancestral culture. This proposition about cultural evolution and diversification over time is supported by the available genetic evidence. For example, Y chromosome, mitochondrial DNA, and whole-genome data all show that Aboriginal Australians and New Guineans share a common ancestry but separate from each other after initial colonization of Sahul, with dates of divergence placed at approximately 50 kya (Bergstrom et al. 2016; 2017; Nagle et al. 2017; Tobler et al. 2017). Evidence from Hepatitis B virus genomes confirms the long separation for New Guinea and Australia. It may additionally provide support for a northern Australian interaction zone because there are two different lineages of HBV/C4 that differentiate Pama-Nyungan and non-Pama-Nyungan speaking populations in Australia (Lilly et al. 2019). These results may indicate that the ancestral community shared the norms and technical procedures for hafting large stone tools and GEAs prior to their arrival in Sahul but that only some groups inhabiting the north of the continent emphasized edge grinding on their hafted tools. Testing this hypothesis is restricted by a lack of complete GEA specimens, as well as by the absence of detailed functional analyses of GEA in northern Sahul and of information about similar technologies within sites of comparable age in Southeast Asia. However, current evidence points to the GEA in particular being a Sahul innovation that perhaps represented the flexibility and innovation of the first colonists. That is, these first colonists likely employed a range of technological techniques to colonize the range of the new and different environments they encountered in their movement across Sahul, and they created regional cultural systems that existed in place for subsequent millennia (Hiscock et al. 2016).

Axes, Agriculture, and Austronesians: Axe Technology in Holocene Papua New Guinea

Elsewhere in the world, ground or polished stone axes have been associated with the concept of the Neolithic—a Holocene cultural package that also includes shifts towards sedentism, agriculture, and pottery (Denham 2019). In Sahul, GEAs are clearly evident from the early stages of occupation in the Pleistocene, indicating that they did not begin as an innovation associated with agriculture. The link between GEA and hunter-gatherer lifestyles continued in Australia up until the first contact with Europeans. In Papua New Guinea, however, shifts in subsistence economies are themselves associated with changes in axe technology. Two of the most significant of these changes in the Holocene period are the emergence of agrarian societies in the Highlands and the introduction of the Neolithic Austronesian cultures, known as the Lapita Cultural Complex, in the island and coastal regions.

Highlands

In Papua New Guinea, the earliest known GEA dates to the Late Pleistocene at Nombe in the Highlands. This find, however, is a chronological outlier, and it is not until the terminal Pleistocene/Early Holocene that additional evidence of ground stone axe technology is present across a wide range of sites in the Highlands (Figure 24.2C), including the sites at Nombe (White 1972), Kiowa (Bulmer 2005; Gaffney, Ford, & Summerhayes 2015), Yuku (Bulmer 2005), Kafiavana (White 1972), Manim (Denham 2019), Waim

(Shaw et al. 2020), and Wanelek (Bulmer 1991). This pattern indicates that in the Highlands, ground stone axes were present during the Last Glacial Maximum (LGM), but in relatively low numbers compared to later periods. Outside of the Highlands region, but also in the montane zone, the earliest ground axe is at the site of Kosipe in the Ivane Valley (White, Crook, & Ruxton 1970), which dates to 4000–8000 cal BP (Summerhayes et al. 2010). Unlike the previously discussed flaked 'waisted' tools, this new technology shows no evidence of hafting modifications, and most of the tools have high levels of grinding or polishing, particularly when compared to the Australian GEA. Commonly, these types of tools have been classified as axe-adzes due to uncertainties in how they were hafted and the nature of the symmetry of the bevels, but they shall be identified as axes here.

Evidence for the independent development of agriculture in the Highlands is largely limited to the site of Kuk Swamp. As early as 10,000 cal BP, forest clearance and plant exploitation occurred on the wetland margins of Kuk, followed by mound cultivation from 7000 cal BP, and the digging of ditches to drain parts of the swamp for cultivation from 4400–4000 cal BP (Denham 2019). Although the agricultural evidence is based on a single site, which is clearly problematical when trying to extrapolate a sequence across the entire Highlands region, there does appear to be a suggestive concurrence between the emergence of the ground/polished axes and the beginning of increased forest clearance and environmental manipulation at Kuk. For example, Golson (2005) argues that the evolution of these ground/polished axes, with more efficient blades and sturdier methods of hafting, was an independent development in New Guinea that resulted from the need to clear forest for cultivation (i.e., the axes were part of the shift towards an agrarian society).

The earliest Highlands axes tended to be lenticular in cross-section and were largely made from local raw materials, mostly river cobbles. Dickson (1981) argued that river cobbles were an efficient use of raw material, as any flaws present within the rock itself should have been 'found out' by the fluvial transport of the cobble. Over time, however, a third shift in axe shape took place in the Highlands with the introduction of planilateral cross-sections (Figure 24.1B), the earliest of which dates to before 4000 years ago. Kafiavana has a possible piece of a planilateral axe that predates 5745–4877 cal BP (White 1972), while Waim has firmer evidence of cut/sawn tool blanks between 4520 and 4150 cal BP (Shaw et al. 2020). There are also undated specimens at Nombe.

The emergence of planilateral axes has been attributed to several causes. Earlier researchers noted their similarities in shape to Austronesian axes in Indonesia and Polynesia, suggesting that they may be representative of contacts with communities from Southeast Asia (Bulmer 1975). Crosby (1973), however, observed that planilateral cross-sections are not generally associated with Austronesian communities in Papua New Guinea. Burton (1984b) suggested that the introduction of planilateral axes should be related to the rise of the modern Highlands quarries rather than to external influences. These large quarries were still in use in 1933, when the Australians made first contact; however, the introduction of steel axes meant that use of many quarries ceased, with only some quarries such as Ganz River continuing to be sporadically worked until the 1970s. Prior to contact, the quarries produced large numbers of axes that were circulated throughout the Highlands and further, reaching north to 'the lower Ramu and the Adelbert Divide, west to Lake Kopiago and south to the deltas of the Papuan Gulf' (Hughes 1973: 101). These axes were traded from community to community in a hand-to-hand exchange, rather than circulated by specialist traders. While most quarries produced work axes, certain quarries such as Dom gaima also produced large ceremonial axes, which were used as display valuables in dances and battles or as payments for bride-price or war reparations (Vial 1940). The ability to obtain large ceremonial axes was considered to be a sign of wealth and status. Axes were therefore an extremely important part of the Highlands' prestige economy, exchanged for other valuables such as pigs, marine shells, or salt, but also in formal ceremonial exchanges, such as the *moka* (Strathern 1969).

All of the major quarries are found within the Wahgi-Chimbu area of the Highlands (for the location of quarries, see Chappell 1966 or Burton 1984a). They have been described as occurring in zones of 'hard contact metamorphic rocks (hornfelses), where intrusive granodiorites have thermally altered Mesozoic sedimentary rocks' (Chappell 1966: 96). Based on his work at the Tuman/Abiamp quarry, Burton (1984a) argued that the natural tabular shape of the blanks quarried from this site may have had a direct influence on cross-section and that during the final grinding process, some axes were not ground on their sides at all, retaining the natural surface, so that they were naturally 'shaped' planilaterally. However, Chappell (1966) noted that most axe blanks were flaked into shape with a 'lens' cross-section, which was then purposefully ground to a quadrate or planilateral cross-section. The exception here is the Kafetu quarry on the Asaro River, which is the only major quarry recorded to have produced axes with an oval cross-section (Chappell 1966). Regardless of purpose or origin, most of these axes were fully polished in their final form.

Despite similarities in raw materials, Burton (1984a) recorded a range of quarrying techniques employed across the different quarry sites, which appeared to vary according to the nature of the source as well as the intended final product, with each quarry producing distinctive axes with subtle differences in shape. Hughes (1973) attributed this variation in style to the aesthetic values of the axe-makers themselves rather than to any differences in raw material.

At the Tuman quarries in the Western Highlands, quarrying took the form of open pits that ranged in size up to 30 metres in width and up to 10 metres in depth (Burton 1984a), as well as underground mining galleries. Visits to the Tuman quarries involved every able-bodied man of the tribe and took place every 4–7 years, lasting 3–5 months. During this time, men involved in quarrying followed 'strict isolation taboos,' such as lack of contact with women (Burton 1984a: 67). Even though the quarries were within easy walking distance of villages, men remained at the quarry site, living in men's houses behind a ritual screen. No gardening was completed nearby, with food brought in daily by women, who would then place the food on wooden platforms outside of the ritual screen. At the end of the quarrying expedition, the women would storm the camp, completing a ritual attack on the site, before burning down the men's houses and returning to their villages.

At the Dom gaima quarry, Vial (1940) observed quarrymen employing a mining shaft up to 10 metres deep, which was shored up with timber to prevent collapse. Other shafts were present nearby, including one where reaching the required axe stone took five months of digging by eight men. The quarrying process involved one man used a digging stick to loosen the shattered stone, while the other men carried discarded stone out of the shaft in baskets. In later research, Burton (1984b) noted that he believed that the shafts were worked over a one- to two-year period because of the depth and thinness of the axe stone seam. In contrast to the Tuman quarries, this quarrying was more time intensive, but it required fewer men to carry out the operation. Burton also noted that to remove the axe stone from the shaft, a fire was built on the top of the thin seam to heat it. Water was then poured on the stone, which exploded into large slabs. The Dom quarries were famous for the production of very large ceremonial bride-price axes, which were much larger than other quarry sites. Vial (1940) recorded that some of the Dom ceremonial axes were 45 cm in length and 15 cm wide, and that when hafted required one man to carry the handle and another to carry the axe blade. The Dom quarries were also unique in their use of sawing rather than percussion flaking to cut the laminar slabs into the large axes.

A different axe stone extraction method was employed at the Ganz River quarry, which is located on a hillside. Here Vial (1940) recorded a water race running along the top of the quarry to wash away surface material and expose the required rock. Once exposed, loose rocks could be prised from the quarry face and then shaped into blanks through percussion flaking. Compared to the Dom gaima or the Tuman quarries, this type of quarrying required less investment of effort; this may account for why Ganz River quarry was utilized for a longer duration than the other quarries in the Highlands postcontact (Burton 1984b).

The time depth of the large Highlands quarries is uncertain, with no dates available for the quarries themselves. As has been noted, the earliest planilateral axes are dated to earlier than 4000 years ago. The earliest conclusive use of raw materials associated with the major quarries are slightly older and appear to come from Nombe, with a piece of Dom gaima material within Stratum B (6300–10,400 cal BP) and a piece from both Dom gaima and Ganz River in Stratum A, which has a basal date of 5650–5480 cal BP (Burton 1984a; Denham & Mountain 2016). Note that Nombe also has undated planilateral axes. Therefore, this technology may be even older than is currently suggested. Manim also has one Tuman quarry sample with an associated date of 3370–3220 cal BP (Denham 2019), while Kafiavana has two pieces of Kafetu quarry material, one of which dates to older than 4877–5745 cal BP (White 1972).

Based on the current dates, there appears to be an association between use of the quarries, introduction of the planilateral axes, and increase in intensity of agriculture and forest clearance from 4000–5000 years ago, although Nombe does appear to predate this. However, this association is still based on very few sites, and further research needs to be undertaken to better understand trajectories in axe technology, production, and exchange in the Highlands, as well as developments towards agrarian-based societies. Identifying the link between the axe quarries and agrarian societies needs to look beyond the use of stone tools for forest clearance and the creation of gardens to include mapping the growth of the wealth and prestige economies in the Highlands and the implications for changes in the sociopolitical complexity of Highlands communities. It is arguable that the development and intensification of agriculture would have allowed for the creation of sufficient agricultural produce to sustain the intensive quarrying expeditions that were required to obtain suitable axe stone, as well as to support large populations of pigs. Both pigs and stone axes were wealth items used in prestige and display events, as well as in trade for other valuables such as shell and salt. Rhoads and Mackenzie (1991) suggested that this prestige economy may be relatively recent; they noted that only within the past 300 years did axes from the Western Highlands reach the Kikori region in the Papuan Gulf, where they were presumably exchanged for marine shell valuables. Rhoads and Mackenzie (1991) argued further that the ceremonial exchange recorded in the Highlands region ethnographically may have been part of an Ipomoean Revolution, where the introduction of the sweet potato (*Ipomoea batatas*) relatively recently was the driver that enabled the buildup of the pig population and the accumulation of wealth and surplus. Burton (1984a), however, argues that use of the axe quarries predates the introduction of the sweet potato. Based on the current uncertainty of dates of both axes and pigs, more research into the emergence of the axe quarries is clearly needed.

Lowlands

A critical dimension of the development and use of axe/adzes in the lowlands of New Guinea is the migration of Austronesians into the island and coastal regions. Linked to the Lapita Cultural Complex, Austronesians in Papua New Guinea first appeared in the Bismarck Archipelago 3300 years ago, bringing with them a package of introductions, including red-slipped dentate pottery, domesticated animals (pigs, dogs, and chickens), the Pacific Rat, and domesticated crops and agriculture (Kirch 2000). Their cultural repertoire included shell and stone adzes. The stone adzes were usually made of imported material, mostly polished, with a range of cross-sections including planilateral, quadrangular, and oval-lenticular, although planilateral and quadrangular are more common and more distinctively 'Lapita' (Green 1991). It is currently not clear what effect the introduction of Lapita adze technology had on the coastal regions of New Guinea, as there are few pre-Lapita axes or adzes in these areas to compare to those from Lapita sites. Even the Lapita adzes are relatively rare; they are found in very low numbers, and many remain unstudied (Sheppard 2010). But there is opportunity here in the future to explore cross-cultural interaction between non-Austronesians ('Papuans') and Austronesians in coastal/lowland New Guinea in terms of the introduction of new axe/adze orms and the establishment of long-distance coastal axe/adze exchange systems.

Early ethnographers recorded several major axe/adze production centres in the lowlands of New Guinea. Available information reflects largely where colonial officials decided to keep records, which often focused on production centres associated with long-distance exchange systems. In reality, axe/adzes are found across New Guinea. This suggests that myriad production systems were developed, although these may have been for local use or for more localized exchange. It is difficult to date the antiquity of these lowlands production centres because in many cases there has not been the same level of archaeological research as with the Highlands. As such, reconstructing the long-term development of these systems draws heavily on anthropological research.

The Suloga quarry on Woodlark Island in the Massim was an important axe/adze production centre, which produced beautiful 'banded' siltstone polished axe/adzes that Sir William MacGregor (1894), then governor of British New Guinea, described as highly sought after and widely distributed (Figures 24.1C and 24.2C). This quarry produced a range of different types of axes and adzes, with the most valued being an easily recognizable dark green material, striped with white lenses of pyroclastic sediments (Bickler & Turner 2002). Within the Massim, Suloga axe/adzes entered local exchange networks (Bickler & Turner 2002) and appear to have been traded alongside, but not as part of, the *kula* regional exchange network made famous by Malinowski (1922). Different types of Suloga axe/adzes were valued for different purposes, with some serving utilitarian roles, while others had ceremonial importance, being used for garden magic and during mortuary feasts (Malinowski 1922: 98). In the Trobriands, Malinowski (1934: 190) recorded that the biggest stone axe/adzes imported from Suloga were kept as items of wealth, becoming heirlooms attached to a particular lineage. He considered the value of these blades to be even higher than that of the shell valuables normally associated with *kula* exchanges, and he noted that they were important tokens used to display wealth and power, and demonstrate social status. Chiefs could also use the blades as gifts in return for services such as sorcery or magic, or at important social occasions such as trading voyages or feasts. Thus, like the Highlands axes discussed above, the Suloga axe/adzes played a vital role in the prestige economy of the Trobriands.

There is some debate over the antiquity of the *kula*, with Egloff (1978) suggesting that the exchange system had its roots around 500 years ago. More recently, both anthropologists and archaeologists have argued that the *kula* as it was known ethnographically was heavily influenced by European colonial pacification, which in decreasing endemic warfare within the region allowed freer travel and greater exchange between the islands (Irwin, Shaw, & McAlister 2019). The evidence from Suloga also points to a recent development of the *kula*, with excavations at the source/production site of Undalai dating use to the late eighteenth and early nineteenth centuries (Bickler, Ivuyo, & Kewibu 1997; Bickler & Turner 2002). However, stone axe/adzes from the Suloga source are also found in other sites on Woodlark Island, dating to possibly 1500 years ago (Bickler & Turner 2002). As such, source use may have started early but did not escalate in scale until more recently, a pattern that fits with both ethnographic and archaeological collections of Suloga stone outside of Woodlark Island. Ethnographically, the Suloga axe/adzes have been found throughout the Massim region, including outside of the *kula* network, which points to the existence of other trading systems within the islands. The axe/adzes were also traded along the north and south coasts of the Papuan mainland, reaching as far west as the Gulf of Papua, though in low numbers (Rhoads & Mackenzie 1991; Seligmann & Joyce 1907).

One of the few examples of Holocene connections and trade between Australia and Papua New Guinea concerns stone axes (McNiven et al. 2004). The Kiwai Island axe has a distinctive 'teardrop' shape with a pointed poll and either a lenticular or oval cross-section. Almost fully polished in their finished state, the only real variation relates to size, ranging between 6 and 53 cm in length (Landtman 1927). Size differentiation has been attributed to different uses, with smaller axes hafted for use in canoe production, while the larger axes may have remained unhafted and were used for ceremonial purposes, including bride-price transactions (Landtman 1927) and grave markers (McNiven 2016). These axes are spread across the Trans-Fly region of Papua New Guinea, with particular concentration at Kiwai Island, at the mouth of the Fly River (McNiven et al. 2004). Originally, these axes were believed to have either been traded from down the Fly River from the interior of Papua New Guinea or across the Torres Strait, with recent petrographic studies of the axe showing that most are fine-grained intrusive rocks associated with the Badu Granite in the Western Islands of the Torres Strait (McNiven et al. 2004). McNiven et al. (2004) suggest that the production of the Kiwai axes in the Torres Strait may be evidence for a symbiotic relationship between these small islands with few natural tree resources and the Papuan mainland, where axes are produced by the Torres Strait islanders and traded to the Trans-Fly region to be used in canoe production, with canoes then traded back to the Torres Strait to support their maritime subsistence economy.

Apart from coastal exchange systems, there is also evidence of the movement of axe/ adzes made in inland regions down to the coastal lowlands. Rhoads and Mackenzie (1991) record trade in axes from the Western Owen Stanley Ranges to the south Papuan coast and then westwards into the Kikori region, where they have been found in archaeological sites as early as 2000 years ago. These stone axes are generally made on volcanic and intrusive rocks that had been metamorphosed to greenschist grade, which gave the axes their distinctive green colour. On the northeast coast of Papua New Guinea, greenish ophicalcite adzes have been recovered from the Collingwood–Holnicote Bay region (Seligmann & Joyce 1907), as well as from the south coast of Papua New Guinea in Cloudy Bay. These nephrite-like adzes have attracted interest due to their colour and jade-like qualities. The source has not yet been found, although early attempts were made to locate the material. For example, Seligmann and Joyce (1907) suggested an inland source in the Gorupu Range. Egloff (1979) recorded examples of this material at Wanigela in Collingwood Bay in deposits dated to 683–972 cal BP.

In summary, in Papua New Guinea changes and intensifications in axe/adze production systems apparently took place throughout the Holocene, both in the Highlands and in the coastal/lowland/island regions. The origins or impetus for these changes differ according to region and cultural context, although in most areas axe/adzes become important parts of the prestige and wealth economies, signaling power and status. In the

Highlands, the growth of axe production and exchange is linked with the independent innovation of agriculture. The coastal/lowland/island axe/adze exchange systems are more of a mystery, particularly in terms of antiquity and long-term development. In some cases, such as the Suloga quarry, it could be argued that the agriculture and long-distance voyaging exchange systems associated with the Lapita Cultural Complex eventually morphed into the *kula* and associated Suloga axe/adze exchange. However, at this point, much of what we know of these production and exchange systems is frozen in time to the ethnographic period. Therefore, much more substantial archaeological work needs to be conducted in order to explore the history and development of these anthropologically recorded exchange systems.

Axe Production and Exchange in Holocene Australia

Similar to the situation in New Guinea, the Late Holocene distribution of GEA is much expanded from the known Pleistocene distribution (Figures 24.2A and 24.2B). In the Pleistocene, GEAs are only known from the tropical northern regions, but by the Late Holocene they were dispersed across most of mainland Australia. However, dispersion of this implement appears to have occurred later in time, near the start of the Late Holocene, probably 3000–4000 BP. This is the maximum antiquity of GEA recovered from archaeological sites in southern Australia, and the absence of the technology from not only the islands of Bass Strait but also large islands close to the mainland, such as Kangaroo Island (with little or no evidence of occupation during the Late Holocene), is consistent with that chronology. The Holocene distribution as presented by Dickson (1981: 17) is puzzling; he thought the absence of axes from the Nullarbor Plain and Great Victoria Desert was to be expected, but axes are present in other gibber and sandy deserts within Australia, and there are temperate woodlands and forests in the far west where GEAs have not been reported. Furthermore, the presence of GEA in the southwest, on the far side of the large region without such specimens, suggests a complex dispersal of the technology, perhaps with axes having been briefly used along at least the western coastline in regions where the technology was then abandoned. Alternatively, the accuracy of the known distribution may be questioned.

Regardless of their ultimate distribution, we know that GEAs could be carried and used for extended periods and sometimes transported over very large distances. The long-distance movement of GEA over hundreds of kilometres has often been explained as the trade from one group to their neighbours, perhaps through a chain of groups. Nineteenth-century ethnographic information obtained from Aboriginal people, sometimes with descriptions of market-based negotiations, is consistent with the proposition that long-distance movement most likely resulted from trade. For all quarries, many GEAs were produced for local use, but it is also clear that some quarries were more specialized and geared for high-level production for purposes of trade. For example, a series of large quarries in the uplands around Mount Isa in northeastern Australia are extremely large in scale and output, and are likely to have supplied a large trade of GEA into the Lake Eyre Basin (Hiscock 2005). One quarry, at Lake Moondara, was estimated to still have 800,000 unfinished blanks remaining on the site, giving a sense of the industrial scale of production. To explore evidence for quarry production, and its possible relationships to trade, politics, and cosmologies, we will now discuss a detailed example from southern Australia.

SOUTHEASTERN EXAMPLE

For over fifty years, studies of axes in Australia's southeast have identified source locations and geographic distributions. As a result, patterning of axes across the landscape is reasonably well understood. However, the quarries at which the axes were made, and the manufacturing processes themselves, have barely been described. Issues with our current understanding of axe quarry production and exchange in Australia are explored in this section, using the Mount William axe quarry as a case study.

In the southeastern section of mainland Australia, particularly in the eastern portions of the states of Victoria and New South Wales and southwestern Queensland, there are many outcrops of igneous rocks that were suitable for production of GEA, especially mafic volcanic sources such as basalt and basaltic rocks like dolerites (or diabase), as well as metamorphic sources such as hornfels. These rocks typically occur as dykes and plugs, and so they are often found as small, dispersed outcrops, with occasional larger outcrops presenting as low rocky ridges. Sometimes this outcropping rock was quarried, but GEAs were also commonly made on cobbles of the same materials that had been eroded and redeposited into rivers. Consequently, raw materials could be obtained in a variety of places, but sources were not evenly distributed across landscapes. Nor were the costs and benefits of exploiting these sources uniform. Quarrying *in situ* sources could be energy expensive, but it could allow craftspeople to invest in regular and high-output production systems. In contrast, exploiting secondary deposits of colluvial debris and redeposited cobbles could significantly reduce production costs but may not have facilitated either high-volume output or standardized shapes and sizes of the artefacts. Here we examine a single example of production to exemplify the evidence and complexities of quarry use.

In the far southeastern corner of Australia, large-scale GEA production has been inferred, and its social and economic context has been discussed at length. More than a dozen 'greenstone' (dolerite) quarries are known in the uplands approximately 70 km northwest of Melbourne. One quarry that has been much discussed is known as the Mt William quarry in reference to its location as a ridgeline on the northeast slope of Mt William (Coutts & Miller 1977). Dolerite crops out on the crest and slopes of the ridge, often as low exposures of fractured bedrock, but occasionally as standing blocks metres high. Hundreds of excavated pits have been reported along the ridge, presumably dug by people searching for suitable blocks of rock. The production process at the quarry has not been reconstructed, but two points can be inferred from the evidence reported. First, the presence of abundant flaking debris, sometimes in the form of well-defined knapping floors, indicates that early-stage reduction was often carried out on-site, near to where the rock was extracted (McBryde & Watchman 1976: 169). However, the absence of ground edges on specimens at the quarry and the absence of grinding grooves in the local area around the quarry indicate that grinding, and perhaps later-stage preparatory flaking, were carried out elsewhere after the unfinished blanks had been transported. The nearest reported grinding grooves are approximately 30 km from the quarry, and so it is likely that blanks were transported at least 30 km prior to grinding. Perhaps they were even exchanged as blanks with little or no grinding to other people in other groups.

Second, some artefacts made at the quarry were carried considerable distances across southeastern Australia. This dispersal has sometimes been taken as evidence for large-volume output from the quarry, but the evidence on such claims is currently equivocal. Certainly, there is evidence for substantial knapping activity at the Mt William quarry, but the number of axes taken from the quarry and traded to other regions, and the time depth over which this trade occurred, are far harder to estimate without intensive study of the site. McBryde undertook studies of the petrography of GEA across the southeast in an attempt to identify source locations and the distance specimens had travelled to the locations where they had been recovered archaeologically in recent times (McBryde 1978, 1984; McBryde & Watchman 1976). Using hand examinations of specimens and thin-section analysis of selected samples, McBryde and her colleagues were able to differentiate a number of source locations and were confident in assigning about 70% of specimens to a specific source (e.g., McBryde 1984). Some quarries, such as Howqua and Jallukar, have specimens distributed only locally, which McBryde interpreted as a signal that production at those quarries had been for local consumption. In contrast, GEA from the Mt William quarry were more widely distributed, some beyond the local area and up to 800 km in a straight line from the quarry. McBryde concluded that production at Mt William was supplying specimens for trade to a large area of southeastern Australia, with local usage a minor component of the production system. She also noticed that Mt William specimens were most numerous about 300 km from the quarry. She interpreted that pattern as evidence of what she labelled as 'redistribution centres', although she did not specify what process may have been involved (McBryde 1984: 269).

However, the distribution of specimens across the landscape is not a good indication of the quantity of GEA entering a trading system. McBryde's sample was only a few hundred specimens, and she identified only 300–400 as being from Mt William, a number that would only require one or two per decade to be made for trade if the quarry had been worked over a couple of thousand years. How should we think about these data? On the one hand, we have no real knowledge of how McBryde's sample relates to the population of GEAs that were made and carried across the southeast, and it is likely that the total number of specimens made and used was very much larger. The output might be estimated if detailed technological reconstructions and dating of the debris at Mt William quarry had been carried out, but such studies have not begun. It is therefore not clear just how many specimens were produced for trade in total or per annum. Given the intractable character of the greenstone as a knapping and grinding material, each GEA would probably have taken considerable time to make, and so there would have been significant labour implications in producing large numbers each year. Broad distribution of items through trading might occur even if production rates were low, especially if demand for the GEAs was linked to their rarity. Hence, high cost and low production rates may underpin the status of Mt William artefacts as rare and valuable in the way that Fabergé eggs or Aston Martins were. We revisit this possibility below.

McBryde's petrographic work established a distribution map for the axes from Mt William. Setting aside sampling questions, such as how accurately the specimens she studied map the total distribution of axes originating from Mt William and whether the transport pathways changed over time, her data are a basis for discussing where axes were discarded, though not for the pathways along which they travelled. Here we make two points about the distribution patterns. First is that McBryde argued that the location of artefacts showed a strong relationship to the geography of languages in the nineteenth century. Figure 24.3A shows the find locations of artefacts she sourced to Mt William and the boundaries of languages that McBryde (1986) employed in her analyses and that she used as a proxy of social boundaries that may have affected the flow of material goods. McBryde inferred the absence of specimens in some language landscapes as evidence for social controls over the dispersion of Mt William GEA. In particular, she posited the social acceptability and desirability of those artefacts within the social landscapes of Kulin and related language speakers but noted the existence of a barrier to the transfer of specimens to Kurnai further east. Her conclusion is incorrect. Her small sample size might well not recover a find spot even if Mt William axes had been present, but more dramatic than that, her own records show multiple axes from Mt William found within the territory of Kurnai speakers, as shown in Figure 24.3A. Hence, the archaeological evidence does not support a Kulin-only distribution model for Mt William specimens.

Distributional evidence is more clearly depicted in Figure 24.3B, which shows the uplands GEA distribution mainly to the east, while what McBryde called the 'distribution array' of Mt William axes extended north and west. Hiscock (2013) used that 'distribution array' to question the association between uplands and the dispersal of axes. But that array plots the maximum distances over which specimens moved and is a poor expression of where most specimens were carried, thereby failing to capture the eastward spread. A better expression of trends in GEA distribution is provided by McBryde's quadrant density data, which is also shown in Figure 24.3B. Those density data reveal specimens travelled in all directions from the quarry, but the greatest numbers were carried into lowland areas to the west of the quarry. This distribution does not support the idea that axes were being supplied in any quantity to the uplands to the east. As

McBryde recognized, there was a distinct pathway along which many specimens flowed, although the ideological context of that flow is unclear.

A powerful economic model of axe dispersion has been framed by Roberts (2017) for axe production in Victoria. He argued that anthropological ideas of exchange focused on mechanisms of balanced reciprocity failed to provide explanations for price/value differences between axe quarries that would explain the greater popularity of specimens

FIGURE 24.3. Distribution of Mt William artefacts. A: The distribution of sourced specimens transported from Mt William and the location of language boundaries as presented in McBryde (1984, 1986). B: The distribution of upland areas relative to the 'distribution array' of McBryde (1984, 1986), and the isopleths show the density of Mt William specimens calculated as the percentage of McBryde's (1984) sample in quadrants 0.5° x 0.5° latitude and longitude.

from the Mt William quarry. Roberts argued that the preferential distribution of specimens from Mt William is better explained by a microeconomic model in which the value or 'price' of the axes in trading was regulated by the availability of this commodity. His proposal is that the high proportion of GEA from Mt William dispersed across far southeastern Australia indicates that the axes from the quarry were assigned high socioeconomic value, and that their high value was based on the conjunction of high demand but low availability. Only a few conditions need to be met for this model to work: restriction of access to quarrying so that other groups cannot directly procure their own axes, the ability to visually distinguish axes from different quarries, and a context in which there was a persistent unmet market demand.

Roberts interpreted the Howitt (1904) ethnography as consistent with low quarry output that resulted in low availability, which in turn promoted a higher value for Mt William GEA compared to GEA from other quarry sources. Whether the low output was a purposeful economic strategy to inflate the value of goods or a simple by-product of infrequent or low-intensity quarrying activity is unclear. However, Roberts' model remains to be tested, and there are a number of avenues by which this could be completed. For example, the issue of whether Mt William axes could be readily distinguished from other sources could be explored through systematic evaluation of factors such as whether the colour, texture, size, or shape of axes could reliably identify the source of an axe. At the same time, there is also little information about how production activities were undertaken at the quarry site itself. Issues of scale and control of production need to be grounded by fieldwork that explores the time depth of quarry use, as well as the scale of quarrying and production activities in order to understand the number of axes being produced at any given time. Refocusing research back upon the axe production sites is therefore clearly needed to better contextualize the distribution patterns of the axes themselves.

Conclusion

The history of GEA in Sahul, which is effectively the history of ground-edge 'axes' in the continent, is long, complex, and quite surprising. It has always been surprising for Australia simply because in nineteenth-century arguments these tools were linked to forest clearance and agricultural economic systems, and yet in the early part of the century there was no agriculture present in Australia. Disjunctions between the observed form and presumptions of a limited range of functions for a form are challenged by both ethnographic and archaeological observations, which reveal that treating all GEAs as having similar uses is unrealistic and too normative (e.g., Attenbrow & Kononenko 2019; Ford 2017). Instead, evidence of usewear and residues, hafting mechanisms, and size and shape of GEA indicates that there were a broad range of uses, including but not restricted to chopping wood, and that we should regard this diverse class of artefacts as portable, maintainable, multipurpose tools.

Those qualities are advantageous for both foragers and agriculturalists who need tools to be available for a variety of purposes as they move around the landscape. One advantage of long-lived, multifunctional tools is that they can be available when required, even when the scheduling of the activity cannot be anticipated. This availability and flexibility makes these kinds of tools especially useful when people are colonizing new landscapes and are not familiar with the location and timing of resources. Sahul has the oldest GEA in the world. Hiscock et al. (2016) noted that the antiquity of GEA is very close to the antiquity of colonization and that exploitation of unfamiliar landscapes was probably the selective context in which GEAs were invented and the technology was dispersed. Subsequent work has also found GEA in the base levels of the oldest sites within Sahul, reinforcing the correlation between these new tools and the occupations of new lands (Clarkson et al. 2017). We therefore argue that this correlation suggests that GEA may have arisen as a response to the economic conditions of the colonizers. The early GEAs from northern Sahul are minimally reported in the literature but appear to have been morphologically diverse, and it is from that pool of variation that regional differences emerged. Regional distinctions appear to have been long-lasting, most noticeably the restriction of GEA to northern Australia for approximately 60,000 years before they were adopted across southern mainland Australia.

New and distinct regional patterns emerged in the Holocene. For example, in Australia this patterning included the expansion of GEA production across many southern regions of the mainland, and in Papua New Guinea the appearance of distinctive planilateral axes in the Highlands represents the emergence of a distinct regional form. These regional systems represent well-recognized norms and procedural patterns that were transmitted between generations and in some cases across space. Expansion and local diversification were probably the consequences of multiple factors, including shifts in subsistence economy, adaptation of tool form to engineering and functional constraints, and the linkage of GEA production to trade systems (see Shaw et al. 2020; Hiscock & Maloney 2017). One element of Holocene shifts that has attracted the attention of archaeologists is the emergence of GEAs as socially valued goods in trade contexts. Archaeologically, this emergence is visible in the transport of GEA over long distances, and especially the preferential distribution of axe/adzes from some sources rather than others. Exploration of the construction of social values and uses for goods has, however, often relied on readings of ethnographic observations. While reference to ethnography has frequently been helpful, particularly in New Guinea where anthropologists and colonial authorities recorded information on axe quarrying, production, and exchange, it is not a replacement for archaeological investigations of quarries, especially because of the high rates of social, economic, and ideological change known in the historical period. GEA production, use, and exchange have a long and diverse history in Sahul, and while we have sketched the emerging information of this history, it is clear that this is an area where much is yet to be learnt through archaeological research.

NOTE

1. All calibrated radiocarbon dates have been presented as originally published by the authors. Dates that were not originally calibrated have been calibrated with OxCal 4.3, using IntCal13 and are reported at 95.4% probability.

REFERENCES

Attenbrow, V., & Kononenko, N. (2019). Microscopic revelations: The forms and multiple uses of ground-edged artefacts of the New South Wales, Central Coast, Australia. *Technical Reports of the Australian Museum, 29*, 1–100.

Bergstrom, A., Nagle, N., Chen, Y., McCarthy, S., Pollard, M. O., Ayub, Q., . . . Tyler-Smith, C. (2016). Deep roots for Aboriginal Australian Y-chromosomes. *Current Biology, 26*, 809–813.

Bergstrom, A., Oppenheimer, S. J., Mentzer, A. J., Auckland, K., Robson, K., Attenborough, R. . . . Tyler-Smith, C. (2017). A Neolithic expansion, but strong genetic structure, in the independent history of New Guinea. *Science, 357*, 1160–1163.

Bickler, S. H., Ivuyo, B., & Kewibu, V. (1997). Archaeology at the Suloga stone tool manufacturing sites, Woodlark Island, Milne Bay Province, PNG. *Archaeology in New Zealand, 40*(3), 204–219.

Bickler, S. H., & Turner, M. (2002). Food to stone: Investigations at the Suloga Adze manufacturing sites, Woodlark Island, Papua New Guinea. *The Journal of the Polynesian Society, 111*(1), 11–43.

Bulmer, S. (1975). Settlement and economy in prehistoric Papua New Guinea: A review of the archaeological evidence. *Journal de la Societe des Oceanistes, 46*(31), 7–75.

Bulmer, S. (1991). Variation and change in stone tools in the Highlands of Papua New Guinea: The witness of Wanelek. In A. Pawley (Ed.), *Man and a half: Essays in Pacific anthropology and ethnobiology in honour of Ralph Bulmer* (pp. 470–478). Auckland: The Polynesian Society.

Bulmer, S. (2005). Reflections in stone: Axes and the beginnings of agriculture in the central highlands of New Guinea. In A. Pawley, R. Attenborough, J. Golson, & R. Hide (Eds.), *Papuan pasts: Cultural, linguistic and biological histories of Papuan-speaking peoples* (pp. 387–450). Canberra: Australian National University.

Burton, J. (1984a*). Axe makers of the Wahgi: Pre-colonial industrialists of the Papua New Guinea highlands* (PhD thesis). Australian National University, Canberra.

Burton, J. (1984b). Field research at the stone axe quarries of Western Highlands and Simbu Provinces, Papua New Guinea. *Bulletin of the Indo-Pacific Prehistory Association, 5*, 83–92.

Chappell, J. (2002). Sea level changes forced ice breakouts in the Last Glacial cycle: New results from coral terraces. *Quaternary Science Reviews, 21*(10), 1229–1240.

Chappell, J. (1966). Stone axe factories in the Highlands of East New Guinea. *Proceedings of the Prehistoric Society, 32*, 96–121.

Clarkson, C., Jacobs, Z., Marwick, B., Fullagar, R., Wallis, L., Smith, M., . . . Pardoe, C. (2017). Human occupation of northern Australia by 65,000 years ago. *Nature, 547*, 306–310.

Clarkson, C., Smith, M., Marwick, B., Fullagar, R., Wallis, L. A., Faulkner, P., . . . Florin, S. A. (2015). The archaeology, chronology and stratigraphy of Madjedbebe (Malakunanja II): A site in northern Australia with early occupation. *Journal of Human Evolution, 83*, 46–64.

Coutts, P. J. F., & Miller, R. (1977). *The Mt. William archaeological area*. Melbourne: Victorian Archaeological Survey.

Crosby, E. (1977). An archaeologically oriented classification of ethnographic material culture. In R. V. S. Wright (Ed.), *Stone tool as cultural markers: Change, evolution and complexity* (pp. 83–96). Canberra: Australian Institute of Aboriginal Studies.

Crosby, E. (1973). *A comparative study of Melanesian hafted edge-tools and other percussive cutting implements* (PhD thesis). Australian National University, Canberra.

David., B., Delannoy, J-J., Mialanes, J., Clarkson, C., Petchey, F., Geneste, J-M., . . . Castets, G. (2019). 45,610–652,160 years of site and landscape occupation at Nawarla Gabarnmang, Arnhem Land Plateau (northern Australia). *Quaternary Science Reviews, 215,* 64–85.

Denham, T. (2019). Reconsidering the 'Neolithic' at Manim rock shelter, Wurup Valley, Papua New Guinea. In M. Leclerc & J. Flexner (Eds.), *Archaeologies of Island Melanesia: Current approaches to landscapes, exchange and practice* (pp. 81–99). Canberra: ANU Press.

Denham, T., & Mountain, M-J. (2016). Resolving some chronological problems at Nombe rock shelter in the highlands of Papua New Guinea. *Archaeology in Oceania, 51,* 73–83.

Dickson, F. P. (1976). Australian ground stone hatchets: Their design and dynamics. *Australian Archaeology, 5,* 33–48.

Dickson, F. P. (1981). *Australian stone hatchets: A study in design and dynamics.* Sydney: Academic Press.

Dickson, F. P. (1972). Ground edge axes. *Mankind, 8,* 206–211.

Dortch, C. E. (1977). Early and late stone industrial phases in western Australia. In R. V. S. Wright (Ed.), *Stone tools as cultural markers: Change, evolution and complexity* (pp. 104–132). Canberra: Australian Institute of Aboriginal Studies.

Egloff, B. (1978). The *kula* before Malinowski: A changing configuration. *Mankind, 11,* 429–435.

Egloff, B. (1979). *Recent Prehistory in Southeast Papua.* Canberra: Australian National University.

Ford, A. (2017). Late Pleistocene lithic technology in the Ivane Valley: A view from the rainforest. *Quaternary International, 448,* 31–43.

Gaffney, D., Ford, A., & Summerhayes, G. (2015). Crossing the Pleistocene-Holocene transition in the New Guinea Highlands: Evidence from the lithic assemblage of Kiowa rockshelter. *Journal of Anthropological Archaeology, 39,* 223–246.

Geneste, J-M., David, B., Plisson, H., Clarkson, C., Delannoy, J-J., Petchey, F., & Whear, R. (2010). Earliest evidence for ground-edge axes: 35,400+/–410 cal BP from Jawoyn Country, Arnhem Land. *Australian Archaeology, 71,* 66–69.

Geneste, J-M., David, B., Plisson, H., Delannoy, J-J., & Petchey, F. (2012). The origins of ground-edge axes: New findings from Nawarla Gabarnmang, Arnhem Land (Australia) and global implications for the evolution of fully modern humans. *Cambridge Archaeological Journal, 22*(1), 1–17.

Golson, J. (2005). The middle reaches of New Guinea history. In A. Pawley, R. Attenborough, J. Golson, & R. Hide (Eds.), *Papuan pasts: Cultural, linguistic and biological histories of Papuan-speaking peoples* (pp. 451–491). Canberra: Australian National University.

Golson, J. (2001). New Guinea, Australia and the Sahul connection. In A. Anderson, I. Lilley, & S. O'Connor (Eds.), *Histories of Old Ages: Essays in honor of Rhys Jones* (pp. 185–210). Canberra: Pandanus Books.

Green, R. (1991). The Lapita Cultural Complex: Current evidence and proposed models. *Bulletin of the Indo-Pacific Prehistory Association, 11,* 295–305.

Groube, L. (1989). The taming of the rain forests: A model for Late Pleistocene forest exploitation in New Guinea. In D. Harris & G. Hillman (Eds.), *Foraging and farming: the evolution of plant exploitation* (pp. 292–304). London: Unwin Hyman.

Groube, L. (1984). Waisted axes of Asia, Melanesia and Australia. In G. Ward (Ed.), *Archaeology at ANZAAS Canberra* (pp. 168–177). Canberra: Canberra Archaeological Society.

Groube, L., Chappell, J., Muke, J., & Price, D. (1986). A 40,000-year-old human occupation site at Huon Peninsula, Papua New Guinea. *Nature, 324*, 453–455.

Hampton, O. W. (1999). *Culture of stone: Sacred and profane uses of stone among the Dani.* College Station: Texas A&M University Press.

Hiscock, P. (2013). Beyond the dreamtime: Archaeology and explorations of religious change in Australia. *World Archaeology 45*, 124–136.

Hiscock, P. (2002). Pattern and context in the Holocene proliferation of backed artefacts in Australia. In R. G. Elston & S. L. Kuhn (Eds.), *Thinking small: Global perspectives on microlithization* (pp. 163–177). Arlington, VA: American Anthropological Association.

Hiscock, P. (2005). Standardised axe manufacture at Mount Isa. In I. Macfarlane, M-J. Mountain, & R. Paton (Eds.), *Many exchanges: Archaeology, history, community and the work of Isobel McBryde* (pp. 287–299). Canberra: Aboriginal History Inc.

Hiscock, P., & Maloney, T. (2017). Australian lithic technology: Evolution, dispersion and connectivity. In T. Hodos (Ed.), *The Routledge handbook of archaeology and globalization* (pp. 301–318). London: Routledge.

Hiscock, P., O'Connor, S., Balme, J., & Maloney, T. (2016). World's earliest ground-edge axe production coincides with human colonization of Australia. *Australian Archaeology, 82*(1), 2–11.

Howitt, A.,W. (1904.) *Native tribes of south-east Australia.* London: Macmillan.

Hughes, I. (1973). Stone-age trade in the New Guinea inland: Historical geography without history. In H. Brookfield (Ed.), *The Pacific in transition: Geographical perspectives on adaptation and change* (pp. 97–126). London: Edward Arnold.

Irwin, G., Shaw, B., & McAlister, A. (2019). The origins of the Kula Ring: Archaeological and maritime perspectives from the southern Massim and Mailu areas of Papua New Guinea. *Archaeology in Oceania, 54*, 1–16.

Jones, R., & Johnson, I. (1985). Deaf Adder Gorge: Lindner site, Nauwalabila I. In R. Jones (Ed.), *Archaeological research in Kakadu National Park* (pp. 165–227). Canberra: Australian National Parks and Wildlife Service.

Kirch, P. (2000). *On the road of the winds.* Berkeley: University of California Press.

Landtman, G. (1927). *The Kiwai Papuans of British New Guinea.* London: Macmillan.

Lilly, K. W. Y., Littlejohn, M., Duchene, S., Edwards, R., Bukulatjpi, S., Binks, P. . . . Locarnini, S. (2019). Tracing ancient human migrations into Sahul using Hepatitis B virus genomes. *Molecular Biology and Evolution, 36*(5), 942–954.

MacGregor, W. (1894). *Annual report on British New Guinea 1893–1894.* Brisbane: Government Printer.

Malinowski, B. (1922). *Argonauts of the Western Pacific.* London: Routledge and Kegan Paul.

Malinowski, B. (1934). Stone implements in Eastern New Guinea. In E. E. Evans-Pritchard, R. Firth, B. Malinowski, & I. Schapera (Eds.), *Essays presented to C. G. Seligmann* (pp. 189–196). London: Kegan Paul, Trench, Trubner and Co.

Maloney, T., O'Connor, S., Wood, R., Aplin, K., & Balme, J. (2018). Carpenters Gap 1: A 47,000 year old record of indigenous adaption and innovation. *Quaternary Science Reviews, 191*, 204–228.

McBryde, I. (1986). Artefacts, language and social interaction: A case study from South-Eastern Australia. In G. N. Bailey & P. Callow (Eds.), *Stone Age prehistory. Studies in memory of Charles McBurney* (pp. 77–93). Cambridge: Cambridge University Press.

McBryde, I. (1984). Kulin greenstone quarries: The social contexts of production and distribution for the Mount William site. *World Archaeology*, 16(2), 267–285.

McBryde, I. (1978). Wil-im-ee Moor-ring: Or, where do axes come from?: Stone axe distribution and exchange patterns in Victoria. *Mankind*, 11(3), 354–382.

McBryde, I., & Watchman, A. (1976). The distribution of green-stone axes in southeastern Australia: A preliminary report. *Mankind*, 10, 163–174.

McNiven, I. J. (2016). Stone axes as grave markers on Kiwai Island, Fly River Delta, Papua New Guinea. *Journal of Pacific Archaeology*, 7(1), 74–83.

McNiven, I. J., Von Gnielinski, F., & Quinnell, M. (2004). Torres Strait and the origin of large stone axes from Kiwai Island, Fly River Estuary (Papua New Guinea). *Memoirs of the Queensland Museum, Cultural Heritage Series*, 3(1), 271–289.

Morwood, M. J., & Hobbs, D. R. (1995). Themes in the prehistory of tropical Australia. *Antiquity* 69, 747–768.

Morwood, M. J., & Trezise, P. J. (1989). Edge-ground axes in Pleistocene Greater Australia: New evidence from S.E. Cape York Peninsula. *Queensland Archaeological Research*, 6, 77–90.

Mountain, M.-J. (1983). Preliminary report of excavations at Nombe rockshelter, Simbu Province, Papua New Guinea. *Bulletin of the Indo-Pacific Prehistory Association*, 4, 84–99.

Nagle, N., Van Oven, M., Wilcox, S., van Holst Pellekaan, S., Tyler-Smith, C., Xue, Y., . . . The Genographic Consortium. (2017). Aboriginal Australian mitochondrial genome variation—an increased understanding of population antiquity and diversity. *Nature Science Reports*, 7, 43041.

O'Connor, S. (1999). *30,000 years of Aboriginal occupation: Kimberley, north west Australia*. Canberra: Australian National University.

O'Connor, S., Maloney, T., Vannieuwenhuyse, D., Balme, J., & Wood, R. (2014). Occupation at Carpenters Gap 3, Windjana Gorge, Kimberley, Western Australia. *Australian Archaeology*, 78, 10–23.

Pétrequin, P., & Pétrequin, A.-M. (2002). *Écologie d'un outil: La hache de pierre en Irian Jaya (Indonésie)*. Nouvelle edition. Monographie du CRA 12. Paris: CNRS Editions.

Pétrequin, P., & Pétrequin, A.-M. (2006). *Objets de pouvoir en Nouvelle-Guinée: Approche ethnarchéologique d'un système de signes sociaux*. Paris: Réunion des Musée Nationaux.

Rhoads, J. W., & Mackenzie, D. E. (1991). Stone axe trade in prehistoric Papua: The travels of *Python. Proceedings of the Prehistoric Society*, 57, 35–49.

Roberts, P. (2017). Revisiting the Mount William Greenstone Quarry: Employment specialisation and a market economy in an early contact hunter-gatherer society. *Australian Aboriginal Studies*, 2017/2, 14–26.

Roberts, R. G., Jones, R., & Smith, M. A. (1993). Optical dating at Deaf Adder Gorge, Northern Territory, indicates human occupation between 53,000 and 60,000 years ago. *Australian Archaeology*, 37, 58–59.

Schrire, C. (1982). *The Alligator Rivers: Prehistory and ecology in western Arnhem Land*. Canberra: Australian National University.

Seligmann, C. G., & Joyce, T. A. (1907). On prehistoric objects in British New Guinea. In W. H. R. Rivers, R. R. Marett, and N. W. Thomas (Eds.), *Anthropological essays presented to Edward Burnett Tylor* (pp. 325–342). Oxford: Clarendon Press.

Shaw, B., Field, J. H., Summerhayes, G. R., Coxe, S., Coster, A. C. F., Ford, A., . . . Kealhofer, L. (2020). Emergence of a Neolithic in highland New Guinea by 5000 to 4000 years ago. *Science Advances, 6*, eaay4573.

Sheppard, P. (2010). Lapita stone tool technology. In C. Sand & S. Bedford (Eds.), *Lapita: Ancetres oceaniens/oceanic ancestors* (pp. 240–251). Paris: Musee du Quai Branly and Somogy Editions d'Art.

Strathern, M. (1969). Stone axes and flake tools: Evaluations from two New Guinea Highlands societies. *Proceedings of the Prehistoric Society, 35*, 311–329.

Summerhayes, G. R., Leavesley, M., Fairbairn, A., Mandui, H., Field, J., Ford, A., & Fullagar, R. (2010). Human adaptation and plant use in Highland New Guinea 49,000 to 44,000 years ago. *Science, 330*, 78–81.

Tobler, R., Rohrlach, A., Soubrier, J., Bover, P., Llamas, B., Tuke, J., . . . Cooper, A. (2017). Aboriginal mitogenomes reveal 50,000 years of regionalism in Australia. *Nature, 544*, 180–184.

Veth, P., Ditchfield, K., Bateman, M., Ouzman, S., Benoit, M., Motta, A. P., . . . Balanggarra Aboriginal Corporation. (2019). Minjiwarra: Archaeological evidence of human occupation of Australia's northern Kimberley by 50,000 BP. *Australian Archaeology, 85*(2), 115–125.

Vial, L. G. (1940). Stone axes of Mount Hagen, New Guinea. *Oceania, 11*(2), 158–163.

White, J. P. (1972). *Ol Tumbuna: Archaeological excavations in the Eastern Central Highlands, Papua New Guinea*. Canberra: Australian National University.

White, J. P., Crook, K. A. W., & Ruxton, B. P. (1970). Kosipe: A Late Pleistocene site in the Papuan Highlands. *Proceedings of the Prehistoric Society, 36*, 152–170.

White, J. P., Flannery, T. F., O'Brien, R., Hancock, R. V., & Pavlish, L. (1991). The Balof Shelters, New Ireland. In J. Allen & C. Gosden (Eds.), *Report of the Lapita Homeland Project* (pp. 46–58). Canberra: Australian National University.

CHAPTER 25

FLAKED STONE TOOLS OF HOLOCENE SAHUL

Case Studies from Northern Australia and Papua New Guinea

TIM RYAN MALONEY

INTRODUCTION

PEOPLE settled the Pleistocene landmass of Sahul, including Australia and New Guinea, before 50,000 years ago (Clarkson et al. 2017; Summerhayes et al. 2010) (Figure 25.1). Australia and New Guinea were subsequently separated by rising sea levels soon after the onset of the Holocene (< 11,700 cal BP). Archaeological research indicates that significant changes occurred within the societies of both Indigenous Australia and Papua New Guinea (PNG) during the Holocene, reflected, among other things, in agriculture, rock art, stone tool technologies, and mobility and settlement patterns. In many cases, the only well-preserved records of this dynamic period are flaked stone tools. Ubiquitous in the archaeological records of humanity's expansion and adaptations across the globe, the latest analytical approaches to stone tools in the strategic region of Sahul are of global relevance to modelling human evolution. While only a small part of humanity's preserved archaeological record, flaked stone tools can provide vivid insights into the lifeways of the past (Andrefsky 2009: 88). Manufactured by reducing cores of siliceous stone, and shaped and resharpened by retouching margins, many different forms of stone tools were developed in the Holocene in response to a range of local and regional environmental and social conditions. The social conditions under which these tools developed include agriculturally focused economies in PNG and mobile forager groups across northern Australia. This chapter reviews illustrative examples of this diversity of tool forms.

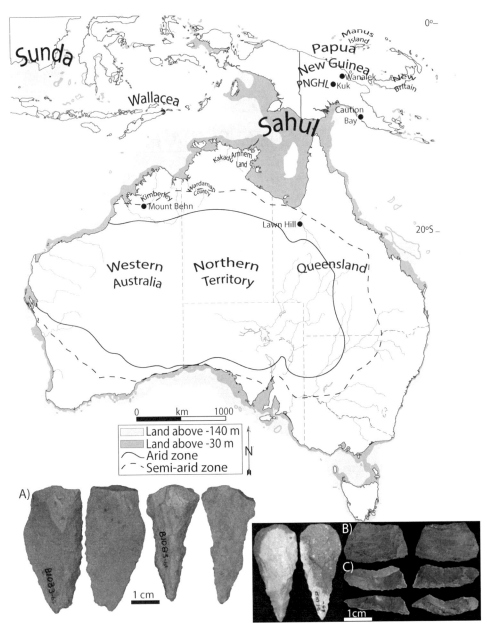

FIGURE 25.1. Location of study area regions in Sahul. A: Unifacial and bifacial direct percussion points, B: Adze tula, and C: Tula slug.

The movement of stone tools from place to place and gradual modification to extend tool use lives and functionality means that tool life histories also reflect their makers' patterns of interaction. Reconstruction of tool life histories is based on quantifying morphological variation amongst flaked stone tool assemblages. Such quantification underpins modelling systemic interactions between tool morphology, reduction intensity, and use wear, with changes in social and ecological factors through time and space (Andrefsky 2009: 70–71; Binford 1964: 425). The general theory underlying these connections, technological organization theory, holds that stone tool technologies are embedded within broader patterns of subsistence and mobility (e.g., Nelson 1991; Spry & Stern 2016; Stiner & Kuhn 2016: 178–179). Technological organization theory attempts to encapsulate the structuring of technology around subsistence, settlement patterns, and social networks (Bamforth & Bleed 1997: 112–113; Torrence 1989: 59). Subsistence patterns are organized around spatial and temporal variations in the availability of desired resources, including food, water, and shelter, with technology highly responsive to the subsistence practices of foragers (Torrence 1989: 58). Binford originally conceived of technological organization as 'the organisational characteristics within a technology which may be manipulated differently to effect acceptable adaptations for different situations' (Binford 1979: 255). Expedient versus highly maintainable tools are common theoretical constructs used to account for patterns of variation amongst flaked stone tools in both PNG and northern Australia.

Models of stone tool use, based on reconstructions of stone tool life histories, have been critical to understanding the mobile forager lifeways of Aboriginal peoples across northern Australia during the Mid- to Late Holocene. Northern Australian Aboriginal peoples innovated flaked stone tools as a technological response to changing environments; a response now argued to reflect a diversity of adjustments to social and economic systems (Hiscock 1994a). Two illustrative examples of this process discussed in this chapter are stone points and Tula adzes. Flaked tools from PNG have often been approached with different analytical foci, including use wear, residue studies, and geochemical sourcing. These analyses have provided a record of flaked stone tool use by highland agriculturists and oceanic voyagers, which also tracks Mid-Holocene developments of expanding social spheres associated with obsidian stemmed tool exchange across near Oceania. Here, researchers also demonstrate the value of experimental reproduction and traceology in the understanding of tool variability. Analysis of use wear and residues preserved on stone artefacts (traceology) reveals details of tool functions beyond that obtained by analysis of tool shape alone.

Analytical approaches to flaked tools from PNG and northern Australia have developed from these different foci and other influences (Lourandos 2008), which, when reviewed together, reveal the latest approaches to understanding ancient, flaked tool technologies and their creators. In both regions, lithic analysts have benefited from direct ethnographic observation of stone tool use by Indigenous peoples in recent times (e.g., Tindale 1965; Watson 1995). Yet these recent observations cannot always directly help understand the role of flaked tools in the ancient past without so-called ethnographic bias (Binford 1972: 86). To help obviate problems associated with direct ethnographic analogy, lithic analysts have developed morphological measures, reduction intensity quantification, and traceology to help understand the factors influencing variability in stone tool form and use in the past. The behavioural practices modelled from flaked stone tools in PNG and northern Australia appear to contrast very different economies and social networks of Holocene Sahul.

Broader influences on these regions' archaeology, associated with the history of contrasting foragers and farmers, have also created different interpretive approaches (Lourandos 2008). A melding of analytical and interpretive approaches in each study area offers a best-practice method for the archaeological discipline as a whole to reveal novel insights into the past lifeways of northern Sahul's Indigenous peoples. This chapter demonstrates that while ecological modelling remains an important analytical focus, social-cultural explanations, once less popular, are now commonplace. The dichotomy between foragers and farmers across northern Sahul is becoming less relevant, particularly for the investigation of flake stone tools, where theoretical modelling increasingly investigates the symbolic underpinnings of stone tool variation.

MODELLING FLAKE TOOL VARIABILITY

Retouched Stone Points of Australia

A review of northern Australian archaeology reveals a range of analytical approaches to stone tools, together with their strengths and shortfalls. New approaches have revealed the causes of technological change associated with retouched stone tools during the Mid- to Late Holocene. Areas of focused technological study include Lawn Hill in Queensland; Arnhem Land, Kakadu, and Wardaman Country in the Northern Territory (Clarkson 2007, 2008; Hiscock 2009, 2011); and the Kimberley region of Western Australia (Maloney 2015, 2019, 2020a) (Figure 25.1). These studies have produced regionally focused models to explain the social and economic roles of retouched flaked tools.

Stone points are recognized by the presence of converging retouched margins (both unifacial and bifacial) produced predominately with direct hard hammer percussion on elongate flake blanks (Figure 25.2A). Thought to have gradually developed from existing flake production strategies of the Early Holocene (Clarkson & David 1995: 40; O'Connor, Maloney, Vannieuwenhuyse, Balme, & Wood 2014: 17), the earliest recovered points date to between 7000 and 5000 cal BP (Hiscock & Maloney 2017), with proliferation dated to between 3000 and 2000 cal BP (Clarkson 2007; Maloney, O'Connor, & Balme 2014). These temporal patterns correlate with environmental change associated with likely changes in foraging risks defined as the probability and severity of subsistence failure (Bamforth & Bleed 1997: 112–113). The latest studies now hold risk-minimization theory as a major explanatory model for point technology producing societies in Holocene Australia.

Earlier studies of stone points were predominately typo-functional and ethnographically focused, particularly in the Kimberley region (Akerman & Bindon 1995; Akerman, Fullagar, & van Gijn 2002; Blundell 1975; O'Connor 1999; Veitch 1999: 363–365). Here a

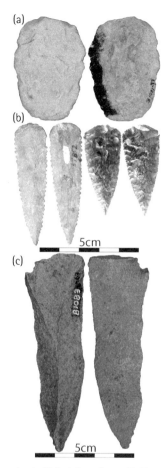

FIGURE 25.2. Late Holocene tools. A: Bifacial preform, B: Pressure flaked bifaces or Kimberley Points, and C: Leilira blade.

vibrant record of historical observations and Indigenous knowledge exists for the manufacture, use, and trade of endemic pressure flaked stone bifaces known as Kimberley Points, later made on European materials such as glass and ceramic (Harrison 2006) (Figure 25.2B). Recent approaches to Kimberley Points suggest a predominately social role, associated with expanding trade and exchange networks over the past millennium (Maloney 2020c, 2019; Maloney et al. 2014; Moore 2015). On the other hand, earlier Mid- to Late Holocene points were produced under different social, economic, and environmental conditions, which the typo-functional approach was poorly suited to explain (Hiscock 2009: 79–81).

Once thought of as mutually exclusive tool types, unifacial and bifacial points of northern Australia have been shown by technological analyses to be part of a single reduction continuum, modified by the gradual resharpening of point edges with retouch. This highly flexible life history created many varied point forms. Such morphological diversity within reduction sequences is argued to result from the need for tool maintainability and extendibility within a mobile foraging population who kept tools usable by continuous resharpening and rejuvenation (Clarkson 2006; Hiscock 2011; Maloney, O'Connor, & Balme 2017).

Critical to these advances in northern Australian point studies was the quantification of tool morphologies using morphological measures (e.g., Clarkson 2006; Hiscock 1994b), and tool reduction intensities using the Kuhn Geometric Index of Unifacial Reduction (Kuhn 1990) and the Index of Invasiveness (Clarkson 2002). These approaches were initially used to refute tool typologies, finding instead that tool variability was chiefly affected by resharpening rates or reduction intensity. As Hiscock (2009: 84) suggested, 'one of the best examples of material conservation and recycling is the production and progressive modification of stone points'. This modification, consistent with the tenets of technological organization theory, varied with transport across the landscape and other subsistence and social factors.

Multifunctionality, as a technological strategy associated with minimizing foraging risk, is also crucial to the latest modelling of northern Australian point technologies. Unlike the previous typo-functional models, modern analysts can only reliably demonstrate tool function through traceology (i.e., the investigation of use-wear/residue traces on stone tools). Traceology studies reveal that the mono-functional role of stone points as hafted projectiles is untenable (Brindley & Clarkson 2015; Maloney 2020a; Maloney, Wood, O'Connor, & Whitau 2015). Instead, traceology supports multifunctionality and only occasional projectile use in the Mid- to Late Holocene. Although few in number, these traceology studies support a multiplicity of wood crafts, plant working, and hunting functions, with interchangeability, rather than a single functional design (Brindley & Clarkson 2015; Maloney 2020a; Maloney et al. 2015; Wallis & O'Connor 1998). Southern and eastern parts of Australia, where backed artefacts (microliths) are prolific, have benefited from traceology studies, similarly documenting multipurpose tool use during the Mid- to Late Holocene (Robertson, Attenbrow, & Hiscock 2009: 249).[1]

Direct percussion points are predominately made on morphologically distinct and standardized flake blanks, resembling blades or lancets with parallel to converging margins and mostly plano-triangular cross-sections. Point blanks are identified as lightly retouched points, where reduction processes have begun but without drastic alteration of tool morphology (e.g., Maloney 2020b). According to morphological and qualitative data, point blanks are standardized across a vast region of northern Australia during the Mid- to Late Holocene (Clarkson 2007: 89; Hiscock 2011: 79; Maloney 2020b; Moore 2011: 3). This emphasis on standardization facilitated predictable retouching patterns, hafting interchangeability, and probably enhanced trade values as a standardized exchange commodity (Hiscock & Maloney 2017).

Point retouch followed standardized patterns of marginal resharpening concurrent with use. As a result, hafting, breakage, rejuvenation, and recycling lead to a variety of distinctive point morphologies at various states of reduction (Clarkson 2007: 104, 109, 2008: 308; Hiscock 2009: 84–85, 2011: 78; Maloney et al. 2017: 10). This quality provided a reliable and flexible technology for foraging, hunting, craft production, and exchange commodities. Other social benefits are likely embedded within this standardized strategy (Weissner 1982: 172–173), including social signalling (Moore 2011: 145). Standardization, both in blank production and predictable tool maintenance, also enhanced people's technological repertoire and potential exchange items at times of increased foraging risk.

Points with a primary role as multipurpose and interchangeable tools supersedes the singular view of points as hafted projectiles during the Mid- to Late Holocene. This finding overturned deeply embedded typo-functional assumptions in Australian archaeology (Davidson & McCarthy 1957: 408; Holdaway & Stern 2004: 266; Mulvaney & Kamminga 1999: 237), which assumed points to be 'spearheads', based on their shape and ethnographic observations. Traceology confirms Mid- to Late Holocene points were used in a multiplicity of functions, and across a diversity of morphologies and reduction intensities, before discard (Brindley & Clarkson 2015; Maloney 2020a; Wallis & O'Connor 1998). The multifunctionality record revealed through traceology supports point technology being highly adaptive, which would have helped mobile foragers be well equipped for situational foraging risks during the Mid- to Late Holocene.

Carrying an array of highly standardized, maintainable, multipurpose, and socially valuable tools represented developments in technological organization responding to periods of likely increased foraging risks (Kuhn 1994; Nelson 1991). Given the increased mobility predicted for the Mid- to Late Holocene foraging populations more broadly (Kuhn 2011: 76), an increase in the frequency and extent of social interconnectedness across northern Australia (Hiscock & Maloney 2017) likely saw points increasingly valued as exchange commodities and possibly as social symbols.

THE AUSTRALIAN TULA ADZE

Another distinctive flaked stone tool of Late Holocene Australia is the Tula adze (Figure 25.1B). As with points, recent understandings of the development of Tula adzes have been modelled with economic and social risk management theory. The Tula is a retouched flake recognized by a prominent bulb of percussion, relatively wide platform, and characteristically steep angled distal retouch (Hiscock & Veth 1991: 333–334; Moore 2004: 66). Tula morphology and reduction sequences are thought of as the signature stone tool of the Australian arid zone (Figure 25.1), widely associated with woodworking (Gould 1980: 70; Hiscock 2008: 200–201; Smith 2013: 186) and endemic to Indigenous Australia. Comprehensive reviews of Tula distribution demonstrate this arid zone concentration (Hiscock 2008: 200–216; Smith 2013: 17–44), although others have found an extension across the nonarid environments of southeast Queensland (McNiven 1993) and the southern Kimberley (Maloney & Dilkes-Hall 2020).

The Tula is continually reduced, progressing through regular resharpening events, until a characteristic exhausted 'slug' is discarded (Figure 25.1C). Morphological measures are used to reconstruct these changes throughout Tula life histories (e.g., Clarkson

2007: 116–121; Hiscock & Veth 1991: 334–335; Maloney & Dilkes-Hall 2020: 226–227; Moore 2004: 64–69), displaying remarkable standardization across their vast distribution and revealing an emphasis on tool extendibility. These reduction sequences have consistently documented radical efforts to resharpen Tulas into tiny slug forms before discard.

Excavations reveal that Tulas date to after 3700 cal BP (Veth, Hiscock, & Williams 2011: 9), implying a widespread and somewhat sudden adoption, with unclear antecedents. In the Kimberley region, the Tula was first widely adopted somewhat later, around 2700 cal BP (Maloney & Dilkes-Hall 2020), at approximately the same time as the neighbouring region of Wardaman Country (Clarkson 2008: 297, 300). Several Indigenous groups manufactured Tulas during the 1960s, using them to produce a range of hardwood objects (Akerman 2006: 339). The initial timing of widespread Tula adoption and the technological qualities revealed through the reconstruction of tool life history are linked to economic risk management models and social exchange networks.

FLAKE TOOLS OF PAPUA NEW GUINEA

Archaeological research in Papua New Guinea (PNG), including the islands of New Britain and Manus (Figure 25.1), highlights a different analytical approach to modelling the role of flake stone tools in the past. Studies of flaked stone tool technology from Holocene PNG are less prolific than studies from Australia. This disparity is probably due in part to the nature of the archaeological record (i.e., generally fewer assemblages dominated by flaked tools) and the apparent decreased economic reliance on flaked stone tools during the Holocene. The foraging risks encountered by Holocene agriculturists were indeed different from those of the mobile foragers of northern Australia. With tuberous agriculture and pig husbandry forming staple foods in some Holocene records of the PNG Highlands (e.g., Lewis, Denham, & Golson 2016: 100), flaked stone tools may have played a less central role in subsistence compared to Australia (Sillitoe & Hardy 2003: 557). Instead, flaked tools may have formed different roles within communities, indicative of more socially derived values, such as establishing and maintaining exchange networks (Torrence 2011). Elsewhere in PNG, flaked chert and obsidian tools were used in more utilitarian (subsistence-related) roles (Pavlides 2004: 103–104).

Possibly as a result of the agricultural phenomenon, and in a reverse of the situation found in Australian archaeology, analysts working on flake stone tools from Holocene PNG have concentrated more on residue and usewear analyses and less on quantifying morphological variation (see Ford 2017; Pavlides 2004: 103–104; Spry 2011). For example, extensive archaeological excavations at Kuk Swamp in the PNG Highlands produced a rich record of Early to Mid-Holocene agriculture (and house sites in some contexts; e.g., Denham et al. 2003). Of the 149 flaked artefacts recovered from Kuk, all eleven flakes and twelve cores revealed signs of edge utilization related to processing wood and other plants, including starchy cultivars (Fullagar & Golson 2017: 374–376).

Traceology studies indicate that 'the range of functions for cores, flakes and utilized fragments appears to overlap considerably through time, mainly covering the cutting and scraping of soft starchy plants and wood' (Fullagar & Golson 2017: 390). Used for resharpening wooden cultivating tools in the field and discarded after use, the flaked tools at Kuk were an expedient technology that was rarely maintained (e.g., retouching and resharpening) (Fullagar & Golson 2017). Indeed, beyond field systems and drainage features, wooden digging sticks are the most common agricultural technology at Kuk (Golson 1977).

The expedient flake tool technology seen at Kuk appears to be present across several other PNG sites (e.g., Bulmer 1966: 108, 132; Strathern 1969; Watson 1995; White & Thomas 1972; White, 1967). For example, coastal regions around Caution Bay have similarly revealed expedient flake tool use (digim'Rina et al. 2016: 162). Here a range of core reduction sequences across multiple Late Holocene sites reveal expedient daily use, as well as specific functions such as shell armband manufacture (digim'Rina et al. 2016: 56). Retouched flakes from Holocene units of Wanalek site were also found to have been used and discarded on-site (Bulmer 1966: 474). Flake tool expediency during the Early to Mid-Holocene, in conjunction with a greater reliance on organic raw materials, may signal a lack of economic importance of flaked stone tools in PNG (Sillitoe & Hardy 2003: 556).

Other areas of the PNG Highlands reveal that retouched flake tools were also hafted (Bulmer 1966: 108; Watson 1995: 91–92). Here, like parts of Australia, researchers have benefited from direct ethnographic observation of stone tool production and Indigenous peoples' knowledge and memory of tool use and significance. Direct observation includes the use of small, hafted, and amorphous flakes, plus occasional use of retouched flakes, to carve wooden arrows and smoking pipes, and to drill holes in shell and wood (Sillitoe & Hardy 2003: 559; Watson 1995). Observation of stone tool use in the 1960s included surgery to remove an arrow from an individual (Bartlett 1964: 669). The antiquity of these various flaked stone tool technologies and their underlying causes in PNG remains largely unknown.

A nonutilitarian role of flaked tools in establishing and maintaining exchange networks between the highlands, valley, and different coastal groups, forms a compelling argument for the underlying causes of Holocene flake tools across PNG (Gaffney & Summerhayes 2018; Torrence et al. 2009; Torrence, Kelloway, & White 2013; Torrence & Swadling 2008). Central to this modelling has been tracking the distribution of stone tools across PNG Island regions and near Oceania (Summerhayes 2017, 2019).

Unlike Australia, Holocene toolmakers in PNG had access to high-quality obsidian—a volcanic lithic material providing extremely sharp edges. Archaeologists in PNG have generated a wide range of obsidian procurement and transport models based on obsidian sourcing and chemical fingerprinting with portable X-ray fluorescence (PXRF) analysis and other methods such as PIXE-PIGME (e.g., Ambrose, Duerden, & Bird 1981; Summerhayes 2009). PXRF uses the unique chemical signature of individual obsidian sources to trace the geological origin of flaked artefacts to known outcrops. This analytical approach tracks the transport of tools across landscapes and between islands, and by implication, between populations in the past (e.g., Specht 2005: 385–386; Torrence & Swadling 2008; White, Jacobsen, Kewibu, & Doelman 2006: 106).

Perhaps the most enigmatic obsidian tools of PNG are stemmed tools (Figure 25.3). Obsidian stemmed tools have a characteristic tang produced by delicate retouch, with lengths varying mostly between 10 and 15 cm (Torrence et al. 2013: 279). Some reduction sequences reveal small, intricate tool shapes resembling fishhooks, possibly reduced from broken stemmed tools (Torrence et al. 2013: 294) as well as smaller stemmed forms (Kononenko, Specht, & Torrence 2010: 22). In some cases, stemmed tools are made from chert (Pavlides 1993). Production of these distinctive retouched flake tools began sometime before 6000 cal BP and ceased by 3000 cal BP (Torrence & Swadling 2008).

Blanks for obsidian stemmed tools were often highly specialized, made by using prismatic blades and Kombewah flakes (Torrence et al. 2013: 279). Production of a Kombewah flake involves the removal of a flake from the bulb of percussion of the ventral surface of a larger parent flake. Traces of this unique form of blank production preserved on stemmed tools are the 'twin' bulbs of percussion or parts thereof, observed on both the dorsal and ventral surfaces of tool blanks. This variety of blank production requires a high level of artisanship and reliable access to raw material (Rath & Torrence 2003) and demonstrates a structured and standardized manufacturing sequence.

The prismatic blades and Kombewah flakes associated with some stemmed tools represent a substantial investment in both time and material, dedicated to perfecting this technique for these elaborate flake tools (Torrence et al. 2013: 5). Subsequent retouch focused on producing the tang and occasionally involved hammer dressing, where the gentle application of hammer force created a pecked surface (Torrence et al. 2009: 122). Retouching the tang and preserving the blank flake termination, as shown in the example depicted in Figure 25.3 from Barema, supported the interpretation of a phallic symbol for these tools, among other symbolic values (Torrence at al. 2013: 6–7). Other smaller tool blanks are known, such as those from the Willaumez Peninsula (Araho,

FIGURE 25.3. Obsidian stemmed tool from Barema (Torrence et al. 2013: 293, fig 10).

Torrence, & White 2002: 69; Kononenko et al. 2010: 22). These studies also documented many less ornate obsidian tools that likely had more utilitarian or expedient roles.

PNG flake tool analysts have tested and verified tool functions with several traceology studies over the past decade (e.g., Field, McGowan, Moss, & Marx 2020; Kononenko, Torrence, & White 2015; Kononenko, Torrence, & Sheppard 2016; Torrence et al. 2018: 61–66). Experimental use of obsidian tools has verified their capacity for chopping and adzing (Kononenko et al. 2015), irrespective of fragility or brittleness (Greiser & Sheets 1979: 296). By replicating obsidian stemmed tool production sequences observed from archaeological contexts, researchers re-created a range of obsidian tool uses (Kononenko et al. 2015: 255) and compared the observed traceology with archaeological specimens from West New Britain. Kombewah flake blanks may have been optimized for cutting roles, and a 'self-sharpening' phenomenon was found to be associated with edge damage on the exposed blank flake termination, not typically retouched in archaeological specimens (Kononenko et al. 2015: 267–268).

Other traceology studies have demonstrated tattooing amongst obsidian tool-using groups from the Mid- to Late Holocene. Examples of small flakes and some retouched flakes used in tattooing possibly reflect cultural links between small and widely spaced communities across near Oceania during the Mid- to Late Holocene (Kononenko et al. 2016; Torrence et al. 2018: 60–63). This traceology analytical focus in PNG and near Oceania has revealed key details on the social roles of obsidian tools. By the Late Holocene, when the Lapita pottery-producing culture spread throughout the region sometime after 3300 cal BP, most flaked stone tools consisted of undiagnostic, unretouched artefacts (e.g., Sheppard 2010; Torrence 2011).

Major research themes with which PNG stone tool analysts continue to grapple include explaining the otherwise scarcity of clearly recognizable Holocene chopping tools used in forest clearance in contexts of shifting agriculture (Kononenko et al. 2015: 268; Lewis et al. 2016). Furthermore, little is known about the stone tools used in the production of advanced watercraft involved in obsidian transport throughout near Oceania islands, from at least 20,000 years ago (e.g., Summerhayes, 2009) and throughout the Holocene. Traceology studies and a theoretical engagement with more socially derived models should reveal new details on these matters.

FLAKED TOOLS AND TECHNOLOGICAL ORGANIZATION

Flaked Tools, Climate, and Risk

New archaeological understandings of northern Australian point technology collectively support response to environmental change as the underlying theoretical cause of innovation and change in this retouched flake technology. This technological response is referred to as the risk reduction model; it focuses on the probability and severity of subsistence failures and how technology helped to mitigate these risks (Bamforth & Bleed 1997: 112–113; Torrence 1989: 59; Winterhalder, Lu, & Tucker 1999: 302). The new analytical approaches to stone points have facilitated the comparison of reduction intensity data and traceology against the proxy records of environmental change linked to economic hardships for foraging populations of northern Australia during the Mid- to Late Holocene. The risk response model suggests that people equipped themselves with technologies that could provide a greater economic return and reduce foraging risks during times of economic hardship and increased mobility. It is predicted that foragers increased their territorial range (and mobility) in response to drier environmental conditions that saw the distribution of subsistence resources such as freshwater, edible plant species, and game animals become more sparsely distributed and less predictable and reliable (Kuhn 2012: 76). In northern Australia, patterns of increased Mid- to Late Holocene aridity are associated with proxy records of El Nino-Southern Oscillation (ENSO) intensification. ENSO intensification moves the intertropical convergence zone to the north, which reduces monsoonal rainfall, overall rainfall, and the predictability of rainfall for northern Australia.

Shifts in ENSO-induced aridity varied in extent and timing across northern Australia. In terms of broad trends, locally varying peaks and troughs in ENSO intensity occurred after 6000 cal BP, with intensified ENSO occurring around 5000 cal BP (Conroy, Overpeck, Cole, Shanahan, & Steinitz-Kannan, 2008; Denniston et al. 2013a; Donders, Haberle, Hope, Wagner, & Visscher 2007; Gagan, Hendy, Haberle, & Hantoro 2004; Moy, Seltzer, Rodbell, & Anderson 2002; Rein et al. 2005). Widespread regional decline in ENSO activity commenced around 1000 years ago (Donders et al. 2007; Gagan et al. 2004), or slightly earlier (Denniston et al. 2013b; McGowan, Marx, Moss, & Hammond 2012).

It is predicted that local and regional aridity patterns increased the foraging risks faced by Aboriginal people of northern Australia during the Mid- to Late Holocene. Aridity decreased the availability and predictability of freshwater resources, with significant roll-on effects on the distribution of other essential subsistence resources such as game animals and plant resources. To mitigate this decrease in resources and concomitant increase in foraging risk, people innovated and adjusted technologies within increasingly mobile and socially interconnected settlement systems. Increasing mobility, such as logistical (specialized, resource-specific) forays, is one way to adapt to new and less reliable resource distributions.

Stone point production patterns, reduction intensities, tool recycling, and rejuvenation rate increases occurred during both regional and local periods of environmental change in the Mid- to Late Holocene. Following gradual adjustments to Early Holocene flake production and the first appearance of retouched points by at least 5500 cal BP, stone points proliferated across northern Australia between 3500 and 1500 cal BP before declining or changing over the past millennium (Allen & Akerman 2015: 90; Clarkson 2008: 302, 2007: 130–142; Hiscock 2006: 90; Maloney et al. 2014). In the Kimberley region, for example, point production, reduction intensity, and rejuvenation rates peak between approximately 3600 and 1600 cal BP (Maloney 2020a: 53–54; Maloney et al. 2017: 11)—congruent with local periods of peak aridity between 2600 and 1300 cal BP (Field et al. 2017; McGowan et al. 2012: 2–4). Here, pressure flaked Kimberley Points only emerged within the past millennium, following a decline in the intensity of direct percussion point retouch (Maloney et al. 2014, 2017). Similar temporal correlations are demonstrated in Wardaman Country (Clarkson 2008: 302) and the Kakadu/Arnhem Land areas (Hiscock 2009: 90) of the Northern Territory. When paired with technological organization theory and concepts such as standardization, multifunctionality, and extendibility, this temporal correlation with proxy records of environmental change and likely subsistence hardships provides a compelling case for stone point technology being a well-preserved element of a wider response to increased foraging risk, including a proliferation of social interconnectedness.

Stone Tools and Social Interconnectedness

In contrast to developments in point technology in the Mid- to Late Holocene documented above, the last millennium saw new stone point technologies emerge in several northern Australia regions linked to both environmental and social change. This shift correlates temporally with a decline in ENSO intensity found in proxy records, as well as with documented shifts in flaked tools away from an emphasis on highly extendable, multipurpose roles. At this time, reduced pressures to maintain points with retouching and rejuvenating have been noted in the Kimberley (Maloney 2020a: 53, 2019: 46), Wardaman Country (Clarkson 2008: 309), and parts of Arnhem Land and Kakadu (Hiscock 1994b: 285–286). The Leilira blade, Wanji biface, and Kimberley Points (Figure 25.2) all developed within the last millennium. Each represents a new form of stone tool production, becoming widespread within expanding exchange networks across northern Australia (Akerman & Bindon 1995: 90–91; Clarkson 2007: 140; Maloney et al. 2014).

The Leilira blade is a large elongate flake, often exceeding 10 cm in length (Figure 25.2C), produced via a specialized and by no means material conserving core reduction strategy (Akerman 2007; Newman & Moore 2013: 2615). Kimberley Points are less economically efficient in terms of raw material conservation than earlier direct percussion points. They were manufactured with a highly staged and complex production sequence (Maloney 2020c, 2019; Moore 2015) involving large bifacial preforms (Figure 25.2A) and the pressure flaking of extremely thin and marginally serrated forms (Figure 25.2B).

The significant investment into these flake tool technologies reveals a change in technological organization whereby the exchange of valuable and socially prestigious flaked tools took on a new and more economically and socially central role (Akerman 2007; Maloney 2020c; Moore 2015). The single traceology study conducted on a sample of ethnographic Kimberley Points (Akerman et al. 2002: 25) found a range of material contacts associated with the manufacture, hafting, painting, and plant wrapping of these highly specialized and symbolic items. Ethnographic (Akerman et al. 2002) and modelled archaeological data (Maloney 2020c, 2019; Moore 2015) indicate that Leilira blades and Kimberley Points were widely traded as prestigious exchange items.

The decreased curation and multifunctionality of northern Australian stone tools over the past millennium (coincident with climatic amelioration) also took place when material conservation of stone was less critical to subsistence. Produced via a staged production system, Kimberley Points require high levels of knapping skill and experience to produce the finely pressure flaked forms. Maloney (2019) argued that Kimberley Point production could have represented a significant shift in time budgeting, made possible by a decline in economic pressure on foragers, and increased value in prestigious trade goods throughout the Kimberley region (Maloney 2020c). An increased emphasis on social networks and alliances associated with the trade and exchange of these elaborate flaked tools of the last millennium is evident across the region.

Tula adze innovation and spread in the Late Holocene have similarly been seen as a response to foraging risk brought on by environmental change (Clarkson 2007; Hiscock & Veth 1991; Maloney & Dilkes-Hall 2020; Smith 2013: 196; Veth et al. 2011). Standardization and extendibility of Tula use-life increased the likelihood that foragers would have a ready toolkit to manufacture and repair wooden tools (Veth et al. 2011: 12). Such change potentially enhanced social interconnectedness via the production and exchange of much desired wooden craft commodities produced by Tulas (Doelman & Cochrane 2012; Maloney & Dilkes-Hall 2020).

Maloney and Dilkes-Hall (2020) argue that the timing of Tula adoption in the southern Kimberley region around 2700 cal BP, and accompanying evidence for woodworking, implied shared technologies in formalized craft production at a time when social groups faced challenging foraging conditions. Increased mobility at this time would have increased intergroup contacts (Kuhn 2011: 76), with wooden craft production and exchange likely forming a social response to enhance intercommunity connections (Doelman & Cochrane 2012; Weissner 1982: 172–173). In short, trade and exchange may have helped offset foraging risks. These behavioural connections in the Kimberley span arid to subtropical zones (Maloney & Dilkes-Hall 2020). Intergroup trade in various wooden craft items was prolific in the southern Kimberley at the commencement of colonial invasion in 1885 (Akerman et al. 2002). Traded wooden objects included boomerangs, digging sticks, spearthrowers, musical instruments, and shields (Akerman 2006). As such, these objects fed into invigorated exchange networks to reaffirm sociocultural cohesion as a response, in part, to the climatic uncertainty of the Late Holocene.

Recent approaches to modelling obsidian tool exchange in PNG during the Mid-Holocene have incorporated artefact morphology, traceology, use wear and residue analysis, and experimental reproduction. Torrence et al. (2013), for example, used both morphological variation and PXRF analysis of tools from New Britain, Manus Island, and mainland PNG to identify multiple stemmed tool groups and evidence of a Mid-Holocene exchange network. Obsidian from two known primary sources, used in the production of these elaborate tools via staged production sequences, implied a wide-spread social interaction between islands (Torrence et al. 2013; Torrence & Swadling 2008). These data reveal that obsidian tool producers travelled the region in advanced watercraft during the Mid-Holocene and exchanged both lithic resources and tool production techniques in social settings. Tool producers may have even 'copied and possibly competed, through the sophisticated manufacture of these large, distinctive, and fragile obsidian artefacts' (Torrence et al. 2013: 306).

Researchers working on PNG flake tools have also employed technological organization theory and risk-minimization models to link changing island settlement with known volcanic eruptions on the Pacific Rim (Lilley 2004: 93; Torrence, Specht, & Fullagar 1990: 463, 1992: 111). That is, exchange networks of obsidian and the elaborate tool forms may have been innovated to enable and maintain social connectedness to mitigate the risks associated with inhabiting regions of increasing volcanic eruptions. People impacted by volcanic threats on the Pacific Rim could have found refuge with connected communities and obsidian exchange partners (Torrence 2014).

DISCUSSION AND CONCLUSION

A melding of current flaked stone tool analytical approaches found in northern Australian and PNG archaeology provides an optimal way to assess the underlying causes and meanings of flake stone tools in the Holocene societies of northern Sahul. In an ideal setting, flake stone tool assemblages would be analysed with morphological quantification, reduction intensity indices, traceology with empirical verification, and geochemical sourcing.

The review of case studies from northern Australia and PNG reveals that this ideal analytical approach cannot be applied to all archaeological contexts. For example, the unique formation processes of igneous lithic materials such as obsidian make them suitable for geochemical sourcing. In contrast, the predominately metasedimentary flaked stone tools of northern Australia currently appear to lack this sourcing suitability, an issue faced in many parts of the world (e.g., Brandl et al. 2018). The analytical value of modelling morphological variability and reduction intensities across space and time (Andrefsky 2009: 88; Hiscock 2009: 84) requires societies with systemic technological use of retouched tools. Some societies of the past did not regularly utilize such tools, such as the Early Holocene societies of the PNG Highlands that employed a more expedient flake tool technology in the context of an agriculturally focused economy.

Understanding the use of obsidian stemmed tools beyond their social exchange roles demonstrates the value of experimental reproduction coupled with traceology studies. Experimental reproduction has established functional roles and documented wear patterns that form on these tools (Kononenko et al. 2015). A variety of adzing, cutting, and chopping functions of softwoods is now known for obsidian tools from the Holocene records of PNG. This experimental analysis is sparse in Australian Holocene archaeology, although it has revealed critical details on the multifunctionality of points (Brindley & Clarkson 2015; Maloney 2020a). There is much promise to expand our knowledge on the functional roles of the Mid- to Late Holocene risk-minimizing tool kits in Australia via traceology and experimental archaeology programs. Both PNG and northern Australian archaeology could benefit greatly from a melding of analytical approaches showcased in each of the study areas reviewed.

Different interpretive influences on the Holocene archaeology of Australia and PNG, as identified by Lourandos (2008), now seem less useful for future interpretations of these records. Lourandos (2008: 69) revealed a history of interpretive models whereby Australian archaeology was primarily shaped by ecological and biological frameworks associated with 'hunter-gatherers' and PNG interpretative models set within an agricultural debate. This review showcases that while both themes remain at the forefront of investigations, the dichotomy between perceived interpretive influences (economic vs social) is less relevant to the current modelling of flake tool variation. Although the reviewed case studies on points from northern Australia primarily engage with ecological modelling, social drivers of change were also discussed (Clarkson 2007: 167, 2008: 311–312; Hiscock 1994b: 277, 2006: 86–87, 2008: 160; Kuhn 2012: 76). Similarly, while investigations into the meaning of observed changes within point and Tula adze assemblages retain the ever-popular and compelling risk-minimization model, social elements are often integrated into the model (e.g., Doelman & Cochrane 2012; Hiscock & Maloney 2017; Maloney & Dilkes-Hall 2020).

Far from being environmentally deterministic, recent approaches to modelling flake tool variation from Mid- to Late Holocene northern Australia explore multiple social dimensions. These social dimensions include trade and exchange (Hiscock & Maloney 2017), teaching and learning (Maloney 2019), prestige good production (Maloney 2020c; Moore 2015), social signalling (Moore 2011), shared craft economies (Maloney & Dilkes-Hall 2020; Doelman & Cochrane 2012), and connections to modern Indigenous social practices (Maloney & Street 2020). In short, a social dynamism is present within this modelling.

Further evidence that the epistemological divide between Australia (hunter-gatherers) and PNG (agriculturalists) identified by Lourandos (2008) is losing traction includes Late Holocene flaked stone tools with cultivar residues in Torres Strait (northeast Australia) (Williams, Wright, Crowther, & Denham 2020: 2–3) and Mid- to Late Holocene aquaculture from Lake Condah (southeast Australia) (McNiven, Crouch, Richards, Dolby, & Jacobsen 2012: 270; Smith et al. 2019: 290–291). The establishment and maintenance of exchange networks involving stone tools such as Kimberley Points and Leilira blades in northern Australia, as well as the obsidian stemmed tools and tattooing flakes from PNG, showcase a recent analytical shift towards more socially derived explanations of flake tool change, irrespective of farming, maritime, or foraging economies.

The numbers of unanswered questions surrounding the Holocene lifeways of northern Sahul are too many to list. However, investigations into the role of flake tools from this dynamic region and period should consider the varied influences and analytical foci explored in this review—morphological, reduction sequence, use wear, residues, experimentation, and geochemical sourcing. Modelling flake tool variation with these approaches across time and space within regularly updated technological organization theory (Stiner & Kuhn 2016) will define the future direction of flake stone tool analysis for Holocene Sahul.

ACKNOWLEDGMENTS

Thank you to Robin Torrence for comments on this manuscript and for providing the image of the Barema tool for Figure 25.3.

NOTE

1. There has been little Australian traceology research on flaked tools over the past few decades (Bordes, Prinsloo, Fullagar, & Roberts 2020; Maloney 2020a; Robertson et al. 2009). These studies represent a combination of usewear and residue analyses, backed by empirical or experimental records (e.g., Fuentes et al. 2020; Rots 2005; Rots & Plisson 2014). Earlier studies did not reveal the same level of detail (Hayden 1977; Kamminga 1977; Fullagar 1998).

REFERENCES

Akerman, K. (2006). High tech-low tech: Lithic technology in the Kimberley region of Western Australia. In J. Apel & K. Knutsson (Eds.), *Skilled production and social reproduction: Aspects of traditional stone-tool technologies* (pp. 20–24). Proceedings of a symposium in Uppsala, August, 2003. Uppsala: Societas Archaeologica Upsaliensis.

Akerman, K. (2007). To make a point: Ethnographic reality and the ethnographic and experimental replication of Australian macroblades known as leilira. *Australian Archaeology, 64*, 23–34.

Akerman, K., & Bindon, P. (1995). Dentate and related stone biface points from northern Australia. *The Beagle, Records of the Museums and Art Galleries of the Northern Territory, 12*, 89–99.

Akerman, K., Fullagar, R., & van Gijn, A. (2002). Weapons and *wunan*: production, function and exchange of Kimberley points. *Australian Aboriginal Studies, 1*, 14–42.

Allen, H., & Akerman, K. (2015). Innovation and change in northern Australian Aboriginal spear technologies: The case for reed spears. *Archaeology in Oceania, 50*, 82–92.

Ambrose, W. R., Duerden, P., & Bird, J. R. (1981). An archaeological application of PIXE-PIGME analysis to Admirality islands obsidians. *Nuclear Instruments and Methods in Physics Research, 191*(1–3), 397–402.

Andrefsky, W., Jr. (2009). The analysis of stone tool procurement, production, and maintenance. *Journal of Archaeological Research, 17*, 65–103.

Araho, N., Torrence, R., & White, J. P. (2002). Valuable and useful: Mid-Holocene stemmed obsidian artifacts from West New Britain, Papua New Guinea. *Proceedings of the Prehistoric Society, 68*, 61–81.

Bamforth, D. B., & Bleed, P. (1997). Technology, flaked stone technology, and risk. In C. M. Barton & G. A. Clark (Eds.), *Rediscovering Darwin: Evolutionary theory in archaeology* (pp. 109–140). Archaeological Papers of the American Anthropological Association. Washington, DC: American Anthropological Association.

Bartlett, H. K. (1964). Note on flint implements near Nipa, Central Papuan Highlands. *Records of the South Australian Museum, 14*, 669–673.

Binford, L. (1972). *An archaeological perspective*. New York: Seminar Press.

Binford, L. (1964). A consideration of archaeological research design. *American Antiquity, 29*(4), 425–441.

Binford, L. (1979). Organizational and formation processes: Looking at curated technologies. *Journal of Anthropological Research, 35*, 255–273.

Blundell, V. J. (1975). *Aboriginal adaptation in northwest Australia* (PhD thesis). University of Wisconsin, Madison.

Bordes, L., Prinsloo, L. C, Fullagar, R, & Roberts, R. G. (2020). A key to identify use-related micro-residues on prehistoric stone artefacts using Raman spectroscopy. *Journal of Archaeological Science: Reports, 31*, 102329.

Brandl, M., Martinez, M. M., Hauzenberger, C., Filzmoser, P., Nymoen, P., & Mehler, N. (2018). A multi-technique analytical approach to sourcing Scandinavian flint: Provenance of ballast flint from the shipwreck 'Leirvigen 1', Norway. *PLoS ONE, 13*(8), e0200647.

Brindley, J., & Clarkson, C. (2015). Beyond a suggestive morphology: were Wardaman stone points exclusively spear armatures? *Australian Archaeology, 80*, 81–92.

Bulmer, S. (1966). *The prehistory of the Australian New Guinea Highlands: Discussion of Archaeological Field Survey and excavations, 1959–60.* (MA thesis). University of Auckland, Auckland.

Clarkson, C. (2002). An index of invasiveness for the measurement of unifacial and bifacial retouch: A theoretical, experimental and archaeological verification. *Journal of Archaeological Science, 29*, 65–75.

Clarkson, C. (2006). Explaining point variability in the eastern Victoria River region, Northern Territory. *Archaeology in Australia, 41*, 97–106.

Clarkson, C. (2007). *Lithics in the Land of the Lightning Brothers: The archaeology of Wardaman country, Northern Territory*. Terra Australis 25. Canberra: ANU E Press.

Clarkson, C. (2008). Changing reduction intensity, settlement, and subsistence in Wardaman Country, northern Australia. In W. Andrefky Jr. (Eds.), *Lithics: Macroscopic approaches to analysis* (2nd edition, pp. 286–316). Cambridge Manuals in Archaeology. New York: Cambridge University Press.

Clarkson, C., Jacobs, Z., Marwick, B., Fullagar, R., Wallis, L., Smith, M., . . . Pardoe, C. (2017). Human occupation of northern Australia by 65,000 years ago. *Nature, 547*(7663), 306–309.

Conroy, J. L., Overpeck, J. T., Cole, J. E., Shanahan, T. M., & Steinitz-Kannan, M. (2008). Holocene changes in eastern tropical Pacific climate inferred from a Galápagos lake sediment record. *Quaternary Science Reviews, 27*(11–12), 1166–1180.

Davidson, D. S., & McCarthy, F. D. (1957). The distribution and chronology of some important types of stone implements in Western Australia. *Anthropos, 52*, 390–458.

Denham, T., Haberle, S., Lentfer, C., Fullagar, R., Field, J., Therin, M., . . . Winsborough, B. (2003). Origins of agriculture at Kuk Swamp in the Highlands of New Guinea. *Science, 301*, 189–193.

Denniston, R. F., Wyrwoll, K.-H., Asmerom, Y., Polyak, V., Humphreys, W., Cugley, J., . . . Greaves, E. (2013a). North Atlantic forcing of millennial-scale Indo-Australian monsoon dynamics during the Last Glacial period. *Quaternary Science Reviews, 72*, 159–168.

Denniston, R. F., Wyrwoll, K.-H., Polyak, V. J., Brown, J. R., Asmerom, Y., Wanamaker, A. D., . . . Humphreys, W. F. (2013b). A stalagmite record of Holocene Indonesian–Australian summer monsoon variability from the Australian tropics. *Quaternary Science Reviews, 78,* 155–168.

Digim'Rina, L. S., Richards, T., David, B., Leavesley, M., Goddard, M., Dutton, T., et al (2016). Koita and Motu landscapes and seascapes of Caution Bay. In T. Richards, B. David, K. Aplin, & I. J. McNiven (Eds.), *Archaeological research at Caution Bay, Papua New Guinea: Cultural, linguistic and environmental setting* (pp. 53–63). Caution Bay Studies in Archaeology 1. Oxford: Achaeopress.

Doelman, T., & Cochrane, G. W. (2012). Design theory and the Australian tula adze. *Asian Perspectives, 51*(2), 251–277.

Donders, T. H., Haberle, S., Hope, G., Wagner, F., & Visscher, H. (2007). Pollen evidence for the transition of the eastern Australian climate system from the post-glacial to the present-day ENSO mode. *Quaternary Science Reviews, 26,* 1621–1637.

Field, E., McGowan, H. A., Moss, P. T., & Marx, S. K. (2017). A late quaternary record of monsoon variability in the northwest Kimberley, Australia. *Quaternary International, 449,* 119–135.

Field, J., Summerhayes, G., Luu, S., Coster, A. C. F., Ford, A., Mandui, H., et al. (2020). Functional studies of flaked and ground stone artefacts reveal starchy tree nut and root exploitation in mid-Holocene highland New Guinea. *The Holocene, 30*(9), 1360–1374.

Ford, A. (2017). Late Pleistocene lithic technology in the Ivane Valley: A view from the rainforest. *Quaternary International, 448,* 31–43.

Fuentes, R., Ono, R., Carlos, J., Kerfant, C., Miranda, T., Aziz, N., . . . Pawlik, A. (2020). Stuck within notches: Direct evidence of plant processing during the last glacial maximum to Holocene in North Sulawesi. *Journal of Archaeological Science: Reports, 30,* 102207.

Fullagar, R. (Ed.). (1998). *A closer look: Recent studies of Australian stone tools.* Sydney University Archaeology Methods Series 6. Sydney: Archaeological Computing Laboratory, School of Archaeology, University of Sydney.

Fullagar, R., & Golson, J. (2017). Kuk stone artefacts: Technology, usewear and residues. In J. Golson, T. P. Denham, P. J. Hughes, J. Muke, & P. Swadling (Eds.), *10,000 years of cultivation: Kuk Swamp and the history of agriculture in the Papua New Guinea Highlands* (pp. 373–402). Terra Australis 46. Canberra: ANU E Press.

Gaffney, D., & Summerhayes, G. R. (2018). Coastal mobility and lithic supply lines in northeast New Guinea. *Archaeological and Anthropological Sciences, 11*(6), 2849–2878.

Gagan, M., Hendy, E. J., Haberle, S. G., & Hantoro, W. S. (2004). Postglacial evolution of the Indo-Pacific warm pool and El Niño–Southern Oscillation. *Quaternary International, 118–119,* 127–143.

Golson, J. (1977). No room at the top: Agricultural intensification in the New Guinea highlands. In J. Allen, J. Golson, & R. Jones (Eds.), *Sunda and Sahul: Prehistoric studies in Southeast Asia, Melanesia and Australia* (pp. 601–638). London: Academic Press.

Gould, R. A. (1980). *Living archaeology.* New Studies in Archaeology. Cambridge: Cambridge University Press.

Greiser, S. T., & Sheets P. D. (1979). Raw materials as a functional variable in use-wear studies. In B. Hayden (Ed.), *Lithic use-wear analysis* (pp. 289–296). New York: Academic Press.

Harrison, R. (2006). An artefact of colonial desire? Kimberley points and the technologies of enchantment. *Current Anthropology, 47*(1), 63–88.

Hayden, B. (1977). Stone tool functions in the Western Desert. In R. V. S. Wright (Ed.), *Stone tools as cultural markers* (pp. 178–188). Prehistoric Material Culture Series 12. Canberra: Australian Institute of Aboriginal Studies; Atlantic Highlands, N.J.: Humanities Press.

Hiscock, P. (2008). *Archaeology of ancient Australia.* New York: Routledge.

Hiscock, P. (2006). Blunt and to the point: Changing technological strategies in Holocene Australia. In I. Lilley (Ed.), *Archaeology in Oceania: Australia and the Pacific Islands* (pp. 69–95). Oxford: Blackwell Publishing.

Hiscock, P. (2011). Point production at Jimede 2, Western Arnhem Land. In J. Specht & R. Torrence (Eds.), *Changing perspectives in Australian archaeology, part VI* (pp. 73–82). *Technical Reports of the Australian Museum, Online, 23*(6), 73–82.

Hiscock, P. (2009). Reduction, recycling and raw material procurement in Western Arnhem Land, Australia. In B. Adams & B. Blades (Eds.), *Lithic materials and Paleolithic societies* (pp.78–93). Oxford: Blackwell.

Hiscock, P. (1994a). Technological responses to risk in Holocene Australia. *Journal of World Prehistory, 8*(3), 267–292.

Hiscock, P. (1994b). The end of points. In A. Webb (Ed.), *Archaeology in the North* (pp. 72–83). North Australian Research Unit. Darwin: Australian National University.

Hiscock, P., & Maloney, T. (2017). Australian lithic technology: Evolution, dispersion and connectivity. In T. Hodos (Ed.), *Routledge handbook of archaeology and globalisation* (pp. 301–318). Abingdon, UK: Routledge.

Hiscock, P., & Veth, P. (1991). Change in the Australian desert culture: A reanalysis of tulas from Puntutjarpa. *World Archaeology, 22*, 332–345.

Holdaway, S., & Stern, N. (2004). *A record in stone: The study of Australia's flaked stone artefacts.* Canberra: Aboriginal Studies Press.

Kamminga, J. (1977). A functional study of use-polished Eloueras. In R. V. S. Wright (Ed.), *Stone tools as cultural markers* (pp. 205–212). Prehistoric Material Culture Series 12. Canberra: Australian Institute of Aboriginal Studies; Atlantic Highlands, N.J.: Humanities Press.

Kononenko, N., Specht, J., & Torrence, R., (2010). Persistent traditions in the face of natural disasters: Stemmed and waisted stone tools in late Holocene New Britain, Papua New Guinea. *Australian Archaeology 70*, 17–28.

Kononenko, N., Torrence, R., & Sheppard, P. (2016). Detecting early tattooing in the Pacific region through experimental usewear and residue analyses of obsidian tools. *Journal of Archaeological Science: Reports, 8*, 147–163.

Kononenko, N., Torrence, R., & White, P. (2015). Unexpected uses for obsidian: Experimental replication and use-wear/residue analyses of chopping tools. *Journal of Archaeological Science 54*, 254–269.

Kuhn, S. (1990). A geometric index of reduction for unifacial stone tools. *Journal of Archaeological Science, 17*, 585–593.

Kuhn, S. (1994). A formal approach to the design and assembly of mobile toolkits. *Antiquity, 59*(3), 426–442.

Kuhn, S. (2011). Are social and operational explanations incompatible? *Australian Archaeology, 72*, 70–71.

Kuhn, S. (2012). Emergent patterns of creativity and innovation in early technologies. In E. Scott (Ed.), *Origins of human innovation and creativity* (pp. 69–87). Developments in Quaternary Science 16. Amsterdam: Elsevier.

Lewis, A., Denham, T., & Golson, J. (2016). Renewed archaeological and archaeobotanical assessment of house sites at Kuk Swamp in the highlands of Papua New Guinea. *Archaeology in Oceania, 51*(1), 91–103.

Lilley, I. (2004). Trade and culture history across the Vitiaz Strait, Papua New Guinea. In V. Attenbrow & R. Fullagar, (Eds.), *A Pacific odyssey: Archaeology and anthropology in the western Pacific* (pp. 89–96). Papers in honour of Jim Specht. Records of the Australian Museum, 29.

Lourandos, H. (2008). Constructing 'hunter-gatherers', constructing 'prehistory'. *Australian Archaeology, 67*, 69–78.

Maloney, T. R. (2015). *Technological organisation and points in the southern Kimberley* (PhD thesis). Australian National University, Canberra.

Maloney, T. R. (2019). Towards quantifying teaching and learning in prehistory using stone artifact reduction sequences. *Lithic Technology, 44*(1), 36–51.

Maloney, T. R. (2020a). Retouched, rejuvenated, recycled and occasionally hafted as projectiles: Stone points of Holocene Australia. *Archaeology in Oceania, 55*(1), 42–56.

Maloney, T. R. (2020b). Experimental and archaeological testing with 3D laser scanning reveals the limits of I/TMC as a reduction index for global scraper and point studies. *Journal of Archaeological Science: Reports, 29*, 102068.

Maloney, T. R. (2020c). Kimberley points of Western Australia: Pressure flaking, projections and prestige. *Journal of Lithic Studies, 7*(1), 1–26.

Maloney, T. R., & Dilkes-Hall, I. E. (2020). Assessing the spread and uptake of tula adze technology in the late Holocene across the southern Kimberley of Western Australia. *Australian Archaeology, 86*(3), 264–283.

Maloney, T., O'Connor, S., & Balme, J. (2017). The effect of retouch intensity on Mid to Late Holocene unifacial and bifacial points from the Kimberley. *Australian Archaeology, 83*(2), 42–55.

Maloney, T. R., & Street, M. (2020). Hot debate: Identifying heat treatment in Australian archaeology using science and modern indigenous knowledge. *Quaternary Science Reviews, 241*(1), 106431.

Maloney, T., O'Connor, S., & Balme, J. (2014). New dates for point technology in the Kimberley. *Archaeology in Oceania, 49*, 137–147.

Maloney, T., Wood, R., O'Connor, S., & Whitau, R. (2015). Directly dated resin hafted stone technology in Australia: Points as composite tools in the mid Holocene. *Australian Archaeology, 81*(1), 35–43.

McGowan, H., Marx, S., Moss, P., & Hammond, A. (2012). Evidence of ENSO mega-drought triggered collapse of prehistory Aboriginal society in northwest Australia. *Geophysical Research Letters, 39*(22), L22702.

McNiven, I. (1993). Tula adzes and bifacial points on the east coast of Australia. *Australian Archaeology, 36*(1), 22–33.

McNiven, I. J., Crouch, J., Richards, T., Dolby, N., & Jacobsen, G. (2012). Dating Aboriginal stone-walled fish traps at Lake Condah, southeast Australia. *Journal of Archaeological Science, 39*(2), 268–286.

Moore, M. W. (2015). Bifacial flint knapping in the Northwest Kimberley, Western Australia. *Journal of Archaeological Method Theory, 22*(3), 913–951.

Moore, M. W. (2011). Simple stone flaking in Australasia: Patterns and implications. *Quaternary International, 285*, 140–149.

Moore, M. W. (2004). The tula adze: Manufacture and purpose. *Antiquity, 78*, 61–73.

Moy, C. M., Seltzer, G. O., Rodbell, D. T., & Anderson, A. M. (2002). Variability of El Niño/Southern Oscillation activity at millennial timescales during the Holocene epoch. *Nature, 420*(6912), 162–165.

Mulvaney, J., & Kamminga, J. (1999). *Prehistory of Australia*. Sydney: Allen and Unwin.

Nelson, M. C. (1991). The study of technological organisation. In M. B. Schiffer (Ed.), *Archaeological method and theory* (pp. 57–100). Princeton, NJ: University of Arizona.

Newman, K., & Moore, M. (2013). Ballistically anomalous stone projectile points in Australia. *Journal of Archaeological Science, 40,* 2614–2620.

O'Connor, S. (1999). *30,000 years of Aboriginal occupation: Kimberley, North West Australia.* Terra Australis 14. Canberra: ANU E Press.

O'Connor, S., Maloney, T., Vannieuwenhuyse, D., Balme, J., & Wood, R. (2014). Occupation at Carpenter's Gap 3, Windjana Gorge, Kimberley, Western Australia. *Australian Archaeology, 78,* 10–23.

Pavlides, C. (2004). From Missil cave to Eliva hamlet: Rediscovering the Pleistocene in interior West New Britain. In V. Attenbrow & R. A. Fullagar (Eds.), *Pacific odyssey: Archaeology and anthropology in the Western Pacific, papers in honour of Jim Specht* (pp. 97–108). Records of the Australian Museum, Supplement 29. Sydney: Australian Museum.

Pavlides, C. (1993). New archaeological research at Yombon, West New Britain, Papua New Guinea. *Archaeology in Oceania, 28,* 55–59.

Rath, P., & Torrence, R. (2003). Producing value: Stemmed tools from Garua Island, Papua New Guinea. *Australian Archaeology, 57,* 119–127.

Rein, B., Lückge, A., Reinhardt, L., Sirocko, F., Wolf, A., & Dullo, W. C. (2005). El Niño variability off Peru during the last 20,000 years. *Paleoceanography, 20*(4), PA4003.

Robertson, G., Attenbrow, V., & Hiscock, P. (2009). Multiple uses for Australian backed artefacts. *Antiquity, 83,* 296–308.

Rots, V. (2005). Wear traces and the interpretation of stone tools. *Journal of Field Archaeology, 30*(1), 61–73.

Rots, V., & Plisson, H. (2014). Projectiles and the abuse of the use-wear method in a search for impact. *Journal of Archaeological Science, 48,* 154–165.

Sheppard, P. J. (2010). Lapita stone tool technology. In C. Sand, S. Bedford, & C. Chambonniere (Eds.), *Lapita: Anc´etres Oceaniens/Oceanic ancestors* (pp. 240–250). Paris: Somogy.

Sillitoe, P., & Hardy, K. (2003). Hardy living lithics: Ethnoarchaeology in Highland Papua New Guinea. *Antiquity, 77*(297), 555–566.

Smith, A., McNiven, I. J., Rose, D., Brown, S., Johnson, C., & Crocker, S. (2019). Indigenous knowledge and resource management as World Heritage values: Budj Bim cultural landscape, Australia. *Archaeologies, 15,* 285–313.

Smith, M. A. (2013). *The archaeology of Australia's deserts.* New York: Cambridge University Press.

Specht, J. (2005). Obsidian stemmed tools in New Britain: Aspects of their role and value in mid- Holocene Papua New Guinea. In I. Macfarlane, R. Paton, & M. Mountain (Eds.), *Many exchanges: Archaeology, history, community and the work of Isabel McBryde* (pp. 373–392). Aboriginal History Monograph 11. Canberra: Australian National University.

Spry, C. (2011). Cache or refuse? A pitchstone artefact assemblage from Pamwak Rockshelter, Manus Island, Papua New Guinea. *The Artefact, 34,* 9–18.

Spry, C., & Stern, N. (2016). Technological organization. In J. L. Jackson (Ed.), *Oxford bibliographies in 'Anthropology'* (pp. 1–16). New York: Oxford University Press.

Stiner, M. C., & Kuhn, S. L. (2016). Are we missing the 'sweet spot' between optimality theory and niche construction theory in archaeology? *Journal of Anthropological Archaeology, 44*(B), 177–184.

Strathern, M. (1969). Stone axes and flake tools: Evaluations from two New Guinea Highland societies. *Proceedings of the Prehistoric Society, 35,* 311–329.

Summerhayes, G. R. (2019). The archaeology of Melanesia. In E. Hirsch & W. Rollason (Eds.), *The Melanseian world* (pp. 43–62). Abingdon, UK: Routledge.

Summerhayes, G. R. (2017). Island Southeast Asia and Oceania interactions. In J. Habu, P. V. Lape, & J. W. Olsen (Eds.), *Handbook of East and Southeast Asian archaeology* (pp. 659–673). New York: Springer.

Summerhayes, G. (2009). Obsidian network patterns in Melanesia—Sources, characterization and distribution. *Bulletin of the Indo-Pacific Prehistory Association, 29*, 110–124.

Summerhayes, G. R., Leavesley, M., Fairbairn, A. S., Mandui, H., Field, J., Ford, A., & Fullagar, R. (2010). Human adaptation and plant use in highland New Guinea 49,000 to 44,000 years ago. *Science, 330*, 78–81.

Tindale, N. B. (1965). Stone implement making among the Nakako, Ngadadjara, and Pitjandjara of the Great Western Desert. *Records of the South Australian Museum, 15*(1), 131–164.

Torrence, R. (1989). Re-tooling: Towards a behavioural theory of stone tools In R. Torrence (Ed.), *Time, energy and stone tools* (pp. 57–66). Cambridge: University of Cambridge Press.

Torrence, R. (1992). What is Lapita about obsidian? A view from the Talasea sources In J. C. Galipaud (Ed.), *Poterie Lapita et peuplement* (pp. 111–126). Noumea: ORSTOM.

Torrence, R. (2011). Finding the right question: Learning from stone tools on the Willaumez Peninsula, Papua New Guinea. *Archaeology in Oceania, 46*, 29–41.

Torrence, R. (2014). Social resilience and long-term adaptation to volcanic disasters: The archaeology of continuity and innovation in the Willaumez Peninsula, Papua New Guinea. *Quaternary International, 394*, 6–16.

Torrence, R., Kelloway, S., & White, P. (2013). Stemmed tools, social interaction, and voyaging in early-mid Holocene Papua New Guinea. *Journal of Island and Coastal Archaeology, 8*, 278–310.

Torrence, R., Kononenko, N., Sheppard, P., Allen, M. S., Bedford, S., Kirch, P., & Spriggs, M. (2018). Tattooing tools and the Lapita cultural complex. *Archaeology in Oceania, 53*, 58–73.

Torrence, R., Specht, J., & Fullagar, R. (1990). Pompeiis in the Pacific. *Australian Natural History, 23*, 457–463.

Torrence, R., & Swadling, P. (2008). Interaction spheres in Mid-Holocene and the spread of Lapita pottery. *Antiquity, 82*, 600–616.

Torrence, R., Swadling, P., Kononenko, N., Ambrose, W., Rath, P., & Glascock, M. D. (2009). Mid-Holocene social interaction in Melanesia: New evidence from hammer-dressed obsidian stemmed tools. *Asian Perspectives, 48*(1), 120–148.

Veitch, B. (1999). *What happened in the mid-Holocene? Archaeological evidence for change from the Mitchell Plateau, northwest Kimberley, Western Australia* (PhD thesis). University of Western Australia, Perth.

Veth, P., Hiscock, P., & Williams, A. (2011). Are tulas and ENSO linked in Australia? *Australian Archaeology, 72*, 7–14.

Wallis, L., & O'Connor, S. (1998). Residues on a sample of stone points from the west Kimberley. In R. Fullagar (Ed.), *A closer look: Recent studies of Australian stone tools* (pp. 150–178). Archaeological Sydney University Archaeology Methods Series 6. Sydney: Archaeological Computing Laboratory, School of Archaeology, University of Sydney.

Watson V. D. (1995). Simple and significant: Stone tool production in Highland New Guinea. *Lithic Technology, 20*(2), 89–99.

Weissner, P. (1982). Risk, reciprocity and social influences on Kung San economics. In E. Leacock & R. Lee (Eds.), *Politics and history in band societies* (pp. 61–84). Cambridge: Cambridge University Press.

White, J. P., Jacobsen, H., Kewibu, V., & Doelman, T. (2006). Obsidian traffic in the southeast Papuan islands. *Journal of Island and Coastal Archaeology 1*, 101–108.

White, J. P. (1967). Ethno-archaeology in New Guinea: Two examples. *Mankind, 6,* 409–414.

White, J. P., & Thomas, D. H. (1972). What mean these stones? In G. Clarke (Ed.), *Models in archaeology* (pp. 275–308). London: Methuen.

Williams, R. N., Wright, D., Crowther, A., & Denham, T. (2020). Multidisciplinary evidence for early banana (*Musa* cvs.) cultivation on Mabuyag Island, Torres Strait. *Nature Ecology and Evolution, 10*(4), 1342–1350.

Winterhalder, B., Lu, F., & Tucker, B. (1999). Risk sensitive adaptive tactics: Models and evidence from subsistence studies in biology and anthropology. *Journal of Archaeological Research, 7,* 330–348.

CHAPTER 26

SHELL VALUABLES AND EXCHANGE SYSTEMS IN NEW GUINEA

KATHERINE SZABÓ

INTRODUCTION

It is difficult to think about the archaeology of shell valuables and associated exchange systems in New Guinea without starting with, thinking through, and drawing upon ethnography. Local ethnographies are almost overwhelmingly rich with examples of shell objects as items of exchange or esteem, or the markers and facilitators of wealth, social bonds, and identity. Best known are the complex and composite necklaces and armshells associated with the *kula* exchange ring of the Massim (Leach & Leach 1983; Malinowski 1922; Munn 1986), the large Gold-lipped Pearl Oyster (*Pinctada maxima*) valves traded into the highlands where they were transformed into *kina* (e.g., Clark 1991; Strathern 1971), the *ndap* and *kê* of Rossel Island (e.g., Liep 2009), and the *tabu* shell money of the Tolai of East New Britain (e.g., Epstein 1968; Parkinson [1907] 2010). Yet these examples offer only the smallest window onto the diversity of shell valuables, and their functions, meanings, and trade across New Guinea.

Anthropologically, the creation, use, and movement of shell valuables make visible key social relationships among groups, individuals, and generations. Making such observations is trickier in archaeology where such relationships must be inferred rather than directly observed. Nevertheless, Pacific archaeology has been charged by anthropology (e.g., Thomas 2012) and often tasked itself (e.g., Kirch & Green 2001) with elucidating the genesis and development of social systems of the sorts that are made manifest and enabled by shell valuables. What are the histories and developmental contexts of shell money systems such as the *kula* and analogous trading networks or specialized centres of shell valuable production? For how long, and over what distances, have shell valuables or their raw materials been traded from coast to interior? Such questions have directly or indirectly underpinned the majority of archaeological inquiries into shell valuables in New Guinea.

Although there are threads of commonality, ethnographic cases vary in their structure, scale, and detail from place to place, with some cases drawing out particular aspects of long-standing interest to archaeologists. The nature of the trade in and use of marine shell in the highlands directly engages with structural relationships between coastal and inland areas, whereas the intensive production of shell valuables in particular locales speaks directly to questions of specialization in craft production. Given these variable issues, I will investigate the way in which shell valuables and the larger exchange systems into which they are embedded manifest across a range of distinct regions via key case studies. For each case study I will also assess how the nature of ethnographic expressions of social linkages have also been embedded into archaeological research agendas. The cases considered will be the trade of marine shell into the highlands of New Guinea, the production of shell valuables of the *kula* ring of the Massim and their antecedents, and the specialized production of beads utilized in the production of currency strands and other shell valuable types at centres on the south coast of New Guinea (see Figure 26.1). Together, these three case studies will form the basis of archaeologically focused reflections on the insights and obstacles of working closely with ethnographies.

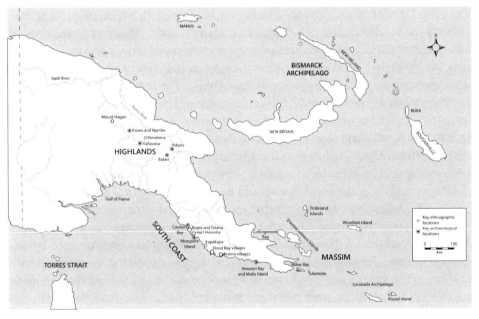

FIGURE 26.1. Map to show the major archaeological and ethnohistorical locations mentioned in the text.

'The Only and Natural Trade': Marine Shell Valuables in the New Guinea Highlands

The first things generally summoned to mind when thinking about shell valuables and their trade in the highlands and highland fringes of Papua New Guinea (PNG) are the striking Gold-lipped Pearl Oyster (*Pinctada maxima*) crescents and plaques so central to wealth and key social transactions.[1] These shells made visible the trade routes from the coast to the interior and then between highland communities, and were mobilized through performative display to accrue and cement influence (e.g., the *moka* discussed by Strathern 1971) (see Figure 26.2). Well-documented examples of highlands groups who imported pearl shells are the Melpa of the Western Highlands Province (e.g., Strathern 1971), the Enga of Enga Province (Feil 1982), and the Wola, Wiru, and Foi of the Southern Highlands Province (Clark 1991; Sillitoe 1979, 1988; Weiner 1988). The widespread recognition and significance of these objects led to the naming of PNG's legal tender after one of its cultural manifestations: *kina*.

Although *kina* are the most well-known of the highland shell valuables, they were neither the most common nor sometimes the most prized. Hughes's (1977) thorough ethnohistorical review of traded items noted (and often introduced) post-contact in the New Guinea highlands reveals a suite of marine shells represented in various combinations and quantities throughout the region. Depending on location, the most valuable shell taxa were the Egg Cowrie (*Ovula ovum*), the baler shell (*Melo* sp.), or the Gold-lipped Pearl Oyster, with the Egg Cowrie predominating in the more easterly zones (e.g., Benabena—Taylor in Hughes 1977: 53) and Gold-lipped Pearl Oyster predominating from the Chimbu River westward into Melpa territory (Hughes 1977: 54). These patterns of use do not appear to be strictly related to availability. According to Taylor, who accompanied the Leahy brothers in early expeditions in the region, those peoples immediately west of the Chimbu River had no interest in the Egg Cowries which were held in such esteem just to the east: 'The egg-cowrie was not to be seen and when offered was unwanted' (Hughes 1977: 54). On other occasions, the Leahy expedition found itself unable to barter for meat through having shells 'of the wrong type' (Hughes 1977: 55). The expedition also failed in its attempt to introduce *Rochia nilotica* [*Trochus niloticus*] as an exchange item to the region (Hughes 1977: 195).

While the most prized marine shell taxa varied from place to place, small cowries (the Money Cowrie *Monetaria moneta* and the gold-ring cowrie *M. annulus*) and diminutive dog whelks (*Nassarius* sp./spp.) were to be found throughout, although in varying quantities. Despite the ubiquity of cowries and dog whelks, the collated ethnohistorical accounts in Hughes (1977: 187–191 and Map 5) indicate that the two taxa followed different pathways into discrete parts of the highlands. These various routes were often reflected in clusters of related names for each shell taxon (Hughes 1977: 184). In most cases,

FIGURE 26.2. Tiki of the Ndika Roklamb wearing a pearl oyster *kina* at the preliminary practice for a *moka* ceremonial exchange near Togoba, Western Highlands (1967). Photograph by M. Strathern. Reproduced by permission of the University of Cambridge Museum of Archaeology and Anthropology (accession number N.132836.MST).

both shell taxa were recognized as the oldest types of imports, and in all but one case, the introduction of cowries antedated that of dog whelks (Hughes 1977: 189).

It is clear that the introduction of large numbers of marine shells into the highlands from the 1930s onwards had a profound impact on local economies, and that the pervasiveness of shell wealth noted throughout the anthropological studies of later decades pivots in large part on this postcontact boom (Gaffney, Summerhayes, Szabo, & Koppel 2019; Hughes 1978). However, as pointed out by Hughes (1977: 45), from the latter part of the nineteenth century through until 1910, coastal peoples of southern PNG were permitted to take part in the pearling industry in the Torres Strait Islands to the southwest. This involvement may have facilitated the movement of pearl oyster and baler shell through local trade networks, even into the highlands (see also Swadling 2010 for interesting insights into trade routes). Thus, European economic activity could have started to impact upon highland trade and social networks decades prior to the arrival of Taylor and the Leahy brothers in the 1930s. Therefore, we must look to archaeology in order to understand the precontact presence, scale, and role of traded marine shells in the highlands.

Although the archaeological record of the highlands stretches back over 40,000 years, marine shell has not been recovered in Pleistocene deposits. Early to Mid-Holocene deposits in inland and highland areas of New Guinea have revealed sporadic examples of marine shell, although numbers are typically low. Small cowries are the most frequent shell taxon recorded, with the earliest examples being several *Monetaria moneta* from the rock shelter site of Kafiavana in the Eastern Highlands (White 1972). Chronological resolution is not tight, but the shells date to between 6000 and 9000 years ago. This antiquity is supported in part by the recovery of another example from Kafiavana (excavated by Cole), estimated to date to around 10,000 years ago (Huff 2016 in Gaffney et al. 2019). This estimation, however, is based on correlations with White's layers and radiocarbon dates, so it does not offer independent corroboration. More recent layers at Kafiavana, dating to the Mid-Holocene (>4690±170 BP), contained an expanded set of taxa, including *Oliva* sp. and *Nassarius* sp., along with *M. moneta* (White 1972: 93).

Kafiavana is part of a broader archaeological signal across much of the highlands where an increasing number and diversity of marine shells appear within the past 5000 years. At Nombe rock shelter, in Simbu Province, very fragmentary pieces of pearl shell occur in a major cultural layer dated to c. 10,400–6300 cal BP (see Denham & Mountain 2016 for confirmation of the site's chronology). For the uppermost layer dating to the past 2000 years, *Monetaria annulus* cowries are present alongside *Pinctada maxima* pearl oyster (Denham & Mountain 2016; Mountain 1991). Less clearly identified marine shell is also present at Batari, in the vicinity of Kafiavana, from around 3000 years ago, but includes a piece of naturally tubular *Dentalium* shell (White 1972: 22). Late Holocene deposits at Ritamauda site in Enga Province include *Monetaria annulus*, various nassarid dog whelks, and *Oliva carneola* from around 3500–3000 years ago, *Pinctada maxima* from around 2000–3000 years ago, and utilitarian estuarine bivalves imported for tool use around 3500 years ago (Swadling & Anamiato 1989).

Within the last thousand years, a range of marine shell taxa, including *Rochia nilotica* (previously known as *Trochus niloticus*), *Monetaria moneta*, the Egg Cowrie *Ovula ovum*, the trumpet shell *Charonia tritonis*, and olivid and nassarid shells were recovered from the upper (~800-year-old) occupation levels of Aibura cave in the Eastern Highlands (White 1972). Recent reanalysis of material originally excavated by Bulmer from Kiowa (Bulmer 1964, 1966; Gaffney et al. 2019) has revealed a pattern similar to that noted by Swadling and Anamiato (1989) for Ritamauda. That is, the introduction of marine bivalves utilized as tools followed by marine shell for adornment only in the most recent deposits. The Kiowa marine shells are represented by the estuarine bivalves *Geloina expansa* (previously known as *Polymesoda/Geloina erosa*) and *Tegillarca granosa* (synonym: *Anadara granosa*), as well as a fragment of *Rochia nilotica* ring, all likely dating to within the last thousand years (Gaffney et al. 2019).

Although patchy with often somewhat broadly defined chronologies, the archaeological record of marine shell importation to the highlands clearly shows that there is considerable antiquity to the trade (and intensifying over the past 3000 years), and that the species encountered largely align with those of notable prominence in the anthropological and historical literature. We already know that the European-mediated spike in the supply of marine shells had a significant impact on highland cultures, and wealth and trade systems, such that the 'ethnographic present' is an expression of postcontact changes (see especially Hughes 1978). How, then, do we assess the nature or degree of potential connectedness between the ethnographic and archaeological records? How far can imported marine shells of the more distant past be construed as 'valuables' or even 'currency'? Combined with the other case studies, I will return to these questions later.

'EPHEMERAL, NEW OR PRECARIOUS'? THE *KULA* RING AND ARCHAEOLOGY OF THE MASSIM

Of all the New Guinea shell valuable systems described by anthropologists, the *kula* is the most iconic.[2] A staple of undergraduate anthropology courses worldwide, its renown also comes via its status as one of the foundational studies of modern 'participant-observer' anthropology deriving from long-term embedded fieldwork (e.g., Malinowski 1922). Taking in a suite of islands and archipelagos off the southeastern tip of the New Guinea mainland (Milne Bay Province, also known anthropologically as the Massim region), two high-status types of shell valuables circulate in a loop around the island nodes in opposing directions: the *soulava* or *bagi* and the *mwali*. Known as *soulava* in the northern Massim and *bagi* in the south, this valuable comprises a strand of typically red shell disc beads manufactured from *Chama* and/or *Spondylus* shell, with other largely standardized shells attached (Liep 1981; Malinowski 1922). *Mwali* are armrings produced from *Conus* shells with a lashed attachment containing combinations of other shells, beads, and nutshells (Kuehling 2005; Malinowski 1922) (Figure 26.3). Alongside the *soulava* and *mwali*, other more utilitarian goods circulated, including foodstuffs and practical items such as earthenware pottery. Through the giving of valuables to established trading partners, a delayed reciprocity system was sustained whereby men could accrue prestige through holding, gifting, and receiving valuables, and increasing their network of trading partners. Although the literature is generally focussed on trading and status of men, key work by Weiner (1976) has explored the important role of women. A century's worth of literature has explored the intricacies and complexities of the *kula* (e.g., Leach & Leach 1983; Mauss [1923–24] 1990; Munn 1986; and very many more),

FIGURE 26.3. *Mwali* from the Massim. Donated by A. von Hügel to the Museum of Archaeology and Anthropology, University of Cambridge. Reproduced by permission of the University of Cambridge Museum of Archaeology and Anthropology (accession Z9342).

and it is unsurprising that one of anthropology's archetypal case studies has prompted questions about the history and development of the *kula*.

Malinowski saw the broad configuration of the *kula* as consistent with a deep-time history and did not believe that a network of such size and complexity, with such intricate magical rites and founding mythology, could arise over the short term (Malinowski 1922: 510). Subsequent research in both anthropology and archaeology, however, has made clear that this conclusion was, to a greater or lesser degree, spurious: the *kula*, its geography, and its core circulating items have expanded, contracted, realigned, been substituted, waxed, and waned continuously over the recent past. Swadling and Bence (2016) draw together historical information from early written accounts, photographs, and museum collections to demonstrate that the rise to prominence of *mwali Conus* armshells happened just prior to Malinowski's fieldwork in the Trobriands in the 1910s. Specifically, *Conus* armshells filled a void left by a prior major class of valuable constructed of circular boar's tusks termed *doga*. *Doga* had progressively left the *kula*, flowing westwards along the southern coast to Port Moresby, where their value in local exchange systems stimulated the production of *Chama* or *Spondylus* shell disc beads used for the production of *soulava* and/or the slightly less fine and non-*kula katudababile* strings then used in the Massim.

In contrast to the work of Swadling and Bence (2016), Irwin, Shaw, & McAlister's (2019) consideration of the origins of the *kula* barely mentions shell valuables beyond an historical recap. Instead, they focus their attentions on the expansions, contractions, and 'leakiness' of the network, as well as periods of connectedness to the north and south mainland coasts evident via shared earthenware pottery styles (see also Egloff 1978). Unlike Swadling and Bence's (2016) concentration on the half century leading up to Malinowski's 1910s fieldwork, Irwin et al. (2019) move through a >2500-year sweep of evidence for regional interconnections from Late Lapita through to what is generally identified as Early Papuan Pottery (EPP) albeit in a localized Massim style they term 'Southern Massim Pottery' (SMP). A roughly analogous approach is taken by Ambrose et al. (2012) in their consideration of elaborately carved *Conus* shells deriving from the Collingwood Bay area but spread across the northern Massim as far as Budibudi Atoll east of Woodlark Island. A series of thirty-two carved *Conus* from a variety of locations clearly match Collingwood Bay art styles visible on ceramics and wood carvings. The *Conus* objects have been radiocarbon dated to Egloff's (1979) 'Expansion Phase' (c. 1000–500 BP), a period characterized by increased archaeological activity (i.e., presence and visibility of archaeological materials) as well as geographical reach (Ambrose et al. 2012; Egloff 1979).

Swadling and Bence's (2016) study is much more closely tied into the minutiae of the *kula* than more standard archaeological approaches, and indeed, as they acknowledge, their approach draws strongly on historical documentation, along with detailed analysis of museum objects, which is akin to that which would be applied to an 'archaeological surface collection' (Swadling & Bence 2016: 2). Although they stress linkages and dynamism in trading and social networks, their focus is on the specific nature of the *kula* itself. In contrast, Egloff (1978, 1979), Ambrose et al. (2012), and Irwin et al. (2019) take a more strictly archaeological approach to *kula* origins and development. Here, the *kula* is construed implicitly or explicitly as a particular constellation of variables in space and time; an ethnographic node in a much longer timeline of expansions, contractions, and reconfigurations in trading and interaction networks. In this guise, and despite its ethnographic fame, the *kula* is conceived of as a trade network akin to any other. Shaw and Langley (2017: 149) in their study of Massim shell artefacts are explicit about this formulation when they say that accounts of traditional exchange such as the *hiri* or *kula* 'often formed an analytical foundation as an "ethnographic endpoint" for archaeological models'.[3] Their study, too, follows this approach, and archaeological shell artefacts across several hundred years are explicitly interpreted within a *kula* valuable (ethnographically conceived) framework.

Taking the 'ethnographic endpoint' as a starting point, and viewing the *kula* as a fair representation of a New Guinea trade network moving prosaic and prestige goods, it is a short step to apply it as a framework for interpretation deeper in time and translocated in space. Leading Pacific archaeologist Patrick Kirch (1988, 1991) has done precisely this with the application of *kula*-based ideas to Lapita assemblages (c. 3300–2700 BP), and it is worth quoting his stance in full:

> Lapita assemblages also contain a variety of shell objects usually classified as beads, pendants, bracelet segments, rings, and similar descriptive categories under the

general rubric 'ornaments'. However, virtually every single one of these artefact classes has direct ethnographic equivalents that functioned as valued items of exchange. Indeed, as the classic shell armrings (*mwali*) and necklaces (*soulava*) of the *kula* network illustrate (Malinowski 1922; Leach & Leach 1983), shell valuables were *frequently the most prestigious* objects of exchange in a given network, and the focus of political intrigue and ritual effort. Since virtually every one of the Lapita archaeological shell object classes has formal equivalents in ethnographically-documented exchange valuables, it is surprising that Oceanic archaeologists have neglected these objects in the context of Lapita prestige-good exchange.

(Kirch 1988: 107–108)

There is a lot to unpack in Kirch's quote. Lapita assemblages, and particularly the Early Lapita assemblages of the Bismarck Archipelago of northeast PNG, incontrovertibly have large and diverse assemblages of shell artefacts. Many of these assemblages also have similar forms, or utilize the same raw materials, as ethnographically known shell valuables deriving from elsewhere in New Guinea. But the next inferential step is more vexed. Can this similarity be translated to direct ethnographic equivalence? If so, can we assume then that Lapita peoples operated a prestige-good exchange network analogous to ethnographic structures? Kirch, of course, expects none of this to be taken at face value and provides a data-driven assessment of Lapita shell artefacts from a sweep of major sites. Acknowledging that the movement of artefacts from centres of production to locations of consumption is needed to establish the presence of a trading network, Kirch (1988) assessed archaeological evidence for production only against evidence for the presence of finished artefacts. The identification of a relatively small number of production centres compared to the number of consumption sites was seen to be consistent with a trade network. While the evidence available at the time supported this interpretation, the excavation of new sites, and the re-excavation and reanalysis of classic sites, has revealed new data patterns and different interpretations. Analysis of the old and new data by Szabó (2018a) revealed evidence of shell artefact production at nearly all sites, with the only divergent pattern noted for Fiji. These data do not lend themselves to an interpretation of centralized production and trade, but, as with Lapita pottery (Summerhayes 2000), suggest a dominant pattern of localized production and consumption.

Whether or not a case for specialized production and exchange in shell valuables can be sustained for Lapita remains to be seen. However, a broader issue exists in the form of the viability of the *kula*-as-model in Pacific archaeology. Here the concern is the detachment of ethnographically observed phenomena such as the *kula* from their historical context, and the ensuing development of abstracted exchange models to be applied globally across different cultures, time periods, and classes of material. This problem is amply demonstrated by a range of international studies which draw upon the *kula* to frame discussions of Mycenaean exchange networks (Voutsaki 1997), British Bronze Age traders (van der Noort 2006), and Bronze Age economies more generally (Earle 2002), to name just a few.

The *Hiri* of Coastal Central and Gulf Provinces: 'Their Object Is to Trade, Not for More Pots, but for Shell Ornaments'

The *kula* of the Massim has important linkages with the *hiri* of the Port Moresby area and the Gulf of Papua to the west.[4] *Hiri* voyages, as recorded in the early years of European colonization, moved earthenware pots produced in the Port Moresby area west to a series of Gulf villages in exchange primarily for sago, although many other items were moved as part of the trade (see Barton 1910; Seligmann 1910: chapter 7). The Western Motu of the Port Moresby area live in a rain shadow, meaning that agricultural production was often mercurial. As such, trade in manufactured goods for foodstuffs seems to have been, to some degree, based on economic imperative. Oram (1982: 10–11) provides supporting evidence for this relationship, outlining that although *hiri* trading expeditions could take place annually, records suggest that in years of good harvest the Motu *hiri* voyages did not proceed (Oram 1982: 10–11, 26–27). Oram (1982: 11) also points out that the *hiri* voyages could be hindered by warfare.

Shell valuables were traded alongside the pots, including (but not necessarily limited to) high-value *toea Conus* armshells, *mairi* crescent-shaped pearl oyster necklaces, and whole pearl oyster valves, along with *tautau Nassarius* dog whelk necklaces (Barton 1910: 109; Seligmann 1910: 93). The majority of Motu villages around Port Moresby specialized in the production of a range of earthenware pottery vessels (for collated references and descriptions of vessel types, see Skelly & David 2017: 26–32). Pottery vessels were produced and owned by women (Groves 1960). Two other villages, Vabukori and Tatana, focussed their efforts on *ageva* red shell bead production (Barton 1910: 114; but see also Swadling & Bence 2016).

While the *hiri* is centred on the Western Motu and coastal villages to the west, generations of scholars have observed and unpicked connections and goods moving predominantly east, linking diverse peoples and places. The close relationship between the Motu and Koita seems to have served to enhance trading connections and access to goods, and Seligmann (1910: 92) itemizes a range of trading partners and items traded along the c. 140 km-long stretch of coast between Port Moresby and Hood Bay in the east (see also Skelly et al. 2018). Whilst list of exchanged goods varied from place to place, there is an overall pattern of *toea* armshells, *tautau* dog whelk valuables, and diverse foodstuffs (yams, coconuts, bananas, betel nut) being traded westwards into Motu-Koita hands, and *ageva* shell beads, sago, and pottery being distributed eastwards in return (Seligmann 1910: 93). Beyond Hood Bay, maritime trade was picked up by the Mailu, who traded at least 125 km west to the Aroma coast and eastwards to the fringes of the Milne Bay area (Irwin 1985: 15–18) (see also McNiven, Coral Sea Cultural Interaction Sphere, this volume).

If we hone in on shell valuables, it is apparent that the goods produced in any given specialist centre were being distributed in multiple directions to serve different ends, and that the bulk of objects such as *toea* utilized in *hiri* trading were amassed from a number of original sources. Oram (1982: 13) states that *toea* were 'obtained from limited local manufacture, especially at Boera, and from the Hood Bay area', while Seligmann (1910: 93) outlines *toea* being obtained in trade with locations to the southeast of Port Moresby including, sequentially, Gaile [Gaire], Kapakapa [Gabagaba], Hula and Kerepunu (Hood Bay), and Aroma. He further states that the *toea* and shell beads acquired in Hula and Aroma came either from the Mailu or from further east via the Mailu (Seligmann 1910: 93). Oram (1982: 19) elaborates on the trading connections between Hood Bay and the Motu, outlining that the Keapara of Hood Bay acquired *Conus* armshells via kinship ties with the Maopa (of Aroma) in trade for pigs. The Aroma themselves are said to have acquired the armshells from Mailu traders in return for the pigs which were used in Mailu affinal exchanges. What tangles such as this may mean for exchange archaeology is explored towards the end of this chapter.

With a squarely material focus in trying to understand trade networks, and the social structures they generated and supported in reticulate fashion, a range of archaeologists have taken hold of these ethnographic leads and explored them in greater depth. Foundational studies of Motu archaeology logically focussed on earthenware pottery sequences in trying to delineate patterns of Motuan and Gulf economy and trade through time, and the early key work of Allen, Bulmer, Vanderwal, and Swadling is usefully summarized in Skelly and David (2017). However, as the focus here is on shell valuables, Allen's work at Motupore is of singular relevance.

At Motupore Island in Bootless Bay, located 16 km to the southeast of Port Moresby, excavations by Allen and colleagues over a series of seasons and years produced large archaeological assemblages of pottery, shell beads, and other classes of material dated to c. 1200 CE (for the most comprehensive overview of findings, see Allen 2017). A total of 440 shell disc beads, of both a smaller, regular type ($n = 371$) and a larger more irregular type ($n = 69$) were recovered from the combined excavation seasons (Allen 2017: 428–429). With abundant evidence of stone drill tips, grinding stones, and beads at various stages in their manufacture, it is clear that Motupore Island was a site at which formalized shell bead production was undertaken (Allen, Holdaway, & Fullagar 1997; Allen 2017: 432–5). Although thought is given to molluscan raw materials, and the small, regular beads are explicitly called *ageva* throughout Allen (2017), the species worked is/are not identified. In their discussion of *ageva* beads, Swadling and Bence (2016) reveal how useful raw material identification can be in untangling narratives of shell bead manufacture and use. Szabó (2018b, 2019) demonstrates how the identification of disc beads—even when strung—is very often possible based on surface textures and the arrangement of microstructures in cross-section.

Overall, it is rather surprising how little attention has been given to shell valuables by archaeologists working along the central and southeast coast given their pervasive and weighty presence in the ethnographic literature on the *hiri* and beyond.[5] The Motupore material at least is interpreted as being an earlier expression of the *hiri* trade, and indeed Allen (2017: 440) explicitly links the various shell artefact classes represented archaeologically to 'ethnographic equivalents'. Despite the analytical short shrift given to worked shell beyond the beads, Allen's (2017: 610) summation draws out the potential dialectic between ceramics and shell valuables in the *hiri* and Melanesian maritime trading systems more generally. In discussing the dichotomy between the anthropological focus on the social side of exchange versus the archaeological focus on the pragmatics of subsistence and utilitarian goods, Allen (2017: 610) states that '[i]t is clear that most or all of the Melanesian maritime trading systems combine elements of both'. It is worth quoting in full where he takes this idea:

> What is clear is that the Motu exchange of pots facilitated the spread of (particularly shell) valuables to groups where they played central roles in local ceremonial activities. Some of these valuables were made on Motupore, but many likely came from further east into the Bootless Bay entrepôt. But in order to access these valuables people further west and inland had to 'buy' pots. Each class of goods provided a conduit for the other.
>
> (Allen 2017: 610)

Only systematic, detailed studies of worked shell from regional sites will allow us to start to explore this fascinating direction, and it is hoped that material from the numerous sites recently sampled at Caution Bay immediately west of Port Moresby, and other locations to the east (e.g., Hood Bay) and west (e.g., Papuan Gulf), will start to facilitate this understanding.

ETHNOGRAPHY AS CATALYST, SOURCEBOOK, AND STRUCTURING DEVICE

When a regional anthropology draws out so fulsomely the rich and important nature of specialized production and exchange, and indeed the central role of material goods in the development and maintenance of social systems, it is hardly surprising that archaeologists would see the opportunity to value-add in this arena where evidence is tangible and available to them. Exactly how archaeologists have proceeded in their investigations of the presence, development, or identification of antecedent exchange systems is variable, as are the classes of evidence which have been privileged in considerations.

Pottery has been the material mainstay of the archaeology of the south coast, taking in the geographical extent of the *hiri* network (e.g., Allen & Rye 1982; Bickler 1997; David et al. 2012; Skelly & David 2017; Vanderwal 1978), through the Mailu trading sphere

(Irwin 1985), and into the Massim stretching around to Collingwood Bay (Egloff 1978, 1979; Irwin et al. 2019). Whether through sourcing, typologies, seriation, or radiocarbon chronologies, stability and change in pottery forms have been plotted through time with sequences sometimes extending over several thousand years.

The other key class of material to receive (somewhat lesser) archaeological focus along the south coast has been obsidian. Its status as a high-value traded material combined with highly refined scientific techniques for establishing sources, has meant that studies of obsidian distributions have been pivotal to assessing the extent and nature of trade connections (e.g., Irwin 1991; Summerhayes & Allen 2007; see also Mialanes et al. 2016).

In all of these pottery and obsidian studies, there is a connection made to an ethnographic trade system—whether *hiri*, *kula*, or the intermediaries at Mailu/Amazon Bay system. This is most frequently step-wise through changing pottery styles. Thus, ethnographic systems are generally seen as the culmination of long-standing trading systems; their development can therefore be tracked through time via the goods that circulate within them. Shaw (2019: 1), from a Massim perspective, states:

> Archaeological research in the Massim has been heavily influenced by anthropological cultural accounts which have provided a historical framework for understanding the deeper past. Because of this, research has predominantly contributed to our understanding of when, how, and why regionally distinct maritime-focused cultural identities developed, including the origins of ethnographically recorded trade networks and social systems.

With specific regards to shell valuables, Allen (2017) refers to the small beads from Motupore as *ageva*, indirectly drawing a straight line from the ethnographic present to the archaeological past. Shaw and Langley (2017) explicitly interpret archaeological shell artefacts from the Massim in an ethnographic framework, often using ethnography as a sort of 'sourcebook' to confer interpretation and meaning based on visual similarities between ethnographic and archaeological shell objects. Drawing attention to this approach is not to say that any particular conclusion drawn via ethnographic analogy is necessarily inaccurate per se. It is rather that the more such correlations are pushed back in time, the more tenuous the assumptions for constancy in use and meaning become, and the more we are potentially missing an opportunity to see change and dynamism through the course of history.

Taking a step back, it seems that exactly what one believes to be the origin point of the *kula* or *hiri* (or equivalent system) depends on what line of archaeological evidence one decides to track, and what one decides to track depends upon what one conceives the *kula* or equivalent, at its core, to be. If it is believed to be a trading system at its essential heart, evidence of trade from far remoter times will be the salient proof required. Regional archaeologists realize that more nuance is vital. Allen (2017: 610) points out that archaeologists have focussed on the economic dimensions of exchange systems whilst anthropologists have emphasized social aspects, but that both lines of insight are necessary and valid. Gosden (1986) argues that New Guinea economies and societies of the ethnographic present are structured as economies of debt, where gift-giving and reciprocal exchange bind groups together, and that trade items and circulating valuables must be understood within this social context. He applies this perspective to the archaeological evidence from the recent past at Mailu, but then proceeds to a crucial second step: a consideration of the earlier ceramic record for Mailu and the south coast Early Papuan Pottery (EPP), which seems to present a picture of a rather different socioeconomic formation. Here, pottery is without regional distinction and seems to be locally produced and unspecialized, but there is evidence for an expansive trade in obsidian which is rarer or absent in later periods (Gosden 1986: 186). Gosden (1986: 186) further observes that this pattern in the early ceramic phase along the south coast does not seem to be unique and has an analogue in Lapita sites in the Bismarck Archipelago and beyond. While Skelly and David (2017: 526) note that aspects of Gosden's (1986) argument must be rethought in light of subsequent research, his critique remains important for what it attempted to do. That is, to conceptualize, theorize, and model what an entirely different system of production may look like to allow us to assess systemic change through time. Although argued differently, similar points are made by Summerhayes and Allen (2007) using a spectrum of evidence for both the south coast and Lapita (see also Skelly & David 2017; Lilley 1987 for the Vitiaz Strait trade system; and Szabó 2018a for Lapita shell artefacts more broadly).

A final point that is often mentioned, and nearly as often falls from view, is the necessity to account for potential colonial disruption to cultural practices, even from the point of first European contact. Numerous studies have demonstrated that exchange systems witnessed and recorded ethnographically were rapidly and dramatically transformed as a result of European colonial contact. For example, Hughes (1978) discusses the significant impact of the colonial flooding of the shell valuable market in the highlands, and of the *hiri*, Oram (1982: 23) says:

> In considering the hiri in 1870, the post-contact changes which occurred afterwards must constantly be borne in mind. The establishment of internal peace led to a radical expansion of trading activities. There is no record of exchanges between the Eastern and Western Motu in the earliest ethnographic accounts, but these developed in post-contact times. The Mailu, who in pre-contact times had not ventured further west than Maopa, regularly began to take armshells to the Western Motu area and, as noted, the Orokolo people began to make return journeys in the 1920s.

While peace could bring enhanced opportunities for safe movement and contact, Irwin et al. (2019: 14) draw on the work of Macintyre (1983) in the Massim to make the important point that significant numbers of shell valuables changed hands during wartime as part of appeasement ceremonies, and the traffic at those times was potentially greater than during the normal transactions of the *kula*.

Looking to the Ethnohistorical Record for More Than Structure and Direct Analogy

Understanding the various roles that shell artefacts may have played in local, regional, and trans-regional exchange systems in New Guinea through time requires assembling a range of archaeological data. Most obvious is accurate documentation of assemblage components and contextual chronostratigraphies, along with secure identification of shell taxa and processes of cultural (and taphonomic) modification. In addition, thought must be given to how shell 'valuables' can be identified without straightforwardly invoking direct ethnographic analogy (a technique which runs the risk of flattening the very history we are trying to elucidate). For example, at what point in its history of production did a *Conus* ring in the Massim become a *mwali*? One hundred years ago? Five hundred? Over three thousand years ago with Lapita? What does it even mean to be a *mwali* rather than any other sort of broad *Conus* ring? These questions require thought, and the answers require analytical and interpretive tools. The regional ethnographic record does indeed provide a tantalizing sourcebook, but an approach more akin to that of Swadling and Bence (2016) with a focus on the detail of the record rather than its general shape may provide some instructive food for thought. Here, I extract just a handful of examples from the ethnohistorical record that serve to confirm, complicate, or challenge standard archaeological assumptions.

Three core go-to lines of evidence for the identification of shell 'valuables' are most visible in the New Guinea archaeological literature: (1) evidence for specialization in production, (2) the degree of working applied, sometimes expressed as labour invested, and (3) the degree of 'exoticism' or distance from the original source. These three lines of evidence are not necessarily mutually exclusive and are often combined in interpretations. Allen (2017; see also Allen et al. 1997) combines evidence from 1 and 2 to make a convincing case for the specialized production of shell beads at Motupore, although the status and extent of *Conus* and *Conomurex luhuanus* working is less clear (Allen 2017; Swadling 2017). As discussed earlier, the argument for specialized trade shell valuable production within Early Lapita sites (Kirch 1988, 1991) remains to be clearly demonstrated with local production and consumption appearing to be the norm (Szabó 2018a).

Overall, while it seems reasonable to assume that intensive, dedicated investment of labour translated to value, either absolute or relative measures of value are harder to quantify. Various early historical texts attempt to provide measures of equivalence to convey the relative or absolute values of particular items (e.g., both Schneider 1905 and Lewis 1929 for shell money). However, in the intervening century or more, we can safely assume that the values of all considered items have shifted. In the case of the *hiri*, Oram (1982: 25) recounted the attempts of Barton to investigate allegations of 'alleged extortion by the Motuans' during *hiri* expeditions. Barton, using a logic based upon labour investment, tried to reconcile the value of sago against wood for canoe hulls and pigs, but eventually gives up stating that 'It is next to impossible, on a European standard, to estimate the value set by natives on this or that article' (Barton 1902–1903 cited in Oram 1982: 25).

The subtle manoeuvring in the acquisition (and redistribution) of wealth is well attested by Parkinson ([1907] 2010) and others for the Tolai of East New Britain, and is fundamental to the processes through which prestige was acquired through the various exchange systems elsewhere in New Guinea (Parry 1989: 86). This social dimension of wealth acquisition in itself implies that value cannot be reduced to calculations of labour input. Nevertheless, archaeological research on shell valuables has made it clear that (at least in a Lapita context) shell artefacts which were more difficult or labour intensive to produce also tended to be the ones which were kept in circulation the longest via mending and remodelling. This curation has been discussed and demonstrated in the case of Lapita *Conus* rings, where the broad rings which were technically trickier and more time-consuming to produce were routinely reshaped and reutilized when broken, whereas the relatively easily produced narrow *Conus* rings were discarded upon breakage (Szabó 2005, 2010, 2018a). The only type of narrow ring regularly refashioned and kept in use was the fully ground and labour-intensive version produced in *Tridacna* giant clam (Szabó 2005). Rath and Torrence (2003) provide another example which is analogous in some respects, demonstrating that the care, complexity, and expertise needed for the production of obsidian stemmed tools in West New Britain contributed to their status as valuables (see Maloney this volume).

Exoticism or rarity is another signifier of inherent value commonly used by regional archaeologists, and this measure of value is easily applied to any evidence of precontact marine shell in the New Guinea highlands (e.g., see Gaffney et al. 2019). Feil (1984) sees rarity as behind the high value of pearl oysters in the highlands, and while this is surely an element, rarity in itself is insufficient to explain the esteem in which these shells were held by various highland societies (Clark 1991). As outlined by Hughes (1977), marine shells (e.g., *Ovula ovum*—Hughes 1977: 191) held to be of high value in some areas of the highlands were completely rejected as trade items in others. Clearly, selection of trade items represented a subjective value judgement. As argued time and time again in anthropological studies, trade/exchange objects and materials do not have an innate, essential value perceived equally by all, but rather are evaluated and appropriated into local cultural systems based on assessments of usefulness and thoughts about the cultural role they may play (e.g., see Ingold 2000; Kroeber 1948: 258; Thomas 1991). This subjectiveness does not mean that rarities or novel objects will not be accepted, kept, or even treasured, but they are likely to hold little currency in exchange and display unless an agreed value has been socially conferred upon them.

A key implication of the cultural integration of trade goods and raw materials is that the meaning and use of each object/material is likely to be variable in different locations. Swadling (1994: 142 drawing on Crittendon 1982) states:

From the Torres Strait pearl shell crescents and pearl shell sliver artifacts were traded to the people of the Trans Fly and to the Papuan Gulf. The communities in the Trans Fly and Middle Fly River regions seem to have considered pearl shells as no more than ornaments. This was not the case with the pearl shell crescents and slivers which were traded up the Kikori and Sirebi rivers, over the slopes of Mount Murray to Samberighi, to the Erave area of the Southern Highlands and thence to the upper Wahgi.

Swadling and Bence (2016) also draw out the relative values of *doga* circular boar-tusk pendants originating in the Massim and their role as a key valuable within the *kula* just prior to Malinowski's fieldwork. As they fell out of use in the *kula*, *mwali* cone shell valuables were elevated in status, and the *doga* were siphoned off into the Motu-Koita trade circles in the Port Moresby area. Here they rapidly became an esteemed valuable central to customary payments and transactions by the time of the Cooke Daniels Ethnographical Expedition to British New Guinea in 1903–1904 (Swadling & Bence 2016: 4). Key take-away points from these two examples are that similar-looking objects can mean different things, hold different values, and function very differently from one society to the next, and that valuables can ascend and descend the value hierarchy rapidly. These are important ethnographic lessons to keep in mind when transposing *kula* specifics to Lapita sites removed in both space and time, or even across several hundred years in places such as the Massim or South Coast.

An additional point is instructively ambiguous and derives from assessments of pearl shell from the historical and anthropological literature on the highlands. The condition of shells appears to be an important criterion in assessing value in some locales, with Hughes (1978: 312–313) outlining that pearl oysters transported in from Manus were considered too worm-eaten to be of value. However, Sillitoe (1979: 143) makes a point of saying that '[i]f a shell is good, wormholes do not detract to any serious extent from its value' in the context of the Wola of the Southern Highlands. As such, we cannot assume a priori that the condition of a shell necessarily feeds into its perceived value.

A final point on which the historical record is instructive speaks to the relative locations of the making and using of objects. It is often assumed in the New Guinea archaeological literature that people will not import a particular class of artefact if they manufacture the same type of object. Indeed, Allen (2017: 604) says this explicitly in the context of pottery: 'It can be assumed that it was the food contents in these pots that was being exchanged rather than the pots themselves, since giving pots to other potters makes no real sense'. The same assumption seems to underpin Kirch's (1988) model for specialized shell artefact production and trade within Lapita, with locations being either donors or recipients. Oram (1982: 13) clearly details how the Motu-Koita, as well as producing *toea* (cone shell valuables) at Boera in limited amounts, also imported *Conus* rings from a suite of other locations to the east as far as Hood Bay and the Aroma Coast. Some *Conus* rings were also coming into the *hiri* system via Mailu traders, who themselves were trading out *mwali* shells formerly moving within the Massim systems. As such, any given *toea* either present in Western Motu villages or traded by them west as part of the *hiri*, may have come from one of any number of locations. Thus, it appears in this instance that the production of *toea* by Western Motu did not preclude the import of visually similar or identical objects to supplement trade. Recognizing this process of producing and importing similar objects opens up interesting possibilities for thinking about archaeological cultures such as Lapita. That is, local production and consumption versus specialized production and distribution may not have to be thought of as a zero sum game.

'A HUGE SPECTRUM OF POSSIBLE WAYS OF DOING MORE OR LESS THE SAME KIND OF THING'

Connectedness is the central element that shines through when looking at the anthropological and historical literature on shell valuable production and exchange in New Guinea.[6] Even exchange systems that are largely distinct at any given point in time, such as the *hiri* or *kula*, tend to have permeable margins with goods such as *Conus* armshells, *doga* boar-tusk pendants, or volumes of shell beads filtering through from adjacent systems. Structures such as the inward trade in marine shells into the highlands and its fringes actively involve the integration of marine shells passing from other areas and peoples. This observation of connectedness is not a new one, with pioneering anthropologists such as Seligmann (1910) and Malinowski (1915, 1922) observing connections along the south coast into the Massim (see discussion in Irwin et al. 2019: 3 for a series of examples and references). Aside from the examples of the *kula*, *hiri*, and highlands briefly discussed here, many other trading systems exist which in effect circle the New Guinea coastline and work inland from the coast. Skelly and David (2017: chapter 17) present a very useful summary and consideration of the literature for a number of these systems, stretching from the Torres Strait network through the *hiri* and Mailu exchange networks of the south coast and onto the Massim, beyond to Collingwood Bay and on to the Vitiaz Strait networks (see also McNiven, Coral Sea Cultural Interaction Sphere, this volume).

Although all of these networks have either been demonstrated to, or can be assumed to have, reconfigured and transformed after European contact, they clearly existed in precontact times linking people and places, and redistributing products and valuables. The early evidence for the translocation of animals and movement of obsidian from at least c. 20,000 BP in the Bismarcks (Allen, Gosden, & White 1989; Summerhayes & Allen 1993) reveals that the spirit of moving things to people rather than people to things has a long history in New Guinea. Unlike highly localized fauna or obsidian which is able to be characterized and matched to specific source areas (see Summerhayes 2009 for an overview of obsidian sourcing and trade), the sources of traded shell valuables are much harder to pin down. Despite patchiness in local availability of many taxa, the majority of species utilized for valuable production (e.g., large *Conus* species, *Rochia nilotica*, and *Tridacna* spp. giant clams) are widely distributed around New Guinea's coast. Especially when levels of production were low, local, low-level supplies of many raw materials could often be presumed to be viable. In some instances, the character of a shell midden deposit may be at odds with the habitats required for supporting shell valuable raw materials, thus pointing to the importation of either finished valuables or raw materials (e.g., the presence of marine shell in highland deposits—Gaffney et al. 2019). However, even in this scenario the original source of the marine shell and the route(s) by which it was transported to the highlands can only be speculative.

Even allowing for these caveats and limitations, what can be observed from at least the Mid-Holocene, and possibly the Early Holocene, is that marine shell was transported over considerable distances, and that ideas and technologies around shell-working are to some degree convergent. For example, *Rochia nilotica* ring fragments are found in preceramic deposits from Caution Bay west of Port Moresby (Szabó, David, McNiven, & Leavesley 2021) to New Ireland (Smith & Allen 1999), the Arawes (Gosden, Webb, Marshall, & Summerhayes 1994), and Buka (Wickler 1990). With regards to more unusual forms, discs hewn in the same manner from valves of the windowpane oyster *Placuna placenta* have been recovered in preceramic/pre-Lapita (3920–4420 cal. BP) contexts from Caution Bay on the south coast (Szabó et al. 2021) and early Lapita deposits in New Ireland (Szabó & Summerhayes 2002). Such similarities suggest some form of cultural link.

There are over 10,000 species of marine shell to be found around the coastline of New Guinea, and it is surely no accident that that same general roster of taxa keep appearing and reappearing in different combinations both across space and through time. On the face of it, there seems to be no particular reason to favour small cowries or *Nassarius* dog whelks over other common, small and robust taxa such as the columbellid dove shells utilized in the Philippines (Fox 1970; Szabó 2005) or diminutive *Pterygia punctata* seen in their multitudes in ethnographic shell valuable strands from parts of the Solomon Islands and Admiralty Islands in particular (see Szabó 2019 for numerous examples). Yet these shell taxa are seemingly absent from the shell valuable inventory of the New Guinea archaeological record. While the consistency of choices in shell raw materials and artefact forms must surely be meaningful, the ethnohistorical records warn us against the seductiveness of assuming that similar-equals-same. *Kula Conus* valuables were used in exchange networks throughout much of the Massim, but they were appropriated as mortuary valuables in Tubetube (Irwin et al. 2019), incorporated into first-born child *heni* ceremonies of the Motu-Koita, and marriage transactions throughout the Gulf of Papua (Oram 1982: 15).

With further archaeological samples anchored by solid identifications, meaningful descriptions, firm contexts and robust chronologies, the shape of these shell distributions should become clearer, allowing more confident and nuanced interpretations. However, even with increasingly better data in hand, we should draw on the ethnographic record cautiously and judiciously in our efforts to grasp the development and dynamism of shell valuable production and exchange systems through time. It seems very hard to believe that long-lived shell artefact forms such as broad *Conus* rings, *Rochia* rings, and *Spondylus* and *Chama* red beads remained static in their meaning and use through several hundred years, let alone over several thousand years and across thousands of square kilometres. As stated by Wagner in Weiner (1988: x), 'projection is the inevitable consequence of unstated assumptions: when it is assumed that the meanings of another culture are self-evident, the only meanings that are evidence at all are one's own!'.

NOTES

1. Subheading is a quote from Mick Leahy (cited in Hughes 1977: 52) upon observing the extent and significance of the trade in shell in Benabena (Eastern Highlands), including that of the Egg Cowrie (*Ovula ovum*), *tambu* (*Nassarius* spp.), and *girigiri* (the Money Cowrie *Monetaria moneta* and gold-ringed cowrie *Monetaria annulus*). This observation prompted him to start procuring commercial quantities to utilize as payment for local labour at very profitable rates.
2. Subheading quote in full: 'Nor can this wide network of social co-relations and cultural influences be considered for a moment as ephemeral, new or precarious' (Malinowski 1922: 510).
3. See also Allen (2017: 617): 'In seeking the prehistory of the *hiri* within the archaeological record the obvious starting point was its ethnographic endpoint'.
4. Subheading quote drawn from Williams (1940: 16) in a mischievously decontextualized manner.
5. With the notable exception of Pam Swadling.
6. Subheading quote from Leach (1983: 537) in talking of the *kula* as observed by Malinowski.

REFERENCES

Allen, J. (2017). *Excavations on Motupore Island, Central District, Papua New Guinea*. Two volumes. University of Otago Working Papers in Anthropology 4. Dunedin: University of Otago.

Allen, J., Gosden, C., & White, J. P. (1989). Human Pleistocene adaptations in the tropical island Pacific: Recent evidence from New Ireland, a Greater Australian outlier. *Antiquity*, *63*, 548–561.

Allen, J., Holdaway, S., & Fullagar, R. (1997). Identifying specialisation, production and exchange in the archaeological record: The case of shell bead manufacture on Motupore Island, Papua. *Archaeology in Oceania*, *32*, 13–38.

Allen, J., & Rye, O. S. (1982). The importance of being earnest in archaeological investigations of prehistoric trade in Papua. In T. E. Dutton (Ed.), *The hiri in history: Further aspects of long-distance trade in Papua* (pp. 99–115). Canberra: Research School of Pacific Studies, Australian National University.

Ambrose, W., Petchey, F., Swadling, P., Beran, H., Bonshek, L., Szabó, K., . . . Summerhayes, G. (2012). Engraved prehistoric *Conus* shell valuables from southeastern Papua New Guinea: Their antiquity, motifs and distribution. *Archaeology in Oceania*, *47*, 113–132.

Barton, F. R. (1910). Annual trading voyages to the Papuan Gulf. In C. G. Seligmann (Ed.), *The Melanesians of British New Guinea* (pp. 96–120). Cambridge: Cambridge University Press.

Bickler, S. H. (1997). Early pottery exchange along the south coast of Papua New Guinea. *Archaeology in Oceania, 32,* 151–162.

Bulmer, S. (1964). Radiocarbon dates from New Guinea. *Journal of the Polynesian Society, 73,* 327–328.

Bulmer, S. (1966). *The prehistory of the Australian New Guinea Highlands: A discussion of archaeological field survey and excavations 1959–1960* (Master's thesis). University of Auckland.

Clark, J. (1991). Pearlshell symbolism in Highlands Papua New Guinea, with particular reference to the Wiru People of Southern Highlands Province. *Oceania, 61,* 309–339.

Crittendon, R. (1982). *Sustenance, seasonality and social cycles on the Nembi Plateau, Papua New Guinea* (PhD thesis). Australian National University, Canberra.

David, B., McNiven, I. J., Leavesley, M., Barker, B., Mandui, H., Richards, T., & Skelly, R. (2012). A new ceramic assemblage from Caution Bay, south coast of mainland PNG: The linear shell edge-impressed tradition from Bogi 1. *Journal of Pacific Archaeology, 3,* 73–89.

Denham, T., & Mountain, M. J. (2016). Resolving some chronological problems at Nombe rock shelter in the highlands of Papua New Guinea. *Archaeology in Oceania, 51*(S1), 73–83.

Earle, T. K. (2002). *Bronze Age economics: The beginning of political economies.* Cambridge, MA: Westview.

Egloff, B. (1978). The *Kula* before Malinowski: A changing configuration. *Mankind, 11,* 429–435.

Egloff, B. (1979). *Recent prehistory in southeast Papua.* Terra Australis 4. Canberra: Department of Prehistory, Research School of Pacific Studies, Australian National University.

Epstein, T. S. (1968). *Capitalism, primitive and modern: Some aspects of Tolai economic growth.* Canberra: Australian National University Press.

Feil, D. (1982). From pigs to pearlshells: The transformation of a New Guinea Highlands exchange economy. *American Ethnologist, 9,* 291–306.

Feil, D. (1984). *Ways of exchange: The Enga-Tee of Papua New Guinea.* St. Lucia: University of Queensland Press.

Fox, R. (1970). *The Tabon Caves.* Manila: National Museum of the Philippines.

Gaffney, D., Summerhayes, G. R., Szabó, H., & Koppel, B. (2019). The emergence of shell valuable exchange in the New Guinea Highlands. *American Anthropologist, 121,* 30–47.

Gosden, C. (1986). The interpretation of Mailu prehistory: The tyranny of distance by G. Irwin. *Archaeology in Oceania, 21,* 180–187.

Gosden, C., Webb, J., Marshall, B., & Summerhayes, G. (1994). Lolmo Cave: A mid- to late Holocene site, Arawe Islands, West New Britain Province, Papua New Guinea. *Asian Perspectives, 33,* 97–119.

Groves, M. (1960). Motu pottery. *Journal of the Polynesian Society, 69,* 3–22.

Hughes, I. (1977). *New Guinea Stone Age trade.* Terra Australis 3. Canberra: Department of Prehistory, Research School of Pacific Studies, Australian National University.

Hughes, I. (1978). Good money and bad: Inflation and devaluation in the colonial process. *Mankind, 11,* 308–318.

Ingold, T. (2000). Culture, perception and cognition. In T. Ingold (Ed.), *The perception of the environment: Essays in livelihood, dwelling and skill* (pp. 157–171). London: Routledge.

Irwin, G. (1985). *The emergence of Mailu: As a central place in coastal Papuan prehistory.* Terra Australis 10. Canberra: Department of Prehistory, Research School of Pacific Studies, Australian National University.

Irwin, G. (1991). Themes in the prehistory of coastal Papua and the Massim. In A. Pawley (Ed.), *Man and a half: Essays in Pacific anthropology and ethnobiology in honour of Ralph Bulmer* (pp. 503–511). Auckland: The Polynesian Society.

Irwin, G., Shaw, B., & McAlister, A. (2019). The origins of the Kula Ring: Archaeological and maritime perspectives from the southern Massim and Mailu areas of Papua New Guinea. *Archaeology in Oceania, 54*, 1–16.

Kirch, P. V. (1988). Long-distance exchange and island colonization: The Lapita case. *Norwegian Archaeological Review, 21*, 103–117.

Kirch, P. V. (1991). Prehistoric exchange in western Melanesia. *Annual Review of Anthropology, 20*, 141–165.

Kirch, P. V., & Green, R. C. (2001). *Hawaiiki, ancestral Polynesia: An essay in historical anthropology*. Cambridge: Cambridge University Press.

Kroeber, A. (1948). *Anthropology: Race, language, culture, psychology, prehistory*. Second edition. New York: Harcourt, Brace, & World.

Kuehling, S. (2005). *Dobu: Ethics of exchange on a Massim Island, Papua New Guinea*. Honolulu: University of Hawaii Press.

Leach, E. (1983). The kula: An alternative view. In J. W. Leach & E. Leach (Eds.), *The kula: New perspectives on Massim exchange* (pp. 529–538). Cambridge: Cambridge University Press.

Leach, J. W., & Leach, E. (Eds.) (1983). *The kula: New perspectives on Massim exchange*. Cambridge: Cambridge University Press.

Lewis, A. B. (1929). *Melanesian shell money in Field Museum collections*. Field Museum of Natural History Publication 268. Chicago: Field Museum.

Liep, J. (1981). The workshop of the Kula: Production and trade of shell necklaces in the Louisiade Archipelago, Papua New Guinea. *Folk, 23*, 297–309.

Liep, J. (2009). *A Papuan plutocracy: Ranked exchange on Rossel Island*. Aarhus: University of Aarhus Press.

Lilley, I. (1987). *Prehistoric exchange in the Vitiaz Strait, Papua New Guinea* (PhD thesis). Australian National University, Canberra.

Macintyre, M. (1983). Warfare and the changing context of Kune on Tubetube. *Journal of Pacific History, 18*, 11–34.

Malinowski, M. (1915). The natives of Mailu: Preliminary results of Robert Mond research work in British New Guinea. *Transactions of the Royal Society of South Australia, 39*, 494–706.

Malinowski, B. (1922). *Argonauts of the Western Pacific*. London: Routledge & Kegan Paul.

Mauss, M. ([1923–1924] 1990). *The gift: The form and reason for exchange in archaic societies*. Trans. W. D. Halls. London: Routledge.

Mialanes, J., David, B., Ford, A., Richards, T., McNiven, I. J., Summerhayes, G. R., & Leavesley, M. (2016). Imported obsidian at Caution Bay, south coast of Papua New Guinea: Cessation of long distance procurement c. 1,900 cal BP. *Australian Archaeology, 82*(3), 248–262.

Mountain, M. J. (1991). *Highlands New Guinea hunter-gatherers: The evidence of Nombe Rockshelter, Simbu with emphasis on the Pleistocene* (PhD thesis). Australian National University, Canberra.

Munn, N. (1986). *The fame of Gawa: A symbolic study of value transformation in a Massim (Papua New Guinea) society*. Cambridge: Cambridge University Press.

Oram, N. (1982). Pots for sago: The *hiri* trading network. In T. Dutton (Ed.), *The hiri in history: Further aspects of Motu long distance trade in Central Papua* (pp. 1–33). Canberra: Australian National University.

Parkinson, R. ([1907] 2010). *Thirty years in the South Seas: Land, custom and traditions in the Bismarck Archipelago and on the German Solomon Islands*. Translated by J. Dennison and edited by J. P White. Sydney: University of Sydney Press.

Parry, J. (1989). On the moral perils of exchange. In J. Parry & M. Bloch (Eds.), *Money and the morality of exchange* (pp. 64–93). Cambridge: Cambridge University Press.

Rath, P., & Torrence, R. (2003). Producing value: Stemmed tools from Garua Island, Papua New Guinea. *Australian Archaeology, 57*, 119–127.

Schneider, O. (1905). *Muschelgeld-Studien*. Dresden: Ernst Engelmann's Nachfg.

Seligmann, C. G. (1910). *The Melanesians of British New Guinea*. Cambridge: Cambridge University Press.

Shaw, B. (2019). Archaeology of the Massim Island region, Papua New Guinea. In C. Smith (Ed.), *Encyclopedia of global archaeology*. Cham: Springer. https://doi.org/10.1007/978-3-319-51726-1_3444-1

Shaw, B., & Langley, M. C. (2017). Investigating the development of prehistoric cultural practices in the Massim regional of eastern Papua New Guinea: Insights from the manufacture and use of shell objects in the Louisiade Archipelago. *Journal of Anthropological Archaeology, 48*, 149–165.

Sillitoe, P. (1979). *Give and take: Exchange in Wola society*. Canberra: Australian National University Press.

Sillitoe, P. (1988). *Made in Niugini: Technology in the Highlands of Papua New Guinea*. London: British Museum Publications.

Skelly, R., David, B., Leavesley, M., Petchey, F., Guise, A., Tsang, R., Richards, T. (2018). Changing ceramic traditions at Agila ancestral village, Hood Bay, Papua New Guinea. *Australian Archaeology, 84*(2), 181–195.

Skelly, R. J., & David, B. (2017). *Hiri: Archaeology of long-distance maritime trade along the south coast of Papua New Guinea*. Honolulu: University of Hawaii Press.

Smith, A., & Allen, J. (1999). Pleistocene shell technologies: Evidence from Island Melanesia. In J. Hall & I. McNiven (Eds.), *Australian coastal archaeology* (pp. 291–297). Canberra: Australian National University.

Strathern, A. (1971). *The rope of Moka: Big-men and ceremonial exchange in Mount Hagen, New Guinea*. Cambridge: Cambridge University Press.

Summerhayes, G. R. (2000). *Lapita interaction*. Terra Australis 15. Canberra, Department of Archaeology and Natural History and the Centre for Archaeological Research.

Summerhayes, G. R. (2009). Obsidian network patterns in Melanesia—Sources, characterisation and distribution. *Bulletin of the Indo-Pacific Prehistory Association, 29*, 109–123.

Summerhayes, G. R., & Allen, J. (1993). The transport of Mopir obsidian to Late Pleistocene New Ireland. *Archaeology in Oceania, 28*(3), 145–149.

Summerhayes, G. R., & Allen, J. (2007). Lapita writ small? Revisiting the Austronesian colonization of the Papuan south coast. In S. Bedford, C. Sand, & S. P. Connaughton (Eds.), *Oceanic explorations: Lapita and Western Pacific settlement* (pp. 97–122). Terra Australis 26. Canberra: Australian National University.

Swadling, P. (1994). Changing shellfish resources and their exploitation for food and artifact production in Papua New Guinea. *Man and Culture in Oceania, 10*, 127–150.

Swadling, P. (2010). The impact of a dynamic environmental past on trade routes and language distributions in the lower-middle Sepik. In J. Bowden, N. P. Himmelmann, & M. Ross (Eds.), *A journey through Austronesian and Papuan linguistic and cultural space papers in honour of Andrew Pawley* (pp. 141–157). Canberra: Pacific Linguistics, Australian National University.

Swadling, P. (2017). Analysis of shellfish excavated from Square N21/II. In J. Allen (Ed.), *Excavations on Motupore Island, Central District, Papua New Guinea*, volume 2 (pp. 451–500). University of Otago Working Papers in Anthropology 4. Dunedin: University of Otago.

Swadling, P., & Anamiato, J. (1989). Marine shells from the Yuat Gorge. In P. Gorecki & D. Gillieson (Eds.), *A crack in the spine: Prehistory and ecology of the Jimi-Yuat Valley, Papua New Guinea* (pp. 224–230). Townsville: James Cook University.

Swadling, P., & Bence, P. (2016). Changes in kula valuables and related supply linkages between the Massim and the South Papuan Coast between 1855 and 1915. *Archaeology in Oceania*, 51(S1), 50–60.

Szabó, K. (2005). *Technique and practice: Shell working in the Western Pacific and Island Southeast Asia* (PhD thesis). Australian National University, Canberra.

Szabó, K. (2010). Shell artefacts and shell-working within the Lapita Cultural Complex. *Journal of Pacific Archaeology*, 1, 115–127.

Szabó, K. (2018a). The impact of the *kula* on archaeological interpretation: The case of Lapita shell ornaments. In H. P. Hahn & G. Schmidtz (Eds.), *Market as place and space of economic exchange* (pp. 115–125). Oxford: Oxbow.

Szabó, K. (2018b). Shell money and context in Western Island Melanesia. In L. Carreau, A. Clark, A. Jelinek, E. Lilje, & N. Thomas (Eds.), *Pacific presences: Oceanic art and European museums, Volume Two* (pp. 25–38). Leiden: Sidestone Press.

Szabó, K. (2019). *Shell valuables from the Bismarck Archipelago and Solomon Islands*. Produced through Monash University for community distribution. Clayton: Monash Publishing.

Szabó, K., David, B., McNiven, I. J., & Leavesley, M. (2021). Preceramic shell-working and the Circum-New Guinea Archipelago. In T. Thomas (Ed.), *Theory in the Pacific, the Pacific in theory: Archaeological perspectives* (pp. 123–144). Oxon: Routledge.

Szabó, K., & Summerhayes, G. R. (2002). Worked shell artefacts: New data from early Lapita. In S. Bedford, C. Sand, & D. Burley (Eds.), *Fifty years in the field: Essays in honour and celebration of Richard Shutler Jr's archaeological career* (pp. 91–100). Auckland: New Zealand Archaeological Association.

Thomas, N. J. (1991). *Entangled objects: Exchange, material culture and colonialism in the Pacific*. Cambridge, MA: Harvard University Press.

Thomas, N. J. (2012). Introduction. In P. Brunt & N. Thomas (Eds.), *Art in Oceania—A new history* (pp. 11–23). London: Thames & Hudson.

Van der Noort, R. (2006). Argonauts of the North Sea: A social maritime archaeology for the 2nd millennium BC. *Proceedings of the Prehistoric Society*, 72, 267–287.

Vanderwal, R. L. (1978). Exchange in prehistoric coastal Papua. *Mankind*, 11, 416–428.

Voutsaki, S. (1997). The creation of value and prestige in the Aegean Late Bronze Age. *Journal of European Archaeology*, 5, 34–52.

Weiner, A. (1976). *Women of value, men of renown: New perspectives in Trobriand exchange*. St Lucia: University of Queensland Press.

Weiner, J. (1988). *The heart of the pearl shell: The mythological dimensions of Foi sociality*. Berkeley: University of California Press.

White, J. P. (1972). *Ol Tumbuna*. Terra Australis 2. Canberra: Department of Prehistory, Research School of Pacific Studies, Australian National University.

Wickler, S. (1990). Prehistoric Melanesian exchange and interaction: Recent evidence from the northern Solomon Islands. *Asian Perspectives*, 29, 135–154.

Williams, F. E. (1940). *Drama of Orokolo*. Oxford: Oxford University Press.

CHAPTER 27

··

BOUNDARIES, RELATIONALITY, AND STYLE PROVINCES IN AUSTRALIAN ROCK ART

··

MADELEINE KELLY AND LIAM M. BRADY

INTRODUCTION

ROCK art holds a unique place in archaeological discourse as a visual expression of social and cultural practices underpinned by relationships to place and people. The fixed location and durability of rock art allow for spatial analyses of sites and motifs that provide insights into past human behaviour and social identity as they are expressed in the landscape (Chippindale & Nash 2004: 7). The study of specific artistic conventions and 'styles'—the individual or combined visual traits of an image or object that can be used to group or differentiate it from other images or objects (i.e., technique, colour, form, subject, or any other artistic conventions)—has been (and continues to be) used by researchers across the globe to detect spatial and temporal continuities and discontinuities in the distribution of rock art imagery (e.g., David & Chant 1995; Domingo-Sanz 2012; Harper 2016; McDonald & Veth 2013; Ross & Travers 2013; Tratebas 2012).[1] Distributions of artistic conventions and styles have, in the past, been theorized as expressions of shared or commonly recognized social and cultural identities and practices. The spatial discontinuities between those artistic conventions and styles are often termed artistic 'boundaries,' which, in turn, are often argued or assumed to represent sociocultural boundaries. In Australia, the spatial data researchers generate from stylistic analyses have tended to define the location of, and interfaces between, discrete style provinces (also often labelled style 'regions' or 'zones') at varied spatial scales (e.g., intrasite, local, regional, continental). As a result, over decades of research, several major rock art provinces have been defined across Australia (e.g., David & Chant 1995;

Flood 1997: 22; Gunn 2011b: 5; Layton 1992: xiii; McDonald 2018: 201; McDonald & Veth 2006: 97; Morwood 2002: 38; Ross 2013; Taçon 2001: 535; Taçon & Ouzman 2004: 43).

Since the 1970s, archaeologists and anthropologists have drawn attention to the challenges of identifying and labelling boundaries in Indigenous Australian contexts and, by extension, Australian rock art provinces (e.g., Cole 2016; Merlan 1989; Munn 1996; Myers 1982; Sutton 1995; Taçon 2013; Winn 2016). In this chapter, we reflect on the history of research into Australian rock art provinces from the 1930s to the present and draw on the anthropological work of Nancy Williams (1982) as a platform to further explore the nature and extent of rock art distributions in relation to contributing social factors. In particular, Williams's book *A Boundary Is to Cross* (1982) has had a major influence on spatial analyses of Australian rock art (e.g., David 1994; Frost, David, & Flood 1992). Here we build on previous works, exploring how notions of 'boundary' in Indigenous epistemologies and ontologies can be useful to rock art research, and in particular focus on how relationality and diversity of rock art provinces can be further examined.

Archaeological Approaches to Rock Art Boundaries

Early Approaches to Continental Styles

Early attempts to identify the spatial extent of rock art styles were largely pan-continental in scale (but see McCarthy 1962) and were often driven by the idea that rock art styles spread across the landscape through the migration or diffusion of cultures, peoples, or ideas over time (see Domingo-Sanz & Fiore 2014; Roberts & Linden 2011). For example, Daniel S. Davidson (2011 [1936]) used site inventory data to summarize regional concentrations of rock art sites across Australia. He did not define distinctive regional concentrations of rock art styles, instead suggesting that 'all Australian artists belong to the same school' as 'there is a fundamental sameness in the murals [rock paintings] of all regions', except for a few 'specialized developments in local areas' (Davidson 2011 [1936]: 15). In contrast, Davidson identified distinctive 'design areas' for portable art (Davidson 2011 [1937]: 136). The spatial boundaries that defined the extent of these design areas of portable art were deliberately overlapping and ephemeral, which Davidson argued was due to the diffusion of cultural traits (e.g., portable art designs) radiating outward from local, isolated origins and replacing earlier traits in the process (Davidson 2011 [1937]: 135).

Other researchers such as Fred McCarthy (1958), Charles Mountford (1959), and Andreas Lommel (1961) followed Davidson with their own summaries of Australian rock art, suggesting regional and pan-continental rock art styles and style sequences. They discussed spatial patterning in rock art styles using explanations similar to

Davidson's description of portable art designs; that is, they were the result of social processes linked to patterns of diffusion and migration. McCarthy, Mountford, and Lommel also equated more naturalistic images in northern Australia to more 'advanced' societal development associated with the migration of people and/or diffusion of artistic traditions from Southeast Asia. Furthermore, an implicit boundary surrounded the distribution of apparently simple geometric rock art imagery in central and southern Australia, preventing the diffusion of naturalistic styles from the north (Lommel 1961: 208, 228; McCarthy 1958: 33; Mountford 1959).

Lesley Maynard (1979) continued the focus on pan-continental sequences and distributions by using large amounts of new data (site records, etc.) to offer an alternative style-based chronological framework to that of Lommel and McCarthy. She divided Australian rock art into three style-based categories: the older and more widespread Panaramitee style, characterized predominantly by geometric and track motifs, followed by Simple Figurative and Complex Figurative imagery, both of which were identified as regionalized and heterogeneous (Maynard 1979: 92–107). While Maynard used diffusionist theory to support her grouping of geographically disparate styles into broad categories for chronological sequencing, she noted that not all categories were evenly distributed across the continent (Maynard 1979: 107, 108). For example, the change from Simple Figurative to Complex Figurative imagery resulted in a 'pattern of considerable regional diversity' (1979: 108) that essentially established a series of geographical styles across the Australian landscape. Thus, her observations represented a slight departure from the culture–history frameworks of her predecessors, and though broad scale in nature, her conclusions drew attention to the transitionary nature of discontinuities between many of the more recent art regions.

Maynard and her predecessors were critical to the development of the present understanding of Australian rock art and its regional distributions. However, the spatial grouping/geographical patterning of rock art in these studies relied largely on artistic conventions and styles observed on (mainly) rock surfaces, rather than on contemporary Indigenous knowledge of what the rock art meant to people, particularly in terms of similarities and differences in the identified style categories. In some cases, the broad style categories were arguably shaped by preconceptions concerning universal models of rock art development (e.g., from abstract to figurative motifs), rather than drawing on ethnographically documented complexities of artistic conventions within Indigenous rock art. As a result, the above studies created implicit spatial and temporal boundaries that homogenized the rock art of a given geographic area and distinguished it from neighboring areas in ways that did not accurately depict distributional nuances.

Recent Approaches to Regional Styles

In the 1980s and 1990s, archaeologists shifted focus from pan-continental style sequences to refining and redefining regional rock art distributions and sequences. Crucial to this change in perspective was Martin Wobst's (1977) information exchange theory, whereby style functioned as a strategy for managing social interaction, signalling group affiliations and boundary-marking. Influential also were newly developed postprocessual interests whereby 'material culture' (such as rock art), as the product of cultural practice, was rephrased as 'material behaviour' in the understanding that objects, styles, and the like were both a product of, and influence upon, sociocultural ways (Appadurai 1988; Conkey 1978; Gamble 1980; Hodder 1982). The work of Australian anthropologists such as Nancy Munn (1973), Howard Morphy (1977, 1991), Peter Sutton and Bruce Rigsby (1982), and Luke Taylor (1987) also played a critical role in discussing Australian Indigenous artistic and symbolic behaviour as part of systems of social organization, control, and communication. Wobst (1977: 328, 332) predicted that regions with higher populations and greater densities of social groups will have greater competition for 'niche-space'. In such settings, a premium is thus placed on group differentiation and boundary maintenance, so that styles in material culture (including rock art) are likely to be more heterogeneous between groups and across space. In contrast, sparsely populated regions were said to place less emphasis on social differentiation and more on communication across large distances, so that styles would be more homogeneous across large distances (see also Smith 1992).

In line with Wobst's conceptualization of social interaction, signalling systems, and boundary-marking, archaeologists in Australia began using the large amounts of quantitative rock art data they had collected to explore in more depth the distribution of artistic conventions and styles in relation to ethnographically known social networks and, in some cases, regions with varying biomass and resource richness (e.g., Brady 2010; David & Chant 1995; David & Cole 1990; Harper 2016; Lewis 1988: 79; McDonald 2008; McDonald & Veth 2013; Morwood 1986; Officer 1992; Ross 2013; Smith 1992; Wade, Wallis, & Woolgar Valley Aboriginal Corporation 2011). For example, more heterogeneous rock art styles have often been linked to fertile, resource-rich environments with high population densities. In this context, people divide into more densely distributed social groups, with rock art styles likened to 'territorial bounding' (Smith 1992: 29) and operating as part of a social system where 'social networks are closed and kinship and territorial systems are relatively rigid' (McDonald & Veth 2006: 98). In contrast, regions with homogeneous rock art styles have been linked to resource-poor environments (e.g., arid or desert-like settings), where rock art serves a 'bonding' function as part of 'open social systems', which are considered to be more flexible and wider ranging given resource scarcity and low population densities (see Smith 1992; Gamble 1982). However, more recent researchers as well as those in the 1990s have noted that environmental conditions and population size were not the only determining factors in the structure of social systems and, furthermore, that a gradient exists between closed and open social systems (David & Chant 1995; David & Lourandos 1998; Franklin 2004; Lourandos 1997; McDonald & Veth 2013).

Many of the archaeologists we have cited note the permeability and ambiguity of social boundaries and stylistic discontinuities in rock art. For example, Bruno David and Harry Lourandos (David & Lourandos 1998: 197)—citing Nancy Williams's work on Australian Indigenous territorial boundaries—pointed out that social "closure' can also be associated with the formalized 'opening' up of relations at other levels (e.g., through ceremony and exchange) . . . Once established, formal boundaries become incorporated within legal frameworks defining conditions of *integration*. Thus, once operationalized, the 'closing' of systems forges more dynamic social relations and formations, as 'boundaries' and social relations, among other things, are negotiated and renegotiated'. However, more often than not, formal style-based approaches to spatial analyses of rock art focus primarily on grouping motifs into statistically similar assemblages that can be temporally and spatially defined. In Wobst's (1999) reflection on his 1977 article on information exchange, he stressed that identifying 'sameness' on the landscape in turn emphasizes distinction and has the potential to silence interrelationships, especially those that might be embedded in the realms of kinship, language, and ceremony (e.g., Brady & Bradley 2014b). Hence, spatial statistical analyses of rock art styles can implicitly reflect a closed system where the distinctions between style regions are emphasized and the relational aspects are obscured.

Efforts to address the limitations of formal statistical-based studies have drawn on ethnography and relational approaches to offer new interpretations of style distributions and discontinuities. For example, David (1992) used ethnography from southeast Cape York Peninsula (northern Queensland) to understand the style-based regional groupings he identified. He showed how hand stencils distributed across specific places in the landscapes could be linked to mortuary practices. Likewise, Paul Taçon (1993) used Indigenous knowledge to explain the frequency and distribution patterns of fish and macropod motifs in western Arnhem Land of northern Australia, especially in terms of the lack of correlation between motif patterning and contemporary language group boundaries. R.G. Gunn (2011a) also suggested an interlanguage group ritual or other cultural practice as the reason for the distribution of two particular styles that cross ethnographically established language boundaries in central Australia. In these studies, the incorporation of ethnography into the initial understanding of style distributions demonstrates that style connects to multiple levels of group identity, which can occur and intersect with one another spatially and temporally, emphasizing a relational network where distinctions and relationships occur simultaneously. In doing so, and as suggested by David and Lourandos (1998: 197), the stylistic discontinuities are shown to transcend territorial social organization. Benjamin Smith and Geoffrey Blundell (2004: 259) also suggested that an underlying assumption, stemming from Western modernist ontologies, links style distributions exclusively to economic and political reasons, such as communicating exclusive ownership and use. These reasons, Smith and Blundell (2004: 259) argue, silence the multitude of ethnographically derived social reasons (e.g., relationality, see below) for the distribution of rock art styles. In restricting the spatial meaning of rock art to the level of territorial group identity, researchers often emphasize a closed system in which rock art style(s) exist in singular and isolated form, highlighting notions of distinctiveness rather than relational aspects of style.

Integrating portable decorative art objects and other decorative media (e.g., sand painting and body modification such as scarring) has continued to expand thinking around the limitations of simply identifying formal discontinuities in rock art contexts (e.g., Munn 1973). In many cases, non-fixed-in-place motifs have further revealed complexities with discontinuities and distribution of distinctive rock art styles across space, including ecological zones (e.g., Best 2003; Buhrich, Goldfinch, & Greer 2016; Hatte 1992; Taçon, South, & Hooper 2003). For example, in northeast Queensland, Liz Hatte (1992) noted that the Wet Tropics or rainforest ecological zone has led to a corresponding cultural demarcation of 'Rainforest Aboriginal people' (see also Buhrich et al. 2016). This area is the only place in Australia where the large iconic, elaborately decorated (linear and geometric designs) 'rainforest shields' were produced. The presence of the distinctive rainforest shield rock art motifs found in the Dry Tropics region, another distinctive ecological zone approximately 30 km south of the Wet Tropics, recently led Alice Buhrich and colleagues to consider why these motifs appeared 'out-of-place'. They identified several reasons for the presence of these motifs outside of the rainforest zone: The rock art motifs 'could represent ceremonial exchange of shields', 'evidence of communication between the painters and those whose designs were represented', as well as 'northern visitors may have made the paintings during gatherings for ceremony and exchange' (Buhrich et al. 2016: 33–34). Yet, what emerges from their research is the realization that the rock art motifs were clearly part of 'exchange relations' involving portable, decorated material objects. In doing so, this interaction created a rock art style boundary that also crossed distinctive ecological boundaries.

Rock Art Provinces

In undertaking style-based studies, a large number of rock art provinces across the continent have been identified, some occupying very large expanses of the landscape, while others are tightly clustered (for a review, see McDonald & Clayton 2016; see also maps in, e.g., Layton 1992; Taçon 2001; Morwood 2002; McDonald & Clayton 2016). For example, Jo McDonald and Peter Veth (2013: 66) have used data collected from the early 1960s to the present to identify a total of nineteen separate rock art provinces from the Pilbara region in Western Australia, some correlating with contemporary language groups and others cross-cutting linguistic boundaries. Other rock art provinces cover vast distances such as the northwest-central Queensland rock art province. This province is characterized by a distinctive style of painted anthropomorphs that developed approximately 1000 years ago and is distributed over 32,000 km^2 (see Davidson et al. 2005; Ross, Valenzuela, Hernández Llosas, Briones, & Santoro 2008).

However, Taçon (2013: 74) recently noted that in the process of refining and redefining rock art provinces, 'there has been relatively little attention to the areas in between now well-described regions and provinces.' This 'has thus led to a distorted impression of rock art change and regionalization across large areas of both countries and continents'. Taçon proposed that researchers focus more attention on those intermediary zones that can themselves be 'small internally consistent rock art bodies' or 'landscapes that can be considered junctions or gateways where different groups of people interacted and left their marks behind or where influence from different directions and provinces changed over time' (Taçon 2013: 74). In a junction area, he suggested there will be fewer sites and images in comparison to the provinces, but an increase in diversity of styles where 'different peoples came in contact with each other or places occupied by different groups at different times' (Taçon 2013: 74). Taçon's description of junction areas represents a key step forward in reconsidering the nature of a closed system by highlighting in greater detail the idea of interrelationships in the context of style-based boundaries.

Given the approaches we have outlined, a key question emerges: How can researchers break down a closed, distinctive representation of Australian rock art and avoid homogenizing and undervaluing diversity? As noted above, Taçon argues that researchers need to shift their focus to the boundaries of provinces as junction or gateway zones. In addition, many archaeologists consider boundaries to be a problematic concept that is often informed by 'colonialist perspectives of territorial expansion, boundary maintenance, and homogenous populations [that] impl[y] that tightly bounded social entities should be visible in the archaeological record' (Lightfoot & Martinez 1995: 478). Thus, we suggest that understanding the nature of boundaries in Indigenous settings could be a useful way to better articulate and characterize rock art discontinuities.

Theorizing Boundaries

Boundaries are Multilayered and Nonexclusive

That boundaries are multilayered and complex is a familiar concept in archaeology. This issue has actually been the focus of research across the globe for some time now and, in many cases, has drawn on ethnographic data (e.g., David & Chant 1995; Green & Perlman 1985; McCarthy 2008; Stark 1998; Stark, Bowser, & Horne 2008; Ulm et al. 2002). An influential text exploring the notion of boundaries in an Indigenous Australian context is Nancy Williams's paper, *A Boundary Is to Cross: Observations on Yolngu Boundaries and Permission* (1982). In this work, Williams presents an in-depth description of the characteristics of Yolngu estate boundaries (Arnhem Land of northern Australia) within the context of Yolngu relationships to land, kin, and 'myth'[2]—a framework we consider useful for archaeologists to contemplate when approaching and characterizing the cultural and relational aspects of graphic systems and boundaries. According to Williams (1982: 139, 142), Yolngu estates were defined by their association with one or more major Ancestral Beings, and ownership of an estate was primarily traced through patrilineal kinship relationships with the specific Ancestral Beings of a particular estate. However, Williams (1982: 138–141) describes several other forms of land ownership legitimized through spirit connections, marriage, matrilineal connections, grants by owners, and other means. These forms of ownership were not exclusive and created a complex system of overlapping and intersecting forms of land ownership at various scales (i.e., country, estate, area, site), as is the case for many Australian Indigenous langu[age groups (e.g., Bradley 1997; Merlan 1989; Rose 1992). Williams (1982) identified geographic boundaries as important markers of these various forms of Yolngu land ownership. Hence, geographic boundaries for many Indigenous peoples are multilayered, overlapping, and intersecting in the landscape.

As mentioned earlier, Williams also argued that the primary function of Yolngu boundaries was not to *exclude* nonowners. The economic benefits of land owning, though important, were not the foundation of Yolngu land ownership, as they are in many modern Western countries. Williams (1982: 149–150; 1986: 220–222) argued that earlier anthropologists' assumptions that boundaries functioned only to delineate and protect exclusive geographic areas of land ownership (private property) were rooted in Western economic structures that amalgamated land ownership and the use of land resources. In the Yolngu case, land use was determined and negotiated through an overlapping and intersecting system of ownership rights, kin relationships, and other cultural laws rather than simply having land use determining ownership. As such, boundaries in a Yolngu sense were amenable to crossing.

Boundaries as Negotiated and Variable

Not only were territorial boundaries frequently crossed in Yolngu society, boundary crossing played a key role in their definition and precision. In many Indigenous contexts, estate and other territorial boundaries vary greatly in their precision (Stanner 1965: 12; Sutton 1995: 51). Williams (1982: 145) observed that well-defined Yolngu boundaries occurred 'in areas frequently or intensively occupied, visited, or traversed'. She argued that 'seeking and granting permission [from the owning group] for specific and/or limited purposes'—such as hunting, fishing, or camping—was the process through which Yolngu boundaries were continuously defined, affirmed, and challenged (Williams 1982: 132). In fact, Williams stated that she did not draw boundaries as lines on maps because 'of a concern that it would contribute to fossilizing, or at least freezing at a particular moment in time, what is for the Yolngu a continuous process of negotiating interests in land' (cited in Sutton 1995: 125). Anthropologist Deborah Bird Rose (1992: 223) echoed Williams's argument, stating that 'boundaries are maintained by being pressed against. This is the metarule of response: To be is to act; to act is to communicate; to communicate is to test and respond. The process of testing and responding affirms relationships'. Williams and Rose posited that boundaries were continually negotiated relationships between owners, users, and others and their interests, gaining definition through interaction.

Boundaries as Relational

The relational contexts associated with boundaries can also be articulated through the movements and actions of Ancestral Beings and their capacity to link people across space. For example, in northern Australia's Victoria River District (VRD), Rose (1992) describes how boundaries follow the tracks of Ancestral Beings—that is, the routes of Ancestral Beings as they travelled across the landscape, creating various landscape features (e.g., rivers, quarries, lakes, and mountain ranges). These tracks can occur at many different geographical scales, from local (e.g., within a specific language group's territory) to vast—often covering considerable distances between one or more language groups, linking specific sites across many hundreds of kilometres. One such example of the latter is from Western Australia and the epic journey of the Seven Sisters Ancestral Beings, who travelled from Roebourne (in the northwest coast of Western Australia) eastward across the Pilbara region and into the vast Western Desert. As they travelled, the Seven Sisters created various features in the landscape (e.g., waterholes, rock shelters), which today are used to link the many different language groups that live along the trackway or storyline (e.g., Neale 2017). Rose (1992: 52–55) described these types of tracks as 'strings' that form 'elaborate webs' cross-cutting one another and interlinking various 'nodes' or specific sites such as the ones noted above. Thus, Dreaming tracks interpenetrate and connect places and people across social boundaries at a variety of geographical scales.

Rose further notes that these tracks not only cross boundaries but are *themselves* boundaries. She states that

> [t]racks and songs are the basis of Aboriginal maps and are often called 'boundaries'. To say that there are boundaries is to say that there are differences; the universe is not uniform. Unlike European maps on which boundaries are lines that divide, tracks connect points on the landscape, showing relationships between points. These are the 'boundaries' that unite. The fact that a Dreaming demarcates differences along the line is important to creating variation, but ultimately a track, by its very existence, demarcated a coming together.
>
> (Rose 1992: 52)

Difference is evident in 'handover points,' which are sites where ownership and responsibility for the tracks of Ancestral Beings are handed over from one group to another (Sutton 1995: 54; Rose 1992: 55). Patrick McConvell and Arthur Palmer (1979: 46) argue that these handover points are the boundaries between land-owning groups in the VRD. Rose describes them as 'a site of convergence, as well as a site of differentiation,' as 'two sets of people defined as different by the fact that the Dreaming changes over, come together because they share the responsibilities' (cited in Sutton 1995: 112). While the structure of boundaries described by McConvell, Palmer, and Rose is different from that described by Williams, the fundamental relational nature of the boundaries is the same.

Discussion

Taking Indigenous worldviews into account, we see that territorial boundaries become integral to social identities and relationships to land. However, territorial boundaries are also contextual, overlapping, continually negotiated, and relational, rather than isolated and exclusionary structures. Boundaries are a site or thread of both difference and coming together.

Placing social identities in their temporal and spatial context is one of the central aims of archaeological and rock art research. However, as discussed above, the relational and intersecting nature of social identities has been obscured by the focus of rock art researchers on mapping sameness onto the landscape. The study of discontinuities in rock art as multilayered, intersecting, and relational boundaries allows researchers to analyse and present both difference and sameness in the spatial distribution of styles. Furthermore, the incorporation of other aspects of Indigenous graphic systems, such as portable art, body art, and ethnographic knowledge (aspects that have historically been excluded from regional statistical analyses), allows for further chains of relationality, connection, and difference to be explored and incorporated into our understanding of interregional boundaries. We now turn to two case studies to explore some of these ideas.

Integrating Rock Art and Portable Art: A Torres Strait Case Study

Located in far northeastern Australia, the Torres Strait Islands are well known in the anthropological and archaeological literature as a transition or intermediary zone between hunter-gatherers of mainland Australia to the south and Melanesian horticulturalists of New Guinea to the north (Walker 1972; see McNiven, Coral Sea Cultural Interaction Sphere, this volume). A rich ethnographic record collected since the 1840s has shown that Torres Strait Islanders were key participants in social interaction and exchange networks across the islands and the neighbouring mainlands. This social interaction is perhaps best characterized through a complex trade and exchange system, social alliances, warfare, oral traditions, language, and kinship (e.g., see Haddon 1904, 1935; Lawrence 1994; Moore 1979).

From the earliest writings about Torres Strait, reference has been made to the decorative arts of the Islanders, in particular portable objects such as elaborate turtleshell masks and headdresses, drums, canoes, and sculpture (e.g., Fraser 1978; Haddon 1912; Moore 1979, 1984). Haddon (1912: 342) drew attention to the challenges of studying the Torres Strait graphic system in a bounded geographical sense:

> The decorative art of the Islanders is so closely connected with that of the natives of the adjacent mainland of New Guinea (Daudai) and of the islands at the mouth of the Fly River, especially Kiwai, that it is impossible to study them apart . . . it must be remembered that many decorated objects have been imported from New Guinea to Torres Strait and possibly a few have passed in the reverse direction.

When the first systematic rock art recording project undertaken in the region between individual Islander communities and archaeologists Ian McNiven and

Bruno David began in 2000, the discovery of similarities between distinctive artistic conventions found in rock art motifs, decorated material culture objects, and scarification artistic conventions signalled an opportunity to explore the widespread geographical distribution of the region's graphic system (McNiven, David, & Brayer 2000; McNiven & David 2004). Subsequent recording and statistical analyses carried out on the Torres Strait rock art assemblage by Liam Brady, based on 990 'determinate' (those that could be formally identified) paintings, revealed a relatively widespread stylistic homogeneity between islands centred around nonfigurative motifs (i.e., open and closed geometrics, linear nonfigurative or abstract) (Brady 2010). These results pointed to a general spread of artistic conventions across the islands, and while at one level Torres Strait could be identified as a discrete rock art province, this conclusion came at the expense of identifying specific, heightened, interisland links, along with links to the Australian and New Guinea mainlands. Using McNiven and David's initial recordings and conclusions, and augmented by Brady's (2008, 2010) later research, a greater geographical distribution of distinctive artistic conventions becomes apparent.

Four-Pointed Star

A distinctive red painted anthropomorph from the Kabadul Kula site on the island of Dauan in northwest Torres Strait was identified by the Daunalgaw (traditional owners of the island) as a *dogai*—an ugly, evil, and potentially dangerous female spirit being with large ears (McNiven, David, Brady, & Brayer 2004: 233; see also Haddon 1904: 353, Laade 1971: xxi; Lawrie 1970: 257). *Dogai* spirit beings are ethnographically known and feared across much of Torres Strait and also among the Kiwai of the southwestern coast of Papua New Guinea at the mouth of the Fly River (see McNiven et al. 2004: 233–236 for a review). The *dogai* motif at Kabadul Kula is depicted in an outlined, X-ray form showing its ribs, with large ears/horns, and a four-pointed star with a circle in the middle painted on its belly. Research into style-based similarities with the *dogai*'s four-pointed star has revealed an extensive geographic distribution of this design (McNiven et al. 2004; see also Brady 2010) (Figure 27.1). Wooden objects depicting anthropomorphs with four-pointed stars on their bellies include a carved wooden stool from the Sepik River region, a bullroarer from the Papuan Gulf, a carving of a human from Kinomere Village (Urama Island, Papuan Gulf), and a skull rack from the Middle Sepik River region. Depictions of this distinctive motif are not restricted to the belly of anthropomorphs; it is also found with stylistic embellishments on wooden objects such as bark belts from the Papuan Gulf, a headdress from Mer (Eastern Torres Strait), a wooden shield from Kiri Village (western Elema area, Papuan Gulf; see also Lewis 1931), a wooden tobacco pipe collected in 1870 at Cape York (Haddon & Rivers 1904: 168), and a carved wooden comb made by Waria of Mabuyag (Haddon 1912: 362). Elsewhere, McNiven et al. (2004: 234) noted that among the Marind-Anim in coastal southeast Papua (Indonesia), a similar star design, representing the morning star, is found on *gari* ritual paraphernalia (headdresses). They also noted similar astrological associations involving *dogai* as certain stars in the night

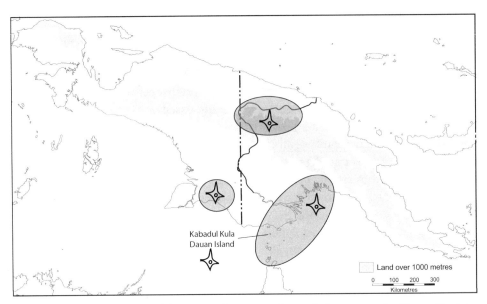

FIGURE 27.1. Distribution of distinctive four-pointed star design across the Torres Strait islands, tip of Cape York Peninsula, Papuan Gulf, Sepik River region, and Papua (Indonesia).

sky, leading them to suggest that these relationships 'may be relevant to the meaning behind the Dauan star depiction given the formal similarities of imagery and frequent contacts between the Marind-Anim and NW Torres Strait Islanders through head-hunting raids as well as through trade' (McNiven et al. 2004: 234).

Analysis of the geographic distribution of the four-pointed star motif via portable material culture is one of the clearest examples of how a distinctive design form found in rock art has correlates that extend much further than its rock art signature. In this case, while the motif only occurs in one instance in rock art, it has a widespread distribution, from the north coast of the Sepik River region in northern Papua New Guinea as far south as Cape York Peninsula.

Faces/Masks

At Mask Cave on the islet of Pulu (midwestern Torres Strait) is a single, red painted face/mask consisting of an outlined, oblong-shaped face with two infilled circles (eyes), an outlined crescent-shaped mouth, and a series of triangles and semi-oval shapes bordering the face/mask. A central line extends from top to bottom, which bisects the mouth and divides the two eyes. McNiven et al. (2006; see also Brady 2010, 2015) noted that this motif shows a striking similarity with distinctive and highly visible carved wooden *gope* (also known as *kwoi* or *hohao*) boards well known from southwestern Papua New Guinea (especially the Fly River estuary) and the Papuan Gulf where they represent spirit ancestors who protected clans and individuals (Beier & Kiki 1970;

Newton 1961; Welsch, Webb, & Haraha 2006). While these boards feature a wide range of design embellishments, their core characteristics of an oblong face with a central line, the position of the eyes and mouth, and perimeter decoration remain consistent across space and between decorative media.

A further seven face/mask motifs—three from Dauan, three from the island of Badu, and one from Mua—feature one or more of three unique artistic conventions, with material culture correlates across the broader region (Figure 27.2A). Concentric circle eyes (two to four circles), concentric circle eyes with the outer circle tapering into a sideways-facing triangle, and interlocked teeth (McNiven et al. 2004; see also McNiven, David, & Brayer 2000; Brady 2010) all frequently occur in some form on material culture objects from southwestern Papua New Guinea, most notably on carved wooden boards decorated with faces collected from Kiwai Island and the Papuan Gulf region (e.g., Brake, McNeish, & Simmons 1979; Gathercole, Kaeppler, & Newton 1979; Lewis 1973; Newton 1961; Serra & Folch 1976). In addition, Carter (2004) describes a carved bone artefact excavated archaeologically from Dauar (eastern Torres Strait) featuring the tapered outer circle design, an example that further widens the geographic distribution of this design form.

Hooked Triangle

The hooked triangle motif—an infilled triangle with two curved lines projecting from either side of the triangle's apex—has been recorded individually or has been laterally linked with other triangles on three midwestern islands of Torres Strait (Zurath, Badu, and Pulu) (Figure 27.2B). A wide range of material culture objects and body scars from across the region and into island Southeast Asia have been located bearing this design, often with stylistic variations while still retaining its core elements. For example, the design is found as an engraving on the upper jaw of *warup*-style drums collected from across Torres Strait (e.g., Saibai, Tudu, Naghir, Muralag, Mer) and southwestern Papua New Guinea (Kiwai Island) (Haddon 1912: 364–365), and a *gama* drum from Mer; bamboo tobacco pipes from Mer and Kiwai Island, a wooden comb from Kiwai Island (Brady 2010: 368–373), a body scar design on women from the eastern Torres Strait that is a sign of mourning (Haddon 1912: 22), and on a decorated pottery sherd collected from Kalumpang in Sulawesi (Glover 1986: 74).

Discussion

In the examples discussed here, a distinctive rock art design convention acted as a platform to reveal the extent of graphic linkages across space. Designs recorded on portable artefacts have been documented from collection locales that cross social and linguistic boundaries. This observation suggests that the interactive sphere involving the exchange of distinctive imagery produced on portable objects circulating between Papua New

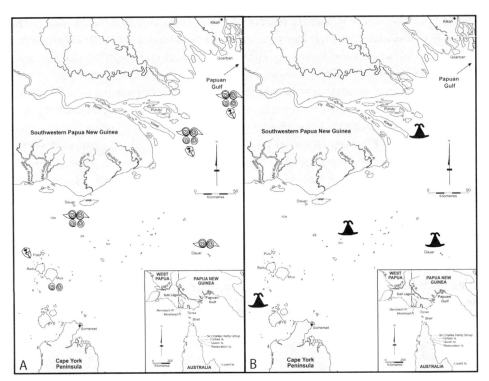

FIGURE 27.2. A: Distribution of concentric circle eye motifs and faces/masks across Torres Strait, southwestern Papua New Guinea, and the Papuan Gulf. B: Distribution map of the hooked triangle motif across Torres Strait and southwestern Papua New Guinea.

Guinea and Torres Strait is much more extensive than previously anticipated. In particular, the New Guinea-based relationships are quite extensive, although this may be due to more collectors having visited these areas rather than Cape York. Furthermore, in tracing multiple specific threads of evidence, various continuities and discontinuities are established which articulate multiple intersecting spatial boundaries within the Torres Strait Islands themselves and across the Torres Strait-New Guinea-Cape York regions more broadly. This multivalent view of boundaries in Torres Strait's rock art provides a more relational and complex understanding of social identity and relationships in the area than was provided by the initial multivariate analysis.

In considering how to integrate portable material culture into style-based geographical distribution analyses, the approach described here used rock art as a geographical anchor from which to conduct a search for comparative portable decorative material. Essential to this process was the role of ethnography as a guide to understanding the nature of people's interregional interaction from the mid-1840s to the present. For example, taking account of the ethnographic boundaries or divisions, such as those recorded between the Eastern, Western, and Central Islanders of Torres Strait at the time of European contact, we can also begin to assess their role in the exchange of artistic conventions and design features within the Torres Strait region artistic system. While some restrictions are associated with this type of approach to style-based geographic distributions (e.g., the short life span of wooden objects in tropical climates, lack of ethnographic data), its usefulness as a research strategy for questions revolving around boundaries and style zones remains an important consideration.

Ethnography and Regional Rock Art Styles: A Gulf of Carpentaria Case Study

As noted earlier, integrating ethnography into regional rock art studies is far less common than a formal style-based analysis. Here we use an example from northern Australia's southwest Gulf of Carpentaria region to show how recent (1980–present) ethnography has been used to offer Indigenous views into regional style labels and provinces by focusing on the cultural and relational understandings of sites and motifs (see Brady & Bradley 2014a, 2014b for further details).

The southwest Gulf country was originally home to six Aboriginal language groups—the Garrwa, Yanyuwa, Binbingka, Wilangarra, Gudanji, and Marra. However, by the early 1900s, the Binbingka and Wilangarra became extinct as a result of frontier violence (see Roberts 2005). Ethnographic research over the past five decades has shown that extensive relationships (e.g., kinship, ceremonial, trade) continue to exist between each of the four remaining language groups, while the paths and songs of many important Ancestral Beings cross-cut the territories of the language groups that further emphasize the connectedness between people (see e.g., Bradley with Yanyuwa Families 2010; Yanyuwa Families, Bradley, & Cameron 2003).

Some acknowledgement of a possible southern 'Gulf style' of rock art has been made in the past, based on a formal style-based comparison of motifs from a handful of small, regionally focussed studies (e.g., Border 1988, 1989; Layton 1992; Walsh 1985; see Brady & Bradley 2014b for a review). However, given the size of the southern Gulf region (approximately 700 km from west to east) and the relatively small amount of rock art research undertaken in the region, there is, at present, a lack of cohesiveness to this label. More importantly, little Aboriginal knowledge concerning the motifs and understanding of regional similarities was incorporated into these studies.

Using ethnographic data collected by John Bradley on rock art in Yanyuwa, Garrwa, Gudanji, and Marra Country from 1980, and a more recent phase (2010–present) of rock art recording involving Brady, Bradley, Amanda Kearney, and each of the four language groups, two examples (see Brady, Bradley, & Kearney 2016; Brady & Bradley 2014a, 2014b for in-depth details of each example) are used here to show how regional relatedness through rock art can be identified using relational understanding.

Ceremony Motifs: Yalkawarru and a-Makurndurna

Yalkawarru is a postfuneral ceremony owned by two of the four clans—Wuyaliya and Wurdaliya—in the southwest Gulf country. The ceremony was last performed in the early 1990s and involved painting a wooden pole representing the recently deceased individual with grid-shaped designs. During the performance, a piece of wood bent into a U-shape (*a-Makurndurna*) is used as a percussion instrument and thumped on the ground (see Bradley 1997; Bradley with Yanyuwa Families 2010; Yanyuwa Families, Bradley, & Cameron 2003 for further details on this ceremony). Rock art featuring the distinctive grid-shapes and U-shape have been documented across the southwest Gulf region since the 1970s: Fourteen monochrome (red or white) grid-shaped motifs have been documented from Yanyuwa Country since 2010 (although many others are known from areas where systematic recording has yet to be undertaken), and interpreted by senior Yanyuwa men and women as depicting the designs from the *Yalkawarru* poles; and eleven monochrome and bichrome U-shaped variants have been recorded from Garrwa, Gudanji, and Binbingka Country, with several others also known from Marra Country (Figure 27.3). In all instances, Traditional Owners identified these motifs as an *a-Makurndurna*. Thus, while a formal, style-based analysis would be unable to identify a relationship between these two stylistically different motifs, their cultural and relational understandings act as indicators of a regional, ceremonial-based grouping based on ethnographic data.

Namurlardajanyngku Spirit Men

Spatially based relationships involving rock art can also be seen in the Sir Edward Pellew Islands (traditionally owned by the Yanyuwa) where two groups of pigment motifs found on Vanderlin Island are intimately related. At the Kammandaringabaya rock shelter on Vanderlin Island are 211 painted, printed, and stencilled motifs, 158 of which are of hands. Senior Yanyuwa men explained to Bradley that the hands were the work of the *namurlardajanyngku* Spirit Men. After creating these motifs, some travelled northward, stopping at different locations to leave additional hand motifs at places such as Liwingkinya, on their way to Muluwa at the northern tip of the island. Here they looked westward and saw another Spirit Man at Wuyakiba near the Roper River in Marra Country (approximately 200 km northwest) and called out to him. This Spirit Man called back to them at Muluwa, and then other *namurlardajanyngku* Spirit Men at Kammandaringabaya called out to the Spirit Man at Wuyakiba. After they called out to each other, some of the *namurlardajanyngku* Spirit Men travelled to Warnngibangirarra where three of them placed their bodies in the rock in the form of paintings (Yanyuwa Families & Bradley 2016: 415–416). In this instance, hand motifs, Spirit Beings, and place are part of a relational nexus, in which rock art plays a key role. Yet, based purely on the style of the motifs, this relationship could not be observed without the ethnographic data.

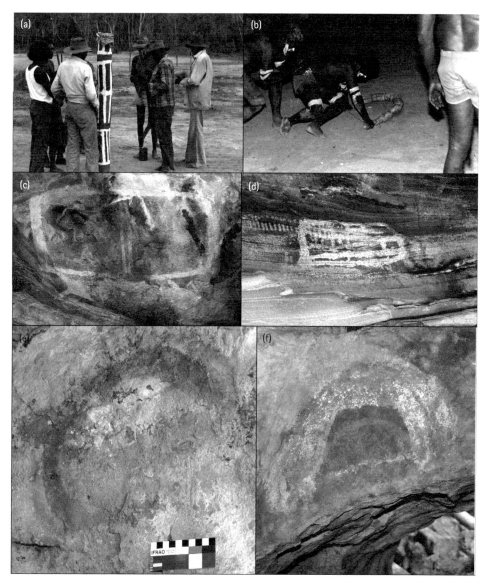

FIGURE 27.3. A: Men singing around the decorated *Yalkawarru* pole at the beginning of the *Yalkawarru* ceremony (photograph courtesy of John Bradley); B: David Douglas dancing with the *a-Makurnduna* during the *Yalkawarru* ceremony (photograph courtesy of John Bradley); C: *Yalkawarru* motif from South West Island (photograph by Liam M. Brady); D: *Yalkawarru* motif from Watson Island (photograph by Liam M. Brady); E: *a-Makurnduna* motif from Wangkalarla (photograph by Liam M. Brady); F: *a-Makurnduna* motif from Wangkalarla (photograph by Liam M. Brady). Images first published in the *Journal of Social Archaeology* 14, No. 3 (2014): 361–382.

Discussion

In describing the ethnographic contexts of rock art from the southwest Gulf country, it is important to note that formal analyses are also beginning to play a role in exploring regional relationships that cross-cut language boundaries. Recent work is beginning to identify white dot outlines as a key stylistic feature that appears across the southwest Gulf country region and also on Groote Eylandt to the north. While the formal, style-based analysis is only in its preliminary stages, it will be useful to contrast it with the ethnographic data in the near future to develop a more comprehensive picture of the nature of regional relationships and potentially the identification of a distinctive rock art province.

However, what is important to take away from these examples is the 'network of ontological and epistemological encounters' within which the rock art of this region is embedded (Brady & Bradley 2014b: 361). In both cases, the images are positioned within ontological and epistemological knowledge relating to ceremony and spiritual beings. Accessing this type of knowledge requires a commitment to understanding, among other things, kinship, ceremony, ritual, and language. Yet, once accessed, this type of information reveals a multivalent spatial understanding of rock art that involves multi-layered social networks and boundaries similar to those described by Williams (1986). In the two examples we have described, social connections across islands and language groups are traced between conventionally disparate rock art motifs through joint ceremonial practices or spiritual beings.

To speak of rock art and regionalism as separate from Indigenous knowledge in this part of Australia would likely overlook the nature of other intimate networks of relationships within which rock art exists. Yet, taken together, research that integrates formal and informed analyses into regionally based studies has the potential to deliver a wealth of information about the complex role rock art plays in understanding social relationships and networks in the past and present.

CONCLUSION

Identifying style-based provinces continues to be an integral part of rock art research in Australia and will most likely continue to be so into the future given its role in helping to better understand the nature of Indigenous graphic systems in their broadest sense. What we have focused on here are the boundaries given to these areas, the challenges that can arise when characterizing and defining these areas, and the implications this process has in understanding the past and present. Our focus here is on the notion of boundaries as threads of connection. Boundaries pinpoint discontinuity, and yet, they cannot be defined without relationships. The case studies presented in this chapter demonstrate the complex nature of boundaries by tracing threads of connection expressed in either specific artistic conventions and designs or ethnographic knowledge. Each of these threads acknowledges difference—different locations, different language groups, different materials, and visually distinct motifs—and yet all emphasize the relational.

Reconsidering what defines and what is defined by rock art provinces may go some way to further exploring Indigenous graphic systems, rock art identities, and different scales of interregional interaction. For example, cultural and relational contexts of rock art could be used to define a province/region/zone by following the path of an Ancestral Being (e.g., Seven Sisters across the Pilbara and Western Desert), or attempting, in very rare instances, the style of motifs produced by known artists such as Nayombolmi in western Arnhem Land (Taçon 1987, 1989). We do, however, acknowledge that portable objects and ethnographic evidence are not always readily available, and they do not have the static, durable qualities so appreciated in rock art. Nevertheless, incorporating the notion that spatial boundaries in rock art are relational and multilayered into research methodologies and following the multilayered threads of connection evidence in specific artistic conventions may shift the focus of research away from past efforts to create and segregate blocs of sameness to emphasizing the complex web of relationships that created and is expressed in rock art.

Acknowledgements

LMB thanks the Yanyuwa and Torres Strait Islander Traditional Owners and custodians he has worked with for permission to carry out research and publish images used in this chapter. MAK thanks the Australian Research Council (ARC) Centre of Excellence for Australian Biodiversity and Heritage (CABAH) for funding academic and professional development. Special thanks to Bruno David, Ian McNiven, and Paul Taçon for providing useful feedback and guidance during various stages of writing this chapter. Funding for aspects of this chapter were generously provided by ARC Discovery grants (DP1093341, DP170101083) and the Australian Institute of Aboriginal and Torres Strait Islander Studies (G2009-7490). Brady's position is funded through an ARC Future Fellow grant (FT180100038). Kelly's position is funded through an Australian Government Research and Training Program (RTP) Scholarship and supported by the ARC Centre of Excellence for Australian Biodiversity and Heritage.

Notes

1. The concept of 'style' and its utility in rock art research has been debated for a long time (e.g., Bednarik 2007; Boast 1997; Conkey 2006; Conkey & Hastorf 1990; Hodder 1990; Sackett 1985; Wiessner 1983). However, 'style' remains a useful tool for exploring patterning in artistic conventions across space.
2. Refers to stories from the 'Dreaming' or Ancestral Past. The Dreaming is the time of world creation and when Ancestral Beings (Dreamings) were present and created the landscape through various actions and events (e.g., see Rose 1992; Stanner 1979).

REFERENCES

Appadurai, A. (Ed.). (1988). *The social life of things: Commodities in cultural perspective.* Cambridge: Cambridge University Press.

Bednarik, R. G. (2007). *Rock art science: The scientific study of palaeoart.* New Delhi: Aryan Books International.

Beier, U., & Kiki, A. M. (1970). *Hohao: The uneasy survival of an art form in the Papuan Gulf.* Melbourne: Thomas Nelson.

Best, A. (2003). *Regional variation in the material culture of hunter gatherers: Social and ecological approaches to ethnographic objects from Queensland, Australia.* British Archaeological Reports International Series 1149. Oxford: Archaeopress.

Boast, R. (1997). A small company of actors: A critique of style. *Journal of Material Culture, 2,* 173–198.

Border, A. (1989). An archaeological survey on Lawn Hill and Bowthorn Stations, north-western Queensland (Unpublished report). Heritage Section, Queensland Department of Environment and Heritage.

Border, A. (1988). An archaeological survey in the Lawn Hill and Musselbrook Creek area, northwestern Queensland Highlands (Unpublished report). Heritage Section, Queensland Department of Environment and Heritage.

Bradley J. J. (1997). *li-Anthawirrayarra, people of the sea: Yanyuwa relations with their maritime environment* (PhD thesis). Northern Territory University, Darwin.

Bradley, J. J., with Yanyuwa Families. (2010). *Singing saltwater country: Journey to the Songlines of Carpentaria.* Crows Nest: Allen and Unwin.

Brady, L. M. (2008). Symbolic language in Torres Strait, NE Australia: Images from rock art, portable objects and human scars. *Antiquity, 82,* 336–350.

Brady, L. M. (2010). *Pictures, patterns and objects: Rock-art of the Torres Strait Islands, north-eastern Australia.* North Melbourne: Australian Scholarly Publishing.

Brady, L. M. (2015). Rock-art from the Mabuyag Islands, Zenadh Kes (Torres Strait). *Memoirs of the Queensland Museum / Culture Heritage Series, 8*(2), 497–530.

Brady, L. M., & Bradley, J. J. (2014a). Images of relatedness: Patterning and cultural contexts in Yanyuwa rock art, Sir Edward Pellew Islands, SW Gulf of Carpentaria, northern Australia. *Rock Art Research, 31* (2), 157–176.

Brady, L. M., & Bradley, J. J. (2014b). Reconsidering regional rock art styles: Exploring cultural and relational understandings in northern Australia's Gulf Country. *Journal of Social Archaeology, 14* (3), 361–382.

Brady, L. M., Bradley, J. J., & Kearney, A. J. (2016). Negotiating Yanyuwa rock art: Relational and affectual experiences in the southwest Gulf of Carpentaria, northern Australia. *Current Anthropology, 57*(1), 28–52.

Brake, B., McNeish, J., & Simmons, P. (1979). *Art of the Pacific.* Oxford: Oxford University Press.

Buhrich, A., Goldfinch, F., & Greer, S. (2016). Connections, transactions and rock art within and beyond the wet tropics of north Queensland. *Memoirs of the Queensland Museum / Culture, 10,* 23–42.

Carter, M. (2004). *North of the cape and south of the Fly: The archaeology of settlement and subsistence on the Murray Islands, Eastern Torres Strait* (PhD thesis). James Cook University, Townsville.

Chippindale, C., & Nash, G. (2004). Pictures in place: Approaches to the figured landscapes of rock-art. In C. Chippindale & G. Nash (Eds.), *The figured landscapes of rock-art: Looking at pictures in place* (pp. 1–36). Cambridge: Cambridge University Press.

Cole, N. (2016). Regions without borders related rock art landscapes of the Laura Basin, Cape York Peninsula. In J. C. Verstraete & D. Hafner (Eds.), *Land and language in Cape York Peninsula and the Gulf country* (pp. 61–84). Amsterdam/Philadelphia: John Benjamins Publishing Company.

Conkey, M. W. (1978). Style and information in cultural evolution: Toward a predictive model for the Paleolithic. In M. Redman, E. Berman, W. T. Curtin, N. Langhorne, M. Versaggi, & J. C. Wanser (Eds.), *Social archaeology: Beyond subsistence and dating* (pp. 61–85). New York: Academic Press.

Conkey, M. W. (2006). Style, design, and function. In C. Y. Tilley (Eds.), *Handbook of material culture* (pp. 355–372). London: Sage.

Conkey, M., & Hastorf, C. A. (Eds.). (1990). *The uses of style in archaeology*. Cambridge: Cambridge University Press.

David, B. (1992). Analysing space: Investigating context and meaning in the rock paintings of the Chillagoe-Mungana limestone belt of north Queensland. In J. McDonald & I. P. Haskovec (Eds.), *State of the art: Regional rock art studies in Australia and Melanesia* (pp. 159–163). Occasional AURA Publication 6. Melbourne: Australian Rock Art Research Association.

David, B. (1994). *A space-time odyssey: Rock art and regionalisation in North Queensland prehistory* (PhD thesis). University of Queensland, Brisbane.

David, B., & Chant, D. (1995). *Rock art and regionalisation in North Queensland prehistory*. Memoirs of the Queensland Museum 37(2). Brisbane: Queensland Museum

David, B., & Cole, N. (1990). Rock art and inter-regional interaction in northeastern Australian prehistory. *Antiquity, 64*(245), 788–806.

David, B., & Lourandos, H. (1998). Rock art and socio-demography in northeastern Australian prehistory. *World Archaeology, 30*(2), 193–219.

Davidson, D. S. (2011 [1936]). *Aboriginal Australian and Tasmanian rock carvings and paintings*. Western Australia: Hesperian Press.

Davidson, D. S. (2011 [1937]). *A preliminary consideration of Aboriginal Australian decorative art*. Western Australia: Hesperian Press.

Davidson, I., Cook, N., Fischer, M., Ridges, M., Ross, J., & Sutton, S. (2005). Archaeology in another country: Exchange and symbols in north-west central Queensland. In I. MacFarlane, M-J. Mountain, & R. Paton (Eds.), *Many exchanges: Archaeology, history, community and the work of Isabel McBryde* (pp. 103–130). Aboriginal History Monograph 11. Canberra: Aboriginal History Incorporated.

Domingo-Sanz, I. D. (2012). A theoretical approach to style in Levantine rock art. In J. McDonald & P. Veth (Eds.), *Companion to rock art* (pp. 306–321). Oxford: Wiley-Blackwell.

Domingo-Sanz, I., & Fiore, D. (2014). Style: Its role in the archaeology of Art. In C. Smith (Ed.), *Encyclopedia of global archaeology* (pp. 7104–7111). Available online: Springer Reference.

Flood, J. (1997). *Rock art of the Dreamtime: Images of ancient Australia*. Sydney: Harper Collins

Franklin, N. R. (2004). *Explorations of variability in Australian prehistoric rock engravings*. British Archaeological Reports 1318. Oxford: BARd.

Fraser, D. F. (1978). *Torres Strait sculpture: A study in Oceanic primitive art*. New York: Garland Publishing.

Frost, R., David, B., & Flood, J. (1992). Pictures in transition: Discussing the interaction of visual forms and symbolic contents in Wardaman rock pictures. In M. J. Morwood & D. R. Hobbs (Eds.), *Rock art and ethnography: Proceedings of the Ethnography Symposium (H), Australian Rock Art Research Association Congress, Darwin, 1988* (pp. 27–32). Occasional AURA Publication No. 5. Darwin: Australian Rock Art Research Association.

Gamble, C. (1980). Information exchange in the Palaeolithic. *Nature, 283*, 522–523.

Gamble, C. (1982). Interaction and alliance in Paleolithic society. *Man (N.S.) 17*, 92–107.

Gathercole, P., Kaeppler, A. L., & Newton, D. (1979). *The art of the Pacific islands*. Washington, DC: National Gallery of Art.

Glover, I. (1986). *Archaeology in eastern Timor, 1966–1967*. Terra Australis 11. Canberra: Research School of Pacific Studies, Australian National University.

Green, S. W., & Perlman, S. M. (1985). Frontiers, boundaries, and open social systems. In S. W. Green & S. M. Perlman (Eds.), *The archaeology of frontiers and boundaries* (pp. 3–13). London: Academic Press.

Gunn, R. G. (2011a). Eastern Arrernte rock art and land tenure. *Rock Art Research, 28* (2), 225–239.

Gunn, R. G. (2011b). Twenty-five years of Australian rock art research. *Rock Art Research, 28* (1), 3–6.

Haddon, A. C. (1904). *Reports of the Cambridge Anthropological Expedition to Torres Straits. Vol. 5. Sociology, magic and religion of the Western Islanders*. Cambridge: Cambridge University Press.

Haddon, A. C. (1912). *Reports of the Cambridge Anthropological Expedition to Torres Straits. Vol. 4. Arts and crafts*. Cambridge: Cambridge University Press.

Haddon, A. C. (1935). *Reports of the Cambridge Anthropological Expedition to Torres Straits. Vol. 1. General ethnography*. Cambridge: Cambridge University Press.

Haddon, A. C., & Rivers, W. H. R. (1904). Totemism. In A. Haddon (Ed.), *Reports of the Cambridge Anthropological Expedition to Torres Straits. Vol 5. Sociology, magic and religion of the Western Islanders* (pp. 153–193). Cambridge: Cambridge University Press.

Harper, S. (2016). Outlining the Port Hedland style: A distinctive local signature within the broader shared iconographies of the Pilbara, northwest Australia. *Journal of the Anthropological Society of South Australia, 40*, 70–107.

Hatte, L. (1992). 'Boring coastal stuff': Rock images of the Townsville district, north Queensland. In J. McDonald & I. Haskovec (Eds.), *State of the art: Regional rock art studies in Australia and Melanesia* (pp. 71–75). Occasional AURA Publication 6. Melbourne: Australian Rock Art Research Association.

Hodder, I. (1982). *Symbols in action: Ethnoarchaeological studies of material culture*. Cambridge: Cambridge University Press.

Hodder, I. (1990). Style as historical quality. In M. W. Conkey & C. A. Hastorf (Eds.), *The uses of style in archaeology* (pp. 44–51). Cambridge: Cambridge University Press.

Laade, W. (1971). *Oral traditions and written documents on the history and ethnography of the northern Torres Strait islands, Saibai-Dauan-Boigu. Vol. 1: adi-myths, legends, fairy tales*. Wiesbaden: Franz Steiner Verlag GMBH.

Lawrence, D. (1994). Customary exchange across Torres Strait. *Memoirs of the Queensland Museum, 34* (2), 241–446.

Lawrie, M. (1970). *Myths and legends of Torres Strait*. St. Lucia: University of Queensland Press.

Layton, R. (1992). *Australian rock art: A new synthesis*. Cambridge: Cambridge University Press.

Lewis, A. B. (1931). *Carved and painted designs from New Guinea*. Anthropology Design Series 5. Chicago: Field Museum of Natural History.

Lewis, A. B. (1973). *Decorative art of New Guinea: Consisting of two complete publications: 'Decorative art of New Guinea: incised designs' and 'Carved and painted designs from New Guinea'*. New York: Dover Publications.

Lewis, D. (1988). *The rock paintings of Arnhem Land, Australia: Social, ecological and material culture change in the post-glacial period*. British Archaeological Reports S415. Oxford: BAR.

Lightfoot, K. G., & Martinez, A. (1995). Frontiers and boundaries in archaeological perspective. *Annual Review of Anthropology, 24*, 471–492.

Lommel, A. (1961). Rock art of Australia. In H. G. Bandi, H. Breuil, L. Berger-Kirchner, H. Lhote, E. Holm, & A. Lommel (Eds.), *The art of the Stone Age: Forty thousand years of rock art* (pp. 205–231). London: Crown.

Lourandos, H. (1997). *Continent of hunter-gatherers: New perspectives in Australian prehistory.* Cambridge: Cambridge University Press.

Maynard, L. (1979). The archaeology of Australian Aboriginal art. In S. Mead (Ed.), *Exploring the visual art of Oceania* (pp. 83–110). Honolulu: University Press of Hawaii.

McCarthy, F. D. (1958). *Australian Aboriginal rock art.* Sydney: Trustees of the Australian Museum.

McCarthy, F. D. (1962). The rock engravings of Port Hedland, northwestern Australia. *Papers of the Kroeber Anthropological Society, 26*, 1–78.

McCarthy, M. (2008). Boundaries and the archaeology of frontier zones. In B. David & J. Thomas (Eds.), *Handbook of landscape archaeology* (pp. 202–209). London: New York: Routledge.

McConvell, P., & Palmer, A. B. (1979). *A claim to an area of traditional land by the Mudbura Traditional Owners, July 1979.* Northern Territory: Northern Land Council.

McDonald, J. (2018). Australia's rock art heritage: A thematic approach to assessing scientific value. In B. David & I. J. McNiven (Eds.), *The Oxford handbook of the archaeology and anthropology of rock art* (pp. 197–220). Oxford: Oxford University Press.

McDonald, J. (2008). *Dreamtime superhighway: Sydney Basin rock art and prehistoric information exchange.* Terra Australis 27. Canberra: ANU E Press.

McDonald, J., & Clayton, L. (2016). *Rock art: A thematic study.* Report to the Department of the Environment and the Australian Heritage Council. Retrieved from https://www.environment.gov.au/heritage/ahc/publications/rock-art-thematic-study.

McDonald, J., & Veth, P. (2006). Rock art and social identity: A comparison of Holocene graphic systems in arid and fertile environments. In I. Lilley (Ed.), *Archaeology of Oceania: Australia and the Pacific islands* (pp. 96–115). Carlton: Blackwell Publishing Ltd.

McDonald, J., & Veth, P. (2013). Rock art in arid landscapes: Pilbara and Western Desert petroglyphs. *Australian Archaeology, 77*(1), 66–81.

McNiven, I. J., & David, B. (2004). Torres Strait rock art and ochre sources: An overview. *Memoirs of the Queensland Museum / Cultural Heritage Series 3* (1), 209–226.

McNiven, I. J., David, B., & Brayer, J. (2000). Digital enhancement of Torres Strait rock-art. *Antiquity, 74*(286), 759–760.

McNiven, I. J., David, B., Brady, L., & Brayer, J. (2004). Kabadul Kula: A rock art site on Dauan Island, Torres Strait. *Memoirs of the Queensland Museum / Cultural Heritage Series, 3* (1), 227–255.

McNiven, I. J., Dickinson, W. R., David, B., Wiesler, M., Von Gnielinski, F., Carter, M., & Zoppi, U. (2006). Mask Cave: Red-slipped pottery and the Australian-Papuan settlement of Zenadh Kes (Torres Strait). *Archaeology in Oceania, 41*, 49–81.

Merlan, F. (1989). The interpretive framework of Wardaman rock art: A preliminary report. *Australian Aboriginal Studies, 1989 / 2*, 14–24.

Moore, D. R. (1979). *Islanders and Aborigines at Cape York: An ethnographic reconstruction based on the 1848–1850 'Rattlesnake' journals of O. W. Brierly and information he obtained from Barbara Thompson.* Canberra: Australian Institute of Aboriginal Studies.

Moore, D. R. (1984). *The Torres Strait collections of A. C. Haddon: A descriptive catalogue.* London: British Museum Publications.

Morphy, H. (1977). *Too many meanings: An analysis of the artistic system of the Yolngu of north-east Arnhem Land* (PhD thesis). Australian National University, Canberra.

Morphy, H. (1991). *Ancestral connections: Art and an Aboriginal system of knowledge.* University of Chicago Press, Chicago.

Morwood, M. J. (1986). The archaeology of art: Excavations at Maidenwell and Gatton Shelters, southeast Queensland. *Queensland Archaeological Research, 3,* 88–132.

Morwood, M. J. (2002). *Visions from the past: The archaeology of Australian Aboriginal art.* Washington, DC: Smithsonian Institution Press.

Mountford, C. P. 1959. *The rock art of Australia* (Unpublished MA thesis). Department of Archaeology, Cambridge University, England.

Munn, N. D. (1973). *Walbiri iconography: Graphic representation and cultural symbolism in a central Australian society.* New York: Cornell University Press.

Munn, N. D. (1996). The figure in the Australian Aboriginal landscape. *Critical Inquiry, 22*(3), 446–465.

Myers, F. (1982). Always ask: Resource use and land ownership among Pintupi Aborigines of the Australian Western Desert. In N. M. Williams & E. S. Hunn (Eds.), *Resource managers: North American and Australian hunter-gatherers* (pp. 131–153). New York: Routledge.

Neale, M. (Ed.). (2017). *Songlines: Tracking the Seven Sisters.* Canberra: National Museum of Australia Press.

Newton, D. (1961). *Art styles of the Papuan Gulf.* New York: University Publishers.

Officer, K. (1992). The edge of the sandstone: Style boundaries and islands in south-eastern New South Wales. In J. McDonald & I. P. Haskovec (Eds.), *State of the art: Regional rock art studies in Australia and Melanesia* (pp. 6–14). Occasional AURA Publication No. 6. Melbourne: Australian Rock Art Research Association.

Roberts, B. W., & Linden, M. V. (2011). Investigating archaeological cultures: Material culture, variability, and transmission. In B. W. Roberts & M. V. Linden (Eds.), *Investigating archaeological cultures* (pp. 1–21). New York: Springer.

Roberts, T. (2005). *Frontier justice: A history of the Gulf country to 1900.* St. Lucia: University of Queensland Press.

Rose, D. B. (1992). *Dingo makes us human: Life and land in an Australian Aboriginal culture.* Cambridge: Cambridge University Press.

Ross, J. (2013). A continent of nations: The emergence of new regionally distinct rock art styles across Australia. *Quaternary International, 285,* 161–171.

Ross, J., & Travers, M. (2013). 'Ancient mariners' in northwest Kimberley rock art: An analysis of watercraft and crew depictions. *The Great Circle, 35*(2), 55–82.

Ross, J., Valenzuela, D. R., Hernández Llosas, M. I., Briones, L., & Santoro, C. M. (2008). More than the motifs: The archaeological analysis of rock art in arid regions of the southern hemisphere / más que motivos: el análisis arqueológico del arte rupestre en regiones áridas del hemisferio sur. *Chungara: Revista De Antropología Chilena, 40,* 273–294.

Sackett, J. R. (1985). Style and ethnicity in the Kalahari. *American Antiquity, 50* (1), 154–159.

Serra, E., & Folch, A. (1976). *The art of Papua and New Guinea.* New York: Rizzoli International.

Smith, B. W., & Blundell, G. (2004). Dangerous ground: A critique of landscape in rock-art studies. In C. Chippindale & G. Nash (Eds.), *The figured landscape of rock-art: Looking at pictures in place* (pp. 239–262). Cambridge: Cambridge University Press.

Smith, C. (1992). The articulation of style and social structure in Australian Aboriginal art. *Australian Aboriginal Studies, 1992 / 1,* 28–34.

Stanner, W. E. H. (1965). Aboriginal territorial organization: Estate, range, domain and regime. *Oceania, 36*(1), 1–26.

Stanner, W. E. H. (1979). *White man got no dreaming: Essays 1938–1973*. Canberra: Australian National University Press.

Stark, M. (Ed.). (1998). *The archaeology of social boundaries*. Washington, DC: Smithsonian Institution Press.

Stark, M. T., Bowser, B. J., & Horne, L. (Eds.). (2008). *Cultural transmission and material culture: Breaking down boundaries*. Tucson: University of Arizona Press.

Sutton, P. (1995). *Country: Aboriginal boundaries and land ownership in Australia*. Aboriginal History Monograph 3. Canberra: ANU Press.

Sutton, P., & Rigsby, B. (1982). People with 'politicks': Management of land and personal on Australian Cape York Peninsula. In N. M. Williams & E. S. Hunn (Eds.), *Resource managers: North American and Australian hunter-gatherers* (pp. 131–153). New York: Routledge.

Taçon, P. S. C. (1987). Internal-external: A re-evaluation of the 'X-ray' concept in western Arnhem Land rock art. *Rock Art Research, 4* (1), 36–50.

Taçon, P. S. C. (1989). *From Rainbow Snakes to 'x-ray' fish: The nature of the recent rock painting tradition of western Arnhem Land, Australia* (PhD thesis). Australian National University, Canberra.

Taçon, P. S. C. (1993). Regionalism in the recent rock art of western Arnhem Land, Northern Territory. *Archaeology in Oceania, 28* (3), 112–120.

Taçon, P. S. C. (2001). Australia. In D. S. Whitley (Ed.), *Handbook of rock art research* (pp. 530). Walnut Creek, CA: Altamira Press.

Taçon, P. S. C. (2013). Interpreting the in-between: Rock art junctions and other small style areas between provinces. *Time and Mind: The Journal of Archaeology, Consciousness and Culture, 6* (1), 73–80.

Tacon, P. S. C., & Ouzman, S. (2004). Worlds within stone: The inner and outer rock-art landscapes of northern Australia and southern Africa. In C. Chippindale & G. Nash (Eds.), *The figured landscapes of rock-art: Looking at pictures in place* (pp. 39–68). Cambridge: Cambridge University Press.

Taçon, P. S. C., South, B., & Hooper, S. B. (2003). Depicting cross-cultural interaction: Figurative designs on wood, earth and stone from south-east Australia. *Archaeology in Oceania, 38*, 89–101.

Taylor, L. (1987). *'The same but different': Social reproduction and innovation in the art of the Kunwinjku of western Arnhem Land* (PhD thesis). Australia National University, Canberra.

Tratebas, A. (2012). North American-Siberian connections: Regional rock art patterning using multivariant statistics. In J. McDonald & P. Veth (Eds.), *A companion to rock art* (pp. 90–102). Hoboken, NJ: Wiley-Blackwell.

Ulm, S., Westcott, C., Reid, J., Ross, A., Lilley, I., Prangnell, J., & Kirkwood, L. (Eds.). (2002). *Barriers, borders, boundaries: Proceedings of the 2001 Australian Archaeological Association Annual Conference*. Tempus 7. St. Lucia: Anthropology Museum, University of Queensland.

Wade, V., Wallis, L. A., & Woolgar Valley Aboriginal Corporation. (2011). Style, space and social interaction: An archaeological investigation of rock art in inland north Queensland, Australia. *Australian Archaeology, 72*(1), 23–34.

Walker, D. (1972). Bridge and barrier. In D. Walker (Ed.), *Bridge and barrier: The natural and cultural history of Torres Strait* (pp. 399–405). Canberra: Australian National University.

Walsh, G. L. (1985). The archaeological significance of Lawn Hill Gorge. Queensland National Parks and Wildlife Service (Unpublished report).

Welsch, R. L., Webb, V-L., & Haraha, S. (2006). *Coaxing the spirits to dance: Art and society in the Papuan Gulf of New Guinea.* Hanover, NH: Hood Museum of Art, Dartmouth College.

Wiessner, P. (1983). Style and social information in Kalahari San projectile points. *American Antiquity, 48* (2), 253–276.

Williams, N. M. (1982). A boundary is to cross: Observations on Yolngu boundaries and permission. In N. M. Williams & E. S. Hunn, (Eds.), *Resource managers: North American and Australian hunter-gatherers* (pp. 131–153). New York: Routledge.

Williams, N. M. (1986). *The Yolngu and their land: A system of land tenure and the fight for its recognition.* Stanford, CA: Stanford University Press.

Winn, N. B. (2016). *Boundaries, connections and cultural heritage management challenges: The rock art of the Chillagoe–Mungana Limestone Belt, Queensland, Australia.* (PhD thesis). Griffith University, Brisbane.

Wobst, H. M. (1999). Style in archaeology of archaeologists in style. In E. S. Chilton (Ed.), *Material meanings: Critical approaches to the interpretation of material culture* (pp. 118–132). Salt Lake City: University of Utah Press.

Wobst, H. M. (1977). Stylistic behaviour and information exchange. In C. E. Cleland (Ed.), *Papers for the Director: Research essays in honour of James B. Griffin* (pp. 317–342). Anthropology Papers Vol. 61. Ann Arbor: Museum of Anthropology, University of Michigan.

Yanyuwa Families & Bradley, J. (2016). *Wuka nya-nganunga li-Yanyuwa li-Anthawirrayarra, langage for us the Yanyuwa Saltwater people: A Yanyuwa encyclopaedia, Volume 1.* North Melbourne: Australian Scholarly Publishing.

Yanyuwa Families, Bradley, J. J., & Cameron, N. (2003). *Forget about Flinders: A Yanyuwa atlas of the south west Gulf of Carpentaria.* Brisbane: J. M. McGregor Ltd.

CHAPTER 28

AUSTRALIAN INDIGENOUS OCHRES

Use, Sourcing, and Exchange

JILLIAN HUNTLEY

INTRODUCTION

ABORIGINAL Australians have long, continuous cultural traditions, as evidenced by archaeological records that contain transported and modified ochres spanning tens of thousands of years. It is very important, however, not to confuse cultural continuity with cultural stasis (David 2000; Head, Trigger, & Mulcock 2005). Cultures are dynamic, and Aboriginal cultures, by virtue of their longevity, are multifaceted and adaptive. Australia's long-term archaeological records provide windows into the social flexibility of diverse Aboriginal cultures, each highly attuned to the environments they inhabited. Against this setting, Australian archaeology holds a unique and privileged place in world cultural studies. Moreover, Australia occupies a rare position in the history of archaeological science. Unlike established regional archaeologies in many other parts of the world, professional university-based archaeology in Australia coincided with the 'radiocarbon revolution', resulting in the integrated deployment of scientific techniques as part-and-parcel of archaeological enquiries (see Urwin & Spriggs, this volume). These developments included ochre studies, which have always had a distinctly archaeometric focus. Indeed, the archaeological accounts of Aboriginal trade and exchange explicitly recognized the need for analytical tools that could provide a spatial dimension to research, suggesting that methods from the physical sciences may illuminate the geographic origin of materials (Mulvaney 1976).

The Archaeological Importance of Ochre Use

Ochres are durable. As with stone artefacts, ochres survive from deep-time archaeological records through to the present. Ochre use is important evidence of the intellectual development of humanity, a material correlate of complex cognition such as planning over both geographic distances and time (Hodgskiss 2013; Wadley 2013). Ochre use is likewise entwined with the archaeological emergence of symbolically mediated behaviours and, more explicitly, the appearance of artistic practices (d'Errico et al. 2003; Henshilwood et al. 2011; Marean et al. 2007). Found in stratified, datable contexts, ochres provide insights into change or stability in cultural and symbolic systems over time (Smith et al. 1998).

It is true that pigments used for burials, body paint, colouring artefacts, or painting rock surfaces involved aesthetic and symbolic dimensions (Mulvaney 2012). However, the presence of faceted, striated, and/or ground ochres in archaeological deposits is not in itself evidence of symbolically mediated behaviour, as the pigmentatious qualities of earth minerals do not mean they were used (solely) as pigments. The selection, collection, and transport of ochres is certainly evidence of forward planning and the material expression of cultural landscapes and social interaction if trade and exchange are implied (Smith et al. 1998).

Ochres that look the same in colour and texture may have distinctive mineral, elemental, and morphological properties. Scientific analysis is therefore required to discern aspects of human–environment interactions and archaeological patterns of trade and exchange. Successful ochre sourcing projects have been able to differentiate local from exotic pigments using a variety of scientific techniques (Dayet, Le Bourdonnec, Daniel, Porraz, & Texier 2016; MacDonald et al. 2013; Scadding, Winton, & Brown 2015; Smith et al. 1998).

Complex symbolism in the form of referential and representational ritual and artistic behaviours (David et al. 2013) should not be assumed from the presence of archaeological ochres alone, especially when a range of alternative, utilitarian functions are recorded (see below). It is, however, unlikely that ochre use was solely utilitarian, especially in Australian Aboriginal societies where landscapes are intertwined with the activities of the ancestral beings who created them, including the formation of ochre sources frequently explained as the spilt bodily fluids of culture heroes (Blundell & Woolagoodja 2005; Head et al. 2005: 257; Morphy 1989, 1991; Scadding et al. 2015; Smith & Fankhauser 2009; Vinnicombe 1997).

Defining Ochre

Ochres are natural earth minerals, the product of geological (chiefly chemical) weathering and the result of landscape-scale processes (Huntley 2014; Watts 2017). Australia is geologically old and consequently highly weathered, with a variety of geomorphic landscapes providing abundant ochre outcrops and other easily accessible sources. These sources occur in primary contexts as conglomerate pebbles, veins (mineral crystallization within rock), and seams (geological strata) in bedrock such as siltstones, shales, and ferruginized sandstones, and as exposed sedimentary deposits. Secondary sources of ochre include loose cobbles in fluvial/beach gravels and nodules in alluvial/colluvial sediments. Ochre sources have unique diagenetic and weathering histories resulting from their specific geomorphic context (Smith & Fankhauser 2009). Large geological seams can create multiple ochre source locations, such as the famed Wilgie Mia and Little Wilgie quarries which lay 3 km apart in the same Banded Iron Formation seam in Wadjari Country (the Weld Range, Western Australia) (Scadding et al. 2015). Ochres are almost always mixed minerals, even where a dominant mineral's properties drive its selection by Aboriginal peoples. This mixture is important as sensitive modern scientific techniques can describe minor mineral constituents, which are fundamental in recognizing the geomorphic contexts of unknown ochre sources to identify likely locations within the landscape, as well as characterizing minute geochemical components to differentiate between neighbouring sources (Brand et al. 2019; Huntley, Brand, Aubert, & Morwood 2014; Scadding et al. 2015).

The term *ochre* conventionally defines ferric-enriched earth minerals, containing 70% or more iron oxide/oxyhydroxide, embedded within matrices of clays, micas, and/or calcite minerals that contain an assortment of other crystals such as quartz and feldspar (MacDonald, Hancock, Cannon, & Pidruczny 2011). Iron-rich earth minerals are predominantly red, purple, yellow, and orange, but they can sometimes appear black, brown, and even green. A focus on iron minerals has led some archaeologists to use the terms *ochre* and *haematite* interchangeably and indiscriminately, despite the fact that less than five weight percent of a mineral by concentration—which may not even be an iron phase—can account for an ochre's colour (Ford, MacLeod, & Haydock 1994; Huntley, Aubert, Ross, Brand, & Morwood 2015; Wallis et al. 2016; Ward, Watchman, Cole, & Morwood 2001). Further, restricting the definition of ochres to red-hued earth minerals is not in keeping with its colloquial use in Australia where Aboriginal people apply the term *ochre* to assorted earth minerals, including those coloured grey, white, and blue (Chalmin & Huntley 2018; Wallis et al. 2016).

Archaeologists also often use the terms *ochre* and *pigment* interchangeably. Ochres are by definition pigmentatious, that is, earth minerals that produce a colour streak upon scraping or grinding, frequently leaving a coloured residue on the skin when touched. Classifications of archaeological ochres commonly define streak geologically, scrapping ochre nodules across unglazed white porcelain tile and describing the colour produced (Hodgskiss 2013; Watts 2017). It is important to bear in mind, however, that just because ochres are by definition pigmentatious, that does not mean that they functioned (solely or even primarily) as pigments. It is equally important to note that, regardless of function, archaeological ochres are evidence of past human–environment interaction, mobility, and material preferences at a variety of scales. Therefore, without assuming function, this chapter uses the terms *ochre, earth minerals, archaeopigment,* and *pigments* to describe the natural minerals selected and used by Australian Aboriginal peoples.

OCHRE USE

The importance of ochre in Indigenous Australia is historically well documented, including in the earliest colonial accounts (Jones 1984; Sagona 1994). Exotic 'high-quality' ochres were (and are) imported via trade networks (Chaloupka 1993; McBryde 1987; McCarthy 1939; McNiven & David 2004), though equally, abundant local ochres were (and are) used (Crawford & Clarke 1976; David, Clayton, & Watchman 1993, David et al. 2019; Huntley et al. 2015; Huntley, Wallis, Stephenson, Karlka Nyiyaparli Aboriginal Corporation, & Davis 2020). Some of the largest, best-known red ochre quarries include Bookartoo/Parachilna in the Flinders Ranges of South Australia; Karrku, Ulpunyali, and Lawa in central Australia; Wilgie Mia and Little Wilgie in the Weld Range of Western Australia; and Tooumbunner in Tasmania (Jones 1984; Sagona 1994; Smith & Fankhauser 2009) (Figure 28.1).

The large, ethnographically documented trade routes that spanned hundreds of kilometres and included a multitude of exchanged materials have received the most archaeological attention (McBryde 1997). Within such routes, dedicated ochre expedition parties of up to 70–80 men were noted as travelling ~450 km through different territories, often fighting their way to distant ochre mines, where they would gather up to 35 kg of ochre each, mixing it with water or urine to form cakes for transport. Such expeditions often collected additional members as they travelled, sending a messenger ahead to seek permission from the ochre mine's owners (Jones 1984; Smith & Fankhauser 2009).

Earth minerals were/are used as a visual/liminal symbol of transitional states; for example red ochre body adornment is used to signal when women have finished menstruating, when a widow exits mourning, and in initiation rites as boys transition to manhood (Jones 1984; Sagona 1994). But red ochres were/are also used in conjunction with other minerals. For example, body paintings were/are executed in two or more colours (red, white, yellow, and black) (Morphy 1991; Rose 1942) and minerals like gypsum were part of a rain maker's tool kit (Jones 1984). White ochres are the most scientifically studied rock art pigments (Huntley, George, Sutton, & Taçon 2018) and were also used as sculptural media, including the enigmatic Toas of central Australia and the mourning caps worn by the bereaved across the continent, both possibly made for some 35,000 years (Davidson 1949; Hamm et al. 2016; Jones 2000; Jones & Sutton 1986) (Figure 28.2).

Ochre was not reserved for ceremonial use. The South Australian Museum (SAM) collection contains Aboriginal ochred children's toys, 'utensils', and weapons, as well as ritual objects (Jones 1984). Ochres were used medically as styptic/antiseptic ointments (on wounds, bruises, and swellings) and to eradicate internal and external parasites; as a skin applicant to protect against sun and wind and to repel insects; and as a preservative for food and wooden implements (Brian 1979; Davies 1846; Jones 1984; Plomley 1966; Sagona 1994: 23). The material properties of particular ochres (greasiness, shine, small particle size, clay content) made certain sources desirable for

FIGURE 28.1. Locations are mentioned in the text. The light grey shaded area is the Lake Eyre Basin. The dark grey shaded area shows the extent of Sahul's landmass during the Last Glacial Maximum around 20,000 years ago.

different purposes. Characteristics such as small grain size or colour (hue and saturation) influenced artists' preferences and selection for ritual practices (Chaloupka 1993; Cole & Watchman 1996; Huntley, Watchman, & Dibden 2011; Sagona 1994). But most importantly for archaeological sourcing, ethnographic evidence shows that an ochre's affiliation within specific cultural landscape features was, and remains, a primary concern in its selection (Blundell & Woolagoodja 2005; Morphy 1989, 1991; Vinnicombe 1997).

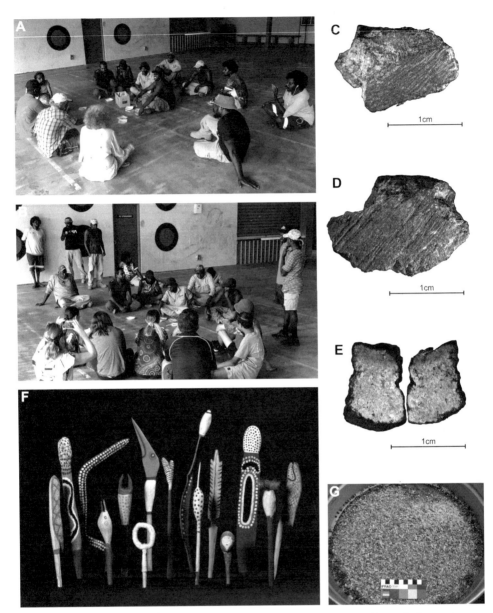

FIGURE 28.2. *A:* Senior Madjedbebe site custodian May Nango along with Djaykuk Djandomerr discussing the materiality of ochres with members of the Djurrubu Ranger team. *B:* Members of the Djurrubu Ranger team teaching Jabiru Area School students about ochres. *C and D:* Ground ochres from Excavation Unit B6 at Madjedbebe dating to ~63,000 years ago. *E:* Red ochre nodules with the flattened (presumably ground) surface painted white and orange, recovered from Excavation Unit B6 at Madjedbebe dating to ~18,000 years ago. *F:* Toa sculptures held in the SAM—object catalogue numbers A6287, A6147, A6149, A6478, A6277, A6245, A6134, A6259, A6117, A6194, A6150, A6182, A6153, A6241, and A6213. *G:* gypsum peds recovered at Warratyi Rock Shelter from strata dated to between 33,000 and 40,000 years old.

What Is Sourcing?

The central tenet of sourcing (provenance) research is that similarity in the composition of artefacts and raw materials is evidence for their common origin (Malainey 2011). First articulated in the late 1970s, the Provenience Postulate was rapidly adopted as the archaeological rationale for compositional analysis of archaeomaterials. It holds that an artefact can be assigned to the geographically restricted source of the materials from which it was manufactured, as long as the difference in chemical composition *between* source materials exceeds, in some recognizable way, the compositional variation *within* a given source (Weigand, Harbottle, & Sayre 1977: 24). A critical qualification is that chemical analyses alone are only capable of systematically eliminating possible sources, given that multiple deposits with identical 'geochemical fingerprints' may exist (Malainey 2011; Wilson & Pollard 2001). Further, earth minerals may have the same chemical profile arranged as distinct crystallographic structures (mineral polymorphs) (Wisseman, Moore, Hughes, Hynes, & Emerson 2002: 690). This nuance led Hector Neff (2002) to restate provenance determination as the possibility of assigning a raw material to its source on the basis that there exists a qualitative or quantitative, chemical or mineralogical, difference between natural sources that exceeds the qualitative or quantitative variation within them—commonly referred to as the Provenance Postulate.

Provenance investigations are important not only in archaeology but also in contemporary cultural studies. A principal motivation for analysing the material properties of Australian earth pigments has been the concept of authenticity in relation to the fine art market, with geochemical procedures designed expressly for authenticating Aboriginal artworks (Green & Watling 2007; Creagh, Lee, Otieno-Alego, & Kubik 2009; O'Neill, Creagh, & Sterns 2004).

Archaeologically, the term *provenience* is used to delineate the precise 'find spot' of an artefact or the discrete geographic extraction location of a raw material. This is distinct from *provenance*, which describes the systematic observation of the chemical/mineralogical composition of an artefact and that characteristic composition's relationship to the physicochemical composition of the raw material(s) from which it has been manufactured (Pollard, Batt, Stern, Suzanne, & Young 2007). Therefore, provenance of archaeological artefacts is often assigned to a raw material source or a group of other artefacts without the establishment of (geographic) 'provenience'.

Provenance investigations are composed of a set of techniques—the mechanics of the approach—and the theoretical frameworks informing research designs and interpretation. Consideration of both aspects is needed for success. In archaeological science, researchers should focus the topic investigated to the point that it can be resolved through the application of physical scientific techniques (Plog 1982). In this vein, the concept of validity addresses whether or not the attributes measured in fact correspond to the archaeological phenomena under study (Frahm 2012: 170). Validity is central to provenance research as 'characterisation requires a bridge between analytical measurements (elemental concentrations, isotope ratios, proportions of mineralogical phases, etc.) and the archaeological concept of interest' (Neff 1998: 323). In other words, the characteristic composition and/or structure being measured needs to be relevant to the problem investigated (Plog 1982: 75).

ANALYTIC METHODS USED TO
ESTABLISH PROVENANCE

Sourcing studies sit firmly in the domain of archaeological science (historically, archaeometry), which blends methods from physics, chemistry, geology, geomorphology, archaeology, anthropology, and art history. Physicochemical characterization is the mainstay of archaeopigment research, describing the physical and chemical properties of ochre in service of archaeological enquiry (Chalmin & Huntley 2018). Physicochemical description of ochres includes their chemistry (usually major, minor, and trace element composition) and their structural (mineral or molecular) and morphological properties (such as matrix constituents and grain sizes).

Earth minerals, including ochres, are challenging for provenance research as they are porous and mineralogically heterogeneous (Killick 2015). Ochres are susceptible to complex geological weathering, resulting in compositional segregation at the material's surface. Physicochemical differences can occur at the exterior of an ochre source/ nodule through interactions with the atmosphere, moisture, biota, and/or sediments (if buried), causing alterations of chemistry/mineralogy at the environment–ochre surface interface. Indeed, there is some suggestion that postdepositional processes such as heating and oxidation have led to an overrepresentation of red ochre in the archaeological record due to mineral phase transitions, particularly from goethite to hematite, which typically expresses visually in a colour change from yellow to red (Cook, Davidson, & Sutton 1990; Smith et al. 1998; Wadley 2010).

No one scientific technique or combination of methods has been shown to definitively provenance archaeological ochres. Indeed, while geochemical methods are most frequently used, there is little consensus as to which elements are diagnostic for ochre sourcing (MacDonald, Fox, Dubreuil, Beddard, & Pidruczny 2018). Research to date shows that ochre sources and provenience locations exhibit distinct, often unique physicochemical characteristics. Therefore, the most successful approaches to provenance have physiochemically characterized pigments and then tailored analyses accordingly.

The techniques used to characterize and provenance ochres may be usefully divided into two broad categories—bulk and surface. First, *bulk techniques* include sourcing study staples such as neutron activation analysis (NAA, also referred to as instrument NAA), inductively coupled plasma spectrometry (ICP, including [atomic emission spectroscopy (AES)], OES [optical emission spectrometry], and MS [mass spectrometry]), and X-ray (powder) diffraction. Such techniques generate data from an area volume of sample, characterizing the whole rather than constituent minerals/grains. Bulk techniques are generally performed on extracted samples that are prepared via mechanical grinding into powder or acid digestion, and sometimes column chemistry (i.e., the use of solvents to separate out constituent fractions for analysis) (Moyo et al. 2016). Historically, bulk techniques have been preferred in provenance investigations, as it is argued that they dilute mineral segregation and other taphonomic effects (Glascock & Neff 2003).

Second, *surface techniques* characterize the outer layer of a sample, generally without preparation of the specimen (though the sample is usually taken back to the laboratory). Depending on the aperture or optic/beam dimensions, surface analyses characterize a circular or ovoid area of microns to millimetres, with similar penetration depths (μ's to mm's). Surface techniques are important for understanding composite earth minerals, quantifying the different constituents of ochres, and describing physicochemical alterations (such as leaching in aqueous or sedimentary environments and oxidation at the sample–atmosphere interface). Examples of surface techniques include chemical (e.g., Laser ablation-inductively coupled plasma (mass spectrometry) [LA-ICP(-MS)], scanning electron microscope–energy dispersive spectroscopy [SEM–EDS], X-Ray fluorescence [XRF]) and structural analyses (e.g., X-Ray diffraction, Raman spectroscopy, and Fourier transform infrared spectroscopy) and can incorporate a mapping function to spatially illustrate chemical/structural features. Due to the heterogeneous nature of ochres across outcrops—associated with mineralogical zoning (i.e., areas of chemical enrichment/depletion) and alteration from postdepositional processes—replicate measurements are important to quantify heterogeneity and ensure that the data from different analyte (or spot) locations are representative of overall composition (Huntley 2014; Scadding et al. 2015). A range of field portable surface analytic instruments have become commercially available in recent years, including raman spectroscopy (Raman), fourier transform infrared spectroscopy (FTIR), portable X-Ray fluorescence (pXRF), and X-Ray diffraction (pXRD). Although most of these are utilized by archaeologists as economical laboratory-based instruments, field-based applications have described the chemistry and structure of pigment-decorated artefacts, rock art, and ochre sources (e.g., Huntley et al. 2020).

A third category of analyses used to complement provenance research is micromorphology—the microscopic study of morphological detail. This is a useful, well-established archaeological method for examining depositional history and postdepositional alterations through the description of site fabrics and their minute features (Goldberg 2018). The morphology of archaeopigments can provide information regarding the geomorphic context of ochre formation, ochre processing (especially understanding composite paints), and postdepositional alteration (Clarkson et al. 2017; Henshilwood, d'Errico, & Watts 2009; Henshilwood et al. 2011, 2018; Huntley 2012; MacDonald et al. 2019). Destructive sampling is most often required for micromorphological investigations as samples are generally mounted into an instrument chamber (Zarzycka et al. 2019), with cross-section preparations common (Huntley et al. 2015; MacDonald et al. 2019). While the visual observations of topographic and morphological details are the primary function of micromorphological ochre studies, element mapping via techniques such as SEM-EDS and LA-ICP-MS can illustrate the spatial extent of chemical constituents and features of interest such as zones of mineral segregation.

Although the volume of geochemical and mineralogical techniques used in past archaeopigment research clearly shows how archaeologically meaningful such investigations are, novel approaches continue to be trailed and evaluated. Most Australian archaeopigment studies have continued to focus on novelty in method development rather than conducting purely applied research, almost exclusively drawing specimens from ethnographically well-known quarry or 'ochre mines' housed in museum and gallery collections (Creagh et al. 2009; Green & Watling 2007; Popelka-Filcoff et al. 2012a, 2012b).

Issues of Scale

Provenance investigations rely on the comparison of compositional data, commonly generating chemical concentrations of major, minor, and trace elements that are scrutinized for trends using multivariate statistics. Typically, transition metals and rare earth elements are used to differentiate groups of ochres (MacDonald et al. 2011; Popelka-Filcoff, Miksa, Robertson, Glascock, & Wallace 2008), although there is little consensus in the literature as to which elements are diagnostic for provenience (MacDonald et al. 2018). A common first step in comparisons is reducing the scale of dominant constituents that swamp analyses, masking trends in components measured in far less abundances (called the dilution effect). Common strategies are logarithmic transformation (usually to base 10) and ratios whereby assays are transformed into fractions of the dominant constituent (Baxter 2008). As the term *ochre* popularly refers to ferric oxides and hydrides, archaeopigment studies frequently ratio (positively correlated) compositional data against iron (Fe), known as iron normalization (Popelka-Filcoff, Robertson, Glascock, & Descantes 2007; Dayet et al. 2016; Huntley 2015; MacDonald et al. 2018). Once transformed, multivariate statistical analyses are performed using provenance study staples such as principal component analysis (PCA), factor, correspondence, and cluster analyses.

Consideration of scale is also vital when selecting specimens for study. Ochre sourcing has generally taken one of two tacks, focusing either on archaeological assemblages to delineate compositional groups (Dayet, d'Errico, & Garcia-Moreno 2014; Pierce, Wright, & Popelka-Filcoff 2020), or on geological features as potential pigment sources to build a database against which future artefact compositions can be compared (MacDonald et al. 2013; Velliky, Barbieri, Porr, Conard, & MacDonald 2019). The ultimate aim of provenance work is of course to integrate the two, thereby tracking the movement of objects and people across landscapes (Dayet et al. 2016; MacDonald et al. 2018). Integrating datasets is fraught, however, because of the different scales at which regional geological and archaeological studies operate (Huntley 2014; Linse 1993; MacDonald et al. 2011).

Historically, two issues have limited the application of scientific provenance methods to archaeological ochres. The primary restriction has been project budgets and the availability of analytical expertise limiting the number of analyses undertaken (Neff 1998: 321). The second is that ochre provenance research is still at an early stage of development, resulting in an understandable bias towards known ochres sources (to validate methods) (Eiselt, Popelka-Filcoff, Darling, & Glascock 2011; Scadding et al. 2015; MacDonald et al. 2018). Indeed, it seems that analytic techniques and sampling methodologies are best targeted to the distinct physicochemical attributes of ochre sources (Scadding et al. 2015; Smith & Fankhauser 2009).

Finally, scale is at the heart of trade and exchange networks. Exchange, particularly customary exchange imbedded within a social network, is seen as a hand-to-hand activity between individuals. Trade operates at a larger scale, requiring a greater investment by hunter-forager communities, where the exchange of goods, perceived to be of equal value, happens between cultural groups and may be part of dedicated trade routes, including down-the-line exchange where commodities pass through multiple cultural groups (Oka & Kusimba 2008).

Conceptualizing Ochre Sourcing

Sourcing investigations aim to document the movement of objects/raw materials across land- and seascapes, with the potential to document change or stability in a cultural group's preferences for, and values placed upon, such objects/raw materials. Establishing that trade and exchange occurred is one thing; conceptualizing the cultural and social significance of these practices is another. Many theoretical frameworks have been offered to help structure and interpret archaeological evidence for the movement of materials, and associated social relationships, over time. Within these frameworks, sourcing studies link people to points in the landscape, a proxy for mobility and evidence of resource provisioning (Ditchfield et al. 2023). Human responses to climatic fluctuations and environmental change have been situated predominantly in ecological constructs like optimal foraging theory and niche construction, interpreting economic/subsistence activities in terms of energy conservation and social behaviours in terms of risk minimization (Hawkes & O'Connell 1992; Laland & O'Brien 2010). In Australian archaeology, extensions of such frameworks, including Late Holocene 'intensification', have been proposed, where human responses to climate amelioration and more-or-less modern environmental conditions saw the increase of social signaling (territorial display) as expressions of population pressures (Lourandos & Ross 1994).

The concept of mobility is critical to the identification of trade and exchange networks in terms of provisioning of materials (e.g., ochre). In its broadest sense, mobility describes seasonal movements by hunter-foragers across their landscape and can be conceptualized in terms of a residential to logistical mobility continuum (Binford 1980). Residential mobility is consistent with the idea of a homeland territory (in Aboriginal societies, Country) throughout which people move, exploiting staple and seasonally available resources. That is, people move from one residential base-camp to the next, foraging for resources within the boundary of their homeland. Logistical mobility takes in residential mobility, but with the additional movement of individuals or small (task) groups in specialized forays from base-camps in order to procure particular resources. Hunter-forager mobility patterns encompass more than just subsistence (resources/seasonality). Foraging is one of a number of factors imbedded within mobility strategies that include the creation and maintenance of social networks, interpreted as provisioning for times of resource scarcity (Kelly 1983; Stewart, et al. 2020) (Figure 28.3).

Australian Aboriginal peoples are amongst the most ethnographically well-described mobile hunter-forager communities on earth. Aboriginal precolonial lifeways were defined by landscape mobility, cultural territoriality (a group's stewardship of their Country), and mythologized (cultural) landscapes encompassing not only one's own Country but also adjoining regions interconnected cosmologically through song-lines, with landscape features representing spiritual 'touch stones', evidence of the creative activities of culture heroes and ancestral beings (McBryde 1997). Of course, Aboriginal peoples were not passive occupants of their territories, at the mercy of their environment. Aboriginal peoples engaged in (archaeologically visible) land management practices (Gammage 2011), and preserved seasonally abundant foods for later consumption and trade (Builth 2014; McNiven, Crouch, Richards, Dolby, & Jacobsen 2012).

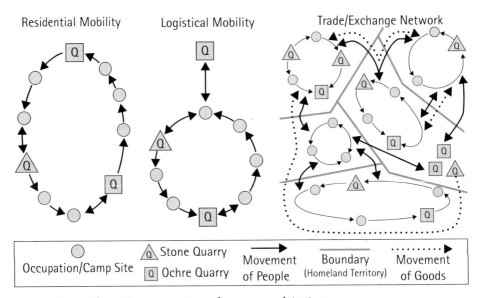

FIGURE 28.3. Schematic representation of resource exploitation.

Subsistence is not only about acquisition, but also the distribution of resources. Australian Aboriginal societies are among hunter-forager communities who engage in demand sharing; an egalitarian practice based on decision-making processes regarding how much, what, and with whom to share resources, including admitting outsiders into homeland territories (Kelly 2013; Peterson 1993). Sharing creates social indebtedness, while at the same time expanding a group's social geography to include materials and resource locations that are storied places, increasing symbolic maps outside of one's Country (McBryde 1997; Rosenfeld 1997).

Provenance studies are integral to these archaeological debates as the description of past social networks, or the tightening of territorial boundaries, relies on evidence of the use of exotic or local materials to establish trade and exchange and intergroup interactions. While the exotic items often command archaeological attention, all groups have some degree of residential mobility, simultaneously engaging in some degree of logistically organized procurement. By identifying the directions and distances involved in the movement of goods and ideas, and focusing on the geographic range of social interactions, sourcing studies can also provide evidence that acquired items and their circulation go beyond utilitarian activities. In most cases, the exchange of exotic materials is interpreted as evidence for contact among separate, otherwise economically independent, groups (Whallon 2006).

Archaeometric provenance studies have always taken explicitly social approaches. Formalist perspectives highlight the individual within the sociopolitical trade and exchange system as determining and constraining the value and distribution of an item, predicting that individuals acquire and redistribute materials in an optimally cost-efficient manner. In contrast, substantivist perspectives emphasize the corporate, viewing procurement and distribution as part of complex social processes that function to maintain inter- and intragroup alliances, often through controlled access to resources (Dillian & White 2010). Substantivist approaches attempt to address the symbolic and ideological aspects of trade and exchange networks and have historically informed archaeological interpretations of ochre movements, centralizing arguments that associate ochre with symbolic/ritual behaviours (McBryde 1997; Mulvaney 1976; Watts 2009).

In Australia, pigment studies have been informed by ethnographic descriptions of ochres exchanged over distances of hundreds of kilometres (e.g., McCarthy 1939; Mulvaney 1976; Smith & Fankhauser 2009). Critically, ethnographies reveal that ochres could be an integral material expression of complex exchange networks and even the subject of dedicated long-distance procurement despite readily available local pigments (McBryde 1987, 1997; Smith & Fankhauser 2009: 1). Such ethnographies not only support substantivist perspectives, they emphasize diffusion as a primary social mechanism evidenced by the movement of 'exotic' goods facilitating intergroup knowledge transfer, with meaning imbedded in 'sacred' places across cultural landscapes (Dillian & White 2010: 11; McBryde 1997). This focus on the exotic has come at the expense of a more nuanced understanding of ochre use in Aboriginal societies which incorporate pigment gathering, grinding, and even art production as part of everyday group activities (Huntley et al. 2020).

ADDITIONAL FRAMEWORKS IN OCHRE SOURCING

In Europe, the investigation of production sequences, or *chaîne opératoire*, is a popular framework that focuses on the technological aspects of a sequence of actions/events and their broader sociocultural context (Farbstein 2011). *Chaînes opératoire* has been applied to the more traditional aspects of geological origins of ochres and also to the description of processing, including grinding, rubbing, and more rarely composite paint and/or the application of pigment to a surface (objects/bodies/rock art) (Chalmin & Huntley 2018; Hensilwood et al. 2011).

The observation of patterning is the primary means by which archaeologists gain insights into the intentional interaction of people with their surroundings and each other. Intentionality is imbedded in every aspect of ochre use, from the selection and procurement of ochre to the processing of pigment and the ways it is applied to objects/bodies/ rock art. Provenance studies are important because just as 'artists can depict anything they wish, but they don't' (David 2004: 71; Smith 1992), ochres can be sourced from almost anywhere and prepared any which way, but they aren't. Archaeomaterials record intention because they are the net result of choices from a series of potential endpoints. Intentionality becomes observable through regularity and archaeological patterning (Russell 2004). Choice is not infinite; rather, it is constrained by culture. Thus, archaeomaterials are evidence of the intentions of individuals and are simultaneously representative of the broader cultural context in which the choices were made (David 2004).

Intentionality and cultural landscapes are conceptual spaces (McBryde 1997; Russell 2004). Cultural landscapes are associative and relational (McBryde 1997), seen by Aboriginal peoples 'as an intimately connected set of phenomena with both material resources for practical usage and encompassing sentient spirituality' (Head et al. 2005: 257). The selection of geological landscape features such as ochres is critical in the archaeological recognition of past cultural landscapes.

A final noteworthy concept is that of 'object biography' (Gosden & Marshall 1999), which places the objects/materials themselves as the central focus to define contextual interpretations, articulating discrete and often dynamic life histories (Dillian & White 2010: 5–6). The attraction of this approach (as with intentionality and cultural landscape approaches) is that it allows fluidity, recognizing that multiple social and cultural contexts can imbue objects/materials with meaning and purpose.

THE AUSTRALIAN OCHRE RECORD IN GLOBAL CONTEXT

Though rare examples suggest earlier hominins utilized ochres, perhaps as far back as 500,000 years ago (Watts, Chazan, & Wilkins 2016), clear evidence for ochre collection, transport, and grinding does not emerge until ~300,000 years ago, in Africa (Brooks et al. 2018; Barham 2002), coincident with the earliest fossil evidence for modern humans (Richter et al. 2017). However, ground earth minerals only become a prominent, consistent feature of archaeological records ~150,000 years ago (Marean et al. 2007). Accordingly, archaeological research has focused on the analysis of ochre associated with early modern human records in Africa (~280–25,000 years ago) and the European Late Pleistocene (130–25,000 years ago), including the material culture of Neanderthals, who also collected and ground ochres (Dayet et al. 2014; Watts 2009).

In contrast to Africa and Europe, Australia was inhabited solely by anatomically modern humans for at least 65,000 years, making our archaeological record globally exceptional. Human settlement of Australia shows that the seafaring peoples who made the difficult water crossing from Island Southeast Asia were already cognitively and behaviourally modern (Davidson 2010; Veth, Stern, McDonald, Balme, & Davidson 2011). The earliest artefact assemblages show that the first Australians engaged in the full suite of varied, complex behaviours that archaeologically define modernity—including the gathering, transport, and grinding of ochres (Clarkson et al. 2017; Davidson 2010).

The unique attributes of the Australian record therefore provide important insights into the material correlates of modern humanity (Brumm & Moore 2005). This is in keeping with the 'traits list' approach to identifying material markers of behavioural modernity (Davidson 2010; McBrearty & Brooks 2000). Initially conceived of as an abrupt cultural florescence, behavioural modernity has been reframed to describe an archaeologically visible 'package' of cultural innovations that gradually assembled in the African Middle Stone Age and then appeared with anatomically modern *Homo sapiens* elsewhere (Brumm & Moore 2005; McBrearty & Brooks 2000). Our region has been at the forefront of recent discoveries of early complex behaviours: art production (Aubert et al. 2018), advanced seafaring (possibly including deep sea fishing) (O'Connor, Ono, & Clarkson 2011), and personal ornamentation (Langley, O'Connor, & Piotto 2016) more than 40,000 years ago. Australian assemblages therefore reflect cultural innovation and adaptation, but not cognitive development, offering scholars all around the world a proxy against which they can critically evaluate earlier/more ambiguous examples of modern, including symbolically mediated, behaviours.

OCHRE SOURCING IN AUSTRALIA—A REVIEW

Following Mulvaney's (1976) observation that scientific analyses may illuminate the spatial extent of a cultural group's movement, there was a flurry of foundation ochre provenance work in the late 1980s to mid-1990s. David et al. (1993) conducted some of the first research, obtaining geochemical signatures via PIXE/PIGE (particle induced X-Ray emission/particle induced gamma-ray emission), analysing thirty-six excavated ochre nodules from Fern Cave in northern Queensland and comparing these with thirty-three ochre nodules from five source locations in the Northern Territory. The trace element profiles distinctly separated in multivariate space; this was an expected result given the different limestone and silicate parent geologies of the excavated and source samples. Importantly, this study provided a proof of concept, which Goodall et al. (1996) expanded to include ninety-one ochre pieces from Fern Cave and sixty-two potential ochre sources from the surrounding region. Goodall et al. (1996) combined elemental with mineralogical analyses (PIXE/PIGE and FTIR) and found a greater variety in the ochres used in the more recent past, with no correlation between element variation and excavation depth. Unfortunately, comparisons between the excavated and potential source ochres could not be made due to unspecified methodological issues. At the same time, Melita Jercher, a geologist at the South Australian Museum (SAM), began analysing ochres using a combination of mineralogy (XRD) and geochemistry (XRF), prosecuting a further proof of concept for ochre source discrimination. Jercher noted that structural analyses were critical in understanding ochre diagenesis and source geomorphology, and in identifying potential source locations within the landscape (Jercher, Pring, Jones, & Raven 1998).

Building on this earlier work, archaeologist Mike Smith began collaborating with Melita Jercher and Australian National University chemist Barry Fankhauser to undertake the largest provenance study of Australian archaeological ochres to date. Their formative work focused on the central deserts of Australia and continues to resonate today, with the analysis of ochres recovered from Puritjarra Rock Shelter, which is widely considered (internationally) as exemplary in ochre sourcing studies. Comparing excavated specimens to ethnographically known ochre mines and other archaeological ochres held in museum collections, Smith et al. (1998) determined provenance via the multivariate analysis of trace element chemistry. Proffering a nested analytic approach, they stated that their interpretations were based on a pilot program of scientific characterizations. Constrained by budget, they selected 32 of 196 ochre specimens (16.3 percent) for analysis via SEM-EDXA (scanning electron microscopy-energy dispersive X-Ray analyses) Choosing red ochres classified as 'high grade', a subset of eight specimens, assumed to be from either the Karrku or Ulpunyali mines, went onto to further XRD and ICP-MS analysis. The results were extrapolated to seven groups of ochres classified on the basis of visual inspections (40x magnification) (Smith et al. 1998: 278–279).

Smith et al. (1998) argued that there was a clear preference for a more distant high-quality ochre source, located in an adjoining clan estate, as opposed to a closer (local) source with equally high-quality ochre. This finding demonstrated the archaeological value of ochre sourcing studies and the alternative perspectives they bring to regional investigations. The sustained impact of Smith et al.'s (1998) work stems from the fact that archaeological studies of this type have not been replicated in other geographic regions within Australia and are rare internationally (though see Eiselt et al. 2011; MacDonald et al. 2013). This foundational ochre research, which used a number of physicochemical techniques, showed that there is no 'magic bullet' in regards to methods for ochre analysis (Mooney, Geiss, & Smith 2003; Smith & Fankhauser 1996, 2009; Smith et al. 1998; Smith, Mooney, & Geiss 2002; Smith & Pell 1997). Further, this work provided a cautionary example of source misattribution where an ochre nodule excavated from Madjedbebe in Arnhem Land was assigned to the same geochemical group as the

Ulpunyali ochre mine in central Australia based on trace element chemistry alone, despite one being vein haematite and the other ferruginized sandstone (Smith & Fankhauser 2009: 41).

Davidson et al. (2005) conducted a PIXE/PIGE program on fourteen rock art motifs and three ochre sources in northwest central Queensland. Their chemical composition results suggested that artists' selection of pigments was not based solely on utility and cost of procurement (Davidson et al. 2005). The clustering of distinctive anthropomorphic motifs with local sources appears to reinforce the findings of Ross (1997) that these geographically restricted anthropomorphs functioned in a different, more bounded way than concentric circle, dot, and line motifs of wider distribution. Although this research was never fully realized, chemical variability within sources appeared less than chemical variance between nonlocal sources.

Technologically focused work has sought to examine different approaches to measuring element concentrations via NAA, selecting ethnographically well-known ochre sources from throughout Australia held in museums (Popelka-Filcoff et al. 2012a, 2012b). Datasets generated independently by the Australian Nuclear Science and Technology Organisation (ANSTO) and Missouri University Research Reactor (MURR) reactors, using k_o-NAA[1] and relative comparator standardization, respectively, were processed using the same multivariate methods, with PCA plots compared. While displaying the same broad trends, element profiles from forty-eight Australian ochre samples showed significant differences between PCA plots for eleven common elements, grouping more tightly in the MURR dataset, while the k_o-NAA data showed significantly more overlap between clusters and greater dispersion. This result is not surprising as their comparison of NIST[2] standards showed significant variation between measured concentrations via each method (Popelka-Filcoff et al. 2012a: 23).

In an applied study using k_o-NAA, Popelka-Filcoff et al. (2012b) characterized thirty-five common elements in sixty-five samples from thirteen ochre quarry locations distributed across South Australia, held in the SAM collection. With between one and fourteen subsamples per quarry, they reported difficulty in comparing data via multivariate methods due to the small subsampling of some ochre sources (< 4). While trends in arsenic (As), antimony (Sb), sodium (Na), and zinc (Zn) were noted, the overall conclusion was that a larger (consistent) number of samples was needed.

From the early 2000s, there was a hiatus in applied Australian pigment provenance studies until Scadding[3] et al. (2015) targeted the famous ochre mines of Wilgie Mia and Little Wilgie, located within the same ore body. Their use of LA-ICP-MS was based on a need for minimal sampling and small spot sizes to facilitate comparison of the quarries with local archaeopigments from rock shelter excavations and open-surface scatter contexts, including local rock art. Their results showed good discrimination between distinctive isotopic lead (Pb) signatures from two mines, something not previously noted via earlier iterations of digestion ICP-MS on the same Weld Range ochres (Smith & Fankhauser, 1996, 2009). Scadding et al. (2015) argued that the hand stencils and excavated ochre nodules derive from the smaller Little Wilgie, whereas all but one of the surface finds were from the larger Wilgie Mia quarry.

Continuing a program that trailed novel methods, Popelka-Filcoff et al. (2014) partnered with the Commonwealth Scientific and Industrial Research Organisation (CSIRO) to test mineral mapping of ochre painted onto six wooded artefacts (shields, boomerangs, and ceremonial 'swords') from the SAM collection using the commercial HyLogger near infrared system. Spatial resolution of the mapping was coarse, but the instrument was sensitive enough to determine nearly all paints mix minerals, with the exception of black pigment, thought likely to be charcoal. Following on from this study, Popelka-Filcoff et al. (2015) undertook synchrotron X-Ray fluorescence (XFM) to chemically characterize and map 165 samples from the same ethnographically known ochres previously examined by NAA (Popelka-Filcoff et al. 2012a, 2012b). Despite providing a table of parts per million (ppm) concentration data, they did not compare assays with multivariate methods, instead presenting element abundance as heat map images alongside conventional light microscopy. While some element trends were discussed, these were cautiously noted as the preparation method for mixing ochres in epoxy resin before slide mounting resulted in varying the dilution of the pigments impeding data comparisons. The same team then tried synchrotron XFM on sections of two polychrome painted objects (from the 2014 infrared trial/SAM collection), a boomerang from north Queensland, and a bark painting from the Northern Territory, direct mounting each into the beamline for scanning. Popelka-Filcoff et al. (2016) presented maps for five elements from a 5 cm x 3 cm square area from each artefact, concluding that the other ten elements measured were not diagnostic. They surmised that both objects were painted with natural earth pigments (not commercially manufactured paints), arguing a proof of concept for nondestructive, high-resolution chemical and morphological analysis of paints (since demonstrated in applied research; see Aubert et al. 2018).

Recently, Lenehan, Tobe, Smith, and Popelka-Filcoff (2017) analysed ochres from museum and private collections relating to four 'major' ochre quarries (Wilgie Mia, Karku, Bookartoo, and Moana) in different parts of Australia. Microbial DNA, 16S rRNA[4] profiles were generated from a single sample from each of the large ochre quarry sites, which were then subsampled three times. The authors compared resulting taxonomic data from sequencing, using various multivariate methods to argue for discrimination between the different sources, and stated that environmental factors were the major influence over ochre microbe communities. It is not clear, however, what microbial differentiation there would be between ochres buried in sediment and the sediment surrounding them, especially in deep-time archaeological deposits where ochres have been preserved for tens of thousands of years.

The Future of Australian Archaeopigment Studies

Archaeopigment studies have much to contribute to Australian archaeology. The assumed exotic context of Pleistocene ochres throughout Australia is cited as evidence for long-distance trade and exchange, intergroup interaction, and identity marking in the form of art production from the time people arrived in Sahul (Veth et al. 2011). Yet archaeometric description of more than sixty known Pleistocene assemblages is very poor (Langley, Clackson, & Ulm 2011: their Table 1). For example, the red ochre associated with the ~ 40,000 BP Mungo III burial in western New South Wales is stated as deriving from 200 km away because that was the nearest ochre source known to researchers (Johnston & Clarke 1998: 117). This hypothesis has yet to be tested using archaeometric analyses.

While there is no consensus on analytical or data interrogation methods, archaeometric pigment studies are thriving, demonstrating they are archaeologically fruitful and popular. However, combining datasets remains complicated because most of them are only internally consistent, specific to particular instrumentation (especially with the uptake of affordable geochemical techniques like pXRF by archaeologists). Without external calibration, directly combining datasets is not possible (Killick 2015; Popelka-Filcoff et al. 2012a). There is, however, no impediment to either comparing data trends or testing broad-scale patterning across regional assemblages. Work to date shows that scientific methods are best targeted to the distinct physicochemical attributes of ochres (Scadding et al. 2015; Smith & Fankhauser 2009). Equally, applied scientific analysis of ochres demonstrates that a variety of technique(s) such as ICP (OES/MS), XRD, pXRF, PIXE/PIGE, NAA, and SEM-EDS can discern archaeological patterning.

Contemporary excavations deliver unprecedented spatial and temporal resolutions, recovering thousands of utilized ochre pieces, such as from the ~65,000-year sequence at Madjedbebe (Clarkson et al. 2017) (Figure 28.2). Rather than continuing the focus on ethnographically well-known sources, current Australian ochre studies have described the geomorphic contexts of smaller, local sources (Huntley et al. 2015; Huntley et al. 2020; Wallis et al. 2016). High-resolution analytic techniques are overcoming the challenges of dealing with paint mixtures, postdepositional processes, and conflated compositional signatures where motifs/artefact pigments have been retouched or overpainted (Huntley et al. 2014; Scadding et al. 2015). The presumed relationship between ochres from excavated, source contexts, and rock art is being examined (Huntley 2015; Scadding et al. 2015). Minimally destructive/noninvasive approaches are common in analyses co-designed with Aboriginal Traditional Owners who hold stewardship over artefacts and site fabrics, including prepared and applied ochres, even droplets resulting from art production and/or ritual activities (David et al. 2017, 2019; Hamm et al. 2016; Huntley et al. 2020; Scadding et al. 2015). And there is untapped potential to undertake regional scale physicochemical mapping of ochre sources to build databases, against which compositional groups from regional archaeological assemblages can be compared.

Although cost remains a perennial issue, noninvasive screening tools can be used to help select ochres for further laboratory analyses (Huntley 2015). Furthermore, the availability of analytical expertise (Dayet et al. 2016; Huntley et al. 2015; MacDonald et al. 2018) is swiftly increasing the number of archaeopigment investigations, and the number of specimens per analytic program. Expanding such work will not only turn attention to underanalysed finds (such as Pleistocene records) but increase applied research as archaeopigment studies become routine in large, multidisciplinary archaeological research programs (David et al. 2017, 2019; Moore et al. 2020).

ACKNOWLEDGMENTS

I am grateful to Brandi MacDonald (MURR's Archaeometry Laboratory) and Iain Davidson (University of New England) for insightful comments on an earlier draft of this manuscript. Figure 28.3 is based on an unpublished illustration by Davidson, adapted with his kind permission. Figure 28.2 photographs A and B were taken by Lynley Wallis, reproduced with permission of the Gundjeihmi Aboriginal Corporation. Photographs C to E were provided by Delyth Cox and reproduced with permission of the Gundjeihmi Aboriginal Corporation. Images in F reproduced with the permission of the South Australian Museum Image, Film and Sound Archive. Photograph G was provided by Giles Hamm and reproduced with the permission of Adnyamathanha Traditional Owners. I thank Emilie Chalmin (Université de Savoie) and an anonymous referee for engaging with the technical aspects of this chapter, as well as editors Ian McNiven and Bruno David for the invitation to contribute to this volume. I am particularly grateful to Ian for helping me sharpen the discussion of theoretical constructs.

NOTES

1. k_0 refers to a specific type of calibration via the measurement of two calibration constants of an internal standard (commonly gold) within a neutron activation analysis dataset.
2. The National Institute of Standards and Technology (NIST) is the longest running laboratory in the United States. NIST manufacture, certify and sell standard reference materials used in analytic programs throughout the world.
3. Nee Green of Green and Watling (2007).
4. Ribosomal ribonucleic acid.

REFERENCES

Aubert, M., Setiawan, P., Oktaviana, A. A., Brumm, A., Sulistyarto, P. H., Saptomo, E. W., . . . Brand, H. E. A. (2018). Palaeolithic cave art in Borneo. *Nature*, 564, 254–257.
Barham, L. (2002). Systematic pigment use in the Middle Pleistocene of south-central Africa. *Current Anthropology*, 43(1), 181–190.
Baxter, M. J. (2008). Mathematics and statistics in archaeometry: The last 50 years or so. *Archaeometry*, 50(6), 968–982.
Binford, L. R. (1980). Willow smoke and dogs' tails: Hunter-gatherer settlement systems and archaeological site formation. *American Antiquity*, 45(1), 4–20.
Blundell, V., & Woolagoodja, D. (2005). *Keeping the Wanjinas fresh*. Fremantle: Fremantle Arts Centre Press.
Brand, H. E. A., Howard, D. L., Huntley, J., Kappen, P., Maksimenko, A., Paterson, D. J., . . . Tobin, M. J. (2019). Research in art and archaeology: Capabilities and investigations at the Australian synchrotron. *Synchrotron Radiation News*, 32(6), 3–10.
Brian, R. (1979). *The decorated body*. London: Hutchison.

Brooks, A. S., Yellen, J. E., Potts, R., Behrensmeyer, A. K., Deino, A. L., Leslie, D. E., . . . Whittaker, S. (2018). Long-distance stone transport and pigment use in the earliest Middle Stone Age. *Science*, *360*(6384), 90–94.

Brumm, A., & Moore, M. W. (2005). Symbolic revolutions and the Australian archaeological record. *Cambridge Archaeological Journal*, *15*(2), 157–175.

Builth, H. (2014). *Ancient Aboriginal aquaculture rediscovered*. Saarbrucken, Germany: LAP Lambert Academic Publishing.

Chalmin, E., & Huntley, J. (2018). Rock art pigment characterisation. In B. David & I. J. McNiven (Eds.), *Oxford handbook of the archaeology and anthropology of rock art* (pp. 885–909). Oxford: Oxford University Press.

Chaloupka, G. (1993). *Journey in time: The world's longest continuing art tradition: The 50,000 year story of the Australian Aboriginal rock art of Arnhem Land*. Chatswood, NSW: Reed.

Clarkson, C., Jacobs, Z., Marwick, B., Fullagar, R., Wallis, L., Smith, M., . . . Pardoe, C. (2017). Human occupation of northern Australia by 65,000 years ago. *Nature*, *547*, 306–310.

Cole, N., & Watchman, A. (1996). Archaeology of white hand stencils of the Laura region, North Queensland, Australia. *Techne: La science au service de l'histoire dae l'art et des civilisations*, *3*, 82–90.

Cook, N., Davidson, I., & Sutton, S. (1990). Why are so many ancient rock paintings red? *Australian Aboriginal Studies*, *1990*(1), 30–33.

Crawford, I. M., & Clarke, J. D. (1976). Aboriginal use of huntite in rock art, Kimberley, Western Australia. Unpublished report prepared for the Australian Institute of Aboriginal Studies, Canberra.

Creagh, D., Lee, A., Otieno-Alego, V., & Kubik, M. (2009). Recent and future developments in the use of radiation for the study of objects of cultural heritage significance. *Radiation Physics and Chemistry*, *78*, 367–374.

David, B. (2000). *Landscapes, rock-art and the Dreaming: An archaeology of preunderstanding*. New York: Leicester University Press.

David, B. (2004). Intentionality, agency and an archaeology of choice. *Cambridge Archaeological Journal*, *14*(1), 67–71.

David, B., Barker, B., Petchey, F., Delannoy J.-J., Geneste, J.-M., Eccleston, M., . . . Whear, R. L. (2013). A 28,000 year old excavated painted rock from Nawarla Gabarnmang, northern Australia. *Journal of Archaeological Science*, *40*(5), 2493–2501.

David, B., Clayton, E., & Watchman, A. (1993). Initial results of PIXE analysis on northern Australian ochres. *Australian Archaeology*, *36*, 50–57.

David, B., Delannoy, J.-J., Gunn, R., Chalmin, E., Castets, G., Petchey, F., . . . Geneste, J.-M. (2017). Dating painted Panel E1 at Nawarla Gabarnmang, central-western Arnhem Land plateau. In B. David, P. S. C. Taçon, J.-J. Delannoy, & J.-M. Geneste (Eds.), *The archaeology of rock art in western Arnhem Land, Australia* (pp. 245–302). Terra Australis 47. Canberra: ANU Press.

David, B., Delannoy, J.-J., Petchey, F., Gunn, R., Huntley, J., Veth, P., . . . Ouzman, S. (2019). Dating painting events through by-products of ochre processing: Borologa 1 Rockshelter, Kimberley, Australia. *Australian Archaeology*, *85*(1), 57–94.

Davidson, D. S. (1949). Mourning-caps of the Australian Aborigines. *Proceedings of the American Philosophical Society*, *93*(1), 57–70.

Davidson, I. (2010). The colonization of Australia and its adjacent islands and the evolution of modern cognition. *Current Anthropology*, *51*(S1), S177–S189.

Davidson, I., Cook, N., Fischer, M., Ridges, M., Ross, J., & Sutton, S. (2005). Archaeology in another country: Exchange and symbols in north-west central Queensland. In M. J. Mountain,

R. Paton, & I. Macfaralane (Eds.), *Many exchanges: Archaeology, history, community and the work of Isabel McBryde* (pp. 103–130). Aboriginal History Monograph 11. Canberra: Aboriginal History Inc.

Davies, R. (1846). On the Aborigines of Van Diemen's Land. *Tasmanian Journal of Natural Science, 2,* 409–420.

Dayet, L., Le Bourdonnec, F. X., Daniel, F., Porraz, G., & Texier, P. J. (2016). Ochre provenance and procurement strategies during the middle stone age at Diepkloof Rock Shelter, South Africa. *Archaeometry, 58*(5), 807–829.

Dayet, L., d'Errico, F., & Garcia-Moreno, R. (2014). Searching for consistencies in Châtelperronian pigment use. *Journal of Archaeological Science, 44,* 180–193.

D'Errico, F., Henshilwood, C., Lawson, G., Vanhaeren, M., Tillier, A.-M., Soressi, M., . . . Julien, M. (2003) Archaeological evidence for the emergence of language, symbolism, and music—an alternative multidisciplinary perspective. *Journal of World Prehistory, 17*(1), 1–70.

Dillian, C. D., & White, C. (2010). Introduction: Perspectives on trade and exchange. In C. Dillian & C. White (Eds.), *Trade and exchange: Archaeological studies from history and prehistory* (pp. 3–16). New York: Springer.

Ditchfield, K., Huntley, J., Ward, I., Webb, J., Doleman, T., & Kurpiel, R. (2023). Sourcing stone and ochre artefacts: Why it matters in Australia (and beyond). In C. A. Speer, R. Parish, & G. Barrientos (Eds.), *Sourcing archaeological lithic assemblages: New perspectives and integrated approaches* (pp. 52–67). Salt Lake City: University of Utah Press.

Eiselt, B. S., Popelka-Filcoff, R. S., Darling, J. A., & Glascock, M. D. (2011). Hematite sources and archaeological ochres from Hohokam and O'odham Sites in Central Arizona: An experiment in type identification and characterization. *Journal of Archaeological Science, 38,* 3019–3028.

Farbstein, R. (2011) Technologies of art: A critical reassessment of Pavlovian art and society, using *chaîne opératoire* method and theory. *Current Anthropology, 52*(3), 401–432.

Ford, B., MacLeod, I., & Haydock, P. (1994). Rock art pigments from the Kimberley region of Western Australia: Identification of the minerals and conversion mechanisms. *Studies in Conservation, 39,* 57–69.

Frahm, E. (2012). Evaluation of archaeological sourcing techniques: Reconsidering and rederiving Hughes' four-fold assessment scheme. *Geoarchaeology, 27*(2), 166–174.

Gammage, B., (2011). *The biggest estate on earth: How Aborigines made Australia.* Sydney: Allen & Unwin.

Glascock, M. D., & Neff, N. (2003). Neutron activation analysis and provenance research in archaeology. *Measurement Science and Technology, 14*(9), 1516–1526.

Goldberg, P. (2018). Micromorphology. In S. L. López Varela (Ed.), *The Encyclopedia of Archaeological Sciences.* Society for Archaeological Sciences. Malden, MA: Wiley Blackwell. https://onlinelibrary.wiley.com/doi/abs/10.1002/9781119188230.saseas0380 1-4

Goodall, R., David, B. & Bartley, J. (1996). Non-destructive techniques for the analysis and characterisation of pigments from archaeological sites: A case from Fern Cave. In S. Ulm, I. Lilley, and A. Ross (Eds.), *Australian archaeology '95: Proceedings of the 1995 Australian Archaeology Association Annual Conference* (pp. 183–187). Tempus 6. Brisbane: Department of Anthropology and Sociology, University of Queensland.

Gosden, C., & Marshall, Y. (1999). The cultural biography of objects. *World Archaeology, 32*(2), 169–178.

Green, R. L., & Watling, J. R. (2007). Trace element fingerprinting of Australian ochre using laser ablation inductively coupled plasma-mass spectrometry (LAICP- MS) for the provenance establishment and authentication of Indigenous art. *Journal of Forensic Science, 52*(4), 851–859.

Hamm, G., Mitchell, P., Arnold, L. J., Prideaux, G. J., Questiaux, D., Spooner, N. A., . . . Coulthard, V. (2016). Cultural innovation and megafauna interaction in the early settlement of arid Australia. *Nature*, *539*, 280–283.

Hawkes, K., & O'Connell, J. F. (1992). On optimal foraging models and subsistence transitions. *Current Anthropology*, *33*, 63–66.

Head, L., Trigger, D., & Mulcock, J. (2005). Culture as concept and influence in environmental research and management. *Conservation and Society*, *3*(2), 251–264.

Henshilwood, C. S., d'Errico, F., van Niekerk, K. L., Coquinot, Y., Lauritzen, S.-E., Jacobs, Z., . . . García-Moreno, R. (2011). A 100,000-year-old ochre-processing workshop at Blombos Cave, South Africa. *Science*, *334*(219), 219–222.

Henshilwood, C. S., d'Errico, F., van Niekerk, K. L., Dayet, L., Queffelec, A., & Pollarolo, L. (2018). An abstract drawing from the 73,000-year-old levels at Blombos Cave, South Africa. *Nature*, *562*(7725), 115–118.

Henshilwood, C. S., d'Errico, F., & Watts, I. (2009). Engraved ochres from the Middle Stone Age levels at Blombos Cave, South Africa. *Journal of Human Evolution*, *57*(1), 27–47.

Hodgskiss, T. (2013). Ochre use in the Middle Stone Age at Sibudu, South Africa: Grinding, rubbing, scoring and engraving. *Journal of African Archaeology*, *11*(1), 75–95.

Huntley, J. (2012). Taphonomy or paint recipe: In situ portable X-ray fluorescence analysis of two anthropomorphic motifs from the Woronora Plateau, New South Wales. *Australian Archaeology*, *75*(1), 78–94.

Huntley, J. (2014). *Messages in paint: An archaeometric analysis Aboriginal pigment use focusing on the production of rock art* (PhD thesis). University of New England, Armidale.

Huntley, J. (2015). Looking up and looking down: Pigment chemistry as a chronological marker in the Sydney Basin rock art assemblage, Australia. *Rock Art Research*, *32*(2), 131–145.

Huntley, J., Aubert, M., Ross, J., Brand, H. E. A., & Morwood, M. J. (2015). One colour (at least) two minerals: A study of mulberry rock art pigment and a mulberry pigment 'quarry' from the Kimberley, northern Australia. *Archaeometry*, *57*(1), 77–99.

Huntley, J., Brand, H., Aubert, M., Ross, J. & Morwood, M. J. (2014). The first Australian synchrotron powder diffraction analysis of pigment from a Wandjina motif in the Kimberley, Western Australia. *Australian Archaeology*, *78*(1), 33–38.

Huntley, J., George, S., Sutton, M.-J., & Taçon, P. S. C. (2018). Second-hand? Paint chemistry and the age, authenticity and conservation/management of hand stencils from the Sunshine Coast, Qld, Australia. *Journal of Archaeological Science: Reports*, *17*, 163–172.

Huntley, J., Wallis, L. A., Stephenson, B., Karlka Nyiyaparli Aboriginal Corporation, & Davis, A. (2020). A multi-technique approach to contextualising painted rock art in the Central Pilbara of Western Australia: Integrating in-field and laboratory methods. *Quaternary International 572*, 52–73, 10.1016/j.quaint.2020.05.032.

Huntley, J., Watchman, A., & Dibden, J. (2011). Characteristics of a pigment art sequence: Woronora Plateau, New South Wales. *Rock Art Research*, *1*(1), 85–97.

Jercher, M., Pring, A., Jones, P. G., & Raven, M. D. (1998). Rietveld X-ray diffraction and X-ray fluorescence analysis of Australian aboriginal ochres. *Archaeometry*, *40*(2), 383–401.

Johnston, H., & Clarke, P. (1998). Willandra Lakes archaeological investigations 1968–98. *Archaeology in Oceania*, *33*(3), 105–199.

Jones, P. (1984). Red ochre expeditions: An ethnographic and historical analysis of Aboriginal trade in the Lake Eyre Basin: A progress report. Part 1. *Journal of the Anthropological Society of South Australia*, *22*, 3–10.

Jones. P. (2000). The Toas of Killlalpaninna. In S. Kleinert, M. Neale, & R. Bancroft (Eds.), *Oxford companion to Aboriginal art and culture* (pp. 245–246). Canberra: Australian National University Press.

Jones, P., & Sutton, P. (1986). *Art and land: Aboriginal sculptures of the Lake Eyre region*. Adelaide: South Australian Museum in association with Wakefield Press.

Kelly, R. (1983). Hunter-gatherer mobility strategies. *Journal of Anthropological Research, 39*(3), 277–306.

Kelly, R. (2013). *Understanding foraging radius and mobility in a high desert*. New York: Cambridge University Press.

Killick, D. (2015). The awkward adolescence of archaeological science. *Journal of Archaeological Science, 56*, 242–247.

Laland, K. N., & O'Brien, M. J. (2010). Niche construction theory and archaeology. *Journal of Archaeological Method and Theory, 17*(4), 303–322.

Langley, M. C., Clarkson, C., & Ulm, S. (2011). From small holes to grand narratives: The impact of taphonomy and sample size on the modernity debate in Australia and New Guinea. *Journal of Human Evolution, 61*, 197–208.

Langley, M. C., O'Connor, S., & Piotto, E. (2016). 42,000-year-old worked and pigment-stained Nautilus shell from Jerimalai (Timor- Leste): Evidence for an early coastal adaptation in ISEA. *Journal of Human Evolution, 97*, 1–16.

Lenehan, C. E., Tobe, S. S., Smith, R. J., & Popelka-Filcoff, R. S. (2017). Microbial composition analyses by 16S rRNA sequencing: A proof of concept approach to provenance determination of archaeological ochre. *PloS one, 12*(10), p.e0185252.

Linse, A. R. (1993). Geoarchaeological scale and archaeological interpretation: Examples from the central Jornada Mogollon. *Geological Society of America Special Paper, 283*, 11–28.

Lourandos, H., & Ross, A. (1994). The great 'intensification debate': Its history and place in Australian archaeology. *Australian Archaeology, 39*(1), 54–63.

MacDonald, B. L., Fox, W., Dubreuil, L., Beddard, J., & Pidruczny, A. (2018). Iron oxide geochemistry in the Great Lakes Region (North America): Implications for ochre provenance studies. *Journal of Archaeological Science: Reports, 19*, 476–490.

MacDonald, B. L., Hancock, R. G. V., Cannon, A., McNeill, F., Reimer, R., & Pidruczny, A. (2013). Elemental analysis of ochre outcrops in southern British Columbia, Canada. *Archaeometry, 55*(6), 1020–1033.

MacDonald, B. L., Hancock, R. G. V., Cannon, A., & Pidruczny, A. (2011). Geochemical characterization of ochre from central coastal British Columbia, Canada. *Journal of Archaeological Science, 38*(12), 3620–3630.

MacDonald, B. L., Stalla, D., He, X., Rahemtulla, F., Emerson, D., Dube, P. A., . . . White, T. A. (2019). Hunter-gatherers harvested and heated microbial biogenic iron oxides to produce rock art pigment. *Scientific Reports, 9*(1), 1–13.

Malainey, M. E. (2011). *A consumer's guide to archaeological science: Analytical techniques*. New York: Springer.

Marean, C. W., Bar-Matthews, M., Bernatchez, J., Fisher, E., Goldberg, P., Herries, A. I., . . . Nilssen, P. J. (2007). Early human use of marine resources and pigment in South Africa during the Middle Pleistocene. *Nature, 449*(7164), 905–908.

McBrearty, S., & Brooks, A. (2000). The revolution that wasn't: A new interpretation of the origin of modern humans. *Journal of Human Evolution, 39*, 453–563.

McBryde, I. (1987). Goods from another country: Exchange networks and the people of the Lake Eyre Basin. In D. J. Mulvaney & P. J. White (Eds.), *Australians to 1788* (pp. 253–273). Broadway: Fairfax, Syme & Weldon Associates.

McBryde, I. (1997). The cultural landscape of Aboriginal long-distance exchange systems: Can they be confined within our heritage registers? *Historic Environment, 13*(3 & 4), 6–14.

McCarthy, F. D. (1939). 'Trade' in Aboriginal Australia, and 'trade' relationships with Torres Strait, New Guinea and Malaya. *Oceania, 9*(4), 405–439, *10*(1), 80–104, *10*(2), 171–195.

McNiven, I. J., Crouch, J., Richards, T., Dolby, N., & Jacobsen, G. (2012). Dating Aboriginal stone-walled fishtraps at Lake Condah, southeast Australia. *Journal of Archaeological Science, 39*(2), 268–286.

McNiven, I. J., & David, B. (2004). Torres Strait rock-art and ochre sources: An overview. *Memoirs of the Queensland Museum, Cultural Heritage Series, 3*(1), 209–225.

Mooney, S. D., Geiss, C., & Smith, M. A. (2003) The use of mineral magnetic parameters to characterize archaeological ochres. *Journal of Archaeological Science, 30*(5), 511–523.

Moore, M. W., Westaway, K., Ross, J., Newman, K., Perston, Y., Huntley, J., . . . Morwood, M. J. (2020). Archaeology and art in context: Excavations at the Gunu site complex, northwest Kimberley, Western Australia. *PloS one, 15*(2), e0226628.

Morphy, H. (1989). Introduction. In H. Morphy (Ed.), *Animals into art* (pp. 1–17). Boston: Unwin Hyman.

Morphy, H. (1991). *Ancestral connections: Art and an Aboriginal system of knowledge*. Chicago: University of Chicago Press.

Moyo, S., Mphuthi, D., Cukrowska, E., Henshilwood, C. S., van Niekerk, K., & Chimuka, L. (2016). Blombos cave: Middle Stone Age ochre differentiation through FTIR, ICP OES, ED XRF and XRD. *Quaternary International, 404*, 20–29.

Mulvaney, D. J. (1976). 'The chain of connection': The material evidence. In N. Peterson (Ed.), *Tribes and boundaries in Australia* (pp. 72–94). Canberra: Australian Institute of Aboriginal Studies.

Mulvaney, J. (2012). Human condition: The Australia evidence. *Antiquity, 86*, 915–921.

Neff, H. (1998). Archaeological investigation of trade and exchange. *Reviews in Anthropology, 27*(3), 317–335.

Neff, H. (2002). Quantitative techniques for analysing ceramic compositional data. In D. M. Glowacki & H. Neff (Eds.), *Ceramic production and circulation in greater southwest: Source determination by INAA and complementary mineralogical investigations* (pp. 15–36). Los Angeles: Costen Institute of Archaeology, UCLA.

O'Connor, S., Ono, R., & Clarkson, C. (2011). Pelagic fishing at 42,000 years before the present and the maritime skills of modern humans. *Science, 334*(6059), 1117–1121.

O'Neill, P. M., Creagh, D. C., & Sterns, M. (2004). Studies of the composition of pigments used traditionally in Australian Aboriginal bark paintings. *Radiation Physics and Chemistry, 71*, 841–842.

Oka, R., & Kusimba, C. M. (2008). The archaeology of trading systems, part 1: Towards a new trade synthesis. *Journal of Archaeological Research, 16*(4), 339–395.

Peterson, N. (1993). Demand sharing: Reciprocity and the pressure for generosity among foragers. *American Anthropologist, 95*(4), 860–874.

Pierce, D. E., Wright, P. J., & Popelka-Filcoff, R. S. (2020). Seeing red: An analysis of archeological hematite in east central Missouri. *Archaeological and Anthropological Sciences, 12*(1), 1–20.

Plog, F. (1982). The integration of archaeometry and archaeological research. In J. S. Olin (Ed.), *Future directions in archaeometry: A round table* (pp. 59–61). Washington, DC: Smithsonian Institution.

Plomley, N. J. B. (1966). *Friendly mission: The Tasmanian historical papers of George Augustus Robinson 1829–1834*. Hobart: Tasmanian Historical Research Association.

Pollard, M., Batt, C., Stern, B., Suzanne, M., & Young, E. (2007). *Analytical chemistry in archaeology*. Cambridge Manuals in Archaeology. Cambridge: Cambridge University Press.

Popelka-Filcoff, R. S., Lenehan, C. E., Glascock, M. D., Bennett, J. W., Stopic, A., Quinton, S. J., . . . Walshe, K. (2012a). Evaluation of relative comparator and k_0-NAA for characterization of Aboriginal Australian ochre. *Journal of Radioanalytical and Nuclear Chemistry*, *291*(1), 19–24.

Popelka-Filcoff, R. S., Lenehan, C. E., Lombi, E., Donner, E., Howard, D. L., de Jonge, M. D., . . . Pring, A. (2015). Microelemental characterisation of Aboriginal Australian natural Fe oxide pigments. *Analytical Methods*, *7*(17), 7363–7380.

Popelka-Filcoff, R. S., Lenehan, C. E., Lombi, E., Donner, E., Howard, D. L., de Jonge, M. D., . . . Pring, A. (2016). Novel application of X-ray fluorescence microscopy (XFM) for the non-destructive micro-elemental analysis of natural mineral pigments on Aboriginal Australian objects. *Analyst*, *141*(12), 3657–3667.

Popelka-Filcoff, R. S., Lenehan, C. E., Walshe, K., Bennett, J. W., Stopic, A., Jones, P., . . . Durham, A. (2012b). Characterisation of ochre sources in South Australia by neutron activation analysis (NAA). *Journal of the Anthropological Society of South Australia*, *35*, 81–90.

Popelka-Filcoff, R. S., Mauger, A., Lenehan, C. E., Walshe, K., & Pring, A. (2014). HyLogger™ near-infrared spectral analysis: A non-destructive mineral analysis of Aboriginal Australian objects. *Analytical Methods*, *6*(5), 1309–1316.

Popelka-Filcoff, R. S., Miksa, E. J., Robertson, J. D., Glascock, M. D., & Wallace, H. (2008). Elemental analysis and characterization of ochre sources from Southern Arizona. *Journal of Archaeological Science*, *35*(3), 752–762.

Popelka-Filcoff, R. S., Robertson, J. D., Glascock, M. D., & Descantes, C. (2007). Trace element characterization of ochre from geological sources. *Journal of Radioanalytical and Nuclear Chemistry*, *272*(1), 17–27.

Richter, D., Grün, R., Joannes-Boyau, R., Steele, T. E., Amani, F., Rué, M., . . . McPherron, S. P. (2017). The age of the hominin fossils from Jebel Irhoud, Morocco, and the origins of the Middle Stone Age. *Nature*, *546*, 293–296.

Rose, F. (1942). Paintings of the Groote Eylandt Aborigines. *Oceania*, *13*(2), 170–176.

Rosenfeld, A. (1997). Archaeological significance of the social context of rock art production. In M. Conkey, D. Stratmann, & N. G. Jablonski (Eds.), *Beyond art: Pleistocene image and symbol* (pp. 289–300). Memoirs of the Californian Academy of Sciences 23. Berkeley: University of California Press.

Ross, J. (1997). *Painted relationships: An archaeological analysis of a distinctive anthropomorphic rock art motif in northwest central Queensland.* BA (Honors) thesis, University of New England, Armidale, NSW.

Russell, L. (2004). Drinking from the pen holder: Intentionality and archaeological theory. *Cambridge Archaeological Journal*, *14*(1), 64–67.

Sagona, A. G. (1994). The quest for red gold. In A. G. Sagona (Ed.), *Bruising the red earth: Ochre mining and ritual in Aboriginal Tasmania* (pp. 8–38). Carlton: Melbourne University Press.

Scadding, R., Winton, V., & Brown, V. (2015). An LA-ICP-MS trace element classification of ochres in the Weld Range environ, Mid West region, Western Australia. *Journal of Archaeological Science*, *54*, 300–312.

Smith, C. (1992). Colonising with style: Reviewing the nexus between rock art, territoriality and the colonisation and occupation of Sahul. *Australian Archaeology*, *34*(1), 34–42.

Smith, M. A., & Fankhauser, B. (1996). An archaeological perspectives in the geochemistry of Australian red ochre deposits: Prospects for fingerprinting major sources. Unpublished report to the Australian Institute of Aboriginal and Torres Strait Islander Studies, Canberra.

Smith, M. A., & Fankhauser, B. (2009). *Geochemistry and identification of Australian red ochre deposits*. Palaeoworks Technical Papers 9. National Museum of Australia, Canberra, and Centre for Archaeological Research, Australian National University, Canberra.

Smith, M. A., Fankhauser, B., & Jercher, M. (1998). The changing provenance of red ochre at Puritjarra rock shelter, central Australia: Late Pleistocene to present. *Proceedings of the Prehistoric Society, 64*, 275–292.

Smith, M. A., Mooney, S. D., & Geiss, C. (2002). The use of mineral magnetic parameters to characterize archaeological ochres. *Journal of Archaeological Science, 29*, 1–13.

Smith, M. A., & Pell, S. (1997). Oxygen-isotope rations in quartz as an indicator of the provenance of archaeological ochres. *Journal of Archaeological Science, 24*, 773–778.

Stewart, B. A., Zhao, Y., Mitchell, P. J., Dewar, G., Gleason, J. D., & Blum, J. D. (2020). Ostrich eggshell bead strontium isotopes reveal persistent macroscale social networking across late Quaternary southern Africa. *Proceedings of the National Academy of Sciences, 117*(12), 6453–6462.

Velliky, E. C., Barbieri, A., Porr, M., Conard, N. J., & MacDonald, B. L. (2019). A preliminary study on ochre sources in southwestern Germany and its potential for ochre provenance during the Upper Paleolithic. *Journal of Archaeological Science: Reports, 27*, 101977.

Veth, P., Stern, N., McDonald, J., Balme, J., & Davidson, I. (2011). The role of information exchange in the colonization of Sahul. In R. Whallon, W. A. Lovis, & R. K. Hichcock (Eds.), *Information and its role in hunter-gatherer bands* (pp. 203–220). Los Angeles: Cotsen Institute of Archaeology Press.

Vinnicombe, P. (1997). Aspects of the value system associated with Wandjina art. In K. F. Kenneally, M. R. Lewis, M. Donaldson, & C. Clement (Eds.), *Aboriginal rock art of the Kimberley: Proceedings of a seminar held at the University of Western Australia, Perth, 8 March 1997* (pp. 13–18). Occasional Paper No. 1. Perth: Kimberley Society.

Wadley, L. (2010). A taphonomic study of ochre demonstrates post-depositional color transformations. *Journal of Taphonomy, 8*(2–3), 267–278.

Wadley, L. (2013). Recognizing complex cognition through innovative technology in Stone Age and Palaeolithic sites. *Cambridge Archaeology Journal, 23*, 163–183.

Wallis, L., Huntley, J., Marsh, M., Watchman, A., Ewen, A., & Strano, A. (2016). PXRF analysis of a yellow ochre quarry and rock art motifs in the Central Pilbara. *Journal of the Anthropological Society of South Australia, 40*, 134–155.

Ward, I., Watchman, A., Cole, N., & Morwood, M. (2001). Identification of minerals in pigments from Aboriginal rock art in the Laura and Kimberley regions, Australia. *Rock Art Research, 18*(1), 15–23.

Watts, I. (2009). Red ochre, body paint and language: interpreting the Blombos ochre. In R. Botha & C. Kight (Eds.), *The cradle of language* (pp. 93–129). Oxford: Oxford University Press.

Watts, I. (2017). Pigments. In A. S. Gilbert (Ed.), *Encyclopedia of geoarchaeology* (pp. 664–671). Netherlands: Springer.

Watts, I., Chazan, M., & Wilkins, J. (2016). Early evidence for brilliant ritualized display: Specularite use in the Northern Cape (South Africa) between ~500 and ~300 ka. *Current Anthropology, 57*(3), 287–302.

Weigand, P. C., Harbottle, G., & Sayre, E. V. (1977). Turquoise sources and source analysis: Mesoamerica and the southwestern USA. In T. K. Earle & J. E. Ericson (Eds.), *Exchange systems in prehistory* (pp. 15–34). New York: Academic Press.

Whallon, R. (2006). Social networks and information: Non-'utilitarian' mobility among hunter-gatherers. *Journal of Anthropological Archaeology, 25*(2), 259–270.

Wilson, L., & Pollard, A. M. (2001). The provenance hypothesis. In D. R. Brothwell & A. M. Pollard (Eds.), *Handbook of archaeological sciences* (pp. 507–584). Chichester: Wiley.

Wisseman, S. U., Moore, D. M., Hughes, R. E., Hynes, M. R., & Emerson, T. E. (2002). Mineralogical approaches to sourcing pipes and figurines from the eastern Woodlands, U.S.A. *Geoarchaeology, 17*(7), 689–715.

Zarzycka, S. E., Surovell, T. A., Mackie, M. E., Pelton, S. R., Kelly, R. L., Goldberg, P., . . . Kent, M. (2019). Long-distance transport of red ochre by Clovis foragers. *Journal of Archaeological Science: Reports, 25,* 519–529.

PART VI

SPECIALIZED SOCIETIES

CHAPTER 29

MARITIME COASTAL AND ISLAND SOCIETIES OF AUSTRALIA AND NEW GUINEA

MICHAEL ROWLAND, BEN SHAW, AND SEAN ULM

INTRODUCTION

COASTS, islands, and marine resources were significant in the peopling of all continents (e.g., Bailey et al. 2015; Leppard & Runnels 2017; Will, Kandel, & Conrad 2019), but they were neither uniformly attractive nor marginal to human dispersal. Rather, they offered a variety of opportunities. Human adaptations to coasts and islands ranged from inland groups fishing on lakes and rivers; to seafaring populations who spent most of their time at sea living off marine resources; and to land-based populations in coastal regions with little or no reliance on marine foods (Bailey et al. 2015). Fishing in open seas, far from land, however, was a significant milestone in human history, requiring skills in watercraft construction and navigation technologies that ultimately opened up opportunities for connectivity and trade between some of the world's most isolated islands (Will et al. 2019).

The remains of coastal resource use are typically found in shell-matrix sites along the world's coastlines and are unique sources of data for reconstructing subsistence practices as well as human adaptations to coastal and island landscapes and to past environmental conditions. Recent studies have also begun to focus on the ceremonial importance of such sites (McNiven 2013; Will et al. 2019). Coastal and island sites are impacted by many processes that differentially damage or remove them from the archaeological record, necessitating complex approaches to understanding their formation, preservation, and functions (Rosendahl, Ulm, & Weisler 2007; Rowland & Ulm 2012).

Australia is an island continent with a coastline of over 59,000 km and over 8000 offshore islands comprising almost 40% of the total length of the coastline. The islands extend through 34 degrees of latitude from the northern tropical islands, reefs, and sandy cays of Torres Strait to the temperate islands of Tasmania in the Southern Ocean. New Guinea, further to the north, is located entirely within tropical latitudes. Most islands were hilltops on the glacially exposed continental shelf, only becoming islands when the continental shelf was flooded during the marine transgression from the end of the Pleistocene and Early Holocene. Other islands that were formed more recently are associated with emerging coral reefs, riverine deltas, and changing sedimentation budgets (McNiven & Ulm 2015: 1). Regional diversity in coastal and island use across such a vast area as Australia and New Guinea is considerable. We have focussed this review on examples drawn from Queensland and New Guinea.

THE ANTIQUITY OF ISLAND AND COASTAL USE

Approximately 70% of the Earth's surface is covered in water. Yet, many archaeologists in the 1970s considered coastal adaptations, seaworthy boats, and maritime dispersals to be late developments in human history, largely occurring within the past 10,000 years (e.g., Cohen 1977; Osborn 1977). Since the 1970s, however, the evidence for early coastal adaptation, seafaring, and island use has increased dramatically, shedding new light on early human dispersals around the world (e.g., Bicho, Haws, & Davis 2011; O'Connor, Ono, & Clarkson 2011).

Neanderthals were using coastal resources in both Eurasia and Africa by ~190–130 ka (Cortés-Sánchez et al. 2011), with potentially earlier use in North Africa by ~254 ka (Ramos-Muñoz et al. 2016), while modern humans (*Homo sapiens*) were making use of coastlines and coastal resources by at least 240–195 ka (Marean 2016). Some researchers regard this early evidence as ephemeral and possibly of limited relevance to human behaviour (e.g., Boivin, Fuller, Dennell, Allaby, & Petraglia 2013: 34), but others view coastal resource use as highly significant to the long-term biological and cultural development of modern humans (e.g., Marean 2016; Will et al. 2019).

The presence of early hominids such as *Homo erectus* and *Homo floresiensis* on Flores and *Homo luzonensis* on Luzon, point to the importance of islands in human history and the early development of watercraft (Détroit et al. 2019; Morwood et al. 2004) (Figure 29.1). *Homo sapiens* reached the island continent of Sahul (the combined landmass of Australia and New Guinea at times of lower sea level) at or prior to 65 ka (Clarkson et al. 2017). The earliest evidence for modern human settlement of the Wallacean Islands, which separate Sahul from Eurasia, dates from 45 ka, although earlier settlement is likely as these islands needed to be crossed to reach Sahul (Hawkins et al. 2017; Kealy, Louys, & O'Connor 2018). The Bismarck Archipelago (New Britain and New Ireland) to the

FIGURE 29.1. Australia, New Guinea, and Wallacea showing places mentioned in the text. Political boundaries sourced from Geoscience Australia, www.ga.gov.au. Bathymetry derived from The GEBCO_2014 Grid, version 20150318, www.gebco.net.

east of mainland New Guinea was colonized by 44 ka and the Solomon Islands by 33 ka, marking the easternmost limits of human dispersal into the Pacific region during the Late Pleistocene (Leavesley 2006; Wickler & Spriggs 1988) (Figure 29.2). Manus Island in the Bismarck Archipelago was colonized as early as 25 ka, and at over 200 km from the nearest landmass it is evidence of the longest Pleistocene-aged open-sea voyaging in the world (Fredericksen, Spriggs, & Ambrose 1993). Recent suggestions of coastally focussed people at Moyjil (Point Ritchie), a cliffed site at the mouth of the Hopkins River at Warrnambool, southeastern Australia, from 100 to 130 ka, and a provisional date of 125 ka on Rottnest Island in southwest Australia, have challenged models for the timing of human colonization. Marine shell remains at these sites are not consistent with a wide range of current evidence, suggesting that coastal resources were not used much before 50 ka, although an association with human activity at these sites remains

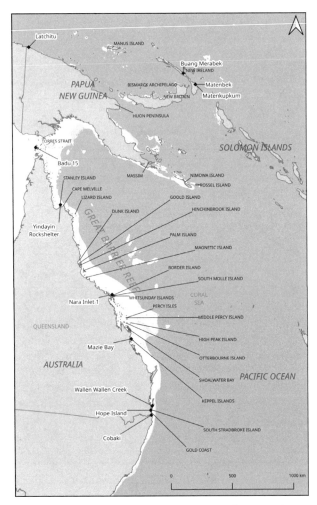

FIGURE 29.2. Northeast Australia and Papua New Guinea showing places mentioned in the text. Political boundaries sourced from Geoscience Australia, www.ga.gov.au. Bathymetry derived from The GEBCO_2014 Grid, version 20150318, www.gebco.net.

contentious (Bowler, Price, Sherwood, & Carey 2018; Hesp, Murray-Wallace, & Dortch 1999; Sherwood, McNiven, & Laurenson 2018; McNiven et al. 2018).

The use of offshore islands has been a significant focus of archaeological research (e.g., Allen 2000; Barker 2004; Beaton 1985; Bowdler 1995; Jones 1976; McNiven, de Maria, Weisler, & Lewis 2014; O'Connor 1992; Rosendahl, Ulm, Tomkins, Wallis, & Memmott 2014; Rowland 2008; Rowland, Wright, & Baker 2015; Shaw 2019; Sim & Wallis 2008; Ulm, McNiven, Aird, & Lambrides 2019). Studies have focussed on when islands were first used and/or permanently occupied; the reasons people started using the islands; how people travelled to the islands; why and when some were abandoned; and cultural responses to insularity, isolation, circumscription, and a range of other issues.

Yet, despite numerous hypotheses developed from the available archaeological record, 'a convincing holistic explanation has yet to be achieved' (Rowland 2008: 89), with explanations likely to differ regionally depending on the distribution and type of islands, as well as distance from the continental coast. Nevertheless, the study of island archaeological sites within the context of sea-level and climate change has provided considerable insights into the interrelationship between environment and culture (Rowland et al. 2015: 154).

REACHING SAHUL AND IMPACT OF THE LAST GLACIAL MAXIMUM

Some researchers propose that modern humans followed a mainly coastal and island route out of Africa eastward to South and Southeast Asia along the Indian Ocean rim and, ultimately, into Sahul (Erlandson & Braje 2015; Veth et al. 2017). Others have argued for a greater role of terrestrial adaptations (Boivin et al. 2013; Rabett 2018). Unfortunately, most of the material evidence for a coastal route is missing due to changes in Pleistocene and Holocene sea levels (Rowland & Ulm 2012). The remains of early underwater coastal sites have to date not been investigated in detail, but the techniques are now available and the potential for investigation is high (Benjamin et al. 2018, 2020; Benjamin & Ulm, this volume; Bailey et al. 2015; Veth et al. 2020).

Watercraft capable of open-ocean voyaging greater than 100 km offshore were always required to get to Sahul. It is likely that people arrived by island hopping through Wallacea and were therefore coastally adapted. Possible multiple colonizations from various entry points have been proposed (Kealy et al. 2018; Norman et al. 2018), along with purposeful and coordinated rather than random voyaging (Bird et al. 2019; Bradshaw et al. 2019) and even return voyaging (Norman et al. 2018: 238). Recent modelling indicates the northwest Australia shelf as the most likely point of entry, perhaps followed by the Bird's Head of west New Guinea (Bradshaw et al. 2019), with minimum founding populations estimated in the order of 1300–1550 people (Bradshaw et al. 2019). Early sites in both Southeast Asia and Sahul (Fujita et al. 2016; O'Connor et al. 2011; Veth et al. 2017) indicate that when people arrived in Sahul, they continued to use the ocean and its resources, while also dispersing further inland to other environments (Balme et al. 2019; Marsh, Hiscock, Williams, Hughes, & Sullivan 2018; Summerhayes, Field, Shaw, & Gaffney 2017; Veth et al. 2020).

Sea-level rise associated with global warming after the Last Glacial Maximum (LGM), ~21 ka, saw sea levels rise by some 130 m and commence flooding of the continental shelf (Ishiwa et al. 2016). Australia and New Guinea were separated by the formation of a shallow sea in the Early Holocene, and one-third of the continental land mass of Australia, or 2.12 million km^2, was drowned by postglacial sea-level rise (Williams, Ulm, Sapienza, Lewis, & Turney 2018). Much of this drowned territory is likely to have been occupied by people. Holocene sea levels peaked +1.0 to +1.5 m above current sea levels between c. 7000 and 7500 and c. 2000 cal BP, before dropping to approximately modern levels (Dougherty et al. 2019; Sloss et al. 2018). Further oscillations occurred around 4800 and 3000 cal BP associated with sea-level falls, which impacted the growth of coral reefs and intertidal shellfish communities (Lewis, Wüst, Webster, & Shields 2008).

Fluctuating sea levels and the extent of coral reefs affected the dispersal of people across Australia, New Guinea, and adjacent islands. Beaton (1985) hypothesized that the coastal zone would have been abandoned with sea-level rise and was only recolonized in the Late Holocene when stable coastal resources were established following sea-level stabilization. However, palaeoenvironmental data indicate that a variety of marine-focussed communities were established across Australia and New Guinea by the end of the marine transgression, and several sites demonstrate the use of coastal resources throughout the marine transgression. Nonetheless, rising seas did impact patterns of human occupation and site survival (Ulm 2011: 445).

LATE PLEISTOCENE COASTAL USE

In northeastern Australia, the near-coastal site of Wallen Wallen Creek on South Stradbroke Island, with a basal date of >20 ka, does not reveal evidence of coastal resource use until c. 4000 BP (Neal & Stock 1986). Similarly, further south in northern coastal New South Wales, the Cobaki site dated from c. 30 ka does not contain marine shell until c. 600 BP (Robins, Hall, & Stock 2015). Nevertheless, evidence of Pleistocene coastal use has now been documented at many rock shelter and cave sites around Australia and New Guinea.

The earliest known, coastally oriented habitation in Sahul comes from the north-west of Australia, preserved in limestone caves on the Montebello and Barrow Islands (Manne & Veth 2015; Veth et al. 2017), at rock shelter sites at Cape Range (Morse 1988; Przywolnik 2005), and at rock shelters in island Melanesia (Leavesley & Allen 1998). At Boodie Cave on Barrow Island, for example, occupation begins between 51.1 and 46.2 ka, with marine resources incorporated into dietary assemblages by 42.3 ka. At times, marine molluscs were transported from 10 to 20 km across the Pleistocene coastal plain from the then distant coast. People continued to transport shellfish to the cave through all periods of occupation, despite fluctuating sea levels and dramatic extensions of the coastal plain. It is likely that other marine mollusc species would also have been processed and consumed closer to the coastline rather than in the cave. Barrow Island, which now lies 60 km from the mainland, was abandoned by 6800 BP when the island became increasingly distant from the mainland (Veth et al. 2017).

Rock shelters and caves in the Bismarck and Solomon archipelagos of island Melanesia yield the only known insular records of coastal adaptations for Pleistocene New Guinea (Leavesley & Allen 1998; Summerhayes et al. 2017). The steep bathymetry of northern New Guinea has meant that the Bismarck Islands have always been separated from Sahul, even during the LGM. In southern New Ireland at Buang Merabek from 44 ka and at Matenkupkum from 41 ka, small, highly mobile groups of hunter-gatherers exploited a range of coastal and inland resources, primarily shellfish and bats. At the Matenbek rock shelter, also in southern New Ireland, dense midden indicates a heavy dietary reliance on reef shellfish and fish from 24 ka onwards, with Pleistocene *Turbo* shell reduction, perhaps for fish hook manufacture, reflecting some of the earliest known shell technology in Sahul (Smith & Allen 1999). It has been argued that bats attracted people to coastal forests and caves in these areas, as caves, rainforests, and therefore bat populations are less prevalent further north on the island where evidence for Late Pleistocene occupation is absent, further highlighting the reliance of early human populations on coastal resources (Leavesley 2006).

Few Pleistocene-aged coastal sites have been preserved in New Guinea, and they have been found only in areas with ideal geomorphological and geological conditions. The uplifted Bobongara terraces on the Huon Peninsula provide a rare glimpse into the technologies of early coastal people. Excavations have revealed waisted stone blades dated to at least 40 ka and possibly as early as 60 ka. They are thought to have been associated with ring-barking, felling, and management of soft trees such as Sago (*Metroxylon* sp.), *Pandanus*, and cycads in areas where fire was not an effective method of rainforest clearance (Groube, Chappell, Muke, & Price 1986). The cave site of Latchitu on the northern coast is the only other known site of a similar antiquity in coastal New Guinea. The cave was first visited from 43 to 36 ka by people consuming nearshore shellfish, notably *Turbo*, and terrestrial fauna likely hunted in the higher elevation inland forests (O'Connor et al. 2011).

Throughout Australia, New Guinea, and Wallacea, evidence for more advanced maritime skills and for offshore fishing is rare before the terminal Pleistocene/Early Holocene. The earliest island sites in New Guinea, mentioned above, contain few fish bones, which suggests that fish capture occurred on shallow reefs, was opportunistic, and probably involved traps and spears rather than hooks (Leavesley 2006). However, an early assemblage of pelagic and other fish species are reported from Asitau Kuru (Jerimalai) shelter in Timor Lesté, dated to 42 ka, along with the earliest definite evidence for fish hook manufacture in the world (O'Connor et al. 2011).

EARLY TO MID-HOLOCENE COASTAL USE

Evidence for coastal resource exploitation becomes more apparent from the Early to Mid-Holocene. Koolan Shelter 2 on Koolan Island on the west Kimberley coast of northwest Australia has evidence for use of coastal resources beginning at 10,500 BP (O'Connor 1999). In central Queensland, Otterbourne Island in Shoalwater Bay was in use from 5200 BP (McNiven et al. 2014), and Nara Inlet 1 on Hook Island in the Whitsunday Islands has evidence of continuous coastal occupation from 8000 BP to the present (Barker 2004). There is also evidence for early coastal use on Border Island, also in the Whitsunday Islands (Barker 2004).

Barker (2004) argued that there was ephemeral use of coastal resources in the earliest levels at Nara Inlet 1, followed by more specialized marine economies focussing on turtle and dugong hunting associated with later more intensive occupation. Close examination of the data from Nara Inlet 1 and Border Island 1, however, suggested to Hiscock (2008: 169–170) a trend towards generalized shore-based foraging and away from the targeting of large marine reptiles and mammals, with the highest rates of discard of turtle bone at Border Island occurring before 6000 BP. On the other hand, Yindayin Rock Shelter on Stanley Island in north Queensland was occupied prior to 6000 BP and is interpreted as indicating complex and nonlinear subsistence and occupation patterns, with periods of increased habitation intensity at the site interspersed with periods of stability and abandonment. Environmental and climate change are argued to have the most significant effects on subsistence behaviours at Yindayin Rock Shelter, while the potential for population-induced economic intensification was only identified within the last 200 years of occupation (Wright 2018). Evidence for the use of marine resources from the Early Holocene in the Whitsunday Island and Stanley Island rock shelters, as well as sites elsewhere in Sahul located near palaeoshorelines (e.g., Torres Strait islands—David et al. 2004; Wright 2011), provide support for the view of continuous use of coastal resources throughout the marine transgression, with people simply following the transgressive coastline (see Hall 1999; Rowland & Ulm 2012; Ulm 2011). Most islands, however, do not appear to have been occupied until after 7000 BP.

Late Holocene Use of Coastal Resources

Coastal and island archaeological sites older than c. 3000 BP are not common in Australia and New Guinea (Ulm 2011: 448) (Figure 29.3). Most archaeological investigations undertaken along the coast have produced evidence consistent with a model of ephemeral use of coastal resources from before the Mid-Holocene and dramatic change in the very Late Holocene towards increased rates of occupation. Explanations for this pattern are diverse. Some have noted that the pattern may be an artefact of preservational bias, with the record skewed towards recent sites (e.g., Bird 1992; Rowland & Ulm 2011). Others have focussed on the importance of environmental factors, particularly resource productivity and availability (e.g., Beaton 1985; Morwood 1987; Rowland 1999a) or the interplay of environmental and cultural factors (Haberle & David 2004; Rowland 1999b). Links have also been made to changes in social structure, especially trends towards socioeconomic intensification, perhaps including population growth (e.g., Barker 2004; Lourandos 1997) and group fissioning (e.g., McNiven 1999;

FIGURE 29.3. Clockwise from top left: Shell midden excavation on Dingaal Country in the Lizard Island Group (Photograph: Sean Ulm); an eroding coastal midden site on Rossel Island, Milne Bay Province (Photograph: Ben Shaw); stone-walled fish trap complex on Kaiadilt Country, Bentinck Island, Gulf of Carpentaria (Photograph: Sean Ulm); large shell mound at Imbuorr, Hey River, near Weipa, within the homelands of Nggoth Custodians (Photograph: Michael Morrison); a Pleistocene-aged coastal cave on the uplifted limestone shores of Panaeati Island, Milne Bay Province (Photograph: Ben Shaw); typical shell midden scatter on Kaiadilt Country, Sweers Island, Gulf of Carpentaria (Photograph: Sean Ulm).

Memmott, Round, Rosendhal, & Ulm 2016), or cultural responses to external contacts (McNiven 2017; Rowland 2018).

Ulm (2000, 2006: 66) identified the emergence of focussed marine resource exploitation from 3500 BP on the mainland coast. Rowland's view that there was a significant change in coastal and island use at 3500 BP developed as a result of excavations undertaken at Mazie Bay on North Keppel Island in central Queensland. Here a distinct environmental 'event' occurred at that time, resulting in distinct differences in fishing, shellfishing, and stone artefacts in layers predating and postdating 3500 BP (Rowland 1996, 1999a, 2008). This interpretation is supported by recent palaeoenvironmental investigations in the Keppel Island Group, with relic barnacle species suggesting environmental change between 4200 and 3200 cal BP (Rowland et al. 2015). David et al. (2004) and McNiven et al. (2006) have also recognized a significant increase in human activity on the Torres Strait Islands at c. 3500 BP; significant changes also occur in Tasmania around this time (e.g., Rowland 1999b; Johnson & Wroe 2003). In the last 3000 years, shell mounds emerged as part of the archaeological landscape across tropical northern Australia, along with extensive stone-walled tidal fishtraps (Holdaway et al. 2017; Kreij, Scriffignano, Rosendahl, Nagel, & Ulm 2018; Rowland & Ulm 2011).

In New Guinea, pottery, a range of animal domesticates, and Austronesian languages were introduced by 3300–3200 BP with the Lapita Cultural Complex, which is linked to agriculturalist seafarers who migrated into the region from island Southeast Asia (Kirch 2001; Ross 1988; Specht 2007; Summerhayes 2007). The earliest Lapita sites have been found in the Bismarck Archipelago, with the appearance of Lapita on small islands in the Massim island region and along the south coast of Papua New Guinea from 3000 to 2900 BP (David et al. 2011; McNiven et al. 2011; Shaw 2019; Skelly, David, Petchey, & Leavesley 2014). Despite the presence of earlier coastal and island settlements in these regions dating to the Mid-Holocene, intensive exploitation of coastal resources is only apparent with the appearance of Lapita settlement (Gosden & Webb 1994). A preference for island and coastal locations, the formation of larger villages, and more intensive exploitation of fish and shellfish contributed to a much higher number of identified sites in New Guinea dating to within the last three millennia (Kirch 1997). Lapita had a profound influence on the organization of many later cultural groups in coastal and island regions of New Guinea, with a notable increase in ornamentation indicating the development of more defined systems of social stratification (Sheppard, Thomas, & Summerhayes 2009; Skelly & David 2017).

The majority of known coastal archaeological sites date to the last millennium (Ulm 2011: 454) and are associated with structural changes in the archaeological record. For example, in Torres Strait, villages only begin to appear in the archaeological record during the period c.1400–700 BP (Ash & David 2008; David & Weisler 2006; Wright 2015), which has been linked with the development of a more intensive engagement with the marine environment (David & Weisler 2006) and reconfigurations of territorial land and seascapes (McNiven et al. 2008; Wright 2015). Significant climatic changes occurred throughout many areas of Australia and the Pacific and worldwide at this time (e.g., Axford et al. 2013; Gliganic et al. 2014), and the implications of these connections have yet to be fully investigated. After 1500 BP, changes in coastal settlement involve a localization of resource use and a trend towards broad-based economies focussed on lower-ranked resources clustered around the shoreline (Ulm 2006, 2011: 454). The role of coastal resources in these economies is part of an ongoing debate, with intensified use of coastal resources seen as largely a Late Holocene phenomenon (Ulm 2013). For example, recent analyses of shellfish assemblages from excavations on Lizard Island in north Queensland showed no evidence for resource depression across the Late Holocene, which is broadly in keeping with previous findings at other locales on the Great Barrier Reef, but contrary to expectations of resource intensification models (Ulm et al. 2019). On the other hand, a recent synthesis of archaeological fish bone assemblages on the Queensland coast showed broadening predation strategies through time in some areas (Lambrides, McNiven, & Ulm 2019). It remains uncertain how these recent changes are connected to synchronous climatic changes. For example, a period of high-frequency El Niño Southern Oscillation (ENSO) events between c. 2500 and 1000 BP, peaking at 1300 BP, is associated with more variable climate, including periods of aridity (Gagan, Hendy, Haberle, & Hantoro 2004; Rowland 1999b; Shulmeister 1999) and coincides with widespread reductions in occupation across southeast Queensland (Ulm 2006). Climate ameliorated in the last 1000 years, with wetter conditions prevailing (Harrison & Dodson 1993).

Settlement and abandonment of small, resource-impoverished islands in the Massim region of southeastern Papua New Guinea demonstrate ENSO-forced behavioural adaptations (Shaw et al. 2020). On Malakai Island, human settlement commenced with the arrival of a Lapita population on a developing coastal fringe from 2500 BP. Low-intensity coastal use ceased between 2500 and 2300 BP, when the island was abandoned during an ENSO-forced period of reduced rainfall, perhaps in favour of more elevated islands where cloud-trapped rainfall occurred more regularly. Within the past 800–550 years, island and coastal populations in the Massim and elsewhere in Papua New Guinea strategically relocated to islands and coastal areas with natural harbours to take advantage of trade opportunities along sheltered sailing routes (Allen 2017; Bulmer 1982; Shaw 2019). Regulated marine trade networks were established around this time, most famously the *hiri* and *kula*, to facilitate the movement of food, pottery, and other locally abundant coastal resources as a risk-reduction strategy to protect populations against the ongoing threat of drought and famine (Rhoads 1982; Skelly & David 2017). Warfare and social tensions between coastal trading communities increased alongside maritime trade over this time as populations grew and competition for resources intensified. Changes in pottery styles and the origins of imported material indicate ongoing fluctuations in trade relations (Allen 2000; Irwin 1985; Lilley 2004). Regular warfare generally diminished within the past two centuries as colonial influences increased in New Guinea, allowing maritime coastal and island trade to reexpand (Irwin, Shaw, & McAlister 2019; Swadling 1981).

Alterations in occupation patterns and broadened coastal resource use in the past 1500 years throughout Australia and New Guinea may therefore have been, in part, a response to more variable climatic conditions, much like the reorganization of settlement–subsistence systems thought to have taken place during the LGM (Williams, Ulm, Cook, Langley, & Collard 2013). However, Rosendahl et al. (2014) found that when these hypotheses are tested at the local level, more nuanced patterns of human–environment interaction emerge. They note, for example, that disjunctions in the timing of the cessation of shell mound construction between the west and east Gulf of Carpentaria may be related, at least in part, to the timing and intensity of external cultural contacts with visiting Macassan seafarers from island Southeast Asia (see also Rowland 2018).

A central point of discussion concerning the occupation of coasts and islands has been the causes of changes in the archaeological record. Coastal erosion can account for the absence of sites in some locations and during certain periods with more frequent destructive weather events. Therefore, archaeologists will at times be constrained by 'missing evidence'. Rowland (e.g., 1996, 1999a, 1999b; Rowland et al. 2015) has long proposed that the scale and amplitude of Holocene environmental changes, particularly those associated with ENSO, must be incorporated into explanations of change in the archaeological record. More recently, ENSO is seen to have impacted stone artefact technology (Hiscock 1994; Veth, Hiscock, & Williams 2011); the occupation of Queensland rainforests (Cosgrove, Field, & Ferrier 2007); precontact population numbers (Williams et al. 2018); rock art styles across northern Australia (Haberle & David 2004); and changes in shellfishing practices in Arnhem Land (Bourke, Brockwell, Faulkner, & Meehan 2007). An alternative view that sees shifts in social and economic behaviour in the Mid- to Late Holocene related to changes in the internal dynamics of social systems (i.e., 'intensification') has proved problematic (e.g., Bourke 2004; Ward 2004; Ulm 2013). However, neither cultural systems nor the environment are static for any length of time, and the two regularly interact. A causal link between culture and environment with different drivers emerging at different times must be considered a valid field of enquiry (e.g., Haberle & Chepstow-Lusty 2000).

The Importance of Islands

In a critical overview, Bowdler (1995: 956) concluded that a 'lack of obvious patterning' in Aboriginal use of islands occurred beyond that most islands came into use within the past 3000 years and were more intensively used in the past 1000 years. Sim and Wallis (2008) found little or no direct evidence for Aboriginal use of small offshore islands during the 'initial post-insulation (island) phase' between approximately 6500 and 4500 BP. Their view is challenged, however, by Barker's (2004) evidence of 8000 years of continuous occupation of the Whitsunday Islands, the date of over 6000 BP from Yindayin Rock Shelter on Stanley Island (Wright 2018), and evidence of Mid-Holocene occupation at Badu 15 in Torres Strait (David et al. 2004). Sim and Wallis (2008: 104) suggest that increased island use across northern Australia during the Late Holocene was 'a direct human response to weather regimes becoming more conducive to coastal habitation and watercraft travel'. However, the presence of a midden on Otterbourne Island, dated at 5200 cal BP (McNiven et al. 2014), is in opposition to this view, and the issue of the development and types of watercraft available is likely more complex than Sim and Wallis allow (Rowland 1995). McDonald and Berry (2017) and Veth et al. (2019) provide midden dates for islands on Murujuga (Dampier Archipelago), which also clearly demonstrate Early to Mid-Holocene use of islands in northwestern Australia.

Islands situated along the temperate southeast coast of Australia exhibit strong evidence for seasonal occupation (Vanderwal 1978; Sullivan 1982; McNiven 2000), whereas islands in northern Australia and in New Guinea have variable signatures in the timing and nature of use throughout the Holocene (Barker 2004; David et al. 2004; Rowland et al. 2015; O'Connor 1992; Sim & Wallis 2008; Wright 2011). A region of important archaeological island studies has been the Queensland coast, with some studies providing results that contrast significantly with island studies from elsewhere. Bowdler (2010: 181) proposed that, rather than the present gentle tropical shore protected by the Great Barrier Reef (GBR), the Queensland Pleistocene coastline consisted of cliffed limestone ridges, rising 100 m or more above sea level, and that the coastal strip may therefore have been 'cold, dry, sparsely vegetated and subject to widespread dust storms'. This important observation has yet to be investigated in detail.

People were using coastal resources during the Late Pleistocene and Early Holocene and followed the coastline inland as sea levels rose from the end of the LGM and some islands were formed at this time. For example, McNiven et al. (2014) note that, among the Shoalwater Bay Islands, High Peak Island at 40 km from the mainland formed at around 11,500 years ago and its modern configuration was reached at 10,000 to 9000 years ago. Otterbourne Island, which is closer to the mainland, probably reached its modern configuration 8000 years ago. Other islands would not have formed until c. 7000 years ago. The recording and excavation of sites on those islands have demonstrated that marine resources were being used prior to 5000 years ago.

Following sea-level stabilization, cyclones, storm surges, and other erosive processes have destroyed many sites (Rowland & Ulm 2012; Williams et al. 2018). Beaton's (1985) earlier suggestion of a significant 'time lag' in the development of coastal economies following the end of the LGM is not supported. It is unlikely, for example, that coastal resources would have taken long to establish following sea-level stabilization, and it is unlikely, too, that these resources would have been overlooked, although resource abundance and availability may have been different than they are today. Population dispersal in response to fluctuating environmental conditions might also account in part for some increase in site numbers after 3500 BP (Rowland 1996: 195), and population increase was also likely. Population increases and decreases are likely to have occurred throughout the Holocene, though such changes are difficult to demonstrate in the archaeological record and changes are likely to have been variable through time and space. Recently, McNiven et al. (2014) have revived Beaton's concept of a 'time lag' (but for a different time period) in explaining the use of Shoalwater Bay Islands. They argue that the development of coral reefs and mangrove systems at c. 3500 cal BP supported green turtle populations and in turn provided the incentive for use of the islands. However, this explanation is of limited general value. Island-specific trajectories of resource exploitation must be considered to effectively model regional patterns of marine biodiversity and food availability. For instance, the first occupation of Otterbourne Island occurred at 5200 cal BP and High Peak Island at 3250 cal BP. Also, coastal resources were being exploited at Mazie Bay prior to 4500 cal BP (Rowland 1999a) and on Lizard Island by 4000 cal BP (Ulm et al. 2019). Nevertheless, an increasing number of coastal island and mainland coastal sites do appear after c. 3500 cal BP (Barker 2004; Beaton 1985; Border 1999; McNiven et al. 2014).

Developing Maritime Economies: Watercraft, Island Location, and Population Size

Depositional changes have occurred in sites in the last 3500 years, as noted at the Mazie Bay site on North Keppel Island (Rowland 1999a), including increases in site numbers and discard rates of cultural material in sites along the coast and on islands in New Guinea and northeastern Australia in the last millennium (Allen 2000; Rosendahl et al. 2014; Shaw 2019; Twaddle et al. 2017; Ulm 2011). Barker (2004) noted the emergence of specialized marine economies at around 600 BP in the Whitsunday Islands. Rowland (1996) thought it likely that the Keppel Islands were permanently occupied only from about c. 700 BP. Specialized marine economies were also apparent along the southern and northern Papua New Guinea coast as well as the Massim Islands from 1000 to 500 BP (Allen 2000, 2017; Shaw 2019). Research across Torres Strait has revealed a distinctive series of cultural changes around 3500 BP (David et al. 2004), but it was not until after 2500 BP that widespread occupation occurred in the form of numerous coastal middens (Barham 2000; Brady & Ash 2018; McNiven et al. 2006). Barham, Rowland, and Hitchcock (2004) associate changes around 2500 BP with the origins of the distinctive marine-oriented societies observed among contemporary Torres Strait Islander communities, while McNiven et al. (2006) associate these changes with the influx of Papuan peoples and the introduction of pottery. Several explanations have been offered for these broader archaeological patterns (see Ulm 2013). Mid- to Late Holocene population restructuring and increasing use of marginal environments ('intensification') have been a predominant explanation for the increasing use of islands in Australia and New Guinea (see Lourandos 1997). Population pressure (Beaton 1985), changes in technology (Beaton 1985), environmental and ecological changes (Rowland 1996, 1999a; Border 1999), and culture contact (Rowland 1995, 2018) are among a range of factors that may explain the use of islands along the Great Barrier Reef, but a convincing holistic explanation (if in fact one exists) awaits formulation. Isolation or semi-isolation is also important in identifying patterns of offshore island use (see Rowland 2008). Island size and distance from the mainland may have determined the extent to which islands in the Great Barrier Reef were seasonally or permanently exploited, but none would have been permanently isolated because of offshore distance (Rowland 1996).

To get to islands and maintain viable populations and economies requires watercraft, but direct archaeological evidence of watercraft is rare, as is true of all artefacts made of perishable materials. Inferences must therefore be drawn from indirect evidence. Bowdler (1995) suggested that watercraft were not made and used anywhere in Australia before the last 3000–2500 years, and despite suggestions that this argument is overly simplistic, Bowdler (2015) argues that it is still tenable (however, see McDonald & Berry 2017; Veth et al. 2019). A possible simplification of seafaring technology following initial colonization has been argued as a positive, fitness-related response to local ecological conditions. In this view, as people followed more terrestrial-based lifestyles after reaching Sahul, oceangoing canoes were no longer required and watercraft technologies became simplified (O'Connell, Allen, & Hawkes 2010). The presence of midden and other habitation sites on islands around Australia and New Guinea since their formation means that watercraft must have been used at least throughout the Holocene.

Watercraft use along the Great Barrier Reef coast of Queensland suggests that a much more complex picture developed in the past. Single-piece bark canoes occurred along most of the Queensland coastline; three-piece sewn bark canoes were known around the Whitsunday Islands; double outriggers extended as far south as Cape Melville; and single outriggers were in use as far south as the Whitsunday Islands and possibly beyond (Rowland 1995, 2018). Little is known regarding the antiquity or capabilities of these canoes. However, South Molle Island quarry was visited from 9000 cal BP and Border Island by cal 7000 BP (Barker 2004); Stanley Island by 6000 cal BP (Wright 2018); Otterbourne Island at 26 km from the mainland by 5200 cal BP (McNiven et al. 2014); North Keppel Island by at least 4200 cal BP; and Lizard Island by at least 4000 cal BP (Ulm et al. 2019). Sites on the Percy Isles demonstrate that 50 km trips from the mainland, or at least a 27 km island-hopping journey to the islands, were possible by at least 3000 BP (Border 1999; Rowland 1984). The innermost of the northwest islands of the Dampier Archipelago appear to have immediate postinsulation reoccupation, with the outermost islands likely included in a seasonal visitation pattern by the Mid- to Late Holocene (McDonald, Dortch, Paterson, & Veth in prep.; Veth et al. 2019).

Sullivan (1982) proposed that people travelled further to islands on the Queensland coast than to islands on the New South Wales coast because it was more sheltered, but this proposal is of limited explanatory value. The Percy Isles are a long way off the coast (over 50 km) and are not well protected from oceanic conditions. They can be reached by island hopping, but a minimum sea crossing of 27 km is still required. The Percy Isles have adequate to abundant coastal resources, minimal terrestrial resources, a few fine-grained stone resources, and turtle nesting sites. Based on the small size of the islands and their limited resources, it is difficult to imagine the islands being particularly attractive given the lengthy and difficult sea crossing (Rowland 1984). However, islands may have been visited for other reasons that are not directly related to the net abundance of food resources, such as for ceremonies, as could be implied, for example, by the large number of stone arrangements recorded on Lizard Island (Fitzpatrick, McNiven, Specht, & Ulm 2018).

Jones (1976) used size and distance criteria to define a dichotomy between the islands occupied permanently and those occupied seasonally off the coast of Tasmania. He found that the minimum island size necessary to support an autonomous population was 77–90 km^2 and that residential islands tended to be closest to the mainland. On the Queensland coast, much smaller islands supported resident populations (Rowland

1996). Limiting distances for Tasmanian watercraft were in the vicinity of 5–8 km, but evidence from the Percy Isles in Queensland suggests that limiting distances were at least four times greater and that the use of other types of watercraft may have substantially extended those distances (Rowland 1984, 1995). At over 50 km offshore, the Percy Isles are the most distant island group off the east coast of Australia, and since they were first visited 3000 years ago, no limiting distance for the extent of watercraft use can be identified in the area. Islands as small as 3 ha and 13 km from the mainland were visited, as were continental islands 50 km from the mainland (Rowland 1996; Rowland et al. 2015; McNiven et al. 2014: 202). Few islands on the Queensland coast may have been permanently occupied following their formation, but may instead have been incorporated into the coastal economies of adjacent mainland groups. However, within the past 2000 years or less, it appears that some of the larger island groups, like Magnetic, Hinchinbrook, Goold, the Keppel, and the Whitsunday Islands, were permanently occupied (Rowland 1996; Rowland et al. 2015). Numerous islands across the Torres Strait were permanently occupied with resident communities within the past 1000 years (e.g., Barham 2000; McNiven 2015; Wright 2015).

Populations may become extinct on islands where the colonizing population is small, where the island area is small, and/or where distance from a source of a new migration is considerable. Jones (1976) proposed that isolated populations whose numbers exceeded 500 could survive indefinitely, while those with fewer than 300 would become extinct. But many factors must be considered (Rowland 2008). The range of watercraft available on the Queensland coast suggests that distance was not a factor that would have led to permanent isolation of any island population. However, linguistic, biological, material cultural, and archaeological evidence from the Keppel Islands, for example, suggests a degree of isolation in a relatively small population over a period of at least 700 years (Rowland 2008). Population densities on Queensland offshore islands have been estimated to be up to 1 person per 25–125 ha (Rowland 1996: Table 11.4, 201). These densities are high in comparison with mainland Australia but can be better explained in terms of the relationship between length of coastline and island area, not island area per se, where coasts and islands offer a territorial advantage of three or four times compared with mainland areas.

Early European explorers on the Queensland coast noted that offshore islands were more densely populated than many mainland areas. Sedentism is suggested by the number of huts observed on Dunk, Palm, Goold, Middle Percy Island, and the Keppel Islands (Rowland 2008), as well as massive fishtraps on Torres Strait Islands and Hinchinbrook Island (Rowland & Ulm 2011). Not all islands on the Queensland coast, however, supported permanent, sedentary populations. Some supported 'sedentary-cum-mobile' economies, in which substantial periods of time were spent on the islands and seasonal visits were made to other islands and the mainland (Border 1999; McNiven et al. 2014; Rowland et al. 2015). The occupation of small islands presents particular challenges largely related to limited terrestrial resources and susceptibility to natural disasters, but the challenges and risks can be offset or overcome through use of maritime technologies and exchange networks (McNiven 2015, 2016; Irwin et al. 2019; Shaw et al. 2020).

The uneven population distribution between islands and across coastal areas can influence linguistic, genetic, and cultural diversity. An example of this process has been documented on Rossel Island in the Massim region of Papua New Guinea where the population is linguistically and genetically distinct from that of neighbouring islands (Shaw 2017). Such a pattern has been argued to have been a result of population isolation since the Late Pleistocene, as smaller islands in the region were abandoned as the postglacial sea-level rise flooded coastlines. Rossel, along with a few other islands in the region, remained large enough to support a pre-agricultural population and were high enough to maintain year-round freshwater supplies.

Islands off the Queensland coast have been viewed as seasonal resource bases for fishing, birding, or turtling, and even as social retreats, although resource availability was central to the nature of their use (McNiven 2000). Island diversity was such that some islands supported permanent or semi-permanent populations. In some cases, there is evidence of more frequent movement within island groups than between the islands and adjacent mainland (Rowland 1996, 2008; Border 1999; Lamb 2011; McNiven et al. 2014). Archaeological and material cultural evidence from several of the islands points to broad-based exploitation of island resources focusing on marine foods. The widespread and distinct adaptation to islands of the Queensland coast (see Rowland 1996) has also been seen as applicable to other northern Australian islands (O'Connor 1992; Barker 2004), yet the timing and development of these island-based economies remain elusive. Despite settlement dating to the Mid-Holocene on North Keppel Island, on South Keppel Island, for example, a larger number of sites date within the past 800 years (Rowland 1999a), so that development of true island-based economies might only be seen to date to the past 1000 years.

CONCLUSION

Coasts and islands, marine resources, and seaborne contacts have been significant in hominid development. As inhabitants of an island continent first occupied over 65,000 years ago, Indigenous peoples in Sahul must have used coasts and islands, and perhaps developed the world's earliest watercraft. Unfortunately, much of the evidence for this use has been drowned by rising seas after the LGM. However, the targeting of relict continental islands (e.g., Barrow Island) and underwater archaeological techniques are now available that would enable these issues to be investigated (Benjamin et al. 2018, 2020; Veth et al. 2019).

There is a critical need to further define the nature of the Pleistocene coastlines and climate regimes of Australia and New Guinea in the context of potential human use. As noted above, Bowdler (2010: 181), for example, has suggested that the Pleistocene coastline of Queensland was 'cold, dry, sparsely vegetated and subject to widespread dust storms'. If this were the case, it would have been unattractive for the development of coastal economies. Yet the coast of Queensland and some offshore islands provide the most compelling evidence available for any part of Australia or New Guinea for continuous, or near-continuous, occupation of island archipelagos over the past 7000 years. The nature of early shellfish collecting on Sahul also needs to be better understood. Contrary to expectations, while the earliest foragers on the continent would have encountered abundant, large, high-ranking shellfish taxa offering relatively high average rates of nutrient return relative to time spent collecting and processing, archaeological data from many coastal shell middens indicate that foraging emphasized smaller, much lower ranked shellfish taxa (Bird, Richardson, Veth, & Barham 2002; Codding, O'Connell, & Bird 2014; Ulm et al. 2019).

There remains a need to identify when coastal resources were first widely used and to determine if there was a time lag in the development of coastal economies as initially proposed by Beaton (1985) and recently revived in a different form by McNiven et al. (2014). Further investigation on the timing of sea-level stabilization and the formation of islands is critical. How well numbers of sites correlate with population also requires ongoing research, as does the nature and development of the Late Holocene specialized island marine-based economies. Numerous mainland and island studies in northeast Australia have demonstrated a significant increase in numbers of coastal sites from the Mid-Holocene. In explaining this increase, some studies have emphasized the primary role of social complexity, but population changes, internal social changes, changes in technology, external cultural contact, and the impacts of insularity all need to be considered in explaining the increase. Site preservation and sampling are also significant in explaining the spatial and temporal distribution of archaeological sites; sea level, climate change, and other environmental variables are also important. Significant cultural changes centre around 3500 BP, along with changes in climate and sea levels. This apparent association can be better understood by developing multidisciplinary studies between archaeologists, environmental scientists, and traditional owner groups. Deterministic models, whether they have an environmental or social focus, must be avoided (McNiven et al. 2014; Rowland et al. 2015; Ulm 2013).

In the past, archaeologists have been more comfortable in accepting the dramatic human impacts of climate and sea-level change during the Pleistocene occupation of Sahul, but they have been less inclined to consider the extent and significance of Holocene environmental change. People in the past, as they do today, responded directly to environmental changes but also indirectly to changes in landscape and resource distribution that were initiated by the changes (Rowland 1999a: 11–12). Human–environment interactions need to be tested at the local level where more nuanced patterns emerge (see Rosendahl et al. 2014). Changes in northern Australia must also take account of the possibility of external cultural contacts with Macassan seafarers and others from island Southeast Asia (Rowland 2018).

Interpretations of marine resource use across Australia and New Guinea must be tempered by the large gaps in archaeological knowledge, reflecting the vast length of the coastline, the small number of archaeologists, and the short history of the discipline in this part of the world. Few coastal regions have been extensively surveyed, and basic chronologies have not been established. These problems are compounded by a poor

MARITIME COASTAL AND ISLAND SOCIETIES   791

understanding of how taphonomic processes have impacted the available sample. Sea-level fluctuations, coastal erosion, cyclones, storm surges, and coastal progradation have resulted in differential destruction and burial of the coastal archaeological record (e.g., Bird 1992; Rowland & Ulm 2012; Skelly et al. 2014). The evidence suggests a very recent origin for virtually all coastal landforms where archaeological studies have been carried out, strongly biasing the known archaeological record of the Late Holocene (Robins et al. 2015; Ulm 2011). While taphonomic and sampling factors are important, so too are social factors. Also, the antecedents of the complex systems recorded ethnohistorically and documented historically for the recent past remain poorly understood. Rowland (1996, 2010) has proposed that much Indigenous cultural heritage, especially that on the coast, continues to be under threat from climate change and sea-level rise, and he has noted that a priority would be to 'discuss with Aboriginal owners the potential impact of greenhouse changes on coastal sites' (Rowland 1992: 31). This issue has been addressed by others (e.g., Carmichael et al. 2017; McIntyre-Tamwoy, Fuary, & Buhrich, 2013; Rowland & Ulm 2012; Rowland et al. 2014), but to date the research has been limited in scope.

As Spriggs (2008) has argued, recent trenchant criticisms of the 'islands as laboratories' concept has been unfortunate. Islands continue to provide a rich source of research on climatic and ecological variability, isolation through distance, navigational skills, population and social structure in small populations, and contrasts with more complex continental situations. Islands are also important models for future sustainability and as corollaries for the survival of humans generally (Fitzpatrick & Erlandson 2018). Aspects of island colonization models will continue to be useful in understanding how islands were used. Insularity should never be an a priori assumption of island use, but it is apparent that isolation was important in human history generally. We all seek to avoid single-factor explanations for events in the past, and at a minimum we must consider the synergies between history, geography, and the environment (Rowland 2008).

In respect to the use of coasts and islands, we have a broad picture of 'what happened', but it is now time to reassess 'how we know what happened'. This will involve a reassessment of previous archaeological results and enable us to develop a better framework for ongoing investigations.

ACKNOWLEDGMENTS

This research was supported by the Australian Research Council Centre of Excellence for Australian Biodiversity and Heritage (project number CE170100015). Damien O'Grady (James Cook University) prepared Figures 29.1 and 29.2.

REFERENCES

Allen, J. (2000). From beach to beach: The development of maritime economies in prehistoric Melanesia. In S. O'Connor & P. M. Veth (Eds.), *East of Wallace's Line: Studies of past and present maritime cultures of the Indo-Pacific region* (pp. 139–176). Rotterdam: A. A. Balkema.

Allen, J. (2017). *Excavations on Motupore Island, Central District, Papua New Guinea.* Vols. 1 & 2. University of Otago, Working Papers in Anthropology No. 4. Dunedin: Department of Anthropology and Sociology, University of Otago.

Ash, J., & David, B. (2008). Mua 22: Archaeology at the old village site of Totalai. *Memoirs of the Queensland Museum, Cultural Heritage Series, 4*(2), 327–348.

Axford, Y., Losee, S., Briner, J. P., Francis, D. R., Langdon P. G., & Walker I. R. (2013). Holocene temperature history at the western Greenland Ice Sheet margin reconstructed from lake sediments. *Quaternary Science Reviews, 59,* 87–100. doi: https://doi.org/10.1016/j.quasci rev.2012.10.024

Bailey, G. N., Devès, M. H., Inglis, R. H., Meredith-Williams, M. G., Momber, G., Sakwllariou, D., & Alsharekh, A. M. (2015). Blue Arabia: Palaeolithic and underwater survey in SW Saudi Arabia and the role of coasts in Pleistocene dispersals. *Quaternary International, 382,* 42–57. doi: https://doi.org/10.1016/j.quaint.2015.01.002

Balme, J., O'Connor, S., Maloney, T., Vannieuwenhuyse, D., Aplin, K., & Dilkes-Hall, I. E. (2019). Long-term occupation on the edge of the desert: Riwi Cave in the southern Kimberley, Western Australia. *Archaeology in Oceania, 54,* 35–52. doi: https://doi.org/ 10.1002/arco.5166

Barham, A. J. (2000). Late Holocene maritime societies in the Torres Strait Islands, northern Australia: Cultural arrival or cultural emergence? In S. O'Connor & P. Veth (Eds.), *East of Wallace's Line: Studies of past and present maritime cultures of the Indo–Pacific region* (pp. 223–314). Modern Quaternary Research in South–East Asia Series No. 16. Rotterdam: AA Balkema Press. http://hdl.handle.net/1885/91320

Barham, A. J., Rowland, M. J., & Hitchcock, G. (2004). Torres Strait *bepotaim*: An overview of archaeological and ethnoarchaeological investigations and research. *Memoirs of the Queensland Museum, Cultural Heritage Series, 3*(1), 1–72.

Barker, B. (2004). *The sea people: Late Holocene maritime specialisation in the Whitsunday Islands, central Queensland.* Canberra: Pandanus Books.

Beaton, J. M. (1985). Evidence for a coastal occupation time-lag at Princess Charlotte Bay (North Queensland) and implications for coastal colonisation and population growth theories for Aboriginal Australia. *Archaeology in Oceania, 20*(1), 1–20. doi: https://doi.org/ 10.1002/j.1834-4453.1985.tb00096.x

Benjamin, J., O'Leary, M., McDonald, J., Wiseman, C., McCarthy, J., Beckett, E., . . . Bailey, G. (2020). Aboriginal artefacts on the continental shelf reveal ancient drowned cultural landscapes in northwest Australia. *PLOS ONE.* 15(7): e0233912. https://doi.org/10.1371/jour nal.pone.0233912

Benjamin, J., O'Leary, M., Ward, I., Hacker, J., Ulm, S., Veth, P., & Bailey, G. (2018). Underwater archaeology and submerged landscapes in Western Australia. *Antiquity, 92*(363), e10. doi: https://doi.org/10.15184/aqy.2018.103

Bicho, N. F., Haws, J. A., & Davis, L. G. (Eds.) (2011). *Trekking the shore: Changing coastlines and the antiquity of coastal settlement.* Secaucus, NJ: Springer. doi: https://doi.org/10.1007/ 978-1-4419-8219-3

Bird, D. W., Richardson, J. L., Veth, P., & Barham, A. (2002). Explaining shellfishing variability in middens on the Meriam Islands, Torres Strait, Australia. *Journal of Archaeological Science, 29,* 457–469. https://doi.org/10.1006/jasc.2001.0734

Bird, M. I., Condie, S. A., O'Connor, S., O'Grady, D., Reepmeyer, C., Ulm, S., & Bradshaw, C. J. A. (2019). Early human settlement of Sahul was not an accident. *Scientific Reports, 9,* 8220. doi: https://doi.org/10.1038/s41598-019-42946-9

Bird, M. K. (1992). The impact of tropical cyclones on the archaeological record: An Australian example. *Archaeology in Oceania, 27*(2), 75–86. doi: https://doi.org/10.1002/j.1834-4453.1992. tb00286.x

Boivin, N., Fuller, D. Q., Dennell, R., Allaby, R., & Petraglia, M. D. (2013). Human dispersal across diverse environments of Asia during the Upper Pleistocene. *Quaternary International, 300,* 32–47. doi: https://doi.org/10.1016/j.quaint.2013.01.008

Border, A. (1999). Aboriginal settlement of offshore islands in the southern Great Barrier Reef province, central Queensland. In J. Hall & I. J. McNiven (Eds.), *Australian coastal archaeology* (pp. 129–139). Canberra: ANH Publication, Department of Archaeology and Natural History, Research School of Pacific and Asian Studies, The Australian National University.

Bourke, P. M. (2004). Three Aboriginal shell mounds at Hope Inlet: Evidence for coastal, not maritime late Holocene economies on the Beagle Gulf mainland, northern Australia. *Australian Archaeology, 59,* 10–22. https://doi.org/10.1080/03122417.2004.11681787

Bourke, P. M., Brockwell, S., Faulkner, P., & Meehan, B. (2007). Climate variability in the mid to late Holocene Arnhem Land Region, north Australia: Archaeological archives of environmental and cultural change. *Archaeology in Oceania, 42*(3), 91–101. https://doi.org/10.1002/j.1834-4453.2007.tb00022.x

Bowdler, S. (1995). Offshore islands and maritime explorations in Australian prehistory. *Antiquity, 69*(266), 945–958. doi: https://doi.org/10.1017/S0003598X0008248X

Bowdler, S. (2010). The empty coast: Conditions for human occupation in southeast Australia during the late Pleistocene. In S. G. Harbele, J. Stevenson, & M. Prebble (Eds.), *Altered ecologies: Fire, climate and human influence on terrestrial landscapes* (pp. 177–185). Canberra: ANU E Press. doi: http://doi.org/10.22459/TA32.11.2010.10

Bowdler, S. (2015). The Bass Strait Islands revisited. *Quaternary International, 385,* 206–218. doi: https://doi.org/10.1016/j.quaint.2014.07.047

Bowler, J. M., Price, D. M., Sherwood, J. E., & Carey, S. P. (2018). The Moyjil site, south-west Victoria, Australia: Fire and environment in a 120,000-year coastal midden—nature or people? *The Royal Society of Victoria, 130*(2), 71–93. doi: 10.1071/RS18007

Bradshaw, C. J. A., Ulm, S., Williams, A. N., Bird, M. I., Roberts, R. G., Jacobs, Z., & Saltré, F. (2019). Minimum founding populations for the first peopling of Sahul. *Nature Ecology and Evolution, 3,* 1057–1063. doi: https://doi.org/10.1038/s41559-019-0902-6

Brady, L. M., & Ash, J. (2018). New radiocarbon dates from Kirriri 4: Extending the 2,500 BP signature for the onset of the Torres Strait Cultural Complex to south western Torres Strait, northeast Queensland. *Australian Archaeology, 84*(1), 1–7. https://doi.org/10.1080/03122 417.2018.1458271

Bulmer, S. (1982). West of Bootless Inlet: Archaeological evidence for prehistoric trade in the Port Moresby area and the origins of the hiri. In T. Dutton (Ed.), *The hiri in history* (pp. 117–130). Canberra: Australian National University.

Carmichael, B., Wilson, G., Namarnyilk, I., Nadji, S., Cahill, J., Brockwell, S., & Bird, D. (2017). Australian Indigenous rangers managing the impacts of climate change on cultural heritage sites. In T. Dawson, C. Nimura, E. López-Romero, & M-Y. Daire (Eds.), *Public archaeology and climate change* (pp. 162–174). Oxford: Oxbow Books. doi: https://doi.org/https://doi.org/10.2307/j.ctvh1dp4n.21

Clarkson, C., Jacobs, Z., Marwick, B., Fullagar, R., Wallis, L., Smith, M., Pardoe, C. (2017). Human occupation of northern Australia by 65,000 years ago. *Nature, 547,* 306–310. doi: https://doi.org/10.1038/nature22968

Codding, B. F., O'Connell, J. F., & Bird, D. W. (2014). Shellfishing and the colonization of Sahul: A multivariate model evaluating the dynamic effects of prey utility, transport considerations and life-history on foraging patterns and midden composition. *Journal of Island and Coastal Archaeology*, *9*, 238–252. doi: https://doi.org/10.1080/15564894.2013.848958

Cohen, M. N. (1977). *The food crisis in prehistory: Overpopulation and the origin of agriculture.* New Haven, CT: Yale University Press.

Cortés-Sánchez, M., Morales-Muniz, A., Simón-Vallejo, M. D., Lozano-Francisco, M., Vera-Peláez, J. L., Finlayson, C., & Bicho, N. F. (2011). Earliest known use of marine resources by Neanderthals. *PLoS ONE*, *6*, e24026. doi: https://doi.org/10.1371/journal.pone.0024026

Cosgrove, R., Field, J., & Ferrier, Å. (2007). The archaeology of Australia's tropical rainforests. *Palaeogeography, Palaeoclimatology, Palaeoecology*, *251*, 150–173. doi: https://doi.org/10.1016/j.palaeo.2007.02.023

David, B., McNiven, I. J., Mitchell, R., Orr, M., Haberle, S., Brady, L., & Crouch, J. (2004). Badu 15 and the Papuan-Austronesian settlement of Torres Strait. *Archaeology in Oceania, 39* (2), 65–78. doi: https://doi.org/10.1002/j.1834-4453.2004.tb00564.x

David, B., McNiven, I. J., Richards, T., Connaughton, S. P., Leavesley, M., Barker B., & Rowe C. (2011). Lapita sites in the Central Province of mainland Papua New Guinea. *World Archaeology*, *43*(4), 576–593. doi: 10.1080/00438243.2011.624720

David, B., & Weisler, W. (2006). Kurturniaiwak (Badu) and the archaeology of villages in Torres Strait. *Australian Archaeology*, *63*(1), 21–34. https://doi.org/10.1080/03122417.2006.11681835

Détroit, F., Mijaries, A. S., Corny, J., Daver, G., Zanolli, C., Dizon, E., & Piper, P. J. (2019). A new species of *Homo* from the Late Pleistocene of the Philippines. *Nature*, *568*, 181–186. doi: https://doi.org/10.1038/s41586-019-1067-9

Dougherty A. J., Thomas, Z. A., Fogwill, C., Hogg, A., Palmer, J., Rainsley, E., & Turney, C. (2019). Redating the earliest evidence of the mid-Holocene relative sea-level highstand in Australia and implications for global sea-level rise. *PLoS ONE*, *14*(7), e0218430. doi: https://doi.org/10.1371/journal.pone.0218430

Erlandson, J. M., & Braje, T. J. (2015). Coasting out of Africa: The potential of mangrove forests and marine habitats to facilitate human coastal expansion via the Southern Dispersal Route. *Quaternary International*, *382*, 31–41. doi: https://doi.org/10.1016/j.quaint.2015.03.046

Fitzpatrick, A., McNiven, I. J., Specht, J., & Ulm, S. (2018). Stylistic analysis of stone arrangements supports regional cultural interactions along the northern Great Barrier Reef, Queensland. *Australian Archaeology*, *84*(2), 129–144. doi: https://doi.org/10.1080/03122417.2018.1507807

Fitzpatrick, S. M., & Erlandson, J. M. (2018). Island archaeology, model systems, the Anthropocene, and how the past informs the future. *Journal of Island and Coastal Archaeology*, *13*, 283–299. doi: https://doi.org/10.1080/15564894.2018.1447051

Fredericksen, C., Spriggs, M., & Ambrose, W. (1993). Pamwak rockshelter: A Pleistocene site on Manus Island, Papua New Guinea. In M. A. Smith, M. Spriggs, & B. Fankhauser (Eds.), *Sahul in review: Pleistocene archaeology in Australia, New Guinea and Island Melanesia* (pp. 144–152). Canberra: Australian National University.

Fujita, M., Yamasaki, S., Katagiri, C., Oshiro, I., Sano, K., Kurozumi, T., & Kaifu, Y. (2016). Advanced maritime adaptation in the western Pacific coastal region extends back to 35,000–30,000 years before present. *Proceedings of the National Academy of Sciences of the United States of America, 113*, 11184–11189. doi: https://doi.org/10.1073/pnas.1607857113

Gagan, M., Hendy, E., Haberle, S., & Hantoro, W. (2004). Post-glacial evolution of the Indo-Pacific Warm Pool and El Niño-Southern Oscillation. *Quaternary International, 118 / 119,* 127–143. doi: https//doi.org/10.1016/S1040-6182(03)00134-4

Gliganic, L. A., Cohen, T. J., May, J-H., Jansen, J. D., Nanson, G. C., Dosseto, A., & Aubert, M. (2014). Late-Holocene climatic variability indicated by three natural archives in arid southern Australia. *The Holocene, 24*(7), 104–117. doi: https://doi.org/10.1177%2F095968361 3515732

Gosden, C., & Webb, J. (1994). The creation of a Papua New Guinean landscape: Archaeological and geomorphological evidence. *Journal of Field Archaeology, 21,* 29–51.

Groube, L., Chappell, J., Muke, J., & Price, D. (1986). A 40,000 year-old human occupation site at Huon Peninsula, Papua New Guinea. *Nature, 324,* 453–455. doi: https://doi.org/10.1038/324453a0

Haberle, S. G., & Chepstow-Lusty, A. (2000). Can climate influence cultural development? A view through time. *Environment and History, 6,* 349–369. doi: https://doi.org/10.3197/096 734000129342334

Haberle, S. G., & David, B. (2004). Climates of change: Human dimensions of Holocene environmental change in low latitudes of the PEPII transect. *Quaternary International, 118–119,* 165–179. doi: https://doi.org/10.1016/S1040-6182(03)00136-8

Hall, J. (1999). The impact of sea level rise on the archaeological record of the Moreton region, southeast Queensland. In J. Hall & I. J. McNiven (Eds.), *Australian coastal archaeology* (pp. 169–184). Canberra: ANH Publications, Department of Archaeology and Natural History, RSPAS, The Australian National University.

Harrison, S. P., & Dodson, J. (1993). Climates of Australia and New Guinea since 18,000 yr BP. In H. E. Wright, Jr., J. E. Kutzbach, T. Webb III, W. F. Ruddiman, F. A Street-Perrott, & P. J. Bartlein (Eds.), *Global climates since the Last Glacial Maximum* (pp. 265–292). Minneapolis: University of Minnesota Press.

Hawkins, S., O'Connor, S., Maloney, T., Litster, M., Kealy, S., Fenner, J. N., & Louys, J. (2017). Oldest human occupation of Wallacea at Laili Cave, Timor-Leste, shows broad-spectrum foraging responses to Late Pleistocene environments. *Quaternary Science Reviews, 171,* 58–72. doi: https://doi.org/10.1016/j.quascirev.2017.07.008

Hesp, P. A., Murray-Wallace, C. V., & Dortch, C. E. (1999). Aboriginal occupation on Rottnest Island, Western Australia, provisionally dated by Aspartic Acid Racemisation Assay of land snails to greater than 50 Ka. *Australian Archaeology, 49,* 7–12. doi: https://doi.org/10.1080/03122417.1999.11681647

Hiscock, P. (1994). Technological responses to risk in Holocene Australia. *Journal of World Prehistory, 8*(3), 267–292. doi: https://doi.org/10.1007/BF02221051

Hiscock, P. (2008). *Archaeology of ancient Australia.* New York: Routledge.

Holdaway, S. J., Fanning, P. C., Petchey, F., Allely, K., Shiner, J. I., & Bailey, G. (2017). Temporal variability in shell mound formation at Albatross Bay, northern Australia. *PLoS ONE, 12*(8), e0183863. doi: https://doi.org/10.1371/journal.pone.0183863

Irwin, G. (1985). *The emergence of Mailu as a central place in coastal Papuan prehistory.* Terra Australias 10. Canberra: Australian National University.

Irwin, G., Shaw, B., & McAlister, A. (2019). The origins of the Kula Ring: Archaeological and maritime perspectives from the southern Massim and Mailu areas of Papua New Guinea. *Archaeology in Oceania, 54*(1), 1–16. doi: https://doi.org/10.1002/arco.5167

Ishiwa, T., Yokoyama, Y., Miyairi, Y., Obrochta, S., Sasaki, T., Kitamura, A., & Matsuzaki, H. (2016). Reappraisal of sea-level lowstand during the last glacial maximum observed in the

Bonaparte Gulf sediments, northwestern Australia. *Quaternary International, 397*, 373–379. doi: https://doi.org/10.1016/j.quaint.2015.03.032

Johnson, C. N., & Wroe, S. (2003). Causes of extinction of vertebrates during the Holocene of mainland Australia: Arrival of the dingo, or human impact? *The Holocene, 13*, 941–948. doi: https://doi.org/10.1191/0959683603hl682fa

Jones, R. (1976). Tasmanian aquatic machines and off-shore islands. In G. d. G. Sieveking, I. H. Longworth, & K. E. Wilson (Eds.), *Problems in economic and social archaeology* (pp. 235–263). London: Duckworth.

Kealy, S., Louys, J., & O'Connor. S. (2018). Least-cost pathway models indicate northern human dispersal from Sunda to Sahul. *Journal of Human Evolution, 125*, 59–70. doi: https://doi.org/10.1016/j.jhevol.2018.10.003

Kirch, P. V. (1997). *The Lapita peoples: Ancestors of the Oceanic world.* Cambridge: Blackwell Publishers.

Kirch, P. V. (2001). *Lapita and its transformations in Near Oceania: Archaeological investigations in the Mussau Islands, Papua New Guinea, 1985–88.* Archaeological Research Facility Contribution 59. Berkeley: University of California Press.

Kreij, A., Scriffignano, J., Rosendahl, D., Nagel, T., & Ulm, S. (2018). Aboriginal stone-walled intertidal fishtrap morphology, function and chronology investigated with high-resolution close-range Unmanned Aerial Vehicle photogrammetry. *Journal of Archaeological Science, 96*, 148–161. doi: https://doi.org/10.1016/j.jas.2018.05.012

Lamb, L. (2011). *Rock of ages: South Molle Island Quarry, Whitsunday Islands: Use and distribution of stone through space and time.* Oxford: Archaeopress.

Lambrides, A. B. J., McNiven, I. J., & Ulm, S. (2019). Meta-analysis of Queensland's coastal Indigenous fisheries: Examining the archaeological evidence for geographic and temporal patterning. *Journal of Archaeological Science: Reports, 28*, 102057. doi: -https://doi.org/10.1016/j.jasrep.2019.102057

Leavesley, M. (2006). Late Pleistocene complexities in the Bismarck Archipelago. In I. Lilley (Ed.), *Archaeology of Oceania: Australia and the Pacific Islands* (pp. 189–204). Carlton, VIC: Blackwell. doi: https://doi.org/10.1002/9780470773475.ch9

Leavesley M., & Allen, J. (1998). Dates, disturbance and artefact distributions: Another analysis of Buang Merabak, a Pleistocene site on New Ireland, Papua New Guinea. *Archaeology in Oceania, 33*(2), 63–82. doi: https://doi.org/10.1002/j.1834-4453.1998.tb00405.x

Leppard, T. P., & Runnels, C. (2017). Maritime hominin dispersals in the Pleistocene: Advancing the debate. *Antiquity, 91*(356), 510–519. doi: https://doi.org/10.15184/aqy.2017.16

Lewis, S. E., Wüst, R. A. J., Webster, J. M., & Shields, G. A. (2008). Mid-late Holocene sea-level variability in eastern Australia. *Terra Nova, 20*(1), 74–81, doi: https://doi.org/10.1111/j.1365-3121.2007.00789.x

Lilley, I. (2004). Trade and culture history across the Vitiaz Strait, Papua New Guinea: The emerging Post-Lapita coastal sequence. *Records of the Australian Museum, 29*, 89–96.

Lourandos, H. (1997). *Continent of hunter-gatherers: New perspectives in Australian prehistory.* Cambridge: Cambridge University Press.

Manne, T., & Veth, P. M. (2015). Late Pleistocene and early Holocene exploitation of estuarine communities in northwestern Australia. *Quaternary International, 385*, 112–123. doi: https://doi.org/10.1016/j.quaint.2014.12.049

Marean, C. W. (2016). The transition to foraging for dense and predictable resources and its impact on the evolution of modern humans. *Philosophical Transactions of the Royal Society B, 371*, 20150239. doi: https://doi.org/10.1098/rstb.2015.0239

Marsh, M., Hiscock, P., Williams, D., Hughes, P., & Sullivan, M. (2018). Watura Jurnti: A 42000–45000-year-long occupation sequence from the north-eastern Pilbara. *Archaeology in Oceania*, *53*(3), 137–149. doi: https://doi.org/10.1002/arco.5152

McDonald, J., & Berry, M. (2017). Murujuga, northwestern Australia: When arid hunter-gatherers became coastal foragers. *The Journal of Island and Coastal Archaeology*, *12*(1), 24–43. doi: 10.1080/15564894.2015.1125971

McDonald, J., Dortch, J., Paterson, A., & Veth, P. (in prep.). Murujuga: Dynamics of the Dreaming. UWA CRARM Monograph Series.

McIntyre-Tamwoy, S., Fuary, M., & Buhrich, A. (2013). Understanding climate, adapting to change: Indigenous cultural values and climate change impacts in north Queensland. *Local Environment*, *18*(1), 91–109. doi: https://doi.org/10.1016/j.quaint.2015.05.062

McNiven, I. J. (1999). Fissioning and regionalisation: The social dimensions of changes in Aboriginal use of the Great Sandy Region, southeast Queensland. In J. Hall & I. J. McNiven (Eds.), *Australian coastal archaeology* (pp. 157–168). Canberra: Australian National University.

McNiven, I. J. (2000). Treats or retreats: Aboriginal island use along the Gippsland coast, southeastern Australia. *The Artefact*, *23*, 22–34.

McNiven, I. J. (2013). Ritualized middening practices. *Journal of Archaeological Method and Theory*, *20*, 552–587. doi: https://doi.org/10.1007/s10816-012-9130-y

McNiven, I. J. (2015). Precarious islands: Kulkalgal reef island settlement and high mobility across 700 km of seascape, central Torres Strait and northern Great Barrier Reef. *Quaternary International*, *385*, 39–55. doi: https://doi.org/10.1016/j.quaint.2014.09.015

McNiven, I. J. (2016). Increase rituals and environmental variability on small residential islands of Torres Strait. *Journal of Island and Coastal Archaeology*, *11*, 195–210. doi.org/10.1080/15564894.2015.1115789

McNiven, I. J. (2017). Edges of worlds. Torres Strait Islander peripheral participation in ancient globalizations. In T. Hodos (Ed.), *The Routledge handbook of globalization and archaeology* (pp. 319–334). New York: Routledge.

McNiven, I. J., Crouch, J., Bowler, J., Sherwood, J., Dolby, N., & Stanisic, J. (2018). The Moyjil site, south-west Victoria: Excavation of a Last Interglacial charcoal and burnt stone feature: Is it a hearth? *Proceedings of the Royal Society of Victoria*, *130*(2), 94–116. https://doi.org/10.1071/RS18008

McNiven, I. J., Crouch, J., Weisler, M., Kemp, N., Clayton Martínez, L., Stanisic, J., . . . Boles, W. (2008). Tigershark Rockshelter (Baidamau Mudh): Seascape and settlement reconfigurations on the sacred islet of Pulu, western Zenadh Kes (Torres Strait). *Australian Archaeology*, *66*, 15–32.

McNiven, I. J., David, B., Richards, T., Aplin, K., Asmussen, B., Mialanes, J., Ulm, S. (2011). New direction in human colonisation of the Pacific: Lapita settlement of south coast New Guinea. *Australian Archaeology*, *72*, 1–6. doi: https://doi.org/10.1080/03122417.2011.11690525

McNiven, I. J., de Maria, N., Weisler, M., & Lewis, T. (2014). Darumbal voyaging: Intensifying use of central Queensland's Shoalwater Bay islands over the past 5000 years. *Archaeology in Oceania*, *49*(1), 2–42. doi: https://doi.org/10.1002/arco.5016

McNiven, I. J., Dickinson, W. R., David, B., Weisler, M., von Gnielinski, F., Carter, M., & Zoppi, U. (2006). Mask Cave: Red–slipped pottery and the Australian–Papuan settlement of Zenadh Kes (Torres Strait). *Archaeology in Oceania*, *41*(2), 49–81. https://doi.org/10.1002/j.1834-4453.2006.tb00610.x

McNiven, I. J., & Ulm, S. (2015). Multidisciplinary approaches to Australian island pasts: Late Pleistocene to historical perspectives on Australian island use. *Quaternary International*, *385*, 1–6. doi: https://doi.org/10.1016/j.quaint.2015.06.032

Memmott, P., Round E., Rosendahl, D., & Ulm, S. (2016). Fission, fusion and syncretism: Linguistic and environmental changes amongst the Tangkic people of the southern Gulf of Carpentaria, Northern Australia. In J-C. Verstraete & D. Hafner (Eds.), *Land and language in Cape York Peninsula and the Gulf Country* (pp. 105–136). Philadelphia: John Benjamins. https://doi.org/10.1075/clu.18.06mem

Morse, K. (1988). Mandu Mandu Creek rockshelter: Pleistocene coastal occupation of North West Cape, Western Australia. *Archaeology in Oceania*, *23*(3), 81–88. doi: https://doi.org/10.1002/j.1834-4453.1988.tb00193.x

Morwood, M. (1987). The archaeology of social complexity in south-east Queensland. *Proceedings of the Prehistoric Society*, *53*, 337–350. doi: https://doi.org/10.1017/S0079497X000006265

Morwood, M. J., Soejono, R. P., Roberts, R. G., Sutikna, T., Turney, C. S. M., Westaway, K. E., . . . Fifield, L. K. (2004). Archaeology and age of a new hominin from Flores in eastern Indonesia. *Nature*, *431*, 1087–1091. doi: https://doi.org/10.1038/nature02956

Neal, R., & Stock, E. (1986). Pleistocene occupation in the south-east Queensland coastal region. *Nature*, *323*, 618–621. doi: https://doi.org/10.1038/323618a0

Norman, K., Inglis, J., Clarkson, C., Faith, J. T., Shulmeister, J., & Harris, D. (2018). An early colonisation pathway into northwest Australia 70–60,000 years ago. *Quaternary Science Reviews*, *180*, 229–239. doi: https://doi.org/10.1016/j.quascirev.2017.11.023

O'Connell, J. F., Allen, J., & Hawkes, K. (2010). Pleistocene Sahul and the origins of seafaring. In A. Anderson, J. H. Barrett, & K. V. Boyle (Eds.), *The global origins and development of seafaring* (pp. 57–68). Cambridge: McDonald Institute of Archaeological Research.

O'Connor, S. (1992). The timing and nature of prehistoric island use in northern Australia. *Archaeology in Oceania*, *27*(2), 49–60. doi: https://doi.org/10.1002/j.1834-4453.1992.tb00284.x

O'Connor, S. (1999). *30,000 years of Aboriginal occupation: Kimberley, north west Australia*. Canberra: Department of Archaeology and Natural History and Centre for Archaeological Research, The Australian National University.

O'Connor, S., Ono, R., & Clarkson, C. (2011). Pelagic fishing at 42,000 years before the present and the maritime skills of modern humans. *Science*, *334*, 1117–1121. doi: https://doi.org/10.1126/science.1207703

Osborn, A. J. (1977). Strandloopers, mermaids, and fairy tales. In L. R. Binford (Ed.), *For theory building in archaeology* (pp. 157–205). New York: Academic Press.

Przywolnik, K. (2005). Long-term transitions in hunter-gatherers of coastal northwestern Australia. In P. Veth, M. Smith, & P. Hiscock (Eds.), *Desert peoples: Archaeological perspectives* (pp. 177–205). Oxford: Blackwell Publishers.

Rabett, R. J. (2018). The success of failed *Homo sapiens* dispersals out of Africa and into Asia. *Nature Ecology and Evolution*, *2*, 212–219. doi: https://doi.org/10.1038/s41559-017-0436-8

Ramos-Muñoz, J., Cantillo-Duarte, J. J., Bernal-Casasola, D., Barrena-Tocino, A., Domínguez-Bella, S., Vijande-Vila, E., & Almisas-Cruz, S. (2016). Early use of marine resources by Middle/Upper Pleistocene human societies: The case of Benzú rockshelter (northern Africa). *Quaternary International*, *407*, 16–28. https://doi.org/10.1016/j.quaint.2015.12.092

Rhoads, J. W. (1982). Prehistoric Papuan exchange systems: The hiri and its antecedents. In T. E. Dutton (Ed.), *The hiri in History* (pp. 131–151). Canberra: Australian National University.

Robins, R., Hall, J., & Stock, E. (2015). Geoarchaeology and the archaeological record in the coastal Moreton Region, Queensland, Australia. *Quaternary International*, *385*, 191–205. doi: https://doi.org/10.1016/j.quaint.2015.02.060

Rosendahl, D., Ulm, S., Tomkins, H., Wallis, L., & Memmott, P. (2014). Late Holocene changes in shellfishing behaviours from the Gulf of Carpentaria, northern Australia. *The Journal of Island and Coastal Archaeology*, *9*(2), 253–267. doi: https://doi.org/10.1080/15564 894.2014.880757

Rosendahl, D., Ulm, S., & Weisler, M. (2007). Using foraminifera to distinguish between natural and cultural shell deposits in coastal eastern Australia. *Journal of Archaeological Science*, *34*(10), 1584–1593. doi: https://doi.org/10.1016/j.jas.2006.11.013

Ross, M. D. (1988). *Proto Oceanic and the Austronesian languages of Western Melanesia*. Canberra: Pacific Linguistics.

Rowland, M. J. (1984). A long way in a bark canoe: Aboriginal occupation of the Percy Isles. *Australian Archaeology*, *18*, 17–31.

Rowland, M. J. (1992). Climate change, sea-level rise and the archaeological record. *Australian Archaeology*, *34*, 29–33. https://doi.org/10.1080/03122417.1992.11681449

Rowland, M. J. (1995). Indigenous water-craft use in Australia. The 'Big Picture' and small experiments on the Queensland coast. *Bulletin of the Australian Institute for Maritime Archaeology*, *19*(1), 5–18.

Rowland, M. J. (1996). Prehistoric archaeology of the Great Barrier Reef Province: Retrospect and prospect. In P. Veth & P. Hiscock (Eds.), *Archaeology of northern Australia: Regional perspectives* (pp. 191–211). St. Lucia: Anthropology Museum, University of Queensland.

Rowland, M. J. (1999a). The Keppel Islands—'a 3000 year' event revisited. In J. Hall & I. J. McNiven (Eds.), *Australian coastal archaeology* (pp. 141–155). Canberra: ANH Publications, Australian National University.

Rowland, M. J. (1999b). Holocene environmental variability: Have its impacts been underestimated in Australian pre-history? *The Artefact*, *22*, 11–40.

Rowland, M. J. (2008). Colonization, environment and insularity: Prehistoric island use in the Great Barrier Reef Province, Queensland, Australia. In J. Connolly & M. Campbell (Eds.), *Comparative island archaeologies* (pp. 85–104). Oxford: British Archaeological Reports.

Rowland, M. J. (2010). Will the sky fall in? Global warming—An alternative view. *Antiquity*, *84*, 1163–1171. doi: https://doi.org/10.1017/S0003598X00067156

Rowland, M. J. (2018). 65,000 years of isolation in Aboriginal Australia or continuity and external contacts? An assessment of the evidence with an emphasis on the Queensland coast. *Journal of the Anthropological Society of South Australia*, *42*, 211–240.

Rowland, M. J., & Ulm, S. (2011). Indigenous fishtraps and weirs of Queensland. *Queensland Archaeological Research*, *14*, 1–58. doi: https://doi.org/10.25120/qar.14.2011.219

Rowland, M. J., & Ulm, S. (2012). Key issues in the conservation of the Australian coastal archaeological record: Natural and human impacts. *Journal of Coastal Conservation*, *16*(2), 159–171. https://doi.org/10.1007/s11852-010-0112-5

Rowland, M., Ulm, S., & Roe, M. (2014). Approaches to monitoring and managing Indigenous Australian coastal cultural heritage places. *Queensland Archaeological Research*, *17*, 37–48. doi: https://doi.org/10.25120/qar.17.2014.231

Rowland, M. J., Wright, S., & Baker, R. (2015). The timing and use of offshore islands in the Great Barrier Reef Marine province, Queensland. *Quaternary International*, *385*, 154–165. doi: https://doi.org/10.1016/j.quaint.2015.01.025

Shaw, B. (2017). Late Pleistocene colonisation of the eastern New Guinea islands? The potential implications of robust waisted stone tool finds from Rossel Island on the long term settlement dynamics in the Massim region. *Journal of Pacific Archaeology, 8*(2), 1–16.

Shaw, B. (2019). Archaeology of the Massim Island Region, Papua New Guinea. In C. Smith (Ed.), *Encyclopedia of global archaeology* (pp. 1–15). New York: Springer Reference.

Shaw, B., Coxe, S., Kewibu, V., Haro, J., Hull, E., & Hawkins, S. (2020). 2500-year cultural sequence in the Massim region of eastern Papua New Guinea reflects adaptive strategies to small islands and changing climate regimes since Lapita settlement. *The Holocene, 30*(7), 1075–1090 doi: https://doi.org/10.1177%2F0959683620908641

Sheppard, P., Thomas, T., & Summerhayes, G. (Eds.) (2009). *Lapita: Ancestors and descendants.* New Zealand Archaeological Association Monograph. Auckland: New Zealand Archaeological Association.

Sherwood, J. E., McNiven, I. J., & Laurenson, L. (2018). The Moyjil site, south-west Victoria, Australia: Shells as evidence of the deposit's origin. *Proceedings of the Royal Society of Victoria, 130*(2), 50–70. doi: 10.1071/rs18006

Shulmeister, J. (1999). Australasian evidence for mid-Holocene climatic change implies precessional control of Walker Circulation in the Pacific. *Quaternary International, 57 / 58*, 81–91. doi: https://doi.org/10.1016/S1040-6182(98)00052-4

Sim, R., & Wallis, L. A. (2008). Northern Australian offshore island use during the Holocene: The archaeology of Vanderlin Island, Sir Edward Pellew Group, Gulf of Carpentaria. *Australian Archaeology, 67*, 95–106. https://doi.org/10.1080/03122417.2008.11681882

Skelly, R., & David, B. (2017). *Hiri: Archaeology of long-distance maritime trade along the south coast of Papua New Guinea.* Honolulu: University of Hawaii Press.

Skelly, R., David, B., Petchey, F., & Leavesley, M. (2014). Tracking ancient beach-lines inland: 2600-year-old dentate-stamped ceramics at Hopo, Vailala River region, Papua New Guinea. *Antiquity, 88*(340), 470–487. doi: https://doi.org/10.1017/S0003598X00101127

Sloss, C. R., Nothdurft, L., Hua, Q., O'Connor, S. G., Moss, P. T., Rosendahl, D., & Ulm, S. (2018). Holocene sea-level change and coastal landscape evolution in the southern Gulf of Carpentaria, Australia. *The Holocene, 28*(9), 1411–1430. doi: https://www.doi.org/10.1177/0959683618777070.

Smith, A., & Allen, J. (1999). Pleistocene shell technologies: Evidence from Island Melanesia. In J. Hall, & I. J. McNiven (Eds.), *Australian coastal archaeology* (pp. 291–298). Canberra: ANH Publications, Australian National University.

Specht, J. (2007). Small islands in the big picture: The formative period of Lapita in the Bismarck Archipelago. In S. Bedford, C. Sand, & S. P. Connaughton (Eds.), *Oceanic explorations: Lapita and Western Pacific settlement* (pp. 51–70). Canberra: ANU E-Press.

Spriggs, M. (2008). Are islands islands? Some thoughts on the history of chalk and cheese. In G. Clark, F. Leach, & S. O'Connor (Eds.), *Islands of inquiry. Colonisation, seafaring and the archaeology of maritime landscapes* (pp. 211–226). Canberra: ANU E Press.

Sullivan, M. E. (1982). Exploitation of offshore islands along the New South Wales coastline. *Australian Archaeology, 15*, 8–19.

Summerhayes, G. R. (2007). The rise and transformation of Lapita in the Bismarck Archipelago. In S. Chui & C. Sand (Eds.), *From Southeast Asia to the Pacific: Archaeological perspectives on the Austronesian expansion and the Lapita Cultural Complex* (pp. 141–169). Taipei: Academic Sinica.

Summerhayes, G., Field, J., Shaw, B., & Gaffney, D. (2017). The archaeology of forest exploitation and change in the tropics during the Pleistocene: The case of Northern Sahul

(Pleistocene New Guinea). *Quaternary International, 448,* 14–30. doi: https://doi.org/10.1016/j.quaint.2016.04.023

Swadling, P. (1981). The settlement history of the Motu and Koita speaking people of the Central Province, Papua New Guinea. In D. Denoon & R. Lacey (Eds.), *Oral tradition in Melanesia* (pp. 241–251). Port Moresby: University of PNG and the Institute of Papua New Guinea Studies.

Twaddle, R. W., Sloss, C. R., Lowe, K. M., Moss, P., Mackenzie, L. L., & Ulm, S. (2017). Short-term late Holocene dry season occupation and sandy-mud flat focused foraging at Murdumurdu, Bentinck Island, Gulf of Carpentaria. *Queensland Archaeological Research, 20,* 9–46. doi: https://doi.org/10.25120/qar.20.2017.3588

Ulm, S. (2000). Evidence for early focussed marine resource exploitation from an open coastal site in central Queensland. *Australian Archaeology, 51,* 66–67. doi: https://doi.org/10.1080/03122417.2000.11681684

Ulm, S. (2006). *Coastal themes: An archaeology of the Southern Curtis coast, Queensland.* Canberra: ANU E Press.

Ulm, S. (2011). Coastal foragers on southern shores: Marine resource use in northeast Australia since the Late Pleistocene. In N. F. Bicho, J. A. Haws, & L. G. Davis (Eds.), *Trekking the shore: Changing coastlines and the antiquity of coastal settlement* (pp. 441–461). New York: Springer. doi: https://doi.org/10.1007/978-1-4419-8219-3_19

Ulm, S. (2013). 'Complexity' and the Australian continental narrative: Themes in the archaeology of Holocene Australia. *Quaternary International, 285,* 182–192. doi: https://doi.org/10.1016/j.quaint.2012.03.046

Ulm, S., McNiven, I. J., Aird, S. J., & Lambrides, A. J. (2019). Sustainable harvesting of *Conomurex luhuanus* and *Rochia nilotica* by Indigenous Australians on the Great Barrier Reef over the past 2000 years. *Journal of Archaeological Science: Reports, 28,* 102017. doi: https://doi.org/10.1016/j.jasrep.2019.102017

Vanderwal, R. L. (1978). Adaptive technology in southwest Tasmania. *Australian Archaeology, 8,* 107–127.

Veth, P., Ditchfield, K., Bateman, M., Ouzman, S., Benoit, M., Motta, A. P., & Balanggarra Aboriginal Corporation. (2019). Minjiwarra: Archaeological evidence of human occupation of Australia's northern Kimberley by 50,000 BP. *Australian Archaeology, 85*(2), 115–125. doi: https://doi.org/10.1080/03122417.2019.1650479

Veth, P., Hiscock, P., & Williams, A. (2011). Are tulas and ENSO linked in Australia? *Australian Archaeology, 72,* 7–14. doi: https://doi.org/10.1080/03122417.2011.11690526

Veth, P., McDonald, J., Ward, I., O'Leary, M., Beckett, E., Benjamin, J., & Bailey, G. (2020). A strategy for assessing continuity in terrestrial and maritime landscapes from Murujuga (Dampier Archipelago), North West Shelf, Australia. *The Journal of Island and Coastal Archaeology, 15*(4), 477–503. doi: https://doi.org/10.1080/15564894.2019.1572677

Veth, P., Ward, I., Manne, T., Ulm, S., Ditchfield, K., Dortch, J., & Kendrick, P. (2017). Early human occupation of a maritime desert, Barrow Island, north-west Australia. *Quaternary Science Reviews, 168,* 19–29. doi: https://doi.org/10.1016/j.quascirev.2017.05.002

Ward, I. (2004). Comparative records of occupation in the Keep River region of the eastern Kimberley, north western Australia. *Australian Archaeology, 59,* 1–9. doi: https://doi.org/10.1080/03122417.2004.11681786

Wickler, S., & Spriggs, M. (1988). Pleistocene human occupation of the Solomon Islands, Melanesia. *Antiquity, 62*(237), 703–706. doi: https://doi.org/10.1017/S0003598X00075104

Will, M., Kandel, A. W., & Conrad, N. J. (2019). Midden or molehill: The role of coastal adaptations in human evolution and dispersal. *Journal of World Prehistory.* doi: https://doi.org/10.1007/s10963-018-09127-4

Williams, A. N., Ulm, S., Cook, A. R., Langley, M. C., & Collard, M. (2013). Human refugia in Australia during the Last Glacial Maximum and terminal Pleistocene: A geospatial analysis of the 25-12ka Australian archaeological record. *Journal of Archaeological Science, 40,* 4612–4625. doi: https://doi.org/10.1016/j.jas.2013.06.015

Williams, A. N., Ulm, S., Sapienza, T., Lewis, S., & Turney, C. S. M. (2018). Sea-level change and demography during the last glacial termination and early Holocene across the Australian continent. *Quaternary Science Reviews, 182,* 144–154. doi: https://doi.org/10.1016/j.quascirev.2017.11.030

Wright, D. (2011). Mid Holocene maritime economy in the western Torres Strait. *Archaeology in Oceania, 46*(1), 23–27. https://doi.org/10.1002/j.1834-4453.2011.tb00096.x

Wright, D. (2015). *Community emergence and development on Mabuyag, western Torres Strait.* British Archaeological Reports International series S2754. Oxford: Archaeopress.

Wright, M. (2018). *Rocky shores, mud, and mangroves: An assessment of economic intensification at the Yindayin Rockshelter, Stanley Island* (Unpublished BA Honours thesis). University of Sydney, Sydney.

CHAPTER 30

SWAMP AND DELTA SOCIETIES OF THE PAPUAN GULF, PAPUA NEW GUINEA

CHRIS URWIN, JAMES W. RHOADS, AND
JOSHUA A. BELL

THE PAPUAN GULF: CULTURAL AND ENVIRONMENTAL HISTORIES

THE Papuan Gulf (aka Gulf of Papua) spans some 400 km of Papua New Guinea's (PNG's) south coast from the Fly River mouth in the west to Hall Sound in the east. The region supports various language and culture groups, and the largest and best known groups in the anthropological literature are the Elema, Purari, Bamu, Kerewo, Gogodala and Kiwai. More than 100,000 people live across the Papuan Gulf (National Statistical Office of Papua New Guinea 2014), and the majority inhabit riverine or coastal lowlands. Foreign anthropologists and artefact collectors brought the lives and material culture of these groups to a global audience in the early colonial era (c. 1884–1940) through museum exhibitions, publications, photographs, and films (see Chalmers 1895; Hurley 1924; Landtman 1933; Williams 1923, 1924, 1940; for histories of these processes, see Bell 2006; Craig 2010; Di Rosa 2018; Welsch, Webb, & Haraha 2006). Early colonial ethnographies and later histories frequently described remarkable Indigenous trading activities of the region. The Motu *hiri*, perhaps the longest and best-known Papuan Gulf exchange system, was observed around the turn of the twentieth century (Bevan 1890: 138; Chalmers 1887: 70; Stone 1880: 62–67). Motu people living in the area now called Port Moresby would sail annually to central and eastern parts of the Gulf of Papua where they traded thousands of earthenware pots and shell ornaments for tonnes of locally made sago and rainforest canoe logs (Barton 1910; Dutton 1982; Mennis 2015; Oram 1982; Skelly & David 2017). Other less spectacular and well-documented trade networks further connected the region with communities beyond the Papuan Gulf. Stone axes were brought through exchange networks from the central highlands to the Purari and Kikori-Omati River Deltas and from Tapini in the Owen Stanley Range to the eastern Papuan Gulf (Hughes 1977: 180–181; Rhoads & Mackenzie 1991). Torres Strait stone axes and shell ornaments were imported to the western Papuan Gulf (Hughes 1977: 44; Landtman 1927: 34; see also Lawrence 1994). Oral tradition and linguistic evidence suggest that traders from eastern Indonesia visited the region during the seventeenth and eighteenth centuries (Laba 1996; Swadling 1996: 153–156).

River deltas in the Papuan Gulf consist of littoral sand and mud landforms that are regularly reworked by erosion and progradation. The sediments originate in PNG's volcanic cordillera c. 150 km to the north. Over the past 10,000 years since the Pleistocene-Holocene transition, large rivers such as the Fly, Kikori, and Purari (Figure 30.1) have washed large quantities of mineral sands, silts, and clays into the Coral Sea (Bird 2010; Howell et al. 2014; Thom & Wright 1983; Walsh & Nittrouer 2004; Wright 1989). A fraction of these sediments is suspended and deposited on the coast by tidal action (Dalrymple & Choi 2007; Löffler 1977: 113; Wright 1989: 499). The sand fractions are distributed and moulded in an east–west drift along the coast and silt-clay sediments are deposited on intertidal mudflats (Bird 2010: 1176; Thom & Wright 1983: 7; Walsh & Nittrouer 2004; Wright 1989: 499). Erosion and progradation of the alluvial coast vary

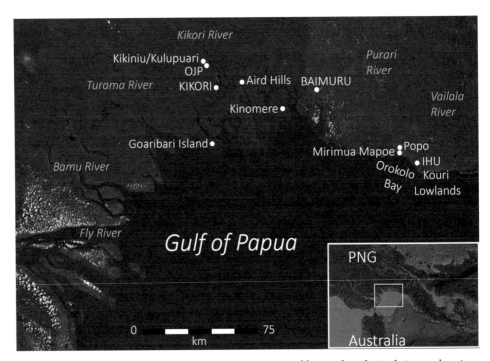

FIGURE 30.1. The Papuan Gulf, showing major rivers and key archaeological sites and regions where excavations have taken place. Colonial station names are capitalized.

(Satellite image courtesy of the U.S. Geological Survey.)

across the region. In the Purari Delta, where mangroves trap sediments, intertidal flats extend southward at a rate of up to 18.5 m per year (Shearman, Bryan, & Walsh 2013). Meanwhile, delta landforms and mangroves of the Fly River have reduced in size since the 1970s, possibly as a result of rising sea levels (Shearman 2010; Shearman et al. 2013: 1179). In the Kikori River Delta, islands situated along the waterways are growing in size, while directly coastal landforms are shrinking at a rate of up to 43 m/year (Shearman et al. 2013: fig. 8). Immediately east of the Vailala River, the predominantly sand coastline developed at different rates during the Holocene. Between c. 2700 and 700 years ago, the coast advanced at c. 1.9 m per year and afterward grew c. 3.9 m per year (Skelly & David 2017: 474–475).

This chapter explores how Papuan Gulf societies inhabited, modified, and made sense of their deltaic world. We begin by outlining the extensive ethnographic evidence of sago use and cultivation in the region. This section is followed by a review of archaeological research in the Kikori River region, focusing on the emergence of sago (*Metroxylon sagu*) cultivation and the role this strategy played in shaping and sustaining Papuan Gulf settlements. We then explore the archaeology of lowland areas of the Purari and Vailala River regions, which leads us into a discussion of the contribution of nuanced spatial histories of migration and place-making. We focus on a case study of the long-lived village site of Popo in Orokolo Bay. Delta landscapes necessitate strategies of migration and settlement relocation by which the opportunities of riverine and coastal life (e.g., access to subsistence zones and exchange networks) can be maximized. Overall, we explore high-potential avenues for historicizing how people made their lives in the Papuan Gulf's littoral environments.

Sago Cultivation in the Gulf of Papua

The sago palm *Metroxylon sagu* is the staple food for people living across much of the New Guinea lowlands coast and inland up to an altitude of about 700 m (Flach 1997: 52). *Metroxylon* forms a natural, permanent woodland in specific lowland freshwater swamp environments. These include locations where (1) the water table lies just below the ground surface, (2) seasonal flooding occurs, and (3) full sunlight easily reaches the palm fronds (Paijmans 1975, 1980). Here mature sago palms grow upwards of 20 m high and comprise the primary canopy vegetation (Figure 30.2d). The plant's suckers, the primary form of natural propagation, form a dense understorey. Among flooded, freshwater swamps, there are also areas of sago woodlands and open *Campnosperma* forest with a dense understory of sago. This vegetation formation dominates the inland reaches of the Purari Delta and the region west to the Wapo River (an area covering more than 80,000 ha), and a much smaller area (approximately 3500 ha) situated northeast of Goaribari Island (Department of Primary Industries PNG 1975). The annual palm starch (dry weight) resource potential of the former area exceeds 550 million kg of sago (Holmes & Newcombe 1980: Table 3; Schuiling 2009: 7, 204).

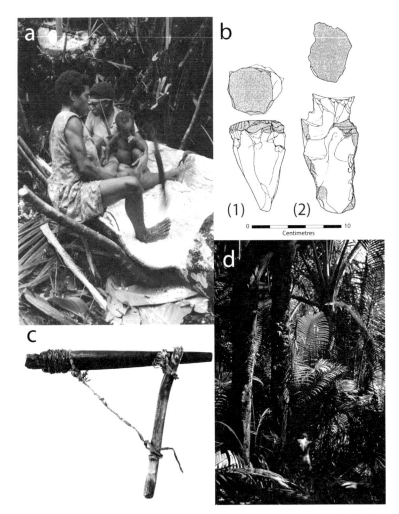

FIGURE 30.2. (a) Nasi Tovi chopping sago at the Waira Swamp 1977. In the background, her eldest son Konimoro tends to her baby boy, Jim; (b) Kulupuari/Kikinu sago choppers, with stippling indicating the location of phytolith polish use wear on the working faces (1. from Recent Phase deposits with the working face partially retouched; 2. a surface find with a heavily retouched lateral margin); (c) contemporary sago chopping implement, Waira Village 1977; (d) Robert Haraha fells a sago palm in 2002, inland of Iuku village, Orokolo Bay.

Images (a) and (c) were photographed by James W. Rhoads, (b) was drawn by Win Mumford (Rhoads 1980: Plate III-9), and (d) was photographed by Joshua A. Bell.

Elsewhere in the river back swamps, sago stands exhibit stunted growth (Paijmans 1975: fig. 1). This stunting occurs because the water table is too high, siting at or above the ground surface. At other localities where the water table lies just below the ground surface during the dry season, herbaceous ground cover is the dominant vegetation and sago palms are rare. Sago palms, albeit as shorter mature plants in small stands, occur naturally in other areas of the Kikori-Purari Delta nearer the sea. Here palms grow in association with mangroves and nipa palms, as sago tolerates brackish soils where sa-linity is less than 7.5 parts per thousand (Cragg 1983). Sago also occurs in swamplands interspersed between prominent coastal beach ridges. In the regions north of the Kikori-Purari Delta, small sago palm clusters are found on well-drained areas of low-land alluvial plains where prolonged wet season flooding occurs.

Even recently, sago palm management in New Guinea was categorized as the semicultivation of wild stands (e.g., Bintoro, Nurulhaq, Pratama, Ahmad, & Ayulia 2018; Flach & Schuiling 1989; Nakamura 2018). The notion that the majority of stands are passively maintained ignores evidence provided by ethnographic studies of sago cultivators (e.g. Rhoads 1981). People throughout New Guinea use a sophisticated range of techniques and strategies to sustain the productivity of small groups of sago palms, increase sago palm density, and create new, relatively large palm stands. These aspects of sago palm management are well documented in areas of the Papuan Gulf and include:

- 'weeding' clusters of sago palm suckers to enhance the succession of a preferred, in-dividual sucker;
- regular clearing of rainforest regrowth from existing sago palm stands thereby eliminating competitive plants encroaching on existing sago palms; and
- removing the rainforest canopy by felling dominant trees species and then transplanting sago palm suckers to the new sunlit areas (Rhoads 1982a; Ulijaszek & Poraituk 1983b).

In summary, the Kikori-Purari Delta possesses wide tracts of both wild and cultivated sago stands that fall under customary patrilineal resource tenure (Williams 1924: 120–124). Sago remains an essential part of the regional diet, providing communities with the bulk of their carbohydrate requirements (Ulijaszek & Poraituk 1983b).

In 1980, Ulijaszek and Poraituk (1983b) studied the subsistence patterns of the Baroi, one of seven tribes of the Purari in the Purari Delta. Their villages are positioned near the transition zone between the mangrove and swamp forests (compare Ulijaszek & Poraituk 1983b: fig. 2 with Shearman et al. 2008: Appendix 4, Map Gulf 2002). Here, mangroves and nipa palms are the dominant vegetation (Cragg 1983). While natural sago stands owned by other Purari speakers are situated farther inland among the fresh-water swamps, these sources are rarely harvested. Instead, people exploit several dif-ferent and much smaller sago stands located closer to villages (Ulijaszek & Poraituk 1983b). Each stand contains only a few sago palms at different stages of development. Over time the continued use of these localities and the transplanting of palm suckers are sufficient to expand and sustain the sago palm community (Ulijaszek & Poraituk 1983b: 581–582).

Building on this research, Bell began ethnographic work in 2000 among Purari speakers—based mainly with the I'ai tribe—and documented aspects of sago cultiva-tion (Purari: *pu*). I'ai oral histories locate the origin of sago as a result of an ancestral gift from the sky to which proper care and respect must be given (Bell 2020; Williams 1924). These histories also connect sago stands to various events in Purari speakers' migrations to the coast, which are commemorated via place names (Bell 2006, 2016). Transplanting of seedlings occurred in the past, and care was taken to manage these stands located close to villages and on other more distant traditional lands. Oral histories suggest that the I'ai planted sago to provide food security and also in anticipation of the trade goods sago would help them secure. As the *hiri* exchange declined in the early 1900s, Europeans and Motuans regularly purchased Papuan Gulf sago to feed plantation labourers in the period 1914–1942 (Bell 2015; Lewis 1996). Across the Purari Delta, the Kabu Movement (1946–1969), an indigenous iconoclastic modernization movement, promoted the resettlement of villages along waterways to facilitate cash-cropping and the exporting of sago (Bell 2006; Maher 1961). The movement resulted in contemporary communities being connected to relatively geographically dispersed stands of sago (an ongoing source of land disputes) and the continued exporting of sago to urban centres of Kerema and Port Moresby. Ulijaszek's (2007) research into the more recent supplying of sago to Port Moresby (in the period 1947–1990) suggests that these colonial economies had regional ecological impacts.

In current practice, I'ai men cut down the sago palm, while women perform the bulk of the labour extracting and processing the palm's pith. This activity typically takes a full day or two, and, on average, the resulting processed sago lasts a family of six a week. Although the extent of male involvement continues to vary among Purari speakers (Williams 1924), sago remains central to subsistence and remains a central regional export. Bell (2020) documented fifteen vernacular names for *Metroxylon sagu* relating to location, taste, and colour after processing, which speaks to the detailed nature of the local knowledge and understanding of this palm. These numerous varieties are matched by around thirty material uses (e.g., providing material for basket weaving, house construction, clothing) of the palm for the I'ai (Bell 2020).

In Orokolo Bay, immediately east of the Purari Delta, sago (Orokolo: *poi*) palms are grown in great numbers. Sago suckers are occasionally transplanted, and the resulting stands can be used as markers for clan or family ownership of land.[1] The missionary Madie Dewdney (1993: 80), who lived in Orokolo Bay in the 1930s–1960s, recorded that 'every time one [sago palm] is cut down for food some of the shoots are planted out. Also each time a child is born into a family more are planted to ensure a constant supply. As with coconut palms, the sago is owned by the people of the villages and everyone knows his own palms.'

According to Dewdney, the biographies of the villagers and their sago palms are in a sense entwined. It is worth noting, too, that Moreas-Gorecki's (1983) ethnobotanical analyses of 1977 suggested that transplanting sago played a role in terraforming swamps. Once established, a new cluster of sago would help anchor swamp sediments (Moreas-Gorecki 1983: 237–238; Kari 1978).

The Kairi (aka Rumu; see Busse, Araho, & Turner 1993: 29), who live along the middle reaches of the Kikori River immediately inland of the Kikori Delta, practice perhaps the most labour-intensive form of sago palm management documented in New Guinea (Rhoads 1981, 1982a). Mature tropical rainforest covers the alluvial plains near Kairi riverside settlements. In selected areas, trees forming the upper canopy are either felled or ring-barked. Sago palm suckers, often obtained from stands near abandoned villages, are then planted at these localities. In 1977, Rhoads (1982a) recorded one new plantation covering more than 18 ha. During the early development of the sago plants, the Kairi conscientiously clear regrowth vegetation from the area. Once established, people occasionally 'weed' vegetation from around those suckers chosen to cultivate for mature palm growth and future starch harvesting.

Sago processing in the Papuan Gulf is typically undertaken once the palm's inflorescence appears, which usually occurs after some 10–15 years of growth. At this time, the trunk contains its maximum starch content. Kairi sago work groups commonly consist of men and women (e.g., Rhoads 1980: 29–30). The work site is prepared by removing low vegetation growing nearby, sometimes including sago palm suckers. After men fell the palm, women process sago from the horizontal-lying trunk using a task-specific chopping tool to cut out and pound the pith, and a special apparatus to wash out the starch (Figures 30.2a and 2c). Traditionally, the chopping tool's striking head is, among delta communities, fashioned from fire-hardened wood, bamboo, or a flaked core tool. The pulverized pith is gathered, placed in either a woven bag or a trough made from a palm leaf stem, and then washed. The starchy water collects in a settling trough manufactured from pliable, palm leaf sheaths and is allowed to stand until the sago starch is deposited in the bottom of the trough. The water is then drained off, and the white pasty starch is either scooped into a carrying bag or stored in a long palm frond container, in which the starch stays fresh for several weeks if stored in a manner that will permit natural fermentation to occur (Greenhill 2006).

Three Papuan Gulf ethnographic studies document palm management and starch harvesting yields. First, the Kairi, who lived at Waira village and cultivated sago palms in the nearby lowland alluvial forest, exploited four stands totalling 36 hectares in 1977–1978 (Rhoads 1980: 30, Tables III-2 & III-3). The starch extracted averaged 130 kg (dry weight) per palm. Second, in 1980, Koravake villagers living in the Purari Delta cultivated several small sago palm stands (Ulijaszek & Poraituk 1983a, 1983b). Each was roughly 20 m² in size and located at varying distances from their village. Fifty kilograms of sago were, on average, extracted from a palm. To add a more general perspective, New Guineans relying on palm starch typically consume 200–300 g (dry weight) per person each day (Ulijaszek & Poraituk 1983a: 561). Therefore, based on a 250 g estimate, people living in a Papuan Gulf village with 50 inhabitants would likely consume in the order of 4500 kg (dry weight) of sago each year. This estimate correlates well with information for the people living at Koravake (population = 31) and at Waira (population = 71) villages. Third, Williams (1940: 12) estimated that a family in Orokolo Bay would produce around 20 kg of sago per day.

Riverine Plains to the Sea: The Archaeology of the Kikori River Region

The archaeological record of the Middle and Lower Kikori River area is among the best understood along Papua New Guinea's south coast. This is largely due to Rhoads's PhD research (1980) and resulting publications (Rhoads 1981, 1982a, 1982b, 1983, 2010) as well as the numerous consultancy projects and research investigations undertaken by David and colleagues (e.g., David 2008; David et al. 2010, McNiven et al. 2010). In brief, two themes characterize this area's archaeological history. First, the archaeology of the middle Kikori River area, situated in the general vicinity of Kopi village, reveals persistent habitation since the terminal Pleistocene and notably includes two periods of intense and relatively lengthy pulses of riverside settlements in the Late Holocene (David 2008). Second, the deltaic area to the south presents a strikingly different picture. Initial occupation began in the delta's northwest and was characteristically episodic over the period from c. 1800 cal BP to c. 600 cal BP. Immediately afterward, several surface sites bearing ceramic deposits appeared in the vicinity of the Aird Hills and Kikori Station. The establishment of large villages along the coast near the mouth of the Kikori River began during early European contact, c. 200 years ago (Barker, Lamb, David, Skelly, & Korakai 2015).[2]

The Papuan Gulf's earliest known site, dating to c. 13,500–11,000 cal BP (David et al. 2007), is a small limestone cave (OJP[3]) located near the base of a limestone hill situated on the Kikori River floodplains south of Kopi village. Its shallow (c. 10 cm) deposits contain plant material, local vertebrate faunal remains, and fresh-to-brackish water shellfish. Over the next 9000 years, human occupation of the area is sporadic, poorly understood, and limited to rock shelter sites—Wokoi Amoho c. 8000 cal BP, KG141 c. 2800 cal BP, and Epe Amoho c. 2700 cal BP (David 2008). *Metroxylon sagu* pollen recovered from Epe Amoho's early sediments confirms that sago palms grew in the Kopi area at this time (McNiven et al. 2010). Two other rock shelters—Rupo and Ouloubomoto— were inhabited near the end of this period (David 2008; Rhoads 1980: 206–207). Faunal remains recovered from both sites indicate seasonal subsistence patterns similar to those found among people living in the area today (Rhoads 1980: 45, 227–228, Plates III-25 & III-26).

The Kulupuari/Kikiniu village site was established c. 1450 cal BP, which marks the commencement of intense occupation of the Kopi region (David 2008; Rhoads 1982b: 140).[4] The settlement spanned almost 500 years until c. 950 cal BP. Evidence from the post holes exposed in the excavations (Rhoads 1980: 127–129, fig. VI-6) is consistent with a large wooden structure, comparable to the region's traditional historic men's houses (Kerewo: *dubu daima*; see Hurley 1924, Plate facing p. 278). The use of temporary camps (*kombati*) at rock shelter and cave sites near the village does not seem to occur for about 200 years. Also, it seems unlikely that open-site *kombati* were in use near Kulupuari/ Kikiniu at this time. The faunal remains recovered from Kulupuari/Kikiniu's earliest deposits (Rhoads 1980: 151, 230–231) are indicative of inhabitation at the start and end of the rainy season (mid-May and late September, respectively), as well as possibly during much of this season. Temporary camps near the village were not ideal staging posts for gathering many food resources due to flooding. Therefore, the village site probably served as a key locality for residency in the riverine environment. Later, villages were also built adjacent to Kulupuari/Kikiniu at Ihi Kaeke (c. 1300 cal BP) and Barauni (c. 1250 cal BP) (David 2008). *Kombati* use reappeared at bush localities: Rupo (c. 1300 cal

BP) (David 2008; Rhoads 1980: 192–195) and Epe Amoho (c. 1100 cal BP) (McNiven et al. 2010). Subsistence remains at temporary camps reflect use of these locales during the dry season, as do those recovered from Kulupuari/Kikiniu (Rhoads 1980: 151–153, 190–194, 204–207, 228–236).

Kulupuari/Kikiniu's flaked stone artefact assemblage is also representative of specific subsistence activities (Rhoads 1980: 140–147). Sago exploitation is indicated by the presence of new, used, and discarded core chopping tools ('sago choppers') that exhibit phytolith polish on their working faces and lateral margins, caused by processing sago palm pith (see Crosby 1976) (Figure 30.2b). Retouch flakes with use wear (phytolith polish) on their dorsal surfaces (probably derived from sago choppers) were also recovered (Rhoads 1980: 143–144).

It is striking that most artefacts found at Kulupuari/Kikiniu originated from distant sources, located between 30 and 300 km away. Pottery analyses (Mackenzie 1980) point to the Port Moresby and Hall Sound regions as source areas for pottery manufacture (see also Bickler 1997; Marsaglia, Kramer, David, & Skelly 2016). Vessel forms and decorations, including a high incidence of red colour slipping or painting (Skelly & David 2017: 70, fig. 41), accord well with pottery from roughly contemporaneous deposits at the Oposisi site on Yule Island (Vanderwal 1973: 106, 107, fig. VI-10; Allen, Summerhayes, Mandui, & Leavesley 2011) and at Nebira 4 near Port Moresby (Allen 1972). Stone axe/adzes at Kulupuari/Kikiniu originated in the Tapini region of the Owen Stanley Mountains located inland from Hall Sound (Rhoads & Mackenzie 1991; Rhoads 2010). Flaked stone artefacts were manufactured from raw materials found at the headwaters of the Omati and Sirebi Rivers, located c. 30 km to the west and northeast, respectively, and from the Baina quarry site situated about 100 km upstream near the Kikori's headwaters (Rhoads 1980: 140; see also David et al. 2015).

Few archaeological sites have been discovered along or relatively near the Kikori River in the Kopi region for roughly 450 years following Kulupuari/Kikiniu's abandonment (David 2008). Those that have been located—OJP, Wokoi Amoho, and Ouloubomoto (all rock shelters), and Eremare (an inland open site)—have limited cultural deposits (David 2008; Rhoads 1980: 207). Rhoads (1980: 249–252) postulates that the availability of exotic goods reaching the area via coastal trading systems likely was the primary stimulus for people to establish villages along major waterways. Other times (e.g., from c. 1000 cal BP to 600 cal BP), people did not leave the Kopi area but instead inhabited the foothills of the karst plateau at least 10–15 km inland from Kulupuari/Kikiniu. Here, the flooding of the alluvial plains did not greatly impact people's subsistence and settlement patterns, and animal resources were generally accessible year round (Aplin & Rhoads 1980). David (2008: 269) suggests that there is 'enough archaeological evidence . . . to indicate the sustained presence of people' in the Kopi area and that the absence of pottery during this time 'may reflect contemporaneous and/or shortly earlier disturbances in sites and cultural sequences further to the east'.

New village settlements appeared in the Kopi region around 600 cal BP (David 2008), with sporadic occupation of Eremare (along Utiti Creek upstream from Kulupuari/Kikiniu) c. 600, 550, and 500 cal BP, and along the Kikori River at Barauni (c. 500 cal BP).

A *kombati* site Leipo (c. 500 cal BP) and three ossuaries—KG141, OJP, and Rupo—were in use from this time (David 2008; David et al. 2008; Rhoads 1980: 194–195). Kulupuari/Kikiniu was occupied again between c. 470 and 180 cal BP. Large and moderate-sized structures were again erected at the site. Subsistence patterns and regional use of *kombati* sites are similar to those observed some 500 years earlier (David 2008; Rhoads 1980: 127–129, 154). Sago choppers and their use-polished retouch flakes were again recovered at Kulupuari/Kikiniu, but not at other analysed archaeological deposits dating to this time. It is, therefore, reasonable to assume that the village was the primary staging point for sago-processing activities, with intentionally cultivated palm stands located nearby. A comparable land-use pattern was observed among present-day Kairi communities in 1977 and documented in historic records (Rhoads 1980: 20, 47–62).

Although potsherds were recovered from the uppermost layers of Kulupuari/Kikiniu, all were badly weathered fragments and no diagnostic rim sherd decorations were distinguishable (Rhoads 1980: Table 8.1). A formal, statistical analysis of rim sherd form attributes was undertaken to determine if pottery found in the upper layer was redeposited.[5] The results reliably confirmed that most rim sherds belonged to the same population (Rhoads 1980: 130–131, Tables VI-4 and VI-5), and those recovered from recent deposits were probably displaced from the early episode of site use, presumably by means of gardening practices and historic settlement activities. Therefore, pottery likely did not arrive in the Kopi region until around the early twentieth century (Rhoads 1980: 131). Regardless, chert raw materials and ground stone axes from Tapini and, now, planilateral forms from the Central Highlands, arrive in the Kopi area. The nearby Ibira open site, dating to c. 600–300 cal BP, is notable for the white glass beads among its finds (Rhoads 1980: 165–168).[6] Historical research (Rhoads 1984) points to China as their likely origin (see also Grave & McNiven 2013) and to traditional exchange systems or the Seram Laut trading network along the southwest coast of New Guinea as the means by which they arrived in the Kikori River area (Swadling 1996: 155–157).[7]

From c. 200 years cal BP, new villages—Baranui, Porokoiu, Ihi Kaeke, and Bageima/Puriau—were established in the mid-Kikori River region (Rhoads 1980: 169–173; David 2008). Subsistence patterns were broadly comparable to those practiced earlier. Kulupuari/Kikiniu finds also include two Murano glass beads dating around the seventeenth century (Rhoads 1980: 148–149, Plate VI-6; Rhoads 1984). These glass beads provide further evidence for coastal trade/exchange networks along New Guinea's southwest coast as the means by which foreign trade goods arrived in the Kopi area (see Swadling 1996: 155–156).

Three sites have been excavated in the Kikori Delta region. The Emo open site at Aird Hills was first occupied c. 1800 cal BP (David et al. 2010; aka Samoa or OAC; see Rhoads 1983), about 1000 years after the first recorded pottery along the south coast of Papua New Guinea at Caution Bay c. 2900 cal BP (David et al. 2011; McNiven et al. 2011). Two other episodes of site use occurred at c. 1550 and 1465 cal BP. Rhoads (1983) and Bickler (1997) postulate that small quantities of fragmented sherds found in each phase of site use arrived in the delta from manufacturing sites eastward along the Papuan coast. Exotic artefacts—chert flakes and shell ornaments—were also recovered. The faunal remains from each occupation phase are broadly similar (David et al. 2010). Intensely exploited shellfish (Thangavelu et al. 2011), supplemented with local fish, comprise important foods. Hunted game was not well represented among the animal remains, and pig and dog bones are present in all but the oldest occupation layer. Interestingly, no evidence of sago palm exploitation was recovered at Emo (David et al. 2010).

Recent Emo deposits (c. 650 cal BP) and those at the adjacent hilltop site Kumukumu 1 (c. 600 cal BP) mark the next habitation phase of the delta region. Emo's occupation was again brief (David et al. 2010: 44), and subsistence remains—shellfish and vertebrate fauna—are comparable to earlier site use. Kumukumu 1's cultural deposits (David et al. 2015) are similar to those at Emo; however, greater quantities of shellfish and fewer potsherds were recovered. Drawing largely on early historic observations (e.g., Haddon 1918), David et al. (2015: 2, 3, 19) propose that Kumukumu's inaccessible location signals a direct and early response to Kerewo headhunting.

Ceramics recovered from seven surface sites in the Aird Hills–Kikori Station area (Rhoads 1983) match pottery styles from Bootless Bay sites near Port Moresby and represent evidence of coastal trade dating from c. 750 cal BP (Allen 2017: 22, 321). Several large coastal village sites dating from c. 200 cal BP were established on and around Goaribari Island at the mouth of the Omati River (just west of the Kikori Delta), and each featured large longhouse (*dubu daima*) structures (Barker et al. 2012, 2015).

Returning to our sago exploitation theme, the archaeology of the Kikori area offers reliable evidence of palm starch's role in human cultural development from early times. The presence of *Metroxylon sagu* pollen in Epe Amoho's earliest deposits c. 2700 'may represent a low-level exploitation' in the Kopi area (McNiven et al. 2010: 46). This form of sago harvesting, if persistent, would have sustained small stands. Moreover, because stable environmental conditions prevailed in the Kikori area since the terminal Pleistocene (Thomas et al. 2018), sago very likely has played a role in peoples' diet for several thousand years.

Understanding Place-Making and the Spatial Histories of Papuan Gulf Villages

We now examine the contribution of nuanced spatial histories to understanding migration and place-making in the Papuan Gulf. After outlining previous studies of these processes in regions currently inhabited by Eleman- and Purari-language speaking communities, we unpack the case study of a village site (Popo), drawing on ethnographic and archaeological research conducted in Orokolo Bay in 2015. We explore how oral traditions of village relocation, along with detailed chronologies and analyses of cultural materials, helped develop new stories about how places coexisted with, and transformed alongside, changing landforms.

Migration and Settlement Patterns in the Purari and Vailala River Regions

Kinomere Village is located on Urama Island, a system of mudflats at the mouth of the Ivi, Wapo, and Era Rivers located 50 km northeast of Goaribari Island (Figure 30.1). Local oral tradition suggests that the village was occupied for approximately seven generations. Frankel and Vanderwal's (1982; Frankel, Thompson, & Vanderwal 1994: 11–12) excavation of a mound at the centre of the modern-day settlement revealed a layer of dense shell deposit and pottery overlying compacted organic material, which they interpreted as a change in 'the structure of the village'. They suggest that the mound area was originally the location of village houses, before later becoming a focus of midden deposition. A radiocarbon date from basal deposits suggests that Kinomere was initially settled c. 500 cal BP. We note, however, that excavations were prematurely cut off at the water table.

The Popo village site is positioned east of the Purari Delta on beach ridges located c. 2.5 km inland of Orokolo Bay. The locality features prominently in the oral traditions of clans of the Eleman language family and is remembered as a beach-fronting village. Upon visiting the site, Rhoads (1994: 53) observed dense cultural material appearing in a 60-cm-deep section exposure running for about 500 m and sparser remains over a further c. 500 m. Rhoads (1994: 54) conducted three small test excavations at Popo in 1976 to document variations in deposition across the site and establish its aerial extent north of the section exposure. Dense shell deposits, pottery sherds, a few stone artefacts, and vertebrate remains were found in only two pits (TP1 and TP3). Pottery rim sherds were decorated using various techniques including incision, drag-relief, shell impressions, and perforations (Rhoads 1994: 57–58, Tables 9 and 10). A single radiocarbon date of c. 450 cal BP and pottery sherds similar in form and decoration to those found by Bulmer (1978) and Allen (1972) in the Port Moresby region led Rhoads to conclude that Popo contained 'early evidence for the Motu *hiri*' dating to sometime in the period 300–600 years ago (Rhoads 1994: 66–67; 1982b; see also Allen 1984).

East of Orokolo Bay and the Vailala River, extensive archaeological research took place in the Kouri Lowlands region during research projects led by Bruno David and colleagues (2009) and Robert Skelly (2014; Skelly & David 2017, xvii–xx; Skelly, David, Barker, Kuaso, & Araho 2010; Skelly, David, Petchey, & Leavesley 2014) (Figure 30.1).[8] From thirteen excavations and sixty-six radiocarbon dates, Skelly and David (2017; Skelly 2014) constructed an occupational and ceramic sequence for the region. The material evidence comprised some 86,051 pottery sherds, numerous animal bones and marine shells, small quantities of stone artefacts and glass beads, and post-hole features. Nine of the thirteen excavations related to places known in local oral traditions. The archaeology of these sites suggested that past village locations were often situated at beach-fronting locations. As progradation occurred in the past, as it does today (Skelly & David 2017: 474–475), people tended to relocate their villages as beach ridges emerged to the south. Here the archaeological evidence ties in well with ethnographic information, suggesting that Eleman communities preferred to occupy near-coastal zones to access trade and important marine resources such as fish and shellfish (Kakare & Karava 1975: 69; Williams 1940: 3).

Occupation of the littoral coastline started c. 2850 cal BP and continued until c. 1200 cal BP. Within this period, Skelly and David (2017: Chapter 15) identified four main radiocarbon-dated phases, which enable us to understand the history of settlement in the region. Human presence is first indicated by a date of c. 2850 cal BP, which occurred in the lower levels of the excavation at Hivo (OKB). The dated charcoal was not associated with pottery and may demonstrate preceramic occupation of the Kouri Lowlands. Approximately c. 2600 cal BP, small deposits of 'pottery displaying Lapita decorative conventions' (Skelly et al. 2014: 485) appeared at the Hopo (OJS) site. Comb dentate-stamped and fingernail impressed pottery sherds, along with obsidian tools sourced to Fergusson Island, are taken to indicate an 'expansive western movement by Lapita seafarers' (Skelly & David 2017: 480). The precise character of this movement (e.g., temporary camp, small settlement) is yet to be defined.

Following initial arrivals of pottery in the Kouri Lowlands, sites dating to c. 2300–1500 cal BP have more extensive deposits of pottery, suggesting 'a period of heightened frequency and/or intensity of interactions among coastal groups' (Skelly & David 2017: 485). At this time, the sites of Kaveharo (OJS) and Iri Kahu (OKA) were in use. Pottery vessels arriving in the region at this time were frequently decorated with impressed shell valve margins (see Skelly & David 2017: 442–444, figs. 182–183). These sherds are similar in form and decoration to those found at various other locations on the south coast of Papua New Guinea; some scholars refer to these styles as Early Papuan Pottery (EPP) (Summerhayes & Allen 2007; see discussion in David, Richards, Skelly, McNiven, & Leavesley 2016: 24). In the era c. 1500–1200 cal BP, new pottery designs occurred at the sites of Hopo (OJS), Kaveharo (OJV), and the hilltop site of Oheo Yopo (OJU). Decorations on the body of pottery vessels in this period often feature red slip/paint and linear incisions. Skelly and David (2017: 470) suggest that the new tradition of pottery occurred 'suddenly' with no 'stylistic antecedents' among older pottery found in the Kouri Lowlands.

None of the sixty-six radiocarbon determinations for the Kouri Lowlands sites occur in the period from c. 1200 cal BP to c. 700 cal BP. Skelly and David (2017: 488–490) suggest that this period was a regional hiatus in human occupation and pottery trade, with a subtly different time frame to the hiatus seen in the archaeological record of the Kikori River region. This period almost certainly saw significant changes in settlement patterns in the Kouri Lowlands. Skelly and David (2017: 489) suggest that, as a result of 'cultural changes', people moved to defensible settlement sites away from the coastline prior to c. 1200 cal BP. Some evidence of changing settlement patterns is provided by the occurrence of the elevated (and thus defendable) occupation at Oheo Yopo c. 1500–1280 cal BP. Skelly and David (2017: 490) suggest that during the period c. 1200–700 cal BP exchange networks encompassing the Papuan Gulf and the Yule Island/Hall Sound and Port Moresby regions broke down, possibly as a result of 'social disruptions . . . closer to the ceramic manufacturing centres to the east'.

Following the 500-year long hiatus, the sites of Iri Kahu (OKA), Kaveharo (OJV), Keveoki 1 (OKE), Meiharo (OKF), and Lui Swamp (OJX) were occupied a little after c. 700 cal BP. This period can be divided into two broad radiocarbon-dated phases: c. 700–300 cal BP and 300–0 cal BP. Coastal village sites were established, and pottery trade into the region resumed (Skelly & David 2017: 447). Pottery sherds found at various sites—especially those from the Lui Swamp site—are decorated with shell-impressed designs resembling those identified at Urourina on Yule Island and Motupore in the Port Moresby region (see Skelly & David 2017: 491). Around 530 cal BP, cultural activity intensified in the Kouri Lowlands. Some 200 years later, in the period 300-0 cal BP, several coastal village sites were in use. Among these are the important oral traditional *hiri*-trading villages of Kaveharo, Hopo, and Hivo. Pottery incoming to these sites in this era resemble ethnographically observed *hiri* pottery (the potsherds were mostly undecorated).

Coastal Change, Trade, and Migration: Case Study of a Papuan Gulf Village

The archaeological site of Popo is a famed ancestral village and provides an excellent case study of Papuan Gulf village biographies. As Indigenous historians Kakare and Karava (1975: 38) state: 'our ancestors migrated from the mountains behind Purari and Vailala Rivers . . . down the Purari River to the ancestral site of Popo'. In the 1920s and 1930s, the anthropologist F. E. Williams (1940: 28; see also Rhoads 1994: 54; Skelly & David 2017: 175) noted that the entire population of Orokolo Bay claimed to originate at Popo. During archaeological fieldwork conducted in 2015, Urwin (2019a, 2019b, 2022; Urwin, Hua, Skelly, & Arifeae 2018) was told many stories about the ancestral place by the current custodians of the site, members of the Larihairu and Kaivakovu village communities.[9] These stories added depth to the sketched (and secondary) 1920s–1930s accounts.

Today Popo is remembered as an important place in a network of twenty-two migration locations (see also Hareavila 1976; Hauka 1978). In local oral traditions, Popo is described as a long-lived village site, which was occupied from ten to sixteen generations ago. Prior to Popo, the ancestors of the Kaivakovu and Larihairu village communities settled at various temporary camps. Oral traditions explain that the opportunity to establish a village was presented by beach progradation. While people were camping in the northerly mountains, they witnessed a beach emerging at the foot of the mountains and 'came down to settle at Popo' (Paul Mahiro in Urwin 2019a: Appendix A, N3a). Motu people began visiting Popo while they were engaged in long-distance trade (*hiri*) expeditions, travelling through creeks connected to the Purari Delta (Williams 1931: NAPNG A447 B2996 ML MSS 5/9 79, 91–95; Urwin 2019a: Appendix A, fig. 3).

Stories told about Popo in 2015 (see Urwin 2019a, 2019b, 2022) suggest a complex spatial history for the village. The place is remembered as having been communally built by various tribes, each of whom established their own estate.[10] Some of the estate boundaries were mapped with Kaivakovu and Larihairu village elders in 2015 (Figure 30.3).[11] The estates have subtly varying oral traditions (see Urwin 2019b). For instance, a cosmological origin story (*lou*) describes the formation of the Aitae Hiru ('crocodile island') estate at a time when Popo was immediately coastal. The estate first formed as an offshore island, and ancestral beings (*lou haera*) directed crocodiles to ferry people between Aitae Hiru and the rest of the mainland village of Popo. Eventually, the once-separate island was physically joined to the rest of the village.

People apparently left Popo six generations ago, precipitated in part by the fact that 'the beach was coming down [prograding southward] very quickly' (Avia Hae in Urwin 2019a: 94–99). Tribal leaders took their people south, settling a riverbank village called Mirimua Mapoe before eventually ending up at the modern-day coastline. These entwined narratives of progradation and migration closely resemble those told by Keuru speakers east of the Vailala River (Skelly & David 2017: 93, 99, 197) and the Purari speakers of the Purari Delta (Bell 2006). Social fissioning also led to the establishment of offshoot villages from Popo. In the early 1900s, it was common for family groups to leave their clan to build a new village and *eravo* (longhouse) elsewhere (Brown 1988: v; Holmes 1903: 128; Skelly & David 2017: 93, 99, 197; Williams 1940: 88). In Popo's case, the size of the village and the diversity of the groups inhabiting it meant that at various times 'the people started to scatter . . . west . . . east . . . and into the mountains' (Paul Mahiro in Urwin 2019a: Appendix A, N3a). Elema and Purari speakers commonly explain their present social group origins through stories of intertribal conflict and fissioning from ancestral village locations (see also Bell 2006; Williams 1940: 28).

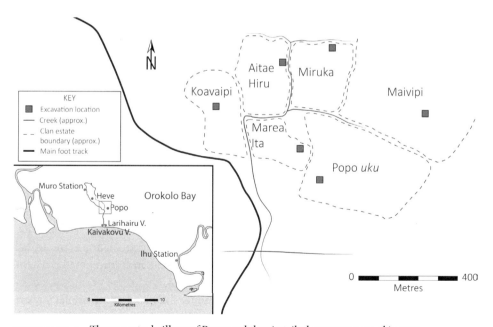

FIGURE 30.3. The ancestral village of Popo and the six tribal estates mapped in 2015.

Complex Site or Site Complex: Archaeological Models of Ancestral Villages

Archaeological research was conducted in February and September–November 2015 to historicize Popo's apparently complex spatial history and to understand the relationships between landform change and village transformation and migration. To examine how the village changed through time—and to build on initial research by Rhoads (1994)—small excavations (1 x 1 m) were carried out at each of the six main tribal estates (Figure 30.3). To investigate when people left Popo and moved south at a time of rapid landform change, an excavation was conducted at Mirimua Mapoe 1.4 km to the south. A Bayesian statistical model comprising thirty-five radiocarbon dates provided a detailed chronology of these places. The structure and results of the model and excavations are detailed in Urwin's (2019a: 255–284, 2022) PhD thesis and subsequent book.

Modelled dates from Popo suggest that the place was occupied for c. 500 years (c. 640–140 cal BP). The results of the archaeological investigation of Popo and Mirimua Mapoe can be distilled into a four-phase spatial history. In the *Initial Settlement period* (c. 640–485 cal BP), people were living at the Miruka and Maivipi estates. Basal deposits of water-borne pumice stone and coarse-grained beach sand suggest that these locations were near-coastal at this time. By c. 500 cal BP, the beach ridges (or offshore islands) on which Popo Uku and Aitae Hiru were later established had just formed but were not intensively occupied. Excavated sherds dating to the Initial Settlement period at Maivipi and Miruka are decorated with distinctive motifs made from small shell margin impressions. The designs bear close resemblance to 'herringbone' motifs identified by Allen (2017: 276) in roughly contemporaneous (and basal) levels of the Motupore site in Bootless Bay 290 km southeast of Popo. The designs—dating roughly to 680 cal BP—have also been found at the Urourina site on Yule Island 170 km southeast of Popo (Vanderwal 1973: fig. VI-12-7). Similar shell-impressed sherds have likewise been found at the Agila site (Hood Bay, c. 95 km southeast of Port Moresby) (Skelly et al. 2018) and Lui swamp (OJX) in the Kouri Lowlands (Skelly & David 2017: fig. 211). The people inhabiting Miruka and Maivipi were clearly connected at this time to 'specialised place[s]' (Irwin 1991: 509) of pottery manufacture and maritime trade located hundreds of kilometres to the east.

In the *Village Expansion period* (c. 425–310 cal BP), Popo grew aerially. Expansion of the village was facilitated by the emergence of stable beach ridges at Marea Ita and Popo Uku. People ceased living at Maivipi and shifted focus to the estates of Marea Ita, Miruka, and Popo Uku. A radiocarbon hiatus of about sixty years separates the Initial Settlement and Village Expansion periods. As there is no break in cultural material deposition and the hiatus is presumably short, we hypothesize that these periods are contiguous. In this period, pottery, charcoal, animal bone, shell, and stone artefacts were being deposited at each estate. At Marea Ita, a series of post holes were uncovered, which Kaivakovu village members interpreted as being evidence of a past *eravo* site; locals had identified the location as such prior to excavation. A charcoal sample from near the base of one of the post holes dates to c. 335 cal BP. Notably, the period of village expansion coincides with a time when long-distance trade was extending in range west of Orokolo Bay to reach the Kikori River and Purari Delta regions (see David 2008; Skelly & David 2017: 496). Transformations were also underway at Motupore where the ancestors of modern-day Motu populations had developed a thriving industry of pottery made for maritime trade (Allen 2017: 606–608).

In the *Moving Estates period* (c. 310–140 cal BP), several relocations took place within the village of Popo. In the period c. 310–265 cal BP, village occupation is in evidence at Popo Uku and Marea Ita. After c. 265 cal BP, people were living at Popo Uku, Aitae Hiru (c. 220 cal BP), and Koavaipi (c. 205 cal BP). Further chronological data is required to better understand this period, but we interpret the present evidence to mean that people were gradually moving southward through the Popo village area. These moves probably relate to landform changes described in the oral traditions about Popo. If beaches had commenced emerging south of Popo in the Moving Estates period, people may have focussed the main zones of village occupation on the southerly estates of Popo Uku and Marea Ita to maintain the opportunities provided by coastal life. These opportunities are materially expressed today by fish and shellfish remains in the Marea Ita assemblage and by raised shell midden features found at Marea Ita and Popo *uku* estates. The variety of faunal remains found in the excavations demonstrates that people were finding food in reef, intertidal, mangrove, and river zones. We suggest that village occupation at Miruka ceased c. 350 cal BP as a result of the place becoming too distant from coastal subsistence zones.

Movements across Popo may also have been motivated by the desire to participate in long-distance maritime trade. In the Moving Estates period, Marea Ita and Popo *uku* were almost certainly more accessible to trading vessels than the Miruka estate. Ethnography and archaeological information suggest that coastal access to trade was a key driver for settlement location in the Eleman region more broadly (Brown 1973: 283; Kakare 1976: 69; Skelly & David 2017: 530–531). This period of occupation at Popo coincides with a time in the Kouri Lowlands when key trading villages were built at Hivo (OKB), Hopo (OJS and OJT), and Kaveharo (OJV), each of which was situated either on the banks of navigable tidal rivers or in sheltered coastal harbours where trading vessels could call in safely. Certainly, large amounts of pottery were incoming to Popo in the Moving Estates period. Two key pieces of evidence suggest that ceramics were being brought to the site as part of a formalized trade:

1. Some of the excavated sherds are decorated with the 'sloping incised band motif' which Allen (2017: 284) has found in levels dating to c. 420–250 cal BP at the Motupore site.[12]
2. Pottery sherds had impressed makers' marks on the internal surface, suggesting that the pottery found at Popo was made specifically for trade. Similar marks can be seen on pottery from Motupore (Allen 2017: 303, fig. 8.24); the Motu were using makers' marks in the early colonial period (Chalmers 1887: 122).

In the final phase of this spatial history, people left Popo and moved to Mirimua Mapoe around 140 cal BP. Of course, archaeological and associated chronological data somewhat oversimplify this move. In oral traditions Mirimua Mapoe was not the only riverbank village occupied after Popo, but it was the longest-lived of these sites. A basal (pre-village occupation) date of c. 300 cal BP from the Mirimua Mapoe excavation shows that beach ridges had formed 1.4 km south of Popo before the end of the Moving Estates period. Oral traditions suggest that the period of beach ridge formation which enabled the Mirimua Mapoe occupation occurred very rapidly. Even today, parts of the system of low-lying beach ridges south of Popo are flooded daily by tidal creeks. We suggest that when the basal piece of charcoal was deposited at Mirimua Mapoe, people were visiting the newly emerged beaches south of Popo, but the land was not dry or stable enough for habitation. Pottery deposited during the village occupation at Mirimua Mapoe was of the almost entirely undecorated ethnographic *hiri* type found at the contemporaneous sites of OJQ and OJY in the Kouri Lowlands.

The spatial history of the ancestral village of Popo reflects the complexity of the oral traditions that describe it. Oral traditions told currently about the site emphasize both fixity and change: expansion of the village, social fissioning, and inward and outward migration through time. In the transforming delta landscapes of the Papuan Gulf, long-lasting villages such as Popo were malleable places. Over the course of 500 years, people moved across the village, presumably seeking to maintain their close relationship with coastal life and the social, subsistence, and exchange benefits that came with it. The ancestors of Orokolo Bay communities—and other clan and/or village groups from the Eleman language family—chose to cease occupying Maivipi to inhabit the estates of Marea Ita and Popo Uku. Later, Miruka was abandoned as people moved towards Aitae Hiru and Koavaipi. Then, as kilometres of land emerged to the south, the ancestors left Popo altogether to inhabit new riverine and coastal villages as the beach ridges grew and stabilized. This research provides new insights into village biographies, but it also makes a case for a landscape approach to similar sites. When sites such as Popo are investigated using single-zone excavations, their material, spatial, and chronological signatures are rendered two-dimensional. Only through excavations and radiocarbon dating across a wide area can an interconnected sense be made of the chronologies and spatial histories of individual places.

IMPLICATIONS FOR ARCHAEOLOGIES OF SWAMP AND DELTA SOCIETIES

In this chapter, we outline two key strategies developed and employed by Papuan Gulf peoples to make delta landscapes home: cultivating sago landscapes and constructing enduring settlements. The two aspects are, of course, closely related. The extensive cultivation of sago stands around large village sites in (at least) the past 1500 years is a form of place-making via cultivation through which settlements become highly productive places and familiar and spatially vast social landscapes are constructed (much like the activity of making a garden). Likewise, the extensive and long-lived settlements we observe archaeologically at Kulupuari/Kikiniu, Kinomere, Popo, and Hopo were almost certainly supported by cultivated sago. Managed sago abundance enabled settlement longevity and allowed inhabitants to dedicate time and effort to social and ceremonial activity, including long-distance trade. In drawing on ethnographic evidence to support our conclusions, we note that research needs to be conducted on the regional ecological impact of increased sago production in the Papuan Gulf during the early 1900s, which occurred to meet the demand of the colonial economy of the Australian Territory of Papua.[13] We are convinced that the avenues of study we have explored are crucial to the region's history and that they can be investigated at greater resolution in future. For instance, there is a need for alternative proxies for sago palm management through time. In Borneo, palynological evidence suggests that *Metroxylon sagu* was introduced from New Guinea in the Early Holocene and was actively managed from this time (Hunt & Rabett 2014). Palaeoecological work in progress at Lake Kutubu will go some way to providing similar information for the highlands of southern New Guinea (Simon Haberle personal communication 2019).

Although the study of Popo demonstrates the potential of conducting multizone excavations to investigate village construction through time, we have only scratched the surface of settlement biographies. Ethnographic documentation reveals that Papuan Gulf villages and landscapes were organized and subdivided according to gender, ceremony, age, and domestic activity (e.g., see Bell 2010; Fowler 2004: fig. 18; Lamb, David, Barker, Pivoru, & Alex 2019; Williams 1924, 1940: 4). Arguably, only Rhoads's (1980: fig. VI-2) aerially extensive excavations were large enough to tackle the spatial complexity of these places. More recent studies have emphasized chronostratigraphic resolution over expansive excavation, from which detailed timelines have been established for local and regional human activity (David 2008; Skelly & David 2017; Urwin 2019a). These approaches should be combined, where possible, in future projects and excavations. For example, the network of post holes exposed by Rhoads's (1980: figs VI-6 & VI-7) excavations at Kulupuari/Kikiniu would have been (had the digs occurred after the advent of AMS dating) excellent candidates for radiocarbon sampling to establish phases of site (and even house) use. The combination of geophysical investigation with targeted excavations also has great potential (see David, Araho, Barker, Kuaso, & Moffat 2009; Moffat et al. 2011).

Despite significant advances in our understanding of the archaeological record of the Papuan Gulf in the past forty years, many foundational questions remain. To echo Rhoads's (1980) thesis title, we still see the region's history as 'through a glass darkly'. There is further work to be done in explaining regional variations in settlement patterns and long-distance trade. If, as environmental records suggest, freshwater swamps of the Purari Delta were naturally abundant in sago in the past 2000 years (and perhaps earlier), why is there so little evidence of extensive pottery trade in the region prior to the *hiri*? By contrast, the mid-Kikori River region—where sago was extensively cultivated—was an important hub and point of articulation for long-distance exchange networks. Further, pulses of long-distance exchange stimulated 'heightened flow-on trade relations with nearby communities' (Skelly & David 2017: 492). The precise nature of these more local exchanges has not yet been teased apart. Oram's (1982) oral tradition research suggested that the ethnographic *hiri* trade seldom reached the Kikori Delta or westerly reaches of the Purari Delta. Further research needs to be dedicated to the networks of pottery redistribution and other forms of regional social exchange, such as the circulation of crabs, coconuts, sago, and betel nut among various Purari-language speaking groups (Williams 1924: 124). Each avenue, of course, requires further archaeological and ethnographic research. From the standpoint of conducting further fieldwork, one area stands out as especially pressing. Little research has been conducted on coastal–hinterland relations (but see Rhoads & Mackenzie 1991). Research in highland and riverine regions north of the Gulf of Papua will elucidate how peoples such as the Anga (Bonnemère & Lemonnier 2009) participated in exchanges linked to (or perhaps independent of) the fluctuations of interconnections along the coast. Understanding these relationships will give crucial context to the history of the swamp and delta societies of the Papuan Gulf.

Notes

1. Orokolo is from the Eleman language family (Rueck, Potter, & Vila 2010).
2. Barker and colleagues (2012: 169) propose that the initial occupation of the Kikori River mouth took place c. 400–500 years ago. This age is based on a single radiocarbon date (Wk-23060) on a piece of charcoal from the Otoia Square 1 excavation. The age closely aligns with the dated occupation of Kinomere village on Urama Island (Frankel et al. 1994: 11–12), which Barker et al. (2012: 169) reference as corroborating evidence. Yet, the Wk-23060 charcoal sample was found in alluvial mud and is not in chronostratigraphic sequence with the other six dated samples (Barker et al. 2012: Table 1). Further, of the ten dates acquired for past village sites on and near Goaribari Island, nine have median ages that cluster at c. 200 years ago (Barker et al. 2012: Table 1; Barker et al. 2015: Table 1). The Wk-23060 date is insufficient evidence of an occupation prior to construction of the longhouses known in local oral traditions. As an alternative explanation, the sample could have been transported into the deposit from an older site upstream.
3. OJP and other site names in this chapter comprising three capitalized letters are codes assigned by the PNG National Museum for their national register of cultural and archaeological sites.
4. Rhoads (1980: 118) reports a conversation with the owner of the site in 1976, during which he was told the site had two names—Kulupuari and Kikiniu—with the latter referring to the ground surface and the former to the soil horizons below. Rhoads's documentary research indicated that a village named 'Hicinu' was established in late April 1917 and abandoned in late 1929. Thirty years later, David (2008) was told the site's name was Kikiniu. Rhoads and David have agreed to refer to the site as Kulupuari/Kikiniu in future.
5. A total of 457 rims were recovered from stratigraphically unbroken excavations across 27 m². These represented three different types of pottery and six quantitative rim attributes, which were used in the analysis.

SWAMP AND DELTA SOCIETIES OF THE PAPUAN GULF, PAPUA NEW GUINEA   823

6. The age range for the Ibira chronology is based on a single radiocarbon determination processed in 1977, prior to the advent of more precise accelerator mass spectrometry (AMS) radiocarbon dating. All other calibrated ages referred to in this chapter are based on AMS determinations.

7. These peoples lived on the Seram Laut islands, situated off Seram's southeast coast. They actively traded along New Guinea's southwest coast as far as the Torres Strait Islands from the mid-seventeenth century and perhaps reached the Papuan Gulf just prior to the eighteenth century (Swadling 1996: 133, 136, 153–156).

8. The people inhabiting the Kouri Lowlands speak an Eleman language called Keuru (aka Keoru-Ahia) (Rueck et al. 2010).

9. See especially the Aripi clan (Larihairu village), Aitaipi Larihairu clan (Larihairu village), and Pakemara clan (Kaivakovu village) oral traditions recorded in Urwin (2019a: 94–99; Appendix A, N1a and N2a).

10. Tribe is the local, English term for their past social group. These tribes appear to be precursors of current clan groups.

11. Each of these estates exhibits considerable complexity within their boundaries. Popo *uku* (*uku* means several) is divided into several smaller estates associated with the modern-day Marepamura, Aripi, and Larihairu clans (all situated within Larihairu village) and with Iuku village.

12. Allen's (2017: 151) proposed chronology for Motupore is imprecise, based partly on radiocarbon dates acquired in the 1970s and 1980s and partly on oral tradition. We infer the chronology to be c. 750–600 cal BP for PAU 6, c. 600–450 cal BP for PAU 5, and c. 450–300 cal BP for PAU 4–1. Our inferences are based on Allen's (2017: 151, 620) preferred start date for the Motupore occupation (c. AD 1200, which is equivalent to 750 cal BP) and his assertion that PAU 6, PAU 5, and PAU 4–1 are 'roughly equal in length to 150 years each'.

13. From 1884 to 1902, the Papuan Gulf was within the colonial protectorate of British New Guinea. From 1902 to 1949, it was part of the Australian Territory of Papua. As of 1975, the region has been encompassed by the Independent State of Papua New Guinea.

References

Allen, J. (1972). Nebira 4: An early Austronesian site in Central Papua. *Archaeology and Physical Anthropology in Oceania, 7*, 92–123.

Allen, J. (1984). Pots and poor princes: A multidimensional approach to the role of pottery trading in coastal Papua. In S. E. Van der Leeuw & A. C. Pritchard (Eds.), *The many dimensions of pottery: Ceramics in archaeology and anthropology* (pp. 407–465). Amsterdam: University of Amsterdam Press.

Allen, J. (2017). *Excavations on Motupore Island, Central District, Papua New Guinea.* University of Otago Working Papers in Anthropology 4. Dunedin: Department of Anthropology and Archaeology, University of Otago.

Allen, J., Summerhayes, G., Mandui, H., & Leavesley, M. (2011). New data from Oposisi: Implications for the early Papuan pottery phase. *Journal of Pacific Archaeology, 2* (1), 69–81.

Aplin, K., & Rhoads, J. W. (1980). Appendix 16: Animal ecology of the Waira region. In J. W. Rhoads, *Through a glass darkly: Present and past land-use systems of Papuan sagopalm users* (PhD thesis). Australian National University, Canberra.

Barker B., Lamb, L., David, B., Korokai, K., Kuaso, A., & Bowman, J. (2012). Otoia, ancestral village of the Kerewo: Modelling the historic emergence of Kerewo regional polities on the island of Goaribari, south coast of mainland Papua New Guinea. In B. David, S. G. Haberle, & D. Walker (Eds.), *Peopled landscapes: Archaeological and biogeographic approaches to landscapes* (pp. 157–176). Terra Australis 34. Canberra: ANU E Press.

Barker, B., Lamb, L., David, B., Skelly, R., & Korakai, K. (2015). Dating in situ longhouse (*dubu daima*) posts in the Kikori River delta: Refining chronologies of the island village occupation in the lower Kikori River delta, Papua New Guinea. *Quaternary International, 385*, 27–38.

Barton, F. R. (1910). Trading voyages to the Gulf of Papua. In C. G. Seligman (Ed.), *The Melanesians of British New Guinea* (pp. 96–120). Cambridge: Cambridge University Press.

Bell, J. A. (2006). *Intersecting histories: Materiality and social transformation in the Purari Delta of Papua New Guinea* (PhD thesis). University of Oxford, Oxford.

Bell, J. A. (2010). Out of the mouths of crocodiles: Eliciting histories with photographs and string figures. *History and Anthropology, 21* (4), 351–373.

Bell, J. A. (2015). The structural violence of resource extraction in the Purari delta. In J. A. Bell, P. West, & C. Filer (Eds.), *Tropical forests of Oceania: Anthropological perspectives* (pp. 127–153). Canberra: ANU Press.

Bell, J. A. (2016). Dystopian realities and archival dreams in the Purari Delta of Papua New Guinea. *Social Anthropology, 24*, 20–35.

Bell, J. A. (2020). The beginnings and ends of basketry in the Purari delta. In T. A. Heslop, & H. Anderson (Eds.), *Basketry and beyond: Constructing cultures*. Norwich: Sainsbury Centre for Visual Arts/University of East Anglia.

Bevan, T. F. (1890). *Toil, travel and discovery in British New Guinea*. London: Kegan Paul.

Bickler, S. H. (1997). Early pottery exchange along the south coast of Papua New Guinea. *Archaeology in Oceania, 32*, 151–162.

Bintoro, M. H., Nurulhaq, M. I., Pratama, A. J., Ahmad, F., & Ayulia, L. (2018). Growing area of sago palm and its environment. In H. Ehara, Y. Toyoda, & D. V. Johnson (Eds.), *Sago palm: Multiple contributions to food security and sustainable livelihoods* (pp. 17–29). Singapore: Springer Nature.

Bird, E. (2010). Papua New Guinea. In E. Bird (Ed.), *Encyclopedia of the world's coastal landforms* (pp. 1175–1186). London: Springer Science.

Bonnemère, P., & Lemonnier, P. (2009). A measure of violence: Forty years of 'first contact' among the Ankave-Anga (Papua New Guinea). In M. Jolly, S. Tcherkézoff, & D. Tryon (Eds.), *Oceanic encounters: Exchange, desire, violence* (pp. 295–334). Canberra: ANU E Press.

Brown, H. A. (1973). The Eleman language family. In K. Franklin (Ed.), *The linguistic situation in the Gulf District and adjacent areas, Papua New Guinea* (pp. 279–376). Canberra: Research School of Pacific Studies, Australian National University.

Brown, H. A. (1988). *Three Elema myths, recorded in Toaripi, translated and annotated by Herbert A. Brown*. Canberra: Research School of Pacific and Asian Studies, Australian National University.

Bulmer, S. (1978). *Prehistoric culture change in the Port Moresby region* (PhD thesis). University of Papua New Guinea, Port Moresby.

Busse, M., Araho, N., & Turner, S. (1993). *The people of Lake Kutubu and Kikori: Changing meanings of daily life*. Port Moresby: Papua New Guinea National Museum and Art Gallery.

Chalmers, J. (1887). *Pioneering in New Guinea*. London: The Religious Tract Society.

Chalmers, J. (1895). *Pioneer life and work in New Guinea*. London: The Religious Tract Society.

Cragg, S. (1983). The mangrove ecosystem of the Purari Delta. In T. Petr (Ed.), *The Purari: Tropical environment of a high rainfall river basin* (pp. 295–324). The Hague: Kluwer.

Craig, B. (2010). 'Scenes hidden from other eyes'—Theodore Bevan's collection from the Gulf of Papua in the South Australian Museum. *The Artefact, 33*, 30–48.

Crosby, E. (1976). Sago exploitation in Melanesia. *Archaeology and Physical Anthropology in Oceania, 11* (2), 138–155.

Dalrymple, R. W., & Choi, K. (2007). Morphologic and facies trends through the fluvial-marine transition in tide-dominated depositional systems: A schematic framework for environmental and sequence-stratigraphic interpretation. *Earth-Science Reviews, 81*, 135–174.

David, B. (2008). Rethinking cultural chronologies and past landscape engagement in the Kopi region, Gulf Province, Papua New Guinea. *The Holocene, 18* (3), 463–479.

David, B., Aplin, K., Petchey, F., Skelly, R., Mialanes, J., Jones-Amin, H., . . . Lamb, L. (2015). Kumukumu 1, a hilltop site in the Aird Hills: Implications for occupational trends and dynamics in the Kikori delta, south coast of Papua New Guinea. *Quaternary International, 30*, 1–20.

David, B., Araho, N., Barker, B., Kuaso, A., & Moffat, I. (2009). Keveoki 1: Exploring the Hiri ceramics trade at a short-lived village site near the Vailala River, Papua New Guinea. *Australian Archaeology, 68*, 11–22.

David, B., Fairbairn, A., Aplin, K., Murepe, L., Green, M., Stanisic, J., . . . Muke, J. (2007). OJP, a terminal Pleistocene archaeological site from the Gulf Province lowlands, Papua New Guinea. *Archaeology in Oceania, 42* (1), 31–33.

David, B., Geneste, J.-M., Aplin, K., Delannoy, J.-J., Araho, N., Clarkson, C., . . . Rowe, C. (2010). The Emo site (OAC) Gulf Province, Papua New Guinea: Resolving long-standing questions of antiquity and implications for the history of the ancestral hiri maritime trade. *Australian Archaeology, 70*, 39–54.

David, B., McNiven, I. J., Richards, T., Connaughton, S. P., Leavesley, M., Barker, B., & Rowe, C. (2011). Lapita sites in the Central Province of mainland Papua New Guinea. *World Archaeology, 43* (4), 580–597.

David, B., Pivoru, M., Pivoru, W., Barker, B., Weiner, J. F., Simala, D., . . . Dop, J. (2008). Living landscapes of the dead: Archaeology of the afterworld among the Rumu of Papua New Guinea. In B. David & J. Thomas (Eds.), *Handbook of landscape archaeology* (pp. 158–166). Walnut Creek, CA: Left Coast Press.

David, B., Richards, T., Skelly, R., McNiven, I. J., & Leavesley, M. (2016). Archaeology in Port Moresby and the southern lowlands of Papua New Guinea: Intellectual and historical contexts for Caution Bay. In T. Richards, B. David, K. Aplin, & I. J. McNiven (Eds.), *Archaeological research at Caution Bay, Papua New Guinea: Cultural, linguistic and environmental setting* (pp. 9–26). Oxford: Archaeopress.

Department of Primary Industries PNG. (1975). *Forest types: Gulf of Papua. Map No. 2687*. Port Moresby: Office of Forests.

Dewdney, M. (1993). *Never the last straw: Memories of Orokolo*. Swaffham: Self Published.

Di Rosa, D. (2018). *Frustrated modernity: Kerewo histories and historical consciousness, Gulf Province, Papua New Guinea* (PhD thesis). Australian National University, Canberra.

Dutton, T. E. (Ed.). (1982). *The hiri in history: Further aspects of long distance Motu trade in Central Papua*. Pacific Research Monograph 8. Canberra: Research School of Pacific Studies, Australian National University.

Flach, M. (1997). *Sago palm. Metroxylon sagu Rottb. Promoting the conservation and use of underutilized and neglected crops*. Institute of Plant Genetics and Crop Plant Research Vol. 13. Rome: International Plant Genetic Resources Institute.

Flach, M., & Schuiling, D. L. (1989). Revival of an ancient starch crop: A review of the agronomy of the sago palm. *Agroforestry Systems, 7*, 259–281.

Fowler, M. (2004). *Papuan transformations: Architectural reflections on colonialism—The modern colony, the Purari, the Orokolo, and the Motu cultural and architectural transactions 1884–1975* (PhD thesis). University of Melbourne, Melbourne.

Frankel, D., Thompson, K., & Vanderwal, R. L. (1994). Kerema and Kinomere. In D. Frankel & J. W. Rhoads (Eds.), *Archaeology of a coastal exchange system: Sites and ceramics of the Papuan Gulf* (pp. 1–48). Research Papers in Archaeology and Natural History 25. Canberra: Research School of Pacific and Asian Studies, Australian National University.

Frankel, D., & Vanderwal, R. L. (1982). Prehistoric research at Kinomere Village, Papua New Guinea, 1981: Preliminary field report. *Australian Archaeology, 14*, 86–95.

Grave, P., & McNiven, I. J. (2013). Geochemical identification of Asian stoneware jars from Torres Strait, northeast Australia. *Journal of Archaeological Science, 40*, 4538–4551.

Greenhill, A. R. (2006). *Food safety and security of sago starch in rural Papua New Guinea* (PhD thesis). James Cook University, Townsville.

Haddon, A. C. (1918). The Agiba cult of the Kerewa culture. *Man 18*, 177–183.

Hareavila, J. S. (1976). Iuku village, Kikori sub-province, Gulf Province. *Oral History, 4* (7), 17.

Hauka, H. (1978). A Legend from Orokolo—Vailala. *Oral History, 6* (8), 71–74.

Holmes, E. B., & Newcombe, K. (1980). Potential and proposed development of sago (*Metroxylon* spp.) as a source of power alcohol in Papua New Guinea. In W. R. Stanton & M. Flach (Eds.), *Sago: The equatorial swamp as a natural resource* (pp. 164–174). The Hague: Martinus Nijhoff.

Holmes, J. H. (1903). Notes on the Elema tribes of the Papuan Gulf. *Journal of the Anthropological Institute of Great Britain and Ireland, 33*, 125–134.

Howell, A. L., Bentley, S. J., Sr., Xu, K., Ferrell, R. E., Jr., Muhammad, Z., & Septama, E. (2014). Fine sediment mineralogy as a tracer of latest Quaternary sediment delivery to a dynamic continental margin: Pandora Trough, Gulf of Papua, Papua New Guinea. *Marine Geology, 357*, 108–122.

Hughes, I. (1977). *New Guinea stone age trade: The geography and ecology of traffic in the interior*. Terra Australis 3. Canberra: Research School of Pacific Studies, Australian National University.

Hunt, C. O., & Rabett, R. J. (2014). Holocene landscape intervention and plant food production strategies in island and mainland Southeast Asia. *Journal of Archaeological Science, 51*, 22–33.

Hurley, F. (1924). *Pearls and savages*. New York: Putnams.

Irwin, G. R. (1991). Themes in the prehistory of coastal Papua and the Massim. In A. Pawley (Ed.), *Man and a half: Essays in Pacific anthropology and ethnobiology in honour of Ralph Bulmer* (pp. 503–511). Auckland: The Polynesian Society.

Kakare, I. (1976). MotuMotu Sariva: Trading voyages from the Gulf to Port Moresby. *Oral History, 4* (10), 69–91.

Kakare, I., & Karava, S. (1975). The Uritai Toaripi. *Oral History, 3*(9), 38–55.

Kari, M. (1978). Sago utilisation amongst the central Elema, Gulf Province, Papua New Guinea. *Oral History, 6* (2), 2–10.

Laba, B. (1996). Oral traditions about early trade by Indonesians in southwest New Guinea. In P. Swadling, *Plumes from paradise: Trade cycles in outer Southeast Asia and their impact on*

New Guinea and nearby islands until 1920 (pp. 299–307). Boroko: PNG National Museum with Robert Brown & Associates.

Lamb, L., David, B., Barker, B., Pivoru, R., & Alex, C. (2019). Female weir fishers of the southern lowlands of Papua New Guinea: Implications for an archaeology of gendered activities. *Australian Archaeology, 85* (1), 48–56.

Landtman, G. (1927). *The Kiwai Papuans of British New Guinea: a nature-born instance of Rousseau's ideal community.* London: Macmillan.

Landtman, G. (1933). *Ethnographical collection from the Kiwai District of British New Guinea in the National Museum of Finland, Helsingfors (Helsinki).* Helsingfors: Commission of the Antell Collection.

Lawrence, D. (1994). Customary exchange across Torres Straits. *Memoirs of the Queensland Museum, 34,* 241–446.

Lewis, D. C. (1996). *The plantation dream: Developing British New Guinea and Papua 1884–1942.* Canberra: The Journal of Pacific History.

Löffler, E. (1977). *Geomorphology of Papua New Guinea.* Canberra: ANU Press.

Mackenzie, D. E. (1980). Appendix 11: Petrographic examination of pottery and stone axe heads from archaeological sites in the Kikori area, Gulf of Papua. In J. W. Rhoads (Ed.), *Through a glass darkly: Present and past land-use systems of Papuan sagopalm users* (PhD thesis). Australian National University, Canberra.

Maher, R. F. (1961). *New men of Papua: A study in culture change.* Madison: University of Wisconsin Press.

Marsaglia, K. M., Kramer, K. G., David, B., & Skelly, R. J. (2016). Petrographic analyses of sand temper/inclusions in ceramics of Kikiniu, Kikori River and modern sand samples from the Gulf Province (Papua New Guinea). *Archaeology in Oceania 51* (2), 131–140.

McNiven, I. J., David, B., Aplin, A., Pivoru, M., Pivoru, W., Sexton, A., . . . Kemp, N. (2010). Historicising the present: Late Holocene emergence of a rainforest hunting camp, Gulf Province, Papua New Guinea. *Australian Archaeology, 71,* 41–56.

McNiven, I. J., David, B., Richards, T., Aplin, K., Asmussen, B., Mialanes, J., . . . Ulm, S. (2011). New direction in human colonisation of the Pacific: Lapita settlement of south coast New Guinea. *Australian Archaeology, 72,* 1–6.

Mennis, M. (2015). *Sailing for survival: A comparative report of the trading systems and trading canoes of the Bel people in the Madang area and of the Motu people in the Port Moresby area of Papua New Guinea.* University of Otago Working Papers in Anthropology 2. Dunedin: University of Otago.

Moffat, I., David, B., Barker, B., Kuaso, A., Skelly, R., & Araho, N. (2011). Magnetometer surveys in archaeological research in Papua New Guinea: Keveoki 1, Gulf Province. *Archaeology in Oceania, 46,* 17–22.

Moraes-Gorecki, V. (1983). Notes on the ownership and utilisation of sago, and on social change, among the Moveave-Toaripi of the Papuan Gulf. *Oceania, 53* (3), 233–241.

Nakamura, S. (2018). Morphogenesis of sago palm. In H. Ehara, Y. Toyoda, & D. V. Johnson (Eds.), *Sago palm: Multiple contributions to food security and sustainable livelihoods* (pp. 169–179). Singapore: Springer Nature.

National Statistical Office of Papua New Guinea. (2014). *Papua New Guinea 2011 National Population and Housing Census: Ward population profile.* Port Moresby: National Statistical Office.

Oram, N. (1982). Pots for sago: The *hiri* trading network. In T. Dutton (Ed.), *The hiri in history: Further aspects of long distance Motu trade in Central Papua* (pp. 1–34). Pacific Research Monograph 8. Canberra: The Australian National University.

Paijmans, K. (1975). *Explanatory notes to the vegetation map of Papua New Guinea*. Land Research Series No. 35. Melbourne: CSIRO.

Paijmans, K. (1980). Ecological notes on sago in New Guinea. In W. R. Stanton & M. Flach (Eds.), *Sago: The equatorial swamp as a natural resource* (pp. 9–12). The Hague: Martinus Nijhoff.

Rhoads, J. W. (1980). *Through a glass darkly: Present and past land-use systems of Papuan sagopalm users* (PhD thesis). Australian National University, Canberra, https://openresearch-repository.anu.edu.au/handle/1885/96947.

Rhoads, J. W. (1981). Variation in land-use strategies among Melanesian sago eaters. *Canberra Anthropology, 4* (2), 45–73.

Rhoads J. W. (1982a). Sagopalm management in Melanesia: An alternative perspective. *Archaeology in Oceania, 17* (1), 20–27.

Rhoads, J. W. (1982b). Prehistoric Papuan exchange systems: The *hiri* and its antecedents. In T. E. Dutton (Ed.), *The hiri in history: Further aspects of long distance Motu trade in Central Papua* (pp. 131–151). Pacific Research Monograph 8. Canberra: Research School of Pacific Studies, Australian National University.

Rhoads, J. W. (1983). Prehistoric sites from the Kikori region, Papua New Guinea. *Australian Archaeology, 14*, 1–5.

Rhoads, J. W. (1984). Pre-contact glass artefacts from Papua New Guinea. *South-East Asian Studies Newsletter, 14*, 1–5.

Rhoads, J. W. (1994). The Popo site. In D. Frankel & J. W. Rhoads (Eds.), *Archaeology of a coastal exchange system: Sites and ceramics of the Papuan Gulf* (pp. 53–69). Research Papers in Archaeology and Natural History 25. Canberra: Research School of Pacific and Asian Studies, Australian National University.

Rhoads, J. W., & Mackenzie, D. E. (1991). Stone axe trade in prehistoric Papua: The travels of python. *Proceedings of the Prehistoric Society, 57* (2), 35–49.

Rueck, M. J., Potter, M., & Vila B. (2010). A sociolinguistic profile of the Tairuma [uar] language group. *SIL Electronic Survey Reports*, http://www.sil.org/resources/publications/entry/9032. SIL International.

Schuiling, D. L. (2009). *Growth and development of true sago palm* (Metroxylon sagu Rottboll)*, with special reference to accumulation of starch in the trunk* (PhD thesis). Wageningen Universiteit, Wageningen.

Shearman, P. L. (2010). Recent change in the extent of mangroves in the northern Gulf of Papua, Papua New Guinea. *Ambio, 39* (2), 181–189.

Shearman, P. L., Bryan, J., Ash, J., Hunnam, P., Mackey, B., & Lokes, B. (2008). *The state of the forests of Papua New Guinea: Mapping the extent and condition of forest cover and measuring the drivers of forest change in the period 1972–2002*. Port Moresby: University of Papua New Guinea.

Shearman, P. L., Bryan, J., & Walsh, J. P. (2013). Trends in deltaic change over three decades in the Asia-Pacific region. *Journal of Coastal Research, 29* (5), 1169–1183.

Skelly, R. (2014). *From Lapita to the hiri: Archaeology of the Kouri Lowlands, Gulf of Papua, Papua New Guinea* (PhD thesis). Monash University, Melbourne.

Skelly, R., & David, B. (2017). *Hiri: Archaeology of long-distance maritime trade along the south coast of Papua New Guinea*. Honolulu: University of Hawaii Press.

Skelly, R., David, B., Barker, B., Kuaso, A., & Araho, N. (2010). Migration sites of the Miaro clan (Vailala River region, Papua New Guinea): Tracking Kouri settlement movements through oral tradition sites on ancient landscapes. *The Artefact, 33*, 16–29.

Skelly, R., David, B., Petchey, F., & Leavesley, M. (2014). Tracking ancient beach-lines inland: 2600-year-old dentate stamped ceramics at Hopo, Vailala River region, Papua New Guinea. *Antiquity, 88,* 470–487.

Skelly, R., David, B., Leavesley, M., Petchey, F., Guise, A., Tsang, R., . . . Richards, T. (2018). Changing ceramic traditions at Agila ancestral village, Hood Bay, Papua New Guinea. *Australian Archaeology, 84* (2), 181–195.

Stone, O. C. (1880). *A few months in New Guinea.* London: William Clows and Sons.

Summerhayes, G., & Allen, J. (2007). Lapita writ large? Revisiting the Austronesian colonisation of the Papuan south coast. In S. Bedford, C. S, & S. P. Connaughton (Eds.), *Lapita and western Pacific settlement* (pp. 97–122). Terra Australia 26. Canberra: Australian National University.

Swadling, P. (1996). *Plumes from paradise: Trade cycles in outer Southeast Asia and their impact on New Guinea and nearby islands until 1920.* Boroko: PNG National Museum with Robert Brown & Associates.

Thangavelu E., David, B., Barker, B., Geneste, J.-M., Delannoy, J.-J., Lamb, L., . . . Skelly, R. (2011). Morphometric analysis of Batissa violacea shells from Emo (OAC), Gulf Provence, Papua New Guinea. *Archaeology in Oceania, 46,* 67–75.

Thom, B. G., & Wright, L. D. (1983). Geomorphology of the Purari Delta. In T. Petr (Ed.), *The Purari: Tropical environment of a high rainfall river basin* (pp. 47–65). The Hague: Kluwer.

Thomas, M. L., Warny, S., Jarzen, D. M., Bentley, S. M., Sr., Droxler, A. W., Harper, B. B., . . . Xu, K. (2018). Palynomorph evidence for tropical climate stability in the Gulf of Papua, Papua New Guinea, over the last marine transgression and highstand (14,500 BP to today). *Quaternary International 467,* 277–291.

Ulijaszek, S. (2007). Bioculturalism. In D. J. Parkin & S. Ulijaszek (Eds.), *Holistic anthropology: Emergence and convergence* (pp. 21–51). New York: Berghahn Books.

Ulijaszek, S., & Poraituk, S. (1983a). Nutritional status of the people of the Purari Delta. In T. Petr (Ed.), *The Purari: Tropical environment of a high rainfall river basin* (pp. 551–564). The Hague: Kluwer.

Ulijaszek, S., & Poraituk, S. (1983b). Subsistence patterns and sago cultivation in the Purari River. In T. Petr (Ed.), *The Purari: Tropical environment of a high rainfall river basin* (pp. 577–588). The Hague: Kluwer

Urwin, C. (2019a). *Building and remembering: Constructing ancestral place at Popo, Orokolo Bay, Papua New Guinea* (PhD thesis). Monash University, Melbourne.

Urwin, C. (2019b). Excavating and interpreting ancestral action: Stories from the subsurface of Orokolo Bay, Papua New Guinea. *Journal of Social Archaeology, 19* (3), 279–306.

Urwin, C. (2022). *Building and remembering: An archaeology of place-making on Papua New Guinea's south coast.* Honolulu: University of Hawaii Press.

Urwin, C., Hua, Q., Skelly, R., & Arifeae, H. (2018). The chronology of Popo, an ancestral village site in Orokolo Bay, Gulf Province, Papua New Guinea. *Australian Archaeology, 84* (1), 90–97.

Vanderwal, R. L. (1973). *Prehistoric studies in coastal Papua* (PhD thesis). Australian National University, Canberra.

Walsh, J. P., & Nittrouer, C. A. (2004). Mangrove-bank sedimentation in a mesotidal environment with large sediment supply, Gulf of Papua. *Marine Geology, 208,* 225–248.

Welsch, R. L., Webb, V-L., & Haraha, S. (2006). *Coaxing the spirits to dance: Art and society in the Papuan Gulf of New Guinea.* New Hanover: Hood Museum of Art and Dartmouth College.

Williams, F. E. (1923). *The collection of curios and the preservation of native culture*. Port Moresby: Government Printer.

Williams, F. E. (1924). *The natives of the Purari Delta*. Port Moresby: Government Printer.

Williams, F. E. (1931). Miscellaneous Orokolo notes. National Archive of Papua New Guinea, Port Moresby (A447 B2996 ML MSS 5/9 79).

Williams, F. E. (1940). *Drama of Orokolo: The social and ceremonial life of the Elema*. Oxford: Oxford University Press.

Wright, L. D. (1989). Dispersal and deposition of river sediments in coastal seas: Models from Asia and the tropics. *Netherlands Journal of Sea Research, 23* (4), 493–500.

CHAPTER 31

THE ARCHAEOLOGY OF SOCIAL TRANSFORMATION IN THE NEW GUINEA HIGHLANDS

DYLAN GAFFNEY AND TIM DENHAM

INTRODUCTION

THE archaeology of highland New Guinea represents the study of how *Homo sapiens* have come to successfully make their livelihoods in montane and subalpine rainforests and grasslands. The distinctive physical geography—a world in the clouds—has helped to shape, and in turn has been shaped by, the productive activities of humans since the very first foraging forays made during the Late Pleistocene, about 40,000–50,000 years ago, through to the emergence of sustained settlement in the Holocene. Living under the canopy and at high altitudes posed unique challenges for people's food procurement, raw material acquisition, locomotion, and thermoregulation (Moore, Fernando Armaza, Villena, & Vargas 2002; Roberts, Boivin, Lee-Thorp, Petraglia, & Stock 2016), and so the successful exploration and inhabitation of these environments give us a window into the distinctly sapient capacities for adaptive flexibility.

The descendant communities that inhabit the highlands today share commonalities in material culture (Bulmer 1975), settlement patterns (Allen 1983), and genetic structure (Bergström et al. 2017), which suggests that the region was, for long periods, relatively isolated from the lowlands. But across the mountain ranges, these groups have come to live out their lives, adapting to the montane and subalpine zones, in myriad locally distinctive ways. It is therefore the archaeologist's task to unravel the social processes that underlay the formation of, first, these similarities, and equally this extreme diversity that we see in social systems (Langness 1964), language (Foley 2000), technology (Pétrequin & Pétrequin 2006), and subsistence practices (Bourke & Harwood 2009). For instance, within the highland zone around 300 mutually unintelligible languages are spoken by communities variably attending to hunting and gathering (e.g., Bulmer 1968), intensive horticulture (e.g., Brass 1941), and producing and trading valuables (e.g., Strathern 1969). Over the past six decades,[1] the archaeology of New Guinea's mountains has sought to trace out the history of these processes and in doing so has helped to redefine our understanding of the human experience, providing (1) some of the earliest global evidence for adaptation to high altitudes, particularly montane rainforests (Summerhayes, Field, Shaw, & Gaffney 2017); (2) deep histories of agriculture and cultivation in the tropics, challenging assumptions about the emergence of food production both regionally and in other domestication centres around the world (Denham 2011); and (3) improved understanding of how incipient social stratification can take form and be transformed by the production and redistribution of material culture, plants, and animals (Golson & Gardner 1990).

In this chapter, we examine these three contributions in further detail. After synthesizing recent developments in highland archaeology and related disciplines, we propose moving away from a study of highland social evolution as homogeneous and linear—an evolution that was intraregionally connected and extraregionally isolated, moving gradually but uniformly from hunting and gathering to intensive agriculture. Instead, we wish to look at this evolution as the generation of a patchwork mosaic, threading together locally peculiar ecologies, social groups, and practices across the landscape. In this way, behavioural and technological trajectories were differently interconnected across the mountains and at times to the lowlands, coasts, and islands as well; each subregion transformed asymmetrically at different rates and scales through time. This approach builds on arguments made originally by Bulmer and Bulmer (1964) and developed by Feil (1987). We stress that the high diversity in highland lifeways observed in the early twentieth century by ethnographers is likely to have arisen over the long term from these asymmetric processes of growth.

ECOLOGICAL VARIABILITY

The theatre for these processes of growth was, and continues to be, the discrete geographical zone of the New Guinea Highlands, which generally refers to the rugged mountain cordillera that runs like a spine through the centre of the island. In this chapter, we consider all montane and subalpine regions of New Guinea over 1200 m above sea level (asl), in particular those of the Central Ranges including the Bismarck-Schrader Range and the Maoke Range, as well as the Owen Stanley Range (Figure 31.1).[2] Along these ranges of steep V-shaped valleys and narrow crested ridges are nestled a series of wide intermontane valleys and basins between 1400 m and 2850 m asl, in which the majority of today's settlements is concentrated (Löffler 1977). In some of these valleys, population density can be as high as $100/km^2$, but in steeper areas it is often below $10/km^2$ (Allen 1983).

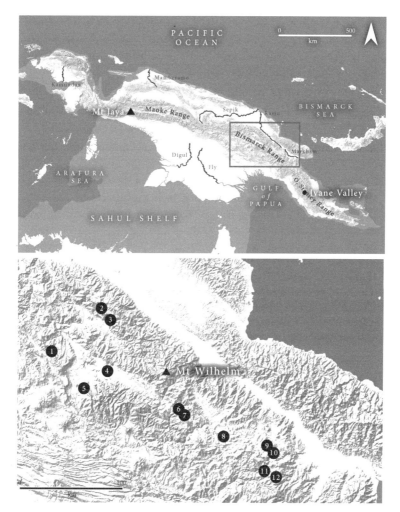

FIGURE 31.1. The island of New Guinea showing the key mountain ranges, river systems, and peaks. The Sahul shelf and the extent of the LGM coastline connecting New Guinea to Australia is shown in the upper map. Archaeological sites mentioned in the text are numbered in the inset map: (1) Yuku; (2) Wañelek; (3) Waim; (4) Kuk; (5) Manim; (6) Kiowa; (7) Nombe; (8) Kafiavana; (9) NFB; (10) Aibura; (11) Batari; (12) NFX.

These ranges are quite unique in the equatorial islands, being subject to sharp ecotonal variation (Figure 31.1). Although, at lower elevations, much of New Guinea is consistently warm and humid, in altitudes above 1500 m asl, air temperatures can reach 0 °C at ground level. There are also periodic frosts, which become even more frequent above 2500 m asl (Brookfield & Allen 1989). This altitudinal variation is mirrored in changes to vegetation, with the present treeline generally no higher than 3000–3600 m asl. In the lower montane rainforests, nut-bearing beech trees (*Nothofagus, Lithocarpus*, and *Castanopsis*) dominate, while in higher altitudes of the subalpine zone, pines

(*Phyllocladus*) and conifers (*Dacrycarpus, Podocarpus*, and *Papuacedrus*) are more common (Walker & Flenley 1979). Above this altitude are more open environments with grasslands, ericaceous shrubs, and herbs usually found in temperate latitudes, while bare rocky ground, snow, and glaciation occur above 4500 m asl (Flenley 1984).

Throughout the period that people have frequented the highlands, the Earth has undergone a series of glacial–interglacial transitions that have dramatically affected climate and vegetation. In the Late Pleistocene (Marine Isotope Stage, MIS-3), and particularly during the Last Glacial Maximum (LGM, MIS-2) when the intermontane valleys were on average 7 °C colder than today, open subalpine grasslands and glaciation were much more extensive and the treeline was compressed down to 2200 m asl (Haberle 1993; see Figure 31.2). Climatic amelioration began shortly after the LGM, with deglaciation occurring from around 15,000 years ago (Flenley & Morley 1978). This amelioration

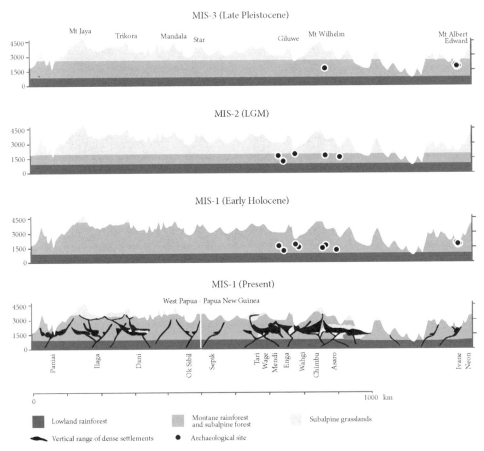

FIGURE 31.2. Changing ecological zones relative to altitude through time. Schematic cross-sections of the highland ranges are adapted from Brookfield and Allen (1989) to include extension showing Owen Stanley Ranges, generated using digital elevation model in Google Earth. Forest growth limits established from Flenley (1984). MIS = Marine Isotope Stage.

was unstable during the terminal Pleistocene, and so the retreat of open terrain and the expansion of scrub and forest land upslope were combined with intermittent but severe drought events and forest fires (Hope 2014). Since the Mid-Holocene and particularly within the past two millennia, clearances of forest cover may have been interrelated with increased climatic variability brought about by El Niño Southern Oscillation (ENSO) events (Haberle & Lusty 2000). El Niño events cause increased aridity and drought, while La Niña conditions encourage heavy frosts, both of which can kill above-ground vegetative growth or delay maturation.

Along with altitudinal changes in ecology through time, there are also longitudinal clines along the highland spine, with the east usually being much more seasonally variable in terms of rainfall and temperature, with some areas experiencing pronounced drought (McAlpine 1983). This variability has implications for the distribution and seasonal availability of edible plant foods such as *Pandanus julianettii,* whose nut production is climate dependent and largely constrained by water stress (Bourke & Vlassak 2004). Moreover, local microclimatic variation in rainfall, atmospheric CO_2, and ambient temperature mean that rates of forest and grassland expansion following the LGM differed markedly in each valley system (Hope & Haberle 2005). These subregional environmental variations are mirrored by notable differences in human subsistence focus, with high-intensity food production occurring year round in the west and lower-intensity, seasonal production in the east (Bulmer & Bulmer 1964; Feil 1995).

HUMAN ADAPTIVE FLEXIBILITY IN HIGHLAND RAINFORESTS AND GRASSLANDS

The initial footsteps into the highlands occurred when New Guinea was still joined to a much larger continent known as Sahul, which connected the landmass to Australia and some of the offshore island groups (Figure 31.1). For Pleistocene foraging communities, the highlands were novel environments, as people were confronted with unfamiliar climatic conditions, new fauna, and different varieties of flora. Previously, they had been adapted to living in lowland tropical rainforests and along equatorial coastlines, using boats to settle Wallacea and the adjacent shores of northwest Sahul (Bird et al. 2019; Gaffney 2020). In this way, studying the behavioural transformations that took place in these highland rainforests and grasslands is important to understanding the rate and scale of adaptive flexibility amongst *H. sapiens* when they began to frequent new and challenging environments. The archaeological record shows that people readily, and perhaps rapidly, learned to live in a diverse array of montane environments, which went hand in hand with innovations in plant collecting, hunting, and stone toolmaking.

It is unclear from which direction people moved into high altitudes, but they likely journeyed along major fluvial systems, such as the Sepik, Markham, Fly, and Ramu Rivers in the east (now Papua New Guinea) and the Kamundan, Mamberamo, and

Digul Rivers in the west (now Indonesian Papua). These routes would have seen foragers moving from the north coast of Sahul or, alternatively, from the tropical woodlands of the Arafura and Torres Plains in the south (Kershaw, van der Kaars, Moss, & Wang 2002). Within rainforests, people often rely on perennial water sources such as rivers, not only for drinking water, but also for navigation (Kawai 2019). Although foragers would not have been constrained to following these rivers, and freshwater can be readily found in the hollows of large bamboo and other plants when moving through the forest, canopy gaps at the banks of rivers often act as 'green oases' where large fauna gather to exploit the increased species richness (Roberts et al. 2016). The movement of people through thinner forest edges is also greatly expedited (Venkataraman et al. 2018).

The earliest archaeological evidence for people in the highlands comes from the east, in the Owen Stanley Ranges, where several sites (Vilakuev, South Kov, and Airport Mound) run along spurs overlooking the swampy Ivane River Basin (see Table 31.1). At these sites, the earliest deposits date to 43,000–49,000 years ago and are found in association with flaked stone artefacts and burnt *Pandanus* sp. drupes from an unknown local variant (Summerhayes et al. 2010). Palaeoecological evidence suggests that the Ivane Valley floor was extensively burnt around 40,000 years ago (Hope 2009), perhaps to facilitate the hunting of megafauna and grassland species (Fairbairn et al. 2006). White, Crook, and Ruxton (1970) originally suggested that the Kosipe site in the same valley was part of a wider landscape of seasonal hunting and *Pandanus* sp. nut exploitation, which would have seen highly mobile rainforest foragers regularly moving between the coast and the mountains (see also Fairbairn et al. 2006). However, although cultivated varieties such as *Pandanus julienetti* are seasonal, found in Holocene levels at the Ivane sites, the wild and unidentified variety present during the Pleistocene probably did not produce in a regular seasonal pattern (see the discussion on the archaeological significance of wild *Pandanus* production in Denham 2007, 2018: 95–100). Despite the marked seasonality in the eastern ranges compared to the west, where rainfall is far less predictable, *Pandanus sp.* nuts were likely available throughout much of the year during MIS-3. It is possible that people in the east may have increasingly specialized in seasonal *Pandanus* collecting throughout the terminal Pleistocene and Holocene, while those people further west adopted a versatile and broad-spectrum approach to collecting plant foods—the beginnings of differential adaptive strategies across the ranges. However, this hypothesis remains to be fully explored with further archaeobotanical research.

At both ends of the highlands, the movement between and through lowland rainforests, fringe highland zones, montane basins and valley systems, and high-altitude cloud forests would have been central to maintaining a broad spectrum of food availability (Denham 2016b). Just as in the present, many groups who are settled in the montane zone continue to lay claim to land in both higher subalpine and alpine areas, often for multiday hunting and collecting expeditions, and in the lowland or foothill rainforests for access to wild forest resources, as well as to maintain trade links to the coast (Hope & Hope 1976). As Bulmer and Bulmer (1964) originally highlighted, the montane mixed-oak forests in particular contained a variety of edible nuts and

Table 31.1. New Guinea highland archaeological sites alongside published ages ranges for occupation. Calibrated ranges BP reported at 2 sigma.

Province	Site Name	Site Code	Type	M asl	~ Distance from Coast	Max age cal. BP	Min age cal. BP	Function/Significance	Source
Central	Vilaukuev	AAXF	Open	2000	80 km	48,687–2973	7142–6799	Ridgeline camp; plant processing	Summerhayes et al. (2010)
	South Kov	AAXE	Open	2000	80 km	45,535–42,756	8328–8179	Ridgeline camp; plant processing	Summerhayes et al. (2010)
	Airport Mound	AAXD	Open	2000	80 km	45,169–42,517	42,257–40,182	Ridgeline camp; plant processing	Summerhayes et al. (2010)
	Kosipe	AER	Open	1950	80 km	41,448–38,697	5857–3265	Ridgeline camp; plant processing	White et al. (1970); Fairbairn et al. (2006)
	Joe's Garden	AAXC	Open	2000	80 km	39,606–37,064	4409–4157	Ridgeline camp; plant processing	Summerhayes et al. (2010)
Chimbu	Nombe	NCA	Cave	1750	95 km	38,781–34,826	253–33	Foraging camp (small game; megafauna)	Mountain (1991b); Denham & Mountain (2016)
	Kiowa	NAW	RS	1500	95 km	12,589–11,630	303–0	Foraging camp (small game)	Bulmer (1964); Denham (2016a); Gaffney et al. (2021)
Western	Manim	MJJ	RS	1770	170 km	22,495–22,081	269–0	Foraging camp (small game)	Christensen (1975); Denham (2019)
	Yuku	MAH	RS	1280	180 km	17,828–17,063	254–32	Foraging camp (small game); burial; ceremonial	Bulmer (1975); Denham (2016a); Gaffney et al. (in prep)

(continued)

Table 31.1. Continued

Province	Site Name	Site Code	Type	M asl	~ Distance from Coast	Max age cal. BP	Min age cal. BP	Function/Significance	Source
	Mugamamp	–	Open	1600	150 km	13,000?	~250	Cultivation and agriculture	Harris & Hughes (1978)
	Kuk	MAB	Open	1560	155 km	10,485–9909	275–0	Cultivation and agriculture	Golson , Denham, Hughes, Swadling, & Muke (2017); Denham (2018)
	Kamapuk	–	RS	2050	170 km	5296–4628	2759–2364	Foraging camp (small game)	Christensen (1975)
	Tambul	–	Open	2170	200 km	4780–4095	4780–4095	Cultivation and agriculture	Golson (1997)
	Kana	–	Open	1480	130 km	3345–2954	518–292	Cultivation and agriculture	Muke & Mandui (2003)
	Tugeri	–	RS	2450	170 km	2716–2353	1705–1386	Foraging camp (small game)	Christensen (1975)
	Warrawau (Manton)	MCS	Open	1600	160 km	2712–2009	2712–2009	Cultivation and agriculture	Golson, Lampert, Wheeler, & Ambrose (1967)
	Minjigina	MCR	Open	2100	160 km	2703–2,117	2695–2008	Cultivation and agriculture	Powell (1970)
	Etpiti	–	RS	2200	170 km	2333–2002	1337–1067	Foraging camp (small game)	Christensen (1975)
	Puki Kumanga	MSP	RS	2200	165 km	1262–912	253–33	Foraging camp	Head & Gillieson (1989)
	Tembinde Kumanga	MSJ	RS	1400	160 km	256–31	256–31	Foraging camp (small game)	Head & Gillieson (1989)

	Rui Kumanga	MSA	RS	1100	160 km	253–33	545–0	Foraging camp (small game)	Head & Gillieson (1989)
Eastern	–	NFX	Open	1550	110 km	23,358–19,594	13,691–13,117	Settlement; stone working	Watson & Cole (1977)
	Batari	NBY	Cave	1300	115 km	21,740–18,642	916–698	Foraging camp (small game)	White (1972)
	Kafiavana	NBZ	RS	1350	90 km	13,309–11,404	5739–4877	Foraging camp (small game)	White (1972)
	–	NGH	Open	1700	100 km	4524–3779	4524–3779	Settlement; stone working	Watson & Cole (1977)
	Aibura	NAE	Cave	1640	100 km	4514–3888	914–555	Foraging camp (small game)	White (1972)
	–	NGG	Open	1680	100 km	3840–3264	3840–3264	Settlement; stone working	Watson & Cole (1977)
	–	NFB	Open	1650	105 km	3472–2991	428–0	Settlement; stone working	Watson & Cole (1977)
Southern	Tumbu's site	LOC	Open	1660	240 km	19,274–17,584	678–330	Cultivation and agriculture	Ballard (1995)
	Baragua	LOA	Open	1670	240 km	14,171–11,101	14,171–11,101	Cultivation and agriculture	Ballard (1995)
	Tari Gap	LOO	Open	1650	240 km	9471–9031	9471–9031	Peat formation; fire disturbance	Ballard (1995)
	Hiribite (Haeapugua)	LOJ	Open	1650	240 km	2967–1871	1291–961	Cultivation and agriculture	Ballard (1995)
	Walobi	LOI	Open	1660	240 km	2695–1526	2695–1526	Cultivation and agriculture	Ballard (1995)

(*continued*)

Table 31.1. Continued

Province	Site Name	Site Code	Type	M asl	~ Distance from Coast	Max age cal. BP	Min age cal. BP	Function/Significance	Source
	Mangobe's site	LOE	Open	1690	240 km	1508–1174	1508–1174	Cultivation and agriculture	Ballard (1995)
	Waya Egeanda	LOQ	Cave	1650	240 km	1516–783	639–0	Foraging camp	Ballard (1995)
	Mabu Yangome	LOF	Open	1650	240 km	1290–1010	1290–1010	Cultivation and agriculture	Ballard (1995)
	Embo Egeanda	LOL	RS	1670	240 km	794–317	426–0	Burial	Ballard (1995)
	Baya's site	LOB	Open	1660	240 km	671–0	671–0	Cultivation and agriculture	Ballard (1995)
	Birimanda	LOH	Open	1660	240 km	429–0	429–0	Ritual centre	Ballard (1995)
Madang	Wañelek	JAO	Open	1650	110 km	19,265–17,199	267–20	Settlement; trade post; gardening; axe manufacture	Bulmer (1977); Gaffney, Summerhayes et al. (2015)
Jiwaka	Waim	WAA	Open	2100	120 km	7421–7279	4288–4088	Settlement; ground stone tool manufacture; plant processing; string bag manufacture	Shaw et al. (2020)
West Papua	Mapala	–	RS	3966	90 km	6475–5928	6475–5928	Foraging camp (small game)	Hope & Hope (1976)
	Let. Kol. Haji Aswar Hamid camp	–	RS	3450	95 km	908–666	666–908	Foraging camp (small game)	Hope & Hope (1976)

seeds, not only *Castanopsis* nuts, but also those of *Elaeocarpus, Sloanea, Finschia,* and *Sterculia.* In higher altitudes between 2000 and 3000 m asl, several species of *Pandanus* would have been variably available (Summerhayes, Leavesley, & Fairbairn 2009), along-side fruits like *Astelia alpina, Podocarpus amarus,* and *Rubus* spp (Fairbairn et al. 2006). Although it has previously been thought that long-term occupation in the montane forests was not possible prior to the cultivation of crops (e.g., Sillitoe 2002), the scope of what we now understand rainforest foragers may have eaten can be expanded to include this wide variety of nuts and fruits, along with leafy vegetal matter, fern shoots and roots, mosses and herbs, terrestrial snails, insects, and grubs.

Starch grains on some of the Ivane stone tools demonstrate that mobile groups potentially provisioned themselves, taking wild yams with them from the coast into the mountains for what must have been multi-day or multi-week trips (Summerhayes et al. 2010). More recently in the Holocene, hunters moving into the high-altitude subalpine grasslands of Mt Jaya provisioned themselves with the nuts of *Pandanus julianettii,* which can be smoked and preserved (Hope & Hope 1976). These foods would have supplemented the ready-to-hand plant foods of the montane beech forests.

It is unlikely that highland vegetal resources alone could have supported human subsistence. The use of snares for capturing hard-to-find rodents, birds, and marsupials (Dwyer 1974), and pit traps for larger animals such as cassowaries (Evans 2000), may have been key to maintaining reliable protein sources as people moved within the montane forests. In open grasslands, several species of large-bodied, but now extinct, marsupial megafauna were likely hunted as a source of animal protein as well as by-products such as fur. At Nombe cave on Mt Elimbari, the earliest archaeological deposits, including a waisted tool, edge-ground axe, and ochre dating to 25,500–19,600 years ago (Mountain 1991a; Denham & Mountain 2016), are tentatively associated with the remains of a diprotodontid, a marsupial wolf (*Thylacinus cynocephalus*), a tree kangaroo (*Dendrologus noibano*), and giant kangaroos (*Protemnodon nombe, Protemnodon tumbuna*) (Flannery, Mountain, & Aplin 1983), while a marsupial wolf (*Thylacinus* sp.) was also identified in Early Holocene levels downslope at Kiowa (van Deusen 1963). Fossil sites from around the highlands also indicate that early hunters overlapped chronologically with a number of other diprotodontids (e.g., *Hulitherium tomasetti, Maokopia ronaldii*), as well as giant kangaroos in the subalpine grasslands, where deliberate burning was likely used as a mode of capture (Hope, Flannery, & Boeardi 1993; Menzies & Ballard 1994). Just prior to the LGM, the largest megafauna all but disappeared from northern Sahul. However, large ground rats (*Mallomys*), bandicoots (*Peroryctes*), echidna (*Zaglossus* spp.), macropods (*Thylogale*), brush turkeys (*Aepypodius* spp.), dwarf cassowaries (*Casuarius benneti*), quails (*Excalfactoria chinensis* and *Coturnix ypsilophora*), and various amphibians and reptiles remained common throughout the Holocene, often up to the subalpine zone, alongside arboreal species such as possums (Pseudocheiridae), cuscus (Phalangeridae), and tree kangaroos (*Dendrologus* spp.). We see many of these animals being preferentially targeted at the majority of rock shelter and cave sites after the LGM and throughout the Early to Mid-Holocene (Sutton, Mountain, Aplin, Bulmer, & Denham 2009). The eggs of many larger birds such as cassowary were also commonly collected, presumably for food or water storage at many rock shelter sites from the Late Pleistocene through to the Holocene (Gaffney et al. 2021). The cave roosts of large fruit bats, in particular, formed fixed nodes across the landscape that would have provided reliable meat, given that these animals can be captured easily using nets, arrows, slings, or stones (Mountain 1979). At Kiowa, for instance, it seems that the mega-bat *Aproteles bulmerae* was hunted extensively in the terminal Pleistocene and Early Holocene until it became locally extinct and people turned to hunting the smaller *Dobsonia magna* (Bulmer 1979).

Following river corridors and being originally familiar with collecting along the littoral zone, early foragers also made use of freshwater shellfish, including mussels, along with fish that can be caught by hand in deep, still waters. At Kiowa and Nombe on Mt Elimbari, we find evidence for freshwater shell in the Early Holocene, while this is increasingly common from the Mid-Holocene at Yuku, Batari, and Aibura (Gaffney, Summerhayes et al. 2019). Freshwater shells are absent in Pleistocene deposits, perhaps due to their fragility. Small fragments of freshwater fishbone have also been recovered from Nombe, but poor stratigraphic integrity impedes further comment (White 1972: 130).

The broad-spectrum monopolization of local highland resources is also visible in the stone tool record. In the Ivane Valley, large-hafted core tools with little modification and shaping were made on schist, quartz, metasediment, and greywacke (Ford 2017). Based on geological surveys, all of these raw materials were collected from the immediate landscape, indicating that the Late Pleistocene toolmakers had rapidly explored and experimented with local lithic resources (Ford 2011). At Kiowa and Nombe in the Central Ranges, lithic sequences from the terminal Pleistocene through to the Late Holocene document a similarly rapid adoption of locally abundant river argillite and basalt, followed by gradual modifications to raw material procurement strategies as people more intensively used the shelters and incorporated wider varieties of local materials into their toolmaking repertoires (Evans & Mountain 2005; Gaffney, Ford, & Summerhayes 2015).

The nature of lithic production itself was ecologically variable and constrained by the underlying lithology. For instance, in the Owen Stanley Range, apart from a baked siliceous metasediment, the area is devoid of high-quality siliceous materials like chert (Ford 2017), while much of the Central Ranges are replete with high-quality argillite, chert, chalcedony, jasper, and limestone, which can be collected from rivers or throughout the forest. Ethnographic descriptions of lithic procurement in the Central Ranges suggest that raw material provisioning is uncommon, as good-quality chert nodules can often be found in a search time of less than ten minutes (Sillitoe & Hardy 2003). This lack of lithic provisioning is mirrored in much of the archaeological evidence both from the Owen Stanley and the Central Ranges (Evans & Mountain 2005; Ford 2017; Gaffney, Ford et al. 2015).

Functionally, most highland lithics can broadly be described as scrapers (White 1969) or amorphous flake and core tools (Evans & Mountain 2005). Many of these tools were likely used within a broader production sequence related to the manufacture and maintenance of wooden, bamboo, and bone implements, which dominate ethnographic assemblages (Sillitoe 1988; Watson 1995). Although there are very few wooden artefacts preserved in highland sites, bone tools are noted from most rock shelters and include awls, points, and needles made from long bones and ribs, and spatulae made from larger splinters often from cassowary (Bulmer 1966a; White 1972). Other lithics were used to butcher animals (Brass 1993; Ford 2017), and, later in time, to carve shell valuables (Bartlett 1964). Larger stone tools, such as 'waisted blades', which are found in most Late Pleistocene sites such as Kosipe, Nombe, and Yuku (Figure 31.3), would likely have been hafted and used for heavy-duty activities, including root clearance, ring-barking, digging for tubers, and grubbing (Bulmer 2005; Groube 1989).

HIGH-ALTITUDE CULTIVATION AND SETTLEMENT

Following postglacial climatic amelioration, people's adaptation to highland landscapes, and the plant resources within them, transformed dramatically. During the Early to Mid-Holocene, some communities came to target economically important, herbaceous plants that had been increasingly managed since the Late Pleistocene, developing forms of cultivation based on the vegetative propagation of aroids (*Colocasia esculenta*), bananas (*Musa* spp.), cane grasses (*Saccharum* spp., *Setaria palmifolia*), leafy vegetables, and yams (*Dioscorea* spp.). Where these transformations took place, as people increasingly tethered their lifeways to cultivation practices, they were associated with major reconfigurations to social life and landscape use (Denham & Haberle 2008; Shaw et al. 2020). However, many subsistence economies remained diverse and included multilayered strategies of arboriculture and tuber exploitation, alongside the collection of plants and animals from the montane rainforests.

Archaeological evidence for Holocene plant exploitation and agriculture in the highlands derives primarily from a single site, Kuk Swamp, situated at 1560 m asl in the Upper Wahgi Valley (Golson 1977; Golson et al. 2017), with supplementary evidence deriving from other sites in the vicinity such as Manton and Mugamamp (Denham & Haberle 2008; Golson 1982). The Upper Wahgi sites indicate that anthropogenic manipulations to wetlands began to expedite plant exploitation around 10,000 years ago, with the incorporation of shifting cultivation throughout the Early Holocene, followed by mounded cultivation from 7000–6400 years ago, and ditched drainage from around 4400–4000 years ago (Denham et al. 2003). However, rather than documenting a linear succession of increasingly complex agronomic technologies, the evidence attests to a sequentially expanding repertoire of subsistence practices, whereby forms of plant exploitation and cultivation of varying duration, intensity, and frequency persisted through many millennia. Today, periodic exploitation of *Pandanus* groves, shifting cultivation in montane rainforest, mounded cultivation in montane grasslands, and ditched

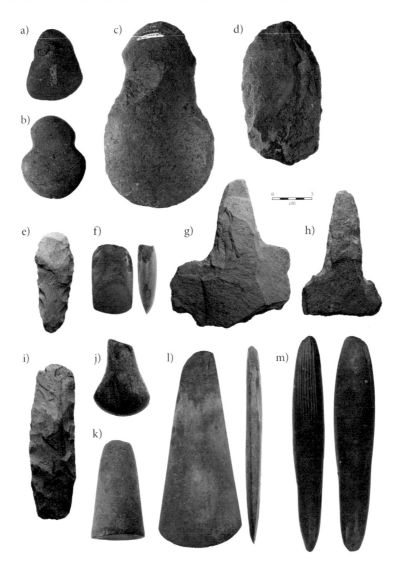

FIGURE 31.3. Formal lithic categories from highland archaeological sites: (a) ground waisted implement, MRK site, Baiyer Valley area, surface collection; (b) Holocene unifacially flaked and ground waisted implement, Yuku, Level 3C-D; (c) Probable Early Holocene waisted implement with unifacial flaking made on large cobble, Yuku, Level 4D-E; (d) Probable Early Holocene large unifacial lithic, Yuku, Level 4D-E; (e) axe preform made on flake, Wañelek, ≥3200–3300 years old; (f) Late Holocene polished lenticular axe, Wañelek; (g) stemmed slate tool, Wañelek, <2950–3850 years old; (h) stemmed slate tool, Kaironk Valley, surface collection; (i) axe preform, Wañelek, ≥3200–3300 years old; (j) pestle fragment with silica gloss on convex working surface, surface collection, Kaironk Valley; (k) pestle fragment with silica gloss on concave working surface, surface collection, Kaironk Valley; (l) recent planilateral axe, collected c. 1973 in Kaironk Valley; (m) recent bark-cloth beater, collected 1960, Chuave, Chimbu Province (artefacts collected by Susan Bulmer; photographs by Dylan Gaffney).

cultivation in wetlands are all practiced by communities living on the floors of the inter-montane valleys (Bourke & Harwood 2009; Denham 2018).

Several key starch-rich plants appeared in 10,000-year-old contexts at Kuk Swamp, including edible bananas, taro, and yams (Bowdery 1999; Fullagar, Field, Denham, & Lentfer 2006; Wilson 1985). However, it is not clear whether these plants were first culti-vated in the highlands or whether they were brought by cultivators from lower altitudes (compare Yen 1995 and Denham 2018). A comparative agricultural chronology has not been reconstructed for the lowlands, which has relied heavily on archaeobotanical evidence of tree fruit and nut exploitation (Fairbairn 2005; Yen 1996). Moreover, the domestication status of many plants cultivated in the highlands itself, in both the past and present, is unclear, and although present-day communities often differentiate be-tween plants grown by people and those that grow themselves (Sillitoe 1983), people also transplant wild and feral plants into gardens and adventitiously incorporate sponta-neous, sexually reproducing progeny into their cultivated stock (Powell 1982; Kennedy & Clarke 2004). Nonetheless, several crops indigenous to New Guinea—diploid ba-nana cultivars, cane grasses, diploid taro cultivars, some yam cultivars, and several leafy vegetables (e.g., *Rungia klossii, Oenanthe javanica*)—were likely domesticated through vegetative propagation on the island, even though there is currently no clear genetic or archaeobotanical evidence tracking the emergence and fixation of domestication traits for any crop through time. The absence of domestication traits largely reflects a lack of archaeobotanical investigation; however, such traits are likely to be more plastic in veg-etatively propagated crops than in most cereals, legumes, fruits, and nuts (Denham et al. 2020).

The elaboration of cultivation practices through time is mirrored in the sequential adoption of crops introduced to the highlands, whether lowland plants or those brought to New Guinea from elsewhere. Although the timing of most plant introductions is un-known, with only a relative chronology inferred from a few radiocarbon dates, wild plant distributions, and degrees of cultural entanglement, ancient introductions likely included gourds (*Lagenaria siceraria, Benincasa hispida*), kudzu (*Pueraria lobata*), and winged bean (*Psophocarpus tetragonolobus*), with slightly more recent introductions having included triploid cultivars of banana and taro, as well as polyploid sugarcane cultivars (*Saccharum officinarum*). Perhaps the most significant crop introduction rele-vant to understanding the character of many modern highland societies is the sweet po-tato (*Ipomoea batatas*), a South American domesticate likely introduced within the past 500 years to New Guinea (Roullier, Benoit, McKey, & Lebot 2013). The incorporation of crops into highland agricultural practices continues today, with maize (*Zea mays*), manioc (*Manihot esculenta*), and potato (*Solanum tuberosum*) introduced within the past hundred years.

No indigenous animal was domesticated in New Guinea. The three animal domesticates present in the Pacific prior to European contact—chicken (*Gallus gallus*), dog (*Canis familiaris*), and pig (*Sus scrofa*)—were all introduced to the circum-New Guinea islands within the past 3500–3000 years (Kirch 1997; Manne et al. 2020). Despite putative early dates for the introduction of dogs and pigs to New Guinea (Bulmer 1966b), these animals were likely marginal to highland subsistence practices until the past 1200 years or so, with chickens being extremely marginal to subsistence until the last few decades (Sutton et al. 2009). Although dogs were largely used for hunting (Sillitoe 2002), pigs became central to the intensification of exchange networks (Strathern 1971), ritual cycles (Rappaport 1968), and low-level stratification in the form of big-man social institutions within the last few hundred years (Modjeska 1982).

Human societies were transformed alongside the changing capacities of specific crops and animals, especially in their potential to maintain sustained year-round settlement and increase the altitudinal limits of production. Although Pleistocene foragers seem to have always moved in and out of the highlands, seasonality and cold temperatures, especially during the LGM, probably discouraged the establishment of year-round settlements in most areas. For instance, the Ivane Valley was abandoned (Summerhayes et al. 2010), whereas other places like the NFX site in the Asaro Valley (Watson & Cole 1977), 500 m lower in altitude, continued to be occasionally frequented. However, as climates warmed at the start of the Holocene and the highlands became increasingly habitable, many rock shelter and cave sites were newly occupied (Figure 31.2), suggesting that mobility ranges gradually shrank, and some populations focussed exclusively on New Guinea's interior. This settlement change is supported by whole-genome sequencing, which suggests that genetic separation from the coast had occurred by at least 10,000 years ago (Bergström 2017: 49).

Although wooden structures may tentatively be present immediately following the LGM at NFX in the Asaro Valley (Huff 2016b: 40; Watson & Cole 1977: 194) and Wañelek in the Kaironk Valley (Bulmer 1973), the first clear archaeological evidence for fixed longer-term settlements at these locations date from c. 5050–3800 years ago (Watson & Cole 1977; Bulmer 1991; Denham 2014; Shaw et al. 2020). The antiquity of these early settlements corresponds, albeit broadly, with the earliest rectilinear ditch networks at Kuk, dating to c. 4400–4000 years ago (Denham 2005), and these Mid-Holocene innovations may be suggestive of increasingly fixed territoriality, as some social groups became embedded in specific parts of the landscape. For example, permanent ditched field systems were probably not ubiquitous. Rather, they would have been focussed on wetlands on the floors of certain intermontane valleys and entailed relatively large investments of labour with recurrent maintenance. Such requirements would have been enabled by, and in turn would have enabled, more permanent occupation of specific places. Conversely, preexisting swidden cultivation in montane forests and mound cultivation in grasslands did not necessarily tie people to fixed locales for extended periods. As yet, contemporary Mid-Holocene settlements have not been documented adjacent to cultivated wetlands, and highly territorial, sedentary groups were probably localized phenomena.

Moreover, the introduction of cold-resistant cultivars encouraged the clearance of forests at higher altitudes as populations shifted upslope, which occurred gradually over the Holocene in many areas (Hope 2014). For instance, the late introduction of sweet potato (*Ipomoea batatas*), a crop that yields better than taro (*Colocasia*) in high elevations and poorer soils (Bayliss-Smith 1985), has allowed cultivators to push more permanent settlements to around 2850 m asl in Chimbu, Enga, and Tari. Later, with the colonial introduction of the potato (*Solanum tuberosum*), Dani groups were able to settle above 3000 m (Mitton 1983).

NETWORKS OF EXCHANGE AND POLITICAL TRANSFORMATION

The physical geography of the highlands was an important factor in shaping exchange networks and intergroup connectivity. A number of precipitous alpine ranges acted as effective isolators—encouraging insularity within the island's interior—while river valleys and ridgelines served as arteries connecting different communities, both within the highlands and between the mountains and the coast. Mapping out the nature of these connections in the past is crucial to understanding how material culture, people, and ideas flowed through the landscape, and also how emergent political and social systems responded to the uneven distribution of these elements.

Early on, Bulmer and Bulmer (1964) conjectured that there were only small-scale population migrations into the highlands after sustained Holocene settlement. The historical record contains abundant examples of these movements, which were usually prompted by warfare or shifting trade networks (Allen 2013). Small groups of secondary dispersers often encounter 'high-density blocking', a process whereby new populations fail to become established genetically due to the overwhelming genetic diversity of original founder populations (Waters, Fraser, & Hewitt 2013). This may account for patterning in the genomic data. One cause for this isolationism, leading to social and biological similarities across the highlands, was likely to be increases in population density throughout the Holocene and concomitant pressures on resource patches. Another likely cause was the prevalence of malaria in lowland forests below 1000 m asl, which would have discouraged the movement of large populations from the malaria-free highland zones (Groube 1993).

Despite this major shift towards demographic isolation, trade and exchange networks were established throughout the highlands, and between the highlands and the coast, meaning that the montane zone was never isolated in a material sense (Summerhayes 2019). In fact, fully polished stone axes came to be traded extensively throughout the highland valleys in the Mid- to Late Holocene from several major quarry sites (Burton 1984; Chappell 1966; Ford & Hiscock, this volume; see fig. 3L) and sometimes interlinked with coastal exchange systems (Rhoads & Mackenzie 1991). Moreover, ground stone pestles and mortars are found throughout the eastern half of the highlands and into the Bismarck Archipelago, indicating maritime interaction networks indirectly connecting highland trade networks to interisland systems during the Mid-Holocene (Swadling, Wiessner, & Tumu 2008; Swadling, this volume; see Figure 31.3j–k). Given the importance of nut-bearing trees in the lower montane forests, Ralph Bulmer (1964) suggested that many of these artefacts were originally associated with cracking acorns from the mixed-oak forests, although they may have taken on a multipurpose role as they were redistributed to fringe highland and coastal areas, for instance in the preparation of taro (Swadling & Hide 2005). Recently excavated pestles from the Waim site in the Jimi Valley, dating to 5050–4200 years ago, may confirm a multifunctional use for the processing of bananas (*Musa* cf. *ingens*), tree nuts (*Castanopsis acuminatissima*), palms (*Hydriastele* spp.), sugarcane (*Saccharum officinarum*), and tubers (*Dioscorea pentaphylla, Dioscorea alata, Pueraria lobata*) (Shaw et al. 2020), while mortars from Joe's Garden in the Ivane Valley indicate the processing of nuts (*Castanopsis acuminatissima*) and tubers (*Pueraria lobata*) during the Mid- to Late Holocene around 4400 years ago (Field et al. 2020).

Marine shell valuables came to be traded up from the coast into the highlands. This trade may have begun in the Early Holocene at Kafiavana, situated along a tributary to the Asaro River Valley, but many other areas, for instance, Chimbu, did not come into the purview of the marine shell trade until the Late Holocene (Gaffney et al. 2019). This difference implies that, rather than accumulating gradually, following cultivation in the Wahgi, contacts with the coast were active in occasional pulses and lend further support to the idea that the emergence of big-men societies, dependent on the accumulation and gifting of shell valuables, along with pigs and other items, may only be a recent phenomenon.

Most cross-country trading involved engaging in frequent local exchanges and tapping into a wider network of extended linkages between the interior, hinterland middlemen, and coastal groups (Denham 2014; see Harding 1967 and Hughes 1977 for ethnographic examples). Several fringe highland zones, for instance, those in the foothills of the Jimi and Yuat Valleys (Gorecki & Gillieson 1989) and those in the Kaironk and Simbai Valleys in Madang (Bulmer 1977) may have been home to middlemen trading communities that redistributed products like polished axes, furs, salt, string bags, and feathers, between the intermontane valleys and lower altitudes. Wañelek, which occupies a strategic position overlooking the Kaironk Valley, may have been home to one such community. At this site, polished oval-lenticular axes (Figure 31.3f), tanged slate hoes (Figure 31.3g–h), drills, and abundant chert debitage (Bulmer 1991) are indicative of local axe production (Figure 31.3e and 3i), alongside horticulture, woodworking, and forest clearance. Pottery that geologically derives from the New Guinea foothills and the northeast coast was also traded into the site from about 3000 years ago (Gaffney, Summerhayes et al. 2015). This evidence is supported by surface finds of Fergusson Island obsidian (Gaffney, Ford, & Summerhayes 2016), which may have been traded up the Yuat, Sepik, and Ramu Rivers from the north coast, having been distributed along maritime networks (Golitko, Schauer, & Terrell 2012). At the nearby Waim site, the exchange of obsidian originally from West New Britain alongside local planilateral and lenticular axe production was active by 5050–4200 years ago (Shaw et al. 2020). During the Mid- to Late Holocene, the high sea stand was raised by several metres, producing a large inland sea at the mouth of the Sepik and Ramu Rivers

(Chappell 2005), which meant that the highlands were substantially closer to the coast than they are today. Pottery that may also date to the third–fourth millennium before present has been described from the Eastern Highlands site of NFB (Huff 2016a), alongside Fergusson Island obsidian (Watson 1986), and indicates similar materials passed into the highlands along the Markham Valley. At other highland sites, ceramics and obsidian are either absent or occur much later in the record, suggesting that not all valley systems were connected with the coastal trade linkages at the same time.

Genetic evidence indicates that there was never substantial direct gene flow between coastal populations with East Asian signatures (a proxy for what is often assumed to represent Austronesian language-speaking pottery makers) and highland groups (Bergström 2017: 41). There is, however, some evidence for minor movements of lowland individuals with East Asian ancestry into the highlands, and the closest genetically related lowlanders derive from the East Sepik region (Bergström 2017: 45). This genetic evidence supports running interpretations that the earliest ceramics to enter into the highlands were traded in from production groups working on the northeast coast and around the Sepik foothills, as opposed to marking the incursion of pottery-making communities that then adapted to the mountains (Summerhayes 2019).

The same trade networks that moved pottery, obsidian, and shells may have also allowed for the exchange of cultivars, which could have been propagated by established vegecultural practices, replanting the cuttings of parts of the plants. These practices have implications for the hypothetical movement of lowland crops into the highlands during the Early Holocene; the movement of mainland crops to the coast and islands during the Mid- to Late Holocene; reconfigurations to ditch networks in the Wahgi Valley (Bayliss-Smith 2007); and the introduction of sweet potatoes (*Ipomoea batatas*) to the highlands. Sweet potato cultivation in particular led to a major transformative period in the long-term social history of the highlands. The agronomic advantages of the sweet potato over preexisting root crops—primarily bananas, kudzu, taro, and yams—provided greater yields to fuel demographic growth and social upscaling, as well as fodder for expanding pig populations. Some consider the character of highland big-man societies to largely result from this 'Ipomoean Revolution' (Ballard, Brown, Bourke, & Harwood 2005), whereby ambitious individuals began to exceed the capacity of home production by recruiting larger numbers of pigs reared from this new crop that grew far more effectively in a variety of soils and altitudes (Golson 1982). The expectation of an increased return (interest) on gifted products meant that the number of debts would far exceed the number of things in circulation (Strathern 1971), obligating people to attend to ongoing pig rearing, as well as the import of valuables from outside of the highlands and the production of axes and other sought-after items within the highlands, as a way to temporarily bring about social equilibrium. Certainly, many elements of social praxis, such as larger-scale exchange ceremonies, as well as more pervasive sexual divisions of labour and residence—with distinctive men's houses and other houses for women, together with children and pigs—either originated or became more marked during this period. For instance, numerous house sites at Kuk dating to the past few hundred years, the post-Ipomoean period, reflect continuities with ethnographically observed designs and functions (Gorecki 1982; Golson 2017). Further, the House A-F and P-Q Complex contains archaeological remains of sweet potato and sugarcane, together with pig bones and a piece of fired ceramic (Lewis, Denham, & Golson 2016).

Discussion: Social Transformations, Tempo, and Asymmetry

As amongst montane and rainforest communities in other tropical regions (e.g., Roberts & Amano 2019; Stewart, Parker, Dewar, Morley, & Allott 2016), people living in the New Guinea Highlands were adaptively flexible and actively engineered new niches for themselves to inhabit by limiting or enabling forest growth, vegetatively propagating crops, digging irrigation channels, rearing domestic animals, quarrying lithic material, trading material objects, and building wooden structures (see Florin & Carah 2018). By investing in these activities throughout the highland ranges, people increasingly focussed their movements within the interior, which came to support a population that today is genetically and linguistically distinct from the coast. However, rather than documenting a linear succession of subsistence thresholds common across the highland ranges, leading highly mobile foragers in the Late Pleistocene to become more sedentary agriculturalists in the Holocene, the archaeological record attests to intraregional variation in the nature and tempo of sociotechnical transformations and a sequential diversification of subsistence practices that overlapped and persisted through time. In the Upper Wahgi during the Early Holocene, hunting and gathering along montane slopes continued even as agronomic technologies emerged in the intermontane valley floor. Forest clearance gradually made its way upslope (Christensen 1975), while in other areas foraging likely remained a primary focus of subsistence, alongside different strategies of arboriculture, into the Mid- to Late Holocene. Although forest clearance occurred during the terminal Pleistocene and Early Holocene in western parts of the Central Ranges, evident at places like Kuk along with several other palaeoenvironmental sites (see Haberle et al., this volume), in the Maoke Range to the west, major clearances only occurred in the Mid-Holocene (Haberle, Hope, & van der Kaars 2001). Similarly, Hope (2014) notes that in areas further east, such as the slopes of Mt Wilhelm, clearances occurred around 1000 years ago and may reflect a late-stage expansion of settlements along the Upper Chimbu Valley. These differential rates of landscape modification are also noted in isotopic studies from the nearby Mt Elimbari, which demonstrate that people continued to hunt forest species under closed canopy even into the Late Holocene (Roberts, Gaffney, Lee-Thorp, & Summerhayes 2017). In contrast, on Mt Jaya there is evidence from the regrowth of shrub overlying previously burnt terrain that hunting using fire may have ceased around 2500 years ago, allowing the slow revegetation of montane forests (Hope & Hope 1976).

Simultaneous to the emergence of these diverse settlement and subsistence strategies, substantial time and energy were spent on generating trade links throughout the highland ranges and between the highlands and the coast, expanding people's material connectivity beyond their range of mobility. In a series of pulses throughout the Mid- to Late Holocene, trade between the coast and the highlands strengthened and may have increasingly encouraged people to attend to exchange relationships as a way of materializing prestige and reconfiguring social order. The degree to which highland groups produced resources from their own land or financed resource acquisition through delayed reciprocal arrangements with others may, in part, relate to the social group's geographic position—whether in highly productive cropping areas, or in more peripheral, low-productivity areas. Moreover, areas of low-population density or those historically geared toward foraging may have become linked in with highland exchange networks later than wide intermontane valleys with large populations practicing wetland cropping.

On a macroregional scale, the highland data attests to asymmetrical transformations to society and landscape use. We can model this development as the generation of a patchwork, formed by threading together different local practices that are individually dynamic but without direction as a whole (following Law & Mol 1995). Paula Brown (1978: 11), describing the Chimbu area during the mid-twentieth century, noted that moving through the highland valleys was to move between a patchwork of forests, grasslands, garden plots, and fallow areas, which hung together in a complex web of social relationships. In this area, the plots attended to by one clan grouping were distributed across different parts of the landscape, meaning that individuals and family groups had access to a wide variety of ecologies: some land for growing crops, some for allowing pigs to roam, some in which economically important trees could grow, and other land for foraging. Similarly, within the New Guinea Highlands generally, locally distinct social trajectories emerged and diversified within different valley systems, which were variably used for hunting and gathering, cultivation, and forest management, with some areas lying abandoned or sparsely frequented and others becoming hubs for intensive agricultural production. Human mobility and trade routes connected these disparate valley systems, which materialized the links in the highland patchwork; some connections endured for many millennia, whereas others were likely to have been fleeting. These asymmetrical processes of diversification and connectivity have contributed to the variability in society, subsistence, and technology that can be observed amongst highland New Guinea societies today.

Acknowledgements

We thank Ian McNiven and Bruno David for the invitation to contribute to the volume, as well the anonymous reviewers for their constructive comments. Thanks also to Glenn Summerhayes for providing in press manuscripts and access to the Bulmer collection.

NOTES

1. Since 1959, when Susan Bulmer, then an MA student at the University of Auckland pioneered systematic survey and excavation. This involved first excavating a small and very recent house site named Yaramanda, followed by more substantial excavations at Yuku starting 1959 and then Kiowa starting in 1960 (Gaffney et al. 2016, citing Bulmer 1966a).
2. This is an ecological rather than an ethnographic approach, and includes not just the 'Highlands' cultural zone, which usually refers exclusively to the peoples of the Central Ranges, but also to all groups living in montane and subalpine areas on the island of New Guinea.

REFERENCES

Allen, B. (1983). Human geography of Papua New Guinea. *Journal of Human Evolution, 12* (1), 3–23.

Allen, B. (2013). Papua New Guinea: Indigenous migrations in the recent past. In I. Ness (Ed.), *The encyclopedia of global human migration* (pp. 1–6). Hoboken, NJ: Blackwell.

Ballard, C. (1995). *The death of a great land: Ritual, history and subsistence revolution in the Southern Highlands of Papua New Guinea* (PhD thesis). Australian National University, Canberra.

Ballard, C., Brown P., Bourke, R. M., & Harwood, T. (Eds.) (2005). *The sweet potato in Oceania: A reappraisal*. Ethnology Monographs 19 and Oceania Monograph 56. Sydney: University of Sydney.

Bartlett, H. K. (1964). *Note on flint implements found near Nipa, Central Papuan Highlands*. Adelaide: South Australian Museum.

Bayliss-Smith, T. (1985). Pre-Ipomoean agriculture in the New Guinea Highlands above 2000 metres: Some experimental data on taro cultivation. In I. Farrington (Ed.), *Prehistoric intensive agriculture in the tropics* (pp. 285–320). Oxford: British Archaeological Reports, International Series 232, Part I.

Bayliss-Smith, T. (2007). The meaning of ditches: Interpreting the archaeological record using insights from ethnography. In T. P. Denham, J. Iriarte, & L. Vrydaghs (Eds.), *Rethinking agriculture: Archaeological and ethnoarchaeological perspectives* (pp. 126–148). Walnut Creek, CA: Left Coast Press.

Bergström, A. (2017). *Genomic insights into the human population history of Australia and New Guinea* (PhD thesis). University of Cambridge, Cambridge.

Bergström, A., Oppenheimer, S. J., Mentzer, A. J., Auckland, K., Robson, K., Attenborough, R., . . . Xue, Y. (2017). A Neolithic expansion, but strong genetic structure, in the independent history of New Guinea. *Science, 357* (6356), 1160–1163.

Bird, M. I., Condie, S. A., O'Connor, S., O'Grady, D., Reepmeyer, C., Ulm, S., . . . Bradshaw, C. J. (2019). Early human settlement of Sahul was not an accident. *Scientific Reports, 9* (8220), 1–10.

Bourke, R. M., & Harwood, T. (Eds.). (2009). *Food and agriculture in Papua New Guinea*. Canberra: ANU E Press.

Bourke, R. M., & Vlassak, V. (2004). *Estimates of food crop production in Papua New Guinea*. Canberra: Land Management Group, Department of Human Geography, Research School of Pacific Studies, Australian National University.

Bowdery, D. (1999). Phytoliths from tropical sediments: Reports from Southeast Asia and Papua New Guinea. *Bulletin of the Indo-Pacific Prehistory Association, 18*, 159–168.

Brass, L. G. (1993). A residue and use-wear analysis of ethnographic and archaeological stone artefacts from the New Guinea Highlands (Unpublished BA Honours thesis). University of Sydney, Sydney.

Brass, L. J. (1941). Stone Age agriculture in New Guinea. *Geographical Review, 31* (4), 555–569.

Brookfield, H., & Allen, B. (1989). High-altitude occupation and environment. *Mountain Research and Development, 9* (3), 201–209.

Brown, P. (1978). *Highland peoples of New Guinea*. Cambridge: Cambridge University Press.

Bulmer, R. N. (1964). Edible seeds and prehistoric stone mortars in the Highlands of East New Guinea. *Man, 64*, 147–150.

Bulmer, S. (1964). Radiocarbon dates from New Guinea. *Journal of the Polynesian Society, 73* (3), 327–328.

Bulmer, S. (1966a). *The prehistory of the Australian New Guinea Highlands* (Unpublished MA dissertation). University of Auckland, Auckland.

Bulmer, S. (1966b). Pig bone from two archaeological sites in the New Guinea Highlands. *Journal of the Polynesian Society, 75* (4), 504–505.

Bulmer, S. (1973). *Notes on 1972 excavations at Wañelek, an open settlement site in the Kaironk Valley, Papua New Guinea*. Auckland: University of Auckland, Department of Anthropology Working Paper 29.

Bulmer, S. (1975). Settlement and economy in prehistoric Papua New Guinea: A review of the archaeological evidence. *Journal de la Société des Océanistes, 31* (46), 7–75.

Bulmer, S. (1977). Between the mountain and the plain: Prehistoric settlement and environment in the Kaironk Valley. In J. H. Winslow (Ed.), *The Melanesian environment* (pp. 61–73). Canberra: ANU Press.

Bulmer, S. (1979). Archaeological evidence of prehistoric faunal change in Highland Papua New Guinea. Unpublished Paper to Australian and New Zealand Association for the Advancement of Science Congress, Section 25A. Auckland.

Bulmer, S. (1991). Variation and change in stone tools in the Highlands of Papua New Guinea: The witness of Wañelek. In A. Pawley (Ed.), *Man and a half: Essays in Pacific anthropology and ethnobiology in honour of Ralph Bulmer* (pp. 470–478). Auckland: Polynesian Society.

Bulmer, S. (2005). Reflections in stone: Axes and the beginnings of agriculture in the Central Highlands of New Guinea. In A. Pawley, R. Attenborough, J. Golson, & R. Hide (Eds.), *Papuan pasts: Cultural, linguistic and biological histories of Papuan-speaking peoples* (pp. 387–450). Canberra: Pacific Linguistics.

Bulmer, R. N. (1968). The strategies of hunting in New Guinea. *Oceania, 38* (4), 302–318.

Bulmer, S., & Bulmer, R. (1964). The prehistory of the Australian New Guinea Highlands. *American Anthropologist, 66* (4), 39–76.

Burton, J. (1984). *The axe makers of the Wahgi* (PhD thesis). Australian National University, Canberra.

Chappell, J. (1966). Stone axe factories in the Highlands of East New Guinea. *Proceedings of the Prehistoric Society, 32*, 96–121.

Chappell, J. (2005). Geographic changes of coastal lowlands in the Papuan past. In A. Pawley, R. Attenborough, J. Golson, & R. Hide (Eds.), Papuan pasts: Cultural, linguistic and biological histories of Papuan-speaking peoples (pp. 525–540). Canberra: Pacific Linguistics.

Christensen, O. A. (1975). Hunters and horticulturalists: A preliminary report of the 1972–4 excavations in the Manim Valley, Papua New Guinea. *Mankind, 10* (1), 24–36.

Denham, T. P. (2005). Agricultural origins and the emergence of rectilinear ditch networks in the Highlands of New Guinea. In A. Pawley, R. Attenborough, J. Golson, & R. Hide (Eds.), *Papuan pasts: Cultural, linguistic and biological histories of Papuan-speaking peoples* (pp. 329–361). Canberra: Pacific Linguistics.

Denham, T. P. (2007). Exploiting diversity: Plant exploitation and occupation in the interior of New Guinea during the Pleistocene. *Archaeology in Oceania, 42,* 41–48.

Denham, T. (2011). Early agriculture and plant domestication in New Guinea and Island Southeast Asia. *Current Anthropology, 52*(S4), S379–S395.

Denham, T. P. (2014). New Guinea during the Holocene. In P. Bahn & C. Renfrew (Eds.), *The Cambridge world prehistory* (pp. 578–597). Cambridge: Cambridge University Press.

Denham, T. (2016a). Revisiting the past: Sue Bulmer's contribution to the archaeology of Papua New Guinea. *Archaeology in Oceania, 51* (S1), 5–10.

Denham, T. (2016b). Socio-environmental adaption to the montane rainforests of New Guinea. In M. Oxenham & H. Buckley (Eds.), *The Routledge handbook of bioarchaeology in Southeast Asia and the Pacific Islands* (pp. 409–426). Oxford: Routledge.

Denham, T. P. (2018). *Tracing early agriculture in the Highlands of New Guinea: Plot, mound and ditch.* Oxford: Routledge.

Denham, T. (2019). Reconsidering the 'Neolithic' at Manim rock shelter, Wurup Valley, Papua New Guinea. In M. Leclerc & J. Flexner (Eds.), *Archaeologies of Island Melanesia: Current approaches to landscape, exchange, and practice* (pp. 81–99). Terra Australis 51. Canberra: ANU Press.

Denham, T. P., Barton, H., Castillo, C., Crowther, A., Dotte-Sarout, E., Florin, A., . . . Fuller, D. Q. (2020). The domestication syndrome in vegetatively propagated field crops. *Annals of Botany, 125,* 581–597.

Denham, T. P., & Haberle, S. G. (2008). Agricultural emergence and transformation in the Upper Wahgi Valley during the Holocene: Theory, method and practice. *The Holocene, 18,* 499–514.

Denham, T. P., Haberle, S. G., Lentfer, C., Fullagar, R., Field, J., Therin, M., . . . Winsborough, B. (2003). Origins of agriculture at Kuk Swamp in the Highlands of New Guinea. *Science, 301,* 189–193.

Denham, T. P., & Mountain, M-J. (2016). Resolving some chronological problems at Nombe rock shelter in the Highlands of Papua New Guinea. *Archaeology in Oceania, 51* (S1), 73–83.

Dwyer, P. D. (1974). The price of protein: Five hundred hours of hunting in the New Guinea Highlands. *Oceania, 44* (4), 278–293.

Evans, B. R., & Mountain, M-J. (2005). Pasin bilong tumbuna: Archaeological evidence for early human activity in the Highlands of Papua New Guinea. In A. Pawley, R. Attenborough, J. Golson, & R. Hide (Eds.), *Papuan pasts: Cultural, linguistic and biological histories of Papuan-speaking peoples* (pp. 363–386). Canberra: Pacific Linguistics.

Evans, W. (2000). The role of the cassowary in adaptive subsistence in prehistoric Highlands New Guinea (Unpublished BA Honours thesis). The Australian National University, Canberra.

Fairbairn, A. (2005). An archaeobotanical perspective on Holocene plant use practices in lowland northern New Guinea. *World Archaeology, 37,* 487–502.

Fairbairn, A. S., Hope, G. S., & Summerhayes, G. R. (2006). Pleistocene occupation of New Guinea's Highland and subalpine environments. *World Archaeology, 38* (3), 371–386.

Feil, D. K. (1987). *The evolution of Highland Papua New Guinea societies.* Cambridge: Cambridge University Press.

THE ARCHAEOLOGY OF SOCIAL TRANSFORMATION   855

Feil, D. K. (1995). The evolution of highland Papua New Guinea societies: A reappraisal. *Bijdragen tot de Taal-, Land-en Volkenkunde, 151* (1), 23–43.

Field, J., Summerhayes, G. R., Luu, S., Coster, A., Ford, A., Mandui, H., . . . Kealhofer, L. (2020). Functional studies of a ground stone mortar reveal starchy tree nut and root exploitation in Mid-Holocene Highland New Guinea. *The Holocene, 30*(9), 1360–1374.

Flannery, T. F., Mountain, M-J., & Aplin, K. (1983). Quaternary kangaroos (*Macropodidae: Marsupialia*) from Nombe rock shelter, Papua New Guinea, with comments on the nature of megafaunal extinction in the New Guinea Highlands. *Proceedings of the Linnean Society of New South Wales, 107* (2), 75–97.

Flenley, J. R. (1984). Late Quaternary changes of vegetation and climate in the Malesian mountains. *Erdwissenschaftliche Forschung, 18*, 261–267.

Flenley, J. R., & Morley, R. J. (1978). A minimum age for the deglaciation of Mt Kinabalu, East Malaysia. *Modern Quaternary Research in Southeast Asia, 4*, 57–61.

Florin, S. A., & Carah, X. (2018). Moving past the 'Neolithic problem': The development and interaction of subsistence systems across Northern Sahul. *Quaternary International, 489*, 46–62.

Foley, W. A. (2000). The languages of New Guinea. *Annual Review of Anthropology, 29* (1), 357–404.

Ford, A. (2011). Learning the lithic landscape: Using raw material sources to investigate Pleistocene colonisation in the Ivane Valley, Papua New Guinea. *Archaeology in Oceania, 46* (2), 42–53.

Ford, A. (2017). Late Pleistocene lithic technology in the Ivane Valley: A view from the rainforest. *Quaternary International, 448*, 31–43.

Fullagar, R., Field, J., Denham, T. P., & Lentfer, C. (2006). Early and Mid Holocene processing of taro (*Colocasia esculenta*) and yam (*Dioscorea sp.*) at Kuk Swamp in the Highlands of Papua New Guinea. *Journal of Archaeological Science, 33*, 595–614.

Gaffney, D. (2020). Pleistocene water-crossings and adaptive flexibility within the *Homo* genus. *Journal of Archaeological Research.*

Gaffney, D., Ford, A., & Summerhayes, G. (2015). Crossing the Pleistocene–Holocene transition in the New Guinea Highlands: Evidence from the lithic assemblage of Kiowa Rockshelter. *Journal of Anthropological Archaeology, 39*, 223–246.

Gaffney, D., Ford, A., & Summerhayes, G. R. (2016). Sue Bulmer's legacy in Highland New Guinea: A re-examination of the Bulmer Collection and future directions. *Archaeology in Oceania, 51* (S1), 23–32.

Gaffney, D., Summerhayes, G. R., Ford, A., Scott, J. M., Denham, T., Field, J., & Dickinson, W. R. (2015). Earliest pottery on New Guinea mainland reveals Austronesian influences in Highland environments 3000 years ago. *PloS One, 10* (9), p.e0134497.

Gaffney, D., Summerhayes, G. R., Szabo, K., & Koppel, B. (2019). The emergence of shell valuable exchange in the New Guinea Highlands. *American Anthropologist, 121* (1), 30–47.

Gaffney, D., Summerhayes, G. R., Luu, S., Menzies, J., Douglass, K., Spitzer, M., & Bulmer, S. (2021). Small game hunting in montane rainforests: Specialised capture and broad spectrum foraging in the Late Pleistocene to Holocene New Guinea Highlands. *Quaternary Science Reviews, 253*, p.106742.

Golitko, M., Schauer, M., & Terrell, J. E. (2012). Identification of Fergusson Island obsidian on the Sepik coast of Northern Papua New Guinea. *Archaeology in Oceania, 47* (3), 151–156.

Golson, J. (1977). No room at the top: Agricultural intensification in the New Guinea Highlands. In J. Allen, J. Golson, & R. Jones (Eds.), *Sunda and Sahul: Prehistoric studies in Southeast Asia, Melanesia and Australia* (pp. 601–638). London: Academic Press.

Golson, J. (1982). The Ipomoean Revolution revisited: Society and sweet potato in the Upper Wahgi Valley. In A. Strathern (Ed.), *Inequality in New Guinea Highland societies* (pp. 109–136). Cambridge: Cambridge University Press.

Golson, J. (1997). The Tambul spade. In H. Levine & A. Ploeg (Eds.), *Work in progress: Essays in New Guinea Highlands ethnography in honour of Paula Brown Glick* (pp. 142–171). Oxford: Peter Lang.

Golson, J. (2017). Houses in and out of the swamp. In J. Golson, T. P. Denham, P. J. Hughes, P. Swadling, & J. Muke (Eds.), *Ten thousand years of cultivation at Kuk Swamp in the Highlands of Papua New Guinea* (pp. 325–350). Terra Australis 46. Canberra: ANU E Press.

Golson, J., Denham, T. P, Hughes, P. J., Swadling, P., & Muke, J. (Eds.). (2017). *Ten thousand years of cultivation at Kuk Swamp in the Highlands of Papua New Guinea*. Terra Australis 46. Canberra: ANU E Press.

Golson, J., & Gardner, D. S. (1990). Agriculture and sociopolitical organization in New Guinea Highlands prehistory. *Annual Review of Anthropology, 19* (1), 395–417.

Golson, J., Lampert R. J., Wheeler, J. M., & Ambrose, W. R. (1967). A note on carbon dates for horticulture in the New Guinea Highlands. *Journal of the Polynesian Society, 76* (3), 369–371.

Gorecki, P. (1982). *Ethnoarchaeology at Kuk: Problems in site formation process* (PhD thesis). University of Sydney, Sydney.

Groube, L. (1989). The taming of the rain forests: A model for Late Pleistocene forest exploitation in New Guinea. In D. Harris & G. Hillman (Eds.), *Foraging and farming: The evolution of plant exploitation* (pp. 292–304). London: Unwin Hyman.

Groube, L. M. (1993). Contradictions and malaria in Melanesian and Australian prehistory. In M. Spriggs, D. Yen, W. Ambrose, R. Jones, A. Thorne, & A. Andrews (Eds.), *A community of culture: The people and prehistory of the Pacific* (pp. 164–186). Canberra: Department Prehistory, Australian National University.

Haberle, S. (1993). Pleistocene vegetation change and early human occupation of a tropical mountainous environment. In B. Frankhauser & M. Spriggs (Eds.), *Sahul in review: Pleistocene archaeology in Australia, New Guinea and Island Melanesia* (pp. 109–122). Canberra: Department of Prehistory, Australian National University.

Haberle, S. G., Hope, G. S., & van der Kaars, S. (2001). Biomass burning in Indonesia and Papua New Guinea: Natural and human induced fire events in the fossil record. *Palaeogeography, Palaeoclimatology, Palaeoecology, 171* (3–4), 259–268.

Haberle, S. G., & Lusty, C. A. (2000). Can climate influence cultural development? A view through time. *Environment and History, 6* (3), 349–369.

Harding, T. G. (1967). *Voyagers of the Vitiaz Strait: A study of a New Guinea trade system*. Seattle: University of Washington Press.

Harris, E. C., & Hughes, P. J. (1978). An early agricultural system at Mugumamp Ridge, Western Highlands Province, Papua New Guinea. *Mankind, 11* (4), 437–444.

Head, J., & Gillieson, D. (1989). Radiocarbon dating - Resolution of contamination problems through stratigraphic correlation. In P. Gorecki & D. S. Gillieson (Eds.), *A crack in the spine: Prehistory and ecology of the Jimi-Yuat Valley, Papua New Guinea* (pp. 123–129). Townsville: James Cook University.

Hope, G. (2009). Environmental change and fire in the Owen Stanley Ranges, Papua New Guinea. *Quaternary Science Reviews, 28* (23–24), 2261–2276.

Hope, G. (2014). The sensitivity of the high mountain ecosystems of New Guinea to climatic change and anthropogenic impact. *Arctic, Antarctic, and Alpine Research, 46* (4), 777–786.

Hope, G., Flannery, T., & Boeardi (1993). A preliminary report of changing Quaternary mammal faunas in subalpine New Guinea. *Quaternary Research, 40* (1), 117–126.

Hope, G., & Haberle, S. (2005). The history of the human landscapes of New Guinea. In A. Pawley, R. Attenborough, J. Golson, & R. Hide (Eds.), *Papuan pasts: cultural, linguistic and biological histories of Papuan-speaking peoples* (pp. 541–554). Canberra: Pacific Linguistics.

Hope, G., & Hope, J. (1976). Man on Mt Jaya. In G. S. Hope, J. A. Peterson, I. Allison, & U. Radok (Eds.), *The equatorial glaciers of New Guinea: Results of the 1971–73 Australian Universities' Expeditions to Irian Jaya: Survey, glaciology, meteorology, biology and palaeoenvironments* (pp. 224–239). Rotterdam: AA Balkema.

Huff, J. (2016a). Revisiting NFB: Ceramic technology in the Eastern Highlands of Papua New Guinea at 3200 cal. BP. *Archaeology in Oceania, 51* (S1), 84–90.

Huff, J. (2016b). *Understanding changes in mobility and subsistence from terminal Pleistocene to Late Holocene in the Highlands of New Guinea through intensity of lithic reduction, changing site types, and paleoclimate* (PhD thesis). University of Washington, Seattle.

Hughes, I. (1977). *New Guinea Stone Age trade.* Terra Australis 3. Canberra: Australian National University, Research School of Pacific Studies.

Kawai, A. (2019). Navigation in the rainforest: The case of the Batek in the Upper Lebir River watershed, Malaysia. *People and Culture in Oceania, 34*, 1–23.

Kennedy, J., & Clarke, W. C. (2004). *Cultivated landscapes of the Southwest Pacific.* Canberra: RMAP, Australian National University

Kershaw, A. P., van der Kaars, S., Moss, P. T., & Wang, X. (2002). Quaternary records of vegetation, biomass burning, climate and possible human impact in the Indonesian-northern Australian region. In P. Kershaw, B. David, N. Tapper, D. Penny, & J. Brown (Eds.), *Bridging Wallace's Line: The environmental and cultural history and dynamics of the Australian-Southeast Asian region* (pp. 97–118). Stuttgart: Schweizerbart Science Publishers.

Kirch, P. V. (1997). *The Lapita peoples.* Oxford: Blackwell.

Langness, L. L. (1964). Some problems in the conceptualization of Highlands social structures. *American Anthropologist, 66* (4), 162–182.

Law, J., & Mol, A. (1995). Notes on materiality and sociality. *The Sociological Review, 43* (2), 274–294.

Lewis, T., Denham, T. P., & Golson, J. (2016). A renewed archaeological and archaeobotanical assessment of house sites at Kuk Swamp in the Highlands of Papua New Guinea. *Archaeology in Oceania, 51*(S1), 91–103.

Löffler, E. (1977). *Geomorphology of Papua New Guinea.* Canberra: Australian National University Press.

Manne, T., David, B., Petchey, F., Leavesley, M., Roberts, G., Szabó, K., . . . Richards, T. (2020). How long have dogs been in Melanesia? New evidence from Caution Bay, south coast of Papua New Guinea. *Journal of Archaeological Science: Reports, 30*, 102255.

McAlpine, J. R. (1983). *Climate of Papua New Guinea.* Canberra: Commonwealth Scientific and Industrial Research Organization in association with Australian National University Press.

Menzies, J. I., & Ballard, C. (1994). Some new records of Pleistocene megafauna from New Guinea. *Science in New Guinea, 20* (2–3), 113–139.

Mitton, R. D. (1983). *The lost world of Irian Jaya.* Oxford: Oxford University Press.

Modjeska, C. M. (1982). Production and inequality: Perspectives from Central New Guinea. In A. Strathern (Ed.), *Inequality in New Guinea Highland societies* (pp. 50–108). Cambridge: Cambridge University Press.

Moore, L. G., Fernando Armaza, V., Villena, M., & Vargas, E. (2002). Comparative aspects of high-altitude adaptation in human populations. In S. Lahiri, N. R. Prabhakar, & R. E. Forster (Eds.), *Oxygen sensing: Molecule to man* (pp. 45–62). Boston, MA: Springer.

Mountain, M-J. (1991a). Bulmer Phase I: Environmental change and human activity through the Late Pleistocene into the Holocene in the Highlands of New Guinea, a scenario. In A. Pawley (Ed.), *Man and a half: Essays in Pacific anthropology and ethnobiology in honour of Ralph Bulmer* (pp. 510–520). Auckland: The Polynesian Society.

Mountain, M-J. (1991b). *Highland New Guinea hunter gatherers: The evidence of Nombe rockshelter, Simbu with emphasis on the Pleistocene* (PhD thesis). Australian National University, Canberra.

Mountain, M-J. (1979). The rescue of the ancestors in Papua New Guinea. *Bulletin of the Institute of Archaeology, 16,* 63–80.

Muke, J., & Mandui, H. (2003). In the shadows of Kuk: Evidence for prehistoric agriculture at Kana, Wahgi Valley, Papua New Guinea. *Archaeology in Oceania, 38* (3), 177–185.

Pétrequin, A. M., & Pétrequin, P. (2006). *Objets de Pouvoir en Nouvelle-Guinée.* Paris: Éditions de la Réunion des Musées Nationaux.

Powell, J. M. (1970). *The impact of man on the vegetation of the Mt Hagen region, New Guinea* (PhD thesis). Australian National University, Canberra.

Powell, J. M. (1982). The history of plant use and man's impact on the vegetation. In J. L. Gressitt (Ed.), *Biogeography and ecology of New Guinea* (pp. 207–227). The Hague: Junk.

Rappaport, R. (1968). *Pigs for the ancestors: Ritual in the ecology of a New Guinea people.* New Haven, CT: Yale University Press.

Rhoads, J. W., & Mackenzie, D. E. (1991). Stone axe trade in prehistoric Papua: The travels of python. *Proceedings of the Prehistoric Society, 57* (2), 35–50.

Roberts, P., & Amano, N. (2019). Plastic pioneers: Hominin biogeography east of the Movius Line during the Pleistocene. *Archaeological Research in Asia, 17,* 181–192.

Roberts, P., Boivin, N., Lee-Thorp, J., Petraglia, M., & Stock, J. (2016). Tropical forests and the genus *Homo. Evolutionary Anthropology, 25* (6), 306–317.

Roberts, P., Gaffney, D., Lee-Thorp, J., & Summerhayes, G. R. (2017). Persistent tropical foraging in the Highlands of terminal Pleistocene/Holocene New Guinea. *Nature: Ecology and Evolution, 1* (3), 1–6.

Roullier, C., Benoit, L., McKey, D. B., & Lebot, V. (2013). Historical collections reveal patterns of diffusion of sweet potato in Oceania obscured by modern plant movements and recombination. *Proceedings of the National Academy of Sciences, 110,* 2205–2210.

Shaw, B., Field, J. H., Summerhayes, G. R., Coxe, S., Coster, A. C. F., Ford, A., . . . Kealhofer, L. (2020). Emergence of a Neolithic in Highland New Guinea by 5000–4000 years ago. *Science Advances, 6*(13), eaay4573.

Sillitoe, P. (1983). *Roots of the Earth.* Kensington: UNSW Press.

Sillitoe, P. (1988). *Made in Niugini: Technology in the Highlands of Papua New Guinea.* London: British Museum Press.

Sillitoe, P. (2002). Always been farmer-foragers? Hunting and gathering in the Papua New Guinea Highlands. *Anthropological Forum, 12* (1), 45–76.

Sillitoe, P., & Hardy, K. (2003). Living lithics: Ethnoarchaeology in Highland Papua New Guinea. *Antiquity, 77* (297), 555–566.

Stewart, B. A., Parker, A. G., Dewar, G., Morley, M. W., & Allott, L. F. (2016). Follow the Senqu: Maloti-Drakensberg paleoenvironments and implications for early human dispersals into mountain systems. In S. C. Jones, & B. A. Stewart (Eds.), *Africa from MIS 6-2: Population dynamics and paleoenvironments* (pp. 247–271). Dordrecht: Springer

Strathern, A. (1969). Finance and production: Two strategies in New Guinea Highlands exchange systems. *Oceania, 40* (1), 42–67.

Strathern, A. (1971). *The Rope of Moka: Big-men and ceremonial exchange in Mount Hagen, New Guinea.* Cambridge: Cambridge University Press.

Summerhayes, G. R. (2019). Austronesian expansions and the role of mainland New Guinea: A new perspective. *Asian Perspectives, 58* (2), 250–260.

Summerhayes, G. R., Field, J. H., Shaw, B., & Gaffney, D. (2017). The archaeology of forest exploitation and change in the tropics during the Pleistocene: The case of northern Sahul (Pleistocene New Guinea). *Quaternary International, 448,* 14–30.

Summerhayes, G. R., Leavesley, M., & Fairbairn, A. (2009). Impact of human colonization on the landscape: A view from the Western Pacific. *Pacific Science, 63* (4), 725–745.

Summerhayes, G. R., Leavesley, M., Fairbairn, A., Mandui, H., Field, J., Ford, A., & Fullagar, R. (2010). Human adaptation and plant use in Highland New Guinea 49,000 to 44,000 years Ago. *Science, 330* (6000), 78–81.

Sutton, A., Mountain, M-J., Aplin, K., Bulmer, S., & Denham, T. (2009). Archaeozoological records for the Highlands of New Guinea: A review of current evidence. *Australian Archaeology, 69* (1), 41–58.

Swadling, P., & Hide, R. (2005). Changing landscape and social interaction: Looking at agricultural history from a Sepik-Ramu perspective. In A. Pawley, R. Attenborough, J. Golson, & R. Hide (Eds.), *Papuan pasts: Cultural, linguistic and biological histories of Papuan-speaking peoples* (pp. 289–328). Canberra: Pacific Linguistics.

Swadling, P., Wiessner, P., & Tumu, A. (2008). Prehistoric stone artefacts from Enga and the implication of links between the Highlands, lowlands and islands for early agriculture in Papua New Guinea. *Journal de la Société des Océanistes, 126–127,* 271–292.

Van Deusen, H. M. (1963). First New Guinea record of Thylacinus. *Journal of Mammalogy, 44* (2), 279–280.

Venkataraman, V. V., Yegian, A. K., Wallace, I. J., Holowka, N. B., Tacey, I., Gurven, M., & Kraft, T. S. (2018). Locomotor constraints favour the evolution of the human pygmy phenotype in tropical rainforests. *Proceedings of the Royal Society B, 285* (1890), 20181492.

Walker, D., & Flenley, J. R. (1979). Late Quaternary vegetational history of the Enga province of upland Papua New Guinea. *Philosophical Transactions of the Royal Society B, 286* (1012), 265–344.

Waters, J. M., Fraser, C. I., & Hewitt, G. M. (2013). Founder takes all: Density-dependent processes structure biodiversity. *Trends in Ecology and Evolution, 28* (2), 78–85.

Watson, V. (1986). *Obsidian as tool and trade: A Papua New Guinea case.* Seattle: Thomas Burke Memorial Washington State Museum.

Watson, V. D. (1995). Simple and significant: Stone tool production in Highland New Guinea. *Lithic Technology, 20* (2), 89–99.

Watson, V., & Cole, D. (1977). *Prehistory of the Eastern Highlands of New Guinea.* Seattle: University of Washington Press.

White, J. P. (1969). Typologies for some prehistoric flaked stone artefacts of the Australian New Guinea Highlands. *Archaeology and Physical Anthropology in Oceania, 4* (1), 18–46.

White, J. P. (1972). *Ol Tumbuna: Archaeological excavations in the Eastern Central Highlands, Papua New Guinea.* Canberra: Department of Prehistory, Research School of Pacific Studies, Australian National University.

White, J. P., Crook, K. A., & Ruxton, B. P. (1970). Kosipe: A late Pleistocene site in the Papuan Highlands. *Proceedings of the Prehistoric Society, 36,* 152–170.

Wilson, S. M. (1985). Phytolith evidence from Kuk, an early agricultural site in New Guinea. *Archaeology in Oceania, 20,* 90–97.

Yen, D. E. (1995). The development of Sahul agriculture with Australia as bystander. *Antiquity, 69* (265), 831–847.

Yen, D. E. (1996). Melanesian arboriculture: Historical perspectives with emphasis on the genus *Canarium*. In B. R. Evans, R. M. Bourke, & P. Ferrar (Eds.), *South Pacific Indigenous nuts* (pp. 36–44). Canberra: ACIAR.

CHAPTER 32

BELOW THE SKY, ABOVE THE CLOUDS

The Archaeology of the Australian High Country

JOANNA FRESLØV AND RUSSELL MULLETT

INTRODUCTION

THE Great Dividing Range (the 'Great Divide'), Australia's longest mountain range that stretches some 3500 km along the east coast, includes the continent's highest mountain peaks (up to 2228 m above sea level [asl] at Mt Kosciuszko). When seen from the lowlands of the inland plains and coastal foothills, the Great Divide forms an impressive and notable feature of the landscape. Ranging between 160 and 300 km in width, by area (2.457 million km^2, or 32% of the nation's 7.692 million km^2), the Great Divide covers a significant part of Australia, with diverse biogeography and broad range of landforms. Yet, and unlike Aboriginal occupation models based on aridity (e.g., Veth 1995), rainfall patterns (e.g., Birdsell 1953), or 'coastal colonisation' (e.g., Bowdler 1977), the Great Divide has not featured as a focal landscape feature in the study of the continent's occupational patterns.

In this chapter, we explore geographical patterns and temporal trends in Aboriginal uses of the High Country, the highest sections of the Great Divide in mainland southeastern Australia. Currently, published understandings of the Aboriginal occupation of the High Country consistently place emphasis on the better-known and chronometrically dated archaeological records of the lowlands and foothills. Archaeological insights into use of the highest elevations are mainly inferred from limited archaeological evidence from north of Mt Kosciuszko, the Monaro Plains (c. 1000 m asl), Tidbinbilla (900–1600 m asl), and Namadgi National Park (900–1900 m asl) in the Australian Capital Territory (ACT), and the lower Snowy River valley (200–1300 m asl) in New South Wales (NSW) and Victoria further to the south, along with, significantly, ethnohistorical accounts (Figure 32.1). The great physical and ethnographic variability of this broad region suggests that patterns of occupation have varied across space and through time. As such, general, all-encompassing models are unlikely to be realistic where few archaeological records are available, such as the Victorian highlands towards the High Country's southern end, or the highest mountain ranges and peaks generally. Similarly, the ethnography of mid-elevations is unlikely to be sufficient, or sufficiently detailed, to account for all of the High Country, let alone for tens of thousands of years of Aboriginal occupation.

THE STUDY AREA

While we briefly consider Tasmania separately in what follows, our main focus is on mainland Australia's alpine, subalpine, and montane regions (including the high plateaux) of the Kosciuszko Ranges and Victorian highlands at the southern end of the study area, which together we refer to as the 'High Country'. This region extends from the Brindabella Mountains in the north to Mt Baw Baw, Lake Mountain, and Mt Buffalo in the south (Figure 32.1). The alpine region is defined as areas above 1850 m asl, the subalpine from 1400 to 1850 m asl, and the montane between 1100 and 1400 m asl, though the plant communities in these zones can vary with rainfall and altitudinally across the three zones (Good 1995; Sahukar, Gallery, Smart, & Mitchell 2003: 219). Across the High Country, the treeline varies with latitude, local temperature, and climate. It lies at 1900 m asl at Mt Jagungal in New South Wales (NSW) and somewhat lower down at 1600 m asl at Mt Howitt in Victoria to the south, with further variation due to local topography and associated conditions such as the presence of cold-constrained wind tunnels (Costin 1972: 2–3; McDougall & Walsh 2007: 2; Ollier 1987). Snowfall in the alpine zone can occur at any time of the year, with consistent fall on the higher peaks (1800–2228 m) in winter lasting around four months (Whetton, Haylock, & Galloway 1996). As such, snow is not permanent in the High Country. With these geographical and climatic variations in mind, this chapter explores the archaeology of the High Country along two intersecting spatial axes: a latitudinal axis from north to south (the Brindabella Range, Snowy Mountains, and Victorian High Country); and an altitudinal axis comprising three zones—alpine, subalpine, and montane landscapes.

The mountain ranges of the High Country are mostly rounded rather than rugged and craggy, with uplifted plateaux, ridges, and peaks (Kirkpatrick 2003: 11; Williams & Costin 1994: 469). The vegetation is largely particular to the region, with summer temperatures, frost frequency, length of snow cover, and solifluction (the slow movement of sediments down a slope) the primary influences on vegetation zonation (Williams & Costin 1994: 467). While the alpine zone above 1850 m is treeless, comprising herbfields and tussock grasslands rich in flowering plants, the subalpine zone is intermediate to the lower-elevation montane zone, featuring moorlands, woodlands, and inverted treeless zones along valleys (Kirkpatrick 2003: 11; Williams & Costin 1994: 467). The cycles of geological-scale glaciations and strongly seasonal climate and wildfires, coupled

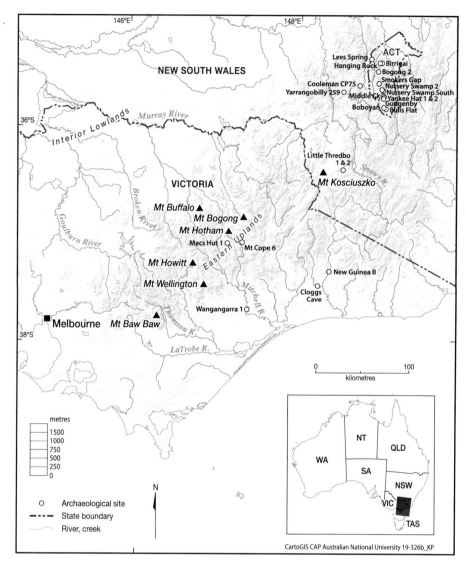

FIGURE 32.1. The study area, showing the location of archaeological sites and key mountain peaks discussed in text.

(Map reproduced with the permission of CartoGIS Services, Scholarly Information Services, The Australian National University.)

with the varied underlying bedrock geology and sediments, and a broad range of topographies, have created a complex array of environments. These environments include treeless moorlands, bogs, and mires in the higher, alpine zone; woodlands and open grassland in the subalpine zone; and woodlands of evergreen trees adapted to bushfires in montane landscapes, although moorlands, bogs, and mires can occur in any zone (Kirkpatrick 2003: 11).

EARLY ARCHAEOLOGICAL RESEARCH IN
THE HIGH COUNTRY

Archaeological research into the Aboriginal occupation of the High Country began when Josephine Flood carried out doctoral research in the southeastern Australian tablelands, the Snowy Mountains, and Brindabella Range in the 1970s. Her work involved a detailed study of ethnohistorical accounts for the Southern Highlands of NSW, which she used to construct a model of highland use for the broader region (see later discussion). Her fieldwork was mainly focused on the ranges towards the northern end of the High Country, but she also carried out some surveys in the south, in the foothills of the Victorian High Country where she investigated a number of rock shelters with excavatable deposits (Flood 1980: Figure 32.2). Flood (1973a) recorded sixty-five sites and excavated twelve small rock shelters and rock shelter complexes (six in the study area) (Flood 1973a: Appendix X). Cloggs Cave, at 72 m asl in the foothills of central-eastern Victoria, was also excavated in 1971–1972 as part of her broader research on the High Country.

Of these sixty-five sites, twenty-two are located above 1100 m asl, with nine in the montane zone (i.e., below 1400 m asl), twelve in the subalpine zone (below 1850 m asl), and only one in the alpine zone. Six rock shelters and a cave were excavated in the study zones: Bogong shelters 1 and 2 and Bogong Cave at 1433 m asl, Rendezvous Creek at 1128 m asl, and Yankee Hat shelters I and II at 1100 m asl, all in the Brindabella Range in the ACT (Flood 1973a: Tables 10:1, 11.1; Flood 1980: Figures 21, 24, 26) (Figure 32.1). The excavation in Bogong Cave, a Bogong moth aestivation site, revealed no cultural materials, while evidence of Aboriginal occupation was found in shallow deposits in Bogong 1 and 2 (Flood 1980: 342). A basal age of 780–1060 cal BP (1000 ± 60 BP, ANU-1050)[1] was obtained for occupation at Bogong 2 (Flood 1980: 342–343). The Rendezvous Creek rock shelter, an art site, is located in the lower elevations of the montane zone. Here, archaeological excavations found relatively sparse evidence of occupation under the overhang, with slightly denser, more disturbed cultural evidence near the entrance (Flood 1973a: Appendix X:18). The occupation deposit was not dated. Yankee Hat I and II are also art sites. At Yankee Hat I, a shallow deposit excavated through five 1 m² 'test pits' (B, D, G, H, S) found evidence of occupation, but the deposit was not dated (Flood 1980: 331). Two test pits were excavated in Yankee Hat II (A and C): one 1 m² and one 1 m × 0.5 m in area (Flood 1973a: Figure Xd). A dense occupation deposit was found between 5 and 30 cm depth in a compact black layer overlying a clay devoid of cultural materials. A basal charcoal sample from Test Pit C gave an age of 460–650 cal BP (550 ± 60 BP, ANU-1048), and a second sample based on dispersed charcoal in Square A gave an age of 510–920 cal BP (770 ± 140 BP, ANU-1051) (Flood 1980: 333).

Fifteen of the seventeen surface sites recorded from the High Country by Flood (1973a, 1980) are artefact scatters, while two are 'ceremonial sites': a ceremonial earth mound (1418 m asl) and the Namadgi stone arrangement (1700 m asl), both in the subalpine

FIGURE 32.2. (A) View from Mt Cope southwest toward Mt Hotham. (B) Subalpine vegetation at Mt Jaitmathang. (C) View from Mt Hotham into lower valley. (D) Mt Howitt Hut, subalpine woodland. (E) Mt Cope 6 rock shelter from near the summit, showing large granite boulder forming the northern side of the rock shelter and tree covering the entrance (yellow rectangle). (F) Internal floor of Mt Cope 6 after small archaeological excavations (near centre of photo) were back-filled, view east. The rocks on the floor are largely rock-fall rather than bedrock. (G) Typical aestivation site of the High Country, with rock walls densely covered by Bogong moths. (H) Bogong moth (*Agrotis infusa*).

(Photos A–F: Joanna Fresløv; G: Eric Warrant; H: Ajay Narendra.)

zone of NSW and the ACT, respectively. Most of these surface artefact scatters are small, with only one large scatter, located at Mt Coree (1174 m asl) in the ACT. Bimberri, a small, undated artefact scatter (1891 m asl) in the ACT, is the only site from the alpine zone reported by Flood.

Flood's research suggested that first occupation of the High Country occurred relatively late. The earliest known deposits were associated with Late Holocene stone artefact types such as 'backed blades' and what was, during the 1970s and early 1980s, referred to as the 'Australian Small Tool Tradition' (Flood 1980: 282). It was also evident that by the time of European colonial settlement in the early to mid-1800s, the whole of the High Country was recognized and used by Aboriginal groups, albeit as altitude increased, population density decreased. Aboriginal people moved about in small groups, and campsites tended to be small (Flood 1980: 276). While Flood observed that it was difficult to delineate 'tribal' (language group) boundaries accurately, coastal groups had long boundaries extending from the coast to the mountains, while inland groups close to the mountains had similarly linear territories extending to the tops of the mountains, reinforcing the importance of mountain resources for mountain as well as lowland groups (Flood 1980: 277).

Flood's (1980: 28, 82) vision of highlands occupation was largely ecological, as was common in 1970s archaeology across Australia (see David et al. 2021a; Lourandos 1985; Veth, O'Connor, & Wallis 2000). In this view, the major driver of highland occupation was the seasonal (spring and summer) exploitation of the 'reliable', abundant, and high-value food resource, the Bogong moth (*Agrotis infusa*), apparently the main and distinctive dietary resource above the treeline where other foods were more marginal (Figure 32.2). Based on ethnohistorical accounts, Flood described how people with estates in the High Country gathered in large multigroup congregations (500 to 700 people) to travel to the mountains as soon as the snow melted (typically October) to feast on Bogong moths (Flood 1980: 63; Helms 1895: 394–395). She argued that moth 'hunting' was predominantly a male activity, and that the seasonal abundance supporting the festive congregations facilitated trade, ceremony, and the exchange of marriage partners (Flood 1980: 82).

Flood's 'moth hunter' thesis holds that 'base camps' were commonly found in lower valleys close to creeks and streams in the foothills and lower valleys below the montane zone, mainly in or near dry sclerophyll forests at the foot of higher ranges. She concluded that these lower-elevation sites were strategically positioned close to forest and woodland resources, and that many were only a day's walk to Bogong moth habitats on the tops of the ranges (Flood 1980: 168). In this scenario, the base camps could have been used in either winter or summer as they lay below the snowline (1525–1675 m asl), and during winter when kangaroo and other game would be driven by the cold and snow (and presumably lack of pasture) to lower altitudes (Flood 1980: 12, 169). Flood interpreted archaeological sites in the montane zone, such as the Mt Coree, Lees Springs (Creek), and Smokers Gap sites in the Brindabella Range, as 'high summer camps' strategically located to exploit the resources of the forests and those of the higher subalpine and alpine zones including Bogong moths (Flood 1980: 164, 169). There were five known sites above the snowline in the Brindabella Range, all small artefact scatters (Flood 1980: 163). These small sites are located in sheltered positions on the lee side of the peaks and close to Bogong moth aestivation sites and abundant starchy tubers such as daisy yams (*Microseris lanceolata*), sites which Flood (1980: 169, 207) described as 'moth hunting camps'. Very few archaeological sites were known above the treeline.

THE BOGONG MOTH IN THE ABORIGINAL OCCUPATION OF THE HIGH COUNTRY

The Bogong moth, around which Flood constructed her interpretations of High Country occupation, is a migratory insect. During spring, they emerge from their pupae in the hotter northern plains of NSW, southern Queensland, and the Western District of Victoria, and migrate at night across enormous distances (up to 1000 km) to aestivate (summer hibernation) in their millions in the cool alpine and subalpine zones (Warrant et al. 2016) (Figure 32.2). In late summer/early autumn, as the highlands cool and frosts become more frequent, the same moths make their return journeys to the warmer lowlands to mate, lay eggs, and die (Common 1954: 225; Warrant et al. 2016). Their initial migratory flight to the foot of the ranges is quite fast, but travel up the range is much slower. Small groups of moths gather at the foot of the ranges for brief periods to feed and rest until the snow melts, after which they continue their travels to the tops of the ranges to aestivate (Warrant et al. 2016: 8). Permanent aestivation sites are generally rocky boulder piles, boulder fields, and deeper crevices in granite rocky tors where the moths can settle in the dark, cool, moist locations protected from the wind (Keaney 2016: 6; Warrant et al. 2016: 10–11). The moths begin to arrive in the foothills of the High Country at the beginning of September, with large numbers arriving at the higher aestivation sites in December and January, peaking in January (Warrant et al. 2016: 9). The return migration begins in February with the number of moths in the high aestivation sites declining rapidly, so that by May only a few stragglers remain (Common 1954: 235; Green 2011: 29; Warrant et al. 2016: 9). When the moths arrive at their return destinations, they are high in fats, making up 62% of their body weight (Common 1954; Green 2011: 26).

Shortly after the publication of her book *The Moth Hunters* (Flood 1980), Flood's model of High Country Aboriginal occupation scheduled around the migratory movements of Bogong moths was questioned by Sandra Bowdler (1981), among others (see also Argue 1991, 1995; Grinbergs 1992). Bowdler's (1981) paper reviewed resource exploitation in the 'uplands' of the Great Divide, specifically examining the likely food staples that underpinned occupation in these areas. In Flood's southeastern High Country, Bowdler argued that Bogong moths were hardly a reliable food source, given that their arrival in the mountains varied from year to year and from area to area, and their numbers were subject to flux (Bowdler 1981: 103–104). Nor were they a staple for the whole group, given that only males, 'the moth hunters', apparently ate them according to the ethnohistorical accounts cited by Flood (1980: 67) and Bowdler (1981: 103). We note that although Jardine (1901: 54) wrote in his recollections of travels in 1844 that, among the 'Manero' (Ngarigo), women were not 'permitted to eat this food', that observation cannot necessarily be applied to all the High Country groups, and it does not necessarily apply to all contexts within a particular Aboriginal group.

To this day, few archaeological sites have been reported from the most elevated areas of the High Country. Those sites that Flood (1980: 169, 207) interpreted as 'moth hunting camps' because they were 'close' to aestivation sites were small, while the larger archaeological sites are located at lower altitude in the purportedly richer resource zones (Bowdler 1981: 104, 107). Rather than Bogong moths being a driver of High Country Aboriginal occupation, Bowdler (1981: 104, 107) concluded that resource exploitation was more likely to have been based on the most abundant and reliable staples available for the 'whole group', in particular the mountain daisy yam (*Microseris lanceolata*), together with other roots and rhizomes (many of which are ubiquitous and available throughout the year at high altitudes) (Bowdler 1981: 104). Like Bogong moth exploitation, plant and tuber harvesting would leave few archaeological traces other than digging sticks and cooking fires (Bowdler 1981: 107), although residue analysis has since developed as a powerful archaeological tool with the potential to reveal considerable new details on the use of stone implements. Bowdler (1981: 104, 109) suggested that Bogong moths, as an easily gathered and prepared food item, may have supported small groups of men while they carried out rituals in seclusion at the higher smaller camps. As such, both Flood's and Bowdler's occupation models for the High Country revolve around high-density foods.

FURTHER EXCAVATION AND DATING OF HIGH COUNTRY SITES IN NSW AND THE ACT

In the 1970s, several Aboriginal occupation sites (including an art site) had been found under rock overhangs in the Nursery Swamp area, in the montane zone of the southern ACT (Flood 1973a, 1980: 136). Flood's (1973a, 1980) excavations at the Yankee Hat I and II and Rendezvous Creek art sites to the south of the Nursery Swamp valley were all in low altitudes of the montane zone. Yankee Hat II was radiocarbon-dated to the past 1000 years (Flood 1980: 248). In the early 1980s, another art site, Nursery Swamp 2 rock shelter, was excavated. Five 0.5 m × 0.5 m pits were dug in c. 5 cm spits to a total depth of c. 55 cm by Andrée Rosenfeld and colleagues (Rosenfeld, Winston-Gregson, & Maskell 1983: 52, Figure 32.3). Four radiocarbon ages were obtained on charcoal, dating the occupational deposits to between 500 and 4410 cal BP. Two radiocarbon determinations were obtained from a dark ashy layer interpreted as accumulated hearths (Spits 1–4) (Rosenfeld et al. 1983: 54). An age of 510–910 cal BP (700 ± 120 BP, ANU-3294) came from Spit 4 of Square 110c, and one of 1300–1530 cal BP (1500 ± 70 BP, ANU-3032) from Spit 5 of Square 120d (Rosenfeld et al. 1983: 54). Two further charcoal samples gave ages of 3080–3580 cal BP (3150 ± 90 BP, ANU-3295) for Spit 6 in Square 115d, and a basal age of 3730–4410 (3700 ± 110 BP, ANU-3033) for Spit 8 in Square 120d (Rosenfeld et al. 1983: Figure 32.2). A small number of 'backed blades' were found throughout the deposit except in the lowest levels (Rosenfeld et al. 1983: 53). The age of the Nursery Swamp 2 deposit suggested that occupation of the High Country began in the Mid-Holocene, earlier than previously thought.

After Flood and Rosenfeld et al.'s pioneering research, little academic work was undertaken on the archaeology of the High Country, although a number of privately funded and largely unpublished cultural assessment surveys associated with ski resort development proposals were carried out in the Snowy Mountains (see later). Archaeological interpretations of such archaeological surveys to this day continue to recycle Flood's Bogong moth interpretations of High Country occupation: Aboriginal people purportedly seasonally moved in small groups to the High Country during the summer months to obtain Bogong moths, soon after returning to lower elevations where most of the community remained and where much of the daily routine took place.

Industry-funded survey projects, such as Johan Kamminga's in the Thredbo Valley of NSW, were useful in locating further evidence of Aboriginal occupation at higher altitudes and in discovering an older than expected antiquity for High Country occupation. In 1988, Kamminga carried out a series of archaeological excavations close to the Thredbo and Little Thredbo Rivers in the then-proposed Lake Crackenback Village in the Snowy Mountains. These excavations were all at open sites located 1100–1200 m asl. Cultural heritage management surveys along the Thredbo Valley and Thredbo ski resort up to 1900 m asl had found more than thirty isolated stone artefacts and, occasionally, stone artefact scatters in sheltered locations above the valley floor. The sites were mainly small, suggesting short-term summer camps given that they are all above the winter snowline (Kamminga, Paton, & Macfarlane 1989: 23–24, 29). During preliminary surveys and subsurface testing, three stone artefact scatters were identified in the Little Thredbo River development area (Kamminga et al. 1989: 26; Paton & Macfarlane 1988). Three radiocarbon ages were obtained from two of the open sites, all of which suggested Mid- to Late Holocene occupation. Two 1 m × 1 m squares (Trench 1, Squares A and C) were excavated at the Little Thredbo 1 archaeological site. The excavations were undertaken in seven spits to a depth of 60 cm and wet sieved through 2 mm mesh (Kamminga et al. 1989: 32). Stone artefacts were located between Spits 3 and 5 (10–40 cm depth). A radiocarbon age of 570–1220 cal BP (940 ± 150 BP, ANU-6866) was obtained from 'very small pieces' of charcoal between c. 10 cm and 30 cm depth of all four quadrants of Square A (Kamminga et al. 1989: 33). A further single square (Trench 4) was excavated to a similar depth of 58 cm. It had stone artefacts in Spits 2 to 5, with the greatest concentration in Spit 3 at 20–30 cm depth (Kamminga et al. 1989: 34). Charcoal from two quadrants in Spit 3 was dated to 2180–2780 cal BP (2460 ± 120 BP, ANU-6868).

A radiocarbon age was also obtained from Little Thredbo 2 (Trench 2, Squares A and C). This trench was excavated in seven spits to a depth of 54 cm (Square A) and 72 cm

(Square C). The ground surface was slightly inclined, and the upper spits followed the inclination (Kamminga et al. 1989: 33). Stone artefacts in these two squares were found between Spits 2 and 6, with the greatest concentrations in Spits 3 and 4 (25 cm to 45 cm depth) of Square A. Stone artefact numbers decreased markedly below this level (Kamminga et al. 1989: 33). An age of 4840–5290 cal BP (4390 ± 80 BP, ANU-6867) was obtained on combined small pieces of charcoal from Squares A and C, from the richest artefact concentration in Spit 4 at no more than 45 cm depth (Kamminga et al. 1989: 33).

While Kamminga et al. (1989: 32; Kamminga pers. comm. 2020) noted that the three Little Thredbo sites are likely to have been affected by a range of subsurface disturbances, including mammal burrowing, uprooting of trees, and bioturbation by invertebrates, such postdepositional taphonomic factors are unlikely to have significantly affected the chronostratigraphy of the occupational horizons. All three charcoal samples used for radiocarbon dating were obtained from the spits with the densest artefact concentrations, with stone artefacts occurring both above and below the samples, providing further evidence that occupation of the Little Thredbo Valley and, therefore, of the High Country, had begun by the Mid-Holocene.

The stone artefacts in the three Little Thredbo sites were made mainly on locally available quartz (96%), followed by small amounts of silcrete, chert, quartzite, and unidentified volcanics (Kamminga et al. 1989: 37). The raw materials were similar to those reported for other sites in the Thredbo Valley (Kamminga et al. 1989: 37). Retouched tools, including small backed artefacts, were made mainly on fine-grained silcrete available from regional river beds, possibly from the Thredbo Valley itself (Kamminga et al. 1989: 38–42). Based on the Little Thredbo sites and the same set of ethnohistoric sources previously used by Flood, Kamminga (1992: 102; Kamminga et al. 1989: 50–56) concluded that it is likely that Aboriginal people lived permanently in the lower valleys of the Snowy Mountains, including near Jindabyne, Wollondibby, and the upper Snowy River. Unlike Flood, however, he suggested that while the Bogong moth was an important food item, a 'broad-spectrum' resource exploitation strategy was more likely to have been employed during the summer months when many food resources were available across much of the High Country.

A New Phase of Archaeological Research in the High Country of NSW and the ACT

Recent research in the montane caves and rock shelters of NSW and the ACT has extended the known antiquity of, and provided further details on, Aboriginal occupation of the High Country (Aplin, Ford, & Hiscock 2010; Theden-Ringl 2018). Ken Aplin and colleagues (2010) excavated a shallow deposit in a cleft in a limestone doline in the Yarrangobilly Caves (1100 m asl), in the Bogong Mountains Wilderness region of NSW.

The cave, Y259, is a Bogong moth aestivation site. It had 'numerous' moth carcasses on its floor at the time of excavation, although it is at a low altitude for an aestivation site (Aplin et al. 2010: 191). A 1 m² pit was excavated as part of a regional survey of 'late to early prehistoric' southeast Australian Alps fauna. The primary aim of the excavation was to obtain vertebrate faunal remains from dateable layers (Aplin et al. 2010: 191). The deposit was excavated in c. 2 cm spits to a depth of c. 35 cm and sieved through 0.5 mm mesh (Aplin et al. 2010: 192, Figure 32.3). Sixteen stone artefacts were found between 20 cm and 35 cm depth in Unit III, in the bottom three spits (7–9) (Aplin et al. 2010: 200–201). None were retouched. Basal radiocarbon ages of 9260–9470 cal BP (8343 ± 43 BP, Wk-18838) from Spit 7, and 9540–9730 cal BP (8668 ± 43 BP, Wk-18839) from Spit 9 were obtained (Aplin et al. 2010: 191, 196). To the northwest of Yarrangobilly, a cave

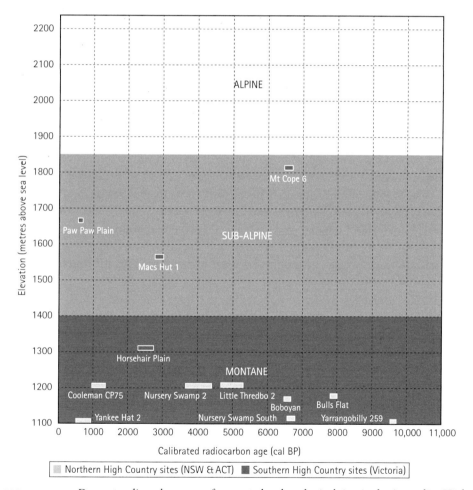

FIGURE 32.3. Deepest radiocarbon ages of excavated archaeological sites in the Australian High Country. The ages were calibrated to 95.4% probability using Calib 7.10 with the IntCal13 curve. The widths of the bars indicate the 95.4% probability age range.

(Graph by Joanna Fresløv)

with Aboriginal skeletal remains, Cooleman CP75 (1200 m asl), has a radiocarbon age of 1070–1370 cal BP (1330 ± 80 BP ANU-6191) (Cooke 1988). The sparse archaeological evidence extends the known occupation of the montane zone in NSW back to the Early Holocene.

Fenja Theden-Ringl's doctoral research in the Namadgi Ranges (ACT) investigated how the chronology of Aboriginal occupation compares and contrasts with that of climate change. She excavated seven rock shelters in NSW and the ACT: Boboyan, Bulls Flat, Nursery Swamp North, Nursery Swamp South, Middle Creek rock shelters, Gudgenby Campsite, and the Wee Jasper cave site (Theden-Ringl 2016, 2018). Four of these sites are below 1200 m asl in the montane zone in the southern Namadgi Ranges: Boboyan (1165 m asl), Bulls Flat (1172 m asl), Nursery Swamp North (1187 m asl), and Nursery Swamp South (1115 m asl). The occupation deposits were sparse, with few stone artefacts found at each site: 135 from 0 to 47 cm depth in a 1.5 m^2 pit at the Boboyan rock shelter; 79 from 0 to 35 cm depth in a 1 m^2 pit at the Bulls Flat site; four from 0 to 25 cm depth in a 1.25 m^2 pit at Nursery Swamp North; and 48 from 0 to 70 cm depth in a 1 m^2 pit at Nursery Swamp South (Theden-Ringl 2016: Table 3; 2017: Table 2).

The excavations provide evidence for occupation of the southern Namadgi Range earlier than previously thought (e.g., Flood 1973a, 1980; Rosenfeld et al. 1983; see earlier). The earliest radiocarbon age for occupation comes from Bulls Flat, where an age of 7840–8010 cal BP (7095 ± 34 BP, D-AMS 3525) is associated with the lowest artefacts at 48 cm depth (Theden-Ringl 2016: 37, Table 4). Two of the other three excavated sites from the montane zone have more recent basal ages associated with the lowermost stone artefacts: 6500–6730 cal BP (5813 ± 31 BP, D-AMS-3521) from Boboyan, and 5910-6170 cal BP (5214 ± 32 BP, D-AMS 3515) from Nursery Swamp South (Theden-Ringl 2016: Table 4). No radiocarbon dating was carried out at Nursery Swamp North rock shelter (Theden-Ringl 2016: 36). At Bulls Flat, the early occupation layers are sparse, with only five stone artefacts associated with the basal age of 7840–8010 cal BP, which is similar in age and content to the early occupation horizon at Yarrangobilly (Y259) where only sixteen stone artefacts came from the basal layers (Aplin et al. 2010: 200; Theden-Ringl 2016: 35). Theden-Ringl (2016: 38) argued that the Early to Mid-Holocene archaeological evidence from the southern Namadgi Ranges sites and Yarrangobilly (Y259) indicates that occupation of the High Country had begun by 9000 years ago, and that the meagre archaeological evidence suggests that there was 'increased exploration and occupation' of the High Country by small groups of Aboriginal people.

The archaeological assemblages of the Namadgi Ranges montane sites are small (all having less than 150 artefacts, although the excavated area in each site was small), so that a total of only 148 stone artefacts date to between c. 7800 cal BP and c. 4800 cal BP, and 114 date to after c. 2100 cal BP (Theden-Ringl 2017: Tables 1–2). The archaeological records of the montane sites of Boboyan, Bulls Flat, and Nursery Swamp South each show significant hiatuses in artefact deposition, as does the site of Gudgenby below the montane zone, although this hiatus is less clear for the other lower altitude site of Middle Creek (Theden-Ringl 2016: 30–37). There is little evidence of occupation for 2100–4800 cal BP, 6700–7800 cal BP, and before 8000 cal BP at the montane sites of Bulls Flat,

Boboyan, and Nursery Swamp South, and at adjacent lower elevations (Theden-Ringl 2016: 37). Theden-Ringl (2016: 38) interpreted these trends as signalling that use of the Namadgi Ranges montane zone was intermittent during the Mid- to Late Holocene, with lower levels of occupation between 4500 and 2000 cal BP, possibly as a result of the onset of ENSO-dominated weather patterns, but with an increase in occupation after 2000 cal BP (Theden-Ringl 2016: 38, 2017: 94). During the Mid- to Late Holocene there was a change from a predominance of quartz artefacts to the use of more diverse and fine-grained raw materials, and the average size of stone artefacts became smaller, particularly after c. 1000 cal BP (Theden-Ringl 2017: 92). Backed artefacts in the southern Namadgi Ranges date from c. 4000 cal BP at Nursery Swamp 2 (Rosenfeld et al. 1983: 54; Theden-Ringl 2017: 94). Archaeological evidence of occupation from both high and lower altitude sites in the Namadgi Ranges increases during the Late Holocene, when more sites (Nursery Swamp 2, Yankee Hat 1 and 2, Bogong 2, and Nursery Swamp 3) were first occupied (Theden-Ringl 2017: 94, 2018: 178–179).

These patterns reveal that first occupation of the High Country in NSW and the ACT began during the Early Holocene, at a time of postglacial climate warming. Stretching back some 9000 years, this early phase is marked archaeologically by intermittent and sparse occupation deposits and a paucity of dates.

INVESTIGATIONS IN THE VICTORIAN HIGH COUNTRY

There can hardly be a greater contrast between the investigations of the High Country regions of NSW and the ACT (see earlier) and those of Victoria to the south. The Victorian High Country has never had any archaeological excavations from academic institutions. Archaeological excavations at two caves, New Guinea II and Cloggs Cave, are often referred to in accounts of the highlands, but these sites are both located in the foothills, below 200 m asl (Flood 1973b, 1980; Ossa, Marshall, & Webb 1995). There has, nevertheless, been several large, landscape-scale, publicly funded, survey investigations in the Victorian High Country since 1998, following wildfires that ravaged wide expanses of country. These investigations, while largely restricted to unpublished but publicly available reports, provide an entirely different archaeological record for the scale and intensity of High Country occupation to that described earlier for NSW and the ACT. The post-wildfire surveys have taken advantage of good ground visibility following the fires, to locate both surface and rock shelter sites otherwise hidden by what is often dense vegetation and outside the disturbance associated with ski resort infrastructures.

One of the early post-wildfire surveys carried out near Mt Wellington in the Victorian Alpine National Park gave the first indication of major differences between northern (NSW and ACT) and southern (Victoria) High Country archaeological records (David, Mullett, & Mullett 1998) (Figure 32.1). Twenty-four surface stone artefact scatters (including one quarry site) were located between 1100 and 1850 m asl, with a large proportion (38%) found at higher altitudes in the subalpine zone. In contrast to the NSW and ACT High Country rock shelters, here the montane and subalpine zones showed no evidence of Bogong moth aestivation sites, signalling that occupation of the sites was probably unrelated to 'moth hunting'. Retouched stone artefacts were infrequently found. Rather than the elongated, asymmetric 'backed blades' found in the NSW and the ACT sites, formal tools were mainly small, backed triangular geometric microliths, all made on locally available fine-grained rhyolite (David et al. 1998: 50).

Since 2000, further large-scale publicly funded studies have been carried out in the Victorian High Country. Of particular interest is the study carried out in the alpine and subalpine zones of the Bogong High Plains, where some of the few documented Bogong moth aestivation habitats in Victoria are located and which shows some similarities to Flood's landscape model for comparative zones of NSW and the ACT (Hughes & Clarkson 2002). The survey found fifty-three surface stone artefact scatters, eleven of which were found in the alpine zone between 1850 m and 1960 m asl, forty in the subalpine zone, and only one each in the montane zone and a lowland valley. As in the High Country of NSW, the higher altitude sites of the Bogong High Plains were generally small, each with less than ten artefacts, although three scatters with twenty to fifty stone artefacts were also found in the subalpine zone (Hughes & Clarkson 2002: Table 1). Sites were found on summit ridges and spur ridges associated with easy lines of movement across the landscape, as well as in more sheltered locations on low rises and knolls and in sheltered snowgum (*Eucalyptus pauciflora*) subalpine woodlands with a grassy understorey (Hughes & Clarkson 2002: 44) (Figure 32.2). Almost all artefacts were made on quartz available from outcrops of schist on the Mt Bogong massif and northern Bogong Plains (Hughes & Clarkson 2002: 32). Potential locations for Bogong moth aestivation sites were limited to the southern parts of the high plains at Mt Jim and between Rocky Knolls and Tawonga Hut Creek (Hughes & Clarkson 2002: 45).

Following huge wildfires across the High Country regions of Victoria in 2003, the Victorian State Government commissioned an extensive survey of the burnt areas in partnership with High Country Aboriginal Traditional Owners. The survey comprised fourteen large study areas between Mt Buffalo in the northeast and the Snowy River in the east (Figure 32.1). A total of 357 archaeological sites were located, with seventy-seven in the montane zone, ninety-seven in the subalpine zone, and three in the alpine zone (Fresløv, Hughes, & Mullett 2004). As in the other large landscape surveys discussed earlier, most (89%) of these sites are surface stone artefact scatters, 63% of which contain less than ten artefacts. Only a few sites (3%) have more than 100 stone artefacts (Fresløv et al. 2004). With good surface visibility, sites were discovered on a wide range of landforms, with those of greatest density, and the largest sites, occurring in sheltered locations below the crests of hills and ridgelines on gentle mid-slopes and breaks of slopes, suggesting that such locations were used repeatedly (Fresløv et al. 2004: 172).

Over and above access to food and water, a wide range of factors would have influenced occupational patterns and, with this, the nature and density of campsite location and artefact discard in alpine and subalpine environments of eastern Victoria. Many of these factors are likely to have constrained occupation in ways that led to the repeated use of favourable landforms: prevailing winds, frost, snow, cold air drainage, altitude, vegetation, tree cover, and fire risk. Occupation sites, as revealed by the archaeology, were indeed located in sheltered locations that would have provided protection from prevailing and sometimes gale-force winds on the high ridges and plains (McDougall & Walsh 2007: 4). The large sites were always located in the warmer zones of the subalpine woodlands, usually well above the colder valley bottoms where temperature inversions cause frequent frosts even in summer (McDougall & Walsh 2007: 2). Inclement weather, such as summer snowstorms, may have influenced the location of larger sites on the high plains. These larger sites, some with many thousands of artefacts, were typically strategically positioned close to gentle spur lines leading to and from lower altitude valleys, providing easy access to warmer montane valleys within a few hundred metres descent. A wide range of factors also influence ground temperature, including aspect, slope, sky view, ground characteristics, and cold-air drainage (Nunez & Colhoun 1986: 14–15). Overnight temperatures in the alpine/subalpine zones in Victoria can reach –6°C during the summer months; there is thus a clear advantage in locating occupation sites along the eastern side of valleys and ridgelines, where maximum advantage can be made of the early morning sun after a cold night. Similarly, locating sites on the edge of snow gum (*Eucalyptus pauciflora*) woodland/grassland interfaces has beneficial advantages, as reported by current GunaiKurnai knowledge holders (Russell Mullett, unpublished cultural knowledge). Trees provide shelter from wind and sun on hotter days in summer, but also north-facing edges receive more sunlight as solar elevation reduces with the progress of the seasons and sunlight penetrates further into the forest canopy edge (Blennow & Persson 1998: 409; Nunez 1983: 155). Temperatures out on the open grasslands are considerably lower than along the forest edge, particularly at night when severe frosts can occur (Blennow & Persson 1998: 410). An added advantage of locating campsites at the interface of woodland and plain is that game can be more easily spotted on the open plains during the day, while nocturnal animals can be more easily seen on moonlit nights. A critical reason for locating summer campsites on the open high plains close to the treeless zone is that, in summer, the high treeless plains are safer than the highly flammable forests of lowland southeastern Australia for both detecting and avoiding wildfires (Russell Mullett, unpublished cultural knowledge).

The 2003 post-bushfire survey sampled most of the Victorian High Country, such that regional and local differences became more apparent than in the spatially more constrained studies carried out in NSW and the ACT. Stone artefacts in the Victorian sites were made on a wide range of raw materials across the region, generally reflecting the local geology, although the use of quartz was ubiquitous (Fresløv et al. 2004: 174). Some raw materials such as chert, rhyolite, and a pale grey quartzite nevertheless show a distinctive distribution, with differences between the southern High Country, where rivers drain south and east into Gippsland, and the northern High Country, where the rivers drain north and west (Fresløv et al. 2004: 174). In the northern High Country, quartz is the dominant artefact raw material, particularly in the granite areas, while in the southern High Country stone artefact raw materials are more diverse. This diversity is most obvious in the high subalpine and alpine regions where larger proportions of silicious artefacts such as chert and hornfels were found right up to the highest peaks (1862 m asl). An example is the diverse raw materials in the stone artefact scatters on the Mt Howitt ridgeline (southern High Country, >1600 m asl) and the quartz stone artefact scatters on the King Billy Range (northern High Country, >1600 m asl) separated by 5 km only. The distribution of stone artefacts made on fine-grained silicious materials, originating from diverse sources, suggests geographical variations in procurement, with people and raw materials moving along lines of access such as ridgelines and river valleys up into the high plains from multiple directions (Fresløv et al. 2004: 174).

There are also regional differences in the retouched artefacts of the southern versus northern High Country sites, with significantly more retouch overall in the southern sites. Asymmetric 'backed blades' and geometric microliths are more common in the southern sites where fine-grained raw materials were commonly used, while geometric microliths have rarely been found in the quartz-dominated assemblages of the northern sites (Fresløv et al. 2004: 175). Edge-ground axes are rare throughout the High Country, only two having been located during systematic surveys so far, one in the subalpine zone and another in the montane zone. In contrast, edge-ground axes are abundant in lowland valley approaches to the High Country, just below the montane zone (e.g., the Mitta Mitta valley and the Snowy River valley) (Fresløv et al. 2004: 176).

The principal difference between the distribution of archaeological sites in the Victorian High Country and that of NSW and the ACT to the north is the less obvious association of archaeological sites with Bogong moth habitats in Victoria. In the Victorian High Country, small, discrete stone artefact scatters are found in sheltered locations in the higher subalpine areas close to known Bogong moth habitats at Mts Cope, Cobberas, Hotham, Tingaringy, and Buffalo (Fresløv et al. 2004; Hall 2002). Away from the known Bogong moth habitats, stone artefacts are distributed as almost continuous low-density 'carpets' along the flatter ridgelines of the alpine/subalpine zones exposed in erosion scours, cleared tracks, and forestry logging areas, suggesting the focus and intensity of Aboriginal occupation in the Victorian High Country was in those areas, rather than in the Bogong moth habitats. Outside of the higher density clusters, the distribution of lower density stone artefact scatters can be regarded as a result of discard from repeated travels along well-worn routes into the highlands along ridgelines, resulting in many small overlapping camps and associated activity areas, together indicating human movement, and social and spatial organization over long periods of time (Fresløv 2005: 33). In the Victorian High Country, movement patterns appear to have been different to those of NSW and the ACT. That is, in Victoria, people travelled mainly along the ridgelines up into the High Country forming very large dense occupation sites in the subalpine zone, unlike NSW where movement was along river valleys and the larger 'campsites' were at lower elevations in the montane zone (Flood 1980: 277; Fresløv 2005: 33).

EXCAVATIONS AND CHRONOLOGY IN THE SOUTHERN VICTORIAN HIGH COUNTRY

Few sites have been excavated and dated in the Victorian High Country. Two sites were excavated after the 2003 wildfires: Mt Cope 6, a rock shelter exposed by the fires near the top of Mt Cope on the boundary of the alpine/subalpine zone at 1817 m asl; and Macs Hut 1, an open site on the Dargo High Plains at 1560 m asl (Fresløv, Shawcross, & Mullett 2005; Shawcross, Mullett, Fresløv, & Tunn 2006). Mt Cope 6 is the highest rock shelter excavated so far in Australia (Figures 32.1 and 32.2). It is a small rock shelter in granite gneiss near the summit of Mt Cope, which rises from the southern edge of the Bogong High Plains. Mt Cope is a known Bogong moth habitat, with the carcasses of moths found in the shelter during the excavation (Keaney 2016: 7; Shawcross et al. 2006: 7; Warrant et al. 2016: 11). A small excavation of two 1 m × 0.5 m squares was undertaken at the back of the rock shelter to a depth of c. 70 cm. The excavated deposits overlay a layer of densely packed angular scree likely to have tumbled as roof-fall during the Last Glacial Maximum (Shawcross et al. 2006: 14, 25, 28). The excavated deposit was dug in c. 5 cm spits and sieved through 2 mm mesh. Six stone artefacts were found on the surface, and a further 37 in small discrete groups down through the occupation deposit (Shawcross et al. 2006: 15–16). All artefacts were made on local quartz, a third of which showed intensive use in the form of edge damage and/or resharpening scars. A basal radiocarbon age of 6500–6720 cal BP (5807 ± 34 BP, Wk-17553) was obtained from the lowest occupation layer at 41.1 cm depth, while an upper, more recent age of 680–780 cal BP (810 ± 31 BP, Wk-17555) came from a depth of 5.8 cm (Shawcross et al. 2006: Table 5). Evidence of Aboriginal occupation was sparse in the oldest occupation layers, with artefact discard rates increasing slightly after c. 3000 cal BP (Shawcross et al. 2006).

Macs Hut 1 is a large and dense artefact scatter extending over 40,000 m^2 of snowgum woodlands with a grassy understorey on the Dargo High Plains west of Mt Hotham. A shallow 3 m × 1 m pit was excavated in 5 to 10 cm spits to bedrock at 22–33 cm depth with sediments sieved through 5 mm mesh (Fresløv et al. 2005: 32). Three charcoal samples from stratigraphic layers 1 and 2 were obtained, each giving near-identical results: 2780–2950 cal BP (2764 ± 33 BP, Wk-17098) from spit 2 at 16.2 cm depth; 2800–3000 cal BP (2807 ± 36 BP, Wk-17100) from spits 3 and 4^2 at 24.8–26.8 cm depth; and 2800–3000 cal BP (2806 ± 36 BP, Wk-17101) from spit 4 at 28.9 cm depth (Fresløv et al. 2005: 35).

Unlike Mt Cope 6 and the excavated sites of the High Country further to the north, stone artefact raw materials were diverse and largely reflect the local geology (Fresløv et al. 2005: 36). A distinctive fine-grained grey quartzite dominates the assemblage (>70%), its source unknown but likely to be local, given its common appearance in stone artefact scatters on the Dargo High Plains. A stone artefact made from the same raw material has been found at another excavated site c. 75 km further south in the High Country foothills, Wangangarra 1 in the lower Mitchell River valley near Bairnsdale (Roberts et al. 2020: 189). Retouched artefacts, including 'backed blades', were present on both the surface and in stratigraphic units 1 and 2 at Macs Hut 1 (Fresløv et al. 2005: 38).

Two further open sites on the high ridgelines have been dated to the Late Holocene: a large, dense open site cluster at Horsehair Plain (1300 m asl) has a basal age of 2350–2720 cal BP (2430 ± 70 BP, Wk-6935); and a small artefact scatter with in situ deposits at Paw Plain, south of Mt Hotham (1660 m asl), has an age of 570–690 cal BP (709 ± 29 BP, Wk-26169) (Muhlen-Schulte 2010; Shawcross 2000: 4; Fresløv et al. 2005: 32).

REGIONAL OCCUPATION CHRONOLOGY

Although few sites have been finely excavated and well dated in the High Country, first occupation of the mountains appears to have been later than in the lowlands, if the limited available results are any indication. Currently, in the foothills of the High Country, the available radiocarbon ages show a pattern of sparse initial occupation at the start of the Last Glacial Maximum. Birrigai rock shelter (730 m asl), in the northern foothills of the Namadgi Ranges, has basal occupation dated to 24,650–25,780 cal BP (21,000 ± 220 BP, Beta-16886) on charcoal from 60.4–71.0 cm depth. The site was sparsely occupied until the Late Holocene (Flood, David, Magee, & English 1987: 16). At the time of its first occupation, Birrigai was above the treeline (then at c. 600 m asl), and permanent ice lay on the Kosciuszko Massif in the Snowy Mountains to the southwest (Barrows, Stone, Fifield, & Cresswell 2001: 186; Kemp & Hope 2014: 786). Further to the south in the southern foothills of the Great Divide, in the Victorian Snowy River valley, Cloggs Cave (72 m asl) was first occupied around 23,000 cal BP, and New Guinea II Cave (100 m asl) before 25,000 cal BP (non-basal age of 23,170–27,140 (21,000 ± 900/+800 BP, SUA 2222)) (David et al. 2021b; Delannoy et al. 2020; Ossa et al. 1995: 28, Table 1). Occupation at Birrigai, Cloggs Cave, and New Guinea II are all more recent than the more southerly occupation of the colder zones of southwestern Tasmania, where first occupation at Bone Cave (400 m asl) is dated at 31,670–38,431 cal BP (29,000 ± 520 BP, Beta-28324), Nunamira (c. 400 m asl) at 31,890–38,430 cal BP (30,750 ± 1340 BP, Beta-25881), and Warreen (c. 200 m asl) at 38,300–40,510 cal BP (34,790 ± 510 BP, Beta-42122B/ETH 7665B) (Allen 1996a, 1996b; Cosgrove 1996). In Tasmania, during the Last Glacial Maximum, small glaciers were present on the West Coast Range (c. 1000–1268 m asl) and Lake Belton, Mt Field (c. 1000 m asl), at lower altitudes than on the mainland. Here subalpine shrubland and herbland environments predominated above c. 200 m asl (Barrows Stone, Fifield, & Cresswell 2002: 20, Table 4; Colhoun, Pola, Barton, & Heijnis 1999: 7, 21). Some sites, such as Bone Cave, were within a few kilometres of the ice sheets, so that cold conditions clearly were no barrier to the use of these landscapes.

There is currently no archaeological evidence for Aboriginal occupation of higher altitudes of the Australian mainland High Country prior to the Early Holocene (Figure 32.3). First occupation of the elevated regions appears in the lower montane zone with the site of Y259 at Yarrangobilly (1100 m asl) to the north of the Snowy Mountains, dated to 9540–9730 cal BP (see earlier). There is more evidence for the occupation of the lower montane zone during the Mid-Holocene after 8000 cal BP, further east at the Bulls Flat site (ACT), but there is no evidence of occupation of the northern High Country above 1200 m asl until after 5000 cal BP. At this time, occupation in the northern High Country montane zone is generally sparse (Theden-Ringl 2016: 37).

The oldest archaeological evidence for the use of the alpine and subalpine zones dates to 6500–6720 cal BP with the first occupation of Mt Cope 6 rock shelter at 1810 m asl in Victoria. Only three other sites have been dated in the subalpine zone, all at lower altitudes than Mt Cope 6. Bogong 2 rock shelter in NSW, at 1433 m asl, just in the sub-alpine zone, has a relatively recent basal age of 780–1060 cal BP. Further south in the Victorian High Country, the open site of Macs Hut 1 (1560 m asl) has a basal age of 2780–2950 cal BP, and Paw Paw Plain south of Mt Hotham (1660 m asl) has a more recent age of 570–690 cal BP. There is thus currently no archaeological evidence for the occupation of the alpine and subalpine zones of southeastern Australia dating to before the Mid-Holocene.

By 14,000–15,000 cal BP, deglaciation of the alpine zones was complete, although there may have been prolonged minor glacial advances. There is thus a long gap of c. 7300 years, from c. 14,000 to 6700 cal BP, between deglaciation and occupation of the alpine and subalpine zones at Mount Cope (Barrows et al. 2001, 2002: 172; Turney et al. 2006: 757). While there are hundreds of large, dense surface artefact scatters, many with subsurface stratified deposits, that have been recorded across the High Country of NSW, the ACT, and Victoria, after fifty years of research very few have been dated and there remain insufficient details to securely determine the apparent late expansion of occupation into the High Country or to discuss the nature and causes of the hiatus, if indeed it withstands the test of time. While Flood's (1980: 276) ecological model stressed a lack or paucity of food resources other than Bogong moths in the High Country, we now know that the region was and continues to be highly diverse, with many different food sources capable of sustaining large populations during the warmer seasons, including important vegetable staples such as the daisy yam, abundant mammals, and Bogong moths. The apparent absence of pre-Mid-Holocene occupation of the alpine and subalpine zones while the climate warmed is difficult to explain and may be due to the limited number of excavated and dated deposits.

Ethnohistory

After five decades of research, the consistent explanatory model for the archaeological record of the Australian High Country seems to repeatedly return to an ecological logic, partly based on chosen ethnohistoric lines of evidence that speak of people seasonally journeying up into the mountains to exploit the fat-rich and 'abundant' food source of the Bogong moth. Yet it is hard to reconcile this logic of persistent occupation with the now-known environmental changes that took place in the High Country over time, and with a more nuanced reading of the ethnohistoric data that incorporates cosmological dimensions of High Country Aboriginal societies.

Flood (1980: 293–297) lists 124 observations of subsistence activities for the early and mid-nineteenth-century colonial period in the northern High Country of NSW and the ACT, only twelve of which refer to the exploitation of Bogong moths. Of these twelve, half are from the mid-nineteenth century (the remainder being later recollections), many years after the arrival of colonial settlers in the 1820s, with the earliest recording dating to December 1832 (Bennett 1834: 266). Of all the observations, Bennett's account is the most compelling, as he had travelled with local Aboriginal people to Bogong moth aestivation sites near Tumut in the Bogong Mountains of NSW. It is clear from his account that at this time Aboriginal people were still exploiting Bogong moth sites, as the party came across recently made hearths and huts (Bennett 1834: 268). Bennett provides some interesting details, including that cooking and processing took place very close to the aestivation sites and that the materials used for gathering, processing, and cooking the moths were all made from organic materials (Bennett 1834: 270–272). These organic materials are unlikely to survive for any depth of time. He provides specific language names for the processed moths and for the tools, and notes that the moths only aestivate in particular places (Bennett 1834: 269). Bennett (1834: 272) also wrote that Bogong moths were so rich and fatty that they induced 'violent vomiting and other debilitating effects' when feasted on following the leaner winter months, and that it took some time for Aboriginal people to get used to the rich seasonal moth diet.

All other accounts of Bogong moths as food are second-hand and date to much later. Bell's 1839 account is not from direct observations at Bogong moth sites, nor did he visit the Bogong moth feasting camps. A new colonist, he provided a brief account of his observations, also from the Tumut valley: 'My own experience of the natives at this time led me to suppose they were a very inoffensive race, for all I had seen had been the Bogong blacks, on the Tumut, who came down in the summer from the ranges, sleek and lazy from the grub or fly of that name which infests that part of the country' (Bell 1853: 171).

In the southern High Country of Victoria, there are no direct observations of Aboriginal people in the mountains. George Augustus Robinson, Chief Protector of Aborigines for the Port Phillip District (Victoria), may have obtained most or all of his information about the High Country from the settlers he stayed with during his travels in southeastern Australia in 1844. Although there is no doubt that he met up with Aboriginal people who spoke English during his travels, he certainly did not reveal the source of his observations about Aboriginal people in the Victorian High Country. When travelling in the Manero district of NSW, Robinson (1844: 328) wrote in his journal: 'The natives of the Low Country and of the Mountains assemble in large numbers in the fine season to collect the *boogong* fly a species of moth found in myriads in the higher altitudes of the mountains. They are extremely nutritious and the natives subsist during the season entirely upon them they are called *cori* by the Omeo, and *boogong* by the Yass blacks'.

Alfred William Howitt (1904), a geologist and magistrate and keen observer and documenter of Aboriginal peoples and their cultures, carried out an extensive study of Aboriginal groups in Gippsland in eastern Victoria, and only cites Helms (1895) when referring to how Aboriginal people lived in the High Country of Victoria. Helms's (1895: 387) report on the 'Omeo Blacks' of the Victorian High Country was based on information from local settlers who had lived in the area for more than forty years and 'who remembered the habits and customs' of the local Aboriginal people (c. 1850–1895). His account of Bogong moth gathering is detailed and similar to that of Bennett's (1834), and he mentions that women were involved in making the fine nets that were used to collect the Bogong moths (Helms 1895: 394–396).

By far the other more interesting, 'non-ecological' aspect of the ethnohistoric accounts and potential future avenues for archaeological research lies in how the Aboriginal peoples of the foothills and inland plains around the mountains invested the High Country with cosmological, social, and magical importance. Recent investigations in the foothills at Cloggs Cave near Buchan in Victoria have revealed how Aboriginal people made sense of their world and landscape beyond the 'food quest' (for details, see David et al. 2021a). A few examples are presented later in this chapter to illustrate this point.

During ethnographic times, the inland peoples of the western side of the Great Divide in Victoria viewed the High Country as a place where the mountains held up the sky on wooden props, and where stone axes from greenstone quarries such as Mt William, north of Melbourne, were invested with meaning and purpose to service the props and stop the sky from falling (Brumm 2010; Howitt 1904: 427). The spatial distribution of the greenstone axes across the Victorian landscape highlights a social divide between the inland groups with access to the High Country on the north and west side of the Great Divide, and those from southeastern Victoria and NSW on the eastern side of the Great Divide, to whom the Mt William axes were rarely traded (McBryde 1978: 363) (see Ford & Hiscock this volume).

In the nineteenth century, the High Country held special significance as a spiritual landscape, imbued with cosmological meaning and a focal location of ceremony and initiation rituals. In his descriptions of the coastal groups of southeastern Victoria and NSW, Howitt (1904: 516–662) repeatedly refers to the 'mountains' and Aboriginal people travelling to the mountains for ceremonies and rituals. Upon initiation, Ngarigo initiates from NSW would be required to spend up to six months in the mountains under the care of an old man or men (Howitt 1904: 563). Early colonial settlers in NSW and the ACT described how large Aboriginal gatherings for ceremonies at the foot of the mountains could not proceed until proper rules, procedures, and ceremonies were carried out. These involved bullroarers 'to frighten the debil debils [spirits] away' (Payten 1949: 1–4). The bullroarer was a flat piece of wood attached to a 'sacred' thread made of red wallaby sinew which was whirled in a circle to make a pulsating, whistling sound. In GunaiKurnai (Gippsland, Victoria) cosmology, the sacred thread was said 'to be let down' from the land beyond the sky by the 'mrarts' or ghosts, by which they descended to earth and then later ascended (Massola 1968: 144). The ceremonies were places where social tensions were resolved, although it needs to be remembered that many were described long after initial colonial settlement and dispossession of Country had severely affected relationships between Aboriginal groups. For example, Bennett (1834: 265–266) described how the close proximity of different 'tribes' led to skirmishes. Dispute resolution was highly formalized, with planned 'battles' where the vanquished lost access rights to parts of the High Country for that season (Bennett 1834: 265–266).

Travelling routes from the foothills to the mountains were marked by cosmological and other cultural associations. The route from the Gippsland foothills north to the Mt Howitt Gathering Place in the High Country was not simply a road to a ceremonial or meeting place. As it climbs into montane and then subalpine regions, the route passes through Countries imbued with meaning. Starting at the meeting place at the confluence of the Macalister (Wirnwirndook/Woonindook) and Wellington (Buk-kewren) Rivers, it passes Baukans Rock (the story rock Baukan, a malevolent spirit), Mt Wellington (Nap-Nappa-Marra), Mt Kent (Nigga-the-rook, meaning 'yellow snake'), Lake Tarli Karrng (Karng-a-Nigothoruk-a, a location where one cannot stay the night), through to the high and rocky plains inhabited by *dulagar* (hairy men), *nial*, and *bruit* (mischievous spirits) to the gathering place at Mt Howitt (Toot-buck-nulluck) (Russell Mullett cultural knowledge; see interview in Fresløv & Goulding 2002: 20; Howitt in Smyth 1878, 2: 190; Howitt, Lucas, & Dendy 1891: 24). Archaeological sites, many of which have been recorded but none excavated, are found at all these named places.

DISCUSSION AND CONCLUSION

Despite the paucity of dated sites, the current archaeological pattern is one of expanding use of the High Country during the Early to Mid-Holocene, although the limited field research done to date may signal an increasing intensity of use rather than an expansion into the mountains. The temporal trend is not easily explained, given the limited archaeological data available for interpretation. With the limited evidence and insufficient chronological resolution at hand, changing patterns of land use cannot readily be attributed to a single driver such as the migration of Bogong moths, climate change, or population pressure. Archaeological evidence for the Aboriginal occupation of the montane, subalpine, and alpine zones is today abundant, but we know very little of its antiquity and even of the details of site contents and regional patterns (Figure 32.3). The inevitable conclusion is that by the late eighteenth and early nineteenth centuries, Aboriginal peoples recognized Country and kin across the highlands from the high alpine regions to the foothills. Oral accounts and limited documentary records from the nineteenth century indicate that by the time of colonial settlement, the High Country was integrated with the foothills and lowland plains in the seasonal round. Most, if not all, lowland groups around the mountains had territorial access to the High Country, so that changes in occupation of the highlands cannot simply be isolated from changes in the lowlands. In such a connected landscape, expansions into the High Country, whenever they happened, link in one way or another with changes in the lowlands, especially when their bonds in Aboriginal cosmologies are taken into account. It is thus worth considering that along the south coast of Victoria, the current littoral zone was sparsely used until c. 3000 cal BP, after which, like the High Country, use of the littoral zone appears to be more intensive (Fresløv & Frankel 1999: 245). While arguments can be made that sea-level changes, biased dating, and alterations to coastal landforms have contributed to the preservation of the more recent sites (e.g., Bird and Frankel 1991; Fresløv & Frankel 1999: 251; Lourandos 1996), such arguments do not readily dispel the current evidence for tandem increases in the use of the coast and its hinterland, large rivers, lakes, and swamps. Inland, between the coast and the High Country, increased use of the foothills during the Late Holocene is evident along the Mitchell River at Wangangarra 1 rock shelter, the Buchan River at Cloggs Cave, and the junction of the Buchan and Snowy Rivers at East Buchan site D (authors and Bruno David, unpublished data), and there is a hint of the long-distance movement of raw materials (stone artefacts) and artefact types (grindstone for the processing of Bogong moths) between the lowlands and the highlands (Stephenson et al. 2020; David et al. 2021a; Delannoy et al. 2020; Flood 1980: 268; Fresløv et al. 2004: 174; Roberts et al. 2020: 20).

Last but not least, 'physical evidence, typically referred to as Aboriginal cultural heritage, requires the stories and traditions of people to give it context' (Ardler 2003: 15). Landscapes are more complex than their material (archaeological) expressions. They are meaningfully, culturally constructed in social life, such as in the travelling route to Mt Howitt noted earlier. Landscapes are networks of places joined by interconnecting pathways 'in' which, rather than 'on' or 'with' which, people move (Ingold 2000: 48, 54; see also Ingold 2007; Lennart 2017; Turnbull 2007), and they involve many ways of walking (e.g., Ingold & Vergunst 2008). As Traditional Owners of the High Country continue to remind us, Country is more than a set of habitats, physical remains, environmental, chronological, or ecological models. The highlands are alive, they are rich in history and in story, and it is these that often draw people to places. They connect kin across Country and through time, the present with the past. Rivers, rocks, lakes, caves, and travel routes have their own language names, creation stories, mystical significance, and spiritual and ancestral beings, very few of which have yet been considered by archaeologists despite current Aboriginal knowledge and in some cases ethnographic records. This is the challenge of High Country archaeology: to go beyond an archaeology that is reduced to ethology, and to engagements with place that go beyond climatology, and that, rather, explores Country as culturally meaningful peopled landscapes.

ACKNOWLEDGMENTS

We are grateful to Bruno David for his help and patience with this chapter. We also thank the Traditional Owners of the High Country for their support, advice, and participation over many years of fieldwork in the mountains; Johan Kamminga and Ingereth Macfarlane for providing additional unpublished information; and Janelle Stephenson and Fenja

Theden-Ringl for clarifying outstanding and puzzling 'data issues'. Thanks also to Taryn Gooley, Fenja Theden-Ringl, and Ian McNiven for their detailed and helpful comments on the final draft.

NOTES

1. Throughout this chapter, radiocarbon ages (all on terrestrial samples) are calibrated to 95.4% probability using Calib 7.10 (Stuiver & Reimer 1993) with the IntCal13 curve (Reimer et al. 2013).
2. A conventional radiocarbon age on charcoal combined from two spits. All other samples were single pieces of charcoal dated by AMS.

REFERENCES

Allen, J. (1996a). Bone Cave. In J. Allen (Ed.), *Report of the Southern Forests Archaeological Project* (pp. 91–122). Bundoora: La Trobe University.

Allen, J. (1996b). Warreen Cave. In J. Allen (Ed.), *Report of the Southern Forests Archaeological Project* (pp. 135–168). Bundoora: La Trobe University.

Aplin, K., Ford, F., & Hiscock, P. (2010). Early Holocene human occupation and environment of the southeast Australian Alps: New evidence from the Yarrangobilly Plateau, New South Wales. In S. Haberle, J. Stevenson, & M. Prebble (Eds.), *Altered ecologies: Fire, climate and human influence on terrestrial landscapes* (pp. 187–212). Terra Australis 32. Canberra: ANU E-Press.

Ardler, J. (2003). Rocks are rocks, mountains are mountains - Aboriginal values of mountains. In *Proceedings of an International Year of Mountains Conference. Jindabyne Australia November 25–28, 2002* (pp. 15–24). Canberra: Australian Alps Liaison Committee.

Argue, D. (1991). *Bountiful Brindabella. Towards an understanding of the prehistory of the Southern Uplands* (BA Honours thesis). Australian National University, Canberra.

Argue, D. (1995). Aboriginal occupation of the Southern Highlands: Was it really seasonal? *Australian Archaeology, 41*(1), 30–36.

Barrows, T. T., Stone, J. O., Fifield, L. K., & Cresswell, R. G. (2001). Late Pleistocene glaciation of the Kosciuszko Massif, Snowy Mountains, Australia. *Quaternary Research, 55*(2), 179–189.

Barrows, T. T., Stone, J. O., Fifield, L. K., & Cresswell, R. G. (2002). The timing of the Last Glacial Maximum in Australia. *Quaternary Science Reviews, 21*(1–3), 159–173.

Bell, D. (1853). Letter. In T. F. Bride (Ed.), (1969). *Letters from Victorian pioneers* (pp. 168–180). Melbourne: Heinemann.

Bennett, G. (1834). *Wanderings in New South Wales, Batavia, Pedir Coast, Singapore and China, being the journal of a naturalist in those countries, during 1832, 1833 and 1834.* London: Bentley.

Bird, C. F., & Frankel, D. (1991). Chronology and explanation in western Victoria and southeast South Australia. *Archaeology in Oceania, 26*(1), 1–16.

Birdsell, J. B. (1953). Some environmental and cultural factors influencing the structuring of Australian Aboriginal populations. *American Naturalist, 87*, 171–207.

Blennow, K., & Persson, P. (1998). Modelling local-scale frost variations using mobile temperature measurements with a GIS. *Agricultural and Forest Meteorology, 89*(1), 59–71.

Bowdler, S. (1977). The coastal colonisation of Australia. In J. Allen, J. Golson, & R. Jones (Eds.), *Sunda and Sahul: Prehistoric studies in Southeast Asia, Melanesia and Australia* (pp. 205–246). New York: Academic Press.

Bowdler, S. (1981). Hunters in the highlands: Aboriginal adaptations in the eastern Australian uplands. *Archaeology in Oceania, 16*(2), 99–111.

Brumm, A. R. (2010). 'The falling sky': Symbolic and cosmological associations of the Mt William greenstone axe quarry, Central Victoria, Australia. *Cambridge Archaeological Journal, 20*, 179–196.

Colhoun, E. A., Pola, J. S., Barton, C. E., & Heijnis, H. (1999). Late Pleistocene vegetation and climate history of Lake Selina, western Tasmania. *Quaternary International, 57*, 5–23.

Common, I. F. B. (1954). A study of the ecology of the adult Bogong moth, *Agrotis Infusa* (Boisd.) (Lepidoptera: Noctuidae), with special reference to its behaviour during migration and aestivation. *Australian Journal of Zoology, 2*(2), 223–263.

Cooke, H. (1988). *An investigation into the prehistory of Blue Water Holes and Cooleman Plains, NSW* (BA Honours thesis). Australian National University, Canberra.

Cosgrove, R. (1996). Nunamira Cave. In J. Allen (Ed.), *Report of the Southern Forests Archaeological Project* (pp. 43–68). Bundoora: La Trobe University.

Costin, A. B. (1972). Characteristics and use of Australian high country. In M. R. Banks (Ed.), *The lake country of Tasmania* (pp. 1–23). Hobart: Royal Society of Tasmania.

David, B., Fresløv, J., Mullett, R., GunaiKurnai Land and Waters Aboriginal Corporation, Delannoy, J.-J., McDowell, M., . . . Green, H. (2021a). 50 years and worlds apart: Rethinking the Holocene occupation of Cloggs Cave (East Gippsland, SE Australia) five decades after its initial archaeological excavation and in light of GunaiKurnai world views. *Australian Archaeology, 87*(1), 1–20.

David, B., Arnold, L., Delannoy, J.-J., Fresløv, J., Mullett, R., Gunaikurnai Land and Waters Aboriginal Corporation, . . . Green, H. (2021b). Late survival of megafauna refuted for Cloggs cave, SE Australia: Implications for the Australian Late Pleistocene megafauna extinction debate. *Quaternary Science Reviews, 253*, 106781.

David, M., Mullett, R., & Mullett, R. (1998). The Caledonia Fire Area, Alpine National Park, Victoria: An archaeological survey and Aboriginal heritage assessment. Unpublished cultural heritage management report to Aboriginal Affairs Victoria, Melbourne.

Delannoy, J.-J., David, B., Fresløv, J., Mullett, R., Gunaikurnai Land and Waters Aboriginal Corporation, Green, H., . . . Wong V. N. L. (2020). Geomorphological context and formation history of Cloggs Cave: What was the cave like when people inhabited it? *Journal of Archaeological Science Reports, 33*, 102461.

Flood, J. (1973a). *The moth hunters: Investigations towards a prehistory of the south-eastern highlands of Australia* (PhD thesis). Australian National University, Canberra.

Flood, J. (1973b). Pleistocene human occupation and extinct fauna in Cloggs Cave, Buchan, southeast Australia. *Nature, 246*, 303.

Flood, J. (1980). *The moth hunters: Aboriginal prehistory of the Australian Alps.* Canberra: Australian Institute of Aboriginal Studies.

Flood, J., David, B., Magee, J., & English, B. (1987). Birrigai: A Pleistocene site in the south-eastern highlands. *Archaeology in Oceania, 22*(1), 9–26.

Fresløv, J. (2005). An Aboriginal archaeological heritage management plan for the Dinner Plain site complex, Victorian Alps. Unpublished cultural heritage management report to Parks Victoria and the Department of Sustainability and Environment, Melbourne, Victoria.

Fresløv, J., & Frankel, D. (1999). Abundant fields? A review of coastal archaeology in Victoria. In J. Hall & I. J. McNiven (Eds.), *Australian coastal archaeology* (pp. 239–254). Canberra: Australian National University.

Fresløv, J., & Goulding, M. (2002). An Aboriginal cultural heritage values assessment of the Howitt Plains area, Alpine National Park, Victoria. Unpublished cultural heritage management report to Parks Victoria, Melbourne, Victoria.

Fresløv, J., Hughes, P., & Mullett, R. (2004). Post wildfire Indigenous heritage survey. Volume 1: Background, survey, results and recommended management options. Unpublished cultural heritage management report to Aboriginal Affairs Victoria, Parks Victoria and the Department of Sustainability and Environment, Melbourne, Victoria.

Fresløv, J., Shawcross, W., & Mullett, R. (2005). An excavation of AAV 8323-0061 (Macs Hut 1), Kings Spur, Dargo High Plains, Victorian Alps. Unpublished cultural heritage management report to Parks Victoria and the Department of Sustainability and Environment, Melbourne, Victoria.

Good, R. B. (1995). Australian Alps. S. D. Davis, V. H. Heywood, & A. C. Hamilton (Eds.), *Centres of plant diversity: Asia, Australasia, and the Pacific* (pp. 458–461). Cambridge: World Wildlife Fund/International Union for the Conservation of Nature and Natural Resources, IUCN Publications Unit.

Green, K. (2011). The transport of nutrients and energy into the Australian Snowy Mountains by migrating Bogong moths *Agrotis infusa. Austral Ecology, 36*(1), 25–34.

Grinbergs, A. (1992). *The myth hunters: Investigations towards a revised prehistory of the south eastern highlands of Australia* (BA Honours thesis). Australian National University, Canberra.

Hall, R. (2002). An archaeological survey of the Snowy River National Park. Unpublished cultural heritage management report to Aboriginal Affairs, Melbourne, Victoria.

Helms, R. (1895). Anthropological notes. *Proceedings of the Linnaean Society of New South Wales, 2*(20), 38–407.

Howitt, A. W. (1904). *The native tribes of south-east Australia*. London: Macmillan.

Howitt, A. W., Lucas, A. H. S., & Dendy, A. (1891). A visit to Lake Nigothoruk and the Mount Wellington District, Gippsland. *Victorian Naturalist, 8*, 17–40.

Hughes, P., & Clarkson, C. (2002). A cultural heritage survey of the Bogong High Plains, Victoria. Unpublished cultural heritage management report to Parks Victoria, Melbourne.

Ingold, T. (2000). *The perception of the environment: Essays on livelihood, dwelling and skill.* London: Routledge.

Ingold, T. (2007). *Lines: A brief history*. London: Routledge.

Ingold, T., & Vergunst, J. L. (Eds.) (2008). *Ways of walking: Ethnography and practice on foot.* Aldershot: Ashgate.

Jardine, W. (1901). Customs of the Currak-da-bidgee tribe, NSW. *Science of Man, 4*(3), 53–54.

Kamminga, J. (1992). Aboriginal settlement and prehistory of the Snowy Mountains. In B. Scougall (Ed.), *Cultural heritage of the Australian Alps* (pp. 101–124). Canberra: Australian Alps Liaison Committee.

Kamminga, J., Paton, R., & Macfarlane, I. (1989). Archaeological investigations in the Thredbo Valley, Snowy Mountains. Unpublished cultural heritage management report to Faraba Pty Ltd, Canberra.

Keaney, B. (2016). *Bogong moth aestivation sites as an archive for understanding the floral, faunal and Indigenous history of the northern Australian Alps* (PhD thesis). Australian National University, Canberra.

Kemp, J., & Hope, G. (2014). Vegetation and environments since the Last Glacial Maximum in the Southern Tablelands, New South Wales. *Journal of Quaternary Science, 29*(8), 778–788.

Kirkpatrick, J. B. (2003). The natural significance of the Australian Alps. In J. Mackay & Assoc. (Eds.), *Proceedings of an International Year of Mountains Conference* (pp. 9–14). Jindabyne: Australian Alps Liaison Committee.

Lennart, A. E. (2017). Place, identity, and relations: The lived experience of two northern worlds. *Artic Anthropology, 54*(2), 83–93.

Lourandos, H. (1985). Intensification and Australian prehistory. In T. D. Price & J. A. Brown (Eds.), *Prehistoric hunters-gatherers* (pp. 385–423). New York: Academic Press.

Lourandos, H. (1996). Change in Australian prehistory: Scale, trends and frameworks of interpretation. In I. Lilley, A. Ross, & S. Ulm (Eds.), *Proceedings of the 1995 Australian Association Annual Conference* (pp. 15–22). Tempus 6. St Lucia: Anthropology Museum, University of Queensland.

Massola, A. (1968). *Bunjil's Cave. Myths, legends and superstitions of the Aborigines of south-east Australia*. Melbourne: Lansdowne Press.

McBryde, I. (1978). *Wil-im-ee Moor-ring*: or, where do axes come from? *Mankind, 11*(3), 354–382.

McDougall, K. L., & Walsh, N. G. (2007). Treeless vegetation of the Australian Alps. *Cunninghamia, 10*(1), 1–57.

Muhlen-Schulte, R. (2010). Hotham–Dinner Plain multipurpose trail Alpine National Park NE Victoria. Unpublished cultural heritage management report to Parks Victoria, Mount Hotham Resort Management Board and Alpine Shire.

Nunez, M. (1983). Estimation of solar radiation received on slopes in Tasmania. *Papers and Proceedings of the Royal Society of Tasmania, 117*, 153–159.

Nunez, M., & Colhoun, E. A. (1986). A note on air temperature lapse rates on Mount Wellington, Tasmania. *Papers and Proceedings of the Royal Society of Tasmania, 120*, 11–15.

Ollier, C. D. (1987). The origin of alpine landforms in Australasia. In B. A. Barlow (Ed.), *Flora and fauna of Alpine Australasia, ages and origins* (pp. 3–27). Melbourne: CSIRO.

Ossa, P., Marshall, B., & Webb, C. (1995). New Guinea II cave: A Pleistocene site on the Snowy River, Victoria. *Archaeology in Oceania, 30*(1), 22–35.

Paton, R. C., & Macfarlane, I. (1988). Results of preliminary salvage excavations at Thredbo Valley. Unpublished cultural heritage management report by ANUTECH Pty. Ltd., to Faraba Pty. Ltd.

Payten, R. F. (1949). The festival of the Bogong moth. Letter to A.S. Le Soeuf, 15 June 1949. Ms (Aa44/3). Sydney: Mitchell Library.

Reimer, P. J., Bard, E., Bayliss, A., Beck, J. W., Blackwell, P. G., Bronk Ramsey, C., . . . van der Plicht, J. (2013). IntCal13 and Marine13 radiocarbon age calibration curves 0–50,000 years cal BP. *Radiocarbon, 55*, 1869–1887.

Roberts, G. L., Mullett, R., David, B., Fresløv, J., GLAWAC, Mialanes, J., . . . Russell, L. (2020). Community research in a public place: Wangangarra 1 rockshelter, Mitchell River National Park, East Gippsland (Australia). *Australian Archaeology, 86*(2), 176–197.

Robinson, G. A. (1844). Report of a Journey of two thousand two hundred miles to the tribes of the coast and eastern interior during the year 1844. In G. Mackaness (Ed.), George Augustus Robinson's Journey into South-Eastern Australia, 1844. *Journal and Proceedings of the Australian Royal Historical Society, 17*(5), 318–349.

Rosenfeld, A., Winston-Gregson, J., & Maskell, K. (1983). Excavations at Nursery Swamp 2, Gudgenby Nature Reserve, Australian Capital Territory. *Australian Archaeology, 17*(1), 48–58.

Sahukar, R., Gallery, C., Smart J., & Mitchell, P. (2003). *The bioregions of New South Wales—Their biodiversity, conservation and history*. Hurstville: National Parks and Wildlife Service (NSW).

Shawcross, W. (2000). The Aboriginal people of the mountains. Unpublished cultural heritage management report for the Hotham Airport and the Mount Hotham Ski Company, Victoria.

Shawcross, W., Mullett, R., Fresløv, J., & Tunn, J. (2006). Mt Cope No. 6 rockshelter. Unpublished cultural heritage management report to Parks Victoria, Melbourne.

Smyth, R. B. (1878). *The Aborigines of Victoria*. Melbourne: Government Printer.

Stephenson, B., David, B., Fresløv, J., Arnold, L. J., Gunaikurnai Land and Waters Aboriginal Corporation, Delannoy J-J., . . . Hellstrom, J., (2020). 2000 year-old Bogong moth (*Agrotis infusa*) Aboriginal food remains, Australia. *Scientific Reports, 10*(1), 1–10.

Stuiver, M., & Reimer, P. J. (1993). Extended ^{14}C database and revised CALIB radiocarbon calibration program. *Radiocarbon, 35*, 215–230.

Theden-Ringl, F. (2016). Aboriginal presence in the high country: New dates from the Namadgi Ranges in the Australian Capital Territory. *Australian Archaeology, 82*(1), 25–42.

Theden-Ringl, F. (2017). A reassessment of technological change models for the Australian high country. *Archaeology in Oceania, 52*(2), 81–97.

Theden-Ringl, F. (2018). *Common cores in the high country. The archaeology and environmental history of the Namadgi Ranges* (PhD thesis). Australian National University, Canberra.

Turnbull, D. (2007). Maps narratives and trails: Performativity, hodology and distributed knowledges in complex adaptive systems - an approach to emergent mapping. *Geographical Research, 45*(2), 140–149.

Turney, C. S., Haberle, S., Fink, D., Kershaw, A. P., Barbetti, M., Barrows, T. T., . . . Hua, Q. (2006). Integration of ice-core, marine and terrestrial records for the Australian Last Glacial Maximum and Termination: A contribution from the OZ INTIMATE group. *Journal of Quaternary Science, 21*(7), 751–761.

Veth, P. (1995). Aridity and settlement. *Antiquity, 69*, 733–746.

Veth, P., O'Connor, S., & Wallis, L. A. (2000). Perspectives on ecological approaches in Australian archaeology. *Australian Archaeology, 50*, 54–66.

Warrant, E., Frost, B., Green, K., Mouritsen, H., Dreyer, D., Adden, A., . . . Heinze, S. (2016). The Australian Bogong moth *Agrotis infusa*: A long-distance nocturnal navigator. *Frontiers in Behavioral Neuroscience, 10*, 77.

Whetton, P. H., Haylock, M. R., & Galloway, R. (1996). Climate change and snow-cover duration in the Australian Alps. *Climatic Change, 32*, 447–479.

Williams, R. J., & Costin, A. B. (1994). Alpine and subalpine vegetation. In R. H. Groves (Ed.), *Australian vegetation* (pp. 467–500). Cambridge: Cambridge University Press.

CHAPTER 33

MURRAY RIVER SOCIETIES IN AUSTRALIA THROUGH THE LENS OF BIOARCHAEOLOGY

JUDITH LITTLETON, SARAH KARSTENS, AND HARRY ALLEN

INTRODUCTION

THE Murray River Valley was identified by Birdsell (1953) as one of the few inland areas in Australia that did not conform to a regular correlation between annual rainfall and the density of Aboriginal linguistic groups. The supply of water and its associated resources meant that this was a high-population region with much linguistic diversity distributed along the river and its tributaries. This contrast to the surrounding country and to the general correlation in the inland between population density and annual precipitation defined the Murray River Valley as a distinct region. Subsequent archaeological and anthropological analyses have often emphasized that riverine unity. In this chapter, we evaluate the unity of Murray River societies in the Holocene period, exploring the tension between regional and local perspectives.

This chapter focusses on the bioarchaeological record because, unlike other areas of Australia, the record of burials and human remains dominates the archaeological narratives of the Murray River Aboriginal experience. The perspective here is an integrated one, where the study of burial practices and the human remains contained within burial sites are brought together within a framework that includes natural history, observations of Aboriginal ethnography, and where possible, other archaeological studies. Different aspects of bioarchaeological analysis (mortuary remains, morphological variation, palaeopathology, and diet) are also discussed in detail.

The Murray River as a Human Environment

The Murray River is Australia's longest river (2500 km). As it flows from the Snowy Mountains to the sea, it passes through a number of ecological–physiographic regions (Figure 33.1): Highlands, Riverine, Central Murray Mallee, Gorge, and the Coastal Lakes and Estuary sections (MacKay & Eastburn 1990) (Table 33.1). For most of this course, the Murray flows roughly east to west until it reaches Morgan in South Australia, where it turns southward towards Lake Alexandrina and the sea. For the greater part of its course, the river moves from an area of higher rainfall (800 to 1200 mm per annum) in the Highlands to a much lower rainfall regime (200 to 400 mm per annum) on the plains through a succession of vegetation zones.

While rainfall is spread over the entire year, summers are hot and evaporation is high, whereas winters are cooler with lower evaporation. This rainfall distribution gives the Murray River Valley an effective Mediterranean climate, with most growth in the natural vegetation occurring during the winter and spring months (Laut et al. 1977a, 1977b; MDBA 2020).

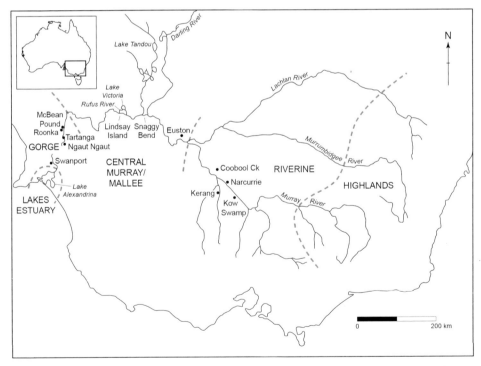

FIGURE 33.1. Map of the Murray River Valley and major tributaries, with the physiographic regions identified along with sites mentioned in the text.

MURRAY RIVER SOCIETIES IN AUSTRALIA   891

Table 33.1. Murray River Sections (List of Murray River Distances, *Wikipedia*, available from: https://en.wikipedia.org/wiki/List_of_Murray_River_distances; MacKay & Eastburn, 1990).

Murray River Major Divisions		Section	
Upper	Mt Kosciusko to Corowa (450 km)	Highland—Headwaters	
Middle	Corowa to Wakool River (810 km)	Riverine	
Lower	Wakool River to the River Mouth (1300 km)	Mallee	Wakool River to Overland Corner (860 km)
		Gorge	Overland Corner to Mannum (280 km)
		Coastal lakes and Estuary	Mannum to the Coorong (160 km)

While much of the Murray Basin is semiarid, the river itself was highly productive in terms of water and food for local Aboriginal communities (Allen, 1972; Humphries, King, & Koehn, 1999; Lawrence, 1968; Walker, Sheldon, & Puckridge 1995). Before the river was controlled through locks and dams, much of its productivity was determined by annual rises associated with spring snowmelt on the mountains and winter and spring water entering the Murray via tributaries, with Aboriginal subsistence varying with the ecological conditions of different river sections (Table 33.1).

Aboriginal people used the entire Murray River to hunt, trap, net, and gather waterfowl, fish, shellfish, aquatic and swamp plants, crustaceans, amphibians, and mammals. On the adjacent plains, they collected a variety of plant foods and organized hunts of large, medium, and small mammals using spears and spearthrowers, fire drives, and nets (Allen 1972). Observing these economic similarities, Pardoe (1995: 704) found a pattern of regional coherence along the entire river, excluding the Highlands. Certainly, communities invested in nets, traps, and weirs to harvest fish and waterfowl in a manner that was common along its central and lower reaches. Large and small bark canoes were ubiquitous, evidenced today by numerous old 'scarred trees'—that is, trees revealing the removal of large sections of bark (Edwards 1972).

This pattern of similar resource reliance begs two questions. First, was this riverine economy equivalent along the river from the Riverine section down to the sea? Second, was this mode of production distinct from that used in other areas of Australia? Lawrence (1968: 85) defined participants in a riverine economy as groups that 'spent at least some seasons of the year in continuous settlement on the rivers, and whose economy . . . showed some specialization in the collection of riverine foods'. In a comparison of Aboriginal lifeways, Keen (2004) found strong similarities in the organization of production across Australia. Similarly, McCarthy (1957) observed that Aboriginal material culture and economy everywhere showed hunting, fishing, and collecting, with variations depending on local circumstances and seasons. Certainly, Murray River Aboriginal people made considerable use of nets, traps, and weirs to harvest fish, and they developed specialized long nets stretched across waterways anchored to trees on adjacent banks to capture large numbers of waterfowl. However, as Satterthwait (1987) and Kelly (2014) point out, the use of large nets for hunting and fishing, and traps and weirs for harvesting fish, was widespread, and what we see in the Murray Valley was the adaptation of generally available material culture to particular circumstances.

Depending on how Aboriginal tribal-linguistic groups are defined, more than 20 Aboriginal groups occupied territories along the Murray River (Table 33.2). Peterson (1976) noted a correlation between high Aboriginal populations and river productivity along the Murray, but he also observed that there was a different language group along every 50 km or so of river frontage. He considered that ease of communication along the river should have brought Aboriginal groups closer together. However, the evidence is that the closest cultural and linguistic ties were with related tribal groups away from the river rather than with immediate riverine neighbours. For example, in a series of papers, Pardoe has attempted to draw multiple factors (landscape, ecology, human biological and social information, population, and productivity) into an evolutionary model to explain this cultural and linguistic diversity (see references in Pardoe 2006). Noting that the greatest ecological contrast was between the river valley and the surrounding semiarid plains, Pardoe contrasted the open boundaries and gene flow between the river and its hinterland with marked divisions along its course, which he links with processes of social exclusion and competition over resources. Pardoe interprets the presence of long-term cemeteries as markers of land ownership.

However, in addition to ecology, historical factors are relevant in explaining diversity along the Murray. The distribution of language groups along the river (Table 33.2) suggests that Upper Murray languages were once continuous along its length. The movement of Kulin speakers from Victoria, and of Bagandji speakers from New South Wales, towards highly productive river frontage territory has disrupted this pattern and created a diverse cultural and linguistic landscape. Other studies show both continuities and discontinuities along the river, such as the common nature of burial locations but with distinctive local mortuary practices (e.g., Littleton & Allen 2020). Hercus (2010: 170) describes the Murray corridor as a 'language cross-roads', quoting A.L.P. Cameron that most Aboriginal people there could speak two or three languages and could understand even more. Hercus further noted that these tribes shared a common social system, which facilitated intermarriage across linguistic lines at the same time that linguistic diversity was emphasized. Such studies emphasize both relatedness and diversity.

Table 33.2. Tribal–linguistic units and language groups along the course of the Murray River from the headwaters to the sea (data after Hercus, 1986, 2010). Note that the orthography of Aboriginal tribal names is highly variable.

Murray River Section	Language Group	Aboriginal Tribe/Linguistic Unit
Highlands–Headwaters	Upper Murray	Dhudhuroa
		Djilamatong
		Bangeran
Riverine		Yorta Yorta
	Kulin	Berabaraba
		Wemba Wemba
		Wadi Wadi
	Upper Murray	Dadi Dadi
Mallee	Kulin	Madi Madi
		Latje Latje
	Upper Murray	Nari Nari
	Bagandji	Gureingi
		Marawara
	Upper Murray–Meru	Ngintait
		Yirawirung
		Ngawait
Mallee	Gorge	Ngaiawang
Gorge	Lakes	Nganguruku
Lakes Estuary	Lower Murray	Ngarrindjeri

MURRAY RIVER SECTIONS

While most commentators consider the Murray to be a unified entity, there is considerable variation in its ecology, physiology, and in the timing of Aboriginal occupation and response across the sections identified in Table 33.1.

The Highlands was an area of medium to high relief, with narrow, fast-flowing streams and eucalypt forest and woodlands. Aboriginal populations were probably small and of low density, with the people highly mobile. The rivers and forests also probably had medium- to low-subsistence potential for Aboriginal hunter-gatherers using fire, spears, and digging sticks. Archaeological evidence for this section is sparse, with some concentration of activity (e.g., stone artefacts) on river flats and mid-latitude valleys. Excavated sites are few, with intermittent dates of occupation beginning c. 25,000 years ago and increased usage in the past 3000 years (Frankel 2017: 179).

The Riverine Plain was created by the Pleistocene Lachlan, Murrumbidgee, and Murray Rivers, where prior streams carried a bedload of sand and gravels and more recent ancestral streams carried clays. It is an area of braided river channels, floodplains, backplains, swamps, lakes, and lunettes, with riparian gum forests, open woodlands, and extensive areas of saltbush and grasslands (Hill, De Decker, von der Borch, & Murray-Wallace 2009; NSW Government, n.d.; Pels 1964). This plain was a productive resource zone, especially during spring when floods overtopped the banks of the many streams to create swamps which lasted through the summer period and into the autumn. These waters carried many fish, turtles, and freshwater crayfish, and, most importantly, bulrush (*Typha* spp.), which was collected and cooked in ground ovens to provide farinaceous carbohydrate in immense quantities (Gott 1999). Archaeological evidence for use of these resources lies in the many earthen mounds situated along the course of the rivers and major creeks, many of which have been mapped and excavated. These mounds are the product of using baked clay in ovens over the past 5000 years, with the result that the mounds themselves became elevated camping places above the floodwater levels (Frankel 2017; Martin 2011). A useful by-product of bulrush was the fibre in its rhizomes. The intensive chewing of this fibre for string used in the manufacture of nets, baskets, bags, and other implements has left distinctive wear marks on the teeth of Aboriginal people from this area (Pardoe 1995: 708). Aboriginal populations in this area were large and of high density, and, at least seasonally, semi-sedentary. Human burials are common in both the mounds and source bordering dunes along the creeks.

In the Central Murray Mallee section, the river moves into a semiarid area dominated by Quaternary dunefields and a floodplain that is between 5 and 25 km wide. Here the Murray River features narrow riparian gum forests along its banks, and mallee woodlands, saltbush, and grasslands on the adjacent plains (Bowler & Magee 1978; Laut et al. 1977b). The slow-flowing and sinuous nature of the river, together with the uniformity of its sediments, means that the Central section is characterized by multiple channels, cutoffs, oxbow lakes, and billabongs that fill when the river floods at overbank stage. As with the Riverine section, this flooding creates highly productive wetlands and swamps. To the north of the Murray within the sand dune belt of southwest New South Wales, the Pleistocene Willandra Lakes have archaeological sites dating to 45,000 BP, while occupation at Lake Tyrrell to the south of the Murray in northwest Victoria goes back 30,000 years (Hiscock 2008; Richards, Pavlides, Walshe, Webber, & Johnston 2007). Along the Murray corridor, archaeological remains consist of freshwater mussel shell middens and areas of multiple heat retainer hearths dating back 15,000 years (Prendergast, Bowler, & Cupper 2009). These ages have been extended by research on the Calpurnum floodplain and Pike cliffs, both close to Renmark on the Murray River. Westell et al. (2020) report single dates on freshwater mussel middens from Pike floodplain back to c. 30,000 BP, with a further spike in dates at about 15,000 BP, slightly later than the final drying period of the Willandra Lakes system (Gillespie 1997: 243). In their totality, dates from these locations indicate human occupation of the Murray corridor intermittently in the Late Pleistocene and probably continuously through the Holocene. Multiple human burials in the Central Murray are often present on remnant dunes rather than earth mounds (Pardoe 1995). One interesting innovation for the sand dune country is the use of shovel-shaped wooden implements to dig animals such as rat-kangaroos out of their burrows (Massola 1959). Plant processing stones, including seed grindstones, are common near creeks.

The nature of the river changes again as it enters a region dominated by limestones overtopped by sands. In the Gorge section, the river channel narrows from c. 5–10 km wide in the Mallee to c. 2–3 km and flows through a trench 30 m below the level of the surrounding drylands. As a result, the area of wetlands in the Gorge section is less than half of that in the Mallee section (Walker & Thoms 1993: 112). Along the river there are riparian forest and swamplands, while on the adjacent Murray Plains there is dry Mallee woodland, open shrubland, and saltbush. The presence of limestone cliffs changes the nature of the archaeology. The Gorge section saw some of the earliest archaeological excavations in Australia at the rock shelter sites of Ngaut Ngaut (Devon Downs), Tungawa (Fromm's Landing 2 & 6), and McBean's Pound, which provided insights into some aspects of the Aboriginal economy between c. 3000 and 7000 years ago (Allen, Karstens, & Littleton 2023; Frankel 2017: 85–89). Both Paton (1983) and Smith (1978) note differences between the ethnographic observations of Aboriginal life on the river and the archaeological evidence from the rock shelters. This, however, is likely to be the result of a bias in both the ethnography and archaeology. A review of the economic evidence from these excavations and surveys along the river revealed differing patterns of exploitation, where multiple resource zones, including the Murray Plains, the riverbanks, and the river itself were used (Allen, Karstens, & Littleton 2023) (Table 33.3). The open, stratified midden site of Tartanga Island, dating to 7000 BP, reveals that quantities of fish were harvested. The greatest deficiency comes from the poor preservation of plant remains where ethnographic observations note the use of *Typha* and other aquatic plants. In his survey, Paton (1983) found little archaeological evidence in the dry country away from the river, although ethnographic recordings indicate that the Murray Plains were utilized to hunt kangaroos, wallabies, and rat kangaroos.

Finally, the river enters its lowermost reaches, the estuary and lakes, before it enters the sea at the Coorong. This final section of the Murray is a more humid environment than the semiarid sections of the river's course. The economy and material culture of Aboriginal people here demonstrate a combination of river and coastal adaptations (Berndt, Berndt, & Stanton 1993; Frankel 2017; Mackay & Eastburn 1990). Again, the archaeological signature of this area varies with the ecology and physiography, consisting of freshwater mussel middens dating between 8000 and 350 BP, and marine shellfish and other coastal foods at the estuary and river mouth (Wilson, Fallon, & Trevorrow 2012).

In the discussion that follows, most attention will be given to the Riverine Plain, the Central Murray Mallee, and the Gorge sections, as these are the areas we are most familiar with and where we have carried out most of our research.

Table 33.3. Summary of economic remains from excavated-survey archaeological sites in the Gorge Section of the Murray River noting the environments exploited and probable means of capture (after Allen, Karstens, & Littleton 2023).

Site Type— Resource Type	Large Mammals	Small to Medium Mammals	Water and Bush Rats Possums	Fish, Turtles Crayfish, Shellfish	Waterfowl	Vegetables
Environment and method of capture	Murray Plains, spear hunting	Murray Plains, nets and fire drives, spear hunting	Riverbanks and water's edge, collecting	Riverbanks and river channel, collecting	Creeks and watercourses, Net and spear hunting	Riverbanks and swamps, collecting
Shelters, Ngaut Ngaut and Tungawa 2 & 6	Present	Major	Major	Major	Present	Present?
Shelters McBean's Pound	Present	Major	Major	Major	Present	Present?
Fishing Camp, Tartanga Island	Major			Major	Present	Present?
Shore Middens, Roonka area			Present	Major	Present	Present?

Mortuary Practices

Information on burial practices along the Murray River comes from diverse archaeological sources (Table 33.4), together with ethnohistoric accounts of specific funerals and monuments observed by Europeans and generalized accounts of normative practice (Meehan 1971; Littleton 2007). Each of these sources is biased in some way: the archaeological survey has a greater potential to identify groups of burials rather than single burials; archaeological finds are biased towards better preserved remains that may result in systematic age biases; and ethnohistoric accounts are more frequently of extended burial rituals. Nevertheless, all forms of burial have been recorded along the Murray Valley: simple inhumations, delayed compound burials, bundle burials, and cremations. The resulting pattern highlights change over time as well as a complex of shared ideas and practices, with considerable spatial and temporal variability.

Even if the population of the Murray remained at only 3000 people for 10,000 years, there would be conservatively one million burials along the Murray River. Not all of these burials would survive, but in this part of Australia where the custom was to bury the dead and not disturb them, and where the soil is calcareous and conducive to good preservation of bone, the discovery of burials on survey and in excavation is inevitable.

Table 33.4. Major surveys and published excavations of Aboriginal burials along the Murray River. The number of burials is indicative only. For a more detailed list, see Littleton (1999).

Fieldwork Type	Number of Burials	Source
Surveys		
Riverine Plain	c. 80	Bonhomme (1990)
Murray-Darling	166	Pardoe (1985, 1988a, 1988b, 1989, 1993) (number excludes Darling River sites)
Mildura Region	176	Clarke & Hope (1985)
Murray-Murrumbidgee	406	Littleton (1997, 1999)
Lake Victoria	304	Littleton, Johnston, & Pardoe (1994)
Katarapko	25	Dowling (1989)
Excavations		
Kow Swamp	c. 40	Thorne et al. (1972)
Robinvale	11	Bowdler (1983)
Chowilla	100	Blackwood & Simpson (1973)
Roonka	142+	Pretty (1977)
Tartanga	3	Hale & Tindale (1930)
Ngaut ngaut (Devon downs)	4	Hale & Tindale (1930)
Tailem Bend	3	Pretty (1967)
Tungawa 2 & 6 (Fromm's Landing)	3	Mulvaney, Lawton, & Twidale (1964)
Swanport	c. 160	Stirling (1911)

The intensity of pastoral occupation causing ground disturbance and erosion has increased the likelihood of burial exposure.

While there are Pleistocene human remains from the Willandra Lakes and the Lachlan River (Pietsch et al. 2019), the oldest remains currently found on the Murray River are those from Coobool Creek, Narcurrie, and Kow Swamp. Precise dating of these remains (now reburied following repatriation) is difficult to determine (Brown 1989; Pardoe 1988a; Stone & Cupper 2003). However, based on the clustering of dates from a small number of burials and shared morphology, it is commonly accepted that the oldest burials date to the Late Pleistocene/Early Holocene (c. 15,000–9000 BP).

The Coobool Creek remains, like those from Kow Swamp, suggest that a significant number of burials occurred within a constrained area.[1] Elsewhere along the Murray, beginning around 9000–5000 BP (Roonka, Chowilla 17, Chowilla 16B, and Barham), burials begin to appear in greater numbers and in areas of higher density (Blackwood & Simpson 1973; Daley 1986; Littleton, Petchey, Walshe, & Pate 2017).

What distinguishes these groups of burials from isolated interments is their presence on particular landforms (generally, source bordering dunes along the Murray River), the density of burials (often more than 1/100 square metres in exposed sites) within restricted areas, exclusivity of use, and formality in the layout of burials. Pardoe (1988a) argued that these burial groupings operated as formal cemeteries serving to symbolize the link between corporate groups and land, following the linkage proposed by Saxe (1970) and Goldstein (1981). In this interpretation, cemeteries are used exclusively by particular descent groups.

The difficulty that arises with the cemetery concept is establishing how burial grounds were used and by whom. Work on the Riverine Plain between the Murrumbidgee and Murray Rivers demonstrates that many clustered burials largely occur in groups of between 3 and 20, with the same characteristics of high density, exclusivity of use, and formal patterns of burial. Within a single area, however, several clusters of burials with different burial orientations and positions may exist (Littleton 2002). The same variability occurs within individual sites (e.g., at Roonka—Pretty 1977) and within adjacent cemeteries (e.g., East Nanyah versus Gecko Island at Lake Victoria—Littleton & Allen 2007).

An alternative argument to groups of burials at high density acting as cemeteries of exclusive territoriality is that clusters of burials represent the accumulation of different processes over time (Littleton & Allen 2007). Places for burial have persistence both in physical terms through the marking of graves but also over a longer period by being recognized as appropriate places for burial. The variability of burials within and between sites suggests that often more than one group uses a particular location. Whether this use is successive or contemporary is unclear.

The burial site of Roonka provides some clues to the cemetery question (Pretty 1977). The earliest burial on the site is radiocarbon dated by charcoal to c. 9000 BP. In the lower level of the site, burials are predominantly males and children. In the upper levels, there are much greater numbers of adult females, and the range of burials has increased, including supine extended burials, flexed burials with people buried on either their right or left side, and a small group of prone burials. All of these groups tend to have preferred orientations although the most frequent position is an extended burial with the head to the northwest. From the dates there is little evidence of successive use and more evidence for synchronous variability (Littleton et al. 2017). This variability could suggest that, rather than burial grounds being exclusive to one social or territorial grouping (i.e., a cemetery), by the Late Holocene multiple burying groups were being incorporated within a single locale. While this is the possible sequence at Roonka, it is not necessarily the same sequence at all burial grounds up the river.

The Roonka site, along with other evidence, still leaves unanswered the questions of who forms the burying group, as well as how many people and what the linkage between them is. The number of burials at any one site is very low relative to past population sizes (e.g., even with an estimated 10,000 burials over 6000 years at Lake Victoria, that is only one or two burials per generation; see Littleton, Johnston, & Pardoe 1994). One way to test underlying demographic models is to progress from the archaeological record and reconstructions of site formation processes to modelling the possible parameters of the contributing population. But the record of burials reflects more than economics and social organization. Underlying how people bury their dead are ontological issues of what it means to be human, relationships between the living and the dead, and associations between the dead and land. The Murray River corridor is an area of both shared ideas and distinct regional variability. With the exception of the mouth of the Murray, primary burial predominated, with relatively few secondary burials (in the form of bundled burials or platform exposures). The exception is the frequently delayed burials of children, which commonly occur with a single adult (Littleton & Allen 2007). Both of these burial practices extend over a wide region, suggesting shared ideas of the relationship between children and death.

Burial monuments as documented in the ethnohistoric record demonstrate regional variability (Littleton & Allen 2020; Meehan 1971). The areas of greatest variation are the major junctions, for example, at the Murray-Darling, which were at the periphery of several groups or reflective of one group with multiple influences in the mid-nineteenth century and therefore key points of interaction (Taçon 2013). This regional distribution lacks hard boundaries.

In terms of burial, the Murray River was an area with internal variability, but it was linked by underlying interaction and some shared practices of temporal and regional depth. Whether this internal diversity is emphasized as exclusivity between neighbours or inclusivity reflecting clinal variation depends both on the marker that is being analysed and on our ability to establish the underlying demographic and economic relationships.

Morphology

Human biological variation results from the interaction of the biological, ecological, economic, and social worlds. Different analyses of human remains capture the interaction of the biological and the social at varying temporal scales, from the lifetime of the individual (e.g., deliberate tooth removal or avulsion) to the pattern of gene flow occurring over thousands of years (e.g., cranial nonmetrics) and potentially longer term adaptation to the environment (e.g., cranial morphology).

Human remains from the Murray River Valley clearly reflect change over time. Brown's (1989) analysis of the Coobool Creek Late Pleistocene remains demonstrates that both crania and teeth were significantly larger and more robust than those in the larger collection of presumed Holocene remains. The difficulty is of course that only the Riverine Plain is represented in this analysis. Conceivably, the same morphology seen in this region was present among people all down the river, but sample sizes are insufficient to be certain. Moreover, people at Coobool Creek and Kow Swamp were actively modifying heads in a way that would help to construct and signal distinctions between groups. The modified crania with their elongated, sloping foreheads would have been a distinctive marker of people from this area (Pardoe 2006).

Later remains from the same area do not show evidence of cranial deformation. However, patterns of gene flow indicated by studies of cranial metric (Pietrusewsky 1979) and nonmetric (discontinuous variants of morphology assumed to be the result of genetic inheritance patterns—Pardoe 1995) characters suggest continuities in the morphological distinctiveness of the Murray Valley and surrounding regions. As a whole, the Murray Valley populations, when considered as broad clusters (e.g., Murray Valley, Roonka, Swanport), are most similar to neighbouring groups in Victoria and South Australia and fit easily into a broad southeastern Australian pattern (e.g., Pietrusewsky 1979).

At a larger scale, however, Pardoe's (1984) analysis of more than 2500 individual human remains from across Australia emphasizes greater intraregional diversity among the Murray River groups compared to the rest of the continent. Effectively, the river serves as a conduit for gene flow, but it does not negate relationships with hinterland populations (often represented by smaller sample sizes from a significantly larger geographic region).

The same pattern occurs in Pleistocene groups; this suggests that the linear (riverine) patterning is of long standing (Pardoe 1984, 2006). Differentiation between Murray groups suggests shorter marriage distances, possible in situations of higher population density. Following Tindale's (1974) distribution of linguistic groups along the Murray, the pattern of greater gene flow between neighbours along the river than with more dispersed populations behind emerges. The extent to which groups interact may result in a pattern consistent with territorial exclusion where there is less gene flow between neighbouring groups than expected given population sizes (Pardoe 1994).

Pardoe's cranial nonmetric analysis (1984) is based on the sample mean, which has the effect of concealing the degree of diversity within each sample. Pardoe's (2006: fig. 2) later analysis demonstrates how, with more than one sample from a single region, there is potentially greater diversity within a 'linguistic group' than between groups, suggesting that while the overall structure of the river corridor dominating gene flow may hold over time, more diverse local processes are occurring. Along the river there are points with marked heterogeneity. The nonmetric analysis demonstrates that the river served to structure relationships, but it does not suggest that a simple model of cultural exclusion explains the Holocene pattern of variation—there is both regional and temporal variation.

While most work has focussed on cranial characteristics, postcranial morphology among Murray Valley human remains has also been studied (Bennett 1995; Hill, Durband, & Walshe 2016, Hill et al. 2020; Macho & Freedman 1987; Pardoe 2006). Similar to cranial morphology, characteristics of the postcrania respond to patterns of gene flow and adaptation to both local and developmental circumstances. Most recently, international studies of long bone shape have revealed a relationship to patterns of mobility and work (Ruff 2008; Stock & Pfeiffer 2001). It is argued, for example, that populations who undertake high rates of walking and running produce (on average) femurs with a more oval than circular cross-section. Hill, Durband, and Walshe (2016) have used this correlation to examine changes over time at Roonka, dividing the sample into pre- El Niño Southern Oscillation (ENSO) period (pre-c. 4000 BP, characterized as warmer and wetter) and post-ENSO period (post-c. 4000 BP) individuals. They argue that the post-ENSO subsample has more oval femoral midshafts indicative of greater mobility (Hill et al. 2016), particularly among females who also show less asymmetry in development of their upper limbs compared to males (Hill et al. 2020). The temporal difference is interpreted as indicative of a trend towards a more diverse diet and the incorporation of 'high handling cost' foods into the diet. The difficulty is that, if use of the burial ground has changed over time, then it is not clear that the two samples originate from the same population in the sense that early use may be biased away from younger males and females, and it is known that patterns of mobility and of work vary by age. Nevertheless, the analysis points to the need to interrogate patterns within samples, which may reveal more fine-grained local changes.

The overarching picture of populations in the Murray Valley is that of biological relatedness held together by patterns of gene exchange. These patterns change over time, and we have relatively little sense of how they vary between areas of the Murray Valley. Some places such as the Murray-Darling junction have marked degrees of diversity, which serve to reflect a major interaction zone. The comparative analysis of large undated samples provides an underlying pattern, but that needs to be tested using multiple techniques (including isotope analyses such as strontium and oxygen) and differing types of dated samples.

PALAEOPATHOLOGY

Human remains reflect the accumulation of life stresses up to the point of death. The interpretation of a person's past life from their remains—an osteobiography—is a window into a very specific event or point of time (e.g., the Mallee Cliffs burial—Pardoe 1988b). While such individual descriptions provide insight, they also incorporate ambiguity due to the nature of archaeological and osteological evidence, as the reinterpretation of a woman from Roonka demonstrates (Littleton & Wallace 2019). These biographies start to build a picture of past life. As they are compared and patterns emerge, both the full range of variability and the relationship between disease, stress, economy, and ecology can be analysed.

Multiple studies have been done of disease and injury in past human remains from the Murray River (Green 1982; Littleton 2005; Pretty & Kricun 1989; Prokopec 1979; Robertson 2003; Sandison 1973), but Webb's (1989, 2009) analysis of museum collections of human remains in the early 1980s is the most extensive regional comparison. With the exception of Late Pleistocene/Early Holocene remains (e.g., Kow Swamp) and the remains from Swanport (Stirling 1911), the majority of the Murray Valley remains analysed originated from the George Murray Black Collection. These were largely undated remains presumed to date primarily from the Mid- to Late Holocene. Beyond biases inherent to an archaeological record (differential preservation, differential burial), the collection was affected by an expressed preference on the part of institutions for particular remains (pathologized, unusual, crania versus postcrania) (Robertson 2007). Most have now been repatriated to traditional owners of the area where the remains originated, though unprovenanced remains continue to be an issue (Pickering 2015; Russell 2010).

The conditions analysed by Webb (1989) were primarily nonspecific indicators of stress (cribra orbitalia, linear enamel hypoplasia, Harris lines, bone infection) and trauma. The underlying premise of palaeopathological analysis was at the time that high rates of such markers upon human remains reflected poor human health. Most notably, Webb found very high rates of cribra orbitalia among children and adults from the Murray samples—particularly his Riverine Plain sample (which he termed central Murray)—and a fairly high frequency of linear enamel hypoplasia. Comparative analysis with frequencies elsewhere in the world suggested that rates of cribra were much higher and comparable to Middle Mississipian (Illinois, USA) rates for children, pointing to a startling similarity between sedentary maize agriculturalists (Cohen & Armelagos 1984a, 1984b) and Aboriginal people residing in the Riverine Plain (the highest rates were recorded at Kerang). The parallel prompted Webb to suggest that the Murray in general, but his Riverine Plain in particular, was 'an infectious environment' inhabited by populations existing at high population density (Webb 1989: 147).

However, the patterns of infection and trauma in the central Murray are not consistent with an interpretation of a stressed, dense population. Dense, sedentary populations tend to experience relatively high rates of nonspecific infection, as wounds heal slowly and pathogens are easily transmitted between individuals. Similarly, interpersonal violence is often assumed to be greater in stressed populations who are competing over resources. Neither of these conditions occurs at higher frequency in the Riverine Plain area (Pardoe, Allen, & Jones 2014; Webb 2009).

Analytical ambiguities in interpreting signs of disease in human remains need to be taken into account. A pivotal article written by Wood, Milner, Harpending, and Weiss (1992) points to the osteological paradox: skeletal samples are not unbiased indicators of the once living but instead comprise nonsurvivors who potentially include the most frail and the most common age group. Furthermore, 'better health makes for worse skeletons'. Conditions that show in the human skeleton are generally a response to chronic conditions, and that response is more likely in a person with a healthy immune system. Acutely ill individuals or individuals unable to mount an immune response are more likely to die before any signs of disease are seen upon the skeleton. Robertson (2003) tackled these issues in relation to interpretation of cribra orbitalia in the Murray region and concluded that the rates recorded among human remains from this area may be overestimated due to temporal mixing and biased collecting practices.

An example of this issue of representation is seen in the analysis of linear enamel hypoplasia in Murray River populations. Both Green (1982) (Rufus River) and Smith (2016) (Roonka) have recorded linear enamel hypoplasia. They both document virtually ubiquitous hypoplasic defects among individuals. However, as Smith and Littleton (2019) show, most people have very few defects, and these defects are not associated with a greater chance of dying. In other words, childhood stressors are present, but the majority of individuals experienced those stressors at defined periods of childhood and survived.

People living on the Murray River existed within an ecology different from elsewhere in Australia. However, this is not a single environment, and not all indicators of disease and injury show a consistent picture. Comparison of the rates of cribra orbitalia from Roonka with the collections studied by Webb shows a startling variation. Rates of cribra orbitalia at Roonka are less than half those recorded in the Riverina area (Webb's Central Murray) and significantly less than those at the Rufus River (Figure 33.2). Over the space of 40 years, even using the same criteria, it is impossible to be assured that there is no difference in recording. But that cannot account for the entire disparity between the two samples—there is significant regional variation.

The rates of disease among human remains along the Murray is clearly a product of particular regional ecologies, but interpreting those rates requires careful consideration of the chronology of the samples. For example, Roonka covers a period (with gaps) between 9000 and 150 BP, including six postcontact individuals who clearly spent at least part of their lives in a rapidly changing ecology. In addition, the samples used in these analyses are not populations; rather, they are samples of human remains from particular sites. The ethnographic record clearly points to different burial locales, depending on an individual's age and gender (Littleton 2007). As such, these samples cannot be treated unproblematically as a palaeodemographic record representative of entire communities. Finally, in order to understand particular lesions, it is necessary to identify the local stressors, the severity of the lesion, and whether it had healed or was active at the time of death?

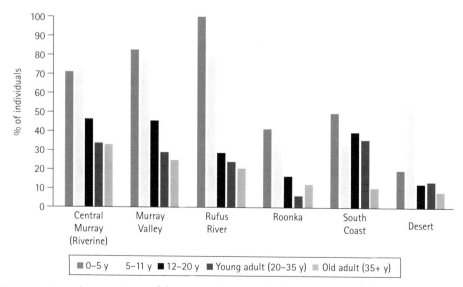

FIGURE 33.2. A comparison of the rates of cribra orbitalia between a single site, Roonka, and the relevant regional groupings of Webb (1989).

Analysis of pathology highlights significant regional differences along the Murray River that are a response to differing subsistence patterns and stressors. There are some striking similarities; for example, linear enamel hypoplasia at Rufus and Roonka is very similar and resembles the historical patterns observed at Yuendummu in central Australia (Smith 2016). There are, however, striking differences, particularly in the level of heterogeneity between different samples. The Riverine Plain samples analysed by Webb (1989) are surprisingly homogeneous, and there is also a reflection of this similarity in some of the dental wear analysis discussed below. The questions then are what are these samples and who do they represent? Detailed contextualized analysis of particular groups of individuals can clarify those patterns and give a clearer idea of both spatial and temporal variation.

DIETARY ANALYSES

Bioarchaeological studies of diet also highlight the nature of variability along the Murray River, indicating that rather than there being a single dietary pattern common to Murray River societies, the types of resources utilized and their relative proportions varied along the length of the river. There is also evidence of dietary variation between individuals buried within a site. However, it is likely that both inter- and intrasite dietary variation is greater than the existing data suggests. This variation is a result of the limitations of certain methods, the nature of the archaeological record on the Murray River, and a focus on population rather than individual-level analyses.

A number of factors may contribute to dietary variation along the Murray River corridor. As discussed earlier, the ecology of the Murray River and its relationship to the surrounding landscape changes as it travels westward from its headwaters in the Great Dividing Range to Lake Alexandrina at its mouth. Such changes also resulted in changes in available resources and in the abundance and seasonality of those resources. Analysis of dental wear patterning suggests regional variation in resource exploitation, particularly in relation to seeds, tubers, and potentially molluscs (Brown 1978; Littleton et al. 2013; Molnar et al. 1989; Richards 1984). For example, while heavy molar wear is seen in all groups analysed along the river, remains from around Euston also had a flat plane of wear on the anterior and central teeth, a pattern not seen in people from Mildura to the Rufus River (Littleton et al. 2013; Molnar et al. 1989). Suggestions regarding the difference in wear planes include a greater reliance on tubers such as the rhizomes of *Typha* on the Riverine Plain, seed-grinding practices in the Central Murray/Mallee, or the greater diversity of ecological zones within the Central Murray/Mallee region (Littleton et al. 2013; Molnar et al. 1989). A number of factors other than diet can impact dental wear patterning. however, and while Molnar et al. (1989) rule out the role of tooth size as an underlying case of variation in wear patterns between groups, nonmasticatory tooth use such as processing fibres, and variability in facial robusticity and occlusal loading are potential additional contributing factors that require further investigation. In addition, Littleton et al. (2013) demonstrate that the use of population averages in analysing dental macrowear can obscure significant differences between individuals. Indeed, analyses of dental wear by age and sex show marked intragroup variability, but notably also that the specific patterns of age- and sex-related wear change by location (see Littleton 2017; Littleton et al. 2013; Richards 1984; Smith, Prokopec, & Pretty 1988). So even when dental wear is uniformly severe, its patterning reflects not just ecological zones and the available resources but also differences in economic organization between those zones.

As Figure 33.3 demonstrates, stable isotope analyses of the remains from Roonka and Swanport also show inter- and intrasite variability in diet (Owen 2004; Pate 1998b, 1998c; Pate & Owen 2014). At both sites, the majority of individuals have isotopic signatures that indicate they were relying primarily on local foods from the Murray River and adjacent Mallee, specifically C3 plants (i.e., those plants that produce a 3-carbon compound during photosynthesis as opposed to a 4-carbon compound, particularly temperate shrubs, trees, and some grasses), freshwater fish and shellfish, and terrestrial animals feeding on C3 plants, but the relative proportions of each of these food sources appears to differ between the sites. The demographic makeup of the respective samples may influence these results, however, as there is also evidence for intrasite variation

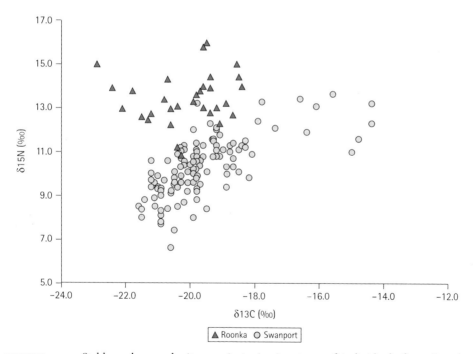

FIGURE 33.3. Stable carbon and nitrogen isotopic signatures of individuals from Roonka ($n = 32$) and Swanport ($n = 121$)

(Source: Pate 1998b)

(Source: Owen 2004).

in diet consistent with cultural practices such as age- and/or gender-restricted foods and division of labour. Differences in the $\delta^{15}N$ values of individuals at Swanport suggest that men were eating foods from higher trophic levels (e.g., large freshwater fish and terrestrial animals) than women, as were adults when compared to nonadults less than 16 years of age (Owen 2004; Pate & Owen 2014). At Roonka, on average, nonadults and adult females had $\delta^{13}C$ values that were ~0.7‰ more negative than those of adult males. This finding suggests that the diets of children and women contained more $\delta^{13}C$-depleted foods such as aquatic and terrestrial plants and freshwater shellfish than men's diets (Pate 1998b).

Dietary reconstructions along the Murray River using stable isotope analysis are, however, highly complex and a number of factors can limit or impact interpretation of data. These and other isotopic analyses of individuals from the Roonka and Swanport sites (e.g., Hobson & Collier 1984; Pate 1995a, 1995b, 1997a, 2000, 2017) have focussed primarily on stable carbon and nitrogen isotopes in bone collagen. In addition to issues of collagen preservation and diagenesis, which are limiting factors (see Pate 1997b, 1998a, 1998c) often skewing samples towards more recent remains, the isotopic values of collagen reflect primarily the protein component of diet rather than total diet (Krueger & Sullivan 1984) and are an average of an individual's diet over the last decades of their life (Eriksson & Liden 2013; Katzenberg 2007; Price 2015; Sealy, Armstrong, & Schrire 1995). Furthermore, within a freshwater environment there are multiple potential sources of carbon and factors that can influence carbon fractionation. Thus, the isotopic signatures of fish being consumed can vary depending on when (season) and where the fish are caught (Cartwright 2010; Hardy, Krull, Hartley, & Oliver 2010; Hecky & Hesslein 1995; Katzenberg & Weber 1999; Zohary, Erez, Gophen, Berman-Frank, & Stiller 1994). Studies have also shown that $\delta^{13}C$ values in terrestrial C3 plants at the base of food chains can vary based on aridity (O'Leary 1988; Pate & Krull 2007). As Pate (2017) emphasizes, as a result of all of these factors, continued analysis of ecological and isotopic data on the food sources available in the vicinity of the riverine zone is vital to improving our understanding of isotopic variability in populations along the Murray River.

Despite these limitations, it is clear that a simple classification of Murray River societies as having a 'riverine diet' is insufficient. While the river undoubtedly plays a significant role in shaping diet, this blanket term ignores the nuances of the variation in diet both between and within Murray River societies. Instead, as the bioarchaeological evidence indicates, discussions of diet and subsistence practices along the Murray River need to be contextualized within a specific local environment. Ongoing analysis of archaeological material, as well as modern flora and fauna, continues to add to our understanding of the variability of the environment, particularly food resources both within and between specific locales along the Murray River. Currently, the role of time in contributing to variation in diet is difficult to assess due to the limited dating evidence for many of the human remains from the Murray Valley. However, technological improvements, particularly in the areas of isotopic analysis and radiocarbon dating, are now allowing for analysis of a wider range of sample types, including in cases where preservation had previously been an issue. Such improvements in the understanding of local ecologies, dating, and analysis of dietary indicators from different time periods within an individual's lifespan (e.g., comparison of isotopic signatures in bone collagen and dental enamel, or the calculation of age-related dental wear gradients) have also led to an increased emphasis on taking an individual-up rather than regional-down approach to dietary research on the Murray River. As a result of these factors, future bioarchaeological studies of diet on the Murray River may more accurately assess the role of time in contributing to dietary variability as well as the true extent of inter- and intragroup variability in diet.

Themes and Debates

This review of the bioarchaeology of the Riverine Plain to the Murray gorge has identified the unifying factors between Murray River societies but has not seen the Murray as a unity. The Murray is both a shared cultural area and heterogeneous—culturally, ecologically, and biologically. While the river served as a conduit for gene flow, people maintained relatively porous boundaries with hinterland groups (as evidenced in linguistic, nonmetric skeletal, burial, and dietary analyses). Populations along the river shared a dependence on riverine resources, but they also had differing emphases (as seen in different proportions of food types and stable isotopes).

The nature of the archaeological record in this region has determined what narratives are drawn. The visibility and survivorship of differing site types, processes of site formation, and the degree of chronological and temporal control, all structure the available data. Particularly in relation to bioarchaeological work, the difference between a sample and a population needs to be remembered. This very partial record is a collection of samples from different locales, not a grouping of populations.

Nevertheless, the integration of the archaeological and bioarchaeological records gives a closer view of the tension between unity and diversity along the Murray River. Developing techniques (e.g., strontium analysis, aDNA, proteomics) all provide new ways of testing existing models and of addressing new questions (e.g., migration, division of labour, the role of different age groups, the structuring of social groups).

Our studies of Murray River peoples concur with the genetic studies by Van Holst Pellekaan, Liu, and Wilton (2010) showing that Darling River peoples were long standing. There are differences between the Pleistocene human remains and the more recent material, but within the Holocene period there appear to be few major changes, with variations the product of multiple and local factors. To a degree, this patterning is at odds with older archaeological interpretations that considered changes in populations, or in cultures, to be the norm. Considerable further work needs to be done in integrating the bioarchaeology with the archaeology and ecology of the region and in considering the implications of differing findings.

However, underlying these differences is the need for joint projects with Aboriginal communities which address Aboriginal priorities as well as scientific priorities.

Nondestructive techniques and recording are always a first step. Future work is not going to be driven by existing collections but from surveys and from individual or small groups of burials exposed through erosion or in the course of development. That places responsibilities on those recording not only to collect and store data in accordance with Aboriginal communities' wishes but also to show how building detailed interpretations in the future is going to depend upon those individual records. Working with the dead entails a sense of long-term obligation as well as a relationship with the dead themselves and with their descendent communities. In this respect, while repatriation has been ongoing, return of human remains does not negate relationships and responsibilities between the institutions and individuals involved and the receiving communities.

The bioarchaeological work done to date along the Murray Valley has been driven by a regional comparative and primarily economic/subsistence focus. It is in the comparison of rates of disease or genetic diversity between the River and elsewhere that the narrative has been drawn. Detailed and contextualized studies of dated burials and individuals serve as a way both to test these grand narratives and to parameterize them—specifically, to define the extent of sedentism, mobility, or exclusivity. These detailed studies can also incorporate a wider range of perspectives, including focus beyond the economic to the social and cultural practices that made the Murray Valley a shared cultural area with significant internal heterogeneity.

ACKNOWLEDGMENTS

This work was undertaken in collaboration with, and the permission of, the River Peoples of the Murray and Mallee Inc. We acknowledge and thank the Ngaiwaing, the Traditional Owners of Roonka, and the Ngaiwait, Nganguruku, Ngingtait, Eraweirung, Ngaralte, and Ngarkat. It is undertaken with ethical clearance from the UAHPEC committee, University of Auckland (010311). Thanks to Caitlin Smith and Ashley McGarry for their editorial help. The research was funded by the Royal Society of New Zealand Marsden Fund (14-UOA-19). Seline McNamee, Anthropology, School of Social Sciences, University of Auckland, drew the maps.

NOTE

1. Coobool Creek remains were collected in 1949 and 1950 by George Murray Black. It is the c. 70 remains from 1950 that are heavily carbonate encrusted and morphologically distinct from more recent remains (see Brown 1989; Pardoe 1988a).

REFERENCES

Allen, H. (1972). *Where the crow flies backward: Man and land in the Darling Basin* (PhD thesis). Australian National University, Canberra.

Allen, H., Karstens, S., & Littleton, J. (2023). Legacy Archaeology: Aboriginal subsistence response to Holocene environmental changes using faunal evidence from archaeological sites on the Murray River, South Australia. *The Holocene, 33*(4),432–445.

Bennett, C. M. (1995). *Morphology of the major limb bones of South Australian Aborigines* (PhD thesis). La Trobe University, Melbourne.

Berndt, R. M., Berndt, C. H., & Stanton, J. (1993). *A world that was: The Yaraldi of the Murray River and lakes, South Australia*. Carlton: Melbourne University Press.

Birdsell, J. B. (1953). Some environmental and cultural factors influencing the structuring of Australian Aboriginal populations. *The American Naturalist, 87*(834), 171–207.

Blackwood, R., & Simpson, K. (1973). Attitudes of Aboriginal skeletons excavated in the Murray Valley region between Mildura and Renmark, Australia. *Memoirs of the National Museum of Victoria, 34*, 99–150.

Bonhomme, T. (1990). Report on burials and sandmining in the Riverine Plain. Report to NSW National Parks and Wildlife Service, Sydney.

Bowdler, S. (1983). Archaeological investigation of a threatened Aboriginal burial site near Robinvale, on the Murray River, Victoria. Report to the Murray Valley Aboriginal Co-operative, Euston, Victoria.

Bowler, J. M., & Magee, J. W. (1978). Geomorphology of the Mallee Region in semi-arid Northern Victoria and Western New South Wales. *Proceedings of the Royal Society of Victoria, 90*, 5–26.

Brown, P. (1978). *The ultrastructure of dental abrasion: Its relationship to diet* (BA Honours thesis). Australian National University, Canberra.

Brown, P. (1989). *Coobool Creek*. Terra Australis 13. Canberra: Department of Prehistory, Australian National University.

Cartwright, I. (2010). The origins and behaviour of carbon in a major semi-arid river, the Murray River, Australia, as constrained by carbon isotopes and hydrochemistry. *Applied Geochemistry, 25*, 1734–1745.

Clarke, P., & Hope, J. (1985). Aboriginal burials and shell middens at Snaggy Bend and other sites on the Central Murray River. *Australian Archaeology, 20*, 68–89.

Cohen, M. N., & Armelagos, G. J. (1984a). Disease and death at Dr Dickson's Mounds. *Natural History, 9*, 12–8.

Cohen, M. N., & Armelagos, G. J. (Eds.). (1984b). *Paleopathology at the origins of agriculture*. New York: Academic Press.

Daley, C. (1986). *The Barham skeletons* (MA thesis). The University of Sydney, Sydney.

Dowling, P. (1989). *Violent epidemics* (MA thesis). Australian National University, Canberra.

Edwards, R. (1972). *Aboriginal bark canoes of the Murray Valley*. Adelaide: Rigby.

Eriksson, G., & Liden, K. (2013). Dietary life histories in Stone Age Northern Europe. *Journal of Anthropological Archaeology, 32*(3), 288–302.

Frankel, D. (2017). *Between the Murray and the sea: Aboriginal archaeology in south-eastern Australia*. Sydney: Sydney University Press.

Gillespie, R. (1997). Burnt and unburnt carbon: Dating charcoal and burnt bone from the Willandra Lakes, Australia. *Radiocarbon, 39*(3), 239–250.

Goldstein, L. (1981). One-dimensional archaeology and multi-dimensional people: Spatial organization and mortuary analysis. In R. Chapman, I. Kinnes, & K. Randsborg (Eds.), *The archaeology of death* (pp. 53–70). Cambridge: Cambridge University Press.

Gott, B. (1999). Cumbungi, Typha species: A staple Aboriginal food in southern Australia. *Australian Aboriginal Studies 1999 /1*, 33–50.

Green, M. K. (1982). *A review of enamel hypoplasia and its application to Australian prehistory* (BA Honours thesis). Australian National University, Canberra.

Hale, H. M., & Tindale, N. B. (1930). Notes on some human remains in the lower Murray Valley, South Australia. *Records of the South Australian Museum, 4*, 145–218.

Hardy, C. M., Krull, E. S., Hartley, D. M., & Oliver, R. L. (2010). Carbon source accounting for fish using combined DNA and stable isotope analysis in a regulated lowland River Weir pool. *Molecular Ecology*, 19, 197–212.

Hecky, R. E., & Hesslein, R. H. (1995). Contributions of benthic algae to lake food webs as revealed by stable isotope analysis. *Journal of the North American Benthological Society*, 14(4), 631–653.

Hercus, L. (1986). *Victorian languages: A late survey.* Pacific Linguistics Series B No 77. Canberra: Australian National University.

Hercus, L. (2010). Aboriginal people and languages of the Murray River in the 1850s. In H. Allen (Ed.), *Australia: William Blandowski's Illustrated Encyclopaedia of Aboriginal Australia* (pp. 169–173). Canberra: Aboriginal Studies Press.

Hill, E. C., Durband, A. C., & Walshe, K. (2016). Risk minimization and a late Holocene increase in mobility at Roonka Flat, South Australia: An analysis of lower limb bone diaphyseal shape. *American Journal of Physical Anthropology*, 161(1), 94–103.

Hill, E. C., Pearson, O. M., Durband, A. C., Walshe, K., Carlson, K. J., & Grine, F. E. (2020). An examination of the cross-sectional geometrical properties of the long bone diaphyses of Holocene foragers from Roonka, South Australia. *American Journal of Physical Anthropology*, 172, 682–697.

Hill, P. J., De Decker, P., von der Borch, C., & Murray-Wallace, C. V. (2009). Ancestral Murray River on the Lacepede Shelf, southern Australia: Late Quaternary migrations of a major river outlet and strandline development. *Australian Journal of Earth Sciences*, 56(2), 135–157.

Hiscock, P. (2008). *Archaeology of ancient Australia.* London: Routledge.

Hobson, K. A., & Collier, S. (1984). Marine and terrestrial protein in Australian Aboriginal diets. *Current Anthropology*, 25(2), 238–240.

Humphries, P., King, A. J., & Koehn, J. D. (1999). Fish, flows and flood plains: Links between freshwater fishes and their environment in the Murray-Darling River system, Australia. *Environmental Biology of Fishes*, 56, 129–151.

Katzenberg, M. A. (2007). Stable isotope analysis: A tool for studying past diet, demography and life history. In M. A. Katzenberg & S. R. Saunders (Eds.), *Biological anthropology of the human skeleton* (pp. 411–441). Hoboken, NJ: John Wiley & Sons.

Katzenberg, M. A., & Weber, A. (1999). Stable isotope ecology and palaeodiet in the Lake Baikal region of Siberia. *Journal of Archaeological Science*, 26(6), 651–659.

Keen, I. (2004). *Aboriginal economy and society: Australia at the threshold of colonisation.* Melbourne: Oxford University press.

Kelly, D. (2014). *Archaeology of Aboriginal fish traps in the Murray–Darling basin, Australia* (Honours thesis). Charles Sturt University, Wagga Wagga.

Krueger, H. W., & Sullivan, C. H. (1984). Models for carbon isotope fractionation between diet and bone. *Stable Isotopes in Nutrition*, 258, 205–220.

Laut, P., Heyligers, P. C., Keig, G., Loffler, E., Margules, G., & Scott, R. M. (Eds.). (1977a). *Environments of South Australia. Province 1. South East.* Canberra: CSIRO Division of Land Use Research.

Laut, P., Heyligers, P. C., Keig, G., Loffler, E., Margules, G., & Scott, R. M. (Eds.). (1977b). *Environments of South Australia. Province 2. Murray Mallee.* Canberra: CSIRO Division of Land Use Research.

Lawrence, R. (1968). *Aboriginal habitat and economy.* Occasional Paper 6, Department of Geography, School of General Studies. Canberra: Australian National University.

Littleton, J. (1997). *Burial sites on the Hay Plain.* Report to the Australian Institute of Aboriginal and Torres Strait Islander Studies, Canberra.

Littleton, J. (1999). East and west: Burial practices along the Murray River. *Archaeology in Oceania, 34*(1), 1–14.

Littleton, J. (2002). Mortuary behaviour on the Hay Plain: Do cemeteries exist? *Archaeology in Oceania, 37*(3), 105–122.

Littleton, J. (2005). Data quarrying in the Western Riverina: A regional perspective on postcontact health. In I. Macfarlane, M-J. Mountain, & R. Paton (Eds.), *Many exchanges: Archaeology, history, community and the work of Isabel McBryde* (pp. 199–218). Aboriginal History Monograph 11. Canberra: Aboriginal History Inc.

Littleton, J. (2007). Time and memory: Historic accounts of Aboriginal burials in south-eastern Australia. *Aboriginal History, 31,* 103–121.

Littleton, J. (2017). Dental wear and age grading at Roonka, South Australia. *American Journal of Physical Anthropology, 163*(3), 519–530.

Littleton, J., & Allen, H. (2007). Hunter-gatherer burials and the creation of persistent places in southeastern Australia. *Journal of Anthropological Archaeology, 26*(2), 283–298.

Littleton, J., & Allen, H. (2020). Monumental landscapes and the agency of the dead along the Murray River, Australia. *World Archaeology, 52*(1), 120–132.

Littleton, J., Johnston, H., & Pardoe, C. (1994). *The Lake Victoria lakebed survey.* Report to NSW National Parks and Wildlife Service, Sydney.

Littleton, J., Petchey, F., Walshe, K., & Pate, F. D. (2017). A preliminary redating of the Holocene Roonka burials, south-eastern Australia. *Archaeology in Oceania, 52*(2), 98–107.

Littleton, J., Scott, R., Mcfarlane, G., & Walshe, K. (2013). Hunter-gatherer variability: Dental wear in South Australia. *American Journal of Physical Anthropology, 152,* 273–296.

Littleton, J., & Wallace, S. (2019). Ambiguity in the bioarchaeological record: The case of "euthanasia" at Roonka, South Australia. *Bioarchaeology International, 3*(2), 103–117.

Macho, G., & Freedman, L. (1987). *A re-analysis of the Andrew A. Abbie morphometric data on Australian Aborigines.* Occasional Papers in Human Biology No. 4. Canberra: Australian Institute of Aboriginal Studies.

Mackay, N., & Eastburn, D. (Eds.). (1990). *The Murray.* Canberra: Murray Darling Basin Commission.

Martin, S. (2011). Palaeoecological evidence associated with earth mounds of the Murray Riverine Plain, south-eastern Australia. *Environmental Archaeology, 16,* 162–172.

Massola, A. (1959). Wooden shovels of the Aborigines of south-east Australia. *Mankind, 5,* 289.

McCarthy, F. (1957). Habitat, economy and equipment of the Australian Aborigines. *Australian Journal of Science, 19,* 88–96.

MDBA (Murray-Darling Basin Authority). (2020). Climate. Accessed at https://www.mdba.gov.au/discover-basin/landscape/climate, 12 February 2020.

Meehan, B. (1971). *The form, distribution and antiquity of Australian Aboriginal mortuary patterns* (MA thesis). University of Sydney, Sydney.

Molnar, S., Richards, L., Mckee, J., & Molnar, I. (1989). Tooth wear in Australian Aboriginal populations from the river Murray Valley. *American Journal of Physical Anthropology, 79*(2), 185–196.

Mulvaney, D. J., Lawton, G. H., & Twidale, C. R. (Eds.). (1964). Archaeological excavation of Rock Shelter No. 6, Fromm's Landing, South Australia. *Proceedings of the Royal Society of Victoria, 77*(2), 479–516.

New South Wales Government. (n.d.). Riverina Landforms. Accessed at https://www.envi ronment.nsw.gov.au/bioregions/Riverina-Landform.htm, 28 February 2020.

O'leary, M. H. (1988). Carbon isotopes in photosynthesis. *Bioscience, 38*, 328–336.

Owen, T. D. (2004). *Of more than usual interest: Bioarchaeological analysis of Aboriginal skeletal material from southeastern South Australia* (PhD thesis). Flinders University, Adelaide.

Pardoe, C. (1984). *Prehistoric human morphological variation in Australia* (PhD thesis). Australian National University, Canberra.

Pardoe, C. (1985). Variation in mortuary patterning along the Darling River. Unpublished report. Australian Institute of Aboriginal and Torres Strait Islander Studies, Canberra.

Pardoe, C. (1988a). The cemetery as symbol. The distribution of prehistoric Aboriginal burial grounds in southeastern Australia. *Archaeology in Oceania, 23*(1), 1–16.

Pardoe, C. (1988b). The Mallee cliffs burial (Central River Murray) and population-based archaeology. *Australian Archaeology, 27*, 45–62.

Pardoe, C. (1989). Archaeology of the western Lindsay Island meander scroll. Unpublished report. Australian Institute of Aboriginal and Torres Strait Islander Studies, Canberra.

Pardoe, C. (1993). Wamba Yadu, a later Holocene cemetery of the Central Murray River. *Archaeology in Oceania, 28*, 77–84.

Pardoe, C. (1994). Bioscapes: The evolutionary landscape of Australia. *Archaeology in Oceania, 29*(3), 182–190.

Pardoe, C. (1995). Riverine, biological and cultural evolution in southeastern Australia. *Antiquity, 69*(265), 696–713.

Pardoe, C. (2006). Becoming Australian: Evolutionary processes and biological variation from ancient to modern times. *Before Farming, 1*, 1–21.

Pardoe, C., Allen, M. W., & Jones, T. L. (2014). Conflict and territoriality in Aboriginal Australia: evidence from biology and ethnography. In M. W. Allen & T. L. Jones (Eds.), *Re-examining a Pacified past: Violence and warfare among hunter-gatherers* (pp. 112–132). Walnut Creek, USA: Left Coast Press.

Pate, F. D. (1995a). Palaeodietary inferences from bone collagen stable carbon isotopes at Roonka Flat, South Australia. *Australian Archaeology, 40*, 57.

Pate, F. D. (1995b). Stable carbon isotope assessment of hunter-gatherer mobility in prehistoric South Australia. *Journal of Archaeological Science, 22*, 81–87.

Pate, F. D. (1997a). Bone chemistry and paleodiet: Reconstructing prehistoric subsistence-settlement systems in Australia. *Journal of Anthropological Archaeology, 16*, 103–120.

Pate, F. D. (1997b). Bone collagen diagenesis at Roonka Flat, South Australia: Implications for isotopic analysis. *Archaeology in Oceania, 32*, 170–175.

Pate, F. D. (1998a). Bone collagen preservation at the Roonka Flat Aboriginal burial Ground: A natural laboratory. *Journal of Field Archaeology, 25*, 203–217.

Pate, F. D. (1998b). Bone collagen stable nitrogen and carbon isotopes as indicators of past human diet and landscape use in southeastern South Australia. *Australian Archaeology, 46*, 23–29.

Pate, F. D. (1998c). Stable carbon and nitrogen isotope evidence for prehistoric hunter-gatherer diet in the lower Murray River Basin, South Australia. *Archaeology in Oceania, 33*, 92–99.

Pate, F. D. (2000). Bone chemistry and palaeodiet: Bioarchaeological research at Roonka Flat, Lower Murray River, South Australia 1983–1999. *Australian Archaeology, 50*, 67–74.

Pate, F. D. (2017). Diet, mobility and subsistence-systems in the late Holocene lower Murray River basin of South Australia: Testing models of Aboriginal seasonal mobility and sedentism with isotopic and archaeological data. *Journal of the Anthropological Society of South Australia, 41*, 123–171.

Pate, F. D., & Krull, E. (2007). Carbon isotope discrimination by C3 pasture grasses along a rainfall gradient in South Australia: Implications for palaeoecological studies. *Quaternary Australasia, 24*(2), 29–33.

Pate, F. D., & Owen, T. D. (2014). Stable carbon and nitrogen isotopes as indicators of sedentism and territoriality in late Holocene South Australia. *Archaeology in Oceania, 49*, 86–94.

Paton, R. C. (1983). *An analysis of Aboriginal subsistence in the lower Murray District, South Australia* (BA Honours thesis). Australian National University, Canberra.

Pels, S. (1964). The present and ancestral Murray River system. *Australian Geographical Studies, 2*(2), 111–119.

Peterson, N. (1976). The natural and cultural areas of Aboriginal Australia: A preliminary analysis of population groupings with adaptive significance. In N. Peterson (Ed.), *Tribes and boundaries in Australia* (pp. 50–71). Canberra: Australian Institute of Aboriginal Studies.

Pickering, M. (2015). Rewards and frustrations: Repatriation of Aboriginal and Torres Strait Islander ancestral remains by the National Museum of Australia. *International Handbooks of Museum Practice, 3*, 455–478.

Pietrusewsky, M. (1979). Craniometric variation in Pleistocene Australian and more recent Australian and New Guinean populations studied by multivariate procedures. *Occasional Papers in Human Biology, 2*, 83–123).

Pietsch, T., Kemp, J., Pardoe, C., Grün, R., Olley, J., & Wood, R. (2019). A multi-method approach to dating the burial and skeleton of Kiacatoo Man, New South Wales, Australia. *Journal of Quaternary Science, 34*(8), 662–673.

Prendergast, A. L., Bowler, J. M., & Cupper, M. L. (2009). Late Quaternary environments and human occupation in the Murray River Valley of northwestern Victoria. In A. Fairbairn, S. O'Connor, & B. Marwick (Eds.), *New directions in archaeological science* (pp. 55–74). Terra Australis 28. Canberra: Australia National University ePress.

Pretty, G. L. (1977). The cultural chronology of the Roonka Flat: A preliminary consideration. In R. Wright (Ed.), *Stone tools as cultural markers* (pp. 288–331). Canberra: Australian Institute of Aboriginal Studies.

Pretty, G. (1967). Rescue excavation of an Aboriginal grave, Tailem Bend, South Australia. *South Australian Naturalist, 41*, 77–80.

Pretty, G. L. & Kricun, M. E. (1989). Prehistoric health status of the Roonka population. *World Archaeology, 21*(2), 198–224.

Price, T. D. (2015). An introduction to the isotopic studies of ancient human remains. *Journal of the North Atlantic, 7*, 71–87.

Prokopec, M. (1979). Demographical and morphological aspects of the Roonka population. *Archaeology and Physical Anthropology in Oceania, 14*(1), 11–26.

Richards, L. C. (1984). Principal axis analysis of dental attrition data from two Australian Aboriginal populations. *American Journal of Physical Anthropology, 65*(1), 5–13.

Richards, T., Pavlides, C., Walshe, K., Webber, H., & Johnston, J. (2007). Box Gully: New evidence for Aboriginal occupation of Australia south of the Murray River prior to the last glacial maximum. *Archaeology in Oceania, 42*, 1–11.

Robertson, S. (2003). *A critical evaluation of the application of cribra orbitalia in Australian archaeology as a correlate of sedentism* (BA Honours thesis). Australian National University, Canberra.

Robertson, S. (2007). Sources of bias in the Murray Black collection: Implications for palaeopathological analysis. *Australian Aboriginal Studies 2007* (1), 116–127.

Ruff, C. B. (2008). Biomechanical analyses of archaeological human skeletons. In M. A. Katzenberg & S. R. Saunders (Eds.), *Biological anthropology of the human skeleton* (2nd edition, pp. 183–206). New York: Wiley-Liss.

Russell, L. (2010). Reflections on Murray Black's writings. In S. Faulkhead & J. Berg (Eds.), *Power and passion: Our people return home* (pp. 56–63). Melbourne: Koorie Heritage Trust Inc.

Sandison, A. T. (1973). Palaeopathology of human bones from Murray River region between Mildura and Renmark, Australia. *Memoirs of the National Museum of Victoria, 34*, 173–174.

Satterthwait, L. (1987). Socioeconomic implications of Australian Aboriginal net hunting. *Man, 22*, 613–636.

Saxe, A. (1970). *Social dimensions of mortuary practices* (PhD thesis). University of Michigan, Ann Arbor, Michigan.

Sealy, J., Armstrong, R., & Schrire, C. (1995). Beyond lifetime averages: Tracing life histories through isotopic analysis of different calcified tissues from archaeological human skeletons. *Antiquity, 69*(263), 290–300.

Smith, C. (2016). *Dental enamel hypoplasia at Roonka flat: A record of hunter-gatherer variability* (MA thesis). The University of Auckland, Auckland.

Smith, C. B., & Littleton, J. (2019). Enamel defects at Roonka, South Australia: Indicators of poor health or the osteological paradox? *Australian Archaeology, 85*(2), 139–150.

Smith, M. (1978). A note on the fauna from Devon Downs shelter. *Australian Archaeology, 8*, 19–21.

Smith, P., Prokopec, M., & Pretty, G. (1988). Dentition of a prehistoric population from Roonka Flat, South Australia. *Archaeology in Oceania, 23*(1), 31–36.

Stirling, E. C. (1911). Preliminary report on the discovery of native remains at Swanport, River Murray: With an inquiry into the alleged occurrence of a pandemic among the Australian Aboriginals. *Transactions of the Royal Society of South Australia, 35*, 4–46.

Stock, J. T., & Pfeiffer, S. K. (2001). Linking structural variability in long bone diaphyses to habitual behaviors: Foragers from the southern African later Stone Age and the Andaman Islands. *American Journal of Physical Anthropology, 115*(4), 337–348.

Stone, T., & Cupper, M. L. (2003). Last Glacial Maximum ages for robust humans at Kow Swamp, southern Australia. *Journal of Human Evolution, 45*(2), 99–111.

Taçon, P. S. (2013). Interpreting the in-between: Rock art junctions and other small style areas between provinces. *Time and Mind, 6*(1), 73–80.

Thorne, A. G., & Macumber, P. G. (1972). Discoveries of late Pleistocene man at Kow Swamp, Australia. *Nature, 238*(5363), 316–319.

Tindale, N. B. (1974). *Aboriginal tribes of Australia: Their terrain, environmental controls, distribution, limits, and proper names*. Canberra: Australian National University Press.

Van Holst Pellekaan, S., Liu, P., & Wilton, A. (2010). Genetic heritage in the Darling River Aboriginal peoples captures ancient presence and post-contact survival. *Before Farming, 4*, 1–17.

Walker, K. F., & Thoms, M. C. (1993). Environmental effects of flow regulations on the Lower Murray River, Australia. *Regulated Rivers Research and Management, 8*, 103–119.

Walker, K. F., Sheldon, F., & Puckridge, J. T. (1995). A perspective on Dryland River ecosystems. *Regulated Rivers Research and Management, 11*, 85–104.

Webb, S. (1989). *Prehistoric stress in Australian Aborigines: A palaeopathological study of a hunter-gatherer population.* Oxford: BAR International Series 490.

Webb, S. (2009). *Palaeopathology of Aboriginal Australians: Health and disease across a hunter-gatherer continent.* Cambridge: Cambridge University Press.

Westell, C., Roberts, A., Morrison, M., Jacobsen, G., & the River Murray and Mallee Aboriginal Corporation (2020). Initial results and observations on a radiocarbon dating program in the Riverland region of South Australia, *Australian Archaeology*, doi: 10.1080/03122417.2020.1787928.

Wilson, C., Fallon, S., & Trevorrow, T. (2012). New radiocarbon ages for the Lower Murray River, South Australia. *Archaeology in Oceania, 47,* 157–160.

Wood, J. W., Milner, G. R., Harpending, H. C., & Weiss, K. M. (1992). The osteological paradox: Problems of inferring prehistoric health from skeletal samples. *Current Anthropology, 33*(4), 343–370.

Zohary, T., Erez, J., Gophen, M., Berman-Frank, I., & Stiller, M. (1994). Seasonality of stable carbon isotopes within the pelagic food web of Lake Kinneret. *Limnology and Oceanography, 39*(5), 1030–1043.

CHAPTER 34

BEYOND THE BARRIERS

A New Model for the Settlement of Australian Deserts

PETER VETH, JO MCDONALD, AND PETER HISCOCK

INTRODUCTION

THE Australian arid zone generally experiences less than 250 mm of annual rainfall and covers over 3.7 million km^2 or 35% of the continent (Figure 34.1). Arid physiographic units include the central Australian ranges that host ancient palm stands, the Western Australian coastline and its jagged calcareous beach ridges, through to the rugged uplands of the Pilbara ironstone province, a region characterized by spring-fed deeply dissected gorges and watered by annual cyclones. To the south is the vast Nullarbor Plain with gibber, heath, and sinkholes, abutting the Great Southern Ocean. The coastal deserts of the northwest comprise ancient limestone and volcanic suites, occurring both on the mainland and also as residual continental islands, abutting some highly productive tropical marine ecosystems. The Western Desert cultural bloc (covering 1.37 million km^2) includes the Great and Little Sandy, Gibson, Great Victoria, Simpson, and Tanami Deserts and is best known for its linear dune fields, saltwater lakes, and remote ranges. Large lake systems occur within and adjacent to the semiarid zone. These include Lakes Gregory and Woods in the north, Lake Eyre in South Australia, and the Willandra Lakes in western New South Wales (NSW). These lakes receive waters from higher rainfall catchments which are recharged variably, from every year through to once in a decade (in the case of Lake Eyre), or were fed by meltwaters (in the case of the Willandra Lakes—Bowler, Huang, Chen, Head, & Yuan 1986). These drainage systems and lakes offer a range of possibilities for human settlers in both an evolutionary adaptive sense and also with respect to settlement trajectories and the suite of materials culture(s) that might be supported.

We have argued that the arid zone of Australia should not be treated as one adaptive zone; instead, our focus has been on differences in environmental structures and rainfall characteristics which provide the canvas for variable cultural landscapes (Hiscock

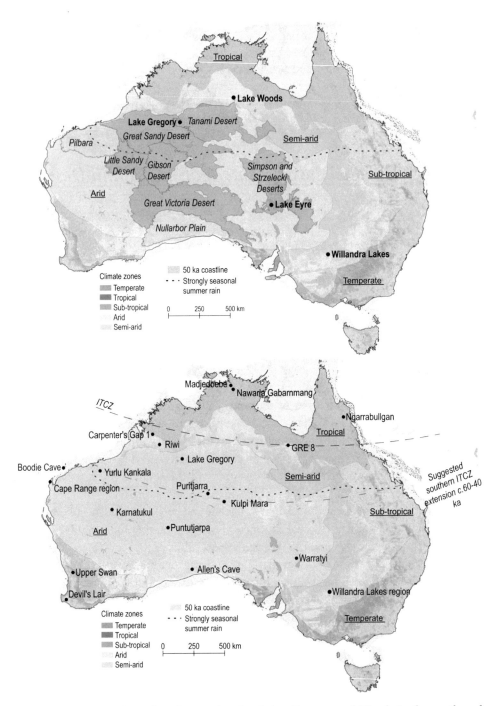

FIGURE 34.1. Top: Australian deserts showing Lakes Gregory and Woods in the north and Lake Eyre and the Willandra Lakes in the south. Climate zones, the 50 ka coastline, and extent of strongly seasonal summer rainfall shown. Bottom: Australia's arid zone, including the arid coastline of the Cape Range region, the Pilbara ranges with sites such as Yurlu Kankala, and the interior Sandy Deserts, showing Lake Gregory in the north and Karnatukul in the south. Other key sites in the 50–45 ka range include Riwi, Warratyi in South Australia, and the Willandra Lakes western NSW are shown, as is the present location of the Inter Tropical Convergence Zone (ITCZ) and its modelled southern extension at 60 ka.

& Wallis 2005; McDonald & Veth 2013a; Veth, Smith, & Hiscock 2005). Indeed it now seems that the level of resource availability and sustainability varies on a very fine scale in modern deserts, making it possible to occupy some patches but rarely use others (Law, Hiscock, Ostendorf, & Lewis 2021). Across these highly varied environments desert peoples show great dynamism in their adaptations to highly variable environments with just some of the responses including the hypermobility of groups, use of long-lived multifunctional tool kits, a strong reliance on lower-ranked and r-selected resources, and ramified kinship systems. These adaptations facilitated access to neighbouring country (clan estates) during droughts and conditions of stress (Veth 1993, 2006), and reveal the capacity of rock art to signal these adaptive responses through multiple symbolic means (providing one of the world's longest records of such behaviour) (Finch et al. 2021; McDonald 2017; McDonald & Veth 2013a; Mulvaney 2015).

While on a global scale Australia is the most arid continent settled by people, the deserts are relatively well vegetated and watered by comparison with other deserts, such as the Atacama Desert in South America (at 15 mm of rainfall on average per annum) and the Skeleton Coast of Namibia (at 10 mm of rainfall on average per annum). Here we will focus on new evidence for use of the arid zone in a transect extending from the coastal deserts of northwest Australia, across the Pilbara uplands, and into the dune fields of the Great and Little Sandy Deserts (Figure 34.1). New chronologies from the dune fields in South Australia near Roxby Down (Hughes, Way, & Sullivan 2020) and from the lake-edge deposits of Lake Mungo (Jankowski, Stern, Lachlan, & Jacobs 2020) add to the increasingly complex picture of this long chronology for human adaptation. Variations in the assemblages of rock art of the northwest and wider arid zone through time are seen to support an approach favouring the dynamics of Australian arid-zone settlement.

WHY EARLY DATES IN THE AUSTRALIAN DESERTS MATTER

The timing of the successful settlement of Australian deserts is critical in hindcasting the southern dispersal of anatomically modern humans from northern Africa, through the Arabian Peninsula, and then across South and Southeast Asia (Hiscock 2013; Breeze et al. 2016). The timing is also important in setting minimum ages for the initial settlement of the north/northwest shores of Sahul (Kealy, Louys, & O'Connor 2018; Norman et al. 2018). Even if the deserts were occupied relatively quickly after first landings, most population models assume that several thousand years would have passed before the southward dispersal of people into all of the deserts (e.g., Bird, O'Grady, & Ulm 2016; Bird et al. 2018; Bradshaw et al. 2021). With increasing evidence for people in the more southerly deserts between 50 and 45 ka, it is clear that revised population modelling is needed to understand the early filling of so many different ecological niches and, as the radiocarbon barrier has been reached in a number of key sites (e.g., McDonald et al. 2018b), that uranium (U-) series, electron spin resonance (ESR), and optically stimulated luminescence (OSL; single-grain or multigrain) must now be routinely used to more effectively encapsulate the earliest ages for Australia's oldest arid zone sites (Veth 2017).

New Records from the Deserts of Northwest Australia and Further Afield

Over the past decade the northwest deserts have been subject to increasingly fine-grained survey and excavation programs. The range of newly dated sites, located in very different arid and semiarid bioregions, include shelters and caves on (now) continental limestone islands of the North West Shelf; limestone caves in the Southern Kimberley Devonian Reef; artefact scatters in lake-edge colluvium at Lake Gregory; and rock shelters in the Pilbara ironstone and Little Sandy Desert ranges. As a result, an increased number of sites have been dated within the 50–45 ka bracket, including Boodie Cave on Barrow Island (Veth et al. 2017), Riwi in the Southern Kimberley (Wood et al. 2016), Parnkupirti at Lake Gregory (Veth et al. 2009,) and Karnatukul in the Little Sandy Desert (McDonald et al. 2018b) (Figures 34.1 and 34.2). Four rock shelters in the Pilbara uplands have recently yielded dates older than 45 ka and include Waturi Jurnti, Yurlu Kankala, HD07, and the ill-fated Juukan-2 site (Morse, Cameron, & Reynen 2014; Reynen, Vannieuwenhuyse, Morse, Monks, & Balme 2018) (Figure 34.2). There is also

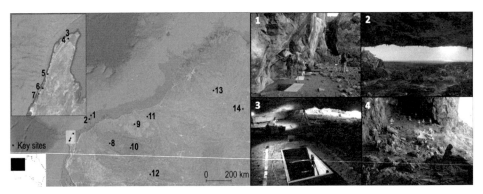

FIGURE 34.2. Early sites noted in text from the Northwest Shelf, the Pilbara ranges, and in the Little Sandy Deserts. Key sites: 1. Noala Cave; 2. Boodie Cave; 3. Jansz; 4. C99; 5. Mandu Creek; 6. Pilgonaman Creek; 7. Yardie Well; 8. Juukan-2; 9. Yurlu Kankala; 10. HD07; 11. Watura Jurnti; 12. Karnatukul; 13. Riwi; and 14. Parnkupirti. Context pictures show 1. Karnatukul, Sandy Desert; 2. Padjari Manu Cave, Cape Range; 3. Boodie Cave, Barrow Island; and 4. Yurlu Kankala, Pilbara.

(Photos 1: Peter Veth; 2: Peter Veth; 3: Peter Veth; 4: Kate Morse.)

an increasing number of sites in the eastern Pilbara uplands with occupation *onset by* 45 ka and showing a shift in site use during the Last Glacial maximum (Cropper and Law 2018; Slack, Law, & Gliganic 2018, 2020).

In the wider arid zone of Australia, only two other site complexes fall within this early age bracket: Warratyi, a perched rock shelter at the northern end of the Flinders Ranges of South Australia (Hamm et al. 2016) and the Willandra Lakes of western New South Wales (Jankowski et al. 2020; see Figure 34.1). In the Roxby dune fields of South Australia, palaeoclimatic evidence from the last c. 60 ka shows fluctuating periods of wet and dry conditions during the Late Pleistocene and Holocene (Hughes, Sullivan, & Hiscock 2017). The pre–Last Glacial Maximum (LGM) archaeological record here is sparse, but cultural records from the LGM through to the Mid-Holocene show that people occupied the dune fields and stony plains during prolonged wet (deglaciation) periods and largely abandoned them during drier (glaciation) phases. From the Late Holocene there were changes in settlement patterns perhaps made possible by social, economic, and technological adaptations which allowed people to occupy what became an increasingly harsh environment. Archaeological understandings of these adaptations were facilitated by discoveries in the Roxby dune fields of buried stratified layers of stone artefacts in dune sands, dated by single-grain OSL. These discoveries indicate the possibility that hitherto unreported cultural sequences, potentially dating back to >50 ka, may be present in many other Australian dune fields (Hughes et al. 2017).

Most archaeologists now accept that occupation of the continent occurred by 50 ka. This consensus is based upon the presence of early sites in the arid zone and others now documented from outside of the arid zone—for example, Minjiwarra and Carpenter's Gap 1 in the Kimberley (Veth et al. 2019; Wood et al. 2016), Nawarla Gabarnmang in the Northern Territory (David et al. 2019a), and Devil's Lair in the southwest of Western Australia (Dortch et al. 2019). This 50 ka onset of occupation dates falls short of the Bayesian modelled estimate of 71–59 ka OSL dates (at 95.4% confidence) for the Northern Territory site of Madjedbebe (Clarkson et al. 2017, 2018); however, it overlaps with this newly proposed earlier timing for desert occupation. Given the groundswell of age estimates at c. 50 ka, it has been recently argued it is time to recast occupation and genomics models to an earlier 60–50 ka bracket for the arrival of people in Sahul (and see recent debate in Allen et al. 2020).

SOME NEW CLIMATIC INDICATORS

A recent analysis of deep-sea cores off South Australia and the northwest Cape (de Deckker et al. 2020) indicates that conditions in northern and central Australia were wet following the end of Marine Isotope Stage (MIS) 4 (71–59 ka), and not simply cold and dry as previously thought. Other records of wetter conditions and enhanced river flow overlapping with a 60–55 ka time bracket come from the Cooper Creek region (Cohen, Nanson, Larsen, Jones, & Price 2010; Maroulis, Nanson, Price, & Pietsch 2007), the Lake

Eyre Basin (Cohen et al. 2015), and the Lower Mungo Unit from the Willandra Lakes (Jankowski et al. 2020).

The southern shift of the Intertropical Convergence Zone (ITCZ)[1] by ~59 ka and intensified monsoon could have facilitated the rapid dispersal of humans into the Australian deserts (Bayon et al. 2017: Fig. 34.1; Bird et al. 2016; Veth et al. 2009, 2017). Large northern lakes, such as Lake Gregory, have extensive catchments and would have been more permanent at this time (Bowler, Wyrwoll, & Lu 2001; Smith 2013: 53). By at least 50 ka, Lake Gregory was 10 times larger than today and supported fish, shellfish, crustaceans, and water birds (Veth et al. 2009). Plant productivity would have been higher and freshwater soaks, waterholes, and springs may have been more active, with seasonal and evaporative stresses different from those experienced today (Smith 2013: 76). The first settlers using these lakes and water points were probably generalized foragers, exploiting a broad suite of plants, reptiles, macropods, emu, and large (now extinct) megapode eggs, as well as marine and lacustrine resources when these were available (Hiscock & Wallis 2005; O'Connor & Veth 2000). Given the possibility of 'hydrological pathways,' a rapid settlement of the arid interior is predicted by c. 60 ka, or soon thereafter.

A New Model for Timing of the Settlement of the Australian Deserts

While colonization of Australia's arid zone was previously seen to occur from 45 ka during a dry phase (Smith 2013: 68), we propose that it occurred significantly earlier and during the wet phase which followed MIS 4. This scenario of an earlier and wide-scale movement of people into desert bioregions builds on the islands in the interior model (Veth 1989, 1993, 2005; see also Hiscock 1989; Smith 1988), deploys propositions consistent with the desert transformation model (Hiscock & Wallis 2005), aligns better with the new climate data, and incorporates a deep-time arid zone rock art chronology based on information exchange theory (McDonald & Veth 2006, 2013a; McDonald 2005, 2017, 2020; following Wobst 1977). The biogeographic/refuge model continues to be a useful heuristic device for understanding larger-scale and dynamic desert settlement through time, as do the changing human occupation and mobility indices wrought by large-scale environmental shifts. This new arid zone settlement model is based on the following testable claims:

- Initial settlement occurred at or slightly after 60 ka with no impediments; unlike previous concepts such as *barrier deserts* (see McDonald et al. 2018b; Veth 2017; and see Smith 1993). The new climatic evidence for an earlier pluvial phase removes any theoretical climatic constraint (and see Smith 2013: 48). The concept of early *corridors* is sustained, however, as these were likely pathways with river systems draining to the Pleistocene exposed coastal shelf and also connecting to large interior lake systems;

- Increasing aridification after 35 ka saw groups reconfiguring, with increasing focus on refuges—both larger (like the Pilbara uplands) and smaller (such as the Carnarvon Ranges in the Little Sandy Desert);
- The LGM (c. 25–19 ka) saw areas 'drop out' of different groups' ranges, but wetter periods (at 24 ka and 23–22 ka) during the LGM could be expected to have seen returned occupation or perhaps increased and/or more focussed occupation in some refugia, being locations with isolated but persistent populations (sensu Veth 1993; after de Deckker et al. 2020; McDonald et al. 2018a);
- By 15–14 ka, with rising sea levels and the re-establishment of the Summer Monsoon, the flooding of the coastal plain (continental shelf) saw a reconfiguration of population. Larger offshore islands were abandoned after 7 ka (e.g., Barrow and Montebello Islands), and there are Early Holocene economic shifts in some refugia (e.g., Murujuga—McDonald & Mulvaney 2023) with changed occupation in the reconfiguring archipelago, and push-on effects through the Pilbara and into the Western Desert;
- Intensification of El Niño Southern Oscillation (ENSO)[2] at c. 4 ka created different drivers for population and technological change; with
- Climatic amelioration during the last millennium underwriting many adaptive changes seen at European contact in the nineteenth and twentieth centuries.

Given the increasing number of sites that date to the terminal Pleistocene from the sandy deserts of the northwest and the southeast of the continent, we now believe that lowland sandy deserts may not have been absolute barriers to initial human colonization. Major dune fields and sand sheets, and other niches where water point sources may have been less frequent or predictable (i.e., area of uncoordinated drainage), most likely had lower carrying capacity, especially during lengthy droughts. Spring-fed water sources in both the Western Desert and Pilbara suggest that this is a 'knowable' landscape—making its utility more predictable to a population which has already mapped onto it. The growing data set continues to suggest shifts in human occupation, mobility, and modes of symbolic production during periods of significant climate change, such as the LGM (25–19 ka), the re-establishment of the Summer Monsoon by 14 ka, intensification of ENSO at c. 4 ka, and climatic amelioration after 1 ka (see Table 34.1).

The concept of smaller, cryptic refugia proposed by Smith (2013: 116), describing pockets of optimal microhabitat (Pepper and Keogh 2021), helps to explain how people could move between points in otherwise coarse-grained, arid landscapes. Chains of water points in small refuges can sustain connectivity deep into the deserts during phases which were drier than today (Veth, Williams, & Paterson 2014). We acknowledge the possibility that the initial movement of people into the arid zone may have been facilitated by hydrological pathways which existed during the early MIS 3 wet phase. There are a number of potential pathways into northwestern Australia—such as the Ord, Fitzroy, and Sturt Rivers in the Kimberley and in the Pilbara by the Fortescue, Ashburton, and De Grey/Oakover Rivers—that link the Western Desert to previous Pleistocene coastlines. Many of the recently dated and early archaeological sites, and

Table 34.1. Comparison of the phased art production correlated with new climate data for Murujuga and the Western Desert, showing suggested behavioural correlates in the broad environmental/temporal phases shown in Figure 34.3.

Posited Age Ranges	Murujuga Phases*	Western Desert Phases†	Behavioural and Signalling Correlates
1500–contact	5b	7,8	Proliferation of distinctive localized style provinces; social signalling in full production (including body painting, sand drawing, and variety of material culture items). Art demarcates broad-scale social cohesion as well as local identifiers. Increase in ceremonial paraphernalia in rock art as well as other forms of symbolic behaviours (shield designs, body painting, stone arrangements) and stone structures.
4–2 ka	5a	6	ENSO shift, longer occupation at key locales; site diversification and increased territoriality and identifying behaviour: headdress figures proliferate as an indicator of local-group identity.
8–6 ka	4	5	Climatic amelioration. Occupation of all parts of the arid zone with emergent territoriality amongst increasingly less mobile but higher density populations. Islandization phase on Murujuga; brief abandonment of outer islands.
12–8 ka	3b	?	Large population groupings on the coast in tandem with decreasing landmass (from sea-level rise) and decreased residential mobility. Territorial pressure at Murujuga with increased art production as signalling behaviour: flow on into the Pilbara but not necessarily reflected into the Western Desert?
15–12 ka	3a	4	People establish new ranges from their refugia; art reflects regional plus local heterogeneity and diminishing long-distance connectivity.
LGM 25–19 ka	2	3	Episodic art production demonstrates continuing long-distance stylistic connection; territorial tethering at refugia. Large outline fauna demonstrates long-distance social connectivity. Larger refuges (Murujuga, Pilbara, Western Desert) show early efflorescence of identity signalling; smaller refugia demonstrate clear stylistic discontinuity, indicating pulses of symbolically motivated behaviours.
<50 ka	1	2	Numerous sites used for the first time; maintenance of low population sizes. Art production (tracks, geometrics) continues; increased focus on permanent settlement at reliable water; stylistic heterogeneity demonstrates regional mapping of deep-time social geography.
>50 ka	?	1	Sporadic art production; small populations at occupation nodes. Cupules, Panaramitee track, and geometrics. Open (homogenous) style graphic across the continent reflecting initial colonizing groups and hypermobile spread.

* Mulvaney 2015; McDonald 2015.

† McDonald & Veth 2013a; McDonald 2017.

now increasingly well-documented rock art provinces, in the northwest are proximal to these hydrological pathways.

New research is required to test these propositions and to track how people responded to changes in climate in patterned and systematic ways through time. For example, how did groups in different desert bioregions respond to a general decrease in the intensity of the Summer Monsoon during the LGM (25–19 ka), its increase by 14 ka, and then later changes in ENSO over the past four millennia, inferred from speleothem and marine cores (Barberena, Méndez, & de Porras 2017; De Deckker, Barrows, & Rogers 2014; Denniston et al. 2013; Fitzsimmons et al. 2013; McBride 2018; Veth 2005). Given this revised model, we identify some central questions about desert occupation which we believe need to be addressed over the next decade.

Grand Desert Themes

In his synthesis of Australian desert archaeology, Smith (2013: 78) noted that with over forty sites now bracketed between 50 and 30 ka, Australia has one of the best records for early occupation of a major global desert. The continued focus over the past decade on research within the northwest has expanded this record, especially for the oldest occupation sites and several deep-time rock art style sequences, allowing a number of themes to be tackled in a more systematic way. Here we discuss and critique a number of conclusions from that seminal volume and assess these against new data and with new methods. These may be broken down into models for change in population and technology from the Australian deserts—and will be expanded on to include symbolic interactions of desert people with their landscapes.

Independently Identifying Population Change in the Deserts

The proposition that population is readily identifiable as an archaeological signature stems from claims first made in the 1980s that the abundance of stone artefacts through time is a proxy for the number of people once living in a site or a landscape. That concept was modified to include other kinds of sites and the number of radiometric dates as proxies for demography in Australia (e.g., Williams et al. 2015). Each of these demographic proxies is strongly advocated by some researchers and interpreted by most advocates of the method to show higher populations in the most recent millennia of Australia's deep-time history because more artefacts/sites/dates have been observed in these time frames. Despite the absence of robust genetic evidence for expanding populations in desert regions, a generation of archaeologists has relied on these proxies. While in some local contexts inferences about demography have been plausible and incorporated into regional narratives, the use of these proxies to identify broad-scale demographic change is not straightforward (see Hiscock & Attenbrow 2005, 2015).

On a broad geographical scale, the use of stone artefacts as an indicator of population densities is implausible, in part because of the generally still-small sample sizes which derive from vast tracts of many arid landscapes. Although there have been no synthetic, metrical studies carried out in Australia, it is clear that there is an overall pattern in the subtropics of an inverse relationship between regional artefact densities and landscape productivity/rainfall (Veth, Harper, & Ditchfield 2021). There certainly are large arte-fact scatters and quarries known in well-watered woodlands of the continental margins to the east and the south, but they are comparatively rare compared to many inland, arid, or semiarid areas where many millions of stone artefacts are sometimes visible per square kilometre (see Hughes et al. 2020). Explaining this general pattern is not an easy matter, since there are distinct density variations within each biogeographical zone. Sedimentation is lower and erosion higher in some arid-semiarid zones than in other environments, leading to greater visibility of the archaeological record. In addition, me-dium- to good-quality knappable stone is sometimes more abundant in those semiarid and arid lands. Notwithstanding those factors, if artefact numbers reflected popula-tion, the higher densities in drylands would not be predicted by many models that have been proposed, because the typical claim about Indigenous Australia is that popula-tion densities were substantially higher in the margins at all or almost all time periods and that deserts were sparsely populated. The recently retrieved artefact densities from Karnatukul (McDonald et al. 2018b), as well as those recovered from the extensive excavations at the high-density Holocene site of Puntutjarpa (Smith, Williams, & Ross 2017), provide additional counterarguments to this assumption of arid zone marginality. At Karnatukul, almost 25,000 artefacts were retrieved from two 1 m × 1 m × c. 65 cm deep excavation squares: 3621 stone artefacts >10 mm (5.98 kg) and 21,375 <10 mm artefacts (1.01 kg) (McDonald et al. 2018b: Table 7, Figure 11). These densities are extremely high, but why? It is plausible that some desert locations had far higher carrying capacity and/or saw people tethered to small refugia, at least in the short term (e.g., Westaway et al. 2021), and that local examples of high artefact density resulted. However, those seem-ingly atypical situations cannot explain the general desert artefact pattern, and hence while increased number of artefacts might have resulted from increases in the number of tools on some occasions, the nature of such a relationship remains underdetermined. Hence we believe other behavioural dynamics contributed to changing abundance of archaeological materials.

Population Models and Dispersal

Discussions of population change in Australia's arid zone often begin with the dispersal of people across the various deserts as a way of establishing initial population sizes and capacities as a baseline. Some dispersion models are specifically linked to hypothesized demographic and mobility patterns. For example, Smith (2013: 72) proposed that there was rapid colonization of the continent starting at 45 ka by small groups of foragers with narrow diet breadth who quickly diminished high-ranked resources and moved further across into the deserts. He proposed that 500 people might spread across the desert in only 150 years, predictions echoing models of Joseph Birdsell (1957) and O'Connell and Allen (2012). While a model of limited diet breadth theoretically drives colonizers onwards, there are other aspects that can be conceptualized further, such as the vulnerability of small isolated groups to unpredictable short-term decreases in resource availability or emergence of detrimental mutations. It is also not a given that a rapid dispersion of this kind would set up viable populations that could persist in all desert regions in less than optimal conditions. Nor is it clear how a single estimated colonization rate, such as 150 years, is likely to be more plausible than longer estimates (Bradshaw et al. 2021).

We have already defined some of the relevant parameters of this new model, such as widespread dispersal of people from soon after 60 ka into most arid landscapes. We note that the dates for both the arrival of people on the continent and rates of dispersals to different environments are imprecise, but that if people are present at c. 60 ka, then existing environmental conditions may not have prevented the widespread movement of people. We suggest that this model can be tested by establishing whether desert occupation was well underway by 60 ka with a targeted survey program. One way of targeting prospective landscapes is to combine remote sensing data of palaeodrainage courses with the distribution of the earliest rock art production nodes, given that the presence of focused art production, with discontinuous stylistic graphics, in deep time is likely to be an indicator of repeated and focused population grouping (McDonald 2017, 2021). Such an approach will allow for targeting of appropriate geomorphic locales where occupation evidence could be co-located and preserved.

Were Arid Zone Settlers Infinitely Adaptable, or Did Entering Deserts during a Wet Phase Constrain Future Adaptation?

The ten different desert sites which are currently dated between 50 and 45 ka show that people were already in the Australian arid zone during the transition from pluvial to drier conditions in MIS 3 (Veth et al. 2017). Where sites have had OSL or other non-^{14}C dating techniques applied to their older units, occupation ages have been comfortably pushed back to c. 50 ka (e.g., Veth et al. 2017). Some desert sites sit at the radiocarbon barrier (after Roberts, Jones, & Smith 1994) and have only been dated through [14]C (e.g., Karnatukul). A new dating program is needed to test the proposition that earlier occupation is widespread in the desert before 50 ka. Suitable new locations will need to be targeted for this dating program (e.g., dunes adjacent to identified palaeo-drainages in the Jilakurru and Kaalpi Ranges, where earlier rock art styles/taphonomy suggest earlier occupation). There is good reason to think this dating boundary 50–45 ka will be pushed back even more with the systematic application of suites of complementary dating methods and techniques (Veth 2017). The revised palaeoclimatic conditions immediately following MIS 4 (de Deckker et al. 2020), whereby conditions were wetter and lakes and water sources recharged, could well have facilitated the earlier movement of groups into the desert. We predict that these earlier colonizers would have been highly mobile and likely possessed many innovative technologies (as evidenced at Riwi and Madjedbebe in the form of ground-stone implements and at Karnatukul with early hafted blade technologies before 40 ka). These technologies could have provided access to resources from the rainforest and savannah country in the tropical north while also equipping people to cover the great distances involved in penetrating more arid interiors (Hiscock, O'Connor, Balme, & Maloney 2016; Veth et al. 2009).

Did Groups Persist in Deserts with the Onset of Different Climate Regimes and Hydrology?

This question was initially addressed by the authors of the *Desert Transformation Model* (Hiscock & Wallis 2005:35) and examines whether desert adaptations evolved *in situ* with increasing aridification of lands that subsequently experienced higher rainfall. Since publication of this model, both the initial occupation of the desert has been pushed back further in time, and it has been demonstrated archaeologically that the earliest colonists possessed a number of technological strategies which were formerly considered to have only developed later in the Holocene (e.g., backed artefacts and seed grinding). There is also new evidence for persistence of occupation at a number of sites during the LGM in the northwest deserts (McDonald et al. 2018a, 2018b; Reynen et al. 2018). However, there are also cases of cessation in site occupation during the LGM (see Barbarena, Méndez, & de Porras 2017), with implied changes in the rock art styles and occupational evidence from rock shelters suggesting changing mobility patterns as groups adapted to changing environmental conditions. The ability to adapt to intensifying aridity *in situ* would imply groups were developing endogenous strategies to maintain residence, and these can include changes in mobility, dietary breath, and the provisioning strategies used to acquire lithics.

The earliest stylistic signalling is evidenced by surviving (engraved) rock art from those locations where multiple arid zone stylistic phases are key to ongoing desert adaptations. In the tropics and the desert, cupules and abraded grooves are thought to appear at or shortly after first settlement (McDonald & Veth 2010; Veth, McDonald, & de Koning 2018; Veth, Myers, Heaney, & Ouzman 2018); followed by the more widespread and pervasive track and geometric repertoire across both the arid and semiarid zones of Australia (Edwards 1968; Maynard 1979; McDonald 2005, 2017; McDonald & Veth 2006, 2010, 2013a). Within these Pleistocene art phases are pulses of episodic production of distinctive art forms (e.g., archaic faces) which demonstrate widespread and long-distance Pleistocene chains of connection (McDonald 2005; Mulvaney 2013), as well as subsequent territorial tethering with local to regional style graphics developing separately, for example, simple archaic faces, which in turn become archaic faces with distinctive additional features (i.e., bodies, with headdresses and accoutrements) in deep time. These persistent and geographically widespread Pleistocene graphic vocabularies, overprinted on the open earlier signalling repertoires of the track and geometric desert assemblages (McDonald & Veth 2010; McDonald 2021), which through time become regionally distinct, are evidence for the ebbs and pulses of arid zone networks through time (see Figure 34.3).

Discontinuous style graphics (e.g., archaic faces, archaic faces with bodies, decorative infilled anthropomorphs, and fat-tailed macropods) have now been recorded in substantial numbers at Murujuga—on the Pilbara coast; in the Hamersley Ranges near Tom Price (e.g., Brown 2018); and at Kaalpi east of the Canning Stock Route (McDonald 2017). The geographic distance between these style provinces and the similarities in several of the earliest graphic productions, and divergent regionalized varieties which follow, argue strongly against Smith's (2013) suggestion that rock art was an arid zone Holocene adaptation—particularly when the more recent style phases in most locations demonstrate both extreme stylistic variability in local and regional signals, and importantly, very disparate modes of signalling in periods of lower mobility (Table 34.1). These regions are today bound by mythological connections which may have provided cultural connections for these discontinuous art graphics in the past (McDonald & Veth 2013b). The ancient and more recent style stratum speak to persistence and resilience but also changes in signalling behaviours which respond to changing environmental conditions through time.

DID ARIDITY CAUSE POPULATION CONTRACTION, BOTTLENECKS, AND EXTINCTIONS AS ARGUED FOR THE NORTHERN HEMISPHERE?

Genetic bottlenecks are evolutionary events that reduce the size and genetic *variation* of populations, sometimes resulting in small founding populations with specific cultural traits in refugia (as suggested by Veth 1993; and see Barbarena, Méndez, & de Porras 2017). Recent genomic studies provide some support for these contractions with evidence for population isolation, reduced genetic drift, and the beginning of regionalism

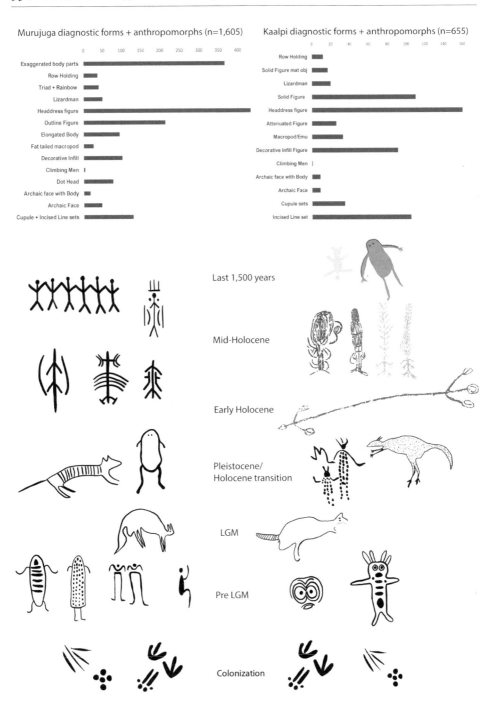

FIGURE 34.3. Persistent Pleistocene graphic connections and Holocene stylistic variabilities—Murujuga and Kaalpi: two sites with large recorded assemblages of anthropomorphic motifs. The graphed diagnostic forms are illustrated by schematic examples below (see Mulvaney 2015 and McDonald 2017 for definitions).

across Australia by approximately 25 ka and coincident with increased aridity of the LGM (Malaspinas et al. 2016).

It remains unclear whether the Pleistocene was consistently a time of smaller social worlds (cf., high population estimates in Bradshaw et al. 2021). However, it is likely that the first groups of people to move into the desert were relatively isolated, at least for a period of time, with smaller groups of closely related people attached to specific locales. The widespread distribution of cupules/abraded grooves (although mainly in the northern arid zone), and then the subsequent superimposed engraved track and geometric repertoire, suggests that these groups may have been extremely mobile—and that they continued to move through the desert, eventually filling all biogeographic zones perhaps within 2000–4000 years. We cannot know what the motivation to keep moving may have been, although depletion of higher ranked sources is often cited by O'Connell and Allen (2012, and others). Yet the presence of sites dated to 50 ka across the northwest and into the central south and southeast currently indicates that the initial groups may have moved rapidly. Contact estimates were that these desert people would have had large foraging ranges/territories and low densities estimated at 1 person per 80–200 km^2. We suggest that this earliest phase of desert occupation was an 'open' system with a focus on long-distance inclusion rather than on exclusive possession of ritual property (as suggested by Smith 2013: 339). During the LGM, societies may have differed from the founding groups as much as they differed from ethnographic desert groups. Smith sees population increases as being delayed until the Mid- to Late Holocene—and that this increase in population introduced new patterns of residence as well as triggering the late efflorescence of rock art production, which we argue against. New ages for the Murujuga Archipelago which demonstrate both a LGM signature and a terminal Pleistocene/Early Holocene efflorescence in occupation evidence (McDonald & Berry 2016; McDonald et al., 2018a; McDonald & Mulvaney 2023) as the sea level approached the current coastline demonstrates an earlier population upswing than envisaged by Smith (2013). Further, given the recently published ages for pigment art in the Kimberley for Infilled Naturalistic depictions from 17 to 13 ka, Gwion anthropomorphs from 12 ka (Finch et al. 2020, 2021), and Wanjina forms in the last several millennia (David et al. 2019b), we argue that Smith's model is unlikely. Instead, we would ask why would the production of rock art, given its modelled role in the colonizing of new landscapes (Balme, Davidson, McDonald, Stern, & Veth 2009), have been delayed in the deserts? Robust dating of earlier desert art is clearly required.

Several sites on the edge of the sandy deserts, including Riwi in the Kimberley (Wood et al. 2016), Murujuga Rockshelter to the west of the Pilbara (McDonald et al. 2018a), and Watura Jurnti (Marsh, Hiscock, Williams, Hughes, & Sullivan 2018) in the northern Pilbara (Figure 34.1 and 34.2), show significant shifts in stone tool reduction strategies during the LGM. In the wider Pilbara, a provisioning strategy involving highly mobile individuals sees cores transported over short distances across the uplands (Reynen 2019). Current data suggest groups had resilience to changing climates and environments once they were established in areas like the Pilbara uplands, with population contractions and bottlenecks remaining a distinct possibility in some desert lowland areas. The artefact assemblages from Karnatukul, in the Little Sandy Desert, show that during the LGM, people were selecting more readily available materials from the adjacent Carnarvon Ranges, which also provided reliable water, high economic plant diversity, and timbers used for fuel such as the *Callitris* pine. This increased focus on local uplands during glacial aridity has been identified at other Australian arid sites occupied during the LGM (Hamm et al. 2016; Maloney, O'Connor, Wood, Aplin, & Balme 2018; Smith 2013; Wood et al. 2016), but not, until this recent excavation, in the Sandy Deserts (McDonald et al. 2018b: Table 11). While good quality chert was utilized for implements for most of the history of site use, there is a marked increase in chert as discard rates increase significantly in the last millennium, while quartz, quartzite, and silcrete usage declined. This increased focus on chert and focussed production and use of backed artefacts and adzes during the last thousand years (McDonald, Reynen, & Fullagar 2018) likely reflected changed technological organizational practices.

Detailed comparative studies are now required of group mobility, early art style provinces, and genetic variance across different desert bioregions to further explore the existence of bottlenecks.

Were People Able to Use Arid Coastlines Continuously Despite Changes in Sea Level and the Resultant Effects on Productivity?

This issue is linked to larger debates about whether coastlines remained productive under conditions of changing sea levels, procumbent versus precipitous coastlines, and the availability of freshwater on the edge of the Pleistocene shelf (see Veth, Ward, & Manne 2017; Veth et al. 2019). In short, there is evidence from the northwest and more widely from Sahul for occupation of coastlines for much of the deep past, obtained largely from sample points on continental islands and precipitous coastlines such as at Barrow Island and Cape Range in the northwest (Figure 34.1). Ditchfield (2017) examined seven Pleistocene stone artefact assemblages from the Montebello and Barrow Islands and the Northwest Cape and reconstructed group mobility for the coastal zone of the (now submerged) Northwest Shelf during the LGM. He concluded that occupation of the Pleistocene coastal landscape involved frequent and small movements by groups focusing on productive marine and coastal habitats, producing dietary assemblages with these fauna as well as arid terrestrial fauna (Ditchfield, Manne, Hook, Ward, & Veth 2018; Veth, Ward, & Manne 2017; Veth, Ward, & Ditchfield 2017; Veth et al. 2017). He argues that seasonal movements from the interior arid lands were made directly to these productive coastal habitats.

Morse (1999) has argued that Pleistocene coasts could have acted as refuges during the LGM, and this seems plausible for other areas where the desert meets the sea, such as the Murujuga/Dampier Archipelago (McDonald et al. 2018a). The Early Holocene record at Murujuga sees people occupying what are now the Murujuga outer islands from around 13,000 years ago (when the coast was estimated to still be c. 15 km distant), with groups transporting mangrove species of shellfish to midden sites several kilometres inland when the coastline remained some distance from its current stand. Recent excavations have shown that occupation of these islands continued into the recent past, with their incorporation after a short passage of time into mainland foraging strategies. The rock art on the archipelago demonstrates changing territorial connections and attachment to land—and different signalling intentions from the deep past up until contact with European explorers and American whalers in the nineteenth century (McDonald & Mulvaney 2023; Paterson et al. 2019a, 2019b).

Models of Population Change and the Deserts

Models of Australia's demographic history have often been presented as simple directional trends depicting either a large population growth soon after human settlement or alternatively an extremely late population increase during the Late Holocene (see Hiscock 2008). For Australia's deserts many researchers currently prefer the idea of a late demographic increase, which implies extremely low population densities for at least the first 40,000–50,000 years (e.g., Smith 2013; Williams et al. 2015). However, here we argue that the 'discontinuous' style chronology for rock art in the Western Desert (McDonald 2017; McDonald & Veth 2013a) and for Murujuga (Mulvaney 2015), and the revised occupation sequence for Karnatukul suggest otherwise. While there is a massive increase in artefact discard in the recent past (particularly the past 1000–1500 years), episodic higher pulses of occupation are indicated earlier on through changing modes of production both in art styles and artefact discard patterns (McDonald et al. 2018a, 2018b; Veth, McDonald, & White 2008). Stylistic similarities and differences in the recent (dated) art phases of two Western Desert rock art provinces—at Kaalpi and Karnatukul (McDonald 2017, 2021; McDonald et al. 2014)—demonstrate a complexity in signalling identifiable in contemporary and recent Western Desert hunter-gatherer social systems. The multiple changes in graphic vocabulary identified in the sequential art phases that *precede* the most recent (dated) pigment art provide support for a long-term genesis of this signalling complexity. Stylistic discontinuities through time and across space provide evidence for arid-zone identity formation—and the presence of substantial assemblages from a number of these sites during the Pleistocene is inferred based on superimposition sequences, theme, and changed placement in the landscape (McDonald 2021). These pulses through time in stylistically distinct graphic repertoires suggest that population sizes at different times in the Late Pleistocene/Early Holocene could have been similar to those recorded throughout the Late Holocene. The recent population modelling by Bradshaw et al. (2021) indicates the potential for relatively high population from soon after settlement.

A settlement model for the desert which proposes an extended delay before sustained population growth, in our view, requires a series of explanations that are not entirely compatible with each other or congruent with existing evidence. Smith (2013: 308–312) suggested there was a coincidence between increased population levels with an increase in carrying capacity created by weakening of ENSO circulation and a strengthening of the Summer Monsoon after 3500 cal BP. We find this proposition, by itself, unpersuasive, as the carrying capacity of various desert patches would have been comparatively high for several extended periods earlier on, not the least at settlement and during the terminal Pleistocene and Early Holocene transition. Even if more productive conditions prevailed in the last few thousand years, there must be some additional demographic drivers involved. Climate drivers are not likely to have been operating equally or evenly across all arid latitudes, so posited uniformity of the timing of population growth is unlikely. Smith argued there is no current evidence to support Pleistocene-aged rock art in the Pilbara or the Western Desert (Smith 2013), despite long relative sequences of styles that plausibly predate and postdate sea-level rise (McDonald et al. 2018b; Mulvaney 2015).

Denying the possibility that symbolic behaviour was part of the earliest and subsequent occupations of Australia's arid zone sits at odds with the increasingly old Pleistocene dates for Kimberley pigment art (Finch et al. 2021) and the dating of pre–45 ka naturalistic art in Sulawesi (Brumm et al. 2021). The suite of human behaviours at this time has been demonstrated to include a number of innovations previously thought to have developed much later (e.g., ground-edge axes, backed artefacts, seed grinding)—and to deny an accompanying symbolic component silences the evidence we believe that rock art can bring to an understanding of changing populations through time. Smith's view of Western Desert early art as 'more typical of the north west with clearly iconic and prominent motifs becoming less frequent with time' (Smith 2013: 253) is inconsistent with the detailed recording from this region (McDonald & Veth 2013a). His interpretation of Archaic Faces being an analogue of ethnographic travelling cults beginning in Pilbara is similarly unsustainable: this art form is clearly not a Late Holocene manifestation, given significant geological alteration, repatination, and relative sequencing (McDonald 2017; Mulvaney 2013). His characterizations of engraved art in the Pilbara having little stylistic variability and being little differentiated (Smith 2013: 260) is incorrect and belies the work that has been done there over several decades which shows high stylistic diversity (e.g., McDonald & Veth 2013a; Vinnicombe 1987; Wright 1968). Equally, Smith argued that the Murujuga art is recent because the highest density of engravings occurs near middens. Yet recent work has shown that art occurs close to both Early Holocene and Late Holocene middens and that several of the earliest art styles occur across the entire landmass of the Archipelago (Berry 2018; McDonald 2015; McDonald & Mulvaney 2023; Mulvaney 2013). In contrast, more recent styles are confined to either the Burrup, or to different islands of the chain, indicating increased territoriality in the Late Holocene (McDonald & Mulvaney 2023). A current rock art dating project (ARC LP LP190100724) is exploring innovative dating techniques (Uranium series, optical surface exposure dating), to enable more direct dating of surface exposure, geocrusts and desert varnish (Gliganic, Meyer, Sohbati, Jain, & Barrett 2019; Green, Gleadow, Finch, Hergt, & Ouzman 2017) and help resolve these differences of interpretation and modelling.

DESERT TECHNOLOGIES AND ECONOMIC BEHAVIOURS

Technologies are multidimensional behavioural systems for creating or modifying objects. Making even comparatively simple artefacts involves multiple different production modules, some of which can be combined in a variety of ways. They have sufficient complexity and diversity that simple depictions of the chronological trends are usually unable to account for the patterns of technological evolution displayed. This is certainly true of desert Australia. We examine a few forms of stone artefact production to illustrate regional and temporal variation in desert artefact production. Ground-edge artefacts, often labelled as 'axes', were made in northern Australia from the earliest periods of visible occupation (Hiscock, O'Connor, Balme, & Maloney 2016; see Ford & Hiscock this volume), but in most desert areas they were not made or traded in from distant regions until the last few thousand years. In some southwestern portions of the continent, they were never made (Dortch et al. 2019). A second ground technology is represented by grinding stones, on which material was processed by abrading it on the surface. These vary in size and shape, were sometimes free-standing and portable, but sometimes comprised grinding surfaces on fixed rock outcrops. Grindstones have been recovered from early occupation levels in both tropical and desert Australia (e.g., Lake Mungo at c. 26 ka), and there are regionally varied patterns of typical grindstone shapes at different times (Hayes 2015). A third kind of artefact is a flake of stone that has further flaking (retouching) to create steep edges in only some parts of the specimens. Called 'microliths' or 'backed artefacts', these kinds of specimens were made at high rates in the start of the Late Holocene across Australian desert regions (c. 4 ka), but there are examples found in earlier dated contexts that suggest they could have been occasionally made for tens of thousands of years before the Holocene 'proliferation' (see McDonald et al. 2018b; McDonald, Reynen, & Fullagar 2018). A fourth technological behaviour does not create specific artefact forms but modifies the stone on which artefacts are made, creating new opportunities. This is called 'heat treatment' because exposing stone to specific heat is the way artisans alter the flaking properties of the material. This production element has a high antiquity across much of the Australian arid zone, beginning with a great emphasis on heat treatment in many arid regions prior to 25,000 years ago;

but over time the employment of this module varied regionally, so that in some locations people continued to use heat treatment as a central element in their technology while in other places people began to use it less until it was rarely or never used (Schmidt & Hiscock 2020). These four examples reveal the regional and chronological diversity of technology across Australian deserts and demonstrate that technologies were neither geographically uniform nor changed over time in discrete stages. Some technological elements are present in the early occupation of deserts, some appear late, some never appear at all, and some persist for a long time but are emphasized for only relatively short periods. Additionally, the specific stone technologies and their evolutionary trajectories vary between Australian deserts. This variable and multidimensional pattern of technological evolution means that arid-zone-wide stadial classifications of technological change are not possible, and that detailed studies of regional evolutionary sequences are needed, as has recently been undertaken for grindstones (Hayes 2015), heat treatment (Schmidt & Hiscock 2020), and rock art (McDonald 2017, 2021).

A significant example of a stadial view for the deserts is the idea that substantial shifts in technology, economy, and social life occurred primarily or only in the Late Holocene. For the Australian arid zone this proposition has been led by researchers such as Lourandos (1985) and Smith (2013), who argued for an extremely delayed, broad spectrum revolution across the continent, suggesting diet breadth increased only in the last few millennia as social networks and population size increased. Part of this late complexity in Smith's model also relates to the production of rock art, which Smith (2013) sees as a Late Holocene introduction. As discussed earlier, independent and direct evidence of population size and the operation of social networks back into deeper time have been hard to obtain. Additionally, direct dietary evidence in the form of preserved plant macrofossils and animal bones is rarely available in Australian deserts for more than a few hundred years (although see Veth, Ward, & Manne 2017 for Barrow Island). Consequently, much of the claim for a late desert broad-spectrum revolution has been based on assertions about stone artefacts. And yet as more research has been carried out and larger and better studied samples obtained, claims for late and uniform increases in diet breadth now seem weak. Certainly, plant residues have been found on Pleistocene flaked artefacts in the Dampier Archipelago—at Murujuga Rockshelter (McDonald et al. 2018a), in all Early Holocene midden sites on the outer islands (Stephenson in Berry 2018; McDonald & Mulvaney 2023), as well as Late Holocene assemblage in this same region. The stone tools on which these residues occur vary from basal grindstones and notched scrapers through to a variety of retouched/utilized flakes; in other words, a wide variety of implements.

A key claim about late broad-spectrum economies is that the use of grass seeds can be identified on the basis of the shape of grindstones, and that 'seed grinder'–shaped specimens called 'millstones' with elongated and pronounced grooves are found only in the last 4000 years or so, with highest numbers in the last 1500 years (Smith 2013: 332). However, current evidence does not support the claim that this is the archaeological pattern across Australian deserts or that it reflects late dietary broadening. For example, these kinds of grindstones have been recovered from Pleistocene levels of sites across

Australia, such as on the Lake Mungo Lunette and at Cuddie Springs in the southeast, from Barrow Island in the northwest, and from Madjedbebe in the extreme northern edge of the continent (Hayes 2015). More significantly, residue and use-wear studies have shown that grindstones in Australia may be used primarily or exclusively for seed grinding regardless of whether they have specific shapes or not (e.g., Balme, Garbin, & Gould 2001; Fullagar & Field 1997; Hayes 2015; Veth, Fullagar, & Gould 1997). Hence rather than looking at the shapes of grindstones, it is residue and use-wear analyses that provide the best insight into whether seed processing was a dominant feature of Late Holocene economies across the arid zone. A recent test of the sequence at Lake Mungo showed that grinding stones recovered from Pleistocene contexts were used exclusively for plant processing, most notably seeds, and that seed processing was not a recent feature of arid foraging but had an antiquity back to at least 15–25 ka (Hayes 2015). We believe the evidence points to seed grinding being a persistent long-term practice in Australia's arid and semiarid areas, with the role of seed use fluctuating geographically and temporally as diet width expanded or contracted depending on regional conditions. This is consistent with a pattern of dynamic and fluctuating adaptation rather than a single invariant trend in regions undergoing different conditions.

SIGNAL SENDING WITH STONE TECHNOLOGY

Technologies are involved in many aspects of peoples' lives. Constructing objects not available in nature can result in tools and weapons with which to harvest resources. But those same objects can be used for many purposes in addition to, or other than as tools, including trade goods and means of storing and transmitting wealth, or as public signals to transmit information. Considering only tool use as an explanation for desert technologies has created very partial explanations in which production systems have been linked simply to environment and economy. When technologies are spread across the entire arid zone, and even across non-drylands regions, the explanatory power of tool function may be minimal as tools in each region need to exploit local environments.

Of course, some tools can have a generic form for an unspecialized and widespread function. But function is an unlikely explanation for specialized and relatively costly technology and standardized objects employed across many environments (Hiscock 2021). We believe this is the case with microliths, as discussed earlier. These ubiquitous small stone artefacts with blunted margins and one sharp edge were spread across much of Australia and throughout all desert areas. These kinds of artefacts were common only for a relatively short period in the Late Holocene and are likely to have been locally standardized because they performed as signals between people, and signals can vary only so much without compromising their recognizability (Hiscock 2021: and see McDonald, Reynen, & Fullagar 2018)- The implication is that this kind of artefact was briefly operating as a key material component of public signal sending system spread across vast tracts of desert landscapes. Expansion and contraction of signalling systems, and replacement of one signal with another, is an indication of the dynamism of information networks across the arid zone, and perhaps their fragility. Such systems sometimes employed portable stone artefacts, but more famously they involved organic artefacts or rock art.

Conclusions about New Perspectives on Desert Dynamics

We have presented a new model for the settlement of Australia's deserts which proposes:

1. Early colonization from after 60 ka when wetter conditions and lake-full conditions prevailed in the north;
2. Rapid dispersal by groups through all bioregions using networks of water source points;
3. Increasing evidence of new and early occupation sites of c. 50 ka age and more from a variety of bioregions, including the edges of sandy deserts and Pleistocene coastlines, illustrating the infinite adaptability of settlers;
4. The development of *in situ* adaptations with increasing aridity through MIS 3 resulting in shifts in mobility and genetic drift variably across different topographies and latitudes of the deserts;
5. Complex responses in lithic technological strategies with a high degree of variation in energy extractive and maintenance tools, including grindstones, tula adzes, and various microlith forms; and
6. The early deployment of art as a symbolic negotiation of new lands and long-distance information exchange. Multiphase art productions shows varying signalling mechanisms through time, with both dated and relative chronologies showing changing environment and social themes from the Pleistocene.

This model builds on many of the different assumptions and scales of the glacial refugia framework (Veth 1989), the desert transformation model (Hiscock & Wallis 2005), the tenets of cryptic refugia (Smith 2013), and the new rapid population growth and dispersal model (Bradshaw et al. 2021). We no longer believe that the heuristic concept of 'desert barriers' is useful in the desert settlement model, though do believe that population retractions are likely to have operated following settlement, leaving substantial tracts of land either 'fallow' or used in archaeologically recognizable ways which are different through time.

We continue to argue that rock art (in particular cupules and abraded grooves followed by geometrics and tracks) was part of the colonizing repertoire and that subsequent discontinuous art systems developed in numerous locations where groups formed longer term connections of country. These deep-time multiphase assemblages, identified from different parts of the arid zone, reveal not only the likely Pleistocene antiquity of signalling behaviour but also demonstrate both the long-distance and then more localized identity signalling behaviour, which is now being disentangled for pigment art in the Kimberley (Finch et al. 2020, 2021). Early regional variants of engraved styles through time are found in adjacent areas of the Pilbara, the Western Desert, central Desert, NW Queensland, and western NSW. An ambitious research program to date the engravings of the Dampier Archipelago is currently underway.[3] Combined with the recent success in dating pigment assemblages in the Kimberley, this work is bound to reset our modelling for the earliest and subsequent occupation of the desert.

While the geographic distributions of different stone tool types are well documented (Hiscock 2008), the timing for their introduction has become far more complex with increased sampling across the deserts and adjacent areas. While microliths/backed artefacts show an efflorescence in production between 4 and 1 ka across the southern arid zone, there are an increasing number of earlier examples now dated to between c. 40 and 10 ka, as well as in the last millennium (McDonald et al. 2018a; McDonald, Reynen, & Fullagar 2018). Formal seed-grinding millstones are more common in the last 1500 years; however, earlier specimens are now documented from the Last Glacial Maximum (Hayes 2015). In contrast, ground-edge axes dated to 46 ka from the Kimberley (Hiscock, O'Connor, Balme, & Maloney 2016) do not enter the southern two thirds of the continent until after the Mid-Holocene (see Ford & Hiscock this volume). Bifacial points are not manufactured in the arid zone, in contrast to unifacial points (Maloney 2015), while tula adzes, used to process hardwoods (Veth, Hiscock, & Williams 2011), are common throughout the entire arid zone and do not date to before c. 4 ka. The systematic use of quarries and lithic provisioning is strongly dependent on patterns of accessible stone supplies and ecotonal complexity near these supplies.

While this emerging complexity is daunting, it does allow archaeologists to focus more on the variability and patterns of different cultural groups and adaptations, an approach which is of more cultural and evolutionary import. It is clear that the previous model of a conservative desert culture, with uniform responses across huge areas and time, is replaced by one that focuses on dynamics and variability in settlement patterns (Veth 1993), art production and identity signalling (McDonald 2017, 2021), and technological and signalling strategies in stone tool production (Hiscock 2021). The previous concept of the 'desert as barrier' gives way to the notion of deserts as 'innovation hubs' which see high levels of experimentation and variability in settlement patterns, material culture, and symbolic behaviours through time. The overwhelming characteristic of desert people is their ability to relocate to exploit localized productive habitats within vast, dynamic, and stochastic landscapes. These high levels of group mobility and economic flexibility are underwritten in at least recent millennia by the 'licence' imbued in long-distance *Tjukurrpa* (Dreamings) which today cosmologically and ceremonially link desert peoples to named water sources and country and with each other, and with groups in adjacent arid and semiarid lands. By using pathways to travel both into, and across vast deserts, this ritual understanding rendered physical barriers permeable and created connectivity between islands of innovation through space and time.

ACKNOWLEDGEMENTS

Figures 34.1 and 34.2 were drawn by Wendy Reynen; Figure 34.3 was compiled by Jo McDonald using data from the CRAR + M database. We acknowledge the Traditional Owners and Custodians for all the deserts sites and cultural landscapes discussed here and for their permissions to work on these.

NOTES

1. ITCZ The Intertropical Convergence Zone is a low-pressure belt centred on the equator which moves north in the Northern Hemisphere summer and south in the Northern Hemisphere winter. The ITCZ drives the wet and dry seasons in the tropics.
2. ENSO (El Niño and the Southern Oscillation) is a periodic fluctuation in sea surface temperature (El Niño) and the air pressure of the overlying atmosphere (Southern Oscillation) across the equatorial Pacific Ocean. It changes global atmospheric circulation, influencing global temperatures and precipitation.
3. Australian Research Council Linkage Project 190100724: 2021–2026; 'Dating Murujuga's Dreaming'; see https://www.crarm.uwa.edu.au/murujuga-dating

REFERENCES

Allen, J., O'Connell, J. F., Clarkson, C., Norman, K., Cox, M., Lambert, D. . . . Veth, P. (2020). A different paradigm for the colonization of Sahul. *Archaeology in Oceania, 55*(1), 1–14.

Balme, J., Davidson, I., McDonald, J., Stern, N., & Veth, P. (2009). Symbolic behaviour and the peopling of the southern arc route to Australia. *Quaternary International, 202,* 59–68.

Balme, J., Garbin, G., & Gould, R. A. (2001). Residue analysis and palaeodiet in arid Australia. *Australian Archaeology, 53,* 1–6.

Barberena, R., Méndez, C., & de Porras, M. E. (2017). Zooming out from archaeological discontinuities: The meaning of mid-Holocene temporal troughs in South American deserts. *Journal of Anthropological Archaeology, 46,* 68–81.

Bayon, G., De Deckker, P., Magee, J. W., Germain, Y., Bermell, S., Tachikawa, K., & Norman, M. D. (2017). Extensive wet episodes in Late Glacial Australia. *Science Reports, 7*(44054), 1–7.

Berry, M. (2018). *Murujuga desert, tide, and dreaming: Understanding early rock art production and lifeways in northwest Australia* (PhD thesis). University of Western Australia, Perth.

Bird, M. I., Beaman, R. J., Condie, S. A., Cooper, A., Ulm, S., & Veth, P. (2018). Palaeogeography and voyage modelling indicates early human colonisation. *Quaternary Science Research, 191,* 431–439.

Bird, M. I., O'Grady, D., & Ulm, S. (2016). Humans, water, and the colonization of Australia. *Proceedings of the National Academy of Sciences, 113*(41), 11477–11482.

Birdsell, J. B. (1957). Some population problems involving Pleistocene man. *Cold Spring Harbor Symposia in Quantitative Biology, 22,* 47–69.

Bowler, J. M., Huang, Q., Chen, K., Head, M. J., & Yuan, B. (1986). Radiocarbon dating of playa-lake hydrologic changes: Examples from China and central Australia. *Palaeogeography, Palaeoclimatology, Palaeoecology, 54,* 241–260.

Bowler, J. M., Wyrwoll, K. H., & Lu, Y. (2001). Variations of the northwest Australian summer monsoon over the last 300,000 years: The paleohydrological record of the Gregory (Mulan) Lakes System. *Quaternary International, 83*, 63–80.

Bradshaw, C. J. A., Norman, K., Ulm, S. G., Williams, A. N., Clarkson, C., Chadoeuf, J., . . . Saltré, F. (2021). Stochastic models support rapid early peopling of Late Pleistocene Sahul. *Nature Communications, 12*(1), 1–11.

Breeze, P. S., Groucutt, H. S., Drake, N. A., White, T. S., Jennings, R. P., & Petraglia, M. D. (2016). Palaeohydrological corridors for hominin dispersals in the Middle East ~250–70,000 years ago. *Quaternary Science Reviews, 144*, 155–185.

Brown, S. (2018). Tales of a fat-tailed macropod. In M. L. Langley, M. Litster, D. Wright, & S. K. May (Eds.), *Archaeology of portable art: Southeast Asian, Pacific, and Australian Perspectives* (pp. 241–257). Oxford: Routledge.

Brumm, A., Oktaviana, A. A., Burhan, B., Hakim, B., Lebe, R., Zhao, J.-X., . . . Aubert, M. (2021). Oldest cave art found in Sulawesi. *Science Advances, 7*(3), 1–12.

Clarkson, C., Jacobs, Z., Marwick, B., Fullagar, R., Wallis, L., Smith, M., . . .Florin, S. A. (2017). Human occupation of northern Australia by 65,000 years ago. *Nature, 547*(7663), 306–310.

Clarkson, C., Roberts, R. G., Jacobs, Z., Marwick, B., Fullagar, R., Arnold, L. J., & Hua, Q. (2018). Reply to comments on Clarkson et al. 2018 Human occupation of northern Australia by 65,000 years ago. *Australian Archaeology, 84*(1), 84–89.

Cohen, T., Jansen, J. D., Gliganic, L. A., Larsen, J. R., Nanson, G. C., May, J.-H., . . . Price, D. (2015). Hydrological transformation coincided with megafaunal extinction in central Australia. *Geology, 43*(3), 195–198.

Cohen, T. J., Nanson, G. C., Larsen, J. R., Jones, B. G., & Price, D. M. (2010). Late Quaternary aeolian and fluvial interactions on the Cooper Creek Fan and the association between linear and source-bordering dunes, Strzelecki Desert, Australia. *Quaternary Science Reviews, 29*, 455–471.

Cropper, D. & W. B. Law (Eds.), (2018). *Rockshelter excavations in the east Hamersley Range, Pilbara Region, Western Australia.* Oxford: Archaeopress.

David, B., Delannoy, J.-J., Mialanes, J., Clarkson, C., Petchey, F., Geneste, J.-M., . . . Chalmin, E. (2019a). 45,610–52,160 years of site and landscape occupation at Nawarla Gabarnmang, Arnhem Land plateau (northern Australia). *Quaternary Science Reviews, 215*, 64–85.

David, B., Delannoy, J.-J., Petchey, F., Gunn, R., Huntley, J., Veth, P., . . . Wong, V. (2019b). Dating painting events through by-products of ochre processing: Borologa 1 Rockshelter, Kimberley, Australia. *Australian Archaeology, 85*(1), 57–94.

De Deckker, P., Barrows, T. T., & Rogers, J. (2014). Land-sea correlations in the Australian region. *Quaternary Science Reviews, 105*, 181–194.

De Deckker, P., Moros, M., Perner, K., Blanz, T., Wacker, L., Schneider, R., . . . Jansen, E. (2020). Climatic evolution in the Australian region over the last 94 ka—spanning human occupancy—and unveiling the Last Glacial Maximum. *Quaternary Science Reviews, 249*, 106593.

Denniston, R. F., Asmerom, Y., Lachniet, M., Polyak, V. J., Hope, P., An, N., . . . Humphreys, W. F. (2013). A Last Glacial Maximum through middle Holocene stalagmite record. *Quaternary Science Reviews, 77*, 101–112.

Ditchfield, K. (2017). *Pleistocene-Holocene coastal mobility patterns in the Carnarvon Bioregion, north-western Australia* (PhD thesis). University of Western Australia, Perth.

Ditchfield, K., Manne, T., Hook, F., Ward, I., & Veth, P. (2018). Coastal occupation before the "Big Swamp": Results from excavations at John Wayne Country Rockshelter on Barrow Island. *Archaeology in Oceania*, 53(3), 163–178.

Dortch, J., Balme, J., McDonald, J., Morse, K., O'Connor, S., & Veth, P. (2019). Settling the West: 50,000 years in a changing land. *Journal of the Royal Society of Western Australia*, 102, 30–44.

Edwards, R. (1968). Prehistoric rock engravings at Thomas Reservoir, Cleland Hills, western central Australia. *Records of the South Australian Museum*, 15(4), 647–670.

Finch, D., Gleadow, A., Hergt, J., Levchenko, V. A., Heaney, P., Veth, P., . . . Green, H. (2020). 12,000-year-old Aboriginal rock art from the Kimberley region, Western Australia. *Science Advances*, 6, 1–9.

Finch, D., Gleadow, A., Hergt, J., Levchenko, V. A., Heaney, P., Veth, P., . . . Green, H. (2021). Ages for Australia's oldest *in situ* rock paintings. *Nature Human Behaviour*, 5(3), 310–318.

Fitzsimmons, K. E., Cohen, T. J., Hesse, P. P., Jansen, J., Nanson, G. C., May, J. H., . . . Larsen, J. (2013). Late Quaternary palaeoenvironmental change in the Australian drylands. *Quaternary Science Reviews*, 74, 78–96.

Fullagar, R., & Field, J. (1997). Pleistocene seed grinding implements from the Australian arid zone. *Antiquity*, 71, 300–307.

Gliganic, L. A., Meyer, M. C., Sohbati, R., Jain, M., & Barrett, S. (2019). OSL surface exposure dating of a lithic quarry in Tibet: Laboratory validation and application. *Quaternary Geochronology*, 49, 199–204.

Green, H., Gleadow, A., Finch, D., Hergt, J., & Ouzman, S. (2017). Mineral deposition systems at rock art sites, Kimberley, Northern Australia—Field observations. *Journal of Archaeological Science: Reports*, 14, 340–352.

Hamm, G., Mitchell, P., Arnold, L. J., Prideaux, G. J., Questiaux, D., Spooner, N. A., . . . Johnston, D. (2016). Cultural innovation and megafauna interaction in the early settlement of arid Australia. *Nature*, 539(7628), 280–283.

Hayes, E. (2015). *What was ground? A functional analysis of grinding stones from Madjedbebe and Lake Mungo, Australia* (PhD thesis). University of Wollongong, Wollongong.

Hiscock, P. (1989). *Prehistoric settlement patterns and artefact manufacture at Lawn Hill* (PhD thesis). University of Queensland, Brisbane.

Hiscock, P. (2008). *Archaeology of ancient Australia*. London: Routledge.

Hiscock, P. (2013). Occupying new lands: Global migrations and cultural diversification with particular reference to Australia. In K. E. Graf, C.V. Ketron, & M. R. Waters (Eds.), Paleoamerican Odyssey (pp. 3–12). Center for the Study of the First Americans, Texas A&M University.

Hiscock, P. (2021). Small signals: Comprehending the Australian microlithic as public signalling. *Cambridge Archaeological Journal*, 31(2), 313–324.

Hiscock, P., & Attenbrow, V. (2005). *Australia's Eastern Regional Sequence revisited: Technology and change at Capertee 3*. BAR International Series 1397. Oxford: Archaeopress.

Hiscock, P., & Attenbrow, V. (2015). Dates and demography: Are radiometric dates a robust proxy for long-term prehistoric demographic change? *Archaeology in Oceania*, 50(1), 29–35.

Hiscock, P., O'Connor, S., Balme, J., & Maloney, T. (2016). World's earliest ground-edge axe production coincides with human colonisation of Australia. *Australian Archaeology*, 82(1), 2–11.

Hiscock, P., & Wallis, L. (2005). Pleistocene settlement of deserts. In P. Veth, M. Smith, & P. Hiscock (Eds.), *Desert peoples: Archaeological perspectives* (pp. 34–57). Malden, MA: Blackwell.

Hughes, P., Sullivan, M., & Hiscock, P. (2017). Palaeoclimate and human occupation in south-eastern arid Australia. *Quaternary Science Reviews, 163*, 72–83.

Hughes, P., Way, A., & Sullivan, M. (2020). Are the widespread scatters of stone artefacts on dune surfaces in southeastern arid Australia really late Holocene in age? *Australian Archaeology, 87*(1), 75–83.

Jankowski, N. R., Stern, N., Lachlan, T. J., & Jacobs, Z. (2020). A high-resolution late Quaternary depositional history and chronology for the southern portion of the Lake Mungo lunette, semi-arid Australia. *Quaternary Science Reviews, 233*, 106–224.

Kealy, S., Louys, J., & O'Connor, S. (2018). Least-cost pathway models indicate northern human dispersal from Sunda to Sahul. *Journal of Human Evolution, 125*, 59–70.

Law, W. B., P. Hiscock, B. Ostendorf, & M. Lewis. (2021). Using satellite imagery to evaluate precontact Aboriginal foraging habitats in the Australian Western Desert. *Scientific Reports, 11*, 10755

Lourandos, H. (1985). Intensification and Australian prehistory. In T. D. Price & J. A. Brown (Eds.), *Prehistoric hunter-gatherers: The emergence of cultural complexity* (pp. 385–423). Orlando, FL: Academic Press.

Malaspinas, A. S., Westaway, M. C., Muller, C., Soussa, V. C., Lao, O., Alves, I., . . . Willerslev, E. (2016). A genomic history of Aboriginal Australia. *Nature, 538*, 207–214.

Maloney, T. (2015). *Technological organisation and points in the Southern Kimberley* (PhD thesis). Australian National University, Canberra.

Maloney, T., O'Connor, S., Wood, R., Aplin, K., & Balme, J. (2018). Carpenters Gap 1: A 47,000 year old record of indigenous adaption and innovation. *Quaternary Science Reviews, 191*, 204–228.

Maroulis, J. C., Nanson, G. C., Price, D. M., & Pietsch, T. (2007). Aeolian-fluvial interaction and climate change: Source-bordering dune development over the past 100 ka on Copper Creek, central Australia. *Quaternary Science Reviews, 26*, 386–404.

Marsh, M., Hiscock, P., Williams, A., Hughes, P., & Sullivan, M. E. (2018). Watura Jurnti: A 42000–45000-year-long occupation sequence. *Archaeology in Oceania, 53*, 137–149.

Maynard, L. (1979). The archaeology of Australian Aboriginal art. In S. M. Mead (Ed.), *Exploring the visual art of Oceania* (pp. 83–110). Honolulu: University Press of Hawaii.

McBride, E. (2018). *Amberat middens and the palaeoenvironmental record* (Master's thesis). Flinders University, Adelaide.

McDonald, J. (2005). Archaic faces to headdresses: The changing role of rock art across the arid zone. In P. Veth, P. Hiscock, & M. Smith (Eds.), *Desert peoples: Archaeological perspectives* (pp. 116–141). Malden, MA: Blackwell.

McDonald, J. (2015). I must go down to the seas again: Or, what happens when the sea comes to you? Murujuga rock art as an environmental indicator for Australia's north-west. *Quaternary International, 385*, 124–135.

McDonald, J. (2017). Discontinuities in arid zone rock art: Graphic indicators for changing social complexity across space and through time. *Journal of Anthropological Archaeology, 46*, 53–67.

McDonald, J. (2020). Serpents Glen (*Karnatukul*): New histories for deep time attachment to Country in Australia's Western Desert. *Bulletin of the History of Archaeology, 30*(1), 1–13.

McDonald, J. (2021). Desert rock art: Social geography at the local scale. In J. Magne and M. Arntzen (Eds.), Perspectives on Difference in Rock Art: *ALTA Conference Proceedings in Honour of Knut Helskog* (pp. 1–23). Alta Norway: Equinox Publishing.

McDonald, J., & Berry, M. (2016). Murujuga, northwestern Australia: When arid hunter-gatherers became coastal foragers. *The Journal of Island and Coastal Archaeology, 12*(1), 24–43.

McDonald J., & Mulvaney, K. (Eds.) (2023). *Murujuga: Dynamics of the Dreaming. A long and short history of this cultural landscape with reference to rock art, stone features, excavations and historical sites recorded across the Dampier Archipelago between 2014–2018.* CRAR+M Monograph No. 2. Perth: UWA Publishing..

McDonald, J., Reynen, W., Ditchfield, K., Dortch, J., Leopold, M., Stephenson, B., . . . Veth, P. (2018a). Murujuga Rockshelter: First evidence for Pleistocene occupation on the Burrup Peninsula. *Quaternary Science Reviews, 193,* 266–287.

McDonald, J., Reynen, W., & Fullagar, R. (2018). Testing predictions for symmetry, variability and chronology of backed artefact production in Australia's Western Desert. *Archaeology in Oceania, 53*(3), 179–190.

McDonald, J., Reynen, W., Petchey, F., Ditchfield, K., Byrne, C., Vannieuwenhuyse, D., . . . Veth, P. (2018b). *Karnatukul* (Serpent's Glen): A new chronology for the oldest site in Australia's Western Desert. *PloS ONE, 13*(9), 1–36.

McDonald, J., Steelman, K., Veth, P., Mackey, J., Loewen, J., Thurber, C. R., & Guilderson, T. P. (2014). Results from the first intensive dating program for pigment art in the Australian arid zone: Insights into recent social complexity. *Journal of Archaeological Science, 46*(1), 195–204.

McDonald, J., & Veth, P. (2006). Rock art and social identity: A comparison of graphic systems operating in arid and fertile environments in the Holocene. In I. Lilley (Ed.), *Archaeology of Oceania: Australia and the Pacific Islands* (pp. 96–115). Oxford: Blackwell.

McDonald, J., & Veth, P. (2010). Pleistocene rock art: A colonising repertoire for Australia's earliest inhabitants. *Préhistoire, art et sociétés: bulletin de la Société Préhistorique de l'Ariège, 65,* 172–178.

McDonald, J., & Veth, P. (2013a). Rock art in arid landscapes. *Australian Archaeology, 77,* 1–16.

McDonald, J., & Veth, P. (2013b). The archaeology of memory: The recursive relationship of Martu rock art and place. *Anthropological Forum, 23*(4), 367–386.

Morse, K. (1999). Coastwatch: Pleistocene resource use on the Cape Range Peninsula. In J. Hall & I. J. McNiven (Eds.), *Australian coastal archaeology* (pp. 73–78). Canberra: ANU Press.

Morse, K., Cameron, R., & Reynen, W. (2014). A tale of three caves. *Australian Archaeology, 79,* 167–178.

Mulvaney, K. (2013). Iconic imagery: Pleistocene rock art development across northern Australia. *Quaternary International, 285,* 99–110.

Mulvaney, K. (2015). *Murujuga Marni: Rock art of the macropod hunters and mollusc harvesters.* CRAR+M Monograph Series No.1. Perth: UWA Press.

Norman, K., Inglis, J., Clarkson, C., Faith, J. T., Shulmeister, J., & Harris, D. (2018). An early colonisation pathway into northwest Australia 70–60,000 years ago. *Quaternary Science Reviews, 180,* 229–239.

O'Connell, J. F., & Allen, J. (2012). The restaurant at the end of the universe: Modelling the colonisation of Sahul. *Australian Archaeology, 74,* 5–31.

O'Connor, S., & Veth, P. (2000). The world's first mariners: Savannah dwellers in an island continent. In S. O'Connor & P. Veth (Eds.), *East of Wallace's Line: Studies of past and present maritime cultures of the Indo-Pacific region* (pp. 99–137). Rotterdam: Balkema.

Paterson, A., Anderson, R., Mulvaney, K., de Koning, S., Dortch, J., & McDonald, J. (2019a). So ends this day: American whalers in Yaburara country, Dampier Archipelago. *Antiquity, 93*(367), 218–235.

Paterson, A., Shellam, T., Veth, P., Mulvaney, K., Anderson, R., Dortch J., & McDonald, J. (2019b). The Mermaid? Re-envisaging the 1818 exploration of Enderby Island, Murujuga, Western Australia. *The Journal of Island and Coastal Archaeology*, 15(2), 284–304.

Pepper, M., & Keogh, J. S. (2021). Life in the "dead heart" of Australia: The geohistory of the Australian deserts and its impact on genetic diversity of arid zone lizards. *Journal of Biogeography*, 48(1), 716–746.

Reynen, W. H. (2019). *Rock shelters and human mobility during the Last Glacial Maximum in the Pilbara Uplands, north-western Australia* (PhD thesis). University of Western Australia, Perth.

Reynen, W. H., Vannieuwenhuyse, D., Morse, K., Monks, C., & Balme, J. (2018). What happened after the Last Glacial Maximum? Transitions in site use on an arid inland island in north-western Australia. *Archaeology in Oceania*, 53(3), 150–162.

Roberts, R. G., Jones, R., & Smith, M. A. (1994). Beyond the radiocarbon barrier in Australian prehistory. *Antiquity*, 68, 611–616.

Schmidt, P., & Hiscock, P. (2020). The antiquity of Australian silcrete heat treatment: Lake Mungo and the Willandra Lakes. *Journal of Human Evolution*, 142, 102744.

Slack, M., Law, W. B., & Gliganic, L. A. (2018). Pleistocene settlement of the eastern Hamersley Plateau: a regional study of 22 rock-shelter sites, *Archaeology in Oceania* 53 (3), 191–204.

Slack, M. J., Law, W. B., & Gliganic, L. A. (2020). The early occupation of the Eastern Pilbara revisited: new radiometric chronologies and archaeological results from Newman Rockshelter and Newman Ore Body XXIX. *Quaternary Science Reviews*, 236, 1–19.

Smith, M. A. (1993). Biogeography, human ecology and prehistory in The Sandridge Deserts. *Australian Archaeology*, 37(1), 35–50.

Smith, M. (1988). The pattern and timing of prehistoric settlement in Central Australia. *Journal of Archaeological Science*, 40(12), 4612–4625.

Smith, M. (2013). *The archaeology of Australia's Deserts*. Cambridge: Cambridge University Press.

Smith, M. A., Williams, A. N., & Ross, J. (2017). Puntutjarpa rockshelter revisited: A chronological and stratigraphic reappraisal of a key archaeological sequence for the Western Desert, Australia. *Australian Archaeology*, 83(1–2), 20–31.

Veth, P. (1989). Islands in the Interior. *Archaeology in Oceania*, 24(3), 81–92.

Veth, P. M. (1993). *Islands in the interior: The dynamics of prehistoric adaptations within the arid zone of Australia*. International Monographs in Prehistory. Archaeological Series 3. Ann Arbor, Michigan.

Veth, P. (2005). Cycles of aridity and human mobility: Risk-minimization amongst late Pleistocene foragers of the Western Desert, Australia. In P. Veth, M. A. Smith, & P. Hiscock (Eds.), *Desert peoples: Archaeological perspectives* (pp. 100–115). Oxford: Blackwell.

Veth, P. (2006). Social dynamism in the archaeology of the Western Desert. In B. David, B. Barker, & I. J. McNiven (Eds.), *Social archaeology of Australian Indigenous societies* (pp. 242–253). Canberra: Aboriginal Studies Press.

Veth, P. (2017). Breaking through the radiocarbon barrier. *Australian Archaeology*, 83(3), 165–167.

Veth, P., Ditchfield, K., Bateman, M., Ouzman, S., Benoit, M., Motta, A., . . . Harper, S. (2019). Minjiwarra: Archaeological evidence of human occupation of Australia's northern Kimberley by 50,000 BP. *Australian Archaeology*, 85(2), 115–125.

Veth, P., Fullagar, R., & Gould, R. (1997). Residue and use-wear analysis of grinding implements from Puntutjarpa Rockshelter in the Western Desert: Current and proposed research. *Australian Archaeology*, 44, 23–25.

Veth, P., Harper, S., & Ditchfield, K. (2021). The case for continuity in the Kimberley occupation and rock art. In A. McGrath, & L. Russell (Eds.), *Routledge companion to Indigenous global history* (pp. 194–220). New York: Routledge.

Veth, P., Hiscock, P., & Williams, A. (2011). Are tulas and ENSO linked in Australia? *Australian Archaeology, 72,* 7–14.

Veth, P., McDonald, J., & S. de Koning (2018). Archaeology and rock art of the north-west arid zone with a focus on animals. In H. Lambers (Ed.) *On the ecology of Australia's arid zone* (pp. 283–305). Dordrecht: Springer.

Veth, P., McDonald, J., & White, B. (2008). Dating of Bush Turkey Rockshelter 3 in the Calvert Ranges establishes Early Holocene occupation of the Little Sandy Desert, Western Australia. *Australian Archaeology, 66,* 33–44.

Veth, P., Myers, C., Heaney, P., & Ouzman, S. (2018). Plants before farming: The deep history of plant-use and representation in the rock art of Australia's Kimberley region. *Quaternary International, 489,* 26–45.

Veth, P. Smith, M., Bowler, J., Fitzsimmons, K., Williams, A., & Hiscock, P. (2009). Excavations at Parnkupirti, Lake Gregory, Great Sandy Desert: OSL ages for occupation before the Last Glacial maximum. *Australian Archaeology, 69,* 1–10.

Veth, P., Smith, M., & Hiscock, P. (Eds.) (2005). *Desert peoples. Archaeological perspectives.* Malden, MA: Blackwell.

Veth, P., Ward, I., & Ditchfield, K. (2017). Reconceptualising Last Glacial Maximum discontinuities: A case study from the maritime deserts of north-western Australia. *Journal of Anthropological Archaeology, 46,* 82–91.

Veth, P., Ward, I., & Manne, T. (2017). Coastal feasts: A Pleistocene antiquity for resource abundance in the maritime deserts of North West Australia. *Journal of Island and Coastal Archaeology, 12,* 8–23.

Veth, P., Ward, I., Manne, T., Ulm, S., Ditchfield, K., Dortch, J., . . . Kendrick, P. (2017). Early human occupation of a maritime desert, Barrow Island, North-West Australia. *Quaternary Science Reviews, 168,* 19–29.

Veth, P. M., Williams, A. N., & Paterson, A. G. (2014). Australian deserts: Extreme environments in archaeology. *Encyclopedia of Global Archaeology, 1,* 654–665.

Vinnicombe, P. (1987). *Dampier archaeological project: Resource document, survey and salvage of Aboriginal sites, Burrup Peninsula, Western Australia.* Perth: Department of Aboriginal Sites, Western Australian Museum.

Westaway, M., Williams, D., Lowe, K. M., Wright, N., Gorringe, J., Kerkhov, R., . . . Collard, M. (2021). Hidden in plain sight: First systematic fieldwork in Mithaka Country, southwest Queensland, reveals an extensive archaeological landscape. *Antiquity, 95*(382), 1043–1060.

Williams, A. N., Veth, P., Steffen, W., Ulm, S., Turney, C. S. M., Phipps, S., . . . Reeves, J. (2015). A continental narrative: Human settlement patterns and Australasian climate change over the last 35,000 years. *Quaternary Science Reviews, 123,* 91–112.

Wobst, H. M. (1977). Stylistic behaviour and information exchange. In C. E. Cleland (Ed.), *For the Director: Research essays in honour of J. B. Griffen* (pp. 317–342). Anthropological Papers 61. Ann Arbor: Museum of Anthropology, University of Michigan.

Wood, R., Jacobs, Z., Vannieuwenhuyse, D., Balme, J., O'Connor, S., & Whitau, R. (2016). Towards an accurate and precise chronology for the colonization of Australia: The example of Riwi, Kimberley, Western Australia. *PLoS ONE, 11*(9): e0160123.

Wright, B. J. (1968). *Rock art of the Pilbara region, north-west Australia.* Canberra: Australian Institute of Aboriginal Studies.

PART VII

CEREMONIES AND RITUALS

CHAPTER 35

HISTORICIZING THE 'DREAMING'

An Archaeological Perspective from Arid Australia

MIKE SMITH

INTRODUCTION

THE 'Dreaming' is an Australian belief system in which elaborate relationships between people and place are religiously sanctioned and articulated in a large body of mythology. This unique place-based ideology is arguably one of the world's major religions, as it once covered an entire continent. It developed autonomously, and by the late eighteenth century it was practised by 750,000 to 1 million people (White & Mulvaney 1987). It is best known from arid Australia where its salient structural features are described in a large corpus of anthropological research (e.g., Mountford 1976; Myers 1986; Spencer & Gillen 1899, 1927; Strehlow 1971; Tindale 1974; Tonkinson 1978). This arid region includes a number of regions of which Central Australia, the Western Desert, and the Pilbara are the best known archaeologically (Smith 2013).

In the Australian desert, landforms and natural features, sacred sites, rock paintings, stone arrangements, and incised *tjurunga* (sacred boards) provide tangible expressions of a totemic geography that underpins a unique system of land tenure. Although the foraging economy in this large region collapsed as a result of the colonial impact in most areas between CE 1870 and 1960, the religious superstructure survived longer, with many aspects of ritual stewardship of the land, or ceremonial practice, and land tenure extending into the twenty-first century. In the 'Dreaming', a large repertoire of landesque mythology (described below) acted to personalize the landscape and thereby provide a framework for localizing people, determining their rights to land.

The history of this religious system and the order in which its key institutions developed are not known in any detail. Bruno David and colleagues initiated systematic study of its archaeology (e.g., David 2002; David, McNiven, Attenbrow, Flood, & Collins

1994). Apart from this research, only a handful of other studies have looked at the archaeology of this system or its ideology (e.g., McDonald & Veth 2011; Smith 2013; Taçon, Wilson, & Chippindale 1996). However, as David (2002: 1) puts it: 'the Dreaming must have a history: it must have arisen out of human practice sometime in the past. . . . as Aboriginal world-views of recent, ethnographic times emerged through the course of history, there surely were times in the past when Aboriginal people thought differently about the world'.

Central Australia, in particular, has a special place in the history of ideas about Palaeolithic societies. Salomon Reinach (1903, 1913; Palacio-Pérez 2010) turned to the rich ethnography from Central Australia (Spencer 1896; Spencer & Gillen 1899), shortly after the antiquity of rock art in Europe was recognized, to understand the religious significance of the art of hunter-gatherers. Spencer and Gillen's detailed accounts (1899) suggested to him that Palaeolithic art had a magical or totemic role. Reinach, therefore, proposed that ancient societies in western Europe were totemic in their form and strongly concerned with the maintenance or increase of species (Reinach 1903). Émile Durkheim also gave Central Australia prominence in his study of elementary religious beliefs, focusing on *tjuringa* (Durkheim 1915). In similar fashion, William Sollas regarded these groups as representatives of ancient societies, deep in the European past, and referred to Central Australian Aboriginal people as 'the Mousterians of the Antipodes' (Sollas 1911). More recent studies have also treated Australian desert groups as analogues for ancient hunter-gatherer socioeconomic systems (e.g., Gould 1980; Hayden 1979; Lee & DeVore 1968). Neither Reinach nor his contemporaries appreciated the strong link between people and place inherent in Australian religious systems, or that Central Australian society might itself have a long history of elaboration and development.

Since the 1980s, archaeological research in Central Australia has demonstrated that this region has been occupied for >30,000 years and that the surrounding desert—including the Pilbara and Western Desert—were first occupied around 45,000–50,000 years ago (Hamm et al. 2016; McDonald et al. 2018; Smith 2013). This deep antiquity allows considerable scope for long-term social evolution in these systems. Also relevant here is research that demonstrates more significant variability in foraging societies, in both their contemporary forms (Kelly 2013) and their histories (Price & Brown 1985; Schrire 1984), than previously thought (Lee & DeVore 1968). Australian religious systems also vary. Although the basic elements of Aboriginal religious life were widely shared across the continent, Ronald Berndt identifies four different religious systems, of which much of arid Australia is marked by the paucity of overarching traditions (those held in common across descent groups) and the relative absence of 'super-totemic' ancestral beings (Berndt 1974). In contrast, arid Australia has a segmented place-based system in which ritual knowledge is jealously held proprietary knowledge controlled by local descent groups.

With these factors in mind, we can best approach Aboriginal societies in Australia's deserts as the historical endpoint of a long trajectory that began around 45,000–50,000 years ago. Any understanding of the archaeology of this belief system must begin with the structure of the 'Dreaming' in its classic nineteenth-century form. Let us begin, therefore, with a brief ethnographic outline of the structural and functional features of the 'Dreaming' before considering its archaeology.

The 'Dreaming'—A Landesque Ideology

History of Thought

The governing ideology in arid Australia is a system of religious belief—and a corpus of scripture—that we now know as the 'Dreaming'. In Central Australia, between 1896 and 1927, Baldwin Spencer and Frank Gillen gave the first formal accounts of the 'Dreaming' (Spencer 1896; Spencer & Gillen 1899, 1927). Gillen (1897: 16) famously wrote: 'there is not a remarkable natural feature in the country without a special tradition—why it is the very breath of their nostrils'.

The term that Spencer and Gillen used—*Dreamtime*—was their attempt to render into English the Arrernte concept of *altyerre* (a concept known by other terms in neighbouring groups—such as *tjukurrpa*). As the words *altyerre, tjukurrpa,* and *jukurrpa* are semantically linked to the word for dream in these languages (Goddard & Wierzbicka 2015; Tonkinson 1978), Spencer's rendering as 'Dreamtime' is understandable. However, the concept was—and remains—widely misunderstood, as the term *Dreamtime* evokes a fabled fairy-tale past, a hazy, deep time footnote to Australia's history. In *The Dreaming and Other Essays*, W. E. H. (Bill) Stanner put it another way. 'The Dreaming', he said, was 'a philosophy in the garb of an oral literature' (Stanner 2010: 62).

We can now see the 'Dreaming' as a major religious system, articulated in an immense web of land-based mythology. In a global context, it is essentially a highly developed form of animism—at least in its structure in the new formulation of animism (Harvey 2006) as opposed to its original, primitivist formulation by E. B. Tylor (1871). Rather than an elementary form of religious belief, it is more likely that the 'Dreaming' is a religious tradition that has developed in its own way to produce a unique landesque ideology that acts to intimately link people and place to an extent not achieved by animist systems anywhere else in the world. T. G. H. Strehlow dubbed this place-based system a totemic geography (Strehlow 1970). In the relatively benign landscapes of Australia, the focus is not on titanic forces of nature (though some totemic sites are dangerous), nor does it hinge on a parallel supernatural world that is entered by trance, as in shamanism. It does, however, share the idea that the fertility of the land needs to be ritually stewarded.

The territorial aspects of this religion structure other aspects of ritual-political life in arid Australia. For instance, land is a form of ritual property; ritual life is strongly male-dominated; place-based religious paraphernalia is more elaborate than that in other areas of Australia (in particular, the sacred boards and engraved stone plaques known as *tjuringa*); totemic ancestors are regarded as eternal and reside in the contemporary landscape; initiation ceremonies are elaborate, with an emphasis on formal instruction of initiates, on long song cycles, and on the number of mythological reenactments. There is also a strongly developed secret-sacred component in these traditions, and the belief system is considered immutable (as it provides the means of linking people to land in an inalienable relationship, colloquially known as 'the law').

Totemic Geography

At the core of this religious system is the idea that the land bears traces of ancestral beings, whose activities create a large web of mythologies, resulting in what is often described as a 'storied' landscape (McBryde 2011). These ancestral beings travelled across the land, leaving traces of their activities, or physical traces of themselves in local landforms, where they are still present and typically regarded as eternal. The natural world is personified in these ancestral beings, with each associated with a plant or animal species as well as a place, and each able to shift shape between animal and human form, or with properties of both latent in their form.

In practice, the 'Dreaming' is a worldview that looks to visible traces in the 'natural' world to verify and validate its governing ideology. The greater part of this totemic geography is vested in landforms or trees, supplemented by rock art or stone arrangements. Rock art and stone arrangements form only a minor component of the symbolic landscape and are widely regarded by Aboriginal people as natural phenomena, as 'significant marks' deriving from the 'Dreaming' itself. 'Dreaming' narratives are foundational. Their importance is taken as self-evident, without the need for explanation, and as fundamental to the world of desert people. In this sense, the 'Dreaming' narratives are a kind of scripture.

'Dreaming' Tracks

The journeys of these ancestral beings intrinsically create a series of mythological trails crisscrossing the landscape, known as 'Dreaming' tracks or 'songlines' (Neale 2017). Many of the associated narratives deal with rites of passage, theft, or tales of lust, revenge, and retribution, or transgressions of marriage rules. The 'Dreaming' tracks and associated narratives also implicitly include a great deal of geographical detail about local landscapes. However, this geographical detail is not their major purpose. Most function primarily as ecclesiastical maps rather than route maps or mnemonic guides to geography and ecology. Most do not cross the landscape in any way that would be sensible to travel on foot; some travel along the centre of large salt lakes, whereas others go underground or involve ancestors that fly through the sky. As a sort of ecclesiastical map, they show the relative positions of totemic sites, a framework primarily concerned with a sacred, rather than secular, landscape.

The majority of 'Dreaming' tracks are local and deal with regional mythologies. In other instances, the tracks concern remarkably long continental narratives (e.g., *Wati Kutjarra*—Two Lizard Men, *Malu*—Red Kangaroo, the *Tingarri* cycle, *Kungkarangkalpa*—Seven Sisters, *Atyelpe*—Native Cat, and *Kipara*—Bush Turkey). These longer mythological tracks probably reflect the greater power and prestige of some traditions, alongside the operation of a syncretic process that connects smaller tracks together to form long narrative trails. Tonkinson (1974: 72) records an Aboriginal view of this dynamic: 'The ancestral beings roamed over wide areas and frequently came into contact with one another. During such meetings they exchanged sacred and non-sacred objects, songlines, rituals, and decorations, thus spreading these cultural elements to the extremes of the desert and beyond'.

Although the vast network of mythological trails framed religious life and ritual interactions, there is little evidence that this network determined recruitment into local descent groups; had broader functional significance in terms of providing a framework for the fall back of desert groups during droughts (Smith 1988); or was an adaptive response to the mobility of desert people.

Mythology and Land Tenure

People's rights to land vary according to their links with the ancestral beings that created or traversed the landscape (Myers 1986; Strehlow 1970, 1971; Sutton 1988). Individuals are linked to specific places through their identification with totemic beings and the activities of these ancestral beings during their travels. As Fred Myers (1993: 45) stresses, '*holding country* primarily consists in control over the stories, objects, and rituals associated with the mythological ancestors of the Dreaming at a particular place'. Sacred knowledge is specific and localized. In this segmented system, desert people have detailed knowledge of only part of a particular 'Dreaming' track. This creates a nexus of place, totemic identity, and land title, captured in the vernacular phrase 'belonging to country'.

The 'Dreaming' is primarily a frame of reference for asserting connections to place and for working out proprietary rights to land, without which there would be the chaos of a *terra nullius*. Essentially, it creates a system of rights obviating the need for arbitrary application of force to determine land ownership.

Every descent group is anchored to an estate by this means, irrespective of whether the relevant tracks are large or small. This accounts for the vast web of mythologies and 'Dreaming' tracks that interlace Central Australia and the Western Desert. The genius of this system is that it managed to underpin the necessity for relatively high levels of residential mobility with an inalienable land tenure.

Time and Tradition

There is no indication that these narratives represent an oral history, a sort of 'folk history' encoding a memory of past events in a community's traditions (Stanner 2010;

Smith 2018). It is relevant here that there is no Indigenous concept for 'historical time'. As Stanner (2010: 57) says: 'A central meaning of The Dreaming is that of a sacred, heroic time ... but neither time nor history as we understand them is involved in this meaning. I have never been able to discover any Aboriginal word for time as an abstract concept. And the sense of 'history' is wholly alien here'. Rather, the 'Dreaming' is seen as eternal, with the totemic ancestors still present in the landscape, in a timeless parallel domain that coexists with the present (what Stanner describes as the 'everywhen'). Although there is an order of events, a before and after, there seems to be no equivalent to the usual Western notion of linear history (Goddard & Wierzbicka 2015; Sutton 1988).

The 'Dreaming' is also seen as immutable. Tonkinson (1978: 112) notes that 'nowhere does their ideology admit structural change as a possibility'. Nevertheless, it is apparent that some of these religious narratives do embed kernels of history (e.g., Smith 2014) and that the resistance to change is more perceived than actual.

Ritual Property and a Political Economy of Knowledge

In these societies, ritual knowledge is a form of property and a major element in a political economy of knowledge. Although the patri-clans responsible for different segments of the same mythological track may coordinate their activities to stage major ceremonies, ritual knowledge is tightly held property.

The connection with land tenure and real estate also helps explain other aspects of this religious system. For instance, the public assertion that the 'Dreaming' is immutable is central to the view that the relationship between people and land is likewise inalienable. Another aspect is the extensive secret-sacred element of these narratives, where people jealously exclude others from their sacred traditions, which can be regarded as analogous to the modern concept of 'commercial-in-confidence'. Although the desert is often seen as an open system in terms of its demographic arrangements and foraging territories, this is not the case in the religious sphere, where ritual property is strongly bounded.

Ceremonies and Access to Knowledge

Throughout Aboriginal Australia, access to religious knowledge was regulated through ceremonies, the most important of which centred on:

1. *Male initiation.* In the desert, initiation ceremonies are particularly elaborate, with an emphasis on formal instruction of initiates. Typically, male initiation is followed by a staggered series of postinitiation revelatory ceremonies that 'served as an introduction to a new discipline, an expansive and expanding area of knowledge, a new way of looking at things within the social, natural and supernatural environments' (Berndt 1974: 4).

2. *'Increase' ceremonies.* These are short ceremonies held to maintain or revitalize the species and natural phenomena personified in the totemic ancestors. These ceremonies operate to sustain the *status quo* and fertility of 'country'. Unlike tropical Australia, where the dominant rites are mortuary rites, in the desert, the dominant rites are concerned with fertility and ritual stewardship of the land. As Berndt (1974: 4) puts it, the 'whole religious corpus vibrated with an expressed aspiration for life, abundant life. Vitality, fertility and growth'.

   'Increase' ceremonies have more to do with ritual stewardship of the land and have little explicit connection to so-called hunting magic, as others have also noted in the case of northern Australia (Kearney, Bradley, & Brady 2019; see McNiven, this volume). In any case, these ceremonies include rites for a wide variety of phenomena, including bush flies, yams, and honey, and are more properly regarded as maintenance ceremonies. This ethic of stewardship associated with 'Dreaming' traditions operates primarily in the ritual domain and less prescriptively in the secular world.

3. *Mythological reenactments.* Other ceremonies revolve around mythological reenactments. These can range from relatively short, discrete performances that are in the public domain to larger, more restricted, ceremonies involving more than a hundred people, lasting more than a month, and involving performance of long song cycles (Kimber & Smith 1987).

Prospects for an Archaeological Investigation of the 'Dreaming'

Religion is an important focus for historical study because of its pervasive role in human experience. As such, it is valid to ask how the 'Dreaming' religious system developed and how ancient the 'Dreaming' is—at least in its classic form. The belief systems of hunter-gatherer societies are notoriously difficult to historicize because their archaeological record is so austere. To reconstruct how the Australian system of codifying relationships between people and land developed, and to explore the history of the 'Dreaming' as a belief system, archaeologists have several options (Table 35.1). As it is unlikely that any single trait will be sufficient to historically track the 'Dreaming' or explore its elaboration over time, the most effective protocol is to approach these as part of an integrated investigation of the system and to avoid dealing with traits in isolation.

Tracking Back

The first option involves investigation of the demographic and economic basis of this system. Historical trajectories can be approached as temporal sequences of

Table 35.1. Examples of options for tracing the history of the 'Dreaming'

1	Tracking back to determine time depth of the ethnographic landscape.
2	Site histories. Changes in the role of key places that are integral to specific 'Dreaming' narratives.
3	Differentiation of rock art, tracking development of a place-based system and/or presence of graphic correlates for this belief system.
4	Dating of stone arrangements that express material dimensions of the totemic geography.
5	Presence of 'associated' ritual practices that show interaction with rock surfaces.
6	An abundance of red ochre.
7	The occurrence of sacred paraphernalia.
8	Lexical age for terminology associated with the 'Dreaming'.

transformations in time or space in cultural systems. One line of inquiry hinging on such trajectories involves a 'tracking-back' approach to establish when critical economic and demographic prerequisites for the 'Dreaming' were in place, allowing estimation of the likely time depth of the belief system recorded in the ethnography (see also David & McNiven's 'Dual Historical Method', 2004: 203).

The ethnographic form of the 'Dreaming' is associated with relatively high population densities in arid Australia that were not in place before 1500 BP (McDonald & Veth 2011; Smith 2013; Smith & Ross 2008; Williams et al. 2015). This has also been observed on the northern fringes of the desert (David et al. 1994). This is a predictable correlation, as we can expect a system of land tenure to be sharpened by higher populations and greater demographic density.

In the ethnographic period (i.e., the past 150 years), large ceremonies also took advantage of episodic fluxes in plant foods, especially the seeds of grasses, chenopods, sedges, and forbs. Such grains—as well as women's labour to process these seed foods—effectively financed the large ceremonial gatherings that were integral to the 'Dreaming' (Hamilton 1980). In Central Australia, the proliferation of worn and typologically distinctive seed-grinders in archaeological assemblages indicates that one of the key economic activities supporting large gatherings was not dominant in this region before 1500 BP (Smith 1986, 2013; Smith & Ross 2008).

Although a nexus of economic and demographic changes may also have resulted from unrelated changes in territoriality and demographic packing, these developments seem fundamental to ceremonial expansion and changes in land tenure in Central Australia.

Site Histories

The second option concerns an analysis of individual site histories to examine changes in the roles of individual places, especially those that relate to reorganization of a cultural landscape, or those integral to specific 'Dreaming' tracks. In Australian archaeology, this approach has particular resonance because religiously sanctioned relationships between people and places are so important. Of course, much hunter-gatherer archaeology could be described as an investigation of history-in-a-locale. Lewis Binford argued that to understand the organization of past cultural systems, archaeologists need to understand 'the organizational relationships among *places*' (Binford 1982: 5, emphasis in the original).

Archaeological research in arid Australia shows significant shifts in patterns of site use during the last few millennia that imply a reorganization of land use in many regions (David et al. 1994). At the broadest interpretation, increasing population appears to have led to demographic packing and more intensive use of foraging territories (Smith & Ross 2008). This means that much of the cultural landscape associated with the ethnography took shape only during the last few millennia.

This period also saw the initiation, or restructuring, of major rock art complexes (e.g., David et al. 1994; Smith 1988; Ross 2003) towards a pattern in which major art sites are surrounded more frequently by satellite sites. The character of painted rock art at some sites also shifted to include larger, more heraldic, or 'signifying' motifs that supplemented an existing graphic vocabulary of tracks, circles, and track-lines (David et al. 1994; Rosenfeld & Smith 2002).

Another line of evidence concerns the direct age of major ceremonial sites, wherever they form an integral part of a 'Dreaming' track. Although little or no intrinsic data distinguishes such sites from other aggregation sites, the ethnography frequently identifies places that have been sites of large ceremonies associated with specific 'Dreaming' tracks. As Smith (1988) found, the age of intensive activity at these sites is relevant to the antiquity and evolution of particular 'Dreaming' tracks. Where there is data, most evidence for ceremonial expansion in Central Australia falls within the past 600 years, somewhat later than shifts in site use at rock art and habitation sites (e.g., Smith & Ross 2008).

Rock Art

In the ethnographic period, the process of 'painting the land' was restricted to those people with core rights in 'country'. Most, if not all, desert rock paintings and engravings are grounded in totemic mythology associated with the 'Dreaming' (e.g., McDonald & Veth 2011; Mountford 1976; Sutton 1988). It is relevant, therefore, that most radiocarbon dates for rock paintings in the arid regions of Australia fall within the last millennium (McDonald & Veth 2011; McDonald et al. 2014). The potential for taphonomic loss of earlier painted art is obviously a factor here, as the few dates for rock engravings show that some form of an inscribed landscape had already developed by the Mid-Holocene in Central Australia and possibly earlier (Smith, Watchman, & Ross 2009).

The iconography of the 'Dreaming' appears to contain few, if any, motifs that represent hallmarks of the system in general, or graphic correlates for it. If widely used emblems do exist, they are yet to be identified. This uncertainty is accentuated by the fact that most central and Western Desert rock art is drawn from a common graphic vocabulary of abstract motifs, where meanings are highly variable and strongly contingent on place and context. Nevertheless, there are some recurring motifs in rock art in the Western Desert, such as snakes and headdress figures (McDonald & Veth 2011). Of these, only the *Wati Kutjarra* figures are sufficiently distinctive to allow this motif to serve as an unambiguous cultural marker, and only then for a specific 'Dreaming' track (Tindale 1936). The few radiocarbon dates for *Wati Kutjarra* figures also fall within the last millennium (McDonald & Veth 2011).

Rock art—and also many stone arrangements (see below)—are essentially an adjunct to natural features that make this totemic geography visible and that are seen as tangible expressions of the 'Dreaming'. Neither rock art nor stone arrangements are widely regarded by Aboriginal people as humanly made. Rather, they are seen as 'natural' features that validate the 'Dreaming' (Berndt 1974; Layton 1992; Mountford & Edwards 1964). This worldview is exemplified by the Warlpiri term, *kuruwari* (lit. 'significant mark'), which applies to any visible mark left by a totemic ancestor. It does not conceptually distinguish rock art from 'natural' marks on rock surfaces. Even where a specific term for rock paintings is used—such as the Western Desert term, *walka* (lit. 'pattern')—this is often an implied comparison with ceremonial body art associated with totemic ancestors. This means that rock art constitutes a nonsystematic fragment of a symbolic system that mostly uses landforms and other 'natural' elements to mark the landscape. Not surprisingly, attempts to use rock art to follow individual 'Dreaming' tracks or to delineate clan estates have been unsuccessful (Gunn 1997, 2011).

The ethic of ritual stewardship leads to curating or restoring ancestral marks, which people do when they repaint or retouch rock paintings, outline and abrade existing motifs, or when a stone arrangement is cleared of vegetation, rebuilt, or extended. A corollary of this is that, once a place has been marked, rock art is likely to be added to the site over an extended period of time, so that rock art tends to accumulate in certain loci irrespective of the totemic importance of a site. Remarking of places is a practice that seems to be of some antiquity, possibly part of the foundations of this belief system and part of an 'agentive' landscape.

An approach that complements direct dating of rock art—one related to the place-based character of the 'Dreaming'—is to analyse changes in intersite differentiation through time. Rock art motifs appear to become more site-specific during the last few millennia as well as more heraldic (emblematic or signifying) in character. The large striped, emblematic designs at Emily Gap are examples of site-specific totemic designs. These emblematic motifs were described by Spencer and Gillen (1899: 632) and are associated with *utnerrengatye* caterpillar ancestors. This design has no counterpart at other sites, although other striped motifs do occur at six or seven other localities.

Increasing site differentiation through time would be expected if the 'Dreaming' was evolving as a more segmented place-based system with mythologies partitioned between different descent groups. Archaeological analyses suggest a significant increase in differentiation of rock art assemblages between sites over the last millennium (using Euclidian distance and motif frequencies to calculate an index of similarity). There appear to be more site-specific motifs during this period, when comparing recent to earlier painted art assemblages (e.g., David et al. 1994; Ross 2003; Smith 2013). Although archaic rock engravings show that an inscribed landscape of some form had already developed in Central Australia by the Mid-Holocene (Smith et al. 2009), intersite differentiation of early engraved assemblages appears to be only moderate at this time (Edwards 1966, 1971; Franklin 2004).

Current analyses are hampered by the need to use a relative chronology, relying on patination, superposition, or condition, to divide painted or engraved assemblages into recent and earlier art datasets, with <50 direct radiocarbon ages on rock paintings for an arid area of 3 million km^2. The current picture of structural changes between sites, and that of temporal changes in graphic vocabulary and style, are likely to change as absolute dates for rock art in Australia's arid regions become more widely available (McDonald et al. 2014). However, the key evidence lies in the structure and differentiation of rock art, and not simply the emergence of an inscribed landscape.

Stone Arrangements

As with rock art, stone arrangements play only a minor role in the symbolic landscape. Also like rock art, stone arrangements are stewarded, leading to their reconstruction over time. Wherever there is ethnographic information on their role, stone arrangements in arid Australia intimately reflect events within 'Dreaming' narratives. In most cases, their form either represents an actual totemic ancestor or deeds associated with their travels and activities (Mountford 1976), such as the raised heads of agitated snakes, the eggs of mythical beings, yams or tubers, or bough shelters built by ancestral beings. Unlike the fishtraps found in coastal regions (see McNiven & Lambrides, this volume), utilitarian stone arrangements, such as hunting hides (Smith 1982), are relatively uncommon. Some arrangements are associated with the performance of particular ceremonies (with positions for seated participants as well as pathways for dancers). Stone arrangements and rock art can be considered complementary approaches to constructing an inscribed landscape and making a totemic geography visible.

Dates on stone arrangements are rare. The few available radiocarbon and optically stimulated luminescence (OSL) dates all fall within the past 500 years (Hook & Di Lello 2010). No archaic stone arrangements have been identified. Most appear to date to the last few millennia, given their geomorphic contexts. There is, however, some evidence for structural changes in individual stone arrangements over time. Some show signs of having been progressively extended, others have been rebuilt on new alignments (Smith & Ross 2007), and yet others are superimposed on disarticulated parts of earlier structures.

The major forms range from large-scale linear and geometric stone alignments to individual cairns or standing stones, stone emplacements, and clusters of small mounds of stones. Figurative stone arrangements or geoglyphs—such as those found in northern

Australia (e.g., Fitzpatrick, McNiven, Specht, & Ulm 2018; MacKnight & Gray 1970)—are not present in Australia's deserts.

Current data on the ages of stone arrangements show that investigation of the evolution of the inscribed landscape associated with the 'Dreaming' requires a greater investment in basic field archaeology, allied with advanced geochronology, than this region has seen so far. Hook and Di Lello (2010) show the potential for systematic investigation of stone arrangements in arid Australia.

Associated Ritual Practices

Some practices associated with this worldview are almost certainly more ancient than the past few millennia. One aspect of the 'Dreaming' is a high level of interaction with rock surfaces and with landscapes, as a form of ritual practice or performance (Ross & Davidson 2006). These practices range from abrading or rubbing rock art surfaces (often over existing rock engravings or paintings) (Mountford 1968) to flaking the edges of rock outcrops or boulders (even where this does not produce useful flakes); pitting rock surfaces; producing cupules or cup marks; making some hand stencils (where the explicit intent is to introduce oneself to an ancestral being resident in a particular place); and curating rock paintings by repainting, overpainting, or retouching. Several of these practices also occur well before 1500 BP (Smith 2010; Watchman, Taçon, Fullagar, & Head 2000).

Another type of formalized ritual behaviour involves adding rocks or branches to small piles when approaching major totemic sites, or calling out to announce one's approach. These activities are seen as necessary to 'interact' with the ancestral beings. There is little archaeological data on these practices. Most surviving traces are assumed to relate to the latest phase of traditional activity in arid Australia. However, it is not unlikely that some practices predate the 'Dreaming' in its classic (ethnographic) form.

Presence of Red Ochre

Red ochre is ubiquitous in archaeological sites in the arid zone of Australia. However, its presence is not an unequivocal proxy for the frequency of ceremonial activity because, apart from its use as body paint during ceremonies, it is also widely used for other purposes (e.g., as decoration of sacred objects, coating of wooden implements, preservative for dried fruit, covering to protect and cool the skin against severe heat, and as a pigment for painting designs on rock surfaces).

Red ochre is present in small amounts (<5 g) in most of the early (Late Pleistocene) sites in the arid zone (Hamm et al. 2016; McDonald et al. 2018; O'Connor, Veth, & Campbell 1998; Smith, Fankhauser, & Jercher 1998; Thorley 1998). It becomes significantly more abundant in the Late Holocene, when the quantity of red ochre substantially increases in most sites. This finding suggests an expansion of its use in ceremonial activities or in production of rock paintings during the last few millennia.

Sacred Paraphernalia

The only type of artefact, or sacra, that represents an unambiguous material correlate of the 'Dreaming' religious system is the *tjurunga,* comprising wooden boards (>1 m long) or elliptical stone plaques (<0.3 m), with elaborate incised totemic designs, often coated with red ochre (Spencer & Gillen 1899: fig. 242). These highly sacred objects are restricted to initiated men. Because of their secret and restricted status, *tjurunga* cannot be explicitly researched or shown in the public domain. It is not improbable, however, that they will be found eventually in dated, archaeological contexts, given that these objects were invariably cached; that caves were often used as ritual storehouses; and that these artefacts were sometimes buried in the sandy floors of rock shelters. As their role is integral to this system of totemic geography, their presence would create an important temporal benchmark for the 'Dreaming' in its classic form.

Within the ethnographic period, changes in the distribution and form of *tjurunga* suggest that they signal recent changes in the formal structure of the 'Dreaming' (Akerman 1995; Davidson 1953). This change suggests that there is potential for research into the evolution of their morphology and iconography to provide yet another perspective on the history of this belief system.

The Lexicon of the 'Dreaming'

Apart from archaeological approaches, historical linguistics also have a role in assessing the lexicon associated with the 'Dreaming'. The Mid-Holocene expansion of Pama-Nyungan languages across the continent, not only replaced an existing linguistic mosaic, but marked a change in the entire semiotic system (McConvell 1996). It follows that, if any of the lexicon of the 'Dreaming' preserves archaic, non-Pama-Nyungan words, this would provide another chronological benchmark for the belief system. In present understanding, terms such as *oltyerre, tjukurrpa,* and *jukurrpa* are entirely Pama-Nyungan and must date after this period of language change.

DISCUSSION

Current archaeological data on the antiquity of the place-based belief system that we know as the 'Dreaming' suggests that the ethnographic form of codifying relations between people and place took shape during the past 1000–1500 years. However, some elements of this elaborate religious system, such as re-marking specific places, abrading or flaking rock surfaces, or creating cup marks (Ross & Davidson 2006; Smith 2010; Watchman et al. 2000) are probably very ancient and presumably derive from a more generalized 'agentive' landscape tradition.

During the past 1000–1500 years, the evidence points to elaboration of an inscribed landscape and indicates that this change coincided with higher populations, demographic packing, new economic practices, and more intensive patterns of land use (e.g., David et al. 1994; Smith & Ross 2008). This period saw changes in totemic referents and in the structure of rock art in arid Australia (McDonald et al. 2014; McDonald & Veth 2011; Rosenfeld & Smith 2002) similar to the pattern that David et al. (1994) found in Wardaman territory on the northern margins of the region. During this period, the arid regions of Australia possibly also saw a degree of ceremonial expansion—a pattern seen in the archaeology of major ceremonial sites and possibly also in the evidence of increased use of red ochre. Although far from definitive, the congruence of these changes indicates that much of the cultural landscape associated with the ethnographic form of the 'Dreaming' only took shape during the past few millennia.

This emerging picture is complicated by the fact that the 'Dreaming' almost certainly changed over time and may have been quite different prior to developing its classic ethnographic form. This dynamism raises questions about what forms the precursors of the 'Dreaming' may have taken prior to 1500 BP and how this belief system morphed into its present form.

At present, research on the archaeology of the 'Dreaming' or its antecedents has been hampered by a relative lack of targeted investigation of this belief system, except for David's pioneering work (2002). To advance study of the 'Dreaming', we need to identify specific cultural markers in art and track structural changes in the rock art of different periods—with explicit investigation of place-based differentiation in art assemblages. To facilitate investigation of the history of this belief system, we also need a secure chronology for desert rock art (both pigment art and rock engravings), stone arrangements, and sites integrally associated with individual 'Dreaming' narratives.

Data are too thin at present to allow reconstruction of the precursors of this system, but a three-phased sequence of developments can be hypothesized.

1. A generalized, 'agentive' approach to land and spirituality with a range of associated ritual practices, mostly involving interaction with rock surfaces in various ways (flaking, abrading, production of cup marks), seems to be an early trait. However, as these practices also form part of the 'Dreaming' in its classic form, even a relative chronology is uncertain. Presumably, this phase was associated with early development of a corpus of mythology, but not necessarily the place-based system of more recent times.

2. An *inscribed landscape*, subsequently developed in Central Australia, or perhaps developed concurrently with (1). Whatever the case, the cultural landscape at this time seems to have lacked a place-based character as intersite variability in rock art was only moderate (Edwards 1966, 1971; Franklin 2004). It is possible that this phase also saw the evolution of short regional mythological tracks. In

Central Australia, some form of inscribed landscape had developed by the Mid-Holocene but was probably in place somewhat earlier in northern Australia (Jones et al. 2017).

3. A highly *territorialized landscape* where larger populations put more stress on rights in land and the prevailing ideology—whatever it may have been—was co-opted to underpin land tenure. Such a change would lead to a more elaborate place-based system. This phase may also be associated with ceremonial expansion and development of longer song cycles. If so, the longer 'Dreaming' tracks probably developed as some regional mythologies were merged.

CONCLUSION

Much of the cultural landscape associated with the ethnographic form of the 'Dreaming' only took shape during the past two millennia. This development coincides with other archaeological evidence that suggests a Late Holocene antiquity for this system of codifying relationships between people and land. Collectively, these data suggest that the classic form of the 'Dreaming' dates within the past 1000–1500 years, although some elements of this elaborate religious system are probably very ancient and may derive from a more generalized belief system associated with an 'agentive' landscape.

None of these data supports the proposition that the 'Dreaming' in its classic form is a relic of an elementary form of religious life, or that it extends back unchanged for 50 millennia. This belief system undoubtedly has a long history of development and elaboration. At present, we cannot determine what the precursors of the 'Dreaming' looked like or how the present form of this land-based belief system developed. We can speculate, however, that the ethnographic form of the 'Dreaming' developed out of earlier religious systems that involved some form of inscribed landscape and an 'agentive' belief system. It is possible that this early belief system was co-opted to support an elaborate system of land tenure as land use intensified during the Late Holocene. At this time, growing populations would have sharpened the need to make land tenure inalienable by anchoring it to the religious system.

More detail could be added to the emerging picture with better data on the intersite differentiation of rock art assemblages over time, as well as identification of motifs in rock art that provide iconographic markers for the 'Dreaming'. Direct dating of rock paintings and rock engravings is the key to understanding structural changes in inscribed landscapes over time. We also need basic data on the field archaeology of stone arrangements (especially archaic structures), constrained by estimates of their ages. Radiocarbon dates for the initiation of large ceremonial gatherings at sites on specific 'Dreaming' tracks would provide some data on development of the network of 'songlines'. Better definition of the lexicon of the 'Dreaming' and its relative position in a sequence of linguistic shifts in arid Australia is also fundamental to reconstructing the history of this religious system.

Acknowledgements

I thank Ian McNiven, Duncan Wright, and Peter Veth for helpful comments on an earlier draft of this manuscript. Sadly, Mike passed away before publication of his chapter (Eds.).

References

Akerman, K. (1995). Tradition and change in aspects of contemporary Australian Aboriginal religious objects. In C. Anderson (Ed.), *Politics of the sacred* (pp. 43–50). Oceania Monograph 45. Sydney: Oceania Publications.

Berndt, R. M. (1974). *Australian Aboriginal religion.* Iconography of Religions Series. Leiden: E. J. Brill.

Binford, L. R. (1982). The archaeology of place. *Journal of Anthropological Archaeology*, *1*(1), 5–31.

David, B. (2002). *Landscapes, rock-art and the Dreaming.* London: Leicester University Press.

David, B., & McNiven, I. J. (2004). Western Torres Strait Cultural History Project. *Memoirs of the Queensland Museum, Cultural Heritage Series*, *3*(1), 199–208.

David, B., McNiven, I., Attenbrow, V., Flood, J., & Collins, J. (1994). Of Lightning Brothers and white cockatoos: Dating the antiquity of signifying systems in the Northern Territory, Australia. *Antiquity*, *68*(259), 241–251.

Davidson, D. S. (1953). The possible source and antiquity of the slate churingas of Western Australia. *Proceedings of the American Philosophical Society*, *97*, 194–213.

Durkheim, E. (1915). *The elementary forms of the religious life.* London: Allen & Unwin.

Edwards, R. (1971). Art and Aboriginal prehistory. In D. J. Mulvaney & J. Golson (Eds.), *Aboriginal man and environment in Australia* (pp. 356–367). Canberra: Australian National University Press.

Edwards, R. (1966). Comparative study of rock engravings in south and central Australia. *Transactions of the Royal Society of South Australia*, *90*, 33–38.

Fitzpatrick, A., McNiven, I. J., Specht, J., & Ulm, S. (2018). Stylistic analysis of stone arrangements supports regional cultural interactions along the northern Great Barrier Reef, Queensland. *Australian Archaeology*, *84*(2), 129–144.

Franklin, N. R. (2004). *Explorations of variability in Australian prehistoric rock engravings.* BAR International Series No. 1318. Oxford: British Archaeological Reports.

Gillen, F. J. (1897). Letter to Baldwin Spencer, 18 June 1897. In J. Mulvaney, H. Morphy, & A. Petch (Eds.), *My dear Spencer* (p. 16). Melbourne: Hyland House.

Goddard, C., & Wierzbicka, A. (2015). What does *Jukurrpa* ('Dreamtime', 'the Dreaming') mean? A semantic and conceptual journey of discovery. *Australian Aboriginal Studies 2015 / 1*, 43–65.

Gould, R. A. (1980). *Living archaeology.* New York: Cambridge University Press.

Gunn, R. G. (1997). Rock art, occupation and myth: The correspondence of symbolic and archaeological sites within Arrernte rock art complexes of Central Australia. *Rock Art Research*, *14*, 124–136.

Gunn, R. G. (2011). Eastern Arrernte rock art and land tenure. *Rock Art Research*, *28*, 225–239.

Hamilton, A. (1980). Dual social systems: Technology, labour and women's secret rites in the eastern Western Desert of Australia. *Oceania*, *51*(1), 4–19.

Hamm, G., Mitchell, P., Arnold, L. J., Prideaux, G. J., Questiaux, D., Spooner, N. A. . . . Johnston, D. (2016). Cultural innovation and megafauna interaction in the early settlement of arid Australia. *Nature*, *539*(7628), 280–283.

Harvey, G. (2006). *Animism: Respecting the living world*. New York: Columbia University Press.

Hayden, B. (1979). *Palaeolithic reflections: Lithic technology and ethnographic excavation among Australian Aborigines*. Canberra: Australian Institute of Aboriginal Studies.

Hook, F., & Di Lello, A. (2010). Gurdadaguji stone arrangements: Late Holocene aggregation locals. In D. Calado, M. Baldia, & M. Boulanger (Eds.), *Monumental questions: Prehistoric megaliths, mounds, and enclosures* (pp. 285–297). British Archaeological Reports International Series S2123. Oxford: Archaeopress.

Jones, T., Levchenko, V. A., King, P. L., Troitzsch, U., Wesley, D., Williams, A. A., & Nayingull, A. (2017). Radiocarbon age constraints for a Pleistocene–Holocene transition rock art style: The northern running figures of the East Alligator River region, western Arnhem Land, Australia. *Journal of Archaeological Science: Reports 11*, 80–89.

Kearney, A., Bradley, J., & Brady, L. M. (2019). Kincentric ecology, species maintenance and the relational power of place in Northern Australia. *Oceania 89* (3), 316–335.

Kelly, R. L. (2013). *The lifeways of hunter-gatherers: The foraging spectrum*. New York: Cambridge University Press.

Kimber, R. G., & Smith, M. A. (1987). An Aranda ceremony. In D. J. Mulvaney & J. P. White (Eds.), *Australians to 1788* (pp. 220–237). Sydney: Fairfax, Syme and Weldon.

Layton, R. (1992). *Australian rock art: A new synthesis*. Cambridge: Cambridge University Press.

Lee, R. B., & DeVore, I. (Eds.). (1968). *Man the hunter*. Chicago: Aldine.

Macknight, C. C., & Gray, W. J. (1970). *Aboriginal stone pictures in Eastern Arnhem Land*. Canberra: Australian Institute of Aboriginal Studies.

McBryde, I. (2011). Travellers in storied landscapes: A case study in exchanges and heritage. *Aboriginal History Journal*, *24*, 152–174.

McConvell, P. (1996). Backtracking to babel: The chronology of Pama-Nyungan expansion in Australia. *Archaeology in Oceania*, *31*(3), 125–144.

McDonald, J., Reynen, W., Petchey, F., Ditchfield, K., Byrne, C., Vannieuwenhuyse, D. . . . Veth, P. (2018). Karnatukul (Serpent's Glen): A new chronology for the oldest site in Australia's Western Desert. *PLOS ONE*, *13*(9): e0202511.

McDonald, J., Steelman, K. L., Veth, P., Mackey, J., Loewen, J., Thurber, C. R., & Guilderson, T. P. (2014). Results from the first intensive dating program for pigment art in the Australian arid zone: Insights into recent social complexity. *Journal of Archaeological Science*, *46*, 195–204.

McDonald, J., & Veth, P. (2011). Western Desert iconography: Rock art mythological narratives and graphic vocabularies. *Diogenes*, *58*(3), 7–21.

Mountford, C. P. (1968). *Winbaraku and the myth of Jarapiri*. Adelaide: Rigby.

Mountford, C. P. (1976). *Nomads of the Australian desert*. Adelaide: Rigby.

Mountford, C. P., & Edwards, R. (1964). Rock engravings in the Red Gorge, Deception Creek, northern South Australia. *Anthropos*, *59*, 849–850.

Myers, F. R. (1986). *Pintupi country, Pintupi self*. Canberra: Australian Institute of Aboriginal Studies.

Myers, F. R. (1993). Place, identity, and exchange in a totemic system: Nurturance and the process of social reproduction in Pintupi Society. In J. Fajans (Ed.), *Exchanging products: Producing exchange* (pp. 33–57). Oceania Monographs. Sydney: University of Sydney.

Neale, M. (Ed.), (2017). *Songlines: Tracking the Seven Sisters*. Canberra: National Museum of Australia Press.

O'Connor, S., Veth, P., & Campbell, C. (1998). Serpent's Glen rockshelter: Report of the first Pleistocene-aged occupation sequence from the Western Desert. *Australian Archaeology, 46*(1), 12–22.

Palacio-Pérez, E. (2010). Salomon Reinach and the religious interpretation of Palaeolithic art. *Antiquity, 84*(325), 853–863.

Price, T. D., & Brown, J. A. (1985). *Prehistoric hunter-gatherers: The emergence of cultural complexity*. New York: Academic Press.

Reinach, S. (1903). L'art et la Magie. A Propos des Peintures et des Gravures de l'age du Renne. *L'Anthropologie, 14*, 257–266.

Reinach, S. (1913). *Repertoire de l'art Quaternaire*. Paris: Tours.

Rosenfeld, A., & Smith, M. A. (2002). Rock-art and the history of Puritjarra rock shelter, Cleland Hills, Central Australia. *Proceedings of the Prehistoric Society, 68*, 103–124.

Ross, J. (2003). *Rock art, ritual and relationships: An archaeological analysis of rock art from the Central Australian arid zone* (PhD thesis). University of New England, Armidale.

Ross, J., & Davidson, I. (2006). Rock art and ritual: An archaeological analysis of rock art in arid Central Australia. *Journal of Archaeological Method and Theory, 13*(4), 304–340.

Schrire, C. (Ed.). (1984). *Past and present in hunter gatherer studies*. London: Academic Press.

Smith, M. A. (1982). Stone hunting hides in the Olary region, S. A. *The Artefact, 7*, 19–27.

Smith, M. A. (1986). The antiquity of seedgrinding in arid Australia. *Archaeology in Oceania, 21*(1), 29–39.

Smith, M. A. (1988). *The pattern and timing of prehistoric settlement in Central Australia* (PhD thesis). University of New England, Armidale.

Smith, M. A. (2010). Hearths, ash lenses and pits. In M. A. Smith (Ed.), *Puritjarra rock shelter: Final report on excavations 1986–1990*. CD. Technical Report 1. Canberra: National Museum of Australia Press.

Smith, M. (2013). *The archaeology of Australia's deserts*. New York: Cambridge University Press.

Smith, M. (2014). Ngintaka's grindstones: An archaeological reading of a Pitjantjatjara-Yankunytjatjara Tjukurpa narrative. In D. James & L. Treganza (Eds.), *Ngintaka* (pp. 148–157). Adelaide: Wakefield Press.

Smith, M. A. (2018). The historiography of Kardimarkara: Reading a desert tradition as cultural memory of the remote past. *Journal of Social Archaeology, 19*(1), 47–66.

Smith, M. A., Fankhauser, B., & Jercher, M. (1998). The changing provenance of red ochre at Puritjarra rock shelter, Central Australia: Late Pleistocene to present. *Proceedings of the Prehistoric Society, 64*, 275–292.

Smith, M. A., & Ross, J. (2007). A re-investigation of the archaeology of Geosurveys Hill, northern Simpson Desert. *Australian Archaeology, 64*(1), 50–52.

Smith, M. A., & Ross, J. (2008). What happened at 1500–1000 BP in Central Australia? Timing, impact and archaeological signatures. *The Holocene, 18*(3), 379–388.

Smith, M. A., Watchman, A., & Ross, J. (2009). Direct dating indicates a Mid-Holocene age for archaic desert rock engravings in arid Central Australia. *Geoarchaeology, 24*(2), 191–203.

Sollas, W. J. (1911). *Ancient hunters and their modern representatives*. London: Macmillan.

Spencer, W. B. (Ed.). (1896). *Report on the work of the Horn Scientific Expedition to Central Australia*. Melbourne: Melville, Mullen and Slade.

Spencer, W. B., & Gillen, F. J. (1927). *The Arunta: A study of a Stone Age people*. London: Macmillan.

Spencer, W. B., & Gillen, F. J. (1899). *The native tribes of central Australia*. London: Macmillan.

Stanner, W. E. H. (2010). The Dreaming. In W. E. H. Stanner, *The Dreaming and other essays*, compiled by R. Manne. Melbourne: Black.

Strehlow, T. G. H. (1970). Geography and the totemic landscape in Central Australia: A functional study. In R. M. Berndt (Ed.), *Australian Aboriginal anthropology* (pp. 92–140). Nedlands: University of Western Australia Press.

Strehlow, T. G. H. (1971). *Songs of Central Australia*. Sydney: Angus & Robertson.

Sutton, P. (Ed.) (1988). *Dreamings: The art of Aboriginal Australia*. Melbourne: Viking.

Taçon, P. S. C., Wilson, M., & Chippindale, C. (1996). Birth of the rainbow serpent in Arnhem Land rock art and oral history. *Archaeology in Oceania, 31*(3), 103–124.

Thorley, P. B. (1998). Pleistocene settlement in the Australian arid zone: Occupation of an inland riverine landscape in the Central Australian ranges. *Antiquity, 72*(275), 34–45.

Tindale, N. B. (1936). Legend of the Wati Kutjara, Warburton range, Western Australia. *Oceania, 7*(2), 169–185.

Tindale, N. B. (1974). *Aboriginal tribes of Australia*. Berkeley: University of California Press.

Tonkinson, R. (1974). *The Jigalong mob: Aboriginal victors of the desert crusade*. Menlo Park, CA: Cummings Publishing Co.

Tonkinson, R. (1978). *The Mardudjara Aborigines. Living the dream in Australia's desert*. New York: Harcourt School.

Tylor, E. B. (1871). *Primitive culture*. London: John Murray.

Watchman, A., Taçon, P., Fullagar, R., & Head, L. (2000). Minimum ages for pecked rock markings from Jinmium, North Western Australia. *Archaeology in Oceania, 35*(1), 1–10.

White, J. P., & Mulvaney, D. J. (1987). How many people? In D. J. Mulvaney & J. P. White (Eds.), *Australians to 1788* (pp. 115–117). Sydney: Fairfax Syme and Weldon.

Williams, A. N., Veth, P., Steffen, W., Ulm, S., Turney, C. S. M., Reeves, J. M. . . . Smith, M. (2015). A continental narrative: Human settlement patterns and Australian climate change over the last 35,000 years. *Quaternary Science Reviews, 123*, 91–112.

CHAPTER 36

ROCK ART MODIFICATION AND ITS RITUALIZED AND RELATIONAL CONTEXTS

LIAM M. BRADY, ROBERT G. GUNN,
AND JOAKIM GOLDHAHN

INTRODUCTION

AUSTRALIA is home to some of the most complex and extensive examples of modified rock art in the world, including superimposed, re-marked, re-touched, re-painted, and re-engraved motifs. For well over a century, Western-trained academics have used modified rock art to develop style-based chronologies, and to explore continuity and change in the lives of those who created and engaged with such rock art (e.g., Chaloupka 1993; Gunn 2018; Harper 2017; Haskovec 1992; Lommel 1952/1997; McCarthy 1974; Morwood, Walsh, & Watchman 2010; Mountford 1968; Motta 2019; Spencer & Gillen 1899; Walsh 1994; Ward 1992; Watchman 1992). Importantly, in Australia, a growing number of Indigenous explanations and perspectives concerning rock art modification have also played a key role in communicating to academic audiences and the general public the contemporary social and cultural significance of rock art (e.g., Blundell & Woolagoodja 2005; Mowaljarlai, Vinnicombe, Ward, & Chippindale 1988; Mangolamara, Karadada, Oobagooma, Woolagoodja, & Karadada 2018). Drawing on this extensive body of literature and our own research, this chapter aims to add another layer of understanding to how we might perceive the production and presence of modified rock art, both as ritualized acts and social practices operating within complex Indigenous networks of relationships and relatedness.

It is generally accepted in archaeological and anthropological discourse that the production and engagement with rock art is a ritual act—a type of repeated, communicative performance or social action that can be used to understand and interpret aspects of culturally ordered social life at various points in time and in a range of contexts (e.g., Goldhahn & Ling 2013; Hays-Gilpin 2004; Ross & Davidson 2006; Whitley 2011). Our aim here is to broaden such understandings to show how the placement, social actions, rules, and structures linked to the modification process are part of a complex relational network that extends across multiple social and cultural realms. In doing so, we continue to build on efforts to highlight how rock art can be viewed as 'images of relatedness' (Brady & Bradley 2014), where individual or groups of motifs and sites exist within a network of Indigenous social and cultural relationships in the past and present. To illustrate our point, we use a series of archaeological and ethnographic examples involving modified rock art from across the Australian continent to identify key themes and contexts where the act of modification of preexisting motifs is undertaken in ritual performance.

Defining Ritual

Rituals form a key part of the social and cultural lives of people across the globe. There are many definitions, explanations, and considerations of "ritual" in anthropological and archaeological literature (e.g., Bell 1992; David 2002; Elkin 1964; Geertz 1973; Goldhahn 2016; Hicks 2010; Morphy 1994; McNiven 2013, 2016; Rappaport 1999; Renfrew 1994; Swenson 2015), but consensus about how best to define ritual has yet to be reached. In this chapter, our core definition of ritual is the performance of a range of repeated, normative behaviours or social actions carried out at specific times or places by individuals or groups. These performances or social actions are usually defined as symbolic and meaningful; they are thought to communicate messages, ideas, and values; and they typically follow some form of set orders or procedures that show that these actions are enmeshed in a nexus of relatedness. The form and duration of these normative behaviours or social actions can be varied and repeated, for example, over a day, a year, or thousands of years. Our approach to the question of whether rock art is ritual in nature relies on rock art meeting our ritual-focused criteria. If, as we described above, a ritual action implies the performance of a range of repeated, normative behaviours or social actions, then where rock art can be clearly embedded in this framework it is by definition ritualistic.

In presenting our definition and description of ritual, we recognize that identifying the meanings or meaningfulness of similar repeated, normative behaviours or social actions performed at specific times or places can be interpreted differently according to their social and cultural contexts. For example, in some countries, hunting is a leisure or recreational activity guided by government regulations concerning set times for hunting throughout the year, limits on animals hunted, and so on, whereas in Indigenous contexts, hunting can be an intimate affair that is grounded in the context of reconnecting with supernatural spiritual or ancestral beings (Brightman 1993; Rose 1992; Villerslev 2007; Viveiros de Castro 2012; see also McNiven, this volume).

Distinguishing ritual from nonritual contexts and actions using an etic analysis that is defined by an ontology founded on naturalism could be construed as ethnocentric. Overcoming ethnocentrism is a key reason why many scholars (including ourselves) now embrace interpretative frameworks acknowledging a broad continuum of ritualized practices from the mundane to profane (i.e., Bell 1992; see Berggen & Nilsson Stutz 2010; Bradley 2005), with a focus on the performative, symbolic, communicative, intentional, relational, repetitive, and agentic aspects of social practices. In the following discussion, we do not focus on whether rock art modifications should be considered "secular" or of a 'magico-religious' nature, but rather on how emic and etic perspectives can broaden understandings of modified rock art.

Ritual and Rock Art

Ritual-based explanations for the production of some (but not all) rock art have been proposed by researchers around the globe for several decades. In most instances, these explanations have relied on the perceived relationship between religious or belief-based rituals and rock art. For example, the neuropsychological model posited that shamans undertaking rituals involving altered states of consciousness illustrated their visions on rock walls (e.g., Clottes & Lewis-Williams 1996; Lewis-Williams & Dowson 1988; Lewis-Williams 1981; Whitley 2000). In Europe, Palaeolithic rock art was previously linked to 'sympathetic hunting magic' by drawing on ethnographic recordings of the ritual creation of rock art in central Australia (e.g., Bégouen 1929; Breuil 1952; Reinach 1903). In analysing these attempts to explain rock art in ritual contexts, Ross and Davidson (2006: 306) point out that

> the quite reasonable inference in many of these studies is that rock art *results from* ritual activity but it may well be that not all art recorded at such locations was produced for ritual purposes or during ritual performance. The ability to separate parts of rock art assemblages that formed an *integral part of ritual performance* from those created in different social contexts, would provide a clearer understanding of the role of rock art in ritual practices.

Ethnography has played a critical role in identifying magico-religious rituals involving rock art. Whitley's (2011) global review of rock art, ritual, and religion provides several examples of rock art's link to magico-religious ritual contexts. Informed by ethnography primarily from the United States and Australia, the direct-historical approach[1], and ethnographic analogy, examples of magico-religious rituals involving rock art abound and include:

- Vision quests by ritual specialists such as shamans (e.g., Lewis-Williams 1981; Whitley 2000);
- Puberty and initiation rites (e.g., Hays-Gilpin 2004; Keyser & Whitley 2006);

- Rites associated with 'power manipulation', such as healing, renewal, fertility, increase, maintenance, sorcery, and rain-making (e.g., Cole 2010: 24; Rose 1942); and
- The modification of existing motifs as part of ceremonies and rituals (e.g., Blundell & Woolagoodja 2012; Spencer & Gillen 1899, 1927).

Ross and Davidson (2006) present the most explicit attempt to link rituals to rock art in archaeological contexts through their Ritual Form Model (RFM), a methodology designed to assess 'the potential for identifying ritual structure in rock art assemblages' (2006: 305). The RFM uses an archaeological lens to identify contexts where rock art can be linked to ritual activity and production. It draws heavily on Rappaport's (1999) seven key structural features of ritual (Ross & Davidson 2006: 312; see also Renfrew 1994) and focuses on identifying key ritual attributes:

- Invariance,
- Repetition,
- Specialized time,
- Specialized place,
- Stylized behaviour/stylized form,
- Performance and participation, and
- Form, which can hold and transfer a canonical message.

An attractive feature of the RFM criteria is that they do not focus solely on a motif in isolation, but also take in its relationships to place, cultural practices, and changes through time. By analysing rock art through these criteria, Ross and Davidson argue that ritual structures or ritual contexts can be identified archaeologically (see below).

Other approaches to describing ritual and rock art draw attention to the practice and implications of re-marking. Morphy (2012: 297) describes the ritual action associated with Australian rock art as iterative, or the "repetitive element of art practice in which variations of a particular design or schema are replicated over time or existing images are redefined or repainted". He also notes that the repeated actions involving re-marking rock art also serve as a means for artists to learn more about the style(s) or design conventions used to make rock art, and the meaning and relationships of motifs to Ancestral Beings (also referred to as Dreamings[2] or other aspects of life) (Morphy 2012: 297).

Elsewhere in Australia, McNiven and Russell's (2002) description of place-marking rituals undertaken by Aboriginal peoples on the colonial frontier is an example of ritualized practices involving rock art. They note that place-marking has been a key feature of resistance activities between Aboriginal people and Europeans, typically undertaken on the "far side" of the frontier, away from Europeans, and designed to 'affect the nature of frontier encounters and control of lands' (2002: 28; see Chaloupka 1993; David & Wilson 2002; Mulvaney 1992). Thus, the repeated and performative elements of place-marking at a specific time and place and as part of a defined cultural context—the colonial frontier—means that rock art in this context can also be considered a ritualized practice.

Superimpositioning, the layering of one motif over another, such that the overlying image interacts with the preexisting image (Gunn et al. 2022), and other techniques of modifying existing rock art also possess the core criteria of ritual action given their performative and repetitive elements. Modifications of distinguishable rock art is recorded across Australia, and in some regions, such as western Arnhem Land in the Northern Territory, and the Kimberley region in Western Australia, they can often feature quite dense layering of motifs (Figures 36.1 and 36.2). Superimpositions are most often used by archaeologists to develop style-based chronological sequences and, as we argue below, superimposition can, in many cases, act as markers of ritualized practices through their intentional placement and repetitive nature. The act of modifying existing motifs through superimpositioning is not an event or activity that occurs by happenstance but by its very nature is an intentional performance.

Unravelling visual layers using formal methods represents a key step to further understanding their ritualistic dimensions and relational contexts of production (see below for examples). While such analyses have been identified as a key element in rock art studies for some time, what is comparatively less well known are the relational networks within which such ritualized practices are embedded[3]. Given that repeated modification fits the definition of a ritual action, what are the contexts of these performative acts, and their relational contexts and networks? To answer these questions, we explore rock art modification using archaeologically and ethnographically informed examples.

FIGURE 36.1. Complex panel of superposed and superimposed rock art from Jawoyn Country, northern Australia.

(Courtesy of the late M. Katherine; photograph by R. G. Gunn).

FIGURE 36.2. Photo-tracing of a superposed panel from Jawoyn Country (northern Australia) showing the layering of motifs.

(By R. G. Gunn).

Rock Art Modification—Formal Perspectives

Katharine Sale (1995: 128; cf. Lewis-Williams 1974) provides one of the first detailed discussions devoted specifically to rock art modification. She notes that the terms archaeologists, ethnographers, and Indigenous communities use to describe modification techniques, such as re-done, freshening, re-paint, renovate, renew, and retouch, are highly variable with different nuances depending on the perceptions and emphases of each researcher. Our definition of rock art modification largely follow Sale's terminology (cf. Gunn 2019; Motta 2019).

Understanding the modification process using a formal perspective begins with identifying superpositioning in the rock art record (e.g., Chippindale & Taçon 1993; Gunn, 2018; Haskovec 1992; McCarthy 1974; Motta 2019). A stratified sequence formed by the layering of motifs signals a relative time sequence from the creation of one rock art motif to another (i.e., the underlying motif (or motif part) was created before the overlying one; Figure 36.2). The time difference between these events can vary from a few moments (e.g., Goldhahn, May, Maralngurra, & Lee 2020) to many thousands of years. At any point in time, an existing motifs can be *re-marked*. Re-marking is an encompassing term that can involve multiple techniques such as re-painting, re-pecking, and re-drawing, and it indicates a clear awareness of the earlier motif. It can be a partial or a complete rendering that by definition must use the same technique and follow closely the outline and form of the original motif, although it is not limited to the use of the same colours. Whereas Sale uses the term *re-marking* in a broad sense to cover a range of re-marking processes, we add further types of re-marking:

Re-touching: the embellishment of an existing motif. Examples include adding an outline and body features (e.g., eyes, claws) or ornamentation (e.g., body designs) or changing the colour of existing features such as eyes.

Alteration: additions that alter the pose or status of a motif, such as the incorporation of weapons or accoutrements. Modification of this type changes the nature of the motif, and possibly its meaning.

Amendment: involves detecting/identifying 'an earlier rendition of an image that differs from the realisation of the final image . . . amendment is present when the final version of a painting is seen to differ from its underlying preparatory outline' (Gunn 2019: 90).

Erasure: where an existing motif has been erased with a uniform wash and then a new motif painted on the washed area.

Retouch by scarring: where an existing motif is scarred to the extent that it can be poorly visible or entirely obliterated, such as later pecking over parts of an earlier motif. This process can involve abrading, direct pounding, or gashing/gouging. In some instances, this can be related to maintenance or increase rituals (e.g., Mulvaney 2009).

While descriptions and definitions of specific methods of modification are important, the key point that emerges is that each modification event is a ritualized practice in itself. By modifying an existing motif, an artist is consciously and intentionally peforming a social action (re-painting, re-pecking, etc.) at a specific place, following a specific procedure (the act of modification) and is being used to communicate some form of message or idea.

ARCHAEOLOGICAL APPROACHES TO RITUAL ROCK ART RELATIONSHIPS

To demonstrate the utility of the RFM, Ross and Davidson (2006) applied Rappaport's (1999) seven criteria for ritualism to a dataset of over 20,000 motifs from 285 rock shelter and open sites from sandridge deserts and gorge complexes in the arid zone of central Australia. In the context of rock art modification, the criterion 'specialised places' was met as extensively layered motifs was fixed in a specific and specialized location of repeated visitation. Ross and Davidson note that 'engravings on some [rock] faces in the region are so dense that it is now impossible to identify individual images suggesting that marking of this panel was either undertaken by large numbers of people or frequently carried out' (2006: 322). The 'performance and participation' criterion was similarly met with superimpositions in the form of '[r]emarking, repainting, outlining and abrading of existing motifs' providing 'the strongest archaeological evidence for participation by people, other than the original artist, in the production of art' (Ross & Davidson 2006: 324).

Other researchers have employed Ross and Davidson's RFM model. For example, Jones and May (2015) focused on a specific motif type—Northern Running Figures (NRF) of western Arnhem Land—to determine whether ritual performance was implicated in the making of rock art. Similar to Ross and Davidson, they used instances of modified rock art, in this case, the intentional placement of paintings of NRF motifs over older motifs, to determine whether NRF met the criteria of Repetition, Specialized Place, and Performance. Their focus on a specific style led them to also meet the Stylized Behaviour/Stylized Form criterion, concluding that 'ritual social function on NRF art is signalled in many ways' (2015: 65).

Quantifying Ritualized Modification Events through Time

The frequency and structure of ritualized modification events can be identified by quantifying the number of motif layers or by dating individual pigment layers on a motif or panel. Such formal methods enable the recognition of multiple acts of motif-making and modification, which we suggest represents a persistent ritualized practice.

At Undiara (Intyeyerre) waterhole, an important ritual site in Arrernte Country[4] in central Australia, a large (545 cm x 205 cm) red and white striped painting is ethnographically known to be associated with the Kangaroo *intichiuma* increase re-painting ritual (Spencer & Gillen 1899, 1927). During visits to the site in the 1990s, one of us (RGG) recorded that the white paint used in the re-painting was 'up to 4 cm thick and produced a three-dimensional relief that cut across the undulations of the vertical rock wall' (Gunn 2000: 117). In the Kimberley region of northwestern Australia, where re-marking events have been extensively documented, Morwood et al. (2010: 6) identified a 'Wandjina-style snake depiction' consisting of thirty-eight superimposed layers, with the lowest and earliest layer dated to 375±35 BP (see also, e.g., Clarke 1976). At Nawarla Gabarnmang in Jawoyn Country on the Arnhem Land plateau, Harris matrices were used to provide a graphic representation of forty-nine superposed layers of painted motifs on one of the site's forty-two art panels (Gunn 2018) (Figures 36.1 and 36.2).

In these examples, the quantification and antiquity of the layered motifs within panels and sites also share attributes of the RFM, namely, Repetition, Specialized Place, and

Performance and Participation, strongly suggesting ritualized practices in connection to modified rock art. Moreover, Morwood et al.'s (2010) documentation of thirty-eight layers of re-painting revealed not only a relatively short time span for the re-marking events on a single motif, but also a good example of Morphy's (2012) iterative, ritual action where replication signalled both continuity and ideology, and the reproduction of knowledge (learning).

Rock Art, Ancestral Beings, and the Spiritual Realm

In many areas of Australia, Ancestral Beings 'placed themselves'[5] onto rock—manifested and materialized as rock art—after completing their epic creative journeys across the landscape. In doing so, the motifs act as reminders to individuals and communities of the existential needs and ritual obligations of life, including obligations to care for these motifs over time (e.g., Arndt 1962; Blundell & Woolagoodja 2005, 2012; Crawford 1968; David 2002; Gunn 1992; Merlan 1989). In an Indigenous Australian context, to physically engage with these rock art materializations typically equates to engaging with associated spiritual powers. The results of this engagement could be both positive and negative. For example, touching rock art could potentially be harmful for uninitiated people who did not follow proper cultural protocols (Chaloupka 1993; Layton 1992), while in other cases, re-marking could have positive outcomes if such protocols were followed (see below). By repeatedly engaging with rock art linked to Ancestral Beings through re-marking, the associated ritual can be viewed as part-celebration, part-commemoration, and part-social obligation.

One of the best-known re-marking events involving Ancestral Beings in Australia concerns the Wanjina of the Kimberley, in the continent's northwest. Here researchers have been documenting Wanjina re-painting events[6] since the 1930s (e.g., Crawford 1968; Elkin 1930, 1948; Lommel 1952/1997; Love 1930; O'Connor, Barham, & Woolagoodja 2008). Upon finishing their creative journeys across the Kimberley landscape, the Wanjina returned to the spirit world by entering the walls of rock shelters and in doing so left their imprints as paintings (Blundell & Woolagoodja 2005, 2012; Crawford 1968; see also Munn 1970). Wanjinas also gave birth to the clans with which people affiliate and relate to each other, and through which obligations and responsibilities were handed down (Utemara & Vinnicombe 1992; Mangolamara et al. 2018). The large, bichrome and polychrome Wanjina motifs have, over many years, been re-painted by the Ngarinyin, Worora, Wunambal and Gaambera clan members on whose land they appear. As sentient Ancestral Beings, the re-painting events keep the Wanjina 'fresh' so that they 'ensure the arrival of the annual rains and instruct their human descendants in their dreams' (Blundell & Woolagoodja 2012: 474).

In central Australia, where motifs of Ancestral Beings are depicted in more or less abstract forms, the situation is similar to the Kimberley region: the paintings are large, bichrome designs in highly visible positions within rock shelters. Many are embedded in *intichiuma* ceremonies designed to reproduce and increase animal populations or other specific features of the environment (e.g., rain, fire, plants). In the late nineteenth century, anthropologists Baldwin Spencer and Frank Gillen (1899, 1927) documented several *intichiuma* ceremonies involving ritual re-painting. The elements common to these ceremonies were as follows:

- The site is usually well known to all members of a community but may be visited only by select individuals and/or only during times of ceremony.
- The site is one of several associated/linked sites dotted across the landscape, and the associated ceremony must not only be attended by the site's owner but also overseen by the site's managers who come from an opposite moiety. Owner and manager groups are defined by kin-based moieties, with the managers assuring that the performance of the owners is undertaken correctly (see the discussion of the role of *junggayi* and *gidjan* below).
- The involvement of a small number of senior men (owners and managers) with appropriate totemic affiliations with the site's associated Ancestral Being.
- A ritualized path approach to the site.
- A number of activities involving tactile handling of ritual objects accompanied by chanting.
- The act of modifying (re-marking, altering, or superimposing) the painted motifs by one or more senior men, accompanied by chanting by other members.
- A ritualized retirement away from the site.

In the Kimberley and central Australian examples, re-painting rituals involving powerful Ancestral Beings are embedded in relational networks that emphasize reciprocal relations with resources (food, rain, etc.), the well-being of people, Aboriginal worldviews, interactions with other clans and moieties, reaffirmation of identity, and links to Country.

Among the Wardaman of the Northern Territory, the painting and subsequent re-marking of *buwarraja* (Dreaming) motifs reaffirmed the identity of the associated Ancestral Beings, connections to clan estates, and in some cases, resistance to European invasion (David & Wilson 2002). Several key locations are associated with highly distinctive *buwarraja* paintings—very large, visually dominating pairs of striped polychrome anthropomorphs of fresh appearance. Based on archival and excavation data, archaeologists have argued that these paintings were created, and in some cases subsequently modified, as a response to the European invasion of Wardaman lands. At Yiwarlarlay (Delamere Station), the re-marking of the Lightning Brothers Ancestral Beings was documented on several occasions during the 1900s (e.g., Arndt 1962; Barrett & Croll 1943; Davidson 1936; Harney 1943; see also David, McNiven, Flood, & Frost 1990), while at Mennge-ya, the home of the White Cockatoo Ancestral Beings, excavations revealed phases of re-painting during the early European-contact period

(David, McNiven, Attenbrow, Flood, & Collins 1994). By re-painting motifs of powerful Ancestral Beings, the paintings have been interpreted as (1) symbols of a resistance-based response to the particularly violent European contact period; and (2) a reaffirmation of people's relationships to lands occupied by Europeans (David & Wilson 2002; cf. Mulvaney 1992). In doing so, the re-painting event can be characterized as a ritualized practice given its performative, intentional, and repetitive nature at a specific place and within a specific temporal context.

Another key aspect of relatedness between Ancestral Beings, rituals, and rock art is the role of pigment[7] and colour (see Huntley, this volume). In the 1980s in western Arnhem Land, Taçon recorded how Aboriginal people used the application of fresh pigments to dull or faded paintings through re-painting to make the paintings 'bright' again and infuse them with the 'power or life-force' of Ancestral Beings. He noted:

> Painting some creatures with brilliant 'rainbow' colour thus enabled Aborigines to tap into the Ancestral force believed to be inherent in the landscape. This is also one of the reasons particular pieces were repainted or superimposed over. The retouching and repainting changed the shelter art back from dull to brilliant, and allowed Aborigines to make contact with the continuing cycle of spiritual and physical existence. In the process it reaffirmed the Aboriginal past and present for the artists and their extended families.
>
> (Taçon 1991: 197)

Taçon noted that fish motifs were frequently repainted. Fish were often given a privileged status in western Arnhem rock art because they were considered 'powerful ancestral species and as symbols of power'[8] (Taçon 1989: 367). They were frequently re-painted as part of ritualized practices: 'when paintings began to fade they had to be renewed with polychrome, rainbow colour or replaced with fresh images' (Taçon 1989: 368). In doing so, the paintings were used to educate younger generations about the power of, and connections to, ancestral forces (Goldhahn et al. 2020; see also Taylor 1996).

Thus, re-painting periodically restored or increased the world's vitality (cf., Mountford 1956: 214–215), and reaffirmed relationships with Country and Ancestral Beings—all are important dimensions of social and existential identity.[9]

KINSHIP AND REAFFIRMING CONNECTIONS WITH COUNTRY

The act of re-marking is also guided by complex rules established through kinship and social organization. For example, re-painting rituals associated with Wanjina are clan-based, relating to the identity of the Wanjina ancestor (see above). In this context, Blundell (1980: 106) notes that 'in order to ensure the continuation of world order, clansmen must annually retouch the paintings in their own estate'; this process not only ensured the maintenance of resources but also reinforced 'ties of clan solidarity'. Blundell (1980: 113) notes that in cases where a clan became extinct, 'the responsibility for the clan estate and its paintings passes 'through the wunan' [world order that connects people and all their material and spiritual associations, including through clan affiliation]' and, as such, 'the responsibility for vacated [clan] estates falls to a clan within the same moiety' (1980: 113; see also Blundell & Woolagoodja 2005: 28–35). Thus, the annual ritual acts of re-painting the Ancestral Beings are also intimately related to the clan-based rules of relatedness.

Likewise, as part of her long-term ethnographic research with the Wardaman, Merlan (1989: 17; see also Kelly, David, & Flood 2021) draws attention to kin-based dimensions of re-marking *buwarrja* paintings, noting structured rules and exceptions[10]:

> [T]hough informants often emphasised that (paintings and other rock art figures) which are *buwarraja* are not of human origin, nevertheless they also emphasise that such figures can and should be painted over by people to make them new . . . Ideally, the renewal of paint at particular sites is said to be the special concern of those patrifiliatively linked to them, but inquiry shows that informants know of renewal done by others (eg, at the Lightning Brothers site).

Smith (1999: 195–196) further highlights such complexities when describing re-painting in the Barunga region of southern Arnhem Land, Northern Territory. She notes that in this part of Australia, patrilineal moieties play a central role in how people order the world, including rock art. When Ancestral Beings created the earth, everything (people, animals, plants, places, colours, and pigments) was positioned into one of two alternating and opposing moieties—Dhuwa or Yirritja. By virtue of their moiety affiliation, all people have a designated responsibility for Country—a reciprocal custodial relationship—either a *gidjan* (owner) or a *junggayi* (custodian or manager). Smith notes that 'the renewal of rock paintings is also subject to the *junggayi* relationship between moieties. Only Yirritja people are permitted to renew (repaint) rock paintings on Dhuwa land, and only Dhuwa people can renew rock paintings on Yirritja land' (Smith 1999: 197). Here the act of re-painting is entirely reliant on *gidjan-junggayi* and Dhuwa-Yirritja relationships.

In western Arnhem Land, a person has particular obligations and responsibilities as *junggayi* in his/her mother's, and mother's mother's, clan Country (Berndt & Berndt 1970; Taylor 1996; see also Maddock 1970). Other-than-human beings, such as some Ancestral Beings, spirits, animals, environmental features, objects, and stars, were also, and continue to be, assigned to specific moieties and semi-moieties (Table 36.1). The rights to paint and re-mark rock art were based on one's relationships to these other-than-human beings. For example, in western Arnhem Land a member of the *ngaraidgu* moiety and *jarijaning* semi-moiety would stand in particular relationships to a range of other-than-human beings to be positioned and authorized to paint and re-paint certain motifs associated with their own semi-moiety (Table 36.1). However, any re-painting of important rock art motifs needed to be sanctioned by senior Traditional Owners of the clan country on which the motif was found. The most suitable artist to execute such ritualized re-marking, a *junggayi* from a moiety that manages the clan's country (estate),

Table 36.1. Example showing the structure of the ngaraidgu moiety, and semi-moieties in the Gunwinggu area of Gunbalanya in western Arnhem Land, and how other-than-human beings (referred to here as "symbols") were placed into the system (Berndt & Berndt 1970: 65).

Moiety	Semi-moiety	Symbol
ngaraidgu	a. jarijaning	*gundung* (sun)
	b. jariburig	*gunag* (fire)

jarijaning, sun: saltwater crocodile (sometimes wrongly called alligator) and freshwater (long-nosed) crocodile; barramundi fish; two varieties of turtle; spotted cat; leech; echidna (in one version): three varieties of goanna, including *galawan;* one variety of wallaby; a round but otherwise scorpion-like creature; several kinds of birds, coastal as well as inland, including pelican; falling star; *mangoidband* 'water peanut'; *djedbar* and *deidjani* roots.

jariburig, fire: shark; small turtle; dugong; dingo; buffalo; bullock; horse; several kinds of bird, including kingfisher and brolga, the *djuri* parakeet whose coloured feathers are used in sacred *maraiin* string; and (in several versions) the *bugbug* pheasant; two varieties of land snake; cicada; *gadderi* wild bee.

would be appointed after necessary negotiations with the *gidjan* of the estate 'owning' moiety (see, e.g., Taylor 1996: 91).

That said, there are few documented examples that reveal how, why, and by whom such re-painting events occurred in western Arnhem Land. The best-documented case took place in the Anbangbang Main Gallery rock shelter at Burrungkuy, also known as Nourlangie Rock in Kakadu National Park, situated in Warramal clan Country (e.g., Chaloupka 1982: 1993). Here the most recent paintings were made by Nayombolmi (c. 1895–1967) and Old Nym Djimongurr (c. 1910–1969) in the 1963/1964 wet season. Nayombolmi was of the Yirritja moiety, and Old Nym Djimongurr was from the Dhuwa moiety. Besides retouching, altering, erasure, amending, and re-painting motifs in the shelter, these senior men also created 'new' motifs consisting of human-like shapes, fish, and Ancestral Beings (Haskovec & Sullivan 1989; May et al. 2019: 13). At the time, Nayombolmi acted as *junggayi* for the area (May et al. 2019), so this performative and intentional event, involving the act of re-marking existing motifs, would most certainly be another example of a ritualized practice of rock art modification that was embedded in the relatedness of the kinship domain.

Rock Art Modification, Ritual, and the Colonial Frontier

An example of ritualized rock art occurring in a colonial setting is the re-marking of existing, traditional motifs with new raw materials. In the south-central Kimberley,

O'Connor et al. (2013) describe two rock art styles and production techniques—black dry pigment motifs and fine scratch-work motifs—in the context of ritual responses to colonial events and continuity of graphic systems. They note that in contrast to the contemporaneous Wanjina motifs, black dry pigment motifs are small, with little structure, and consist largely of linear designs, irregular shapes, hand outlines, and anthropomorphs (2013: 544). Such pigments are frequently used to retouch 'existing motifs by outlining the painted figures or highlighting or refreshing certain features of painted figures' (e.g., Wanjinas) or to amend anthropomorphs by adding new features (e.g., headdresses) (O'Connor et al. 2013: 544–545). The fine scratch-work motifs are shallow incisions likely made by using metal tools (e.g., screwdrivers, knife blades, fencing wire) (O'Connor et al. 2013: 548). At the Stumpy Soak 1 site, O'Connor et al. observed that 'in all cases where painted motifs and scratch-work overlap, the scratch-work images are executed over the painted art. The fact that the scratch-work anthropomorphs are clearly superimposed over red painted figures but appear to re-produce the subject and posture of the painted anthropomorphs indicates they were created after the painted art but reference the same stylistic and symbolic system' (2013: 549).

Both the black dry pigment and fine scratch-work motifs typically occur as the most recent layer on panels throughout the region, and they have been placed into the most recent phase of the Contact period in the Kimberley rock art sequence (O'Connor et al. 2013: 540). Yet, rather than motifs depicting introduced subject matter, O'Connor et al. suggest that the overwhelming focus on re-marking and/or creating 'pre-European'-style motifs formed part of maintenance rituals performed to reinforce or reemphasize connections to traditional subject matters and graphic expressions (see also Frederick 1999; Taçon, Kelleher, King, & Brennan 2008). As such, Kimberley artists and their communities actively reinforced their connections with traditional graphic systems by adapting ritualized modification practices of rock art to include black dry pigment. In doing so, they were using ritual modification as a symbol of resistance to intrusions into Country by Europeans.

Increase rituals involving rock art modification in contact-themed settings have also been documented elsewhere (see McNiven & Russell 2002). For example, on Groote Eylandt, Rose (1942: 175) described how one painted axe motif featured fresh white paint on its sharper cutting end. When he asked an Aboriginal man accompanying him why the fresh paint was applied, the man replied to 'make 'em sharp', and reported that 'an Aborigine had painted the axe-edge afresh in order to make his own axe sharp, presumably by suggestive magic'.

Elsewhere, modification rituals involving sorcery and depictions of Native Police have been documented from Cape York Peninsula in north Queensland. Trezise (1993: 51) reported how seven white hand stencils superimposed over a painting of a snake injecting poison into Native Police were 'the signatures of the small guerrilla band harrying the Black Police'. At a rock art site at Mingaroo Hill, Cole (2010: 24) similarly recorded a line of 'shallow, pounded marks' superimposed over paintings of Native Police. George Musgrave, a senior Kuku Thaypan man working with Cole (2010: 24), interpreted these marks as being made by 'flogging the rock with a stone while singing, clapping and using special words'—another indicator of a ritualized practice based on its performative and intentional nature undertaken at a specific place and laden with specific meaning and symbolism.

CONTESTATION, CONTROVERSY, AND POLITICAL MATTERS IN ROCK ART MODIFICATION

The issue of rock art modification catapulted into the public's consciousness in the late 1980s when a series of re-painting events occurred in the Kimberley region of Western Australia. In 1987, the Ngarinyin Cultural Continuity Project, funded by the Australian government, set out to re-paint Wanjina sites as part of a training program for younger generations of Ngarinyin and 'rejuvenate ritual and ceremonial practices for the Ngarinyin people' (Mowaljarlai & Peck, 1987: 71). Opposition came from some archaeologists, rock art enthusiasts, pastoral owners, and members of the public who considered these acts of re-painting by youths with 'non-traditional' pigments as 'desecration' or 'defacement' of 'universal heritage' (e.g., Walsh 1992; see Bowdler 1988 for a review; see also Ward 1992). As noted above, such criticisms overlooked the role that ritual participation played in the Wanjinas' meeting of social obligations and responsibilities (Blundell & Woolagoodja 2012: 474; Mangolamara et al. 2018). It also bypassed Traditional Owner concerns for the mentoring of youths into important dimensions of culture, including cultural continuity, knowledge transfer, and the health and well-being of the Ngarinyin community.

More recently, the ritual of re-painting has been documented in relation to Native Title concerns and contested landscapes. In 2017, the Wabubadda Aboriginal Corporation (representing the Jirrbal language group) invited Alice Buhrich to record the Snake Cave site in Silver Valley (Cape York Peninsula, Queensland), where a re-painting event had occurred in 2014. In recording the site, Buhrich documented a deteriorated but visible snake motif that had been painted over with a new, considerably larger, red and white snake motif measuring over 24 m in length (Buhrich 2017: 151). Buhrich noted that the Snake Cave site was situated in an area over which the Jirrbal had recently placed a Native Title claim and of which they were in dispute over ownership with another Aboriginal community. The Jirrbal had no knowledge of the snake having been re-painted and interpreted the unauthorized re-painting as a 'statement of ownership by one group over another in a contested native title landscape' (Buhrich 2017: 217). The implications of the re-painting involving a powerful visual symbol were set in a volatile political context where the intentional superimpositioning of a new snake to 'replace' an earlier, faded version was employed[11]. In this case, the large, visually dominating painted symbol had multiple layers of meaning, reaffirming cultural identity but also contesting connections to Country. This politically motivated event can be interpreted as a ritual action, given its performative and intentional dimensions undertaken at a specific place and laden with specific symbolism.

CONCLUSION

As noted above, the act of modifying rock art in Australia through re-marking and superpositioning is not an event or activity that occurs by happenstance. Rather, it is an intentional and repeated performance or social action shaped by a range of cultural factors, including the persisting importance of particular subjects such as Ancestral Beings. The act of modifying existing motifs has, as David (2002: 50) writes, a 'performative dimension' and something that implies 'a conscious awareness of the act, and intentional actions *for* something'. Yet the products of such intentional and performative events—modified motifs—visually show only some outcomes of the ritualized acts. Embedded also are complex connections that guide the inner workings of decision making and ritual orchestrations. In considering how ritualized practices relate to rock art as a meaningful phenomenon, the examples discussed here reveal the depth of overlap in the themes identified (relationships to Ancestral Beings and the spiritual realm, kinship, connections to Country, colonial frontiers, and contestation and politics), supporting the idea that rock art modification implicates deeper, socially performative processes. Hence, Wardaman rock art of relatively recent times expresses experiences with Europeans, clan and kinship-based networks of reciprocity and obligations, and the reaffirmation of group identity and connections with Country (for further details, see Kelly et al. 2021). Such interrelated dimensions of rock art modification further highlight the central role relatedness plays in the lives of Aboriginal peoples. Rose (2001: 105) captures the essence of connections when she notes that 'relatedness is the meat of life, situating people's bodily presence in shared projects that link human and nonhuman interests around intersecting and crosscutting contexts of tracks, countries, totems, and sites. Every discrete category is linked to other discrete categories through kinship, and is crosscut by other discrete categories'. As an event involving the intentional and repeated performance of a social action, the modification of rock art is likewise steeped in networks of relationships, traditions, and change.

As a final point, what is also important to recognize in the examples presented here is that the ritual action of re-marking involves subject matter (e.g., specific Ancestral Beings) that are regionally specific. That is, Wanjina appear only in the Kimberley, the Lightning Brothers only in the Victoria River District, and so on. What remains to be seen is whether patterns of re-marking can also be identified within groups linked by songlines involving Ancestral Beings who traveled great distances (e.g., Arndt 1965). By doing so, we may add another element to understanding the nature of ritual practices and the interrelatedness of rock art across space.

Acknowledgments

Special thanks to Ian McNiven and Bruno David for their invitation to contribute to this volume and to the reviewers for useful comments and insights. JG thanks Jeffrey Lee (senior Traditional Owner of Djok clan country), Parks Australia in Kakadu National Park, and Paul Taçon and Sally K. May at PERAHU (Griffith University) for fruitful research collaborations over the past decade. Brady's position is funded through an ARC Future Fellow grant (FT180100038).

Notes

1. The direct-historical approach is an interpretive method that draws on the ethnographic record to understand past human behaviour through its archaeological record. It relies primarily on documenting continuities in the material correlates of cultural activities (e.g., stone artefact manufacture, iconography).
2. In Aboriginal Australia, the Dreaming was a time of world creation where Ancestral Beings or Dreamings shaped and named all parts of the land and waterways and transformed parts of their bodies, knowledge, and creative forces into landscape features, animals, plant, and natural phenomena such as stars and the moon (among other things). Aboriginal people consider Ancestral Beings to be alive with an active and creative presence in the landscape and seascape.
3. Relational networks are the webs of connections that link and structure the many different aspects of people's lives such as kinship, language, ceremony, relationships to land, and interaction with others.
4. 'Country; in an Aboriginal sense, is a concept that refers to a 'bounded geographical area consisting of interrelated, interdependent elements including people, animals, plants, Ancestral Beings . . . and other types of spirits . . . that act together to create a life-sustaining whole" (Brady & Bradley 2016: 85; see also Rose 1996).
5. Sometimes referred to as leaving their 'shadows' on the rocks (see, e.g., Blundell 1980 for the Kimberley, and Arndt 1962 for the Victoria River District).
6. O'Connor and Arrow (2008) have identified other examples of contact-themed modified (re-painted) rock art in the Kimberley (e.g., schooners, ketch-rigged vessels).
7. In some cases, specific pigments related to Ancestral Beings (e.g., red ochre as the blood of an Ancestral Being) were used to create rock art and infuse it with power (e.g., Chaloupka 1993: 83–86; Taçon 2004).
8. For example, the Barramundi Ancestral Being is known for its creative power and is responsible for creating the East Alligator River (Gunn 1992).
9. Similar examples concerning the power and symbolism of colour can be found in bark paintings from the Arnhem Land region (e.g., Morphy 1989; Taylor 1996).
10. See also Smith (1999) for an example from the Barunga region (Northern Territory) where the patrilineal moiety system guides the re-marking process.
11. A similar example was observed by RGG when, during a Native Title claim in the Northern Territory, a bichrome turtle motif that he previously recorded was erased by a competing claimant group. The turtle was the totem animal of the main claimant group, and the act of erasure was seen by the main claimant group as a sign of the competing claimant group's rights to the land.

REFERENCES

Arndt, W. (1962). The interpretation of Delamere lightning paintings and rock engravings. *Oceania, 32*(3), 163–177.

Arndt, W. (1965). The Dreaming of Kunukban. *Oceania, 35*(4), 241–259.

Barrett, C., & Croll, R. H. (1943). *The art of the Australian Aboriginal.* Melbourne: The Bread and Cheese Club.

Bégouen, H. (1929). The magic origin of prehistoric art. *Antiquity, 3,* 5–19.

Bell, C. (1992). *Ritual theory, ritual practice.* Oxford: Oxford University Press.

Berndt, R. M., & Berndt, C. H. (1970). *Man, land and myth in North Australia: The Gunwinggu people.* Sydney: Ure Smith.

Berggren, Å., & Nilsson Stutz, L. (2010). From spectator to critic and participant: A new role for archaeology in ritual studies. *Journal of Social Archaeology, 10*(2), 171–197.

Blundell, V. (1980). Hunter-gatherer territoriality: Ideology and behaviour in northwest Australia. *Ethnohistory, 27*(2), 103–117.

Blundell, V., & Woolagoodja, D. (2005). *Keeping the Wanjinas fresh.* Fremantle: Fremantle Press.

Blundell, V., & Woolagoodja, D. (2012). Rock art, Aboriginal culture, and identity: The Wanjina paintings of northwest Australia. In J. McDonald & P. Veth (Eds.), *A companion to rock art* (pp. 472–487). Malden, MA: Blackwell.

Bowdler, S. (1988). Repainting Australian rock art. *Antiquity, 62,* 517–523.

Bradley, R. (2005). *Ritual and domestic life in prehistoric Europe.* London: Routledge.

Brady, L. M., & Bradley, J. J. (2014). Images of relatedness: Patterning and cultural contexts in Yanyuwa rock art, Sir Edward Pellew Islands, SW Gulf of Carpentaria, northern Australia. *Rock Art Research, 31*(2), 157–176.

Brady, L. M., & Bradley, J. J. (2016). 'That painting now is telling us something': Negotiating and apprehending contemporary meaning in Yanyuwa rock art. In L. M. Brady & P. S. C. Taçon (Eds.), *Rock art in the contemporary world: Navigating symbolism, meaning and significance* (pp. 83–106). Boulder: University Press of Colorado.

Breuil, H. (1952). *Four hundred centuries of cave art.* Montignac: Centre d'Etudes et de Documentation Préhistoriques.

Brightman, R. (1993). *Grateful prey: Rock Cree human-animal relationships.* Berkeley: University of California Press.

Buhrich, A. (2017). *Art and identity: Aboriginal rock art and dendroglyphs of Queensland's Wet Tropics* (PhD thesis). James Cook University, Townsville.

Chaloupka, G. (1982). *Burrunguy: Nourlangie rock.* Darwin: Northart.

Chaloupka, G. (1993). *Journey in time, the world's longest continuing art tradition: The story of the Australian Aboriginal rock art of Arnhem Land.* Chatswood: Reed.

Chippindale, C., & Taçon, P. S. C. (1993). Two old painted panels from Kakadu: Variation and sequence in Arnhem Land rock-art. In J. Steinberg, A. Watchman, P. Faulstich, & P. S. C. Taçon (Eds.), *Time and space: Dating and spatial considerations in rock-art research* (pp. 32–56). Melbourne: Australian Rock Art Research Association (Occasional AURA Publication No. 8).

Clarke, J. (1976). Two Aboriginal rock art pigments from Western Australia: Their properties, use and durability. *Studies in Conservation, 21,* 134–142.

Clottes, J., & Lewis-Williams, J. D. (1996). *The shamans of prehistory: Trance magic in the painted caves.* New York: Abrams.

Cole, N. (2010). Painting the police: Aboriginal visual culture and identity in colonial Cape York Peninsula. *Australian Archaeology, 71,* 17–28.

Crawford, I. (1968). *The art of the Wandjina: Aboriginal cave paintings in Kimberley, Western Australia*. Melbourne: Oxford University Press.

David, B. (2002). *Landscapes, rock-art and the Dreaming: An archaeology of preunderstanding*. London: Leicester University Press.

David, B., McNiven, I., Attenbrow, V., Flood, J., & Collins, J. (1994). Of Lightning Brothers and White Cockatoos: Dating the antiquity of signifying systems in the Northern Territory, Australia. *Antiquity, 68*, 241–251.

David, B., McNiven, I., Flood, J., & Frost, R. (1990). Yiwarlarlay 1: Archaeological excavations at the Lightning Brothers site, Delamere station, Northern Territory. *Archaeology in Oceania, 25*(2), 79–84.

David, B., & Wilson, M. (2002). Spaces of resistance: Graffiti and Indigenous place markings in the early European contact period of northern Australia. In B. David & M. Wilson (Eds.), *Inscribed landscapes: Marking and making place* (pp. 42–60). Honolulu: University of Hawaii Press.

Davidson, D. S. (1936). *Aboriginal Australian and Tasmanian rock carvings and paintings*. Memoirs of the American Philosophical Society Vol. 5. Philadelphia: American Philosophical Society.

Elkin, A. P. (1948). Grey's northern Kimberley cave-paintings re-found. *Oceania, 19*(1), 1–15.

Elkin, A. P. (1964). *Australian Aborigines: How to understand them*. 4th edition. Sydney: Angus & Robertson.

Elkin, A. P. (1930). Rock paintings of north-west Australia. *Oceania, 1*(3), 257–279.

Frederick, U. (1999). At the centre of it all: Constructing contact through the rock art of Watarrka National Park, central Australia. *Archaeology in Oceania, 34*, 132–144.

Geertz, C. (1973). *The interpretation of culture*. New York: Basic Books.

Goldhahn, J. (2016). *Sagaholm: North European Bronze Age rock art and burial ritual*. Oxford: Oxbow Books.

Goldhahn, J., & Ling, J. (2013). Scandinavian Bronze Age rock art—contexts and interpretations. In H. Fokkens & A. Harding (Eds.), *Handbook of European Bronze Age* (pp. 270–290). Oxford: Oxford University Press.

Goldhahn, J., May, S. K., Marlangurra, J., & Lee, J. (2020). Children and rock art: A case study from western Arnhem Land, Australia. *Norwegian Archaeological Review, 53*(1), 59–82.

Gunn, R. G. (1992). Mikinj: Rock art, myth and place. Unpublished report to the Australian Institute of Aboriginal and Torres Strait Islander Studies (Canberra), and the Northern Land Council (Darwin).

Gunn, R. G. (2000). Central Australian rock art: A second report. *Rock Art Research, 17* (2), 111–126.

Gunn, R. G. (2018). *Art of the ancestors: Spatial and temporal patterning in the ceiling rock art of Nawarla Gabarnmang, Arnhem Land, Australia*. Oxford: Archaeopress Publishing.

Gunn, R. G. (2019). Degrees of change: Amendment and alteration in Australian Aboriginal rock art. In J. Huntley & G. Nash (Eds.), *Aesthetics, applications, artistry and anarchy: Essays in prehistoric and contemporary art: A festschrift in honour of John Kay Clegg* (pp. 87–97). Oxford: Archaeopress Publishing.

Gunn, R.G., B. David, J.-J. Delannoy, B. Smith, A. Unghangho, I. Waina, Balanggarra Aboriginal Corporation, L. Douglas, C. Myers, P. Heaney, S. Ouzman, P. Veth and S. Harper (2022). Superpositions and superimpositions in rock art studies: Reading the rock face at Pundawar Manbur, Kimberley, northwest Australia. *Journal of Anthropological Archaeology, 67*(2022), 101442..

Harney Snr, W. (1943). *Taboo*. Sydney: Australasian Publishing Co.

Harper, S. (2017). *Inside the outline: Understanding inclusive and exclusive identity in Marapikurrinya (Port Hedland) rock art* (PhD thesis). University of Western Australia, Perth.

Haskovec, I. P. (1992). Mt Gilruth Revisited. *Archaeology in Oceania, 27*(2), 61–74.

Haskovec, I. P., & Sullivan, H. (1989). Reflections and rejections of an Aboriginal artist. In H. Morphy (Ed.), *Animals into art* (pp. 57–74). London: Unwin Hyman.

Hays-Gilpin, K. (2004). *Ambiguous images: Gender and rock art*. Walnut Creek, CA: Altamira Press.

Hicks, D. (2010). *Ritual and belief: Readings in the anthropology of religion*. 3rd edition. Lanham, MD: Altamira Press.

Jones, T., & May, S. K. (2015). Rock art and ritual function: The Northern Running Figures of western Arnhem Land. *The Artefact, 38*, 53–66.

Kelly, M., David, B., & Flood, J. (2021). Scene but not heard: Seeing scenes in a northern Australian Aboriginal site. In I. Davidson & A. Nowell (Eds.), *Making scenes: Global perspectives on scenes in rock art* (pp. 162–178). New York: Berghahn Books.

Keyser, J. D., & Whitley, D. S. (2006). Sympathetic magic in western North American rock art. *American Antiquity, 71*(1), 3–26.

Layton, R. (1992). *Australian rock art: A new synthesis*. Cambridge: Cambridge University Press.

Lewis-Williams, J. D. (1974). Superpositioning in a sample of rock-paintings from the Barkly East District. *The South African Archaeological Bulletin, 29*(115/116), 93–103.

Lewis-Williams, J. D. (1981). *Believing and seeing: Symbolic meaning in southern San rock paintings*. London: Academic Press.

Lewis-Williams, J. D., & Dowson, T. A. (1988). Signs of the times: Entoptic phenomena in Upper Palaeolithic art. *Current Anthropology, 29*, 210–245.

Lommel, A. (1952 [1997]). *The Unambal: A tribe in northwest Australia* (translated by I. Campbell). Carnarvon Gorge: Takarakka Nowan Kas Publications.

Love, J. R. B. (1930). Rock paintings of the Worora and their mythical interpretation. *Royal Society of Western Australia Journal 16*, 1–24.

Maddock, K. (1970). Imagery and social structure at two Dalabon rock art sites. *Anthropological Forum, 2*(4), 444–463.

Mangolamara, S., Karadada, L., Oobagooma, J., Woolagoodja, D., & Karadada, J. (2018). *Nyara pari kala niragu (Gaambera), Gadawara ngyaran-gada (Wunambal), Inganinja gubadjoongana (Woddordda): We are coming to see you*. Derby: Dambimangari Aboriginal Corporation & Wunambal Gaambera Aboriginal Corporation.

May, S. K., Maralngurra, J. G., Johnston, I. G., Goldhahn, J., Lee, J., O'Loughlin, G., . . . Taçon, P. (2019). 'This is my father's painting': A first-hand account of the creation of the most iconic rock art in Kakadu National Park. *Rock Art Research, 36*(2), 1–15.

McCarthy, F. D. (1974). Space and superimpositions in Australian Aboriginal Art. In A. K. Ghosh (Ed.), *Perspectives in palaeoanthropology* (pp. 113–128). Calcutta: Firma K L Mukhopadhyay.

McNiven, I. J. (2013). Ritualized middening practices. *Journal of Archaeological Method and Theory, 20*, 552–587.

McNiven, I. J. (2016). Increase rituals and environmental variability on small residential islands of Torres Strait. *Journal of Island and Coastal Archaeology, 11*(2), 195–210.

McNiven, I. J., & Russell, L. (2002). Ritual response: Place marking and the colonial frontier in Australia. In B. David & M. Wilson (Eds.), *Inscribed landscapes: Marking and making place* (pp. 27–41). Honolulu: University of Hawaii Press.

Merlan, F. (1989). The interpretative framework of Wardaman rock art: A preliminary report. *Australian Aboriginal Studies 1989 / 2*, 14–24.

Morphy, H. (1989). From dull to brilliant: The aesthetics of spiritual power among the Yolngu. *Man, 24*, 21–39.

Morphy, H. (1994). The interpretation of ritual: Reflections from film on anthropological practice. *Man, 29*(1), 117–146.

Morphy, H. (2012). Recursive and iterative processes in Australian rock art: An anthropological perspective. In J. McDonald & P. Veth (Eds.), *A companion to rock art* (pp. 294–305). Malden, MA: Blackwell.

Morwood, M. J., Walsh, G. L., & Watchman, A. L. (2010). AMS radiocarbon ages for beeswax and charcoal pigments in north Kimberley rock art. *Rock Art Research, 27*(1), 3–8.

Motta, A. P. (2019). From top down under: New insights into the social significance of superimpositions in the rock art of northern Kimberley, Australia. *Cambridge Archaeological Journal, 29*(3), 479–495.

Mountford, C. P. (Ed.). (1956). *Records of the American-Australian Scientific Expedition to Arnhem Land 1: Art, myth and symbolism*. Melbourne: Melbourne University Press.

Mountford, C. P. (1968). *Winbaraku and the myth of Jarapiri*. Adelaide: Rigby.

Mowaljarlai, D., & Peck, C. (1987). Ngarinyin cultural continuity: A project to teach the young people our culture, including the repainting of Wandjina rock art sites. *Australian Aboriginal Studies, 1987/2*, 71–78.

Mowaljarlai, D., Vinnicombe, P., Ward, G. K., & Chippindale, C. (1988). Repainting of images on rock in Australia and the maintenance of Aboriginal culture. *Antiquity, 62*(237), 690–696.

Mulvaney, K. (1992). Who paints for a killing: Gurindji sorcery paintings of Palngarrawuny. In J. McDonald & I. P. Haskovec (Eds.), *State of the art: Regional rock art studies in Australian and Melanesia* (pp. 216–225). Occasional AURA Publication No. 6. Melbourne: Australian Rock Art Research Association.

Mulvaney, K. (2009). Dating the Dreaming: Extinct fauna in the petroglyphs of the Pilbara region, Western Australia. *Archaeolgy in Oceania, 44*, 40–48.

Munn, N. (1970). The transformation of subjects into objects in Walbiri and Pitjantjatjara myth. In R. Berndt (Ed.), *Australian Aboriginal anthropology* (pp. 141–163). Perth: University of Western Australia Press.

O'Connor, S., & Arrow, S. (2008). Boat images in the rock art of northern Australia with particular reference to the Kimberley, Western Australia. In G. Clark, F. Leach, & S. O'Connor (Eds.), *Islands of inquiry: Colonisation, seafaring and the archaeology of maritime landscapes* (pp. 397–409). Canberra: ANU E-Press.

O'Connor, S., Balme, J., Fyfe, J., Oscar, J., Oscar, M., Davis, J., . . . Surprise, D. (2013). Marking resistance? Change and continuity in the recent rock art of the southern Kimberley, Australia. *Antiquity, 87*, 539–554.

O'Connor, S., Barham, A., & Woolagoodja, D. (2008). Painting and repainting in the west Kimberley. *Australian Aboriginal Studies, 2008/1*, 22–38.

Rappaport, R. A. (1999). *Ritual and religion in the making of humanity*. Cambridge: Cambridge University Press.

Reinach, S. (1903). L'art et la magie. À propos des peintures et des gravures de l' Age du Renne. *L'Anthropologie, 14*, 257–266.

Renfrew, C. (1994). The archaeology of religion. In C. Renfrew & I. E. Zubrow (Eds.), *The ancient mind* (pp. 47–54). Cambridge: Cambridge University Press.

Rose, D. B. (1992). *Dingo makes us human: Life and land in an Australian Aboriginal culture.* Cambridge: Cambridge University Press.

Rose, D. B. (1996). *Nourishing terrains: Australian Aboriginal views of landscape and wilderness.* Canberra: Australian Heritage Commission.

Rose, F. (1942). Paintings of the Groote Eylandt Aborigines. *Oceania, 13*, 170–176.

Rose, D. B. (2001). Sacred site, ancestral clearing, and environmental ethics. In A. Rumsey & J. F. Weiner (Eds.), *Space, narrative, and knowledge in Aboriginal Australia and Papua New Guinea* (pp. 99–119). Honolulu: University of Hawaii Press.

Ross, J., & Davidson, I. (2006). Rock art and ritual: An archaeological analysis of rock art in arid central Australia. *Journal of Archaeological Method and Theory, 13*(4), 305–341.

Sale, K. M. (1995). Making the old brighter: Aboriginal re-marking of rock pictures. In G. K. Ward & L. A. Ward (Eds.), *Management of rock imagery* (pp. 128–140). Occasional AURA Publication No. 9. Melbourne: Australian Rock Art Research Association.

Smith, C. (1999). Ancestors, place and people: Social landscapes in Aboriginal Australia. In P. J. Ucko & R. Layton (Eds.), *The archaeology and anthropology of landscape: Shaping your landscape* (pp. 189–205). London: Routledge.

Spencer, B., & Gillen, F. J. (1899). *The native tribes of central Australia.* London: Macmillan.

Spencer, B., & Gillen, F. J. (1927). *The Arunta: A study of a Stone Age people.* London: Macmillan.

Swenson, E. (2015). The archaeology of ritual. *Annual Review of Anthropology, 44*, 329–345.

Taçon, P. S. C. (1989). *From rainbow snakes to "x-ray" fish: The nature of the recent rock painting tradition of western Arnhem Land, Australia* (PhD thesis). Australian National University, Canberra.

Taçon, P. S. C. (1991). The power of stone: Symbolic aspects of stone use and tool development in western Arnhem Land, Australia. *Antiquity, 65*, 192–207.

Taçon, P. S. C. (2004). Ochre, clay, stone and art: The symbolic importance of minerals as life-force among Aboriginal peoples of northern and central Australia. In N. Boivin & M. A. Owoc (Eds.), *Soils, stones and symbols: Cultural perceptions of the mineral world* (pp. 31–42). New York: Routledge.

Taçon, P. S. C., Kelleher, M., King, G., & Brennan, W. (2008). Eagle's reach: A focal point for past and present social identity within the Northern Blue Mountains World Heritage Area, Australia. In I. S. Domingo, D. Fiore, & S. K. May (Eds.), *Archaeologies of art: Time, place identity* (pp. 195–214). Walnut Creek, CA: Left Coast Press.

Taylor, L. (1996). *Seeing the inside: Bark painting in western Arnhem Land.* Oxford: Oxford University Press.

Trezise, P. (1993). *Dream road: A journey of discovery.* St Leonards: Allen & Unwin.

Utemara, D., & Vinnicombe, P. (1992). North-western Kimberley belief systems. In M. J. Morwood & D. R. Hobbs (Eds.), *Rock art and ethnography* (pp. 25–26). Occasional AURA Publication No. 5. Melbourne: Australian Rock Art Research Association.

Villerslev, R. (2007). *Soul hunters: Hunting, animism and personhood among the Siberian Yukaghirs.* Berkeley: University of California Press.

Viveiros de Castro, E. (2012). *Cosmological perspectivism in Amazonia and elsewhere: Four lectures given in the Department of Social Anthropology, University of Cambridge, February–March 1998.* HAU: Masterclass Series.

Watchman, A. (1992). Repainting or periodic-painting at Australian Aboriginal sites: Evidence from rock surface crusts. In G. K. Ward (Ed.), *Retouch: Maintenance and conservation of Aboriginal rock imagery* (pp. 26–31). Occasional AURA Publication No. 5. Melbourne: Australian Rock Art Research Association.

Walsh, G. L. (1994). *Bradshaws: Ancient rock paintings of north-west Australia*. Geneva: Bradshaw Foundation.

Whitley, D. S. (2000). *The art of the shaman: The rock art of California*. Salt Lake City: University of Utah Press.

Whitley, D. S. (2011). Rock art, religion, and ritual. In T. Insoll (Ed.), *The archaeology of ritual and religion* (pp. 307–326). Oxford: Oxford University Press.

CHAPTER 37

DUGONGS AND TURTLES AS KIN

Relational Ontologies and Archaeological Perspectives on Ritualized Hunting by Coastal Indigenous Australians

IAN J. MCNIVEN

INTRODUCTION

ANTHROPOLOGICAL and archaeological research, especially in the Arctic and sub-Arctic of Eurasia and North America, reveals that the hunting of animals by people for food is not just a technical exercise. Anthropological research indicates that Indigenous hunting, especially of large animals, has major ontological and moral implications in terms of killing what are often considered to be sentient beings, nonhuman persons, and kin. While archaeological investigations of past hunting practices emphasizing technology and subsistence and calories are not invalid, neglecting the ontological dimensions of big-game hunting provides a secular view of the past that underplays past cultural difference and worldviews. This underplay is not limited to hunting practices but brings in a much bigger and more fundamental issue of how peoples of the past understood what it meant to be human vis-à-vis animal, and how such a separation and proximity was negotiated, navigated, manipulated, and expressed ritually and materially. Archaeological investigation of ritualized hunting practices provides a rare opportunity to engage with such worlds and ontological boundaries of self and other.

Archaeologies of past hunting rituals are an important dimension of the 'ontological turn' in archaeology (Alberti 2016) and specifically relational ontologies (Watts 2013). Central to these ontological explorations are human–animal relationships, both past and present. These relationships are not imposed but are inherent qualities that people know to be true. While 'ontology' refers not to a belief system or religious cosmology, but to reality as it is known, inherent qualities of phenomena are often understood and validated cosmologically. With relational ontologies, entities such as 'human' versus 'animal' do not exist in that form, as if essentially separate but relatable to one another, for the very identity of each is contingent on the relationship itself. The notion of 'relational ontologies' thus means that the relations between things comes first, that an entity cannot be known without first understanding how it is existentially connected with something else in a given worldview (i.e., in a given ontology). In this sense, hunting rituals that relate humans to animals are not symbolic representations of the two categories, but rather a key dimension of the generative expression of the relationship that connects them.

This chapter explores issues of relational ontologies and human–animal relationships through rituals of increase/maintenance and hunting associated with dugongs and marine turtles as practiced by coastal Indigenous Australians. I set the conceptual scene for this exploration with a brief discussion of ontologies of animate worlds (animism) and sentient and kin-centric ecologies as keys to understanding spiritual and ritual relationships between hunters and dugongs and marine turtles. This type of archaeological research requires a critical reading of ethnographic information to help archaeologists know what to look for and know the ontological and epistemological frameworks within which ritualized hunting practices and associated objects and sites operated. Most importantly, approaches that consider relational ontologies provide opportunities for archaeologists to create understandings of the past that are more sympathetic and commensurate with the ontologies and epistemologies of the Indigenous communities with whom they collaborate.

ANIMATE WORLDS AND RELATIONAL ONTOLOGIES: THE FOUNDATIONS OF RITUALIZED HUNTING

Anthropological research informs us that all peoples see the world in a relational sense whereby people and other lifeforms exist through connected life forces. Critically, many peoples, especially Indigenous peoples, know the world as infused with interdependent sentience and agency. Such 'animate' (animistic) worlds contrast with an ontological separation of 'nature' from 'culture' and a 'mechanistic' view of the world subject to the 'laws of nature' as devised and conceptualized by Western philosophers during the Enlightenment in the seventeenth and eighteenth centuries (Descola 2013; Henry 2004). It also differs from ancient Greek views of nature (e.g., Aristotelian), which did not encompass a separate ontological category of an external and mechanistic nature but an internal nature (as in the 'nature of' or 'essence of' phenomena) and organismic nature that was 'alive' and 'intelligent' and in possession of a 'soul' (Collingwood 1945: 3–4). A mechanistic nature is the ontological and epistemological foundation of Western scientific research (Descola 2013: 63). For most Enlightenment philosophers and scientists, a mechanistic view of the world was not inconsistent with a belief in the existence of God, at least in a metaphysical sense. Indeed, most Westerners know the world as comprising tangible and intangible elements, both secular and spiritual (Latour 1993). For the seventeenth-century philosopher René Descartes, humans (created by God) were dualist beings with a body separate from a rational soul and a self-reflective and thoughtful mind (a special and unique creation by God), whereas animals (similarly created by God) were relegated as 'mechanical automata' and instinctive creatures (Cottingham 2018: xxviii, xxx). For Indigenous peoples, the world and the 'environment' are multidimensional, where the tangible includes the spiritual realm and animals are thoughtful and sentient. Taken together, these ontological (worldview and reality) and epistemological (construction of knowledge and understanding) aspects present Indigenous worlds where people are intimately connected to animals in very particular ways, especially animals hunted for food. Fundamentally, hunting is much more than a technological act of procuring prey for food but also a spiritual act of reciprocity and morality whereby hunters propitiate spiritual forces to entice prey animals to come close to hunters. In some cases, these spiritual forces are external to prey, as with many circumpolar societies where a spiritual provider or guardian, following appropriate rituals of etiquette and reciprocity, will entice prey towards prospective hunters. In other cases, spiritual forces are part of the prey themselves, and again through special ritual performances, hunters and prey enter into dialogue such that the prey may present itself to a hunter for killing if the hunter meets appropriate and respectful conditions (see later discussion).

Hunting practices are ritualized because of the intimate spiritual connections between people and animals. Many anthropologists argue that such ritualization is an expression of animistic ontologies that challenge Cartesian dualist dichotomies (at least in an idealized Western scientific guise) between the categories of human versus animal, culture versus nature, tangible versus intangible, spiritual versus secular, body versus mind, and so on (Anderson 2000; Berkes 2008; Bird-David 1999; Brightman 1993; Descola 2013; Hallowell 1960; Ingold 2000; Scott 1989; Tanner 1979; Viveiros de Castro 1998; Willerslev 2007). In the wake of the 'animal turn' in anthropology (Anderson 1997), an ontology of 'sentient ecology' (Anderson 2000) took centre stage whereby sentience is a characteristic of the world and not the sole (exceptional) prerogative of humans. With sentient ecologies, humans and so-called natural phenomena (e.g., the elements such as wind, and certain animals and plants) have consciousness, agency, and the capacity for dialogue, mutual understanding, and judgement. This perspective is encapsulated nicely in anthropologist Eduardo Kohn's (2013: 21–22) evocative phrase 'How forests think' to convey the essence of animistic ontologies of the Runa of Ecuador's Upper Amazon. In such worlds, the engaged social arena of people includes certain animals, plants, elements, and landscape features, in addition to the animate and inanimate, the tangible and intangible, and the living and the dead. Furthermore, sentient ecologies not only concern landscapes and the terrestrial domain, they also concern seascapes and the marine domain for many coastal communities (McNiven 2004, 2008).

McNiven (2010: 215–216) posits that conceptualizing the divide between humans and animals 'as a liminal and at times fluid and permeable boundary' is central to the capacity for dialogue and mutual understanding and goes to the heart of many hunting rituals. That is, 'hunters often enter into an interpersonal dialogue with prey such that prey agree either to be killed or at least to be drawn in closer to allow hunters to effect a successful kill' (McNiven 2010: 218). Special and highly specific ritual performances increase the permeability of the human–animal divide and decrease the ontological distance between humans and animals such that a spiritual dialogue, or more specifically a 'killing dialogue' (Bradley 1997: 9), can occur. This killing dialogue is often ritually enhanced and mediated by objects (often referred to as hunting charms) that either are animal body parts or incorporate animal body parts (McNiven 2010: 217).

For many Indigenous peoples, the deep spiritual and intimate relationship between people and animals does not start and end with the practice of hunting. People often have spiritual roles to play in the creation of animals and in the maintenance and rejuvenation of animal populations. Such roles are validated due to an understanding that people and animals are kin, with shared connections of existence and shared roles and obligations of regeneration. Such roles also involve rituals often referred to in the anthropological literature as 'increase ceremonies'. Australia is the focus for much of this literature, and it has been since the pioneering anthropological research by Baldwin Spencer with Aboriginal communities in Central Australia during the late nineteenth century (Spencer & Gillen 1899: chap. 6, 1904: chap 9). These rituals were undertaken by ritual specialists with appropriate connections to the species being rejuvenated. As social anthropologists have long been at pains to point out, the phrase 'increase ceremony' is a misnomer as the role of such rituals was not strictly about propitiating increased numbers of animals (but also plants, rain, etc.) but about maintaining a cosmic order through ritualized human participation (Meggitt 1962: 221; Rose 1996: 53; Swain 1995: 26). As anthropologist Peter Elkin (1981: 228) explained, increase rituals are 'not an attempt to control nature by magical means' but about ensuring that the 'normal order of nature should be maintained. . . . It is not an attempt to bring about the irregular and extraordinary, but to maintain the regular'. However, anthropologist John Morton (1987: 459, 461) points out that increase rituals are 'not simply designed to maintain natural species' but fundamentally concern reinvigorating the 'spirituality of humans' and human totemic relationships with animals etc. In terms of relational ontologies, some of these rituals 'also guarantee human reproduction and this may be their primary aim' (Morton 1987: 461). In a Melanesian context, anthropologist Chris Ballard (1998: 73) points out that the life forces of the world are in a constant state of 'decline and dissipation rather than increase and accumulation'. The process of 'entropic decline' can be reversed by adherence to 'appropriate moral behaviour' and 'repeated acts of ritual replenishment' (Ballard 1998: 74, 76).

Anthropologist Amanda Kearney and colleagues (2019) discuss Australian Aboriginal 'maintenance rituals' using Salmón's (2000) notion of 'kin-centric ecology'.

Kin-centric ecologies are relational ontologies whereby ancestral presence and power underpin how people, phenomena (e.g., animals), and places are intimately connected and co-constituted though agentive bonds of mutually prescribed and understood sentience, reciprocity, and morality. In short, the well-being of people and the well-being of phenomena (e.g., animals) and places are interdependent (Kearney, Bradley, & Brady 2019: 326). Maintenance rituals are an expression of this interdependency and are part of 'maintaining an order that implicates much more than beneficial return in the form of food resources' (Kearney et al. 2019: 331). It needs to be emphasized that a 'kin-centric ecology' perspective presupposes that 'sentience' is everywhere but is not a characteristic of everything. The critical point is that sentience is a characteristic of phenomena with an ancestral spiritual presence (Rose 2001: 104; cf. Peterson 2011). In such sentient and kin-centric worlds, the ontological status of humans and certain animals is inherently interdependent and co-constituted, and antithetical to human exceptionalism and anthropocentrism that dominates Western ontologies (see Plumwood 2003; Weitzenfeld & Joy 2014).

Rituals of hunting are often termed 'hunting magic' and/or 'magico-religious' rites by anthropologists (e.g., Brown 1984; Carneiro 1970; Frazer 1911; Hallowell 1926) and archaeologists (e.g., Freikman & Garfinkel 2009; Keyser & Whitley 2006; McGranaghan & Challis 2016; McNiven & Feldman 2003; Turpin 1993). Following on from anthropologist James Frazer's (1911) conceptualization of 'sympathetic magic', McNiven and Feldman (2003) identified two forms of 'hunting magic' rituals from the literature—'immobilisation rituals' (aimed at halting or minimizing the movement of prey) and 'allurement rituals' (aimed at attracting prey towards the hunter). Yet is it clear in much of this literature of the past two decades that a tension exists in the appropriateness of the term 'hunting magic' for a range of theoretical, substantive, and ethical reasons. Indeed, some archaeologists do not use the term 'magic' in relation to hunting rituals (e.g., Äikäs, Puputti, Núñez, Aspi, & Okkonen 2009; Emery & Brown 2012). Although I have employed the term 'hunting magic' in the past (e.g., McNiven & Feldman 2003), I endorse its removal from hunting rituals discourse. Early anthropological literature often represented the magical practices of small-scale communities (e.g., Western and non-Western) pejoratively as expressions of superstition and a primitive mentality, and juxtaposed these to the proclaimed rationality of Christian religious practices of divine causality and metropolitan science's 'laws of nature' (Tambiah 1990). For example, pioneering anthropologist Edward B. Tylor (1871, I: 101) described the 'belief in magic' as 'one of the most pernicious delusions that ever vexed mankind'. Frazer (1911: 53) saw magic as 'a spurious system of natural law as well as a fallacious guide of conduct; it is a false science as well as an abortive art'. Anthropologist Susan Greenwood (2009: 4) states, 'Magic has been associated with backwardness and primitivism, a negative trope in constructions of the primitive other'. Kearney et al. (2019: 324) robustly make the point that the term 'magic' conjures notions of the 'esoteric' and smothers the complexity of causative pathways associated with hunting rituals and sidelines issues of morality and reciprocity central to relational ontologies. As such, 'there are ethical shortcomings in casting Indigenous knowledge and practice as esoteric, and/or magical'

(Kearney et al. 2019: 330). Similarly, anthropologist Philippe Descola (2013: 84) notes that 'hunting magic' is a misnomer and is not associated with an ontology where 'such actions are invested with an operational efficacy'. For example, in relation to the *anent* (hunting) ritual of Achuar hunters of the Amazon, he notes:

> The magic incantation is not operational because it is performative or because it may bring about the result that it suggests or make this seem possible in the eyes of the singer. It is operational because it helps to characterize and therefore to render effective the relationship that is established at a particular moment between one particular man and one particular animal; it recalls the links between the hunter and other members of the animal's species, it describes those links using the language of kinship, and underlines the ties of solidarity between the two parties that are present; in short, it picks out from the attributes of each party those that will impart to their confrontation a greater existential reality. So a hunting *anent* cannot be isolated as a symbolic dross that accompanies a technical process.
>
> (Descola 2013: 84)

From archaeological and anthropological perspectives, research on the ritualization of hunting has focused on marine mammal hunting (seals and whales) by Arctic and sub-Arctic peoples of Siberia and North America. In this context, archaeologist Erica Hill (2011: 408) makes the observation that sea mammal 'interactions with humans are relational, interpersonal and intersubjective'. Within Arctic and sub-Arctic animistic ontologies, marine mammals are sentient and self-conscience and possess the capacity to exercise intentionality and agency and to make morally prescribed value judgements on the behaviours and attitudes of hunters and their communities. Hunters similarly view their interactions with marine mammals as centring on respectful, reciprocal, interdependent, and morally proscribed social relationships (Fienup-Riordan 1990; Gadamus & Raymond-Yakoubian 2015; Lowenstein 1994; Pelly 2001). Seals and whales would exercise their agency and only make themselves available to human hunters if they knew hunters had previously treated their marine mammal kin with respect. Expressions of respect included skilful hunting, formalized processing and caching of remains (particularly skulls) to allow reincarnation, morally prescribed sharing of meat and fat products, and broader adherence to strict and gendered protocols, taboos, and rituals. Respectful hunting also enhanced marine mammal numbers, thus blurring the boundary between rituals of hunting and rituals of maintenance. In this guise, hunting was less a technological act and more a social and moral contract built around mutual respect, trust, etiquette, and reciprocal exchange (Armstrong Oma 2010; Hill 2018: 40; Nadasdy 2007). Harvey (2006: 99) makes the broader point that 'respectful engagement is the central moral imperative' of the new, reinvigorated conceptualization of animism (see also Descola 2013).

Within an Australian context, archaeological and anthropological research on marine hunting rituals has similarly focused on marine mammals, in this case dugongs (or sea cows) by Torres Strait Islanders and Aboriginal peoples of tropical Northeast Australia. However, considerable ethnographic information is also available on marine turtle hunting and associated rituals by Aboriginal peoples and Torres Strait Islanders. Indeed, coastal communities that hunt dugongs also tend to hunt turtles. The remainder of this chapter provides an overview of this dugong and turtle research. Although the focus is Indigenous Australia, it is acknowledged that complementary ethnographic information is available on dugong and turtle hunting rituals by communities along the southwest coast of Papua New Guinea adjacent to Torres Strait (e.g., Eley 1988; Landtman 1927; McNiven 2013a; Stasch 1996).

Hunting Dugongs

The dugong or sea cow (*Dugong dugon*) is a marine mammal herbivore growing up to 3.3 m in length and 570 kg in weight (Marsh, O'Shea, & Reynolds 2011: 6). Dugongs are distributed discontinuously across shallow coastal tropical and subtropical waters from East Africa through to the Southwest Pacific (Marsh et al. 2011: 8). They occur within coastal waters of the northern half of Australia and were and remain an important and prestigious food source for many Aboriginal and Torres Strait Islander communities (Bradley 1991; Johannes & MacFarlane 1991; Mitchell 1996; Rouja 1998; Thomson 1934). Anthropologist Donald Thomson (1934: 238) pointed out that hunting of dugongs was 'undoubtedly the most dangerous and spectacular occupation' practised by Indigenous Australians. The earliest known evidence for hunting of dugongs by Indigenous Australians is 4000 years (Berberass, western Torres Strait) and possibly 6000 years (Shea's Creek, New South Wales) (Crouch, McNiven, David, Rowe, & Weisler 2007; Haworth, Baker, & Flood 2004). Dugong is an important totem (*awgadh* in western Torres Strait language) in Torres Strait, with important dugong rituals the responsibility of senior members of the dugong clan on various islands (Haddon 1904: 154–156, 182–183). A deep spiritual kinship connection exists between a person and their totem. Haddon was told 'emphatically' that '*Augud* [sic] all same as relation he belong same family' (1904: 184). A similar agentive totemic relationship and ancestral spiritual kinship exists between numerous northern coastal Aboriginal peoples and dugongs (e.g., Bradley 1991, 1997, 1998; Buku-Larrngay Mulka Centre 1999; Memmott & Trigger 1998; Rigsby & Chase 1998; Thomson 1934).

Ritualized Maintenance

Formalized maintenance rituals focused specially on dugongs have not been recorded anthropologically amongst Torres Strait Islanders and their Kiwai neighbours of coastal Papua New Guinea to the immediate northeast (McNiven & Feldman 2003: 176). In contrast, anthropologists have recorded a variety of dugong maintenance rituals used by Aboriginal peoples of northeastern Australia. Government Protector and anthropologist Walter Roth (1903: 27) recorded that Princess Charlotte Bay Aboriginal people knew that 'if the bones or skulls of the dugong be not put away in a heap or otherwise preserved, no more will be caught. Some of these bone-heaps are of comparatively large size: on the other hand, I have seen dugong skulls hidden singly under bushes on Flinders Island' (Roth 1903: 27). In the same region, anthropologist Norman Tindale recorded 'dugong increase charm[s]' in the form of dugong bone 'heaps' on the islands and mainland of Princess Charlotte Bay. Some of the piles contained 'only one or two animals' but one large example was 'six feet in length, three feet in width, and about three feet in height' and contained 'all the major bones' of the dugong (Hale & Tindale 1933: 92–93). To the immediate north, Thomson (1934: 252) was informed by the Koko Yao (Kuuku Ya'u) people of a ceremony 'for the purpose of increasing the number of dugong' that took place at the 'dugong totem centre' featuring a special 'dugong stone' (see also Rigsby & Chase 1998: 207). Men of the dugong clan walk around the stone, 'striking' it with bunches of leaves and uttering '*Ampimbo! Ampi'! Ampi'! Ampi'!* (You come plenty! Come plenty! Come plenty! Come plenty!)' (Thomson 1933: 501, 1934: 252). The ritual was performed when 'people noticed a falling off in the number of dugong' (Thomson 1933: 501).

Anthropologist John Bradley (1991: 102–104) recorded that the Mara and Yanyuwa peoples of the Gulf of Carpentaria (southwest of Cape York Peninsula) perform 'dugong increase rituals' at a special dugong cosmological site (known as Wunubarryi) to send forth dugongs into the sea. The site consists of a 'herd' of male and female 'metamorphosed dugong' (quartzite boulders) and the maintenance ritual included striking or rubbing 'female dugongs' with hammerstones (see also Spencer & Gillen 1904: 313). Bradley (1997: 205) added that each 'fragment of rock that comes off a dugong stone . . . is a potential dugong'. The Yanyuwa also butcher a dugong on the water's edge with its head facing the sea 'to enable the spirit of the dugong to return to the sea' (Bradley 1991: 97). More specifically, the seaward-facing head relates to increasing the fecundity of sea grass (dugong food) which helps maintain dugong populations (John Bradley, pers. comm. 2020).

No archaeological research has focused explicitly on dugong maintenance sites in Australia or elsewhere in the world. Bradley (1991: 103) noted that a number of 'female dugongs' at the Wunubarryi site feature 'deep grooves and depressions in them indicating that the rites of increase are of some antiquity'. Archaeologist Monica Minnegal (1984a) undertook a faunal analysis of seven small dugong bone deposits at Princess Charlotte Bay from a butchering perspective. Site 6 stood out as different to the four 'initial butchering sites' and two 'consumption sites'. It consisted of a 'cache' of ribs and mandibles 'stacked in a heap', the purpose of which 'must remain a matter for speculation' (Minnegal 1984a: 70, 1984b: 19). No reference was made to Site 6 resembling bone 'heaps' associated with 'dugong increase' recorded ethnographically in the same area by Hale and Tindale (1933).

Ritualized Hunting

Comparatively little ethnographic information is available on dugong hunting rituals of Aboriginal peoples compared to Torres Strait Islanders. The Yolngu of Arnhem Land

(Northern Territory) visit a 'pile of coral representing Ngulmi Ngulmi', a 'spirit woman' located on the beach in Blue Mud Bay, and offer a lit cigarette or a small amount of food and 'call out the names of the animals they hope to catch, often prefaced by a cry "Brrr!"' in order 'to ensure a good hunt' for dugong and turtle (Barber 2005: A53). Yanyuwa hunters would insert into their ears water or specially prepared leaves to 'make the dugong deaf to the hunter's movements' (Bradley 1997: 326). After feasting on dugong, the Yanyuwa deposit all remains back into the ground oven pit for burning, knowing that 'failure to dispose of the bones correctly will result in a cessation of successful hunting' (Bradley 1991: 100, 1997: 314–315). The skull of the dugong ('deemed sacred') is usually thrown back into the sea or river (Bradley 1991: 100).

The Kuuku Ya'u of eastern Cape York Peninsula place much importance on dugongs, 'emphasized by a wealth of magic and ritual which is associated not only with its capture, but also with the subsequent disposal of every part of the animal' (Thomson 1934: 250). For example, after a meal of dugong the bones were collected and placed into water, where at intervals they were assembled into 'heaps' (Thomson 1934: 253). In at least one instance, hundreds of dugong bones were carefully arranged and placed on the grave of a *wataychi* (harpooner) with dugong skulls placed at the head of the grave, which was located 'on a low headland looking out to sea' (Thomson 1934: 254). Similar graves were visible along the coast up until the 1970s (Rigsby & Chase 1998: 207). Thomson (1934: 252) also recorded that ritual consumption of human calf muscles would 'give special prowess in dugong hunting'. To the immediate south, a grave marked by dugong bones was recorded on Flinders Island near Princess Charlotte Bay in the 1970s (Peter Sutton, pers. comm. 2020).

The material dimensions of hunting rituals in Torres Strait consisted of fixed sites and mobile 'charms' (see McNiven 2010 and McNiven & Feldman 2003 for detailed overviews). In terms of fixed sites, large trees ornamented with dugong bones and shells described as 'propitiatory offerings' to 'a spirit possessing the power of giving or withholding success in dugong hunting' were recorded in western and central Torres Strait (Gill 1876: 203, 302; see also Haddon 1935: 59). One of these tree shrines was located on Mabuyag at the coastal village of Dabangay, which was described by anthropologist Alfred Haddon as the totemic 'headquarters' of the island's dugong clan and the place where 'the magical ceremony took place, which had for its object the constraining of the dugong to come towards the island to be caught' (1904: 182). The body of the 'first dugong of the season' was placed on a bed of plants with ritual properties on the beach with its head facing inland to lure other dugongs towards the island (Haddon 1901: 134, 1904: 183). Graves of famous dugong hunters were also visited to enlist ancestral power to increase hunting success (Nietschmann & Nietschmann 1981: 61). Skulls of ancestors were also consulted to help bring luck in dugong hunting (Gill 1876: 302; Haddon 1935: 78). In this sense, rituals of dugong hunting were activated by what McNiven (2013a: 98) calls a 'dialogical matrix' involving the living (humans and dugongs) and the dead (humans and dugongs).

Dugong hunting 'charms' were manufactured by Torres Strait Islanders from wood, stone, or parts of dead dugong (Figure 37.1). These wood/stone 'charms' were finely

FIGURE 37.1. Top: *dhangal kula* (dugong stone) portable dugong hunting charm, Tudu, Central Torres Strait. Collected by Alfred C. Haddon in 1888. (L = 22 cm)

(© The Trustees of the British Museum oc,89 + .184).

Bottom: Wooden dugong hunting "charm" with cavity for placement of special substances. Collected by Alfred Haddon from Mabuyag in 1898. (L = 49 cm).

(© Reproduced by permission of Museum of Archaeology & Anthropology, Cambridge Z.9678.)

executed and realistic representations of dugongs and were clearly carved by people with detailed understanding of the form of dugongs, gained through extensive experience with observing, hunting, and butchering them. The form of these carvings suggests that a relationship existed between anatomical correctness and the ritual efficacy of carved 'charms'. Indeed, it is possible that both hunters and dugongs associated anatomical correctness of 'charms' with respect for dugongs, which enhanced communication between hunters and prey, and therefore enhanced hunting success.

Small carved wooden dugong effigies were used on Mabuyag in western Torres Strait and Mer in eastern Torres Strait (Haddon 1904: Pl. 16; 1908: 217, Pl. 20). In some cases the ritual efficacy of dugong charms was enhanced by an abdominal cavity into which was placed 'chewed' vegetal matter 'mixed with dugong grass, dugong fat, and red paint' (Haddon 1890: 352–353, 1904: Pl. 16). Haddon (1890: 352, 1908: 217) recorded that 'a wooden or stone image of a dugong' was hung from a hunting platform (erected over shallow water) 'to serve as a charm to ensure the approach of the animal' and to 'make him come straight'. One such charm from the island of Mua had attached the fibulae of the sorcery man who originally made the charm to 'greatly' increase its 'efficacy' (Haddon 1904: 338, Pl. 16; Moore 1984: 50). Charms were also made from the 'nose and anterior part of the face of a dead dugong' and the 'larynx and trachea . . . stuffed' with a range of plant products (including sea grass) so 'dugong he smell him, he come quick' (Haddon 1904: 338). On the island of Boigu in northern Torres Strait, 'dugong skulls were stuffed with plants and used' as hunting charms (Raven 1990: 140). Boigu also had a portable dugong stone (in the shape of a dugong) activated by a ritual specialist through the application of coconut oil, charcoal, and red ochre. Next to the stone were placed dugong bones (arranged in their 'correct order'), a post suspending a *damab* (dugong's trachea stuffed with flowers), and sea grass (dugong food). The operator could 'call up' dugongs out in the sea through song and by whispering into the ear of the dugong stone and orienting the stone in certain ways. Finally, the *damab* was placed on the hunting platform to 'waft the dugong towards the hunter' (Lawrie 1970: 236; Tobi 1991: 35). On Ugar in eastern Torres Strait is a stone with a carved face representing a dugong. The blood from the first dugong caught by a young man was poured over the stone to ensure that he 'would become a great dugong hunter like his father and his ancestors' (Teske 1987: 48–49). In recent times, Mua Islanders placed a small sachet of dugong meat in a dinghy such that it 'steered the dinghy straight to the dugong' (Manas, David, Manas, Ash, & Shnukal 2008: 396). In addition, Mua hunters ate dugong brain and trachea to bring them closer to dugongs. As Fr. John Manas explained: 'That throat pipe makes you see where the dugongs are, it leads you there, it calls you to there where they are. That throat pipe is a road, when you eat it you know that road. That throat pipe is *yabu* [road], it's the path taken by dugong' (Manas et al. 2008: 391).

McNiven (2010: 222) states that 'hunting charms in the form of dugong body parts gave hunters sensory access to the cognitive agency of dugongs through an ontology of shared and permeable personhood'. That is, 'an interpersonal cognitive and sensory consubstantiation was established and enabled that directed hunters towards dugongs and dugongs towards hunters' (McNiven 2010: 222). Furthermore, 'interpersonal dialogue between hunters and prey is founded upon an ontology of prey as kin and shared and permeable personhood ritually enhanced for the hunt and mediated by material culture' (McNiven 2010: 225–226).

The Kaurareg and Goemulgal of western Torres Strait placed dugong bones on graves similar to the Kuuku Ya'u of eastern Cape York Peninsula. For example, in 1791, Captain Edward Edwards observed a Kaurareg site on the island of Muralag in southwestern Torres Strait consisting of 'a heap of bones. There were amongst them two human skulls, the bones of some large animals [dugong], and some turtle-bones. They were heaped together in the form of a grave, and a very long paddle, supported at each end by a bifurcated branch of a tree, was laid horizontally alongside it' (Hamilton 1793: 121). In 1844, naturalist Joseph Beete Jukes (1847, I: 149–150) similarly recorded on Muralag a 'quite recent' mounded grave adorned with dugong skulls. In the early 1880s, naturalist Otto

Finsch counted at least sixty dugong skulls on a grave on the island of Mabuyag in central western Torres Strait (Howes 2015: 234).

Considerable archaeological research has taken place on dugong hunting rituals in Torres Strait. This research has been heavily informed by ethnographic information (see earlier) and has focused on large mounds of dugong bones. Ethnographic and historical information makes no link between dugong bone mounds and hunting rituals (Figure 37.2). Haddon (1912: 131–132) stated simply that 'dugong and turtle skulls and bones were formerly, and often still are, massed in heaps or placed in rows by the Western Islanders; this was done for ceremonial purposes . . ., or merely to keep count of the number of animals caught in any one season, in the latter case they were subsequently distributed and soon crumbled away'. Archaeologist Barbara Ghaleb made the first tentative links between archaeological mounds with high amounts of dugong bones and hunting rituals based on excavations at the ancestral village site of Goemu on the island of Mabuyag. Familiar with Haddon's ethnographies, Ghaleb (1990: 209, 363) surmised that the mounds were 'symbolically significant' and represented the 'loci of past ceremonial activity'. More specifically, Ghaleb (1990: 379) concluded that 'it seems conceivable' that the mounds 'may represent past "shrines" which symbolized some sort of power or magic (perhaps related to hunting, warfare, or to individual men?)' and that 'some of the features may have been related to burial practices, or to honouring the dead'.

Following excavation of dugong bone mounds on the islands of Tudu and Pulu, McNiven and Feldman (2003) made the formal link between archaeological mounds of

FIGURE 37.2. Ceremonial dugong bone mounds with ribs and skulls, Tudu, central Torres Strait, recorded by the Dumont d'Urville expedition in 1840 (Dumont d'Urville 1846: pl. 189). Originally described as a 'grave' by Dumont d'Urville, archaeological research across western and central Torres Strait indicates a functional association with dugong hunting rituals.

(© The Trustees of the British Museum.)

dugong bones and dugong 'hunting magic'. Of particular significance was the recovery of numerous disarticulated dugong ear bones (tympano-periotic complex) from the bone mounds (which consisted mostly of fragments of dugong ribs and skull bones). These ear bones had been purposefully and forcefully extracted from the robust skulls of dugong, leading McNiven to hypothesize a possible function as dugong hunting charms connected with the acute hearing of dugongs. Subsequent interviews with senior Torres Strait Islanders confirmed the ritual role of dugong ear bones in dugong hunting. Described variously as 'wireless bones' or 'radar bones', dugong hunters 'would "talk to bones" before a hunting expedition to assist communication with dugongs and help lure these animals towards a boat for harpooning' (McNiven & Feldman 2003: 186). Subsequent detailed analysis of dugong bone mounds on the island of Koey Ngurtai revealed purposeful extraction of ear bones from dugong skulls (Skelly, David, McNiven, & Barker 2011).

Twelve dugong bone mounds have been excavated to various degrees on six islands in western and central Torres Strait—Tudu (McNiven & Feldman 2003), Pulu (McNiven & Feldman 2003; McNiven, David, Goemulgau Kod, & Fitzpatrick 2009), Woeydhul (Wright et al. 2021), Mabuyag (McNiven & Bedingfield 2008; Urwin, McNiven, Clarke, Macquarie, & Whap 2016; Wright 2015; Wright et al. 2016), Koey Ngurtai (David et al. 2009; Skelly et al. 2011), and Zurath (Joe Crouch, pers. comm.). Dugong bone mounds have also been recorded on three other islands—Saibai (Teske 1988: 40) in northern Torres Strait, and Kuykusoegay (Redfruit Island) (Harris & Ghaleb-Kirby 2015: 293) and Maurura (Wednesday Island) (Haddon 1935: 66) in western Torres Strait. Radiocarbon dating suggests that the tradition of dugong bone mound elaboration commenced 400–500 years ago and was thus a recent development in the 9000-year human history of the region (David et al. 2004). Objects of 'European' origin throughout the Tudu bone mound (McNiven & Feldman 2003) and in the upper levels of the Dabangay bone mound on Mabuyag (McNiven & Bedingfield 2008) and one of the Koey Ngurtai bone mounds (David et al. 2009) indicate construction in the late nineteenth and early twentieth centuries. Such is the complexity of dugong bone mounds that an overarching explanation for their late development in Islander history has eluded archaeologists. The issue of complexity centres on the polyvalent quality of dugong bone mounds as expressions of the interrelated and in part overlapping domains of ritual power and social agency, totemic clan identity and social reproduction, and status and social inclusion. Understanding the historical emergence of dugong bone mounds requires teasing out the intersecting historical development of each of these three domains. Thus, we currently have the what and when but not the why.

In terms of *ritual power and social agency*, McNiven and Feldman (2003: 188) and McNiven (2010: 227) note that ear bones within dugong bone mounds had ongoing social agency by continuing to mediate dialogue between hunters and dugongs and attracting dugongs to hunters. Indeed, the 'ritual gravity' of a mound would gradually increase as the mound incrementally increased in size (McNiven & Feldman 2003: 188). The very large (9 × 13 × 1 m high) dugong bone mound at Dabangay on Mabuyag contains thousands of dugong ear bones and potentially the remains of 10,000–11,000 dugongs (McNiven & Bedingfield 2008). All dugong bone mounds are located strategically near the edge of the sea overlooking major dugong hunting areas. The formal act of curating the skeletal remains of dugongs would be seen by dugongs as fulfilling the moral contract of respect and reciprocity and contribute to the desire of dugongs to make themselves available to hunters.

In terms of *totemic clan identity and social reproduction*, McNiven et al. (2009) tie the development of the large communal ceremonial site complex (*kod*) on the sacred islet of Pulu with the establishment of a new totemic clan structure for the Goemulgal people on the adjacent residential island of Mabuyag. This *kod* site features two named dugong bone mounds linked directly with the moiety structure of the Goemulgal. Critically, the incremental accumulation of bone mounds with each dugong bone depositional event positioned these structures as 'work-in-progress' with ever-emergent qualities. McNiven et al. (2009) link this ever-emergent quality recursively with the ever-emergent quality of totemic clans. That is, the continued development of dugong bone mounds through time was positioned as an expression and legitimization of the continued reproduction of totemic clans by each generation. Bani (2004: 151) makes the point that Torres Strait totems are 'one of the main elements that hold the society together'. Thus, 'around 300–400 years ago the Goemulgal created the *kod* as a "structuring structure" and since that time the *kod* has continued to create and legitimize the Goemulgal through mutual emergence' (McNiven, David, Goemulgau Kod, & Fitzpatrick 2009: 314).

In terms of *status and social inclusion*, McNiven and Feldman (2003: 187) argue that a dugong bone mound had broader socially generative meaning 'beyond the sum of its parts'. That is, the physical structure of a mound was also an expression of the morally prescribed and sanctioned social structure of a community. Mound contents (i.e., dugong bones) were expressions of successfully organized and executed hunting expeditions and associated gendered power relations (McNiven & Feldman 2003: 188). Furthermore, the centralized discard of dugong bones on a mound gave emplaced material expression of the transformation of a successful dugong hunt (an exclusive adult male act associated with personal status) into a feast (an inclusive generational and gendered act associated with food sharing, community welfare, and solidarity) (McNiven & Feldman 2003: 188; see also Smith & Bliege Bird 2000). Dugong bone mounds thus 'articulate individual acts of hunting success with collective history and identity' (McNiven & Feldman 2003: 188). McNiven et al. (2009: 310) add that these mounds embody the Goemulgal 'collective memory' as 'structuring structures' that help formulate a sense of history for the Goemulgal (see also Bradley 2002).

Hunting Turtles

The most commonly hunted marine turtle by Indigenous Australians (of northern Australia) is the herbivorous green turtle (*Chelonia mydas*), which weighs up to 200 kg. Green turtles inhabit tropical and subtropical waters of northern Australia and continue to be an important and prestigious source of food for many coastal Indigenous communities (e.g., Bradley 1991; Johannes & MacFarlane 1991; McCarthy 1955; Mitchell 1996; Rouja 1998). The earliest known archaeological evidence for the hunting of marine turtles in Australia is 6000–7000 years (Dabangay, western Torres Strait), 7000 years (Border Island, central Queensland), and 7000–8000 years (Boodie Cave, Western Australia) (Barker 2004; Veth et al. 2017; Wright 2011). Green turtle is a major totem in Torres Strait, with important turtle rituals the responsibility of senior members of the turtle clan who know turtle to be kin (Haddon 1904: 154–156, 183–184). A similar agentive totemic relationship and ancestral spiritual kinship exists between numerous northern coastal Aboriginal peoples and marine turtles (e.g., Bradley 1991, 1997, 1998; Buku-Larrngay Mulka Centre 1999; Palmer 1984).

Ritualized Maintenance

The Bardi coastal people of northern Western Australia have terrestrial 'ritual places' that are 'used both as viewing platforms to observe turtles prior to hunting, and also as increase centres where rituals are performed to ensure an adequate supply' (Green 1988: 23). As with dugongs, most ethnographic information on turtle increase/maintenance sites is available for northeastern Australia. For example, Bradley (1997: 207–208) reports on three turtle maintenance sites of the Yanyuwa. All are located on islands of the Sir Edward Pellew Group and all were activated by ritual specialists brushing green foliage across certain rock formations. These ritual specialists have the power to activate these sites by maintaining a special relationship with turtles through a wide range of ceremonies. Appropriate treatment of turtle body parts after butchering and consumption was important in helping to maintain turtle populations as 'wrong disposal' was 'associated with a depletion in the number of turtles' (Bradley 1997: 321).

A series of Aboriginal stone cairns located on headlands around Cape York at the northeast tip of mainland Australia are associated with turtle increase/maintenance rituals. However, as with some dugong ritual sites, the boundary between turtle increase/maintenance rituals and hunting rituals is blurred and arbitrary for many of these Aboriginal sites. In 1848/49, naturalist John MacGillivray on the HMS *Rattlesnake* expedition visited Albany Rock (near Cape York) during the turtling season (October and November) and observed a stone cairn with turtle and human bones that was actively used by a 'turtling party to ensure success' (1852, II: 22). Artist Oswald Brierly, also on the HMS *Rattlesnake*, recorded that the Kaurareg/Gudang of southwestern Torres Strait and the adjacent mainland coast around Cape York constructed 'piles of stones and turtle heads at different points where they look out for turtle. They say that these heads will bring the other turtle about. They call these places *agoo* [*agu*]. There is one on Cape York Island—Wamalug' (cited in Moore 1979: 168, 226). Brierly recorded another active turtle shrine in the same area in the form of a stone cairn with turtle skulls, some painted with red ochre, and human bone, located on Tree Island (Moore 1979: 88–89). On the sandy island of Poruma in central Torres Strait was a *zogo* (ritual) shrine 'to ensure the abundance of turtle' in the form of a giant clam shell containing a 'globular black stone, *babat*' that was activated in November by the application of 'turtle oil' (Haddon 1935: 87). No other published ethnographic records are known for sites associated with turtle increase/maintenance across Torres Strait (McNiven 2016a: 204).

Ritualized Hunting

Most ethnographic records of turtle hunting rituals of Indigenous Australians focus on Torres Strait. Many of these rituals took place during the *surlal* or turtle breeding/hunting season (October and November) when turtles are frequently seen mating on the surface of the sea.[1] As with dugong hunting rituals, rituals of turtle hunting involved portable items (e.g., charms) and emplaced shrines. In terms of charms, the Kaurareg Aboriginal people of southwestern Torres Strait attached a 'magic bundle' (*marki mabaar* or *mabaaroub*) to the bow of a canoe and said to it in a 'supplicatory tone . . . "Friend, send turtle floating near for us"' (Brierly 1849 cited in Moore 1979: 184). The Gudang Aboriginal people of the adjacent coast of Cape York rubbed the 'eye' of a stone representing a turtle, located on Peak Point near Evans Bay, to bring 'good luck' in turtle hunting (McIntyre-Tamwoy & Harrison 2004: 37). Further to the north on Mabuyag in central western Torres Strait, ritual preparations for turtle hunting included applying and attaching spiritually charged plant products to canoe hulls. Outside of *surlal* season, 'the head, oesophagus and probably trachea of a turtle stuffed with [special plant products] . . . were fixed in the bow of the canoe . . . to prevent the turtles from sinking' (Haddon 1904: 330). On returning to Mabuyag, the carapaces of butchered turtles were placed in a row on a long wooden platform (*agu*) from which were suspended large bullroarers (*bigu*). *Bigu* were swung over canoes before setting out on a turtle hunt, taken in canoes during the hunt, and swung over the *agu* upon returning from the hunt (Haddon 1904: 331–333). Other turtle hunting charms used by Torres Strait Islanders included a small wooden effigy of a turtle attached to the bow of a canoe by Tudu Islanders of central Torres Strait (Haddon 1904: 333, Pl. 16).

Turtle hunting shrines are known in the western Torres Strait (Mabuyag and Pulu), central Torres Strait (Warraber, Iama, Naghir, and Masig), and northern Torres Strait (Dauan). A *wiwai* turtle hunting shrine was located at the ancestral village site of Goemu on Mabuyag. The shrine featured a large spherical granite boulder (circumference = 152 cm) surrounded by three small stone columns. Rituals at the *wiwai* shrine during the *surlal* season were 'to ensure success in catching turtle' (Haddon 1904: 334–336). The Goemulgal also performed a turtle hunting ritual at the ceremonial site complex (*kod*) on Pulu using a waterspout pole (see later) (Haddon 1904: 333–334). On the sandy island of Warraber, a shrine consisting of 'a block of introduced stone, *bau*' was used 'as part of a cult for ensuring success in turtle hunting' (Haddon 1935: 86–87, 361). On Iama was a *wiwai* stone associated with rituals for catching turtles (Haddon 1904: 335, 1935: 353, 360). A large stone was also associated with the turtle hunting shrine on Naghir (see later) (Haddon 1935: 69). Turtle shrines featuring turtle carapace and/or skulls, probably related to turtle hunting rituals, were recorded on Naghir (see later), Masig (Haddon 1935: 92–93), and Dauan (see later).

Turtle hunting shrines are documented also in eastern Torres Strait on the Murray Islands (Mer, Dauar, and Waier) and to the north on Erub. A portable turtle stone (in the shape of a turtle's head) known as *nam kerem* (turtle head) is on Erub and with ritual application of 'oil' (turtle oil?) and recitation of 'special words' it brings turtles to the island (Teske n.d.: 46–47). The *nam kerem* was taken by Murray Islanders to Mer but has since been returned to Erub (Teske n.d.: 46). The *buz nam zogo* on Mer consisted of effigies of a male and female turtle and was 'effective in helping men to catch turtle' (Haddon 1935: 154; see also Haddon 1908: 46–52). The *nam zogo* at Giar pit on Dauar consisted of a basket containing 'three effigies of the heads of turtle, one male, two female'. The heads were anointed with turtle oil and placed on a board looking out to sea where they would attract turtles and 'ensure successful turtle hunting' (Haddon 1935: 155–156). A *zogo* stone on Waier in the form of a 'black stone representing a man' (*waipĕm*) was given food offerings to provide 'plenty turtle' for hunters (Haddon 1908: 216, 1935: 158; see also Hunt 1899: 8). Haddon (1935: 158) concluded that 'the ritual of the *zogo* ensures an abundance of turtle', thus blurring the boundary between rituals of maintenance and rituals of hunting.

As with dugong hunting, 'success in catching turtle depended on the help of the spirits of deceased men, especially those of former successful hunters' (Haddon 1935: 69). A remarkable shrine expressing this relationship was recorded by the HMS *Rattlesnake* expedition when it visited the island of Naghir in December 1849 (Figure 37.3). The shrine featured a 'large smooth stone painted red and black, and partly embedded in the earth, and beside it were some painted human leg and arm bones, shells and other ornaments' (MacGillivray 1852, II: 37). Immediately behind, 'ten human skulls—of former members of the tribe, as we were informed—were arranged upon a plank raised on stones a foot or so from the ground' (MacGillivray 1852, II: 36). Backing the human skulls 'some thirty

FIGURE 37.3. Turtle hunting shrine, Naghir, central Torres Strait. Drawing by Oswald Brierly, 4 December 1849, during the HMS *Rattlesnake* expedition. Front row of human skulls backed by multiple rows of turtle skulls.

(Courtesy: Mitchell Library, State Library of New South Wales, PXA510 054.)

or forty skulls of turtle were arranged on the ground in several rows forming a triangle' (MacGillivray 1852, II: 37). In late November, at the end of the turtle season in 1875, explorer Luigi D'Albertis visited Dauan in northern Torres Strait and counted sixty-five turtle carapaces and rotting turtle 'eggs and entrails' at a shrine house that contained 'bones and skulls' of turtles, along with skulls painted with red ochre of 'two famous turtle-hunters, held in great veneration'. The turtle shells were aligned in a row extending from the shrine to the beach, reminiscent of *agu* on Mabuyag (1880, II: 7–8, 210; see also Haddon 1904: 333).

The dead were also invoked for turtle (and dugong) hunting through an association with waterspouts, which are created and used by the dead (*markai*) to 'spear and suck up turtle and dugong' (Haddon 1935: 354). Wooden effigies of waterspouts were used in turtle hunting ceremonies. They took the form of either a pole or board and featured relief carvings of human faces probably representing *markai* (Haddon 1935: 354). For example, a waterspout pole (*baiu*) was placed in the ground next to the *bau* stone on Warraber (Haddon 1935: 86–87, 354). On the beach at Giar pit on Dauar, two 3–3.4 m-long waterspout boards (*zogo baur*), representing male and female, were placed into the ground on either side of the neck of a freshly caught turtle (Haddon 1908: 214–216). Adorning the two boards were relief carved faces; human bones (ribs, clavicles, fibulae, and especially pelvic bones) and shells, all painted with red ochre; dog tooth necklaces, and cassowary and bird-of-paradise feathers, all imported from New Guinea (Haddon 1908: 216). At the ceremonial *kod* site on Pulu during the *surlal* season, a *baiu* (3–4.5 m long) with a carved human face was erected and from it were suspended two elaborately carved boards (1.5 m long), while around the base were placed 'recently caught turtles and dugongs' (Haddon 1904: 333–334).

Of the little archaeological research undertaken on sites associated with rituals of turtle hunting in Australia, all has focused on the Torres Strait region. In 1984, archaeologists David Harris and Barbara Ghaleb-Kirby (2015: 297–299) excavated a small mounded midden feature (Mound No. 52) at Goemu on Mabuyag. To their surprise the mound contained a series of cylindrical stones identical in form to those seen in an 1898 photograph taken by Haddon of the *wiwai* turtle hunting shrine (see earlier). The spherical granite stone in the photo was missing from the excavated site but was identified resting at the steps of St Mary's church on Mabuyag. The excavated 'midden' deposit contained bones of turtle, dugong, and fish; shells; angular fragments of rock; hammerstones, and an ovoid-shaped piece of coral. In 2007, archaeologist Susan McIntyre-Tamwoy (2011: 22–23) excavated a midden deposit associated with an *agu* stone arrangement (see earlier) on Tree Islet (Moebunum) located off the tip of Cape York. The shallow deposit consisted of densely packed turtle bone and a few shells. Two turtle bone samples produced radiocarbon dates of modern (past fifty years) and 470–280 cal BP, suggesting use up to c. 400 years ago and continuing through to recent times. Numerous other stone arrangements on the adjacent mainland at Evans Point were identified as *agu*, suggesting that the headland 'may have functioned as an important turtle increase centre' (McIntyre-Tamwoy 2011: 22; see also McIntyre-Tamwoy & Harrison 2004). Archaeologist Shelley Greer and colleagues (2011: 6) added that 'while we do not currently have a fine-grained understanding of the way that these sites are related to one another in time, we believe that this pattern of sites could be at least 500–1000 years old'.

CONCLUSION

Australian archaeological research on rituals associated with increase/maintenance and hunting of dugongs and turtles provides a rare and special opportunity to explore Indigenous ontologies. This opportunity centres on close working relationships with contemporary Indigenous communities and rich ethnographic records. Developing relationships with Indigenous communities provides opportunities for mutual development of new understandings of the form and ontological context of ritual sites. For archaeologists, new understandings not only help fill in gaps in the available ethnographic record but also allow development of innovative conceptual frameworks to understand the spiritual and ritual dimensions of past lives. For Indigenous peoples, new research insights often allow better understanding of the enduring materiality of past rituals and the potential of archaeological remains to provide historical insights into the ritual practices of their ancestors. As such, collaborative research partnerships allow creation of research projects of meaning and relevance to contemporary Indigenous communities.

Archaeologies of increase/maintenance/hunting rituals are examples of the recursive relationship between anthropology and archaeology whereby anthropological information informs archaeological insights and archaeological information informs anthropological insights. For archaeology, this recursive relationship moves beyond the issue of simple ethnographic analogy, as anthropological information is not taken at face value but reviewed critically through the lens of archaeological information. Furthermore, use of ethnographic texts is filtered through contemporary Indigenous communities who are in a position to undertake their own critical assessment of the validity of these texts. The final result is an understanding of the past that expresses the fruits of a critical analysis and synthesis of both ethnographic and archaeological information. This process enriches both contemporary Indigenous oral histories and the archaeological research process and results. Anthropologically informed archaeological research produces richer understandings of Indigenous pasts, beyond the reach of standard material readings of the past. Critically, these new understandings encompass ontologies other than the researchers' that not only increase the scope and capacity of archaeology to understand past peoples and their worldviews but also resonate more meaningfully with contemporary Indigenous epistemologies.

In an Australian context, archaeological research on rituals of hunting have focused on Torres Strait with little uptake of the associated theoretical concepts and approaches to mainland Australia, despite a diverse and rich ethnography on the topic. It is for this reason that the Torres Strait research, especially that on rituals of dugong hunting, has developed in something of a local theoretical vacuum. In its stead, this research has engaged theoretically with international literature on the anthropology and archaeology of rituals of hunting, much of which is dominated by Arctic and sub-Arctic studies. The paucity of theoretical interest in exploring issues of relational ontologies and epistemology associated with rituals of increase/maintenance and hunting in Australia beyond Torres Strait represents a lost opportunity, particularly given the availability of relevant ethnographic records.

Limited interest in exploring the archaeology of rituals of increase/maintenance/hunting in Australia beyond Torres Strait also has important ethical and moral dimensions. Avoiding or under-representing the ontological and epistemological dimensions of such rituals and past Indigenous kin-centric relationships with animals colonizes Indigenous pasts with Western dualisms, secularism, and anthropocentrism (Boyd 2017; McNiven 2016b: 35). As David (2006: 65) notes cogently, 'To understand the past meaningfulness of things requires situating objects in past worldviews'. The Australian archaeological profession needs to broaden its intellectual gaze to explore the ontological dimensions of human–animal relationships as expressed through rituals of increase/maintenance and hunting, and this has implications also for how to understand the place of nonritual, 'domestic' sites in the broader landscape (see McNiven 2013b; McNiven & Wright 2008). While many regions of Australia may not have the ethnographic detail that is available for Torres Strait, the Torres Strait archaeological literature provides conceptual and analytical clues on how archaeologies of increase/maintenance/hunting rituals can be explored and expanded in other cultural contexts.

ACKNOWLEDGMENTS

Thanks to Joe Crouch for unpublished information on dugong bone mound excavations. I thank John Bradley for many conversations over the years on the ontology and epistemology of Australian Aboriginal dugong and turtle hunting rituals, and for helpful comments on an earlier draft of this chapter. Thanks also to Peter Sutton for insightful comments that improved the chapter. All remaining errors of fact or interpretation are my own.

NOTE

1. Mating turtles are also referred to as 'turtlefast' (i.e., 'turtles fastened together'—Johannes & MacFarlane 1991: 54) and *totol pas* (*totol* = turtle, *pas* = 'to stick' or 'get stuck', in Torres Strait creole—Shnukal 1998: 178, 216).

REFERENCES

Äikäs, T., Puputti, A. K., Núñez, M., Aspi, J., & Okkonen, J. (2009). Sacred and profane livelihood: Animal bones from Sieidi sites in Northern Finland. *Norwegian Archaeological Review, 42*(2), 109–122.

Alberti, B. (2016). Archaeologies of ontology. *Annual Review of Anthropology, 45*, 163–179.

Anderson, K. (1997). A walk on the wild side: A critical geography of domestication. *Progress in Human Geography, 21*(4), 463–485.

Anderson, D. G. (2000). *Identity and ecology in Arctic Siberia: The number one reindeer brigade.* Oxford: Oxford University Press.

Armstrong Oma, K. (2010). Between trust and domination: Social contracts between humans and animals. *World Archaeology, 42*(2), 175–187.

Ballard, C. (1998). The sun by night: Huli moral topography and myths of a time of darkness. In L. R. Goldman & C. Ballard (Eds.), *Fluid ontologies: Myth, ritual and philosophy in the Highlands of Papua New Guinea* (pp. 66–85). Westport: Bergin & Garvey.

Bani, E. (2004). What is a totem? In R. Davis (Ed.), *Woven histories, dancing lives: Torres Strait Islander identity, culture and history* (p. 151). Canberra: Aboriginal Studies Press.

Barber, M. (2005). *Where the clouds stand: Australian Aboriginal relationships to water, place, and the marine environment in Blue Mud Bay, Northern Territory* (PhD thesis). Australian National University, Canberra.

Barker, B. C. (2004). *The sea people: Late Holocene maritime specialisation in the Whitsunday Islands, Central Queensland.* Terra Australis 20. Canberra: Research School of Pacific & Asian Studies, Australian National University Press.

Berkes, F. (2008). *Sacred ecology* (2nd ed.). New York: Routledge.

Bird-David, N. (1999). "Animism" revisited: Personhood, environment, and relational epistemology. *Current Anthropology, 40*(S1), S67–S91.

Boyd, B. (2017). Archaeology and human–animal relations: Thinking through anthropocentrism. *Annual Review of Anthropology, 46*, 299–316.

Bradley, J. J. (1991). 'Li-Maramaranja': Yanyuwa hunters of marine animals in the Sir Edward Pellew Group, Northern Territory. *Records of the South Australian Museum, 25*(1), 91–110.

Bradley, J. J. (1997). *Li-anthawirriyarra, people of the sea: Yanyuwa relations with their maritime environment* (PhD thesis). Northern Territory University, Darwin.

Bradley, J. (1998). 'We always look north': Yanyuwa identity and the marine environment. In N. Peterson & B. Rigsby (Eds.), *Customary marine tenure in Australia* (pp. 125–141). Oceania Monograph 48. Sydney: University of Sydney, Oceania Publications.

Bradley, R. (2002). *The past in prehistoric societies.* London: Routledge.

Brightman, R. (1993). *Grateful prey: Rock Cree human-animal relationships.* Regina: Canadian Plains Research Centre, University of Regina.

Brown, M. F. (1984). The role of words in Aguaruna hunting magic. *American Ethnologist, 11*(3), 545–558.

Buku-Larrngay Mulka Centre. (1999). *Saltwater people: Yirrkala bark paintings of sea country. Recognising Indigenous sea rights.* Buku-Larrngay Mulka Centre in association with Jennifer Isaacs Publishing.

Carneiro, R. L. (1970). Hunting and hunting magic among the Amahuaca of the Peruvian Montaña. *Ethnology, 9*(4), 331–341.

Collingwood, R. G. (1945). *The idea of nature.* Oxford: Clarendon Press.

Cottingham, J. (2018). General introduction: The Meditations and Cartesian philosophy. In J. Cottingham (Ed.), *René Descartes. Meditations on First Philosophy with selections from the Objections and Replies* (pp. xix–xliv). Cambridge: Cambridge University Press.

Crouch, J., McNiven, I. J., David, B., Rowe, C., & Weisler, M. (2007). Berberass: Marine resource specialisation and environmental change in Torres Strait over the past 4000 years. *Archaeology in Oceania, 42*(2), 49–64.

D'Albertis, L. M. (1880). *New Guinea: What I did and what I saw.* 2 vols. London: Sampson Low, Marston, Searle, & Rivington.

David, B. (2006). Archaeology and the Dreaming: Toward an archaeology of ontology. In I. Lilley (Ed.), *Archaeology of Oceania: Australia and the Pacific Islands* (pp. 48–68). Carlton, Victoria: Blackwell.

David, B., McNiven, I. J., Mitchell, R., Orr, M., Haberle, S., Brady, L., & Crouch, J. (2004). Badu 15 and the Papuan-Austronesian settlement of Torres Strait. *Archaeology in Oceania*, 39(2), 65–78.

David, B., McNiven, I. J., Crouch, J., Mura Badulgal Corporation Committee, Skelly, R., Barker, B., . . . Hewitt, G. (2009). Koey Ngurtai: The emergence of a ritual domain in Western Torres Strait. *Archaeology in Oceania*, 44(1), 1–17.

Descola, P. (2013). *Beyond nature and culture.* Chicago: The University of Chicago Press.

Dumont d'Urville, J. (1846). *Voyage au Pole Sud et dans l'Oceanie. Atlas pittoresque* (Vol. 2). Paris: Gide et J. Baudry.

Eley, T. F. Jr. (1988). *Hunters of the reefs: The marine geography of the Kiwai, Papua New Guinea* (PhD thesis). University of California, Berkeley.

Elkin, A. P. (1981). *The Australian Aborigines.* London: Angus & Robertson.

Emery, K. F., & Brown, L. A. (2012). Maya hunting sustainability: Perspectives from past and present. In R. J. Chacon & R. G. Mendoza (Eds.), *The ethics of anthropology and Amerindian research: Reporting on environmental degradation and warfare* (pp. 79–116). New York: Springer.

Fienup-Riordan, A. (1990). The bird and the bladder: The cosmology of Central Yup'ik seal hunting. *Études Inuit Studies*, 14(1–2), 23–38.

Frazer, J. G. (1911). *The golden bough: A study in magic and religion. Part 1: The magic art and the evolution of kings* (Vol. 1, 3rd ed.). London: Macmillan.

Freikman, M., & Garfinkel, Y. (2009). The zoomorphic figurines from Sha'ar Hagolan: Hunting magic practices in the Neolithic Near East. *Levant*, 41(1), 5–17.

Gadamus, L., & Raymond-Yakoubian, J. (2015). A Bering Strait indigenous framework for resource management: Respectful seal and walrus hunting. *Arctic Anthropology*, 52(2), 87–101.

Ghaleb, B. (1990). *An ethnoarchaeological study of Mabuiag Island, Torres Strait, northern Australia* (PhD thesis). University College London, London.

Gill, W. W. (1876). *Life in the Southern Isles.* London: The Religious Tract Society.

Green, N. (1988). Aboriginal affiliations with the sea in Western Australia. In F. Gray & L. Zann (Eds.), *Traditional knowledge of the marine environment in northern Australia* (pp. 19–29). Townville: Great Barrier Reef Marine Park Authority.

Greenwood, S. (2009). *The anthropology of magic.* Oxford: Berg.

Greer, S., McIntyre-Tamwoy, S., & Henry, R. (2011). Sentinel sites in a cosmo-political seascape. In *ISIC 7-2011 7th International Small Islands Conference*, *12–15 June 2011, Airlie Beach, QLD, Australia.* http://sicri-network.org/.

Haddon, A. C. (1890). The ethnography of the western tribes of Torres Straits. *Journal of the Anthropological Institute of Great Britain and Ireland*, 19, 297–446.

Haddon, A. C. (1901). *Head-hunters: Black, white and brown.* London: Methuen.

Haddon, A. C. (Ed.) (1904). *Reports of the Cambridge Anthropological Expedition to Torres Straits. Vol. V. Sociology, magic and religion of the Western Islanders.* Cambridge: Cambridge University Press.

Haddon, A. C. (Ed.) (1908). *Reports of the Cambridge Anthropological Expedition to Torres Straits. Vol. VI. Sociology, magic and religion of the Eastern Islanders.* Cambridge: Cambridge University Press.

Haddon, A. C. (Ed.) (1912). *Reports of the Cambridge Anthropological Expedition to Torres Straits. Vol. IV. Arts and crafts.* Cambridge: Cambridge University Press.

Haddon, A. C. (1935). *Reports of the Cambridge Anthropological Expedition to Torres Straits. Vol. I. General ethnography.* Cambridge: Cambridge University Press.

Hale, H. M., & Tindale, N. B. (1933). Aborigines of Princess Charlotte Bay, North Queensland. *Records of the South Australian Museum, 5*(1), 63–116.

Hallowell, A. I. (1926). Bear ceremonialism in the northern hemisphere. *American Anthropologist, 18*(1), 1–175.

Hallowell, A. I. (1960). Ojibwa ontology, behavior and world view. In S. Diamond (Ed.), *Culture in history: Essays in honor of Paul Radin* (pp. 19–52). New York: Columbia University Press.

Hamilton, G. (1793). *A voyage round the world in His Majesty's frigate Pandora, performed under the direction of Captain Edwards in the years 1790, 1791, and 1792.* Berwick: W. Phorson.

Harris, D. R., & Ghaleb-Kirby, B. (2015). Mabuyag (Torres Strait) in the mid-1980s: Archaeological reconnaissance of the island and midden excavations at Goemu. *Memoirs of the Queensland Museum–Culture, 8*(2), 283–375.

Harvey, G. (2006). *Animism: Respecting the living world.* New York: Columbia University Press.

Haworth, R. J., Baker, R. G. V., & Flood, P. J. (2004). A 6000 year-old fossil dugong from Botany Bay: Inferences about changes in Sydney's climate, sea levels and waterways. *Australian Geographical Studies, 42*(1), 46–59.

Henry, J. (2004). Metaphysics and the origins of modern science: Descartes and the importance of laws of nature. *Early Science and Medicine, 9*(2), 73–114.

Hill, E. (2011). Animals as agents: Hunting ritual and relational ontologies in prehistoric Alaska and Chukotka. *Cambridge Archaeological Journal, 21*(3), 407–426.

Hill, E. (2018). Personhood and agency in Eskimo interactions with the other-than-human. In E. Harrison-Buck & J. A. Hendon (Eds.), *Relational identities and other-than-human agency in archaeology* (pp. 29–50). Denver: University of Colorado Press.

Howes, H. (2015). Between wealth and poverty: Otto Finsch on Mabuyag, 1881. *Memoirs of the Queensland Museum–Culture, 8*(1), 221–251.

Hunt, A. E. (1899). Ethnographical notes on the Murray Islands, Torres Straits. *The Journal of the Anthropological Institute of Great Britain and Ireland, 28*(1/2), 5–19.

Ingold, T. (2000). *The perception of the environment: Essays on livelihood, dwelling and skill.* London: Routledge.

Johannes, R. E., & MacFarlane, J. W. (1991). *Traditional fishing in the Torres Strait Islands.* Hobart: CSIRO Division of Fisheries.

Jukes, J. B. (1847). *Narrative of the surveying voyage of H.M.S. Fly.* 2 vols. London: T. & W. Boone.

Kearney, A., Bradley, J., & Brady, L. M. (2019). Kincentric ecology, species maintenance and the relational power of place in northern Australia. *Oceania, 89*(3), 316–335.

Keyser, J. D. & Whitley, D. S. (2006). Sympathetic magic in western North American rock art. *American Antiquity, 71*(1), 3–26.

Kohn, E. (2013). *How forests think: Toward an anthropology beyond the human.* Berkeley: University of California Press.

Landtman, G. (1927). *The Kiwai Papuans of British New Guinea.* London: Macmillan.

Latour, B. (1993). *We have never been modern.* Cambridge, MA: Harvard University Press.

Lawrie, M. (1970). *Myths and legends of Torres Strait.* St. Lucia: University of Queensland Press.

Lowenstein, T. (1994). *Ancient lands, sacred whales: The Inuit hunt and its rituals.* New York: Farrar, Straus & Giroux.

MacGillivray, J. (1852). *Narrative of the voyage of H.M.S. Rattlesnake*. 2 vols. London: T. & W. Boone.

Manas, J., David, B., Manas, L., Ash, J., & Shnukal, A. (2008). An interview with Fr John Manas. *Memoirs of the Queensland Museum Cultural Heritage Series*, 4(2), 385–418.

Marsh, H., O'Shea, T. J., & Reynolds, J. E. (2011). *Ecology and conservation of the Sirenia: Dugongs and manatees*. Cambridge: Cambridge University Press.

McCarthy, F. D. (1955). Aboriginal turtle hunters. *Australian Museum Magazine*, 11(9), 283–288.

McGranaghan, M., & Challis, S. (2016). Reconfiguring hunting magic: Southern Bushman (San) perspectives on taming and their implications for understanding rock art. *Cambridge Archaeological Journal*, 26(4), 579–599.

McIntyre-Tamwoy, S. (2011). Hunting magic, maintenance ceremonies and increase sites: Exploring traditional management systems for marine resources in Northern Cape York Peninsula. *Historic Environment*, 23(2), 19–25.

McIntyre-Tamwoy, S., & Harrison, R. (2004). Monuments to colonialism? Stone arrangements, tourist cairns and turtle magic at Evans Bay, Cape York. *Australian Archaeology*, 59(1), 31–42.

McNiven, I. J. (2004). Saltwater people: Spiritscapes, maritime rituals and the archaeology of Australian indigenous seascapes. *World Archaeology*, 35(3), 329–349.

McNiven, I. J. (2008). Sentient sea: Seascapes as spiritscapes. In B. David & J. Thomas (Eds.), *Handbook of landscape archaeology* (pp. 149–157). Walnut Creek, CA: Left Coast Press.

McNiven, I. J. (2010). Navigating the human-animal divide: Marine mammal hunters and rituals of sensory allurement. *World Archaeology*, 42(2), 215–230.

McNiven, I. J. (2013a). Between the living and the dead: Relational ontologies and the ritual dimensions of dugong hunting across Torres Strait. In C. Watts (Ed.), *Archaeologies of relationality: Humans, animals, things* (pp. 97–116). London: Routledge.

McNiven, I. J. (2013b). Ritualized middening practices. *Journal of Archaeological Method and Theory*, 20(4), 552–587.

McNiven, I. J. (2016a). Increase rituals and environmental variability on small residential islands of Torres Strait. *Journal of Island and Coastal Archaeology*, 11(2), 195–210.

McNiven, I. J. (2016b). Theoretical challenges of Indigenous archaeology: Setting an agenda. *American Antiquity*, 81(1), 27–41.

McNiven, I. J., & Bedingfield, A. C. (2008). Past and present marine mammal hunting rates and abundances: Dugong (*Dugong dugon*) evidence from Dabangai Bone Mound, Torres Strait. *Journal of Archaeological Science*, 35(2), 505–515.

McNiven, I. J., & Feldman, R. (2003). Ritually orchestrated seascapes: Hunting magic and dugong bone mounds in Torres Strait, NE Australia. *Cambridge Archaeological Journal*, 13(2), 169–194.

McNiven, I. J., & Wright, D. (2008). Ritualised marine midden formation in western Zenadh Kes (Torres Strait). In G. Clark, F. Leach, & S. O'Connor (Eds.), *Islands of inquiry: Colonisation, seafaring and the archaeology of maritime landscapes* (pp. 133–147). Terra Australis 29. Canberra: ANU ePress.

McNiven, I. J., David, B., Goemulgau Kod, & Fitzpatrick, J. (2009). The great *kod* of Pulu: Mutual historical emergence of ceremonial sites and social groups in Torres Strait, NE Australia. *Cambridge Archaeological Journal*, 19(3), 291–317.

Meggitt, M. J. (1962). *Desert people: A study of the Walbiri Aborigines of Central Australia*. London: Angus & Robertson.

Memmott, P., & Trigger, D. (1998). Marine tenure in the Wellesley Islands region, Gulf of Carpentaria. In N. Peterson & B. Rigsby (Eds.), *Customary marine tenure in Australia* (pp. 109–124). Oceania Monograph 48. Sydney: University of Sydney, Oceania Publications.

Minnegal, M. (1984a). Dugong bones from Princess Charlotte Bay. *Australian Archaeology*, *18*, 63–71.

Minnegal, M. (1984b). A note on butchering dugong at Princess Charlotte Bay. *Australian Archaeology*, *19*, 15–20.

Mitchell, S. (1996). Dugongs and dugouts, sharptacks and shellbacks: Macassan contact and Aboriginal marine hunting on the Cobourg Peninsula, north western Arnhem Land. *Bulletin of the Indo-Pacific Prehistory Association*, *15*, 181–191.

Moore, D. R. (1979). *Islanders and Aborigines at Cape York*. Canberra: Australian Institute of Aboriginal Studies.

Moore, D. R. (1984). *The Torres Strait collections of A.C. Haddon*. London: British Museum Publications.

Morton, J. (1987). The effectiveness of totemism: "Increase ritual" and resource control in Central Australia. *Man*, *22*(3), 453–474.

Nadasdy, P. (2007). The gift in the animal: The ontology of hunting and human–animal sociality. *American Ethnologist*, *34*(1), 25–43.

Nietschmann, B., & Nietschmann, J. (1981). Good dugong, bad dugong; bad turtle, good turtle. *Natural History*, *90*(5), 54–63, 86–87.

Palmer, K. (1984). Ownership and use of the seas: The Yolngu of North-East Arnhem Land. *Anthropological Forum*, *5*(3), 448–455.

Pelly, D. F. (2001). *Sacred hunt: A portrait of the relationship between seals and Inuit*. Vancouver: Duncan & McIntyre.

Peterson, N. (2011). Is the Aboriginal landscape sentient? Animism, the New Animism and the Warlpiri. *Oceania*, *81*(2), 167–179.

Plumwood, V. (2003). Decolonizing relationships with nature. In W. M. Adams & M. Mulligan (Eds.), *Decolonizing nature: Strategies for conservation in a post-colonial era* (pp. 51–78). London: Earthscan.

Raven, M. M. (1990). *The point of no diminishing returns: Hunting and resource decline on Boigu Island, Torres Strait* (PhD thesis). University of California, Davis.

Rigsby, B., & Chase, A. (1998). The Sandbeach People and dugong hunters of eastern Cape York Peninsula: Property in land and sea country. In N. Peterson & B. Rigsby (Eds.), *Customary marine tenure in Australia* (pp. 192–218). Oceania Monograph 48. Sydney: University of Sydney, Oceania Publications.

Rose, D. B. (1996). *Nourishing terrains: Australian Aboriginal views of landscape and wilderness*. Canberra: Australian Heritage Commission.

Rose, D. B. (2001). Sacred site, ancestral clearing, and environmental ethics. In A. Rumsey & J. Weiner (Eds.), *Emplaced myth: Space, narrative, and knowledge in Aboriginal Australia and Papua New Guinea* (pp. 99–119). Honolulu: University of Hawaii Press.

Roth, W. E. (1903). *Superstition, magic, and medicine*. North Queensland Ethnography Bulletin No. 5. Brisbane: Government Printer.

Rouja, P. M. (1998). *Fishing for culture: Toward an Aboriginal theory of marine resource use among the Bardi Aborigines of One Arm Point, Western Australia* (PhD thesis). Durham University, Durham.

Salmón, E. (2000). Kincentric ecology: Indigenous perceptions of the human-nature relationship. *Ecological Applications*, *10*(5), 1327–1332.

Scott, C. (1989). Knowledge construction among Cree hunters: Metaphors and literal understanding. *Journal de la Société des Américanistes*, *75*, 193–208.

Shnukal, A. (1998). *Broken: An introduction to the creole language of Torres Strait*. Pacific Linguistics C-107. Canberra: Research School of Pacific and Asian Studies, The Australian National University.

Skelly, R., David, B., McNiven, I. J., & Barker, B. (2011). The ritual dugong bone mounds of Koey Ngurtai, Torres Strait, Australia: Investigating their construction. *International Journal of Osteoarchaeology, 21*(1), 32–54.

Smith, E. A., & Bliege Bird, R. L. (2000). Turtle hunting and tombstone opening: Public generosity as costly signalling. *Evolution and Human Behavior, 21*, 245–261.

Spencer, B., & Gillen, F. J. (1899). *The native tribes of Central Australia*. London: MacMillan & Co., Ltd.

Spencer, B., & Gillen, F. J. (1904). *The northern tribes of Central Australia*. London: MacMillan.

Stasch, R. (1996). Killing as reproductive agency. Dugong, pigs, and humanity among the Kiwai, circa 1900. *Anthropos, 91*(4/6), 359–379.

Swain, T. (1995). Part 1. Australia. In T. Swain & G. Trompf (Eds.), *The religions of Oceania* (pp. 17–118). London: Routledge.

Tambiah, S. J. (1990). *Magic, science, religion, and the scope of rationality*. Cambridge: Cambridge University Press.

Tanner, A. (1979). *Bringing home animals: Religious ideology and mode of production of the Mistassini Cree hunters*. London: E. Hurst.

Teske, T. (Ed.) (n.d.). *Darnley Island of Torres Strait*. Cairns: Far Northern Schools Development Unit.

Teske, T. (Ed.) (1987). *Stephens Island of Torres Strait*. Cairns: Far Northern Schools Development Unit.

Teske, T. (Ed.) (1988). *Saibai Island of Torres Strait*. Cairns: Far Northern Schools Development Unit.

Thomson, D. F. (1933). The hero cult, initiation and totemism on Cape York. *Royal Anthropological Institute Journal, 63*, 453–537.

Thomson, D. F. (1934). The dugong hunters of Cape York. *Royal Anthropological Institute Journal, 64*, 237–262.

Tobi, G. (1991). Dhugama's dugong stone. In Boigu Island Community Council (Eds.), *Boigu: Our history and culture* (pp. 35–36). Canberra: Aboriginal Studies Press.

Turpin, S. A. (1993). Hunting camps and hunting magic: Petroglyphs of the Eldorado divide, west Texas. *North American Archaeologist, 13*(4), 295–316.

Tylor, E. B. (1871). *Primitive culture: Researches into the development of mythology, philosophy, religion, art, and custom* (Vols. 1 & 2). London: John Murray.

Urwin, C., McNiven, I. J., Clarke, S., Macquarie, L., & Whap, T. (2016). Hearing the evidence: Using archaeological data to analyse the long-term impacts of dugong (*Dugong dugon*) hunting on Mabuyag, Torres Strait, over the past 1000 years. *Australian Archaeology, 82*(3), 201–217.

Veth, P., Ward, I., Manne, T., Ulm, S., Ditchfield, K., Dortch, J., . . . Kendrick, P. (2017). Early human occupation of a maritime desert, Barrow Island, North-West Australia. *Quaternary Science Reviews, 168*, 19–29.

Viveiros de Castro, E. (1998). Cosmological deixis and Amerindian perspectivism. *Journal of the Royal Anthropological Institute, 4*, 469–488.

Watts, C. (Ed.) (2013). *Archaeologies of relationality: Humans, animals, things*. London: Routledge.

Weitzenfeld, A., & Joy, M. (2014). An overview of anthropocentrism, humanism, and spe-ciesism in critical animal theory. In A. J. Nocella III, J. Sorenson, K. Socha, & A. Matsuka (Eds.), *Defining critical animal studies: An intersectional social justice approach for liberation* (pp. 3–27). New York: Peter Lang.

Willerslev, R. (2007). *Soul hunters: Hunting, animism, and personhood among the Siberian Yukaghirs*. Berkeley: University of California Press.

Wright, D. (2011). Mid-Holocene maritime economy in the Western Torres Strait. *Archaeology in Oceania, 46*(1), 23–27.

Wright, D. (2015). *The archaeology of community emergence and development on Mabuyag in the western Torres Strait*. BAR International Series 2754. Oxford: Archaeopress.

Wright, D., Samper Carro, S. C., Nejman, L., van der Kolk, G., Litster, M., Langley, M. C., . . . Repu, C. (2021). Archaeology of the Waiat mysteries on Woeydhul Island in Western Torres Strait. *Antiquity 95* (381), 791–811.

Wright, D., Stephenson, B., Taçon, P. S., Williams, R. N., Fogel, A., Sutton, S., & Ulm, S. (2016). Exploring ceremony: The archaeology of a men's meeting house ('kod') on Mabuyag, Western Torres Strait. *Cambridge Archaeological Journal, 26*(4), 721–740.

PART VIII

VISITORS AND COLONIZERS

CHAPTER 38

CROSS-CULTURAL INTERACTION ACROSS THE ARAFURA AND TIMOR SEAS

Aboriginal People and Macassans in Northern Australia

CHRIS URWIN, LYNETTE RUSSELL, AND LILY YULIANTI FARID

INTRODUCTION

THE 'Macassan'[1] fishers visited the northern Australian coastline annually to collect trepang (or *teripang* in Indonesian)—edible sea cucumbers (holothurians), also known as *bêche-de-mer*, or sea slugs. Leaving Makassar around December with the western monsoon, the fishers would work the trepang grounds of northern Australia until March or April when they would return home on the east trade winds (Chaloupka 1996; Earl 1846; Langton & Sloggett 2014: 8; Macknight 1976; Máñez & Ferse 2010). These fishers sailed their *praus* to the northern Australian coastal waters, spending time in Arnhem Land and the Gulf of Carpentaria (Northern Territory) and the Kimberley (Western Australia). From at least the 1700s onwards (until the closing of the industry in c. 1907), the trepang trade was controlled by the Macassans, working with other men from various Southeast Asian ports, and trading out of Makassar in Sulawesi. For the Macassans the Australian coastline was known as Kayu Jawa (Kimberley, Western Australia) and Marege' (Arnhem Land, Northern Territory) (Clark & May 2013: 1–2).

The processing of trepang involved collecting, boiling, drying, and then smoking, before storage and transport to Makassar. Archaeologically, Macassan trepang processing sites are most often identified by stone fireplaces, traces of smokehouses, and tamarind trees (*Tamarindus indica*) (Crawford 1969: 202–204; Macknight 1976: 61–82;

Morwood & Hobbs 1997). Other evidence of the industry includes Asian pottery sherds, glass, coins, metal fishhooks, clay smoking pipes, fragments of metal (Macknight 1976: 59, 78, 80–81; May, Wesley, Goldhahn, Lamilami, & Taçon 2021: 130), and burials (Theden-Ringl, Fenner, Wesley, & Lamilami 2011). The trepang trade was dependent on the Chinese market, and in addition to sea cucumbers the Macassan crews collected other trade goods, including turtle and pearl shell, ironwood, and beeswax (Clarke 2000; Clark & May 2013: 2; Howard 2009; Macknight 1976). These sustained trade activities over the centuries resulted in strong social and cultural relationships developing with local peoples, including with the Yolŋu of eastern Arnhem Land. According to Yolŋu oral tradition, when the Macassans arrived on the coast, they would look out for the fluttering of specific Aboriginal clan flags which would indicate that they had been granted permission to enter the clan estates (Corn & Marrett 2011: 75). This chapter draws on historical, oral traditional, and archaeological evidence to explore the timing, location, and nature of Aboriginal–Macassan interactions. After six decades of research, an increasingly nuanced picture is emerging of cross-cultural encounters on north Australian shores, in which Aboriginal people selectively engaged in exchange with Macassans and adopted maritime technologies which enabled new modes of coastal engagement. Research to date has focussed on the Arnhem Land region. We argue that sites in the Kimberley and Gulf of Carpentaria should be prioritized for future research, to understand how interaction varied across these regions.

INTERACTIONS BETWEEN MACASSANS AND ABORIGINAL PEOPLE IN NORTHERN AUSTRALIA: ORAL AND WRITTEN HISTORIES

The Macassans traded cloth, knives, sugar, tobacco, rice, and alcohol with Aboriginal peoples of coastal northern Australia. Relationships with Aboriginal clan groups were reciprocal and negotiated (Langton 2011). These reciprocal relationships included the trepangers taking some young Aboriginal men to Makassar where they stayed for extended periods (Lydon 2014). Socially, while stationed in Australia or Kayu Jawa/ Marege' as they knew it, the Macassans were included in ceremonies and made clan members. Borrow words or a mixed language developed, including among the Yolŋu of eastern Arnhem Land (Evans 1992: 46; Urry & Walsh 1981: 93). Aboriginal people adopted the dugout canoe and wooden tobacco pipes (Brady 2013). The depth of relationships between Yolŋu and Macassans has been well documented, and Yolŋu art, song, and stories continue to celebrate the connection over a century after the industry was closed (Bilous 2015a: 906–907; 2015b).

Yolŋu oral histories of Aboriginal-Macassan contact speak of light-skinned travellers from Asia who visited their lands prior to the trepangers. They call these people the

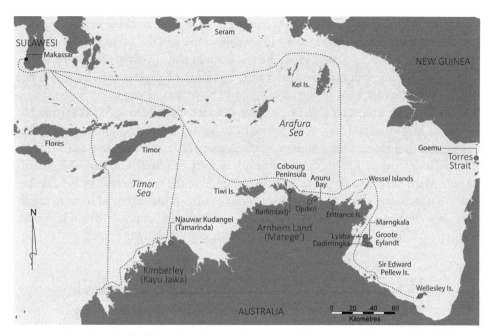

FIGURE 38.1. For details of sites from Groote Eylandt, see Clarke (1994: Figure 7.1). For Cobourg Peninsula sites, see Mitchell (1994: Figure 9-1). For the west Kimberley, see Crawford (1969: Map 1). Macknight (1976: Figure 2) provides details of known sites located between the Cobourg Peninsula in the west and the Sir Edward Pellew Islands in the east. Dashed lines indicate the approximate trajectories of Macassan seafaring to northern Australia.

(After Bulbeck & Rowley 2001: 56; Oertle et al. 2014: Figure 1).

Bayini. There has been much debate about the Bayini; Macknight (2008) states that this oral tradition is relatively recent and dates to Yolŋu visits to Makassar in the nineteenth century. Others have suggested that the Sama Bajau or Bajau Laut, colloquially known as the 'Sea Gypsies' or 'Sea Nomads' (Fox 1977: 460), were earlier visitors to the Northern Australian trepang grounds. Ian McIntosh (2011, 2013) argues that the identity of these pre-Macassans will always be an enigma, even though the Bayini feature extensively in Yolŋu cosmology (see also Clark & May 2013: 4–5). McIntosh (2011) suggests that until recently the identity of the Bayini was kept secret amongst the Yolŋu and was not discussed with outsiders (see also Bilous 2015a).

Much of the oral history research conducted on Macassan voyages to Marege' has been concerned with Aboriginal, especially Yolŋu, memories, narratives, and stories. This research only gives part of the story and focusses on the impact of cross-cultural interaction rather than the motivation or impetus for it. One of the earliest genealogical studies of Macassan trepangers was conducted in Makassar in 1977 by Darwin-based historian Peter Spillet, who collected family stories from a trepanger named Mangngellai Daeng Maro. Spillet compiled stories of Mangellai's great-grandfather,[2] who began to set sail to Australia around the time of the 1667–1669 war between the Vereenigde Oost-Indische

Compagnie (VOC)[3] and Makassar. According to Mangellai, working as trepangers in Australia was his family's main job for four generations, and the wartime story was vividly remembered by his family. When he was born in 1888, his father was in Australia, working and living with his Aboriginal wife. From his Aboriginal wife, his father had four children (Spillet 1988: 5). Regionally, the VOC-Makassar war led to increased instability. The VOC, together with Bugis allies, defeated the joint kingdoms of Gowa and Tallo near Makassar, and this prompted many to flee throughout Southeast Asia to find new economic opportunities (Andaya 1995: 3; Andaya & Andaya 2015: 213–214). This defeat, and its after-effects in the early eighteenth century, may well be linked with an early stage of Makassar's new explorations to the south, into the new shores and beaches beyond VOC's monopoly system. The oral histories, rock art research, and some of the archaeology can be seen to provide tentative support for an earlier phase of incipient trade occurring before establishment of the trepang industry proper in the 1700s.

WHEN AND WHERE DID ABORIGINAL PEOPLE AND MACASSANS INTERACT?

Investigations of trepang processing sites and other locations of Aboriginal–Macassan interaction commenced in the very earliest years of Australian archaeology (see May 2011; Urwin & Spriggs 2021). In the 1920s, W. Lloyd Warner (1932) excavated sites located near tamarind trees on Milingimbi (or Yurruwi) Island, and Tindale (1926) identified trepang processing sites on Groote Eylandt and the Gulf of Carpentaria (Figure 38.1). Anthropologists Ronald Berndt and Catherine Berndt (1947) collected exotic pottery found at Arnhem Land sites and recorded Aboriginal songs related to the items. On the 1948 American-Australian Expedition to Arnhem Land, Frederick McCarthy and Frank Setzler (1960: 215) hoped to recover 'dateable objects of Malay or European origin in direct association with an aboriginal horizon'. Although radiocarbon dating was yet to be developed, Warner (1932: 488) suggested that visits by 'Malay' people were of considerable age, citing exotic tamarind trees which were partially 'covered with refuse shell . . . well packed and hardened by time'. These were not the first interpretations of Macassan sites and material culture. Aboriginal people depicted Indonesian visitors in rock art and Yolŋu men built stone pictures representing *praus* and trepang fishers' fireplaces (Figure 38.2; Chaloupka 1996; Macknight 1976: 53, Plate 15; Macknight & Gray 1970; May, Taçon, Wesley, & Travers 2010; May, Wesley, Goldhahn, Lamilami, & Taçon 2021; Taçon & May 2013a, 2013b; Wesley, McKinnon, & Raupp 2012). These depictions reflect extensive Aboriginal knowledge of the Macassan world, and they materialize memories of shared experiences during the trepang fishing era.

In the 1960s, Campbell Macknight (1969, 1976) used historical literature, aerial photographs, and surveys to identify coastal sites used by Macassans in Arnhem Land.

FIGURE 38.2. A stone arrangement called Garanhan, built by Yolŋu men to represent Macassan trepang boiling fireplaces. Photograph from 1967, reproduced with permission of Campbell Macknight (from Macknight 1976: Plate 15). This site was observed by one of us (Russell) in 2021, and it has become a well-curated tourism site.

He conducted extensive excavations at Anuru Bay A (or Malara), Entrance Island, and Lyäba (see Figure 38.1). These were major trepang processing sites, all located on open beaches (Macknight 1969: 112–129; Mitchell 1994: Figure 8-1). In Arnhem Land, trepang processing sites are most often characterized by stone lines and hearths (constructed so that the trepang could be boiled in cauldrons), pit features where trepang were buried after boiling, and circular traces of smokehouses, along with tamarind trees and scatters of cultural materials (shell, bone, glass, metal, and pottery) (Figure 38.3; see Macknight 1976: 54–56, 62–82; Wesley, Jones, O'Connor, & Dickinson 2014: 18, Figure 4). There is also an enigmatic circular stone feature located at Warruwi in the intertidal zone near South Goulburn Island which may be a Macassan trepang 'holding pond' (see Dobson 2015). A few sites have Macassan graves, marked by rectangular stone arrangements (Macknight 1976: 60; Macknight & Thorne 1968; Theden-Ringl et al. 2011). In the Kimberley, some 800 km to the west, Crawford (1969) excavated the large trepang processing site of Tamarinda at Napier Broome Bay, known to local Aboriginal people as Njauwar Kudangei ('the beach with the black stones'). The surface signature of the Kimberley and Gulf of Carpentaria trepang fisheries is limited to stone lines, wells, tamarinds, and artefact scatters (Crawford 1969; Morwood & Hobbs 1997: 205; Oertle, Leavesley, Ulm, Mate, & Rosendahl 2014). These sites can be challenging to identify and investigate, as they are seasonal beach camps in erosional landscapes (see Mitchell 1995); crews stayed only a few days or weeks in each location (though some locations were reused, year on year) (Macknight 1976: 59).

FIGURE 38.3. (A) Macassan trepang processing site on an island in Raffles Bay, 1839 ('Pècheurs de tripang a la Baie Raffles'; image by Louis Le Breton; lithograph by Emile Lassalle in 1846—National Library of Australia, PIC Volume 594, #S11251). (B) The Macassans at Victoria, Port Essington, 1845 ('The trepang fishery of the northern coast of Australia' by Harden S. Melville—British Library, BL3279600).

Anne Clarke (1994: i) and Scott Mitchell (1994: 173) adopted new approaches to contact archaeology on Groote Eylandt and the Cobourg Peninsula regions, respectively. Clarke (1994: 152) aimed to investigate 'Aboriginal land use in the context of Macassan contact' by excavating Aboriginal shell middens and rock shelters located close to the coast (sometimes adjacent to stone lines and tamarinds). Of the eighteen sites excavated for Clarke's (1994: 463, Figure 7.1) doctoral research, six were interpreted as evidence of

CROSS-CULTURAL INTERACTION   1029

'wet season aggregation of people in places close to Macassan activities'. Mitchell (1994: 173), too, elected to investigate Aboriginal midden sites—as well as Macassan stone lines at Barlambidj on Copeland Island—which could provide evidence of Aboriginal practices spanning the precontact and postcontact eras.

In the past decade, archaeological investigations have focused on western Arnhem Land, re-excavating, dating, and analysing cultural material from the Anuru Bay A site (McKinnon, Wesley, Raupp, & Moffat 2013; Wesley 2014; Wesley & Litster 2015; Wesley et al. 2014; Wesley, O'Connor, & Fenner 2016) and recording Aboriginal depictions of Macassan people, *praus*, and material culture in Wellington Range rock art (Taçon & May 2013a, 2013b; Taçon et al. 2010; Wesley & Viney 2016; Wesley et al. 2012). Across each era of archaeological research, key sites were revealed to researchers by Aboriginal people: they are clearly key places for maintaining social memories of encounter and exchange.

British, Dutch, and Indonesian historical records suggest that trepanging visits to northern Australia commenced in the seventeenth century (Bulbeck & Rowley 2001; Macknight 1969, 1976). Yet based on his reading of Matthew Flinders' early nineteenth-century ethnohistoric accounts and following Knaap and Sutherland's (2004) archival research, Macknight (2011: 133–134; 2013: 20–21) has recently argued that the industry commenced after CE 1780 in Arnhem Land and shortly before CE 1754 on the Kimberley coast, precipitated by growing Chinese demand for trepang.[4] Several lines of archaeological evidence confirm that Macassans were visiting northern Australia at this time. Coins minted in the period CE 1742–1838 (e.g., *duits* of the Dutch East India Company) have been found at contact sites in Arnhem Land (Macknight 1976: 73; Mitchell 1994: 49, Table 3-4; Mulvaney 1966: 453), and a single CE 1823 coin was recovered from the Kimberley trepang fishery site of Tamarinda (Crawford 1969: 169). Glass and stone beads brought through Asia probably entered Aboriginal exchange networks after the early eighteenth century (Wesley & Litster 2015: 13). South Sulawesi earthenware pottery and Chinese or Vietnamese bowl sherds recovered from trepang fishery sites date (stylistically) almost exclusively to the seventeenth century onwards (Bulbeck & Rowley 2001; Key 1969; Macknight 1969: 387; 1976; Mitchell 1994: 50; Wesley et al. 2014: 23). The best-established exception to this pattern is from Torres Strait, where a sixteenth-century Chinese sherd found in an excavation at Goemu village site (Mabuyag Island) suggests the presence of 'some Southeast Asian traders, possibly including Chinese traders' in the Coral Sea at this time (Grave & McNiven 2013: 1616). This small sherd hints at an early expansion of Asian trade networks in the Coral and Arafura Seas, and potentially ties Australia into the emergent 'silk road' and spice route trade systems (McNiven 2017).

Several radiocarbon dates obtained from trepang processing sites, rock shelter sites, and rock art sites in Arnhem Land calibrate earlier than CE 1780. Of six dates acquired by Macknight (1969, 1976; Macknight & Thorne 1968)—all from distinct hearth or ash lenses associated with Macassan stone lines—five calibrate significantly older than CE 1780, and three calibrate to c. CE 1000–1300 (see Mitchell 1994: Figure 3-6; Wesley et al. 2016: 174–178, Table 2). Most researchers have rejected these early ages, arguing either that the wood (possibly mangrove) had absorbed old carbon from the environment (Macknight 1976: 98–99; but see Wesley et al. 2016: 177) or had inbuilt age, being from trees already hundreds of years old when they were cut down (Bulbeck & Rowley 2001: 55; Mitchell 1994: 49–56). At the Groote Eylandt rock shelter of Dadirringka, a small, friable earthenware sherd was recovered from a depth of 48 cm below the surface, in levels underlying a piece of charcoal dating to c. CE 1000–1250 (Clarke 1994: 399; Clarke & Frederick 2011: 151). Yet Clarke (1994: 399; see also Grave & McNiven 2013: 4550) has stated that this sherd could have been relocated from overlying stratigraphy through trampling or other taphonomic processes. The other radiocarbon dates acquired by Clarke (1994: 463, Table 6.3) for stratigraphy containing postcontact (introduced) cultural materials—at Marngkala Cave, Marngkala Rockshelter, Lerrumungumanja Rockshelter, Lerrumungumanja Midden, Makbumanja, Aburrkbumanja (Test Pit 2), and Malmudinga—all calibrated within 'the period of historically documented Macassan contact'. Two radiocarbon ages from stratigraphy associated with the Macassan trepang fishery at Barlambidj on Copeland Island calibrate to c. CE 1835 and c. CE 1900 (Mitchell 1994: 313–314, Table 12-11).[5]

A single date for an Aboriginal *prau* depiction, and recent efforts to redate the Anuru Bay A site, have bolstered arguments for pre–CE 1780 Macassan visits. In the Wellington Range of western Arnhem Land, Taçon et al. (2010) radiocarbon dated several contact-era motifs by sampling beeswax covering or underlying the depictions. Two *prau* depictions produced median age distributions clustering in the late seventeenth and eighteenth centuries (Taçon et al. 2010: Table 1), well within the era of historically documented visits for trepang collection. However, dating of a yellow *prau* painting at the rock art site of Djulirri resulted in a probable *terminus ante quem* age of CE 1664.

For the Anuru Bay A site, Wesley et al. (2016: 179; see also Theden-Ringl et al. 2011) used Bayesian statistical modelling to calibrate eighteen new AMS radiocarbon ages. The samples were pieces of charcoal and shell adhered to pottery and parts of stone lines, along with teeth from two Macassan burials. Their model gave a 50% probability that site use commenced before CE 1622, suggesting that 'Macassan visits . . . most probably began in the third decade of the seventeenth century' (Wesley et al. 2016: 188). The main period of site use at Anuru Bay A dates to the middle of the eighteenth century until sometime prior to CE 1880 (Wesley et al. 2016: 191). Their new excavations and chronology led Wesley, O'Connor, and Fenner (2016: 188–190) to argue that the more ancient dates acquired by Macknight probably derived from precontact Aboriginal 'shell-charcoal hearth feature[s]' underlying (or mixed with) strata formed during the trepang fishery (cf. Macknight 1976: 98).

Two lines of evidence from the well-dated Anuru Bay A site help confirm documentary evidence that the trepang fishers came from South Sulawesi. Two male individuals, aged in their twenties or thirties, were buried beneath a stone arrangement at the northern edge of the site. The upper burial crosscut the lower, with the most recently buried individual placed on their right side facing northwest, the direction of Makassar and the approximate direction of Mecca (Macknight 1976: 60; Macknight & Thorne 1968). Strontium and carbon stable isotope analyses of the individuals' teeth suggest they are 'non-local'; the results fit within the range of Sulawesi geological strontium isotope signatures (Theden-Ringl et al. 2011: 46). We should note, though, that the two people 'did not necessarily share a common childhood origin' (Theden-Ringl et al. 2011: 46), and the precise location of their developmental years is not yet clear. Pottery from the site is predominantly earthenware; petrological analysis of these sherds indicated that all the pottery originated from volcanic South Sulawesi islands (Wesley et al. 2014: 22–23). These findings support earlier petrological studies showing that the pottery found at Macassan sites (mostly globular pot sherds) predominantly originated in South Sulawesi, and probably Makassar (Key 1969; Macknight 1976; Rowley 1997). Yet Key (1969: 105), studying sherds from 'several different' sites investigated by Macknight (1969) located between the Tiwi Islands and the Gulf of Carpentaria, and Rowley (1997), examining Goulburn Island and Tamarinda pottery, both identified some diversity in the pottery's mineralogical signatures. Key (1969) suggested that one earthenware sherd (containing hornfels) originated in the Kei Islands, and Rowley (1997) identified a group of shell-tempered pottery (Tamarinda Group 1) which was probably not made in South Sulawesi.

In broad terms, the long and short chronologies for Indonesian–Aboriginal interaction are not incompatible. It is entirely possible that *encounters* (occasional visits and glimpses of boats from islands north of Australia) took place from c. CE 1664 or earlier, and meaningful cultural *exchange* (of language, ideas, and things) took place after c. CE 1780 when the Macassan trepang industry as documented in written records was in full swing (Bulbeck & Rowley 2001: 56; Clarke 2000: 327; Macknight 1976: 97; Wesley et al. 2016: 190). It is worth noting that Aboriginal people depicted European ships prior to sustained contact, presumably based on fleeting encounters or offshore sightings (Taçon et al. 2010: 4). Establishing fine-grained chronologies for multiple sites will be crucial because these dates affect how we understand interaction through time. These understandings in turn affect how recent transformations of Aboriginal social and ceremonial landscapes are explained and characterized. For example, Daryl Wesley (2014: 333–334) has drawn on long chronology dates to suggest that Aboriginal customary worldviews transformed in response to pre-Macassan contact. Likewise, Clarke (1994: 181) tentatively suggested that changes in subsistence patterns at the Groote Eylandt site of Malmudinga could have been precipitated by contact with people from Indonesia c. 900–800 years ago. More reliable regional chronologies are required before these proposals can be tested.

UNDERSTANDING CROSS-CULTURAL ENCOUNTERS THROUGH ARCHAEOLOGY

> ... the sandy, shelving beaches of the rich trepang grounds ... took on a dual identity for Aboriginal people—simultaneously the centre of clan estates and a window to other worlds of knowledge and experience accessed through the maritime technologies, language and cultural practices of the Macassan visitors.
>
> (Clarke 2000: 316)

Places with archaeological evidence of trepang processing have not always been characterized as meeting points of Aboriginal and Macassan 'worlds of knowledge and experience' (Clarke 2000: 316; Clarke & Frederick 2011: 155). Some interpretations have focussed more closely on the Macassan world: on fluctuations of Asian trade networks in the Arafura and Timor Seas, the origins of transported pottery, and on Macassan experiences of Kayu Jawa and Marege' (e.g., see Bulbeck & Rowley 2001; Macknight 1969, 1976). Macknight (1976: 74)[6] saw the archaeology of trepang processing sites as being of 'little use in determining the circumstances in which Aborigines and Macassans came into contact'. Yet these sites are undeniably places of encounter and were to some extent co-formed by Macassans and Aboriginal people. Aboriginal people from Arnhem Land are known to have worked in the industry, participated in the daily activities of the camps, and sailed to and from the port of Makassar in the *praus* (see Worsley 1955). How did people with different languages, cosmologies, cultural practices, and even differing understandings of trade and exchange interact? When were metal, pottery, and glass items incorporated into local exchange networks, and how did Aboriginal people use and modify these exotic materials? Archaeology is uniquely positioned to investigate the silences of early ethnographic documents, and to establish when specific historically documented patterns of exchange and interaction emerged. The material evidence is especially crucial for understanding cross-cultural interaction on the Kimberley and Gulf of Carpentaria coasts, for which there are fewer ethnographic sources compared to Arnhem Land (Crawford 1969: 9–10).

The archaeological record suggests that aspects of Indigenous social landscapes changed during the era of coastal interaction with Macassans (e.g., see Clarke 1994: 463). Groote Eylandt midden deposits containing contact materials and dating to the past c. 200–300 years also contain a large variety of sand- and mud-dwelling shellfish gathered to feed 'aggregated populations' near wet season trepang processing sites (Clarke 1994: 463–465; 2000: 331), or possibly to sustain people gathered during the dry season to prepare items for later exchange with Macassans (see Worsley 1955). Similarly, postcontact midden sites on the Cobourg Peninsula are significantly larger than those from the precontact era (Mitchell 1994: Tables 14-10 & 14-11).[7] These transformations may reflect intensification of coastal site use during the era of Aboriginal–Macassan interaction (Mitchell 1994, 1996; see also Rose 1960; Schrire 1972). Mitchell (1994: 397) attributed the process of coastal settlement aggregation to either 'new opportunities for marine exploitation opened up by the adoption of the dugout canoe', destruction of inland vegetation by introduced feral animals (causing people to focus on marine resources), or mitigation of the risk of conflict brought about by 'foreign contact'. Similar patterns have been observed farther inland at the Wellington Range in northwest Arnhem Land. May, Taçon, Wesley, and Travers (2010: 64) have suggested there was a 'significant reorganization of local residential mobility strategies' involving a 'contraction of residential mobility' over the past c. 250 years to regulate access to exchange with Macassans and coastal Aboriginal communities.

Archaeological and ethnographic records provide evidence for selective uptake of materials and technologies. As McNiven (2021) has argued, in the context of two-way object flows across Torres Strait, 'Every directional movement of objects and ideas involves selectivity and agency by both provider and recipient' (see also Clarke 2000:

322; Rowland 2018: 216–217; Torrence & Clarke 2000: 18–20; Wesley & Litster 2015). Well after the establishment of European extractive economies in Arnhem Land, local Aboriginal communities chose to continue to supply Macassans visitors with turtle shell and preferred to participate in the Indonesian trepang industry in the 1870s–1880s (Mitchell 1994: 113). The seasonal visitors were not just harvesting trepang, but sought to acquire tortoise shell, pearls, pearl shell, sandalwood, and other timber from Aboriginal lands (Berndt & Berndt 1954; Clarke 2000: 317; Macknight 1976: 44–45; Warner 1932). Clay smoking pipes and tobacco, belts, string, alcohol, rice, and tamarind fruit moved in the opposite direction, brought on *praus* to northern Australia (Macknight 1972: 306). Despite at least five and probably more than nine generations of cross-cultural contact, 'very few items of [Macassan] material culture were permanently adopted' by Aboriginal people (Macknight 1976: 90; 1986).[8] Pottery, glass, and metal were evidently acquired, used and 'carefully curated' by Aboriginal people, who deposited the items at rock shelter and midden sites (Clarke 1994: 296, 464; Mitchell 1994: 40). Aboriginal communities sought to sustain exchange with Indonesian visitors to their shores and decided which things and ideas should be shared or received on their shores.

Aboriginal people's decisions to participate in cross-cultural exchange were probably driven, in part, by the desire to fuel existing regional relationships. The arrival of exotic materials such as iron has been implicated in the intensification of regional Indigenous exchange networks after Macassan contact (Clarke 1994: 464; Mitchell 1994; Thomson 1949: 82–94; Warner 1932: 490). The middens of the Cobourg Peninsula, including those at Barlambidj, contained larger quantities of nonlocal stone artefacts in levels and sites dating to the period of Macassan contact (Mitchell 1994: 269, 369). At Groote Eylandt, volcanic rock (used in the manufacture of ground-edge axes) and silcrete were first brought to the site of Marngkala Cave in the postcontact era (Clarke 1994: 464). We should caution, however, that regional chronologies yet lack the resolution to distinguish between levels dating to the Macassan and European contact eras.

There is some evidence that coastal exchange on the northern Australian coast had a flow-on effect. For example, glass beads entered western Arnhem Land exchange networks c. CE 1800, with Aboriginal people likely making 'beads a specific demand item for Indigenous co-operation and involvement' in 'non-customary enterprises' like working to harvest and process trepang (Wesley & Litster 2015: 13; cf. Wesley & Viney 2016). Recent research on glass beads and 'beaded objects' in the collections of Museums Victoria found that these items were commonly collected from 'a discrete corridor' of northern Australia which includes the Wellington Range (Allen, Babister, Bonshek, & Goodall 2018). Trace element analyses conducted with a portable X-ray fluorescence unit suggested significant similarities between the Arnhem Land items and glass beads collected in Papua New Guinea (Allen et al. 2018: 72). These preliminary analyses suggested a common manufacturing source or sources (probably European or Southeast Asian) for the glass beads and provide an intriguing link between the trade routes which reached Arnhem Land, and those which looped in Papua New Guinea's coast.

Perhaps the most significant of the technological adoptions or exchanges was that of the sailing dugout canoe. Aboriginal people were obtaining canoes from Macassans in the early nineteenth century and were making these canoes locally by the late 1830s–1840s (e.g., see Earl 1846: 77; Lewis 1922: 152; see Mitchell 1994: Table 6-1 for a summary). Several Aboriginal language groups—especially the Anindilyakwa speakers of Groote Eylandt—acquired a great deal of Macassan seafaring vocabulary and extensive knowledge of *prau* construction (Evans 1992: 52; 2002; see also Crawford 1969: 298–300; Macknight 1972: 297–298, Table 1; Macknight & Gray 1970). New aspects of ceremonial performance were developed alongside the exchange of maritime technology and language. Mortuary ceremonies in eastern Arnhem Land incorporated representations of *praus*, anchors, flags, and masts, along with songs originally performed by Macassans when they were due to leave Australian shores each year (Macknight 1972: 314–315; Warner 1932: 492). The adoption of sailing dugout canoes may have seen an intensification of existing Aboriginal marine hunting practices and other maritime engagements (Mitchell 1994: 135–141; 1996; see also Mulvaney 1975: 39; Rose 1960; Urry & Walsh 1981). New dugong and turtle hunting grounds farther offshore were probably made accessible by sailing dugouts (Baker 1988: 181, 183; Bradley 1991; Macknight 1972: 305; Mitchell 1994, 1996; Rowland 2018: 229–230). The archaeology of the Cobourg Peninsula provides some material support for these ideas, as dugong and turtle bone deposits seem to have increased in postcontact-era middens, perhaps signalling the increased hunting efficacy of iron harpoon heads (Mitchell 1994: 269, 369). Sailing canoes and intensifying maritime hunting may likewise have made coastal settlement more attractive and strategic (see discussion of coastal aggregation above; Mitchell 1994: 139–140).

Rock art sites which include unequivocal images of Macassan material culture, such as *praus*, knives, and smoking pipes present tangible evidence of contact and cross-cultural engagements. Other images include containers, rope, and even a purported monkey (Chaloupka 1996). Sally May and colleagues have demonstrated that one of the dominant motifs is 'watercraft', particularly in the past '500 years in northwest Arnhem Land' (May, Taçon, Paterson, & Travers 2013, May, Taçon, Wesley, & Pearson 2013; May et al. 2021; Roberts 2004; Taçon & May 2013a). Recent work by May et al. (2021) has suggested that the relatively harmonious and long-term relationships with Macassans—in contrast with the later British arrivals—is demonstrated by most of the images being of European ships rather than Macassan *praus*. The authors argued that these rock art sites might be read as statements of sovereignty (May et al. 2021). The Macassans were known as visitors, allies, and trading partners as opposed to invaders, and so their watercraft were less often recorded. They convincingly argue that 'the archaeological silence' can be read as evidence for deep cultural engagements sustained over a long period, 'far longer than current research suggests', and a different mode of interaction to the permanent European settlements (May et al. 2021: 139). As noted earlier, one *prau* motif in the Wellington Range was probably painted before CE 1664 (Taçon et al. 2010). When taken with the archaeology, the oral histories (both Aboriginal and Macassan) suggest that we are yet to fully understand the timeframe of contact between Southeast Asian peoples and Aboriginal peoples of northern Australia.

Material Silences and Future Avenues for Research

Evidence of Aboriginal–Macassan interactions is often described as 'unknown' or 'surprising' by popular media. However, after more than six decades of archaeological and historical study the trepang trade has 'become one of the most celebrated chapters in Australia's history [and it] continues to attract great interest' (Clark & May 2013: 3). Despite decades of investigation, some fundamental questions remain concerning the nature of cross-cultural interactions across time and place. As we have discussed, the evidence derives from locations on or near the Arnhem Land coast, including trepang processing camps, Aboriginal middens and rock shelters on Groote Eylandt and the Cobourg Peninsula, and rock art sites on Groote Eylandt and western Arnhem Land. Investigations in the Kimberley and Gulf of Carpentaria regions have been comparatively few, and chronological information for these regions is very limited. We must also consider how representative the selected sites are for phases of cross-cultural interaction and regional chronologies. By far the most reliable radiocarbon chronology has been obtained for the Macassan burials and stone lines of Anuru Bay A (Wesley et al. 2016). Yet well-preserved trepang processing sites like Anuru Bay A may not necessarily hold the key to understanding when Macassan visits first occurred. Rather, the oldest evidence for interaction may come from sites which are today highly degraded or mostly buried, having been subject to centuries of tidal action, cyclones, and storm surges. This potentially self-fulfilling cycle of site selection has been identified for the archaeology of Gunditjmara stone houses in western Victoria: archaeologists tend to select well-preserved structures for investigation, and these less degraded structures are probably among the most recent (McNiven, Dunn, Crouch, & Gunditj Mirring Traditional Owners Aboriginal Corporation 2017: 193). Aboriginal middens and rock shelters adjacent to Macassan sites will also be key to historicizing the longue durée of cross-cultural interaction.

A paucity of research in some parts of northern Australia has caused chronological and material silences, which have in turn impacted our understanding of Aboriginal–Macassan interactions through time. As Crawford (1969) suggested, there were markedly different modes of engagement and exchange between the Kimberley and Arnhem Land regions (see also Evans 1992: 48–53; Macknight 1972: 289; Paterson & Wilson 2009). Based on limited surveys and excavations, sites with Macassan material culture in the Kimberley and Gulf of Carpentaria appear to be more ephemeral than those of the Arnhem Land coast, including Groote Eylandt (Morwood & Hobbs 1997; Oertle, Leavesley, Ulm, Mate, & Rosendahl 2014). There are, however, linguistic clues to the intensity and nature of interaction. Unlike Kaiadilt speakers of the Wellesley Islands, the Marra and Yanyuwa languages of the southern Gulf of Carpentaria have numerous Macassan linguistic influences, indicating some extended contact (Evans 1992: 52–53). Likewise, Indonesian loanwords occur extensively in the Iwaidja and Maung languages of the Cobourg Peninsula and Wellington Range, and Yolŋu farther to the east (Evans 1997, 2002, 2009; Harris 1985). These patterns provide rich grounds for future archaeological research in the Kimberley and Gulf of Carpentaria regions. Did Macassan visits occur later than those in Arnhem Land? If they were 'low intensity and most likely sporadic' (Oertle, Leavesley, Ulm, Mate, & Rosendahl 2014: 70), how did patterns of Indonesian activity between regions affect the nature of interactions?

Interactions between Macassans and Aboriginal people also need to be understood in the wider context of Asian exchange networks in the Timor, Arafura, and Coral Seas. Asian exchange networks north of Australia do appear to have expanded in the seventeenth century. A Chinese ceramic sherd reached western Torres Strait by c. CE 1500–1600 (Grave & McNiven 2013; McNiven 2017), and Seramese traders were probably active in the Gulf of Papua after c. CE 1645 (Rhoads 1980: 149; Swadling 2019: 155). Sustained research on the Coral Sea Cultural Interaction Sphere (McNiven 2015, 2017, 2021) is likely to shed light on the role of northern Australia in the broader economic systems loosely referred to as the spice and silk trade routes. Building on the work of McIntosh (1996, 1999, 2006, 2008), future research is planned to explore what were the economic and social mechanisms for increased Asian engagement in these new locations, and how these interactions with Indigenous people differed across these spheres. Another avenue for future research being developed by the authors, with botanical and DNA researchers, is a deep history of the tamarind trees of northern Australia (cf., Diallo, Joly, McKey, Hossaert-McKey, & Chevallier 2007). These trees, almost always associated with Macassan sites, have yet to be properly studied. Early insights from a preliminary study of some of the large tamarind trees of Arnhem Land indicate that these are potentially very old and may yield valuable evidence for timing of Macassan visits. Importantly, the trees, places, and exchanges which we seek to investigate archaeologically are known through rich extant networks of oral traditional knowledge on either side of the Arafura and Timor Seas. Close engagement with these oral traditions will be key to developing rich, collaborative historical narratives and making sense of the (sub)surface as it relates to Aboriginal–Macassan encounters and relationships.

ACKNOWLEDGMENTS

Sadly, our co-author and colleague Lily Yulianti Farid passed away earlier this year. She was passionate about this history. We thank Campbell Macknight for allowing us to reproduce his photograph of the Garanhan site (Figure 38.2). Buku-Larrŋgay Mulka provided advice on cultural permissions. The National Library of Australia and the British Library permitted us to reproduce Figures 38.3a and 3b. Campbell Macknight and Sue O'Connor provided insightful and constructive reviews.

NOTES

1. Following the conventions first established by Campbell Macknight (1976, 2008, 2011, 2013), we are using the term 'Macassan' when describing the archaeology of the trepang fishers and

their activities harvesting and processing trepang. Most of these men were, culturally and linguistically, Makasars from the South Sulawesi port of Makassar. However, Macknight (1976, 2008, 2011, 2013) suggests that 'Macassan' (with a c) is a better collective term as some crew members were drawn from other islands and ports in the Southeast Asian archipelago. Unlike Macknight, and following Ronald Berndt and Catherine Berndt (1947), we also use this term for the trepang processing sites in the Kimberly region of Western Australia.

2. It is highly likely that there may be generational compression here; it was possibly a great-great-grandfather.

3. Vereenigde Oost-Indische Compagnie (VOC) was a Dutch government supported military-commercial enterprise. The Company had its Asian base in Batavia (Jakarta), and other bases in Japan and throughout the Indian Ocean and Southeast Asia (Boxer 1965).

4. Macknight (1969: 97; 1976: 69; 2011: 133–134) had earlier proposed that the industry commenced sometime in the period CE 1650–1750.

5. A detailed review of all key Aboriginal-Macassan contact site chronologies is overdue (previous efforts have focused on specific regions or especially 'old' dates), but exhaustive age recalibrations and detailed discussion of these are beyond the scope of the present chapter. We have opted to refer to estimated ages based on previously published calibrations, except for two dates from the upper strata of the Barlimbidj stone lines (BETA 41415 and BETA 47217), as Mitchell has not provided a calibration for BETA 47217 (BETA 41415 was calibrated as 'modern'). Our estimated ages of CE 1835 (BETA 47217) and CE 1900 (BETA 41415) are medians calibrated using a mixed (50/50) SHCal20 (Hogg et al. 2020) and IntCal20 (Reimer et al. 2020) curve in OxCal 4.4.

6. Macknight's (1976: 1–2) arguments do not preclude cross-cultural co-construction of trepang processing sites, as he included Aboriginal participants in his definition of the term 'Macassans'.

7. Mitchell (1994) defined postcontact sites as containing metal, glass, or pottery, or dating after CE 1720.

8. Our estimate of contact duration was worked out using an assumed twenty-five-year generational spacing. The range derives from Macknight's (2011: 133–134) conservative CE 1780 date for first contact, and Taçon et al.'s (2010) preferred pre–CE 1664 date.

References

Allen, L., Babister, S., Bonshek, E., & Goodall, R. (2018). Finding the signatures of glass beads: A preliminary investigation of Indigenous artefacts from Australia and Papua New Guinea. *Journal of the Anthropological Society of South Australia*, 42, 48–80.

Andaya, B. W., & Andaya, L. Y. (2015). *A history of early modern Southeast Asia, 1400–1830*. Cambridge: Cambridge University Press.

Andaya, L. Y. (1995). The Bugis-Makassar diaspora. *Journal of the Malaysian Branch of the Royal Asiatic Society*, 68(1), 119–138.

Baker, R. (1988). Yanyuwa canoe making. *Records of the South Australian Museum*, 22(2), 173–188.

Berndt, R. M., & Berndt, C. H. (1947). Discovery of pottery in northeastern Arnhem Land. *The Journal of the Royal Anthropological Institute of Great Britain and Ireland*, 7(2), 133–138.

Berndt, R. M., & Berndt, C. H. (1954). *Arnhem Land: Its history and its people*. Melbourne: F. W. Cheshire.

Bilous, R. H. (2015a). "All mucked up" sharing stories of Yolŋu–Macassan cultural heritage at Bawaka, north-east Arnhem Land. *International Journal of Heritage Studies, 21*(9), 905–918.

Bilous, R. H. (2015b). Making connections: Hearing and sharing Macassan-Yolŋu stories. *Asia Pacific Viewpoint, 56*(3), 365–379.

Boxer, C. R. (1965). *The Dutch seaborne empire, 1600–1800*. New York: Alfred Knopf.

Bradley, J. J. (1991). "Li-Maramanja": Yanyuwa hunters of marine animals in the Sir Edward Pellew group, Northern Territory. *Records of the South Australian Museum, 25*(1), 91–110.

Brady, M. (2013). Drug substances introduced by the Macassans: The mystery of the tobacco pipe. In M. Clark & S. K. May (Eds.), *Macassan history and heritage: Journeys, encounters and influences* (pp. 141–158). Canberra: ANU E Press.

Bulbeck, D., & Rowley, B. (2001). Macassans and their pots in northern Australia. In C. Fredericksen & I. Walters (Eds.), *Altered states: Material culture transformations in the Arafura region* (pp. 55–74). Darwin: Northern Territory University Press in association with the Centre for Southeast Asian Studies, Northern Territory University.

Chaloupka, G. (1996). Praus in Marege: Makassan subjects in Aboriginal rock art of Arnhem Land, Northern territory, Australia. *Anthropologie, 14*(1–2), 131–142.

Clark, M., & May, S. K. (2013). Understanding the Macassans: A regional approach. In M. Clark & S. K. May (Eds.), *Macassan history and heritage: Journeys, encounters and influences* (pp. 1–18). Canberra: ANU E Press.

Clarke, A. (1994). *Winds of change: An archaeology of contact in the Groote Eylandt archipelago, Northern Australia* (PhD thesis). Australian National University, Canberra.

Clarke, A. (2000). The "Moormans trowsers": Macassan and Aboriginal interactions and the changing fabric of indigenous social life. In S. O'Connor & P. Veth (Eds.), *East of Wallace's Line: Studies of past and present maritime cultures of the Indo-Pacific region* (pp. 315–335). Modern Quaternary Research in Southeast Asia 16. Rotterdam: A.A. Balkema.

Clarke, A., & Frederick, U. (2011). Making a sea change: Rock art, archaeology and the enduring legacy of Frederick McCarthy's research on Groote Eylandt. In M. Thomas & M. Neale (Eds.), *Exploring the legacy of the 1948 Arnhem Land Expedition* (pp. 135–155). Canberra: ANU E Press.

Corn, A., & Marrett, A. (2011). To proclaim they still exist: The contemporary Yolŋu performance of historical Macassan contact. In M. Langton (Ed.), *Trepang: China and the story of Macassan-Aboriginal trade* (pp. 72–80). Melbourne: The Centre for Cultural Materials Conservation.

Crawford, I. M. (1969). *Late prehistoric changes in Aboriginal cultures in Kimberley, Western Australia* (PhD thesis). University of London, London.

Diallo, B. O., Joly, H. I., McKey, D., Hossaert-McKey, M., & Chevallier, M. H. (2007). Genetic diversity of *Tamarindus indica* populations: Any clues on the origin from its current distribution? *African Journal of Biotechnology, 6*(7), 853–860.

Dobson, G. T. (2015). *The Warruwi Pond enigma: Pre-European aquaculture in Arnhem Land?* (PhD thesis). Australian National University, Canberra.

Earl, G. W. (1846). *Enterprise in tropical Australia*. London: Madden & Malcolm.

Evans, N. (1992). Macassan loanwords in top end languages. *Australian Journal of Linguistics, 12*(1), 45–91.

Evans, N. (1997). Macassan loans and linguistic stratification in western Arnhem Land. In P. McConvell & N. Evans (Eds.), *Archaeology and linguistics: Aboriginal Australia in global perspective* (pp. 237–260). Melbourne: Oxford University Press.

CROSS-CULTURAL INTERACTION   1039

Evans, N. (2002). Country and the word: Linguistic evidence in the Croker sea claim. In J. Henderson & D. Nash (Eds.), *Language in native title* (pp. 53–99). Canberra: Aboriginal Studies Press.

Evans, N. (2009). Doubled up all over again: Borrowing, sound change and reduplication in Iwaidja. *Morphology, 19*(2), 159–176.

Fox, J. J. (1977). Notes on the southern voyages and settlements of the Sama-Bajau. *Bijdragen Tot De Taal-, Land- En Volkenkunde, 133*(4), 459–465.

Grave, P., & McNiven, I. J. (2013). Geochemical provenience of 16th–19th century C. E. Asian ceramics from Torres Strait, northeast Australia. *Journal of Archaeological Science, 40*(12), 4538–4551.

Harris, J. (1985). Contact languages at the Northern Territory British military settlements 1824–1849. *Aboriginal History, 9*(2), 148–169.

Hogg, A. G., Heaton, T. J., Hua, Q., Palmer, J. G., Turney, C. S. M., Southon, J., . . . Wacker, L. (2020). SHCal20 Southern Hemisphere calibration, 0–55,000 years cal BP. *Radiocarbon, 62*(4), 759–778.

Howard, P. (2009). *Past and present; An ethno-historical and archaeological study of the North Australian trepang industry* (Honours thesis). University of Wollongong, Wollongong.

Key, C. (1969). Archaeological pottery in Arnhem Land. *Archaeology & Physical Anthropology in Oceania, 4*(2), 103–106.

Knaap, G., & Sutherland, H. (2004). *Monsoon traders: Ships, skippers and commodities in eighteenth-century Makassar*. Leiden: KITLV Press.

Langton, M. (2011). Trepang. In M. Langton (Ed.), *Trepang: China and the story of Macassan-Aboriginal trade* (pp. 14–71). Melbourne: The Centre for Cultural Materials Conservation.

Langton, M., & Sloggett, R. (2014). Trepang: China and the story of Macassan-Aboriginal Trade—Examining historical accounts as research tools for cultural materials conservation. *AICCM Bulletin, 35*(1), 4–13.

Lewis, J. (1922). *Fought and won*. Adelaide: Thomas.

Lydon, J. (2014). Picturing Macassan–Australian histories: Odoardo Beccari's 1873 photographs of the "Orang-Mereghi" and Indigenous authenticity. In J. Carey & J. Lydon (Eds.), *Indigenous networks: Mobility, connections and exchange* (pp. 140–165). London: Routledge.

Macknight, C. C. (1969). *The Macassans: A study of the early trepang industry along the Northern Territory coast* (PhD thesis). Australian National University, Canberra.

Macknight, C. C. (1972). Macassans and Aborigines. *Oceania, 42*(4), 283–321.

Macknight, C. C. (1976). *The voyage to Marege'*. Melbourne: Melbourne University Press.

Macknight, C. C. (1986). Macassans and the Aboriginal past. *Archaeology in Oceania, 21*(1), 69–75.

Macknight, C. C. (2008). Harvesting the memory: Open beaches in Makassar and Arnhem Land. In P. Veth, P. Sutton, & M. Neale (Eds.), *Strangers on the shore: Early coastal contacts in Australia* (pp. 133–147). Canberra: National Museum of Australia.

Macknight, C. C. (2011). The view from Marege': Australian knowledge of Makassar and the impact of the trepang industry across two centuries. *Aboriginal History Journal, 35*, 121–143.

Macknight, C. C. (2013). Studying trepangers. In M. Clark & S. K. May (Eds.), *Macassan history and heritage: Journeys, encounters and influences* (pp. 19–40). Canberra: ANU E Press.

Macknight C. C., & Gray, W. J. (1970). *Aboriginal stone pictures in Arnhem Land*. Canberra: Australian Institute of Aboriginal Studies.

Macknight, C. C., & Thorne, A. G. (1968). Two Macassan burials in Arnhem Land. *Archaeology and Physical Anthropology in Oceania, 3*(3), 216–222.

Máñez, K. S., & Ferse, S. C. A. (2010). The history of Makassan trepang fishing and trade. *PLoS ONE, 5*(6), e11346.

May, S. K. (2011). Piecing the history together: An overview of the 1948 Arnhem Land expedition. In M. Thomas & M. Neale (Eds.), *Exploring the legacy of the 1948 Arnhem Land expedition* (pp. 171–188). Canberra: ANU E Press.

May, S. K., Taçon, P. S. C., Paterson, A., & Travers, M. (2013). The world from Malarrak: Depictions of Southeast Asian and European subjects in rock art from the Wellington Range. Australia. *Australian Aboriginal Studies, 2013-1*, 45–56.

May, S. K., Taçon, P. S. C., Wesley, D., & Pearson, M. (2013). Painted ships on a painted Arnhem Land landscape. *The Great Circle: Journal of the Australian Association for Maritime History, 35*(2), 83–102.

May, S. K., Taçon, P. S. C., Wesley, D., & Travers, M. (2010). Painting history: Indigenous observations and depictions of the "other" in northwestern Arnhem Land, Australia. *Australian Archaeology, 71*(1), 57–65.

May, S. K., Wesley, D., Goldhahn, J., Lamilami, R., & Taçon, P. S. C. (2021). The missing Macassans: Indigenous sovereignty, rock art and the archaeology of absence. *Australian Archaeology, 87*(2), 127–143.

McCarthy, F. D., & Setzler, F. M. (1960). The archaeology of Arnhem Land. In C. P. Mountford (Ed.), *Records of the American-Australian scientific expedition to Arnhem Land 1948: 2, anthropology and nutrition* (pp. 215–295). Melbourne: Melbourne University Press.

McIntosh, I. S. (1996). Allah and the spirit of the dead: The hidden legacy of pre-colonial Indonesian/Aboriginal contact in north-east Arnhem Land. *Australian Folklore, 11*, 131–138.

McIntosh, I. S. (1999). The ship's mast. The legacy of the Macassan presence in Northern Australia. *The Beagle: Records of the Museums and Art Galleries of the Northern Territory, 15*, 155–165.

McIntosh, I. S. (2006). A Treaty with the Macassans? Burrumarra and the Dholtji Ideal. *The Asia Pacific Journal of Anthropology, 7*(2), 153–172.

McIntosh, I. S. (2008). Pre-Macassans at Dholtji?: Exploring one of north-east Arnhem Land's great conundrums. In P. Veth, P. Sutton, & M. Neale (Eds.), *Strangers on the shore: Early coastal contacts in Australia* (pp. 165–180). Canberra: National Museum of Australia.

McIntosh, I. S. (2011). Missing the revolution! Negotiating disclosure on the pre-Macassans (Bayini) in north-east Arnhem Land. In M. Thomas & M. Neale (Eds.) *Exploring the legacy of the 1948 Arnhem Land Expedition* (pp. 337–354). Canberra: ANU E Press.

McIntosh, I. S. (2013). Unbirri's pre-Macassan legacy, or how the Yolngu became black. In M. Clark & S. K. May (Eds.), *Macassan history and heritage: Journeys, encounters and influences* (pp. 95–105). Canberra: ANU E Press.

McKinnon, J. F., Wesley, D., Raupp, J. T., & Moffat, I. (2013). Geophysical investigations at the Anuru Bay trepang site: A new approach to locating Macassan archaeological sites in northern Australia. *Bulletin of the Australasian Institute for Maritime Archaeology, 37*, 106–112.

McNiven, I. J. (2015). Precarious islands: Kulkalgal reef island settlement and high mobility across 700 km of seascape, central Torres Strait and northern Great Barrier Reef. *Quaternary International, 385*, 39–55.

McNiven, I. J. (2017). Edges of worlds: Torres Strait Islander peripheral participation in ancient globalizations. In T. Hodos (Ed.), *The Routledge handbook of globalization and archaeology* (pp. 319–334). New York: Routledge.

McNiven, I. J. (2021). Coral Sea cultural interaction sphere. In I. J. McNiven & B. David (Eds.), *The Oxford handbook of the archaeology of Indigenous Australia and New Guinea*. Oxford: Oxford University Press. https://doi.org/10.1093/oxfordhb/9780190095611.013.28

McNiven, I. J., Dunn, J. E., Crouch, J., & Gunditj Mirring Traditional Owners Aboriginal Corporation (2017). Kurtonitj stone house: Excavation of a mid-nineteenth century Aboriginal frontier site from Gunditjmara Country, south-west Victoria. *Archaeology in Oceania, 52,* 171–197.

Mitchell, S. (1995). A transient heritage: Trepanging sites on the Cobourg Peninsula. *Historic Environment,* 11(2–3), 37–46.

Mitchell, S. (1996). Dugongs and dugouts, sharptacks and shellbacks: Macassan contact and Aboriginal marine hunting on the Coburg Peninsula, northwestern Arnhem Land. *Bulletin of the Indo-Pacific Prehistory Association, 15,* 181–191.

Mitchell, S. R. A. (1994). *Culture contact and Indigenous economies on the Coburg Peninsula, northwestern Arnhem Land* (PhD thesis). Northern Territory University, Darwin.

Morwood, M. J., & Hobbs, D. R. (1997). The Asian connection: Preliminary report on Indonesian trepang sites on the Kimberley coast, N. W. Australia. *Archaeology in Oceania,* 32(3), 197–206.

Mulvaney, D. J. (1966). Beche-de-mer, Aborigines and Australian history. *Proceedings of the Royal Society of Victoria,* 79(2), 449–457.

Mulvaney, D. J. (1975). *The prehistory of Australia.* Melbourne: Penguin.

Oertle, A., Leavesley, M., Ulm, S., Mate, G., & Rosendahl, D. (2014). At the margins: Archaeological evidence for Macassan activities in the South Wellesley Islands, Gulf of Carpentaria. *Australasian Historical Archaeology, 32,* 64–71.

Paterson, A., & Wilson, A. (2009). Indigenous perceptions of contact at Inthanoona, northwest Western Australia. *Archaeology in Oceania,* 44(S1), 99–111.

Reimer, P. J., Austin, W. E. N., Bard, E., Bayliss, A., Blackwell, P. G., Bronk Ramsey, C. . . . Talamo, S. (2020). The IntCal20 Northern Hemisphere radiocarbon age calibration curve (0–55 cal kBP). *Radiocarbon,* 62(4), 725–757.

Rhoads, J. W. (1980). *Through a glass darkly: Present and past land-use systems of Papuan sagopalm users* (PhD thesis). Australian National University, Canberra https://openresea rch-repository.anu.edu.au/handle/1885/96947.

Roberts, D. A. (2004). Nautical themes in the Aboriginal rock paintings of Mount Borradaile, western Arnhem Land. *The Great Circle: Journal of the Australian Association for Maritime History,* 26(1), 19–50

Rose, F. G. G. (1960). *Classification of kin, age structure and marriage amongst Groote Eylandt Aborigines.* Berlin: Akademie Verlag.

Rowland, M. J. (2018). 65,000 years of isolation in Aboriginal Australia or continuity and external contacts? An assessment of the evidence with an emphasis on the Queensland coast. *Journal of the Anthropological Society of South Australia, 42,* 211–240.

Rowley, B. (1997). *The Makassar connection: A descriptive analysis and comparison of Macassan and Makassar earthenwares* (BA Honours thesis). The University of Western Australia, Crawley.

Schrire, C. (1972). Ethno-archaeological models and subsistence behaviour in Arnhem Land. In D. L. Clarke (Ed.), *Models in archaeology* (pp. 653–670). London: Methuen.

Spillet, P. (1988). *Gotong Royong: Hubungan Makassar–Marege* (Working together: Makassar–Marege relationship). *Bulletin of Indonesian Cultural and Educational Institute,* 5(1), 3–16.

Swadling, P. (2019). *Plumes from paradise: Trade cycles in outer Southeast Asia and their impact on New Guinea and nearby islands until 1920*. Sydney: Sydney University Press.

Taçon, P. S. C., & May, S. K. (2013a). Ship shape: An exploration of maritime-related depictions in Indigenous rock art and material culture. *The Great Circle: Journal of the Australian Association for Maritime History, 35*(2), 7–15.

Taçon, P. S. C., & May, S. K. (2013b). Rock art evidence for Macassan–Aboriginal contact in northwestern Arnhem Land. In M. Clark & S. K. May (Eds.), *Macassan history and heritage: Journeys, encounters and influences* (pp. 127–139). Canberra: ANU E Press.

Taçon, P. S. C., May, S. K., Fallon, S. J., Travers, M. E., Wesley, D., & Lamilami, R. (2010). A minimum age for early depictions of southeast Asian praus in the rock art of Arnhem Land, Northern Territory. *Australian Archaeology, 71*(1), 1–10.

Theden-Ringl, F., Fenner, J. N., Wesley, D., & Lamilami, R. (2011). Buried on foreign shores: Isotope analysis of the origin of human remains recovered from a Macassan site in Arnhem Land. *Australian Archaeology, 73*, 41–48.

Thomson, D. (1949). *Economic structure and the ceremonial cycle in Arnhem Land*. Melbourne: McMillan & Co.

Tindale, N. B. (1926). The natives of Groote Eylandt and the west coast of the Gulf of Carpentaria. *Records of the Australian Museum, 3*(2), 61–143.

Torrence, R., & Clarke, A. (2000). Negotiating difference: Practice makes theory for contemporary archaeology in Oceania. In A. Clarke & R. Torrence (Eds.), *The archaeology of difference: Negotiating cross-cultural engagements in Oceania* (pp. 1–32). London: Routledge.

Urry, J., & Walsh, M. (1981). The lost "Macassar language" of northern Australia. *Aboriginal History, 5*, 91–108.

Urwin, C., & Spriggs, M. (2021). The development (and imagined re-invention) of Australian archaeology in the twentieth century. In I. J. McNiven & B. David (Eds.), *The Oxford handbook of the archaeology of Indigenous Australia and New Guinea*. Oxford: Oxford University Press. https://doi.org/10.1093/oxfordhb/9780190095611.013.44

Warner, W. L. (1932). Malay influence on the Aboriginal cultures of north-eastern Arnhem Land. *Oceania, 2*(1), 476–495.

Wesley, D. (2014). *Bayini, Macassans, Balanda, and Bininj: Defining the Indigenous past of Arnhem Land through culture contact* (PhD thesis). Australian National University, Canberra.

Wesley, D., Jones, T., O'Connor, S., & Dickinson, W. R. (2014). Earthenware of Malara, Anuru Bay: A reassessment of potsherds from a Macassan trepang processing site, Arnhem Land, Australia, and implications for Macassan trade and the trepang industry. *Australian Archaeology, 79*, 14–25.

Wesley, D., McKinnon, J. F., & Raupp, J. T. (2012). Sails set in stone: A technological analysis of non-Indigenous watercraft rock art paintings in north western Arnhem Land. *Journal of Maritime Archaeology, 7*(2), 245–269.

Wesley, D., & Litster, M. (2015). "Small, individually nondescript and easily overlooked": Contact beads from northwest Arnhem Land in an Indigenous-Macassan-European hybrid economy. *Australian Archaeology, 80*(1), 1–16.

Wesley, D., O'Connor, S., & Fenner, J. N. (2016). Re-evaluating the timing of the Indonesian trepang industry in north-west Arnhem Land: Chronological investigations at Malara (Anuru Bay A). *Archaeology in Oceania, 51*(3), 169–195.

Wesley, D., & Viney, J. (2016). South East Asian influences in western Arnhem Land rock art decorative infill. *Journal of the Anthropological Society of South Australia, 40*, 35–69.

Worsley, P. M. (1955). Early Asian contacts with Australia. *Past & Present, 7*, 1–11.

CHAPTER 39

WHALING AND SEALING IN NINETEENTH-CENTURY AUSTRALIA

MARTIN GIBBS AND LYNETTE RUSSELL

INTRODUCTION

THE maritime industries of whaling and sealing largely grew out of the eighteenth-century industrial revolution and the Western need for oil to light the darkness of cities and grease the wheels of machinery (Morton 1982). For over eighty years beginning in 1776, the Southern Whale Fishery (SWF) was perhaps the most successful and profitable fishery in the world, taking in the Pacific, Indian, and Atlantic southern waters. The British dominated the SWF once they had lost access to the North America whaling grounds; a consequence of the American War of Independence (Chatwin 1996: 4). These Southern oceans teamed with cetaceans, both the Mysticeti or baleen, and the Odontoceti or toothed whales, of which the Sperm (*Physeter macrocephalus*) was the largest.

Conventional histories have tended to emphasize official exploration of the Indian-Pacific maritime frontiers (e.g., Dolin 2008; Tønnessen & Johnsen 1982), with more recent attention being paid to the spread of settler-colonialism. However, over the past three decades, there has been increasing interest in the extent and nature of mercantile and industrial maritime enterprises as colonial entities (Gibbs 1996; Gojak 1998; Russell 2012). Of particular interest is the way these different types of enterprises engaged with and affected Indigenous communities. This chapter focuses on Antipodean whaling and sealing through the late eighteenth and nineteenth centuries, examining social and economic impacts through the lenses of the overlapping themes of mobility, opportunity, and marginality. However, it is worth noting that while the archaeological implications are often clear, explicit archaeological investigation to identify Indigenous involvement in these industries has been limited, while for reasons that will become evident in the section "Archaeologies of Aboriginal Connections with, and Involvement in, Whaling and Sealing" below, disentangling that presence within the archaeological record may in many instances be difficult.

WHALING

Late eighteenth- and nineteenth-century whaling and sealing were two allied extractive industries encompassing a range of approaches. Whaling was primarily aimed at the harvesting of oil rendered from the fat or blubber of any number of marine mammal species. This oil was used extensively for high-quality illumination and lubrication until the mid-nineteenth century, when the development of refined mineral oils made the harvesting of whale oil largely redundant. The baleen mouth plates, largely from humpback (*Megaptera novaeangliae*) and Southern right (*Eubalaena australis*) whales, were extracted for use as a semi-flexible material in a range of products from umbrella and corset stays to carriage springs, riding crops, and even fishing rods (Lauffenburger 1993). Baleen was harvested well into the twentieth century until sophisticated flexible plastics emerged as alternatives. Far more rarely, the extremely valuable ambergris from sperm whales was extracted as a fixative for perfume (Cousteau & Paccalet 1988). Whaling and sealing were, in many ways, interchangeable with the labour force capable of working both industries often seasonally. Both industries were staffed with polyglot crews of 'natives' and 'newcomers', to borrow Bruce Trigger's phrase (Trigger 1986). The Australian industries were dominated by Europeans, Lascars from the Indian subcontinent, Polynesians (including Maori), and others.

In the period under consideration, whaling was carried out in specialized boats carrying eight to ten men who rowed up to a whale before the harpooner 'fixed' (stabbed into it) a toggle-headed harpoon that attached a line from whale to boat. There would usually follow a period of the enraged animal dragging the boat at speed as it fled or dived, although once it was exhausted and had slowed, the line would be used to pull the whaleboat close enough for the headsman to stab the animal with a long, razor-sharp lance until it died. Harpooning and lancing whales was a dangerous task and required heroic levels of skill and strength. As experienced spearhunters, Aboriginal men were highly suited to work as harpooners, and many were employed in both shore-based and pelagic operations (Russell 2012: 34, 37, 65, 70, 140). Once lanced, the dead whale would then be towed back to ship or shore and flensed of its blubber and commercially valuable body parts (Haley 1948; Hohman 1928). The blubber was rendered in large metal try-pots heated with coal or wood fires. The oil was stored in large wooden kegs (Bennett 1840; Cheever 1853).

Large-scale commercial whaling was carried out using pelagic vessels equipped to undertake two- to three-year-long voyages. Such duration was necessary to traverse the globe following the whales' seasonal migration routes, as knowledge of the distributions and habits of the whale populations was constantly refined. Each whaleship had the boats and infrastructure to chase, kill, and process whales while at sea (Dolin 2008).

The United States of America, Britain, several European nations, and, to a lesser extent, colonial Australian fleets operated at various times within Australian waters. While the pelagic sperm whale was the primary target, whaleships would periodically return to shore for food, fuel, and water, and in some circumstances engage in hunting of coastal species such as Humpback and Right whales. Alternatively, hunting of Humpbacks and Right whales was carried out from fixed-location shore stations (Gibbs 2010). These shore-based whalers operated out of camps or stations, bringing the whale back to shore for processing. The industrial processes of both pelagic and shore-based parties are well documented (e.g., Creighton 1995; Currie 2001; Gibbs 2010; Nash 2003; Pearson 1983). In both pelagic and shore-based operations, the meat from whales was of no commercial or practical use and would be discarded, with the flensed carcass cut free from the whaleship and allowed to sink or float away, or if at a shore station, then towed back out to sea or simply left in place on the shore.

The range of whaling industrial operations was truly global and often well beyond the accepted boundaries of either settlement or official exploration. The presence of whalers in far-flung and remote parts of the globe, their industrial and trade activities, and the collection of intelligence became factors in the geopolitical intentions and expansion of the European and American powers, and has been termed by historians the 'whaling frontier' (Gibson & Whitehead 1993: x; Weeks 2006: 73). By the mid-1770s, American whalers had commenced operations in the Australian region, soon to be joined by Britain and other European nations.

Traditional Aboriginal Whale Relations

There was no tradition of offshore whaling within precontact Australian Aboriginal economies, although whales did figure in Dreaming stories and as totem animals. In addition, stranded or dead whales on the shore provided situational superabundances of food and opportunities for feasting. Archaeological finds, including whale teeth, are known from several sites (e.g., Barker 2004: 79) but represent equivocal evidence for precontact whaling. Around 1817, colonial artist Joseph Lycett painted an Awabakal communal feast as a beached whale is butchered and the meat is distributed to family groups. The image relates to the New South Wales coast near the mouth of the Hunter River (Figure 39.1). An interesting set of sandstone engravings in the Sydney region of New South Wales show people inside whale bodies. Stanbury and Clegg (1990: 22–23) suggest that the drawing may be of 'singing whales', where 'the man is a magician performing a rite to entice the whale to become stranded so that the tribe may feast'. It is also possible that this is a visual rendering of a traditional healing practice. The man 'may be lying in the whale to cure himself of an illness—a custom of those Aboriginal tribes that lived near the eastern seaboard' (Stanbury & Clegg 1990: 23; see also Attenbrow 2002).

FIGURE 39.1. 'Aborigines cooking and eating beached whales, Newcastle, New South Wales, ca. 1817'.

(Watercolour by Joseph Lycett. Private Collection.)

Beached whales would offer a superabundance of food and would enable groups to engage in interregional gatherings. In 1770, Sir Joseph Banks, on Captain James Cook's voyage of discovery, first recorded that Aboriginal people feasted on stranded whales (Beaglehole 1963: 54). Two decades later (7 September 1790), First-fleet observer Watkin Tench noted that:

> a party of men, went in a boat to Manly Cove, intending to land there and walk on to Broken Bay. On drawing near the shore, a dead whale in the most disgusting state of putrification was seen lying on the beach, and at least two hundred Indians surrounding it, broiling the flesh on different fires and feasting on it with the most extravagant marks of greediness and rapture.
>
> (Cited in Flannery 1996: 24)

Emphasizing the value of a whale stranding, Tench further observed: 'Whereas every sun awakes the native of New South Wales (unless a whale be thrown upon the coast) to a renewal of labour, to provide subsistence for the present day' (1793, cited in Flannery 1996: 134–136).

Based on nineteenth-century ethnographic observations from southwest Victoria, archaeologist Harry Lourandos noted that during 'winter months, when seas were high, large numbers of whales were either washed up or lured ashore . . . these formed the resource base upon which large-scale intergroup communal and ceremonial occasions were held, with up to 1000 people attending' (Lourandos 1988: 278).

Whales, ubiquitous in pre-European contact Australian waters, served many roles and uses in Aboriginal society. They were a resource, food source, healing practice, and part of the Aboriginal known world. George French Angas, visiting South Australia in 1844, recorded the use of whale ribs supporting boughs and leaves creating a shelter or 'encampment' (Figure 39.2).

Although Aboriginal people did not traditionally hunt whales with harpoons and the like, Ian McNiven (2010) has suggested that ritual engagement with whales, which Aboriginal people attest caused the whales to strand and hence be available for whale feasts and ceremonies, might be thought of as a kind of hunting 'using spiritual technology' (McNiven 2010: 220). Singing the whales ashore is an application of this spiritual technology.

It is almost certain that with the emergence of commercial whaling along the Australian coasts from the late 1780s, the number of cast-off whale carcasses washing ashore would have increased significantly, influencing Aboriginal seasonal mobility patterns. However, it was the establishment of colonial shore-based stations and the semi-regular supply of masses of meat that drew Aboriginal people towards the coast during the winter months of the whale season. This meat was available to Aboriginal communities, given, as noted above, that nineteenth-century European whalers had no economic (or dietary) use for whale meat and flensed whale carcasses. At stations close to European settlements, this alternative (and abundant) food supply also came at a time

FIGURE 39.2. 'Natives of Encounter Bay', South Australia, c. 1846.
(Lithograph by George French Angas (from Angas 1847: Plate 16). Private Collection.)

when land alienation by colonists reduced access to traditional terrestrial food sources. Historical descriptions of colonial whaling stations frequently mention this Aboriginal presence, as well as implying the presence of campsites nearby.

It is not surprising that Aboriginal people and non-Aboriginal whalers, especially at more distant locations, were progressively drawn into various types of economic and social engagements and entanglements. Aboriginal hunters could provide food to supplement station diets, while Aboriginal women were party to short- and long-term sexual and domestic arrangements (Russell 2007; numerous references in Russell 2012; see also Kostaglou 1995; Kostaglou & McCarthy 1991; Paterson & Wilson 2019). Soon after their arrival, whaling station operators both recognized and harnessed the skills of local Aboriginal men, including their keen eyesight, stamina, and marksmanship. Young Aboriginal men (and in the earliest periods possibly Aboriginal women as well) were hired on as boat hands, and some eventually rose in status to become harpooners and headsmen, the most respected positions aboard a whaleboat crew (Chamberlain 1988: 120). Perhaps following international tradition, there is historical evidence that their status within the camps and crews was as equals, and as senior crew they were empowered to give orders to non-Aboriginal hands (Gibbs 2003; Lawrence 2006). In Western Australia, there were times when Aboriginal whalers may have made up as much as 30% of the total workforce (Gibbs 1996: 446). Aboriginal whalers were paid in cash and in trade goods, depending on the station (Staniforth, Briggs, & Lewczak 2001; Russell 2008, 2012). This economic bounty was distributed among the local Aboriginal community and clearly had significant social impacts (e.g., Gibbs 2003; Russell 2007, 2008).

Historian Henry Reynolds has noted that maritime industries such as whaling were 'probably less disruptive of Aboriginal life than either mining or pastoralism' and fitted easily into the accustomed pattern of Aboriginal seasonal use of coasts (Reynolds 1982: 175). Although whalers were often only a seasonal presence and generally did not extend their terrestrial activities to areas much beyond the immediate surrounds of stations, violence could still ensue between Aboriginal and non-Aboriginal groups, for a range of reasons (Paterson & Wilson 2019). The most notorious of these incidents was the Convincing Ground massacre of 1833–1834, when an argument over ownership of a beached whale led to whalers near Portland (southwest Victoria) brutally slaughtering members of the local Gunditjmara clan (Clark 2011).

George Augustus Robinson, guardian and protector of Aborigines in Tasmania and, later, the Port Phillip District in southeastern Australia, now the state of Victoria, visited Portland in May 1841. He described a nearby piece of land that local colonial settlers referred to as the 'Convincing Ground'. Robinson was told of the origin of this name, which he recorded in his personal daily journal:

> It is stated that the natives fought the whalers. Now, the cause of this fight, if such an unequal contest can be so designated, firearms are certain death against spears, was occasioned by the whalers going to get the whalebone from the fish, when the natives, not knowing their intentions and supposing they intended to take away the

fish which the natives considered theirs and which it had been for 1000s of years previous, they of course resisted the aggression on the part of the white men; it was the first year of the fishery, and the whalers having used their guns beat them off and hence called the spot the Convincing Ground. That was because they convinced them of their mistake and which, but for their firearms they perhaps could not have done.

(Clark 1988: 211)

In his official notes, Robinson made the following, more measured observation:

Among the remarkable places on the coast, is the "Convincing Ground," originating in a severe conflict which took place a few years previous between the Aborigines and Whalers on which the occasion a large number of the former were slain. The circumstances are that a whale had come on shore and the Natives who feed on the carcase claimed it was their own. The whalers said they would "convince them" and had recourse to firearms. On this spot a fishery is now established. It is unsurprising that there would be disputes over the ownership of whales and whale meat, as this was a resource that the Aboriginal people were used to harvesting, albeit infrequently.

(Clark 1988: 19)

The historical veracity of the Convincing Ground massacre has been much debated, however, as the meticulous forensic research of geographer Ian Clark has shown, although the 'actual date of the massacre is uncertain, and we may never know the numbers of Aboriginal people killed . . . the evidence that it took place is overwhelming' (Clark 2011: 103). The archaeological implications of this event have yet to materialize.

While colonial shore-based whaling was often closely aligned with other forms of settlement activity and maritime interests, pelagic whaling had a very different complexion. In particular, pelagic whalers had a long tradition of multiracial crews, although the degree to which peoples of different ethnic backgrounds were treated well varied from ship to ship (Melville 1851; see also Bolster 1990; Chappell 1997; McKissack & McKissack 1999). However, there is good evidence that numerous Aboriginal men were signed aboard whaleships (Chamberlain 1988). The best known of the Aboriginal pelagic whalers was a Tasmanian Palawa man named William Lanné (Russell 2008, 2012), although historical accounts record other men returning from voyages of several years or more.

SEALING

Although often discussed in the same context as whaling, sealing was a very different industry in its scope and scale, primarily focussed on obtaining skins, although in some instances oil might also be extracted. As for whaling, sealing was an international industry with vessels searching out sealing grounds, sometimes in conjunction with whaling operations. Sealing groups might remain for a period of days and weeks, slaughtering animals within one colony or area. In some instances, sealers were dropped off for a period of weeks or months before being collected. Traditionally, Aboriginal people hunted Fur seals (*Arctocephalus forsteri*) and Sealions (*Neophoca cinera*) along the southern Australian coast and offshore islands (Russell 2012). European sealers hunted these species, along with the oil-rich Southern Elephant seal (*Mirounga leonina*) which is occasionally found in Australian coastal waters, but more frequently in the sub-Antarctic seal grounds. Colonial sealers based on islands such as those of Bass Strait were serviced by vessels periodically dropping off supplies and taking away the skins. However, there was also a segment of the sealing industry where much more permanent camps and settlements were established.

In contrast to whales, seals were a traditional food source actively sought by Aboriginal communities along the coasts and nearby offshore islands of the southern parts of Australia. Aboriginal women in Tasmania were skilled hunters, using clubs to stun and kill seals (Plomley 1966; Plomley & Henley 1990). Russell (2007, 2012) has argued that this proficiency in the industrial processes of seal hunting, rather than the accepted narratives of sexual exploitation, may explain why Aboriginal women were a significant and valued group in the early colonial sealing industry. From the later years of the eighteenth century and through the first decades of the nineteenth century, Aboriginal women, especially those from Tasmania, were transported as part of sealing crews to coasts and islands far beyond Bass Strait, including westward to Kangaroo Island and even further west to the Archipelago of the Recherche off southeast Western Australia (Russell 2012: 43, 156).

According to Lourandos (1988: 278), numerous archaeological sites along the southwest Victorian coast show evidence of seal hunting, especially of fur seals (see also Bowdler & Lourandos 1982; Gill 1967; Mulvaney 1962). Perhaps the best studied of all Australian sealing grounds is that of Kangaroo Island (Clarke 1996; Taylor 1996, 2000, 2002; Walshe 2014; Walshe & Loy 2004). Neale Draper, in a report on archaeological excavations at Cape du Couedic Rock Shelter, noted that in pre-European times the occupants of Kangaroo Island hunted, butchered, and consumed sea lions. The site, dated to between 7500 and 5500 years BP, shows evidence for the processing and consumption of sea lion adults, subadults, and pups (Draper 2006: 27).

Despite the interest in Kangaroo Island, there is relatively little archaeological literature that is revealing of the lives of the historic-period sealers (although see Russell 2007; Walshe 2014; Walshe & Loy 2004). European sealers were often characterized accurately as being a combination of escaped or former convicts, or social misfits, living well beyond the normal boundaries of European settlement, often in open relationships with Aboriginal women (Taylor 2000, 2002). This social and physical marginality to mainstream colonial society, as well as the hybrid cultural (European and Aboriginal) nature of these groups, saw them create unique, semi-permanent settlements in remote locations (Russell 2012). The sealing communities on the Bass Strait islands of King and Flinders, and further west to Kangaroo Islands were sizeable and took on a multigenerational aspect (Russell 2005).

Archaeologies of Aboriginal Connections with, and Involvement in, Whaling and Sealing

The sheer size of the whales that were stranded or washed ashore meant that meat could be readily carved off without the arduous task of sawing through bones, leaving no obvious evidence (such as bone fragments) to indicate whale as a dietary element in pre- or postcontact archaeological sites. However, there are a few examples of whale bones being found on sites, possibly opportunistically salvaged from carcasses washed ashore (e.g., Barker 2004: 79). One such object is a smoothed whale vertebral epiphysis that was collected in the late 1890s from an Aboriginal site near Kalgoorlie in southern Western Australia, more than 300 km inland (Dortch 1988). While this object almost certainly indicates active trade connections between coastal and inland communities, whether the object was utilitarian or symbolic, or whether pre- or postcontact, is unknown (Anderson 2016: 131). A similar question hangs over the several teeth from a sperm whale found in a precontact midden site excavated in South Australia in the 1920s (Clarke 2001: 22). Another signifier of whales worth exploring in an Australian context is the potential presence of whale barnacles (see Bianucci et al. 2006). The potential for eDNA evidence of cetaceans in the soil of these sites has yet to be explored (see Thomsen & Willerslev 2015).

During the 1980s and 1990s, there was a surge of interest by Australian historical and maritime archaeologists in locating and, in some instances, excavating shore-based whaling stations, with the result that it is in relative terms a highly studied aspect of Australia's maritime industrial past (e.g., Lawrence & Staniforth, 1998; Stuart, 1998). While many of these studies recognized the strong connections between whaling activity and Aboriginal men and women, as well as the place of whaling as an agent of cultural contact, very few identified archaeological evidence of these engagements and entanglements. As noted above, the increased availability of whale meat during the shore-based whaling season actively drew Aboriginal people towards the coasts to a degree that was not usual for the winter seasons. For Aboriginal groups whose country included shore-based whaling stations, the norm was to establish a fringe camp nearby for the several months or more of the whaling season, although in some instances access to the station settlement itself was prevented (Gibbs 2003; Staniforth et al. 2001).

It is not unreasonable to suppose that economic exchanges between shore-based whalers and Aboriginal groups, as indicated in the historical record, might manifest in the archaeological records of fringe campsites. Most archaeological studies of the 1980s–1990s focussed on the industrial processes and lifeways of the stations themselves and did not make any particular effort to find or investigate associated Indigenous fringe camps. Of the Aboriginal campsites located near to whaling stations that have been recorded, objects include modified European materials in the form of flaked glass and ceramics, although whether these are indicative of contemporary economic interactions or later salvage of materials from abandoned station sites is unclear (Staniforth et al. 2001). Recent work by archaeologists in the northwest of Western Australia has documented rock engravings made by American whalers that interact with, indeed overlap, Aboriginal petroglyphs (Paterson et al. 2019). In this region, the archaeological team also identified a possible whaler's grave that had incorporated Aboriginal rock art (Paterson 2006; Souter, Paterson, & Hook 2006). Beyond these sites, little further evidence has been forthcoming on direct social interactions between whalers and local Aboriginal people.

Archaeological excavations within whaling settlement sites have not yet been able to identify unambiguous evidence of Aboriginal cohabitation. Aboriginal men working within the crews and Aboriginal women in domestic situations with whalers would presumably have been housed within the huts of the station and would have had access to European goods, such that distinguishing their presence is difficult, if not impossible. The presence of the remains of native fauna within station middens may be indicative of economic interactions between cultures (Gibbs 1996, 2005; Lawrence 2001), but might also be explained by other processes (e.g., hunting by Europeans). This is not to say that archaeological evidence of Aboriginal connections to these sites has not been found. Lawrence's (2006) several excavations in Tasmania found that whaling stations were not infrequently located on what had been places of Aboriginal occupation.

Although few sealing sites have been subjected to sustained scholarly archaeological interest, with Anderson's work on Middle Island in the Archipelago of the Recherche being one of the rare examples (Anderson 2016), there is good reason to consider these as potentially rich sources for knowledge on the early contact relations, economy, and cross-cultural complexity of the maritime industry.

Conclusion

Aboriginal participation in the whaling and sealing industries ranged from entrepreneurial and egalitarian through to brutal and exploitative. Their presence in and around whaling stations is undeniable, with excellent historical and ethnographic evidence for shifting patterns of residential occupation as Aboriginal populations took advantage of the whale meat by-products of the industry as a dietary resource. In so doing, these communities were extending their traditional maritime activities and harvesting marine mammal remains, albeit on a larger scale. As George Augustus Robinson observed in the 1840s in southwest Victoria, Aboriginal people had been using beached whale products for thousands of years. The continuity of traditional activities can be also deduced from those instances where Aboriginal men engaged in long-distance voyaging on-board whaleships. As skilled harpooners and hunters, they were key members of the industry. Similarly, the sealing industry relied on the skills of Aboriginal women as an essential part of its productivity. The impact of these industries on the contact-period landscapes of Aboriginal peoples and the nature of these complex social, economic, and exchange relationships are all potentially archaeologically visible, yet await dedicated attention.

Although this chapter has focussed on the late eighteenth and nineteenth centuries, it should be recalled that whaling did continue into the last quarter of the twentieth century and the era of overly efficient powered whaleships, explosive harpoons, and large industrial processing plants. Aboriginal people continued to be involved in whaling at stations such as Frenchman's Bay, Carnarvon, and Point Cloates (Western Australia), as well as at Byron Bay (NSW) and Tangalooma (Qld) (Gibbs 2010). However, these histories and archaeologies of Aboriginal industrial participation and the labour conditions they experienced have yet to be documented.

References

Anderson, R. (2016). *Beneath the colonial gaze: Modelling maritime society and cross-cultural contact on Australia's Southern Ocean frontier—the Archipelago of the Recherche, Western Australia* (PhD thesis). University of Western Australia, Perth.

Angas, G. F. (1847). *South Australia illustrated*. London: Thomas McLean.

Attenbrow, V. (2002). *Sydney's Aboriginal past: Investigating the archaeological and historical Sydney*. Sydney: University of New South Wales Press.

Barker, B. (2004). *The Sea People: Late Holocene maritime specialisation in the Whitsunday Islands, central Queensland*. Canberra, ACT: Pandanus Books.

Beaglehole, J. (Ed.) (1963). *The Endeavour Journal of Joseph Banks: 1768–1771*. Sydney: Angus and Robertson.

Bennett, F. D. (1840). *Narrative of a whaling voyage round the globe from the year 1833 to 1836: Comprising sketches of Polynesia, California, the Indian Archipelago, etc. with an account of southern whales, the sperm whale fishery, and the natural history of the climates visited* (Vol. 1). London: R. Bentley.

Bianucci, G., Landini, W., & Buckeridge, J. (2006). Whale barnacles and Neogene cetacean migration routes, *New Zealand Journal of Geology and Geophysics*, 49(1), 115–120.

Bolster, W. J. (1990). 'To feel like a man': Black seamen in the northern states, 1800–1860. *Journal of American History*, 76(4), 1173–1199.

Bowdler, S., & Lourandos, H. (1982). Both sides of Bass Strait. In S. Bowdler (Ed.), *Coastal archaeology in eastern Australia: Proceedings of the 1980 Valla Conference on Australian Prehistory* (pp. 121–132). Canberra: Australian National University.

Chamberlain, S. (1988). *The Hobart whaling industry 1830 to 1900* (PhD thesis). La Trobe University, Melbourne.

Chappell, D. (1997). *Double ghosts: Oceanian voyagers on Euroamerican ships*. Armonk, NY: M. E. Sharpe.

Chatwin, D. (1996). *A trade so uncontrollably uncertain: A study of the English southern whale fishery from 1815 to 1860* (Unpublished Master's thesis). Australian National University, Canberra.

Cheever, H. T. (1853). *The whale and his captors; or, The whalemen's adventures, and the whale's biography as gathered on the homeward cruise of the 'Commodore Preble'*. New York: Harper.

Clark, I. (1988). *The Port Phillip journals of George Augustus Robinson: 8 March–7 April 1842 and 18 March–29 April 1843*. Monash Publications in Geography 34. Melbourne: Department of Geography, Monash University.

Clark, I. D. (2011). The Convincing Ground Aboriginal massacre at Portland Bay, Victoria: Fact or fiction? *Aboriginal History, 35,* 79–109.

Clarke, P. A. (1996). Early European interaction with Aboriginal hunters and gatherers on Kangaroo Island, South Australia. *Aboriginal History, 20,* 51–81.

Clarke, P. A. (2001). The significance of whales to the Aboriginal people of southern South Australia. *Records of the South Australian Museum, 34*(1), 19–35.

Cousteau, J., & Paccalet, Y. (1988). *Whales*. New York: Harry N. Abrams Publishers.

Creighton, M. S. (1995). *Rites and passages: The experience of American whaling, 1830–1870.* New York: Cambridge University Press.

Currie, S. (2001). *Thar she blows: American whaling in the nineteenth century*. Minneapolis: Lerner.

Dolin, E. J. (2008). *Leviathan: The history of whaling in America*. New York: W. W. Norton.

Dortch, C. E. (1988). The Kalgoorlie whale bone: A probable example of long range Aboriginal transport of a marine object. *Records of the Western Australian Museum, 14*(1), 145–149.

Draper, N. (2006). Mid-Holocene hunters of Kangaroo Island: The perspective from Cape du Coudeic Rockshelter. In S. Ulm & I. Lilley (Eds.), *An archaeological life: Papers in honour of Jay Hall* (pp. 27–46). Brisbane: Aboriginal and Torres Strait Islander Studies Unit, University of Queensland.

Flannery, T. (Ed.). (1996). *Watkin Tench, 1788*; comprising a narrative of the expedition to Botany Bay and a complete account of the settlement of Port Jackson. Melbourne: Text Publishing Co.

Gibbs, M. (1996). *The historical archaeology of shore-based whaling in Western Australia, 1836–79* (PhD thesis). University of Western Australia, Perth.

Gibbs, M. (2003). Nebinyan's song—the Aboriginal whalers of south-western Australia. *Aboriginal History, 27,* 11–20.

Gibbs, M. (2005). The archaeology of subsistence on the maritime frontier. *Australasian Historical Archaeology, 23,* 115–122.

Gibbs, M. (2010). *The shore whalers of Western Australia: Historical archaeology of a maritime frontier*. Studies in Australasian Historical Archaeology 2. Sydney: Sydney University Press.

Gibson, A., & Whitehead, J. (1993). *Yankees in paradise: The Pacific Basin frontier*. Albuquerque: University of New Mexico Press.

Gill, E. D. (1967). Evolution of the Warrnambool-Port Fairy coast and the Tower Hill eruption, western Victoria. In J. N. Jennings & J. A. Mabbutt (Eds.), *Landform studies from Australia and New Guinea* (pp. 340–364). Canberra: Australian National University.

Gojak, D. (1998). An historical and archaeological overview of the whaling industry in New South Wales and Norfolk Island. In S. Lawrence & M. Staniforth (Eds.), *The archaeology of whaling in southern Australia and New Zealand* (pp. 11–20). Sydney: Australasian Society for Historical Archaeology.

Haley, N. C. (1948). *Whalehunt. The narrative of a voyage by Nelson Cole Haley, harpooner in the ship* Charles W. Morgan, *1849–1853*. New York: Washburn.

Hohman, E. (1928). *The American whaleman; a study of life and labor in the whaling industry*. New York: Longmans, Green.

Kostaglou, P. (1995). *Shore based whaling in Tasmania archaeological research project*. Hobart: Tasmanian Parks and Wildlife Service.

Kostaglou, P., & McCarthy, J. (1991). *Whaling and sealing sites in South Australia*. Special Publication No. 6. Australian Institute for Maritime Archaeology.

Lauffenburger, J. A. (1993). Baleen in museum collections: Its sources, uses, and identification. *Journal of the American Institute of Conservation, 32*(3), 213–230.

Lawrence, S. (2001). Foodways on two colonial whaling stations: Archaeological and historical evidence for diet in nineteenth century Tasmania. *Journal of the Royal Australian Historical Society, 87*(2), 209–229.

Lawrence, S. (2006). *Whalers and free men: Life on Tasmania's colonial whaling stations*. Melbourne: Australian Scholarly Publishing.

Lawrence, S., & Staniforth. M. (Eds.). (1998). *The archaeology of whaling in southern Australia and New Zealand*. The Australasian Society for Historical Archaeology and The Australian Institute for Maritime Archaeology, Special Publication 10.

Lourandos, H. (1988). Seals, sedentism and change in Bass Strait. In B. Meehan & R. Jones (Eds.), *Archaeology with ethnography: An Australian perspective* (pp. 277–285). Occasional Papers in Prehistory no. 15. Canberra: Research School of Pacific Studies, The Australian National University.

McKissack, P. C., & McKissack, F. L. (1999). *Black hands, white sails: The story of African-American whalers*. New York: Scholastic Press.

McNiven, I. J. (2010). Navigating the human-animal divide: Marine mammal hunters and rituals of sensory allurement. *World Archaeology, 42*(2), 215–230.

Melville, H. (1851). *Moby Dick; or, the whale*. 1967 reprint. New York: W. W. Norton.

Morton, H. (1982). *The whale's wake*. Dunedin: University of Otago Press.

Mulvaney, D. J. (1962). Archaeological excavations on the Aire River, Otway Peninsula, Victoria. *Proceedings of the Royal Society of Victoria, 75*, 1–15.

Nash, M. (2003). *The bay whalers: Tasmania's shore based whaling industry*. Canberra: Navarine.

Paterson, A. (2006). Towards a historical archaeology of Western Australia's northwest. *Australasian Historical Archaeology, 24*, 99–111.

Paterson, A., Anderson, R., Mulvaney, K., de Koning, S., Dortch, J., & McDonald, J., (2019). 'So ends this day: American whalers in Yaburara Country, Dampier Archipelago.' *Antiquity, 93*(367), 218–235.

Paterson, A., & Wilson, C. (2019). Ngarrindjeri whaling narratives and reconciliation at Encounter Bay, South Australia. *RCC Perspectives: Transformations in Environment and Society, 5*, 91–98.

Pearson, M. (1983). The technology of whaling in Australian waters in the 19th century. *Australian Journal of Historical Archaeology, 1*, 40–54.

Plomley, B., & Henley, K. K. (1990). The sealers of Bass Strait and the Cape Barren Island community. *Papers and Proceedings of the Tasmanian Historical Research Association, 37*(2–3), 37–127.

Plomley, N. J. (Ed.). (1966). *Friendly mission: The Tasmanian journals and papers of George Augustus Robinson, 1829–1834*. Hobart: Tasmanian Historical Research Association.

Reynolds, H. (1982). *The other side of the frontier*. Melbourne: Penguin.

Russell, L. (2005). Kangaroo Island sealers and their descendants: Ethnic and gender ambiguities in the archaeology of a creolised community. *Australian Archaeology, 60*(1), 1–5.

Russell, L. (2007). 'Dirty domestics and worse cooks': Aboriginal women's agency and domestic frontiers, southern Australia 1800–1850. *Frontiers: An Interdisciplinary Journal of Women's Studies, 28*, 18–47.

Russell, L. (2008). 'A New Holland half-caste'. The remarkable life of sealer and whaler Tommy Chaseland: Diaspora, autonomy and hybridity. *History Australia*, 5(1), 08.1–08.15.

Russell, L. (2012). *Roving mariners: Australian Aboriginal whalers and sealers in the Southern Oceans 1790–1870*. Albany: State University of New York Press.

Souter, C., Paterson, A. G., & Hook, F. (2006). The assessment of archaeological sites on Barrow Island and the Dampier Archipelago, Pilbara, Western Australia: A collaborative approach. *Bulletin of the Australasian Institute of Maritime Archaeology*, 30, 85–92.

Stanbury, P., & Clegg, J. (1990). *A field guide to Aboriginal rock engravings, with special reference to those around Sydney*. Sydney: Sydney University Press.

Staniforth, M., Briggs, S., & Lewczak, C. (2001). Archaeology unearthing the invisible people: European women and children and Aboriginal people at South Australian shore-based whaling stations. *Mains'l Haul: A Journal of Pacific Maritime History*, 36(3), 12–19.

Stuart, I. (1998). Sealing and whaling seascapes. In S. Lawrence & M. Staniforth (Eds.), *The archaeology of whaling in southern Australia and New Zealand* (pp. 98–102). The Australasian Society for Historical Archaeology and The Australian Institute for Maritime Archaeology, Special Publication 10.

Taylor, R. (1996). *Sticking to the land: A history of exclusion on Kangaroo Island, 1827–1996*

Taylor, R. (2000). Savages and saviours: The Australian sealers and Aboriginal survival. *Journal of Australian Studies*, 66, 73–84.

(Unpublished Master's thesis). University of Melbourne, Melbourne.

Taylor, R. (2002). *Unearthed: The Aboriginal Tasmanians of Kangaroo Island*. Adelaide: Wakefield Press.

Thomsen, F. P., & Willerslev, E. (2015). Environmental DNA—An emerging tool in conservation for monitoring past and present biodiversity. *Biological Conservation*, 183, 4–18.

Tønnessen, J. N., & Johnsen, A. O. (1982). *The history of modern whaling*. Berkeley: University of California Press.

Trigger, B. G., (1986). *Natives and newcomers: Canada's 'heroic age' reconsidered*. Manchester: Manchester University Press.

Walshe, K. (2014). Archaeological evidence for a sealer's and wallaby hunter's skinning site on Kangaroo Island, South Australia. *The Journal of Island and Coastal Archaeology*, 9(1), 130–143.

Walshe, K., & Loy, T. (2004). An adze manufactured from a telegraph insulator, Harvey's Return, Kangaroo Island. *Australian Archaeology*, 58, 38–40.

Weeks, W. (2006). American expansion 1815–60. In R. Schulzinger (Ed.), *A companion to American foreign relations* (pp. 64–78). New York: Wiley-Blackwell.

CHAPTER 40

FATAL FRONTIER

Temporal and Spatial Considerations of the Native Mounted Police and Colonial Violence Across Queensland

LYNLEY A. WALLIS, HEATHER BURKE, BRYCE BARKER, AND NOELENE COLE

Introduction

ARCHAEOLOGICAL research on Indigenous–European[1] 'contact' in Australia initially focused on the European experience (e.g., Allen 1973; Birmingham 1992), reflecting a disciplinary divide between what was then known as prehistoric (Aboriginal) and historical (European) archaeology. Recent scholarship on the archaeology of rock art, missions, pastoral stations, and fringe camps has considered Indigenous agency so as to better encompass a more holistic view of contact cultural interaction (e.g., Brown, Avery, & Goulding 2002; Byrne 2003; Cole 2010; David, McNiven, Attenbrow, Flood, & Collins 1994; Griffin 2010; Harrison 2004, 2007; Lydon 2009a, 2009b, 2009b; McNiven 2018; McNiven & Russell 2002; Paterson 2006; Smith 2000; Wesley 2013). Even so, archaeological studies rarely explore the conflict that often underpinned cross-cultural encounters. Instead, the examination of frontier conflict in Australia has largely remained the domain of historians (e.g., Allbrook & Jebb 2009; Bottoms 2013; Connors 2015; Critchett 1990; Evans, Saunders, & Cronin 1975; Green 1995; Loos 1982; Lydon 1996; Manne 2003; Ørsted-Jensen 2011; Reynolds 1981; Richards 2008; Ryan 2008, 2010, 2013). Historians have shown conclusively that frontier violence was ubiquitous and enacted by 'colonists', the military, and various forms of policing forces reliant on Aboriginal labour ('Native Police'). Despite this close attention, the silence of the documentary record has confounded such studies, with Finnane and Richards (2004: 85) lamenting that 'the reality of settlement at the boundaries of colonial rule challenges reconstruction'.

The potential for archaeology to address this silence and to contribute new perspectives to the discourse was recognized nearly two decades ago (Attwood & Foster 2003: 23), but until recently it remained largely untapped, despite long-established interests in conflict archaeology internationally (e.g., Fox & Scott 1991; Zimmerman 2009). Hitherto, most published studies of frontier conflict sites in Australia by archaeologists have been restricted to heritage assessments or historical treatments, with little or no detailed archaeological investigation (e.g., Godwin & L'Oste Brown 2002; Murray & Williamson 2003; but for an exception see Rowland 2004). In part, this limitation may stem from the peculiar difficulties surrounding the identification of conflict events in the Australian archaeological record, made more challenging by the furtive manner in which many killings were carried out. The first systematic steps toward understanding such material signatures were by Barker (2007) and Litster and Wallis (2011), who argued that perpetrators often targetted small numbers of people in short-lived punitive expeditions highly dispersed across sometimes large distances, leaving a very light 'footprint'. The archaeological signature of such events has also been strongly affected by the treatment of victims after death, which regularly involved leaving the bodies on the surface and/or burning rather than interment. As a consequence, large-scale massacres resulting in concentrations of bodies buried in a single location, such as are recorded elsewhere in the New World from conflict encounters (e.g., Greene & Scott 2004; National Parks Service 2000a, 2000b; Nicklisch, Ramsthaler, Meller, Friederich, & Alt 2017; Zimmerman 2009; Zimmerman & Whitten 1980), are unlikely to occur in the Australian context. Combined with the effects of natural transformation processes, this light footprint has sometimes led to inconclusive archaeological results (e.g., Smith, Raven, Walshe, Fitzpatrick, & Pate 2017; Wallis, Wright, Moffat, Domett, & Woolgar Valley Aboriginal Corporation 2005; but see Genever, Duncan, Derksen, & Tranter 1996).

Given the establishment of various Native Police forces utilizing Aboriginal labour in all colonies across Australia from the 1830s onward (e.g., Fels 1988; Nettlebeck & Ryan 2018; O'Connor 2002), an alternative lens through which to examine frontier conflict is the more obvious and abundant material signatures evidenced by the camps of such forces. In particular, the paramilitary Queensland Native Mounted Police[2] force—the longest-lasting and most brutal of all Australian Native Police forces—offers a window into the form, nature, and spatial location of frontier violence across more than fifty years of colonial settlement in the northeast quarter of the continent (e.g., Burke & Wallis 2019; Burke et al. 2018; Cole 2004; Cole, Musgrave, George, George, & Banjo 2002; Lowe et al. 2018; Wallis et al. 2017, 2018). Formed in 1848 in what was then the northern districts of New South Wales and before the separation of Queensland as a self-governing colony in 1859, the Queensland Native Mounted Police comprised detachments of usually four to fifteen Aboriginal men ('troopers') drawn from distant areas and led by a White officer. Their role was to protect European populations on the extreme limits of colonial settlement by ostensibly establishing and promoting the rule of British law (Nettelbeck & Ryan 2018; Richards 2008; Skinner 1975). In practice, this meant carrying out extrajudicial killings, destroying property, and forcibly removing

Aboriginal people from their traditional lands. Such was the level of Aboriginal resistance that the Queensland authorities found it necessary to deploy their force from more than 150 different camps across the state. As bases for detachments whose preemptive and/or retaliatory attacks systematically devastated local Aboriginal communities, the camps serve as a proxy for frontier violence. Using an archaeological landscape approach, Queensland-wide material associated with the remains of Native Mounted Police bases provide rich potential for shedding fresh light on Australia's 'dark' colonial past (cf. Lennon & Continuum 2002; Sharpley 2005).

CONTEXTUALIZING THE CAMPS

Following a short stint as a penal convict depot, 'free' European settlement in Queensland commenced in 1842 with the opening of the Moreton district in the southeast,[3] though what the new arrivals thought of as virgin country was, of course, already occupied and had been for tens of thousands of years (Figure 40.1). In the southeast, pastoralism (initially involving sheep and later cattle) quickly emerged as the main industry, with the first shipment of wool departing Moreton Bay in 1851 (State Government of Queensland 2019). Through to the declaration of the pastoral districts of Gregory North and Gregory South in 1873, the opening of successive regions provided further impetus for influxes of land-hungry settlers, effectively completing assertion of colonial control over the entire colony. As the European presence in distant locales increased, other potential industries ripe for development were identified. Although not as large as those elsewhere in Australia, the discovery of several important minerals (predominantly gold, but also tin and copper) led to intense, though relatively short-lived, mining rushes in Queensland. Commencing with Canoona in 1858, the fields of Gympie (est. 1867), Cape River (est. 1867), Ravenswood (est. 1868), Gilbert River (est. 1869), Etheridge (est. 1870), Charters Towers (est. 1871), Palmer River (est. 1873), Herberton (est. 1875), and Hodgkinson (est. 1876) were proclaimed, encouraging colonists to settle in regions that had hitherto been of limited European interest (Bolton 1972). In the northeast, colonial expansion was also connected to the development of sugar plantations replete with imported cheap labour from the South Pacific Islands after 1863 (Griggs 2011) and commercial timber-getting in the rainforests after the 1870s (Frawley 1991). Beche-de-mer and pearlshell fishing industries along the north Queensland coastline in the latter decades of the nineteenth century opened further opportunities for exploitation and violence (e.g., Ganter 1994; Loos 1974, 1982; Mullins 1995).

Each of the primary industries placed different demands on land and water resources, with concomitantly varying expressions in terms of settlement, infrastructure development, and ensuing conflict with local Indigenous communities (Loos 1982). Pastoralism involved relatively small numbers of people but large numbers of stock spread over extensive areas of country. Once settled, pastoralists were heavily invested in staying on the 'runs' they had secured. In contrast, mining involved large numbers of people in

1060   LYNLEY A. WALLIS ET AL.

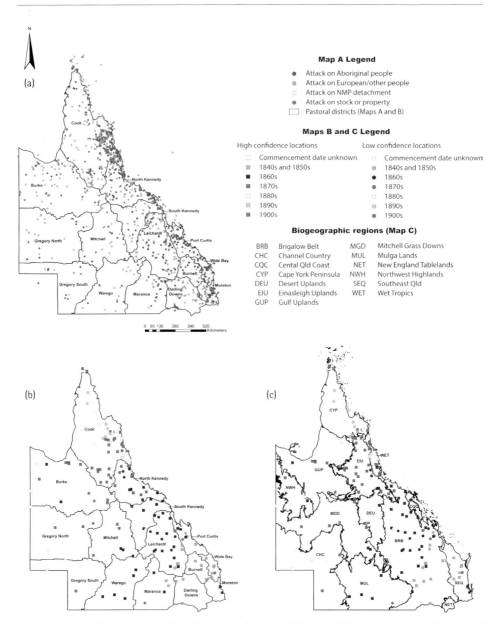

FIGURE 40.1. (a) Frontier conflict 'events' and pastoral districts; (b) NMP camps and pastoral districts; and (c) NMP camps and biogeographic regions (based on data in Burke & Wallis 2019 as of 8 October 2019; see updated online database referenced in Burke & Wallis 2019).

relatively concentrated locations for shorter, more intense periods of time, who soon decamped once the easily secured resources had been depleted. The mining fields were often situated in rugged country that pastoralists largely avoided and that had otherwise afforded Aboriginal people refuge. In contrast, while involving smaller numbers of people than mining, both timber-getting and agriculture required extensive clearing across large tracts of land, causing massive ecological impacts. Like pastoralists, farmers and plantation owners were heavily invested in remaining in place rather than decamping when sought-after resources had been depleted. In the tropical northeast, the seemingly impenetrable rainforests that were the focus of both timber-getting and agriculture had afforded Aboriginal people some means of respite from colonial impact, as well as a context for resistance and continued conflict. Fishing industries, though restricted to coastal regions and/or offshore islands, also involved relatively small numbers of entrepreneurs (far fewer than mining but probably many more than pastoralism in the adjacent inland areas). Many colonial fishers developed a violent and abusive relationship with their cheap Aboriginal labour force.

Invariably, regardless of the specific industry involved, initial European incursions were tied to reliable water sources, thus placing invaders in immediate conflict with Aboriginal landholders who both directly and indirectly relied on such resources. Once it was clear to Aboriginal people that the newcomers, with their impacts on resources and sacred cultural places, were determined to take up long-term residency, concerted resistance against the invaders was inevitable. This took the shape of attacks on people—usually more isolated and vulnerable individuals—and the running off, spearing, and maiming of stock, with occasional attacks on property or theft of unguarded supplies, equipment, and/or crops. Such resistance led to increased calls by colonists for police protection, which in many cases provoked further confrontation. Typically, this conflict resulted in an increasingly vicious spiral until Aboriginal opposition was either defeated or, as happened in rare cases, the colonists moved on.

Although mapping such conflict is challenging, increasingly sophisticated geospatial interfaces are allowing spatial representations of such events beyond static dots on maps. For example, Ryan (2019) recently released an online interactive 'map, timelines, and information about massacres in Central and Eastern Australia from 1794 . . . until 1930'. With stringent criteria regarding the number of victims (six or more) and the level of confidence in whether the alleged incident actually took place, Ryan's map (as at early 2020) shows approximately sixty-five massacre events across Queensland. While valuable, the limited scope of the events depicted in this map belies the complexity of the frontier, where larger-scale killings were rare and were usually the culmination of weeks or months of smaller-scale events.

Adopting a more holistic approach to include all frontier conflict 'events', regardless of whether these resulted in large (or any) numbers of deaths, provided Burke and Wallis (2019) with a more nuanced view of the ebb and flow of violence on the Queensland frontier (cf Barker 2007). Attacks were categorized as against either (1) Aboriginal people, (2) Europeans/others, (3) property and/or stock, or (4) Native Mounted Police detachments. Sourced primarily from historical documents, over 1800 such events have been plotted to at least an approximate location across Queensland (Burke & Wallis 2019; note that as at 19 July 2023 the figure is now more than 2500) (Figure 40.1a and Table 40.1). This dataset has several limitations, principally its documentary bias that privileges accounts of European deaths over those of Aboriginal people and the fact that many accounts (both oral and written) provide insufficient locational or temporal information to allow mapping with any degree of confidence. Further complications are the limited number of literate Europeans and the often sporadic reporting of frontier conflict in newspapers, letters, and diaries, as a result of which some areas or time periods appear to have few or no events. As such, areas with few events are more likely to reflect a lack of written sources relating to that region rather than an absence of conflict per se. Despite its shortcomings, the data provide a damning visualization of the extent of conflict across colonial Queensland. Adjusting figures to account for the differences in size of each pastoral district, Table 40.1 reveals that, relatively speaking, the southeast pastoral districts of Wide Bay and Moreton were by far the most 'violent' based on the number of conflict events, followed closely by Cook, Port Curtis, and North Kennedy. It is in light of the extent and nature of frontier conflict events that the establishment of Native Mounted Police camps can be better contextualized.

Table 40.1. Summary of frontier conflict events across Queensland (based on data in Burke & Wallis 2019 as at 8 October 2019).

Pastoral District	Size of District (ha)	Attacks against Aboriginal People	Attacks against Europeans/ Others	Attacks against NMP	Attacks against Property/ Stock	Total Attacks	Km^2 per Attack
Burke	30,169,230	17	55	3	26	101	2987
Cook	28,590,338	66	277	7	253	603	474
Gregory North	25,858,835	9	19	0	1	29	8916
Warrego	18,494,334	6	16	2	1	25	7398
Mitchell	16,646,136	7	21	0	5	33	5044
Gregory South	16,118,345	5	8	0	2	15	10,745
Leichhardt	14,941,282	54	85	8	15	162	922
Maranoa	12,690,413	16	15	1	8	40	3172
North Kennedy	9,659,535	46	52	1	69	168	575
South Kennedy	9,351,043	11	36	1	29	77	1214
Darling Downs	8,031,241	11	39	1	9	60	1339
Port Curtis	4,515,403	33	39	1	10	83	544
Burnett	3,950,967	11	18	2	5	36	1097
Wide Bay	2,827,047	25	43	0	55	123	230
Moreton	2,666,229	17	51	1	46	115	231
Other*		25	75	0	16	116	
TOTAL		**359**	**849**	**28**	**550**	**1786**	

* These are events that fall outside the pastoral district polygons, predominantly occurring on vessels or offshore islands.

The Geographic and Temporal Distribution of Camps

Biogeography, hydrology, and geology are key factors in understanding the nature of Aboriginal occupation of a region and the interests that Europeans subsequently developed in such areas. These factors also influenced the conflict that occurred between people and, in turn, the establishment of Native Mounted Police camps. Although initially squatters[4] seemed to have dealt with Aboriginal resistance themselves, many took good note of the lessons learned from the Myall Creek case, when eleven Europeans were tried and seven hanged for the murder of at least twenty-eight Aboriginal people in New South Wales in the late 1830s. The trials and punishment of the perpetrators set a judicial precedent and led to a more clandestine culture surrounding the killing of Aboriginal people (see papers in Lydon & Ryan 2018). Queensland squatters whose stock, staff, and property were targetted appealed consistently and loudly to the Colonial Secretary to establish a Native Police force, and then for detachments to regularly patrol their 'runs' to 'disperse'[5] Aboriginal people. As such, the timing of the establishment of Native Mounted Police camps followed in a general sense the establishment of pastoral districts (Figure 40.1b and Table 40.2).

In the first decade of European colonization in Queensland, Native Mounted Police detachments had few permanent bases, being regularly on the move as they responded to written and verbal requests for assistance. In 1849, the first 'permanent' camp was established at Callandoon (Goondiwindi), followed by others in the Lower Burnett (Walla) in 1851 and on Tchanning Creek (Wandai Gumbal) in 1853 (Burke & Wallis 2019).[6] All three camps were built on pastoral properties, with Wandai Gumbal constructed specifically by squatters to enable a police presence. This heralded what became a common practice of squatters making pastoral outbuildings temporarily available for police use and even erecting bespoke temporary barracks to entice Native Mounted Police detachments to visit certain runs. Other Native Mounted Police camps established in the early 1850s were less permanent but no less connected to the patronage of squatters. In all, some 43% of camps across the lifetime of the Native Mounted Police were associated with either current or former pastoral runs.

Of 174 known Native Mounted Police camps with secure locational data, 168 have relatively secure establishment and cessation dates (Burke & Wallis 2019). These dates range from a maximum of fifty-one years at Coen on Cape York Peninsula to less than a year at other locations, with an average duration of thirteen years overall. Such camp durations suggest that it took approximately a decade to quell Aboriginal resistence in any given region, transforming the myth of the 'peaceful' colonization of Queensland into an account of a long, drawn-out war in which the 'battleground' was expansive and ever shifting. It also expands the scope of Evans and Ørsted-Jensen's (2014) calculation of frontier Aboriginal death rates, based as they were on an estimated seven-year average for each camp. Once the camp duration is extended to thirteen years, their minimum

1064   LYNLEY A. WALLIS ET AL.

Table 40.2. Pastoral districts, their size, opening dates, and numbers of Native Mounted Police camps, and information about the density of camps per district.

District	Gazettal Date	Size of District (ha)	Total Number of NMP Camps	Area (ha) per Camp	Density Ranking*
Burke	1865	30,169,230	18	1,676,068	9
Cook	1864	28,590,338	54	529,451	3
Gregory North	1873	25,858,835	6	4,309,806	15
Warrego	1864	18,494,334	5	3,698,867	13
Mitchell	1859	16,646,136	6	2,774,356	12
Gregory South	1873	16,118,345	4	4,029,586	14
Leichhardt	1854	14,941,282	24	622,553	5
Maranoa	1848	12,690,413	5	2,538,083	10
North Kennedy	1863	9,659,535	22	439,070	1
South Kennedy	1858	9,351,043	7	1,335,863	8
Darling Downs	1843	8,031,241	3	2,677,080	11
Port Curtis	1854	4,515,403	8	564,425	4
Burnett	1848	3,950,967	3	1,316,989	7
Wide Bay	1847	2,827,047	6	471,175	2
Moreton	1842	2,666,229	3	888,743	6
Total			174		

* 1 is the distict with the highest number of camps per unit area and 15 is the lowest.

and parsimonious estimate of a potential death rate of 41,040 Aboriginal people killed at the hands of the Native Mounted Police between 1859 and 1897 significantly advances in size to over 100,000.

The shift to State-funded camps, coupled with the separation of Queensland from the colony of New South Wales in 1859 and an ever-expanding European population, saw the number of camps double in the first half of the 1860s, remaining high for the following decade before slowing down after the mid-1870s (Table 40.3). The number of camps declined rapidly in the 1890s as the heart of Aboriginal resistance was largely broken and the then police commissioner, David Seymour, followed by his successor, William Parry-Okeden, deliberately wound down the Native Mounted Police and repositioned them within and behind the civilian police force. 'Troopers' became 'trackers', and many of the remaining officers were either transitioned to the regular force or let go.

Just as the timing of establishing Native Mounted Police camps was structured and systematic, so too was their geographic distribution, reflecting the sheer scale and ambition of the colonial project. The size of pastoral districts varied considerably, with the three largest located in the far west and north (Burke, Gregory North, and Cook) and

Table 40.3. Dates of establishment of Native Mounted Police camps across Queensland (based on data in Burke and Wallis 2019 as at 8 October 2019; note that four camps whose establishment year is not known have been excluded).

Time Period (typically in five-year increments)	Number of Native Mounted Police Camps Established
pre-1855	12
1856–1860	14
1861–1865	28
1866–1870	26
1871–1875	29
1876–1880	21
1881–1885	19
1886–1890	12
1891–1895	5
1896–1904	4
Total	170

the three smallest (Moreton, Wide Bay, and Burnett) in the southeast (Figure 40.2b and Table 40.2). Accordingly, the number of camps varied within each district, from just three in the smallest district to as many as fifty-four in Cook. While this relationship appears superficially to be a straightforward one, related directly to district size, one of the largest districts—Gregory North—in fact had only six camps, suggesting that other forces were at play.

To understand this variability, a more useful measure is the number of Native Mounted Police camps adjusted to account for the different sizes of the districts. As shown in Table 40.2, this reveals that the 'densest' district in terms of the Native Mounted Police presence was North Kennedy (the ninth largest district), with an average of 1 camp/439,070 ha. This was followed by Wide Bay, the second smallest district (1 camp/471,175 ha), and Cook, the second largest district (1 camp/529,451 ha). In contrast, the least dense districts of Gregory South (1 camp/4,029,586 ha) and Gregory North (1 camp/4,309,806 ha) were the sixth and third largest districts, respectively. The high density of camps in the North Kennedy and Cook districts is likely due to a complex mix of factors, including the European industries in each, the density of Aboriginal populations, and the nature of the local terrain. Here, mountainous and/or heavily forested regions countermanded the advantages of coverage and speed belonging to a mounted force, while at the same time affording Aboriginal people safe havens. The high density of camps in Wide Bay, which opened within five years after free settlement

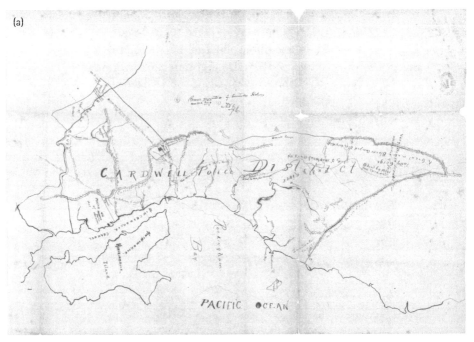

FIGURE 40.2. (a) Map showing the location of the Native Mounted Police camp at Cardwell in respect to Aboriginal travel routes and bora (ceremonial) ground (Queensland State Archives ID 629688; © State of Queensland [Department of Natural Resources, Mines and Energy] 2020; reproduced with permission) and (b) Photograph of Waterview Native Mounted Police camp (image reproduced with permission of the State Library of Queensland, collection ID 156880).

began, is a particularly interesting case. Its denser Native Mounted Police presence was likely due to the expansion of wealthy pastoral interests, many of whom were members of the Queensland Parliament and so had greater influence over the decision-making processes regarding funding and resources allocated to the force. Further, the especially unchecked violence of the Native Mounted Police in its first decade or so of operation (culminating in a Select Committee enquiry in 1861; Queensland Legislative Assembly 1861) was arguably a prime factor in the heightened resistance and retaliation of Aboriginal peoples in the Wide Bay district.

A spatial analysis of camp distribution against biogeographic regions is even more revealing (Figure 40.1c and Table 40.4). By this measure, the four regions with the greatest densities of camps are the Wet Tropics and Einasleigh Uplands (both dominated by forestry and agriculture, and, in the north of the latter, mining), South East Queensland (dominated by early pastoralism), and Cape York Peninsula (dominated in the south by mining). The regions with arguably the lowest economic value and European population densities—the Mitchell Grass Downs, Mulga Lands, Desert Uplands, and Channel Country, all in the southwest of the state—are those with the lowest densities of camps and, by default, the greatest distances between camps. Generally speaking, these latter four regions are characterized by open and topographically featureless plains, which are ideal for pursuit on horseback and provide little in the way of physical refuge for Aboriginal people. Here the ease of mounted travel enabled detachments to patrol a far greater area than was possible in, for example, the rugged sandstone ranges of the Einasleigh Uplands and Cape York Peninsula. Furthermore, in the more arid areas of southwest Queensland, Aboriginal fisher-gatherer-hunters were particularly closely tethered to seasonal and permanent water sources, making their movements more predictable and therefore easier for detachments to track and thus quell any resistance they might have attempted. The Native Mounted Police camps at Cooper's Creek (214 km), Boulia/Burke River (160 km), and Birdsville (160 km) in southwestern Queensland were the most isolated camps,[7] whereas Glenroy, Palmerville, Puckley Creek, and East Normanby in Cape York Peninsula were all just 7 km from another camp (Burke & Wallis 2019). The average distance between camps across the state was 53 km (~32

Table 40.4. Sumary of information about the size of biogeographic regions and the number of camps per region.

Biogeographic Region	Size of Region (ha)	Number of Camps	Approximate Area (ha) per Camp within Region	Density Ranking
Brigalow Belt	36,528,110	49	745,472	5
Mitchell Grass Downs	24,162,330	11	2,196,575	9
Channel Country	23,217,290	6	3,869,548	12
Gulf Plains	21,910,940	11	1,991,904	8
Mulga Lands	18,605,810	6	3,100,968	10
Cape York Peninsula	12,305,220	21	585,963	4
Einasleigh Uplands	11,625,730	31	375,024	2
Northwest Highlands	7,343,640	5	1,468,728	6
Desert Uplands	6,941,100	2	3,470,550	11
Southeast Queensland	6,248,420	12	520,702	3
Wet Tropics	1,992,900	19	104,889	1
Central Queensland Coast	1,484,280	1	1,484,280	7
New England Tableland	774,800	0	NA	NA

mi), which was theoretically the average distance that could be travelled comfortably on horseback if the horses were well conditioned; it was a regular lament that Native Mounted Police horses were anything but well conditioned (e.g., Anon. 1866; Kellet, R 1865).

Other interesting patterns emerge when the distribution of Native Mounted Police camps is plotted against Aboriginal language groups.[8] This reveals the extent to which some groups bore the brunt of police brutality, suffering multiple camps in their territory, particularly so for the clans in southeast Cape York Peninsula. Of course, the absence of a Native Mounted Police camp in any clan group's country did not protect them from violence, as detachments typically ranged widely, and reprisals at the hands of settlers operating outside the law were still possible. Nonetheless, groups with fewer camps, or without camps in their core territory, may have been slightly better insulated from violence than others.

ARCHAEOLOGICAL SIGNATURES OF NATIVE MOUNTED POLICE CAMPS

The duration of a Native Mounted Police camp conditioned the extent of violent attacks and reprisals that were possible in its vicinity but could also be assumed to affect the potential archaeological signature of the force's presence. Yet even at the longest occupied sites, field investigations have revealed that material evidence of occupation is often sparse (Barker et al. 2020). Since camps were never intended to be permanent and were always constructed and maintained with government parsimony uppermost in mind, they mostly consisted of timber slab and bark constructions with few permanent foundations. Only rarely and in the latest decades of the nineteenth century were sawn timber and corrugated iron used to build structures, and in most cases any reusable building materials were routinely moved to the next camp when the detachment received orders from headquarters to relocate. Surviving architectural features are therefore rare to nonexistent. Some features that do remain, such as ant bed flooring, are subsurface and only detectable through the use of geophysical survey or excavation (Lowe et al. 2018). Other remaining surface features include remnant house or yard posts, stone lines demarcating pathways, and stone fireplaces.

Some stone features visible at Native Mounted Police camps imply nonstructural and nondomestic activities of a localized nature. Camps at Burke River (western Queensland), Mistake Creek (central Queensland), and possibly Puckley Creek (Cape York Peninsula) all have stone features that were almost certainly constructed by Aboriginal people as part of an earlier ceremonial presence at these sites, given their form and the absence of associated nineteenth-century artefact assemblages. The siting of Native Mounted Police camps in such significant Aboriginal locations is unlikely to have been coincidental, although their need for reliable water would have caused geographic synchronicity with previous Aboriginal use regardless. Historical evidence bears out at least some element of deliberate placement vis-a-vis key Aboriginal places. A hand-drawn map of the police district of Cardwell, for example, shows the placement of the Native Mounted Police camp at Attie Creek not only in relation to the major European road, but also to Aboriginal travel routes and a bora (ceremonial) ground (Figure 40.2a). In this sense, the choice to locate camps in relation to established Aboriginal networks of communication and ceremonial nodes was a classic technique of colonial discipline and surveillance (Hannah 1997: 175–176). The Native Mounted Police force as a technology of power (sensu Foucault 1979) functioned in this capacity at several levels.

Apart from the choice of location for their camps, the spatial mechanics of surveillance were enacted at a landscape scale by the Native Mounted Police through regular patrolling by detachments to create a visible colonial authority presence on Aboriginal lands. Within the camps themselves, elements of spatial discipline were created through daily practices and the hierarchy of the force. Although there is some variety in camp layouts, from linear to quadrangular, they nonetheless contained various mechanisms for ensuring disciplinary control, such as locating the camp sergeant in closer relation to the troopers, placing officers' quarters separate from those of subordinates and at one end of a parade ground, or physically elevating the accommodation of the officer(s) above that of subordinates. This strategy is more visible at some camps than others (e.g., Waterview; Figure 40.2b).

Architectural forms of spatial confinement, such as lockups or palisades, were absent from the camps themselves; of course, when the unofficial policy was to 'take no prisoners', lockups were redundant. In this arrangement, the Native Mounted Police camps differed from military encampments in that observational hierarchies were generally minimal, and not reinforced by enclosing walls, watchtowers, or other devices for overtly exercising surveillance. Although permeable boundaries surrounded each camp, at least some degree of enclosure still operated in the sense that troopers were displaced from their own traditional country and thus automatically surrounded by an enemy's territory. This was a deliberate tactic to reinforce troopers' reliance on their own detachment, prevent collusion with local Aboriginal people, and inhibit desertion (Richards 2008: 10, 120–182). The fact that there were, nevertheless, many instances of resistance in the form of desertion and sometimes open rebellion against officers merely highlights the imperfect nature of the Queensland Native Mounted Police as a disciplinary institution.

At the most personal level, applicable to the individual troopers, the structure and nature of the force was designed to inculcate European notions of personal discipline, including dress, deportment, and hygiene, reinforced through hierarchy and punishment to create obedient, active troopers. Many camps featured neat rows of bark huts that served as the modest residences of troopers, their wives, and their children (Figure 40.2b). As women had often been captured from local Aboriginal groups and the men were often frontier conflict victims themselves (Burke et al. 2018), the huts cloak a very sinister installation with a thin veneer of European respectability and domesticity.

Conclusion

One repercussion of feminist and postcolonial archaeology (e.g., Gero & Conkey 1991; Lydon & Rizvi 2010; Silliman 2005; Spector 1993) has been the challenging of conventional (gendered and colonialist) narratives. It is in this context that frontier conflict associated with the British diaspora has proven fertile ground for such approaches, both domestically and abroad. The Native Mounted Police camps from which government-sanctioned paramilitary forces led patrols to 'disperse' the Aboriginal peoples of Queensland are perhaps the most visible archaeological manifestations of the frontier wars in Australia. The use of such phrasing as 'the other *side* of the frontier' in Reynolds's (1981) seminal book on the topic has in part contributed to the notion that there was in fact some particular line in the landscape, on one side of which lay safety but beyond which both Aboriginal and non-Aboriginal people were at extremely high risk. Following from this approach came the misconceived idea that the location of the 'frontier' was in some ways well known and thus allowed for specific places to be patrolled with relative ease and ultimately controlled. Various researchers have challenged this overly simplistic notion (e.g., Godwin 2001; Russell 2001; Wolski 2001), and studies of the Queensland Native Mounted Police add weight to these arguments.

Unlike frontier military camps in other contexts (e.g., the nineteenth-century gaucho 'fortlets' in Argentina [Romero 2002], the military camps on the U.S. frontier [Watson 1999], or those camps associated with the American War of Independence [Starbuck 1999]), Native Mounted Police camps in Queensland did not form a defensive cordon of structures akin to a 'frontier line'. Nonetheless, the location of such camps undoubtedly demarcated a malleable frontier 'zone' that was contested, precarious, and violent. The frontier was a place of ever-shifting relationships, as invaders and defenders attempted to retain, gain, or maintain control over country and resources. Places that might have been 'safe' for several years could easily become the scene of new confrontations, as demands on resources shifted and tenuous accommodations and relationships that might previously have been reached were retested and found wanting. Accordingly, the establishment of Native Mounted Police camps fluctuated, moving generally outward from the southeastern corner of Queensland, but persisting longer in some areas than others, and requiring some camps to be reestablished in 'once-pacified' areas when it became apparent that Aboriginal people were still willing and able to actively defend their lands and communities.

Further, just as Native Mounted Police camps in Queensland presented a less clear-cut 'line' of defense than that seen in other settler nations, neither were they routinely associated with battlefields of the type that lend themselves to the kinds of 'battlefield archaeology' increasingly common in the United States and United Kingdom (e.g., Freeman & Pollard 2001; Fernández-Götz & Roymans 2017; Scott & McFeaters 2011). While there certainly were some instances of large-scale physical confrontations in Queensland, the frontier and the nature of frontier conflict there were more nebulous and oftentimes clandestine, leaving a more challenging archaeological signature to be identified and interpreted.

The result is that the archaeology of the colonial frontier in Australia is not the usual 'archaeology of war'. As yet, there are no mass graves with skeletal remains of victims showing evidence of violent death, and even if some were to be identified in the future, they would be the exception rather than the rule. However, the archaeological footprint of Native Mounted Police camps across Queensland provides unequivocal evidence of the scale and enduring nature of the Native Mounted Police's operations. The fact that so many camps were required at various locations for a period of seventy-nine years provides clear evidence of the persistent and determined resistance of Aboriginal peoples to the theft of their land and the bloodshed that resulted. Such sites raise core questions about the paradox of 'civilization' achieved through violence (Atkinson 2003). How could a society that depended on a foundation of law and refined moral sensibilities to justify its colonial worth (Nettelbeck & Ryan 2018; Rowse & Waterton 2018)—achievements that are still celebrated today in various ways—also encompass a concept such as the deliberate extermination of Aboriginal people through a mechanism as brutally efficient and as routinely organized as the Native Mounted Police?

Acknowledgements

This research was supported by an Australian Research Council Grant (DP160100307). In a project of this extent it is impossible to thank everyone individually, so we give our thanks to the many Aboriginal corporations, communities, and individuals who have assisted us over the years, and to the colleagues, students, and volunteers who have similarly offered their support. In particular, we thank Wayne Beck for his assistance with mapping, and Glen Maclaren, Troy Mallie, and Steve Wealands from Environmental Systems Solutions for their assistance with database development. Thanks also to Alistair Paterson, Lyndall Ryan, and Ian McNiven for reviewing this chapter, though the viewpoints presented remain those of the authors.

Notes

1. Although we use the term *European*, we note that colonizers included peoples of varied cultural backgrounds, including large numbers of Chinese peoples who were particularly involved in the mining industry.
2. Known variously as the Native Police, the Native Mounted Police, and the Black Police.
3. While commonly known as 'pastoral districts', it is recognized that in some instances pastoralism was not the key European land-use industry, such as in Cook, where mining was more common, and North Kennedy, where timber-getting and agriculture dominated.
4. A large-scale sheep or cattle farmer.
5. A nineteenth-century colonial euphemism that is widely accepted as having meant to kill.
6. Native Mounted Police camps were often referred to as 'barracks'. Today this term implies a degree of permanence and substance, with a formal structure and layout that many of the camps did not in fact have—some 'barracks' were nothing more than a collection of canvas tents.

7. The values in parentheses are distances to the next closest camp.
8. While recognizing the serious limitations of the linguistic mapping of Tindale (1974) and Horton (1994), it serves here as the basis for crudely demonstrating that the various clan groups of Queensland were likely unequally impacted by the Native Mounted Police presence, rather than necessarily accurately reflecting group territories. Readers are directed to Monaghan (2003), who provides a detailed critique of some of the flaws in Tindale's mapping of linguistic groups in northwest South Australia, elements of which are equally applicable to Queensland, such as his boundaries being somewhat arbitrary determinations reflective of Western and colonial concepts rather than Indigenous worldviews and based on very few knowledgeable informants.

References

Allbrook, M., & Jebb, M. A. (2009). *Hidden histories: Conflict massacres and colonisation of the Pilbara*. Port Hedland: Wangka Maya Pilbara Aboriginal Language Centre.

Allen, J. (1973). The archaeology of nineteenth-century British imperialism: An Australian case study. *World Archaeology, 5* (1), 44–60.

Anon. (1866). *Brisbane Courier*, 26 March 1866, p. 3.

Atkinson, A. (2003). Historians and moral disgust. In B. Attwood & S. G. Foster (Eds.), *Frontier conflict: The Australian experience* (pp. 113–119). Canberra: National Museum of Australia.

Attwood, B., & Foster, S. G. (Eds.). (2003). *Frontier conflict: The Australian experience*. Canberra: National Museum of Australia.

Barker, B. (2007). Massacre, frontier conflict and Australian archaeology. *Australian Archaeology, 64*, 9–14.

Barker, B., Wallis, L. A., Burke, H., Cole, N., Lowe, K., Artym, U., . . . Zimmerman, L. (2020). The archaeology of the 'Secret War': The material evidence of conflict on the Queensland frontier 1849–1901. *Queensland Archaeological Research, 23*, 25–41.

Birmingham, J. (1992). *Wybalenna: The archaeology of cultural accommodation in nineteenth century Tasmania—A report on the historical archaeological investigation of the Aboriginal establishment on Flinders Island*. Sydney: The Australian Society for Historical Archaeology.

Bolton, G. C. (1972). *A thousand miles away: A history of North Queensland to 1920*. Canberra: Australian National University Press.

Bottoms, T. (2013). *Conspiracy of silence: Queensland's frontier killing times*. Sydney: Allen and Unwin.

Brown, S., Avery, S., & Goulding, M. (2002). Recent investigations at the Ebeneezer mission cemetery. In R. Harrison & C. Williamson (Eds.), *After Captain Cook: The archaeology of the recent Indigenous past in Australia* (pp. 147–170). Sydney: Archaeological Computing Laboratory, Sydney University in association with NSW National Parks and Wildlife Service.

Burke, H., Barker, B., Cole, N., Wallis, L. A., Hatte, E., Davidson, I., & Lowe, K. (2018). The Queensland Native Police and strategies of recruitment on the Queensland frontier 1849–1901. *Journal of Australian Studies*, https://doi.org/10.1080/14443058.2018.1474942.

Burke, H., & Wallis, L. A. (2019). *Frontier conflict and the Native Mounted Police in Queensland database*, https://doi.org/10.25957/5d9fb541294d5.

Byrne, D. (2003). The ethos of return: Erasure and reinstatement of Aboriginal visibility in the Australian historical landscape. *Historical Archaeology, 37* (1), 73–86.

Cole, N. (2004). Battle Camp to Boralga: A local study of colonial war on Cape York Peninsula, 1873–1894. *Aboriginal History, 28*, 156–189.

Cole, N. (2010). Painting the police: Aboriginal culture and identity in colonial Cape York Peninsula. *Australian Archaeology, 21*, 17–28.

Cole, N., Musgrave, G., George, L., George, T., & Banjo, D. (2002). Community archaeology at Laura, Cape York Pensinsula. In S. Ulm et al. (Eds.), *Barriers, borders, boundaries: Proceedings of the 2001 Australian Archaeological Association annual conference* (pp. 137–150). St Lucia: University of Queensland.

Connor, J. (2002). *The Australian frontier wars, 1788–1838*. Sydney: UNSW Press.

Connors, L. (2015). *Warrior: A legendary leader's dramatic life and violent death on the colonial frontier*. Sydney: Allen and Unwin.

Critchett, J. (1990). *A distant field of murder: Western District frontiers 1834—1848*. Carlton: Melbourne University Press.

David, B., McNiven, I. J., Attenbrow, V., Flood, J., & Collins, J. (1994). Of Lightning Brothers and white cockatoos: Dating the antiquity of signifying systems in the Northern Territory, Australia. *Antiquity, 68*, 241–251.

Evans, R., & Ørsted-Jensen, R. (2014). 'I cannot say the numbers that were killed': Assessing violent mortality of the Queensland frontier. Unpublished paper presented at The Australian Historical Association 33rd Annual Conference, University of Queensland, St Lucia, Australia, 7–11 July 2014.

Evans, R., Saunders, K., & Cronin, K. (Eds.). (1975). *Race relations in colonial Queensland: A history of exclusion, exploitation and extermination*. Brisbane: University of Queensland Press.

Fels, M. H. (1988). *Good men and true: The Aboriginal police of the Port Phillip District 1837–1853*. Carlton: Melbourne University Press.

Fernández-Götz, M., & Roymans, N. (Eds.). (2017). *Conflict archaeology: Materialities of collective violence from prehistory to late antiquity*. London: Routledge.

Finnane, M., & Richards, J. (2004). 'You'll get nothing out of it'? The inquest, police and Aboriginal deaths in colonial Queensland. *Australian Historical Studies, 35*, 84–105.

Foucault, M. (1979). *Discipline and punish. The birth of the prison* (trans. A. Sheridan). New York: Vintage Books.

Fox, R. A., & Scott, D. D. (1991). The post-Civil War battlefield pattern: An example from the Custer Battlefield. *Historical Archaeology, 95* (2), 92–103.

Frawley, K. J. (1991). Queensland rainforest management: Frontier attitudes and public policy. *Journal of Rural Studies, 7* (3), 219–239.

Freeman, P. W. M., & Pollard, A. (Eds.). (2001). *Fields of conflict: Progress and prospect in battlefield archaeology*. British Archaeological Reports, International Series 958. Oxford: Archaeopress.

Ganter, R. (1994). *The pearl-shellers of Torres Strait: Resource use, development and decline, 1860s–1960s*. Melbourne Melbourne University Press.

Genever, G., Duncan, R., Derksen, T., & Tranter, H. (1996). *Failure of justice. The story of the Irvinebank massacre*. Millaa Millaa: Eacham Historical Society.

Gero, J. M., & Conkey, M. W. (Eds.). (1991). *Engendering archaeology: Women and prehistory*. Oxford: Blackwell Press.

Godwin, L. (2001). The fluid frontier: Central Queensland 1845–63. In L. Russell (Ed.), *Colonial frontiers: Indigenous-European encounters in settler societies* (pp. 101–118). Manchester: Manchester University Press.

Godwin, L., & L'Oste-Brown, S. (2002). A past remembered: Aboriginal 'historical' places in central Queensland. In R. Harrison & C. Williamson (Eds.), *After Captain Cook: The archaeology of the recent Indigenous past in Australia* (pp. 191–212). Sydney: Archaeological Computing Laboratory, Sydney University in association with NSW National Parks and Wildlife Service.

Green, N. (1995). *The Forrest River massacres*. Fremantle: Fremantle Arts Centre Press.

Greene, J. A., & Scott, D. D. (2004). *Finding Sand Creek: History, archeology, and the 1864 massacre site*. Norman: University of Oklahoma Press.

Griffin, D. (2010). Identifying domination and resistance through the spatial organization of Poonindie Mission, South Australia. *International Journal of Historical Archaeology, 14,* 156–169.

Griggs, P. D. (2011). *Global industry, local innovation: The history of cane sugar production in Australia, 1820–1995*. Bern: Peter Lang.

Hannah, M. G. (1997). Space and the structuring of disciplinary power: An interpretive review. *Geografiska Annaler: Series B, Human Geography, 79* (3), 171–180.

Harrison, R. (2004). *Shared landscapes: Archaeologies of attachment and the pastoral industry in New South Wales*. Sydney: University of New South Wales Press.

Harrison, R. (2007). Materiality, 'ambiguity', and the unfamiliar in the archaeology of intersocietal confrontations: A case study from northwest Australia. In P. Cornell & F. Fahlander (Eds.), *Encounters, materialities, confrontations: Archaeologies of social space and interaction* (pp. 42–57). Newcastle: Cambridge Scholars.

Horton, D. (1994). *The encyclopaedia of Aboriginal Australia: Aboriginal and Torres Strait Islander history, society and culture*. Canberra: Aboriginal Studies Press.

Kellet, R. (1865). Letter to Colonial Secretary John Wickham dated 26 January 1865. Queensland State Archive ID number 846794, In letter 65/499, Microfilm Z6410.

Lennon, J., & Continuum, M. F. (2002). Dark tourism: The attraction of death and disaster. *Annals of Tourism Research, 29* (4), 1188–1189.

Litster, M., & Wallis, L. A. (2011). Looking for the proverbial needle: The archaeology of Australian colonial frontier. *Archaeology in Oceania, 46* (3), 105–117.

Loos, N. (1974). Aboriginal resistance on the mining, rainforest and fishing frontiers. In B. J. Dalton (Ed.), *Lectures on North Queensland history* (pp. 163–175). Townsville: James Cook University of North Queensland.

Loos, N. (1982). *Invasion and resistance: Aboriginal-European relations on the north Queensland frontier 1861–1897*. Canberra: Australian National University Press.

Lowe, K. M., Cole, N., Burke, H., Wallis, L. A., Barker, B., Hatte, E., & Rinyirru Aboriginal Corporation. (2018). The archaeological signature of 'ant bed' mound floors in the northern tropics of Australia: Case study on the Boralga Native Mounted Police Camp, Cape York Peninsula. *Journal of Archaeological Science: Reports, 19,* 686–700.

Lydon, J. (1996). 'No moral doubt . . . ': Aboriginal evidence and the Kangaroo Creek poisoning, 1847–1849. *Aboriginal History, 20,* 151–175.

Lydon, J. (2009a). *Fantastic dreaming: The archaeology of an Aboriginal mission*. Lanham, MD: AltaMira Press.

Lydon, J. (2009b). Imagining the Moravian mission: Space and surveillance at the former Ebenezer mission, Victoria, southeastern Australia. *Historical Archaeology, 43* (3), 5–19.

Lydon, J., & Rizvi, U. (Eds.). (2010). *Handbook of postcolonial archaeology*. Walnut Creek, CA: Left Coast Press.

Lydon, J., & Ryan, L. (Eds.). (2018). *Remembering the Myall Creek massacre*. Sydney: NewSouth Publishing.

Manne, R. (Ed.). (2003). *Whitewash: On Keith Windschuttle's fabrication of Aboriginal history*. Melbourne: Black Inc. Agenda.

McNiven, I.J., & Russell, L. (2002). Ritual response: Place marking and the colonial frontier in Australia. In B. David & M. Wilson (Eds.), *Inscribed landscapes: Marking and making place* (pp. 27–41). Honolulu: University of Hawaii Press.

McNiven, I. J. (2018). Ritual mutilation of Europeans on the Torres Strait maritime frontier. *Journal of Pacific History, 53* (3), 229–251.

Monaghan, P. E. (2003). *Laying down the country: Norman B. Tindale and the linguistic construction of the north-west of South Australia* (PhD thesis). University of Adelaide, Adelaide.

Mullins, S. (1995). *Torres Strait: A history of colonial occupation and culture contact, 1864–1897*. Rockhampton: Central Queensland University Press.

Murray, T., & Williamson, C. (2003). Archaeology and history. In R. Manne (Ed.), *Whitewash: On Keith Windshuttle's fabrication of Aboriginal history* (pp. 311–336). Melbourne: Black Inc. Agenda.

National Parks Service. (2000a). *Sand Creek Massacre Project: Volume one—site location study*. Denver, CO: National Parks Service.

National Parks Service. (2000b). *Sand Creek Massacre Project: Volume two—special resources study*. Denver, CO: National Parks Service.

Nettelbeck, A., & Ryan, L. (2018). Salutary lessons: Native Police and the 'civilising' role of legalised violence in colonial Australia. *The Journal of Imperial and Commonwealth History, 46*(1), 47–68.

Nicklisch, N., Ramsthaler, F., Meller, H., Friederich, S., & Alt, K. W. (2017). The face of war: Trauma analysis of a mass grave from the Battle of Lützen (1632). *PLoS One, 12* (5), e0178252, https://doi.org/10.1371/journal.pone.0178252.

Ørsted-Jensen, R. (2011). *Frontier history revisited: Colonial Queensland and the 'history war'*. Brisbane: Lex Mundi Publishing.

Paterson, A. (2006). Towards a historical archaeology of Western Australia's northwest. *Australasian Historical Archaeology, 24*, 99–111.

Queensland Legislative Assembly. (1861). *Report from the Select Committee on the Native Police Force and the condition of the Aborigines generally together with the proceedings of the Committee and minutes of evidence*. Brisbane: Fairfax and Belbridge.

Reynolds, H. (1981). *The other side of the frontier: Aboriginal resistance to the European invasion of Australia*. Sydney: University of New South Wales Press.

Richards, J. (2008). *The secret war: A true history of Queensland's Native Police*. St Lucia: University of Queensland Press.

Romero, F. G. (2002). Philosophy and historical archaeology. Foucault and a singular technology of power development at the borderlands of nineteenth-century Argentina. *Journal of Social Archaeology, 2* (3), 402–429.

Rowland, M. J. (2004). Myths and non-myths: Frontier 'massacres' in Australian history—The Woppaburra of the Keppel Islands. *Journal of Australian Studies, 81*, 1–16.

Rowse, T., & Waterton, E. (2018). The 'difficult heritage' of the Native Mounted Police. *Memory Studies*, 1–5, https://doi.org/10.1177/1750698018766385.

Russell, L. (2001). Introduction. In L. Russell (Ed.), *Colonial frontiers: Indigenous-European encounters in settler societies* (pp. 1–15). Manchester: Manchester University Press.

Ryan, L. (2008). Massacre in the Black War in Tasmania 1823–34: A case study of the Meander River region, June 1827. *Journal of Genocide Research, 10* (4), 479–499.

Ryan, L. (2010). Settler massacres on the Port Phillip frontier, 1836–1851. *Journal of Social Archaeology, 34* (3), 257–273.

Ryan, L. (2013). Untangling Aboriginal resistance and the settler punitive expedition: The Hawkesbury River frontier in New South Wales, 1794–1810. *Journal of Genocide Research, 15* (2), 219–232.

Ryan, L. (2019). *Colonial frontier massacres in central and eastern Australia 1788–1930*,https://c21ch.newcastle.edu.au/colonialmassacres.

Scott, D. D., & McFeaters, A. P. (2011). The archaeology of historic battlefields: A history and theoretical development in conflict archaeology. *Journal of Archaeological Research, 19* (1), 103–132.

Sharpley, R. (2005). Travels to the edge of darkness: Towards a typology of 'dark tourism'. In C. Ryan, S. J. Page, & M. Aicken (Eds.), *Taking tourism to the limits: Issues, concepts, and managerial perspectives* (pp. 215–226). London: Elsevier.

Silliman, S. W. (2005). Culture contact or colonialism? Challenges in the archaeology of Native North America. *American Antiquity, 70* (1), 55–74.

Skinner, L. E. (1975). *Police on the pastoral frontier: Native Police, 1849–1859.* St Lucia: University of Queensland Press.

Smith, P. A. (2000*). Station camps: The ethnoarchaeology of cultural change in the post-contact period in the southeast Kimberley region of Western Australia* (PhD thesis). Flinders University, Adelaide.

Smith, P. A., Raven, M. D., Walshe, K., Fitzpatrick, R. W., & Pate, F. D. (2017). Scientific evidence for the identification of an Aboriginal massacre at the Sturt Creek sites on the Kimberley frontier of north-western Australia. *Forensic Science International, 279,* 258–267.

Spector, J. D. (1993). *What this awl means: Feminist archaeology at a Wahpeton Dakota village.* St Paul: Minnesota Historical Society Press.

Starbuck, D. R. (1999). *The great warpath: British military sites from Albany to Crown Point.* Hanover: University Press of New England.

State Government of Queensland. (2019). Queensland's history 1800s. https://www.qld.gov.au/about/about-queensland/history/timeline/1800s.

Tindale, N. B. (1974). *Aboriginal tribes of Australia: Their terrain, environmental controls, distribution, limits, and proper names.* Canberra: Australian Institute of Aboriginal Studies.

Wallis, L. A., Burke, H., Barker, B., Cole, N., Bateman, L., Artym, U., . . . Hatte, E. (2018). The archaeology of the 'secret war' in colonial Queensland, 1849 to 1904. *Signals, 124,* 14–19.

Wallis, L. A., Cole, N., Burke, H., Barker, B., Lowe, K., Davidson, I., & Hatte, E. (2017). *Rewriting the history of the Native Mounted Police in Queensland.* Broome: Nulungu Research Institute.

Wallis, L. A., Wright, R., Moffat, I., Domett, K., & Woolgar Valley Aboriginal Corporation (2005). Investigating the Woolgar Aboriginal massacre, northwest Queensland: A preliminary report. Unpublished paper presented at the Australian Archaeological Association Annual Conference, Fremantle (December 2005).

Watson, D. R. (1999). *An archaeological investigation of an 1867 military camp in the South Platte River Valley.* Lincoln: University of Nebraska State Museum.

Wesley, D. (2013). Firearms in rock art of Arnhem Land, Northern Territory, Australia. *Rock Art Research, 30* (2), 235–247.

Wolski, N. (2001). All's not quiet on the western front—rethinking resistance and frontiers in Aboriginal historiography. In L. Russell (Ed.), *Colonial frontiers: Indigenous-European encounters in settler societies* (pp. 216–236). Manchester: Manchester University Press.

Zimmerman, L. (2009). Crow Creek site and massacre. In F. P. McManamon, L. S. Cordell, K. G. Lightfoot, & G. R. Milner (Eds.), *Archaeology in America: An encyclopedia* (pp. 252–254). Westport, CT: Greenwood Press.

Zimmerman, L. J., & Whitten, R. (1980). Mass grave at Crow Creek in South Dakota reveals how Indians massacred Indians in 14th century attack. *Smithsonian, 11* (6), 100–109.

CHAPTER 41

THE ARCHAEOLOGY OF AGRARIAN AUSTRALIA

ALISTAIR PATERSON

INTRODUCTION

THE arrival of the British in Australia in 1788 heralded the start of new forms of farming that were to clash with Indigenous economies and practices, as well as impact upon Australian ecosystems and environments. These dramatic changes were part of a spectrum of changes occurring globally since the fifteenth century. For North America, Crosby described the translocation of European farming practices, technology, pathogens, and human populations as the 'Colombian Exchange' (Crosby 1986: 2003). While no similar term popularly exists for Australia, for environmental historian Tom Griffiths, 1788, like 1492, was 'a momentous date in world ecological history [when] . . . Australia . . . experienced colonization and industrialization almost coincidentally, a compressed, double revolution' (Griffiths 1996: x). The traditional view of colonialism in Australia focusses on the transportation of convicts, the establishment of Western practices and institutions, and the extent of dependency of colonies on Britain. However, equally significant were attempts to establish industries (mostly extractive in nature), and the relationship between agrarian farming and local Indigenous peoples. An archaeology of agrarian Australia (Paterson 2018) has been suggested as a corollary to colonial farming in other parts of the world (Castillo 2014).

The story of agrarian Australia is part of the global story of agriculture. Only one animal—the dingo—had been introduced to Australia in the Holocene prior to European colonization. The arrival of non-Aboriginal others meant the deliberate introduction and promotion of multiple animal species, including horses, camels, donkeys, cattle, sheep, goats, buffalos, pigs, dogs, cats, chickens, and foxes—amongst others ranging from fire ants to rats. Introduced plants species also postdate 1788, with the First Fleet carrying wheat and corn seeds, and a mix of plants with both decorative and culinary uses collected from Cape Hope (South Africa) en route—quince, apple, pear, strawberry, fig, bamboo, sugar cane, oak, and myrtle.[1] Aboriginal people in the early colonial world would probably have encountered introduced animals before they met the newcomers (Davidson 1989).

Agrarianism was integral to European colonization and colonialism: farming and pastoralism being the largest uses of land in Australia. In 2021, pastoral leases covered 44% of Australia, while lands with legally recognized Native Title covered 40%. Across the world pastoralism developed due to several factors, including the presence of rangelands dominated by plant species suitable for animal grazing—these were typically in semiarid regions; suitable animal species made available through either domestication or, in the case of Australia and many other settler societies, diffusion; and human population densities (Blench 2001: 2). In Australia, pastoralism was inherently part of colonialism and represented the usurpation of traditional Indigenous country and land-use practices following introduction of domesticated species and clearing of forests for the establishment of grassland pastures. Interestingly, forms of medieval land management suited to the open range were common in semiarid Australia, with the animals tended by shepherds with infrequent corralling (Paterson 2008).

Prior to the arrival of Europeans, Aboriginal Australians managed different plants and animals by various means—this is a story of hunter-foraging lifeways. Increasingly, studies of Aboriginal land management allow us to respond to concepts based on rejected evolutionary ideas of economic development formed in Europe, wherein societies develop from hunter-foraging to farming in a hierarchy of development. We now see ways in which the manipulation of the environment by Aboriginal people is part of a larger story of anthropogenically transformed landscapes and human interactions with companion species.

This chapter provides an overview of archaeological research in Australia relevant to agrarian history. It begins with a review of the current debate regarding the nature of Aboriginal resource management and foodways around Australia prior to the arrival of European invaders. A central part of these discussions relates to concepts like 'agriculture' and 'hunter-gatherers'—these types of terms have not been constant over time in their use and have come to reflect racist and evolutionary worldviews. A challenge today is to continue to understand how Aboriginal people lived effectively in Australia prior to the arrival of European farmers, and the consequences of that history. Many of the early archaeological studies of agrarian Australia presented in this chapter have overlooked the Aboriginal dimensions of farming, rather focussing instead on industrial and white settler histories. However, recent decades have seen a substantial effort by archaeologists to explore the cross-cultural dimensions of agrarian Australia and its heritage. A more recent challenge, identified here in a couple of studies, is to integrate the evidence available through archaeology with environmental sciences to better understand the ways in which Australian ecologies and environments were transformed by the interdiction of European farming.

ABORIGINAL LAND AND RESOURCE MANAGEMENT PRIOR TO CONTACT

The topic of Aboriginal and Torres Strait Islander land and resource management prior to the arrival of Europeans has become part of a national discourse in recent years—fuelled by publications claiming that Aboriginal Australians practiced forms of agriculture (Gerritsen 2010; Pascoe 2014). Much of the evidence for these claims comes from a reading of historical accounts by European explorers from across colonial Australia that suggest that 'Aborigines were building dams and wells, planting, irrigating and harvesting seed; preserving the surplus . . . and manipulating the landscape' (White 2019: 63 citing Pascoe 2014: 2) as well as forms of sedentism (see also Gammage 2011). There are various responses to this thesis (e.g., Keen 2021; Paterson 2013; Sutton & Walshe 2021; White 2019), which, in its attempt to highlight accounts of Aboriginal innovation, risk falling back on evolutionary thinking that sees agriculture as a more developed form of subsistence than hunter-forager lifeways. Sutton and Walshe (2021: 18–19) note: 'We also take issue with the notion that recognizably European 'settled' ways of living, focused on material and technical 'development' in food production, are in any way to be valued more than the ways of living that existed in Australia before invasion'.

Another problem with the use of Gammage and Pascoe is that the literature generalizes for the whole of Australia, rather than recognizing regional variations. Hiscock (2008) and Ulm (2012) argue that pan-Holocene and pan-Australian trends should be considered cautiously, instead arguing that regional diversity reflects a mosaic of independent cultural trajectories based on continuous adjustments to local physical and social exigencies (Ulm 2012: 189). Pascoe's *Dark Emu* has raised debate regarding the definition of agriculture. White finds that the activities cited by Pascoe are 'hard to describe . . . as other than agricultural' (White 2019); however, contrary to Pascoe, Keen (2021: 106) finds that the sum of evidence suggests that there is another conclusion to draw: that Aboriginal people in 1788 were hunter-gatherers, and along rivers, lakes, and the coast, they were also fishers, and that Aboriginal languages lack vocabularies associated with gardening and agriculture, which would be expected from long-term agriculturalists (Keen 2021, citing Sutton & Walshe 2021). Archaeological and anthropological evidence accumulated over several decades does, however, support 'The current consensus in archaeology . . . that before the British colonisation of Australia, Aboriginal people engaged in practices to do with the intensification of food resources. These included some replanting and transplantation, and some rudimentary sowing' (Keen 2021: 111). These practices and those of harvesting and storage are not necessarily forms of cultivation, and the translocation of plants does not mean domestication. However, any hard distinction between forager and farmer is too rigid, and instead food production can be seen to be complex and diverse across Aboriginal Australia (Keen 2003). Sutton and Walshe (2021: 172) prefer the term 'hunter-gatherers-plus' for economic activities that occurred in some regions. Hynes and Chase (1982) propose alternate terms such as *domiculture*, in their study for Cape York food production; while Denham (2009) proposes a practice-based approach, building on Bourdieu, which advocates looking at the practices around plant exploitation over time locally, whether undertaken by foragers or farmers (Denham's example here being drawn from the Highlands of Papua New Guinea).

At contact, Aboriginal Australians relied on diverse food resources managed through a variety of means, such as the use of fire, the promotion of certain plant and animal species, the use of physical structures such as traps and barriers to direct resources, and through the timing of activities (see McNiven, Manne, & Ross this volume). The anthropogenic use of fire is known from historical sources, Aboriginal knowledge and practice, and palaeoecological records (Paterson 2013: 7; see Rowe et al. this volume). Certain accounts have been well cited, such as Edmund Curr: 'there was another instrument in the hands of these savages which must be credited with results which it would be difficult to over-estimate. I refer to the *fire-stick*. . . . he tilled his land and cultivated his pastures with fire' (Curr 1883: 189–190, quoted in Gammage 2011: 2). It is the selective use of historical accounts such as this in *Dark Emu* that is critiqued by Sutton and Walshe (2021). In fact, a reading of settler accounts reveals that there were very few references to Aboriginal gardens or farms; rather, the absence of agriculture among Aboriginal people was used by the invaders to justify white claims to land ownership (Gammage 2011; Gott 1982).

Accounts such as that by Curr inspired archaeologist Rhys Jones's (1969) work on 'fire stick farming' to describe burning as a resource management tool. This work was followed by other archaeologists (e.g., Hallam 1975), and ecologists and historians (e.g., Burrows, Burbidge, Fuller, & Behn 2006; Gott 2002; Gill, Williams, & Bradstock 2002; Head 1994; Latz 1995; Pyne 1998). Fire-modified landscapes were sometimes beneficial to Europeans and their farming (see Gammage 2011 for a review of historical sources), something observed by colonial administrators (e.g., Ward 1998 for southwest Western Australia). The use of fire as a management tool to promote biodiversity and manage fire regimes is a contemporary concern, leading to experimental research and long-term studies of the consequences of human burning practices (Bliege Bird, Bird, Codding, Parker, & Jones 2008).

The evidence from archaeology and palaeoecology for management of plant species remains challenging, largely reflecting the paucity of survival of plant remains in archaeological sites and the dramatic changes in land forms across Australia since European arrival. However, studies have revealed the intensive reliance on various 'wild' plants (Beck, Clarke, & Head 1989; Denham, Donohue, & Booth 2009; Denham 2008; Gott 1982, 1983) and their social implications (Antolin et al. 2016).

Other forms of land modification reveal the intensive quest for food—restricted to specific localities. The use of fish traps, nets, and canals to assist the capture of fish is demonstrated in some inland rivers and along the coast (see McNiven & Lambrides this volume). The most widely recognized example is the World Heritage Listed Budj Bim Cultural Landscape in southwest Victoria, where the ancestors of the Gunditjmara excavated channels to funnel water into low-lying areas to create new habitats for eels and other freshwater fish in the Late Holocene and into the contact period (Builth 2014; Clarke 1994; McNiven et al. 2012).

The only domesticated animal to precede European contact was the dingo, introduced as a domesticated species over 3500 years ago; it has long been realized that Aboriginal people maintained a close relationship with dingoes (Balme & O'Connor 2016, this volume). Recently, Adam Brumm (2021) has argued that Aboriginal peoples' interactions with dingoes involved management and domestication processes, but not as conventionally defined (i.e., controlled breeding and artificial selection). This new view builds on critiques of binary understandings of domestication (i.e., animals having their breeding controlled by humans) versus nondomestication (i.e., animals having no interaction with humans) (Fijn 2018).

A heterogeneous image of the continent at the threshold of European arrival has emerged from the history, archaeology, and palaeoecology of lifeways and intensities of resource use in diverse regions. As Ulm (2012: 189) cogently notes:

> we might conceive of a landscape in which at any point in time there might be a range of higher-density populations distributed across resource-rich areas separated by lower-density populations. Not every society needs to be complex and we should not have the expectation that this will be the case. This is not denying anyone agency or ability; it simply recognizes the fact that different people developed different ways of living to meet particular needs in particular circumstances shaped by what came before (i.e. historical contingency).

AGRARIAN AUSTRALIA

Substantial and dramatic changes occurred across Australia in the century after European arrival in 1788. The ecology of the entire continent was reworked by the disruption of fire regimes and the destruction of Aboriginal societies, the introduction of plough agriculture, the wholesale clearance of forests, and the spread of exotic plant and animal species into every ecological zone (Lawrence & Davies 2018: 230). Agrarian Australia involved forms of crop farming and pastoralism, but for much of semiarid and arid Australia the only form of farming was sheep and cattle pastoralism (Paterson 2005a, 2005b, 2018) (Figure 41.1a).

The study of agrarian Australia has a long history; pastoral history until the 1950s was the central component of the general history and 'national narrative' of Australia, which was said to ride on the sheep's back (Pearson & Lennon 2010: ix) (Figure 41.1b). The themes of exploration, squatters, and the national wool industry were at the heart of the national psyche—fuelled by commercial dominance, literature, and art. Historical (Barnard 1962; Bean 1912) and architectural overviews of the pastoral industry have highlighted certain historical narratives and the heritage primacy of built infrastructure, especially of homesteads, woolsheds, and other iconic structures such as windmills

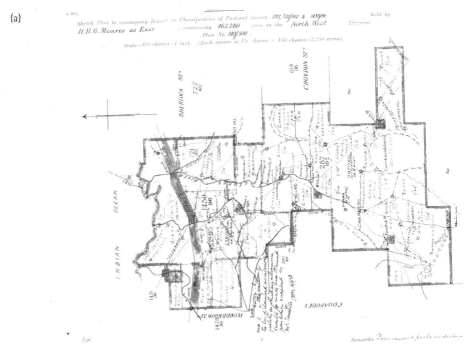

FIGURE 41.1. Pyramid Station, Pilbara, Western Australia. (a) Pastoral lease map showing landscape features, pastures, water sources, stock routes, and improvements (1920, Map to accompany Inspector's Report on Classification of Pastoral Leases, Government Surveyors Office). (b) Loading wool bales for transport at Pyramid Station, 1925–1930.

(Courtesy of the City of Karratha Local History Office, 2005.389).

(Pearson & Lennon 2010). The historical ecology of agrarian Australia has been largely the domain of environmental historians, environmental scientists, and geographers; however, the informative potential for historical archaeology and industrial archaeology is emerging (Lawrence & Davies 2018).

A significant element of farming is industry, as the history of Australian society was intrinsically linked with industrial processes. Pastoralism and mining drove the expansion of Europeans into the interior of the continent. Extractive primary industries—agriculture, pastoralism, mining, whaling, and timber-getting—created raw materials for consumption and export and were the main contributors to the economy (see Gibbs & Russell this volume). As argued by Casella (2006), there are three aspects of industrial archaeology: (1) the origin of industries, equipment, and technology; (2) adaptation of industries to Australian conditions; and (3) Australian industrial innovations—all themes relevant to agriculture and pastoralism (Winter & Paterson in press). Ireland (2002) explores how British industrial archaeology in the 1970s and 1980s influenced the study of mining and pastoralism in Australia.

Pastoralism was the vehicle for the expansion of the colonial frontier, initially in the early eighteenth century with convicts as shepherds then developing other forms of labour, including Aboriginal labour (Davidson 1994). Twinned to this expansion was the development of transport infrastructure (riverine, maritime, and overland), energy production (initially steam and also wind, and to a lesser extent water), the development of specialist work sites (for example, woolsheds, wool scours, yards, fenced paddocks, etc.), new forms of water management (leading to the development of artesian bores), inland settlements, and related mercantile and commercial sites (wool stores, banks, telegraph and post facilities) (Figures 41.2a and 41.2b). It is difficult then to state exactly where colonialism 'ends', given its deep articulations with farming and pastoralism. Accordingly, agriculture and its associated work sites also represented colonialism and relate directly to sites of governance, policing, health, and incarceration of Aboriginal peoples. For example, a survey of Aboriginal historical places in central Queensland includes pastoral sites such as droving sites in a wider range of historical places that take in sites related to massacres, Native Police, yambas (camping), ceremonies, resource gathering, missions, and reserves, and events such as birthing places (Godwin & L'Oste-Brown 2002).

Historical archaeology has long been interested in the sites and relics of industry, including faming and pastoral sites (e.g., Birmingham, Jack, & Jeans 1979; Walker & Forrest 1995). In the 1970s, Connah (1977) conducted landscape-level work at Saumarez Station, in New South Wales, leading to later work on colonial estates (Connah 2007). An interest in technology and adaptation around water fuelled much earlier work, with investigations of woolscours (Figure 41.2b) and woolsheds (Cannon 1992; Cummins 1989; Partridge 1984), water-powered flour mills (Connah 1994; Pearson 1996), and access to water over time (Godwin & L'Oste-Brown 2012; Paterson 2003), including Aboriginal waterholes (Grimwade 1998) and artesian springs (Paterson 2005c). Early farms have been examined by historical archaeologists using microfossils, sedimentology, archaeological features, anthrocology, and archaeobotany

FIGURE 41.2. (a) Australian Agricultural Company's Coal Works, Port Stephens, New South Wales (attributed to J. C. White) (SSV1B/NEWC/1840-9/1, State Library, New South Wales). (b) Wool scour at Strangways Springs, Western Australia, ca. 1870 (B1491, State Library of South Australia).

to better understand the origins of European farming landscapes at colonial Parramatta (Macphail & Casey 2008) and Albany (Winter, Forsey, Dotte-Sarout, & Paterson 2016).

Homesteads were mainly studied by heritage architects, although after the 1970s these were subject to archaeological investigation, especially at the residences of rural elites (e.g., Connah, Rowland, & Oppenheimer 1978; Connah 1986). However, other social and political aspects relevant to life on farms have been explored. Dimensions of early agricultural companies have been touched upon by archaeologists at the Australian Agricultural Company at Port Stephens, New South Wales (Bairstow 1985) (Figure 41.2a) and the Van Dieman's Land Company in northwest Tasmania (Murray 1988), both English joint-stock companies. At the Kinchega Pastoral Station in western New South Wales, Allison used archaeology (particularly ceramics) and documentary evidence to explore domestic behaviour in rural Australia in the late nineteenth and early twentieth centuries, highlighting the activities of women and children (Allison 2003; Allison & Esposito 2020). Terry's (2013) study of Caboonbah, a pastoral property in the Brisbane Valley of Queensland in the late nineteenth and early twentieth centuries, excavated domestic waste to highlight how a middle-class family maintained their values in a remote setting. Egloff, O'Sullivan, & Ramsay (1991) used archaeology to study the 1891 shearer's war and the main strike camp at Barcaldine, Queensland. In the Pilbara, the attempts made by the foundation pastoral families from the 1860s to demonstrate their aesthetics are revealed in material choices, such as expensive and tasteful building materials and musical instruments (Paterson 2006; Smith 2008). Farming settlements were also significant for Chinese settlers; there is a rich tradition of historical archaeological research into the Chinese in Australasia. Despite the focus on mining and urban life, the Chinese migrants also often maintained market gardens, such as Ah Toy's garden on the Palmer River goldfield (Jack, Holmes, & Kerr 1984). In contrast, some forms of farming have had almost no archaeological attention, such as the dairy industry which—with the exception of Casey's (1999) analysis of a home dairy at the Brickfields site—has undergone significant developments worthy of archaeological research, such as technological innovations and the shift from household-level herd ownership and management to larger corporate farms.

Historical archaeologists have moved beyond a site-based approach to consider landscape and environmental transformations. Most notably, Lawrence and Davies (2019; Davies & Lawrence 2015) have used archaeological evidence to demonstrate the ways that the Victorian goldfields resulted in the mass movement of sediments, transformed hydrology, and landforms—and tied these changes into an archaeological approach to the Anthropocene (Lawrence, Davies, & Turnbull 2016). Similar to mining, both farming and pastoralism transformed landscapes, ecosystems, and environments through removal/elimination of native plant and animal species, changes to topsoil through tilling and animal treadage, increased erosion, changes to hydrology, and various structural changes, such as roads, fences, bores, wells, dams, canals, and built structures—termed 'improvements'. In the recent volume *Historical Archaeology and the Environment* (Torres de Souza & Costa 2018), Murray (2018) maps out an archaeology of pastoralism in the Great Artesian Basin in southeast Australia that defines the diverse themes of an archaeology of pastoralism at a regional level: contributing to ecological history, treating wool as a global commodity, the impact of new technologies (particularly bores), and Aboriginal dispossession (see later). Lawrence and Davies (2018: 230–231) see a central role for historical archaeology and settler history in Anthropocene studies and provide a comprehensive review of studies of settler-driven anthropogenic change as they relate to archaeology: 'Environmental data from disciplines such as ecology, palynology and geomorphology have yet to be fully integrated into the human narrative. . . . [and] It is historical archaeology, working with documentary as well as material sources, that can integrate the multiple lines of evidence needed to understand what has happened to the environment in the 200 years since European arrival'.

Aboriginal People and Agrarian Australia

The evidence for the presence of Aboriginal people on farms and pastoral stations represents a larger body of archaeological work, growing from the 1980s onwards. This is due to the growth of archaeological work on culture contact and Aboriginal experiences in the colonial world. It followed and built on revisionist history (particularly that of Henry Reynolds and others) concerned with the forms of Aboriginal engagement with settlers on the frontier (Reynolds 1972, 1990)—which for much of Australia involved agrarian dimensions—and the ways that these histories were hidden, obscured, and forgotten (Reynolds 1998). Work on frontier violence by historians (Dwyer & Ryan 2012; Reynolds 2001) is equally relevant to archaeological approaches to the pastoral frontier (Burke et al. 2018; Wallis et al. this volume).

It goes without saying that farms and pastoral stations were created on Aboriginal peoples' Country. Farms can be read as a palimpsest that often acted to obscure the evidence for Aboriginal people. Archaeological material in farming landscapes for Aboriginal people's past occupation became subject to colonial collecting processes (Griffiths 1996). In some instances, pastoralists removed, destroyed, and obscured the evidence for Aboriginal people as well excluding and restricting Aboriginal people's access (Liebelt 2016).

The archaeological evidence for the historical presence of Aboriginal people on farms and pastoral stations is important evidence for the strategies of survival and negotiation deployed by Aboriginal people. Archaeology reveals how farmers, pastoralists, and government policies variously relied upon, constrained, and excluded Aboriginal people in farming landscapes over time—from the nineteenth century through the twentieth century until the land rights movement of the 1960s. As such, the historical legacies of power relations are represented in archaeological sites on farms. In Liebelt's (2019) innovative study of affective and emotional responses to the material properties of Aboriginal grindstones on Narungga Country on Guuranda/Yorke Peninsula, South

Australia, and Yandruwandha Yawarrawarrka Country in the Strzelecki Desert (northwest South Australia and southwest Queensland), she highlights how Aboriginal peoples and Australian rural settler-descendants are reminded of history by archaeological sites and artefacts within farming landscapes.

Aboriginal people were often present on farms as they accessed their Country, laboured as workers and visited kin, and in some cases as they became farmers themselves (Paterson 2018) (Figure 41.3). The archaeological evidence for settlements of Aboriginal labourers and their kin has been studied across pastoral Australia (see Castle & Hagan 1988). In the Kimberley region of northern Western Australia, Harrison's work at Old Lamboo Station highlighted the material evidence for negotiated Aboriginal access to labour and resources (Harrison 2002a, 2002b, 2004a; see also Smith 2001). Head and Fullagar (1997) used evidence from site locations and contents, rock art, stone tools, and plant food use to reveal how Kimberley Aboriginal people have maintained links with sites on Country and negotiated their interaction with pastoral colonization and attachments to places. Feakins (2019) reveals how buffalo hunting in what is now Kakadu National Park involved Aboriginal men and women, as revealed through buffalo camps and oral history—challenging the dominant colonial legend of the white male and commemorating Bininj/Mungguy heritage of the historical past.

In the Pilbara of Western Australia, the remains of the earliest sheep stations established in the 1860s have been recorded, revealing the presence of Aboriginal people and the connections between the pastoral settlers on a remote frontier (Paterson 2006, 2008, 2011). The pastoral settlement on West Lewis Island in the Dampier Archipelago of Western Australia appears to have attempted to bridge both pearlshell fishing and sheep (Souter, Paterson, & Hook 2006). The Northern Territory pastoral frontier relied on cattle—the earliest period remains largely unstudied (however see Anthony 2004), although mid-twentieth century archaeological sites have been studied through the lens of biography for the Murchison and Davenport Ranges (Gill, Paterson, & Murphy 2005; Gill & Paterson 2007). In Central Australia, sheep stations were established from the 1860s, with archaeological work at Strangways Station (Paterson 2005c, 2008) and Killalpaninna Mission, which had a small number of animals (Birmingham & Wilson 2010).

In southeastern Australia a rich body of work has focussed on the heritage values of Aboriginal sites in pastoral landscapes, driven by the leadership of National Parks and Wildlife Service staff (at the time), including Denis Byrne, Steven Brown, and Rodney Harrison, whose 'shared landscape' approach reflected and inspired contemporary archaeological and heritage thinking (Brown 2010, 2011; Byrne 2003; Byrne & Nugent 2004; Harrison 2003, 2004b). A correlate to this research is work into the archaeology of missions, remembering that some missions like Coranderrk (Lydon 2002) and New Norcia (Shellam 2015) were focussed on producing Aboriginal gardeners and farmers. The presence of Aboriginal people on pastoral work sites has been presumably overlooked, an issue highlighted in Wolski's (2000) study on the pastoral frontier in western Victoria. Wolski compared outstations (shepherd's huts) with other 'contact' sites to explore details of Indigenous technological and subsistence practices previously

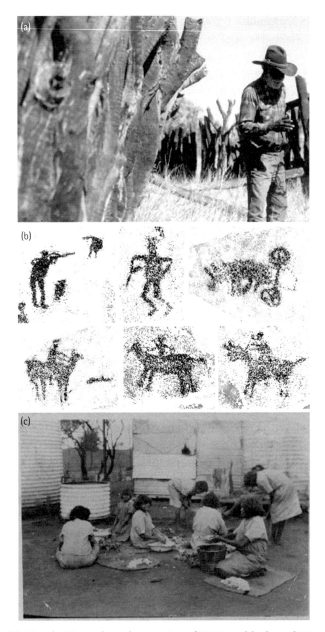

FIGURE 41.3. (a) Murphy Kennedy at the remains of Tjinjarra block yard, Murchison Ranges, Northern Territory (which operated in the 1930s), 2000 (photography by A. Paterson). (b) Aboriginal rock art images at 1860s sheep station, Springs Station, inland from Roebourne, Pilbara, western Australia (digitally enhanced by A. Paterson). (c) Girls washing wool at Mt Margaret Mission, Western Australia, ca. 1930 (BA1340/ERA3/16D, State Library of Western Australia).

inaccessible to archaeological research—particularly the potential of modified glass artefacts to act as indicators of Aboriginal 'everyday resistance' (see Loy & Wolski 1999). At a similar type of site on the Tasmanian pastoral frontier, Murray (1993) excavated a shepherd's hut of the Van Dieman's Land Company (VDL) that colonized northwest Tasmania after 1825 and found Aboriginal glass and stone artefacts in the hut. Rather than being Aboriginal workers on the frontier, Murray argued that 'It is a reasonable conjecture that the people who left the Aboriginal artefacts found at Burghley . . . fought the guerrilla actions against the VDL after 1836' (Murray 1993: 514). At Budj Bim in southwestern Victoria the first detailed excavation of an Aboriginal stone hut house (site KSH-1) discovered bottle glass artefacts and a cache of thirty-four iron nails (McNiven, Dunn, Crouch, & Gunditj Mirring Traditional Owners Aboriginal Corporation 2017). The stratigraphic evidence suggests multiple, short-term occupation events between the 1840s and 1870s, a period when Aboriginal people variously resisted and negotiated the pastoral invasion.

Diet and economic considerations related to Aboriginal people are implied in archaeological studies of colonial agrarianism, given the evidence for shifts from traditional foods to new foods, although few studies are specifically focussed on diet (see, however, Smith 2000; Zeanah, Codding, Bird, Bliege Bird, & Veth 2015). The institutional practice of providing rations to Aboriginal people dates from the earliest period of contact through to Citizenship, and it has been explored in terms of its relationship to protectionism, assimilation policies, historical Aboriginal settlements, welfare, and Aboriginal agency (e.g., Rowse 1998). On pastoral stations rations were provided on behalf of governments as a distribution to Aboriginal people deemed in need of support, and also to employees as a form of payment (Rowse 1987). Rationing supported extended families beyond the immediate recipients, the material expression is Aboriginal settlements in relation to pastoral sites. At Strangways Springs, for example, the archaeological record reveals a spatial trend where certain Aboriginal camps reveal a wide range of material culture largely derived from rationing as payment for labour. At camps more distant from the central pastoral work sites the amount of rationed material decreases, yet the range of material—clothing, food, tobacco, and tools—remains constant, suggesting that Aboriginal people across the pastoral landscape had similar access to rations, probably through Aboriginal intermediaries 'inside' the pastoral domain (Paterson 2003).

A range of studies across Australia have linked archaeological evidence such as rock art to the consequences of pastoralism—in some instances rock art provides evidence for Aboriginal perceptions of change related to pastoralism. For example, in Central Australia, Frederick (1999) tracks the emergence of charcoal motifs to the new world of pastoral work. In the Kimberley, O'Connor et al. (2013) related contact-era rock art to forms of resistance on the colonial frontier. In the Pilbara on Ngarluma people's Country, rock art and archaeological evidence at sheep stations reveal the presence of resident groups of Aboriginal workers. At several sheep stations Aboriginal rock art depicts pastoral work (Figure 41.3b) (Paterson & Wilson 2009) as well as work on pearl shell luggers owned by the white pastoralists (Paterson & van Duivenvoorde 2014).

These studies provide tantalizing glimpses into early perceptions of Aboriginal people to the arrival and realities of pastoral colonialism.

Conclusion

To date, archaeology has only begun to gain a significant sense of its potential to reveal the ecological, social, cultural, and heritage dimensions of agrarian Australia. However, the field remains cleaved between Aboriginal and non-Aboriginal histories, and it has yet to develop a broad interdisciplinary methodology. There exist major opportunities for close-disciplinary collaboration and integration. The amount of literature on the topic of the archaeology of the Anthropocene is growing quickly as the challenges of climate change and its mitigation come into focus (Boivin & Crowther 2021; Lawrence & Davies 2019). Most definitions of the start of the Anthropocene focus on recent centuries or the twentieth century (Bashford 2013). Settler Australia and its associated environmental impacts are central to these time frames and relevant to issues of environmental and social justice.

The first opportunity is the further integration of ecological records with archaeological evidence. The significant history of overlapping archaeological and ecological approaches is reviewed in Lawrence and Davies (2018) and, despite some studies suggesting the effectiveness of such efforts, such as the multidisciplinary investigation of the nineteenth settlement of Willunga Plains, South Australian (Denham, Lentfer, Stuart, Bickford, & Barr 2012), overall there are few truly integrated projects. This opportunity leads directly to the second—specifically, the relevance of archaeology to our understanding of human-environmental histories. Future projects will hopefully contribute to regional research programs, such as those undertaken by Lawrence and Davies, to validate the potential of using archaeological thinking to shift the frame of evidence from smaller sites to whole landscapes. Furthermore, research into farming and pastoralism through an environmental history lens invites broadening the frame to consider agrarian Australia similarly to emerging historical archaeologies of geoheritage, mining, and other extractive processes (Lawrence & Davies 2018), and the archaeology of the movement of industrial contaminants like mercury (Lawrence & Davies 2020). Legacies of farming and pastoralism include environmental damage, species extinction and replacement, and contaminants (i.e., waste at work sites and farm/pastoral settlements), although there is little archaeological engagement with these topics. Similarly, environmental research into grasslands and rangelands rarely includes archaeological perspectives, if at all. Recent work in the social sciences shifts the focus from humans to consider nonhuman species, such as anthropologist Anna Tsing's (2015) exploration of how the lives of fungi reveal problems with narratives of progress. This type of research invites rethinking on how categories of wild, feral, and domestic relate to animal 'management' in cross-cultural settings in Australia.

The third, and related, opportunity is to better understand the relationship between Aboriginal economies at the time of the arrival of the British to determine how they were altered by colonization and to develop histories which privilege Indigenous innovation rather than argue for ways that this resembled agriculture elsewhere. Perhaps more so than any continent, the relatively recent and rapid transition from hunter-foraging to farming and pastoralism in Australia provides potential insights into processes that occurred earlier elsewhere (Paterson 2018). White (2019: 64) reminds us that this transition requires asking: How did Aboriginal agriculture differ from what the European invaders were used to? This questioning makes an important link between Aboriginal perceptions of agriculture and landscape and wider ideas and histories of agriculture in Australia, with implications for the future of land management in Australia. Finally, looking forward, the future of maintaining the multispecies landscapes that have nurtured humans, among others, will require farming, pastoralism, and other industrial actions to be considered, along with precolonial Aboriginal environmental management.

NOTE

1. https://www.thecultureconcept.com/fantastic-flora-in-australia-first-fleet-to-federation; accessed 24 March 2021.

REFERENCES

Allison, P. M. (2003). The Old Kinchega Homestead: Doing household archaeology in outback New South Wales, Australia. *International Journal of Historical Archaeology*, 7(3), 161–194.

Allison, P. M. & Esposito, V. (2020). *Who came to tea at The Old Kinchega Homestead?: Tablewares, teawares and social interaction at an Australian outback pastoral homestead.* BAR International Series 2964. Oxford: BAR.

Anthony, T. (2004). Labour relations on northern cattle stations: Feudal exploitation and accommodation. *The Drawing Board: An Australian Review of Public Affairs*, 4(3), 117–136.

Antolín, F., Berihuete, M., & López, O. (2016). Archaeobotany of wild plant use: Approaches to the exploitation of wild plant resources in the past and its social implications. *Quaternary International*, 404(Part A), 1–3.

Bairstow, D. (1985). *The Australian Agricultural Company at Port Stephens: An archaeological contribution to history.* Cremorne: self-published.

Balme, J., & O'Connor, S. (2016). Dingoes and Aboriginal social organization in Holocene Australia. *Journal of Archaeological Science: Reports*, 7, 775–781.

Barnard, A. (1962). *The simple fleece: Studies in the Australian wool industry.* Parkville: Melbourne University Press in association with The Australian National University.

Bashford, A. (2013). The Anthropocene is modern history: Reflections on climate and Australian deep time. *Australian Historical Studies*, 44(3), 341–349.

Bean, C. E. W. (1912). *On the wool track.* London: Alston Rivers.

Beck, W., Clarke, A., & Head, L. (1989). *Plants in Australian archaeology*. Tempus 1. St. Lucia: Anthropology Museum, University of Queensland.

Birmingham, J., Jack, I., & Jeans, D. N. (1979). *Australian pioneer technology: Sites and relics*. Richmond: Heinemann Educational Australia.

Birmingham, J., & Wilson, A. (2010). Archaeologies of cultural interaction: Wybalenna settlement and Killalpaninna mission. *International Journal of Historical Archaeology*, *14*(1), 15–38.

Blench, R. (2001). 'You can't go home again': Pastoralism in the new millennium. Food and Agriculture Organisation, United Nations: Animal Health and Production Series, No 150. London: Overseas Development Institute.

Bliege Bird, R., Bird, D. W., Codding, B. F., Parker, C. H., & Jones, J. H. (2008). The "fire stick farming" hypothesis: Australian Aboriginal foraging strategies, biodiversity, and anthropogenic fire mosaics. *Proceedings of the National Academy of Sciences of the United States of America*, *105*(39), 796–801.

Boivin, N., & Crowther, A. (2021). Mobilizing the past to shape a better Anthropocene. *Nature Ecology & Evolution*, *5*, 273–284.

Brown, S. (2010). *Cultural landscape: A practical guide for park management*. Sydney: Department of Environment, Climate Change, and Water.

Brown, S. (2011). Documenting pastoral landscapes—Connecting archaeology, history, and communities. *Heritage & Society*, *4*(1), 33–58.

Brumm, A. (2021). Dingoes and domestication. *Archaeology in Oceania*, *56*, 17–31

Builth, H. (2014). *Ancient Aboriginal aquaculture rediscovered*. Saarbrucken, Germany: LAP Lambert.

Burke, H., Barker, B., Cole, N., Wallis, L. A., Hatte, E., Davidson, I., & Lowe, K. (2018). The Queensland Native Police and strategies of recruitment on the Queensland frontier, 1849–1901. *Journal of Australian Studies*, *42*(3), 297–313.

Burrows, N. D., Burbidge, A., Fuller, P. J., & Behn, G. (2006). Evidence of altered fire regimes in the Western Desert region of Australia. *Conservation Science Western Australia*, *5*(3), 14–26.

Byrne, D. (2003). The ethos of return: Erasure and reinstatement of Aboriginal visibility in the Australian historical landscape. *Historical Archaeology*, *37*(1), 73–86.

Byrne, D., & Nugent, M. (2004). *Mapping attachment: A spatial approach to Aboriginal post-contact heritage*. Sydney: Department of Environment and Conservation.

Cannon, A. (1992). Woolsheds and catastrophe theory: The lower Lachlan experiment. *The Australian Journal of Historical Archaeology*, *10*, 65–74.

Casella, E.C. (2006). Transplanted technologies and rural relics: Australian industrial archaeology and questions that matter. *Australasian Historical Archaeology*, *24*, 65–75.

Casey, M. (1999). Local pottery and dairying at the DMR Site, Brickfield, Sydney, New South Wales. *Australasian Historical Archaeology*, *17*, 3–37.

Castillo, J. A. Q. (2014). Agrarian archaeology in Early Medieval Europe. *Quaternary International*, *346*, 1–6.

Castle, R., & Hagan, J. (1988). Settlers and the state: The creation of an Aboriginal workforce in Australia. *Aboriginal History*, *22*, 24–35.

Clarke, A. (1994). Romancing the stones. The cultural construction of an archaeological landscape in the Western District of Victoria. *Archaeology in Oceania*, *29*(1), 1–15.

Connah, G. (1977). Wool, water and settlement: The archaeological landscape of Saumarez Station. *Armidale and District Historical Society*, *20*, 117–127.

Connah, G. (1986). Historical reality: Archaeological reality. Excavations at Regentville, Penrith, New South Wales, 1985. *The Australian Journal of Historical Archaeology, 4*, 29–42.

Connah, G. (1994). Bagot's Mill: Genesis and revelation in an archaeological research project. *Australasian Historical Archaeology, 12*, 3–55.

Connah, G. (2007). *The same under a different sky? A country estate in nineteenth-century New South Wales*. BAR International Series 1625. Oxford: British Archaeological Reports.

Connah, G., Rowland, M., & Oppenheimer, J. (1978). *Captain Richards' house at Winterbourne: A study in historical archaeology*. Armidale: Department of Prehistory and Archaeology, University of New England.

Crosby, A. W. (1986). *Ecological imperialism: The biological expansion of Europe, 900–1900*. Cambridge: Cambridge University Press.

Crosby, A. W. (2003). *The Columbian exchange: Biological and cultural consequences of 1492*. Westport, CT: Praeger.

Cummins, R. D. (1989). Scouring the clip: Boom and burn on Woolscour Lane. *Australian Journal of Historical Archaeology, 7*, 23–28.

Curr, E. M. (1883). *Recollections of squatting in Victoria, then called the Port Phillip District (from 1841 to 1851)*. Melbourne: G. Robertson.

Davidson, B. R. (1994). The development of the pastoral industry in Australia during the nineteenth century. In C. Chang & H. A. Koster (Eds.), *Pastoralists at the periphery: Herders in a capitalist world* (pp. 79–95). Tucson: The University of Arizona Press.

Davidson, I. (1989). Escaped domestic animals and the introduction of agriculture to Spain. In J. Clutton-Brock (Ed.), *The walking larder: Patterns of domestication, pastoralism and predation* (pp. 59–71). London: Unwin-Hyman.

Davies, P., & Lawrence, S. (2015). Dams and ditches: Cultural landscapes of colonial water management in the highlands of Victoria. *Historic Environment, 27*(3), 36–47.

Denham, T. (2008). Traditional forms of plant exploitation in Australia and New Guinea: The search for common ground. *Vegetation History and Archaeobotany, 17*, 245–248.

Denham, T. (2009). A practice-centred method for charting the emergence and transformations of agriculture. *Current Anthropology, 50*(5), 661–667.

Denham, T., Donohue, M., & Booth, S. (2009). Horticultural experimentation in Northern Australia reconsidered. *Antiquity, 83*, 634–648.

Denham, T., Lentfer, C., Stuart, E., Bickford, S., & Barr, C. (2012). Multi-disciplinary investigation of 19th century European settlement of the Willunga Plains, South Australia. In S. Haberle and B. David (Eds.), *Peopled landscapes: Archaeological and biogeographic approaches to landscapes* (pp. 393–412). Terra Australis 34. Canberra: ANU E-Press.

de Souza, M. A. T., & Costa, D. M. (2018). *Historical archaeology and environment*. New York: Springer.

Dwyer, P. G., & Ryan, L. (2012). Theatres of violence, massacre, mass killing and atrocity throughout history. *War and Genocide, 11*, 299.

Egloff, B. J., O'Sullivan, M., & Ramsay, J. (1991). Archaeology of the 1891 shearer's war: The main strike camp at Barcaldine, Queensland. *Australian Historical Archaeology, 9*, 63–75.

Feakins, C. (2019). Buffalo shooting in the 'wild' north: The hidden heritage of Kakadu National Park. *Historic Environment, 31*(1), 10–26.

Fijn, N. (2018). Dog ears and tails: Differential ways of being with canines in Aboriginal Australia and Mongolia. In H. A. Swanson, M. E. Lien, & G. B. Ween (Eds.), *Domestication gone wild: Politics and practices of multispecies relations* (pp. 72–93). Durham, NC: Duke University Press.

Frederick, U. (1999). At the centre of it all: Constructing contact through the rock art of Watarrka National Park, Central Australia. *Archaeology in Oceania, 34*(3), 132–143.

Gammage, B. (2011). *The biggest estate on earth: How Aborigines made Australia*. Crows Nest: Allen & Unwin.

Gerritsen, R. (2010). Evidence for Indigenous Australian agriculture. *Australasian Science August 2010*, 1–3. http://australasianscience.com.au/article/issue-july-august-2020/evidence-indigenous-australian-agriculture.html

Gill, A. M., Williams, J. E., & Bradstock, R. A. (2002). *Flammable Australia: The fire regimes and biodiversity of a continent*. Cambridge: Cambridge University Press.

Gill, N., & Paterson, A. G. (2007). A work in progress: Aboriginal people and pastoral cultural heritage in Australia. In R. Jones & B. Shaw (Eds.) *Loving a sunburned country? Geographies of Australian heritages* (pp. 113–131). Aldershot: Ashgate.

Gill, N., Paterson, A., & Murphy, M. (2005). 'Murphy, do you want to delete this?' Hidden histories and hidden landscapes in the Murchison and Davenport ranges, Northern Territory, Australia. Faculty of Science Papers, http://ro.uow.edu.au/scipapers/19. Wollongong: University of Wollongong.

Godwin, L., & L'Oste-Brown, S. (2002). A past remembered: Aboriginal 'historical' places in central Queensland. In R. Harrison & C. Williamson (Eds.), *After Captain Cook: The archaeology of the recent indigenous past in Australia* (pp. 191–212). Archaeological Methods Series 8, Archaeological Computing Laboratory. Sydney: University of Sydney.

Godwin, L., & L'Oste-Brown, S. (2012). Water, water everywhere: Attempts at drought-proofing properties using surface water infrastructure in central west Queensland in the early 1880s. *Australian Archaeology, 74*, 55–70.

Gott, B. (1982). Ecology of root use by the Aborigines of southern Australia. *Archaeology in Oceania, 17*, 59–67.

Gott, B. (1983). Murnong—*Microseris scapigera*: A study of a staple food of Victorian Aborigines. *Australian Aboriginal Studies, 2/1983*: 2–17.

Gott, B. (2002). Fire-making in Tasmania: Absence of evidence is not evidence of absence. *Current Anthropology, 43*, 650–56.

Griffiths, T. (1996). *Hunters and collectors: The antiquarian imagination in Australia*. Melbourne: Cambridge University Press.

Grimwade, G. (1998). The Canning Stock Route: Desert stock route to outback tourism. *Australasian Historical Archaeology, 16*, 70–79.

Hallam, S. J. (1975). *Fire and hearth: A study of Aboriginal usage and European usurpation in south-western Australia*. Canberra: Australian Institute of Aboriginal Studies.

Harrison, R. (2002a). Archaeology and the colonial encounter: Kimberley spearpoints, cultural identity and masculinity in the north of Australia. *Journal of Social Archaeology, 2*(3), 352–377.

Harrison, R. (2002b). Australia's Iron Age: Aboriginal post-contact metal artefacts from Old Lamboo Station, Southeast Kimberley, Western Australia. *Australasian Historical Archaeology, 20*, 67–76.

Harrison, R. (2003). The archaeology of 'lost places': Ruin, memory and the heritage of the Aboriginal diaspora in Australia. *Historic Environment, 17*(1), 18–23.

Harrison, R. (2004a). Contact archaeology and the landscapes of pastoralism in the north-west of Australia. In T. Murray (Ed.), *The archaeology of contact in settler societies* (pp. 109–143). Cambridge: Cambridge University Press.

Harrison, R. (2004b). *Shared landscapes: Archaeologies of attachment and the pastoral industry in New South Wales*. Sydney: UNSW Press.

Head, L., & Fullagar, R. (1997). Hunter-gatherer archaeology and pastoral contact: Perspectives from the northwest Northern Territory, Australia. *World Archaeology, 28*, 418–428.

Head, L. (1994). Landscapes socialised by fire: Post contact changes in Aboriginal fire use in northern Australia, and implications for prehistory. *Archaeology in Oceania, 29*(3), 172–181.

Hiscock, P. (2008). *The archaeology of ancient Australia*. London: Routledge.

Hynes, R. A., & Chase, A. K. (1982). Plants, sites and domiculture: Aboriginal influence upon plant communities in Cape York Peninsula. *Archaeology in Oceania, 17*, 38–50.

Ireland, T. (2002). Giving value to the historic past: Historical archaeology, heritage, and nationalism. *Australasian Historical Archaeology, 20*, 15–25.

Jack, I., Holmes, K., & Kerr, R. (1984). Ah Toy's garden: A Chinese market-garden on the Palmer River goldfield, North Queensland. *Australian Journal of Historical Archaeology, 2*, 51–58.

Jones, R. (1969). Fire stick farming. *Australian Natural History, 16*, 224–228.

Keen, I. (2003). Aboriginal economy and society at the threshold of colonisation: A comparative study. *Before Farming, 3*(2), 1–24.

Keen, I. (2021). Foragers or farmers: *Dark Emu* and the controversy over Aboriginal agriculture. *Anthropological Forum, 31*(1), 106–128.

Latz, P. K. (1995). *Bushfires and bushtucker: Aboriginal plant use in Central Australia*. Alice Springs: I.A.D. Press.

Lawrence, S., & Davies, P. (2018). Archaeology and the Anthropocene in the study of settler Australia. In M. A. T. de Souza & D. M. Costa (Eds.), *Historical archaeology and the environment* (pp. 229–251). Berlin: Springer.

Lawrence, S., & Davies, P. (2019). *Sludge: Disaster on Victoria's goldfields*. Melbourne: Black.

Lawrence, S., & Davies, P. (2020). Historical mercury losses from the gold mines of Victoria, Australia. *Elementa: Science of the Anthropocene, 8*, 35, doi:10.1525/elementa.432.

Lawrence, S., Davies, P., & Turnbull, J. (2016). The archaeology of Anthropocene rivers: Water management and landscape change in 'Gold Rush' Australia. *Antiquity, 90*(353), 1348–1362.

Liebelt, B. (2016). *Aboriginal occupation traces in agricultural assemblages* (PhD thesis). University of Western Australia, Perth.

Liebelt, B. (2019). Touching grindstones in archaeological and cultural heritage practice: Materiality, affect and emotion in settler-colonial Australia. *Australian Archaeology, 85*, 267–278.

Loy, T. H., & Wolski, N. (1999). On the invisibility of contact: Residue analyses on Aboriginal glass artefacts from western Victoria. *The Artefact, 22*, 65–73.

Lydon, J. (2002). 'This civilising experiment': Photography at Coranderrk Aboriginal Station during the 1860s. In R. Harrison & C. Williamson (Eds.), *After Captain Cook: The archaeology of the recent indigenous past in Australia* (pp. 59–74). Archaeological Method Series 8, Archaeological Computing Laboratory. Sydney: University of Sydney.

Macphail, M. K., & Casey, M. (2008). "News from the Interior": What can we tell from plant microfossils preserved on historical archaeological sites in colonial Parramatta? *Australasian Historical Archaeology, 26*, 45–69.

McNiven, I. J., Dunn, J. E., Crouch, J., & Gunditj Mirring Traditional Owners Aboriginal Corporation. (2017). Kurtonitj stone house: Excavation of a mid-nineteenth century Aboriginal frontier site from Gunditjmara country, south-west Victoria. *Archaeology in Oceania, 52*, 171–197.

McNiven, I. J., Crouch, J., Richards, T., Dolby, N., Jacobsen, G., & Gunditj Mirring Traditional Owners Aboriginal Corporation. (2012). Dating Aboriginal stone-walled fishtraps at Lake Condah, Southeast Australia. *Journal of Archaeological Science, 39,* 268–286.

Murray, T. (1988). Beyond the ramparts of the unknown: The historical archaeology of the Van Diemen's Land Company. In J. Birmingham, D. Bairstow, & A. Wilson (Eds.), *Archaeology and colonisation: Australia in the world context* (pp. 99–108). Sydney: The Australian Society for Historical Archaeology.

Murray, T. (1993). The childhood of William Lanne: Contact archaeology and Aboriginality in Tasmania. *Antiquity, 67,* 507–519.

Murray, T. (2018). Towards an archaeology of extensive pastoralism in the Great Artesian Basin in Australia. In M. A. T. de Souza & D. M. Costa (Eds.), *Historical archaeology and environment* (pp. 109–127). Berlin: Springer.

O'Connor, S., Balme, J., Fyfe, J., Oscar, J., Oscar, M., Davis, J., . . . Surprise, D. (2013). Marking resistance? Change and continuity in the recent rock art of the southern Kimberley. *Antiquity, 87*(336), 539–554.

Partridge, M. (1984). The excavation of the Mount Wood woolscour, Tibooburra, New South Wales. *Australian Journal of Historical Archaeology, 2,* 38–50.

Pascoe, B. (2014). *Dark Emu: Aboriginal Australia and the birth of agriculture.* Broome: Magabala Book.

Paterson, A. G. (2003). The texture of agency: An example of culture contact in central Australia. *Archaeology in Oceania, 38*(2), 52–65.

Paterson, A. G. (2005a). Hunter-gatherer interactions with sheep and cattle pastoralists from the Australian arid zone. In M. A. Smith & P. Veth (Eds.), *Desert peoples: Archaeological perspectives* (pp. 276–292). Oxford: Blackwell.

Paterson, A. G. (2005b). Historical interactions between Aborigines and European pastoralists in Australia's drylands. In M. A. Smith & P. Hesse (Eds.), *23 degrees south: Archaeology and environmental history of the southern deserts* (pp. 267–280). Canberra: National Museum of Australia.

Paterson, A. G. (2005c). Early pastoral landscapes and culture contact in Central Australia. *Historical Archaeology, 39*(3), 28–48.

Paterson, A. G. (2006). Towards a historical archaeology of Western Australia's northwest. *Australasian Historical Archaeology, 24,* 99–111.

Paterson, A. G. (2008). *The lost legions: Culture contact in colonial Australia.* Lanham, MD: AltaMira Press.

Paterson, A. G. (2011). Considering colonialism and capitalism in Australian historical archaeology: Two case studies of culture contact from the pastoral domain. In S. Croucher & L. Weiss (Eds.), *The archaeology of capitalism in colonial contexts: Postcolonial historical archaeologies* (pp. 243–267). New York: Springer.

Paterson, A. G. (2013). Enduring contact: Australian perspectives in environmental and social change. *Occasion: Interdisciplinary Studies in the Humanities 5* (March 1). https://arcade. stanford.edu/occasion/enduring-contact-australian-perspectives-environmental-and-soc ial-change

Paterson, A. G. (2018). Once were foragers: The archaeology of agrarian Australia and the fate of Aboriginal land management. *Quaternary International, 489,* 4–16.

Paterson, A. G., & van Duivenvoorde, W. (2014). The sea, inland: Aboriginal rock art depictions of boats from the western Pilbara. *Great Circle, 35*(2), 30–54.

Paterson, A. G., & Wilson, A. (2009). Indigenous perceptions of contact at Inthanoona, northwest Western Australia. *Archaeology in Oceania, 44*, 98–110.

Pearson, M., & Lennon, J. (2010). *Pastoral Australia: Fortunes, failures and hard yakka. A historical overview 1788–1967*. Collingwood: CSIRO.

Pearson, W. (1996). Water power in a dry continent: The transfer of watermill technology from Britain to Australia in the nineteenth century. *Australasian Historical Archaeology, 14*, 46–62.

Pyne, S. J. (1998). *Burning bush: A fire history of Australia*. Seattle: University of Washington Press.

Reynolds, H. (1972). *Aborigines and settlers: The Australian experience, 1788–1939*. North Melbourne: Cassell Australia.

Reynolds, H. (1990). *With the white people*. Ringwood: Penguin.

Reynolds, H. (1998). *This whispering in our hearts*. St. Leonards: Allen & Unwin.

Reynolds, H. (2001). *An indelible stain?: The question of genocide in Australia's history*. Ringwood: Penguin.

Rowse, T. (1987). 'Were you ever savages?' The Aboriginal insiders and pastoralists' patronage. *Oceania, 58*(1), 81–99.

Rowse, T. (1998). *White flour, white power: From rations to citizenship in Central Australia*. Melbourne: Cambridge University Press.

Shellam, T. (2015). On my ground: Indigenous farmers at New Norcia, 1860s–1900s. In A. Lester & Z. Laidlaw (Eds.), *Indigenous communities and settler colonialism: Land holding, loss and survival in an interconnected world* (pp. 62–85). London: Palgrave.

Smith, P. A. (2000). Station camps: Legislation, labour relations and rations on pastoral leases in the Kimberley region, Western Australia. *Aboriginal History, 24*, 75–97.

Smith, P. A. (2001). Station camps: Identifying the archaeological evidence for continuity and change in post-contact Aboriginal sites in the south Kimberley, Western Australia. *Australian Archaeology, 53*, 23–31.

Smith, S. (2008). *Early Pilbara headstations: Spatiality and social relations* (Honours thesis). University of Western Australia, Perth

Souter, C., Paterson, A. G., & Hook, F. (2006). The assessment of archaeological sites on Barrow Island and the Dampier Archipelago, Pilbara, Western Australia: A collaborative approach. *Bulletin of the Australasian Institute of Maritime Archaeology, 30*, 85–92.

Sutton, P., & Walshe, K. (2021). *Farmers or hunter-gatherers? The Dark Emu debate*. Melbourne: Melbourne University Press.

Terry, L. (2013). Caboonbah: The archaeology of a middle class Queensland pastoral family. *International Journal of Historical Archaeology, 17*(3), 569–589.

Tsing, A. (2015). *The mushroom at the end of the world: On the possibility of life in capitalist ruins*. Princeton, NJ: Princeton University Press.

Ulm, S. (2012). 'Complexity' and the Australian continental narrative: Themes in the archaeology of Holocene Australia. *Quaternary International, 285*(2013), 182–192.

Walker, M., & Forrest, P. (1995). *Pastoral technology and the National Estate*. Australia ICOMOS.

Ward, D. (1998). *Fire, flogging, measles and grass: Nineteenth century land use conflict in southwestern Australia*. Perth: Department of Conservation and Land Management.

White, P. (2019). Book review: *Dark Emu. Aboriginal Australia and the birth of agriculture*, by Bruce Pascoe. Magabala Books, Broome, Western Australia, New Edition, 2018. *Archaeology in Oceania, 55*, 63–64.

Winter, S., Forsey, C., Dotte-Sarout, E., & Paterson, A. (2016). The settlement at Barmup: Britain's first farm in Western Australia. *Australasian Historical Archaeology, 34*, 32–43.

Winter, S., & Paterson, A. (in press). Australian colonial land settlement. In M. Nevell & E. C. Casella (Eds.), *Handbook of industrial archaeology*. London: Oxford University Press.

Wolski, N. (2000). *Brushing against the grain: Excavating for Aboriginal-European interaction on the colonial frontier in Western Victoria, Australia* (PhD thesis). University of Melbourne, Melbourne.

Zeanah, D. W., Codding, B. F., Bird, D. W., Bliege Bird, R., & Veth, P. M. (2015). Diesel and damper: Changes in seed use and mobility patterns following contact amongst the Martu of Western Australia. *Journal of Anthropological Archaeology, 39*, 51–62.

CHAPTER 42

'PREHISTORY' AND THE INDIGENOUS ARCHAEOLOGY OF MISSIONS AND RESERVES IN AUSTRALIA AND NEW GUINEA

JEREMY ASH

INTRODUCTION

CRITICAL reviews of Australasian and Pacific mission archaeology include studies of the intellectual history and historiography of Australian missions (Lydon & Ash 2010), comparisons of Australian and Pacific-style missions (and colonial experiences and cross-cultural situations within missions) (Middleton 2008, 2010, 2018), the role of First Nations peoples in shaping mission archaeology and the historical archaeology of the recent past (Lawrence & Davies 2010; see also McNiven & Russell 2005), links between missions with maritime archaeology (Fowler 2013), and critical summaries of works in the broader Pacific region (Bedford, Flexner, & Jones 2020; Flexner 2013). This chapter draws on several themes described in these syntheses and charts the diverging approach and tradition of mission archaeology (and historical archaeology more generally) in Australia and New Guinea.

Scholars have long critiqued the archetypes structuring archaeological theory and history-telling in the region, expressed as hunting and gathering Aboriginal societies and horticultural Melanesian societies (David & Denham 2006; Lourandos 2008; McNiven & Russell 2005). While this hard division is now recognized as an ethnographic and colonial construct (e.g., Denham, Donohue, & Booth 2009; Denham, Fullagar, & Head 2009; Florin & Carah 2018; Gosden & Head 1999; Harris 1995; Lourandos 1980, 1983; McNiven & Russell 2005), the archetypes nevertheless continue to provide the theoretical underpinnings of the discipline across the region (David & Denham 2006; Lourandos 2008). To summarize the general argument, archaeology in New Guinea emphasizes dynamic historical processes of internally derived change in 'agricultural' societies. In contrast, Australian archaeology has tended to emphasize ecological models of relatively stable 'hunter-gatherer' societies (David & Denham 2006; Lourandos 2008). The result is that 'prehistory' in New Guinea is characterized as historical, genealogical, and internally generative. In contrast, change in Aboriginal 'prehistory' generally involved environmentally and climatically derived 'nudges' charting new courses for otherwise stable but ultimately 'ahistoric' societies (cf. David et al. 2021).

However, the comparative critique of the discipline has centred largely on precolonial situations. Yet the division can be extended to the colonial era, whereby First Nations peoples (particularly in settler colonial Australia but also in comparable settings elsewhere) essentially only entered into history/linear time, and thus encountered 'modernity', following European invasion (after Fabian 1983; see also Attwood 1992; Byrne 1996; Comaroff & Comaroff 1986, 1991, 1997; Lydon 2009a; McNiven & Russell 2005). Nineteenth-century missionaries and missions were informed by and productive of the progressivist (social evolutionary) thinking underpinning the notion of prehistory (Barker 1996; e.g., McFarlane 1888), dismissing traditional life as 'prehistoric' and primitive, and teaching Western culture as progress and the future.

There is now a relatively established tradition of 'mission archaeology' in Australia, most of which has been directed to grappling with these fundamental problems of colonial time keeping: modernity, history and prehistory, rupture, and connection (Hemming, Wood, & Hunter 2000; see also Langford 1983; Pardoe 1990; Colley & Bickford 1997). Mission archaeology in New Guinea, however, appears to have taken a somewhat different pathway. With the exception of investigations at the nineteenth-century 'Papuan Mission' sites of the London Missionary Society in Torres Strait (Ash & David 2008; Ash, Brooks, David, & McNiven 2008), there have not been any published archaeological studies undertaken on missions in New Guinea. This is not to say there is no tradition of archaeological research at missions in the region: there is a long and interesting history of missionaries at archaeological sites, and, vice versa, archaeologists at mission sites (e.g., Dotte-Sarout & Howes 2019; Haddow 2019; Haddow, Dotte-Sarout, & Specht 2020; Howes 2017; see also Summerhayes this volume). What appears to have emerged is a distinctive inversion of the temporal and spatial thinking framing many of the Australian studies, where:

1. In spite of a surprisingly high number of excavations occurring within mission villages, the 'surface event' of the mission has largely been bypassed for explorations of deeper cultural sequences; or,
2. Mission histories have been incorporated into studies of ancestral landscapes of current communities (e.g., Ash 2014; David et al. 2008).

This chapter explores these diverging traditions in mission archaeology to consider whether and to what degree the broader disciplinary issues framing archaeological approaches to 'prehistoric' Australia and dynamic, historical New Guinea are replicated in archaeologies of the recent past. I conclude with a brief reflection on the persistent use of the term 'historical archaeology' (and its geographical and temporal circumscription) and suggest that a more inclusive approach to First Nations communities' short and long-term histories might be best imagined within the general theoretical and ethical possibilities of what has become known as 'Indigenous archaeology' (Atalay 2006; Colwell-Chanthaphonh et al. 2010; McNiven 2016a; Nicholas 2010; Silliman 2009). Indigenous archaeology is defined here as a style of collaborative archaeology that seeks to develop theoretical and methodological approaches compatible or sympathetic with the worldviews, epistemologies, political and cultural aspirations, and ethics of Indigenous peoples (Atalay 2006; McNiven 2016a; Nicholas 2008; see also Wilson, Smith, and Brady this volume). As a collaborative practice, Indigenous archaeology requires a certain level of reflection about how the discipline has historically engaged with Indigenous histories, and an openness to building new ways of knowing and telling material stories of relevance to Indigenous communities.

Defining Missions

As Elizabeth Graham (1998) observed for the northern American mission setting, the remarkable breadth of evangelical encounters and practices poses major problems for defining 'missions'. The sheer range of styles and evangelical organizations, First Nations groups, and religious experiences in Australia and New Guinea is remarkable. Mission styles range from the established to ephemeral. Established missions include the carceral-style institutions (e.g., Palm Island Mission in Queensland), the household-style missions in Torres Strait (northeast Australia) and southern coastal Papua New Guinea in the late nineteenth century (Beckett 2014; Prendergast 1968), and the model kampung (model village, such as Okaba and Merauke) in western New Guinea (Indonesia). Periodic or ephemeral missions include the rotating village teacher system in western New Guinea or even missions operated from the back of travelling lorries or over the side of boats. For some Aboriginal communities, 'mission' refers to government-run or approved reserves or stations. Discriminating between the missions, government stations and reserves (gazetted lands set aside for Aboriginal people), and the innumerable and poorly documented settlements such as 'fringe camps' (First Nations settlements that developed on the fringes of settler townships), is not clear-cut. Some were gazetted settlements overseen or visited by a missionary; others were only occasionally visited by missionary, superintendent, Protector, or police. All, however, form part of the morally fraught geographies and system of governance that developed in the latter half of the nineteenth century (e.g., Boucher & Russell 2012; McLisky, Russell, & Boucher 2015) and the forced labour and the widespread, systematic child removal policy that devastated Aboriginal families and communities in the late nineteenth and twentieth centuries (e.g., Kidd 1997). Such is the breadth of the idea of 'mission', the range of local meanings attached to the word, and the range of complex relationships among missions, Church, state, colonialism, and identity (e.g., Etherington 2005; Harris 1994; Lake 2018; Swain & Bird Rose 1988), that the category only begins to makes sense, for the purposes of any regional review, at its most polythetic.

AUSTRALIA

Mission archaeology in Australia has expanded exponentially in the five decades since Judy Birmingham's (1976, 1992, 1993) pioneering excavations at Wybalenna, the Pallawah Tasmanian Aboriginal station on Flinders Island in the Bass Strait, and Jim Allen and Rhys Jones's (1980) surface collection at putalina (the settlement known for many years as Oyster Cove in southeast Tasmania). Since that time, there have been field investigations at numerous Aboriginal and Torres Strait Islander missions and reserves across Australia. The most well-known is the series of archaeological studies at Ebenezer mission in Wotjobaluk Country in northwest Victoria (see Brown, Avery, & Goulding 2004; Lydon 2005, 2009a, 2009b, 2014; Lydon & Burns 2010) and other Victorian missions (e.g., Rhodes 1986). Major studies have also been undertaken in South Australia (e.g., Birmingham 2000; Birmingham & Wilson 2010; Brockwell, Gara, Colley, & Cane 1989; Fowler 2013, 2015, 2019; Fowler, Roberts, & Rigney 2016; Griffin 2010; Hemming et al. 2000), mainland Queensland (e.g., Morrison, McNaughton, & Shiner 2010; Morrison, McNaughton, & Keating 2015; Sutton 2003, 2014; Sutton et al. 2013; Sutton, Conyers, Pearce, St Pierre, & Nichols Pitt 2020), and Torres Strait in far north Queensland (e.g., Ash 2014; Ash, Manas, & Bosun 2010).

Rupture and (Pre)history in the Archaeology of Australian Missions

Numerous scholars have remarked upon the problem encapsulated in the Western tradition of separating First Nations peoples' pasts into prehistories and postcontact or post-European histories (Byrne 1996; Flexner 2017; Lightfoot 1995; Panich 2013; Russell 2016; Silliman 2001, 2005). As McNiven & Russell (2005) argue, Western processes of alienation and 'antiquation' (representing Indigenous peoples as 'living fossils') are key to the expression of settler colonial power over Indigenous worlds. Such processes are important ways modern liberal postcolonial states realize or militate Indigenous land expropriation, labour, rights, and heritage (e.g., Birch 2005; Byrne 1996; Langford 1983; Wolfe 1994, 2006). Archaeology has had (and in some ways continues to have) an interest in cultivating this boundary or rupture in First Nations histories. However, its previously unproblematic position as the legitimate way to know and narrate First Nations (particularly deep-time) histories is transforming. The archaeology of missions confronts this problem in quite immediate and intimate ways because it is often the product of deep collaborative research partnerships between researchers and descendent communities, engaging with living and vital places historically involved in the systematic dispossession of individuals, families, and Nations (e.g., Ash 2014; Hemming et al. 2000; Lydon 2009b; Morrison et al. 2010; Fowler & Rigney 2017).

However, bridging the gap between 'prehistory' and 'history' has proved a difficult, and at times impossible, task because the binary is not so easily resolved as simply connecting two disjointed chronological periods into a coherent story. On the contrary, the problem is about connecting two fundamentally incompatible ideas about the past. In practice, the task involves engaging with and slipping between contradictory ideas, imaginings, and spiritual and philosophical differences that the West has used (and uses) to organize and frame narratives about First Nations peoples.

Two key problems emerged in disciplinary approaches to cultural dynamism in 'prehistory' and 'history'. Firstly, Lourandos (2008; see also 1980, 1983, and Lourandos & Ross this volume) and David and Denham (2006) perceptively note that the notion of 'prehistory' in the Australian tradition, with roots in cultural ecology, is founded on the understanding that past Aboriginal hunting and gathering societies were inherently stable cultural systems. Archaeological histories explained cultural change as human adaptations to external environmental flux. This approach contrasts with the New Guinea situation where socio-cultural explanations for change in the archaeology of hunter-gatherers was considered by many to be quite reasonable because 'the interpretations of archaeologists conformed to the traditional "towards horticulture" paradigm and narrative' (Lourandos 2008: 3). The prehistory of Aboriginal societies was, in this conception, a complex expression of human-environment interactions, but nevertheless still ultimately comprised of 'ahistoric' social groups distinct from the dynamic socio-evolutionary pathway taken by societies in New Guinea.

Secondly, the notion of 'postcontact' mission Aboriginal histories in archaeology struggled to articulate a theory of cultural change and historical dynamism outside the twinned colonial strategies of missionaries to civilize and Christianize Aboriginal people. While the expression of and philosophies underpinning these colonial ideas evolved over time and differed between religious denominations, the missions typically saw themselves as implementing change within Aboriginal societies focused on spirituality (towards Christianity) but also in terms of settlement (towards agriculture), labour (towards godly industry), gender and class (towards a nuclear family and work discipline), and containment and the colonial expropriation of territory (humanitarianism and the emergence of sedentism and new village and nuclear family-based households and communities).[1]

Judy Birmingham's work at Wybalenna (1833–1847) on Flinders Island, Bass Strait, southeast Australia, was the first to tackle this problem of cultural change in Australian mission archaeology; however, her early efforts were stymied by a lack of theory from the then nascent discipline of historical archaeology in Australia in the late 1960s. Indeed, Birmingham would only publish her ground-breaking monograph after Mark P. Leone's and Parker B. Potter's work on domination and resistance became available to scholars, some two decades following the 1971 excavations at the village (e.g., Leone and Potter 1988). Inspired by these models of resistance and strategic accommodation to colonial domination that were developing in the United States, Birmingham analysed the excavation data of the 1830s cottages of the Tasmanian Aboriginal people to assess the ideological 'acceptance' (i.e., accommodation) or resistance of the inhabitants to the 'Christianizing' and 'civilizing' ideology of the settlement's manager, George Augustus Robinson (cf. Stevens 2017). The problems of the binary model of accommodation and resistance are well known (Russell 2016), particularly how tradition (as resistance) and change (as accommodation) were conceptualized in the analyses of material culture from the cottages replicated within archaeological theory and interpretation Robinson's view on stadial change. The agencies, lives, and complex social worlds of Tasmanian Aboriginal people on the southeastern maritime frontier were lost, not in the rupture between past and present but in the *association* between a Western idea of Aboriginal 'prehistory' (as tradition/static) and Western 'history' itself (as dynamic).

So what does it mean exactly to bridge this conceptual and epistemological gap between 'prehistory' and postcontact history? Or, from another perspective, where are the interpretive frameworks from 'prehistory' that can guide archaeological interpretations of mission landscapes?

Some of these issues are illuminated in Birmingham's (2000; see also Birmingham & Wilson 2010) other landmark mission study: the Killalpaninna Lutheran Mission in Dieri Country in Central Australia (1867–1928). This study refined some of her earlier thinking from Wybalenna, though also introduced hybridity (namely, creolization; cf. Russell 2005 on hybridity and Dalley & Memmott 2010 on the intercultural) and optimal foraging theory and risk minimization theory to Australian historical archaeology to examine social interactions between mission and non-mission-dwellers living in the vicinity of the mission across Lake Killalpaninna. The novel application of elements of optimal foraging theory and risk minimization theory to understanding patterns in material culture between 'traditional' and 'mission' dweller camps across this semiarid mission landscape is significant, if flawed, as it was the first such Australian study to provide a model to interpret spatial patterns of 'traditional' non-mission-dwellers. Similar to Lourandos's (2008) critique of Australian prehistory, the optimal foraging theory approach essentially located the mission—for 'traditional' Dieri—within the 'broad spectrum involving food quest, food preparation, clothing, wages and tool manufacture' (Birmingham 2000: 409). In other words, the study spatialized the temporal *disassociation* of prehistory and history; the mission became merely another ecological niche in the worlds of Dieri.

Nevertheless, Birmingham's landscape approach represented a landmark departure from earlier site-based approaches that directed scholarly attention to postcontact era Aboriginal geographies. Birmingham's landscape approach importantly directed attention *away* from mission compounds (e.g., Walshe, Malone, Telfer, & Gully 2019) and anticipated several major landscape-level studies of missions within Indigenous land- and seascapes (e.g., Fowler 2019; Fowler & Rigney 2017; Fowler et al. 2016; Morrison & Shepard 2013; Morrison et al. 2010; Morrison et al. 2015; see also Clarke 2000; Panich & Schneider's 2015 arguments for the significance of landscape perspectives for mission archaeology in northern American settings).

Vital and Contemporary Places

Several significant community collaborations between archaeologists and First Nations community members working on mission sites in Victoria, New South Wales, Queensland, and South Australia resist narratives of stadial progress by destabilizing some of the epistemological boundaries between historical archaeology and critical heritage studies, contemporary archaeology, and Indigenous orality and historicism (e.g., Fowler & Rigney 2017; Ireland 2010; Lydon & Burns 2010). Critical heritage approaches are proving particularly valuable in providing new narratives to build archaeological stories.

The series of archaeological excavations at Ebenezer Mission on the Traditional Country of the Wergaia-speaking people (the Wotjobaluk) of northwestern Victoria, for example, had the effect of challenging the 'romanticisation and manicuring' of this place as a Western ruin that had developed via the early efforts of conservationists. From the 1950s, efforts to 'preserve' the mission landscape strategically conserved only certain fabrics and structures, 'and their assessment of its significance mirrored the missionaries' own values, centring upon their work of conversion and redemption, and the patriarchal authority of the mission-house' (Lydon & Burns 2010: 43). The less durable Aboriginal houses and material traces were lost from the surface of the place; a process of progressive and selective erasure of Aboriginal pasts and presences that persist in colonialist and heroic representations of pastoral frontiers (see Birch 2005; Griffiths 1996).

Significantly, the transfer of land title back to the Wotjobaluk community in the early 1990s, and the later recognition of Native Title, meant that the archaeological works at the Ebenezer Mission came to be defined within the worldviews of the community. Acknowledging the complex location of the mission for those people with ties to this place (in terms of the mission's association with dispossession, connection, evangelism, spiritual elaborations or transformations, and community strength), the archaeological excavations brought to the surface (both literally and metaphorically) those things which had been hidden by the earlier heritage works. The archaeological research process was a complex exercise of encounter, memory, and narrative. The Wotjobaluk community invested 'these remains', as Lydon and Burns (2010) reflect, 'with their own ambivalent meanings, happy and sad; and in the words of Wotjobaluk Elder Nancy Harrison, "sort of half and half".'

Ancestral Resting Places

Missions are, as is frequently said, homes and homelands (McNiven & Russell 2005); 'complex' places occupying 'an important place in Aboriginal memory, as sites of recent memory, ancestral resting-places, historical landmarks, and the focus of social action in the present' (Lydon & Burns 2010: 39; see Attwood 1989; Barwick 1963, 1988; Blake 2001; Brock 1993; Choo 2001). On Mua (in Western Torres Strait), the mission cemetery continues to be a vital and active place of engagement for contemporary community members with the ancestors; people often return to visit, sometimes to repaint the headstones and maintain the graves, or at other times to sit and reflect. The great Mualgal and Kaurareg leader, Mr Wees Nawia—who as a boy was forced along with other Kaurareg community members to relocate to Poid Mission on Mua by the Queensland State government in the 1920s—later reflected that he could not bring himself to leave Mua and return to his homeland of Kirriri: 'I love the place where I was born [Kirriri, southwest Torres Strait]; better I live on the place I was born. But I can't leave Moa just because my mother's buried there [at Poid cemetery]. One thing that I can't leave Moa for now, because if not for my mother I never see this world' (cited in Sharp 1992: 127). In his work with repatriation of the Old People, Michael Aird (2004: 308) reports on the repatriation of ancestral remains and their reburial at the old mission cemetery on Stradbroke Island in southeast Queensland. Luke Godwin and Scott L'Oste-Brown (2004: 198) note the 'substantial ceremonial activity involving people gathering from across the region and elsewhere to partake in ceremonies imbued with great significance in terms of asserting association with country and returning "the old people" to their home country' at the Taroom Mission cemetery in central Queensland (see also L'Oste-Brown, Godwin, & Yelf 1996).

Of singular importance in historical archaeology and contact archaeology in general is the recognition of various forms of Aboriginal and Torres Strait Islander legal title in land (and later sea) from the early 1990s and the gradual transfer of select powers from state to First Nations communities (Lydon & Burns 2010; see works in Harrison & Williamson 2004). The transfer of title over some missions and reserves to Aboriginal organizations signified important state recognition of Indigenous self-determination and of missions as the ancestral homes and homelands of communities displaced by European colonization. These transfers also meant that Aboriginal and Torres Strait Islander corporate bodies were now the recognized organizations with legal rights over these missions (McNiven & Russell 2005: 227; Weir 2009), including the resting places of the Old People.

In Victoria (southeast Australia), the emergence of Aboriginal organizations as controlling bodies led to a number of important archaeological projects at several Victorian missions in the 1990s, and to a shift in the idea and application of mission archaeology. These projects focused on mission cemeteries, and in particular on identifying (unmarked) ancestral resting places within cemeteries. The projects used surface survey (Rhodes 1996), a range of noninvasive remote sensing techniques, including ground magnetic surveys (e.g., von Strokirch 1999; Long 1998; Long & MacKinnon 1999, 2000) and ground-penetrating radar (Brown et al. 2004; McDougall, Massie, & Cull 1997). They also included the mapping of surface topography (Long & McKinnon 1999), surface survey (Rhodes 1996), and plant distributions (e.g., mapping the surface distribution of iris bulbs) to locate unmarked ancestral grave sites at Ebenezer in western Victoria (Brown et al. 2004; Rhodes 1998). Similar survey programmes in Victoria were conducted at the Western Port Aboriginal Protectorate Station and Native Police Corps Headquarters (Rhodes 1998), the Goulburn River Protectorate Station (Lomax 1991; Long & McKinnon 1999), and the Lake Condah Mission (Lomax & Long

1991). Elsewhere in Australia, remote sensing cemetery surveys were undertaken at Wybalenna (Ranson & Egloff 1988), Bowraville (Stanley 1999) and Forster in New South Wales (Stanley & Connah 1977), and at Taroom Aboriginal Reserve in Queensland (L'Oste-Brown & Godwin 1995; Yelf & Burnett 1995). More recently, Mary-Jane Sutton and colleagues (2013) used noninvasive geophysical techniques at the cemetery of the former mission village of Mapoon (Western Cape York Peninsula, north Queensland) to identify unmarked burial sites threatened by town housing (see also St Pierre et al. 2019; Sutton 2014; Sutton et al. 2020). At Lake Condah Mission cemetery in southwest Victoria, where there are numerous unmarked graves, university researchers and the Gunditj Mirring Traditional Owners Aboriginal Corporation have been using ground penetrating radar as a way to find suitable areas for *future* internments for community members (Moffat et al. 2018).

In these applied archaeology frameworks, researchers do not address academic research questions, or apply methodologies and historical narratives defined by the academy. On one level, many of these studies are technical descriptions of methods and findings. But they are the outcome of place-based—emplaced—non-traditional research programmes guided by Indigenous communities and designed to address questions directly relevant to the political, ontological, ancestral, and pragmatic contexts of communities. It is worth noting that in the fifty years since the inception of historical archaeology in Australia, there have been only four excavations at Australian missions: Jane Lydon's collaborative research with the Wotjobaluk community at Ebenezer in Victoria (Lydon 2009b); my project with the Mualgal community at the twentieth century village of Poid on the island of Mua in western Torres Strait in Queensland (Ash 2014); David Rhodes' (1986) excavations at Lake Condah Mission dormitory in Victoria; and Judy Birmingham's excavations at Wybalenna in Tasmania (which occurred in the days before community involvement, consent and/or participation) (Birmingham 1992). All other published field investigations at Australian missions have been surface surveys or noninvasive subsurface survey. This relatively long history of applied work at missions anticipates Claire Smith and colleagues' (2019: 537) interesting recent reflections on collaborative research agendas where they suggest that '[t]he challenge lies in the shift from working with Indigenous peoples to working for Indigenous peoples as part of a process in which social justice outcomes are a product, rather than a by-product, of archaeological research.'

It is perhaps to be expected that some of the earliest expressions of First Nations communities shaping the discipline of historical archaeology in Australia occurred at missions. It is entirely consistent with missions as places of intense political action and agency (Attwood & Markus 1999; Horton 2012), direct community connections with their ancestral pasts (Ireland 2010; Lydon & Burns 2010), and because these places were often sites for some of the first real wins in Aboriginal land rights movements in the southeast of the continent (Weir 2009). In this sense, Indigenous control over research processes and outcomes redefine the starting point for historical archaeology, because the historical narrative is not organized around some conjectural point of contact between the Old People and Settlers. Rather, the starting point for any work is the present, in full recognition of the historical processes of settler colonialism and in full recognition of the contemporary significance of the work for the community today and into the future.

Papua New Guinea

Permanent missions were first established in Dutch New Guinea (western New Guinea) in the 1850s, and German New Guinea and British New Guinea (northeast and southeast New Guinea respectively) in the 1870s (Figure 42.1). While mission organizations usually had the tacit support of the colonizing state—indeed, colonial governance of the territories often relied upon mission infrastructure and social networks in the mission's allocated sphere of influence—the individual missions typically maintained some separation and local autonomy (MacGregor 1912).

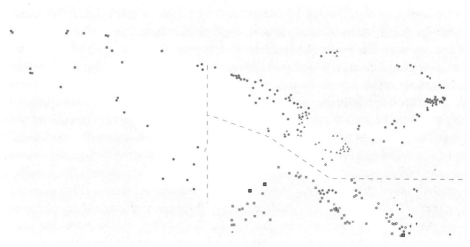

○ Anglican
▪ London Missionary Society
▲ Lutheran
+ Methodist
⊙ Other

• Roman Catholic
• Roman Catholic - Missions of the Sacred Heart, and allied orders
× Seventh Day Adventist
▪ Utrechtse Zendings Vereniging, and allied groups

FIGURE 42.1. Map showing the location and denominations of known mission stations in the New Guinea region (including New Britain, New Ireland, and offshore islands), 1855–1945. Boundary lines separate west New Guinea (Dutch New Guinea) (now Indonesia), and northeast (German) and southeast (British) New Guinea (now Papua New Guinea). Data compiled from maps and information in Aritonang and Steenbrink (2008), Dersken (2016), McFarlane (1888), Prendergast (1968), and Naval Intelligence Division [British] (1945). The Catholic and Protestant missions marked within the Indonesian provinces of Papua and West Papua in western New Guinea do not show the location and network of village-based mission teachers (artwork: Jeremy Ash).

While sharing common ideas on Christianization, the location of missions within local worlds differed to what would become the reserve-based systems in settler colonial Australia (e.g., Barker 2013). In the region that would become British New Guinea, for example, London Missionary Society (LMS) missions were originally established within existing coastal villages, or close to settled areas, in negotiation with local leaders and sometimes at their request. Some missionaries and missionary families were European (British, German, and Dutch), and their voices are clear in the archives and published literature. Most missionaries, however, were Pacific Islanders trained at seminaries in Samoa and Vanuatu. In contrast to European missionaries, their testament is largely missing from archives and publications. There is, as well, the general lacunae of archaeological research west of the 141st meridian (Indonesia–Papua New Guinea border), though with exceptions in West Papuan Christian missiology (e.g., Derksen 2016; Rutherford 2006). As such, western New Guinea is not explored in this chapter (but see Ballard 1999; Wright, Denham, Shine, & Donohue 2013 for reviews of published and archival sources). However, Protestant missionaries of the Utrechtse Zendings Vereniging were active from the mid-nineteenth century at the sacred Christian island, Mansinam and surrounds, while Roman Catholics were active in the southwest (Fakfak) and southeast (Merauke and Okaba) from the late nineteenth and early twentieth centuries, respectively (see Aritonang & Steenbrink 2008). The post-1871 LMS missions in Torres Strait are included under 'New Guinea' in spite of annexation by the Colony of Queensland, and given that these missions were essentially the southern and western extensions of the LMS's Papuan Mission to what is now the southern coast of Papua New Guinea.

The general absence of an established mission archaeology in the New Guinea region is striking, given the key roles and high numbers of missions in the precolonial and colonial administration (e.g., MacGregor 1912; McFarlane 1888) and because of the social, economic, political, moral, ecological, spiritual, and cosmological influences in the region (e.g., Ballard 2000; Barker 2014; Beckett 2014; Eves 1996; Handman 2014; Hughes 1978; Kahn 1990; Mosko 2010; Robbins 1995, 2001a, 2001b). At first glance, it would appear that archaeology has left this domain to anthropology (and to a lesser degree, history, and material culture studies), even if anthropology has struggled at times to articulate the problem of an 'anthropology of Christianity' (Barker 2008; Cannell 2006; Robbins 2007, 2014). This dearth of archaeological research is despite the fact that missionization was a deeply material process involved in the creation of new village and settlement systems, the rebuilding and erasure of local ceremonial and other cultural places, the transformation of trading networks, and the incorporation and circulation of new materials and goods, among other material expressions of religious and spiritual life (e.g., Ash 2020; Barker 2001; David et al. 2008; Hermkens 2014; Kahn 1990; McNiven 2016b; Schieffelin 2002; Torrence & Clarke 2016).

Continuity and Pre(history) in the Archaeology of Missions in the New Guinea Region

Senses and experiences of time and temporality in Christian evangelical contexts were and are complex and locally mediated (e.g., Ballard 2000; Schieffelin 2002). A key element of Christian evangelism in mission-based intercultural settings in New Guinea involved reframing how converts experienced time and temporality. Missionary ontologies of time commonly focused on the tropes of darkness and light (e.g., Barker 2013; Schieffelin 2002) to represent the spiritual—and temporal—transition from primordial Other to Christian awakening.

Part of this 'transition', as Miriam Kahn (1990) classically observed at Wamira in Milne Bay (southeast Papua New Guinea), involved mission-based or inspired assaults on the 'physically represented past' embedded in cultural landscapes, such as cementing ancestral, sentient, and mobile stones face-down in the structure of churches. Such interventions were, however, complex, dialogical, and locally variable. Missionaries found themselves implicated within (and not directing) quite subtle and multifaceted object-based encounters and negotiations with local peoples within cultural landscapes and seascapes (e.g., Bell 2013; Clarke & Torrence 2011; Schieffelin 1981; Tippett 1967; Urwin 2018; see also Bedford, Haskell-Crook, Spriggs, & Shing 2020 for results of excavations at such a site in Vanuatu). Moreover, mission landscapes in New Guinea—as they were also in Australia (if rarely acknowledged)—were spiritually blurred and cosmologically complex landscapes. Kahn (1990) goes on to recount how Tauribariba, the ancestral Wamiran stone, refused to be shackled by the missionary in the pulpit of the church; at night, Tauribariba would leave the church to return to his fellow stones on the beach. Tauribariba finally succumbed, however, to rest 'together with stones sent from Abbeys and Cathedrals in England, there to be silent witnesses to the Faith which has proclaimed that God alone is Giver of all good things' (cited in Kahn 1990: 58; see Ash 2020 for Torres Strait examples of complex, multidimensional spiritscapes).

While not directly equivalent, this change from dark to light parallels the change underpinning social evolutionism in the prehistory/history duality of the Western archaeological tradition. Some missionaries dabbled in deeper time conjectural histories of migration and diffusion (e.g., McFarlane 1888). Some, however, were quite serious in these pursuits and were among the first Westerners to conduct archaeological research in the region (see Summerhayes this volume). Father Otto Meyer, the German-born Sacred Heart missionary, conducted archaeological excavations on Watom Island in the Bismark Archipelago, and his work with the Marist Patrick O'Reilly and the Musée de l'Homme in Paris (Green & Anson 2000; see Dotte-Sarout & Howes 2019) is now recognized as producing the earliest known Western descriptions of Lapita pottery (Howes 2017). On the mainland of Papua New Guinea, Sue Bulmer (1976: 173), in her pioneering archaeological study in the Highlands, encountered lay workers from the Kondiu Catholic Mission in Chimbu excavating a rock shelter (Gumbe) during her 1959 visit to the area. Unfolding recent research into the history of archaeology in the broader region is revealing numerous missionary-archaeological practitioners, including the Anglican lay missionary Rev. P. J. Money at Wanigela Mission (Egloff 1979); Charles Elliot Fox of the Melanesian Mission in the Solomon Islands (Haddow 2019); Frederick Gatherer Bowie of the Free Church of Scotland Mission in Vanuatu (Haddow 2019); and the Methodist Missionary Rev. A.H. Voyce in North Solomon Islands (now the Autonomous Region of Bougainville) (Haddow et al. 2020). The vibrancy and number of missionary-archaeological practitioners led Eve Haddow (2019) to describe this milieu as an 'Anglophone missionary archaeology'. Reflecting on the exchanges of information between Meyer and O'Reilly about the early Lapita pottery findings, Emilie Dotte-Sarout and Hilary Howes (2019: 377) cogently note that these 'exemplify the central role played by men of the cloth in the history of "modern" anthropology and archaeology until the mid-20th century, despite the very cautious expression of ideas they allowed themselves according to the codes of conduct recommended for missionaries. Their long-standing presence in the islands, as well as their extensive international and plurilingual networks, provided essential data.'

The network of missions across the region also provided the infrastructure necessary to support the development of archaeological research into New Guinea's 'prehistory'. Sue Bulmer's first steps in the New Guinea Highlands, for example, relied on missions and plantations to support field surveys for her thesis research (Bulmer 1960, 1976). Indeed, the mission grounds themselves would become sites of enquiry. In fact, archaeologists have undertaken field investigations at a surprisingly high number of missions:

1. Excavations at the Wanigela Anglican Mission in Collingwood Bay, southeast Papua New Guinea. Medical practitioner and anthropologist Rudolf Pöch undertook excavations in ceramic-rich earthen mounds cut into during construction of the mission in 1905. It is one of the first archaeological excavations into New Guinea 'prehistory' (Howes 2017). The site was re-excavated by Brian Egloff between 1967 and 1969 (Egloff 1979).

2. The famous excavations at the Kosipe Sacre Coeur Mission in 1964 and 1967. The site was originally reported to archaeologist J. Peter White by the Catholic missionary, Fr. L. Willem via the Assistant District Officer, following the discovery of axes and waisted blades during excavations for the new Church foundations (White 1967; White, Crooke, & Ruxton 1970; see also Hope 2009).

3. Excavations at the LMS mission at Samoa site (site OAC) and Kumukumu (site OAI) in the Aird Hills, Kikori River region in southern Papua New Guinea in 1976 (Rhoads 1983) and 2008 (David et al. 2010, 2014).

4. A series of surveys and excavations of obsidian sources and cultural sequences excavated at the Bitokara Catholic Mission, New Britain, northeast Papua New Guinea in 1988 (Specht, Fullagar, Torrence, & Baker 1988; Torrence 1992).

5. Excavations of earthen mounds bearing pottery, obsidian, and shell at the Lasigi sites (site ELT) associated with the Catholic Mission compound, New Ireland, northeast Papua New Guinea in 1985 (Golson 1991).

6. Excavations at Kainapirina (site SAC) on the Reber Mission station on Watom Island, northeast Papua New Guinea in 1985 (Green & Anson 1998).
7. Excavations at a coastal midden (site FCL) comprising pottery, obsidian, and shell at Poi Mission, Willaumez Peninsula, New Britain in 1988 (Lilley 1991).
8. Excavations of possibly Middle to Late Lapita ceramic sequences and obsidian artefacts at the Feni Catholic Mission (site ERG) on Ambitle in the Anir Islands in the Bismarck Archipelago in 1995, 1997, and 1998 (Summerhayes 2000).
9. Site surveys and preliminary excavations at a complex of earthen mounds at Lavongai Mission, New Ireland in 1999 (Leavesley 2001).
10. Excavations at the LMS mission at Totalai (site Mua 22), Mua Island, western Torres Strait between 2004 and 2006 (Ash & David 2008).
11. Test pitting at Mt Mario rock shelters on the grounds of the Catholic Mission at Aitape, northwest Papua New Guinea in 2014 (Golitko, Cochrane, Schechter, & Kariwiga 2016).

These field investigations have each contributed insights on various aspects of Papua New Guinea regional 'prehistories' (including on Lapita histories, social networks on the south coast, and Pleistocene settlement of the Highlands). But with the exception of the Torres Strait work, none was intended to address questions about the missions themselves. On a certain level, the high number of excavations occurring at missions— but not *of* missions—probably reflects a combination of priorities in Western academic research topics; mission infrastructure supporting research (e.g., Bulmer 1960); the circulation of knowledge within Western intellectual circles and networks (e.g., White et al. 1970); the training of most archaeologists operating in New Guinea as 'prehistorians'; the fact that missions were often emplaced within existing villages and settlement areas (e.g. Ash 2014; David et al. 2008, 2010, 2014); and, perhaps, the perception that mission histories were too recent to be of interest.

Nevertheless, archaeological projects combining oral histories, fine-grained excavation techniques, and refinements in building archaeological chronologies (e.g., Ash 2014; David et al. 2008; Urwin 2018, 2019) are beginning to reveal important archaeological stories on and below the surfaces of missions and other recent cultural places. On the Papua New Guinea mainland, for example, Bruno David and colleagues' (2008) investigations at numerous cultural places (including villages, hunting camps, and ossuaries) in the Kikori River in the Gulf Province of Papua New Guinea reveal quite profound changes and elaborations in the organization of Rumu landscapes and expressions of the afterlife since the arrival of the LMS. Chris Urwin's (2018) work at the village of Popo in Orokolo Bay (Gulf Province) reveals the past and present making of a living ancestral place and landscape. In Torres Strait, my work at the ancestral village of Totalai on Mua in Torres Strait reveals the emplacement of the LMS station within an existing ancestral village and cultural landscape populated by petrified culture heroes (Ash 2014). Here, archaeological excavations reveal a near-continuous 1300-year-history of dwelling from ancestral village to LMS mission (Ash & David 2008). Elsewhere in Torres Strait, researchers are revealing transformations in various practices within the cultural seascapes and spiritscapes of Torres Strait Islanders since missionization (e.g., David et al. 2009; Harris & Ghaleb Kirby 2015; McNiven, David, Goemulgau Kod, & Fitzpatrick 2009; McNiven et al. 2015; Wright & Ricardi 2015). Much of this work occurs within the geographical region defined by the LMS's Papuan Mission: the region encompassing Torres Strait and much of the southern Papua New Guinea coast. Common to these approaches are collaborative archaeological research programmes developed through discussion with local communities, and a blurring of archaeology, social anthropology, ethnography, and oral histories that is informing understanding of these places as living ancestral places of encounter.

DISCUSSION AND CONCLUSION: TOWARDS AN INDIGENOUS ARCHAEOLOGY OF MISSIONS

There are major differences in how archaeologists conceptualize missions and recent Indigenous pasts in Australia and New Guinea. These different approaches are historical (relating to the expression and trajectories and practices of colonialism across the region) and structural (relating to the histories and emergence of the disciplines), and centre to varying degrees on the relationship to 'prehistory'. Australian approaches are grounded in the historical archaeology that emerged alongside, but discrete from, 'Indigenous archaeology' (i.e., 'prehistory') in the late 1960s and 1970s (see Jack 2006; Ireland, Casey, & Birmingham 2006). As such, archaeological approaches to missions and reserves developed in isolation from longer-term Indigenous (pre)histories and cultural landscapes. Critically, however, Australian approaches are sympathetic to the structural problems presented by settler colonialism, including co-developing methods and agendas designed to explore relationships between descendant communities and the Old People. New Guinea (including Torres Strait) approaches, on the other hand, are less constrained by these binaries or agendas, typically focusing on continuity and elaborations of traditions and the emplacement of missions within historically inscribed worlds. They are less bound to the traditional dualism presented in Australian studies (prehistory/history), but risk, without care, losing sight of the contemporary relevance of such research for communities today.

What is the future of mission archaeology? Should the various traditions of mission archaeology developed in Australia and New Guinea come together? Clearly, any archaeology of missions and reserves best occurs in full regard of the aspirations, worldviews, and political realities of communities. Rather than advocate for a cohesive subarea termed 'mission archaeology', it may be productive to recast the area in light of the possibilities presented by Indigenous archaeology. Indigenous archaeology—as an approach designed to bring together Indigenous ontologies with Western scientific insights of the past (Atalay 2006; see, e.g., Colwell-Chanthaphonh et al. 2010; Nicholas 2010; McNiven 2016a; Silliman 2009, 2010)—creates opportunities to reimagine the categories discussed earlier and to develop novel approaches that suit Indigenous agendas. While there are numerous ways to blur disciplinary boundaries, I briefly canvass three here (not all of which are unique to mission archaeology but apply to archaeologies of the recent past more generally).

Blurring the Temporal Divide: A Two-Way Street

Indigenous archaeology redefines the long-criticized disciplinary boundary between history and prehistory (Lightfoot 1995), and indeed Australian researchers have been at the vanguard of the critique (e.g., Harrison & Williamson 2004; McNiven 2016a: 33; Wolski 2000). Most commonly, researchers explore the continuity of ancestral cultural practices into mission settings (e.g., Ash et al. 2010; Dalley & Memmott 2010; Lydon 2005) though rarely do researchers work back the other way. Curiously, mission archaeology (and equally archaeology at other recent Indigenous sites) is rarely used to inform interpretations of older cultural sites predating missions; indeed, archaeologists are far more likely to engage with Western ethnographies collected at missions than with the archaeology of the mission dwellers themselves. Nevertheless, mission studies do have much to contribute the 'other way', especially in light of the considerable work done on social space, as well as the array of oral histories, ethnographies, and, often, rich archival materials that so often provide intimate insights into these dynamic social milieus. For example, Lydon's (2005, 2009a) work on social space, Indigenous aurality, and collective personhood at missions in southeast Australia has profound, albeit untested, applications for interpreting the archaeology of Indigenous social spaces not just within missions themselves, but indeed other pre-mission-era contexts.

Blurring the Spiritual and Secular Divide: Materials and Materialization

Part of the theoretical and ethical challenge and aim of Indigenous archaeology is to extend the ontological reach and understanding of the discipline (Atalay 2006). As McNiven (2016a: 35) points out, '[e]ngaging with the spiritual dimensions of culture is a critical theoretical undertaking for Indigenous archaeology' for '[s]piritual dimensions and associated ritual practices provide rare and revealing insights into ontologies and worldviews'. He notes a number of Indigenous researchers have 'voiced concerns about the capacity of many archaeologists to understand and appreciate the spiritual and sacred dimensions of the past, especially given the secularist approach of Western academia' (McNiven 2016a: 35). Christian missions, spiritual expressions, evangelism, and syncretism are themes rarely explored, often subsumed by secular readings of Indigenous resistance and (in Australia) settler colonialism. Yet, in many cases, Indigenous people, often Christians, are deeply interested in exploring these serious dimensions of their worlds (but see Flexner's 2016 study of the archaeology of Christianity in Vanuatu).

Materials and the materialization of missions may offer insight into such blurred (spiritual-secular) worlds. Whereas mission archaeology often conceptualizes mission landscapes in terms of compounds, habitus, and proxemics, a refocus of attention to the materials and materialization of missions can provide insights into the worldviews and agencies of the Old People dwelling and making the village. Miriam Kahn's (1990) important study of the dialogical nature of building the Anglican Church at Dogura in Milne Bay is a case in point. There are innumerable other examples. In the Trobriand Islands, southeast Papua New Guinea, Malinowski (1922: 196) described how missionary teachers always 'put a mass of stones to fill the space beneath their [pylon] houses' for fear of the *bwaga'u* (sorcerer) creeping below. For the 'saltwater peoples' of Torres Strait (see McNiven 2004), the nineteenth and early to mid-twentieth-century churches were generally built from a rock and lime cement matrix of corals, marine shells, and pebbles that women and men had collected from intertidal areas and the sea floor. Baptismal fonts are often giant clamshells, and church bells are often salvaged bells from shipwrecks. Similar examples of such 'Saltwater Missions' occur in South Australia (Fowler 2019; Fowler, Roberts, & Rigney 2019), and in the shimmering brilliance of the mother of pearl shell embedded in the side altars and chancel walls of the Sacred Heart Church at Beagle Bay in the Kimberley, northwest Australia (Ganter 2015: 13). At the Mapoon mission on Cape York Peninsula, 'native pigments mixed with water are used for paint' (Department of Native Affairs 1901: 14). In some cases, Indigenous materials clearly possessed significant cosmological properties. At the Killalpaninna mission in Dieri Country investigated by Birmingham (2000; Birmingham & Wilson 2010), the gypsum used to plaster walls of the mission buildings came from *tudnapiti* (gypsum mines), 'rare enough to be distinctively named sites with mythological associations; one of these, to the east of the mission, was still being used as a source of gypsum in [missionary] Reuther's time' (Jones 2007: 241). Similarly, anthropologist Diane Austin-Broos (2009: 51ff) describes the complex meaning and significance of sacred water that was pumped by pipeline from the Western Arrente underground springs called Kaporilya, Central Australia—a 'big place' (i.e., a powerful cosmological place)—to irrigate the gardens at Hermannsburg mission following a devastating drought between 1926 and 1930.

Blurring the Spatial Divide: Indigenous Historicism and Landscapes

Indigenous historicism is another major dimension of Indigenous archaeology that may radically reshape the field, particularly in terms of resituating missions in broader cultural landscapes (see Clarke 2000). Lydon's (2004) exploration of photography and archival materials documenting (and recreating) the epic journey of Kulin peoples (Victoria, southeast Australia) to Coranderrk Aboriginal Station, outside Melbourne, is a telling portrait of movement, dispossession, and agency across the 1860s frontier. In Torres Strait, it is geography (place), not linear time, that frames history (Nietschmann 1989). Mualgau narratives documenting the arrival of the LMS in the 1870s and the government reserves c. 1904 to the island of Mua take the metaphor of the road (*yabugad* or *yabu* in Kala Lagaw Ya, the language of Western Torres Strait). The *yabugad* structures how people narrate (and know) the sequence of historical movements of the community as they relocated to each mission village on the island over the past ~150 years. The *yabugad* also informs archaeological theory in that it doubles as a powerful ethics-based Islander theory of cultural transmission and change linking generations through time (Ash 2014).

Much has yet to unfold regarding the exciting prospect of an Indigenous archaeology of the recent past involving missions. The area, as a field of deep collaborative exploration, will of course find multiple expressions through multiple communities. The area leaves open the possibility for the ongoing creative encounters, discoveries, and revelations about the past in the present. Within such an approach, interpretations of the past are not, by definition, limited by the narrow straightjackets of prehistory/history or rupture/continuity but are instead emergent from the enduring relationships and engagements between Indigenous people and their ancestors as mediated by their objects, patterns, and processes that comprise the archaeological record.

ACKNOWLEDGEMENTS

Many thanks to Ian McNiven and Bruno David for the invitation to contribute to this Handbook. Many thanks to Jane Lydon and Ian McNiven for insightful comments and edits on a draft of this chapter. I also extend thanks and acknowledgement to the Mualgal in Torres Strait, especially the late Father John Manas, the late Mrs Manas, the late Mr Osa Bosun, and Mrs Lilian Bosun, for the invitation and trust to explore their ancestral village missions. *Big eso*. Monash Indigenous Studies Centre at Monash University and the Centre of Excellence for Australian Biodiversity and Heritage (CE170100015) provided support to Ash.

NOTE

1. Missionary ideologies of directional change reinforced the circular logic of colonialist tropes: for even as the term hunter-gatherer as a 'colonial trope' helped to legitimize the dispossession of First Nation societies in settler-colonial Australia (McNiven & Russell 2005: 38–41), the emergence of agricultural societies within missions was instrumental in realizing it.

References

Aird, M. (2004). Developments in the repatriation of human remains and other cultural items in Queensland, Australia. In C. Fforde, J. Hubert, & P. Turnbull (Eds.), *The dead and their possessions: The repatriation in principle, policy and practice* (pp. 303–311). One World Archaeology Series 43. New York: Routledge.

Allen, J., & Jones, R. (1980). Oyster Cove: Archaeological traces of the last Tasmanians and notes on the criteria for the authentication of flaked glass artefacts. *Papers and Proceedings of the Royal Society of Tasmania, 114,* 225–233.

Aritonang, J. S., & Steenbrink, K. (2008). Christianity in Papua. In J. S. Aritonang & K. Steenbrink (Eds.), *A history of Christianity in Indonesia* (pp. 345–381). Leiden: Brill.

Ash, J. (2014). *Change in continuity: An archaeology of Mualgal missions, Western Torres Strait, Northeastern Australia* (PhD thesis). Monash University, Melbourne.

Ash, J. (2020). A typology of erasure: The involvement of evangelical missionaries in the generative spiritscapes of Torres Strait and southern central New Guinea. *Journal of Pacific Archaeology, 11*(2), 90–100.

Ash, J., & David, B. (2008). Mua 22: Archaeology at the old village site of Totalai. *Memoirs of the Queensland Museum / Culture, 4*(2), 327–348.

Ash, J., Manas, L., & Bosun, D. (2010). Lining the path: A seascape perspective of two Torres Strait missions, northeast Australia. *International Journal of Historical Archaeology, 14*(1), 56–85.

Ash, J., Brooks, A., David, B., & McNiven, I. J. (2008). European-manufactured objects from the 'early mission' site of Totalai, Mua (Western Torres Strait). *Memoirs of the Queensland Museum / Culture, 4*(2), 349–367.

Atalay, S. (2006). Indigenous archaeology as decolonizing practice. *The American Indian Quarterly, 30,* 280–310.

Attwood, B. (1989). *The making of the Aborigines.* Sydney: Allen and Unwin.

Attwood, B. (1992). Introduction. *Journal of Australian Studies, 16*(35), 1–16.

Attwood, B., & Markus, A. (1999). *The struggle for Aboriginal rights: A documentary history.* London: Routledge.

Austin-Broos, D. J. (2009). *Arrernte present, Arrernte past: Invasion, violence, and imagination in Indigenous Central Australia.* Chicago: University of Chicago Press.

Ballard, C. (1999). Blanks in the writing: Possible histories for West New Guinea. *The Journal of Pacific History, 34*(2), 149–155.

Ballard, C. (2000). The fire next time: The conversion of the Huli apocalypse. *Ethnohistory, 47*(1), 205–225.

Barker, J. (1996). Way back in Papua: Representing society and change in the publications of the London Missionary Society in New Guinea, 1871–1932. *Pacific Studies, 19,* 107–142.

Barker, J. (2001). Dangerous objects: Changing Indigenous perceptions of material culture in a Papua New Guinea Society. *Pacific Science, 55,* 359–75.

Barker, J. (2008). Toward an anthropology of Christianity. *American Anthropologist, 110*(3), 377–381.

Barker, J. (2013). Anthropology and the politics of Christianity in Papua New Guinea. In M. Tomlinson & D. McDougall (Eds.), *Christian politics in Oceania* (pp. 146–170). ASAO Studies in Pacific Anthropology 2. New York: Berghahn Books.

Barker, J. (2014). The one and the many: Church-centred innovations in a Papua New Guinean community. *Current Anthropology, 55*(S10), S172–S181.

Barwick, D. (1963). *A little more than kin: Regional affiliation and group identity among Aboriginal migrants in Melbourne* (PhD thesis). Australian National University, Canberra.

Barwick, D. (1988). Aborigines of Victoria. In I. Keen (Ed.), *Being Black: Aboriginal cultures in 'settled' Australia* (pp. 27–32). Canberra: Aboriginal Studies Press.

Beckett, J. (2014). Mission, church and sect: Three types of religious commitment in the Torres Strait islands. In J. Beckett (Ed.), *Encounters with indigeneity: Writing about Aboriginal and Torres Strait Islander peoples* (pp. 150–167). Canberra: Aboriginal Studies Press.

Bedford, S., Flexner, J., & Jones, M. (2020). The archaeology of missions and missionisation in Australasia and the Pacific. *Journal of Pacific Archaeology, 11*(2), 7–10.

Bedford, S., Haskell-Crook, D., Spriggs, M., & Shing, R. (2020). Encounters with stone: Missionary battles with idols in the Southern New Hebrides. *Journal of Pacific Archaeology, 11*(2), 21–33.

Bell, J. A. (2013). 'Expression of kindly feeling': The London Missionary Society collections from the Papuan Gulf. In L. Bolton, N. Thomas, E. Bonshek, J. Adams, & B. Burt (Eds.), *Melanesia: Art and encounter* (pp. 57–63). London: British Museum.

Birch, T. (2005). 'Death is forgotten in victory': Colonial landscapes and narratives of emptiness. In J. Lydon & T. Ireland (Eds.), *Object lessons: Archaeology and heritage in Australia* (pp. 186–200). Melbourne: Australian Scholarly Publishing.

Birmingham, J. (1976). The archaeological contribution to nineteenth-century history: Some Australian case studies. *World Archaeology, 7*(3), 306–317.

Birmingham, J. (1992). *Wybalenna: The archaeology of cultural accommodation in nineteenth-century Tasmania: A report on the historical archaeological investigation of the Aboriginal establishment on Flinders Island.* Sydney: Australasian Society for Historical Archaeology.

Birmingham, J. (1993). Engendynamics: Women in the archaeological record at Wybalenna, Flinders Island 1835–1840. In H. du Cros & L. Smith (Eds.), *Women in archaeology: A feminist critique* (pp. 121–128). Occasional Papers in Prehistory No. 23. Canberra: Department of Prehistory, Research School of the Pacific and Asian Studies, The Australian National University.

Birmingham, J. (2000). Resistance, creolization or optimal foraging at Killalpaninna Mission, South Australia. In R. Torrence & A. Clarke (Eds.), *The archaeology of difference: Negotiating cross-cultural engagements in Oceania* (pp. 360–405). London: Routledge.

Birmingham, J. & Wilson, A. (2010). Archaeologies of cultural interaction: Wybalenna settlement and Killalpaninna mission. *International Journal of Historical Archaeology, 14*(1), 15–38.

Blake, T. (2001). *A dumping ground: A history of the Cherbourg settlement.* Brisbane: University of Queensland Press.

Boucher, L., & Russell, L. (2012). 'Soliciting sixpences from township to township': Moral dilemmas in mid-nineteenth-century Melbourne. *Postcolonial Studies, 15*(2), 149–165.

Brock, P. (1993). *Outback ghettoes: A history of Aboriginal institutionalisation and survival.* Cambridge: Cambridge University Press.

Brockwell, S., Gara, T., Colley, S., & Cane, S. (1989). The history and archaeology of Ooldea Soak and Mission. *Australian Archaeology, 28*, 55–78.

Brown, S., Avery, S., & Goulding, M. (2004). Recent investigations at the Ebenezer Mission cemetery. In R. Harrison & C. Williamson (Eds.), *After Captain Cook: The archaeology of the recent Indigenous past in Australia* (pp. 147–170). Walnut Creek, CA: AltaMira Press.

Bulmer, S. (1960). *Report on archaeological fieldwork in the New Guinea Highlands October 1959 to May 1960 sponsored by the American Museum of Natural History.* Auckland: Anthropology Department, University of Auckland.

Bulmer, S. (1976). *The prehistory of the New Guinea Highlands*. Oceanic Prehistory Records 1. Auckland: University of Auckland Press.

Byrne, D. (1996). Deep nation: Australia's acquisition of an indigenous past. *Aboriginal History, 20*, 82–107.

Cannell, F. (Ed.) (2006). *The anthropology of Christianity*. Durham, NC: Duke University Press.

Choo, C. (2001). *Mission girls: Aboriginal women on Catholic missions in the Kimberley, Western Australia, 1900–1950*. Perth: University of Western Australia Press.

Clarke, A. (2000). Time, tradition and transformation: The negotiation of cross-cultural engagements on Groote Eylandt, northern Australia. In A. Clarke & R. Torrence (Eds.), *The archaeology of difference: Negotiating cross-cultural engagements in Oceania* (pp. 146–186). One World Archaeology Series 38. London: Routledge.

Clarke, A., & Torrence, R. (2011). Archaeology and the collection: Tracing material relationships in colonial Papua from 1875 to 1925. *Journal of Australian Studies, 35*(4), 433–448.

Colley, S., & Bickford, A. (1997). 'Real' Aborigines and 'real' archaeology: Aboriginal places and Australian historical archaeology. *World Archaeological Bulletin, 7*, 5–21.

Colwell-Chanthaphonh, C., Ferguson, T. J., Lippert, D., McGuire, R. H., Nicholas, G. P., Watkins, J. E., & Zimmerman, L. J. (2010). The premise and promise of Indigenous archaeology. *American Antiquity, 75*(2), 228–238.

Comaroff, J., & Comaroff, J. (1986). Christianity and colonialism in South Africa. *American Ethnologist, 13*(1), 1–22.

Comaroff, J., & Comaroff, J. (1991). *Of revelation and revolution, Volume 1: Christianity, colonialism, and consciousness in South Africa*. Chicago: University of Chicago Press.

Comaroff, J., & Comaroff, J. (1997). *Of revelation and revolution, Volume 2: The dialectics of modernity on a South African frontier*. Chicago: University of Chicago Press.

Dalley, C., & Memmott, P. (2010). Domains and the intercultural: Understanding Aboriginal and missionary engagement at the Mornington Island Mission, Gulf of Carpentaria, Australia from 1914 to 1942. *International Journal of Historical Archaeology, 14*(1), 112–135.

David, B., Aplin, K., Petchey, F., Skelly, R., Mialanes, J., Jones-Amin, H., . . . Lamb, L. (2014). Kumukumu 1, a hilltop site in the Aird Hills: Implications for occupational trends and dynamics in the Kikori River delta, south coast of Papua New Guinea. *Quaternary International, 385*, 7–26.

David, B., & Denham, T. (2006). Unpacking Australian history. In B. David, B. Barker, & I. J. McNiven (Eds.), *The social archaeology of Australian Indigenous societies* (pp. 52–71). Canberra: Aboriginal Studies Press.

David, B., Fresløv, J., Mullett, R., GunaiKurnai Land and Waters Aboriginal Corporation, Delannoy, J.-J., McDowell, M., . . . Green, H. (2021). 50 years and worlds apart: Rethinking the Holocene occupation of Cloggs Cave (East Gippsland, SE Australia) five decades after its initial archaeological excavation and in light of GunaiKurnai world views. *Australian Archaeology, 87*(1), 1–20.

David, B., Geneste, J.-M., Aplin, K., Delannoy, J.-J., Araho, N., Clarkson, C., . . . Rowe, C. (2010). The Emo site (OAC), Gulf Province, Papua New Guinea: Resolving long-standing questions of antiquity and implications for the history of the ancestral *hiri* maritime trade. *Australian Archaeology, 70*(1), 39–54.

David, B., McNiven, I. J., Crouch, J., Mura Badulgal Corporation Committee, Skelly, R., Barker, B., . . . Hewitt, G. (2009). Koey Ngurtai: The emergence of a ritual domain in Western Torres Strait. *Archaeology in Oceania, 44*(1), 1–17.

David, B., Pivoru, M., Pivoru, W., Green, M., Barker, B., Weiner, J. F., ... Dop, J. (2008). Living landscapes of the dead: Archaeology of the afterworld among the Rumu of Papua New Guinea. In B. David & J. Thomas (Eds.), *Handbook of landscape archaeology* (pp. 158–166). Walnut Creek, CA: Left Coast Press.

Denham, T., Donohue, M., & Booth, S. (2009). Horticultural experimentation in northern Australia reconsidered. *Antiquity, 83*(321), 634–648.

Denham, R., Fullagar, R., & Head, L. (2009). Plant exploitation on Sahul: From colonisation to the emergence of regional specialisation during the Holocene. *Quaternary International, 202*(1–2), 29–40.

Department of Native Affairs. (1901). *Annual reports of the Chief Protector of Aboriginals*. Votes and Proceedings of Queensland Parliament. Brisbane: Government Printer.

Derksen, M. (2016). Local intermediaries? The missionising and governing of colonial subjects in south Dutch New Guinea, 1920–42. *The Journal of Pacific History, 51*(2), 111–142.

Dotte-Sarout, E., & Howes, H. (2019). Lapita before Lapita: The early story of the Meyer/O'Reilly Watom Island archaeological collection. *The Journal of Pacific History, 54*(3), 354–378.

Egloff, B. J. (1979). *Recent prehistory in Southeast Papua*. Terra Australis 4. Canberra: Department of Prehistory, Research School of Pacific Studies, The Australian National University.

Etherington, N. (2005). Introduction. In N. Etherington (Ed.), *Missions and empire* (pp. 1–18). Oxford: Oxford University Press.

Eves, R. (1996). Colonialism, corporeality and character: Methodist missions and the refashioning of bodies in the Pacific. *History and Anthropology, 10*(1), 85–138.

Fabian, J. (1983). *Time and the other: How anthropology makes its object*. New York: Columbia University Press.

Flexner, J. L. (2013). Mission archaeology in Vanuatu: Preliminary findings, problems, and prospects. *Australasian Historical Archaeology, 31*, 14–24.

Flexner, J. L. (2016). *An archaeology of early Christianity in Vanuatu: Kastom and religious change on Tanna and Erromango, 1839–1920*. Terra Australis 44. Canberra: ANU Press.

Flexner, J. L. (2017). Reform and purification in the historical archaeology of the South Pacific, 1840–1900. *International Journal of Historical Archaeology, 21*(4), 827–847.

Florin, S. A., & Carah, X. (2018). Moving past the 'Neolithic problem': The development and interaction of subsistence systems across northern Sahul. *Quaternary International, 489*, 46–62.

Fowler, M. (2013). Aboriginal missions and post-contact maritime archaeology: A South Australian synthesis. *Journal of the Anthropological Society of South Australia, 37*, 73–89.

Fowler, M. (2015). *'Now, are you going to believe this or not?' Addressing neglected narratives through the maritime cultural landscape of Point Pearce Aboriginal Mission/Burgiyana, South Australia* (PhD thesis). Flinders University, Adelaide.

Fowler, M. (2019). *Aboriginal maritime landscapes in South Australia: The Balance Ground*. London: Routledge.

Fowler, M., & Rigney, L. I. (2017). Collaboration, collision, and (re)conciliation: Indigenous participation in Australia's maritime industry—a case study from Point Pearce/Burgiyana, South Australia. In A. Caporaso (Ed.), *Formation processes of maritime archaeological landscapes* (pp. 53–77). Cham: Springer.

Fowler, M., Roberts, A., & Rigney, L. I. (2016). The 'very stillness of things': Object biographies of sailcloth and fishing net from the Point Pearce Aboriginal Mission (Burgiyana) colonial archive, South Australia. *World Archaeology, 48*(2), 210–225.

Fowler, M., Roberts, A., & Rigney, L. I. (2019). The sounds of colonization: An examination of bells at Point Pearce Aboriginal Mission Station/Burgiyana, South Australia. In T. Äikäs & A.-K. Salmi (Eds.), *The sound of silence: Indigenous perspectives on the historical archaeology of colonialism* (pp. 15–38). New York: Berghahn.

Ganter, R. (2015). Helpers—sisters—wives: White women on Australian missions. *Journal of Australian Studies*, 39(1), 7–19.

Godwin, L., & L'Oste-Brown, S. (2004). A past remembered: Aboriginal 'historical' places in central Queensland. In R. Harrison & C. Williamson (Eds.), *After Captain Cook: The archaeology of the recent Indigenous past in Australia* (pp. 191–212). Walnut Creek, CA: AltaMira Press.

Golitko, M., Cochrane, E. E., Schechter, E. M., & Kariwiga, J. (2016). Archaeological and palaeoenvironmental investigations near Aitape, northern Papua New Guinea, 2014. *Journal of Pacific Archaeology*, 7(1), 139–150.

Golson, J. (1991). Two sites at Lasigi, New Ireland. In J. Allen & C. Gosden (Eds.), *Report of the Lapita Homeland Project* (pp. 244–259). Occasional Papers in Prehistory No. 20. Canberra: Department of Prehistory, The Australian National University.

Gosden, C., & Head, L. (1999). Different histories: A common inheritance for Papua New Guinea and Australia? In C. Gosden & C. Hather (Eds.), *Prehistory of food: Appetites for change* (pp. 227–245). London: Routledge.

Graham, E. (1998). Mission archaeology. *Annual Review of Anthropology*, 27, 25–62.

Green, R. C., & Anson, D. (1998). Excavations at Kainapirina (SAC), Watom Island, Papua New Guinea. *New Zealand Journal of Archaeology*, 20, 29–94.

Green, R. C., & Anson, D. (2000). Archaeological investigations on Watom Island: Early work, outcomes of recent investigations and future prospects. *New Zealand Journal of Archaeology*, 20, 183–197.

Griffin, D. (2010). Identifying domination and resistance through the spatial organization of Poonindie Mission, South Australia. *International Journal of Historical Archaeology*, 14(1), 156–169.

Griffiths, T. (1996). *Hunters and collectors: The antiquarian imagination in Australia.* Cambridge: Cambridge University Press.

Haddow, E. (2019). Island networks and missionary methods: Locating Charles E. Fox and Frederick G. Bowie in the history of Pacific archaeology. *The Journal of Pacific History*, 54(3), 330–353.

Haddow, E., Dotte-Sarout, E., & Specht, J. (2020). Reverend Voyce and Père O'Reilly's excavated collection Bougainville: A case study in transnational histories of archaeology in the Pacific. *Historical Records of Australian Science*, 32(1), 15–28.

Handman, C. (2014). Becoming the Body of Christ: Sacrificing the speaking subject in the making of the colonial Lutheran Church in New Guinea. *Current Anthropology*, 55(S10), S205–S205.

Harris, D. R. (1995). Early agriculture in New Guinea and the Torres Strait divide. *Antiquity*, 69, 848–854.

Harris, D. R., & Ghaleb Kirby, B. (2015). Mabuyag (Torres Strait) in the mid-1980s: Archaeological reconnaissance of the island and midden excavations at Goemu. *Memoirs of the Queensland Museum, Cultural Heritage Series*, 8(2), 283–375.

Harris, J. W. (1994). *One blood: 200 years of Aboriginal encounter with Christianity: A story of hope.* Sutherland: Albatross Books.

Harrison, R. & Williamson, C. (Eds.) (2004). *After Captain Cook: The archaeology of the recent Indigenous past in Australia.* Walnut Creek, CA: AltaMira Press.

Ireland, S., Wood, V., & Hunter, R. (2000). Researching the past: Oral history and archaeology at Swan Reach. In A. Clarke & R. Torrence (Eds.), *The archaeology of difference: Negotiating cross-cultural engagements in Oceania* (pp. 339–367). One World Archaeology Series 38. London: Routledge.

Hermkens, A. K. (2014). The materiality of missionisation in Collingwood Bay, Papua New Guinea. In H. Choi & M. Jolly (Eds.), *Divine domesticities: Christian paradoxes in Asia and the Pacific* (pp. 397–427). Canberra: ANU Press.

Hope, G. (2009). Environmental change and fire in the Owen Stanley ranges, Papua New Guinea. *Quaternary Science Reviews, 28*(23–24), 2261–2276.

Horton, J. (2012). Rewriting political history: Letters from Aboriginal people in Victoria, 1886–1919. *History Australia, 9*(2), 157–181.

Howes, H. (2017). Early German-language analyses of potsherds from New Guinea and the Bismarck Archipelago. *Journal of Pacific Archaeology, 8*(1), 35–46.

Hughes, I. (1978). Good money and bad: Inflation and devaluation in the colonial process. *Mankind, 11*, 308–318

Ireland, T. (2010). From mission to *Maynggu Ganai*: The Wellington Valley convict station and mission site. *International Journal of Historical Archaeology, 14*(1), 136–155.

Ireland, T., Casey, M., & Birmingham, J. (2006). Judy Birmingham in conversation. *Australasian Historical Archaeology, 24*, 7–16.

Jack, I. (2006). Historical Archaeology, heritage and the University of Sydney. *Australasian Historical Archaeology, 24*, 19–24.

Jones, P. (2007). *Ochre and rust: Artefacts and encounters on Australian frontiers*. Adelaide: Wakefield Press.

Kahn, M. (1990). Stone-faced ancestors: The spatial anchoring of myth in Wamira, Papua New Guinea. *Ethnology, 29*(1), 51–66.

Kidd, R. (1997). *The way we civilise: Aboriginal affairs, the untold story*. St Lucia: University of Queensland Press.

Lake, M. (2018). *The bible in Australia: A cultural history*. Sydney: University of New South Wales Press.

Langford, R. F. (1983). Our heritage—your playground. *Australian Archaeology, 16*(1), 1–6.

Lawrence, S., & Davies, P. (2010). *An archaeology of Australia since 1788*. Berlin: Springer Science & Business Media.

Leavesley, M. G. (2001). Earth mounds of New Hanover, Papua New Guinea: Distribution and function. In G. R. Clark, A. J. Anderson, & T. Vunidilo (Eds.), *The archaeology of Lapita dispersal in Oceania* (pp. 203–209). Terra Australis 17. Canberra: ANU Press.

Leone, M., & Potter, P. (Eds.) (1988). *The recovery of meaning*. Washington, DC: Smithsonian Institution Press.

Lightfoot, K. G. (1995). Culture contact studies: Redefining the relationship between prehistoric and historical archaeology. *American Antiquity, 60*(2), 199–217.

Lilley, I. (1991). Lapita and post-Lapita developments in the Vitiaz Straits—West New Britain area. *Indo-Pacific Prehistory Association Bulletin, 11*, 313–322.

L'Oste-Brown, S., & Godwin, L. (with Henry, G., Mitchell, T., & Tyson, V.) (1995). *'Living under the Act': Taroom Aboriginal Reserve 1911–1927*. Cultural Heritage Monograph Series No. 1. Brisbane: Department of Environment and Heritage.

L'Oste-Brown, S., Godwin, L., & Yelf, R. (1996). Taroom Aboriginal Reserve cemeteries: Their history and investigation. In S. Ulm, I. Lilley, & A. Ross (Eds.), *Australian Archaeology '95:*

Proceedings of the 1995 Australian Archaeological Association annual conference (pp. 207–217). Tempus Volume 6. Brisbane: Anthropology Museum, University of Queensland.

Lomax, K. (1991). *Murchison Police Paddocks archaeological survey*. Unpublished report to Rumbalara Aboriginal Co-operative Ltd and Aboriginal Affairs Victoria, Melbourne.

Lomax, K., & Long, A. (1991). *Lake Condah Mission cemetery investigations*. Unpublished report to the Kerrup Jmara Elders Aboriginal Corporation, Melbourne.

Long, A. (1998). *Ebenezer Mission cemetery: Micro-topographic and surface vegetation study, Stage 2*. Unpublished report to Aboriginal Affairs Victoria, Melbourne.

Long, A., & MacKinnon, A. (1999). *Goulburn River Protectorate Station, Murchison: Management plan*. Unpublished report to Aboriginal Affairs Victoria, Melbourne.

Long, A., & MacKinnon, A. (2000). *Ebenezer Mission cemetery: Micro-topographic and surface vegetation study, Stage 3*. Unpublished report to Aboriginal Affairs Victoria, Melbourne.

Lourandos, H. (1980). Change or stability? Hydraulics, hunter-gatherers and population in temperate Australia. *World Archaeology, 11*(3), 245–264.

Lourandos, H. (1983). Intensification: A late Pleistocene-Holocene archaeological sequence from southwestern Victoria. *Archaeology in Oceania, 18*, 81–94.

Lourandos, H. (2008). Constructing 'hunter-gatherers', constructing 'prehistory': Australia and New Guinea. *Australian Archaeology, 67*, 69–78.

Lydon, J. (2004). 'This civilising experiment': Photography at Coranderrk Aboriginal Station during the 1860s. In R. Harrison & C. Williamson (Eds.), *After Captain Cook: The archaeology of the recent Indigenous past in Australia* (pp. 59–74). Walnut Creek, CA: AltaMira Press.

Lydon, J. (2005). 'Our sense of beauty': Visuality, space and gender on Victoria's Aboriginal Reserves, south-eastern Australia. *History and Anthropology, 16*(2), 211–233.

Lydon, J. (2009a). Imagining the Moravian mission: Space and surveillance at the former Ebenezer Mission, Victoria, southeastern Australia. *Historical Archaeology, 43*(3), 5–19.

Lydon, J. (2009b). *Fantastic dreaming: The archaeology of an Aboriginal mission*. Lanham, MD: AltaMira Press.

Lydon, J. (2014). Intimacy and distance: Life on the Australian Aboriginal mission. In N. Ferris, R. Harrison, & M. V. Wilcox (Eds.), *Rethinking colonial pasts through archaeology* (pp. 232–250). Oxford: Oxford University Press.

Lydon, J., & Ash, J. (2010). The archaeology of missions in Australasia: Introduction. *International Journal of Historical Archaeology, 14*(1), 1–14.

Lydon, J., & Burns, A. (2010). Memories of the past, visions of the future: Changing views of Ebenezer Mission, Victoria, Australia. *International Journal of Historical Archaeology, 14*(1), 39–55.

MacGregor, W. (1912). Introduction. In J. H. P. Murray (Ed.), *Papua or British New Guinea* (pp. 1–2). London: T. Fisher Unwin.

Malinowski, B. (1922 / 1994). *Argonauts of the western Pacific: An account of native enterprise and adventure in the archipelagoes of Melanesian New Guinea*. London: Routledge.

McDougall, M., Massie, D., & Cull, J. (1997). *Ground penetrating radar investigation; Former Ebenezer Mission cemetery*. Unpublished report to Aboriginal Affairs Victoria, Melbourne.

McFarlane, S. (1888). *Among the cannibals of New Guinea: Being the story of the New Guinea Mission of the London Missionary Society*. Philadelphia: Presbyterian Board of Publication and Sabbath-School Work.

McLisky, C., Russell L., & Boucher, L. (2015). Managing mission life, 1869–1886. In L. Boucher & L. Russell (Eds.), *Settler colonial governance in nineteenth-century Victoria* (pp. 117–138). Canberra: ANU Press.

McNiven, I. J. (2004). Saltwater people: Spiritscapes, maritime rituals and the archaeology of Indigenous seascapes. *World Archaeology, 35*(3), 329–349.

McNiven, I. J. (2016a). Theoretical challenges of Indigenous archaeology: Setting an agenda. *American Antiquity, 81*(1), 27–41.

McNiven, I. J. (2016b). Stone axes as grave markers on Kiwai Island, Fly River Delta, Papua New Guinea. *Journal of Pacific Archaeology, 7*(1), 74–83.

McNiven, I. J., David, B., Goemulgau, K., & Fitzpatrick, J. (2009). The great *kod* of Pulu: Mutual historical emergence of ceremonial sites and social groups in Torres Strait, northeast Australia. *Cambridge Archaeological Journal, 19*(3), 291–317.

McNiven, I. J., & Russell, L. (2005). *Appropriated pasts: Indigenous peoples and the colonial culture of archaeology.* Lanham, MD: AltaMira.

McNiven, I. J., Wright, D., Sutton, S., Weisler, M., Hocknull, S., & Stanisic, J. (2015). Midden formation and marine specialisation at Goemu village, Mabuyag (Torres Strait) before and after European contact. *Memoirs of the Queensland Museum – Culture, 8*(2), 377–475.

Middleton, A. (2008). *Te Puna – A New Zealand mission station: Historical archaeology in New Zealand.* New York: Springer.

Middleton, A. (2010). Missionization in New Zealand and Australia: A comparison. *International Journal of Historical Archaeology, 14*(1), 170–187.

Middleton, A. (2018). Missionization and mission archaeology in New Zealand and Australia. In C. Smith (Ed.), *Encyclopaedia of global archaeology.* Cham: Springer.

Moffat, I., Garnaut, J., Jordan, C., Vella, A., Bailey, M., & Gunditj Mirring Traditional Owners Corporation. (2018). Ground penetrating radar at the Lake Condah Mission Cemetery: Locating unmarked graves in areas with extensive subsurface disturbance. *The Artefact, 39,* 8–14.

Morrison, M., & Shepard, E. (2013). The archaeology of culturally modified trees: Indigenous economic diversification within colonial intercultural settings in Cape York Peninsula, northeastern Australia. *Journal of Field Archaeology, 38,* 143–160.

Morrison, M., McNaughton, D., & Shiner, J. (2010). Mission-based Indigenous production at the Weipa Presbyterian Mission, Western Cape York Peninsula (1932–66). *International Journal of Historical Archaeology, 14*(1), 86–111.

Morrison, M., McNaughton, D., & Keating, C. (2015). 'Their God is their belly': Moravian missionaries at the Weipa Mission (1898–1932). *Archaeology in Oceania, 50*(2), 85–104.

Mosko, M. (2010). Partible penitents: Dividual personhood and Christian practice in Melanesia and the West. *Journal of the Royal Anthropological Institute, 16,* 215–240.

Naval Intelligence Division. (1945). Western Pacific. In the *Geographical handbook series.* Volume IV, B.R. 519C. Great Britain: Naval Intelligence Division.

Nicholas, G. P. (2008). Native peoples and archaeology. In D. M. Pearsall (Ed.), *Encyclopedia of archaeology, Vol. 3* (pp. 1660–1669). New York: Academic Press.

Nicholas, G. P. (2010). Seeking the end of Indigenous Archaeology. In C. Phillips & H. Allen (Eds.), *Bridging the divide* (pp. 233–252). Walnut Creek, CA: Left Coast Press.

Nietschmann, B. (1989). Traditional sea territories, resources and rights in Torres Strait. In J. Cordell (Ed.), *A sea of small boats* (pp. 60–94). Cambridge, MA: Cultural Survival Inc.

Panich, L. M. (2013). Archaeologies of persistence: Reconsidering the legacies of colonialism in Native North America. *American Antiquity, 78*(1), 105–122.

Panich, L. M., & Schneider, T. D. (2015). Expanding mission archaeology: A landscape approach to indigenous autonomy in colonial California. *Journal of Anthropological Archaeology, 40*, 48–58.

Pardoe, C. (1990). Sharing the past: Aboriginal influence on archaeological practice, a case study from New South Wales. *Aboriginal History, 14*, 208–23.

Prendergast, P. A. (1968). *A history of the London Missionary Society in British New Guinea, 1871–1901* (PhD thesis). University of Hawai'i, Honolulu.

Ranson, D., & Egloff, B. (1988). Application of earth-resistivity surveys in Australian archaeological sites. *Australian Journal of Historical Archaeology, 6*, 57–73.

Rhoads, J. W. (1983). Prehistoric sites from the Kikori region, Papua New Guinea. *Australian Archaeology, 16*(1), 96–114.

Rhodes, D. (1986). *The Lake Condah Aboriginal Mission dormitory: An historical and archaeological investigation* (MA thesis). La Trobe University, Melbourne.

Rhodes, D. (1996). *The history of the Ramahyuck Aboriginal Mission and a report on the survey of the Ramahyuck Mission Cemetery.* Occasional Report 47. Melbourne: Aboriginal Affairs Victoria.

Rhodes, D. (1998). *An archaeological survey of Ebenezer Mission.* Unpublished report to Aboriginal Affairs Victoria, Melbourne.

Robbins, J. (1995). Dispossessing the spirits: Christian transformations of desire and ecology among the Urapmin of Papua New Guinea. *Ethnology, 34*, 211–224.

Robbins, J. (2001a). God is nothing but talk: Modernity, language and prayer in a Papua New Guinea society. *American Anthropologist, 103*, 901–912.

Robbins, J. (2001b). Secrecy and the sense of an ending: Narrative, time and everyday millenarianism in Papua New Guinea and in Christian fundamentalism. *Comparative Studies in Society and History, 43*, 525–551.

Robbins, J. (2007). Continuity thinking and the problem of Christian culture: Belief, time and the anthropology of Christianity. *Current Anthropology, 48*(1), 5–38.

Robbins, J. (2014). The anthropology of Christianity: Unity, diversity, new directions: An introduction to Supplement 10. *Current Anthropology, 55*(S10), S157–S171.

Russell, L. (2005). 'Either, or, neither nor': Resisting the production of gender, race and class dichotomies in the pre-colonial period. In E. Casella & C. Fowler (Eds.), *The archaeology of plural and changing identities* (pp. 33–51). Boston, MA: Springer.

Russell, L. (2016). Fifty years on: History's handmaiden? A plea for capital H History. *Historical Archaeology, 50*(3), 50–61.

Rutherford, D. (2006). The Bible meets the idol: Writing and conversion in Biak, Irian Jaya, Indonesia. In F. Cannell (Ed.), *The anthropology of Christianity* (pp. 240–272). Durham, NC: Duke University Press.

Schieffelin, B. B. (2002). Marking time: The dichotomizing discourse of multiple temporalities. *Current Anthropology, 43*, S5–S17.

Schieffelin, E. L. (1981). *The end of traditional music, dance, and body decoration in Bosavi, Papua New Guinea.* Institute of Papua New Guinea Studies Discussion Papers 30–32.

Sharp, N. (1992). *Footprints along the Cape York sandbeaches.* Canberra: Aboriginal Studies Press.

Silliman, S. (2001). Agency, practical politics and the archaeology of culture contact. *Journal of Social Archaeology, 1*(2), 190–209.

Silliman, S. W. (2005). Culture contact or colonialism? Challenges in the archaeology of native North America. *American Antiquity, 70*(1), 55–74.

Silliman, S. W. (2009). Blurring for clarity: Archaeology as hybrid practice. In P. Bikoulis, D. Lacroix, & M. Peuramaki-Brown (Eds.), *Postcolonial perspectives in archaeology* (pp. 15–25). Calgary: University of Calgary and Chacmool Archaeological Association.

Silliman, S. W. (2010). Indigenous traces in colonial spaces: Archaeologies of ambiguity, origin and practice. *Journal of Social Archaeology, 10*(1), 28–58.

Smith, C., Burke, H., Ralph, J., Pollard, K., Gorman, A., Wilson, C., . . . Jackson, G. (2019). Pursuing social justice through collaborative archaeologies in Aboriginal Australia. *Archaeologies, 15*, 536–569.

Specht, J., Fullagar, R., Torrence, R., & Baker, R. (1988). Prehistoric obsidian exchange on Melanesia: A perspective from the Talasea sources. *Australian Archaeology, 27*, 3–16.

St Pierre, E., Conyers, L., Sutton, M.-J., Mitchell, P., Walker, C., & Nicholls, D. (2019). Reimagining life and death: Results and interpretation of geophysical and ethnohistorical investigations of earth mounds, Mapoon, Cape York Peninsula, Queensland, Australia. *Archaeology in Oceania, 54*(2), 90–106.

Stanley, J. (1999). *A geophysical investigation at the Bowraville Mission grave site, Bowraville, NSW, Australia*. Unpublished report to New South Wales National Parks and Wildlife Service, Sydney.

Stanley, J., & Connah, G. (1977). Magnetic evidence of an Aboriginal burial ground at Forster, NSW. In P. Coutts & R. Brooks (Eds.), *A collection of papers presented to ANZAAS 1977* (pp. 37–50). Memoirs of the Victorian Archaeological Survey 2. Melbourne: Victorian Archaeological Survey.

Stevens, L. (2017). *"Me write myself": The free Aboriginal inhabitants of Van Diemen's Land at Wybalenna, 1832–47*. Melbourne: Monash University Publishing.

Summerhayes, G. R. (2000). Recent archaeological investigations in the Bismarck Archipelago, Anir–New Ireland Province, Papua New Guinea. In P. Bellwood, D. Bowdery, D. Bulbeck, D. Baer, V. Schinde, R. Shutler, & G. Summerhayes (Eds.), *Indo-Pacific prehistory: The Melaka papers. Bulletin of the Indo-Pacific Prehistory Association, 19*(3), 167–174). Canberra: Australian National University.

Sutton, M. J. (2003). Re-examining total institutions: A case study from Queensland. *Archaeology in Oceania, 38*, 78–88.

Sutton, M. J. (2014). *Remembering the mother mission: Exploring trauma, cultural heritage values and identity at Mapoon, a former mission village in western Cape York, Queensland* (PhD thesis). University of Queensland, Brisbane.

Sutton, M. J., Conyers, L. B., Day, A., Flinders, H., Luff, F., Madua, S., . . . Busch, W. (2013). Understanding cultural history using ground-penetrating radar mapping of unmarked graves in the Mapoon Mission Cemetery, Western Cape York, Queensland, Australia. *International Journal of Historical Archaeology, 17*, 782–805.

Sutton, M. J., Conyers, L. B., Pearce, S., St Pierre, E., & Nichols Pitt, D. (2020). Creating and renewing identity and value through the use of non-invasive archaeological methods: Mapoon unmarked graves, potential burial mounds and cemeteries project, western Cape York Peninsula, Queensland. *Archaeology in Oceania, 55*(2), 118–128.

Swain, T., & Rose, D. (Eds.) (1988). *Aboriginal Australians and Christian missions: Ethnographic and historical studies*. Bedford Park: Australian Association for the Study of Religion.

Tippett, A. R. (1967). *Solomon Islands Christianity: A study in growth and obstruction*. London: Lutterworth Press.

Torrence, R. (1992). What is Lapita about obsidian? A view from the Talasea sources. In J. C. Galipaud (Ed.), *Poterie Lapita et peuplement: Actes du colloque Lapita, Nouméa, Nouvelle-Calédonie, Janvier 1992* (pp. 111–126). Nouméa: ORSTROM.

Torrence, R., & Clarke, A. (2016). Excavating ethnographic collections: Negotiations and cross-cultural exchange in Papua New Guinea. *World Archaeology, 48*(2), 181–195.

Urwin, C. (2018). *Building and remembering: Constructing ancestral place at Popo, Orokolo Bay, Papua New Guinea* (PhD thesis). Monash University, Melbourne.

Urwin, C. (2019). Excavating and interpreting ancestral action: Stories from the subsurface of Orokolo Bay, Papua New Guinea. *Journal of Social Archaeology, 19*(3), 279–306.

von Strokirch, T. (1999). *A report on a ground magnetic survey over the Ebenezer Mission cemetery and surrounds.* Unpublished report to Aboriginal Affairs Victoria, Melbourne.

Walshe, K., Malone, G., Telfer, K., & Gully, G. (2019). Aboriginal historical archaeological site, Kanyanyapilla camp, McLaren Vale, South Australia. *Australian Archaeology, 85*(2), 196–209.

Weir, J. K. (2009). *The Gunditjmara Land Justice Story.* Native Title Research Unit Monograph Series. Canberra: Australian Institute of Aboriginal and Torres Strait Islander Studies.

White, J. P. (1967). *Taim bilong bipo* (PhD thesis). Australian National University, Canberra.

White, J. P., Crooke, K. A. W., & Ruxton, B. P. (1970). Kosipe: A late Pleistocene site in the Papuan Highlands. *Proceedings of the Prehistoric Society, 36*, 152–170.

Wolfe, P. (1994). Nation and miscegenNation: Discursive continuity in the Post-Mabo era. *Social Analysis, 36*, 93–152.

Wolfe, P. (2006). Settler colonialism and the elimination of the native. *Journal of Genocide Research, 8*(4), 387–409.

Wolski, N. (2000). *Brushing against the grain: excavating for Aboriginal—European interaction on the colonial frontier in Western Victoria, Australia* (PhD thesis). University of Melbourne, Melbourne.

Wright, D., & Ricardi, P. (2015). Both sides of the frontier: The 'contact' archaeology of villages on Mabuyag, western Torres Strait. *Quaternary International, 385*, 102–111.

Wright, D., Denham, T., Shine, D., & Donohue, M. (2013). An archaeological review of Western New Guinea. *Journal of World Prehistory, 26*, 58–73.

Yelf, R., & Burnett, A. (1995). *Ground penetrating radar survey of unmarked cemeteries at Taroom Aboriginal Reserve, Bundulla, Queensland.* Unpublished report for Department of Environment and Heritage, Rockhampton.

Index

For the benefit of digital users, indexed terms that span two pages (e.g., 52–53) may, on occasion, appear on only one of those pages.

Note: Tables and figures are indicated by *t* and *f* following the page number

abandonment
  of Boodie Cave, 254
  of coastal zones, 778
  ditches and field systems, 467–468
  frequency during LGM, 531
  of islands, 776, 783, 789, 923
  of Ivane Valley, 846
  of Kuk Early Agricultural Site, 450, 452–454
  of large-scale fish traps, 509
  of mortars and pestles, 634
  of Orokolo Bay communities, 820
  of Wahgi Valley, 452
Aboriginal agency, 30, 337, 351, 1091
Aboriginal languages, 175, 1081
Aboriginal-Macassan cross-sea interactions
  archaeological understanding of, 1031–1034
  future research avenues, 1035–1036
  introduction to, 1023–1024
  oral and written histories, 1024–1026, 1025f
  radiocarbon dating, 1029–1030
  rock art sites, 1034
  trepang/trepangers, 20, 1024–1027, 1027f, 1028f
  when and when, 1026–1031, 1027f, 1028f
Aboriginal people
  agrarian Australia and, 1088–1092, 1090f
  death of, 3
  future research opportunities, 1092–1093
  introduction to, 3–9
  primitivism and colonialist ideologies, 9–10, 329, 997
  whaling and sealing, 1045–1049, 1046f, 1047f, 1051–1053
Aboriginal Tasmanians, 60
The Aborigines of Victoria and Riverina (Beveridge), 57

The Aborigines of Victoria (Smyth), 57, 63
accelerator mass spectrometry (AMS)
    radiocarbon dating, 567–568, 600, 823n6
Adam, Leonhard, 99
aDNA, 302, 308, 316, 907
adornments, 20, 120, 225, 262, 598, 606, 697, 746, 1003, 1010
adzes
  distinction from axes, 643–644
  Lapita adze, 653
  Lapstone Creek excavations, 115–116
  Tula adzes, 671, 675–676, 682–684, 938–939
  Wanigela excavation, 98
agency and social justice in archaeology
  Ancestral Beings, 140–147
  development of, 150–153
  Elders, 147–150
  introduction to, 137–139
  Ngarrindjeri epistemologies, 148–150
agentive approach to land and spirituality, 962
agrarian Australia
  Aboriginal people and, 1088–1092, 1090f
  introduction to, 1079–1080
  land and resource management, 1081–1083
  overview of, 1083–1088, 1084f, 1086f
agriculture/agriculturalists. *See also* eel-based aquaculture
  barbarians as, 55
  cultural differences, 332
  firestick farming, 15, 335–336, 489, 505, 1082
  introduction to, 18
  in New Guinea highlands, 843–847, 844f
  oyster farming, 347, 501
  systems of, 23, 449, 452–454

INDEX

agronomic technologies, 449, 469, 843, 849–850

Aitape skull, 100–101

Allen, Harry, 121, 124

Allen, Jim, 102

alpine environments, 23

alterations in rock art modifications, 975

amateur *vs.* professional research, 120–125

amendment in rock art modifications, 975

American Anthropologist, 85

ancestral agency. *See* agency and social justice in archaeology

Ancestral Beings

  agency of, 140–142

  mimis (spirit beings), 142–143, 143*f*

  namurlanjanyngku, 146–147

  ngabaya, 146–147

  Old People, 144–145

  revelations by, 140–145

  rock art boundaries and, 724–725

  rock art modifications and, 977–979, 985n2 985n8

  spiritual beings, 72, 140, 142–145, 152, 417, 734

ancestral remains, 110, 118, 122, 125–126, 137, 138, 147, 305, 1108

ancestral resting places, 1107–1110

Angas, George French, 1047

animal domesticates, 845–846

animal habitats, 15, 338, 341

anthropogenic burning, 15, 291, 336, 388

Anthropological Society of Victoria, 112, 121

anthropomorphic face mortars, 631

Anthropos, 87

Antipodes, 2, 56, 950

antiquarian archaeology in colonial Victoria

  anthropological approaches, 58–59

  archaeological approaches, 60–61

  ceremonial sites, 72–74

  fossilized human impressions, 74–75

  geological approaches, 59–60

  implement sites, 62–67

  introduction to, 53–54

  nineteenth century practices and, 54–55

  occupation sites, 67–70

  origin approaches, 58–61

  resource extraction sites, 70–71

  social context of, 55–58

  summary of, 76

antiquarianism, 9–10, 25, 53, 56–62, 67–76, 110, 191

Approximate Bayesian Computation, 307

aquaculture, eel-based. *See* eel-based aquaculture

aquaculture, oyster, 347, 501

archaeometric provenance studies, 743, 755, 761

archaeomorphological research, 477, 481, 484, 488

ARIMA (auto-regressive integrated moving average) models, 526

art. *See also* ochre/ochre sourcing; rock art

  on mortars and pestles, 633

  portable art, 726–731

  rock engravings, 528, 564, 573, 580, 957–963, 1052

  stone figurines, 96–98

atomic emission spectroscopy (AES), 750

Austen, Leo, 94

Australian Aborigines (Dawson), 57, 59

Australian Archaeological Association, 31–32

Australian archaeology in twentieth century

  amateur *vs.* professional research, 120–125

  brief history of, 109–111

  cross-cultural research, 117–120

  lessons from historical excavations, 125–127

  professionals in, 111–117

  in Willandra Lakes and Mildura regions, 120–125

Australian high country

  Bogong moths, 866–868, 880, 882

  chronology of, 877–879

  early research in, 864–867, 865*f*

  ethnohistory, 879–882

  excavations in, 877–878

  introduction to, 861–862

  investigations in, 873–876

  new phase of research, 870–873, 871*f*

  patterns of expanding use of, 882–883

  research study area, 862–863, 863*f*

  site dating, 868–870

Australian Institute of Aboriginal Studies (AIAS), 110

Australian Intensification debate. *See* complexity in hunter-gatherer Intensification Model

Australian Museum in Sydney, 91, 94

Australian Museums and Galleries Association (AMaGA), 188

Australian National University (ANU), 110

Australian Nuclear Science and Technology Organisation (ANSTO) reactor, 759

The Australian Race (Curr), 57

axes. *See* stone axes

Baker, Richard, 330

Banks, Joseph, 1046

Bass Strait fire studies, 399–400, 400*f*

Bassani, Florrie, 196

Bassani, Sunlight, 196

Bayliss-Smith, Tim, 451, 453

behavioural ecology, 498–499, 507

Berg, Jim, 126

Berndt, Catherine H., 117–118

Berndt, Ronald M., 117–118

Beveridge, Peter, 57

The Biggest Estate on Earth (Gammage), 489

Bindon, Peter, 338

bioarchaeology. *See* Murray River Valley societal bioarchaeology

bird pestles, 96, 99, 631, 633

Birmingham, Judy, 1104, 1105–1106, 1109

Blaeu, Joan, 2

Blandowski, William, 70

blood-group distribution studies, 596–597

Blundell, Geoffrey, 721

Bogong moths, 866–868, 880, 882

Bolton, Brian, 335

bone artefacts, 61, 66–67

Boodie Cave site, 254–255

Borologa 1 site, 481–483, 482*f*

bossed bowls, 631

A Boundary Is to Cross: Observations on Yolngu Boundaries and Permission (Williams), 723–724

Bowler, Jim, 121, 123–124

Bradley, John, 139, 146, 731

Bramell, Elsie, 115

Briggs, Asa, 56

Briggs, Donald, 342

British colonialism, 3, 28–30, 78–79

British New Guinea, 3, 90, 95, 654, 709, 823n13 1110–1111

Brumm, Adam, 1083

Budgeongutte Swamp, 16, 16*f*, 342

building and construction of sites

archaeomorphological research, 477, 481, 484, 488

as architecture, 474–488

Borologa 1 site, 481–483, 482*f*

Cloggs Cave, 483–488, 485*f*, 487*f*

cultural knowledge of, 473–474, 488

introduction to, 473–474

Nawarla Gabarnmang, 476–480, 479*f*, 480*f*

phantomization, 477, 484

social construction and, 477, 481, 488–489, 513

Builth, Heather, 342

bulk techniques, 750–751

Bunjilaka Aboriginal Centre at Melbourne Museum, 188

burial sites, 896–899, 897*t*

buried deposits, 118

burning practices on vegetation, 15, 335, 386, 392, 1082

Burrill Lake excavations, 115

Carpenters Gap 1 site, 253–254

cartographers, 2, 4

Casey, Dermot, 88, 112, 116

Castanospermum australe (Fabaceae) mtDNA data, 316

caves

building and construction in, 475–476

Chauvet Cave, 560, 564, 567

Cloggs Cave, 483–488, 485*f*, 487*f*

Fern Cave, 757–758

limestone caves, 254, 255–256, 282, 363, 572–575, 778, 810, 920

Mask Cave, 604, 605, 728–729

ritual caves, 61, 72, 484

rock art dating, 560

ceramics

art styles on, 700

Chinese sherds, 1036

for cooking, 627

in earthen mounds, 1113

1134 INDEX

ceramics (*cont.*)
  from highland sites, 849–850
  Hopo ceramics, 603
  lime-filled dentate stamped, 88
  repurposing of, 30
  rings of, 96–97
  from surface sites, 810, 813–816, 819
  for tools, 30
  trading in, 603–604, 673, 704, 706, 1052
ceremonial architecture, 476
ceremonial practices, 25–28, 122–123, 734,
  949, 983
ceremonial sites, 61, 72–74, 436, 864, 957, 962,
  1006, 1008
ceremonies. *See* Dreaming/Dreaming
  narratives; ritualized hunting; rituals;
  rock art modifications
chaîne opératoire approach, 477–478, 480, 756
charcoal studies, 384, 386. *See also* fire and
  charcoal studies
Chauncy, Philip, 57
Chauvet Cave, 560, 564, 567
Childs, Terry, 192–193
Clark, Grahame, 543
Clark, Ian, 1049
Clarke, Anne, 1028, 1031
Clear Swamp, 16, 16*f*, 342
Cloggs Cave, 483–488, 485*f*, 487*f*
coastal middens, 22, 781*f*, 786, 1114
coasts, islands, and marine societies
  in antiquity, 774–777, 775*f*, 776*f*
  development of maritime economies,
  786–789
  Early Holocene impact on, 779–780
  importance of islands, 784–786
  introduction to, 773–774
  Last Glacial Maximum impact on, 777–778
  Late Holocene impact on, 780–784, 781*f*
  Late Pleistocene impact on, 778–779
  Mid-Holocene impact on, 779–780
  significance in hominid development,
  789–791
colonialism, 3, 28–31, 78–79, 302, 317, 654, 705,
  866. *See also* antiquarian archaeology in
  colonial Victoria
colonial violence and conflict
  contextualization of, 1059–1062, 1060*f*, 1062*t*

frontier violence, 10, 30, 529, 731, 1057–1059,
  1088
geographic and temporal distribution of,
  1063–1068, 1064*t*, 1065*t*, 1066*f*, 1067*t*
introduction to, 1057–1059
Native Mounted Police, 162, 166, 169,
  1058–1059, 1061–1071, 1064*t*, 1065*t*, 1066*f*,
  1071n6 1072n8
Native Police forces, 1058, 1063, 1071n2
repercussions of, 1070––1071
colonization
  European colonization, 341, 361, 388–389,
  397, 702, 1063, 1079–1080, 1108
  human colonization, 382
  museum collections as, 194
Commonwealth Scientific and Industrial
  Research Organisation (CSIRO), 760
Complex Figurative imagery, 719
complexity in hunter-gatherer
  Intensification Model
  changing perceptions of, 502–503
  critique of, 507–510
  early explanatory models, 498–499
  evidence for, 505–507
  exchange systems, 502
  introduction to, 497–498
  landscape management, 505
  overview of, 499–503
  social dynamics of, 503–505
  sociostructural change paradigms, 510–512
  spatiotemporal trends, 500–502
confidence interval (CI), 242, 244, 385, 597
continental landmass, 4, 226, 528, 641
Continuous Cultures, Ongoing Responsibilities
  (Museums Australia), 188
Conus shells, 92–94, 602, 698–700
Convincing Ground massacre, 1049
Cook, James, 1046
Cootamundra Shoals survey, 545–546
Coral Sea Cultural Interaction Sphere (CSCIS)
  archaeological evidence, 600–601
  archaeological time depth, 601–605
  chronology, 601–604
  ethnographic evidence, 598–599
  introduction to, 591–592
  maritime exchange networks, 594–596
  overview of, 592–593, 594*f*

research framework, 605–607
shared biology, 596–597
shared material culture, 597–601, 599*f*
cosmogenic nuclide dating, 562–566, 565*f*
cosmographers, 2
cowries, 632, 695–697, 711, 712n1
cranial deformation, 900
cranial elements, 216, 222
craniometrics, 596–597
Crawford, Tony, 197
Creation myths, 170
Cuddie Springs site, 285
cultivation patterns in New Guinea highlands, 843–847, 844*f*
cultural change
development of, 110
ethnohistorical evidence of, 500, 506
in human population, 548, 786, 1105
of hunter-gatherers, 331
introduction to, 15, 18–19, 22, 30–32
in Mid-Holocene, 790
processual archaeology and, 15, 499–500, 720
settlement patterns, 815
cultural differences and practices
Australian cross-cultural research, 117–120
in Dreaming/Dreaming narratives, 963
hunter-gatherer societies, 332
Indigenous cultural heritage, 581, 791
introduction to, 30–31
in museum collection legacies, 187, 189–190, 194, 196–198, 204–205
in submerged landscapes heritage management, 551–552
cultural diversity, 25, 31, 789
cultural dynamics, 20–21, 32, 498, 505, 591, 1105
cultural ecology, 116, 498–499, 1105
cultural knowledge, 26, 148, 151, 172, 196, 473–474, 488, 875, 882
cultural patrimony, 187, 189–190, 194, 196–198, 204–205
Curr, Edward M., 57

Dampier Archipelago (Murujuga), 547–548
Dark Emu Black Seeds: Agriculture or Accident? (Pascoe), 334, 1081, 1082
Darwin, Charles, 4, 54

Davidson, Daniel, 118, 592
Dawkins, Boyd, 543
Dawson, James, 57, 59, 67, 69
decolonization, 34, 179, 189
Deep History of Sea Country (DHSC) project, 547–549, 548*f*
Deep Time Dreaming (Griffiths), 109
deglaciation, 834, 879, 921
delta societies. *See* swamp and delta societies of Papuan Gulf
demographic and population changes. *See also* population densities
change and territoriality, 501–502
expansion, 502
introduction to, 523–525
radiocarbon dating measuring, 525–526, 531–533
time series analysis, 527–531, 528*f*, 530*f*
demographic packing, 19, 529, 956–957, 962
Denisovan genome, 306–308
Descartes, René, 995
Descola, Philippe, 998
desert settlements in Australia
adaptability of, 927–928
climactic indicators, 921–925
dynamics of, 938–939
impact of aridity, 929–932, 930*f*
importance of early dates, 919–920, 920*f*
introduction to, 917–919, 918*f*
new records from, 920–921
persistence of, 928–929
population change identification, 925–926
population dispersal models, 926–927, 933–935
sea level changes effect on productivity, 932–933
signal sending stone technology, 937–938
technology impact on economic behaviours, 935–937
timing of, 922–925, 924*t*
wet phases, 927–928
detrital Thorium contamination, 576
Deutsch Neu-Guinea (Neuhauss), 96
Devil's Lair site, 255–256
dietary analyses, 904–907, 905*f*
diffusionism, 101, 116, 592–593, 719
Digital Elevation Models (DEMs), 415

dingoes
arrival of, 367–370, 368*f*
human interaction with, 370–373
introduction to, 361–364, 362*f*
origins of, 364–366
role in Holocene, 370–373
Diprotodon optatum, 256, 275, 276*f,*
283–385
direct percussion points, 670*f,* 674, 681
diseases and injury, 3, 122, 524, 529, 901–904,
903*f,* 908
ditches. *See* Huli ditches and field systems in
swampland
diversity loss of megafauna, 281
Dixon, Robert, 171–172
djalambu photographs, 197–204
Djäwa Dhäwirriŋu, 199–200
DNA sequencing, 302, 318n1 365
dogai spirit, 727–728, 728*f*
dog mtDNA data, 313, 315
Dom gaima quarry, 652
domiculture, 7–8, 505, 1082
Dong Son cultures, 94–95
Dotte-Sarout, Emile, 1113
double outrigger canoes, 597–601, 599*f*
Draper, Neale, 1050
Dreaming/Dreaming narratives
Ancestral Beings and, 140–142
archaeological investigation of, 955–963
cultural landscape associated with, 963
historical linguistics, 961
historical time and, 953–954
historical trajectories, 955–956, 956*t*
history of thought, 951–952
ideology of, 951–955
introduction to, 25–27, 949–951
mythology in, 953
oral traditions of, 160, 167–168, 167*t,* 171
red ochre and, 960–961
research challenges, 961–963
ritual knowledge of, 954–955
rituals associated with, 960
rock art of, 957–959
site histories, 956–957
stone arrangements and, 959–960
Tjukurrpa, 939
tjurunga use, 961

totemic geography of, 952
tracks/songlines, 952–953
Dromornis stirtoni, 256, 275–276, 278
drought conditions, 17, 254, 288, 291–292,
340–341, 350, 388, 457, 783, 835, 919, 923,
953, 1117
droveways, 461–462
Dry Temperate zone, 388, 395–396
Dry Tropic zone, 390–393
dugong/sea cow *(Dugong dugon)* ritualized
hunting, 999–1006, 1002*f,* 1004*f*
dung fungi, 277, 278, 283, 291–292
Dutch cartographers, 2
dying race ethos, 57

Early Papuan Pottery (EPP), 700, 706, 815
earthen (oven) mounds, 67–69, 68*f*
earthenware pottery, 698, 700, 702–703, 803,
1029–1031
ecosystem engineering, 330, 351
edge-ground axes, 250, 252–253, 259–261, 263,
477, 841, 876
eel-based aquaculture
farming of, 344, 417, 425, 437
harvesting devices, 16, 342
resource use for, 501
social dynamics of, 503–504, 506
trapping devices, 344–345, 395–396, 417, 437
waterscapes for, 16–17, 17*f*
eggshell fossils, 256, 277–280, 283, 285–286, 560
Eglinton, Ernest, 169
Elders agency, 147–150
Elkin, Peter, 119, 996
El Niño Southern Oscillation (ENSO), 371,
508, 529, 680, 783–784, 835, 901, 923,
934, 940n2
Enlightenment philosophy era/philosophy, 19,
27, 994–995
environmental determinism, 15–16, 497, 507,
510, 512
environmental enhancement and engagement
aquaculture channels, 332
building and construction of sites as
engagement, 475
ecosystem engineering, 330, 351
flaked stone tools, 679–681
freshwater resources and, 341–346

in hunter-gatherer societies, 331–334
introduction to, 329–331
irrigation channels, 332–333, 850
landscape burning, 15, 332, 335–336, 341
marine resources and, 346–350
protected rearing, 341, 343–346, 348–349
replanting process, 332, 849, 1081
resource enhancement, 330, 333, 338, 350–351,
   435, 436–439
restocking depleted animal species, 340–341
shelter creation, 337–338, 348
substrate enhancement, 346–347
translocation of animals, 338–340, 342–343,
   348
transplanting process, 332, 807–808, 1081
waterhole enhancement, 336–337
weirs, 16, 332, 343–345, 414–418, 421, 422*f*,
   425–431, 435, 891–892
erasure in rock art modifications, 975
ethnoarchaeology, 109, 128n11 158
ethnographic observations, 21, 25, 61, 67, 151,
   415, 662, 675, 895, 1046
ethnography/ethnohistory
   Australian high country, 879–882
   Coral Sea Cultural Interaction Sphere,
     598–599
   on hunter-gatherers, 224
   of magico-religious rituals, 971–972
   oral history and tradition, 159–161
   research information, 20, 158, 418, 421, 425,
     428, 432, 498, 559, 595, 606, 625, 656, 814,
     959, 994, 998–1004, 1007
   shell valuables and exchange systems,
     704–706
European colonialism, 28–31, 317, 654, 705, 866
European colonization, 341, 361, 388–389, 397,
   702, 1063, 1079–1080, 1108
evolutionary ecology, 498–499, 512
exchange networks/systems. *See* shell
   valuables and exchange systems
Expansion Phase (1000 to 500 BP), 92, 94,
   602, 700
Eylandt, Groote, 1032

faunal remains, 87–88, 222, 253, 256, 284–286,
   316, 414, 810, 819, 871
Fern Cave, 757–758

field systems. *See* Huli ditches and field
   systems in swampland
Finsch, Otto, 93
fire and charcoal studies
   Arid zone, 388, 393–394
   biogeography of, 386–389, 389*f*
   constructing records of, 383–386, 385*f*
   Dry Temperate zone, 388, 395–396
   Dry Tropic zone, 390–393
   human interaction, 381–382
   introduction to, 381–383
   island environments, 397–400
   Wet Temperate zone, 396–397
   Wet Tropic zone, 388, 390
firestick farming, 15, 335–336, 489, 505, 1082.
   See also landscape burning
First Nations histories, 1104–1106
First People of Australia
   Boodie Cave site, 254–255
   Carpenters Gap 1 site, 253–254
   debates about dates, 242–244, 243*f*
   Devil's Lair site, 255–256
   introduction to, 241–242
   Karnatukul site, 255
   Lake Mungo site, 256–257
   Madjedbebe site, 248–250
   Minjiwarra site, 252
   Nauwalabila 1 site, 251
   Nawarla Gabarnmang site, 252
   oldest sites, 244–257, 245*t*–247*t*, 249*f*
   population size, 258–259
   Riwi site, 254
   subsistence economy of, 261–262
   symbolism of, 262
   technology of, 259–261, 259*f*, 260*f*
   Warratyi site, 256
fishing facilities, 16–18, 344, 434–436
fish traps/trapping, 71, 343–346. *See also*
   eel-based aquaculture; stone-walled
   fish traps
Fison, Lorimer, 57–58
fissioning, 228, 780–781, 817–818, 820
flaked stone tools
   analytical approaches, 61, 683–685
   in Cuddie Springs site, 285
   environmental change and, 679–681
   highland use, 836

1138 INDEX

flaked stone tools (*cont.*)
    introduction to, 669–672, 670*f*
    Leilira blade, 681–682, 684, 773*f*
    modelling variability, 672–675
    overview of, 65–66
    of Papua New Guinea, 676–679, 678*f*
    retouched stone points, 672–675, 673*f*
    social interconnectedness and, 681–683
    for subsistence activities, 811
    technological organization, 263, 679–681
    Tula adzes, 671, 675–676, 682–684, 938–939
Flinders, Matthew, 3, 1029
Flood, Josephine, 483, 864–865
food remains, 253, 484
food supplies, 15, 1047–1048
foot mortars, 632
foragers/foraging
    coastal-based, 254–255
    colonization by, 927
    demand sharing by, 755
    ideological characteristics of, 501
    increased range of, 680
    introduction to, 6–7
    maritime-based, 223
    of rainforest, 836, 841
    risks of, 675–676
    seasonal movements by, 753–754, 836, 846, 850
    shellfish collecting, 790, 842
    subsistence practices of, 671–672, 922, 1081–1082
    tools of, 662, 669
    trade goods, 682, 753
Fourier transform infrared spectroscopy (FTIR), 386, 751
four-pointed star, 727–728, 728*f*
Fox, Charles Elliot, 1113
Frazer, James, 58
freshwater practices, 341–346, 418–425
frontier violence, 10, 30, 529, 731, 1057–1059, 1088
fur seals (*Arctocephalus forsteri*), 1050
Fysh, Hudson, 169

Gaisseau, Pierre-Dominique, 455–456, 463
Gammage, Bill, 489
gana, 456*f*, 459–466
Ganz River quarry, 652

genetic data
    aDNA, 302, 308, 316
    Denisovan genome, 306–308
    diversification within Australia, 314–317
    diversification within New Guinea, 312–314
    DNA sequencing, 302, 318n1
    evidence of adaptations, 311
    introduction to, 301–306, 303*t*–305*t*
    isolation data, 311–312
    mitochondrial DNA, 244, 258, 301–302, 307–316, 310*f*, 318n2 361, 364–365, 597
    New Guinea highlands, 849
    nuclear DNA, 318n1 597
    Out-of-Africa migrations, 301, 306–311, 317
    technological developments in research, 317–318
genome, defined, 318n1
Genyornis, 287
geoarchaeological analyses, 249, 251, 547, 550
German New Guinea, 3, 90, 1110
Ghaleb, Barbara, 1004
Gillen, Frank, 57, 951
Gilmore, Mary, 336–337
Gnielinski, Friedrich von, 606
Gogodala Cultural Centre at Balimo, 197
Gold-lipped Pearl Oyster (*Pinctada maxima*), 693, 695
Golson, Jack, 94, 102, 452, 453
Göttingen Zoological Museum, 62
Gough, Julie, 192, 193, 194, 205
Graham, Elizabeth, 1103
Great Barrier Reef (GBR), 783, 785–787
Great Dividing Range, 23, 861, 904
Greater Australia, 6, 248, 255, 382–383, 387–388, 400
green turtle (*Chelonia mydas*) ritualized hunting, 1006–1011, 1009*f*
Greer, Shelley, 606, 1010–1011
Gregory, A. C., 474
Gregory, John, 59, 111–112
Grey, George, 338
Griffiths, Billy, 109–110
grindstones, 250–251, 260, 262, 483, 486, 529, 883, 895, 935–938, 1088–1089
Grist, Mark, 13
ground-edge artefacts (GEAs). *See* stone axes
group identity, 21, 24, 721, 984

Gulf of Carpentaria case study, 731–734, 733*f*
Gulf of Mexico, 544
Gumbula, Joe, 198–204
Gunditjmara People, 60, 71
Gunn, Aeneas, 345
Gunn, Ben, 721
Gupapuyngu Daygurrgurr clan, 198–204

Haddon, Alfred, 93, 592
Haddow, Eve, 1113
Hafner, Diane, 194–195
Hale, Herbert, 112–113
Hamlyn-Harris, Ronald, 592
Head, Lesley, 400
Heinsohn, Tom, 340
Hepatitis B virus (HBV) genomes, 314
highlands/high country. *See also* Australian
    high country; New Guinea highlands
  hunter-gatherers in, 832
  material culture in, 831
  mortars and pestles in, 620–626, 621*f*, 623*f*,
    630–632
  radiocarbon dating of ditches and field
    systems, 453
  stone axes of, 649–653
Hiri shell valuables and exchange systems,
    702–704
Historical Archaeology and the Environment
    (Torres de Souza, Costa), 1087–1088
historical emergence, 26, 158–159, 1005
Homo erectus, 224, 306–308, 381, 774
Homo floresiensis, 224, 307–308, 774
Homo luzonensis, 224, 774
Homo sapiens, 14, 215, 219*t,* 241, 244, 288–289,
    302, 306, 757, 774, 831, 835
hooked triangle motif, 729
Hopo ceramics, 603
Howes, Hilary, 1113
Howitt, Alfred, 57–58
Hughes, Ian, 627
Huli ditches and field systems in swampland
  aesthetics of, 463
  as boundaries, 463–465
  cosmology of, 466
  for gardens, 460–461
  as history, 465–466
  idea of, 449–451, 450*f*

New Guinea highlands, 451–455, 454*f*
  reclamation and abandonment, 467–468
  technology of, 458–459
  types of, 459
  walkways and droveways, 461–462
  warfare and, 462–463
human adaptations, 773, 919, 1105
human cognition, 559–560
human colonization, 9, 382, 775, 923
Human Genome Diversity Project, 302
humanitarianism, 56, 152, 1105
human occupation sites
  in antiquarian colonial Victoria, 67–70
  earthen (oven) mounds, 67–69, 68*f*
  Murray River Valley societal
    bioarchaeology, 890–892, 890*f,* 891*t,* 893*t*
  shell middens, 69–70
  stone houses, 70
human remains
  ancestral remains, 110, 118, 122, 125–126, 137,
    138, 147, 305, 1108
  mortuary practices, 896–899, 897*t*
  skeletal remains, 10, 61, 67, 87, 122, 223–225,
    230, 277, 597, 872, 1006, 1071
  Wanigela excavation, 91, 97
human symbolic evolution, 560
humpback whale *(Megaptera novaeangliae),*
    1044
hunter-gatherers. *See also* complexity in
    hunter-gatherer Intensification Model;
    ritualized hunting
  demographic data on, 228–229
  dingoes, as aid to, 368–369
  environmental enhancement and
    engagement, 331–334
  ethnographic data on, 224
  in highlands, 832
  introduction to, 6–8, 18
  mission archaeology and, 1101–1102
hunting magic, 997–998, 1005
Huxley, Thomas, 62
hydrological engineering, 17, 332
hyperdiffusionism, 116
hyper-variable region (HVR), 312

I'ai tribe, 807–808
imperialist archaeologies, 54–55

inclusionism, 188, 224, 931, 1005–1006

increase ceremonies, 955

Indigenous archaeology, 137–139, 139*f*, 140–145, 150–153

Indigenous architecture, 32–33, 33f, 474–488. *See also* building and construction of sites

Indigenous cultural heritage, 581, 791

Indigenous independence movement, 3

Indigenous ontologies, 27, 138, 148, 188, 205, 1011, 1115–1116

Indigenous Roadmap (Janke), 188

infant/ child mortality, 372

information exchange theory, 922

infrared stimulated luminescence (IRSL), 577–578

inhabited world *(oikoumene)*, 2

Initial Settlement period (c. 640-485 cal BP), 308, 311, 818–819, 919

injuries. *See* diseases and injury

inscribed landscape, 962–963

intensification of resource use, 501

intensified resource production, 504

interactions. *See* Aboriginal-Macassan cross-sea interactions; Coral Sea Cultural Interaction Sphere; interregional gatherings; megafauna interactions

interchanges/interchangeability, 593, 606, 674–675, 745, 1044

interregional gatherings, 330, 435–437, 1046

intertidal zones, 346–347, 428, 547, 550–552, 778, 804–805, 819, 1027, 1117

Intertropical Convergence Zone (ITCZ), 680, 922, 940n1

intichiuma ceremonies, 978

Into the Heart of Tasmania (Taylor), 109

introgression, 225, 302, 306–308, 319n3

irrigation channels, 332–333, 850

islands/island environments. *See also* coasts, islands, and marine societies; Torres Strait Islands/Islanders

abandonment of, 776, 783, 789, 923

Bass Strait, 399–400, 400*f*

fire and charcoal studies, 397–400

Keppel Islands, 782, 786–789

Lizard Island, 33, 593, 598, 605–607, 781*f*, 783, 785–787

stepping stone islands, 224, 226–230, 232–233

Torres Strait, 398–399

Trobriand Islands, 94, 654, 1117

Watom Island excavation, 87–90, 89*f*

Island Southeast Asia (ISEA), 365

isotope analyses, 364, 901, 905–906, 905*f*, 1030

Jones, Jonathon, 202–204

Jones, Rhys, 335, 1082

Joyce, Thomas, 91–92

Kahn, Miriam, 1112

Kamilaroi and Kurnai (Howitt, Fison), 57–58

Kamminga, Johan, 869

Karnatukul site, 255

Kasprusch, Alios, 98–99

Kearney, Amanda, 146, 996–997

Keble, Robert A., 116

Keipte Kuyumen clan, 35n1

Kenniff Cave excavations, 13, 242

Keppel Islands, 782, 786–789

Kewibu, Vincent, 93

Kikori River Delta, 805–807, 809–813

Kimberley Basin, 561–562

Kimberley Points, 252, 372, 673, 673*f*, 681–682, 684

kina exchanges, 693, 695, 696*f*

kin-centric ecology, 996–997

Kiowa excavations, 13, 85, 643*f*, 697, 841–842

Kirch, Patrick, 700–701

Kohn, Eduardo, 995

kombati site, 812

Kombewah flakes, 678–679

Kuhn Geometric Index of Unifacial Reduction, 674

Kuk Swamp, 313, 451–453, 464–465, 650, 676, 843, 845

kula exchanges, 594, 601, 654, 693–694, 698–702, 699*f*

Lake Menindee site, 284–285

Lake Mungo site, 256–257

Lamalama people, 195–196

Lampert, Ron, 102, 453

landscape burning, 15, 332, 335–336, 341, 1082. *See also* firestick farming

landscapes. *See also* desert settlements in
Australia; Huli ditches and field systems
in swampland; submerged landscapes
constructed, 14–18, 16*f*
hunter-gatherer management of, 505
inscribed landscape, 962–963
living landscapes, 138, 140–145, 151–152
territorialized landscape, 963
language groups, 20, 56, 175, 722–725, 731–735,
892, 893*t*, 1034, 1068
Lapita adze, 653
Lapita Cultural Complex, 22, 313, 649, 653,
656, 782
Lapita pottery, 33, 86*f*, 88, 89*f*, 90, 314, 600, 633,
679, 701, 1112–1113
Lapita shell artefacts, 701, 706
Lapstone Creek excavations, 115–116
Last Glacial Period, 170, 222, 226–227, 283,
399, 548
Latz, Peter, 335–336, 340–341
Leask, Maurice, 100
Leilira blade, 681–682, 684, 773*f*
Leone, Mark P., 1105–1106
Lévi-Strauss, Claude, 7
Liddy, Harry, 195
Liddy, Karen, 195
Lilley, Ian, 606
limestone caves, 254, 255–256, 282, 363, 572–575,
778, 810, 920
linguistic diversity, 1, 889, 892
lithic resources
artefact collections, 190, 192–194, 644
in highlands, 842, 844*f*
igneous materials, 683
of obsidian tool producers, 683
production from, 842–843
quarrying material, 850, 939
stone tool use and, 671
in submerged sites, 547–548, 548*f*
technology of, 256, 261, 938
volcanic material, 677
living fossils, 76, 1104
living landscapes, 138, 140–145, 151–152
Lizard Island, 33, 593, 598, 605–607, 781*f*, 783,
785–787
lizard traps, 338, 339*f*
Lofgren, Mancel, 338

Logaueng mortar, 96–97
Lommel, Andreas, 718–719
London Missionary Society (LMS), 31, 1111,
1114–1115
long-distance interactions. *See* Aboriginal-
Macassan cross-sea interactions;
Coral Sea Cultural Interaction Sphere;
interregional gatherings; megafauna
interactions
The Lost World (Part 2) project (Gough), 193
low-oxygen environments, 544
Lubbock, John, 54, 65
luminescence dating, 9, 242, 251, 285,
580. *See also* infrared stimulated
luminescence; optically stimulated
luminescence; thermoluminescence

Mabo v. Queensland (no. 2) (1992), 158
Macassan pottery, 117–118
Macassans. *See* Aboriginal-Macassan
cross-sea interactions
MacGillivray, John, 598
MacIntosh, Neil W. G., 117, 119
Macknight, Campbell, 1026–1027
MacPherson, Peter, 474
macrobotanic record, 248, 253
Madjedbebe site, 248–250
magico-religious rites, 997
Mahony, Daniel J., 111
Mainland Southeast Asia (MSEA), 365
maintenance rituals, 996–997
male initiation ceremonies, 954
Manabaru, Peter, 144
Mandui, Herman, 13
Mankind, 122
Marine Isotope Stage (MIS), 216, 223, 250, 263,
523–524, 834, 834*f*, 921
marine practices. *See* stone-walled fish traps;
whaling and sealing
marine resource enhancement, 346–350
marine resources, 22, 222, 262, 341, 346–350,
437–438, 529, 545, 773, 778, 780, 785,
789, 815
marine transgression, 22, 546, 628, 774,
778, 780
maritime economies, 786–789
maritime exchange networks, 594–596

maritime migration
    from Africa, 216–217
    archaic encounters, 224–226
    dispersal corridors, 226–229, 226f
    earliest human presence in Sunda, 217–224, 218f, 219t–221t
    geographical gaps, 230–232
    introduction to, 215, 217f
    stepping stone islands and, 224, 226–230, 232–233
maritime societies, 22
Mask Cave, 604, 605, 728–729
mass spectrometry, 567–568, 600, 750–751
Mathew, John, 59
Matthews, Jacqueline, 337–338
Maynard, Lesley, 719
McBryde, Isabel, 109, 659–660
McCarthy, Frederick D., 115, 117, 118, 592, 593, 718–719
McCarthy, John, 550
McCartney, Joslyn, 141–142, 144
McConnel, Ursula, 595
McConvell, Patrick, 725
megafauna interactions
    Cuddie Springs site, 285
    defined, 274
    Diprotodon optatum, 256, 275, 276f, 283–385
    Dromornis stirtoni, 256, 275, 278
    drought conditions, 254, 288, 291–292
    dung fungi, 277, 278, 283, 291–292
    eggshell fossils, 256, 277–280, 283, 285–286, 560
    evolution and diversity, 274–277
    extinctions, 280–283, 282f, 290–292
    human interaction with, 279–291
    human subsistence from, 841–842
    information sources on, 277–278
    introduction to, 273–274
    Lake Menindee site, 284–285
    mammals, 274–275
    Palorchestes azael, 275, 276f
    Pleistocene megafauna, 274–278, 276f, 278f
    Procoptodon goliah, 275, 276f, 292
    reptiles, 277
    rock art of, 286–287
    skeletal remains, 277
    Warratyi rock shelter site, 285

megalithic stone circles, 73–74, 74f
megapodes, 274, 276–278, 280, 285–286, 290–291, 922
Melanesian DNA, 307, 314
Melanesian dogs, 366
memory recovery, 198, 202
The Menace of Colour: A Study of the Difficulties Due to the Association of White and Coloured Races (Gregory), 75–76
Mesolithic of Northern Europe (Clark), 543
Meston, Archibald L., 112
Meyer, Otto, 86f, 87, 1112
microbial DNA, 760
micromorphological investigations, 751–752
migration patterns, 301, 306–311, 317, 814–817. *See also* maritime migration
Mildura and District Anthropological Group (MDAG), 121–124
Miles, Gerald, 98
mimis (spirit beings), 142–143, 143f
mineral accretions, 562, 567–569, 572–577
Minjiwarra site, 252
mission archaeology
    ancestral resting places, 1107–1110
    archaeologists-community collaborations, 1107
    in Australia, 1104–1110
    continuity and prehistory in, 1112–1115
    ideologies of directional change, 1118n1
    introduction to, 30, 1101–1103
    missions, defined, 1103–1104
    in Papua New Guinea, 1110–1115, 1110f
    research discussion on, 1115–1118
    rupture in First Nations prehistory, 1104–1106
    spatial divide, 1117–1118
    spiritual-secular divide, 1116–1117
    temporal divide, 1116
Missouri University Research Reactor (MURR), 759
Mitchell, Myles, 338
Mitchell, Scott, 1028
mitochondrial DNA (mtDNA), 244, 258, 301–302, 307–316, 310f, 318n2 361, 364–365, 597
Monckton, Charles, 91, 95–96
Money, P. J., 1113

Morgan, Lewis Henry, 58
Morphy, Howard, 720
mortars and pestles
  anthropomorphic faces, 631
  of antiquity, 619–620, 620t
  art on, 633
  bird pestles, 96, 99, 631–632, 633
  bossed bowls, 631
  coastal lowland areas, 626–627, 630–632
  distribution process, 629–630
  foot mortars, 632
  of former inland sea, 627–629
  functions of, 620–627, 621f, 623f
  in highlands, 620–626, 621f, 623f, 630–632
  importance of, 633–634
  introduction to, 617–619, 618f, 619f
  multifunctional use of, 848
  with nipple-like base, 632
  regional variations of form, 630–632
  in vicinity of inland sea, 629
  Wanigela excavation, 98–99
mortuary practices, 896–899, 897t
Motu-Papuan Gulf network, 594–595
Mountford, Charles, 718–719
Moving Estates period (c. 310-140 cal BP), 819
Mt Elephant stone circle site, 73–74, 74f
Mt William quarry, 657–661, 660f
mud wasp nests, 570–571, 570f
Müller, Ferdinand von, 62
multifunctionality, 644, 674–675, 681–684
multivocality, 498, 512
Mulvaney, John, 13
Munn, Nancy, 720
Munro, Neil G., 92
Murphy, John, 97–98
Murray River Valley societal bioarchaeology
  dietary analyses, 904–907, 905f
  human occupation, 890–892, 890f,
    891t, 893t
  introduction to, 889
  morphology of, 899–901
  mortuary practices, 896–899, 897t
  paleopathology, 901–904, 903f
  unity and diversity within, 907–908
  variation among sections, 893–895, 896t
Murujuga Aboriginal Corporation, 547
museum collection legacies

cultural patrimony of, 187, 189–190, 194,
  196–198, 204–205
decolonizing of, 189–190, 198
impact of collecting, 191–192
inclusionism of, 188, 224, 931, 1005–1006
introduction to, 187–191
as intrusions of colonization, 194
memory recovery, 198, 202
multidimensional nature of, 204–205
reconnecting to and recovering, 197–201
stone artefact collections, 192–194
visiting collections as ancestors, 194–196
Museum of Archaeology and Anthropology
  (MAA), 193
Mwali armrings, 698–699, 699f, 701, 707,
  709–710
mythological reenactments, 955

namurlanjanyngku spirit beings, 146–147
namurlardajanyngku Spirit Men, 732
National American Graves Protection and
  Repatriation Act (NAGPRA), 188
National Geographic Society, 117
nationalist archaeologies, 54
National Museum of Australia in Canberra, 188
National Museum of the American Indian
  Act, 188
National Museum of Victoria (NMV), 88,
  110, 122
Native Mounted Police, 162, 166, 169, 1058–1059,
  1061–1071, 1064t, 1065t, 1066f, 1071n6
  1072n8
Native Police forces, 3, 30, 982, 1057–1058,
  1063, 1071n2 1085, 1108
Native Title rights, 158, 164, 983, 985n11
  1080, 1107
The Native Tribes of Central Australia
  (Spencer, Gillen), 57, 58
The Native Tribes of South-East Australia
  (Howitt), 57, 58
Nauwalabila 1 site, 251
Nawarla Gabarnmang site, 252, 476–480,
  479f, 480f
Neale, Margo, 162
Neanderthal genome, 306–308
Neanderthal man, 62, 560
Netherlands New Guinea, 3

Neuhauss, Richard, 96–97
neutron activation analysis (NAA), 750, 762n1
New Guinea highlands
cultivation and settlement, 843–847, 844*f*
ecological variability, 832–835, 833*f*, 834*f*
exchange networks, 847–850
human adaptive flexibility, 835–843,
838*t*–840*t*
introduction to, 831–832
political transformations, 847–850
social transformation, 850–851
New Guinea singing dogs (NGSDs), 365–366
ngabaya, 146–147
Ngarrindjeri Nation, 11, 148–150
Nicholas, George, 150
non-Aboriginal law, 158
non-Indigenous histories, 168–169
Noone, Herbert, 592–593
Northern Running Figures (NRF), 976
nuclear DNA (nDNA), 318n1 597
Nunn, Patrick, 170, 172, 173–174, 174*t*

object biography, 756
obsidian axe, 95–96
obsidian tools, 95–96, 100, 629, 632, 676,
678–679, 682–683, 815
occupational deposits, 26, 118, 868
Oceania, 97
ochre/ochre sourcing
additional frameworks, 756
analytical methods for provenance, 750–752
archaeological importance, 744
bulk techniques, 750–751
conceptual sourcing, 753–755, 754*f*
defined, 744–745
First People of Australia, 262
future of studies on, 760–762
global record on, 756–757
introduction to, 743
overview of, 746–748, 747*f*, 748*f*
red ochre and Dreaming, 960–961
review of, 757–760
scale of dominant constituents, 752–753
sourcing (provenance) research, 749–750
surface techniques, 751
symbolism in, 744
Tangtangjal cave, 119–120

O'Connell, James, 5–6
old charcoal problem, 559–560
Old People, 144–145, 190, 195–205, 484–488, 487*f*
On the Origin of Species (Darwin), 54
open-air sites, 254, 475–476, 546
optical dating, 577–580
optical emission spectrometry (OES), 750
optically stimulated luminescence (OSL),
216, 244, 248–249, 252, 277, 570, 577–578,
920, 959
oral history and tradition
challenges with, 169–170
ethnography of, 159–161
geography of, 171–175, 174*t*
of I'ai tribe, 807–808
introduction to, 157–159
Macassans and Aboriginal cross-sea
interactions, 1024–1026, 1025*f*
non-Indigenous histories and, 168–169
personal cases of, 161–168, 163*f*, 164*f*, 165*f*
principal genres of, 175–179, 176*t*
time depth of, 11–12
use for future research, 179–180
O'Reilly, Patrick, 88, 90, 1112
orphan collections in museums, 192–193
Ortiz de Retez, Ynigo, 2
Out-of-Africa migrations, 301, 306–311, 317
oven mounds. *See* earthen (oven) mounds
oyster farming, 347, 501

paleopathology, 901–904, 903*f*
Palmer, Arthur, 725
Palorchestes azael, 275, 276*f*
Papua New Guinea archaeological history
Aitape skull, 100–101
early excavations, 87–95
introduction to, 85–87
modern archaeology in, 101–102
summary of, 102
surface collection and excavation, 95–100
Wanigela excavation, 90–95
Watom Island excavation, 87–90, 89*f*
Pardoe, Colin, 126
Pascoe, Bruce, 334
pastoralists/pastoralism, 3, 54–57, 166, 169, 195,
331, 1048, 1059–1061, 1067, 1071n3 1080,
1083–1085, 1087–1088, 1091–1093

Perry, William, 116
pestles. *See* mortars and pestles
petroglyphs, 546, 568, 1052
phantomization, 477, 484
Phillips, Ruth, 188
PIXIE/PIGE program, 758, 759
place-making strategies, 21, 805, 813–821
place-marking strategies, 21, 972–973
plasma oxidation, 568
plasma spectrometry, 750
Pleistocene landmass, 4, 8, 215, 669
Pleistocene megafauna, 274–278, 276f, 278f
PNG National Cultural Council (NCC), 197
Pöch, Rudolf, 90–91, 93
population densities
   agrarianism and, 1080
   among hunter-gatherers, 502–503
   availability of fish, 17
   in biogeographic regions, 1067
   boundary-marking and, 720
   desert models of, 933–935
   dingoes and, 371
   Dreaming association and, 956
   ecological variability and, 832
   environmental enhancement and
     engagement, 329, 334, 336
   exchange networks and, 847, 851
   fire and charcoal studies of, 392
   group interactions and, 900–902
   in highlands, 866
   isolation impact on, 788
   in Papua New Guinea, 617
   radiocarbon dating measuring, 525–526,
     531–533
   sea-level rises and, 541–543
   spatiotemporal trends, 500–502, 507
   in specialized societies, 22
   stone artefact use and, 926
   stone-walled fish traps and, 17, 437
   time series analysis, 527–531, 528f, 530f
   water access and, 889
portable art, 726–731
portable X-ray fluorescence (pXRF), 677,
   682, 751
Potter, Parker B., 1105–1106
pottery
   Early Papuan Pottery, 700, 706, 815

earthenware pottery, 698, 700, 702–703,
   803, 1029–1031
Lapita pottery, 33, 86f, 88, 89f, 90, 314, 600,
   633, 679, 701, 1112–1113
Macassan pottery, 117–118
Macassans and Aboriginal cross-sea
   interactions, 1031
migration and settlement patterns and,
   814–816, 822
Southern Massim Pottery, 700
Wanigela excavation, 91–92, 94
Watom Island excavation, 88
prehistoric archaeology, 10, 53
Prehistoric Japan (Munro), 92
Prehistoric Times (Lubbock), 54, 65
A Prehistory Australia, New Guinea and Sahul
   (O'Connell, White), 5
Pretty, Graeme, 100
Previous Possessions, New Obligations
   (Council of Australian Museum
   Associations), 188
Primitive Culture (Tylor), 54
primitive hunter-gatherers, 54–55
primitivism and colonialist ideologies, 9–10,
   329, 997
primordialism, 9–10, 65, 76, 331, 1112
prismatic blades, 678
probability distribution function, 525
processual archaeology, 15, 499–500, 720
Procoptodon goliah, 275, 276f, 292
protected rearing, 341, 343–346, 348–349
provenance, defined, 749
provenance research, 749–752
provenience, defined, 749
Purari Delta, 805–809, 814, 816–819, 821–822
Pythagorean tradition, 2

radiocarbon dating
   accelerator mass spectrometry, 567–568,
     600, 823n6
   Australian high country, 868–870
   demographic and population changes,
     525–526, 531–533
   direct dating of motifs, 567–568
   First People of Australia, 242, 244, 248–249,
     251–252
   highland ditches and field systems, 453

radiocarbon dating (*cont.*)
  of inland seas, 628
  Macassans and Aboriginal cross-sea
      interactions, 1029–1030
  megafauna, 277
  methodology, 566–567
  for migration and settlement patterns,
      815–816
  mineral accretions in, 562, 567–569, 572–577
  plasma oxidation in, 568
  of rock art, 566–572, 570*f*, 571*f*, 957–959
  of shell valuables and exchange systems, 700
  stone arrangements, 959
rainforest contraction, 222
rainwater diversion, 337
raman spectroscopy, 751
reclamation, 30–31, 467–468
Regional Continuity Model, 306
Reich, David, 307
Reid, Nick, 172, 173–174, 174*t*
repatriation of Elders, 147–150
Replacement Model, 306
replanting process, 332, 849, 1081
Republic of Indonesia, 3
resource enhancement, 330, 333, 338, 350–351,
    435, 436–439
resource extraction sites, 61, 70–71, 371, 417
restocking depleted animal species, 340–341
retouched stone points, 672–675, 673*f*
re-touching in rock art modifications, 975
Reynolds, Henry, 1048
Rhodes, David, 1109
Rigsby, Bruce, 195, 720
ritual caves, 61, 72, 484
Ritual Form Model (RFM), 972, 976–977
ritualized hunting
  archaeological research on, 1011–1012
  of dugong/sea cow (*Dugong dugon*), 999–1006,
      1002*f*, 1004*f*
  foundations of, 994–999
  green turtle (*Chelonia mydas*), 1006–1011,
      1009*f*
  introduction to, 993–994
  power and social agency, 1005–1006
  social reproduction, 1006
  status and social inclusion, 1006
  totemic clan identity, 1006

ritual knowledge, 160, 164, 166–167, 950, 954
rituals
  in Dreaming/Dreaming narratives, 960
  introduction to, 17, 21, 25–28
  magico-religious rites, 997
  maintenance rituals, 996–997
  for marine fish catches, 431–432
  of rock art modifications, 970–974, 975–977,
      981–983
  singing whales, 1045
river deltas, 23–24, 595, 804–805
Riwi site, 254
Robinson, George Augustus, 16, 71, 344–345,
    1048–1049, 1052, 1106
rock art
  Borologa 1 site, 481–483, 482*f*
  buried deposits and, 118
  in ceremonial sites, 72–73
  Dreaming/Dreaming narratives, 957–959
  introduction to, 19, 717–718
  of Macassan material culture, 1034
  mapping of, 21
  of megafauna, 286–287
  physical modification of, 27
  representations in, 30
  of submerged landscapes, 546
  Tangtangjal cave, 119–120
  Wanigela excavation, 94
rock art boundaries
  Ancestral Beings and, 724–725
  archaeological approaches to, 718–723
  early approaches to continental styles,
      718–719
  four-pointed star, 727–728, 728*f*
  Gulf of Carpentaria case study, 731–734, 733*f*
  hooked triangle motif, 729
  introduction to, 717–718
  as multilayered and nonexclusive, 723–724
  namurlardajanyngku Spirit Men, 732
  as negotiated and variable, 724
  as portable art, 726–731
  provinces, 722–723, 734–735
  recent approaches to regional styles,
      719–722
  as relational, 724–725
  research discussions, 725–726, 729–731,
      730*f*, 734

theorizing about, 723–726
Yalkawarru ceremony motifs, 732, 733*f*
rock art dating
   challenges, 580–581
   by cosmogenic nuclides, 562–566, 565*f*
   introduction to, 559–561
   optical dating, 577–580
   radiocarbon dating, 566–572, 570*f*, 571*f*,
     957–959
   Uranium-Thorium (U-Th) dating, 560,
     572–577
rock art modifications
   Ancestral Beings and spiritual realm,
     977–979, 985n2 985n8
   events and time quantifications, 976–977
   formal perspectives on, 974–975
   introduction to, 969–970
   kinship connections, 979–981, 981*t*
   opposition and controversy surrounding,
     983–984
   re-marking, 975
   rituals of, 970–974, 975–977, 981–983
rock engravings, 528, 564, 573, 580, 957–963, 1052
rock shelters
   building and construction of, 475–480
   coastal adaptations of, 778–779
   creation of, 337–338, 348
   Nawarla Gabarnmang, 476–480, 479*f*, 480*f*
   rock art dating, 561–562
   Warratyi rock shelter site, 285
roots/root crop remains, 253, 343, 627, 841, 843,
   849, 868
Roscoe, Paul, 6
Rose, Deborah Bird, 162, 724, 725
Royal Anthropological Society of Australasia
   (RASA), 64–65
Royal Society of Victoria, 66

sago (*Metroxylon sagu*) cultivation, 805–813,
   806*f*, 821–822
scanning electron microscopy (SEM), 386
scarring in rock art modifications, 975
Schrire, Carmel, 646
Science of Man, 74
scratch-work in rock art modifications, 982
seafaring technology, 542–543
sea-level rise. *See also* submerged landscapes

effect on productivity in desert settlements,
   932–933
   geographic examples of, 173
   introduction to, 541–543, 542*f*
   narratives of, 172–173, 175
   postglacial rise, 11, 19, 22, 541
sealions (*Neophoca cinera*), 1050
Seligmann, Charles, 91–92, 96
SEM-EDXA (scanning electron microscopy-
   energy dispersive X-Ray analyses), 758
sentient ecology, 995, 997
settlement patterns, 814–816, 843–847, 844*f*.
   See also desert settlements in Australia
Setzler, Frank, 117, 118
Seymour, David, 1064
shared material culture, 597–601, 599*f*
Sharpe, Margaret, 171
shellfish species, 254–255, 261–262
shell middens, 54, 61, 69–70, 112, 118, 119*f*, 121,
   123–124, 347, 509–510, 546, 711, 781*f*, 790,
   819, 894, 1028
Shellshear, Joseph L., 114–115
shell valuables and exchange systems
   connectedness of, 710–712
   cowries, 632, 695–697, 711, 712n1
   ethnography of, 704–706
   ethnohistorical record of, 707–710
   of Hiri, 702–704
   introduction to, 693–694, 694*f*
   kina exchanges, 693, 695, 696*f*
   kula exchanges, 594, 601, 654, 693–694,
     698–702, 699*f*
   Lapita shell artefacts, 701, 706
   Mwali armrings, 698–699, 699*f*, 701, 707,
     709–710
   in New Guinea highlands, 695–698, 696*f*,
     847–850
   radiocarbon dating of, 700
signal sending stone technology, 937–938
Signor-Lipps Effect (SLE), 281
Simons Genome Diversity Project, 308–309
Simple Figurative imagery, 719
single-nucleotide polymorphisms
   (SNPs), 319n4
skeletal elements, 216, 217, 222
skeletal remains, 10, 61, 67, 87, 122, 223–225,
   230, 277, 597, 872, 1006, 1071

Skelly, Robert, 603–604
skulls
  Aitape skull, 100–101
  cranial deformation, 900
  craniometrics, 596–597
  Victorian skulls, 62
  Western Port skull, 62
smallpox, 524, 529
Smith, Benjamin, 721
Smith, Grafton Elliott, 116
Smithsonian Institution, 118
Smyth, Robert Brough, 57, 63
social archaeology and Intensification Model,
    511–512
social construction, 477, 481, 488–489, 513
social evolutionism, 9, 54, 58, 61–62, 65, 76, 112,
    331, 592, 596
social justice, 56, 137, 139, 151, 1092, 1109. *See also*
    agency and social justice in archaeology
social networks, 20, 24, 502–503, 671–672, 682,
    697, 700, 720, 734, 753–755, 936, 1110, 1114
socio-demographics, 18
sourcing (provenance) research, 749–750
South Australian Museum (SAM), 112, 117, 746
southeastern stone axes, 657–661, 660f
Southern Elephant seal *(Mirounga leonina)*,
    1050
Southern Massim Pottery (SMP), 700
Southern right whale *(Eubalaena australis)*, 1044
Southern Whale Fishery (SWF), 1043
Spanish cartographers, 2
spatial history, 818–820
Specht, Jim, 102
specialized societies, 22–24
Spencer, Baldwin, 57, 66, 951
spiritual beings, 72, 140, 142–145, 152, 417, 734
spiritual realm of rock art modifications,
    977–979
squattocracy, 56
Stanley, Evan, 88
Statham, E. J., 474
stepping stone islands, 224, 226–230, 232–233
stone arrangements, 959–960
stone artefacts, 115–116, 192–194, 868–870
stone axes
  of antiquarian colonial Victoria, 62–65, 64f
  defined, 642–644, 643f

edge-ground axes, 250, 252–253, 259–261,
    263, 477, 841, 876
first makers of, 644–649, 645f
of highlands, 649–653
introduction to, 641–642
of lowlands, 653–656
obsidian axe, 95–96
production and exchange, 656–657
resource extraction sites, 70–71
southeastern examples, 657–661, 660f
surprising qualities of, 661–662
technology of, 649–656
Trobriands tools, 654
stone circles, 73–74, 74f, 191
stone club heads, 92, 97–99, 101, 595, 606
stone figurines, 96–98
stone houses, 70, 488
stone pillars, 96
stone points, 21, 260, 263, 671, 672–675, 673f, 680
stone tools. *See also* adzes; flaked stone tools
  Aboriginal skulls and, 76
  associated with copper mining, 63
  Kimberley Points, 252, 372, 673, 673f,
    681–682, 684
  obsidian tools, 95, 100, 629, 632, 676,
    678–679, 682–683, 815
  signal sending stone technology, 937–938
  social interconnectedness and, 681–683
  waisted blades, 85, 647, 843, 1113
  Wero Sisira, 35n1
stone-walled fish traps
  archaeology of, 414–418
  construction of, 434–435
  freshwater practices, 418–425
  interregional gatherings and, 435–436
  introduction to, 413–414
  marine practices, 425–434
  new understandings of, 439
  ownership exclusivity, 438
  protected rearing, 345–346
  resource enhancement, 436–438
  social dimensions, 417–418
  sociality of, 434–439
  technical dimensions, 414–416
  tropical and temperate Australia, 421, 422f,
    423t–424t, 424–425
  tropical New Guinea, 418–421, 419t–421t

Strehlow, T. G. H., 951
Submerged Forests (Dawkins), 543
submerged landscapes
    cultural heritage management, 551–552
    cultural landscapes, 544–545
    evidence of, 545–548, 548*f*
    future research directions, 548–551, 549*f*
    international archaeological context,
       543–544
    introduction to, 541–543, 542*f*
subsistence patterns, 25, 88, 334, 671, 807, 810,
    812, 904, 1031
subsistence strategies, 222, 261–262, 334, 851
substrate enhancement, 346–347
Suloga quarry, 654, 656
Sunda, earliest human presence in, 217–224,
    218*f*, 219*t*–221*t*
superimpositioning in rock art modification,
    973, 974*f*
surface exposure dating, 563, 580, 935
surface techniques, 751
Sutton, Peter, 720
Sutton, Stephen, 170
swamp and delta societies of Papuan Gulf
    archaeological village models, 818–820
    cultural and environmental histories,
       803–805, 804*f*
    implications for archaeologists, 820–822
    Kikori River Delta, 805–807, 809–813
    migration and settlement patterns, 814–816
    place-making in, 813–820
    Purari Delta, 805–809, 814, 816–819,
       821–822
    river deltas, 23, 595, 804–805
    sago cultivation, 805–813, 806*f*, 821–822
    spatial history, 818–820
    trade and migration, 816–817
swamp/swampland. *See also* Huli ditches and
    field systems in swampland
    Budgeongutte Swamp, 16, 16*f*, 342
    Clear Swamp, 16, 16*f*, 342
    Kuk Swamp, 313, 451–453, 464–465, 650,
       676, 843, 845
symbolic behaviour, 259*f*, 263, 559, 720, 934, 939
symbolism, 17, 241–242, 262, 453, 744, 983–984,
    985n9
sympathetic magic, 971, 997

Tamaki Makau-rau Accord on the Display
    of Human Remains and Sacred
    Objects, 188
Taming the North (Fysh), 169
taskscape construction, 434
Tasmanian culture, 113–114, 128n8
Taylor, Luke, 720
Taylor, Norman, 348
Taylor, Rebe, 109
technological organization theory, 671, 674,
    681, 683, 685
temporal frequency distribution, 525–526
Te Papa Tongarewa, 188
territorialized landscape, 963
Territory of Papua, 3, 90, 94, 821, 823n13
Terry, Mitchell, 338–339
thermoluminescence (TL), 216, 242
Thomas, Nicholas, 197, 203
Thomas, William, 57
Thompson, John, 119
Thomson, Donald, 195–204, 595
Thorne, Alan, 4, 306
Thorpe, William W., 115
Thousand Genomes Project, 302
3D contour topographic models, 415
Thylacoleo, 287
time series analysis, 527–531, 528*f*, 530*f*
Tindale, Norman, 112–114
Tjukurrpa (Dreamings), 939
Tjurunga use in Dreaming, 961
Tonkinson, Robert, 160
Torres Strait Cultural Complex (TSCC), 606
Torres Strait Islands/Islanders
    clam gardens, 348–349, 437
    colonialism of, 3
    dugong/sea cow *(Dugong dugon)* ritualized
       hunting, 999–1006, 1002*f*, 1004*f*
    exchange/trade, 595, 709, 804
    fish traps, 432–433, 438
    green turtle *(Chelonia mydas)* ritualized
       hunting, 1006–1011, 1009*f*
    fire studies, 398–399
    introduction to, 3–9
    missions, 1108, 1114–1115, 1118
    pottery, 33, 603–604, 1036
    rock art boundaries, 726–731
totemic clan identity, 1006

1150 INDEX

trade/trade networks
  in ceramics, 603–604, 673, 704, 706, 1052
  exchanged materials, 746
  of foragers, 682, 753
  of Hiri, 702–704
  in New Guinea highlands, 849–850
  swamp and delta societies of Papuan Gulf,
    814–817
Traditional Owner groups, 10–11, 34
traits list identity approach, 757
translocation of animals, 338–340, 342–343, 348
transplanting process, 332, 807–808, 1081
trepang/trepangers, 20, 1024–1027, 1027f, 1028f
Trigger, Bruce, 54
Trobriand Islands, 94, 654, 1117
tropical Australia, 421, 422f, 423t–424t, 424–425,
    428–434, 429f, 430t–431t, 433f
tropical New Guinea, 418–421, 419t–421t, 425,
    426t–427t, 427–428
Trueman, Will, 342
Tula adzes, 671, 675–676, 682–684, 938–939
Tuman quarries, 651–652
Tumu, Akii, 159
Tunbridge, Dorothy, 171
Tylor, Edward, 54, 58, 65

United Kingdom's Museums Association, 188
Uranium-Thorium (U-Th) dating
  applications, 573–574
  criticisms and limitations, 574–576
  desert settlements in Australia, 920
  detrital Thorium contamination, 576
  future research directions, 577
  megafauna, 277
  methodology, 573
  mineral accretions, 575–577
  mineral deposition timing, 575
  of rock art, 560, 572–577
U-series age, 216–217, 222, 225, 230–231, 255–256

Van Dieman's Land Company (VDL), 1091
vegetation remains, 253
Vereenigde Oost-Indische Compagnie
  (VOC), 1025–1026
Vermillion Accord on Human Remains, 188
Victoria. *See* antiquarian archaeology in
  colonial Victoria

Victorian Archaeological Survey, 124
Victoria River District (VRD), 474, 725, 984
Village Expansion period (c. 425-310 cal BP),
  818–819
village models, 818–820
Voyce, A.H., 1113

waisted blades, 85, 647, 843, 1113
Wallace, Alfred Russel, 4
Walter, Charles, 203
Wanigela excavation, 90–95
Warratyi rock shelter site, 256, 285
Warrnambool Museum, 74–75
water controls, 17, 499, 501–503
watercraft, 307, 364, 679, 683, 773–774, 777, 784,
  786–789, 1034
waterhole enhancement, 336–337
waterscapes. *See* Huli ditches and field systems
  in swampland
Wati Kutjarra figures, 958
Watom Island excavation, 87–90, 89f
Watson, Judy, 192, 193, 194
weirs, 16, 332, 343–345, 414–418, 421, 422f,
  425–431, 435, 891–892
Wells, Edgar, 199
We of the Never-Never (Gunn), 345
Western Australian Museum, 110
Western District Aboriginal people, 57, 59
Western Port skull, 62
wet phases in deserts, 927–928
Wet Temperate zone, 396–397
Wet Tropic zone, 388, 390, 722, 1067
whaling and sealing
  Aboriginal connections and involvement,
    1051–1053
  introduction to, 1043–1044
  sealing, overview, 1049–1050
  traditional Aboriginal relations, 1045–1049,
    1046f, 1047f
  whaling, overview, 1044–1045
White, Peter, 5–6, 102
White Australia Policy, 76
Wiessner, Polly, 159
Williams, Elizabeth, 339, 345
Williams, Francis Edgar, 94, 452
Williams, Nancy, 720–721
Wiseman, Chelsea, 550

Wiynjorroc, Lamjerroc, 144–145, 145*f*
Wiynjorroc, Phyllis, 144–145, 145*f*
Wobst, Martin, 719–720
Wohlt, Paul, 453
Wolpoff, Milford, 306
women
    partnership with dingoes, 371–372
    seal hunting and, 1050, 1052–1053
    whale hunting and, 1048
wooden objects, 263, 682, 727, 731
Wood-Jones, Frederic, 112
World Archaeological Congress (WAC),
    188

World Archaeology, 121
World Hunter-Gatherer Conferences, 510–511
worm consumption, 347
Worsnop, Thomas, 71
Wright, Duncan, 603
written histories of cross-sea interactions,
    1024–1026

X-ray diffraction (pXRD), 750, 751

yabugad narration, 1118
Yalkawarru ceremony motifs, 732, 733*f*
Yolngu boundaries, 724